The Earth As Transformed by Human Action

The Earth As Transformed by Human Action

Global and Regional Changes in the Biosphere over the Past 300 Years

Edited by

B. L. TURNER II
Graduate School of Geography,
Clark University

WILLIAM C. CLARK
John F. Kennedy School of Government,
Harvard University

ROBERT W. KATES
Alan Shawn Feinstein World Hunger Program,
Brown University

JOHN F. RICHARDS
Department of History,
Duke University

JESSICA T. MATHEWS
World Resources Institute

WILLIAM B. MEYER
Graduate School of Geography
Clark University

With computer graphics by Montine Jordan

CAMBRIDGE
UNIVERSITY PRESS

PUBLISHED BY THE PRESS SYNDICATE OF THE UNIVERSITY OF CAMBRIDGE
The Pitt Building, Trumpington Street, Cambridge CB2 1RP, United Kingdom

CAMBRIDGE UNIVERSITY PRESS
The Edinburgh Building, Cambridge CB2 2RU, United Kingdom
40 West 20th Street, New York, NY 10011-4211, USA
10 Stamford Road, Oakleigh, Melbourne 3166, Australia

First published 1990
First paperback edition 1993
Reprinted 1994, 1995, 1997

Printed in the United States of America

Typeset in Times

A catalogue record for this book is available from the British Library

Library of Congress Cataloguing-in-Publication Data is available

ISBN 0-521-44630-9 paperback

Contents

Foreword

The Relativity of Time and Transformation

ROBERT McC. ADAMS

This volume concentrates on the impacts of human activities on the "faces and flows" of the global environment over the past three centuries or so. Its choice of subject implies that the impacts are, to an important degree, unidirectional. But merely to describe them in these terms is to acknowledge almost at once the need for important qualifications, if not an outright denial, of the implication.

Any such choice of wording and subject has, we should frankly recognize, positivist or whiggian overtones. Probably there are also Malthusian roots to the apparent assumption that changes in human societies and behavior autonomously generate environmental impacts. World population, having taken several million years to rise to the 1 billion level about two centuries ago, probably passed 5 billion sometime in 1986. The now-exponential rate of increase can be projected to lead to the level of 10 billion by A.D. 2150 (chap. 1). This increasingly massive physical presence of humanity, even apart from its still more rapidly growing, technologically based transformative potential, makes a vivid if not wholly compelling case for pressures being generated that can be thought of as originating within society itself.

Somewhat marginal, although surely not inconsistent with the main theme of the volume, is the important question of the extent to which the ways in which we have understood the world have themselves been transformed over the same period. Our sources of data have been shaped in subtle and not-so-subtle ways, by these same demographic and technological trends as well as by others. That being so, they must have shaped the sequence of historical impressions on which we consciously or unconsciously draw.

Similarly marginal and yet worthy of attention is the rather elementary proposition that neither human society nor the global environment can really be regarded as an independent entity. The impact of one on the other can be understood only by inquiring at the same time into their reciprocal effects. Human society and the global environment obviously form a dynamically interacting system.

We are fortunate that scientific means are available by which to establish at least some objective measures (e.g., pollen analysis, glacial cores) of the historical changes in the environment that have occurred in the past. Such measures play a central part in our proceedings. But while considering the degree to which recorded changes may have been products of changing aggregate forms of human activity (e.g., the Industrial Revolution, population growth), we should remember that perception of these events has passed through a cultural filter and does not come down to us as an objective record.

Had a five-century interval instead of the three-century focus of this volume been chosen, its beginning would have closely coincided with the Columbian discoveries of the new world whose quincentenary will be celebrated in 1992. The world-circling expansion of Europe would then be the process defining, if not precipitating, the subject of our inquiry. That implies that either the deep, unresolved crisis of World War I or the more extensive and permanent political reconfigurations that emerged after World War II brought it to an end. Colonial empires, and the asymmetrical flows of resources inward toward the metropolitan powers that they compelled, were dominant features. Plausibly, we could regard the Industrial Revolution as having been at least partly encapsulated within these larger structures, since it was profoundly stimulated by both the new wealth and the new markets acquired through first mercantilist and then colonial expansionism. Of course, this is not to deny that industrial activity later began to develop a shape and dynamic of its own.

Accompanying the very first phases of this epoch of a five-century European diaspora were other dispersals. The devastating impacts of epidemic diseases on native human populations of the New World, long known in general outline, are an increasingly important theme of study. Just as sweeping and even more direct in their ecological effects were dispersals of domesticated plants and animals, weeds, insects, and other cohabitors of the zones of disturbance accompanying European life. These related, often abrupt, and surprisingly little recognized processes of dispersal contributed decisively to the European conquest of the New World and some of the great archipelagos of the Pacific (Crosby 1986).

This alternative five-century schema, centering on a

Europe-centered dynamic, implies that the onset of a post-colonial world in 1945 ranked as another historical turning point of major importance. Perhaps that will turn out to be the case, although the sense of drift and periodic crisis currently pervading most former colonial possessions thus far has failed to signal a major new release of creative energies. Instead, it can plausibly be argued that while directly imposed colonial rule disappeared almost completely and without a protracted struggle, the pathologically polarized pattern of development and dependency that was left behind perpetuates some of the earlier, underlying economic relationships in all but name.

Contrary to the belief succinctly expressed by Rostow (1960: 166) a generation ago that the "tricks of growth are not all that difficult," ensuing experience has disclosed formidable barriers not only to the attainment of developed status but even to consistent progress toward it. Whether in health, housing, education, adequacy of diet, per capita income, or productivity, the idea that there is a familiar, unilineal path that all can follow is widely rejected today. Pressures resulting from population growth, regional political rivalries, erosion of popularly based political leadership and the repeated threat of its replacement by authoritarian military regimes, and outright planning failures at home; and from a variety of direct and indirect foreign influences that include shifting relative prices in world markets, the periodic lack of access to investment capital, and the cumulative burden of indebtedness – all have contributed to recursive stresses and instabilities that have largely dispelled initial optimism.

The tendency has been to separate these disturbing trends in postcolonial political and socioeconomic settings from their equally disturbing environmental concomitants. A temporal framework focusing on the challenges before developing countries has the useful side effect of forcing us to view both societal and environmental trends in their intimate inter-relationship. Ethiopia's periodically calamitous famines and protracted civil war, for example, are surely part of a syndrome of systemically related processes that also includes its consistently decrepit and authoritarian rule over a long period of time and its devastated landscape. Its annual loss of topsoil per hectare, to cite merely one index, is nearly ten times the annual rate in the United States – even though our rate, too, is viewed as a serious, long-range problem. Political instability in the Sahel (most recently exemplified by a violent, regressive coup in Burkina Faso) is surely related to ongoing, unchecked desertification, to population pressure on its fragile resources, and to resultant mass migrations across national borders that have Africa accounting for well over half of the world's refugees.

Nor is the New World immune to symptoms of the same syndrome. Haiti's tragic problems are clearly a compound of overpopulation, political misrule, and overwhelming degradation of agricultural lands. El Salvador's persistent schisms and instability cannot be separated from the fact that it suffers from the region's most serious population pressures, deforestation, and loss of agricultural productivity. As Norman Myers (1987: 17) has recently and aptly generalized:

There is hardly any agent more destructive of natural resources – notably soil cover, grasslands, and forests – than the subsistence cultivator who cannot procure enough to eat by cultivating traditional farmlands... Of course, he is no more to be "blamed" for his actions than is a soldier to be held responsible for starting a war: the subsistence cultivator is often impelled by forces of political structures, economic systems, and/or institutional factors, of which he may have little understanding and over which he exercises virtually no influence. But the result is the same: widespread deforestation, soil erosion, and the spread of deserts. Another result is the growing incapacity of the natural-resource base to sustain ever-increasing numbers of people with a growing sense of desperation.

This is not to deny that impressive improvements and records of cumulative capital formation can be found in a number of formerly undeveloped countries. Even where they have occurred, however, they have usually been subject to serious distortions and constraints. Large proportions of the benefits typically are confined to geographic locations dictated by export production and to the emergence of swollen "primate" cities into which are channeled a disproportionate share of the benefits of international trade. Little in the way of multiplier effects has proved to be generated by import substitution, price restraints on agricultural products, and other common inducements to such growth, which have weakened the economy of more peripheral districts by mobilizing savings only for centralized investment. Steep income gradients between rural and urban sectors then encourage an overconcentration of trained labor and professional and entrepreneurial elements, further intensifying a damaging asymmetry of resource flows. That a differently oriented cycle succeeded the demise of colonialism is thus apparent. The means by which much of the Third World will ultimately find its way past the new forms of dependency are still obscure.

It bears repeating here that the advantages of our developed status and the problems of dependency are linked. Sharing one set of global resources, we cannot absolve ourselves of responsibility for contributing to worldwide development goals by merely turning our attention to our own, internally preferred set of priorities. Yet who can deny, to take the most egregious and important case, that we have powerfully stimulated a worldwide trend toward increased military expenditures, paralleled by a trend in the opposite direction with regard to the alleviation of poverty, investment in basic economic infrastructures, and the protection of natural resources?

If the Great Powers finally have brought themselves to the brink of a slowdown or reversal of the arms race, as seems hearteningly possible, what can we do to assure that at least a portion of the funds thus saved is made available to our less fortunate global cohabitors? What inducements can we provide to extend this reversal of suicidal military investment to smaller countries that are even less able than we to sustain the risks and costs of modern armaments?

This alternate five-century option in periodization thus raises provocative questions. It has the virtue of focusing our attention on fundamental imbalances that stand in the way of any more equitable, less reckless apportionment of the world's resources. It is important that the theme of equity, in particular, not be wholly submerged by a preoccupation with inanimate "faces and flows."

Let me briefly outline still another option for periodization, resting on different criteria and having different consequences. Consider the transformative processes that would have been salient, had we chosen a ten-century span. Europe as a culturally defined whole does not even appear to have been recognized prior to the coining of the term by an obscure Arab scholar in the eighth century A.D. Ten centuries ago much of its northern and western parts was just emerging from the grip of Viking raids. Essentially all of Europe, save the immediate environs of Byzantium, was still far short of the levels of population and economic and cultural activity that had characterized the late classical epoch.

Choice of this interval of a millennium would contravene the widely held, supposedly modernist assumption that a barbarian "free" Europe with its own unique potential for dynamic growth must have had historic roots virtually as deep as those of what we all too readily characterize as a static, despotic Orient. Ten centuries ago the advanced centers of civilized life lay well to the south – in resplendent Islam along the southern shores of the Mediterranean and in the Near East, and in the central Mexican, Mayan, and Peruvian civilizations in the New World that had no temperate-zone counterparts. Viewed across a millennium, the inconstancy of regional superiority, as exemplified by the northward shift coinciding with the beginning of the Renaissance and then consummated by the wave of European conquests, would have commanded our attention.

The subsequent shift westward to the North American continent could well be seen as merely a continuation of the same theme. It would leave us unsurprised that this, too, may well be transitory. Implicit in a millennium-long temporal scale is a readiness to view with something approaching historical inevitability the prospect of a further movement of centers of dynamic growth and prosperity – for example, to the western Pacific rim.

No less than the two alternatives I have described, the three-century span for the volume rests on its own assumptions and strategies of inquiry. It attaches unique and central importance to the Industrial Revolution as a profound contributor to the transformation of our environment. Our attention tends to be drawn more to the inevitability of technology's outward spread, and correspondingly less to colonialism's characteristically rigid asymmetries of wealth and power, even though advancing technology surely accompanied, sustained, and sometimes even precipitated the latter. The transformative thrust if not irresistibility of technological advance, largely divorced from the social institutions and relationships that associated it with divergent meanings and values in different settings, would seem to be the message of our chosen focus on a three-century period.

Much depends, in other words, upon our choice of scale. Three hundred years adequately frames the Industrial Revolution as at least the immediate cause of some of the more lasting human impacts on the earth and its environment.

Apart from fairly localized areas of siltation, alluviation, and downcutting, and from patches of salinization and some fairly extensive areas of deforestation that were at least partly reversible, such impacts were few and essentially negligible before the Industrial Revolution. Its onset, on the other hand, was accompanied by irreversible increases in fossil-fuel consumption, signaled in recoverable samples by an initially slight increase in levels of atmospheric carbon dioxide. That increase very gradually accelerated into the more steeply rising curve we are viewing with growing concern today, whose consequences cannot yet be foreseen for temperature and precipitation patterns, for submerged ports and receding shorelines, and for complex plant successions affecting human subsistence and thus possibly even the fate of nations.

The CO_2 problem is, of course, merely a shorthand symbol for a rapidly growing mass of other, often much more proximate and dangerous disturbances and contaminants with which we are all more or less familiar. The extent to which they have moved from headline treatment in the media to perfunctory reports on the inside pages of only a few major newspapers is one of the more depressing signs of the prevailing shortsightedness and complacency of our times. Most recently representing these threats, after all, are examples as truly grave as the discovery of oxygen-depleted dead zones even in open, continental-shelf waters of the western Atlantic, of a massively poisoned, reportedly virtually moribund Adriatic Sea, and of the alarming chlorofluoro-carbon-induced declines in Antarctic ozone.

A view three centuries in temporal depth admittedly encourages us to view this process with appropriate regard for the long-term technological changes that have led to it. But its corresponding defect is that it fails to call sufficient attention to the rapidly accelerating rate of destructive impacts within our own lifetimes. To achieve the latter end, we would need a scheme of periodization in which successive epochs are dramatically foreshortened rather than lengthened. Such a scheme presumably would focus primarily on nonrenewable resources beyond reach of easy and economical substitution. Oil is preeminent among such resources, of course; yet the public's awareness that its supply might be in any way limited is not yet a decade and a half old – and sufficiently casual to have left little or no permanent imprint on the behavior of markets. Nondegraded or undesertified croplands and rangelands are other, large and variegated but ultimately nonsubstitutable resources, especially in tropical settings. After huge increases in the supply of both within the last century or so, both are nearing the upper asymptotes of their potential global extents – at least without further, catastrophic losses of biodiversity consequent upon an even more massive attack on primary forests than is already under way.

The point to be driven home, for which a three-century frame of reference is clearly too coarse-meshed, is that changes are now beginning to compound themselves interactively in ways that challenge even near-term prediction. Market mechanisms can provide for substitution or other adaptations to scarcity only with more time than in some cases may any longer be available. Smoothly proceeding parallel changes and adaptive countermeasures, always inherently unlikely, are still less believable as we begin to recognize that we confront complex, unstable, nonlinear systems that are far from equilibrium and moving in indeterminate ways.

Consideration of this question of alternative scales of time thus calls attention to a pervasive problem whose increasing urgency I am sure we all recognize. It is the disparity between the demonstrable consequences of the massive environmental transformations in which we are now almost routinely engaged and the very limited means we have to ameliorate or counteract them – in most cases without our having monitored them adequately, and, in some, virtually without our ever having noticed them. I speak, to be sure, not of what might be done optimally but in the narrowly pragmatic sense of what we in this country have generally regarded as politically or economically realistic.

Perhaps the key deterrent to more effective action is a matter of scalar disparity. We live in an unprecedentedly interdependent, highly interactive world that is beset by processes of disturbance and transformation that are proceeding on many different spatial and temporal scales. But the units within which decisions must be made are still the traditional nation-states whose boundaries – and whose bounded spheres of recognized responsibility for their actions – are products of earlier historical epochs that made more limited demands.

How do we face this set of new, sometimes conflicting, often poorly understood challenges of global scale and complexity when solutions must be hammered out within such units? Each country characteristically tends to consider only those manifestations that fall within its own partisan frame of reference, and calculates its risks and opportunities against political calendars that heavily discount the longer-term future. In this sense, our chosen three-century span may well be excessively leisurely. It cannot be given sufficient emphasis that not only the scale and urgency but the political intractability of the problems facing us are mounting exponentially. They have clearly entered a domain of irretrievable losses and almost incalculable further risks for which historical precedents provide little guidance.

Profoundly complicating our assessment of past human impacts on the environment, or estimates of future ones, is the prevalence of indirect, or second-order, interactions.

Much recent policy-oriented research makes us increasingly conscious of them and of resultant uncertainty as to the connection – if any – between intentions and outcomes. In the social sciences, reductionist paradigms are giving way to more pessimistic appraisals of the extent to which the results of large-scale planning and intervention are ever truly predictable. Also shrinking our horizons of certainty is the growing recognition that unambiguous, determinate boundaries, in both time and space, are lacking in almost all of the systems we propose to examine – let alone to alter.

I will conclude by suggesting that the real meaning of the historic overview to which this symposium commits us is that we must understand and grapple with a very broad, complex, and irregular series of interacting changes. We face the painful triage of choices that physicians confront in major emergencies. Some processes of transformation seem to be on the whole neutral if not positive, and for this reason need little attention. Some are tragically negative but essentially irreversible, and cannot benefit from more than palliative assistance. Then there are those that are potentially but not certainly subject to redirection and fundamental improvement. It is those processes that deserve the fullest commitment of newly focused efforts that this volume may help to stimulate.

Only with the lengthy time perspective of historically ordered change can the complex considerations be disentangled in order for particular changes to be correctly assigned to one of this triad of categories. Perhaps the central burden of my own message is that the social and ecological dimensions of change form a single, embracing system that must be holistically addressed. What makes its history relevant is that a fuller understanding of the past not only changes our image of this attainable future but also helps to instill the needed sense of responsibility and commitment with which to work together for its realization.

References

Crosby, A. E. 1986. *Ecological Imperialism: The Biological Expansion of Europe, 900–1900.* Cambridge: Cambridge University Press.

Myers, N. 1987. Population, environment, and conflict. *Environmental Conservation* 14.

Rostow, W. W. 1960. *The Stages of Economic Growth: A Non-Communist Manifesto.* Cambridge: Cambridge University Press.

Preface

To explain a project and volume as complex in its development and ambitious in its purpose as *The Earth As Transformed by Human Action*, it is perhaps best to begin at the beginning.

The Background

In 1982, the Director of the Graduate School of Geography, Clark University, asked the faculty members of the program to begin to think about an activity that the school could undertake as part of the University's 1987–1988 centennial celebrations. At the beginning of my directorship of the School in 1983, Robert W. Kates (now of the Alan Shawn Feinstein World Hunger Program, Brown University) stepped forward to suggest a major project for the centennial that would examine the human transformation of the earth. The initial rationales for such a project were several. The world's population was about to reach twice its level at the time of 1955 Princeton Wenner-Gren symposium that produced the noted volume *Man's Role in Changing the Face of the Earth*, and this situation, along with others, was propelling massive changes in the nature of our planet-home; yet a comprehensive and authoritative survey of the changes wrought by humankind had not been undertaken since the posthumous appearance in 1885 of the final edition of George Perkins Marsh's brilliant work, *The Earth As Modified by Human Action* (first published in 1864 under the title *Man and Nature*). Bob's suggested subject, though interdisciplinary in scope, was inherently geographic in the kind and scale of synthesis demanded; and the wide-ranging synthesis of human-environment relationships has been a long-established research forte of the School and other branches of the institution, especially the Center for Technology, Environment, and Development. Bob and I had several discussions of this kernel of an idea, but no immediate action was taken.

In the fall of 1984, William C. Clark visited the School to present the annual Wallace W. Atwood, Jr. lecture. An ecologist by training, Bill had extended his interests to the human alteration of the earth, and was at the time the leader of the "Sustainable Development of the Biosphere" project at the International Institute of Applied Systems Analysis,

Laxenburg, Austria. Bill and Bob had established research links and were committed to formalizing studies of human-induced changes in the biosphere as part of the several national and international initiatives directed toward the subject of the transformation of the earth that were under discussion at that time.

Bill's visit proved a catalyst for discussions on the conceptual rudiments of a symposium and volume; these discussions included Leonard Berry, past Director of the School and then Provost of Clark University. A loose framework was conceived. We agreed that another "brainstorming" session was needed immediately with an expanded set of experts to advise us. Bill agreed to coordinate a meeting at the American Academy of Arts and Sciences in October 1984. Among those also in attendance was John Richards, an environmental historian at Duke University, who joined the steering committee of the project. Discussion centered on elaborating the goals and the rationale for the pending project.

Following this meeting, the School began work on the project in earnest. Two graduate students, William B. Meyer and Andrew Schultz, were enlisted as the initial staff; planning documents were prepared and revised by the then five-member steering committee. This activity culminated in a meeting early in February 1985 at Clark in which a first-draft formal document detailing the effort was adopted. The School, with the assistance of IIASA, would raise the funds for a major interdisciplinary symposium to be held at Clark University in the fall of 1987 and for a subsequent volume or volumes on the subject of *The Earth As Transformed by Human Action*. The title, a paraphrase of Marsh, embodied the notion that the scale of changes on the earth was indeed of a radical kind, that humankind had so fundamentally altered the biosphere that for all practical purposes much of it had been genuinely transformed or was nearing that condition. The purpose of the "Earth Transformed," or "ET," effort would be: (1) to document these changes over the past 300 years at a global scale; (2) to contrast the global patterns of change to those experienced at the regional level; and (3) to explore the major human forces that have driven these changes. A preliminary proposal was developed, including lists of the principal biospheric variables to be examined. This document was circulated to about fifty experts from a variety of countries and disciplines for their advice.

On February 13, 1985, four of the steering committee met in Washington, D.C. to refine the preliminary proposal and to solicit funding to assist in the intensive planning and development stages to follow. James G. Speth, President of World Resources Institute (WRI), provided a one-time allocation to get us going, and discussion with Dr. Barry Bishop, Program Director of the National Geographic Society (NGS), proved most promising. The NGS ultimately provided development support for three consecutive years. Dr. Jessica Mathews, Vice-President of WRI, was added as the sixth member of the steering committee, and Dr. Yuri Badenkov, then Deputy Director of the Institute of Geography, U.S.S.R. Academy of Sciences, was made an ex officio member.

Armed with the responses to our preliminary proposal, the ET steering committee (Berry, Clark, Kates, Mathews, Richards, and Turner) met in September 1985 to undertake revisions. Potential authors were contacted for many sections of the study. An advisory committee of distinguished authorities was established to provide guidance on the structure and content of the symposium and its publications and on potential authors and participants. Headed by Gilbert White, and including Mohammed Kassas, Ester Boserup, Paul Crutzen, Francesco DiCastri, and Martin Holdgate, this group met with the steering committee at IIASA in Laxenburg, Austria in January 1986. Yuri Badenkov was represented in this meeting by L. Kairiukstis and V. Kaftanov.

The outcomes of this meeting were several. A developmental framework was explicitly adopted: the symposium and publications from it would emerge through a dynamic process, such that the symposium itself would serve as one stage in the revisions leading to the ultimate publications. The steering committee defined and orchestrated the papers for the symposium, identifying the major or critical changes in the biosphere, the range of regional case studies, and the major human driving forces of change, while adding background papers on long-term environmental and population change, the recent history of environmental awareness, and the role of social theory for understanding environmental transformation. The steering committee also developed a paragraph-length outline of the envisioned basic content of each paper. In some instances, discussions with the chosen authors subsequently led to changes in paper content and direction.

A second envisioned product was "a lay volume," to be a single authored, condensed work based on the professional volume but geared to a larger audience, including secondary and lower-division higher education. Much discussion ensued during the IIASA meetings on the pros and cons of various approaches to its development. It was decided that the author should be someone familiar with the subject, and preferably intimate with the development and content of the professional volume, and, of course, with experience in writing for the intended audience. Fortunately, the ET Program had

such an individual on its staff, William B. Meyer, who is preparing that volume as this one goes to press.

After the IIASA meeting, major efforts were devoted to commissioning authors for the papers and to fundraising with the assistance of the Office of University Resources, Clark University. That work need not be reviewed in detail here. It is sufficient to note that in addition to the initial development grants and assistance from the National Geographic Society (NGS), World Resources Institute, and the International Institute for Applied Systems Analysis (IIASA), other funding followed in this order: NGS provided additional developmental funds during 1986 and 1987; a National Science Foundation grant supported travel for the symposium participants; basic symposium funds were allocated by the United States Information Agency (with the assistance of the National Oceanic and Atmospheric Administration and the Office of the U.S. Geographer); and the Joyce Mertz-Gilmore Foundation contributed support funds for the development of the popular volume now in preparation. In addition, the Andrew W. Mellon Foundation conferred a very generous award to support work on the general theme of environmental transformation, portions of which have been used to prepare this volume and to support the larger, ongoing ET Program at Clark University, which now includes several international research projects, partial spinoffs of the ET symposium and volumes.

By the summer of 1986, a core ET staff of three was based at Clark through which all activities of the project passed. The steering committee met in December 1986 to finalize the structure of the project, and again several weeks before the symposium itself to confirm the sequence of paper presentations and to select a publisher – Cambridge University Press – from among several that had expressed interest in publishing the volumes.

The "Earth as Transformed by Human Action" symposium was held on the campus of Clark University, Worcester, Massachusetts from Sunday, October 25, through Friday, October 30, 1987 during Clark's centennial-year celebration. Paper sessions began on Sunday morning, following a welcome from Dr. Richard P. Traina, President of Clark University. The afternoon saw the official opening of the symposium, held at Mechanics Hall in downtown Worcester. There Dr. Robert McC. Adams, Secretary of the Smithsonian Institution, delivered an opening address, which was followed by a lecture on the meaning and scope of the symposium presented by William C. Clark.

What followed was a most intensive week-long symposium, averaging about four sessions each day. Full-length drafts of most of the papers had been delivered in advance and circulated to the participants; only abbreviated versions were presented orally at the symposium. Most of each paper session was devoted to discussion, first by commentators and then by the symposium participants in general. Working rooms were provided, adjacent to the main meeting room in Jefferson Hall, in which final adjustments to presentations were made and to which the steering committee retired to make modifications in the program as needed. On Thursday afternoon, the symposium participants visited the Harvard Forest in nearby Petersham, Massachusetts, one of the classic examples of environmental transformation and management. The symposium ended with a Friday afternoon session in which Martin Holdgate, then Chief Scientist of the United Kingdom Department of the Environment, and William L. Thomas, Jr., editor of the 1955 Princeton symposium's volume *Man's Role in Changing the Face of the Earth*, provided summary comments and insights. A closing banquet followed.

After catching our breaths, we members of the steering committee took action to finalize the content of the volume, allocate editorial responsibilities, and discuss publishers. Related sets of papers were assigned to members of the steering committee for conceptual editing, based on points raised in the discussion, and for return to the authors. Revised papers were reviewed by specialists selected by the individual section editors, many drawn from the ranks of the symposium participants. When necessary, additional modifications to the papers were requested. Once accepted by the section editor, individual papers were forwarded to Clark University, where they were edited again for basic conformity in the style and technical aspects of the volume. All figures were redrafted under the supervision of the Clark Cartography Laboratory to insure coordination and visual consistency. The authors and steering committee adhered surprisingly closely to this ideal development sequence. A late withdrawal and the absence of certain critical themes from the original outline required the committee to commission four papers post facto. They dealt with urbanization, the coastal zone, flora, and cultural–human ecology as a perspective on human-induced transformation. Leonard Berry had left Clark by this time and his new responsibilities prevented his full participation; William B. Meyer, associate coordinator of the project, took his place on the steering committee.

Structure of the Volume

The text is composed of an introduction and four principal sections. Each of the four begins with an introduction by the section editor(s). The introductory chapter of the volume establishes the intellectual ancestry of the subject of *The Earth As Transformed by Human Action* and briefly traces some of the basic views of the human–nature relationships of the past 300 years. It then summarizes the major findings of the volume as a whole, assessing the major trends in the transformation variables and the major patterns found in the regional case studies.

Section I, **Changes in Population and Society**, examines five major human forces of change over the past 300 years: population, technology, institutions/organization/culture, location of production and consumption, and urbanization. The stage for these five studies is set by the lead chapter of the section, which examines long-term, regional population changes, and the section is set in intellectual context by a concluding chapter on the history of beliefs regarding transformation,

which themselves may also be seen as real or potential human forces of environmental change.

Section II, **Transformations of the Global Environment**, consists of eighteen papers that address the principal objective of the volume, a stocktaking of the major transformations of the biosphere wrought by human action over the past 300 years. Again, the first chapter of the section establishes the context by assessing long-term changes in the biosphere of natural origin. The other papers attempt to trace the changes in the components of the biosphere, either a single variable or a set of variables. They are arranged in subsections: land, water, oceans and atmosphere, biota, and chemicals and radiation.

Section III, **Regional Studies of Transformations**, is comprised of twelve case studies that document the multiple-variable interactions of environmental change over a 300-year period for specific areas, serving as spatial and conceptual comparisons for the global papers. Two of the fourteen studies presented could not be published. Of the rest, one provides a long-term perspective; the others have been grouped according to socioeconomic and environmental criteria as tropical frontiers, highlands, plains, populous south, and populous north.

Section IV, **Understanding Transformations**, briefly examines a range of perspectives and theories that purport to explain human actions in regard to the biosphere. Three papers address such themes as they emanate from the realms of meaning, social relations, and human ecology.

In addition, the opening and closing public lectures of the symposium, revised for the volume, constitute the foreword and postscript of the text, respectively. The foreword by Robert McC. Adams sets the stage of the ET effort in terms of some of the contemporary social conditions of humankind and places the 300-year time frame in perspective. The postscript by Martin Holdgate speculates on the future of the transformation of the biosphere and discusses some of the implications of the volume for environmental policy.

Acknowledgments

Neither the ET symposium nor this volume could have been achieved without the assistance of a large number of individuals, programs, and agencies. Lest anyone be omitted below, the ET Program extends its deepest appreciation to all who were involved.

The 1987 symposium and this volume were originally inspired by the steering committee, especially by Robert W. Kates and William C. Clark, and admirably assisted by the advisory committee, particularly though Gilbert F. White, on whom we drew for guidance throughout this project. We were also generously assisted by the lead institutions – the Graduate School of Geography of Clark University, the International Institute of Applied Systems Analysis, the World Resources Institute, and the Institute of Geography, USSR Academy of Sciences – which facilitated our efforts in a number of critical ways. Yuri Badenkov was essential to the

Soviet involvement in the project. The time and effort of the members of both committees and each of these institutes are deeply appreciated.

Of course, a program and project of this kind requires considerable funding, and here we were assisted by Clark's then new office of University Resources. Eight public and private foundations and agencies, mentioned earlier, provided the funding for the ET symposium and volumes. We are indebted to each for its faith in this project. We are also deeply grateful for the advice and assistance given by Congressman Joseph Early of Worcester and by Dr. Charles H. W. Foster.

The Clark "family" and the various staffs of the contractual parties used by ET were not only efficient; they also served beyond the call of duty, staging the 1987 symposium almost without a hitch. At Clark, special recognition should be given to food services (DAKA), Physical Plant, Communications, and Audio/Visual Services, to the planning and hosting of Roma Josephs, and to the translations provided by Dr. Tatyana McAuley, Sam Dickinson, Joshua Searle, and Lisbet White. Jody DiLeo's service as coordinator of travel was untiring. The staff and students of the Graduate School of Geography responded to our needs more than we could have ever asked of them. We are indebted to Jean Heffernan, Maureen Hilyard, Madeleine Grinkis, and Dana Morton of that staff. John Thompson and Jimmy Levy served as project assistants during the planning stages. Anthony J. Bebbington coordinated all travel arrangements between Boston and Worcester and the services of the graduate and undegraduate students of Geography who met the ET participants at various airports, hosted a hospitality suite at the local hotel, and monitored the daily activities of the symposium. We thank Usama Abdelgadir, Peter Ahlfeld, Simon Batterbury, Brooks Bitterman, Jim Boisse, Elizabeth Brooks, John Courville, Tom Downing, Wei Du, Tom Estabrook, Joseph Guardiano, Andrew Goodale, Elaine Hartwick, Mark Johnson, Samantha Kaplan, Sean King, Pam Lee, Nina Littinger, David Mazambani, Jeffrey Mitchell, Steve Sadlier, Jennifer Santer, David Sauri, Camilla Schamaun, Nocembo Simelane, Amadou Thiam, John Thompson, Thomas Whitmore, Cara Williams, and Fang Xu. A special thank you to Michael Zimmer and Jim Lyons for providing entertainment at the closing banquet.

Of course, we are indebted to the cooperation of all the symposium participants and paper authors who accepted in good spirits the challenges, cajoling, and editing of the steering committee. Clark's Word Processing Office provided valuable assistance. Anne Gibson, Head of the Cartography Laboratory, and Montine Jordan deserve special recognition for their efforts in coordinating the volume's graphic design and managing that endeavor so as to relieve an overburdened ET staff.

The ET core staff – William B. Meyer and Linda Finan – at Clark University has always functioned as if were much larger than it is; without the scale and quality of their efforts the success of the symposium and the production of this volume would not have been possible. Linda joined the staff as Administrative Assistant just in time to have the entire weight of the symposium thrust upon her. Throughout, she rose resourcefully to a wide range of unusual and unexpected challenges. The entire project is deeply indebted to Bill Meyer, Associate Coordinator of the ET Program, who worked behind the scenes to assist a harried Program Coordinator throughout the symposium and the volume's production: No one has been more important to the actual production of this volume than has he.

B. L. TURNER II

The Earth As Transformed by Human Action

SYMPOSIUM AND VOLUME PARTICIPANTS

STEERING COMMITTEE

Yuri P. Badenkov*
USSR Academy of Science
Robert W. Kates*
Brown University
John F. Richards*
Duke University

Leonard Berry*
Florida Atlantic University
Jessica Mathews
World Resources Institute
B. L. Turner II*
Clark University

William C. Clark*
IIASA; Harvard University
William B. Meyer*
Clark University

ADVISORY COMMITTEE

Ester Boserup*
Switzerland
Martin Holdgate*
Department of the Environment, U.K.

Paul Crutzen*
Max Planck Institute, FRG
Mohammed Kassas
Cairo University, Egypt

Francesco DiCastri*
Centre Louis Emberger, France
Gilbert F. White*
University of Colorado, Boulder

VOLUME AUTHORS

A. A. Afolayan, *University of Ibadan, Nigeria*
E. B. Alayev, *Institute of Geography, USSR Academy of Science*
O. O. Areola, *University of Ibadon, Nigeria*
J. O. Ayoade, *University of Ibadan, Nigeria*
Robert Ayres*, *Carnegie-Mellon University*
Roger Barry, *University of Colorado, Boulder*
Patrick Bartlein, *University of Oregon*
John Bennett*, *Washington University*
A. K. Borunov, *Institute of Geography, USSR Academy of Science*
Harold Brookfield*, *The Australian National University*
Halina Brown*, *Clark University*
Karl Butzer*, *University of Texas, Austin*
Roy Carpenter, *University of Washington*
Michael Chisholm*, *University of Cambridge, U.K.*
Kenneth Dahlberg*, *Western Michigan University*
Paul Demeny*, *The Population Council*
William Dickens*, *Thames Water Authority; Essex Water Authority, U.K.*

Ian Douglas*, *University of Manchester, U.K.*
Merril Eisenbud*, *New York University Medical Center*
Jacque Emel*, *Clark University*
Exequiel Ezcurra*, *Universidad Nacional Autonoma de Mexico*
Thomas Gottschang*, *College of The Holy Cross*
Thomas Graedel*, *Bell Laboratories*
Torsten Hagerstrand*, *University of Lund, Sweden*
Daniel Headrick*, *Roosevelt University*
Ray Hilborn*, *University of Washington*
Richard Houghton*, *Woods Hole Research Center*
Janja Djukic Husar, *Washington University*
Rudolf Husar*, *Washington University*
Jill Jäger, *FRG*
Timothy Jickells*, *University of East Anglia, U.K.*
Douglas L. Johnson*, *Clark University*
Nina Karavaeva*, *Institute of Geography, USSR Academy of Science*
Roger Kasperson*, *Clark University*
Low Kwai-Sim, *Universiti Malaya*

Laurence Lewis*, *Clark University*
Francis Jana Lian, *Universiti Brunei Darussalam*
Peter Liss, *University of East Anglia, U.K.*
Ulrik Lohm, *University of Linköping, Sweden*
Thomas Lovejoy, *World Wildlife Fund, U.S.; Smithsonian Institution*
David Lowenthal*, *University of London, U.K.*
Mark I. L'vovich, *Institute of Water Problems, USSR Academy of Science*
Anatoly Mandych*, *Institute of Geography, USSR Academy of Science*
Carolyn Merchant*, *University of California, Berkeley*
Paul Messerli, *Universität Bern, Switzerland*
D. S. Orlov, *Institute of Geography, USSR Academy of Science*
Richard Perritt*, *Clark University*
Robert Peters*, *World Wildlife Fund, U.S.*
Christian Pfister*, *Universität Bern, Switzerland*
Lesley Potter*, *University of Adelaide, Australia*
Ghillean Prance, *Royal Botanic Gardens, U.K.*
Susan Raymond*, *Clark University*
William Riebsame*, *University of Colorado, Boulder*
Peter Rogers*, *Harvard University*
Boris Rozanov, *Moscow State University, USSR*
Robert Sack*, *University of Wisconsin, Madison*
Eneas Salati*, *Fundacao Salim Farah Maluf, Brazil*
Harry Schwarz*, *Clark University*
David Skole*, *University of New Hampshire*
Vaclav Smil*, *University of Manitoba, Canada*
Viktor Targulian*, *Institute of Geography, USSR Academy of Science*
Joel Tarr, *Carnegie-Mellon University*
John Thompson*, *Clark University*
Reuben Udo*, *University of Ibadan, Nigeria*
G. Voropaev*, *Institute of Water Problems, USSR Academy of Science*
H. J. Walker, *Louisiana State University*

Thompson Webb III*, *Brown University*
Thomas Whitmore*, *Clark University*
Cara Williams*, *Clark University*
Michael Williams*, *University of Oxford, U.K.*
Peiyuan Zhang*, *Academia Sinica, People's Republic of China*
Dakang Zuo*, *Academia Sinica, People's Republic of China*

OTHER SYMPOSIUM PARTICIPANTS

Ronald Abler*, *National Science Foundation; Pennsylvania State University*
Robert McC. Adams*, *Smithsonian Institution*
William Denevan*, *University of Wisconsin, Madison*
Michael Farrell*, *Oak Ridge National Laboratories*
Andrew Friedland*, *Dartmouth College*
Abe Goldman*, *International Institute of Tropical Agriculture, Nigeria*
Arturo Gomez-Pompa*, *MEXUS, University of California, Riverside*
Alan Grainger*, *Resources for the Future; University of Salford, U.K.*
James Hagen*, *Duke University*
Christoph Hohenemser*, *Clark University*
C. S. Holling*, *University of British Columbia, Canada*
Viktor Kovda*, *Moscow State University, USSR*
William McNeill*, *University of Chicago*
J. M. Melillo*, *NSF*
Robert Mitchell*, *Clark University*
Timothy O'Riordan*, *University of East Anglia, U.K.*
Samuel Ratick*, *Clark University*
Gaston Schaber*, *International Institute for Studies in Technology Environment, Nature and Development, Luxembourg*
Allen Solomon*, *IIASA, Austria*
Michael Steinitz*, *Clark University*
William Thomas*, *California State University at Hayward*
Michael Watts*, *University of California, Berkeley*

*Asterisk denotes individuals who attended the ET symposium.

1

The Great Transformation

ROBERT W. KATES   B. L. TURNER II   WILLIAM C. CLARK

The collection of phenomena must precede the analysis of them, and every new fact, illustrative of the action and reaction between humanity and the material world around it, is another step toward the determination of the great question, whether man is of nature or above her.   George Perkins Marsh, 1864 [1965: 465]

We live in a special period in history. Sometime between June 1986 and June 1987, the human population of the earth reached 5 billion. It took almost all of human history for the number of our species to reach 1 billion, about 175 years ago. Since then, each new billion has been gained at rapidly decreasing time intervals – 115 years, 35 years, 15 years, and 11–12 years. Even if growth rates decline as predicted, the earth's population will double to 10 billion by A.D. 2050.

It appears inevitable that global population will continue to increase rapidly into and through the next century and that the demands upon nature will reach scales never before imagined. Humanity faces fundamental questions regarding the future of the biosphere and the capacity of both nature and society to sustain life. To identify the character and dimensions of the sustainable development of the earth requires choices informed by the best insight that science and the humanities can provide.

The ability of our species to change landscapes or physical environments at the local and regional scales is ancient (Darby 1956; Sauer 1956; Meiggs 1982). The use of fire by hunter-gatherers altered flora and fauna; incipient cultivators spread domesticates and cut forests; early civilizations transformed deserts through irrigation. Some early activities may have led to wide and lasting transformations, as in the possible role of Pleistocene hunters in the eradication of megafauna in the Western Hemisphere (Martin and Klein 1984). Others produced major alterations subsequently erased by natural recovery, as in the afforestation of the central Maya lowlands after its abandonment between A.D. 800–1000 (chap. 2).

The human role in changing the face of the earth has grown continually. During the past 300 years, on which we focus here, the scales, rates, and kinds of environmental change have been fundamentally altered as humanity has passed through an era of rapid population growth and the development of a fossil-fuel-based industrial society. The results are unprecedented. For example:

1. The net loss of the world's forests due to human activity since preagricultural times is on the order of 8 million km^2, an area about the size of the continental United States. Of this amount, more than three-quarters has been cleared since 1680.
2. The human contribution to the world's sulfur budget is now about 150 million tons per year – about the equivalent of the natural flux of sulfur. This contribution was practically negligible at the beginning of the twentieth century.
3. The annual human withdrawal of water from natural circulation is now about 3,600 km^3 – an amount exceeding the volume of Lake Huron. In 1680, annual withdrawal was less than 100 km^3.

To transform is to effect fundamental change in appearance or nature. In our judgment, albeit a subjective one, the biosphere has accumulated, or is on its way to accumulating, such a magnitude and variety of changes that it may be said to have been transformed. Most of the change of the past 300 years has been at the hands of humankind, intentionally or otherwise. Our ever-growing role in this continuing metamorphosis has itself essentially changed. Transformation has escalated through time, and in some instances the scales of change have shifted from the locale and region to the earth as a whole. Whereas humankind once acted primarily upon the visible "faces" or "states" of the earth, such as forest cover, we are now also altering the fundamental flows of chemicals and energy that sustain life on the only inhabited planet we know.

Professionals and much of the public recognize the protean character of this transformation and the critical need for understanding it. Numerous studies have been undertaken of specific types of transformations and of the current global condition of the biosphere. A major new scientific effort, the International Geosphere-Biosphere Programme, has recently been launched to study the basic processes underlying global environmental change per se (IGBP 1988). But since the publication, more than 30 years ago, of *Man's Role in Changing the Face of the Earth* (Thomas 1956), no effort has been made to document and understand the interaction of human and environmental systems from a long-term, global perspective.

This volume reports the early results of one such effort. It is based on the proposition that the capability now exists: (1) to monitor human transformations of the biosphere at a global scale; (2) to estimate their trajectories over the past several centuries with some degree of confidence; (3) to identify some of the broad, direct processes underlying them; and (4) to understand the interactions of these processes at the regional scale. In formulating the study we have drawn upon three significant, indeed profound, developments of science – developments that have gained prominence since the *Man's Role* effort: (1) new ways to conceptualize the unity of the biosphere, symbolized by the wide currency of the term itself; (2) new ways and collective efforts to acquire data and analyze their detail and complexity; and (3) reassessment of some of the avenues that link social behavior with environmental transformations.

We draw upon these advances to provide the rudiments of a new stocktaking of the transformed earth. These concepts, abilities, and assessments, however, are part of a deeper, more fundamental search for the meaning of earth transformation, an ancient search that is central to our endeavors: What is and ought to be the relationship of humans to the earth?

Nature and Humanity

The nature–human relationship has been the subject of discourse since antiquity, generating lively, even heated, debate within different countries and different intellectual currents. It is interesting, however, that three broad perspectives, already elaborated in premodern culture have continued to dominate modern discourse (e.g., Glacken 1967: vii–viii). These are humanity (society) in harmony with nature, humanity as determined by nature, and humanity as modifier of nature.[1]

The perspective of humanity in harmony with nature can be discerned in arcadian, romantic, and biocentric/ecocentric views of the eighteenth, nineteenth, and twentieth centuries, respectively (e.g., Worster 1977; O'Riordan 1981; also Weiner 1988). At least two versions exist: one prescriptive (humankind ought to act in harmony with nature) and one descriptive (human activities are necessarily in harmony with nature), although elements of both can often be found within the same work, argument, or school of thought. This perspective has an ancient history: flourishing as physico-theology in the West (e.g., Glacken 1967: chaps. 8 and 11) and in the philosophy of Taoism in the East (Needham 1951); implicit in almost spiritualized descriptions of the environment (Ritter 1822–59; Reclus 1869); explicit in the early twentieth century, antimodernist, pastoralist views of Ivan Borodin and others in Russia (Weiner 1988: 12) and in Teilhard's (1958; 1959) noösphere; and revived in cybernetic and ecosystemic views of biospheric self-regulation, such as the Gaia hypothesis (Lovelock 1979; Lovelock 1988) and in evolutionary discussions on the inability of humanity to divorce itself from the "nature" in which it emerged (e.g., Iltis 1973).[2] The key themes are the holistic unity of nature and society, peaceful (or at least ecologically wise) coexistence with nature, and

preservation. Of the three, this perspective has most often addressed ethical, moral, and even spiritual issues.

Humanity as determined by nature is a view whose roots extend at least as far back as Hippocrates' *Airs, Waters, and Places* (Glacken 1967: 82–88). During the nineteenth century it found expression in climatic and environmental (geographical) determinism and was used both to justify the global aspirations of imperial societies and to oppose colonial expansion into novel environments. It lingered within geography until the 1940s (e.g., Semple 1911; Huntington 1945) and occasionally resurfaces in various forms in other disciplines (e.g., Meggers 1954). The key themes are the role of nature in shaping social (and even individual) characteristics, from livelihood to creativity, and empirical-theoretical approaches to the study of these influences.

The view of humanity as modifier of nature has assumed no less diverse forms than the other perspectives. It too can be identified in premodern cultures, some of which held that even thought can directly affect the surrounding world (Douglas 1966). The origins of such a prescription in Western thought have been traced to the book of Genesis and a Christian doctrine in which humans are called upon to subdue the earth (White 1967). Such a sense of mission underlay both some European justifications of colonial expansion and some twentieth-century humanistic and technocratic visions, even if modern uses rarely draw upon the biblical message. Vernadsky (1929; 1945) envisioned humankind as having the potential through science and technology to control even the biogeochemical cycles, albeit within the limits set by the biosphere; his noösphere – a future "state of equilibrium between mankind and biota, created by the rational action of man" (Annenkov 1988: 77) – was both "'human creating' and 'created by humans'" (Serafin 1987: 5). Ecosystemic views emphasizing the transforming role of humankind can be seen as variants of these positions. The "utilitarian" view in Russia and the U.S.S.R. called for the sustainable or wise use of the earth, in recognition of humankind's powerful tendencies to abuse it, whereas the "conservationist's" position in the same country was more extreme, emphasizing civilization's almost inevitable disruption of "nature's balance" to the point of the destruction of humankind (Weiner 1988: 230; Yanshin 1988).[3] The so-called Cassandra view (Ehrlich and Holdren 1988) in the West predicts this same destruction, unless action is immediately taken. In general, the "modification" perspective separates society from nature more than do the other two; humans are seen as having the power, and in some versions the right or even the obligation, to mold nature.[4,5]

As far as these three themes remain perspectives on the nature–society relation, they do not exclude one another. Indeed, most arguments contain elements from more than one. Recognition of human power to degrade the earth, for example, is readily used to underpin the prescription for existence in harmony with natural processes. Current analytical approaches acknowledge that the relationship is always one of mutual determination and interaction and that the degree of dominance is context-specific (e.g., Bennett 1976: chap. 10; Ellen 1982). For some, this has led to the use of a "selective eclectic" approach to nature–society theory that makes no explicit claim about the overarching or macrotheory of the relationships (e.g., Kates 1988). Others rely on a variety of explicitly elaborated positions, ranging from ecosystemics (e.g., Bennett 1976) to realism (Sayer 1979) and Marxism (Smith 1984; Strenz et al. 1988).

The various lineages and perspectives have converged, though incompletely, on an emerging, widely shared ethic: to do minimal harm to the biosphere.[6] The origins and justifications of this ethic remain diverse – in an ontology of the unity of nature (e.g., Vernadsky 1929 and 1945; Teilhard 1958; Lovelock 1979), in a morality that demands human stewardship (e.g., Timonov 1922; Black 1970), or in a pragmatism that acknowledges our dependence on nature's life-support systems (e.g., Clark and Munn 1986). Each of these and their many variants implies a different sense of the sustainable development of the biosphere, both in amount and kind. Here moral theory can call on science to illuminate, although surely not settle, these differences. How greatly have we transformed the earth? How do these transformations change our relationship with nature? How do these transformations and changes affect human life?

Previous Stocktakings

Our effort to provide insights into these questions is the third attempt at a long-term, global stocktaking and follows many more limited efforts. Our two precursors are *Man and Nature; or Physical Geography as Modified by Human Action* by George Perkins Marsh, and *Man's Role in Changing the Face of the Earth*, edited by William L. Thomas, Jr.

The Earth Modified

Man and Nature, first published in 1864, was received enthusiastically by academic and lay audiences in North America and Europe. It subsequently has become a classic among works challenging the notion of an inexhaustible earth. A scholar and diplomat, Marsh drew upon his wide experiences, from his Vermont boyhood to his Mediterranean travels, to show how humankind has modified nature. His goal was:

to indicate the character and, approximately, the extent of the changes produced by human action in the physical conditions of the globe we inhabit; to point out the dangers of imprudence and the necessity of caution in all operations which, on a large scale, interfere with the spontaneous arrangements of the organic or the inorganic world; to suggest the possibility and the importance of the restoration of disturbed harmonies and the material improvement of waste and exhausted regions; and, incidentally, to illustrate the doctrine, that man is, in both kind and degree, a power of a higher order than any of the other forms of animated life... (Marsh 1965: 3).

Marsh straddled two of the great environmental philosophies of his time – the Arcadian/Romantic notion of a harmonious nature and the Victorian notion of man above nature – as indicated by the initial title of his book, "Man the Disturber of Nature's Harmonies" (Lowenthal 1965: xxiii). Even so, he firmly believed that humanity ought to transform and subdue the earth. His survey was a prodigiously learned discussion of the modifications of the flora and fauna and of

the destruction wrought on forests, waters, soils, and sands. While the state of knowledge at the time precluded any systematic assessment of the magnitudes of impact, he drew examples from around the world and described them vividly. Marsh also touched upon such features as population, land use, and climate. He ended with an assessment of some of the major transformations projected for his time (a sea-level Panama Canal, the drainage of the Zuider Zee, artificial rainmaking, and the prevention or mitigation of earthquakes), speculating on their possible environmental consequences.

Dubos (1972: 171) calls Marsh "the first American prophet of ecology." The importance of *Man and Nature* lies less in the individual impacts that it catalogued (almost all of which had long been recognized) than in a grouping and wide-ranging synthesis that emphasized their interrelations and traced the innumerable distant effects of human action. The work was cited by many early conservationists, especially foresters (Lowenthal 1965; Thomas 1956), and influenced views of nature–society relationships well beyond Marsh's native shores (e.g., in the Soviet Union [see Weiner 1988: 8, 256] and in New Zealand [see Wynn 1979]). This influence, however, was neither unadulterated nor immediate. Marsh stressed the breadth and gravity of the unintentional human impacts, and thus the need to understand the complex interactions of natural processes prior to human intervention; in contrast, early citations tended only to draw out individual strands from Marsh's finely woven fabric for use in narrowly technical discussions. Subsequent, briefer surveys in the same vein (Rolleston 1879; Voeikov 1901) met much the same fate. Conservationists in the West and utilitarians in the Soviet Union in particular focused more on management strategies aimed at maximizing or sustaining the yields of particular resources for human use than on ecological complexities (e.g., Worster 1977; Weiner 1988). Marsh also saw the transformation of the environment, if properly done, as almost entirely desirable (as opposed to Ivan Timonov's view that society was destroying nature [Weiner 1988: 79]) – a message that many conservationists chose to ignore (James and Martin 1981). The full impact of Marsh's work in America awaited later events: the shock of the Dust Bowl, the emergence of a science of ecology, and the creation of various professional forums through which ideas could be systematically transmitted (James and Martin 1981). Indeed, only since the middle part of this century has Marsh's work again been widely acknowledged in the Western world, perhaps as the ecological movement has sought to substantiate its antecedents (Gade 1983).

The Earth Changed

In 1955, some 90 years after Marsh's effort, a second assessment was undertaken by an international symposium held in Princeton under the auspices of the Wenner-Gren Foundation for Anthropological Research. The results were published in the following year under the title *Man's Role in Changing the Face of the Earth*. The project was initiated by the Foundation, with William L. Thomas, Jr. as principal organizer and with the cooperation of Carl O. Sauer (symposium chair), Marston Bates, and Lewis Mumford. Such guidance gave a strong historical and anthropological tinge to an interdisciplinary exploration of "what had happened and is happening to the earth under man's impress" (Thomas 1956: xxxviii). Yet the orientations of *Man's Role* are more difficult to define than those of *Man and Nature* because the later work does not represent the views of a single individual. Some have noted the absence from its pages of a unifying concept of nature–society relations (Williams 1987). It was, moreover, less an orchestrated, empirical investigation of the major changes than a collection of the research and reflections of individual scholars, brilliant as many of them were.

In identifying the human forces that had changed the states or faces of the biosphere, *Man's Role* drew upon a much broader store of knowledge than did its predecessor, although systematic documentation remained sparse. Papers dealt at length or in passing with various components of the biosphere: population, land use, water management, climate, marine and terrestrial biota, forests, carbon and other elements, earth materials, water quality, and nuclear radiation. Several aspects of society responsible for changes in these were discussed directly or indirectly, especially technology, urbanization, and trade.

The impact of *Man's Role* is difficult to assess. The volume did not directly herald a new generation of environmental research, even among scholars within the two main disciplines involved, anthropology and geography. *Man's Role* seems at least to have anticipated the ecological movement of the 1960s, although direct links between the two have not been demonstrated. Its dispassionate, academic approach was certainly foreign to the style of that movement, a portion of which Sauer apparently labeled the "ecological binge" (Leighly 1987). Rather, *Man's Role* appears to have exerted a much more subtle, and perhaps more lasting, influence as a reflective, broad-ranging, and multidimensional work that informed and sometimes inspired several generations of scholars in the natural sciences, social sciences, and humanities.

Subsequent Efforts

Global environmental assessments have multiplied in type and number since the 1960s, with a particular growth in perspectives from the natural sciences and from agencies and institutions committed to positions of advocacy. Table 1-1 lists some seventeen works published in English since 1956 that meet the following criteria: (1) an emphasis on human-induced change in biosphere, earth, environment, or nature; (2) a global-scale perspective; (3) concern with multiple sectors, areas, states, or flows; and, (4) an assessment, inventory, or stocktaking of change.

Compared to *Man and Nature* and *Man's Role*, these works pay little attention to the history of modification, change, or transformation. They do, however, draw upon an increased understanding both of the quantitative aspects of human-induced transformation and of the processes responsible for it. At the time of the Princeton symposium in 1955, planning was underway for the International Geophysical Year (IGY) – the beginning of today's worldwide scientific efforts to identify and monitor the key global processes and to measure

Table 1-1 *Global Studies of Human-Induced Environmental Transformation, 1957–1987*

1969
Farvar, M. T. and J. P. Milton, eds. *The Careless Technology: Ecology and International Development*. London: Stacey.

1970
Study of Critical Environmental Problems. *Man's Impact on the Global Biosphere*. Cambridge: Massachusetts Institute of Technology. (Companion volumes: W. H. Matthews, W. W. Kellogg, and G. D. Robinson (eds.), 1971, *Man's Impact on the Climate* and *Man's Impact on Terrestrial and Oceanic Ecosystems*.)

1971
Detwyler, T. R., ed. *Man's Impact on Environment*. New York: McGraw-Hill.

1971
Singer, F., ed. *Global Effects of Environmental Pollution*. New York: Springer Verlag.

1972
Meadows, D. H., D. L. Meadows, J. Randers, and W. Behrens. *The Limits to Growth*. New York: Universe Books.

1980
United States Council on Environmental Quality and Department of State. *The Global 2000 Report to the President of the United States: Entering the 21st Century*. Washington, D.C.: Government Printing Office.

1982
Goody, R. M. *Global Change: Impacts Upon Habitability. A Scientific Basis for Assessment*. Pasadena: California Institute of Technology.

1982
Holdgate, M. W., M. Kassas, and G. F. White, eds. *The World Environment 1972–1982: A Report by the United Nations Environment Programme*. Dun Laoghaire, Ireland: Tycooly International.

1984 and subsequent years
Brown, L. et al. *State of the World: A Worldwatch Institute Report on Progress Toward A Sustainable Society*. London: W. W. Norton.

1984
Malone, T. F. and J. G. Roederer, eds. *Global Change*. Cambridge: Cambridge University Press.

1984
Myers, N., ed. *GAIA: An Atlas of Planet Management*. New York: Anchor Press.

1984
Simon, J. and H. Kahn, eds. *The Resourceful Earth: A Response to Global 2000*. New York: Basil Blackwell.

1985
Repetto, R., ed. *The Global Possible: Resources, Development, and the New Century*. New Haven: Yale University Press. (companion volume: *World Enough and Time*, 1986.)

1985
Southwick, A. *Global Ecology*. Sunderland: Sinauer Associates.

1985
Clark, W. and R. Munn, eds. *Sustainable Development of the Biosphere*. Cambridge: Cambridge University Press.

1986 and subsequent years
World Resources Institute & International Institute for Environment and Development. *World Resources 1986*. New York: Basic Books.

1987
World Commission on Environment and Development. *Our Common Future*. Oxford: Oxford University Press.

Collections of reports with environmental and global perspectives of note:

S.C.O.P.E. Reports. Chichester: John Wiley. *State of the Environment Reports*. U.N.E.P. *Natural Resources and the Environment Series*.

systematically the effects of human activity. Thirty years later, the results of the IGY and its successors in the natural sciences have laid the foundations for a vastly more ambitious and comprehensive International Geosphere-Biosphere Program, now in its early stages. Advances in basic data have also occurred in environmental history, geography, ecology, and anthropology.

The development of new technologies of data gathering and analysis has been instrumental in making available a quantity and quality of information about the biosphere once unimaginable. New integrative systems of data storage, display, and analysis facilitate the examination of multiple variables in various data arrays. Developments of the past 30 years include growth in the international system for the gathering and dissemination of contemporary data on many aspects of the human system relevant to its interactions with the environment; increasing computerization of such data bases; emergence of geographic information systems (GIS) and their use in dynamic modeling of the environment; and an explosion of satellite imagery that allows monitoring of the global environment on a continuing basis. New means of recovering information on past environmental changes have also been developed, including atmospheric samples trapped in ice bubbles, vegetation change recorded in pollen cores, and a variety of other methods described in the relevant chapters of this volume. Our compilation benefits from all of these developments. It is clear, however, both that the record of change is still punctuated by large gaps and that the stock of existing information nonetheless often exceeds the capacity of specialists to analyze it and of generalists to synthesize it.

The information garnered by recent technological achievements provides useful answers only when the right questions are asked, and it is theory and related conceptual frameworks that direct our interrogation. Several relevant bodies of thought have been greatly amplified or altered since the 1955 stocktaking. In the natural sciences, simple equilibrium models and theories have been replaced by more sophisticated views of dynamic systems and multiple or punctuated states (e.g., Gould 1984; Lorenz, 1984; Holling 1986; McElroy 1986). The identification and measurement of energy fluxes and biogeochemical flows now complements the venerable emphasis on landscape change (e.g., Bolin and Cook 1983). In the human sciences, a better understanding has emerged of the relationships among the various spatial and temporal scales of social activities and environmental processes (e.g., Clark 1987), along with a useful debate on the nature of "sustainable development" (WCED 1987; cf. B. Brown et al. 1987). Growing interest in the large- and long-scale regularities of human history is evident in studies of world systems, center-periphery patterns, and long waves of economic and technological change (Wallerstein 1974; McNeill 1976; Rostow 1978; Braudel 1981–4; Ausubel and Sladovich 1989).

Above all, however, there is a growing recognition of the global and interactive character of nature–society relationships and of the need to develop frameworks that merge the roles of human agency, social relations, and adaptation in the transformation of the earth (e.g., Bennett 1976; Sayer 1979; Butzer 1982; Clark 1989). At present, no general theories of

societies' behaviors in transforming the biosphere dominate; no accepted "paradigm" rules. Perhaps more importantly, most social theories seem to search for explanations based on those qualities that make us distinct from other species. Efforts to tackle issues of human agency and social relations in the transformation of the biosphere have therefore been leading to increasingly deeper investigations that strive to look beyond the direct interactions of nature and humanity (e.g., chaps. 40–42, this volume).

The Earth Transformed

Planning for the present volume – a third global inventory of the long-term changes wrought by humanity on the biosphere – began in 1984. Out of the initiative of the Graduate School of Geography, Clark University and the International Institute for Applied Systems Analysis, and later, the World Resources Institute and the Institute of Geography, USSR Academy of Sciences, an international and interdisciplinary project evolved.[7] Under the title *The Earth as Transformed by Human Action*, this project has attempted to document the major transformations in the faces and flows of the biosphere since the late seventeenth century on a global scale, to address some of the immediate social causes of these changes, and to examine their interplay through regional case studies. The objective was not to provide the final word on these subjects. Rather, it was to catalyze and capture synthetic thinking on the human transformation of the earth at a time when both concern for and understanding of global environmental change are rapidly expanding. In the remainder of this introductory chapter, we attempt to sketch some of the major patterns of transformation that emerge through the detailed topical chapters that follow.

Transformations of the Global Environment

The biosphere – that thin, life-supporting layer of planet Earth – is a complex system of life forms, habitats, and fluxes. Marsh and the Princeton symposium reported primarily on the so-called faces of the earth – those aspects of the biosphere that largely are fixed in place or can be effectively examined in place. These are the "landscapes" of classical geography. Since the time of the Princeton symposium, scholarship has complemented this early focus on faces with increasing attention to the "flows" of materials and energy that are in constant movement or flux through the biosphere. The "*Earth Transformed*" inventory combined the face and flow perspectives to address the components of the biosphere summarized in Table 1-2. One component, human population, is both a biological component of the biosphere and a fundamental human driving force of change in most of the other components. Throughout this volume, it is treated in both contexts.

Patterns of Global Transformation

Humankind has altered or transformed virtually every element of the biosphere. Quantifying the history of these transformations is difficult because of data and projection (retrojection) problems, and our attempts to supply such es-

Table 1-2 *Nineteen Components of the Biosphere*

Land	**Biota**
Land transformation	Terrestrial fauna
Forests	Marine biota
Soils	Flora
Sediment	Human population
Water	**Chemicals and Radiation**
Water management	Carbon
Water quality and flows	Sulfur
Coastal environment	Nitrogen and phosphorus
	Trace pollutants
Oceans and Atmosphere	Ionizing radiations
Atmospheric trace constituents	
Marine environment	
Climate	

timates must be weighed cautiously. This caveat made, insights into the pattern of transformation can be gained by comparing the magnitudes and trajectories of change for various components of the biosphere.

Magnitudes   The overall magnitude of the human impact on the biosphere has been considerable, though varying by the component examined. Inasmuch as this subject has garnered considerable attention in the literature, it is only briefly reviewed based upon the evidence marshaled within the subsequent chapters of this book.

The lands of the earth bear the most visible, if not necessarily the most profound, imprints of humankind's actions: in an area the size of France submerged by artificial reservoirs; in the 15% of all plant species now estimated to be threatened with extinction; in the estimated threefold increase in sediment load in typical large rivers and eightfold increase in small rivers within regions of major human activity; and in the net 8 million km^2 cleared of forest during the Holocene, much of it added to the 15 million km^2 that is now used for cropland.

While changes in the biogeochemical flows that sustain the biosphere may not be visible, the impacts of these changes can be dramatic, even life-threatening, as in the depletion by industrial and other gases of the protective ozone shield in the atmosphere. These impacts also extend to much less obvious components. For example, averaged annually across the earth, the human release of energy is only 1/10,000 of the solar radiation received at the surface, but in the major urban-industrial areas of North America and Europe, the human releases during the winter months are comparable to the natural input. High-temperature industrial emissions alone now multiply the annual natural releases of arsenic by 3, of cadmium by 7, of mercury by 10, and of lead by 25. Even substantial flows of substances not present in nature, such as synthetic organic chemicals, have been created by human action.

The significance of change is not, of course, necessarily measured by its gross magnitude. As noted already, the annual human contribution to the global sulfur cycle is now approx-

mately equal to the natural, while to the carbon cycle, on the other hand, it is still less than 10% of even the natural flows directly involved in photosynthesis and respiration. Yet the human impact on the atmosphere's carbon content has been magnified beyond this level in an approximate doubling of methane concentrations since the mid-eighteenth century and a 20% increase in CO_2 levels over the preindustrial background. Because of the key roles that these gases play, even at their small concentrations, in regulating the global climate, increases that may seem modest when compared in percentage terms with the changes wrought on other components may still be of great importance in the secondary impacts that they produce.

Trajectories   The studies reported elsewhere in this volume have allowed us to make quantitative comparisons of the impact of human activity on ten component indicators of the biosphere listed in Table 1-3 and illustrated in Fig. 1.1 and 1.2. For each component, we defined total net change clearly induced by humans in its global value to be 0% for 10,000 years ago, and to be 100% for 1985.[8] We then estimated dates by which each component had reached successive quartiles (i.e., 25%, 50%, and 75%) of its 1985 total change (Figs. 1.1; Table 1-3a). Finally, to help put the results of this global stocktaking in perspective relative to its predecessors, we calculated the percent of each component's present transformation that had been reached at approximately the times of the Marsh and Princeton studies. Results are summarized in Table 1-3b.

Only four of the components for which we have quantitative estimates (human population growth, forest clearing, carbon, and extinction of terrestrial vertebrates) had reached the first quartile of change by Marsh's time (Table 1-3; Figs. 1.1 and 1.2). The spread and growth of population acting as a major driving force created major land use changes that substantially reduced the world's forests and vertebrates – the latter through habitat destruction, overkill, and domestication. In contrast, the papers in *Man's Role* were undertaken at a time by which half the components had reached or were reaching their second quartile of change, and two had reached their third quartile. It follows that about half of the components in Table 1-3 have changed more in the single generation since the period of the Princeton symposium than in all of human history before 1950.

These data, though approximate, illustrate the cumulative nature of the human transformation of the biosphere. Simultaneously, however, they emphasize the dramatic changes in the rate and locus of transformation associated with the great twentieth-century increase in the human population and its development of the so-called modern world of science, technology, and mass consumption. Forest depletion and (probably) vertebrate extinctions are the only two components for which we have numerical estimates to have attained their first quartile of human-induced global change during the eighteenth century. Human population and emission of carbon to the atmosphere reach their first quartile of change in the nineteenth century. For all other components, even the first quartile of change is a twentieth-century phenomenon.

Table 1-3 *Selected Forms of Human-Induced Transformation of Environmental Components: Chronologies of Change*

A. Quartiles of change from 10,000 B.C. to mid-1980s

	Dates of quartiles[1]		
Form of transformation	25%	50%	75%
Deforested area	1700	1850	1915
Terrestrial vertebrate diversity[2]	1790	1880	1910
Water withdrawals[3]	1925	1955	1975
Population size	1850	1950	1970
Carbon releases[4]	1815	1920	1960
Sulfur releases[5]	1940	1960	1970
Phosphorus releases[6]	1955	1975	1980
Nitrogen releases[4]	1970	1975	1980
Lead releases[4]	1920	1950	1965
Carbon tetrachloride production[4]	1950	1960	1970

B. Percent of change by the time of Marsh and the Princeton symposium

	% Change	
Form of transformation	1860	1950
Deforested area	50	90
Terrestrial vertebrate diversity[2]	25–50	75–100
Water withdrawals[3]	15	40
Population size	30	50
Carbon releases[4]	30	65
Sulfur releases[5]	5	40
Phosphorus releases[6]	<1	20
Nitrogen releases[4]	<1	5
Lead releases[4]	5	50
Carbon tetrachloride production[4]	0	25

Notes:

[1] Calculations assume a baseline or pristine biosphere about 10,000 BP and 100% change as of the mid-1980s. Percentages refer to the total of the later or 100% figure.

[2] Number of vertebrate species that have become extinct through human action since 1600. Does not include possible waves of Pleistocene and earlier Holocene human-induced extinctions, because of continuing controversy over their nature and magnitude.

[3] Total amount of water now withdrawn annually for human use.

[4] Total mass mobilized by human activity.

[5] Present human contribution to the sulfur budget.

[6] Amount of P mined as phosphate rock.

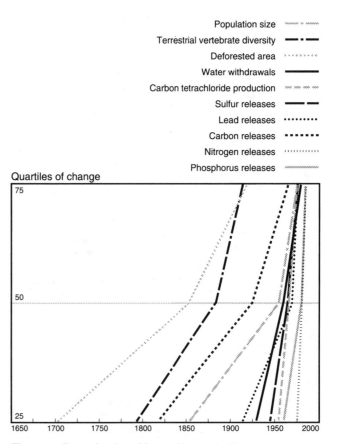

Figure 1.1 Trends in selected forms of human-induced transformation of environmental components.

Attaining the second quartile of change is even more exclusively a twentieth-century event, exceptions being (again) forest depletion and vertebrate extinctions. The third quartile of change is reached only in the twentieth century and, for eight of the ten components we examined, only in the second half of that century.

Patterns of change in these ten components of the biosphere can usefully be classified along two dimensions relating to the recency of change and the rate of change. Figure 1.2 plots each component (including others for which quantitative estimates are not available) according to whether it achieved 50% of its present transformation in the nineteenth or twentieth centuries, and whether its rate of transformation has accelerated or decelerated since roughly the time of the Princeton symposium. Four extreme trajectories of change are possible. The first, long-established and decelerating, is reflected in the depletion of vertebrate biotic diversity. The second, long-established and accelerating, is reflected by the development of global deforestation. The third, recently established and decelerating, is reflected in the emissions of lead, sulfur, and carbon tetrachloride – now all heavily regulated in parts of the world. Finally, the fourth trajectory of recently established and still accelerating transformations is reflected in the global diversion of water flows. These four trajectories of change can be applied, albeit with less confidence, to some of the other components or subcomponents of the biosphere examined in this volume. The results, also plotted in Fig. 1.1, suggest both the tendency of most changes, whether novel or long-established, to accelerate and the potential for management to effect visible improvements in some areas.

This characterization of the patterns of change in components of the biosphere not surprisingly provides support for the existence of at least three patterns or modes of environmental transformation that are associated with the three great technopolitical economies of the past 300 years – the agrarian, the industrial, and the advanced industrial.[9]

The agrarian mode of transformation refers to situations in which preindustrial subsistence to small-surplus agriculture is predominant. Here, the faces of the earth – its landscapes and much of its flora and fauna – are primarily involved, either directly through the conversion of land for plant cultivation,

1980 vs 1955 Rates of Change

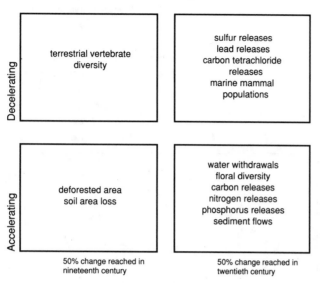

Figure 1.2 Recency and rate of change in human-induced transformation of environmental components.

stockrearing, and the harvesting of wood for fuel and construction material, or indirectly through the secondary effects of these changes. This mode dominated the world through the eighteenth century and remained important in various regions into the twentieth century. Today it is found primarily in the remaining frontiers of the tropics, usually mixed or in conflict with other modes.

The industrial mode of transformation involves fossil-fuel-based and mechanized agriculture and manufacturing, largely related to the rise of modern capitalist and socialist economies. In general, it is characterized by continuing changes of the faces noted above, by the mobilization of energy and materials from the reservoirs of the earth, and by the creation of new chemicals. This mode began in Europe and North America in the nineteenth century, although many of its major impacts were not detected until the late twentieth century. Today it is spreading to new regions, while declining in some of its initial centers. It is strongly associated with increased levels of per capita consumption.

The advanced industrial mode of transformation refers to those circumstances in which much of the mass-polluting industry has been controlled or converted and the service sector of the economy has increased in comparison to the manufacturing sector. This mode is characterized by the decrease in the rates of transformations in many of the components of the biosphere, although the total amount of transformation may continue to rise. It is associated with conditions of relative affluence, a growing service sector, population stabilization, and technological advances that lessen the impacts of traditional industrial effluents (although new, unforeseen impacts associated with mass consumption may be created). These conditions have emerged in the latter half of this century in many of the same regions that spawned the industrial transformation. It is not yet clear to what degree these changes are independent of a transfer of environmental

transformation to those regions of the world in which extractive or industrial economies remain dominant.

These three modes of environmental transformation are not intended to imply a universal sequence experienced by every region of the world. Nor do they presume a linkage with theories of economic growth, the dynamics of which are much disputed. Regions and nations have experienced one or all of the modes at different times and in different global contexts. For example, agrarian transformation may characterize a region within a larger political unit that is in an industrial economic phase. Today, all three modes of environmental transformation contribute to change in the biosphere; in some cases, a single region may be experiencing more than one mode.

Patterns of Regional Transformation

Global trends in environmental change have not been experienced uniformly across the earth; different regions have had different experiences. To explore this variation, we examined twelve regional case studies (chaps. 28–39). These studies represent a broad range of environmental and socioeconomic conditions in the past and present, from interior tropical forest to coastal near-Arctic zones and from sparsely settled frontiers to centers of population and industry in both capitalist and socialist states (Fig. 1.3). Analyzing these cases in terms of their current modes of transformation and population densities and in terms of the general paths of these two variables over the past 300 years allows the identification of seven broad trajectories of regional environmental transformation. These trajectories are tentative and imprecise, and would vary according to the criteria employed by the interpreter. We have found the exercise to be useful, however, in focusing attention on the considerable spatial and temporal variation within the overall global situation without treating each regional history as unique.

Figure 1.4 shows these trajectories and the groupings by region. "Population density" is self-explanatory. "Mode of transformation" refers to the general nature (quality and quantity) of environmental change as described above for which simple quantitative measures do not exist. Here, indicators of wealth and urbanization are used as broad surrogates.[10] Because such information is not readily available at a regional scale, national level data are substituted but adjusted for regions that clearly differ from the national average (e.g., Amazonia within Brazil). Placement of a region by its current mode of environmental transformation must therefore be viewed as subjective but guided by these broad criteria.

The first trajectory represents the relatively densely populated regions of the "developed" world that have entered an advanced industrial phase, represented here by the Hudson-Raritan region and the country regions of Switzerland and Sweden. (The last region is much closer to the other two in terms of population density if only the highly developed parts of southern Sweden are considered.) These regions industrialized early and have been leaders in the post–World War II move toward a service economy with virtually zero population growth rates. Much of their rural landscape has re-

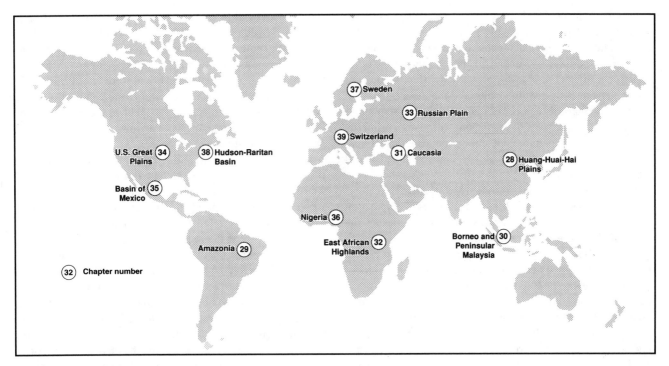

Figure 1.3 Locations of regional case studies.

verted to forest, the area devoted to farming has decreased, dispersed suburban settlement has expanded rapidly, and various forms of controls have apparently begun to lower the emission of some air and water pollutants. On the other hand, waste products from mass consumption have become a new problem. The immediate future of these regions appears to be one of very slow population growth, increased service activities, and probable decreases in the rates of production and the release of pollutants of all kinds. This trajectory is probably typical of most of the long-industrialized regions of the world.

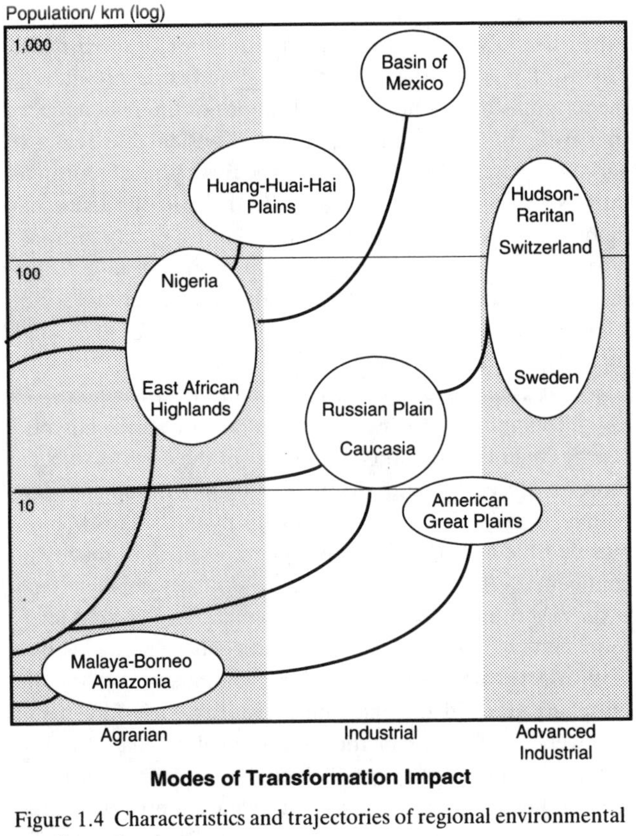

The second trajectory is characterized by the American Great Plains – relatively low population densities sustained by industrial agriculture, but situated within a larger advanced industrial economy. The Great Plains were occupied throughout the eighteenth century by relatively small numbers of paleolithic peoples who were abruptly replaced in the mid-nineteenth century by a sparsely settled, commercial agricultural system. Rapid transformation occurred up to the 1930s. The area cultivated has continued to increase, while most of the major problems of environmental degradation, some of which have been profound, such as the Dust Bowl, have been addressed through various means for nearly 50 years. The two keys to sustained or decreased rates of environmental change are the regional problems of groundwater depletion and soil erosion and the global one of climatic change. If the first two are controlled and the third does not occur, then the immediate future is probably one of relatively moderate to slow growth and environmental change. This trajectory seems appropriate for a number of regions invaded by industrial-settler expansion in the late eighteenth and nineteenth centuries.

The Russian Plain and Caucasia have followed a third, albeit complex, trajectory. Both regions of ancient occupation, they were relatively late to enter an industrial phase and they continue to experience considerable population growth, although the overall population densities remain moderate. The twentieth century has been a time of considerable growth in industry and commercial agriculture, such that many indicators show substantial change in both the faces and the flows

Figure 1.4 Characteristics and trajectories of regional environmental transformation.

of the environment. This has been offset somewhat, however, by a centrally planned economy that has constrained mass consumption and the effluents that accompany it.[11] The picture here is, perhaps, more complex than in some of the other regions because of the wide diversity in activity and settlement across the extent of both the plains and the mountains. Two futures may mark this case, both accompanied by moderate population growth: parts of the regions will remain primarily in commercial agriculture (not unlike the American Great Plains) and others will move slowly towards an advanced industrial situation.

The Basin of Mexico displays a fourth distinctive trajectory. Here the concentrations and the growth rates of population are exceptionally high. Moreover, industrial activities for the entire nation have been concentrated at this locale. In this regard, the Basin resembles many "primate" cities or metropolitan regions of the developing world. Unlike some of those regions, however, the Basin has had a relative high population density over the past 300 years, but has entered the industrial phase in a major way only during the latter half of this century. The growth and density of population and industry in this highland basin, coupled with a burgeoning economy of mass consumption, has led to one of the most transformed landscapes imaginable and some of the most serious atmospheric pollution and water problems on earth. The immediate future portends even more people, and stability or slow growth in industrial activities.

The Huang-Huai-Hai Plains of China represent a fifth trajectory. They are characterized by somewhat less wealthy conditions than exist in the Basin of Mexico, in part because they include large rural areas. Here, highly concentrated rural settlement has existed for centuries, but the latter half of the twentieth century has been marked by the rapid rise of industry, typically concentrated within urban areas. Current environmental change, therefore, has not involved landscape modifications (apart from continuing water management efforts) so much as it has the degradation of rural lands owing to extreme land pressures and the generation of industrial effluents. While the rate of population growth appears to have fallen in this region, the move to a fully industrial-commercial agricultural economy will be slow. The future most likely will combine the industrial and agrarian modes of environmental transformation.

Nigeria and the East African Highlands offer another trajectory of transformation. The population and the economy remain primarily agrarian, although resource extraction (especially oil in Nigeria) and centers of industry (usually in primate cities) have grown in the latter half of this century. Population growth is extremely high by any standard. Environmental transformation focuses on landscape change, with land expansion and the opening of "marginal" lands for small-holder agriculture. The results have included desertification, massive deforestation, and major problems of soil erosion. Localized industrial activities have been highly polluting, in part because the regions are not sufficiently developed to enforce controls on wastes and byproducts. The current conditions and recent past seem to mimic those exhibited several stages earlier by regions in trajectory five

(Huang-Huai-Hai Plains), but the longer histories are much different. Nigeria and the East African Highlands entered the eighteenth century in a paleotechnic stage, were sparsely to moderately populated by world standards (although Nigeria had nodes of dense occupation), and were late to rid themselves of colonialism and move toward a more industrial stage. The immediate future apparently involves a continuation of the current transformations, in part owing to the continued growth in population.

The seventh transformation trajectory involves the vast tropical forest regions of Malaya-Borneo and Amazonia, which, along with other such environments, appear to constitute the next and perhaps last great settlement frontiers. The trajectories here are relatively simple and pronounced. Until very recently, the regions supported extremely sparsely settled, paleolithic populations. Intrusions by the industrial world were largely confined to mining and small nodes of plantations. This has changed dramatically in the past twenty years as large-scale timber extraction and "pioneer" clearing for agriculture and livestock raising have invaded the forest lands with great speed. This mix of subsistence and industrial agriculture and resource extraction has led to a temporal-spatial scale of landscape transformation perhaps never before witnessed on earth, the full environmental consequences of which are unclear. The loss of forest and species is certain, as are the regional problems of sedimentation and destruction of the soil. The global climatic effects of transforming these great reservoirs of carbon and moisture are less predictable. Both regions, which are probably characteristic of most tropical forest zones remaining on earth, will most likely follow their current paths into the foreseeable future.

These seven regional transformation trajectories are not exhaustive. They do, however, capture some of the broader classes of regional trends in the kind and scale of environmental transformation. The implications of the regional perspectives are simple but significant. Considerable regional variation in transformation exists. The regions most representative of the global pattern may be those in the industrial mode. And as technology has increased, especially in transportation, the scale and kind of transformation in a region increasingly need not reflect the local demographic and socioeconomic conditions.

Social Processes of Transformation

The most fundamental and dramatic environmental changes over the 4-billion-year history of the earth have been those produced by natural forces, probably including a few cosmic interventions. Such dramatic metamorphoses have included the creation of the biosphere itself, movements of continents and oceans, the evolutionary development and extinction of millions of plant and animal species, and long-term shifts in climatic conditions and zones. The forces that gave rise to these transformations continue to act on the biosphere through tectonic and geomorphologic forces and relatively short-term climatic change, or flux (chap. 9). The last major climatic shift, the Pleistocene-Holocene transition, marked the rise of our species as a significant presence in the biosphere, ultimately joining the other forces as a major agent of transformation. Humanity has become such a force that it is now difficult to characterize many changes or transformations of the biosphere independent of it. Conversely, though, many human impacts are difficult to specify against a fluctuating natural backdrop.

Humankind, of course, transforms the biosphere in its effort to satisfy real and perceived needs and desires, and it is the conceptualization of these "human dimensions of global environmental change" that has become the focus of scholarly attention among the social sciences and humanities. A set of common basic components or classes of components has emerged from numerous assessments of the human "dimensions," "causes," or "driving forces" of global environmental change, although the ordering and intricacies of their relationships remain controversial, with suggested resolutions relying upon common-sense, theoretical, or ideological arguments.

We can envision these dimensions of change as the expression through human driving and mitigating forces of the underlying behavior of humankind (Turner 1989) (Fig. 1.5). Driving forces are those actions that change nature from its conditions independent of humankind, whereas mitigating forces are those countervailing influences that operate to reduce or alter the driving forces or their impacts. Behavior refers to the underlying rationales, both conditions and choices, for the actions that give rise to these two sets of forces.

The primary components (or classes of components) of driving forces are population, technological capacity, and sociocultural organization. Of these, the first constitutes an almost universally recognized component, whereas the other two have received varied attention. Formally at least since Malthus (1798), and much longer in vernacular thought,

population has been seen as a prime transforming agent, because our species demands basic levels of food, water, fuel, clothing, and shelter for subsistence. Therefore, as population size increases, so does basic biological demand.

Technological capacity involves both the elaboration of technical knowledge and the social conditions for its mobilization. It can be viewed as a driving force in at least two ways: by influencing demand for resources through changes in their affordability or accessibility and by the secondary, unintended environmental consequences that it can create.

Sociocultural organization is sufficiently diffuse that it might best be considered a class of driving-force components involving economic and political structures, and social values and norms. As yet, empirical documentation of the role of any of these components at a global scale is rudimentary at best. Nevertheless, it is generally recognized that sociocultural organization has a major impact on demand, in affecting, for example, both the expected material standard of living in modern mass consumption society and the means for reaching it.

Changes in these three components affect the demand for and supply of resources, the distribution of or access to the supply, and hence, the transformation of the biosphere. The three have broad associations, at least over the long sweep of human history, such that it is often difficult to separate their respective roles. Moreover, the primacy afforded to any one of the three has had much to do with the question asked or the perspective used.

This said, it is difficult not to conclude that population growth has been the first-tier driving force of environmental change throughout the history of humankind for the simple biological reasons already stated. Regardless of the technology employed or the sociocultural organization that dominates, increases in the number of our species mean that more resources are required.

Ranking the other two driving forces is a bit more problematic because of the synergism between technological capacity and sociocultural organization. It appears, however, that the grand technological epochs of history (tool, agricultural, and industrial) and technological capacity within any epoch crosscut multiple forms of sociocultural organization. For example, modern industrialism and its impacts on the environment are apparently similar in mass-consumption, capitalist societies and in centrally planned and controlled socialist societies. For this reason, we are led to place technological capacity second in the tier of order to population growth at this time. Sociocultural organization, at least by measure of what little comparative work exists on the subject, may have much greater impact on the means by which transformation takes place and the differential impacts of the transformation than on the kinds and scales of change operating at any moment.

A number of efforts have been made to relate the course of human population and technological growth to the global demands on resources and, to a lesser extent, the resulting transformations of the biosphere (e.g., Meadows et al. 1972; Repetto 1987). They argue for a strong association among the rise in population, the increases in demands, the ability to

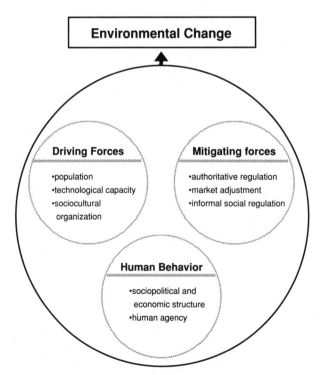

Figure 1.5 Human forces of environmental change.

meet demands in the short run, and the changes in the biosphere created in the course of satisfying those demands.

For example, the rise and spread of an agrarian-based population across the earth led to significant global changes in several components of the biosphere even before the advent of the industrial revolution and the third outbreak of global population growth (Deevey 1960). For the most part, these changes involved those indicators of the landscape central to the agricultural base (Table 1-3) – indicators that track the clearing of woodlands, the draining of wetlands, and the plowing of grasslands. Much of this transformation was spatially concentrated in the great floodplains, basins, and lowlands that housed the development of sophisticated agricultural systems. It was associated with urbanization, the development of states, and the enlargement of empires in China, Europe, and elsewhere. Some transfer of impacts also occurred; for instance, at the beginning of the Christian era, Rome turned North Africa into a breadbasket for its 1 million urban inhabitants, transporting 200,000 tons of grain across the Mediterranean in a fleet of upwards of 1,000 ships each season (Rickman 1980).

Just preceding the industrial revolution, populations in Europe and China began to grow rapidly, and the emerging empires of Britain, France, Holland, Portugal, and Spain became truly global in scale. The patterns of flora and fauna, especially domesticates, were, perhaps for the first time, transformed on a global scale (chaps. 20 and 22; Crosby 1986). But with the advent of fossil-fuel-based industry in Europe, this synergy of population growth, expansive socioeconomic organization, and more powerful technologies continued, making possible new types and levels of transformation, creating demands on even larger and more distant environments. The move to coal-based industry in Europe now swelled the carbon emissions that had previously been affected primarily by deforestation. Over the long term, substantial quantities of sulfur and heavy metals would be released to the atmosphere and concentrate in the soil. The ability to fix nitrogen and to synthesize existing chemicals and to create new ones fundamentally altered the flows of energy and materials in the biosphere. Transformation of the biosphere was no longer primarily confined to landscape changes.

In this century, and particularly in the past 40 years, these trends have come together and accelerated. In seven of our ten quantified components, half of the total transformation wrought by humankind occurred after World War II. From the middle of this century until the present, human population, water withdrawals, and cumulative releases of sulfur, phosphorus, nitrogen, lead, and a variety of organic chemicals have doubled and more, although several of these have slowed in very recent years. The growth in population and the even larger growth in material and energy consumption mirrored in these indicators have been accompanied by unprecedented movements of materials and concentrations of people.

Resource extraction, production, and consumption have become spatially disassociated, promoting a virtual explosion in commodity flows. By 1984, the tonnage of international seaborne freight per capita increased threefold from 1950

levels (chap. 6), much of the increase due to the shipment of crude oil. The burning of fossil fuels that drives the industries and transportation of the modern world, coupled with the depletion of the world's forests for resources and land, has not only altered the critical chemical flows of the biosphere, but may also be changing the very functioning of the atmosphere through the so-called greenhouse effect of global climate change (e.g., Schneider 1989).

Transformations of population and technology have been accompanied by major changes in the nature of society itself. Almost the entire world population was rural 300 years ago, and behaved by the social norms, values, and structures that accompany this "traditional" or agrarian settlement and lifestyle. By 1985, more than 40% of the world's population was urbanized (chap. 7), concentrated at high population densities, requiring alterations in social organization and, presumably, stimulating dramatic changes in the fabric of society itself.[12] The immediate environmental consequences of this concentration have tended to be local or regional (chaps. 7 and 19). The indirect consequences are of a larger scale, today reaching a global dimension. This is so because the urban and urbane societies of the industrial nations tend to drive demand on a per capita basis to levels exceeding those of rural and preindustrial societies, although this distinction may be disappearing as the twenty-first century approaches.

As population, technology, and settlement have been transformed over the past 300 years, so has the global political economy (e.g., Wallerstein 1974; Braudel 1981–84). Much of the extensive literature on this subject focuses on the regional and class imbalances in wealth and well-being created by the clash of capitalism with other economies, little of it on the resulting consequences for the environment. The implication, at least, is strong that capitalism and mass consumption inflate the levels of demand by the population in question (chap. 40), and that greater stress is thereby placed on the physical environment. Yet it remains an open question whether the levels of transformation currently underway would not have resulted from any workable form of socioeconomic organization incorporating the levels of population and technology that humankind has now reached.

The changes in driving forces briefly sketched here have been matched by changes in mitigating forces. Inasmuch as considerable attention has been given to this subject (e.g., Schnaiberg 1980: Part 3; Jodha and Mascarenhas 1985), it need not be elaborated here. It is sufficient to note that the basic types of mitigating forces are authoritative regulation, market adjustments, and informal social regulation. Over the long sweep of history, informal social regulation may have diminished in importance in comparison to the other two types, while institutions with authoritative powers relevant to the environmental field have proliferated.

The emergence of a large global population, a technologically advanced and urbanized society, and an international political economy, indeed, has been accompanied by the development of a vast structure of social, economic, and political institutions that control and order human activity. Many of society's impacts on the physical environment, global or otherwise, are mediated through this complex, and often conflicting, hierarchy (chap. 5). Some institutions promote the very change that other institutions attempt to regulate. Public awareness and attitudes (chap. 8) may play an important role in prompting institutional responses to environmental issues, but how far are those attitudes themselves shaped by institutions and how important are the institutional responses? Empirical assessments of their nature and impacts are virtually nonexistent (Clark 1989). Have transformation, on the one hand, and societal knowledge about and responses to environmental issues, on the other, changed much because of the characteristics or roles of these institutions, or do the institutions simply mirror deeper societal forces?

Finally, to understand the processes of global and regional environmental change it is necessary not only to address the roles of direct and indirect driving and mitigating forces of change, but to place these forces within the context of human and social rationales of action, or human behavior, as indicated in the "theory" papers (chaps. 40–42). Despite this recognition, the indirect linkages from the why of human action to the kind and scale of environmental transformation have not been well developed beyond the obvious, and debate has largely remained at the theoretical level. This situation exists, in part, because the competing perspectives about the nature of human behavior do not necessarily agree even on the ground rules for assessing the validity of their assertions. An emergent theme is the need to integrate human agency with social structure – that is, decisions and the context in which they are made – although how this synthesis may be achieved remains unclear.

And beyond this need to understand the human behavior of transformation is human nature itself. Those distinctive qualities of humankind, those that might separate homo sapiens from the other species that share the biosphere, have been questions of wonder, sins of pride, and studies of science – ever since Prometheus. The oft-heralded human qualities of prolonged gestation and care of the young, toolmaking and using, information preserving and transmitting, exploration and adaptation to varied environments, and collective social action – all affect and contribute to human-induced earth transformation.

Transformation Lessons

The examination of the human-induced transformation of the biosphere, briefly summarized here and detailed in the subsequent chapters of this book, illuminates several key themes or lessons about the transformation process and our ability to understand it. While these lessons are not necessarily new, several of them have not been sufficiently appreciated and warrant much more consideration than they have received. For the most part, these lessons involve perspectives gained from expanding the range of temporal and spatial considerations of environmental change.

1. The magnitude of human-induced environmental change at the global scale is enormous. Transformed, managed, and utilized ecosystems constitute about half of the ice-free earth; human-mobilized material and energy flows rival those of nature. The greater part of change in most of these components of the biosphere over the last three centuries has been human-induced.

2. Most global-scale impacts of human-induced change have been quite recent, particularly those dealing with biogeochemical flows of the biosphere. Only a few of the components of the biosphere examined in this volume attained 50% of their current level of change before the twentieth century, and probably the majority attained this level around or after the midpoint of this century.

3. The history of human-induced change has witnessed a shift from the agricultural transformation of the surface of the earth, to industrial mobilization of materials and energy, to the current mix of agricultural, industrial, and advanced-industrial transformation. As this range has expanded, so has the secondary interaction among the changes, and hence the complexity of the problems that they pose. The recent and stark increases in the changes of biogeochemical flows can have impacts on the very composition of the biosphere, such as its climate and atmospheric protection from radiation.

4. A downward shift in the rate of change for some components of the biosphere has recently been observed even while others are still accelerating. Much of what deceleration has occurred can be traced to awareness of harmful impacts prompting management initiatives for their mitigation. Deceleration of some deeper forces of change, such as global population growth (as predicted by recent estimates), may be offset by the rise in demand for material consumption.

5. Overall earth transformation is mirrored poorly within its regions; these vary significantly from global averages. In these regions, agricultural, industrial, and advanced-industrial activities mix, population densities vary by an order of magnitude, and activity and density are mediated by the details of the physical environment. In a simple example, some areas have been reforested, whereas others are now experiencing the greatest levels of deforestation in their history.

6. These broadly different patterns of regional transformation lead to variable perceptions of, interest in, and responses to this change, compounded by the socioeconomic conditions within any region. Thus the view from Sahelian Africa is not that from the northern plains of Canada, in regard to both current and projected transformation. These differences make difficult a global consensus as to courses of action to take in regard to the transformation of the biosphere.

7. The global transformation of the biosphere is driven first by population growth, followed by technological capacity and sociocultural organization. More empirical-based study is needed to document the specific ordering of these forces of change within specific regions and historical periods.

8. A generally accepted theory of human–environment relationships has not been developed, but its rudiments are emerging. Such a theory of human-environment relationships needs to conceptualize the relations among the

driving forces of human-induced change, their mitigating processes and activities, and human behavior and organization.

Cautionary Tales

It is difficult to be in the midst of change and to understand it: to separate the deep structures from the shallow constructions, the long rhythms from time's embellishments, or the profound understandings from the current enthusiasms. And we are very much in the midst of change.

We again recall this moment in history. If the demographers' consensus holds true, we are about halfway towards a level population of between 8 and 12 billion people, barring a major catastrophe, such as nuclear war or a global pandemic. The conventional wisdom forecasts of most international studies estimate that an increase in the world population to 10 billion would be accompanied by a three- to fourfold increase in agricultural production and a six- to eightfold increase in energy consumption (Svedin and Aniansson 1987). These multipliers would allow, in the case of agriculture, for humankind to move higher on the food chain and improve dietary intake and to meet the inevitable increase in the demand for specialty crops and organic industrial materials, and in the case of energy, for much of the Third World to enjoy increased consumption. Given the role of population and its demand for food, fiber, and energy in environmental transformation, these projections are sobering. Crudely translated, they suggest that the enormous transformations of the last three centuries will be doubled, trebled, or more in the centuries to come (Ehrlich and Holdren 1988). But we have more to learn from the past record than the scope, magnitude, and driving forces of human-induced transformation. We have some lessons to learn about "conventional wisdom" as we ponder the meaning and implications of history.

Our first cautionary tale begins at the turn of the century at the Harvard Forest in Petersham, Massachusetts (some 50 km from Worcester, the site of the "Earth Transformed" symposium). Harvard Forest was a pioneer research and education program and an early American center for experiments with new notions of sustainable yields and multiple use in forestry. As a major research station, it drew upon the very best in scientific forestry; as a gift to Harvard University, it was required to be self-supporting. Both science and industry failed in important and cautionary ways.

The early managers tried to maintain the forest as they found it, but what they had found was a forest in transition between the cleared fields and pastures of mid-nineteenth-century central Massachusetts in its golden age of agriculture, and a returning, mature conifer-beech-maple forest similar to that encountered by the original European settlers a century and a half earlier. Of the marketable timber, 90% was old-field white pine less than 70 years old. To maintain the sustainable yield of the pine, managers lavished great effort in removing the competing hardwoods from the moist upland sites that favored them, not understanding at that time that they were actually trying to stabilize a forest in succession. Even where they succeeded in maintaining pine stands, they husbanded them, cutting only an equivalent to the portion grown on a sustainable basis from year to year.

The bulk of this carefully maintained inventory was lost in the hurricane of 1938. The economic worth of the forest fared just as poorly. When Harvard took over the forest, it was within the center of the country's wooden-box industry. The timber continued to grow in value, to a high in 1923, but was worth virtually nothing by 1940.

From this cautionary tale, we draw a lesson. The very best scientists of any time may only poorly understand the fundamental processes governing nature, society, and the relationships between them; in this case, which trees are edaphic, how species composition changes, how demand for species changes, and how catastrophic surprise can occur. Our attempts to understand the current transformation of the earth and the various transformation trajectories will surely offer many examples of failure to understand process or to anticipate surprise.

A second cautionary tale begins in a country parish in England, where a 32-year-old curate named Thomas Robert Malthus wrote his *Essay on the Principle of Population*, published anonymously in 1798. A regional concern for the adequacy of agricultural land and food production for England and Wales would expand by the 1860s to cover energy and material resources. By the 1960s the scope would include the amenities and pollution-absorbing qualities of the environment. Today, it has added concerns with species diversity and the sustainability of the biosphere. As the numerator of the Malthusian equation expanded from food, to resources, to environment, to the biosphere, so did the denominator, from the country parish of Oakwood to the world. This volume is another way station continuing along that trajectory.

Of course, Malthus was proven wrong, but Malthusian concerns persist. While he underestimated the ability of population to grow, he surely underestimated the ability of society to augment the resource base in various ways. And, if we take his warnings as his expectations, then he grossly underestimated technological progress and the ability of society to undertake corrective or ameliorative action (preventive checks), partly in response to his own expressed concerns. Subsequently, however, almost each generation seems to rediscover Malthus, to revise the nature of the numerator of concern, and to extend the denominator of population. And within each generation, this rediscovery is rejected by those attempting to prove that the latest set of doomsday fears is unwarranted. Indeed, since the Princeton symposium on "Man's Role in Changing the Face of the Earth," we have experienced such a refutation (Barnett and Morse 1963; Potter and Christy 1962; Landsberg, Fischman, and Fisher 1963), a renewal (Ehrlich and Ehrlich 1970; Meadows et al. 1972), and another refutation (Simon 1981).

What should we learn from this cautionary tale, a chapter to which this volume contributes? Perhaps there are three lessons. First, the fundamental question of the adequacy of the earth to sustain its population is a profound one. It is not dispelled by attack on either its factual base or its ideological roots; rather, it recurs as the scale of transformation enlarges, as our definition of the essentials of life expands, and as our place in the natural order seems paradoxically to grow both larger and smaller. Second, many of one generation's great fears are remembered by the next generation, if they are remembered at all, as quaint curiosities. Surely some of the concerns that we feel for the transformations of the biosphere or for the fate of its elements will baffle future generations. Third, and perhaps most importantly, predictions are not falsified only because the concerns were ill-founded or the hypothesized relationships were wrong. On the contrary, the gloomiest of forecasts may not be realized because society takes them seriously and acts upon them.

This volume thus takes a place in the continuing process by which our species, so powerful in its ability to understand and transform the world, struggles to understand and control itself.

Notes

1. Tracing and categorizing theoretical and ideological lineages is a notoriously difficult endeavor. We make no claim to expertise on this subject, but maintain at least that the works cited in this brief overview are representative of the perspective in question.

2. "Noösphere," as used by Teilhard (1958), refers to the "... total pattern of thinking organisms and their activity, including patterns of their interrelations" (Serafin 1988: 128), as opposed to the "noösystem" that Huxley (1958) identified as the medium for humankind.

3. The pastoralist, utilitarian, and conservationist views have been identified as the three main nature–society themes in twentieth-century Russia and the Soviet Union (Weiner 1988).

4. This theme has appeared in many guises: for some others, see Brunhes (1910), Gerasimov (1983), Leiss (1972), Schmidt (1971), Smith (1984), and Voeikov (1901).

5. An extreme variant of the "modifier" perspective tends to see humankind as divorced from nature. While rarely stated directly, this belief dwells in the implication that humanity, through inventiveness and technology, has broken the bounds of nature (e.g., Simon 1981). Inasmuch as this perspective largely dismisses nature's importance in human affairs, it is not considered here as a perspective on nature–society relationships per se.

6. The past roles of philosophies, ideologies, or religions on humankind's impact on the biosphere have been left largely undocumented. Many take their importance for granted, whereas others would call it into question. Western capitalist states have been roundly criticized for their supposedly destructive, cavalier attitudes toward nature. But Smil (1984) and Weiner (1988) demonstrate that modern Marxist–Leninist and Maoist states have radically altered their environments, often with the same reliance on "technological fixes" that has marked the Western countries. Tuan (1968) has argued that despite the prescription to live in harmony with nature in dominant Taoist philosophies, ancient China also modified its landscapes as much or more than did comparable civilizations.

7. Details of the development of "The Earth As Transformed by Human Action" symposium and this volume are found in the preface.

8. While this effort focuses primarily on human-induced changes in the biosphere over the past 300 years, changes in various components of the biosphere had taken place previously. Our effort in these tables and figures is to provide a perspective on the total time frame of major human-induced transformation in order that the more recent magnitudes and trajectories of change could be compared.

9. A standard terminology with which to distinguish the broad socio-economic and technological "orders" that have existed from the eighteenth century onward does not exist. Socioeconomic categories, such as precapitalist and capitalist, do not adequately capture the technological basis. Other problems exist with the use of such technological categories as modern, neotechnic, and scientific, which imply little about the larger political economy. A merger of the two, as in the term "industrial capitalism," has not been developed into a complete typology or classification. The terms used here – agrarian, industrial, and advanced industrial – focus on the basic technologies that support the economy and transform the environment.

10. "Advanced industrial" denotes per capita Gross National Product in excess of US $10,000 and a population more than 60% urbanized. "Industrial" has a per capita GNP of between $5,000 and $10,000 and is more than 50% urbanized. "Agrarian" falls below the lower limits given for the industrial case.

11. Environmental transformation in East Bloc countries has not been open to the same level of scrutiny as it has been elsewhere, in part because the data were not publicly available. This situation has begun to change dramatically of late (e.g., Micklin 1988; Environment 1988).

12. Generally, "urban" implies a higher settlement density than does "rural." Yet in some cases, agrarian or rural densities may exceed urban ones; farming areas in parts of South Asia and China range up to 1,000 people/km^2. Therefore, other criteria are important in distinguishing urban from rural areas, including the functions performed. One of the more important for our examination is the change from so-called traditional or rural social structure to modern or urbane ones. This change has been related to dramatic shifts in patterns of consumption and values – patterns that may have major impacts on the global environment, albeit largely unexplored.

Acknowledgment

We thank Anthony J. Bebbington for his assistance in the initial stages of the development of this chapter. Subsequently, William B. Meyer provided invaluable insights and contributions; we are indebted to Bill's time, attention, and intellect.

References

Annenkov, V. V. 1988. Noösphere: historico-geographical approach. *Historical Geography of Environmental Changes*, ed. V. V. Annenkov and L. Jelecek, 73–88. Prague: Institute of Czechoslovak and World History of the Czechoslovak Academy of Sciences.

Ausubel, J. H., and H. E. Sladovich, eds. 1989. *Technology and Environment*. Washington, D.C.: National Academy Press.

Barnett, H. J., and C. Morse. 1963. *Scarcity and Growth: The Economics of Natural Resource Availability*. Baltimore, MD: Johns Hopkins University Press.

Bennett, J. W. 1976. *The Ecological Transition: Cultural Anthropology and Human Adaptation*. New York: Pergamon Press.

Black, J. N. 1970. *The Dominion of Man: The Search for Ecological Responsibility*. Edinburgh: J. Black.

Bodde, D. 1957. Evidence for "laws of nature" in Chinese thought. *Harvard Journal of Asiatic Studies* 20: 709–27.

Bolin, B., and R. B. Cook, eds. 1983. *The Major Biogeochemical Cycles and Their Interactions*. New York: John Wiley and Sons.

Braudel, F. 1981–84. *Civilization and Capitalism, 15th–18th Century*. 3 vols. New York: Harper & Row.

Brown, B. J., M. E. Hanson, D. M. Liverman, and R. W. Meredith, Jr. 1987. Global sustainability: towards definition. *Environmental Management* 11: 713–19.

Brunhes, J. 1910. *La géographie humaine: Essai de classification positive*. Paris: Alcan.

Butzer, K. W. 1982. *Archaeology as Human Ecology*. Cambridge: Cambridge University Press.

Clark, W. C. 1987. Scale relationships in the interaction of climate, ecosystems, and societies. In *Forecasting in the Natural and Social Sciences*, ed. K. C. Land and S. H. Schneider, 337–78. Dordrecht, Holland: D. Reidel.

———. 1989. The human ecology of global change. *International Social Science Journal* 41: 315–45.

Clark, W. C., and R. E. Munn, eds. 1986. *Sustainable Development of the Biosphere*. Cambridge: Cambridge University Press.

Crosby, A. W. 1986. *Ecological Imperialism: The Biological Expansion of Europe, 900–1900*. Cambridge: Cambridge University Press.

Darby, H. C. 1956. The clearing of the woodland in Europe. In *Man's Role in Changing the Face of the Earth*, ed. W. L. Thomas, Jr., 183–216. Chicago: University of Chicago Press.

Deevey, E. S. 1960. The human population. *Scientific American* 203: 195–204.

Douglas, M. 1966. *Purity and Danger: An Analysis of Concepts of Pollution and Taboo*. London: Routledge and Kegan Paul.

Dubos, R. 1972. *A God Within*. New York: Charles Scribner's Sons.

Ehrlich, P., and A. Ehrlich. 1970. *Population, Resources, Environment*. San Francisco: W. H. Freeman and Co.

Ehrlich, P., and J. P. Holdren. 1988. *The Cassandra Conference*. College Station, TX: Texas A&M University Press.

Ellen, R. 1982. *Environment, Subsistence and System: The Ecology of Small-Scale Social Formations*. Cambridge: Cambridge University Press.

Environment Magazine. 1988. Glasnost and ecology: Three reports from the Soviet Union. *Environment* 30(10): 1–35.

Gade, D. W. 1983. The growing recognition of George Perkins Marsh. *Geographical Review* 73: 341–44.

Gerasimov, I. P. 1983. *Geography and Ecology: A Collection of Articles, 1971–1981*. Moscow: Progress Publishers.

Glacken, C. 1967. *Traces on the Rhodian Shore*. Berkeley: University of California Press.

Gould, S. J. 1984. The Ediacarian experiment. *Natural History* 2: 14–23.

Holling, C. S. 1973. Resilience and stability of ecological systems. *Annual Review of Ecology and Systematics* 4: 1–23.

———. 1986. The resilience of terrestrial ecosystems: local surprise and global change. In *Sustainable Development of the Biosphere*, ed. W. C. Clark and R. E. Munn, 292–317. Cambridge: Cambridge University Press.

Huntington, E. 1945. *Mainsprings of Civilization*. New York: John Wiley and Sons.

Huxley, J. 1958. Introduction. In P. Teilhard de Chardin, *The Phenomenon of Man*. London: Collins Fountain Books.

Iltis, H. H. 1973. Can one love a plastic tree? *Bulletin of the Ecological Society of America* 54: 5–7, 19.

International Geosphere-Biosphere Program. 1988. *The International Geosphere-Biosphere Program: A Plan For Action*. IGBP Report No. 4. Stockholm: IGBP Secretariate, Royal Swedish Academy of Sciences.

James, P., and G. J. Martin. 1981. *All Possible Worlds: A History of Geographical Ideas*. 2d ed. New York: John Wiley and Sons.

Jodha, N. S. and A. C. Mascarenhas. 1985. Adjustments in self-provisioning societies. In *Climate Impact Assessment*, ed. R. W. Kates, J. H. Ausubel and M. Berberian, 437–64. New York: John Wiley and Sons.

Kates, R. W. 1988. Theories of nature, science and technology. In *Man, Nature and Technology: Essays on the Role of Ideological Perception*, ed. E. Baark and U. Svedin. Houndsmill, U. K.: MacMillan Press.

Landsberg, H. H., L. L. Fischman, and J. L. Fisher. 1963. *Resources in America's Future: Patterns of Requirements and Availability 1960–2000*. Baltimore, MD: Johns Hopkins University Press.

Leighly, J. 1987. Ecology as metaphor: Carl Sauer and human ecology. *The Professional Geographer* 39: 405–12.

Leiss, W. 1972. *The Domination of Nature*. New York: George Braziller.

Lorenz, E. N. 1984. Irregularity: A fundamental property of the atmosphere. *Tellus* 36A: 98–110.

Lovelock, J. E. 1979. *Gaia: A New Look at Life on Earth*. Oxford: Oxford University Press.

———. 1988. *The Ages of Gaia: A Biography of Our Living Planet*. New York: Norton.

Lowenthal, D. 1965. Introduction. In George Perkins Marsh, *Man and Nature; Or, Physical Geography as Modified by Human Action* (orig. 1864), ix–xxix. Cambridge, MA: Belknap Press of Harvard University Press.

Malthus, T. R. 1798. *An Essay on the Principle of Population*. London: Johnson.

Marsh, G. P. 1965. *Man and Nature; Or, The Earth As Modified by Human Action* (orig. 1864). Cambridge, MA: Belknap Press of Harvard University Press.

Martin, P. S., and R. G. Klein. 1984. *Quaternary Extinctions: A Prehistoric Revolution*. Tucson: University of Arizona Press.

McElroy, M. 1986. Change in the natural environment of the earth: the historical record. In *Sustainable Development of the Biosphere*, ed. W. C. Clark and R. E. Munn, 199–212. Cambridge: Cambridge University Press.

McNeill, W. H. 1976. *Plagues and Peoples*. Garden City, NY: Anchor Press.

Meadows, D. H., D. L. Meadows, J. Randers, and W. W. Behrens III. 1972. *The Limits to Growth*. New York: Universe Books.

Meggers, B. J. 1954. Environmental limitations on the development of culture. *American Anthropologist* 56: 801–24.

Meiggs, R. 1982. *Trees and Timber in the Ancient Mediterranean World*. Cambridge: Cambridge University Press.

Micklin, P. P. 1988. Desiccation of the Aral Sea: A water management disaster in the Soviet Union. *Science* 241: 1168–76.

Needham, J. 1951. Human laws and laws of nature in China and the West. *Journal of the History of Ideas* 12: 3–32, 194–230.

O'Riordan, T. 1981. *Environmentalism*. 2d ed. London: Pion.

Potter, N., and F. T. Christy, Jr. 1962. *Trends in Natural Resource Commodities*. Baltimore, MD: Johns Hopkins University Press.

Reclus, E. 1869. *La Terre: Description des phénomènes de la vie du globe*. Vol. 2. Paris: Hachette.

Repetto, R. 1987. Population, resources, environment: an uncertain future. *Population Bulletin* 42(2): 1–43.

Rickman, G. 1980. *The Corn Supply of Ancient Rome*. Oxford: Oxford University Press.

Ritter, K. 1822–59. *Die Erdkunde*. 19 vols. Berlin.

Rolleston, G. 1879. The modifications of the external aspects of organic nature produced by man's interference. *Journal of the Royal Geographical Society* 49: 320–92.

Rostow, W. W. 1978. *The World Economy: History and Prospect*. Austin, TX: University of Texas Press.

Sauer, C. O. 1956. The agency of man on the earth. In *Man's Role in Changing the Face of the Earth*, ed. W. L. Thomas, Jr., 49–69. Chicago: University of Chicago Press.

Sayer, R. A. 1979. Epistemology and conceptions of people and nature in geography. *Geoforum* 10: 19–44.

Schmidt, A. 1971. *The Concept of Nature in Marx*. London: New Left Books.

Schnaiberg, A. 1980. *The Environment from Surplus to Scarcity*. Oxford: Oxford University Press.

Schneider, S. H. 1989. The greenhouse effect: science and policy. *Science* 243: 771–80.

Semple, E. C. 1911. *Influences of Geographic Environment*. New York: Henry Holt and Company.

Serafin, R. 1987. *Vernadsky's Biosphere, Teilhard's Noösphere, and Lovelock's Gaia: Perspectives on Human Intervention in Global Biogeochemical Cycles*. Laxenburg, Austria: IIASA.

———. 1988. Noösphere, gaia, and the science of the biosphere. *Environmental Ethics* 10: 121–37.

Simon, J. 1981. *The Ultimate Resource*. Princeton: Princeton University Press.

Smil, V. 1984. *The Bad Earth: Environmental Degradation in China*. Armonk, NY: M. E. Sharpe, Inc.

Smith, N. 1984. *Uneven Development: Nature, Capital, and the Production of Space*. Oxford: Basil Blackwell.

Strenz, W., G. Narweileit, H.-J. Rook, and H. Thummler. 1988. The influence of society on the biosphere during the period from the industrial revolution to the transition to imperialism. In *Historical Geography of Environmental Changes*, ed. V. V. Annenkov and L. Jelecek, 37–72. Prague: Institute of Czechoslovak and World History of the Czechoslovak Academy of Sciences.

Svedin, U., and B. Aniansson. 1987. *Surprising Futures: Notes from an International Workshop on Long-Term World Development*. Stockholm: Swedish Council for Planning and Coordination of Research, Report 87:1.

Teilhard de Chardin, P. 1958. *The Phenomenon of Man*. London: Collins Fountain Books.

———. 1959. *The Future of Man*. London: Collins Fountain Books.

Thomas, W. L., Jr. 1956. *Man's Role in Changing the Face of the Earth*. Chicago: University of Chicago Press.

Timonov, V. E. 1922. Okhrana prirody pri inzhenernykh rabotakh. *Priroda* #1-2: cols. 72–86.

Tuan, Y.-F. 1968. Discrepancies between environmental attitude and behavior: Examples from Europe and China. *Canadian Geographer* 12: 176–91.

Turner, B. L., II. 1989. The human causes of global environmental change. In *Global Environmental Change and Our Common Future: Results of a Forum*, eds. R.S. DeFries and T. Malone, 91–99. Washington, D.C.: National Academy of Sciences.

Vernadsky, W. I. 1929. *La Biosphere*. Paris: Felix Alcan. 33: 1–12.

———. 1945. The biosphere and the noösphere. *American Scientist*

Voeikov, A. 1901. De l'influence de l'homme sur la terre. *Annales de géographie* 10: 97–114, 193–215.

Wallerstein, I. 1974. *The Capitalist World-System*. New York: Academic Press.

Weiner, D. R. 1988. *Models of Nature: Ecology, Conservation, and Cultural Revolution in Soviet Russia*. Bloomington, IN: Indiana University Press.

White, L., Jr. 1967. The historic roots of our ecologic crisis. *Science* 155: 1203–207.

Williams, M. 1987. Sauer and 'Man's Role in Changing the Face of the Earth.' *Geographical Review* 77: 218–31.

World Commission on Environment and Development. 1987. *Our Common Future*. Oxford: Oxford University Press.

Worster, D. 1977. *Nature's Economy: A History of Ecological Ideas*. Cambridge: Cambridge University Press.

Wynn, G. 1979. Pioneers, politicians, and the conservation of forests in early New Zealand. *Journal of Historical Geography* 5: 171–88.

Yanshin, A. L. 1988. Reviving Vernadsky's legacy: Ecological advances in the Soviet Union. *Environment* 30(10): 6–9, 26–27.

I

Changes in Population and Society

Editorial Introduction

Over the past three centuries humanity itself has undergone its most profound transformation, as documented by Demeny in this section. Having grown steadily from 350 million in A.D. 1400 to 680 million in 1700, suddenly humankind has entered into a new, explosive, growth cycle. During the past three centuries, human numbers have soared in the eighteenth century to over 900 million by 1800, in the next century to 1650 million in 1900, to an estimated 5,000 million as of the late 1980s. The doubling time for world population growth has dropped from over three centuries to mere decades. This single brute fact – the exponential curve of rising numbers in the past 300 years – needs little discussion. Today human numbers have become so great in most parts of the world that the effects of crowding on the environment seem more and more obvious and frightening.

The current trend is so powerful that we assume – and perhaps hope – that it will continue almost indefinitely. (One suspects that human societies have a deep-rooted bias in favor of population expansion.) Whatever its possible costs, population expansion is preferable to decline for almost any human group. These perceptions and attitudes demand cautious reexamination from a longer time perspective. Systematic examination of earlier population trends at the regional scale suggests that the modern episode of growth is not unique. Whitmore and colleagues draw this conclusion after reconstructing population growth patterns in the Egyptian Nile Valley, the Tigris-Euphrates lowlands, the Basin of Mexico, and the central Maya lowlands over the very long term. Population growth is associated with environmental transformations, but growth is accompanied by decline as well. Unquestioning assumptions that global populations will spiral upward indefinitely must be qualified – at least from this perspective. What is unique about the present world trend, however, "is the scale, rapidity, and global interdependence of modern growth" and its impact upon the global environment.

As population has risen, so has the cumulative impact of human economic activity upon the biosphere. Nearly all indices of environmental change mimic the same exponential curve over the past three centuries. Basic human needs drive the world economy. Greater numbers permit application of human energy and intellect toward production on far greater levels of intensity than ever before. It is tempting, therefore, to explain any and all changes humanity has wrought in the world's environment over the past three centuries by means of population growth. Unfortunately, this option is too simplistic. To confront the complexities of environmental change in the modern world, we must accurately describe and analyze changes in social organization. In spite of dazzling feats of science and technology, humankind's most significant technological advance has been in large-scale complex organizations. Over the past 300 years human societies, grown enormously larger, have responded to this growth by fostering galaxies of new organizations – more efficient, more complex, and more self-conscious than any in previous history. Mobilizing individual energy and intellect in bureaucratic structures (in the broadest sense) is the mark of modernity. We cannot understand environmental transformations until we better understand changes in human institutions.

The essays included in this section address several significant aspects of the evolution of institutions and organization: the growth of cities, the universalist modern state, technical innovation, the mechanisms of long-distance trade, and rising environmental consciousness. Discussion of market systems, although not treated separately, forms an important theme in each contribution. In keeping with the tenets of the volume, the authors adopt a long-term global perspective. Each essay examines the changing interaction between environment and society in the context of world time.

Rapid population growth has been marked by unprecedented levels of urbanization. As Berry points out, between A.D. 1700 and 1900 an expanding network of world cities provided the nodes for expansion of commodity production in agriculture, forestry, and mining. At the turn of the twentieth century, only 16 cities exceeded 1 million in population and just over one-quarter of the world's population lived in cities. As consumers of energy and other resources, the populations of these cities did contribute to massive changes in the world's environment. Direct environmental effects on climate, water, and soils of these urban concentrations for the most part were local. In the decade of the 1980s, 400 cities have populations larger than 1 million, and nearly half of humanity lives in cities. The largest metropolitan areas generate enough heat, gaseous and solid airborne pollutants, and wastewater to have effects on wider regions. Mitigating or coping with these impacts requires new institutions, new human behavior, and heavy investment.

Human social organization has undergone a similar transformation as societies have struggled to cope with rapid, frightening increases in their numbers. The size, complexity, and territorial reach of all types of human organization have burst their former bounds. Of necessity these institutions have turned to the tasks of producing goods and services, maintaining order, and nurturing cultural life. Around the world human societies have coped more or less adequately with the tasks of "development" to keep pace with rising numbers. Productivity, as we are quick to assert, has soared in the modern industrial age. Our ability to mobilize energy and human intellect in new ways has made it possible for population to rise so dramatically in the twentieth century. Unfortunately, our ability to assess and mitigate the environmental consequences of economic growth has not matched rises in productivity. Intensifying land degradation and multiplying industrial wastes are but two indices of the lack of fit between our economic and environmental capability. Human concerns for survival have driven economic advances; only recently has the same motive begun to drive improvements in environmental management.

Throughout the past three centuries, humanity has been involved in the Industrial Revolution, the most recent of five great transitions in human history. Bennett and Dahlberg review the transitions by which the dominant human institution has become the universalist modern state. It is the state that has fostered production by its ever-increasing spatial reach and by its support of widening markets or exchange networks and of the notion of property, which "creates a fictional domain over nature." Modern property thereby defines the natural world as a resource that can be tapped to gain energy and materials for human use. The elements of nature – air, water, soil, animals, minerals – become natural resources, which have monetary value. Their use must be regulated by the state through allocation of property rights to individuals, corporations, or to the state itself.

Nature is incorporated into society, and the natural world becomes an object for human use. Consequently, the modern state neglects or ignores changes in the environment in its anxiety to exploit natural resources. What Bennett and Dahlberg term highly centralized "modern resource regimes" have strong structural inclinations toward the incorporation and exploitation of resources or nature. Despite the panoply of presumably preservationist and protectionist state agencies – national parks, environmental protection agencies, among others – the overall thrust has been toward economic development at virtually any environmental cost.

Undergirding the modern state is the dramatic climb in technical innovation in the modern world. In his essay,

Headrick examines the progression of technical invention in industry, from the emergence of the textile and iron industries of the eighteenth century to the electronics and service sectors of our own time. Fossil-fuel energy sources have freed humanity from the tyranny of distance on land, at sea, and even in the air. The power thus released has permitted global exploitation of natural resources in timbering, mining, and agriculture. Humanity's most impressive technical feat has been to apply new technology (including species transfer) to grow more food around the world. Our capacity to store, retrieve, and disseminate new knowledge has improved, but has barely kept pace with technical innovation. Unfortunately, as Headrick stresses, the consequences of each invention are often unforeseen and unexpected. Certainly the environmental effects of new technical advances have been overlooked in the rush to seize new opportunities for enhanced production.

Chisholm, in his discussion of the global trend in separation of production and consumption, observes that trade in basic commodities (both absolute and per capita) has followed the steeply inclined developmental curve. Prior to World War I, the modern world saw a dramatic expansion in primary produce supply zones for the industrialized nations of Europe and North America. Their ability to exploit natural resources worldwide was a significant aspect of rising productivity and environmental stress in the eighteenth and nineteenth centuries. More recently, a decided shift has occurred. By far, the majority of goods transferred are manufactured goods rather than primary products. Comparative advantage in this more complex trading pattern rests as much on human energy and skill as on natural resources. The implications of this change for environmental pressures need further exploration.

Lowenthal traces the trajectory of attitudes toward environmental changes over the past three centuries. Not surprisingly, the shape of this curve, if plotted out, would resemble that of the exponential curve for world population, discussed earlier. Manifest alterations in the landscape of North America in the nineteenth century, for example, inspired the warnings of George Perkins Marsh at midcentury. Marsh was confident that damage done to the land could be repaired if full recognition were given to those large processes of change so evident in his lifetime. More recently, conservationists still believed that humanity should subdue nature and freely use its wealth in the belief that human technical capacity could restore that wealth. In the past few decades, however, the new environmental movement has gained numbers and passion. Recent public opinion has had a more pessimistic outlook than before. Human technology has harmed the natural world, and it is not at all certain that it can be put right again. Fueled by direct perception of environmental degradation as well as by technical indices generated by the use of new measuring techniques, the general public has pressed hard for remedial action – especially by the state.

Human attitudes and institutions, so carefully attuned to the immediate needs of survival – food, shelter, clothing, physical security, and cultural expression – until very recently have ignored all but the most localized impact of these activities upon the environment. As the cumulative effect of production has altered the natural world, social attitudes have begun to respond. An emerging world culture and increasingly interdependent social institutions now struggle to reconcile the conundrum of economic growth and sustainability of the biosphere.

JOHN F. RICHARDS

2

Long-Term Population Change

THOMAS M. WHITMORE   B. L. TURNER II   DOUGLAS L. JOHNSON
ROBERT W. KATES   THOMAS R. GOTTSCHANG

No aspect of understanding transformations of the biosphere is more fascinating or important than that of the patterns of human population change. It is fascinating because population is simultaneously a constituent of the biosphere and an agent of transformation. It is important because the scale and, in some cases, the kind of environmental transformations have been ascribed to population dynamics. At no time has this association seemed more important than in the recent period of global transformation and population growth. Indeed, the uniform pace and magnitude of modern population growth, along with the paucity of data for earlier periods, may color perceptions of the patterns of population change and of the nature of population-transformation relationships.[1]

This study places these patterns and linkages in a broader perspective through an exploration of long-term population change at several spatial and temporal scales, focusing on the patterns of millennial-scale population change in four regions. Some tentative exegeses are offered of patterns of long-term population change at these temporal and spatial scales and of their association with some of the more fundamental changes in regional environments. A basic thesis of this study is that the scale of analysis can strongly influence interpretations of the subject.

Global Perspectives

We possess at least three major interpretations of global population trends over the millennia. The arithmetic-exponential, perhaps the dominant perspective, views the history of global population as a two-stage phenomenon. The first stage consists of infinitesimally slow, monotonic growth up to the so-called Industrial Revolution. The second stage covers the recent, staggering acceleration in global population growth rates (Fig. 2.1a). The resulting long-term trajectory forms an exponential growth-like curve. While several versions of this curve exist, most indicate that about 90% of the world's population growth from its base is the product of the past 350 years. This period of most rapid growth is less than 1% of the vast interval and is commonly held responsible for the current stress on global resources and the associated transformations of the biosphere.

Another view, the logarithmic-logistic, is associated with Deevey (1960; but see Hassan 1981) (Fig. 2.1b). It divides 1 million years of population history into three disjunctive paths (see Menard 1987 for a similar division). Each of the population outbreaks associated with the "Tool, Agricultural, and Industrial Revolutions" is envisioned as a logistic-like curve in which the population "revolution" is, or is projected to be, followed by a leveling of population at a new, higher plateau. In this view, humankind has increased the carrying capacity of the earth at least thrice. It is presumed that each sociotechnological adjustment has been associated with qualitative and quantitative changes in environmental transformations.

A third view, an arithmetic-logistic, describes global population history from 10,000 B.C. as a set of three cycles (Fig. 2.1c) (McEvedy and Jones 1978: 343–51). In this case, an even finer division is made. The past 12,000 years are divided into three periods, chosen to focus on the growth-overshoot-stabilization patterns associated with two continental-scale changes in carrying capacity. The resulting continental-scale population "explosions" account for the change in global population.

These interpretations sacrifice detail to capture the long-term patterns of human occupance at a global scale. They draw our attention to the great inflections in the demographic trajectory of our species. A central message is that global growth spurts have accompanied sociotechnological expansion of the carrying capacity of the earth. Four characteristics of long-term growth are implied: (1) significant population "outbreaks" are limited to only one (the arithmetic-exponential) or three (the logarithmic-logistic and the arithmetic-logistic) sociotechnological transformations of humankind; (2) population variations about these trends within each technological-demographic phase are insignificant; (3) population decline is relatively insignificant; and (4) the general trend of population is coincident for all regions participating in a particular

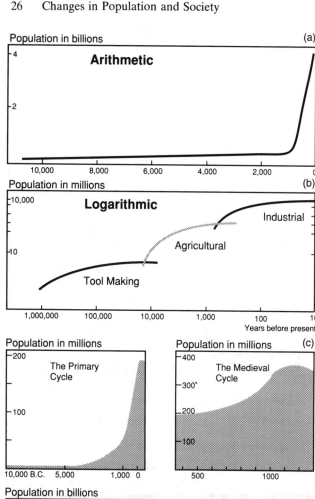

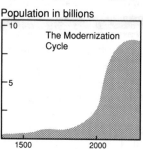

Figure 2.1 Global population paths.

technological-demographic phase (the arithmetic-exponential and logarithmic-logistic).

Regional Perspectives

In contrast, assessments of regions, albeit of varying size, indicate considerable diversity in population patterns, particularly during the premodern, or "agricultural," phases of human occupance. Examples may be found in McEvedy and Jones' (1978) comparison of populations over the past 1,475 years (A.D. 500–1975), in which at least four types of logistic curves can be identified (Fig. 2.2) (see Menard [1987: 14] for a tabular interpretation of McEvedy and Jones' data).[2]

The first curve resembles the global arithmetic-exponential curve (Fig. 2.2a) in its slow population increase, single inflection, and subsequent exponential growth. Although the inflection occurs at different times, the curve typifies the reconstructions for every region in Europe and most regions in the Americas, six in Asia, and five in Africa. A second

curve type (Fig. 2.2b) consists of an initial 500-year period of no or marginal growth, followed by differing degrees of inflection (shallow to steep) to exponential growth. This reconstruction is found for the regions of Australia, Canada, Soviet Asia and Siberia, and the Arabian Peninsula.

The third curve (Fig. 2.2c) has three parts: initial population growth, a significant pause or decrease in that growth, and an inflection to exponential growth. With some temporal variability, it typifies the reconstructions for Africa and the regions of Mongolia, Oceania, Central America, and Melanesia. The fourth curve (Fig. 2.2d) involves an initial wave of growth and decline between A.D. 1000–1500, followed by an inflection to exponential growth. It typifies the Islamic realm of the estern Mediterranean and North Africa.

Most of these reconstructions incorporate subcontinental sized expanses. The use of smaller spatial units (e.g., regions or countries) presumably would increase further the variability of the curves. Indeed, several subtypes of curves may become evident at this scale of analysis. Nevertheless, two common elements of these reconstructions emerge. Ultimately, every curve reaches an exponential growth phase – for example, the well-known twentieth-century population explosion. In contrast, the reconstructions for previous eras strongly suggest asynchronous regional variability in population trends, including the possibility of significant regional population declines. These possibilities should be illuminated by an examination of more compact, homogeneous regions over a longer period than that used by McEvedy and Jones. Such illumination is the goal of our long-term regional studies.

Long-Term Regional Population Reconstructions

Four reconstructions, two each for the Eastern Hemisphere and the Western Hemisphere, have been undertaken

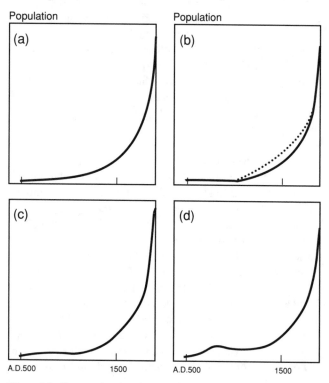

Figure 2.2 Classes of regional population paths.

as a preliminary exploration into the nature of population trends if space is held constant at the regional scale and time frames span several millennia. These regions are the Egyptian Nile Valley, the Tigris-Euphrates lowlands, the Basin of Mexico, and the central Maya lowlands of Mexico and Guatemala.[3]

Definitions

Here, the regional boundaries are constant through time and are based on a spatial congruency between a particular culture and a distinctive physical environment, at least during the first phases of Neolithic occupation (the first phases of the reconstructions). In this case, "region" does not imply a particular size range, although an arbitrary target range of about 10,000–50,000 km^2 was chosen initially. This scale was chosen to augment the archive of long-term regional population histories, and on the premise that for the majority of the reconstruction history, population dynamics and environmental transformations were largely played out within such cultural-ecological regions.

A temporal unit shorter than that of the total record is required to examine variability within the reconstructed paths. But since regional records are not of similar length and the reconstructed population patterns are not of similar shape, an arbitrary time scale for all cases is not feasible. To overcome this problem, and because the initial reconstructions revealed recurrent phases of population growth and decline, we decided to highlight portions of the record in which the population minimally doubles from its preexisting level or is minimally halved from its intervening apex. This criterion of amplitude divides each record into a series of aperiodic fluctuations. These wavelike undulations of differing length and amplitude are called *millennial long waves*. These dimensions were selected to accommodate the rather wide confidence intervals that are necessarily part of precensus population estimates and to increase the probability that a long wave is a characteristic of the population rather than an artifact of the uncertainty. For reasons of confidence, analysis focuses on the patterns traced by long waves rather than on shorter-term patterns.

Data and Procedures

The general problems of reconstruction involved: (1) using estimates derived from different types of data (e.g., archaeological and documentary); (2) selecting from competing estimates within a specific time frame by determining their demographic probability, quality of source data, and validity of estimation technique; and (3) estimating values for key time intervals for which estimates were lacking or unsuitable by means of a "qualitative best fit" approach.

In general, the types of data are similar for all the case studies. The archaeological surrogate data record ceramic and/or habitation site remains and convert these measures into population estimates. The historical-documentary data are also typically surrogate and no more comprehensive than the archaeological, at least in the early historical periods. The primary type of documentary data is taxation records of several kinds. Data from census documents were modified to

reflect the boundaries of our case-study areas. The unique problems associated with data acquisition and estimation procedures for each case cannot be detailed here; the technical papers cited in the text should be consulted.

Tigris and Euphrates Lowlands

The alluvial lowland of Iraq between the Tigris and Euphrates rivers is an exceedingly flat, desert landscape that boasts comparatively few indigenous physical resources other than the exotic streams that cross its expanse. Agriculture and human settlement are closely bound to water availability. Nevertheless, identifiable human settlement in Mesopotamia goes back at least 6,000 years.

No distinct physiographic border separates the formerly inhabited floodplain from the surrounding, comparatively unused areas, and different segments of the floodplain were used in different eras. For these reasons, defining the Mesopotamian settlement region is difficult. Here, an area encompassing Mesopotamian settlement in all periods – about 55,260 km^2 – is defined as the region (Fig. 2.3).

Data and Procedures   Both the Tigris and Euphrates rivers flood frequently and unpredictably, and the combination of gentle gradient and high sediment load produces abrupt shifts in stream channels. Hence, patterns of human habitation in Mesopotamia are complex and ephemeral. Further, the gradual (but sometimes abrupt) shifts in the courses of the Tigris and Euphrates rivers and their associated distributaries and canals have fostered a shifting pattern of human settlement. Regions that are now easily reached by gravity-fed irrigation water were, in former times, likely uninhabited periphery. Similarly, much of the heartland of ancient Mesopotamian civilizations now lies abandoned, far from the current rivers and canals. These difficulties have prevented the survey of all the area ever settled within the region (Fig. 2.3). The extensive settlement surveys of Adams (1965; 1981) and his colleagues (Jacobsen and Adams 1958; Adams and Nissen 1972) form the basis for the premodern population reconstruction.[4] Similarly, the relatively rich documentary materials of Mesopotamia are spatially and temporally fragmentary. Extrapolations from individual primate or capital-city populations are hindered by the uncertainty of the "rural" record.

Reasonably reliable census enumerations are twentieth-century phenomena. Johnson and Whitmore (n.d.) detail these and other problems, outline the procedures used to create these estimates, and analyze the sources for the reconstruction.

Population-Path Reconstruction   As early as 4100 B.C., an agricultural society thinly populated (0.45 people/km^2) the Mesopotamian lowlands. For the next 2,200 years, population grew from this base as agriculture and settlement spread gradually along the main natural watercourses of the southern alluvium (Fig. 2.4a and Table 2-1). By 1900 B.C., the population reached a peak of 630,000 (11.4 people/km^2). Following this, the population plummeted for 300 years, reaching a nadir of 270,000 (4.9 people/km^2) in 1600 B.C.

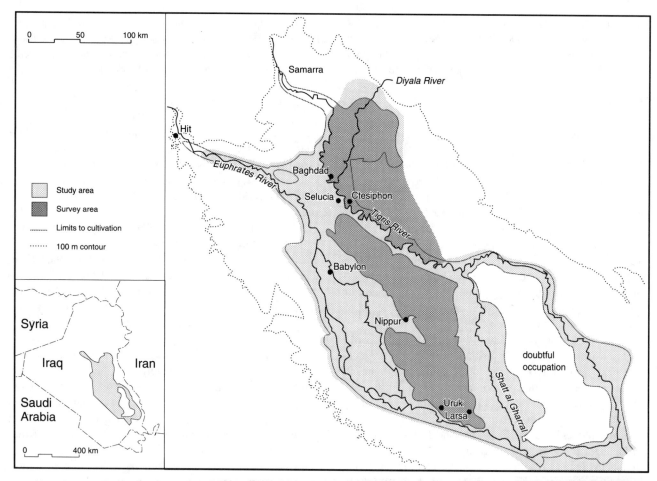

Figure 2.3 Tigris-Euphrates study area.

For the better part of the following millennium, populations rose and fell within rather narrow limits, never exceeding 350,000 (6.3 people/km²) (Fig. 2.4a and Table 2-1). After the Persian conquest of the lowlands, population growth began, and continued for a millennium. Settlement and the centralized, sophisticated organization of irrigation were now concentrated more in the north-central parts of the study area. The high point of this population growth occurred in the period encompassing the Sassanian and Abbasaid administrations (A.D. 550 to A.D. 800), during which 1.5 million people (27.1 people/km²) inhabited the study area (Fig. 2.4a and Table 2-1).

Beginning soon after the Arab invasion, the next 450 years were a period of sustained and rapid depopulation (Fig. 2.4a and Table 2-1). The population dropped to only one-tenth of its previous peak – 140,000 (2.5 persons/km²) – by A.D. 1300.

For 200 years, the Tigris-Euphrates lowlands remained relatively depopulated. By A.D. 1500, the total regional population had climbed to only 240,000 (4.3 people/km²). Slightly less rapid growth ensued for 250 years, as the regional population soared to 440,000 (8.0 people/km²) by A.D. 1850. Modern growth rates have exceeded 1.0%/year since A.D. 1850, and the A.D. 1982 regional population was in excess of 7,676,000 (138.9 people/km²).

Population-Path Characteristics A broad pattern of two millennium-length waves of population growth and decline,

followed by unprecedented modern growth, is evident in this reconstruction. The earliest wave, and by far the longest, at 3,650 years, sustained an average annual rate of growth of 0.15%. Its initially rapid (0.28%/year) 300-year decline was followed by 1,150 years of approximate population stasis (the overall rate of decline was 0.08%/year), reaching a nadir in 450 B.C.

The second great wave of growth and decline lasted 1,650 years (450 B.C. to A.D. 550). In it, almost a millennium of growth sustained an average annual growth rate of 0.22%. Unlike the first wave, the 750-year-long decline phase (A.D. 550 to A.D. 1250) of the second wave was continuous and rapid, averaging 0.32%/year.

The final partial wave of Tigris-Euphrates population dynamics is characterized by moderate-to-average growth (0.27 to 0.17%/year) for 550 years to A.D. 1850 and by very rapid exponential growth (averaging 2.2%/year) to the present.

Analysis of the long waves in population in the Tigris-Euphrates lowlands indicates a pattern of decreasing "wavelength," increasing "amplitude," and increasing rapidity of change over the millennia. In particular, the relatively restrained population path in the first wave has been replaced by more energetic change (both growth and decline) in the subsequent years. Viewed in its entirety, the long-term trajectory of population in Mesopotamia is typical of the pattern exhibited by regional reconstructions of the Islamic realm of

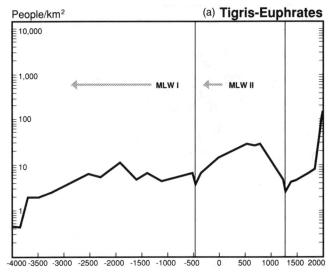

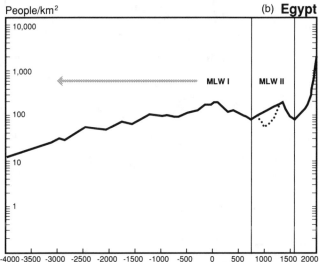

Figure 2.4 Tigris-Euphrates lowlands and Egyptian Nile Valley population densities.

North Africa and the eastern Mediterranean, except that in the Tigris-Euphrates lowlands, the initial arch of population growth and decline occurs earlier (Figs. 2.2d and 2.4a).

The Tigris-Euphrates population reconstruction may be characterized further in ecological system terminology. Here, the trajectory of population history suggests a "resilient" pattern – one capable of absorbing change, fluctuating greatly, yet persisting (Holling 1973: 17). This is in contrast to a "stable" pattern – one in which the population disturbances are small and the population rapidly returns to an equilibrium after a temporary disturbance. Further, the pattern of long waves suggests that the Tigris-Euphrates population exhibits increasing resilience and decreasing stability.

Transformations The population paths in the Tigris-Euphrates alluvium reflect a struggle to convert a meteorological desert into an agrarian landscape. The environmental transformations engendered by this conversion were designed to capture water resources through gravity flow irrigation, to minimize environmental hazard from damaging floods, and to cope with environmental degradation.

Initially, conversion to irrigated agriculture involved the replacement of existing riparian vegetation. As canal-based irrigation expanded, relatively barren desert lands were transformed. Beginning at least by 4100 B.C., irrigation was tied to natural watercourses of the Euphrates and its branches. Throughout the growth periods, these systems were expanded in area by use of canal networks. This expansion did not encompass the entire floodplain.[5] Rather, from 2000 B.C. to A.D. 500, there was a gradual movement northward of the "center of gravity" of the irrigated ecumene (Adams 1965, 1981; Adams and Nissen 1972). The incorporation of Tigris water was well underway by 300 B.C. to A.D. 226, and the second major growth period took place under an irrigation regime dominated by Tigris water.

Beginning with the earliest water diversion, overzealous watering apparently promoted both salinization and the growth of marshes at the tails of the water-distribution system. Drainage canal systems, built to alleviate waterlogging and salinization, added to the scale of transformation. By at least 1700 B.C., severe salinization appeared in some settled areas at the distal ends of the irrigation system (Jacobsen and Adams 1958). These areas were so degraded that they were abandoned as the locale of settlement, and transformation slowly migrated upstream. In addition, siltation has been a perennial managerial problem with the canals, one that was exacerbated by the increasing use of Tigris water.

Table 2-1 *Tigris-Euphrates Lowlands Population Reconstructions: 4100 B.C. to A.D. 1982*

Date	Density (people/km²)	Population	Immediate rate of change (percent/year)
4100 B.C.	0.45	25,000	—
3850	0.45	25,000	+0.00
3700	1.99	110,000	+0.99
3500	1.99	110,000	+0.00
3250	2.53	140,000	+0.10
2500	6.52	360,000	+0.13
2300	5.43	300,000	−0.09
1900	11.40	630,000	+0.19
1600	4.89	270,000	−0.28
1375	6.52	360,000	+0.13
1100	4.34	240,000	−0.15
500	6.33	350,000	+0.06
450	3.62	200,000	−1.10
350	6.33	350,000	+1.10
0 A.D.	13.57	750,000	+0.22
550	27.14	1,500,000	+0.13
700	24.43	1,350,000	−0.07
800	26.78	1,480,000	+0.09
1250	4.52	250,000	−0.40
1300	2.53	140,000	−1.16
1400	4.16	230,000	+0.50
1500	4.34	240,000	+0.04
1750	6.15	340,000	+0.14
1850	7.96	440,000	+0.26
1947	46.15	2,550,000	+1.80
1976	123.16	6,806,000	+3.40
1982	138.91	7,676,000	+2.00

A third type of transformation was necessary to protect these complex hydrologic systems against damaging floods. Throughout the time period, natural levees were raised and strengthened, and artificial barriers were erected to protect settlements. These geomorphological alterations, canals, levees, and drainage works have surprising persistence. Even in nearly abandoned areas of desert scrub, traces of ancient engineering works crisscross the landscape.

Indeed, the contemporary population of the region continues to use ancient canals and thus perpetuates the five-millennium-long tradition of transformation. And while the goals of transformation are similar, the technology and impacts have multiplied. Dams have been constructed to control the floodwaters of Tigris tributaries and to divert and store excess runoff. The resulting large-scale water distribution and drainage systems have raised, once again, the problem of salinization and waterlogging. Massive urban growth, particularly in Baghdad, Basra, Kirkuk, and Mosul, has increased air pollution and groundwater contamination. Thus productive transformations in this region carry with them costs (negative impacts) that may have been partly responsible for population decline in the past.

Egyptian Nile Valley

The linear oasis of the Egyptian Nile Valley is a nearly ideal laboratory in which to study population history. Despite early and important stimuli from Mesopotamia and other Near Eastern regions, the Egyptian Nile Valley has been largely isolated from outside contact by the barriers of desert and sea for much of its long history. For thousands of years it remained a self-contained, autonomous, and stable cultural unit.

There is an extremely close fit between the spatial core of Egyptian culture and the physiographic province of the Nile Valley (Fig. 2.5). For the overwhelming bulk of its history, this elongated ecumene encompassed approximately 27,300 km^2, which is roughly the maximum extent of land open to agriculture and habitation in a non–fossil-fuel economy.

Data and Procedures   Egyptian cultural continuity provides a relatively rich array of data with which to recreate the population history of the region. At the same time, the core of the Valley has been reused for thousands of years, and much of the physical evidence of the past has been lost, destroyed, or modified. This shortcoming is particularly important for the reconstruction of the period from 4000 B.C. to A.D. 100, since it is based largely on archaeologically derived surrogates of population density, and for the reconstruction of the period from A.D. 100 to A.D. 1800, since it is based largely on documentary surrogates for population data. The arguments and data elaborated by Butzer (1976) form the basis of the reconstruction for the former period, whereas the most important sources for the latter period are Russell (1958, 1966) and Dols (1977).[6] The contemporary-period data begin with the French census in A.D. 1798, although a modern census was not taken until A.D. 1882. For this period, we have been guided by McCarthy's (1976) analysis. Johnson

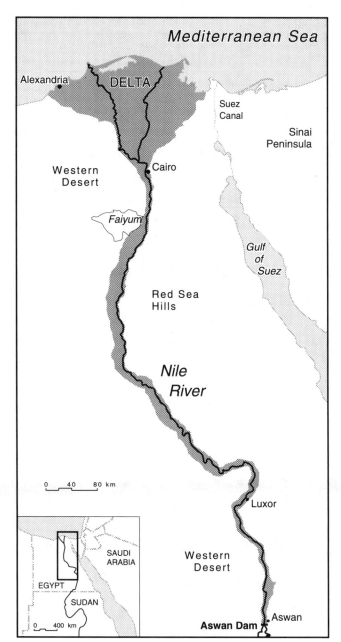

Figure 2.5 Egyptian Nile Valley study area.

and Whitmore (1987) detail the procedures, problems, and sources involved in producing this reconstruction.

Population-Path Reconstruction   The Egyptian population path begins as early as 4000 B.C., when a part agrarian, part hunting-and-gathering society had achieved the relatively high population density of 11 people/km^2 (350,000) (Fig. 2.4b and Table 2-2). From this base, population grew, and agriculture and settlement expanded throughout the Nile Valley for 4,100 years. This slow rise was not uniform, however, as is indicated by four episodes of decline (3000–2900 B.C., 2500–2100 B.C., 1800–1600 B.C., and 1250–1000 B.C.), totaling 850 years (Fig. 2.4b). The slow growth that characterized the Pharaonic dynasties was accelerated from 500 B.C. to 150 B.C. (Fig. 2.4b). In the 350 years of Persian and early Ptolemaic rule, population grew from 3 million to 4.9 million (179 people/km²). This rapid growth slowed in the later Ptolemaic and early Roman periods, when the Egyptian population reached its ancient maximum of 5.2 million (190 people/km²) in A.D. 100.

In contrast to the small variability of the first 4,100 years, the next 1,500 years are marked by a sequence of decline-growth-decline phases. From the A.D. 100 zenith, the Egyptian population plummeted for 600 years, apparently without interruption, to an A.D. 743 minimum of 2.2 million (81 people/km²). An alternative reconstruction extends this decline to a population minimum of only 1.5 million (55 people/km²) by A.D. 1000 (Fig. 2.4b and Table 2-2). The middle phase of this trio shows a population rebounding strongly from this late Byzantine–early Islamic minimum. By A.D. 1370, the population of 5.1 million (187 people/km²) virtually matched the Roman maximum. This upward movement was truncated by the Black Death after A.D. 1370. A second precipitous population decline ensued from A.D. 1370 to A.D. 1600.

From this nadir, Egyptian population has grown continuously to the present. This growth was slow until the mid-nineteenth century, when the population again matched the ancient maximum. Fueled by growth rates that have not fallen below 1.0%/annum since A.D. 1882, the Egyptian population has expanded to 44.3 million (1,623 people/km²) in A.D. 1983.

Population-Path Characteristics The broad outline of two and one half millennium-long waves of population growth and decline can be discerned in this reconstruction. The first wave is by far the longest at 4,743 years (or 5,100 years in the alternate reconstruction). It is marked by moderate rates of change, an average growth rate of 0.06%/annum, and an average rate of decline of 0.13%/annum (or 0.14%/annum in the alternative reconstruction). The second wave traces 857 years (or 600 years in the alternative reconstruction) of growth and decline. In this wave, the rates of change are greater than in the first; the average rate of growth equals 0.13%/annum (or 0.33%/annum), whereas the decline phase averages 0.38%/annum. This acceleration is shown even more clearly in the third wave's growth phase, thus far lasting 383 years. To date, growth has averaged 0.79%/annum.

In this case, the slow movement of the earlier population numbers in the first long wave has given way to more rapid and profound changes in the second long wave and in the initial portion of the third. The fluctuations in population have grown greater. Using the ecological system analogue, the Egyptian population reconstruction suggests a pattern characterized by decreasing stability and increasing resilience.

Viewed in its entirety, the Egyptian case study, perhaps better than any of the other case studies, mimics a global pattern – the logistic growth associated with Deevey's model (Fig. 2.1b). This view portrays a population expanding (4000 B.C. to A.D. 100) to a preindustrial "limit" (A.D. 100 to A.D. 1850). This limit is exceeded only when a renewed surge of exponential growth (A.D. 1850 to present) is engendered by the transformations of the modern age (Fig. 2.4b).

Table 2-2 *Egyptian Population Reconstructions: 4000 B.C. to A.D. 1983*

Date	Density (people/km²)	Population	Immediate rate of change (percent/year)
4100 B.C.	12.82	350,000	—
3150	25.64	700,000	+0.08
3000	31.87	870,000	+0.14
2900	29.30	800,000	−0.08
2500	58.61	1,600,000	+0.17
2100	51.28	1,400,000	−0.03
1800	73.26	2,000,000	+0.12
1600	64.10	1,750,000	−0.07
1320	91.58	2,500,000	+0.13
1250	106.23	2,900,000	+0.11
1000	95.24	2,600,000	−0.04
900	98.90	2,700,000	+0.04
750	91.58	2,500,000	−0.05
664	91.58	2,500,000	0.00
500	109.89	3,000,000	+0.07
300	128.21	3,500,000	+0.15
181	164.84	4,500,000	+0.21
150	179.49	4,900,000	+0.27
50	172.16	4,700,000	−0.04
14 A.D.	183.15	5,000,000	+0.10
100	190.48	5,200,000	+0.05
300	117.22	3,200,000	−0.24
400	124.54	3,400,000	+0.06
600	95.24	2,600,000	−0.13
650	87.91	2,400,000	−0.16
743	80.59	2,200,000	−0.09
*884	86.45	2,360,000	+0.14
*975	64.47	1,760,000	−0.32
*1000	54.95	1,500,000	−0.21
*1090	61.65	1,683,000	+0.13
*1189	86.08	2,350,000	+0.34
*1300	153.85	4,200,000	+0.52
869	96.70	2,640,000	(from 743) +0.14
1050	124.54	3,400,000	+0.14
1170	146.52	4,000,000	+0.13
1300	171.25	4,675,000	+0.12
1370	186.81	5,100,000	+0.12
1420	131.87	3,600,000	−0.74
1500	91.58	2,500,000	−0.45
1600	78.76	2,150,000	−0.15
1800	141.14	3,853,000	+0.29
1846	163.96	4,476,000	+0.33
1882	287.18	7,840,000	+1.56
1897	356.56	9,734,000	+1.44
1907	413.44	11,287,000	+1.48
1917	467.07	12,751,000	+1.16
1927	519.34	14,178,000	+1.06
1937	583.19	15,921,000	+1.16
1947	695.09	18,976,000	+1.76
1960	955.50	26,085,000	+2.45
1966	1101.94	30,083,000	+2.38
1976	1341.61	36,626,000	+1.97
1980	1549.05	42,289,000	+3.59
1983	1624.29	44,343,000	+1.59

*Alternate reconstruction for A.D. 743–1300 period.

Transformations Throughout history, Egypt's environmental transformations have been directed to increasing agricultural output. The rachet-like growth trajectory in the first 4,100 years, a dynamic equilibrium about an upward-tending trend line, was made possible by the Nile's relatively stable replenishment of resources. For this reason, the environmental transformations of this period were directed toward the more effective capture of the resources annually pulsed through the system: Nile floodwater and its soil-renewing silt. The resource base was expanded throughout the period as irrigated cultivation spread at the expense of grazing and "natural" riverine vegetation.

This spatial expansion (internal colonization) was supplemented by technological innovations that further transformed the Valley and served to intensify output. The first of these, artificial basin irrigation (utilizing controlled flooding and drainage in dike-constrained basins), was established by 3000 B.C. in Upper Egypt (Butzer 1976: 107). Limited expansion and intensification was made possible by the introduction of the *shaduf* (pole-lever bucket lifter) about 1300 B.C. (Butzer 1976: 46). The complex system of winter and summer cropping characteristic of Egyptian agriculture emerged after the introduction of the *saquia* (animal-powered waterwheel) in Ptolemaic times (about 300 B.C.). The early Islamic period (A.D. 800–1300) witnessed additional intensification and expansion of agriculture using new cultigens and rotations that demanded more intensive water management (Watson 1981).

The rapid population growth evident in the Egyptian record since A.D. 1850 has been associated with what are, perhaps, the most significant transformations – barrages, high dams, and chemical inputs to agriculture. These innovations made possible the conversion from predominantly flood-basin irrigation to perennial, multicrop agriculture. A range of environmental impacts including salinization, nutrient replacement loss, erosion, fisheries disruption, and pollution has accompanied this most recent transformation.

Basin of Mexico

The Basin of Mexico is an elevated, enclosed hydrographic unit, situated at the southern end of the central Mexican plateau. The basin floor, 2,240 m above sea level, is circumscribed by high mountains or rugged hills. This naturally demarcated region is small enough to facilitate population reconstructions, yet large enough to have been a heartland for several major Amerindian civilizations and currently to hold the huge metropolis of Mexico City.

As delimited here, the Basin occupies 6,650 km² (Fig. 2.6). For much of its settlement history, the center of the Basin contained a large lacustrine system of freshwater lakes on the southern margin, a major saline lake, Texcoco, in the center, and a brackish lake in the north. A combination of urban buildup and the completion of a drainage canal has greatly diminished the Basin's lacustrine system.

Data and Procedures Reconstruction of the Basin's population history is facilitated by the level of attention given to the region because of its sociopolitical significance to Mexican

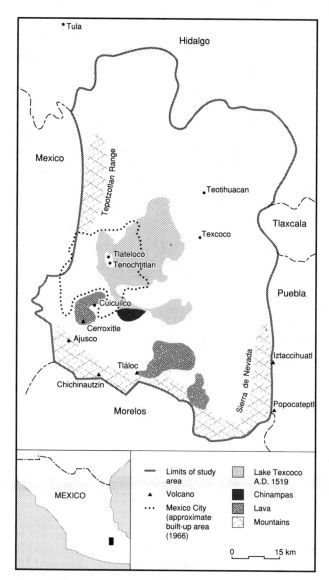

Figure 2.6 Basin of Mexico study area.

history and prehistory. The population reconstruction for the pre-Hispanic period (1150 B.C. to A.D. 1519) is based almost completely on the extensive surface survey and detailed analysis of the Basin of Mexico Project (Sanders, Parsons, and Santley 1979).[7] The colonial-period (A.D. 1520 to A.D. 1800) reconstruction is based on interpretations of various documentary sources, which record partial populations or surrogates for population (e.g., Cook and Simpson 1948; Cook and Borah 1960; Gibson 1964; Gerard 1972; Borah 1976: 18–22; Denevan 1976: 7–11; and Sanders 1976: 94–98, 112–14).[8] Modern period data begin with the A.D. 1793 census, although true censuses did not begin until the Mexican government assumed full control of the process in A.D. 1900 (Kicza 1980). Details of the procedures and of problems encountered in all facets of the reconstruction are described by Whitmore and Turner (1986).

Population Reconstruction The Basin was occupied as early as 3000 B.C., although the first population estimate – about 5,000 (0.75 people/km²) – is associated with the appearance of agrarian settlements in the south as early as 1150 B.C. (Fig. 2.7a and Table 2-3).

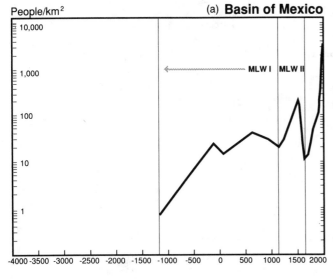

People/km² (a) **Basin of Mexico**

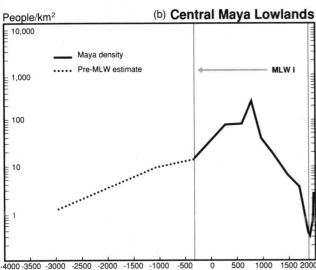

People/km² (b) **Central Maya Lowlands**

— Maya density
····· Pre-MLW estimate

Figure 2.7 Basin of Mexico and central Maya lowlands population densities.

Table 2-3 *Basin of Mexico Population Reconstructions: 1150 B.C. to A.D. 1985*

Date	Density (people/km²)	Population	Immediate rate of change (percent/year)
1150 B.C.	0.72	5,000	—
650	3.76	25,000	+0.32
300	11.28	75,000	+0.31
100	21.81	145,000	+0.32
100 A.D.	12.03/16.54	80,000/110,000	−0.29/0.13
650	37.59	250,000	+0.20/0.14
950	27.07	180,000	−0.10
1150	19.55	130,000	−0.16
1250	26.32	175,000	+0.29
1519	180.45	1,200,000	+0.77
1530	150.38	1,000,000	−1.40
1548	135.34	900,000	−0.66
1565	52.63	350,000	−4.70
1580	37.59	250,000	−2.80
1595	22.56	150,000	−2.40
1620	11.02	73,300	−2.75
1643–44	11.58	77,000	+0.22
1692	13.23	88,000	+0.28
1742	22.56	150,000	+1.07
1787–94	41.35	275,000	+1.21
1797–1804	45.11	300,000	+0.87
1838	61.65	410,000	+0.82
1856–57	71.43	475,000	+0.82
1869–70	76.69	510,000	+0.59
1878–80	91.73	610,000	+1.96
1889	105.26	700,000	+1.53
1900	140.90	937,000	+2.65
1910	179.55	1,194,000	+2.42
1940	315.79	2,100,000	+1.88
1970	1,473.23	9,797,000	+5.10
1980	2,150.38	14,300,000	+3.78
1985	2,721.81	18,100,000	+4.70

The settlement spread across the Basin, and population grew to 145,000 by 100 B.C. During a decline of 200 years, the population fell to between 80,000 and 110,000. This trend was reversed by A.D. 100, and new growth culminated in the development of the large city-state of Teotihuacán (150,000) before A.D. 650. The Basin population reached 250,000 (37.6 people/km²) at this time. A major depopulation followed the collapse of Teotihuacán (A.D. 650), and the Basin's population declined for 500 years to 130,000 by A.D. 1150.

From this nadir, the population grew again for approximately 350 years, culminating in the Aztec state. By A.D. 1500, the population of the Basin was 1.2 million (180 people/km²), with perhaps 150,000–200,000 located on the island capital of Tenochtitlán-Tlatelolco (Fig. 2.7a). The Spanish arrival in A.D. 1519 set off a major depopulation in the Basin as a whole that lasted for a little more than 100 years. The population collapsed at the average annual rate of 2.8%, and by A.D. 1620/25, the Basin's population numbered only 73,000. Such a collapse (part of the general Amerindian collapse) has few parallels elsewhere, although the prehistoric

collapse of the classic Maya (below) appears to have been of a similar magnitude.

A new period of growth began in the seventeenth century and has continued to the present. It was not until the early 1900s that the Basin fully recovered from its fifteenth-century losses. Nevertheless, the phenomenal twentieth-century growth rates (averaging over 3.5%/annum) have pushed the Basin population to over 18 million (2,721 people/km²) in A.D. 1985 (Table 2-3).

Population-Path Characteristics The Basin of Mexico has witnessed two and one-half millennium-length waves of growth and decline over the past 3,000 years. The first wave is at least 2,300 years in duration. It is characterized by an average growth rate of 0.22%/annum and an average rate of decline of 0.13%/annum. The second wave involved only 470 years, but the population grew at the higher average rate of 0.6%/annum and plummeted even more rapidly, at an average rate of 2.8%/annum. In the 360 years (to date) of the latest wave, the average rate of growth is 0.5%/annum. This pattern

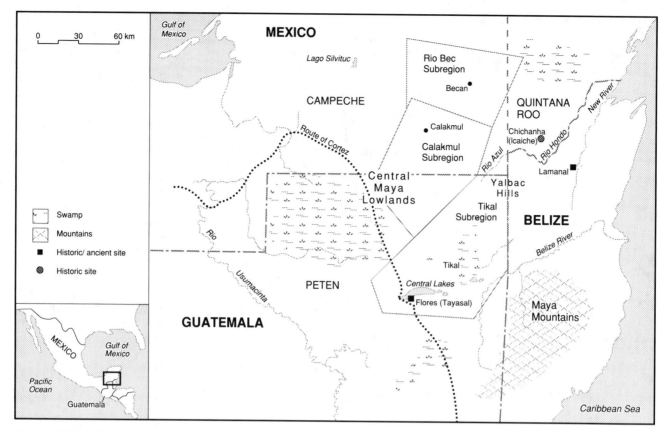

Figure 2.8 Central Maya lowlands study area.

of declining wavelength, increasing amplitude, and increasing rates of change suggests a pattern of increasing resilience and low stability.

Viewed as a single long-term trajectory, the Basin reconstruction mimics approximately that of the global arithmetic-exponential path (Figs. 2.1 and 2.7a). The Basin curve records moderate, steady growth from the earliest times (about 1150 B.C.) up to an inflection in the sixteenth century. An accelerated rate of exponential growth marks the period since that turning point.

Transformations   There have been three fundamentally different transformations of the Basin. The first of these was marked by the extension of agriculture throughout the Basin, but especially in the northeastern section (near Teotihuacán), where terracing and irrigation were prevalent. The fall of that city-state doubtless reduced the scale and pace of transformations in the Basin. There is no evidence of agrarian or environmental collapse in the Basin, however; rather, the political and economic deevolution of Teotihuacan may have triggered the population decline.[9] The dramatic population increase associated with the rise of the Aztec state led to extensive alterations of the southern lakes Xochimilco and Chalco for wetland agriculture. This transformation included partitioning them from saline Lake Texcoco by a dike.

The second set of transformations was less evolutionary. The Spanish conquest destroyed the Aztec capital, altered the Basin's economy, forced migration, and introduced diseases. During this period, the *chinampa*, or wetland system of agriculture, was dramatically reduced in favor of *haciendas*, whose introduced European livestock and cultivation practices altered the preexisting human landscape.

The final transformations of the Basin have been the most profound. They have been engendered by an industrial revolution and by both in-migration and natural population increase. By A.D. 1900, the central lakes were largely drained. By the second half of this century, this reclaimed land and much of the rest of the Basin were consumed by a massive metropolis. The once open, lacustrine Basin is now literally paved over by urban sprawl. The industrial transformations that have facilitated this concentration of population have led to other transformations as well, including serious water and air pollution (chap. 35).

Central Maya Lowlands

The central Maya lowlands are located at the base of the Yucatan Peninsula in northeastern Petén, Guatemala, and southern Campeche and Quintana Roo, Mexico. This 22,715 km² region is delimited by a composite of cultural and physiographic criteria (Turner 1983a) (Fig. 2.8). The region, the so-called heartland of the classic period Maya civilization, once contained three subcultures, as distinguished by three distinct architectural zones: Tikal, Calakmul, and Rio Bec (Adams and Jones 1981). This tripartite cultural region corresponds closely to the distinctive interior ridgeland of the peninsular area. This rolling terrain of seasonal tropical forests, interspersed with seasonally inundated depressions, or *bajos*, ranges between 50 m and 300 m in elevation.

Data and Procedures   The population reconstruction for the central Maya lowlands used three distinctive data sets. Population data for the pre-Hispanic period (before A.D. 1500) are derived from archaeological studies of the remains of several large settlements, such as Tikal and Becan, and rural or intersite surveys (e.g., Bullard 1960; Coe 1965; Haviland 1965; 1969; 1972; Puleston 1973; 1974; Eaton 1975; Turner 1978; 1983a; Rice and Rice 1980; Ford 1982; Adams et al. 1984).[10] The reconstruction developed here accounts for density differences between rural and urban settlement through the use of rank-order assumptions about Maya settlements (Adams and Jones 1981; Turner n.d.). The historic period reconstruction (A.D. 1500 to A.D. 1880) requires manipulation of the rather sparse archival data, consisting primarily of Spanish observations (Thompson 1966; Bolland 1977; Hellmuth 1977; Jones 1977). Decadal censuses are not available for the entire region until A.D. 1930, and there are problems of fit between the regional and the census boundaries (see Turner 1986).[11] The problems and procedures for all facets of the reconstruction are discussed by Turner (1986).

Population-Path Reconstruction Agrarian settlements existed on the peripheries of the central Maya lowlands as early as 3000 B.C. (Hammond 1977), and presumably were within the region as well by that time. This reconstruction begins, however, at 300 B.C., with an estimated population of 242,000 (10.65 people/km^2) (Fig. 2.7b and Table 2-4). The subsequent 600 years were marked by overall growth, culminating in an A.D. 300 population of 1,020,000 (44.9 people/km^2). A brief hiatus of very slow or no growth followed for 300 years. Rapid population growth (0.45–0.58%/annum) resumed from A.D. 600 to A.D. 800, resulting in an apex population of between 2.6 million and 3.4 million people (117.2–151.2 people/km^2).

From this classic period zenith, very rapid (0.8 to 0.93%/annum) depopulation led to an A.D. 1000 population of 536,000 (23.4 people/km^2) (Fig. 2.7b and Table 2-4). While the subsequent rates of depopulation declined, the central Maya lowlands population continued to plummet for 900 more years. A nadir population of 6,800 (0.3 people/km^2) was reached about A.D. 1900. Very rapid modern growth, especially since 1960, pushed the population to 48,700 (2.1

people/km^2) in 1970 – a figure that is less than 2% of the regional population of 1,000 years earlier.

Population-Path Characteristics The pattern of population change in this case study differs radically from the regional or global models; unlike all the others, the "modern era" population in the central Maya lowlands has failed (to date) to exceed or even match its earlier maximum. For that reason, the long-term trajectory does not mimic any global- or large-scale pattern. Similarly, while there is a millennial-long wave (300 B.C. to A.D. 1900), no pattern of waves exists. This arciform curve suggests little stability or resilience.

Transformations The pattern of environmental transformation in the central Maya lowlands parallels the uniqueness of its population pattern. During its long period of growth, the central Maya lowlands emerged dominant in the Maya world – at least in terms of monumental architecture and other material manifestations of civilization. As in the other case studies, this population growth resulted in dramatic environmental changes. Certainly before A.D. 300, much of the vast tropical forest had been cut and species composition altered (Turner 1983a; Turner and Miksicek 1984; Pohl 1985). During the later stages of the growth phase, perhaps as much as 75% of the region (both wetland and ridgeland) had been altered for intensive cultivation. Unlike the other cases, the 1,100-year-long population collapse was accompanied by a return to the preexisting environment, tropical forest, albeit in an altered state. This great expanse of forest and wetland is once again under siege for timber, agriculture, and grazing by a small (but rapidly growing) population on its margins.

Reconstruction Patterns and Inferences

Regional-scale population reconstruction patterns may be characterized best as aperiodic fluctuations that include repetitive phases of growth and decline (Figs. 2.4 and 2.7). These patterns are not well correlated in time, even for situations of roughly similar technological order. They do not, however, appear to be simply random; rather, they suggest wavelike patterns.

These waves decrease in length through time; the mean length of the first wave (about 3,600 years) is over twice the mean length of the second (about 1,500 years). The growth phase of the third wave (still in progress) averages 378 years to date.

The growth phases of the waves are temporally dominant, comprising about 70% of the reconstructions. It is important to note, however, that while the decline phases are shorter than growth phases (except in the Maya case), they are not precipitous. Even including the extraordinary sixteenth-century population collapse in the Basin of Mexico, declines in the second waves average over five centuries in duration. The first waves' declines are even longer.

Within the waves, the rates of population growth show an acceleration over time – not a surprising result, given the increasing peak densities and decreasing wavelengths. The average rate of growth for the first wave (0.14%/annum) is about half of that for the second (about 0.30%/annum).[12]

Table 2-4 *Central Maya Lowlands Population Reconstructions, 1000 B.C. to A.D. 1970*

Date	Density (people/km^2)	Population	Immediate rate of change (percent/year)
1000 B.C.	7.09	161,000	—
300	10.65	242,000	+0.06
300 A.D.	44.90	1,020,000	+0.24
600	47.41	1,077,000	+0.02
800	117.24/151.22	2,663,000/3,435,000	+0.45/0.58
1000	23.60	536,000	−0.80/0.93
1200	12.55	285,000	−0.32
1500	4.58	104,000	−0.34
1700	2.73	62,000	−0.26
1850	0.35	8,000	−1.37
1900	0.30	6,800	−0.33
1950/1960	0.65	14,800	+1.41
1970	2.14	48,700	+7.94

From the nadir of the second waves, modern growth rates average 1.43%/annum. This acceleration is shown even more clearly in the decline rates. The mean rate of decline in the first wave (0.11–0.12%/annum) is less than one-eighth as rapid as the second's (1.0–1.01%/annum). A good deal of this remarkable acceleration, however, is due to the sixteenth-century Amerindian population collapse in the Basin of Mexico.

With the exception of the Maya case – an anomaly in many ways – the rapidity of large-amplitude population change increases through time for each reconstruction. This pattern suggests an "evolution" of the respective populations toward reduced stability and increased resilience, consistent with Holling's (1973: 18–19) notion that complex systems may fluctuate more than less complex ones. In our reconstructions, greater regional population fluctuations appear to coincide with incorporation into more complex political economies, both spatially and hierarchically.

Viewing the overall population trajectories, only one case, the Basin of Mexico, mimics reasonably well the widely cited arithmetic-exponential model. Similarly, two cases, the Egyptian Nile and the Tigris-Euphrates lowlands, superficially resemble the logarithmic-logistic model. The Maya case fits none of the global or larger regional models. That regional reconstructions only vaguely resemble global models is not surprising because the global models presumably reflect summation of regional patterns. These results emphasize the pitfalls of assuming that global patterns are reproduced at smaller scales.

Implications for Environmental Transformations

Global and regional models of long-term population change imply environmental transformation because population requires resources and is a transforming agent. Indeed, these global models and regional population reconstructions act as partial surrogates from which inferences about environmental transformation can be made, if only because population change is typically related to changes in settlement and cultivated areas.

The patterns of environmental transformation associated with global models differ. The arithmetic-exponential global path (Fig. 2.1a) implies a gradual, cumulative, or expansive transformation of the earth's "faces" and "flows" until the population outbreak of the modern era. This outbreak implies qualitative changes in the fundamental faces and flows of the environment to accommodate the unique scale and pace of growth. It is also associated with the quantitative shifts in the global interconnectivity of flows in particular (e.g., the role of carbon dioxide flows in global atmospheric warming). In contrast, the logarithmic-logistic global model (Fig. 2.1b) identifies three "revolutionary" population outbreaks in which environmental transformations of the earth took place. Each of these revolutions presumably entailed qualitative and quantitative changes in the nature of environmental transformation. Alteration of the earth's faces and flows was mostly local or regional in the first two global transformations, but has been global in the third. These episodes are linked by

periods of less profound environmental change. Finally, the arithmetic-logistic pathways of the past 10,000 years (Fig. 2.1c) suggest three major periods of transformation. The first and second are marked by the expansion of human activity and changes in both the faces and the flows of the biosphere at local or regional scales (McEvedy and Jones 1978: 343). The third is the modern era, in which fundamental changes in both the faces and the flows are taking place.

The message implicit in the latter two global models is that major environmental transformations had taken place before the modern (industrial) era. Most of them were played out largely at local or regional scales, although the impacts may have been panregional or even continental in scale. Also, for most of human history, these transformations were related largely to the dynamics of the local and regional populations, particularly within any great technological phase of society, although the relationship need not have been direct or linear. Inasmuch as long-term population trends in different regions have not been coincidental, it follows that regional transformations of the biosphere have not been either, although regional-scale transformations may have contributed to long-time-scale, global cumulative transformations.

In the four regional case studies, major alterations in the regional environments accompanied the growth phases of the initial population waves. These alterations involved primarily spatial expansion of settlement and cultivation, and therefore, were most likely concentrated in the faces of regional biomes. Beyond this, the broad relationships between population trends and transformations are somewhat less regular and undoubtedly more complex. Intensification of land use was a major factor contributing to transformations, but the relationship was mediated by cultural, socioeconomic, and/or technological changes. Indeed, in some cases, transformation continued while populations declined, and owing to regional variation in regional environmental opportunities and constraints, specific levels of population need not have resulted in similar scales of transformation.[13] Even the long-term impacts of the changes have differed.

Examples from the four case studies help to clarify these points:

1.. The first population decline in the Tigris-Euphrates lowlands (1900–1600 B.C.) has been associated, by some scholars (e.g., Jacobsen and Adams 1958), with widespread soil salinization due to the very transformation that sustained population growth: widespread, intensive canal irrigation. Regardless of the ultimate cause of this degradation, it was of such magnitude that the subsequent decrease in population and relocation of farming activities did not result in a recovery of the environment; the transformation persisted.

2. The sustained period of population decline in Egypt during the Byzantine period (A.D. 100–743) and during the Islamic fifteenth and sixteenth centuries seems not to have been accompanied by significant changes in the scale or character of environmental transformation. While some lands were abandoned during epidemics, to be sure, it is not clear that the fundamental patterns of agricultural practice

were much modified. Nor is it certain that the area under human management greatly decreased.

3. The central Maya lowlands were radically altered, such that well before the large populations of the Classic period (A.D. 600–1000), the tropical forest had been largely eradicated and many wetlands altered for agriculture (Turner 1983a). Unlike the experience in the Tigris-Euphrates area, this transformation did not persist. Once the population declined in a major way, the forest returned, albeit altered somewhat in terms of species composition. Even today, the expanse of tropical forest in the region is greater than that found during the classic peak, A.D. 800–1000.

4. Each indigenous population growth phase in the Basin of Mexico was accompanied by a new level of environmental change. But the Basin of Mexico also witnessed significant, if not radical, environmental transformations during the catastrophic population collapse of the sixteenth century. They were precipitated both by the massive reduction in labor available to sustain the production systems that had been in place and by the cultural and political-economic changes introduced by the Spanish. The conquerors – bearers of new technologies and biota – drained wetlands and introduced livestock and other exogenous fauna and flora that changed the landscape (Simpson 1952).

These examples demonstrate the complexity of the interactions between population and environment that give rise to environmental transformations in any locale. They indicate the danger of invoking simple, direct correlations between fluctuations in population and environmental transformations, and the need for caution in using population as a simple surrogate for environmental transformation.[14] Nevertheless, it is interesting to note that in the three cases in which the population patterns exhibit decreased stability, both radical and cumulative environmental transformations persist. In these cases, the time scales of population variability are asynchronous with those of environmental transformation and recovery. The persistence of those environmental transformations need not be in phase with the population trajectories. It is unclear if fluctuating populations are responsible for persistent transformations, nor is it certain that cumulative environmental changes lie behind the decreased stability of the local population systems.

Conclusion

Returning to our central task, to place in perspective the current era of population-transformation by drawing upon analogs and inferences from the past based on different scales of analysis, we need look no further than the logarithmic-logistic global model to demonstrate that major explosions in global population are not unique to the modern era. What is unique, of course, is the scale, rapidity, and global interdependence of modern growth – beginning about A.D. 1650 with a world population estimated at 545 million (McEvedy and Jones 1978: 342) and projected to peak by A.D. 2155 at about 10–11 billion (Vu 1985: 3) – that carries with it the ability to transform basic flows of the biosphere.

Examination of long-term population records at the regional scale reveals a common pattern of significant episodic growth and decline. Hence, within the known worlds of earlier generations, population change and regional transformation of significant magnitude occurred, albeit at rates slower than today's. These transformations were concentrated on the faces of the regional biospheres but included radical changes at times. Nevertheless, these regional population changes were only loosely linked to the accompanying environmental transformations for most of the record.

The most important inference from the past, though, may be for the future. The regional case studies indicate that what went up – population – sometimes came down, often dramatically and significantly. This view leads us to speculate that the predicted global-scale zero rate population growth (ZPG) would need not necessarily be achieved by persistent ZPG at regional scales. The warning is that regional population declines are possible, potentially brutal, and even likely, accompaniments to ZPG on a global scale.

For the most part, regional-scale transformations have persisted, despite population fluctuations. Since we are now in the midst of a long period of global-scale population growth and environmental transformation, with rapid change occurring in all but a few regions, this observation is important. If the experience of past regional population changes and their accompanying environmental transformations has relevance for the future, the projected global-scale population "leveling out" need not diminish the scale and profundity of global environmental change. This is particularly true on the regional or local scale, where global ZPG (of population or transformation) need not be accompanied by local or regional equilibrium.

Notes

1. We wish to thank the following individuals who offered suggestions and criticisms of this work at various stages of its progress: R. McC. Adams, K. W. Butzer, W. M. Denevan, D. Dumond, J. Parsons, and T. Webb.

2. We are aware of the range of error and of the various controversies that surround the regional reconstructions in the 1978 *Atlas of World Population History*. An example is the low population estimate for the Americas in A.D. 1500. This 14 million estimate is considered by most regional specialists as a rock bottom figure for a population that could have been as high as 72 million (Denevan 1976: 291). The strength of the *Atlas* lies not in its detail, but in its breadth of survey and comparison.

3. These studies stem from the "Millennial Long Waves in Human Occupance" project, undertaken by the authors with support from the National Science Foundation. Additional funds were provided by a MacArthur Foundation award to R. W. Kates. The regions were selected on the basis of the length of the population record, the quality of the data, and the expertise of the authors. The project was designed to draw upon existing population reconstructions or interpretations, not to create new ones per se.

4. R. McC. Adams (personal communication) provided a speculative reconstruction for the population of the alluvium.

5. The boundaries of this study area encompass all of the floodplain area believed to have been settled and cultivated at any period. Even so, it is scarcely one-half of the total area of the floodplain (Fig. 2.3). Further, at no time in antiquity was all of the study area cultivated or occupied.

6. K. W. Butzer (personal communication) notes, and we concur, that the most reliable method of estimating ancient Egyptian popu-

lations is to use archaeological-site-size data, coupled with site hierarchy, to compile an "urban" population for each period. Some of the data necessary for such an approach are found in Butzer (1976). We believe, however, that these surrogate-based estimates are sufficient to indicate the broad path of population and are, therefore, adequate for the purposes of this paper.

7. The basic survey methodology involved sampling surface sherd densities, converting these into habitation figures, and from these figures, estimating population numbers. The pros and cons of this method are detailed in Sanders, Parsons, and Santley (1979) and in Whitmore and Turner (1986).

8. The methodologies used to create population estimates from these data are complex and controversial (e.g., Sanders 1976: 94–98, 112–14; Denevan 1976: 7–11; Borah 1976: 18–22). Here, a best-fit method was used to reconcile differing estimates (Whitmore and Turner 1986).

9. The fall of Teotihuacán may have involved movement of much of the population to another city-state, Tula, just outside of the Basin. At least one argument suggests that Teotihuacán was dependent on trade, including food, from the greater central Mexican zone. Loss of control of this trade, therefore, would have weakened that city-state in any number of ways (Sanders 1976).

10. Population estimates based on area of settlement are typically derived by sampling to derive occupational frequency by time phase, assuming a constant number of occupants per structure.

11. In addition to the problems of fit, the distributions of the populations within census districts are highly skewed. In most cases, the large majority of the population in each census district lives outside the regional boundaries used in this study.

12. Rates of growth are figured using the equation, $P2 = P1 \times e^{rt}$ (where $P2$ = subsequent population, $P1$ = initial population, e = base of natural logarithms, r = annual rate of growth, and t = number of years in the interval), and solving for r.

13. This reasoning follows from work on population and agricultural transformations (Brookfield 1962; Brush and Turner 1987; Turner, Hanham, and Portararo 1977) and has been applied to the Maya lowlands by Turner (1983a).

14. Lee (1987), however, argues that, in the long term, the population-resource-transformation nexus is dominated by a homeostatic relationship between population and food availability or economic productivity. He argues that a fluctuating population may be in equilibrium with a fluctuating economic product if the relative ratio between the two is stable. This relationship is complicated by factors independent of the population-food relation per se. Influences on population dynamics such as epidemic disease or external forcing factors that alter the "carrying capacity" of the system (for example, environmental fluctuations) act independently of the homeostatic relation – and in most cases are of significantly greater importance in explaining shorter-run variability (Lee 1987: 455, 452). Further, Lee (1987: 452–453) argues that as long as there is any trace of a homeostatic relationship (i.e., a negative-feedback relationship), its influence, by virtue of its persistence, will come to dominate human population dynamics over the long run. This homeostatic relationship is weakened greatly, however, in the modern age (Lee 1987: 452).

References

Adams, R. E. W., and R. C. Jones. 1981. Spatial patterns and regional growth among Classic Maya cities. *American Antiquity* 46: 301–22.

Adams, R. E. W., G. D. Hall, I. Graham, F. Valdez, S. L. Black, D. Potter, D. J. Cannell, and B. Cannell. 1984. *Final 1983 Report. Rio Azul Project Reports No. 1*. Center for Archaeological Research, University of Texas at San Antonio.

Adams, R. McC. 1965. *Land Behind Baghdad: A History of Settlement on the Diyala Plains*. Chicago: University of Chicago Press.

———. 1981. *Heartland of Cities*. Chicago: University of Chicago Press.

Adams, R. McC., and H. Nissen. 1972. *The Uruk Countryside: The Natural Setting of Urban Societies*. Chicago: University of Chicago Press.

Bolland, O. N. 1977. The Maya and the colonization of Belize in the nineteenth century. In *Anthropology and History in Yucatan*, ed. G. D. Jones. Austin: University of Texas Press.

Borah, W. W. 1976. The historical demography of aboriginal and colonial America: An attempt at perspective. In *The Native Population of the Americas in 1492*, ed. W. M. Denevan. Madison: University of Wisconsin Press.

Brookfield, H. C. 1962. Local study and comparative method: An example from Central New Guinea. *Annals of the Association of American Geographers* 52: 242–58.

Brush, S. P., and B. L. Turner II. 1987. The nature of farming systems and themes of their change. In *Comparative Farming Systems*, ed. B. L. Turner II and S. P. Brush. New York: Guilford Press.

Bullard, W. W. 1960. Maya settlement patterns in Northeastern Peten, Guatemala. *American Antiquity* 25: 355–72.

Butzer, K. W. 1976. *Early Hydraulic Civilization in Egypt: A Study in Cultural Ecology*. Chicago: University of Chicago Press.

Coe, W. 1965. Tikal: Ten years of study of a Mayan ruin in lowland Guatemala. *Expedition* 8: 5–56.

Cook, S. F. and W. W. Borah. 1960. *The Indian Population of Central Mexico 1531–1610*. Ibero-Americana 44. Berkeley: University of California Press.

Cook, S. F. and L. B. Simpson. 1948. *The Population of Central Mexico in the Sixteenth Century*. Ibero-Americana 31. Berkeley: University of California Press.

Deevey, E. S. Jr. 1960. The human population. *Scientific American* 203(3): 194–204.

Denevan, W. M. 1976. Introduction. In *The Native Population of the Americas in 1492*, ed. W. M. Denevan. Madison: University of Wisconsin Press.

Dols, M. W. 1977. *The Black Death in the Middle East*. Princeton: Princeton University Press.

Eaton, J. D. 1975. *Ancient Agricultural Farmsteads in the Rio Bec Region of Yucatan*. Contributions of the University of California Archaeological Research Facility, Berkeley. No. 27.

Ford, A. 1982. Los Mayas en El Petén: Distribucion de las poblaciones en el Periodio Clasico. *Mesoamerica* 3: 124–44.

Gerard, P. 1972. *A Guide to the Historical Geography of New Spain*. Cambridge Latin American Studies, No. 14. Cambridge: Cambridge University Press.

Gibson, C. 1964. *The Aztecs under Spanish Rule: A History of the Indians of the Valley of Mexico 1519–1810*. Stanford: Stanford University Press.

Hammond, N. 1977. The earliest Maya. *Scientific American* 236: 116–33.

Haviland, W. A. 1965. Prehistoric settlement at Tikal, Guatemala. *Expedition* 7: 14–23.

———. 1969. A new population estimate for Tikal, Guatemala. *American Antiquity* 34: 424–33.

———. 1972. Family size, prehistoric population estimates, and the ancient Maya, *American Antiquity* 37: 135–39.

Hassan, F. A. 1981. *Demographic Anthropology*. New York: Academic Press.

Hellmuth, N. 1977. Cholti-Lacondon (Chiapas) and Petén Itzá agriculture, settlement patterns, and population. In *Social Processes in Maya Prehistory*, ed. N. Hammond. New York: Academic Press.

Hollings, C. S. 1973. Resilience and stability of ecological systems. In vol. 4, *Annual Review of Ecology and Systematics*, ed. R. F. Johnson. 1–23. Palo Alto, CA: Annual Reviews Inc.

Jacobsen, T., and R. McC. Adams. 1958. Salt and silt in ancient Mesopotamian agriculture. *Science* 128: 1251–8.

Johnson, D. L., and T. M. Whitmore. 1987. *Population Reconstruction of the Egyptian Nile Valley: 4000 B.C. to Present*. Technical Paper No. 3, Millennial Long Waves of Human Occupance Project, Clark University, Worcester, MA.

———. n.d. *Population Reconstruction of the Tigris–Euphrates Lowlands: 4100 B.C. to Present*. Technical Paper No. 4, Millennial Long Waves of Human Occupance Project, Clark University, Worcester, MA.

Jones, G. D. 1977. Levels of settlement alliance among the San Pedro Maya of western Belize and eastern Peten, 1857–1936. In *Anthropology and History in Yucatan*, ed. G. D. Jones. Austin: University of Texas Press.

Kicza, J. E. 1980. Mexican demographic history of the nineteenth century: Evidence and approaches. In vol. 21, *Statistical Abstract of Latin America*, ed. J. W. Wilkie and S. Haber. Los Angeles: U.C.L.A. Latin American Center Publications.

Lee, R. D. 1987. Population dynamics of humans and other animals, *Demography* 24(4): 443–65.

McCarthy, J. A. 1976. Nineteenth century Egyptian population, *Middle Eastern Studies* 12(3): 1–39.

McEvedy, C., and R. Jones. 1978. *Atlas of World Population History*. New York: Penguin Books.

Menard, S. W. 1987. Regional variations in population histories. In *Perspectives on Population*, ed. S. W. Menard and E. W. Moen. New York: Oxford University Press.

Pohl, M., ed. 1985. *Prehistoric Lowland Maya Environment and Subsistence Economy*. Papers of the Peabody Museum of Archaeology and Ethnology, vol. 77. Harvard University.

Puleston, D. E. 1973. *Ancient Maya Settlement Patterns and Environment at Tikal, Guatemala: Implications for Subsistence Models*. Unpublished Ph.D. dissertation, University of Pennsylvania.

———. 1974. Intersite areas in the vicinity of Tikal and Uaxactun. In N. Hammond, ed., *Mesoamerican Archaeology. New Approaches*. London: Duckworth.

Rice, D. S., and P. M. Rice. 1980. The northern Peten revisited, *American Anthropologist* 45: 432–54.

Russell, J. C. 1958. Late ancient and medieval populations, *Transactions of the American Philosophical Society* 48(3): 5–148.

———. 1966. The population of medieval Egypt, *Journal of the American Research Center in Egypt* 5: 69–82.

Sanders, W. T. 1976. The population of the central Mexican symbiotic region, the Basin of Mexico, and the Teotihuacan Valley in the sixteenth century. In *The Native Population of the Americas in 1492*, ed. W. M. Denevan. Madison: University of Wisconsin Press.

Sanders, W. T., J. R. Parsons, and R. S. Santley. 1979. *The Basin of Mexico: Ecological Processes in the Evolution of a Civilization*. New York: Academic Press.

Simpson, L. B. 1952. *Exploitation of Land in Central Mexico in the Seventeenth Century*. Ibero-Americana 36. Berkeley: University of California Press.

Thompson, J. E. S. 1966. *The Rise and Fall of Maya Civilization*. 2d ed. Norman: University of Oklahoma Press.

Turner B. L. II. 1978. The development and demise of the swidden thesis of Maya agriculture. In *Pre-Hispanic Maya Agriculture*, ed. P. D. Harrison and B. L. Turner II. Albuquerque: University of New Mexico Press.

———. 1983a. *Once Beneath the Forest. Prehistoric Terracing in the Rio Bec Region of the Maya Lowlands*. Dellplain Latin American Studies, No. 13. Boulder, CO: Westview Press.

———. 1983b. Comparisons of agrotechnologies in the Basin of Mexico and the Central Maya Lowlands: Formative to the Classic Maya collapse. In *Highland–Lowland Interaction in Mesoamerica: Interdisciplinary Approaches*, ed. A. G. Miller. Washington, D.C.: Dunbarton Oaks Residence Library and Collection.

———. 1986. *Population Reconstruction of the Central Maya Lowlands, 1000 B.C. to Present*. Technical Paper No. 2, Millennial Long Waves of Human Occupance Project, Clark University, Worcester, MA.

———. n.d. Population reconstruction of the Central Maya lowlands: 1000 B.C. to A.D. 1500. In *Precolumbian Population History in the Maya Lowlands*, ed. T. P. Culbert and D. S. Rice. Albuquerque: University of New Mexico Press.

Turner, B. L. II, R. Q. Hanham, and A. V. Portararo. 1977. Population pressure and agricultural intensity, *Annals of the Association of American Geographers* 67: 384–96.

Turner, B.L. II, and C. H. Miksicek. 1984. Economic plant species associated with prehistoric agriculture in the Maya lowlands, *Economic Botany* 38: 179–93.

Vu, M. T. 1985. *World Population Projections, 1985*. Baltimore, MD: The Johns Hopkins University Press for the World Bank.

Watson, A. M. 1981. A medieval Green Revolution. In *The Islamic Middle East, 700–1900: Studies in Economic and Social History*, ed. A. L. Udovitch. Princeton: The Darwin Press, Inc.

Whitmore, T. M. and B. L. Turner II. 1986. *Population Reconstruction of the Basin of Mexico, 1150 B.C. to Present*. Technical Paper No. 1, Millennial Long Waves of Human Occupance Project, Clark University, Worcester, MA.

3

Population

PAUL DEMENY

Nature, the ancients held, makes no jumps. The proposition, with little qualification, also applies to human history, including its demographic component. Sharp demarcations of epochs and stages within the story of population change as it unfolds over time are thus necessarily arbitrary. They can be defended only, first, by invoking the need to make such demarcations for orderly discussion of any subject and, second, by choosing break points on the time scale that recommend themselves both as practical and as least vulnerable to counterarguments.

The aim of the discussion that follows is to present an outline of demographic history in the modern era. The discussion will focus on changes in population size globally and in major regions, and on describing the factors, demographic and social, underlying those changes. It will take 1700 as the starting point, a choice that satisfies the criteria just noted. Reasonably accurate estimates of the size of the population of the world and of its major geographic subdivisions have been pushed back to that date by historians of human demography with some success. For earlier points in time, population estimates become increasingly conjectural. The beginning of the eighteenth century also marks the onset of an acceleration of the rate of global population growth and most of its major regional components. Earlier periods did show examples of shifts in the balance of births and deaths, causing spurts in population size. Invariably, however, such increases proved episodic, or if they were sustained for longer periods, the average rate of increase attained remained modest, such as a small fraction of one percent per year. In contrast, from 1700 on, the rate of growth followed a nearly unbroken upward trend for over two and a half centuries, culminating at the unprecedentedly high global level of 2 percent during the decade centering on 1970. Finally, and most importantly, the acceleration of population increase after 1700 reflected the beginning of a decisive qualitative shift away from the theretofore dominant demographic regime, which was characterized by a precarious balance between high levels of fertility and mortality. The putative endpoint of that secular shift, characterized by low levels of fertility and mortality, has now been reached in some parts of the world's population, is more or less dimly discernible in other parts, and can be at least conjectured as a plausible future in all remaining populations. In other words, and in round figures, 1700 is the best reference date to mark the beginning of what has come to be called the modern demographic transition.

Consideration of the nearly 300 years of demographic history bracketed between 1700 and the present can be conveniently divided into two periods of unequal length: one prior to, the other following the end of World War II – or, for practical purposes, the year 1950. For each of these two periods, the discussion will focus on, first, overall changes in population size and the implied characteristics of demographic growth. Second, using the notion of demographic transition as a frame of reference, it will briefly examine the proximate demographic changes underlying population growth and the factors that explain them. A closing section will comment on likely future demographic developments. This will be done not so much with the intent to prognosticate but rather as a means to complement the description of the existing demographic situation of the world and its major regions. Barring extreme assumptions concerning future fertility, mortality, and migration, demographic inertia assures that current demographic characteristics and near- and medium-term population futures are tightly linked. Population projections represent not just a necessarily tentative prediction of what is to come, but a report about demographic potential – coiled, as it were, in the existing demographic makeup.

Population Change, 1700–1950

The single most important demographic information about a population of a given area is size. A time series of such data provides two crucial indexes of population dynamics: the rate of growth over time (usually expressed as annual change per hundred population), and – an indicator often more pertinent as far as resource use and environmental impact are concerned – absolute change in population size over a given time period. Unequal rates of change between components of a population aggregate lead to shifts in population structure reflected in growing or declining shares of the various components within the total. In the short term, population changes represented by these indicators tend to appear negligible, even when population growth is "rapid." By any historical standard, 2 percent annual growth amply qualifies for such characterization, yet in a year-to-year perspective, such change tends to be barely perceptible on the aggregate level. But, over time, seemingly glacial change can rapidly cumulate into major shifts in size and structure. Two populations, starting with the same initial stock but one growing at a 2 percent annual rate and the other stationary, will be, in 100 years, in a 7:1 numerical ratio to each other. In 250 years, the growing population would be 148 times larger than the stationary population. In the long run, population numbers shape human history and set a crucial term in the equation determining humankind's impact on its physical and social environment.

Size and Growth

The first modern attempts to estimate the size of the world's population were made at the end of the seventeenth century, just a few years from the beginning of the period under discussion here. Sir William Petty, father of "political arithmetick," made his pioneering calculation concerning global numbers in 1682 (Petty 1698). Lacking population data, he started with the by then quite accurately known land areas of the world and combined these with estimates of what today would be called carrying capacity. Astute as this approach was, the resulting global estimate, 320 million, was badly off the mark: probably well below 50 percent of the actual figure. Although a few years later, in 1695, the statistician Gregory King arrived at what present-day demographic historians would consider a quite accurate figure – between 600 and 700 million – these early efforts underscore the uncertainty of statistical estimates in the absence of data derived either from comprehensive censuses of the population or from continuously maintained registers of inhabitants in a given territory. But the practice of conducting censuses – enumerations that, unlike administrative records kept for

various purposes, such as taxation, seek to cover the population as a whole – began only in the mid-eighteenth century in continental Europe (notably in Scandinavia and in Austria-Hungary), in 1790 in the United States, and in 1801 in Britain. It is only during the nineteenth century that more or less regular census-taking became institutionalized in all European countries (with Russia the last, in 1897), as well as in a number of countries of Latin America. The first modern census in India, albeit of less than adequate coverage, was taken in 1867 to 1872, and in Japan, only in 1920. The majority of Asia's population was still not covered by a full enumeration at the close of World War II, as was true for the population of Africa (Glass 1966).

Population estimates covering the 250 years following 1700 thus must rely to a significant degree on information deficient in coverage and quality. Most often such information consists of results of partial enumerations and of statistics on households, dwellings, or hearths. Estimates may also involve manipulation of supplementary socioeconomic information and the drawing of inferences from sundry demographic data. Skillful application of statistical estimating techniques (such as "backward projections") permits, nevertheless, valid reconstruction of population time series for individual countries. The reliability of the resulting estimates of course will vary considerably between regions, and it is likely to diminish as the time distance from the present lengthens. Pioneering work on preparing estimates for the period 1700–1950 has been done by Willcox (1931) and Carr-Saunders (1936) and, more recently, by Durand (1967, 1977), Clark (1967), and Biraben (1979), and for the period 1920 to 1950, by the United Nations (1966). McEvedy and Jones (1978) offer a valuable compendium containing detailed long-term historical series disaggregated to the country level.

The relatively high degree of consistency of the time series presented by the various authors should not, in itself, inspire confidence in their accuracy. The consistency is often built-in: apart from the fact that later work often tends to draw heavily

Table 3-1 *Population of the World and of Major Areas (Millions), 1700–1985, and Projected Population in 2020*

	1700	1750	1800	1850	1900	1950	1985	2020
World total	679	769	957	1,260	1,650	2,515	4,853	8,061
Africa	107	106	107	111	133	224	557	1,441
Asia[a]	435	498	630	801	925	1,375	2,834	4,680
China	—	*200*	*323*	*430*	*436*	*555*	*1,060*	*1,460*
Japan	—	*30*	*30*	*31*	*44*	*84*	*121*	*130*
Rest of Asia	—	*268*	*277*	*340*	*445*	*736*	*1,653*	*3,090*
Europe[a]	92	109	145	208	294	393	492	514
USSR	30	35	49	79	127	180	277	343
Northern America[b]	2	3	5	25	90	166	265	327
Latin America[c]	10	15	19	34	75	165	404	719
Oceania	3	3	2	2	6	13	25	37

Notes: [a] Excluding the USSR
     [b] Canada and the United States
     [c] South and Central America, Mexico, and the Caribbean
     — = Not available

Source: Compilation based on Durand 1967, 1979, Biraben 1979, and United Nations 1989.

Millions

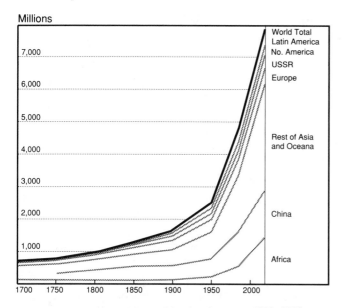

Figure 3.1 Population of the world and major areas, 1700–1985; Projected population in 2020. *Source:* see Table 3-1.

subcomponents. Figure 3.1 depicts these time series in the form of a line diagram in which the course of the changing global population is shown as the aggregate of continental layers. (In this graph, Oceania, demographically too small to be shown separately, is included with "Rest of Asia.") The continental divisions shown in the table and in the graph treat the present territory of the Soviet Union as a separate unit, hence define Europe and Asia as excluding that country. Also, in the case of Asia (which around 1800 contained almost two-thirds of the world's population), further detail is provided by showing China and Japan, hence the rest of Asia, separately. Tables 3-2 and 3-3 give the average rates of annual population increase and the absolute amounts of population change for each of the 50-year time periods defined by the series in Table 3-1. Table 3-4 (p. 44) and Figure 3.2 (p. 50) display the shifting composition of the global population with respect to major geographic areas. (For reference in the discussion below, in each of these tables, as in Fig. 3.1, estimates for the year 1985 and projected populations for the year 2020 are also shown.)

Clearly, viewed in an evolutionary perspective, the 250 years between 1700 and 1950 have witnessed extraordinary success of the human species in terms of expanding numbers, a success that invokes the image of swarming. It took countless millennia to reach a global 1700 population of somewhat under 700 million. The next 150 years, a tiny fraction of humankind's total history, roughly matched this performance. By 1950 global human numbers doubled again, to surpass 2.5 billion. The average annual rate of population growth was 0.34% in the eighteenth century; it climbed to 0.54% in the nineteenth century, and to 0.84% in the first half of the twentieth. In absolute terms, the first five decades following 1700 added 90 million to global numbers. Between 1900 and 1950, notwithstanding two world wars, an influenza pandemic, and a protracted global economic crisis, the net addition to population size amounted to nearly ten times that much.

Participation in this spectacular global expansion has differed greatly from continent to continent, and has done so in a pattern that has shifted appreciably over time. The most conspicuous contrast between the demographic map of 1700 and that of the mid-twentieth century is the result of rapid

on earlier estimates, similarity is also generated by authors' tendency to work backward from the relative terra firma of more recent and more reliable data by using similar simplifying assumptions. Durand (1977: 260) offers an insightful evaluation of the quality of historical population estimates in terms of "indifference ranges of estimates" for each world region. He defines those ranges not as indicators of the limits of possible errors (which would be wider), but as limits, within which, in his judgment, "there seems to be little ground for preference between lower and higher figures." Thus, for example, Durand professes indifference between 735 million and 805 million as estimates of the global population in 1750, or between 400 and 450 million as estimates of the population of China in 1900. Wide as these ranges are, they do not necessarily bracket the single-point estimates of various authors for some of the regions most deficient in reliable statistics, notably for Africa.

Estimates, based on Durand (1967, 1977) and Biraben (1979) for 1700–1950, spaced at 50-year intervals are presented in Table 3-1 for the global population and for its continental

Table 3-2 *Average Annual Rates of Population Increase (Percent). Estimates: 1700–1985; Projection: 1985–2020*

	1700–1750	1750–1800	1800–1850	1850–1900	1900–1950	1950–1985	1985–2020
World total	.25	.44	.55	.54	.84	1.88	1.45
Africa	.0	.0	.1	.4	1.0	2.6	2.7
Asia[a]	.3	.5	.5	.3	.8	2.1	1.4
China	—	*1.0*	*.6*	*.0*	*.5*	*1.9*	*.9*
Japan	—	*.0*	*.1*	*.7*	*1.3*	*1.0*	*.2*
Rest of Asia	—	*.1*	*.4*	*.5*	*1.0*	*2.3*	*1.8*
Europe[a]	.3	.6	.7	.7	.6	.6	.1
USSR	.3	.7	1.0	1.0	.7	1.2	.6
Northern America[b]	.8	1.0	3.2	2.6	1.2	1.3	.6
Latin America[c]	.8	.5	1.2	1.6	1.6	2.6	1.6
Oceania	—	—	—	—	1.6	1.9	1.2

Notes and Source: See Table 3-1.

Table 3-3 *Absolute Increase in Population Size (Millions). Estimates: 1700–1985; Projection: 1985–2020*

	1700–1750	1750–1800	1800–1850	1850–1900	1900–1950	1950–1985	1985–2020
World total	90	188	303	390	865	2,338	3,208
Africa	−1	1	4	22	91	333	884
Asia[a]	63	132	171	124	450	1,459	1,846
China	—	123	107	6	119	505	400
Japan	—	0	1	13	40	37	9
Rest of Asia	—	9	63	105	291	917	1,437
Europe[a]	17	36	63	86	99	99	22
USSR	5	14	30	48	53	97	66
Northern America[b]	1	2	20	65	76	99	62
Latin America[c]	5	4	15	41	90	239	315
Oceania	0	−1	0	4	7	12	12

Notes and Source: See Table 3-1.

population increase in the Western Hemisphere. At the beginning of the seventeenth century, the combined populations of Northern America (i.e., the United States and Canada) and of Latin America (the rest of the Western Hemisphere) was about one-tenth of the population of Europe, including Russia. Northern America, in comparative terms a virtual demographic vacuum in 1700, increased its population during the next 250 years eightfold: from about 2 million to some 166 million. Latin America, which in precolumbian times had a population more than ten times larger than that of northern America, suffered a major demographic catastrophe in the sixteenth and seventeenth centuries. The precipitous decline in the size of the Amerindian population of the region bottomed out around 1700, with a population less than one-third of its size 200 years earlier. The recovery from this low point has been rapid, although the rate of population growth during the first 200 years of this period remained distinctly below that of northern America. By around 1850, Latin America's population surpassed its precolumbian peak, and in the first 50 years of the twentieth century, Latin America (along with the demographically much smaller Oceania) became the world's fastest growing region. By midcentury, with a population of 165 million, Latin America's demographic weight equaled that of the United States and Canada.

Stagnation, and perhaps even retrogression, characterized demographic change in Africa for a longer period than was the case in Latin America, post-Columbus. The point applies with particular emphasis to Africa south of the Sahara. There the onset of rapid population growth was a phenomenon delayed until the first half of the twentieth century, when it reached an average annual rate of about 1%. In 1950, the population of Africa was not much more than twice its size in 1700, thus registering the lowest overall rate of increase among the continents during the entire 250-year period. As a result, the share of Africa's population in the world's total dropped from about 16% in 1700 to about 9% in 1950.

The strongest impact on the world's changing demographic makeup was due, however, to combinations of rapid population growth and large initial demographic weight. The joint populations of Europe and of the area which is today the Soviet Union amounted to some 18% of the world's total in 1700. In the next 250 years, Europe's population more than quadrupled, and that of the USSR grew sixfold. Furthermore, the growth of European stock was much larger than these figures suggest. Perhaps nine-tenths of the population increase in Northern America and Oceania and two-thirds of that in Latin America could be directly attributed to European outmigration to, and to the subsequent rapid growth of

Table 3-4 *Distribution of the World Population by Major Areas (Percentage). Estimates: 1700–1985; Projection: 2020*

	1700	1750	1800	1850	1900	1950	1985	2020
World total	100.0	100.0	100.0	100.0	100.0	100.0	100.0	100.0
Africa	15.8	13.8	11.2	8.8	8.1	8.9	11.5	17.9
Asia[a]	64.1	64.8	65.8	63.6	56.1	54.7	58.4	58.1
China	—	26.0	33.8	34.1	26.4	22.1	21.8	18.1
Japan	—	3.9	3.1	2.5	2.7	3.3	2.5	1.6
Rest of Asia	—	34.9	28.9	27.0	27.0	29.3	34.1	38.3
Europe[a]	13.6	14.2	15.2	16.5	17.8	15.6	10.1	6.4
USSR	4.4	4.6	5.1	6.3	7.7	7.2	5.7	4.3
Northern America[b]	.3	.4	.5	2.0	5.5	6.6	5.5	4.1
Latin America[c]	1.5	2.0	2.0	2.7	4.6	6.6	8.3	8.9
Oceania	.4	.4	.2	.2	.4	.5	.5	.5

Notes and Source: See Table 3-1.

European migrant populations within, Europe's demographic offshoots in the vast, formerly thinly populated, lands of the Americas, Oceania, and northern Asia. Altogether, the areas of European settlement that comprised 20% of the world's population in 1700 claimed 36% of that total by the middle of the twentieth century.

Perhaps as remarkable as this European growth performance was the spectacular expansion of the population of China in the eighteenth century. Between 1750 and 1800 China's annual rate of population growth averaged 1% – nearly twice as high as that of Europe. (This rapid growth, in all probability, was a continuation of sustained demographic increase during the preceding two centuries.) The expansion continued in the first half of the nineteenth century, but came to a virtual halt in the second half, followed by a weak reemergence of growth between 1900 and 1950. As a result of these shifting growth trends, the share of the population of China within the world's total climbed from 26% in 1750 to as high as 34% in 1850, but dropped to 22% by 1950.

Thus, 250 years of rapid if uneven demographic growth brought about major changes in the world's demographic makeup. Most of the areas suitable for human settlement under the existing state of technology became inhabited. The sharpness of the gradient of population density (admittedly only a very rough index of the relationship of human populations to their physical environment) between the Old World and the New has greatly diminished. In 1700 all but a small fraction of the world's population was rural. By 1950, nearly 30% lived in urban areas, and the proportion urban was 64% in Northern America, 56% in Europe, and 41% in Latin America (United Nations 1988). The ten largest cities of the world, ranging from 5 to 12 million in size, had a combined population of 75 million (United Nations 1985).

Writing in 1955, John von Neumann (1986) saw the globe in a "rapidly maturing crisis," caused by an environment that has become "both undersized and underorganized." Contemplating a diminished *Lebensraum*, he lamented the loss of a safety factor due to the expanding geographic scope of man's activities: "At long last, we begin to feel the effects of the finite, actual size of the earth in a critical way.... Literally and figuratively, we are running out of room" (p. 118). Such pessimism, as later demographic developments would suggest, was perhaps rather premature. Yet, as world population has passed the 2.5 billion mark, looking backward from the vantage point of the middle of the twentieth century, a feeling of creeping claustrophobia was hardly unfounded.

Demographic Transition

Population growth is a residual: it is a reflection of the balance of accretion and decay; of births and deaths. This simple accounting identity becomes more complicated in a population that can grow not only through "natural increase" (births minus deaths), but also through migration: entries from, and exits to, the "outside." The global population, of course, is by definition a closed system; there, natural increase is the only possible source of demographic growth. The smaller the population unit considered, however, the greater is the likely influence of migration on population change.

Indeed, looking at growth at the level of broad continental aggregates conceals much of that influence because a large share of migration is certain to take place within these regions.

Over the long pull of human history, migration powerfully shaped the population of all continents. In the modern era, too, intercontinental migration – much of it voluntary, but in the eighteenth and nineteenth centuries, much also forced, or involving movement of indentured labor – was important in the peopling of the New World and parts of Africa. Such movements had important direct and long-lasting indirect impacts on the population of the receiving areas. While typically of less relative weight in the sending countries (which were generally populous), migration was nevertheless important in moderating or even blocking natural population growth in parts of the Old World. Thus, it is estimated that between the late 1840s and the early 1930s, some 52 million migrants left Europe (including Russia) for destinations overseas, most of them for the Americas. The peak of this mass movement was registered in the decade just before the outbreak of World War I, during which time over 13 million Europeans emigrated (Carr-Saunders 1936). Data on return migration, by no means a negligible phenomenon, are much less certain.

During the period we are considering, even when intercontinental migration was at its peak, the number of migrants was far surpassed by the numbers generated by natural increase. As to the important indirect effects of migration on population growth, they are exerted through migrants' affecting the balance of births and deaths in the sending and receiving areas. Thus, understanding the proximate causes of population growth must concentrate primarily on understanding the levels of fertility and mortality and their changes over time.

"Demographic transition" is a frame of reference for organizing the mass of historical experience that has accumulated on these matters since the sixteenth century. More ambitiously, it is also a theory – a set of propositions incorporating generally valid relationships that can be extracted from that experience: relationships between either various components of the demographic growth process (for example, between mortality and fertility trends) or facets of socioeconomic change and demographic behavior (for example, between urbanization and changes in family size). Such relationships can be used to discern and predict the direction of change in demographic growth and its proximate determinants, or more optimistically, even quantitative features of such changes (for example, the timing of the onset and the tempo of an expected change).

There is abundant empirical evidence to confirm the proposition that premodern demographic regimes are regimes of high fertility and high mortality. Indeed, given the latter, the former is a logical necessity. For example, as stable population models (models incorporating the assumption of constant fertility and mortality over time) demonstrate, with an expectation of life at birth of 20 years, a population cannot survive unless women have, on the average, 6.5 births (Coale and Demeny 1983). Any actually observed population of low expectation of life thus had to possess institutions that generated and sustained high average levels of fertility.

But such institutions and, indeed, the underlying proclivities of the human race for procreation shaped by evolution also could result in levels of fertility that more than compensated for mortality, generating rapid population growth. Malthusian theory (Malthus 1966) was above all concerned with that eventuality. In Darwin's paraphrase of Malthus, "there is no exception to the rule that every organic being naturally increases at so high a rate, that if not destroyed, the earth would be soon covered by the progeny of a single pair" (1968: 117). The equilibrating mechanism that would relieve the pressure that sustained population growth would in due course inevitably put on the environment – on the "means of subsistence" – was thus identified as mortality; set into motion, directly or indirectly, by some mixture of "war, pestilence, and famine." Premodern demographic history amply documents the workings of these three scourges of humankind.

But low mortality is universally desired, and if attainable, a demographic regime that seeks to secure and preserve it will be socially and individually preferred. Such a regime also has inevitable consequences for the level of fertility. For example, if expectation of life at birth is 75 years (a level now well surpassed in a number of populations), combining it with a fertility of 6.5 children per woman would generate a stable growth rate of 4% per annum. Within a single century, such a growth rate would increase a population fifty-five-fold. Clearly, such a combination of fertility and mortality could not be sustained. Given low mortality, a zero rate of population growth (a logical necessity in the long run) would require an average fertility of just 2.1 children per woman.

The demographic transition is the process of adjustment over time from a premodern mortality-fertility regime to a low mortality–low fertility regime. Evidently, the specific patterns of fertility and mortality change that can accomplish such a transition can vary greatly; hence, they can have greatly varying demographic and socioeconomic implications. In the classic pattern, pictured in stylized representations of the demographic transition, mortality plays the role of precipitating the onset of the process. As mortality decreases while fertility remains at its premodern level, a gap opens up between birth rates and death rates, generating population growth. Fertility decline follows, according to this classic scenario, with a more-or-less extended time lag, thus beginning to moderate transitional growth. Eventually the decline of mortality levels off, no longer providing further impetus toward population growth. (Indeed, such leveling-off is not strictly a requirement for attaining long-run equilibrium. Beyond an expectation of life at birth of about 70 years, further improvements of mortality have little effect on the chances of survival to the childbearing ages, hence little effect on the long-run population growth rate.) The process of transition is completed as fertility descends to a level just sufficient to secure a zero rate of growth.

That this stylized model captures some essential features of demographic history between 1700 and 1950 is evident. Mortality typically led the process of change, fertility decline

lagged, and the growth potential inherent in premodern fertility levels was triggered. The result, as described earlier, was the nearly fourfold increase of the global population. It is equally clear, however, that the pattern of transitions, country by country or region by region, exhibited variations too great to permit simple generalizations about the path already traveled, let alone to encourage confident predictions concerning developments to come.

In western Europe, where the transition began the earliest and where that process seemed to have been completed essentially by the 1930s, initial levels of both mortality and fertility were lower than in the rest of the world. Thus, other things equal, the potential effect of mortality decline on population growth was less. Also, lower fertility reflected, in part, a system of control characterized by strict limitations of nonmarital fertility, relatively late age of marriage, and in a number of instances, high proportions that remained celibate. The fertility levels generated by such a system of fertility control were highly responsive to changing economic conditions, as is demonstrated, in particular, by the especially well researched demographic history of England (Wrigley and Schofield 1981). This system of fertility control could be expected to be sensitive also to pressures that declining mortality might bring about through accelerating population growth. Indeed, in the instance of France, the decline of mortality was nearly simultaneous with the decline of fertility. French demographic history demonstrates, as a result, that transitional population growth can be kept at a relatively low level.

Even when the onset of the secular decline of fertility lagged far behind that of mortality (as was the case in much of Europe), growth seldom surpassed the 1% level. (As in France, in the United States a steady decline of fertility began early in the nineteenth century, although from a very high initial level. The rate of increase, as noted earlier, remained very rapid in the United States throughout the 1800s.) This is not surprising, since mortality change was slow, and in particular, infant mortality rates remained high until the late nineteenth or early twentieth century (Chesnais 1986, Vallin 1988). Mortality change in Europe was an autochthonous process, generated by gradual successes – some hard earned, some fortuitous – in reining in war, famine, and pestilence. The emergence of strong and stable states in much of Europe reduced losses from armed conflict and created a hospitable frame for the spread of industry and economic growth. The nutritional status of the population improved, reflecting such factors as advances in agriculture (greatly facilitated by the adoption of plants originating from the New World, notably maize and the potato), improvements in animal husbandry (creating a buffer that diminished the potential shock from crop failures), better transportation and storage facilities, and increasing access to overseas sources of food supply. Exogenous climate changes – the onset of a warming trend in the eighteenth century after the "little ice age" of the 1600s – may also have played a part in increasing crop yields, a factor that might provide the expansion for the puzzling simultaneity of the seemingly unrelated accelerations of population growth in western Europe and in China (Galloway 1986). As to pestilence, standards of housing and sanitation gradually improved, and partly as a result of this and partly due to subtle ecological changes, the virulence of epidemic diseases (such as smallpox, plague, typhus, and measles) has gradually diminished, and the lethality of infections, apart from among children, became much more moderate (McNeill 1976, Crosby 1986). Medical interventions played only a marginal role in this process of improvement (with some notable exceptions, such as the discovery and application of a vaccination against smallpox) until quite late in the nineteenth century (McKeown 1976).

Steady progress in reducing death rates over a period of 200 years eventually translated into great improvements. In the major countries of western Europe, expectation of life at birth around 1830 had reached about 40 years. On the eve of World War I it was 50 years or higher, and by the middle of the century it was appreciably above 60 years.

Improvements outside western Europe and Northern America were also appreciable: yet with some exceptions (such as Japan and Oceania), the lag between leaders and followers, already marked around 1700, generally increased. Around 1950, life expectancy at birth in Africa was still below 40 years; in Asia as a whole it was only modestly higher. These levels may have been about twice as high as they were in 1700, but they also represented a level surpassed by the leading countries more than 100 years earlier. Latin America fared better. There, at midcentury, life expectancy was already above 50 years, corresponding to a lag of about four decades behind the vanguard.

Similar comparisons cannot be made for fertility trends. In western Europe and Northern America and in a few other countries outside these areas, fertility had declined to near- or even below-replacement levels by the economically depressed 1930s. (In some instances, such as in France or in the urban population of the eastern United States, this stage of the demographic transition had been reached several decades earlier.) This process reflected the uncoordinated voluntary choices of individual couples who found themselves confronted with an interrelated complex of social, economic, and cultural pressures that made it advantageous for them to limit the size of their families. By the middle of the twentieth century, however, the large majority of the world's population remained unaffected by a similar shift in reproductive behavior. In Asia, Latin America, and Africa "modernization," if it influenced fertility at all, caused it to increase as a byproduct of improvements in health and mortality. Attempts by contemporary demographers to discern the crucial ingredients of socioeconomic change that might be expected to trigger fertility declines in what came to be labeled as the economically less developed countries (LDCs) seemed to yield no useful results. Alternatively, and perhaps more commonly, they suggested skepticism about the possibility that early fertility declines in these areas could occur at all.

Population Change, 1950–1985

In terms of the rate of global population growth, the roughly one-third of a century between 1950 and 1985 has been unique in mankind's history. Not only was the prevailing global rate unmatched by the rate of demographic growth for any past time of similar duration; it is also virtually certain that at no time in the future will such a global rate be attained again.

Demographers were rather slow to adjust their thinking to the sudden changes in demographic trends that materialized following World War II. This was the case, first of all, in the regions that either had already achieved very low levels of fertility prior to 1940 or were approaching such levels. Expert opinion assumed that the sharp upturn of birth rates that were registered in the immediate postwar years (or in some cases already in the early 1940s) represented only a temporary disturbance rather than a genuine shift in preferences concerning family size. Some of the upturn, quickly dubbed a "baby boom," was attributed to the making-up of births that were postponed during the depression and World War II, and some of it was explained as mere borrowing on future fertility or as a transient effect of the large marriage cohorts of the immediate post–World War II years. But fertility trends in the Western world refused to conform to the timetable that such interpretations would have prescribed. Instead of running out of steam quickly, the baby boom gathered momentum for more than a decade after the end of World War II. When demographic theorizing finally adjusted to this wholly unexpected development, fertility trends once again shifted, first in the United States and later in western Europe, rapidly converging to or even sinking below the low levels attained a few decades earlier. By the end of the period under consideration, the baby boom was history, and the implications of below-replacement fertility were once again in the forefront of demographers' research agendas and policy deliberations (Davis, Bernstam, and Ricardo-Campbell 1987).

In the countries affected by the post–World War II baby boom, statistical data on demographic trends were generally up to date; it was agreed-upon interpretation that lagged badly behind the observed events. In the less developed countries, sheer demographic description, too, was tardy. Thus, well into the first postwar decade, most discussions of demographic trends and prospects in Asia, Africa, and Latin America showed little awareness of the radical acceleration of population growth. In particular, the possibility that precipitous declines of death rates might occur, even in relatively poor countries, was greatly underestimated. When the "population explosion" finally was discovered and sized up, it was in full bloom, and most demographic interpretations tended to consider the high birth rates that sustained it a phenomenon more resistant to change (whether spontaneously generated or policy-induced) than in fact turned out to be the case.

Indeed, the historical turning point in world demographic transition, signaled by the peaking of the global growth rate, and simultaneously with it, by the peaking of the growth rate in the less developed world, went unnoticed until well after its actual occurrence. But once it was belatedly discovered that growth rates slowly had begun to recede, and as evidence accumulated on a widespread fertility decline in the less-developed world, demographers became increasingly confident that such declines were imminent everywhere and that once declines had begun, their tempo was bound to accelerate over time. In this instance, interpretation, instead of lagging behind the facts, may have been rushing ahead of them without sufficient warrant, possibly setting the stage for another painful reappraisal of world demographic trends some time in the future.

Size and Growth

The shifting and often unhappy fortunes of demographic theorizing should not obscure, however, the very real progress achieved in demographic description during the last four decades. The improvement is a result of a combination of influences. Regular census-taking became institutionalized in virtually all countries. Progress in Africa, achieved with effective international assistance, was particularly important in this regard, even though, in regional comparisons, the quality of African demographic statistics remains the weakest. Three Chinese censuses and the publication and critical analysis of many of their results have gone a long way toward filling in the largest blank spot on the world's demographic map. In many countries, statistics derived from population censuses came to be complemented usefully by information obtained through specialized sample surveys, often as a result of international technical cooperation. Advances in demographic analysis sharpened the focus and increased the pertinence of quantitative investigations of demographic dynamics. Newly developed techniques of demographic estimation often succeeded in compensating for deficiencies in raw statistical data. International organizations, in particular the Population Division of the United Nations, have greatly contributed to the timely gathering, analysis, and dissemination of population statistics and of related information and have begun to issue detailed and authoritative population estimates on a regular basis.

As a result of these developments, the changing contours of the world's demographic situation are mapped now with greater accuracy, detail, and speed than ever before. Estimates of population size for 1985 entered in Table 3-1, drawing extensively on the most recent population estimates prepared by the United Nations (1989), carry forward the basic historical time series on the population of the world's major regions discussed earlier. Tables 3-2, 3-3, and 3-4 show relative and absolute population changes between 1950 and 1985 in regional detail, in juxtaposition to similar indexes characterizing the previous 250 years. Figure 3.1 also depicts global and regional population growth between 1950 and 1985 as a continuation of preceding time trends.

The global values of these indexes are particularly striking. The estimated 1985 population, 4.8 billion, is nearly double the global figure of 35 years earlier. (Modest extrapolation of this estimate has the world population passing the 5 billion mark in 1987 and reaching 5.3 billion in 1990.) The 1985 estimate implies an average annual growth rate of 1.88% during the period 1950 to 1985 – more than twice the average level attained during the first half of the century. It also indicates that the absolute net addition to the world's population between 1950 and 1985 was over 2.3 billion – about the size of the global population at the close of World War II.

Detailed figures indicate acceleration of growth in every major region, with the exception of Japan and Europe. Compared to growth rates in the first half of the century, the acceleration of growth in the 1950–1985 period was particularly sharp in Asia (from an average annual rate of 0.8% to 2.1%), in Africa (from 1% to 2.6%), and in Latin America (from 1.6% to 2.6%). Because these high rates (which in earlier times occurred only in combination with populations of modest demographic size or of thin settlement) were experienced by already large populations, they generated very substantial increases as reckoned in absolute terms. For example, the net addition to the population of China between 1950 and 1985 was more than three times as much as the total population of Northern America in 1950. The net increase of Africa's population was as large as the total population of Europe at the time of World War I. As a result of unequal rates of demographic expansion, changes in the regional composition of the world's population also were marked, despite the brevity of 35 years, if time is measured on a historical scale. For example, Asia outside Japan and China increased its share of the global total from 29% to 34%. Europe's share dropped from 15.6% to 10.1%. In 1950, the size of the population of Northern America was the same as that of Latin America. Net increases in these two regions during the 35 years that followed were 100 million and 240 million, respectively. As a result, and despite the countervailing influence of significant south-to-north migration, by 1985 Latin America had a population more than 50% larger than northern America.

Migration did affect population dynamics to some extent also outside the Western Hemisphere. Europe, for the first time in its modern history, became a region of net inmigration during the post–World War II decades. But the overall direct demographic significance of global interregional migration has remained marginal in comparison to the impact of natural increase, determined by the balance of births and deaths. The volume of transcontinental migration, cited earlier, that was recorded during Europe's nearly century-long period as a region experiencing major outmigration was equivalent to only about eight months' natural increase around 1985 in the less-developed world.

A more detailed picture of population change during the period 1950–1985 is offered in Table 3-5, which shows global and regional population estimates spaced at five-year intervals. Table 3-6 extracts some of the information contained in these time series in the form of average annual rates of growth relating to 1955–1965 and to the two subsequent decade-length periods. The last three columns of the table translate these data into decadal estimates of the absolute population increase in each region. As Table 3-6 shows, the global rate of population growth peaked between 1965 and 1975, at the average annual rate of just over 2%. The less-developed world experienced a peak rate during the same decade, at 2.5%. (Through closer scrutiny of the figures given in Table 3-5, the peak rates of growth of the global population and of the population of the LDCs can be further pinpointed as having occurred in the quinquennium 1965–1970, at the annual rates of 2.06% and 2.54%, respectively.) In the developed countries, in contrast, the highest growth rates

Table 3-5 *Population of the World and of Major Areas (Millions), 1950–1985*

	1950	1955	1960	1965	1970	1975	1980	1985
World total	2,515	2,751	3,019	3,335	3,698	4,079	4,450	4,853
Africa	224	250	281	318	363	415	481	557
Asia[a]	1,375	1,512	1,667	1,860	2,101	2,353	2,583	2,834
China	*555*	*609*	*657*	*729*	*831*	*927*	*996*	*1,060*
Japan	*84*	*90*	*94*	*99*	*104*	*112*	*117*	*121*
Rest of Asia	*736*	*813*	*916*	*1,032*	*1,166*	*1,314*	*1,470*	*1,653*
Europe[a]	393	408	425	445	460	474	484	492
USSR	180	196	214	231	243	255	266	277
Northern America[b]	166	182	199	214	226	239	252	265
Latin America[c]	165	190	218	250	285	323	362	404
Oceania	13	14	16	18	19	21	23	25
More-Developed Countries[d]	832	887	945	1,003	1,049	1,096	1,136	1,174
Less-Developed Countries[e]	1,683	1,864	2,074	2,332	2,648	2,984	3,313	3,680

Notes: [a] Excluding USSR

      [b] Canada and the United States

      [c] South and Central America, Mexico, and the Caribbean

      [d] Japan, Europe, USSR, North America, Australia and New Zealand

      [e] Africa, Asia (excluding Japan), Latin America, and Oceania (excluding Australia and New Zealand)

Source: United Nations 1989.

during the period occurred between 1955 and 1965, and monotonically decreased thereafter. (Such steady decline of population growth from decade to decade has also been experienced by Latin America and Oceania, but in each case, starting from a high initial rate.) The dynamics of population growth in Africa had this pattern reversed; there, the rate climbed from an estimated initial level of 2.4% per year to 2.7%, and then to 3.0%. For the more-developed countries as a whole, the growth rate was 1.22% during the first decade, 0.89% during the second, and 0.69% during the third.

Even when the rates of population growth exhibited an up-down time trend, the down-step was not decisive enough to cancel the effect of increasing population size on the magnitude of absolute population increase. (China and Japan, however, are exceptions to this rule.) Thus, for example, for

the total LDC population the rate of growth was the lowest (2.1%) during the last decade (1975–85) shown in Table 3-6, but the size of the absolute increase was still the highest then: an average of 69.6 million per year.

Demographic Transition

As the preceding discussion indicates, global and regional rates of population growth exhibited considerable change over the period 1950 to 1985. Yet these changes conceal much of the dramatic transformation in mortality and fertility, which jointly determine population growth. This is because the effects on growth exerted by mortality and fertility changes in recent decades tended to offset each other. Since the middle of the twentieth century, demographic transition has become a worldwide process, with virtually all areas of the world experiencing growth-enhancing reductions

Table 3-6 *Average Annual Rates of Population Growth (Percent) and Increases in Absolute Population Size (Millions), 1955–1985*

	1955–65	1965–75	1975–85	1955–65	1965–75	1975–85
World total	1.93	2.01	1.74	584	744	774
Africa	2.42	2.66	2.95	68	97	142
Asia[a]	2.07	2.35	1.86	348	493	481
China	*1.80*	*2.40*	*1.33*	*120*	*198*	*133*
Japan	*.96*	*1.20*	*.80*	*9*	*13*	*9*
Rest of Asia	*2.39*	*2.42*	*2.30*	*219*	*282*	*339*
Europe[a]	.86	.63	.38	37	29	18
USSR	1.63	.99	.83	35	24	22
Northern America[b]	1.64	1.09	1.03	32	25	26
Latin America[c]	2.78	2.54	2.24	60	73	81
Oceania	2.13	1.88	1.53	4	3	4
More-Developed Countries[d]	1.22	.89	.69	116	93	78
Less-Developed Countries[e]	2.24	2.46	2.10	468	652	696

Notes and Source: See Table 3-5.

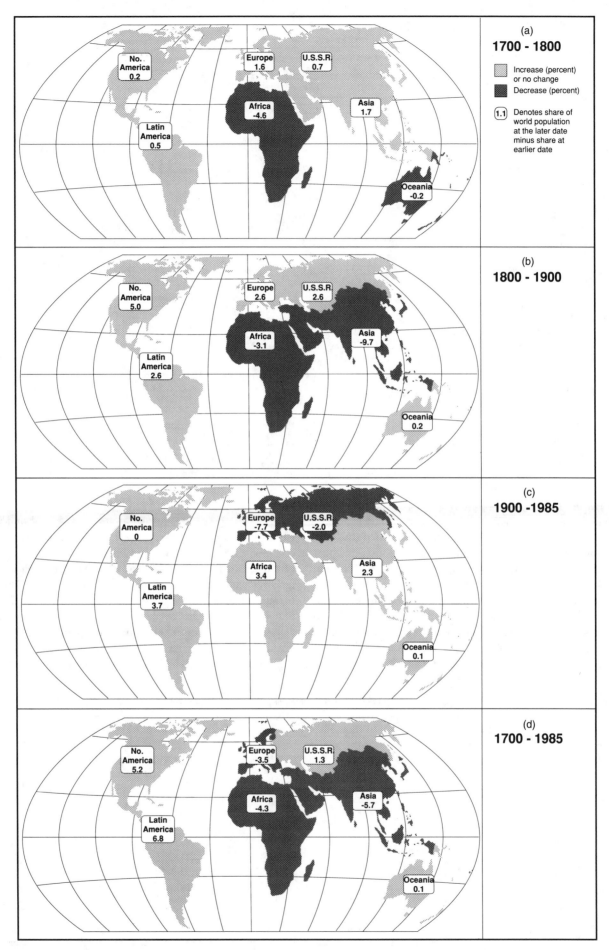

Figure 3.2 Changes in percentage distribution of the world's population by major areas. (a) 1700–1800; (b) 1800–1900; (c) 1900–1985; (d) 1700–1985. *Source:* see Table 3-4.

in mortality, and a large share of the world's population experiencing growth-checking declines in fertility.

Thus, for example, at midcentury the overall global rate of population growth was 1.8%, a rate generated by a crude birth rate of about 38 per 1,000 population and a crude death rate of 20 per 1,000 population. Three and a half decades later, the global growth rate was essentially the same – 1.8% – but it resulted from global birth and death rates of 28‰ and 10‰, respectively. Demographers call such rates "crude" because they reflect not just the underlying "true" levels of fertility and mortality, but also the transient shape of the age distribution of the population. Since age distributions can differ considerably from region to region, the detailed regional patterns of mortality and fertility transition between 1950 and 1985 are represented in Figs. 3.3 and 3.4 by means of indexes, already referred to above, that are unaffected by such differences. The expectation of life at birth measures the average length of life that a cohort of newborn children would experience if during his or her lifetime that person were subject at each age to the same chances of dying that characterize the year (or, in the present instance, the five-year period) to which the index refers. (Thus, its name notwithstanding, "expectation of life" implies no hint of prediction as to future mortality change. When mortality is declining, newborn children, in fact, are expected to live, on average, longer lives than the index would suggest.) The total fertility rate is a similar hypothetical construct: it measures the average

number of children women would have if they lived through their entire reproductive lifetime and experienced the age-specific fertility rates prevailing during the year to which the index refers.

As Fig. 3.3 indicates, rapid improvement in mortality has become a worldwide phenomenon since 1950. The rate of advance, both in relative and in absolute terms, was fastest in regions with initial high levels of mortality (that is, low expectations of life): in Africa, Latin America, and especially, Asia. The tempo at which expectation of life increased from low levels had far exceeded the tempo experienced by the developed countries at similar stages of mortality. In record-holder Asia, the average gain in expectation of life sustained during three decades was as high as 0.6 year per annum. As in the earlier historical experience, improvements in the standard of living – in housing, sanitation, and nutrition – have played a significant role. Thus, increases in expectation of life and overall economic performance (as measured, for example, by the growth in per capita income) continued to be broadly correlated. But the level of mortality associated with particular levels of living has shifted appreciably upward compared to the historical experience. Much of the explanation for this shift is supplied by advances in medicine, pharmacology, and public health – advances made particularly potent in developing countries by favorable combinations of cultural patterns and public policies, including vigorous promotion of education, particularly of women (Caldwell 1986). On a broad regional basis, by the 1980s, with the exception of Africa, the major part of the contribution that mortality reduction could make to long-term population growth had been exploited.

In areas in which relatively low levels of mortality had been achieved by midcentury, the scope for further improvements was necessarily more limited. Nevertheless, gains in expectation of life were considerable during the ensuing decades, exceeding most predictions. By around 1985, the most advanced countries had life expectancies in the neighborhood of 75 or more years. These and any further advances will have little influence on long-term population growth, but will contribute increasingly to the growth of the old-age population; hence, in combination with low fertility, will accelerate the process called "population aging," a process defined by an increasing share of persons of advanced age within the population as a whole.

Regional fertility trends, depicted in Fig. 3.4, highlight the sharp contrast between the developed and the less developed areas that continued to persist during the decades beyond midcentury, but also the significant trend toward convergence to common low levels that occurred in all regions, again with the notable exception of Africa. Such a tendency toward convergence is especially remarkable in view of the fact that in the developed regions, following the protracted postwar baby booms, the trend toward lower fertility resumed, and fertility appears to have stabilized well below the average of 2.1 children per woman that would be required for long-term population stability. But the fertility declines experienced by the developed countries have been eclipsed, both in relative and in absolute terms, by the declines registered in Asia and

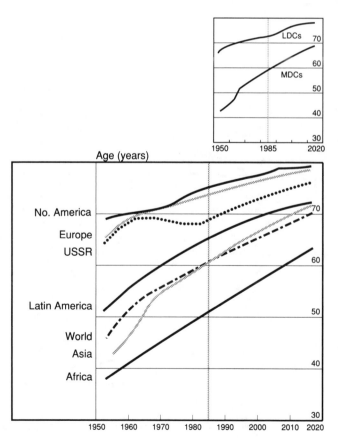

Figure 3.3 World mortality trends: Expectation of life at birth (e_0), for both sexes, 1950–1985: estimates; 1985–2020: projections.
Source: United Nations 1989.

in Latin America. In both of these regions, average levels of the total fertility rate (which, however, conceal a great deal of within-area variation) were about 6 around 1950. If the conceptual resting point of the fertility transition is taken as the replacement level – that is, a total fertility rate of 2.1 – both Asia and Latin America as a whole have covered somewhat more than half of the distance from high to low fertility, much of it in the brief span of the 20 years between 1965 and 1985.

In retrospect, the pattern of the ongoing fertility transition in the less developed world is broadly consistent with what might have been expected from transition theory. Fertility declines observed in the postwar period continued to be strongly correlated with conventional measures of economic development, such as increases in income per capita, urbanization, structural changes in the labor force, increasing literacy, and, in general, increasing schooling, lower infant and child mortality, and improvement in the status of women. Change in each of these areas has been remarkably rapid. For example, the proportion of the population of the less developed countries living in urban areas was 17% in 1950; by 1985 the proportion exceeded 31% (United Nations 1988). As in earlier fertility transitions, the macrolevel indicators signaling such changes were paralleled by shifts on the microlevel in the terms of the implicit cost-benefit calculus that underlies parental attitudes toward childbearing. As the economic functions of the family weaken, children's direct economic value to parents decreases or disappears, while the cost of investment in children's human capital mandated by a variety of economic pressures and mobility aspirations grows rapidly. Broadening options for women to participate in the labor force increase the opportunity costs of childrearing. At the same time, acting on the emerging desire to limit family size has been facilitated by the increasing availability of efficient and low-cost methods of birth control, reflecting technological advances and public policies aimed at providing easy access to such methods. Adoption of the practice of birth control in some countries, most notably in China, has also been accelerated by the introduction of systems of incentives designed to promote lower fertility deemed to be in the collective interest.

Prospects for Population Change, 1985–2020

The broad correspondence between development trends and population policies, on the one hand, and trends in mortality and fertility on the other, does not provide us with adequate guidance on the likely future dynamics of demographic change in particular countries or regions, or even globally. Nevertheless, demographic structures and behaviors have a high degree of inertia that, short of catastrophic events that are necessarily unpredictable, permits some reasonably safe propositions concerning future population change. Thus, for example, if the existing distribution of a population is heavily biased toward the young age groups, rapid population growth is a certainty even under highly "conservative" assumptions as to the factors determining growth: mortality and fertility. Should mortality improvement cease or should fertility instantaneously drop to replacement level, popula-

tion growth would still continue for a long time to come, generating an eventual population size that might be, in the case of contemporary high-fertility populations, endowed with young age distributions, twice the size of the original population or more. (For calculations indicating the "population momentum" of each country under the assumption of instant achievement of replacement fertility, see World Bank 1988.)

Less unrealistic assumptions concerning future fertility and mortality change provide the basis of more interesting conjectures. Both the United Nations and, with more regularity, the World Bank have undertaken long-range calculations (to the year 2100 and beyond) indicating the population of the world and its component parts under well-specified assumptions as to future fertility and mortality – assumptions that stipulate a plausible evolution, in some instances including several variants, of present fertility and mortality levels and recent trends (United Nations Secretariat 1983: Zachariah and Vu 1988). Plausibility is assured by anticipating no sharp break in past trend lines and, equally important, by avoiding assumptions that would generate either implausibly large eventual population sizes or declining populations. This is achieved by stipulating a more or less rapid convergence of fertility and mortality to levels that would lead to an eventually stabilized population size, and requiring that once such a level is attained, fertility and mortality remain constant. Clearly, although the formulation appeals to a stylized demographic transition model, it also rests on circular reasoning.

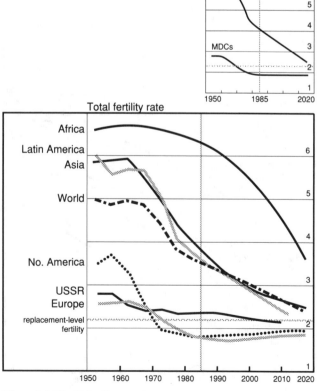

Figure 3.4 World fertility trends. Number of children per woman (total fertility rate), 1950–1985: estimates; 1985–2020: projections. *Source:* United Nations 1989.

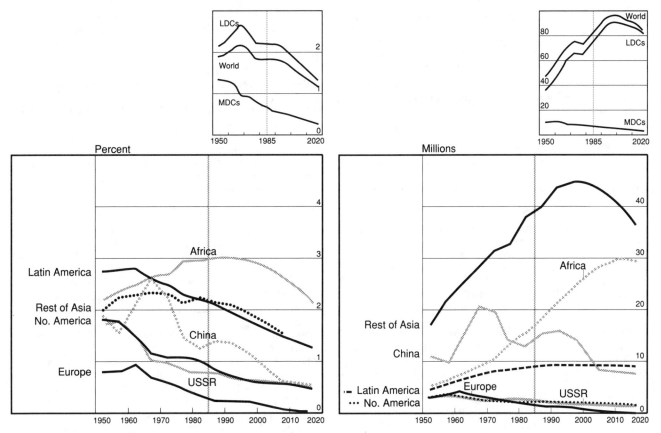

Figure 3.5 Average annual rates of population increase (percent), 1950–1985: estimates; 1985–2020: projections. *Source:* United Nations 1989.

Figure 3.6 Average annual population increase (millions), 1950–1985: estimates; 1985–2020: projections. *Source:* United Nations 1989.

Its aim is to predict future population size, but the prediction is the outcome of stipulations dictated by what is considered acceptable prediction.

Projections into the less remote future can command a greater degree of confidence as to the general orders of magnitude of their results. Tables 3-1 to 3-4 and Figs. 3.3 to 3.6 present selected results of the United Nations "medium" projections to the year 2020, thus extending the time horizon from 1950–85, considered in the preceding section, by an additional 35 years. According to these projections, the global population in 2020 will exceed 8 billion, implying an average annual rate of growth of 1.45% during the period 1985–2020 (compared to a rate of 1.88% during the preceding 35 years) and an absolute increase of 3.2 billion (compared to an increase of 2.3 billion in the preceding 35 years). Regional shares in this growth will continue to be highly unequal; indeed, the regional differentials will be sharpened. Thus, for example, the rate of growth in Africa will be 2.7%, in contrast to Europe's 0.1%; absolute increase in Africa will be 884 million, in contrast to Europe's 22 million. Africa's share in the world's population will grow from 11.5% in 1985 to 17.9% in 2020; Europe's share will drop from 10.1% to 6.4%.

How plausible are these and other numerical results detailed in Tables 3-1 to 3-4? Their authority, or lack of it, rests on the underlying mortality and fertility assumptions pictured in the right-hand segments of Figs. 3.3 and 3.4. The anticipated changes in mortality, arguably, are highly conservative. They

assume continuation of the favorable mortality trends observed prior to 1985, but such trends will still leave life expectancy in the less developed world in 2020 no higher than the level achieved in Northern America some 70 years earlier. They also assume a leveling-off of mortality improvement in the developed world at below 80 years of expectation of life at birth. More optimistic assumptions on either score would result in more rapid population growth than described in Table 3-1.

The projected changes in fertility are, in comparison, less firmly grounded, drawing as they do on the historical experience of a vanguard that the followers may be reasonably expected to retrace. Africa, where fertility decline has barely started, is assumed to embark on a rapid-paced fertility transition, covering about two-thirds of the way toward replacement-level fertility by 2020. The rest of the less developed world is expected virtually to complete the fertility transition by that date. En route to that stage no reversals – no temporary baby booms – are permitted. As to the developed world, fertility is assumed to stay appreciably below replacement level during the entire 35-year period. None of these assumptions is implausible, but, arguably, any deviations from the anticipated paths are likely to entail an upward revision of the 8 billion global forecast for 2020 (and of the remaining population growth momentum beyond that date) rather than a revision in the opposite direction.

A detailed picture of the implied regional differences in

the 1985–2020 projected rate of population growth and in the absolute population increases is presented, against the background of the preceding 35 years, in Figs. 3.5 and 3.6. A gradual moderation of the rate of growth can be anticipated with confidence. Almost certainly, in terms of absolute increases, the brunt of the global population explosion is yet to come.

References

Biraben, J.-N. 1979. Essai sur l'évolution du nombre des hommes. *Population* (Paris). 34: 13–25.

Caldwell, J. C. 1986. Routes to low mortality in poor countries. *Population and Development Review* 12: 171–220.

Carr-Saunders, A. M. 1936. *World Population: Past Growth and Present Trends*. Oxford: Oxford University Press.

Chesnais, J.-C. 1986. *La transition démographique*. Travaux et documents No. 113. Paris: Presses Universitaires de France.

Clark, C. 1967. *Population Growth and Land Use*. New York: St. Martin's Press.

Coale, A. J., and P. Demeny, with B. Vaughan. 1983. *Regional Model Life Tables and Stable Populations*. 2d ed. New York: Academic Press.

Crosby, A. W. 1986. *Ecological Imperialism: The Biological Expansion of Europe, 900–1900*. Cambridge: Cambridge University Press.

Darwin, C. [1859] 1968. *The Origin of Species*. London: Penguin Books.

Davis, K., M.S. Bernstam, and R. Ricardo-Campbell, eds. 1987. *Below-Replacement Fertility in Industrial Societies: Causes, Consequences, Policies*. Cambridge: Cambridge University Press.

Durand, J. D. 1967. The modern expansion of world population. *Proceedings of the American Philosophical Society*. 111: 136–59.

———. 1977. Historical estimates of world population: An evaluation. *Population and Development Review* 3: 253–96.

Galloway, P. R. 1986. Long-term fluctuations in climate and population in the preindustrial era. *Population and Development Review* 12: 1–24.

Glass, D. 1966. World population, 1800–1950. In *The Cambridge Economic History of Europe*. Vol. VI, ed. H. J. Habakkuk and M. Postan. pp. 56–138. Cambridge: The University Press.

McEvedy, C., and R. Jones. 1978. *Atlas of World Population History*. New York: Penguin Books.

McKeown, T. 1976. *The Modern Rise of Population*. New York: Academic Press.

McNeill, W. H. 1976. *Plagues and Peoples*. Garden City, NY: Anchor Press/Doubleday.

Malthus, T. R. [1798] 1966. *First Essay on Population 1798*. (A Reprint in Facsimile). London: Macmillan.

Neumann, J. von. [1955] 1986. Can we survive technology? Reprinted in *Population and Development Review* 12: 117–26.

United Nations. 1966. *World Population Prospects as Assessed in 1963*. New York.

———. 1985. *World Population Trends, Population and Development Interrelations and Population Policies*. 1983 Monitoring Report. I, Population Policies. New York.

———. 1988. *World Demographic Estimates and Projections, 1950–2025*. New York.

———. 1989. *World Population Prospects: 1988*. New York.

United Nations Secretariat. 1983. Long-range global population projections, as assessed in 1980. *Population Bulletin of the United Nations*. 14: 17–30.

Vallin, J. 1988. *La mortalité en Europe de 1720 à 1914*. Dossiers et recherches, No. 18. Paris: INED.

Willcox, W. F. 1931. Increase in the population of the earth and of the continents. In *International Migrations*. Vol. II, Interpretations. New York: National Bureau of Economic Research.

World Bank. 1988. *World Development Report 1988*. New York: Oxford University Press.

Wrigley, E. A., and R. S. Schofield. 1981. *The Population History of England 1541–1871*. Cambridge, MA: Harvard University Press.

Zachariah, K. C., and M. T. Vu. 1988. *World Population Projections 1987–88 Edition. Short- and Long-Term Estimates*. Published for the World Bank. Baltimore, MD: The Johns Hopkins University Press.

4

Technological Change

DANIEL R. HEADRICK

Technology is a means whereby humans use nature for their own benefit. Although this is often described as production, it also involves two other, less desirable outcomes: in order to produce objects or energy, humans must consume natural resources, in some cases depleting them; furthermore, both production and consumption create wastes. Although both resource depletion and waste disposal are recurring themes in the economic and technological history of the world, it is only now, at the very end of the twentieth century, that these problems have assumed global and perhaps irreversible dimensions. Yet their causes date back several centuries.

The motives behind technological innovations are familiar ones: power over nature (to go faster, to light the darkness, to do more work with less effort, to extract wealth from the earth) and power over people (to defeat enemies, to outwit competitors, to control others). The latter motive gives rise to competition as a most powerful motive for change, and the international and commercial rivalries that characterize Western civilization have been a major engine of technological transformation.

In the past 200 years, technology has changed in kind and complexity, and the rate at which it has done so has accelerated sharply. As a result, technology has been increasingly misunderstood and feared. It is viewed by some as a sorcerer's apprentice, a force growing out of control and threatening to destroy its human masters (Ellul 1954; Winner 1977). Even the creators of technology frequently are surprised by its consequences. For example, the development of the atomic bomb certainly was not designed to render the United States vulnerable to sudden and total destruction, yet that is what it did.

The reason for these surprises is not the technology itself, but the linear way in which it is commonly perceived. Inventors and their backers generally think of an innovation as a line-segment joining the device or process to its intended effect, and they ignore its side-effects. Unlike cultures that conceived of nature as animate and feared the retribution of the gods or spirits, Western culture since the Middle Ages has denied the idea of the spirits of nature and underemphasized humankind's responsibility toward the natural world (White 1967).

For most people in the Western world, nature serves our purposes, and the act of technological innovation is commonly divorced from any responsibility for its environmental impacts.

The consequences of technology do not stop at original intentions, however, but form cycles and feedback loops. In our own lifetimes, technology has become so powerful that we now feel and measure the feedback in the form of resource depletion, environmental degradation, and threats to life itself. It is the growing chasm between the intended purpose and the actual consequences of technology that promotes the fear that technology may be running amok. This is true not only of the nuclear arms race, but also of the exponential increases in resource depletion and environmental pollution that have marked our times.

Contemporary environmental problems can be traced to the sudden acceleration in the rate and power of innovations that began with the Industrial Revolution in late-eighteenth-century England. Here, the story can be examined only through eight great "clusters" of technological innovations and some of their unintended consequences, drawing upon a vast literature that is overwhelmingly biased toward the industrialized nations.

Industrialization

Industrialization was not a smooth process, but occurred in spurts. Economies went through boom-and-bust cycles, and societies adjusted in erratic patterns of reform, reaction, and revolution. Associated with these complex changes were several clusters of industrial innovations. Although these innovations were not the original causes of social and economic changes, they nonetheless serve as a means of ordering the complex events of the Age of Industry. It is important to note, however, that a new cluster of innovations by no means replaces the old: automobiles are no less important just because we have entered the "information age." Rather, the technological world becomes more complex.

The first of these clusters, the "classic" British Industrial Revolution, involved the introduction of cotton mills and the boom in iron production in the last third of the eighteenth

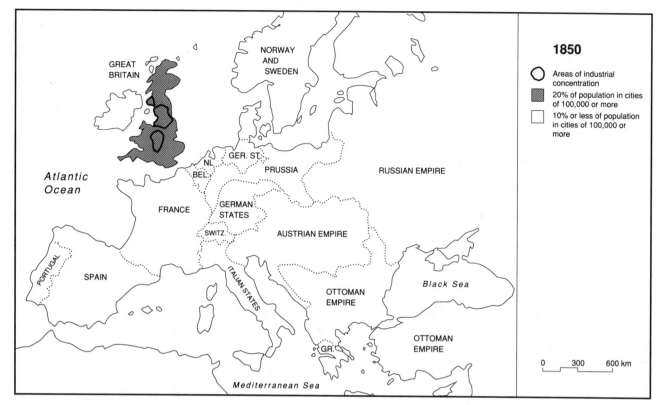

Figure 4.1 European industrialization ca. 1850.

century and the beginning of the nineteenth (Ashton 1962; Mokyr 1985). This phenomenon, though economically important, was limited to the Midlands and Lancashire, barely touching the rest of England (Fig. 4.1).

The second phase, which occurred in the middle of the nineteenth century, had a much greater impact. It involved the application of the steam engine (the first device to produce energy on demand independent of the weather), first to pumping, then to turning machines, then to moving boats and ships, and finally to the railroads. It spread throughout Europe in the mid- and late nineteenth century (Landes 1969) (Fig. 4.2).

The next phase of industrialization was marked by the appearance, in the last third of the nineteenth century, of three new industries: steel, chemicals, and electricity. The Bessemer and Siemens-Martin processes transformed steel from a rare and costly product to the cheapest and most useful of metals, an ideal material for rails, bridges, and weapons. Its usefulness is evident from the tremendous growth in steel production shown in Table 4-1. Electricity and the mass production of chemicals from salt, coal-tar, and even air created myriad new products and services. This phase of industrialization, like its predecessor, was associated with a new geographical distribution. Newcomers like Germany and the United States surpassed Great Britain, while Russia and Japan began their own transformation (see Fig. 4.3).

The fourth phase, like the second and third phases, is also associated with a new source of energy: the internal combustion engine. It transformed existing means of transportation (shipping and railroads), and more importantly, led to the introduction of automobiles and aircraft. While few new countries were added to the roster of industrialized nations, these technologies greatly enhanced the position of the United States, Japan, and Russia in relation to their western European predecessors.

We are currently in the fifth phase of industrialization, which began some time after World War II. Until recently, energy consumption has been a good indicator of economic development, but now energy consumption has leveled, even in growing economies. The older "smokestack" industries, still glorified on stock certificates, are in decline. Taking their place are two interrelated activities: the production of electronic devices (e.g., computers and television) and a plethora of services (e.g., education, entertainment, defense, finance) that make heavy use of these devices. Here again, the locus of these activities is shifting to the Pacific rim (California, Japan, Korea, Taiwan), with even newer centers emerging in Latin America, the Mideast, and Asia (Fig. 4.4).

Table 4-1 *World Raw Steel Output, 1860–1975* (in 1,000 metric tons)

1860	1.6	1890	12,368	1920	71,784	1950	186,733
1865	4	1895	16,831	1925	88,931	1955	266,257
1870	253	1900	28,146	1930	94,071	1960	345,645
1875	2,163	1905	44,843	1935	99,816	1965	591,824
1880	4,265	1910	59,824	1940	143,853	1970	591,824
1885	6,150	1915	78,146	1945	112,482	1975	640,470

Sources: Mitchell 1975: 420–25; Mitchell 1982: 336–37; Mitchell 1983: 457–59.

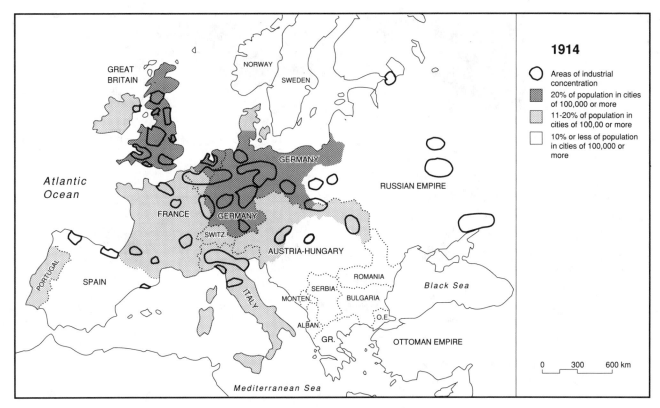

Figure 4.2 European industrialization ca. 1914.

Industrialization has also been marked by uneven, episodic acceleration. Statistical series (Tables 4-1 and 4-2) show the enormous increase in world industrial potential, beginning very slowly, then taking off in the late nineteenth century, slowing down in the early twentieth century, but then taking off even more spectacularly after World War II. This growth occurred in the familiar sequence of industrializing countries: first Britain, then Germany and the United States, then the Soviet Union, then Japan (Table 4-3). Less familiar (and more controversial) is the dramatic decline of traditional manufacturing in the Third World in the nineteenth century, the Age of Imperialism. This was not just a relative delay, but

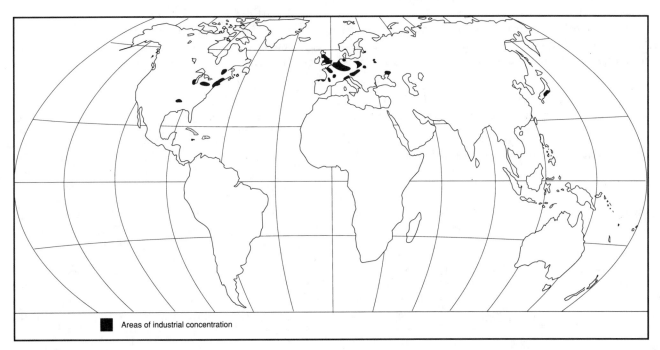

Figure 4.3 World industrialization in 1914.

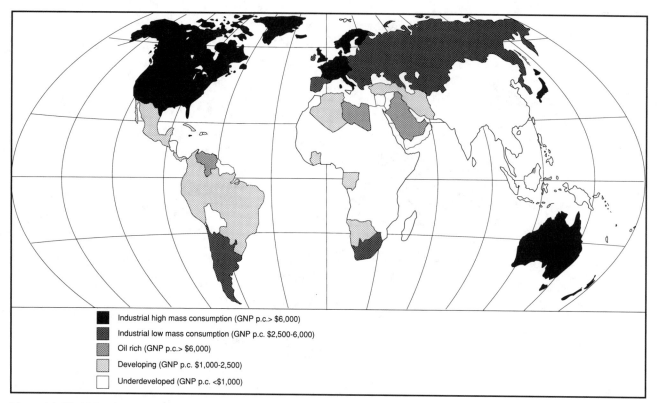

Industrial high mass consumption (GNP p.c.> $6,000)

Industrial low mass consumption (GNP p.c. $2,500-6,000)

Oil rich (GNP p.c.> $6,000)

Developing (GNP p.c. $1,000-2,500)

Underdeveloped (GNP p.c. <$1,000)

Figure 4.4 World development in the 1980s.

an absolute collapse, as western imports replaced local manufactures and were paid for by exports of agricultural and mineral products (Bairoch 1963).

This summary of technological progress and economic change; of production, distribution, and consumption; of urbanization, recessions and booms, labor problems; and other social adjustments is a familiar but myopic view of industrialization.

From a global perspective and from that of the biosphere, the story of industrialization also includes unintended and unanticipated consequences that have accumulated faster than our comprehension of them. The mass production of goods requires massive inputs of raw materials, and these resources are not always found near industries or their consumers. This spatial incongruence has had worldwide impacts of both a social and an ecological sort, as demonstrated throughout this volume.

Knowledge

Industrialization also required a great deal of new knowledge, and new ways of creating, storing, and retrieving it as well. The transition was not instantaneous. In the first stages

Table 4-2 *Total Industrial Potential, 1750–1980* (U.K. in 1900 = 100)

	1750	1800	1830	1860	1880	1900	1913	1928	1938	1953	1963	1973	1980
DEVELOPED	34	47	73	143	253	481	863	1259	1562	2870	4699	8432	9718
U.K.	2	6	18	45	73	100	127	135	181	258	330	462	441
Germany	4	5	7	11	27	71	138	158	214	180	330	550	590
France	5	6	10	18	25	37	57	82	74	98	194	328	362
Italy	3	4	4	6	8	14	23	37	46	71	150	258	319
Russia/U.S.S.R.	6	8	10	16	25	48	77	72	152	328	760	1345	1630
U.S.A.		1	5	16	47	128	298	533	528	1373	1804	3089	3475
Japan	5	5	5	6	8	13	25	45	88	88	264	819	1001
THIRD WORLD	93	99	112	83	67	60	70	98	122	200	439	927	1323
China	42	49	55	44	40	34	33	46	52	71	178	369	553
India	31	29	33	19	9	9	13	26	40	52	91	194	254
WORLD	127	147	184	226	320	541	933	1356	1684	3070	5138	9359	11041

Source: Bairoch 1982: 292, 299.

Notes: These figures include handicrafts as well as industrial manufacturing. Figures are rounded off. Triennial annual averages except for 1913, 1928, and 1938. India includes Pakistan.

Table 4-3 *Relative Shares of Different Countries and Regions in Total World Manufacturing Output, 1750–1980* (in percentages)

	1750	1800	1830	1860	1880	1900	1913	1928	1938	1953	1963	1973	1980
DEVELOPED	27.0	32.3	39.5	63.4	79.1	89.0	92.5	92.8	92.8	93.5	91.5	90.1	88.0
U.K.	1.9	4.3	9.5	19.9	22.9	18.5	13.6	9.9	10.7	8.4	6.4	4.9	4.0
Germany	2.9	3.5	3.5	4.9	8.5	13.2	14.8	11.6	12.7	5.9	6.4	5.9	5.3
France	4.0	4.2	5.2	7.9	7.8	6.8	6.1	6.0	4.4	3.2	3.8	3.5	3.3
Italy	2.4	2.5	2.3	2.5	2.5	2.5	2.4	2.7	2.8	2.3	2.9	2.9	2.9
Russia/U.S.S.R.	5.0	5.6	5.6	7.0	7.6	8.8	8.2	5.3	9.0	10.7	14.2	14.4	14.8
U.S.A.	0.1	0.8	2.4	7.2	14.7	23.6	32.0	39.3	31.4	44.7	35.1	33.0	31.5
Japan	3.8	3.5	2.8	2.6	2.4	2.4	2.7	3.3	5.2	2.9	5.1	8.8	9.1
THIRD WORLD	73.0	67.7	60.5	36.6	20.9	11.0	7.5	7.2	7.2	6.5	8.5	9.9	12.0
China	32.8	33.3	29.8	19.7	12.5	6.2	3.6	3.4	3.1	2.3	3.5	3.9	5.0
India	24.5	19.7	17.6	8.6	2.8	1.7	1.4	1.9	2.4	1.7	1.8	2.1	2.3

Source: Bairoch 1982: 292, 299.

Notes: These figures include handicrafts as well as industrial manufacturing. Figures are rounded off. Triennial annual averages except for 1913, 1928, and 1938. India includes Pakistan.

of the British Industrial Revolution, innovations were devised by trial and error, produced by craftsmen, and taught by the traditional apprenticeship system; thus Newcomen, inventor of the atmospheric steam engine in the early eighteenth century, left no technical treatises or engineering drawings behind. By the end of the century, however, curiosity and technical difficulties turned crafts technology into engineering and then into science. Nowadays, science is intermingled with technology at every level, and education has become a prerequisite for almost every technical craft. This shift has made the economic development of Asia, Africa, and Latin America more difficult than was the diffusion of industrialization to Europe and North America 150 years ago (Bairoch 1963).

Governments – repositories of power over people – were involved in the process of technological innovation a long time ago, and have become more involved ever since. As early as the seventeenth century, they encouraged the increase in knowledge and power over nature. Examples include the patent system introduced in England in 1623, the Royal Society chartered in 1662, the Académie Royale des Sciences in 1666, the Society of Arts in 1754, the Conservatoire National des Arts et Métiers and the Ecole Polytechnique, the last two founded during the French Revolution.

Since the eighteenth century, institutions devoted to the acquisition of knowledge about nature – laboratories, universities, research foundations – have proliferated. Governments also have subsidized means of storing and transmitting knowledge of every sort, such as agricultural extension services, libraries, the postal service, telecommunications and, recently, computers and their data banks. As a result, the knowledge and information industry has become the largest in the world. Unlike other industries, it does not make profits, but is subsidized by governments and other industries, paying them back in knowledge. Although technology is not the only beneficiary of this process, it has produced the most spectacular results, and has justified the sums invested in it.

It is clear also that the craving for new knowledge is not uniform. It was especially intense in western Europe until the mid-nineteenth century, then in America, Russia-U.S.S.R.,

and Japan, and only recently has it begun spreading to other areas of the world. Of all the money invested in research worldwide in the early 1980s, the United States was spending one-third, western Europe and Japan another third, the Soviet Union and eastern Europe almost as much, and the rest of the world (Asia, Africa, and Latin America) only 3% (Norman 1981: 67). Insofar as technology is knowledge of nature and how to manipulate it for human ends, it follows that countries with the most information are also the most able to develop their economies and transform the land. Knowledge is both cause and effect of economic growth, and the information industry has been the primary cause of the acceleration of technological change in the past 200 years.

Mining

In the first century of industrialization, large-scale mining was concentrated in its traditional locales – Britain, Germany, and Sweden. Until the 1880s, Welsh anthracite, for instance, was shipped as far as India and South America as fuel for steamships and railroad locomotives. By the mid-nineteenth century, however, the increasing demand for industrial raw materials led to the discovery and exploitation of new sources ever more distant from the industrialized regions. To fuel the steam engines that transported the rising flood of goods around the world, coal was mined not only in industrializing areas like Pennsylvania, Japan, and South Africa, but also in places that otherwise lacked industry of any sort, like Borneo and the Sahara. Table 4-4 shows the rise in coal output in the late-nineteenth and early-twentieth centuries, when it was the most important industrial fuel. Great Britain's coal extraction peaked in the period 1910–14, France's in 1925–29, Germany's in 1940–44. Their successors were the more recently developing countries: the United States, the Soviet Union, Japan, China, Poland, and others.

Industrializing economies were built on metal, especially iron and steel. Iron-ore extraction shifted from Britain and Germany to the United States, the Soviet Union, and numerous other countries – some of them quite distant from the

Table 4-4 *World Coal Output, 1825–1975* (in million metric tons)

1825	26	1865	181	1905	941	1945	1,265
1830	27	1870	220	1910	1,151	1950	1,800
1835	37	1875	283	1915	1,211	1955	2,113
1840	48	1880	340	1920	1,319	1960	2,624
1845	66	1885	405	1925	1,358	1965	2,787
1850	76	1890	511	1930	1,401	1970	3,018
1855	111	1895	583	1935	1,333	1975	3,257
1860	139	1900	762	1940	1,686		

Sources: Mitchell 1975: 381–89; Mitchell 1982: 282–86; Mitchell 1983: 399–405.

original centers of industry, like Spanish Morocco, South Africa, or Australia.

The same was true of nonferrous metals. With the advent of a mass market for canned food, tin from Malaya and Bolivia overshadowed English production after 1870. Similarly, the electrical industry's voracious appetite for copper led to the opening of mines in Michigan, Montana, Chile, the Belgian Congo (now Zaire), and Northern Rhodesia (now Zambia).

In other words, the global spread of mining activity resulted not only from the spread of industrialization, but also from a demand for minerals by the industrializing economies that far outstripped their own capacity to produce. Actually, when applied to minerals, the words output and production are misnomers, for the process is really one of extraction and depletion. The depletion of mineral reserves elicited two responses. One was the search for new deposits, a process closely tied to the imperialist push of the turn of the century and also to the rise of large corporations able to raise capital in London and New York to spend half a world away. The other was the development of new methods of extracting and processing ores of ever lower grades, at depth, and in harsh environments; they included giant steam and electric shovels and dredges, dynamite for blasting, electrolysis and flotation, and reverberatory furnaces.

Mineral extraction could take place in countries that had little or no industry because the technologies involved were easy to transfer geographically. In remote areas, mining companies brought in equipment; built railway lines, power plants, and suburban-style bungalows for the managers and engineers; and hired local inhabitants primarily for unskilled jobs. In many places, mining was an "enclave" economy – creating towns, railways, and harbors that were more closely connected to distant markets than to the surrounding countryside. When the minerals were exhausted, only ghost towns and open pits remained.

Even more external to the local economy was petroleum extraction, which began in the mid-nineteenth century but only took off at the beginning of the twentieth, with the advent of the automobile. The oil industry was so capital-intensive and used so little unskilled labor that several oil-producing countries like Mexico and Burma saw their resources depleted with almost no national impact. Not until the 1970s did underdeveloped but oil-rich countries in the Middle East, Africa, and Latin America receive benefits from their resources comparable to those that the industrialized customers had long been enjoying.

Transportation

New means of transportation played a role in every aspect of the transformation of the earth. They were a key factor in the expansion of both industry and agriculture in the nineteenth century and in their intensification in the twentieth, for they linked farms, factories, and mines to their customers and suppliers. Lower transport costs, combined with mass production, led to regional specialization on a global scale; this was beneficial to the industrial economies, but left the nonindustrial ones dependent on a few exports to pay for imported manufactured goods.

Boats and ships, the first vehicles, remain to this day the most cost-effective means of transporting bulk cargoes slowly. It is no coincidence that most great cities arose on rivers or lakes or near the sea and that much of their surface was devoted to harbors.

All new means of transportation that have appeared in the past 150 years are based on the two engines mentioned earlier: the railroad and steamships on the steam engine, and automobiles and airplanes on the internal combustion engine. The railroad, which appeared in England in the 1830s and quickly spread, was the most revolutionary device ever created up to its time. It used great tracts of land, both in cities and in the country, and hastened the coming of many other land-consuming activities: bridges and tunnels, coal and iron mines, foundries and steel mills, rail mills, factories, and repair shops. Whole industries arose that were primarily devoted to serving its needs (Burlingame 1967; Ferguson 1967; Williams 1967).

Even more space is occupied by the automobile. Streets and parking lots, highways and interchanges stand out in the landscapes of industrial countries as much as in the cities themselves. In Los Angeles – an extreme case but a premonition of the future – roadways occupy more space than buildings and green spaces together. Even cities built in the railroad age, like London, are encircled by belts of suburbs in which the automobile has filled in the rural spaces between the fingers of railway urbanization. And as a secondary effect, automobiles bring forth yet more mines and factories, workshops, filling stations, and junkyards (Rae 1967).

Airplanes are also major consumers of land. For example, Chicago's O'Hare Airport is much larger (about 28 km^2) than the city's central business district (about 8 km^2). Finally, other means of transportation also consume much space. Electric power lines run straight across the landscape over 200-foot-wide paths kept clear of trees and buildings. To supply cities with their necessary liquids and gases, pipelines, reservoirs, and refineries take up space along their edges. Even the ethereal telecommunications networks, the telephone lines and radio/television transmitters that carry information and entertainment from place to place, leave patterns and lines on the landscape.

Transportation systems have become, after agriculture, humankind's most extensive consumer of land, and are also themselves major industries and customers of other industries, especially mining and steel. As such, they not only occupy a large place in industrial economies, but they also have a major impact on the environment. Vehicles consume most of the world's oil, as they once consumed coal, and many of today's environmental problems – air pollution and possibly acid rain and the greenhouse effect – can be traced to industrial civilization's dependence on mechanized transportation.

Timber Extraction

The ability to cull and remove both timber and forests is ancient and can be achieved even with primitive technology. Global industrial economies have had a profound effect on timber extraction in at least two ways: by increasing the demand for wood and by increasing technologies that facilitate its extraction and delivery. On the demand side, the rise of paper products, especially newsprint, opened a vast market for softwoods, as did frame houses and railroad ties. Mechanized sawmills and the technology to make paper from softwoods transformed the supply side. The nineteenth century witnessed steam-powered clear-cutting of temperate forests, creating "cut-over" regions in such places as Minnesota, Wisconsin, and Michigan (Wilkinson 1973: 165). In the Western world, timber extraction is now largely controlled, with considerable effort expended on forest regeneration for future cutting (Vale 1982). The modern version of the cut-over process has been shifted largely to the last tropical forests of the world, spurred by the demand for hardwoods and wood pulp and by the new technologies of the portable power saw and the lumber truck that can deliver the products cheaply to the nearest harbors (Richards 1973). The biospheric effects of this extraction and deforestation may be global, the subject of various chapters in this volume.

Agriculture: Species Transfers and Biotechnology

Of all technologies, those related to agriculture have been most land-consuming and have altered vast quantities of the earth's surface. Agricultural technologies are, of course, ancient and include the ability to adjust soil, slope, and water at various scales and to breed plants and animals. Remarkable early examples of local technological transformations of the biosphere abound, such as the *chinampas* of the Basin of Mexico (chaps. 2 and 35); despite this antiquity, both the scale and kind of agricultural technology have changed dramatically since the eighteenth century. Species transfers – another ancient form of agricultural transformation – were radically altered between the sixteenth and eighteenth centuries. In what Alfred Crosby (1972; 1986) calls the "Columbian exchange" and "ecological imperialism," the patterns of world food crops – as well as diseases and nonagricultural biota – were reshaped by European global expansion. Staples such as maize (corn), potato, and manioc (cassava) were introduced from America to the Old World, whereas rice, wheat, and other grains were taken to the New World, Australia, and elsewhere. Major exchanges of fruits, vegetables, medicinal plants, and weeds were also made. In addition, horses, cattle, pigs, sheep, chicken, and rats, among others, were introduced to the Americas, whereas sheep and rabbits were important introductions to Australia.

In eighteenth-century Europe, the interest in plants had crystallized into the science of botany, and plant transfers became a carefully planned, government-subsidized activity. From the beginning, botanical gardens were centers of scientific and technological research. The earliest were "apothecary" gardens, created to provide the courts of Europe with drugs. The first botanical gardens were founded in Pisa and Bologna in the sixteenth century; later they were begun in Leipzig, Leiden, Montpellier, and many other places. In the eighteenth century, several of them – notably the Royal Botanic Garden at Kew near London and the Jardin des Plantes in Paris – grew into scientific research establishments. Closely connected with them were the tropical gardens of Mauritius (founded 1735), Bourbon (1769), St. Thomas (1764), Calcutta (1786), and Jamaica (1793). Like space exploration today, botanical research was practically a monopoly of the two major world powers of the time, France and England.

The task of the botanical gardens was not only to collect and classify all plants, but also to transfer plants for agricultural purposes. A celebrated instance of such a transfer is the voyage of HMS *Bounty* in 1789, which was sent from England to bring breadfruit and sugar cane from Tahiti to Jamaica; though delayed by a mutiny, the expedition fulfilled its mission.

By the nineteenth century, botany had become a major activity in several countries of the world. The invention in 1826 of the Wardian case, or terrarium, greatly increased the chances of keeping delicate seedlings alive during long ocean voyages. Under government sponsorship, botanic gardens and botanizing expeditions accelerated the rate of plant transfers. The Bourbon variety of sugar cane from Tahiti was diffused throughout the tropics. Tea, once a Chinese monopoly, was transplanted to Java in 1826 and to India ten years later. By the midcentury almost every domesticated plant had been transferred, at least experimentally, to every likely environment on earth.

At that point, botanists turned to the infinitely richer wild plant kingdom. As Europeans sought to advance into tropical Africa in the mid-nineteenth century, malaria restrained their imperialistic impulses. While this disease did not prevent Africans from inhabiting these regions – for no part of the world is medically unfit for human habitation – it caused such high death rates among newcomers that even explorers hesitated to penetrate them. To overcome this obstacle, they needed quinine, an antimalarial drug extracted from the bark of the cinchona tree, which grew wild in the Andes (Headrick 1981: 58–76). In 1854 and 1861, Dutch and English expeditions succeeded in smuggling cinchona seeds out of South America and transplanting them to Java and India (Brockway 1979: 103–39).

Similarly, the demand for natural rubber led to attempts to smuggle the *Hevea brasiliensis* tree out of the Amazon rain forests. In the 1870s, the British government sent expeditions to smuggle *Hevea* seeds from Brazil to Kew Gardens and on to Singapore, where they eventually formed the basis for the vast rubber plantations of Southeast Asia. Numerous other useful species or varieties of plants were similarly transferred to new environments where ecological or political circumstances made their exploitation more profitable than in their native habitats (Brockway 1979; Dean 1987; Headrick 1988).

Thus whole regions were opened up to the new agriculture, as forests were felled, grasslands plowed under, and swamps drained to make room for commercial estates. Regions that began the nineteenth century with a few traditional farmers scattered throughout a vast wilderness entered the twentieth century covered with huge plantations. Many tropical countries became dependent on one or two export crops: sugar and tobacco in Cuba, bananas in Guatemala, tea in Ceylon, rice in Burma, and coffee in Colombia. All this activity in turn depended on the new modes of transportation, especially the railroad and the steamship, which linked the tropical farms to the markets of Europe and America.

The same processes – economic botany and transportation – also transformed the agriculture of the temperate zone. New wilderness areas were tamed and vast regions opened specifically to produce plants and animals brought in from elsewhere. The American Midwest, the Argentine pampas, and the Russian steppe became the granaries of the industrial world. Australia and parts of the Americas produced wool and meat, and the southern United States provided the textile industries with most of their cotton. The transformation of these vast landscapes for human purposes was the most extensive in history and was intimately connected with the growing demand of industrializing societies for their products.

Important differences, however, separate the agricultural transformation of the tropics from that of the temperate zone. In the latter, agriculture remained varied but became highly mechanized, and the displaced farm population found work in the burgeoning industrial cities. The commercial agriculture in the poorer and weaker countries of the tropics was more specialized and was subject to the fluctuations of the world market, and it remained labor intensive. This technical and economic difference was reinforced by political pressures. The dominant powers of the world in the temperate zone controlled parts of the tropics or annexed them outright. Almost all technological innovations originated in the industrial world; some of them, to be sure, were transferred to the tropics, but selectively and with many political controls. The result reinforced a trend that had begun in the Age of Discoveries: whereas the temperate zone became modern and industrial, the tropics were transformed from traditional to underdeveloped societies (Headrick 1988: chaps. 1 and 11).

By the early twentieth century, almost all the world's primary arable lands were under the plow. Nonetheless, attempts continue to bring ever more marginal lands under cultivation, often at a high ecological and social price; examples include the virgin lands of Soviet Kazakhstan and the rain forests of the Amazon and of Sumatra and Borneo. The difficulties encountered indicate that we may be approaching the limit of the economically and ecologically efficient arable land, given current technology. Only new sources of cheap water are likely to extend the area of the world's farmlands in the foreseeable future.

There is, however, another method of increasing agricultural production, namely intensification. While new discoveries of commercially useful wild plants have almost ceased, agricultural research is more productive than ever. This process began at the turn of the twentieth century, when experiment stations were set up to concentrate the attention of several related sciences on plant species, in contrast to the botanic gardens that applied one science to a multitude of plants. Instead of transferring plants from one area to another, scientists now manipulate familiar plants, adjusting their characteristics to human requirements and to specific environments. Geneticists have replaced the traditional domesticated plants with new and far more productive varieties, while soil scientists, agricultural chemists, plant pathologists, and entomologists have learned to improve the environment in which the plants can grow. The process began showing results in the 1920s with the introduction of nobilized sugar cane and hybrid maize, and continued after World War II with dwarf wheat in the 1950s and the "green revolution" varieties of wheat and rice introduced into the tropics in the 1960s. Modern biotechnology has affected virtually every region of the world, but this technical achievement has been accompanied by startling paradoxes: overproduction in the advanced countries, and famines in the underdeveloped ones. Agricultural productivity today has less to do with rich soils than with costly inputs from outside the agricultural sector (Evenson 1974).

Agriculture: Mechanical and Chemical Technology

The mechanization of agriculture has involved the introduction both of machines into the processes of agriculture themselves and of new linkages between the farms and their markets and suppliers. Since the 1850s, North America has been at the forefront of agricultural innovation. Several devices helped farmers plow the rich but difficult lands of the prairie. The steel plow, or "prairie breaker," patented by John Deere in 1837, was the first mechanical device able to cut through the tough sod formed by millennia of prairie grass roots. The McCormick reaper boosted the process of harvesting grain to the same labor-productivity as plowing and sowing. The horse-drawn rake, patented in 1856, provided fuel for the teams of farm animals, the engines of agriculture in those days. By the mid-nineteenth century, even horses could not provide all the energy required by the larger farms. Steam engines, long used for stationary power, were put on wheels to form the first tractors. They also powered the combines which, by the end of the century, could harvest up to 12 ha of wheat a day.

During the twentieth century, steam and horses were replaced by more efficient gasoline and diesel engines. By the 1920s, large modern farms in North America boasted equipment costing as much as the land itself. Their example was widely imitated, especially in the Soviet Union, where Stalin sought to replace peasant initiative with a blend of coercion in collective farms and mechanization through Machine Tractor Stations.

Tropical agriculture remained labor intensive and relatively unmechanized until World War II. Since then, however, there has been a substantial rise in the number of tractors and trucks, and even more so of smaller, more "appropriate" devices such as electric pumps and mills, plastic pipes, metal storage sheds, and rototillers.

Mechanization, however, required much closer bonds between farms and cities than had ever existed before. The machines were urban products, paid for by a constant flow of farm products to ever more distant markets. Sea trade in cheap and bulky products like grain, timber, and salt had been common along the coasts of Europe and Asia from the Middle Ages on, but before the mid-nineteenth century, only costly and relatively imperishable products (sugar, tea, tobacco, cotton, and opium) had been shipped across oceans. In the last third of the nineteenth century, the introduction of the railroad, steam shipping, and the Suez Canal revolutionized agricultural markets. Even grain could now be shipped profitably halfway around the world. After 1880, refrigeration opened up long-distance trade to perishables like meat, fruit, and dairy products. Argentinian beef and Australian mutton became staples of the European diet, along with wheat from the Ukraine, the Punjab, and the American Midwest.

The transportation revolution begun in the mid-nineteenth century was intensified in the twentieth. In the 1920s, the automobile and the truck increasingly tied farms to local markets and to railroad lines. After World War II, long-haul trucks and freight airplanes opened distant markets to the most delicate products (fresh fruits and vegetables, flowers, seafood), which until then had been strictly regional and seasonal items of consumption.

By the late eighteenth century, "natural" methods of maintaining and conserving soil fertility were considered insufficient by progressive farmers in England, who sought faster ways of replenishment. Marling and liming restored the chemical balance of the soil. In addition, farmers applied ground-up bone from slaughterhouses, and from the 1830s on, guano from Peru and nitrates from Chile. The role of chemicals, especially nitrates, in plant growth was first investigated by Baron Justus von Liebig (1803–1873). By the end of the nineteenth century, potash (potassium carbonate) and phosphate rock became additional tools of farming. In the twentieth century, the synthetic fixing of nitrogen from the air provided new supplies of fertilizer for the industrial countries. New hybrid plants were especially dependent on chemical fertilizers. Indeed, they were created specifically to transform chemicals into crops more efficiently, that is to say, with less land and labor than their "primitive" predecessors. At the same time, the new varieties of plants were more vulnerable to droughts, fungi, insects, and other traditional scourges of farming. Hence, they required irrigation and pesticides to reach their full potential.

Chemical pesticides were introduced in the mid-nineteenth century. Complex compounds of copper, lead, and arsenic (e.g., Paris green, London purple, lead arsenate) were used with varying degrees of success against the phylloxera of the vine, wheat rust, sugar-cane borers, and other ills. These inorganic compounds were helpful but costly. The major breakthrough came with the introduction of organic compounds into agriculture. The most effective was DDT, discovered in 1939 and widely used after World War II, not only in agriculture but also in global malaria-eradication campaigns. By suppressing malaria for a generation, DDT prolonged life expectancy in tropical countries like Sri Lanka by some twenty years – more than any other measure undertaken before or since. It thus contributed to a sudden surge of population and further pressure on the land.

DDT was soon followed by a series of chlorinated hydrocarbons (Chlordane, Dieldrin) and organic phosphates (Malathion). These chemicals were not only highly effective against their target-pests, but they were also toxic to many other forms of life such as bees, wildlife, domestic animals, and humans. As most of them were chemically stable, they remained in the food chain long after their original task was accomplished. In the 1960s, when their side-effects became better known, they were either banned or severely restricted. Meanwhile the search continues for the "magic bullet" that hits only its designated target.

Water Control

Since antiquity, three types of water control have had a major impact on landscapes: irrigation, drainage, and impoundment. The first two controls are used primarily for agricultural purposes and, therefore, can involve large areas of land: the third is also associated with direct human consumption and industrial-urban uses. Impoundment of this kind has grown dramatically, especially in the twentieth century (see chap. 14). Here, however, we focus on irrigation and drainage.

Much, if not most, of ancient irrigation centered on small-scale systems constructed and controlled by local communities. In some of the great river valleys in which early civilizations were centered, such as the Nile, large systems of the basin or inundation type emerged that apparently did not require state-level involvement (Butzer 1976). True "hydraulic civilizations" (Wittfogel 1957) may have been rare, though perhaps reflected in the radial irrigation systems of Mesopotamia or in the complex canal systems of Peru, where water was impounded and/or transported long distances by considerable feats of engineering. This situation changed dramatically in the nineteenth century as demand for foods grew and the ability of governments to utilize new methods of large-scale construction increased.

New hydraulic engineering techniques developed in the second half of the nineteenth century improved on the inundation system. They originated in the 1830s in India, where British engineers rebuilt abandoned canals and weirs dating from the Mogul Empire. With the confidence gained from those tasks, they began a series of new irrigation works in Hindustan and in the eastern Deccan that involved learning about flows, silting and scouring, and the construction of aqueducts and barrages. In the 1870s and 1880s, irrigation engineers tackled more difficult challenges: flushing and draining salty land, settling farmers on former desert lands, and moving water from one watershed to another through tunnels and across rivers. The first decades of this century saw the scope of their projects increase yet again, with multiriver projects in the Punjab, and the enormous Sukkur Barrage across the Indus.

Hydrological techniques evolved slowly – more by trial and error than by scientific calculation. Most of the work was done by masses of unskilled labor using techniques that would have been familiar to the Moguls and the Romans. Not until the 1920s did the engineers begin using bulldozers and reinforced concrete. Beyond the engineering aspects of the question, they faced many political and economic questions: creating regional multiriver, multipurpose development projects overlapping several jurisdictions; distributing water fairly among competing users; and most difficult of all, persuading farmers to adjust their agricultural practices to make the best use of new water supplies (Harris 1923; Hart 1956; Michel 1967).

By the turn of the century, India had about one-quarter of the world's irrigated land, and by 1940 the big government irrigation projects watered an area as large as England. Inundation irrigation gave way to perennial irrigation, in which water was stored and released gradually throughout the year, allowing two or even three growing seasons.

The techniques developed in India in the late-nineteenth century were carried to other parts of the world by the migration of engineers and the diffusion of knowledge. By the end of the century, major irrigation projects were undertaken in Egypt, the United States, Australia, Mexico, South Africa, and central Asia. Since then, modern irrigation has spread to China, Southeast Asia, the Middle East, and tropical Africa – in other words, to all the arid zones with agricultural potential. These great projects have many nonagricultural uses as well: hydroelectric power, fish breeding, navigation, recreation, and urban water supply.

Irrigation efforts have accelerated since World War II, both in the developed countries and as part of a worldwide campaign to alleviate hunger in the tropics. The world's irrigated area rose from 98 million ha in 1949 to almost 240 million ha in 1984 (Framji and Mahajan 1969: 1: cxiv; Kurian 1984: 123). New technologies have been instrumental in achieving this remarkable growth, especially reinforced concrete dams like the Aswan High Dam in Egypt and computers to control the extremely complex operations of regional water-control projects. By the mid-twentieth century, the best opportunities for the use of big dams and canals had apparently been exploited, except in Africa.

The big projects suffered from two flaws: their high fixed cost and their dependence upon gravity to distribute the water. Meanwhile, it was known that much fresh water lay below the level of good agricultural land. The result was a shift to new technologies, based on new materials and sources of energy, that would provide water to places outside the command areas of the big irrigation schemes. Pipelines and pumping stations made it possible to move water where it would not flow of its own accord. Tubewells, with their diesel or electric pumps, brought water up from the water table; in certain places, rising energy costs, however, have led to a resurrection of that ancient technology, the windmill. To avoid the waste of water inherent in surface irrigation, farmers turned to aluminum and plastic pipes and to sprinkler systems such as the center-pivot irrigator, which creates green circles on the landscapes of the western United States.

The most recent techniques and the most sparing of water are the drip-irrigation systems and the polyethylene-covered greenhouses found in intensively cultivated areas like southern California, Israel, and Catalonia. These new methods are so expensive and complex that they can be justified in growing only costly fruits, vegetables, and seeds.

For a century, agronomists and engineers have experimented with two other forms of water supply: hydroponic agriculture, in which plants grow in water that is constantly recycled; and desalination, which turns seawater into fresh. So far the costs of these techniques make them prohibitive, except where they are subsidized for military or political reasons: Guantanamo Naval Base, Ascension Island, parts of Arabia. If they ever become commercially remunerative, they will surely transform the earth as much as all previous types of irrigation (Postel 1986).

The counterpart to irrigation, in places where there is too much rather than too little water, is drainage. Though not as visible as irrigation, drainage has had a major impact on certain areas of the world. Along the lower reaches of the Nile, Tigris, and Euphrates rivers, ancient engineers had dug canals to dry out land waterlogged by excessive irrigation. More recently, engineers have learned to control (although not prevent entirely) the salt deposits that irrigation water leaves on the soil; this lesson was learned through bitter experience after the Egyptian cotton crop of 1909 failed because of salination and waterlogging in the Nile delta.

Drainage is also applied to nonirrigated land. The Romans and medieval Europeans drained swamps like the Pontine Marshes and the English Fens – a practice common also throughout the Americas and Oceania. For centuries the Dutch have been reclaiming land from the sea itself. In drainage, as in irrigation, the technologies of the industrial age have hastened the process. In mid-nineteenth-century Holland, steam engines replaced the ubiquitous windmills, except those preserved for tourists. More recently, diesel and electric pumps have taken over the task of draining polders. When rain-watered land must be drained, the preferred method is by underground pipes, a system first used in Scotland in the 1840s and now common in the United States, Canada, and the U.S.S.R. (Framji and Mahajan 1969: 1: cxx).

Irrigation is perhaps the most spectacular example of humankind's interference with the flows that make the earth's surface a living biosphere. River irrigation supplies plants with water that would otherwise run off into the sea; the flow is diverted rather than broken. More serious is the mining of groundwaters, like the Ogallala Aquifer, which lies under the Great Plains of North America and now sinks deeper every year. As for the grand projects that are periodically proposed – to divert the waters of the Ob and Irtysh to Kazakhstan, the Saskatchewan to the American Southwest, or the Congo to the Sahel – their impact on the world's climate is simply unknowable.

Unintended Consequences of Modern Technology

The more important technological achievements of modern society have had at least two major objectives. Each innovation, each engineering project has been designed to achieve a specific goal: to link one place to another, to irrigate a certain piece of land, to immunize against a particular disease, and so on. In addition, the whole package of innovations known as the Industrial Revolution has carried grander intentions: raising living standards and enhancing national power. On the whole, these objectives have been attained: the earth now sustains unprecedented numbers of people, many at unprecedented material standards of consumption.

But these achievements have not come without costs – many the result of surprise impacts or consequences of technological change. Until recently, these surprises were felt primarily in the social and political realms: social turmoil, labor strife, and revolutions associated with economic development in one locale and underdevelopment in another. Major surprises now include the responses of the environment, even at a global scale. Such consequences are, in part, a result of the "linear perspective" of technological development, the emphasis on solving the immediate problem without regard to the larger context in which it exists. The history of these consequences, however, suggests that changes of any kind, including technological ones, involve surprises (Kates 1978).

Today, the unintended impacts of industrialization on local environments and the global biosphere appear to be severe, even dangerous. Industry, especially the "smokestack" variety, creates waste products both at the point of production and at the end of the consumption cycle. Mines have left tailings and acid runoff, the steel industry has created slag heaps and atmospheric pollution, textile manufacturers have polluted rivers, consumers have created sewage and waste – the examples are innumerable.

These results are a product of both the "linear view" of production and the economies of mass consumption (chap. 40). Previous to the Industrial Revolution, relatively low and subsistence-oriented populations could produce and consume in such ways that the scars of production and the wastes of consumption would mostly disappear within nature. The unintended consequences to the environment were generally small and could be alleviated without cost or action. In the industrial age, mass consumption of cheap iron and steel, and later, plastics, led to a "throw-away" economy; growing cities produced more waste then they could treat and more smoke than could be carried away by the winds.

The consequences were soon noticeable. By the early nineteenth century, there were many complaints in Britain about air pollution, sewage, and the spoilation of the countryside. It was difficult, however, to identify the waste producers and make them pay the cost of cleaning up. Instead of being part of the production-consumption cycle, waste disposal was allowed to become a social cost and a burden on the environment.

Compounding the difficulties was the tendency of industrial economies and their waste-disposal systems to take their wastes further away and disperse them more widely. Although the mines and mills of the eighteenth century and before affected small areas intensely, a cleaner environment was usually available within walking distance. In the nineteenth and early twentieth centuries, waste-disposal problems were becoming regional: greater London, the Ruhr, and other industrial regions suffered from smog (or pea-soup fog) and sewage affected whole watersheds. Every advance in productive technology brought with it an increase in waste problems. Since the 1870s, the steel industry, with its outpouring of rails, automobiles, tin cans, and other disposable metal objects, produced a significant jump in the quantity of slag and air pollution and new forms of nondegradable garbage. The products of the chemical industry (pesticides, fertilizers, solvents, and so on) have proved to be even harder to control, since they are usually liquids or gases and are dispersed by the air and water over wide areas.

In the second half of the twentieth century, the problems have spread beyond localized regions to involve whole nations and even groups of nations. Although acid rain crosses national boundaries, governments find it difficult to accept responsibility for a problem occurring in a foreign country; among the consequences is the poisoning of forests (*Waldsterben*) in Europe and North America. Municipal officials search further and further for places to dump garbage. In an ironic twist, poor countries are now seen not only as suppliers of raw materials and consumers of industrial products, but also as recipients for the wastes of the rich. Industrial wastes and byproducts now affect the entire planet; the greenhouse effect is but one sign of this trend.

Industrial wastes are not simply growing in quantity, but are becoming more varied, more toxic, and more difficult to degrade or dispose of. This is especially true of the wastes from the petrochemical industries that arose in the mid-twentieth century and produce pharmaceuticals, plastics, synthetics, and organic fertilizers and pesticides. Their products and byproducts which are either indestructible (like plastics) or toxic (like mercury, PCB, and dioxin), accumulate in garbage dumps and in estuaries, lakes, and groundwaters. Most dangerous of all is the nuclear industry, with its ever-accumulating stockpiles of radioactive wastes. Not only is the impact of these substances more widespread and difficult to assess, but it also is accumulating over large areas in ways that are poorly understood; acid rain and coastal pollution are two recent examples of this cumulative effect.

Although modern industrial technology can be blamed for much of the world's pollution, it should be noted that technology also can be applied to the prevention or disposal of pollutants, as shown in the development of catalytic converters, scrubbers and electrostatic precipitators, and biodegradable detergents, to name a few. In comparison to the growing dangers to the environment from other industrial processes, however, these protective technologies are only palliatives.

In addition to chronic environmental problems, the world has recently been hit with a series of industrial catastrophes: the oil spill of the tanker *Exxon Valdez*, the poison gas leak in Bhopal, India, and most spectacular of all, the Three Mile Island and Chernobyl nuclear reactor accidents. The scale and complexity of modern industry seems to make such periodic catastrophes almost inevitable.

Some technologies press on the environment in indirect ways, by facilitating the growth of population. Much of the pressure on contemporary landscapes is a consequence of rapid population growth – a growth that has been spawned, in part, by biomedical technologies. These technologies primarily were intended to make life healthier and longer, but they also have created conditions in which population growth outstrips the economies of support (Keyfitz 1967).

Conclusion

The grand sweep of technological change over the past 300 years has been marked by a movement from a global agrarian, organic-based system to an industrial, machine-based one. The history of the development of industrial technology is well known. It was not uniform in time and space. Emerging in northwest Europe in the nineteenth century, it spread first to other parts of Europe and North America, and subsequently to various nodes and regions throughout the world, especially in the midlatitudes. Obviously linked to the political economy, this technological transformation permitted a rapid rise in material consumption and in the power of certain regions. Ultimately, those regions could not supply the amount of raw products demanded by the new socio-economic and technological system, and they used their power to extract those resources from elsewhere. The amount and kind of environmental transformation associated with the overall system were unparalleled.

A linear view of production and consumption apparently has dominated industrial technology, solving the immediate problem without necessarily assessing the wider impacts of that solution. This and the tendency of surprise to follow change have led to unsuspected environmental consequences at the local, regional, and global levels. Waste and pollution have exceeded nature's ability to absorb them effectively, and diverse industrial activities can mutually reinforce impacts, as seen in the predicted global climatic change related to atmospheric pollution and tropical deforestation. Fortunately, a less linear, less simplistic "cyclical," or "systems," view may be emerging in the advanced stages of industrialization – a view that has as much to do with the attitudes of those who control technology as with the technology itself.

Industrial technology, which is powerful enough to break the self-renewing cycles of nature, is also capable of protecting the biosphere from its own excesses; modern forestry is an example of this process. In the past decade, the world's consumption of energy has stabilized, despite the continued growth of the industrial economies. The results are visible in the stagnation of the oil and nuclear-power industries and of the energy-voracious railroad, shipping, and automobile industries. Smokestack industries that feed on coal and other raw materials are also stagnant, in boom years as well as in recessions. The new leading sectors – information, electronics, health, and other high-technology industries – are more sparing in their use of energy and gentler on the environment than their predecessors. They are evidence that the industrial age is passing and that a new technological era – one based on services and information – is in the process of being born (Beniger 1986; Quinn, Baruch, and Paquette 1987).

References

Ashton, T. S. 1962. *The Industrial Revolution, 1760–1830*. New York: Oxford University Press.

Bairoch, P. 1963. *Revolution industrielle et sous-développement*. Paris: Société d'édition d'enseignement supérieur.

———. 1982. International industrialization levels from 1705 to 1980. *Journal of European Economic History* 11:269–333.

Beniger, J. R. 1986. *The Control Revolution: Technological and Economic Origins of the Information Society*. Cambridge, MA: Harvard University Press.

Brockway, L. H. 1979. *Science and Colonial Expansion: The Role of the British Royal Botanic Gardens*. New York: Academic Press.

Burlingame, R. 1967. Locomotives, railways, and steamships. In *Technology in Western Civilization*, ed. M. Kranzberg and C. W. Pursell, 1: 425–37. New York: Oxford University Press.

Butzer, K. W. 1976. *Early Hydraulic Civilization in Egypt: A Study in Cultural Ecology*. Chicago: University of Chicago Press.

Crosby, A. W., Jr. 1972. *The Columbian Exchange: Biological and Cultural Consequences of 1492*. Westport, CT: Greenwood Press.

———. 1986. *Ecological Imperialism: The Biological Expansion of Europe, 900–1900*. Cambridge: Cambridge University Press.

Dean, W. 1987. *Brazil and the Struggle for Rubber: A Study in Environmental History*. Cambridge and New York: Cambridge University Press.

Ellul, J. 1954. *La technique ou l'enjeu du siècle*. Paris: Librairie Armand Colin.

Evenson, R. 1974. International diffusion of agrarian technology. *Journal of Economic History* 34: 51–73.

Ferguson, E. S. 1967. Steam transportation. In *Technology in Western Civilization*, ed. M. Kranzberg and C. W. Pursell, 1: 284–302. New York: Oxford University Press.

Framji, K. K., and I. K. Mahajan. 1969. *Irrigation and Drainage in the World: A Global View*. 2d ed. 2 vols. New Delhi: International Commission on Irrigation and Drainage.

Harris, D. G. 1923. *Irrigation in India*. London: Oxford University Press.

Hart, H. C. 1956. *New India's Rivers*. Bombay: Orient Longmans.

Headrick, D. R. 1981. *The Tools of Empire: Technology and European Imperialism in the Nineteenth Century*. New York: Oxford University Press.

———. 1988. *The Tentacles of Progress: Technology Transfer in the Age of Imperialism, 1850–1940*. New York: Oxford University Press.

Kates, R. W. 1978. *Risk Assessment of Environmental Hazard*. Chichester, NY: Wiley.

Keyfitz, N. 1967. National population and the technological watershed. *Journal of Social Issues* 23: 62–78.

Kurian, G. T. 1984. *The New Book of World Rankings*. New York: Facts on File.

Landes, D. S. 1969. *The Unbound Prometheus: Technological Change and Industrial Development in Western Europe from 1750 to the Present*. Cambridge: Cambridge University Press.

Michel, A. A. 1967. *The Indus Rivers: A Study of the Effects of Partition*. New Haven and London: Yale University Press.

Mitchell, B. R. 1975. *European Historical Statistics 1750–1970*. New York: Facts on File.

———. 1982. *International Historical Statistics: Africa and Asia*. New York: New York University Press.

———. 1983. *International Historical Statistics: The Americas and Australasia*. Detroit: Gale Research Co.

Mokyr, J., ed. 1985. *The Economics of the Industrial Revolution*. Totowa, NJ: Rowman and Allanhead.

Norman, C. 1981. *The God That Limps: Science and Technology in the Eighties*. New York: Norton.

Postel, S. 1986. Increasing water efficiency. In *State of the World 1986*, ed. L. R. Brown et al., 40–61. New York: Norton.

Quinn, J. B., J. J. Baruch and P. C. Paquette. 1987. Technology in services. *Scientific American* 257: 50–58.

Rae, J. B. 1967. The internal combustion engine on wheels. In *Technology in Western Civilization*, ed. M. Kranzberg and C. W. Pursell, 2: 119–37. New York: Oxford University Press.

Richards, P. W. 1973. The tropical rain forest. *Scientific American* 229: 58–67.

United States Bureau of the Census. *Historical Statistics of the United States, Colonial Times to 1970*. Washington, D.C.: U.S. Department of Commerce, Bureau of the Census.

Vale, T. R. 1982. *Plants and People: Vegetation Change in North America*. Washington, D.C.: Association of American Geographers.

White, L., Jr. 1967. The historical roots of our ecologic crisis. *Science* 155: 1203–207.

Wilkinson, R. G. 1973. *Poverty and Progress: An Ecological Model of Economic Development*. London: Methuen.

Williams, E. W., Jr. 1967. Rail and water transport. In *Technology in Western Civilization*, ed. M. Kranzberg and C. W. Pursell, 2: 137–53. New York: Oxford University Press.

Winner, L. 1977. *Autonomous Technology: Technics-out-of-Control As a Theme in Political Thought*. Cambridge, MA: MIT Press.

Wittfogel, K. A. 1957. *Oriental Despotism: A Comparative Study of Total Power*. New Haven, CT: Yale University Press.

5

Institutions, Social Organization, and Cultural Values

JOHN W. BENNETT   KENNETH A. DAHLBERG

The extensive transformations of the earth described elsewhere in this book raise fundamental questions about the capacity of humans to change their ways so as to guard the environmental heritage for future generations. It is all too easy to adopt a pessimistic position: that because the contemporary situation is the product of the drift of human activities and behavior since the appearance of *Homo sapiens*, any attempt to reverse directions is naive; and that each individual and group must seek its own protection in an increasingly dangerous world.

Easy optimism is the other side of the coin: that humans have the necessary intelligence and will to solve problems and redress wrongs; that if the world must be changed, it is in our power to change it because we have learned to see ourselves as the source of good as well as evil; and that science and technology give us the tools for such positive change. Both positions ignore the importance of modern institutions in shaping possibilities, actions, and values. Thus, if we are to go beyond easy pessimism and optimism, we must diagnose how social institutions channel the direction of modern society, and perhaps discover what needed and desirable changes are within institutional capabilities. Our objective is to provide a broad overview, not to present detailed suggestions.

Underlying our presentation is a paradox involving continuity and change in the human condition. On the one hand, the continuities in human behavior – purposefulness, the ability to find means to accomplish ever-more complex and difficult ends, and the vitality of values – lead to change. On the other hand, the results of change – the construction of elaborate institutions and organizations – create structures that resist change. Each of the earlier great transitions reviewed in the first section had this dynamic. In the current era we find a new combination — where increasing institutional capabilities and rigidities blend to transform radically humankind's relationship to the earth, in both values and action.

Basic institutional differences – past and present – in patterns of resource use are then examined in terms of the great resource domains of air, water, and land. Then we trace the more specific organizational and ideological patterns arising in the industrial era – focusing on the modern resource regimes of agriculture, energy, and minerals. In tracing the implications of these patterns, we conclude that the present world system, projected into the future, cannot be sustained either ecologically or socially over the long run. Fundamental change will occur. Any successful attempt to give it some direction will have to take account of basic institutional trends and characteristics.

The Great Transitions

Since the emergence of *Homo sapiens*, ecological history may be written as a series of transitions in the relationships between human society and the physical environment (Bennett 1976). Each transition has witnessed a progressive incorporation of natural substances into culture, thus extending the dominion of humankind over the earth and its creatures. This process has been accompanied by an exponential growth of both human population and the amount of energy extracted from nature and used in human endeavor.[1] The process has reached a point in the last quarter of the twentieth century at which the "dominion" of the species has begun to assume menacing and contradictory proportions. Exploitation of the environment and continued population growth threaten human existence through resource degradation and the release of manmade substances injurious to all living things. While the seeds of this situation extend far back into human history, the most critical phase – coinciding with the steep upswing of the exponential curves – has taken place in the past 300 years.

Historians and anthropologists suggest five transitions. The *first* is the change from simple subsistence foraging by family units to hunting and gathering carried out by larger band groups as a directed and organized undertaking. This change did not occur in any one time or place in the Old World, but was a tendency manifest in foraging itself, and the transition could have occurred many times in early hominid history.[2] Sociostructural innovations were crucial, although tools and weapons were also improved. The key development seems to have been a superior method of group hunting, providing a more reliable food supply than individual action or uncoordinated foraging could afford.

The *second* transition is the change from organized nomadic hunting to semisedentary life and the intensive exploitation of natural foods and products in a particular territory. Territories had become increasingly important in the hunting-gathering transition, as methods of harvesting food became more efficient and comprehensive. In many localities in the Old and the New Worlds, this led to specialized subsistence regimes within forests and in areas close to water (lakes, streams, and the ocean margin). This permitted a more settled life in what were not full-fledged villages, but certainly long-term encampments.[3]

While the first evidence for the great transitions came from Old World paleontology and archaeology, the same transitions occurred in the New World among Amerindian populations, although the timing differed and they did not pass through identical steps (Ford 1985; Jennings 1983). Also, while many populations moved into new transitions, some remained in earlier ones. The point is that we are dealing not with an inevitable or lawful evolutionary process, but with an historically contingent search by hominids with rising intelligence and skill to ensure food for slowly growing regional populations.

The *third*, and perhaps most significant transition of the prehistoric past, was the change from the previous methods of exploitation of natural substances to the actual raising of plant foods and the breeding of animals – the so-called agricultural revolution, associated with the traditional rubric "Neolithic," and accompanied by population increases (Cohen 1977). This third transition is probably the first in which a decided change in technological proficiency was the major feature, but it also was accompanied by an intensification of sedentary life through the emergence of the more or less autonomous *village community*. Food *producing* required detailed contextual knowledge of how to select hardy plants and their seeds for cultivation, and productive and docile animals for breeding. The change, a genuine innovation, no matter how gradual, is fully comparable in its ecological significance to the development of independent sources of power in the Industrial Revolution (see Blum 1982 for an historical review).

The village was a new form of human association and coordination in which people were required to create their own environment: the precursor of the "built environment" of the industrial transition. By constructing houses, storerooms, and ceremonial chambers, people were creating a milieu different from anything found in nature. The technology of food production plus the creation of a communal environment to some extent removed those groups from the intimate, dependent contact with the physical environment required for hunters and gatherers. The village became an enduring form of cultural ecology, however, and its staying power can be explained by its transitional or compromise status: it is several steps removed from nature, but at the same time, the raising of plants and animals keeps humans in reasonable contact with natural cycles and processes. In some respects, the country village is the most "successful" of the

transitions insofar as it conferred a degree of autonomy on humans, yet did so without drastic environmental intervention or degradation (see Sims 1920 and Homans 1942 for classic descriptions of village life).

The *fourth* transition involved, once again, a major *social* development, along with some new skills and techniques. This was the rise of intercommunal trade and craft manufacturing as a response to steady population growth and the necessary nucleation of populations engaged in trade, that is, the *city*. V. Gordon Childe (1950; 1951) called it the urban revolution (also see Adams 1966). But cities were not invented as cities; initially, at least, they were a technodemographic response to the need to concentrate craft and commercial activities in the desert river valleys of Southwest Asia and the Middle East. This eventually created mutual dependence of growing population aggregates at considerable distance from each other. The physical environment between such trade-related entities became open to exploitation from both sides, and of course competition for control of this space immediately arose. Although conflict over territory had always existed, something new was added: the idea of possession, not mere occupancy.

The *fifth* transition – and the one we are, on the whole, still within – is the Industrial Revolution, which is based on the discovery and refinement of technological means to extract and concentrate energy in quantities vastly greater than in any preceding period.[4] In some respects, it is the most technically determined transition of the five. Social organization initially followed, rather than led, the developments of the industrial and power age. Today, those institutions and organizations that reinforce the extractive and expansive tendencies of industry have more than caught up, whereas regulatory and control systems to protect the common good and the environment continue to lag far behind.

The *modern state*, rather than the local community, is the key social organizational expression of the transition, and this is of course a direct reflection of the increasing need for control over growing populations, increasing technological complexity, and the expanding territorial scope of human involvement with the environment.[5] It is, in some respects, the culmination of the social administration of space and resources through property, although there are indications that it is being gradually supplanted by an emerging world system made up of multinational corporations and international organizations, banks, and communications networks. The modern state still can be considered to be the ultimate possessor, however, regardless of locally varying forms of tenure. The state apparatus is the final arbiter and landlord because it alone has the effective power to defend its territory.[6]

This brief review of the great transitions in the human engagement with the terrestrial environment has introduced several key points: (1) The increase of technological control over resources was important, but it varied from one transition to another. Of equal importance throughout were particular forms of human association, coordination, and nucleated assembly. (2) Every change in technology was accompanied by some change in social organization, but these correlative changes were not necessarily symmetrical or adaptive. (3)

Ecological arrangements made by human societies have covered an increasing spatial range. As both technology and the control functions of human ecology expand, the spatial coordinates increase in size and in their potential for conflict and competition. (4) The definition of "resources" has expanded in complexity. The term itself is a recent one, becoming cogent only in the industrial transition. The contrast is seen by comparing the ceremonial customs of the organized hunters of the first transition – aimed at pacifying the natural species needed for food (here humans were part of nature, using it, but apologizing for the use) – with the contemporary era, in which natural substances are defined almost exclusively as sources of energy and gratification for humans.[7] Conservation movements seek to protect and conserve such resources, but in so doing, define them as cultural phenomena to be guarded for future needs or for such interests as beauty, the enjoyment of nature, and recreation.

Institutional Dynamics, Patterns, and Trends

The specific societal pattern emerging from any of the great transitions can be seen to reflect complex interactions and tensions among: (1) the basic behavioral proclivities of *Homo sapiens* toward gratification and order; (2) the embodiment of those proclivities in technologies and institutions, which then take on a life of their own; and (3) the survival need (and capability) of human groups to adapt to major changes in their larger environment.[8] Historically, there have been many examples of societies that so heavily institutionalized the social drives for gratification and order that they found it difficult to adapt to major changes, whether social or environmental. Imperial China is a classic example.

Today, humankind faces a difficult – and perhaps historically unique – situation. First, the drives toward gratification and predictable control (order) are more strongly and widely institutionalized than ever before. Second, modern institutional forms, while offering great productive capacity, are more rigid and vulnerable to failure when overstressed than traditional institutions. Third, modern institutions systematically neglect or obscure larger changes in the natural environment – in part because, conceptually, nature increasingly has been absorbed into industrial culture. Thus, fundamental questions regarding humankind's capacity to adapt to emerging global environmental and resource threats are raised. To address them we need to understand better these institutional problems and their sources.

Resource-Related Institutions

Institutions can be classified in a variety of ways.[9] In this brief review we choose to focus on three key resource-related institutions that are useful in exploring resource use and management: (1) institutions of *property*; (2) *regulatory* institutions, which serve the "control function" in human society and are crucial to our use and governance of physical resources; and (3) institutions of *exchange* and their associated concepts of *value*.[10]

The first institutional construct is that of possession, or *property*. In the Industrial Revolution, humans created a fictional dominion over nature, defining possession not fundamentally in terms of respect for nature, but with emphasis on ways to transfer to humans the energy and materials residing in nature's "resources" (Black 1970). In other words, the conditions of possession are defined primarily on the basis of existing social conventions. The ownership of a resource, such as water, is made analogous to ownership, say, of jewels, factories, or weapons. Although the nature of the resource itself does influence the institutional rules (see below), there is a strong compulsion to shape the rules by existing precedents within the social system. In the last analysis, the most dominant and pervasive points to be derived from the study of humankind's ecological history are the drive toward autonomy and the increasing institutional absorption of nature into culture.

The *regulatory institutions* have three main forms: control by force, control through bargaining, and control through legislation. We already have referred to the long history of warfare over territory and the importance of the state in this activity. Internally, "possession is nine-tenths..."; i.e., occupancy is recognized as creating a right. But in cases of disputes, bargaining takes place, money may change hands, and a market for the resource emerges. Force can be used occasionally or as a last resort, usually by states or their agents. Seizure by force by the *modern state* is difficult to treat as illegal, and recompense or redress is difficult to come by. The control over minerals, grazing lands, water rights, air rights, corporations, and so on are subject to these interlocking and overlapping conventions of force, threats, and bargaining and dealing. In the course of such interaction, regulatory institutions that confer power on the controllers or owners proliferate in all civilizations – generally until the mass of laws and rules becomes top-heavy and is overturned by people who no longer believe in them. Embedded in the regulatory function, then, are arms, military action, customary law, legislated law, courts, regulatory agencies, formal and informal devices to threaten malefactors, and other conflict-resolving and award-granting agencies. All of these agencies treat natural substances as elements of human property. Few exceptions are made for natural phenomena simply because they are part of nature.

This underlines the next concept of significance: *value*. This is a behavioral element, rooted in the mental characteristics of *Homo sapiens* and not found in any other species. The latter may exhibit strong attachments to physical phenomena, but they cannot express *degrees* of this attachment in words, nor can they effectively compare the value placed on one resource with the value of another. The manifestation of value in human behavior leads to economics, or more specifically, ordered exchange. Such exchange is based on *expectations* of certain outcomes: transactions are not random or idiosyncratic, but are based on conventional beliefs and values. This is also a way of defining *culture*: a useful term referring to the shared and communicated expectations of social behavior in defined contexts and their symbolic storage in language.

Natural substances, when transformed mentally into resources, can thereby be assigned value, which may also be expressed monetarily – an abstract summation of that value.

Resources are thus placed in comparative value contexts with other objects and social phenomena and absorbed into the general culture. Once an aspect of nature is incorporated into the cultural system in this manner, it is extremely difficult to extract it or to change its value assignment. To do so, one must proceed according to the same social procedures or rituals used for any other cultural value or form of property.

Value, conceived as a major principle of thought and action, and embedded in economic theory as an ultimate reality, creates the phenomenon of *market exchange*. Markets always existed, but the great increase of population and the necessity of keeping these populations supplied with food and goods, has heightened their significance in the industrial era. It also has facilitated the creation of abstract values like money. Markets or exchange institutions are universal in industrial society, regardless of the particular form of political economy – capitalist or socialist. Each produces valued commodities, tangible and intangible, for the purpose of distribution and sale – a process that increases markets. The system tends to flow into every realm of human activity in which some kind of "output" is generated, whether or not the thing produced is appropriately defined as an economic good. Natural substances thus become both resources and goods and are absorbed into the system of production and distribution as human-created objects. One of the most striking examples is the attempt by economists in benefit-cost analyses to find monetary values for intangible resources like "natural beauty" (see Hufschmidt and Hyman 1983). At present, it is only by taking nature into culture in this manner that there is any hope of protection. In the longer term, it would appear that industrial societies will have to find ways to exclude various life-supporting systems and resources from the economic calculus, just as they attempt to do with human life. Such environmental *exceptionalism* is found in all societies, but more so in earlier ones, and is linked to concepts of the "sacred."[11]

Institutional Patterns and Trends

To illustrate the basic differences between the institutional patterns and trends of modern industrial society and those of all the previous transitions, we will draw upon ideas from the tradition of historical sociology, inaugurated by Max Weber and expanded upon by Talcott Parsons (1951). Two pairs of contrasting concepts will be used to depict: (1) different cultural conceptualizations of institutions and organizations; and (2) different societal patterns for structuring work roles.

The first pair – *contextualism* versus *universalism* – involves two different ways of conceptualizing the basic institutions of society (e.g., laws, property, regulations, threats, and the exchange system). *Contextual* approaches, which were dominant in all earlier transitions, define these institutions and their associated phenomena – people, rules, customs, resources – in terms of their local and particular interrelationships. Both contextual concepts and institutions tend to be particularistic and mutually reinforcing, thus encouraging tradition. Because social change often occurs at different rates in different parts of a society, one may find

particularistic manifestations of earlier patterns still present today.[12]

Universalism, on the other hand, is a way of generalizing the applicability of institutions to all classes of people, regardless of contextual particularities. As a social process, it is particularly associated with the state or any central government ruling over a diverse population or social system. Both contextualism and universalism have been found in ancient as well as modern civilizations, but an historic trend is perceptible: in the age of industry, the movement has been increasingly toward *universalistic treatment*. This is expressed by such things as human rights, universal scientific "laws," mimimum wage laws, provisions of the welfare state, the universal voting franchise, and the myriad rules and regulations of business and industry. Violations are common, but if discovered, may be brought to justice on the basis of the universalistic principles of the modern state. Contextual and particularistic arrangements can be transformed into universalistic regulations, of course, but they first must pass through a formal legislative or regulatory procedure. It is this formal, public procedure that has become the hallmark of modern universalistic society.

With respect to physical resources and natural phenomena generally, the trend has been to include them in the universalistic paradigm. An example can be noted in the contemporary controversy over national parks in the United States and the desire by some to preserve their natural features from the pressure of public, or "multiple," use. On the one hand, the concept of public use as a right is based upon universalistic assumptions and the aforementioned incorporation of nature into society. These concepts conflict with the wilderness approach, which seeks to preserve these particular features in their natural (traditional) form for aesthetic reasons, for posterity, or for the intangible benefit of nature itself. Other examples are visible in controversies to protect the genetic diversity of tropical forests from development, sacred tribal lands from agricultural development, or scenic coastlines from off-shore oil drilling. These controversies are often couched in terms of public versus private rights but usually involve deeper differences in values.

The second pair of concepts – *multifunctionalism* versus *functional specialization* – involves contrasting ways of allocating tasks and functions in social organizations. Both are important in all cultures, but again, an historic trend appears to exist. Prior to the expansion of science and engineering, technical and economic activities were carried out with less specificity, and organizational structures were not as bureaucratically subdivided. Multifunctionalism refers to the tendency for individuals to perform an indefinite number of roles – particularly in contextually structured societies – depending on needs and their own energy and interests. Functional specialization, which seems to be a logical corollary to universalism, refers to modern organizational practices whereby individuals are trained, certified, and assigned to specific tasts. The archetypical example is the Western industrial assembly line, where each individual worker has one assigned task.[13]

This pair of concepts relates to the environment in terms of the way physical resources are placed under organizational control and exploitation. The more functional specialization, the less any one technical division or administrative agency is in full control over any given resource; hence, responsibility is divided. In the exploitation of minerals, the effects on the land surface, water, subsoil, local residents, and wildlife are likely to be the official concerns of many different agencies or individuals. Thus, no single entity has the responsibility of deciding whether or not the particular exploitative venture is desirable or undesirable in general. This system leads to competition and conflict, which societies attempt to adjudicate through both informal and legal procedures. The environment, rather than being treated holistically, is thus subdivided according to the organizational principles of the social system, not the natural world.

Subdivision also intersects the property system, creating frequent conflicts over ownership. For a given tract of land, mineral rights may belong to one group, water rights to another, the soil to a farmer, and the wildlife to the "public" as represented by the conservation department. Any use-activity concerning any one of these resource factors inevitably will infringe on the property rights of a group "owning" another resource. In any resulting legal dispute, specific experts on particular resource domains must be called in to give testimony as to possible effects. In large-scale activities, the benefit-cost mode of analysis is often used to attempt to forecast the different economic costs and benefits.[14]

The universalistic, functionally specialized constructs just described constitute the underlying institutional and organizational order of modern industrial civilization as it has evolved in the West over the past 300 years. The differences from previous transitions can be seen from Table 5-1, which summarizes the main points of the argument.[15] From the standpoint of nature, there are two major implications: (1) Increasingly, environment becomes culture; that is, things of nature are absorbed into the sociocultural system of humankind. (2) Increasingly, nature is seen to possess no value of its own – only that which humans decide to give it. This means that there is no automatic exception made for nature in modern industrial society. Although exceptionalism has emerged as an ideal of the conservation and environmental movements and is gaining increasing sympathy from the larger society, it is opposed vigorously by many powerful interests. This means that until a greater value consensus can be built for exceptionalism, nature, in order to be protected (whether for its own sake or for human posterity) must be treated as any other object of differential value and defended with the same rules and devices used for any other article of human possession.

The Great Resource Domains

Anything in nature, society, or culture can become a "resource" when humans incorporate it into institutions of purposeful accomplishment; however, in this section we are concerned only with the three resources that ensure biological existence: the great domains of *air*, *water*, and *land*. Humans living during the earlier transitions were concerned mainly with subsistence. Manufacturing to provide surplus goods for trade or sale was not of sufficient magnitude to threaten the supply and integrity of physical resources.

Human existence remains dependent on the great domains that permit biological functioning. Science and technology have found no substitutes for air, water, or land, although their capacity to support human populations has been enhanced through fertilizer, irrigation, and desalinization. This technological enhancement, however, does not increase the basic supply, and the enhancement processes themselves often contribute to degradation.

The uses of air, water, and land are shaped by two things: the physical nature of the resource itself, and the social institutions of property, exchange, and regulation. The first is fixed: air is a gas, water a liquid, land a particulate solid. The second system is variable: institutions can take many forms, each intersecting the qualities of the resource in differing ways. Some institutions appropriately safeguard the resource against degradation; others accelerate the process. There is no universal imperative to apply institutional and technological means to ensure environmental quality and sustainability; the main objective through most of human history (and especially in the past three centuries) has been to make the resource available for current needs and demands.

With respect to property and exchange, our contemporary economic institutions distinguish between three principal concepts: resources as *free goods*, *private goods*, and *public goods*. The three concepts are fundamental in the social ecology of industrialism and the culture of consumer gratification: people are seen to be entitled to satisfy their appetites at whatever level deemed appropriate by the culture (see Barkley and Seckler 1972, Krutilla and Fisher 1976, and Olson 1965 for classic analyses of key economic concepts in their environmental contexts). This entitlement has always been subject to a degree of qualification with respect to the common good, however, which means that conversion of the resource into property or into an article of exchange, or its treatment by individuals without concern for its supply or quality, can go just so far. At the point of jeopardy, the idea of public good comes into play: If pollution of an entire airshed by toxic gases reaches a point at which the health of citizens who must breathe the air is endangered, the air is "seized" by the regulatory authorities and redefined, in whole or in part, as public property, and attempts are made to bring the dangerous practices under control. The problem always has been precisely how to define this point of jeopardy, as well as what environmental and human costs are tolerable as a price of continuing the practices.[16]

Although we focus on air, water, and land, the analysis could be extended to any other physical substance needed or used as a resource. New "resources" constantly are being added as culture and technology expand. *Light* is one of the more recent additions. Light, like air, has been historically a free good, but in cities, as the built environment begins to alter the pattern of light, it can be given exchange value and redefined as an economic good.[17]

A major issue not dealt with in detail is the problem of

Table 5-1 *Major Aspects of Institutions*

Features	Earlier transitions	Industrial societies and the emerging world system
Cultural Conceptualization of Institutions	Contextual and indigenous on the whole.	Universalistic and cross-cultural with some segregated contextual exceptions.
Dominant Pattern of Role Performance	Multifunctional, overlapping roles.	Functional specialization of roles is the public norm.
Relation to Resources and Natural Phenomena	Sustaining: with some major exceptions. Limits respected on the whole since wants are limited.	Dominance, control, and exploitation with few exceptions made for natural phenomena. Little regard for environmental limits.
Patterning of major institutions	Earlier transitions	Industrial societies and the emerging world system
Property	Customary and particularistic; contextual and localized.	Legal, rational, and bureaucratic; universalistic and cross-cultural.
Exchange	Customary and particularistic; often informal.	Monetary and economic institutions are formal and separated from society and ritual. Increasing commodification of all phenomena, natural and cultural.
Regulation	An extension of existing social and ritual arrangements; some use of force; contextual control of behavior.	Legal; integrated into economy and government; resource use controlled overtly, not through implicit or contextual values.

resource depletion. While the issue is more relevant to extractable substances like minerals, it is becoming a matter of increasing concern as aquifers are drained for public and agricultural use, as soil is degraded by excessive use and erosion, or as air is made less breathable. As resources are degraded or depleted, their cost rises and their inclusion in economic systems as ascertainable goods is accelerated. The depletion of fossil fuels poses the greatest threat to the continuance of modern industrial institutions, while the depletion and/or degradation of air, water, and land poses the greatest threat to the earth's biological systems.

Air

The unique property of air is its invisible fluidity. It surrounds us. It is necessary to all plant, animal, and human life, yet it cannot be seen and its movements cannot be controlled by technology. Historically, it has been considered – implicitly or formally – a free good, available to everyone who can breath or ingest the gases. Also, as a free good, it usually has not been subject to control over what is discharged into it.

Since their movements are not amenable to human intervention, air masses can move freely with the weather, and substances discharged into them at one geographical location will make themselves felt at some farther point. This basic indeterminance of movement creates a problem for legal institutions, which require proof of commission. This is seen in the contemporary acid-rain controversy: if dangerous and largely invisible pollutants are inserted into the atmosphere from multiple sources and cause damage to forests and lakes hundreds of miles away, how does one assign responsibility for damage?[18]

The problem of *local* airsheds polluted by open combustion was relatively easy to solve: because the assignment of responsibility was a matter of local political decision and the source of the effluents was relatively obvious, air was converted, by civic action, from a free to a public good. The community's political institutions took responsibility for safeguarding the public's interest in clean (if not pure) air. The concept of public good may eventually be used with respect to the more complex problem of acid rain, but because sovereign countries are involved – whether in the North American case or in the European and Nordic countries – the legal and regulatory measures are intricate and are subject to diplomatic negotiation.

Air largely has escaped institutionalization as property, since its use by private entities for, say, chemical manufacture, has been a minor matter.[19] The case of chlorofluorocarbonic erosion of the ozone layer may by implication, at least, raise the issue of ownership and price in a different way, insofar as the companies manufacturing the destructant could be "charged" for the damage. In a sense, by causing the emission of the gas, they are appropriating the ozone portion of the atmosphere. On the other hand, it could be argued that the laws of property are irrelevant and that the agencies causing the contamination simply should be subject to government regulation as endangering public health and the quality of a public good. The same argument applies even more to issues of human-induced climate change – whether carbon-dioxide-induced warmings or "nuclear winters" – but is complicated by the transnational character of the problems.[20]

These contrasting definitions of what constitutes "good" air, a "clean" atmosphere, and "normal" climatic conditions have been generated by the practices and institutions of technological society. In the traditional societies of the earlier transitions, air was simply an informal free good. No better illustration of the progressive incorporation of natural substances into culture can be found: now even air and atmospheric processes must be given institutional cognizance and regulation.

Water

Water, like air, is fluid and can move freely. But unlike air, it is visible and can also be channeled, impounded, pumped, bottled, and poured. Fresh water is as important to life as air. Unlike air, however, it has been treated as a good of some kind ever since the agricultural transition, due to the necessity of providing fresh water for domesticated plants and animals. Water rights are as old as the first Neolithic farmers, who diverted streams to their own use.

Traditionally, water (unlike air) had much in common, institutionally speaking, with land: i.e., the supply needed for agriculture was subject to measurement by volume. The concept of acre feet of water, often used in irrigation, attests to the affinity with land – the areal extent of a given depth of water is used as a quantity measure. While the concept of water rights gave water some of the characteristics of property by legally affirming that individuals or communities had a right to obtain a given measure of water, it also has retained some aspects of a public good.

This is because the fluidity of stream flow and the transiency of water supply, due to variations in weather and climate, lead to scarcity situations that call forth public-good conceptualizations – in which individuals have the right to obtain only a certain amount. In this sense, the status of water today hovers somewhat uncertainly between private property and public good. This uncertainty is documented in the many controversies and experiments with water rights for agricultural land in climates of differing moisture capacities and in populations of varying size. Conflicts over water rights and entitlements between urban and agricultural districts have been equally urgent – and especially complex because property rights, business interests, genuine public and private needs, real estate development, and many other issues and institutions are involved in such disputes. Rivers have furnished rights struggles on monumental scales: pollution, salmon fisheries, and irrigation impoundments with dubious geological, ecological, and economic effects have proliferated in the twentieth century (Reisner 1986 and Worster 1985 contain examples).

If the exercise of individual or group rights to water results in diminished or irregular supply to others, the response can be violent and third parties may need to intervene. The nature of water as a substance requires a degree of universalism simply because of its vital physiological function. Yet the needs of agricultural producers and industrialists for water require an element of contextual assignment. The institutions governing water use and management contain a tension between these two sets of patterns.[21]

Therefore, the vital needs served by water and its fluidity and transiency require a perennial degree of public concern and guardianship. Although "responsible management agencies may be divided between those that are predominantly private, and those which are predominantly public,"

there are "only a very few water management undertakings which are exclusively private" (White 1969: 11). The public character of management usually means "government" in large nations. But in many rural areas in all countries, and in developing countries only a few generations removed from agrarianism, the pattern is one of many local cooperative groups of users – often with usufruct claims on particular watersheds. "Agricultural development" in these countries usually has meant that the traditional local rights and cooperative systems gradually give way to government-operated or adjudicated schemes. Some see this trend as undesirable because it removes water from local control and husbandry.

The tendency for the control and distribution of water to become a dominant concern in large-scale, agrarian-based societies has led some analysts to define "irrigation civilizations" (Steward et al. 1955) and "hydraulic societies" (Wittfogel 1957) as major forms of political economy in human history. The degree to which reliance on water becomes a key to political institutions is unclear. Wittfogel argued that the organizational requirements of creating and managing large-scale water infrastructures led to despotism, but others point to the reverse causal linkage: despotic rule led to the extending of government control over water (Adams 1966). Either way, the ancient Orient and Middle East had many examples of this type of state control and management of water systems in early urbanized kingdoms and empires dependent on irrigated agriculture. With increasing population and use of water, it is conceivable that this tendency will reassert itself in the non-market economy nations and in many developing countries in moisture-deficient climates.

The foregoing implies that increasing population and the increasing use of technologies that require water will almost certainly result in: (1) greater competition between users; (2) increasing regulation by governments of water supply and use; and (3) increasing adjudication of water uses on an international basis. A fundamental change in our concepts of water as a commodity or a good thus can be expected. At present, most countries consider water to be scarce only in arid and semiarid regions, and the solution to scarcity has taken the form of large-scale projects designed to bring the water from better-endowed regions into drier regions. This practice is coming to be increasingly questioned as water becomes scarce everywhere; that is, as the demand begins to press against supplies.[22]

Thus, a trend toward greater collective management can be expected. This is consistent with the already mentioned collective and cooperative water institutions that have been a major and consistent theme in all social systems, at whatever level. Even so, they always were subject to qualification or modification by individual needs and objectives. The peculiarities of water as a resource have demanded collective management perhaps to a greater extent than other physical resources. Thus, careful examination of the way human institutions have accommodated water management should tell us a good deal about the limits and possibilities of conservationist action. In general, it would seem that when the nature of the resource permits – as in the case of purely extractive substances like metallic ores – the tendency toward private property management and exploitation is very strong. When the substance is necessary to life and fluid/transient as well, tendencies toward public and collective management will be strong.

Land

The physical properties of land include depth, surface (soils and topography), and space. These properties are institutionalized in tenure and commodity systems. Physically, the substratum is composed of the bulk solids forming the planet. From beneath the surface, we take fossil fuels, ores, and chemicals. The surface layers of soil provide the particulate minerals, the remains of plants and animals, and the medium for raising food plants. We use the surface itself for transportation and recreation, and the spatial expanse of the surface provides room for human endeavor and the built environment. Land is fixed in space, although increasingly, as the technology emerges, we remodel the surface to suit human needs and interests. Land may be, as Henry George (1955) and other philosophers believed, the ultimate source of all economic value, the prime good. At the very least, increasing human population and urbanization calls attention to the escalating value of space, surface, and the commodities produced on or extracted from land.

Land tenure represents the institutional or commodity aspect of land. Some form of rights over land has existed within and between all human groups, and it may be rooted in pre-sapiens behavior. *Territoriality* is a basic adaptation found in birds and mammals, and there is little doubt that some sort of continuity into the hominid order exists. But the *sapiens* version – tenure – is something far more elaborate and cognitively organized. It is institutionalized as part of culture and is linked to other forms of behavior and organization. Thus, land tenure may be an aspect of a religious imperium, as it was in the temple-dominated city-states of the Bronze Age. Or it may be a facet of extended kinship, as it was in the tribal-peasant agricultural societies of both the Old and the New World. Or it may be a matter of political economy – involving treaties between land users – as in the case of some Middle Eastern and African pastoralists.

The specific forms of tenure differ greatly, but all involve three main variables: the particular uses of the land permitted; the duration of control or use; and the complex issue of who may use or own land. The concept of full private/individual ownership, or freehold tenure as it has been called, is characteristic of the Euro–North American institutional system and is obviously linked to values concerning the rights of individuals and groups to determine their own destinies. It is also part of the history of an industrializing economy that for three centuries permitted an outflow of excess population from rural areas, easing pressure for acquisition of land. Even so, no Euro–North American nation lacks concepts of residual rights, such as eminent domain, condemnation proceedings, establishment of reserves for various purposes, and many local contextual rules conferring power on government or civic bodies to control land uses.

Freehold, or absolute private ownership tenure, is relatively uncommon on a global basis. More widely distributed are usufruct systems, in which the right to use the land is granted on the basis of a particular need or use. Transfer of such rights to others is contingent upon other aspects of tenure, principally the degree to which land is alienable or which other agencies may have residual rights. Most traditional systems did not consider land as saleable, since final tenure resided in the community, kin groups, cooperatives, or the state. In such cases, usufruct was a gratuity, subject to revocation depending on circumstances. In general, use-rights in land continued as long as the use continued.[23]

Land-tenure systems, in which a substantial portion of land is held in common, are also a worldwide institution. The medieval European systems are well documented (e.g., Bloch 1967; Dahlman 1980). One of the most frequent arrangements was found in agricultural villages in which the upland areas were owned in common by the entire community and used mainly for grazing livestock, while the lower elevations and stream or lake bottomlands were divided into family-owned cropping and domiciliary strips. "Commons" systems have been ubiquitous in Third World countries and are presently in transition toward "enclosure," either as privately or state-owned land. "Common property institutions" – the current scholarly term for land and water arrangements held in common – are being investigated in the search for more responsible resource practices and as an antidote to the pressures in developing countries to modify or outlaw common resource tenures (see Hardin 1968; National Research Council 1986).

Although most theories of land use and land tenure are based on the concept and practice of fixed abode or sedentary existence, another set of tenure arrangements pertains to transient, or "nomadic," adaptations, which involve combinations of usufruct and common land. Two groups are involved: (1) the food collectors, now nearly extinct remnant populations of the earliest ecological transitions; and (2) the pastoralists, a specialized offshoot of the agricultural transition who are still an important demographic and economic segment of the arid/semiarid lands of Africa and Southwest Asia.[24]

Transient land tenure is a form of usufruct, but is rooted mainly in "customary law." It involves a continual round of negotiation among the pastoralists and the farmers through whose fields they must frequently pass. No one really owns land, but many people and groups may have rights to use the land – its forage and its water – at different times and under differing circumstances. This dynamic form of tenure often engenders conflict because the boundaries are flexible and because group needs may change as herd size, human population, and/or weather patterns change, or as the entrepreneurial drives of individual herd owners lead to expansion of their operations. Over the centuries, herding groups have dealt with such conflicts through negotiation, threats, and when necessary, intergroup warfare.

Universalistic institutions in modern societies with democratic traditions tend to define land tenure and all its ancillary rules and rights in terms that are uniform for all persons and groups. In the United States, freehold tenure underlies the whole system of private property and corporate freedom. The contemporary problem of toxic-waste dumps illustrates the resistance to regulation.[25] Dangerous substances dumped on land have found their way into aquifers, creating health hazards. Invariably, the companies or the government bureaucracies involved have denied dumping, have blamed others, or more commonly, have questioned whether such seepage in aquifers is a serious or real problem. That is, there is resistance to admit that practices conducted on owned land (private or public) can have consequences for which one can be held accountable. Under public pressure, accountability is taking a familiar form: regulation of threatened land as a "public good."[26]

What about *soil*? Everywhere, it has been equated with land, and we find no instance of soil being treated as a resource subject to control or ownership independent of the land surface and expanse. Thus, control of land means control of the surface layers of soil (but often not of the mineral rights). Soil popularly is perceived simply as the nutrient content of the land. Modern soil science distinguishes between soils of varying quality, however, and agricultural land taxes are frequently calculated on the basis of soil type. Even so, this method of valuing soil quality independent of spatial qualities is flawed because even "poor" soils can produce valuable crops, given the right choice of crop or the right treatment. Light, sandy soils in the Great Plains or in the grassland regions of Asia are discounted with reference to grain crops, but can produce forage for animals.[27]

Let us review the broad patterns. The institutions regulating use of the great resource domains were forged in earlier eras – when the expansion of the human population and the activities and technologies to satisfy their needs were generally of modest scale. Their form was generally contextual. Since the Industrial Revolution, huge infrastructures and the universalism of industrial growth have come to be considered heroic and emblematic of progress. Freedom to exploit these and other resource domains has been maximized, and possible future costs or difficulties have been ignored until recently. Universalistic concepts and practices relating to human rights, elections, and bureaucracy were also essential in the expansion of democracy and of the nation-state.

As a result, modern institutions have come to reflect less and less of the particular and peculiar characteristics of each basic resource, and find it difficult to deal with variability. Air has gone from being almost completely part of nature, to a free good, to a commodity subject to public regulation or control under certain circumstances. Water, a subject of social control since the agricultural transition, has become a source of controversy between public and private interests. The increasing scarcity of clean water will bring about additional legal and instituional redefinitions. Land, being stable and not fluid, always has been more subject to the practices of ownership, property, and exchange. Today, land is organized uniformly and geometrically in most countries through standardized survey, mapping, and registration systems – in contrast to the enormous variability of the land itself in terms of surface configurations, seasonal capabilities, and soil types. Older forms of tenure were more cognizant of these irregularities and permitted property lines or use-boundaries to

vary depending on season, access to water, and suitable landforms. It is a tragedy that these more flexible – and typically ecologically sounder – boundary systems have been abridged in many developing countries in the interest of "agricultural development" or "modernization," something that has often meant an effort by the state to gain control of these resources for large-scale exploitation, rarely with serious concern for conservation (Little et al. 1987).

The Growth of Modern Industrial Resource Regimes

The previous sections of this chapter have described the basic structural and institutional patterns found among the different transitions, as well as how modern institutional patterns have altered the treatment of the great resource domains of air, water, and land. Just as with other economic sectors, these domains have been progressively incorporated into modern resource regimes over the past 300 years and, more broadly, into an emerging world system. This section describes the process, using the examples of agriculture, energy, and minerals.

Modern resource regimes are defined here in infrastructural, as well as institutional and organizational, terms (for a discussion of the latter, see Young 1982). They are the organized energy-, food-, and material-providing components of the modern state. They depend upon: (1) extensive, complicated, and usually centralized physical infrastructures (i.e., roads, railroads, ports, and energy extraction and distribution systems); and (2) equally complicated and centralized institutional and organizational patterns. Our definition goes well beyond typical norm-based and decision-based definitions found in the international relations literature (see Krasner 1985: 5) and points to the longer-term interactions of physical infrastructures with institutions and organizations. It also facilitates an examination of the impacts of any given regime upon the natural environment.

Institutions, Organizations, Values, and Ideologies

The discussion that follows is based on several ideas. The first is that as physical infrastructures are expanded in scale, more highly centralized controlling organizations are required to manage them. In turn, such institutions and organizations develop vested interests that make them more rigid, unadaptive, and prone to error and collapse. This is not a new phenomenon: it occurred first in the Bronze Age, in the "irrigation civilizations" cited previously. Still, relatively little analysis of the situation in contemporary civilization is available.[28] One reason for this concerns the Western cultural value or myth of *neutrality of technology*.[29] Another involves the associated belief that the general application of science and technology to society leads to progress. Both ideas tend to discourage critical scrutiny of the ways in which the costs and benefits of large-scale technological enterprises are distributed within society and with reference to the environment.

These values thus serve what Mannheim (1936) termed ideological functions; that is, they tend to protect vested economic and intellectual interests through symbolic reassurance. In contrast, there are utopian values and visions, which challenge the status quo and its interests in the name of social justice, salvation, nationalism, or revolution. Ironically, values that were utopian at the beginning of the industrial era have now become ideologies. For example, the vision of an urban society governed by reason (and economic rationality), and achieving progress through the applications of science and technology challenged the status quo of religious kingdoms, landed aristocracies, and mercantilist empires (Mumford 1959). Today, these values have become fixed ideologies, protecting corporations and bureaucracies, reassuring people that all is well and that "business as usual" will continue to provide "progress."

Various new social movements – environmentalism, feminism, religious revitalization movements, the peace movement, and the regenerative agriculture movement – challenge the status quo and suggest basic changes in social priorities, though not the underlying institutional and organizational patterns (de Moll et al. 1977; Theobald 1987). Their emphasis is on the "good place," that is, the contextual quality of the local social and physical environments, rather than on the rational and universal qualities of Thomas More's utopia (no place/ideal place).[30]

The combination of these ideological and cultural factors with the increasing universalism and functional specialization of the past 300 years has compounded significantly the problem of trying to understand and protect the natural environment. The urban and industrial aspects of society are emphasized, while rural and informal aspects are neglected and undervalued (Blum 1982; Lipton 1977). Much of the natural environment is thus systematically filtered out. The narrowness of functionally specialized agencies and scholarly disciplines further blocks out large areas of awareness and understanding, a process reinforced by the vested interests and ideologies growing up around them. Thus, modern institutions and organizations operate with strong positive feedback loops that continually reinforce their structural tendencies to incorporate and exploit nature. What negative feedback exists with reference to adaptation, conservation, and a recognition of limits comes from groups outside the elite systems, though they often share many of the same basic predilections (see Cummings 1980 and Laszlo 1972 on systems theories).

This process is particularly visible in the changing role of economic theory. As suggested earlier, modern economic doctrines were originally utopian. They were also an important social innovation helping to realize the Industrial Revolution. However, today much – although certainly not all – economic theory is bent on preserving the status quo. Indeed, it has contributed to the larger process of "commodifying" the physical environment, thereby also reinforcing tendencies toward exploitation. And although significant differences exist between neoclassical and neo-Marxist economics, particularly over questions of the distribution of economic proceeds among the various groups in society, both exhibit little interest in the condition of the terrestrial environment, which is the ultimate source of all value.

Modern Agricultural Regimes

Traditional agricultural systems are characterized by their great contextual variability, where climatic, weather, soil, topographic, resource, cultural, social, and institutional variation all profoundly affect their structure and viability. The ways in which many of them have been transformed into modern regimes and have been incorporated into industrial society illustrate many of the tensions between contextualism and universalism. On the one hand, contextual approaches are required to understand fully and manage properly the traditional agricultural systems (Altieri 1983). On the other hand, most modern researchers and analysts tend to view agriculture – and such related, biologically based regimes as forestry and fisheries – through universalistic lenses, which filter out local contextual and environmental variations.[31]

This tendency is also visible in historical studies of the development and transformation of modern agriculture. Studies of the development of modern agriculture in Europe have focused on identifying the key element leading to the agricultural revolution. This is variously seen (Grigg 1984) to be social (involving changes in land tenure), technological (involving new farming methods and implements), or economic (involving the application of modern economic approaches).

Rather than focusing on any single element, our approach stresses the gradual transformations occurring within agriculture, which reflect, and later reinforce, outside pressures for its incorporation into national economies (Dahlberg 1990; Polanyi 1957). In the process, agriculture has been transformed from a highly contextual and multifunctional set of operations into a major transnational industrial sector. This transformation has involved the gradual replacement of labor with both capital (mechanization) and energy (fertilizers). Mechanization was emphasized in nineteenth-century United States agriculture because of the need to farm large areas with few laborers. Fertilizers were emphasized in nineteenth-century Europe, where land was scarcer and labor was somewhat more plentiful. Since World War II, both of these substitutes for labor have been promoted in both regions and in the Third World, along with a variety of scientific and technological inputs.

Linked with this has been the decline in the numbers of farmers in the population – even though employment in the total food system has been much more stable. The result has been the creation of agricultural systems that are dependent upon foreign markets, fossil fuels, and a host of technologies generated by the industrial sectors.

This transnational industrial system may not be either ecologically or socially sustainable. A range of recent studies point to the high ecological, social, and health costs of modern industrial agriculture (Dahlberg 1986), its vulnerability to major fluctuations – whether in markets or in climate (Parry 1986) – and its dependence upon nonrenewable resources (Gever et al. 1986). Two fundamental questions emerge from these studies. First, are institutional adaptations possible that will make agriculture more sustainable and/or regenerative? Second, if modern industrial agriculture is obsolescent and/or obsolete, is it ethically justifiable to continue to promote its export to Third World countries?

Some cross-cultural and historical perspective may help in addressing these questions. Many of the processes, trends, and practices involved in the transformation of agriculture and its incorporation into modern industrial society are visible especially in the imposition of Western ideas, institutions, technologies, and infrastructures upon the non-Western world – first, through the conquest of the New World, and then, through Asian and African colonialism. Throughout, the assumption and rationale was that Western culture and institutions were superior, thus justifying the use of the West's genuinely superior military technology to impose or encourage them. Many of these ethnocentric attitudes are still found in postindependence approaches to development and technology transfer.

These attitudes were reflected most clearly in the treatment of the indigenous peoples of Africa, America, and Oceania, who were either physically expelled from desirable lands or forced to become subservient. After some sort of legal rationale for control was established, these formerly self-sufficient peoples were forced into both labor and economic markets through head taxes, labor levies, and trade monopolies. Attempts were made not only to convert them to Christianity, but also to discourage or prohibit traditional religious practices. Formal, Western-style education, with its implicit rejection or denigration of indigenous knowlege and oral cultures, was also promoted (for descriptions, see Bodley 1982).

The great trading companies of the seventeenth and eighteenth centuries were supplanted by colonial governments as European nationalism and great-power rivalry increased. Colonial infrastructures – roads, railroads, and telegraph lines – were built in funnel-shaped patterns that focused on the major ports, thus facilitating the shipping of minerals or cash crops to the metropolitan country. The lands were also overlaid with geometrically constructed political boundaries and land surveys. Administrative structures were designed to maintain law and order and to facilitate exploitation of the colony's resources while also opening markets for processed goods. As higher education was gradually introduced, the urban, elite, and academic model prevalent in nineteenth-century Europe simply was transferred.

Western methods were also exported and applied to agriculture. Tropical crops such as sugar cane, indigo, coffee, tea, groundnuts, and rubber were developed along industrial lines. Large-scale production facilities (plantations) displaced small-scale, local, subsistence producers through land expropriation. Labor also was handled in an industrial manner – resulting in the creation of a dependent work force. The scale, structure, and management of these plantations reflected Western notions of industry and economic rationality. Their direct linkage with the factories and markets of the metropolitan country was a major factor in creating the dual economy of most colonies.

In the white-settler enclaves, precursors to the Green Revolution could be seen in the practice of importing temperate-zone crops, animals, and cultivation techniques, not to mention Western-style agricultural research institutions (Dahlberg 1979: chap. 2). Settlers and colonial administrators clearly believed in the superiority of these imports over local crops and practices. Yet they also shared the Western cultural belief in technological neutrality: that is, that technologies

can be transfered to other locations, with the expectation that they should work as well there as in their place of origin.[32]

The initial impact of these enclaves of Western agriculture on the vast majority of peasants, nomads, and villagers was very small. The foundations for the later rapid expansion of the Green Revolution lay more in the creation of centralized administrative control systems that enabled relatively small Westernized enclaves – symbolized by Western-style cities – to penetrate the colonies and extract their resources (Crosby 1986). After independence, these centralized systems were progressively expanded through "development" programs in order to exert full control over the countryside (Pearson 1987).

In addition to the transformation and incorporation of traditional agricultural systems into national economies, there has been the larger process of incorporating Third World economies into a global economy, or what Wallerstein (1974; 1978) and others call the world system. This means not only the need for both First and Third World farmers to worry about production levels, fluctuations, and trends abroad, but the tendency of governments – especially those in the First World – to see agriculture and food as integral "power" components in their economic and strategic planning (Wallensteen 1986).

The destabilization of locally self-sufficient food economies has had serious environmental as well as human costs. While making local populations more vulnerable to the uncertainties of pricing and markets, intensive commercial agricultural "development" also has contributed to the massive destruction of tropical forests, severe soil erosion, disruption of natural watersheds and groundwater supplies, and the elimination of many useful wild plants and animals – processes that have their parallels in the industrial countries.[33] Local, subsistence agricultural systems are usually diverse – their human-made diversity paralleling the diversity of nature (Turner and Brush 1987: Part II). In both cases, nature is permitted to experiment with varying genotypes, which later may be found useful in generating new cultivated varieties. The replacement of natural and traditional cultural diversity by commercial monocultures is a way of destroying, not creating, new resources (Klee 1980; Little et al. 1987).

Some slowing-down and even reversals of these trends have been evident in recent years. The failure of many agricultural development schemes has focused attention on the deleterious social and ecological consequences of interrupting traditional subsistence systems (Bunker 1985; Spooner 1984). International development agencies and national ministries have begun to modify policies and programs to allow for more local autonomy and more benign pricing and marketing arrangements. Yet considerable damage – much of it irreversible – has been done to the economic and ecological basis of food production in both the North and the South, and only the future will tell if a more sustainable system can be achieved.

Energy and Mineral Regimes

The evolution of modern industrial society reflects both scientific and technological advancement and the development of energy and mineral regimes. In this process, one can see a gradual – and often competitive – overlay of earlier regimes with newer ones, with each regime having depended for its development upon both technological and social innovations.

The earliest modern resource regimes grew up around coal and iron. Although they initially drew upon traditional wind, water, and wood technologies and fuels, their greater productive power soon largely supplanted the traditional systems. The later development of petroleum and chemical regimes was facilitated by the scientific and technological capabilities generated during the coal and iron age (Peach and Constantin 1972). Social innovations in the form of new university curricula based on individual disciplines and the creation of engineering schools played an important part in this development. In turn, the capabilities and knowledge generated by these regimes and their associated disciplines encouraged the later creation of the electronics and nuclear regimes. Currently, we appear to be in the initial stages of developing and adding a new regime: biotechnology. Most of these resource-concentrating regimes have been based upon nonrenewable fossil fuels. The most significant question regarding biotechnology is whether or not in the long run it offers any realistic prospect of production based on renewable, instead of increasingly costly nonrenewable, resources.[34]

This question highlights the dependence of modern industrial society upon its current energy and mineral regimes (Adams 1988). Not surprisingly, such regimes have become a large part of the "national security" of modern states. Unfortunately, understandings thereof have been severely limited by the institutional and ideological factors outlined previously. Rather than focusing upon the issues of conservation, sustainability, and renewable energy, the emphasis has been upon guaranteeing access to petroleum and the so-called strategic minerals so important to the military. Governments have developed policies for monitoring supplies and even stockpiling reserves of these minerals. Analysis in this area suffers both from disciplinary specializations and from special interests that derive strength by invoking "national security" concerns and fears (McCartan 1985). Thus, debates and discussions are carried on primarily in terms of Great-Powers politics and military needs, and not ecology.

There also has been increasing recognition of the importance of petroleum in the world system, as can be seen in the close attention given by governments and the financial community to OPEC and its pricing policies. While the United States government has sought to reduce the short-term risks of future embargoes through the creation of a strategic petroleum reserve, the political power of the United States oil industry has discouraged longer-term oil conservation measures and has encouraged the rapid exploitation (i.e., depletion) of both privately owned and government-leased reserves. At a more fundamental level, there is a need for a long-term strategy to develop new and less environmentally destructive systems based upon renewable resources (Clark and Munn 1986; IUCN 1980). This will require a gradual shift away from the complex overlay of physical infrastructures, economic and social institutions, and political organizations

that encourage current centralized approaches. Such a strategy ultimately will have to be international and will require a reconceptualization of resources and resource regimes that will better comprehend their associated environmental and social costs.

Global Implications and Conclusions

There are several clear implications of our analysis. The first is that the current momentum of centralized industrial institutions toward a world system is unlikely to be sustainable. This is because a continuation of current high levels of energy use is ultimately unsustainable in two very different ways. The fossil fuels upon which these institutions have been built and totally depend will become scarcer and more expensive, eventually leading to major changes or collapse. Even in the unlikely event that replacement high-energy sources were developed (e.g., fusion energy, or the so-called hydrogen economy), the environmental and social impacts of continued high-energy use are also unsustainable. On the one hand, a continuation of current patterns of energy use will increase threats of global environmental disruption, whether from climate change, acid rain, soil exhaustion, or the loss of genetic diversity. On the other hand, the continued externalization of the social and economic costs of these systems through international trade and financial structures will likely feed back in the form of a global debt crisis, a depression, or major social disorders.[35] The closing of global feedback loops that is occurring now is thus generating a new and significant set of risks and threats that logically call for a fundamental rethinking and restructuring of current industrial models and patterns.

The second implication of the analysis is that this fundamental rethinking and restructuring is impeded by a combination of powerful centralized institutions, functionally specialized divisions of labor, and their accompanying political and economic ideologies – all of which make adaptive social change difficult, perhaps more so than at any point in human history. In trying to answer the question of what may be done, a threefold strategy is suggested by our analysis. First, there is a need to recognize that a profound cultural shift may be occurring. The visions of a smaller-scale, more localized, more environmentally sound, and more socially just future shared by a number of new social movements reflect both a fundamental questioning of current institutions and ideologies and a search for a more sustainable or regenerative type of society. Second, there is a need to recognize the value of traditional resource systems and their people, both in their own right and in terms of protecting the global diversity of both habitats and cultures.[36] Third, there is a need to attack the institutional blockages that make adaptive change difficult.

There are several important issues involved in adaptive social change. There is a need to make institutions more responsible; that is, to reduce their ability either to obtain hidden subsidies or to externalize major costs of their operation. This requires both better ways to assess the environmental consequences of their proposed actions and also a more general challenge to economic modes of thought that neglect environmental and other informal systems. Along with this, there is a need to challenge the myth of the neutrality of technology, which has become an ideology protecting the power of large institutions and resource regimes.

One dilemma is that the academic world itself suffers from the same bureaucratic and professional specialization as other sectors. It is divided into many exclusive fraternities of knowledge with separate languages and problems, making cumbersome a cooperative attack on the problems we have described (Dahlberg and Bennett 1986). Also, many disciplines have developed direct linkages with particular industries or government sectors (like the military) and have come to share their vested interests. It is thus difficult to mount vigorous fact-finding programs to ascertain the real conditions of pollution, toxicity, or species extinction – let alone to establish significant cross-disciplinary remedial and reform programs. Yet the pressures of spiraling populations, environmental damage, and resource depletion, as well as the protest movements emerging from them, suggest that major changes will occur. The question is whether they will be adaptive or maladaptive.

In the future, a vision that is based upon diversity and the generation of new systems and institutional patterns is a vital necessity. Rather than simply projecting into the future the patterns and forces that have created the problem, we should strive to transform our institutions in scale, structure, and content. That is, the problem boils down to institutional ideology and rigidity: our institutions have reified old values, and because of their structure, cannot capture emerging values of a new context. They tell us that the things we do to nature are not evil; or that they can be easily corrected; or that they are not our fault. Institutions need to be painfully restructured to capture the basic understanding of most previous cultures and the new social movements: that nature must be viewed not as something there for the taking, but as the soul of the planet – our heritage and our guarantee of a continuous social existence.

Notes

1. This is clear when longer time horizons are employed (see Deevey 1960 on population, and Starr 1971 and Hubbert 1969 on energy), although even here – as in the futures literature – there are differences of interpretation depending upon the underlying assumptions of the historians/modelers (see Hughes 1985: chaps. 4 and 6 for a useful discussion). The great value of recent global modeling efforts has been to link population, resources, and environment more systematically. Even so, there has been a strong tendency for demographers and modelers to look only at human populations, ignoring the increases in livestock populations and the pressures they place upon food, water, and other resources (see Borgstrom 1965, in which he develops and applies a concept of population equivalents for livestock, which he then adds to the human populations of various countries). Also, there is a tendency to focus only on population numbers (which are concentrated in the Third World) as the source of environmental pressure, while ignoring its real source in resource use per person. When so understood, it is clear that the environmental pressures generated by intensive resource use in the industrial countries of the North are as significant, if not more so. The implication is that in developing new strategies for sustainable development, the stabilization – if not reduction – of both population levels and resource consumption must be addressed.

2. It is now generally recognized that the appearance of early hominids like the Australopithecines marks the beginning of foraging,

several millions of years in the past. Organized hunting emerges in the Middle Paleolithic era, perhaps around 200,000 years ago, coincident with the appearance of *Homo sapiens* varieties. However, many problems remain. The specific archaeological issue is the making of tools, since by manufacturing implements not found naturally, hominids or humans took the first step in transforming nature. Recently tool making has possibly been pushed back to the Australopithecines, giving the capability much greater antiquity than previously acknowledged (Susman 1988). Heretofore it had been assumed to be a *sapiens* behavioral capacity. Another issue of contention is the apparent association of specific types of stone tools with specific hominid and *sapiens* fossil varieties (Foley 1988). Whatever the early history of hominid interventions in nature, it is an established archaeological fact that our species (called by some *Homo sapiens sapiens*) is responsible for the rapid evolution of culture since the Paleolithic and for the exponential increase in energy utilization since the food-producing transition of some 10,000 years or so ago. For surveys of prehistory and the earlier transitions, see Hawkes and Woolley 1963; and Redman 1978. A pioneer synthesis of available ethnological and archaeological knowledge concerning the organized hunting systems of early man and contemporary tribalists is Lee and DeVore 1968.

3. The traditional term used in Old World archaeology for this period was Mesolithic – a misnomer, of course, as is the term Paleolithic – because social and residential innovations were fully as significant as technological ones.

4. Some scholars consider that we have now entered a *second* Industrial Revolution characterized by: (1) the production of consumer goods for the masses; and (2) multinational corporations using automated methods that minimize human labor. The first Industrial Revolution created the proletariat; the second created the global "consumer classes." This sort of historical refinement can go on indefinitely. In a brief overview, it is sufficient to speak of one Industrial Revolution, characterized by powered machinery and volume production, gradually supplanting localized handicraft production.

5. The two terms "state" and "nation" are often combined or confused. A nation is, properly, a population with a common cultural heritage and self-identity. The modern state (which emerged with the Treaty of Westphalia in 1648) is a legal entity with population, territory, a government, and sovereignty. Thus, the nation-state is only one of several combinations of nations and states. Much of international conflict derives from attempts to readjust the legal boundaries of the state to fit "national" or "ethnic" boundaries. These territorial conflicts also often involve conflicts over the control of resources. In the era of the industrial transition, the state has generally expanded its control at the expense of nations, tribes, ethnic groups, etc. This has meant that the physical resources associated with these sub- or cross-state groups have fallen increasingly under the control of the state and its aspirations and bureaucracies. However, as we note, countervailing powers may be emerging.

6. War has enlarged and expanded its functions since the hunting transition, and while it remains a final court of decision regarding the internal control of a state's land and its resources, the role of military power today – at least for the great powers – is more that of preventing the disruption of the complex international system of economic, corporate, and legal organizations through which states seek access to the resources of other states.

7. The anthropological field of "cultural ecology" is concerned with ways tribal peoples use resources and achieve a reasonable balance with nature. In technical terms, this means that such societies become parts of natural ecosystems, supporting and rationalizing their sustainable strategies with cultural values and ceremonials (see Ellen 1982 for a review of the theoretical issues). It should be remembered that equilibrium was achieved mainly because of small and slowly growing human populations, however, that demanded little from the environment. This systemic fusion of a small population, limited wants, and modest technology could persist for long periods due to relative cultural isolation and limited trade and social contact. In any

case, the transition to more dynamic cultures and larger populations began with the Bronze Age and has since spread globally. While the ecosystemic practices of tribal groups cannot be used directly as a recipe for modern conservationist strategy, the underlying principles are worthy of detailed study, particularly in terms of agroecosystems.

8. Our arguments ultimately are based on a definition of human behavior that emphasizes the impressive drive toward gratification and the superlative (as compared with other species) ability to relate means to ends. Interests and values tend to be strongly influenced by culture; that is, what people learn from each other and how the interests and outlooks of the others influence the cultivation of similar ideas in their egos. See Bennett (1980) for an attempt to define the behavioral aspect of human ecology.

9. Any established set of rules, procedures, and rationalizations concerned with any sector of human existence is an institution by definition. However, institutions tend to fall into a few large sets. Some are concerned with biological maintenance – food production, reproduction, and health. Others are involved with the maintenance of meaning and motivation – religion, faith, systems of value, and belief. Still others are organizational, providing social coordination. The term is a useful heuristic one, typical of most sociological concepts (see Eisenstadt 1968).

10. Our review takes a global point of view; i.e., that the problems associated with the human use of physical resources are worldwide. While we cite below a number of recent examples from North America, we would argue that they are generally representative of the currently dominant trends, even though there are obviously variations by country and region. The most interesting longer-term question is whether or not the cultural and civilizational values of other industrial and industrializing countries (e.g. Japan and China) will moderate or transform current institutional patterns of resource use and abuse.

11. Although traditional concepts of the "sacred" are currently in decline everywhere, a number of religious and secular groups are seeking new or revitalized concepts of the sacred – even if they are not so labeled. Indeed, concern among scientists over the loss of genetic and biological diversity has led to pronouncements carrying strong overtones of a new science-based "natural law," which would restrict societal actions threatening these basic sources of life (Lovelock 1979). In addition, Thomas (1983) describes what he calls the "sensibility" toward nature that he believes has been slowly evolving in Western civilization and is currently beginning to "clash" with material values. Let us hope so, but the values conflict by itself will not resolve the issues. The basic problem of creating an exceptionalist status for aspects of nature is the necessary convergence of several dimensions: sentiments, aesthetic motives, legal arrangements, social fictions like the "rights" of nature, and appropriate property conceptions. No one dimension (e.g., positive values for nature alone) will do the job. Extensive institutional change is necessary, and such change will take place more slowly than the changes in sensibility values, as can be seen in the current popularity of environmentalist positions as compared to continued activities degrading nature. For other visions of the exceptionalist future, see Jonas 1984; and Valaskakis et al. 1979.

12. For example, some workmen in Italy, Japan, and other countries still receive wages adjusted to their own unique circumstances (e.g., family size) instead of standard amounts pegged to the particular task or job definition, something characteristic of universalistic paradigms.

13. The obvious effectiveness of Japanese modes of industrial organization, which are less functionally specialized and more multifunctional, has led to some rethinking of the more elaborate divisions of labor in the West. However, the typical approach is one that seeks the transference of management techniques, rather than an examination of the cultural differences (i.e., the longer time horizons employed in Japan and the greater emphasis on investing in human capital).

14. Requirements to perform social and environmental impact assessments are now standard in many countries. Even in the United States, where such assessments are rigorous, economic considerations clearly take precedence over social costs, which in turn tend to take precedence over environmental impacts.

15. Due to the extreme brevity of the presentation, we have not tried to be rigorously consistent in the use of terms, and in any event, since the social order is itself fluid, there is no particular virtue in slavish consistency over concepts that blend into one another in the give-and-take of any social system.

16. Modern industrial processes add other problems as well. One is that the cause-effect nexus is often widely separated in space and/or time so that assessing or evaluating the effects of pollutants discharged either long ago (e.g., the Love Canal toxic waste site) or at a long distance (see the following discussion on acid rain) is often difficult. Also, the spreading scale of impacts and their magnitude raise fundamental questions about democratic control – which ultimately assumes that people can learn from and correct mistakes. What can modern society do to maintain democratic control over society-wide and society-threatening technologies and processes when protective judgments and actions must be taken before rather than after an "accident"?

17. Residents of Tokyo in the 1970s attracted attention with their successful suits against developers who constructed buildings blocking sunlight. The increase of ultraviolet radiation that accompanies ozone depletion is another example of how light is changing its institutional identity as the result of technological activity.

18. There is, however, an important precedent in the 1935 Trail Smelter dispute between the United States and Canada. A pre-existing international institution, the International Joint Commission, presented evidence leading to the establishment of an international tribunal, which awarded the United States $350,000 in damages. This dispute was much simpler than the acid-rain issue because it involved only a single source, which had clear and measurable agricultural impacts. The Trail Smelter precedent was expanded in Principle 21 of the Stockholm Declaration in 1972 to include the liability of states for negligent damage not only to other states, but also to areas outside of national jurisdiction (the upper atmosphere, outer space, the oceans and deep sea beds, and Antarctica). See Caldwell 1984: 104–106, for a detailed discussion.

19. It is not beyond possibility, however, that seizure of air and extractions of useful gases could become a major affair, jeopardizing its gaseous balances and quality. If this happened, then air would enter the realm of economics as a priced commodity. In a sense, this already exists in the form of bottled oxygen, hydrogen and so on, but the price charged is not really for the gases, but for the service and costs of the extraction and packaging.

20. Another, and somewhat different, instance of changing concepts of resource rights and goods is seen in the compaigns against smoking tobacco, particularly cigarettes. Originally antismoking campaigns focused on the health damage done to the individual smoker himself; now they encompass antismoking regulations enforced by public law. The campaigns in effect create a new legal right: the right to breathe air in the immediate vicinity that is not contaminated by an effluent coming from a voluntary action by another person. In effect, this adds another dimension – that of air as a personal good – to the notion of air as a public good. Given the economic significance and power of the vested interests that the antismoking movement is challenging, we have a prime example of how a basic physical resource – air – gets entangled in human behavior and habit, corporate power, and legal institutions.

21. A simple, yet revealing example can be found in the endless competitive interplay over water rights in the American West. The rule of prior appropriation, which governed the assignment of private rights to ranchers in the early, unpopulated days, has had to be

modified continually and adjudicated as the number of users has increased or as holders of early, high-yielding rights have underused or abused their privilege (for an historical survey of water in cultural history, see Bennett 1974).

22. The situation is analogous to energy, where there is conflict between the production orientation of large-scale generating plants and the conservation approaches based on increasing the efficiency of use. Thus, we still find controversial attempts to "produce" more water by moving it. The Garrison Diversion of Missouri River water in North Dakota is an example: sending much of the Missouri flow out of the Mississippi and into the Hudson Bay watershed. Another is the proposal to tap the Great Lakes to provide water for the Southwest United States. It is imperative that such schemes be viewed in the largest possible economic and ecological context, measured against conservation alternatives, and not planned piecemeal as incremental fixes.

23. In some cases, use-rights continue only as long as the user does not abuse them. For example, government-granted grazing leases in some Western American states and Canadian provinces can be revoked if it can be shown that the leaseholder is either overgrazing or undergrazing. In such instances, leasing land is in many respects a form of usufruct, even though the cultural concepts of the system tend to use ownership language.

24. There are various estimates of numbers of people, ranging from 1 to 3 million, who subsist on some form of transient livestock pasturing. While these people are currently under strong pressures to establish sedentary ranching regimes, the climatic and edaphic context of life in these vast regions of the Old World makes this very difficult. Some form of transient pasturing of these marginal lands will probably persist – or will experience a resurgence as the agricultural development schemes fail. For a survey of pastoralists and their "political ecology," see Bennett et al. 1986.

25. Other examples include traditional controversies over the power and extent of local zoning boards and more recent battles to establish legislation protecting wetlands.

26. Such controversies highlight several points: (1) that the unrestricted practices of industry are establishing complex linkages between the three great domains and a corresponding set of issues of public responsibility; (2) that there are growing similarities in the regulation of environmental threats to land, water, and air through "public good" limitations on tenure rights, water rights, and air rights; and (3) that these complex linkages are not reflected yet in any sort of integrated regulatory effort to manage the various ways in which air, water, and land pollution and degradation are interactive and often synergistic. Bureaucratic specialization still prevails.

27. Heightened concern for soil quality has become evident in the twentieth century in connection with extractive surface mining of minerals, chiefly coal. Since reclamation of the land surface does not always restore useful soil quality, separate efforts are required in some cases to restore the soil profiles to viable crop production. Similar issues pertain to toxic-waste dumps, at which cleanup requires removal of the poisoned soils and replacement by soils of equivalent quality. In these cases, the exchange values assigned to soil are separate from those assigned to the land surface and contours. Methods for calculating such values have been worked out in benefit-cost analysis procedures. It is conceivable that as these problems increase, a general trend toward valuing soil quality apart from land surface and bulk may evolve. In order to deal with environmental problems of this kind, it is necessary to assemble interdisciplinary teams – a practice being followed by the National Academy of Sciences and the National Research Council. For an example of such a teamwork approach, see National Research Council 1981, which provides a study of the impacts of strip mining on soils, land surface, water, and the associated legal and tenure problems.

28. For some exceptions, see the work of Lovins and Lovins (1982) on the vulnerability of highly centralized energy infrastructures and

that of Worster (1985) on the ways in which irrigation systems in the Southwest United States have developed into bureaucratic empires.

29. Technologies are not neutral in at least three ways: (1) they reflect their physical environments (e.g., a Midwestern plow reflects the deep and moist soils of the region); (2) they reflect their social environments (e.g., a Midwestern plow reflects the large acreages owned by individuals); and (3) they reflect their basic design principles. More controversial is the question of whether or not they are morally neutral.

30. Maynard Kaufman (1972) has termed these new movements eutopian (which means the "good place"), to contrast the differences between them and more traditional utopian movements.

31. In this, they are reflecting the larger universalism and rationalism of modern science, technology, and industry – which generally encourage "blueprint" approaches, whereby local variation is fitted to abstract conceptual or organizational designs.

32. If they do not, the explanation is that "politics" or the "stupidity" or "traditionalism" of the peasants prevented the proper adoption and application of the technology.

33. The separation among specialists working on environment, development, and agriculture is shown by the few general references on the environmental costs of commercial agriculture in the Third World. The few that exist are usually more general cries of alarm (Borgstrom 1969; Dumont 1975) or general overviews of the environmental costs of development (IUCN 1980; WCED 1987) than detailed analyses. The latter tend to come in the form of specialized studies by natural scientists concerned about specific problems, such as the loss of tropical forests (Myers 1984), the loss of genetic and biological diversity (Wilson 1988), and soil erosion (ASA 1982).

34. One of the key aspects is whether or not present rates of fossil fuel use are so simplifying and undermining renewable resource systems (such as agriculture, grazing, forestry, and fisheries) and their supporting habitats, biodiversity, and basic elements (such as soil, fresh water, and clean air) that without major efforts at their conservation and preservation now, there later will be an insufficient natural resource base upon which to develop whatever potentialities biotechnology might prove to have.

35. This is because the progressive alienation of human beings from nature, induced by technology and the industrial system and its institutions, is paralleled by increasing alienation of human beings from one another, and the consequent spread of social tensions, protest, and revolution – exacerbated by the rise of the modern state and its insistence on power and autonomy. Thus, the ecological problem is simply one side of a coin: the social problem of the modern world system is the other. This means, for example, that attempts at regulating or controlling our use of natural substances inevitably become entangled in the questions of freedom, control, and rights of humans.

36. In this regard, it can be suggested that the goal should be a globe of villages rather than a global village.

References

Adams, R. N. 1988. Evolution and development. In *Production and Autonomy: Anthropological Studies and Critiques of Development*, ed. J. W. Bennett and J. R. Bowen. Lapham, MD: University Press of America.

Adams, R. McC. 1966. *The Evolution of Urban Society: Early Mesopotamia and Prehispanic Mexico*. Chicago: Aldine.

Altieri, M. 1983. *Agroecology: The Scientific Basis of Alternative Agriculture*. Division of Biological Control. Berkeley: University of California.

American Society of Agronomy. 1982. *Soil Conservation and Erosion in the Tropics*. ASA Special Publication No. 43. Madison, WI: American Society of Agronomy.

Ashby, E. 1978. *Reconciling Man with the Environment*. Stanford: Stanford University Press.

Barkley, P. W., and Seckler, D. W. 1972. *Economic Growth and Environmental Decay*. New York: Harcourt Brace Jovanovich.

Bennett, J. W. 1974. Anthropological contributions to the cultural ecology and management of water resources. In *Man and Water: the Social Sciences in Management of Water Resources*, ed. L. D. James, chap. 2. Lexington: The University Press of Kentucky.

———. 1976. *The Ecological Transition: Cultural Anthropology and Human Adaptation*. New York: Pergamon Press.

———. 1980. Human ecology as human behavior: A normative anthropology of resource use and abuse. In *Human Behavior and Environment*. Vol. 4, *Environment and Culture*, ed. Irving Altman et al. New York: Plenum.

———. 1981. *Of Time and the Enterprise: North American Family Farm Management in a Context of Resource Marginality*. Minneapolis: University of Minnesota Press.

———. 1984. Ecosystems, environmentalism, resource conservation and anthropological research. In *The Ecosystem Concept in Anthropology*, ed. Emilio Moran. Boulder, CO: Westview Press.

Bennett, J. W., S. W. Lawry, and J. C. Riddell. 1986. *Land Tenure and Livestock Development in Sub-Saharan Africa*. AID Special Evaluation Study No. 39. Washington, DC: Agency for International Development.

Berger, P. L. 1976. *Pyramids of Sacrifice: Political Ethics and Social Change*. Garden City, NY: Anchor Books.

Bijker, W. E., T. P. Hughes, and T. J. Pinch, eds. 1987. *The Social Construction of Technological Systems: New Directions in the Sociology and History of Technology*. Cambridge, MA: MIT Press.

Black, J. 1970. *The Dominion of Man: The Search for Ecological Responsibility*. Edinburgh: The University Press.

Blaikie, P. 1985. *The Political Economy of Soil Erosion in Developing Countries*. New York: Longman.

Bloch, M. 1967. *Land and medieval Europe*. Berkeley: University of California Press.

Blum, J., ed. 1982. *Our Forgotten Past: Seven Centuries of Life on the Land*. London: Thames and Hudson.

Bodley, J. H. 1982. *Victims of Progress*. Palo Alto, CA: Mayfield.

Borgstrom, G. 1965. *The Hungry Planet: The Modern World at the Edge of Famine*. New York: Macmillan.

———. 1969. *Too Many: A Study of the Earth's Biological Limitations*. New York: Macmillan.

Boulding, K. E. 1964. *The Meaning of the Twentieth Century: The Great Transition*. New York: Harper & Row.

Bruce, J. W. 1986. *Land Tenure Issues in Project Design and Strategies for Agricultural Development in Sub-Saharan Africa*. Land Tenure Centre. Madison, University of Wisconsin.

Bunker, S. G. 1985. *Underdeveloping the Amazon: Extraction, Unequal Exchange, and the Failure of the Modern State*. Chicago: University of Chicago Press.

Burton, M. L., G. M. Schoepfle, and M. L. Miller. 1986. Natural resource anthropology. *Human Organization* 45: 261–69.

Caldwell, L. K. 1984. *International Environmental Policy: Emergence and Dimensions*. Durham, NC: Duke University Press.

Castle, E. N., and K. A. Price, eds. 1983. *U.S. Interests and Global Natural Resources: Energy, Minerals, Food*. Baltimore, MD: Johns Hopkins University Press.

Chambers, R. 1983. *Rural Development: Putting the Last First*. London: Longman.

Childe, V. G. 1950. The urban revolution. *Town Planning Review* 21: 3–17.

———. 1951. *Man Makes Himself*. London: Watts.

Clark. W. C., and R. E. Munn, eds. 1986. *Sustainable Development of the Biosphere*. Cambridge: Cambridge University Press.

Cohen, M. N. 1977. *The Food Crisis in Prehistory: Overpopulation and the Origins of Agriculture*. New Haven, CT: Yale University Press.

Crosby, A. W. 1986. *Ecological Imperialism: The Biological Expansion of Europe, 900–1900*. New York: Cambridge University Press.

Cummings, T. G. 1980. *Systems Theory for Organizational Development*. New York: Wiley.

Dahlberg, K. A. 1979. *Beyond the Green Revolution: The Ecology and Politics of Global Agricultural Development*. New York: Plenum.

———, ed. 1986. *New Directions for Agriculture and Agricultural Research: Neglected Dimensions and Emerging Alternatives*. Totowa, NJ: Roman & Allanheld.

———. 1987. Redefining development priorities: genetic diversity and agroecodevelopment. *Conservation Biology* 1(4): 311–22.

———. 1990. The industrial model and its impacts on small farmers: The Green Revolution as a case. In *Agroecology and Small Farm Development*. ed. M. Altieri and S. Hecht, 81–88. Boca Raton, FL: CRC Press.

Dahlberg, K. A., and J. W. Bennett, eds. 1986. *Natural Resources and People: Conceptual Issues in Interdisciplinary Research*. Boulder, CO: Westview Press.

Dahlman, C. J. 1980. *The Open Field System and Beyond: A Property Rights Analysis of an Economic Institution*. Cambridge: Cambridge University Press.

Deevey, E. S., Jr. 1960. The human population. *Scientific American* 203(3): 194–205.

de Janvry, A. 1981. *The Agrarian Question and Reformism in Latin America*. Baltimore, MD: The Johns Hopkins University Press.

de Moll, L., T. Bender, S. Johnson, L. Johnson, and R. Epstein, eds. 1977. *RAINBOOK: Resources for AT*. New York: Schocken.

Diwan, R. K., and D. Livingston. 1979. *Alternative Development Strategies and Appropriate Technology: Science Policy for an Equitable World Order*. New York: Pergamon Press.

Dover, M., and L. Talbot. 1987. *To Feed the Earth: Agro-Ecology for Sustainable Development*. Washington, D.C.: World Resources Institute.

Dumont, R. 1975. *La Croissance...de la Famine! Une Agriculture Repensee*. Paris: Editions du Seuil.

Durrenburger, F. P., and G. Palsson. Ownership at sea: fishing territories and access to sea resources. *American Ethnologist* 14: 508–22.

Edgerton, R. B. 1971. *The Individual in Cultural Adaptation*. Berkeley: University of California Press.

Ehrenfeld, D. W. 1978. *The Arrogance of Humanism*. New York: Oxford University Press.

Ehrlich, P. R., and A. H. Ehrlich. 1981. *Extinction: The Causes and Consequences of the Disappearance of Species*. New York: Random House.

Ehrlich, P. R., C. Sagan, D. Kennedy, and W. O. Roberts. 1984. *The Cold and the Dark: The World after Nuclear War*. New York: W. W. Norton.

Eisenstadt, S. N. 1968. Social institutions: the concept. In *The International Encyclopaedia of the Social Sciences*, ed. D. L. Sills, 409–21. New York: Macmillan and Free Press.

Ellen, R. 1982. *Environment, Subsistence and System: the Ecology of Small-Scale Social Formations*. Cambridge: Cambridge University Press.

Ellul, J. 1964. *The Technological Society*. New York: Knopf.

Feder, E. 1983. *Perverse Development*. Foundation for Nationalist Studies, Quezon City, Philippines.

Foley, R. 1988. Hominid species and stone-tool assemblages. *Antiquity* 61: 380.

Ford, R., ed. 1985. *Prehistoric Food Production in North America*. Anthropological Papers No. 75. Museum of Anthropology. Ann Arbor, MI: University of Michigan.

George, H. 1955. *Progress and Poverty*. New York: Robert Schalkenbach Foundation.

Georgescu-Roegen, N. 1971. *The Entropy Law and the Economic Process*. Cambridge, MA: Harvard University Press.

Gever, J., R. Kaufmann, D. Skole, and C. Vorosmarty. 1986. *Beyond*

Oil: The Threat to Food and Fuel in the Coming Decades. Cambridge, MA: Ballinger.

Grigg, D. B. 1984. The agricultural revolution in Western Europe. In *Understanding Green Revolutions*, ed. T. P. Bayliss-Smith and S. Wanmali, chap. 1. Cambridge: Cambridge University Press.

Hanks, L. 1972. *Rice and Man: Agricultural Ecology in Southeast Asia.* Chicago: Aldine.

Hardin, G. 1968. The tragedy of the commons. *Science* 162: 1243–48.

Hawkes, J. G. 1983. *The Diversity of Crop Plants.* Cambridge, MA: Harvard University Press.

Hawkes, J., and L. Woolley. 1963. *Prehistory and the Beginnings of Civilization.* New York: Harper & Row.

Hirsch, F. 1976. *The Social Limits to Growth.* Cambridge, MA: Harvard University Press.

Homans, G. C. 1942. *English Villages and the Thirteenth Century.* Cambridge, MA: Harvard University Press.

Hubbert, M. K. 1969. Energy resources. In *Resources and Man*, National Academy of Sciences–National Research Council, 170–84. San Francisco: W. H. Freeman.

Hufschmidt, M. M., and E. L. Hyman, eds. 1983. *Economic Approaches to Natural Resource Management and Environmental Quality Analysis.* Dublin: Tycooly International.

Hughes, B. B. 1985. *World Futures: A Critical Analysis of Alternatives.* Baltimore, MD: The Johns Hopkins University Press.

Illich, I. 1973. *Tools for Conviviality.* New York: Harper & Row.

International Union for the Conservation of Nature and Natural Resources (IUCN). 1980. *World Conservation Strategy.* Gland, Switzerland: IUCN.

Jennings, J. D., ed. 1983. *Ancient North Americans.* New York: W. H. Freeman.

Jonas, H. 1984. *The Imperative of Responsibility: In Search of an Ethics for the Technological Age.* Chicago: The University of Chicago Press.

Kaufman, M. 1972. The new homesteading movement: From utopia to eutopia. In *The Family, Communes and Utopian Societies*, ed. S. TeSell, 63–82. New York: Harper Torchbooks.

Kempton, W. and M. Neiman, eds. 1987. *Energy Efficiency: Perspectives on Individual Behavior.* Washington, D.C.: American Council for an Energy-Efficient Economy.

Klee, G. A. 1980. *World Systems of Traditional Resource Management.* New York: Wiley.

Krasner, S. D. 1985. *Structural Conflict: The Third World against Global Liberalism.* Berkeley: University of California Press.

Krutilla, J. W., and A. C. Fisher. 1976. *The Economics of Natural Environments.* Baltimore, MD: The Johns Hopkins University Press.

Lal, R. 1987. Managing the soils of sub-Saharan Africa. *Science* 236: 1069–76.

Lazlo, E. 1972. *An Introduction to Systems Philosophy.* New York: Science Publishers.

Lee, R. B., and I. DeVore, eds. 1968. *Man the Hunter.* Chicago: Aldine.

Leiss, W. 1972. *The Domination of Nature.* New York: George Braziller.

Lipton, M. 1977. *Why Poor People Stay Poor: Urban Bias in World Development.* Cambridge, MA: Harvard University Press.

Little, P. D., M. M. Horowitz, and A. E. Nyerges. 1987. *Lands at Risk in the Third World: Local Level Perspectives.* Boulder, CO: Westview Press.

London, J., and G. F. White, eds. 1984. *The Environmental Effects of Nuclear War.* Boulder, CO: Westview Press.

Lovelock, J. E. 1979. *Gaia: A New Look at Life on Earth.* New York: Oxford University Press.

Lovins, A. B. 1977. *Soft Energy Paths: Towards a Durable Peace.* Cambridge, MA: Ballinger.

Lovins, A. B., and L. H. Lovins. 1982. *Brittle Power: Energy Strategy for National Security.* Andover, MA: Brick House.

Lowrance, R., B. R. Stinner, and G. J. House, eds. 1984. *Agricultural Ecosystems: Unifying Concepts.* New York: John Wiley & Sons.

Mannheim, K. 1936. *Ideology and Utopia.* New York: Harcourt, Brace.

Margalef, R. 1968. *Perspectives on Ecological Theory.* Chicago: University of Chicago Press.

McCartan, B. 1985. Resource wars: the myth of American mineral vulnerability. *Defense Monitor* 14(9): 1–8.

McNeill, W. H. 1982. *The Pursuit of Power.* Chicago: The University of Chicago Press.

Mumford, Lewis. 1934. *Technics and Civilization.* New York: Harcourt, Brace & Co.

———. 1959. *The Story of Utopias.* Gloucester, MA: P. Smith.

———. 1974. *The Myth of the Machine: Technics and Human Development.* New York: Harcourt, Brace, and World.

Myers, N. 1984. *The Primary Source: Tropical Forests and our Future.* New York: W. W. Norton.

National Academy of Sciences. 1988. *Biodiversity: Proceedings of the Forum on Biodiversity.* Washington, D.C.: National Academy Press.

National Research Council. 1981. *Surface Mining: Soil, Coal and Society.* Washington, D.C.: Commission on National Resources, National Academy Press.

National Research Council. 1986. *Common Property Resource Management: Proceedings of the Conference.* NRC Panel on Common Property Resource Management. Washington, D.C.: National Academy Press.

Odum, H. T. 1971. *Environment, Power and Society.* New York: John Wiley.

Olson, M. 1965. *The Logic of Collective Action.* Cambridge, MA: Harvard University Press.

Olson, M., and H. H. Landsberg, eds. 1973. *The No-Growth Society.* New York: W. W. Norton.

Ophuls, W. 1977. *Ecology and the Politics of Scarcity.* San Francisco: Freeman.

Pacey, A. 1983. *The Culture of Technolgy.* Oxford: Basil Blackwell.

Parry, M. L. 1986. Some implications of climatic change for human development. In *Sustainable Development of the Biosphere*. ed. W. C. Clark and R. E. Munn, 378–407. Cambridge: Cambridge University Press.

Parsons, T. 1951. *The Social System.* New York: Harper.

Peach, W. N., and J. A. Constantin. 1972. *Zimmermann's World Resources and Industries.* New York: Harper & Row.

Pearson, C. S., ed. 1987. *Multinational Corporations, Environment, and the Third World.* Durham, NC: Duke University Press.

Perdue, P. C. 1987. *Exhausing the Earth: State and Peasant in Hunan, 1500–1850.* Cambridge, MA: Harvard University Press.

Petulla, J. M. 1987. *Environmental Protection in the United States.* San Francisco: San Francisco Study Center.

Pfister, C. 1986. *Bevoelkerung, Klima und Agrarmodernisierung 1525–1860.* Bern: Paul Haupt.

Pimentel, D., and M. Pimentel. 1979. *Food, Energy, and Society.* London: Edward Arnold.

Polanyi, K. 1957. *The Great Transformation.* Boston: Beacon Press.

Rambo, T., K. Gillogly, and K. A. Hytterer, eds. 1988. *Ethnic Diversity and the Control of Natural Resources in Southeast Asia.* Ann Arbor, Michigan, Papers on South and Southeast Asia, No. 32.

Redman, C. L. 1978. *The Rise of Civilization: From Early Farmers to Urban Society in the Ancient Near East.* San Francisco: Freeman.

Reisner, M. 1986. *Cadillac Desert: The American West and Its Disappearing Water.* New York: Viking Penguin.

Schumacher, E. F. 1973. *Small Is Beautiful.* New York: Harper Torchbooks.

Seidenberg, R. 1974. *Posthistoric Man: An Inquiry.* New York: Viking Press.

Simon, J. L., and H. Kahn, eds. 1984. *The Resourceful Earth: A Response to Global 2000.* New York: Basil Blackwell.

Sims, N. L. 1920. *The Rural Community: Ancient and Modern.* New York: Charles Scribner's Sons.

Singer, C., E. J. Holmyard, A. R. Hall, and T. I. Williams. 1954–1974.

A History of Technology. 5 vols. Oxford: Clarendon Press.

Spooner, B. 1984. *Ecology in Development: A Rationale for Three-Dimensional Policy.* Tokyo: The United Nations University.

Starr, C. 1971. Energy and Power. *Scientific American* 225(3): 36–49.

Steward, J., J. H. Steward, R. M. Adams, D. Collier, A. Palermo, K. A. Wittfogel, and R. L. Beals. 1955. *Irrigation Civilizations: A Comparative Study.* Washington, D.C.: Pan American Union.

Stone, R. D. 1985. *Dreams of Amazonia.* New York: Viking Penguin.

Stroup, R. L., and J. A. Baden. 1988. *Natural Resources: Bureaucratic Myths and Environmental Management.* San Francisco, CA: Pacific Research Institute for Public Policy.

Susman, R. L. 1988. Hand of Paranthropus Robustus from member 1, Swartkrans: fossil evidence for tool behavior. *Science* 240: 781–83.

Tawney, R. H. 1938. *Religion and the Rise of Capitalism.* London: Penguin.

Theobald, R. 1987. *The Rapids of Change.* Indianapolis, IN: Knowledge Systems Inc.

Thomas, K. 1983. *Man and the Natural World: A History of the Modern Sensibility.* New York: Pantheon.

Thomas, W. L., Jr., ed. 1956. *Man's Role in Changing the Face of the Earth.* Chicago: University of Chicago Press.

Turner, B. L., II, and S. B. Brush, eds. 1987. *Comparative Farming Systems.* New York: Guildford.

U.S. Congress, Office of Technology Assessment. 1987. *Technologies to Maintain Biological Diversity.* OTA-F-330. Washington, D.C.: U. S. Printing Office.

U. S. Department of State. 1982. *Proceedings of the U. S. Strategy Conference on Biological Diversity, November 16–18, 1982.* Washington, D.C.: U. S. Department of State.

Valaskakis, K., P. S. Sindell, J. G. Smith, and I. Fitzpatrick-Martin. 1979. *The Conserver Society: A Workable Alternative for the Future.* New York: Harper Colophon.

Wagner, P. 1960. *The Human Use of the Earth.* Glencoe, IL: The Free Press.

Wallensteen, P. 1986. Food crops as a factor in strategic policy and action. In *Global Resources and International Conflict: Environmental Factors in Strategic Policy and Action,* ed. A. H. Westing, 143–58. Oxford: Oxford University Press.

Wallerstein, I. 1974 and 1978. *The Modern World System.* 2 vols. New York: Academic Press.

Weber, M. 1951. *The Theory of Social and Economic Organization.* Tr. by T. Parsons and A. M. Henderson. New York: Oxford University Press.

Welch, S., and R. Miewald, eds. 1983. *Scarce Natural Resources: The Challenge to Public Policy Making.* Beverly Hills, CA: Sage Publications.

Westing A. H., ed. 1986. *Global Resources and International Conflict: Environmental Factors in Strategic Policy and Action.* Oxford: Oxford University Press.

Westney, D. E. 1987. *Imitation and Innovation: The Transfer of Western Organizational Patterns to Meiji Japan.* Cambridge, MA: Harvard University Press.

White, G. F. 1971. *Strategies of American Water Management.* Ann Arbor: University of Michigan Press.

White, L., Jr. 1969. The historical roots of our ecological crisis. In *The Subversive Science,* ed. P. Shepard and D. McKinley, 341–51. Boston: Houghton Mifflin.

Williams, T. I., ed. 1978. *A History of Technology,* vols. 6 and 7. Oxford: Clarendon Press.

Wilson, E. O., ed. 1988. *Biodiversity.* Washington, D.C.: National Academy Press.

Wittfogel, K. A. 1957. *Oriental Despotism.* New Haven, CT: Yale University Press.

Wolf, E. C. 1987. *On the Brink of Extinction: Preserving the Diversity of Life.* Worldwatch Paper 78. Washington, D.C.: Worldwatch Institute.

World Commission on Environment and Development (WCED). 1987. *Our Common Future.* Oxford: Oxford University Press.

Worster, D. 1985. *Rivers of Empire: Water, Aridity, and the Growth of the American West.* New York: Pantheon.

Young, O. R. 1982. *Resource Regimes: Natural Resources and Social Institutions.* Berkeley: University of California Press.

6

The Increasing Separation of Production and Consumption

MICHAEL CHISHOLM

Only in a completely self-sufficient community could it be said that production and consumption occur at the same place. Where there is less than full self-sufficiency, some transfers of resources must occur, i.e., the separation of production and consumption. Such transfers may take the form of traditional "exchange" systems, as visualised by Polanyi (1944) and Wilkinson (1973), or involve trade for profit. With the evolution of the world economy, especially following the Industrial Revolution, it is generally supposed that traditional, "precontact" societies have progressively been penetrated by trading systems geared to profit, as a response to the needs of the industrialized countries. For this reason, some would argue, the Industrial Revolution has created an entirely new situation.

In practice, it appears that virtually all societies have engaged in trade, as distinct from exchange, throughout the past 300 years, and in fact since long before. Latham (1978) has assembled persuasive evidence to show the remarkably widespread use of currencies from very early times, in support of his contention that trade has been the norm rather than the exception. Boserup's (1981) study makes the identical point. Therefore, although contact with Europe and European needs in the nineteenth and twentieth centuries transformed the scale of trading relationships worldwide, this change was quantitative rather than qualitative. The central task in this essay is to explore the nature and the scale of resource transfers during the past 300 years.

Data problems are serious. Only with the formation of the League of Nations in 1919 were sustained and systematic efforts made to collect, collate, and publish data pertaining to the global economy. Broadly speaking, we may say that since 1945 the supply of information has been quite good, whereas before 1914 data are exiguous. Therefore, it will be necessary to piece together disparate information. In so doing I will take the liberty of using data for periods before 1687, where these throw useful light on the situation at the beginning of the study period.

Approaching the available data, we must beware of two biases. In much of the literature for periods before about 1800, trade in exotic goods seems to have attracted dispro-portionate attention. No doubt there has been, and will continue to be, a fascination with strange places and the frontiers of discovery, and the associated products. It appears, though, that because of this bias, traffic in the basic necessities of life has been given less prominence than would be warranted by its importance.

In contrast, from about 1800, the frontiers of European expansion were in the temperate lands – North America, Argentina, Australia, New Zealand, and elsewhere. Grain, wool, meat, and dairy products were their staple exports, for which good records exist. It is very easy, therefore, to exaggerate the growth of traffic in basic commodities from about 1800 relative to such trade in earlier years.

The second bias is more serious. It is the Euro-centric view of the world, which dominates the literature. This point was forcibly expressed by Latham (1978: 13). He attended a conference in 1973, entitled "Britain in the World's Economy, 1860–1914," of which he has the following to say:

... while many sophisticated papers were heard, it was frankly staggering to witness the myopia of British and American economic historians, who, almost without exception, seemed to believe that the world economy at the end of the nineteenth century consisted mainly of Britain and the United States, with Asia and Africa hardly figuring at all in the discussions.

Nevertheless, the myopia persists, as witness the influential work of Wallerstein (1974; 1980). In this two-volume study of the world economy to 1750, everywhere outside the European core is relegated to the status of periphery or semiperiphery. To appreciate the scale and nature of global trading relations, it is essential to raise one's eyes from the European scene.

Nevertheless, it is convenient to begin with the conventional view of Europe's expansion, especially in the nineteenth century. We then will consider how that picture must be amended, first by examining earlier patterns of trade in the European domain, and then by considering Asia, Latin America, and Africa. This will give us a perspective from which to examine the growth of global trading in the nineteenth and twentieth centuries and the evolution of theoretical discussion about trade. Finally we will briefly consider the implications of the increased separation of production and

Table 6-1 *Estimates of World Population, Selected Dates (Millions)*

Region	A.D. 0	1000	1500	1750	1900	1975
China	70–90	50–80	100–150	190–225	400–450	800–900
India, Pakistan, Bangladesh	50–100	50–100	75–150	160–200	285–295	740–765
Southwestern Asia	25–45	20–30	20–30	25–35	40–45	115–125
Japan	1–2	3–8	15–20	29–30	44–45	111
Remainder of Asia, exc. USSR	8–20	10–25	15–30	35–55	110–125	435–460
Europe, exc. USSR	30–40	30–40	60–70	120–135	295–300	470–475
USSR	5–10	6–15	10–18	30–40	130–135	255
Northern Africa	10–15	5–10	6–12	10–15	53–55	80–82
Remainder of Africa	15–30	20–40	30–60	50–80	90–120	315–335
North America	1–2	2–3	2–3	2–3	82–83	237
Central and Southern America	6–15	20–50	30–60	13–18	71–78	320–335
Oceania	1–2	1–2	1–2	2	6	21
Total	270–330	275–345	440–54	735–805	1165–1710	3950–4050

Source: Durand 1977: 259.

consumption. As background to this discussion, Table 6-1 provides estimates of the world's population at selected dates, in total and for the major regions.

The Conventional View – the Expansion of Europe

The Industrial Revolution was initiated in England in the mid-eighteenth century and quickly spread to Europe. As the nineteenth and twentieth centuries unfolded, North America, the USSR, and Japan in particular have become industrialized also, along with several other smaller, non-European nations. As industrialization has proceeded, so has the demand expanded for raw materials and fuels, a demand that has triggered development elsewhere. As Chisholm and Wrigley (both writing in 1962 but quite independently) point out, this process can be visualized as the expansion of supply zones in a dynamic version of von Thünen's theory of agricultural location.

As Wrigley (1962) very aptly notes, in 1776 the traditional world of Adam Smith and his forebears was about to be ruptured. Hitherto, the perceived "natural order" had been for a town to trade with its surrounding area, exchanging manufactures for industrial materials and food. In this scheme of things, long-distance trade was confined mainly to exotic commodities, such as silks and spices, of a high value relative to weight (see Chisholm 1979). With the onset of the Industrial Revolution, quite basic commodities came to be traded over long distances, even worldwide (e.g., coal and iron ore, grain and meat, in the present day).

Britain in the nineteenth century, and Europe more generally, was a major and rapidly expanding market for agricultural products and raw materials. The expansion of the supply zones, treated in terms of a dynamic von Thünen model, has been documented by Peet (1969; 1972; see also Chisholm 1961; 1962).

Even by the early eighteenth century, well before Britain could be said to be industrialized, the growth of the London food market had seriously affected the agriculture of areas two to three hundred miles [320 to 480 km] away. For example, Wales and northwestern England

engaged in rearing animals intended eventually for the London market, whereas the northeastern coast shipped cheese and salt butter. Permanent agricultural *imports*, however, came only with the rapid growth of manufacturing industry in the 1780's and 1790's. (Peet 1969: 293–94)

Between 1870–1876 and 1910–1914, the proportion of temperate agricultural products drawn from abroad rose from 26% to 46% of apparent consumpton in the United Kingdom. At the same time, as supply zones expanded, the average distance over which these imports were drawn increased sharply, from 2,929 km in the period 1831–35, to 9,463 km in the period 1909–13 (see Table 6-2 for details).

As Malenbaum (1953: 96) points out with respect to wheat: "If production was to be increased, expanding acreage was generally more economical than expanding yields per acre." Consequently, notwithstanding steady yield increases in the main European importing countries from 1885–89 onward, the greater part of rising demand for wheat was met by expansion of the cultivated area overseas. The same was true for other temperate agricultural products. The demand for foodstuffs and agricultural raw materials created by expansion in Europe, and particularly in Britain, provided a major stimulus to development in the supplying regions – mainly European-settled temperate states, such as Canada, Argentina, and Australia. The effect on tropical economies came later and was less pronounced (Lewis 1970).

A Euro-centered view of development from the early to mid-nineteenth century focuses on the following features: Europe as the main market for foodstuffs and primary produce generally; the expansion in that demand and the consequential widening of supply zones; and the fact that long-distance trade is no longer confined to luxury or semiluxury goods, but includes bulky raw materials on a massive scale. This conventional view has been expressed by Woodruff (1966: 267–68) in the following terms:

Whereas in the fifteenth and sixteenth centuries the spice trade had been the source of wealth in international commerce and had later been displaced by the growing demand for colonial products, the period after 1850 is marked by the growing trade in the bulky articles

Table 6-2 *Average Distance from London to Regions from Which British Agricultural Imports Were Derived*[1] *(Kilometers)*

Commodity	1831–35	1856–60	1871–75	1891–95	1909–13
Fruit and Vegetables	0[2]	521	861	1,851	3,025
Live animals	0[2]	1,014	1,400	5,681	7,242
Butter, cheese, eggs, etc.	422	853	2,156	2,591	5,021
Feed grains	1,384	3,267	3,911	5,214	7,773
Flax and seeds	2,446	5,230	4,458	6,566	6,276
Meat and tallow	3,219	4,667	6,019	8,127	10,058
Wheat and flour	3,911	3,492	6,759	8,288	9,575
Wool and hides	3,750	14,210	16,093	17,718	17,541
Weighted average	2,929	5,874	6,920	8,127	9,463

Source: Peet 1969: 295.

[1] "Imports" from Ireland not included.

[2] No significant imports.

of commerce: grain, minerals, raw textile materials, timber, and perishable commodities like fruit and meat.

This view of the evolution of the world economy is consistent with the history of transport improvements, deriving from European inventions and technological improvements, the effect of which has been to reduce transport costs and reduce transit times (see Chisholm 1982; Clark and Haswell 1970; Kindleberger 1956; North 1968). And, as technological advances have occurred, the volume of materials needed per unit of output has fallen throughout the nineteenth and twentieth centuries (Chisholm 1966: 158).

Prior to 1687, major improvements had already occurred in the construction and rigging of sailing ships, in the accuracy of the compass and of the astrolabe (and equivalent instruments for measuring the altitude of heavenly bodies so that latitude can be determined). At the same time, charts and globes were being much improved as knowledge accumulated. However, it was not until the second half of the eighteenth century that a reasonably cheap chronometer became widely available. Such a timepiece is essential for the accurate determination of longitude; until its use became general, long-distance oceanic navigation remained very hazardous. Notwithstanding improvements to river navigations, the first major change in modern times in the ability to carry goods overland came with the construction of canals, especially with the 1681 completion of the Canal du Midi. Thereafter, throughout much of Europe the ability to move bulky goods long distances overland improved dramatically.

Important though these developments were, it was the application of steam power that wrought the most profound changes. Between 1825 and about 1914, railway networks were built across Europe, North America, India, and elsewhere, in part complementing river and canal transport, in part replacing carriage by water. Horse and cart gave reasonably convenient access for distances up to about 30 km from railheads or wharfs. The railway transformation of overland movement was more dramatic than the changes in the preceding canal era, and brought most continental interiors into actual or potential contact with the worldwide trading systems, whereas previously, such contact had been limited to navigable rivers and the areas that could be served by canal.

The combination of iron construction and steam propulsion revolutionized ocean shipping during the nineteenth century, though sailing vessels fought a long and surprisingly successful rearguard action. Britain, with the world's largest fleet of commercial vessels, had a bigger tonnage of sail than of steam until 1884 – barely a century ago. With the opening in 1869 of the Suez Canal and of the Panama Canal in 1914, distances on many voyages were cut dramatically.

In parallel with these developments came the telegraph, initially an essential adjunct to the operation of railway systems, but quickly applied to intercontinental communications with the success of the first trans-Atlantic cable, laid in 1866. During the next 20 years, the skeleton of a worldwide system was established, putting buyers and sellers into direct contact. During the last two decades of the nineteenth century, the introduction of refrigerated vessels opened up worldwide markets for perishable commodities such as butter and beef.

After World War I, motor vehicles and aircraft began yet further revolutions, although the latter has been much less significant for freight traffic than for passengers. Initially, lorries were used for local collection and delivery, replacing horse and cart. By the 1930s, however, intercity road traffic – passenger and freight – had expanded so much that major road improvements had become urgent in the more advanced nations. In most cases, though, it was not until after 1945 that major programs of road construction were undertaken, consolidating the role of the internal combustion engine for both local and long-distance freight movement. At the present time, roads handle 90% of the tonnage of inland freight in Japan, 80% in Great Britain, but only 40% of the combined road-plus-rail freight tonnage of Canada.

Associated with the technological changes sketched in preceding paragraphs has been the increase in scale of transport units – whether individual vessels, railway wagons, or lorries. Speeds have been increasing and the reliability of schedules improving, making for greater economy in transport. Finally, specialized facilities have been extended beyond refrigeration to include the bulk carriage of many substances, especially liquids, which were previously difficult or impossible to transport; oil and gas pipelines now play a significant part in transport systems, and electricity transmission obviates the need to shift oil or coal.

There is no doubt that over the past 300 years, transport technology has been transformed, creating opportunities to separate production and consumption on a scale hitherto not imagined. Nevertheless, this should not blind us to the fact that surprisingly large amounts of traffic in basic commodities have occurred for a very long time. Although the past 150 years have witnessed a remarkable expansion in absolute volume of trade over considerable distances, it is a mistake to suppose that the spatial separation of production and consumption is really such a recent phenomenon.

The Conventional View Amended

Early European Trade in Basic Commodities

In the fifteenth century, Europe could be divided broadly into two trading zones – the north, focusing on the Baltic and North seas, and the south, focusing on the Mediterranean. There was extensive trade within both zones, and also between them. Darby (1961: 41) characterized the northern trade as dominated by the necessities of life, whereas that of the south was composed of luxuries. There is no doubt that trade in the Baltic/North Sea region was predominantly of wool and cloth, fish (salted and dried), grain, timber, and similar necessities. But these necessities also entered the trade of the Mediterranean world to provision the major trading cities. And, as the centuries passed, trade between the two regions became increasingly important; olive oil, wine, and salt, for example, moved northward in exchange for grain and cloth.

These traffics have been especially well described in several volumes of the New Cambridge Modern History, by Glamann (1971; 1977) and by Braudel (1982). We have considerable detail concerning the range of commodities traded and the geographical extent of the traffic, but much less complete detail concerning the quantities being moved. Nevertheless, it is apparent that the tonnage of basic commodities shifted in Europe in medieval times and later must have been considerable. While Icelandic fish was brought to England (Wilson 1933), cattle from eastern Europe might walk 1,000 km to market. For some of these traffics, surprisingly good statistics are available from quite early dates, one such being the toll records of the Kingdom of Denmark and the Duchy of Schleswig (Glamann 1977). These records span the period from 1497 to 1783 in the case of Baltic shipping, and from 1483 to 1640–41 in the case of cattle (being driven southward to market). In the first half of the seventeenth century, approximately 138,000 metric tons of grain passed through the Sound each year – enough to feed about 0.75 million people. The maximum transit of cattle recorded was 52,350, in the year 1612.

Specifically with respect to grain passing through the Sound, Glamann (1977: 231–32) expresses the opinion that it was marginal to Europe's needs. The principal destination for the Baltic grain was Holland, with a population in 1622 estimated at 671,000 (de Vries 1974: 86). Estimates vary as to the proportion of this population that was fed by imports. Slicher van Bath (1963: 241) and Boserup (1981: 104) put the proportion depending on foreign grain at between 12% and 17%, but de Vries (1974: 172) states that "well over half" the population was fed in this way (this is with reference to a population of 1.0 million in Holland and adjacent areas). Furthermore, for a period at least, three-quarters of the grain imported into Holland was reexported (Glamann 1971: 39). Summarizing the evidence for Holland, de Vries (1974: 172–73) has this to say:

These diverse statistics are sufficient to show that the region [Holland] was much more than marginally dependent on foreign grain. The dense population and specialized economy could not have arisen had the region not been able to draw upon all of Europe, and Poland in particular, for its grain.

Probably the main reason for the difference of opinion between Glamann and de Vries lies in the distinction between foreign grain and grain that passed through the Sound. A large proportion of the Baltic supplies were in fact off-loaded at Lübeck for trans-shipment at Hamburg. Thus, during the first half of the seventeenth century, the average grain export from Danzig (which was the largest exporter) amounted to some 220,000 metric tons per annum (Price 1970: 837) – considerably in excess of the amount recorded as passing through the Sound.

It is equally clear that there were other major movements of foodstuffs. The grain trades in England and France have been described carefully in two classic works (Gras 1915; Usher 1913). Although these texts do not provide statistical data that can be compared readily with the traffic through the Sound, nobody could doubt the large scale of the grain trades and the considerable areas over which they were articulated. As for cattle, we may compare the 52,350 head already mentioned for the year 1612 with Ireland's annual export to England. During the first half of the seventeenth century, the number fluctuated between 60,000 and 100,000 head (Peet 1972: 5). Or Paris, provisioned mainly by French producers, consumed 67,600 oxen, 426,000 sheep, and 100,000 calves in 1707, drawing these supplies from far afield (Braudel 1982: 39).

The wine trade was also of major importance as early as the fourteenth and fifteenth centuries. According to James (1951; 1971), exports from southwest France (essentially Bordeaux) reached their peak in 1308–09, at the astonishing level of 77,000 to 92,500 metric tons (there is some doubt concerning the modern equivalent of the unit used). Given that Europe's population was about 70 million early in the fourteenth century (Table 6-3), this wine export trade amounted to between 1.1 and 1.3 kilograms per person. For comparison, some 300 years later, the grain traffic through the Sound amounted to about 1.4 kilograms for every European inhabitant. When account is taken of the total movement of cattle, fish, salt, olive oil, timber, cloth, and a multitude of other commodities, it is certain that international traffic within the European domain amounted to considerably more than 1–2 kilograms per person in the seventeenth century – probably well in excess of 10 kilograms.

Table 6-3 *Estimates of Europe's Population, Selected Dates (millions)*

Year	Population	Year	Population
1000	42	1500	69
1050	46	1550	78
1100	48	1600	89
1150	50	1650	100
1200	61	1700	115
1250	69	1750	140
1300	73	1800	188
1350	51	1850	266
1400	45	1900	401
1450	60		

Source: Bennett 1954: 9.

N.B.: These figures include European Russia.

Copper was important for coinage, for cannons, and for more general purposes. Early in the seventeenth century, Sweden was Europe's biggest supplier. However, as early as 1620, the idea was first aired of bringing copper from Japan, copper being one of the staples of Japan's export trade. In 1624, the Dutch East India Company ordered between 91 and 136 metric tons of copper in annual shipments. This trade reached its peak in 1672–75, when Japanese copper imports to Europe were equivalent to between one-third and one-half of Swedish exports. For the years 1671–75, Dutch imports were equivalent to 30% of Japan's exports of copper (Glamann 1958: 175). Although Japanese copper figured on the Amsterdam price lists between 1669 and 1688, the copper trade with Europe was secondary to Japan's exports to the Asiatic factories of the Dutch East India Company.

Two other commodities are worthy of special note. Before 1600, a highly competitive trade in cloth was already established within Europe. Indian, and subsequently Chinese, cloth then became a major component, especially Indian cotton goods. According to Glamann, these imports had their heyday in the second half of the seventeenth century:

Large quantities of cheap Indian cloth were sold in Europe... in the second half of the seventeenth century, not only for clothing, especially underclothing, handkerchiefs and the like, but also for such domestic uses as bedspreads, curtains and so on. (Glamann 1977: 205)

Peak imports amounted to over 2 million pieces for England and about one-tenth that level for Holland (Harrison 1961: 400).

In the following century, another overseas import made its mark:

The circulation of crockery and porcelain expanded very markedly in the eighteenth century upon the introduction into the European market of large quantities of Chinese wares. (Glamann 1977: 203)

These trades became so important that several words have passed into everyday usage in European languages. "Muslin" is the term for high-quality, light-weight cotton fabrics, originally from Mosul, situated on the upper reaches of the Tigris River in Iraq, whereas "calico" describes a thicker cotton fabric from Calicut in southwest India. A third example is the use of "china" to denote good-quality tableware.

In his study of trade between Asia and Holland, Glamann (1958: 13) tabulates the value of cargoes dispatched from Asia and also of sales in Amsterdam. By 1698–1700, spices and pepper had been displaced from their leading position by textiles, silks, and cottons, which together accounted for over half the value of goods consigned westward. A further 22% was accounted for by tea and coffee, drugs and dyestuffs, saltpeter and metals. In other words, the bulk of the trade was in manufactures, raw materials, and exotic beverages, and was much more prosaic than is conjured by the shorthand term, the "spice trade."

Imports of both cotton goods and china became so large and sustained that European entrepreneurs sought ways to manufacture equivalent goods that would compete in both quality and price. Delft in Holland and Stoke-on-Trent in England became early centers of this import and reexport substituting manufacture of chinaware, just as Lancashire cottons replaced the Indian trade in textiles. In both industries, import and reexport substitution proved to be a major element in the Industrial Revolution pioneered in England and Europe.

Trade in the Asiatic Realm

At the time of direct European contact by sea, much of Asia, and especially India, China, and Japan, were far ahead of Europe in many of the material aspects of civilization. Indeed, as Fairbank et al. (1973: 243) put it: "...the expansion of the Europeans reflected not only their greed, curiosity, zeal and patriotism but also in some ways their backwardness." McNeill (1983) attributes Asia's lead, at least in part, to the dramatic technological changes that occurred in China from about A.D. 1000, the associated commercialization of China's economy, and the rapid expansion of trade that occurred throughout the Asiatic realm. For example, as early as 1078, some 127,000 metric tons of iron were made in China, with the aid of coke, at a time when the population was about 100 million – giving 1.3 kilograms per person.

China's influence had waned prior to the European incursion, and something of a power vacuum existed. Nevertheless, quite extensive regional trading systems continued and thrived in which basic commodities were integral. A picture of what was going on can be pieced together, though only in broad outline (e.g., Chaudhuri 1985; Curtin 1984; Spate 1979). Of key importance was Japan, if only as the major source of silver in which trade could be settled. However, silver supplies were inadequate. The Europeans had virtually no manufactures that tempted Asian buyers. On the other hand, the silver of the New World was as acceptable as any other, and this silver reached Asia either via Europe or directly across the Pacific. Equipped with silver, Europeans could enter the marketplace to buy silks, spices, and porcelain, some of which reached Europe from the west, and some via central America, where trans-shipment was necessary.

Ships' manifests and traders' records allow glimpses of the Asiatic trade into which European traders locked, showing two things of particular interest in the present context: (1)

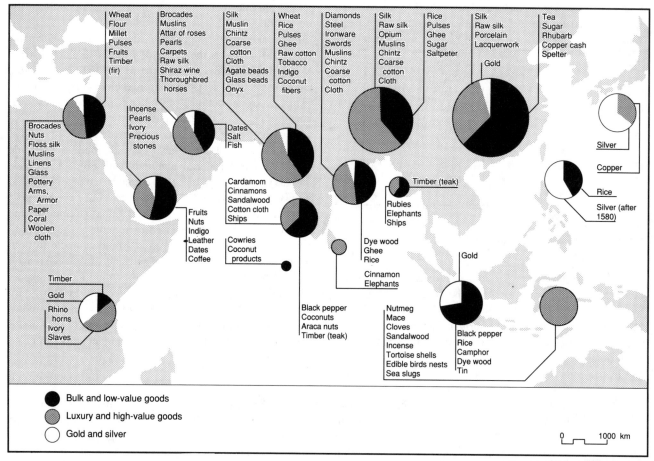

Figure 6.1 Main regional exports of Afro-Asia before 1750. *Source:*
Chaudhuri 1985: 186–87.

European purchases were not confined to luxury items, and
(2) much Asiatic trade was in the staples of life.

The first of these points is illustrated by an example given
by Borah (1954: 117). In 1582, a vessel arriving at Callao
(Peru) from Manila had on board, in addition to silks,
porcelain, and spices, a quantity of iron. The second point has
been documented by Chaudhuri (1985).

Figure 6.1 reproduces a map from Chaudhuri that demonstrates the wide range of goods that entered Asiatic
trade before 1750. In private correspondence, I asked Prof.
Chaudhuri whether he could supply a scale for the pie-graphs,
as a guide to absolute as distinct from relative quantities;
unfortunately, the nature of the raw data does not permit
this. However, some flesh can be put on these bare bones for
Makassar, a port near the southern end of the southwest
peninsula of Sulawesi (formerly Celebes). According to
Chaudhuri's map, this island was a source of luxury and high-
value goods. Nevertheless, in the early part of the seventeenth century, prior to seizure by the Dutch in the 1660s, the
indigenous trading system had the following characteristics:

The economic base was partly entreport trade, but South Sulawesi
also produced a rice surplus that was shipped to the Malukus, to
Timor and Solor in the Lesser Sunda Islands, and even to northern
Australia. Timor and Solor produced sandalwood, in great demand
in China for incense. Spices went to China and westward toward
India and Europe. Since the voyage from Makassar to Timor, or to a
port like Ternate in the Spice Islands, was just over 1000 kilometres,

this was trade in high-bulk, low-value commodities over a considerable distance. (Curtin 1984: 160–61)

Simkin (1968: 256) also remarks on the same point, noting the
"short distance" trade in rice, dates, dried fish, fruits, and
vegetables; Malaya and Indonesia frequently needed to import rice to compensate for poor harvests. From the 1630s
onward, trade between China and Siam expanded rapidly,
based on the sale of such Chinese manufactures as porcelain
and silk in exchange for Siamese rice and timber (Curtin
1984: 168). Finally, the Chinese and Arab scholars who
recorded the conditions of their time:

. . . knew perfectly well that the staple products of the trading regions
entered the flow of long-distance exchange as much as did the luxury
goods. These commodities did not share the prestige in possession
conferred by the latter, but each writer took pains to describe the
main agricultural crops and their role in trade. (Chaudhuri 1985: 191)

The trade networks extended far inland. According to
Steensgaard (1973; see also Curtin 1984), a unique document
records every transaction by an Armenian trader between
1682 and 1693. One Hovannes was based in New Julfa
(Isfahan) in Iran. During the period in question, he traveled
through India, Nepal, and Tibet as far as Xining in China.
The key characteristic of this trading journey can be described
thus:

Where trade by sea a century or so ago had been essentially a peddling trade, where the merchant had to travel with his goods, this was no longer required. Hovannes was able to send goods back and forth to his principals in New Julfa without actually making the trip himself. Money had been easy to transfer in Mughal India since the late sixteenth century. (Curtin 1984: 196)

Furthermore, in making his extensive journeys, Hovannes was able to travel from one group of Armenian merchants to another, or to merchants known to the Armenians – a fact that indicates the established nature of the long-distance overland trading systems.

There can be little doubt that throughout the Asiatic realm the European interlopers found extensive and well articulated trading systems that were handling basic commodities as well as luxuries. What we do not know is the aggregate volume of trade or the relationship of that trade to the volume of production. In the case of Portugal's pepper trade with southwest India during the first decade of the seventeenth century, the minimum annual output in the producing region was 12,900 metric tons, of which only 10% was shipped to Europe. The remaining 90% entered the regional trade of Asia (Disney 1978: 36). More generally, there is sufficient evidence of extensive trade in basic commodities as well as luxuries, over land and by sea, to suggest that the impact of the expansion of demand, in Europe first and then elsewhere, was to increase the scale and the scope of commerce, and thereby the degree of separation between production and consumption. But a significant degree of separation had existed for a long time before the Industrial Revolution.

Latin America

The arrival of the Europeans in Latin America led to the rapid decline of indigenous trading systems (Chapman 1957). In the present context, therefore, both the regional and trans-Atlantic trading systems are European creations. We are apt to picture this traffic as being dominated by the silver from Peru and Mexico, the sugar of Brazil and the Caribbean, tobacco, and the westward traffic in slaves. Although these were of inestimable importance, to concentrate on these commodities is to lose sight of much of the reality. Portugal's initial expansion into the Atlantic, to Madeira and the Azores, was triggered in part by shortages of wheat and timber. Subsequently, although the New World could not supply wheat until much later, timber quickly became one of the principal exports from Brazil to Portugal (Mauro 1960). Furthermore, in the early years of European conquest and settlement, all the basic necessities of life had to be shipped to the colonists – wine, olive oil, flour, soap, and nails (Chaunu 1955–1959; Connell-Smith 1950; Fuentes 1980; Mauro 1960; Pike 1966; Sanz 1979; 1980). According to Borah (1970: 724), the largest fleet sailing from Spain to the New World occurred in 1608, with, it is estimated, 45,720 metric tons of general wares. The volume of the westward traffic was, therefore, considerable.

Given the considerable costs of transporting goods across the Atlantic and overland to their final destination in the Americas, local production and manufacture of the necessities and luxuries of life quickly began. Within the Spanish realm,

Mexico soon emerged as the main center for this import-substituting manufacturing, in particular to supply goods to the main silver-producing center – Peru. Thereby was established the basis for regular sailings between Mexico and Peru, traffic that matured by 1550 and remained fairly stable until 1585 (Borah 1954). However, toward the end of the sixteenth century, goods from China, Japan, and elsewhere in the Orient began to move eastward across the Pacific, dwarfing the established intercolonial traffic. By 1728–42, this Pacific traffic had become so extensive that Guzmán-Rivas (1960) devotes four pages to listing the items unloaded at Acapulco. He categorises the items as follows:

Food, preserves, spices, etc.
Raw materials
Manufactured items
Jewelery, ornaments, etc.
Furniture, wood pieces, etc.

The raw materials included iron; the main manufactures were textiles.

It is abundantly clear, therefore, that although silver, sugar (and subsequently other plantation crops), and slaves provided the basis for European trade with and within Latin America, considerable quantities of prosaic goods also were shipped across the Atlantic and the Pacific from very early times. In this respect, there are close parallels with the Asiatic trade, which we have already considered.

Africa

For the present purpose, I will confine myself to three main points. Trans-Saharan trade began as early as 1000 B.C. and has continued to the present day, albeit on a diminished scale and now using lorries instead of camels (Hopkins 1973). Between the eleventh and seventeenth centuries, West Africa was the main supplier of gold to the international economy, and all of it found its way northward across the Sahara. For a time, Seville in Spain became the main European center for dealing in gold. In addition to this precious metal, many other goods were traded across the desert, contributing to the fortunes of Timbuctoo, Kano, and other major cities.

With European penetration along the coasts of Africa from the fifteenth century, contacts with the inhabitants were limited almost entirely to the coastal trading posts, until the nineteenth century. As is well known, the primary European interest was to purchase slaves for the American plantations, and along the West African coast slaves were the main export until the abolition of this traffic provided the incentive to seek other export commodities – the Ashanti cocoa growers being the most notable example. So for the Europeans, Africa remained a largely unknown continent until very recently.

Nevertheless, within Africa there were extensive trading systems, of a wholly indigenous nature and also linking to the trans-Saharan commerce and the coastal slaving traffic. Hopkins (1973) provides ample evidence for the scale of these trading links, which have been especially carefully documented in the case of desert salt (Lovejoy 1986). Thus, as Fieldhouse (1973: 133) put the matter:

...Africans in most parts of the coast were commercially minded, had long specialized in the Saharan trade or the slave trade, and were very willing to co-operate with Europeans. For example, the Jack-Jacks on the Ivory Coast and the Brassmen in the Oil Rivers can best be described as political groups organised as professional middlemen; and elsewhere larger states, such as Dahomey and Benin, were prepared to control and profit by transit trades, whether in slaves or [vegetable] oil. So long as the power and efficiency of these African organizations survived it was obviously expedient for the European merchant to come to terms with them.

Ballast

Seaborne trade presents the problem that some legs of the voyage may have to be undertaken in the absence of a full cargo. Even if a full cargo is available, it may not provide the requisite trim. Therefore, to maintain seaworthiness, ballast must be taken on board. If possible, this ballast should be saleable, to provide some revenue. To meet this need, low-value and bulky commodities can be transported, often over great distances. For example, Glamann (1971: 39) refers to the considerable scale of manufacture in Holland of ballast wares – flagstones, tiles, and bricks. In the Asiatic realm, Chaudhuri (1985: 191) refers to the transport of dressed stone in the same manner, and also black pepper from Indonesia and Malabar. One of the more remarkable examples is provided by some of the islands off southwest Norway. Stripped of their soils by glacial action, farmland was created by the transport of Dutch soil as ballast in Norwegian sailing vessels returning home (E. Boulding, at a meeting held at Friiberghs Herrgard, Sweden, January 1986). It seems likely that the scale of traffic in ballast of all kinds prior to the Industrial Revolution was considerably greater than the scanty extant records might suggest.

The Growth of International Trade in the Nineteenth and Twentieth Centuries

Many countries have kept good records of their international freight transactions (visible trade) for a very long time. In contrast, information about intranational goods traffic is patchy and incomplete, so that we are not able to assess, on a global scale, the relative importance of international and intranational freight movements. As an example, however, Great Britain in 1969 may be cited. By any standard, Britain has a very open economy; in 1969, foreign trade (the sum of imports plus exports) amounted in value to 41% of the gross domestic product. For the same year, the tonnage of international freight was equivalent to only 12% of the tonnage of goods moved inland (Chisholm and O'Sullivan, 1973: 20; see also Pitfield, 1978: 668). Most other economies are much less dependent on international trade. Therefore, it seems likely that, for the world as a whole, the volume of international visible trade (imports plus exports) measured in tonnage terms is less – probably much less – than 10% of the volume of inland freight movements.

On the other hand, given that trading circuits have been expanding, freight movements that were formerly intranational in scope have become international, and consequently recorded in the international trade data. Therefore, international trade data will exaggerate the temporal growth in

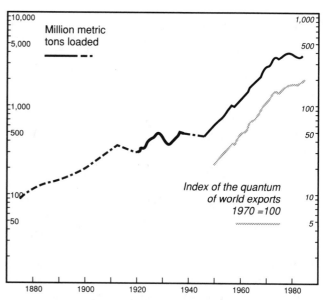

Figure 6.2 Growth in the tonnage of seaborne international freight and of the quantum of world trade. (1) Million metric tons of freight (left-hand scale). (2) Quantum of world exports, 1970 = 100 (right-hand scale). *Sources:* Farnie 1969: 754; G.A.T.T. 1986: Table A1; *United Nations Statistical Yearbook*, various issues.

trade, merely because a growing proportion of total traffic has been recorded as consignments that now cross international frontiers, whereas previously they did not.

The Tonnage of Trade

Figure 6.2 shows the growth in tonnage of international seaborne freight since 1875. So far as I am aware, comparable data for the sum of railway, inland waterway, road, pipeline, and air traffic are not available, and therefore it is difficult to know whether seaborne freight provides an adequate index of total movements.[1] However, as Fig. 6.2 shows, the index of the quantum of world trade has behaved in a manner very similar to the tonnage of international seaborne freight, so it seems reasonable to believe that the behavior of the one yardstick is a good guide to the other.

The tonnage of international seaborne freight has been increasing much faster than world population. For the year 1900, world population has been variously estimated at be-

Table 6-4 *Tonnage of Seaborne International Freight in Relation to World Population, 1950–1984*

Year	World population (millions)	Freight (million metric tons)	Freight per person (kilograms)
1950	2,516	550	219
1960	3,019	1,100	364
1965	3,335	1,670	501
1970	3,693	2,605	705
1975	4,076	3,072	754
1980	4,450	3,676	826
1984	4,760	3,415	717

Source: As for Fig. 6.2, and United Nations 1987: 131.

tween 1,550 million and 1,668 million (Clark 1967: 108; Clarke 1965: 147); by 1984, the total had reached 4,760 million (United Nations 1987: 131). Meantime, freight increased from 182 million metric tons (in 1899) to 3,415 million in 1984. Thus, somewhat over 100 kilograms were moved for each inhabitant at the beginning of this century, compared with about 700 kilograms at the present time. Most of this increase has occurred since World War II; in 1950, international seaborne freight amounted to about 220 kilograms per inhabitant – barely two-sevenths of the figure subsequently reached in less than three and one half decades (see Table 6-4). However, in recent years, this growth has faltered, and there actually has been a small decline in the tonnage per person.

The Value of Trade

The evidence cited in the previous section implies that national economies have become, and continue to become, more "open." However, this inference is only partially correct. According to *The Times* (London) (1978: 256), the value of world trade (imports plus exports) was 3% of world output in 1800, rising to 33% in 1913. The latter figure is comparable to that given by Nurkse (1961: 13). The classic studies of Kuznets (1966), Maizels (1963), and Yatès (1959), supplemented by Robinson's (1954) study of Britain, indicate that most of the increase in trade relative to output had occurred by about 1870 or 1880. Furthermore, these studies show that between the two world wars, visible trade declined sharply as a proportion of world output. Since World War II, the relative importance of trade has recovered to near the level of 1913; according to data published by G.A.T.T. (1986: 139) and the World Bank (1986: 155), the global trade proportion in 1984 was 30.5%.

Two recent papers have explored this history in some detail (Beenstock and Warburton 1983; Grassman 1980). The picture that emerges is much affected by the choice of current or constant values. Grassman argues that over a long period, it is more useful to use current values – a view with which I concur. His data are broadly comparable with the figures cited earlier. Over the period 1875–1975, the ratio of trade to GNP, for a selection of countries, has certainly *not* increased in a dramatic manner. There was some increase for Italy and Norway, but a decline for Great Britain, Sweden, Denmark, and the United States. In every case except the United States, there was a sharp increase in the relative importance of trade after 1945, to reach levels in the 1970s comparable to those of 1913.

The Commodity Composition of Trade

Figure 6.3 shows that for both agriculture and manufacturing, world export volumes have risen consistently faster than the respective output volumes over the entire period 1950–85, although the manufacturing sector has expanded more quickly than agriculture. Minerals and fuels present a different picture. Until 1973, exports were rising more rapidly than output. Although production continued to rise until 1979, since then output has fallen somewhat; exports fell much more sharply, declining to the 1970 level by the mid-

1980s. In its 1986 report on trade, G.A.T.T. refers to the relatively slow growth in the share of agricultural output that is traded internationally, compared with the change for manufactures. Representative data are shown in Table 6-5. Given the persistence of the trends shown for agriculture and industry in Figure 6-3, notwithstanding the 1973–74 and subsequent oil-price shocks and the post-1979 recession, it seems likely that the global trade proportion will continue to increase to levels markedly above the 1913 level. To an increasing extent, however, this global trade proportion will be trade in manufactures rather than in primary produce.

Table 6-5 *International Trade Volume As a Percentage of World Output (Selected goods)*

	Primary products			Manufactured goods[1]		
	Rice	Wheat	Sugar	Steel	Passenger cars	Trucks
1961–65	3.0	20	33	9	18	14
1970–75	2.7	19	30	14	30	18
1980–83	3.0	22	31	20	39	33

Source: G.A.T.T. 1986: 35.
[1] Data refer to 1963, 1973, and 1983.

In his perceptive Wicksell lectures, delivered in 1959, Nurkse (1961) was one of the first scholars to draw attention to the unique characteristic of nineteenth-century international trade, when the demand for primary produce was

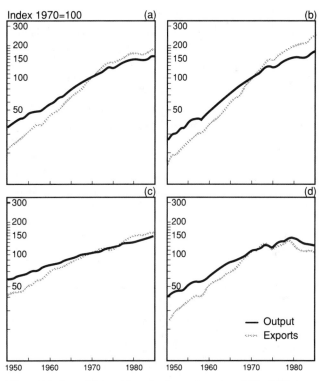

Figure 6.3 Growth in world production and exports, 1950–1985; 1970 = 100. (a) total; (b) manufactures; (c) agriculture; (d) minerals.
Source: G.A.T.T. 1986: Table A1.

Table 6-6 *World Merchandise Exports by Commodity Class and Trade Areas, 1984*

	Percentage distribution			
Commodity class	Developed countries	Developing areas	Eastern trading bloc	World
Food	10.8	13.5	7.2	11.1
Raw materials	3.4	3.5	5.0	3.6
Ores and minerals	1.6	2.3	1.8	1.8
Fuels	7.8	46.8	30.3	19.8
Nonferrous metals	2.3	1.8	1.6	2.1
Total primary products	25.9	67.9	45.9	38.4
Iron and steel	4.3	1.6	3.8	3.6
Chemicals	10.8	2.8	5.9	8.3
Other semimanufactures	5.4	2.9	2.2	4.4
Engineering products	42.8	12.5	28.6	33.8
Textiles	2.8	3.0	2.8	2.8
Clothing	1.6	4.5	2.9	2.5
Other consumer goods	4.9	4.2	3.0	4.5
Total manufactures	72.6	31.5	49.4	59.9
Others	1.5	0.6	4.7	1.7
Total	100.0	100.0	100.0	100.0
Billion dollars f.o.b.	1,231.60	465.00	210.00	1,906.60

Source: G.A.T.T. 1986: Table A12.

the major "engine of growth" for many countries. Primary produce accounted for over three-fifths of world exports throughout the last quarter of the nineteenth century and up to 1937 (Yates 1959: 37). In contrast, as Table 6-6 shows, primary goods accounted for less than two-fifths of world trade in 1984. The comparison is affected by changes in classification, but the transformation shown is nevertheless real and not an artifact of the rules governing the statistics. While it is true that primary commodity exports are more important for the developing areas than for the developed countries (67.9% and 25.9%, respectively), the difference is almost entirely attributable to petroleum. With the exception of petroleum supplies, the less developed nations collectively have ceased to be preeminently suppliers of raw materials to the industrial nations. The petroleum-exporting nations are generally highly dependent on the one export, and some other countries – mostly quite small – are also highly specialized in one or two primary export commodities. A fundamental shift in world trading patterns has occurred since 1945, and looks likely to be consolidated in the oncoming decades (see Moore 1985).

The Evolution of Trade Theory

If there have been dramatic changes in world trading patterns over the past 300 years, there have been equally striking developments in the way commerce is conceptualized. While it would be wrong to present the evolution of theory as a linear progression, some fundamental themes are easily recognizable. First, does the world have a finite stock of resources and goods, such that trade is essentially a zero-sum game? If so, there will be both gainers and losers. Or are we faced

with a nonfinite situation, in which case there may be either (1) gainers and losers or (2) all gainers, but possibly (probably) in different proportions? Is trade to be regarded as essentially benign for all parties, or does it provide a mechanism whereby some are exploited by others? It is with these questions in mind that we will review briefly the evolution of ideas concerning the reasons for, and the advantages to be gained from, trade.

In the days of Mercantilist thought, prior to the publication of Adam Smith's *The Wealth of Nations* in 1776, it was widely held that trade was essentially a zero-sum game, that overseas possessions were to be exploited for the benefit of the metropolitan nation, and that the primary object of trade was to increase the national stock of specie. Adam Smith, building on the work of earlier theorists, challenged these ideas in a number of ways. Directly, he argued that it was both wrong and impossible for Britain to try to rein in the development of the American colonies (the United States and Canada). He also adumbrated the division of labor and the importance of the size of the market, with the clear implication that labor resources are not finite. And he articulated the idea that trade should be based on differences in production costs, in the version we now know as the doctrine of absolute advantage. Thereby, he visualized that incomes could rise from their then-present levels, but that the natural resource base set an upper limit to the level that incomes could reach. Thus, although total resources were conceived to be finite, the world of Adam Smith was well within those limits, and trade would provide a mechanism for achieving the income levels that were realizable.

Forty-one years later, David Ricardo formulated the more powerful concept of comparative advantage. This provides a rationale for trade between two countries when one has an absolute advantage in both (all) the commodities involved. Ricardo laid the foundation for all subsequent mainstream economic theorizing on trade. Until the early 1950s, trade theory was dominated by the assumption that technology remains fixed and unchanging. Since then, additional reasons for trade have been accepted, arising from recognition of the fact of technical change.

The first major development from Ricardo's comparative advantage theorem is associated with Heckscher, Ohlin, and Samuelson, whose contributions spanned the period 1914–49 (see Greenaway 1983). Although Ricardo had hinted that "artificial" advantages might be important, he clearly had considered trade to arise from "natural" advantages such as location, climate, and mineral resources, which would affect the productivity of labor and capital. The theorem developed by the three twentieth-century scholars, known as the factor proportions theorem, asks the following question: even if factor productivity is identical in various nations, can trade between them nevertheless arise? If labor and capital must be combined in the production process, if each commodity has its own production function, if production functions are identical in both (all) countries, trade will arise if the endowment of labor and capital varies between nations. These differential initial endowments are taken as given.

In two seminal papers, Leontief (1953; 1956) sought unsuccessfully to substantiate the factor proportions trade theorem. His lack of success stimulated a serious rethinking of the reasons for trade. Attention began to focus on the previously neglected fact that technical change and development is ongoing. As Nurkse (1961: 34) put it:

No useful purpose is served by continuing to discuss matters of trade and development on the classical assumption of a constant stock of productive factors.

Product and process innovations are a continuing feature of the world economy, and the quality of fixed capital and human capital is being improved. Therefore, although the factor-proportions explanation for comparative advantage remains valid as *one* explanation for trade, it is clearly inadequate as a complete account.

In the present context, four main features of technical change as it relates to trade should be noted. The most general concept is that of the technology gap, advanced by Posner (1961). Subsidiary aspects of this idea are the product cycle (Vernon 1966), product differentiation, and scale economies. Over many years, Balassa has drawn attention to the role of intrasector trade arising from the nonhomogeneity of products, and according to Greenaway, Adam Smith's ideas regarding scale economies have entered trade theory only in the late 1970s, although this attribution ignores the explicit treatment given by Ohlin (1933) and others to this topic.

Two things deserve emphasis in the tradition that has been outlined in the previous paragraphs. First, manmade, or artificial, advantages are now accorded a place, alongside "natural" advantages, as a basis for trade. This raises the important question, which so far as I know has not been adequately addressed, regarding the relative importance of the manmade advantages in trade compared with the advantages that accrue from natural resource endowments. Second, whatever the ultimate limits to growth set by the availability of natural resources, the fact that artificial advantages are now recognized implies that trade need not be viewed as a zero-sum game, if, indeed, that was ever an appropriate concept.

A third matter is of considerable importance. It appears possible that technical change will continue apace for the foreseeable future and that manufacturing will provide an increasing share of world output and trade. With product differentiation, larger amounts of embodied labor, and continuing economy in the use of materials to achieve desired ends, the scope for long-distance trade will continue to expand. Whereas in the nineteenth century this increasing scope crucially depended on transport innovations and the reduction in transport costs, for the present and the future, it is the rising unit value of goods that will be the key enabling factor. As Fig. 6.3 shows, world output and trade in manufactures is expanding much faster than the two primary commodity sectors. The worldwide trade proportion, which has regained the level approximately of 1913, is therefore likely to continue to grow, for a combination of reasons:

1. There are still considerable gains to be had from the static comparative advantage–factor proportions reallocation of production and trade for countries at the earlier stages of development.

2. The increasing relative importance of manufacturing, and technical change in this sector, implies widening scope for trade, as well as constant shifts in the comparative advantage of nations.

Trade Equals Exploitation?

Dependency analysts consider that the arguments just presented are wrong. Two versions of these ideas are relevant in the present context. The more general idea is that the terms on which international trade is conducted are systematically biased, so that a net transfer of resources occurs from the poorer to the richer nations. The mechanism whereby this is said to occur is that of "unequal exchange," which is portrayed as a characteristic of the capitalist mode of production. Stripped of the jargon, the "theory" of unequal exchange is a derivative of the labor theory of value, and says no more than that the productivity of labor varies from one nation to another (Chisholm 1982: 70–71). As a consequence, when two countries engage in trade, the goods obtained from the high-productivity economy will embody fewer hours of direct work than the compensating flow from the low-productivity nation.

A variant of the exploitation thesis casts multinational companies as villains. The driving force for these companies, it is said, is the maximization of profits, which are transferred to the location that gives the greatest fiscal advantages, in order to maximize the value of profits retained. Such firms will have no compunction in transferring their productive facilities from one location to another if they perceive more profitable opportunities – often equated with wages that are lower for a given level of labor efficiency. This view depends on the absence of countervailing powers that will modify the behavior of multinational companies. Since 1945, especially in the exploitation of minerals and fuels, most governments all over the world have sought to put the screws on multinational companies, with a view to extracting better terms. The final sanction, expropriation, has been used. Although it may well be the case that too small a proportion of the benefits from development has been and is retained by the host countries, the balance undoubtedly has shifted toward the host nations, and may well shift further.

Epilogue

The nature of the material that has been reviewed is such that to treat the final paragraphs as a "conclusion" would be inappropriate. Instead, it seems more suitable to consider if any general implications, arising from the fact of increasing separation between the location of production and consumption, can be discerned.

In this essay we have shown that for the greater part of humanity – from 1687 and much earlier – trade in basic commodities has been the norm rather than the exception. The past 300 years have seen a very great increase in the absolute and per-person volumes of freight movement. At the same time, the proportion of freight moving over substantial distances has almost certainly increased considerably. The

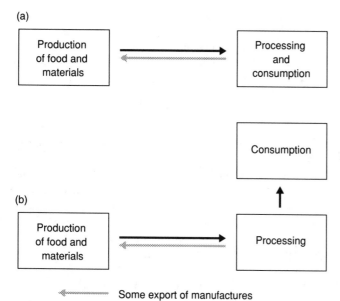

(a)

(b)

Some export of manufactures

Figure 6.4 Schematic representation of changing trading patterns.

fact of separation between production and consumption is not the important one; the primary issue is the magnitude of the separation and what it implies. As far as the quantitative changes go, two main periods can be distinguished. The first lasted until World War I, and was dominated by the expansion of primary produce-supply zones, primarily to provision Britain and mainland Europe. At the same time, trade in manufactures expanded, but primary produce accounted for about three-fifths of international trade in the late nineteenth century. The second clearly defined period dates from the end of World War II, and is marked by the very fast increase in the output of and trade in manufactures, such that primary produce now accounts for less than two-fifths of world trade. This recent change in the character of the separation of consumption from production is probably every bit as important as the quantitative change that has occurred over the past 300 years, and especially since 1945.

These changes can be represented schematically, as in Fig. 6.4. Prior to the Industrial Revolution – and for a considerable time thereafter – the dominant pattern was that shown as (a). Basic materials were exported to the main manufacturing centers, which in turn were the principal centers of consumption, though exporting manufactures to pay for the primary produce. As industrial output grew, the flow of primary produce increased in volume and extended geographically. Now, manufacturing has become considerably more economical in the use of resources, a very wide range of primary produce may be needed for the manufacture of an article, albeit in small quantities, and finished products are becoming more heterogeneous in character. As a consequence, a greater proportion of trade has the character portrayed as (b) in Fig. 6.4. The evidence we have cited suggests that this shift will continue. Because international trade is increasingly of the character (b) rather than (a), further increases in the trade proportions will not necessarily be matched by an equivalent further separation between the

point of initial production of primary goods and the point at which they are consumed.

For the purpose of argument, we could propose that "precontact" societies, living in equilibrium with the resources provided by their environments, treated those environments in ecologically sensitive and responsible ways. Superficially, such a proposition makes sense. At one level, it is of course a tautology, in that the concept of equilibrium implies the maintenance of the system and all subsystems. Setting that semantic problem aside, it may be presumed that a society that is "close to nature" will understand the ecology of its environment and will exploit it in a conserving way. Against this image we can set innumerable examples of the devastation wrought by uncaring and/or ignorant exploitation of resources for commercial gain. It is believed by some that serious desertification occurred along the North African littoral zone 2,000 years ago in response to grain cultivation to feed Rome. The Dust Bowl catastrophe that occurred in the United States between the two World Wars, immortalized in Steinbeck's *The Grapes of Wrath*, is something every school child is taught. And the destruction that is currently going on in Amazonia as the rain forest is cleared makes somber reading.

But this antithesis is flawed, since it ignores a whole range of variables, not least the fact that for over 300 years very few societies have been immune to internal and external pressures for change, of which trade is but one. Four sets of consideration must be taken into account:

1. What is the rate of change?
2. What time-scale is considered by the relevant decision makers?
3. Who are the decision makers?
4. With what knowledge of the implications of development and with what ability to rectify ill effects are the decision makers equipped?

All four of these sets of considerations have been, and continue to be, subject to change.

We have no objective way in which to measure the overall rate of change, although probably a consensus exists that change has been accelerating, and will continue so to do. If this is indeed the case, it carries the implication that mistakes may occur and inadvertent damage to ecosystems be caused. Whether or not this happens, and how generally, will depend on the interaction of time scales on which the decision makers operate, the framework of financial and legal incentives and constraints within which they work, and the knowledge they possess. Two quite general trends appear to be relevant in this context. On the one hand, the scale of multinational operations has been growing dramatically, both in absolute and relative terms. It can be argued that multinationals are primarily, if not exclusively, interested in maximizing their overall profitability and that profits are transferred from the overseas operations to company headquarters. Hence, it may be argued that multinationals feel no sense of responsibility for the welfare of the host country. On the assumption that multinationals operate with "hypermobile" capital, they will move elsewhere as and when it suits them. This view of the multinational company implies that there are zero, or near-zero, costs in moving operations from site to site, or from country to country – an implication that is implausible. Even if the view taken by multinationals cannot be described as long term, it certainly extends beyond one or two years. For the extraction of minerals and fuels, a relatively short-term view is often appropriate, geared to the life of the deposits. However, it is notable how the mining companies concentrate their attentions on countries with reasonable prospects of political stability, because there must be some certainty about recouping the considerable capital expenditure. In any case, multinationals are increasingly involved in the manufacturing sector, in which the cost of establishing an operation is far from zero. Thus, however true it may be that multinational companies are constantly reviewing the spatial disposition of their operations, their freedom to relocate is constrained in some degree by purely commercial considerations.

At least as important has been the establishment of sovereign nations in former colonial possesions and the general evolution of concepts and practices concerning the role of governments. Notwithstanding the substantial disengagement in economic activities upon which several countries have embarked since the late 1970s, the general and long-term trend is for governments to assume more rather than fewer powers. Therefore, the freedom that an individual, a national company, or a multinational company has to pursue self-interested ends is limited in some degree by the legislative and fiscal framework within which they operate. In no way is this a new phenomenon; whether absolute monarchies or elective democracies, governments have always been concerned about raising revenue and fostering that which is deemed to be in the national interest. For example, Queen Elizabeth I of England sought to preserve the supply of oak trees suitable for building ships for the navy.

To an increasing extent, therefore, we must consider the role of governments in creating and maintaining a suitable legal and fiscal framework within which individuals and companies operate. Given the interdependence of the world economy, this will necessarily involve collaboration between governments to complement national provisions. In practice, sustainable use of the environment will depend on an evolving consensus that will be based on the interplay of scientific investigation and practical experience, plus political horse-trading.

In general, humankind's scientific capability has improved greatly and will continue to improve. This means that the ability to predict the effects of particular forms of exploitation and to devise remedial measures where these are necessary is improving rapidly. Therefore, we may make the following proposition: if the increasing separation of production and consumption implies that there are greater risks that ecologically unsound practices will be employed, the growth of scientific knowledge provides the potential to find partial or complete remedies. To the extent that these remedies may depend on the intervention of governments, either directly or indirectly, governments have an interest and a duty to foster the requisite science and to ensure that they are equipped to follow good scientific advice.

These remarks lead me to my final comment. The significance of the increasing separation of production and consumption is not a matter that can be treated in *a priori* terms, in isolation from other changes. To examine the interaction of overall rates of change, the role of decision makers, the role of governments, the level of scientific knowledge, and how all of them interact with the production-consumption system in its spatial dimension, would require extended discussion that is beyond the scope of this paper and also beyond my competence.

Acknowledgments

I am deeply grateful to the organizers of the ET Symposium for the challenge they presented by asking me to prepare this paper. Although the reading that I did was fascinating, it leaves me aware that I have but scratched the surface. An early draft was read by Judith Shackleton, and I am indebted both for the helpful comments and the encouragement that she gave me. In addition, the draft as prepared for the symposium elicited very helpful comments from several readers; these comments have in varying degree been incorporated in the revised version. In particular, I am indebted to: Ron Abler, Alan Baker, K. N. Chaudhuri, Robin Donkin, David Fieldhouse, and John Richards. However, to the extent that there are errors of commission or omission, mine alone is the responsibility. I am also indebted to Mike Young for preparing the illustrations and to Maria Constantinou and Alison Chalkley for their patience in converting my manuscript into clean typescript.

Note

1. Historical data series are available for many countries in official publications, such as *Historical Statistics of the United States, Colonial Times to 1970*, U.S. Department of Commerce, Bureau of the Census. Much of the data has been collated by Mitchell (1981; 1982; 1983). However, although railway traffic is generally well documented, inland-waterway data are much less complete. More important, although good data exist for the number of road vehicles, information on the amount of work done by road hauliers is available for a limited number of countries and generally only since World War II, notwithstanding that already by 1939 road-freight transport was very significant. Indeed, Mitchell does not even attempt to collate the existing data on tonnage and ton-km of road freight. To analyze the available information on inland transport by all modes, including air freight and pipelines, would be a major undertaking, but necessarily would be incomplete.

References

Beenstock, M., and P. Warburton. 1983. Long-term trends in economic openness in the United Kingdom and the United States. *Oxford Economic Papers* 35: 130–35.

Bennett, M. K. 1954. *The World's Food. A Study of the Interrelations of World Populations, National Diets and Food Potentials*. New York: Harper and Brothers.

Borah, W. 1954. *Early Colonial Trade and Navigation between Mexico and Peru*. Berkeley: University of California Press.

———. 1970. Latin America 1610–60. In Vol. IV, *The New Cambridge Modern History*, ed. J. P. Cooper, 707–26. Cambridge: Cambridge University Press.

Boserup, E. 1981. *Population and Technology*. Oxford: Blackwell.

Braudel, F. 1982. *Civilization and Capitalism 15th–18th Century*. Vol. II, *The Wheels of Commerce*. London: Collins.

Chapman, A. C. 1957. Port of trade enclaves in Aztec and Maya civilizations. In *Trade and Market in Early Empires: Economies in*

History and Theory, ed. K. Polanyi, C. M. Arensberg, and H. W. Pearson, 114–53. New York: The Free Press.

Chaudhuri, K. N. 1985. *Trade and Civilization in the Indian Ocean. An Economic History of the Rise of Islam to 1750*. Cambridge: Cambridge University Press.

Chaunu, H., and P. Chaunu. 1955–59. *Seville et l'Atlantique (1504–1650)*, 8 vol. Paris: Travaux et Memoires de l'Institut des Hautes Etudes de l'Amerique Latine.

Chisholm, M. 1961. Agricultural production, location and rent, *Oxford Economic Papers* 13: 342–59.

———. 1962. *Rural Settlement and Land Use. An Essay in Location*. London: Hutchinson.

———. 1966. *Geography and Economics*. London: Bell.

———. 1979. Von Thünen anticipated. *Area* 11: 37–39.

———. 1982. *Modern World Development. A Geographical Perspective*. London: Hutchinson.

Chisholm, M., and P. O'Sullivan. 1973. *Freight Flows and Spatial Aspects of the British Economy*. Cambridge: Cambridge University Press.

Clark, C. 1967. *Population Growth and Land Use*. London: Macmillan.

Clark, C., and M. Haswell. 1970. *The Economics of Subsistence Agriculture*, 4th ed. London: Macmillan.

Clarke, J. I. 1965. *Population Geography*. Oxford: Pergamon Press.

Connell-Smith, G. 1950. English merchants trading to the New World in the early sixteenth century, *Bulletin of the Institute of Historical Research* xxiii: 53–67.

Curtin, P. 1984. *Cross-Cultural Trade in World History*. Cambridge: Cambridge University Press.

Darby, H. C. 1961. In *The New Cambridge Modern History*. Vol. I, *The Face of Europe on the Eve of the Great Discoveries*, 20–49, ed. G. R. Potter. Cambridge: Cambridge University Press.

Disney, A. R. 1978. *Twilight of the Pepper Empire. Portuguese Trade in Southwest India in the Early Seventeenth Century*. Cambridge, MA: Harvard University Press.

Durand, J. D. 1977. Historical estimates of world population: an evaluation, *Population and Development Review* 3: 253–96.

Fairbank, J. K., E. O. Reischauer, and A. M. Craig. 1973. *East Asia: Tradition and Transformation*. London: Allen and Unwin.

Farnie, D. A. 1969. *East and West of Suez: the Suez Canal in History*. Oxford: Clarendon Press.

Fieldhouse, D. K. 1973. *Economics and Empire 1830–1914*. Ithaca, NY: Cornell University Press.

Fuentes, L. G. 1980. *El comercio Espanol con America 1650–1700*. Seville: Escuela de Estudios Hispano-Americanos de Sevilla.

General Agreement on Tariffs and Trade. 1986. *International Trade 85–86*. Geneva: G.A.T.T.

Glamann, K. 1958. *Dutch-Asiatic Trade, 1620–1740*. Copenhagen: Martinus Nijhoff.

———. 1971. *European Trade 1500–1750*, Fontana Economic History of Europe. London: Collins.

———. 1977. The changing patterns of trade. In *The Cambridge Economic History of Europe*. Vol. V: *The Economic Organization of Early Modern Europe*, ed. E. E. Rich and C. H. Wilson, 185–289. Cambridge: Cambridge University Press.

Gras, N. S. B. 1915. *The Evolution of the English Corn Market from the Twelfth to the Eighteenth Century*. Cambridge, MA: Harvard University Press.

Grassman, S. 1980. Long-term trends in openness of national economies, *Oxford Economic Papers* 32: 123–33.

Greenaway, D. 1983. *International Trade Policy. From Tariffs to the New Protectionism*. London: Macmillan.

Guzmán-Rivas, P. 1960. Geographic influences of the galleon trade on New Spain, *Rivista Geografica* XXVII: 5–81.

Harrison, J. B. 1961. In *The New Cambridge Modern History*. Vol. V, *Europe and Asia: The European Connection with Asia*, 398–416, ed. F. L. Carsten. Cambridge: Cambridge University Press.

Hopkins, A. G. 1973. *An Economic History of West Africa*. London: Longman.

James, M. K. 1951. The fluctuations of the Anglo-Gascon wine trade during the fourteenth century. *Economic History Review*, 2d ser. IV: 170–96.

———. 1971. *Studies in the Medieval Wine Trade*. Oxford: Clarendon Press.

Kindleberger, C. P. 1956. *The Terms of Trade: A European Case Study*, New York: MIT Press/Wiley.

Kuznets, S. 1966. *Modern Economic Growth. Rate, Structure and Spread*, New Haven, CT: Yale University Press.

Latham, A. J. H. 1978. *The International Economy and the Underdeveloped World 1865–1914*. London: Croom Helm.

Leontief, W. 1953. Domestic production and foreign trade: the American capital position re-examined. *Economia Internazionale* 7: 3–32.

———. 1956. Factor proportions and the structure of American trade: further theoretical and empirical analysis. *Review of Economics and Statistics* 38: 386–407.

Lewis, W. A. 1970. *Tropical Development 1880–1913: Studies in Economic Progress*. London: Allen & Unwin.

Lovejoy, P. E. 1986. *Salt of the Sun. A History of Salt Production and Trade in the Central Sudan*. Cambridge: Cambridge University Press.

McNeill, W. H. 1983. *The Pursuit of Power*. Oxford: Blackwell.

Maizels, A. 1963. *Industrial Growth and World Trade. An Empirical Study of Trends in Production, Consumption and Trade in Manufactures from 1899–1959 with a Discussion of Probable Future Trends*. Cambridge: Cambridge University Press.

Malenbaum, W. 1953. *The World Wheat Economy 1885–1939*. Cambridge, MA: Harvard University Press.

Mauro, F. 1960. *Le Portugal et l'Atlantique au XVIIe Siècle (1570–1670)*. Paris: École Pratique des Hautes Études.

Mitchell, B. R. 1981. *European Historical Statistics 1750–1975*, 2d ed. London: Macmillan.

———. 1982. *International Historical Statistics. Africa and Asia*. London: Macmillan.

———. 1983. *International Historical Statistics. The Americas and Australasia*. London: Macmillan.

Moore, L. 1985. *The Growth and Structure of International Trade Since the Second World War*. Brighton: Wheatsheaf Books.

North, D. C. 1968. Sources of productivity change in ocean shipping, 1600–1850. *Journal of Political Economy* LXXVI: 953–70.

Nurkse, R. 1961. *Patterns of Trade and Development*. Oxford: Blackwell.

Ohlin, B. 1933. *Interregional and International Trade*, rev. ed. 1967. Cambridge, MA: Harvard University Press.

Peet, R. 1969. The spatial expansion of commercial agriculture in the nineteenth century: a von Thünen interpretation. *Economic Geography* 45: 283–301.

Peet, R. 1972. Influences of the British market on agriculture and related economic development in Europe before 1860. *Transactions*. Institute of British Geographers 56: 1–20.

Pike, R. 1966. *Enterprise and Adventure. The Genoese in Seville and the Opening of the New World*. Ithaca, NY: Cornell University Press.

Pitfield, D. E. 1978. The volume of internal and external trade: is Britain a closed economy? *Regional Studies* 12: 665–82.

Polanyi, K. [1944] 1975. *The Great Transformation*. New York: Octagon Books.

Posner, M. V. 1961. International trade and technical change, *Oxford Economic Papers* 13: 323–41.

Price, J. M. 1970. In *The New Cambridge Modern History*. Vol. VI, *Economic Activity: The Map of Commerce*, 1683–1721, 834–74, ed. J. S. Bromley. Cambridge: Cambridge University Press.

Robinson, E. A. G. 1954. The changing structure of the British economy, *Advancement of Science*, 182–93.

Sanz, E. L. 1979 and 1980. *Comercio de España con America en la Epoca de Felipe II*, 2 vol. Valladolid: Servicio de Publicaciones de la Diputacion Provincial de Valladolid.

Simkin, C. G. F. 1968. *The Traditional Trade of Asia*. Oxford:

Oxford University Press.

Slicher van Bath, B. H. 1963. *The Agrarian History of Western Europe A.D. 500–1850*. London: Arnold.

Spate, O. H. K. 1979. *The Spanish Lake*. London: Croom Helm.

Steensgaard, N. 1973. *Carracks, Caravans, and Companies: The Structural Crisis in the European-Asian Trade in the Early seventeenth Century*. Copenhagen: Scandinavian Institute of Asian Studies.

The Times. 1978. *Times Atlas of World History*. London: *The Times*.

United Nations. 1987. *Demographic Yearbook 1985*. New York: United Nations.

Usher, A. P. 1913. *The History of the Grain Trade in France 1400–1700*. Cambridge, MA: Harvard University Press.

Vernon, R. 1966. International investment and international trade in the product cycle. *Quarterly Journal of Economics* 80: 190–207.

de Vries, J. 1974. *The Dutch Rural Economy in the Golden Age, 1500–1700*. New Haven, CT: Yale University Press.

Wallerstein, I. 1974, 1980. *The Modern World System*, 2 vols. New York: Academic Press.

Wilkinson, R. G. 1973. *Poverty and Progress. An Ecological Model of Economic Development*. London: Methuen.

Wilson, E. M. C. 1933. The Icelandic trade. In *Studies in English Trade in the Fifteenth Century*, ed. E. Power and M. M. Postan, 155–82. London: Routledge.

Woodruff, W. 1966. *Impact of Western Man. A Study of Europe's Role in the World Economy, 1750–1960*. London: Macmillan.

World Bank. 1986. *World Development Report 1986*. New York: Oxford University Press.

Wrigley, E. A. 1962. The supply of raw materials in the industrial revolution. *Economic History Review* XV: 1–16.

Yates, P. L. 1959. *Forty Years of Foreign Trade. A Statistical Handbook with Special Reference to Primary Products and Underdeveloped Countries*. London: Allen & Unwin.

7

Urbanization

BRIAN J. L. BERRY

How has the concentration of the world's population in urban settlements changed in the past 300 years? Where and when has urban growth occurred, and why? What has happened to the distribution of cities by size? The first purpose of this chapter is to answer these questions by laying out the evidence on urban growth since 1700.

Has this urbanization resulted in environmental change? Is further urbanization likely to do so in the years ahead? Neither the social nor the physical sciences have answered these questions, yet the broad outlines of an answer certainly can be sketched. Until the middle of the twentieth century, urbanization levels were too low and the number of large cities was too small for there to be anything other than local climatic and hydrologic impacts. To the extent that urbanization produced environmental modification, it was in urban-centered gradients of agricultural land use and mineral and forest exploitation as urban demands diffused into the surrounding countryside. As late as 1900, there were barely 43 cities in the world exceeding 500,000 population, of which only 16 exceeded 1,000,000.[1] But since 1950, the number of large cities has increased very rapidly – close to 400 now exceed 1,000,000. Sprawling metropolitan areas have formed even larger agglomerations, and some very large urban regions with populations in the tens of millions have emerged. The question that arises in these cases is whether or not changes in the biosphere are unfolding at a regional scale that, in turn, might have global impacts. There is little to suggest that historic urban developments were active agents in climatic change. There is significant evidence that the modern metropolis has climatic and hydrologic consequences that increase with city size and urban densities. There is at least the suggestion that these consequences may be compounded at a regional scale in the largest agglomerations. But if our analysis is correct, regional-scale impacts may be more likely in the years ahead in Third World nations, where very large urban agglomerations are emerging, rather than in the most economically advanced countries, where a transformation is unfolding that is resulting in dispersed and relatively low-density urban networks. The very regions in which environmental alterations are most likely are those regions in which increasing shares of the world's population are concentrating.

Urbanization in 1700: City-Centering of World Economies

The world of 1700 was largely agrarian. Urban populations were less than 10% of the whole. Yet in Fernand Braudel's view, this world was divided into a number of *city-centered world economies*: "economically autonomous sections of the planet able to provide for most of their own needs, sections to which their internal links and exchanges gave a certain organic unity" (Braudel 1984: 22). World economies, he said, centered on *world cities* that were in perpetual political and economic rivalry with each other, some rising and some falling. Each world city was surrounded by an immediate *core region* within which modification of the earth was greatest, a fairly developed *middle zone*, and a vast and relatively untouched *periphery* (Braudel 1984: 39). The core contained the concentration of everything that was most advanced and diversified, lying at the heart of the middle zone, the settled area of the state.

Thus, in the seventeenth century, Amsterdam was the "warehouse of the world" and the United Provinces were the middle zone. In this zone, urbanization levels rose to more than 30% (Wrigley 1987: 183); a high degree of agricultural specialization in cash crops for both the urban consumer and the industrial market developed; agriculture became close to gardening; ingenious methods of crop rotation were developed that were also to transform the English agricultural landscape; new drainage technologies were developed that enabled Holland's cultivable area to be increased and the British fenland to be settled; and the new middle-class spirit of Protestantism linked to capitalism was fostered, carrying with it associated ideas of man's dominion over nature. The closer to Amsterdam, the greater the degree of cash-crop specialization and the greater the extent of environmental modification to support agricultural development. The pattern was universal: the further from the world city, the less the clearance of the woodlands for ships' timbers, fuelwood, and

Table 7-1 *Urban Centers of the World Economies in 1700*

France		Britain-Holland	
Paris	550,000	London	550,000
Lyon	97,000	Dublin	80,000
Marseille	75,000	Edinburgh	35,000
Rouen	63,000	Norwich	29,000
		Bristol	25,000
		Amsterdam	210,000
		Leiden	56,000
		Rotterdam	55,000
		Haarlem	48,000
		The Hague	36,000

Ottoman Empire		Spanish Empire	
Constantinople	700,000	Naples	207,000
Cairo	175,000	Palermo	124,000
Smyrna	135,000	Milan	113,000
Adrianople	85,000	Madrid	105,000
Damascus	70,000	Seville	80,000
Aleppo	67,000	Brussels	70,000
Bursa	60,000	Antwerp	67,000
Mecca	50,000	Mexico City	85,000
Baghdad	50,000	Potosi	82,000
Bucharest	50,000	Puebla	63,000
Belgrade	40,000		
Salonika	40,000		

German States		Portugal	
Hamburg	63,000	Lisbon	188,000
		Oporto	23,000

Austria		Russia	
Vienna	105,000	Moscow	114,000
Prague	48,000		

China		Japan	
Peking	650,000	Yedo	688,000
Hangchow	303,000	Osaka	380,000
Canton	200,000	Kyoto	350,000
Sian	167,000	Kanazawa	67,000
Soochow	140,000	Five more over	50,000
Nanking	140,000		
Wuchang	110,000	Korea	
Kingtehchen	100,000	Seoul	158,000
Niaghsia	90,000	Pyongyang	55,000
12 more over	50,000		

Moghul Empire		Persia	
Ahmedabad	380,000	Isfahan	350,000
Aurangabad	200,000	Tabriz	75,000
Dacca	150,000	Qazvin	60,000
Srinagar	125,000		
Patna	100,000	Siam	
Benares	75,000	Ayutia	150,000
Agra	70,000		
Delhi	60,000		

Source of data: Chandler 1987.

farming. The more the city grew, the more intense the modification of the core and the wider the ring of diffusion into the middle zone. Furthest from the world city was the periphery, "with its scattered population, representing on the contrary backwardness, archaism, and exploitation by others" (Braudel 1984: 39; also Wallerstein 1974).

Tertius Chandler's statistics provide graphic evidence of the city-centeredness of Europe's world economies of 1700 (Chandler 1987; see also Table 7-1). What is impressive is both the sharpness of the primacy of most of Europe's world cities, many times the sizes of the other towns within their world economies, and the smallness of the capitals themselves, even though they accounted for a large share of the total urban population. Europe's six significant world economies centered on physically compact world cities that ranged in population from 200,000 to 700,000. Their surrounding core regions were equally small, as were the zones of active environmental modification.

This pattern was repeated elsewhere in the world. In China, new Manchu rulers had by 1700 restored the state apparatus of the Ming Dynasty. The Ching state (1644–1911), managed by competitively selected literati, engaged in economic planning to assure adequate supplies and effective distribution of foodgrains, presiding over a flexible market structure linking urban areas to the rural economy. Water management for both irrigated agriculture and transportation was one of the central administration's main duties, and was the measure of the efficiency of the state (Wittfogel 1957). The key component of the Chinese urban system was the establishment of a capital city – the emperor's seat and supreme political and spiritual authority of the empire – dominating and controlling the entire kingdom and concentrating the power of the bureaucracy. Beneath the capital city was an echelon of military-administrative centers, and beneath them the *Hsien* (county) capitals, which fulfilled the administrative roles of tax collection, military garrison, and dispensing public functions (Eisenstadt and Shachar 1987: 130).[2]

Similarly, in India, the Mogul Empire had been firmly established under the rule of Akhbar (1556–1605), who instituted a well organized central administration that was the cornerstone of governance over the next centuries and the basis of primate-city dominance. A similar dominance was evidenced in Japan even before reunified national political authority was asserted during the Tokugawa Shogunate (17th to 19th centuries). Japan's major cities were not simply political-administrative centers, but also centers of trade, tightly controlled by wholesale and retail monopolies and by the guilds.[3] As in Europe, Asian world cities and the *ecumene* were small. The world urban map of 1700 was nearly empty. Only 5 cities exceeded 500,000 population, and only 34 exceeded 100,000.

Beyond Europe and Asia, in Central and South America, the largest urban places were those of the Spanish and Portuguese empires. Outside the Ottoman Empire, the largest of Africa's cities were Muslim – Algiers, Fez, Meknes, Tunis, and Sale-Rabat exceeded 50,000 in the Mahgreb, whereas the principal south Moslem centers were Katsina, Kazarganu, and Zaria. Only Oyo reached 50,000 in Black Africa. A few small dots on the map contained the majority of the world's urban population (Fig. 7.1).

Eighteenth-Century Quickening: Britain Emerges

The first example of urban-led economic growth that brought urbanization levels above 10% was that of the Nether-

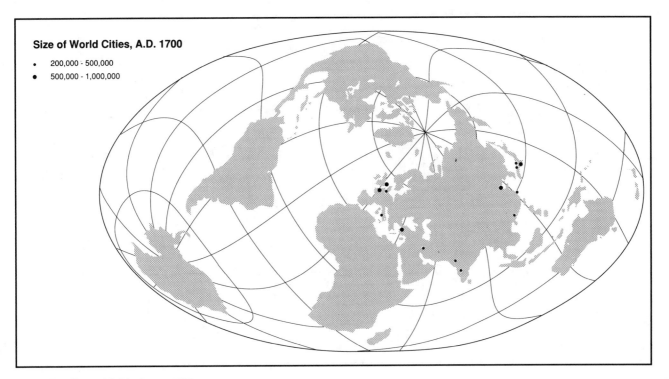

Figure 7.1 The world cities in A.D. 1700.

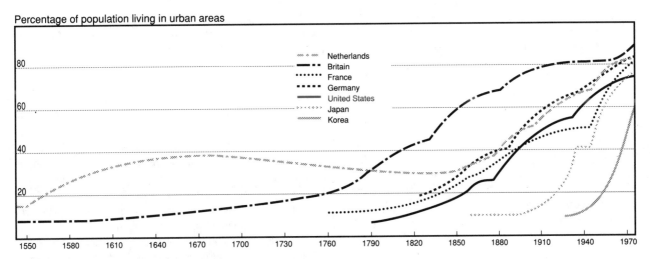

Figure 7.2 Changing levels of urbanization, 1550–1980: The
Netherlands, Britain, the United States, France, Germany, Japan,
and Korea.

lands from the early sixteenth century through their great age
of economic supremacy in the seventeenth century (Braudel
1984; DeVries 1981; also see Fig. 7.2). The next example was
that of Britain, whose navies and trading companies established their ascendancy during the eighteenth century as
European nation-states reached outward to expand their world
economies, establishing colonial outposts to exploit the resources of the peripheries and setting in motion the expansion
of pioneer settlement frontiers. Radiating outward, there
were waves of clearance, drainage, conversion, and extraction, with the extent of environmental modification – of
human dominion over nature – patterned by gradients of

accessibility to the world cities. London grew to be the largest
city in Europe. Its food market radically changed the agri-
cultures of the Kentish and East Anglian core. Its wealthy
merchants bought country estates and hired the landscape
gardeners who created England's rural landscape. The wealthy
merchant classes of the core became the principal dissenters
who set in motion Europeans' drive to master the North
American wilderness. Yet by 1800, the world's urban map
had scarcely changed (Fig. 7.3). Chandler's statistics show
that the number of cities in the world with greater than
500,000 population had increased only from 5 to 6 and that
the number of additional places exceeding 100,000 had in-

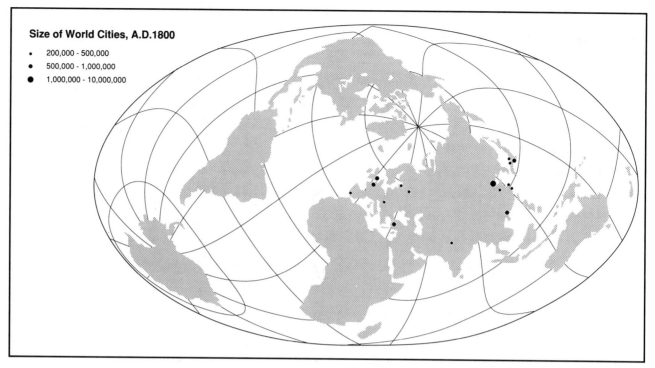

Figure 7.3 The world cities in A.D. 1800.

Table 7-2 *Changes in City-Size Distributions, 1700–1975*

	Numbers of Cities Exceeding Specified Sizes (population in thousands)					
	>100	>200	>500	>1,000	>10,000	>20,000
1700[a]	34	14	5			
1800[a]	50	17	6	1		
1900[a]	287	142	43	16	1	
1950[b]	950	N.E.	179	76	N.E.	
1975[a]	N.E.	N.E.	422	191	7	1
2000[b]	1,699	N.E.	859	440	N.E.	N.E.

[a] Adapted from Chandler 1987: 521.
[b] United Nations 1980.
N.E.: not estimated.

creased only from 29 to 44 (Tables 7-2 and 7-3).

In contrast to the stationary state of Holland in the eighteenth century, it was Britain's growth that had been quickening. As a result, the urbanization of the population had been increasing since the mid-seventeenth century. But the pattern still was one of world-city concentration as mercantile expansion took place. Britain's urban percentage rose from 8.25% in 1600 to 17.0% in 1700, and London's share of the national population increased from 5% to 11.5% (Wrigley 1987: 163), justifying James I's fear that "soon London will be all England." The concentration of Britain's urban population in London increased from 60% in 1600 to 67% in 1700. The city's net population increase of 275,000 from 1650 to 1750, at a time when its death rates exceeded its birth rates, was achieved by absorbing the natural increase of a population of 5 million people, in which the surplus of births over deaths was 5 per 1,000 per annum (Wrigley 1987: 135–36). Capital-city concentration was a feature not only of English urban growth; during the eighteenth century fully 80% of European urban growth took place in its capital cities (DeVries 1981: 88).

It was Britain that first broke with the pattern of world-city urban concentration. From 1700 to 1800, the degree of urbanization in England increased from 17.0% to 27.5%, but London's share of the national population remained constant at around 11.0%, while its share of the urban population dropped from 67% to 40%. Urban growth accelerated outside London, with the main burst of expansion occurring in the last quarter of the century in such cities as Manchester, Liverpool, Birmingham, and Glasgow, and a second echelon in the 20,000-to-50,000 range that included Leeds, Sheffield, Newcastle, Stoke, and Wolverhampton. The English share of European urban growth had been 33% in the seventeenth century, but was over 70% in the second half of the eighteenth century (Wrigley 1987: 177), and this increased share was concentrated outside London in the newly industrializing north.

This was, of course, the initial wave of the Industrial Revolution, brought about by major advances in the cotton and iron industries, the first flush of factory building, significant improvements in waterborne transportation, and also colonial policies that systematically destroyed Indian cotton-textile production and guaranteed imperial markets to Lancashire's producers. As a result of the quickening of growth, there were already heavy pressures on land use for bread grains and pasturage early in the century, to which one response was the Enclosure Movement. There was need for timber for shipbuilding, oaks for the Royal Navy, and wood

Table 7-3 *Major Cities in the World Economies of 1800*

Britain[a]		British Empire		Portugal		Austria-Hungary	
London	861,000	Lucknow	240,000	Lisbon	237,000	Vienna	231,000
	(959,000)	Murshidabad	190,000	Oporto	67,000	Venice	146,000
Dublin	165,000	Benares	179,000			Prague	77,000
Glasgow	84,000	Hyderabad	175,000	**Holland**			
Edinburgh	82,000	Patna	170,000	Amsterdam	195,000	**Russia**	
Manchester	81,000	Calcutta	162,000	Rotterdam	60,000	Moscow	248,000
	(89,000)	Bombay	140,000			St. Petersburg	220,000
Liverpool	76,000	Surat	120,000	**Ottoman Empire**			
	(83,000)	Madras	110,000	Constantinople	570,000	**Japan**	
Birmingham	71,000	Dacca	106,000	Smyrna	125,000	Yedo	685,000
	(74,000)			Damascus	90,000	Osaka	383,000
				Adrianople	80,000	Kyoto	377,000
France				Aleppo	72,000	Nagoya	92,000
Paris	547,000					Kanazawa	71,000
Lyon	111,000	**French Empire**		**Chinese Empire**			
Bordeaux	92,000	Cairo	186,000	Peking	1,100,000	**Marathas and Rajputs**	
Marseille	83,000			Canton	800,000	Delhi	140,000
Rouen	80,000			Hangchow	387,000	Ujjain	100,000
Nantes	70,000			Soochow	243,000	Ahmedabad	89,000
				Sian	224,000	Baroda	83,000
Spain				Kingtehchen	164,000	Jodhpur	75,000
Madrid	182,000	**Spanish Empire**		Wuchang	160,000	Bharatpur	75,000
Barcelona	113,000	Mexico City	128,000	Tientsin	130,000	Nagpur	74,000
Seville	96,000	Manila	77,000	Foshan	124,000		
Cadiz	87,000			Chengdu	97,000	**Burma**	
				Langchow	90,000	Amarapura	175,000
Italian States				Changsha	85,000		
Naples	430,000	**German States**		Ningpo	80,000	**Korea**	
Rome	142,000	Berlin	172,000	Kaifeng	80,000	Seoul	194,000
Palermo	135,000	Hamburg	117,000	Hsuchow	75,000	Pyongyang	68,000
Milan	122,000	Warsaw	75,000				

Source: Chandler 1987.

[a] The alternative populations placed in parentheses are those appearing in Wrigley 1987: 160.

ash for the alkalies used in the bleaching process by the textile industry. But above all, an energy shortage afflicted the economy at midcentury, calling forth the key inventions of Cort and Watt: the development of a substitute (coal) for progressively scarcer wood (the production of 10,000 tons of charcoal-iron required the felling of 40,000 hectares of forest; Wrigley 1987: 79); the need to drain the coal mines (steam engine); and the need to transport the coal (canals). Coal output increased in Britain from 3 to 10 million tons in the eighteenth century, particularly in the northeast, with easy access by sea to the London market.

The origins of the factory system were in another crisis: the shortage of spinners to supply the hand-loom weavers. The water frame and spinning jenny came into use in the 1770s. Water-powered scribbling mills were introduced in the 1780s, taking over the tasks of teazing and carding, but they were as dispersed as the weaver-crofters. It was only after 1800 that factory production concentrated on the coal fields, rivers, and canals; when steam began to replace the power of the overshot water wheel; and when the scribbling mill, the power mule, the dyehouse, the fulling mill, the warehouse, and the cropping shop were incorporated under a single roof. Only then did industrial urbanization begin in

earnest, coal-field-oriented, with housing developments confined to walking distance of the mills, and it was reinforced after the turn of the century by the railroad and the steamship.

Long Waves of Industrial Urbanization

The late-eighteenth-century burst of industrial growth was concentrated in Britain, and ended in the sharp depression that followed the Napoleonic Wars and the War of 1812. From initial acceleration to a peak in 1792, followed by a turnaround into deceleration to depression, the wave of growth lasted about 55 years. This 55-year pattern has been repeated three more times in modern history. Each growth upswing quickened urbanward migration; each slowdown was followed by a lower rate of urban growth. From the 1820s on, the rhythms were sharpest in the United States, where the urbanward migrants came not only from America's farms, but from Europe too. The waves of emigration to the New World that increased in good times and decreased in bad times flattened the 55-year rhythms of European urban growth.

Urban growth, of course, has two components: natural increase and net migration. It is in urbanward migration that the 55-year long-wave rhythmicity of urban growth is revealed. If this rhythmicity is compared with the long swings of

Average annual growth rate (percent)

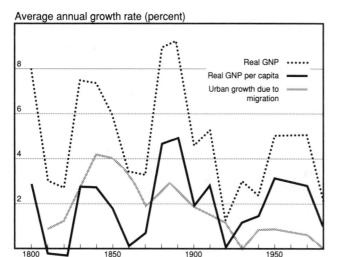

Figure 7.4 Long waves of economic growth and urbanward migration in the United States, 1790–1980.

economic growth (as measured by the average annual growth rates of real GNP and of real GNP per capita), it is clear that the urbanward migrants were simply responding to economic opportunity; the waves of urban growth in the United States were sympathetic and somewhat lagged responses to waves of economic growth (Fig. 7.4). Each burst of economic growth called forth a rush of urbanward migrants and raised the level of urbanization.

It was the Soviet economist Nikolai Kondratiev who first drew attention to the 55-year-long-wave phenomenon (Kondratiev 1935; like all such ideas, this one had antecedents, for example van Gelderen 1913). As enriched by growth theorists such as Schumpeter (1934), the theory of long waves centers on the role of key innovations that become the leading sectors in growth. In the eyes of these theorists, clusters of innovations produce accelerated expansion until markets are saturated; there is then a recessionary turning point, acceleration turns to deceleration, and deceleration turns to stagnation and collapse in a depression. Venture capitalists then look for new sources of profit, investing in new technologies that become the leaders for the next wave of growth. The span from depression to depression averages some 55 years.

Following this argument, the late-eighteenth-century growth that was Britain's alone (the "first Kondratiev") was sparked by innovations in the water-powered textile industries. Britain's second wave of growth (the "second Kondratiev") was coal-based and steam-powered, marked by mechanization of the textile factories, initial railroadization, and the growth of the iron industry. It was in this wave that Britain became the "workshop of the world" and the center of the Atlantic economy. Around 1830, jerry-builders hit upon an ingenious house design that could save both land and building materials and that produced increasing urban concentration – the back-to-back house. Built in double rows under a single roof, with a standpipe for water supply at the end of the streets and a couple of earth closets devoid of privacy for each 150 people, this design could cram large numbers of houses into small

spaces, without either sunlight or ventilation. The result was "...the despair of medical officers...(with) a mortality rate greater by 15 or 20 percent...the absence of a general system of sewerage, the imperfect conditions of the streets and roads, the confined courts, the open middens and cesspools, stagnant ditches and insufficient water supply" (F. Tillyard, quoted in Aldridge 1915).

It was apparent that the new urbanization was creating unhealthy environments – environments that persisted long into the twentieth century and were responsible for the growth of the modern public health and urban planning professions. Even in 1913 in Birmingham

200,000 people were housed in 43,366 buildings of the back-to-back type already long condemned or injurious to health because of lack of ventilation. In the worst six wards, from 51 percent to 76 percent were back-to-backs. Even more serious was the fact that 42,020 houses had no separate water supply, no sinks, no drains, and 58,028 no separate w.c., the closets being communal and exposed in the courts. This meant that over a quarter of a million people lived in cavernous conditions. The real objection to back-to-back houses lies not so much in their method of construction as in the degrading and disgusting condition of their out-buildings, which frequently made decency impossible and inevitably tended to undermine the health and morals of the tenants (Bourneville Village Trust 1941: 16).

There was lagged emulation of both the best and the worst of Britain's second-Kondratiev growth, in which factory chimneys and smoky atmospheres were the mark of progress. Victorian England became the hub of a worldwide economy. Liverpool and Manchester became the first noncapital cities in the world ever to rival in size the capital cities of the world empires. Railroadization and both industrial and urban growth diffused outward, finally reaching the world's furthest peripheries late in the twentieth century (Berry, Conkling, and Ray 1987: 415–16).

As the Victorian boom began in Britain, the first wave of United States industrial and urban growth also took place, but it was predominantly water-powered (Fig. 7.5; Borchert 1967); this was the epoch in which the northeastern mill towns grew. Only toward the end did the railroads and the iron industries expand. It was not until after the Civil War that the locus of initiative shifted to the United States and to continental Europe as the leading growth regions (Fig. 7.6). Urban growth rates in Britain slowed down, and were further depressed by the magnitude of emigration. It was the third Kondratiev that was the principal epoch of coal-based steam power in the United States (later supplemented by gas and electricity), of steel rails and ships, and of the growth of the chemical industry. New steel-frame technologies enabled urban densities to be increased by going upward at the same time that the balloon frame enabled rapid construction of workers' housing further outward. New communications technologies enabled the head office to be separated from the factory floor, and the office skyscraper core of the modern central business district was born. Large-scale mass production gave rise to the essence of urbanization, "a process of population concentration" (Tisdale 1942), characterized by increasing size of cities, increasing population densities, and the increasing heterogeneity of their immigrant populations

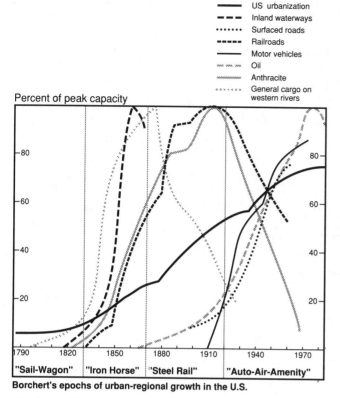

Figure 7.5 Changing levels of urbanization in the United States compared with the dominant mode of transportation, 1790–1980.

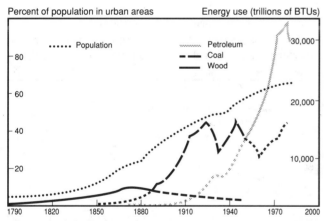

Figure 7.6 Dominant sources of energy compared with the level of urbanization, 1790–1980.

the present century is the concentration of population in cities" (Weber 1899: 1). Chandler's statistics reveal a fivefold increase in the cities exceeding 125,000 population and an eightfold increase of those exceeding 500,000 between 1800 and 1900 (Table 7-2). The ancient Asian urban hierarchies of 1800 were replaced by a map dominated by major cities within Northern-hemisphere industrial regions, linked by overseas gateways to colonial empires (Fig. 7.7).

Britain's urban map was dominated in 1900 by nine major cities and a constellation of smaller industrial towns:

London	6,480,000
Manchester	1,435,000
Birmingham	1,248,000
Glasgow	1,015,000
Liverpool	940,000
Newcastle	615,000
Leeds	430,000
Sheffield	402,000
Edinburgh	400,000

Eight urban complexes marked out Germany's industrial heartland:

Berlin	2,707,000
Hamburg	895,000
Ruhrgebiet	766,000
Dresden	540,000
Leipzig	532,000
Munich	499,000
Cologne	437,000
Breslau	427,000

Paris (3,330,000) still dominated France, but Lyon (508,000) and Marseille (410,000) had grown. Barcelona (552,000) now rivaled Madrid (539,000) in Spain, and Italy's first wave of industrialization had seen the rise of Milan (491,000), alongside Naples (563,000) and Rome (438,000). And instead of small mercantile centers on the eastern seaboard of North America in 1800, there now was the northeastern manufacturing belt marked out by major urban centers:

New York	4,242,000
Chicago	1,717,000
Philadelphia	1,418,000
Boston	1,075,000
St. Louis	614,000
Pittsburgh	562,000
Baltimore	508,000
Cincinnati	417,000

Standing in a dependent relationship to this heartland, radiating out across the national landscape, were resource-dominant regional hinterlands. But whereas within the United States the resources of the hinterlands had been brought within the nation's boundaries during the course of the nineteenth century by purchase and conquest, many of Europe's resource hinterlands were parts of overseas empires, and major cities had grown at the points of colonial penetration. To be sure, San Francisco (439,000) was a gateway to the West, but in the zones of active European settlement in the

(Wirth 1938). Radiating rail lines and omnibuses, originally horse-drawn but soon steam- (and later electric-) powered, first enabled owners and managers (and later the workers) to commute to residences beyond the confusion and smoky atmospheres of the concentrated core. By the end of the nineteenth century, the modern metropolis as we know it had been born.

When, in 1899, he wrote his monumental study *The Growth of Cities in the Nineteenth Century*, Adna Ferrin Weber concluded that "the most remarkable social phenomenon of

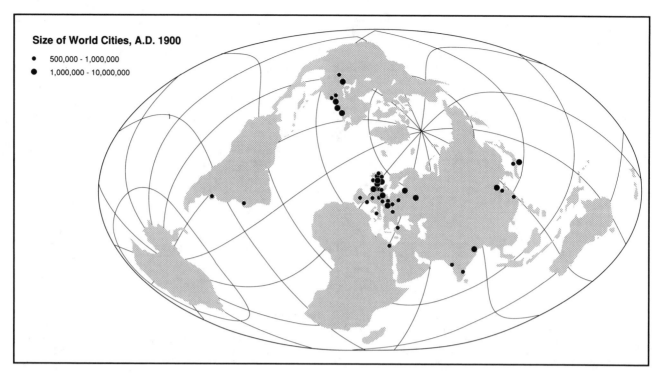

Figure 7.7 The world cities in A.D. 1900.

Southern Hemisphere, comparable gateway cities included Buenos Aires (806,000), Rio de Janeiro (744,000), Melbourne (485,000), and Sydney (478,000). Cairo's growth (595,000) reflected the flow of world commerce through the Suez Canal. Calcutta (1,085,000), Bombay (780,000), and Madras (505,000) were the gateways through which British Imperial domination of India was exercised, and even though Peking (1,100,000) remained China's largest city, external influence through Tientsin (700,000), Shanghai (619,000), Canton (585,000), and Hankow (480,000) dictated the dissolution of that imperial system. The balance of the world's urban map in 1900 was the more familiar one of the centers of the world empires: Europe's other capitals had grown [St. Petersburg (1,439,000), Moscow (1,112,000), Constantinople (900,000), Warsaw (724,000), Brussels (561,000), Amsterdam (510,000), and Copenhagen (462,000)]; and Tokyo (1,497,000) and Osaka (970,000) were still dominant in Japan; but there was a great gulf between them and lesser cities within their regions.

As impressive as these numbers may be, the change had not yet produced any truly urbanized societies, save perhaps Great Britain. Only 43 cities in the world exceeded 500,000 population in 1900, although 16 of them were now more than a million. Barely ten nations had more than 25% of their populations living in urban centers of more than 10,000 people in 1900 (Great Britain, Belgium, the Netherlands, Germany, France, the United States, Turkey-in-Europe, plus Australia, Argentina, and Uruguay) – a level of urbanization that was surpassed in 1985 by all but a few of the very poorest of the world's nations (Figs. 7.8 and 7.9).

What was significant about late-nineteenth-century growth was not that it urbanized the world, but that it produced a new scale and texture of world empires: the heartland (core)

and hinterland (periphery) pattern of regional specialization in which multiechelon hierarchies of urban places played the critical structuring role. In the United States this involved the concentration of big cities in the northeastern manufacturing belt, the great heartland nucleation of industry and the national market, the focus of large-scale national-serving industry, the seedbed of new industry responding to the dynamic structure of national final demand, and the center of high levels

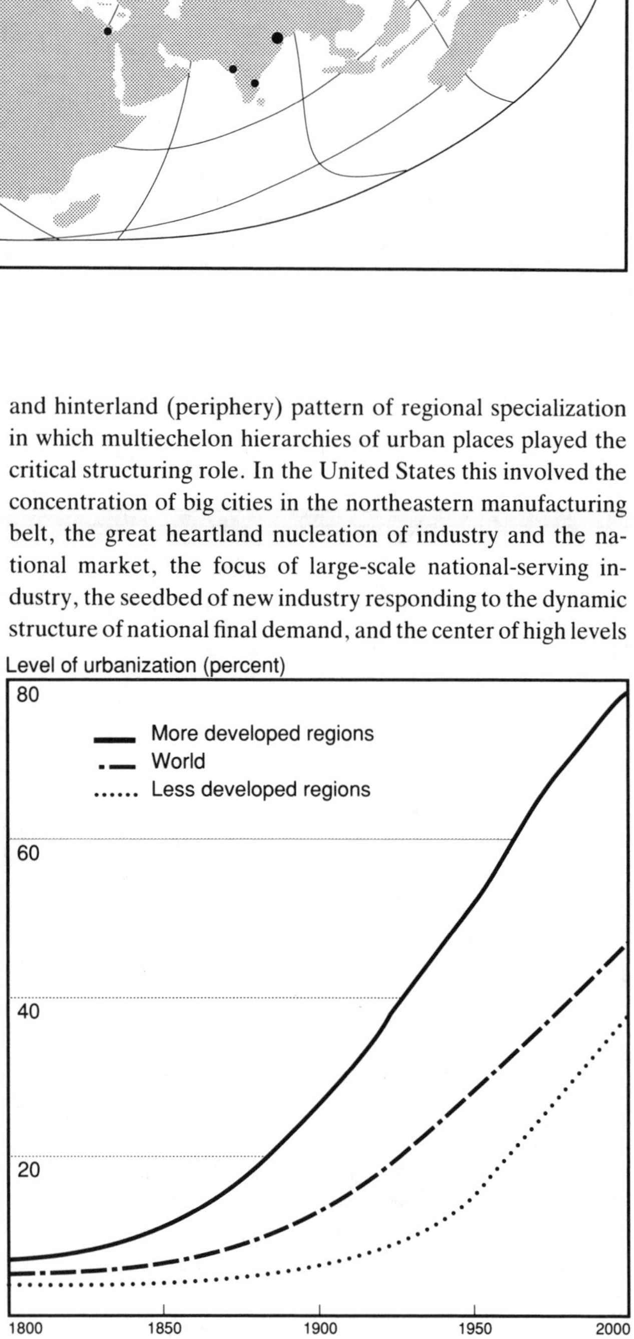

Level of urbanization (percent)

More developed regions
World
Less developed regions

80

60

40

20

1800   1850   1900   1950   2000

Figure 7.8 Increases in the level of urbanization in the world's more- and less-developed regions, 1800–2000.

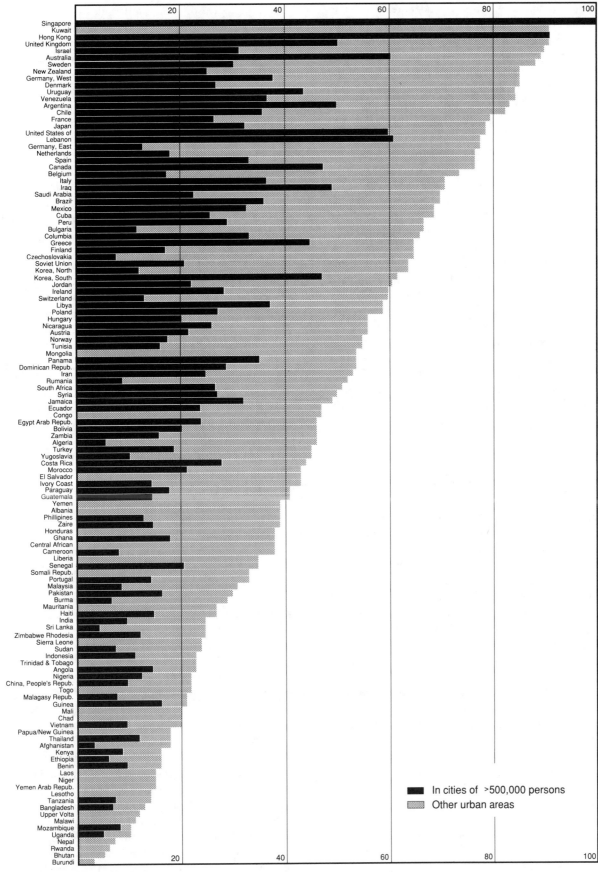

Figure 7.9 World urbanization levels in 1985.

of per capita income. Standing in a dependent relationship to the heartland, radiating out across the national landscape there developed resource-dependent regional hinterlands specializing in the production of raw material and intermediate outputs for which the heartland reached out to satisfy the input requirements of its great manufacturing plants. In the hinterlands, resource endowment was a critical determinant of the particular cumulative advantage of the region and hence its growth potential. In each case, the basic conditions of regional growth were set by the heartland. It was the lever for successive development of newer peripheral regions by reaching out to them as its input requirements expanded, and it thereby fostered specialization of regional roles in the national economy. The heartland experienced cumulative urban-industrial specialization, while each of the hinterlands found its comparative advantage based on narrow and intensive specialization in a few resource subsectors – diversifying only when the extent of specialization enabled the hinterland region to pass through that threshold scale of market necessary to support profitable local enterprise. Flows of raw materials inward and finished products outward articulated the whole. Large cities grew at the center of each region and at the top of each regional hierarchy – centers of activity and of innovation, focal points of the transport and communications networks, locations of superior accessibility, at which firms could most easily reap economies of scale and at which industrial complexes could obtain economies of localization and urbanization, encouraging labor specialization and efficiency in the provision of services.[4]

The urban-industrial system that evolved within the expanding national boundaries of the United States was duplicated globally by each of Europe's imperial powers. Each developed an economic heartland and each reached out globally for resource-dependent hinterlands, in the core-periphery pattern described by V. I. Lenin's "colonial model." Only imperial Russia mirrored the United States by bringing its peripheries within the frontiers of the nation-state. For Britain, France, Germany, Italy, Spain, and Portugal, the mother-country, urban-industrial cores reached out both for colonial raw materials and for safe colonial markets. Systems of imperial preference cemented the relationship, along with active European settlement of more temperate areas, from which the indigenous populations were relatively easily displaced. Urban-centered interconnections held the colonial networks together – networks that were to be disconnected in the twentieth century by two global wars separated by a profound depression. World War I disassembled the ancient Habsburg and Ottoman empires. World War II stemmed Germany's ultimately unsuccessful search for *lebensraum* and Japan's attempt to create its "greater East Asia co-prosperity sphere" by military means, but the price to the victors also was a loss of empire.

The Great Depression marked another technological watershed – from coal, steam, and rail to petroleum and the internal combustion engine. The base for new rounds of urban growth was the kind of city that had emerged in the nineteenth century, built on productive power, massed population, and industrial technology, and credited with the creation of a system of social life founded on entirely new principles. "Urbanization," wrote Tisdale (1942) "is a process of population concentration. It proceeds in two ways: the multiplication of the points of concentration and the increasing in size of individual concentrations.... Just as long as cities grow in size or multiply in number, urbanization is taking place.... Urbanization is a process of becoming. It implies a movement ... from a state of less concentration to a state of more concentration." It was these concentrated urban environments that produced the local climatic and hydrologic alterations discussed in the section that follows.

In part, the reason for agglomeration was the concentration of large-scale production facilities at strategic points on efficient interregional transportation networks. It resulted partly from the specialization of functions that large-scale industry made possible, with external economies to be reaped within the agglomerations. But relatively poor intraregional transportation (still predominantly foot and horse until the Great Depression) meant that externalities could be captured only in the most central locations within the agglomerations. Supported by new building technologies, high-rise central business districts developed at the urban cores, surrounded by inner-city manufacturing, and then by high-density rings of workers' housing. Only the upper classes could escape the perceived ills of the core-oriented concentrations as street railways, tramways, and the omnibus provided access to more pleasant and lower-density environs.

A new concept was needed to capture the scale of the largest agglomerations. The authors of a report issued by the United States Bureau of the Census (1932) in the 1930s wrote that "the population of the corporate city frequently gives a very inadequate idea of the population massed in and around that city, constituting the greater city. [The boundaries of] large cities in few cases limit the urban population which that city represents or of which it is the center. If we are to have a correct picture of the massing or concentration of population in extensive urban areas it is necessary to establish *metropolitan districts* which will show the magnitude of each of the principal population centres." Spelling out the idea further, the Bureau of the Budget's Committee on Metropolitan Area Definition (1967) wrote: "The general concept of a *metropolitan area* is one of an integrated economic and social unit with a recognized large population nucleus."

The situation was both fluid and dynamic, however, and the form of the metropolis changed rapidly in the period of accelerating economic growth that followed World War II, facilitated by the new technologies that assumed ascendancy at this time. The concentrated industrial metropolis developed because proximity meant lower transportation and communication costs for those interdependent specialists who had to interact with each other frequently or intensively. But shortened distances meant higher densities and the costs of congestion, polluted environments, high rent, loss of privacy, and the like. The technological developments implemented in the fourth Kondratiev had the effect of reducing the constraints of geographic space and the costs of concentration. Modern transportation and communications made it possible for each succeeding generation to live farther apart, producing first, accelerated suburbanization and urban sprawl, and later, real deconcentration. In 1902 H. G. Wells had speculated about the possibility:

Many of [the] railway-begotten "giant cities" will reach their maximum in the coming century [and] in all probability they . . . are destined to . . . dissection and diffusion. . . . [T]hese coming cities will not be, in the old sense, cities at all; they will present a new and entirely different phase of human distribution [italics added] [T]he social history of the middle and latter third of the nineteenth century . . . [has been] the history of a gigantic rush of population into the magic radius of – for most people – four miles. . . . But . . . [n]ew forces, at present so potently centripetal in their influence, bring with them the distinct promise of a centrifugal application. . . . Great towns before this century presented rounded contours and grew as puff-ball swells; the modern Great City looks like something that has burst an intolerable envelope and splashed . . . the mere first rough expedient of far more convenient and rapid developments. . . . We are . . . in the early phase of a great development of centrifugal possibilities . . . [A] city of pedestrians is inexorably limited by a radius of about four miles . . . a horse-using city may grow out to seven or eight . . . [I]s it too much . . . to expect that the available area for even the common daily toilers of the great city of year 2000 . . . will have a radius of over one hundred miles? . . . [T]he city will diffuse itself until it has taken up . . . many of the characteristics of what is now country . . . [T]he country will take itself many of the qualities of the city. The old anti-thesis will . . . cease, the boundary lines will altogether disappear.[5]

These predictions were certainly realized in the United States. After 1950, growth of the service sector, increase in the number of "footloose" industries (including final processing of consumer goods using manufactured parts, and the aircraft, aerospace, and defense industries), rapid emergence of a "quaternary" sector of the economy (involving, for example, the research and development industry), expansion and interregional migration of the non–job-oriented population (for example, of retirees to Florida, Arizona, and California), rising governmental expenditures and overall rising real incomes, plus modern highways and the automobile – all served to produce yet another transformation of the economy and the urban system that confirmed H. G. Wells' forecasts. Not only did urban areas grow and disperse into sprawling metropolitan regions; advantages for economic growth were found during the fourth Kondratiev in former hinterland regions around the "outer rim" of the country as changing communications technology reduced the time and costs involved in previous heartland-hinterland relationships.

The changes were cumulative. First, regional growth within the context of the national pattern of heartland and hinter-land brought outlying regions to threshold sizes for local production of a wide variety of goods and services. But then, they developed alternative bases of expansion as changes in the definition of urban resources made their rapid advance, free of the traditional constraints of heartland-hinterland leverage, possible. Hence, the explosive metropolitan growth of the South, Southwest, and West, led by the tertiary and quaternary sectors. The outcome was that it became possible, by the end of the 1960s, to interpret the spatial structure of the United States as a pattern consisting of (1) metropolitan areas and (2) the intermetropolitan periphery. Except for thinly populated parts of the American interior, the inter-metropolitan periphery included "all the areas that intervened

among metropolitan regions and that were the reverse image of the trend towards large scale concentrated settlement. . . . Like a devils' mirror . . . the periphery . . . developed a socio-economic profile that perversely reflects the very opposite of metropolitan virility" (Friedmann and Miller 1965).

Even by 1960, much of the United States territory was covered by the daily commuting areas of its metropolitan centers, as the far-flung suburbs made possible by the auto-mobile and by superhighway construction spread across the national landscape. The Greek planner Constantinos A. Doxiadis called these urban regions *daily urban systems* (Berry 1968). The coalescence of expanding metropolitan areas along the northeastern seaboard of the United States led Jean Gottman (1961) to coin a new term for the phenom-enon – *megalopolis* – and a later author, somewhat face-tiously, to call three such alleged developments "BosWash," "ChiPitts," and "SanSan." Peter Hall (1973) went on to document the extent of megalopolitan development else-where in the world, arguing that similar processes were unfolding in every economically advanced area.

It is these metropolitan regions that have been the subjects of extensive environmental analysis in the past half century, and it is from this analysis that we have been able to develop an understanding of the impacts of urbanization upon the biosphere.

Environmental Effects of Metropolitan Growth

Urban modification of the atmospheric environment can occur at three geographic scales (Berry and Horton 1974: 39ff):

1. Locally, by altering in the nature of the effective surface: the replacement of the natural surface of soil, grass, and trees by the multiplicity of urban surfaces of brick, con-crete, glass, and metal at different levels above the ground. These artificial materials change the nature of the reflecting and radiating surfaces, the heat exchange near the surface, and the aerodynamic roughness of the surface.
2. Regionally, by generating large amounts of heat artificially and by altering the composition of the atmosphere via emission of gaseous and solid pollutants. At certain times of the year in midlatitude cities, artificial heat input into the atmosphere by combustion and metabolic processes may approach or even exceed that derived indirectly from the sun. The heat island that results serves as a trap for pollutants.
3. Potentially, globally, through urban contributions to the sulfur budget or to CO_2, and thus to the greenhouse effect, to global warming, and to sea-level changes that are likely to be of greatest consequence for major coastal cities.

Leopold (1968) records four interrelated but separable effects of local land-use changes on the hydrology: changes in peak-flow characteristics; changes in total runoff; changes in water quality; and changes in hydrologic amenities. Stream flows following rainstorms may be characterized by unit hydrographs that capture both the peakedness and the lags in the rainfall-discharge relationship (Fig. 7.10). After urban-ization, runoff occurs more rapidly and with a greater peak

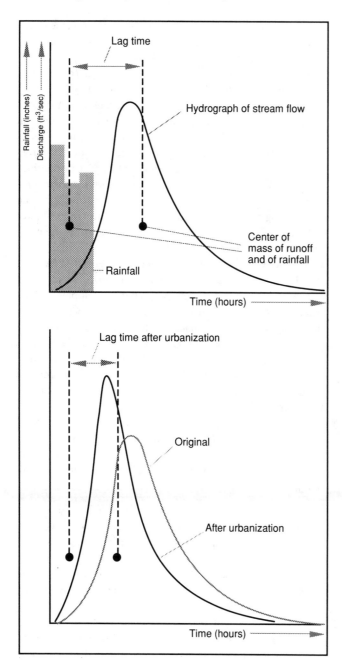

Figure 7.10 Unit hydrographs before and after urbanization.

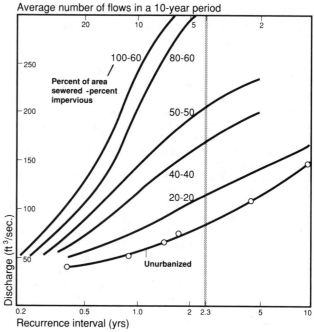

Figure 7.11 Increasing flood frequencies as urbanization progresses.

flow than under nonurban conditions. Urbanization increases the impervious land area, and the urban area may be served by storm sewers. Both increase the peak discharge: maximum sewerage and imperviousness results in peak discharges that are more than six times greater than in unurbanized conditions. In their turn, sharper peak discharges increase flood frequencies (Fig. 7.11) and the ratio of overbank flows. Urbanization, then, increases the flood volume, the flood peak, and the flood frequency, and the flushing effect increases turbidity and pollutant loads, although sediment loads may fall and the channel response will therefore shift from aggradation to bank erosion (Wolman 1967). Water pollution, in its turn, changes the quality of the downstream resource, the ecology of the riverine environment, and the amenity value of the river bank or estuary. The effects become pronounced

downstream of the larger cities, where natural flushing is incapable of preventing long-term damage.

At the scale of the metropolitan region, Landsberg's 1981 summary of the major changes in climates is, of course, well known (Table 7-4), but it needs to be discussed because it provides on-average estimates rather then insights into variations with city size.

The most dramatic effect of metropolitan growth is the creation of the urban heat island, which serves as a trap for atmospheric pollutants. Ceteris paribus, the temperature differential between the city core and the rural periphery increases with city size; the differences are small and ephemeral in places of 250,000 or less population, but are both substantial and longer-lasting in larger places. The heat island expands and intensifies as the city grows, and stronger and stronger winds are needed to overcome it. Wind speeds of $5 \, \text{m/sec}^{-1}$ can eliminate the heat island in a city of 250,000, but speeds of $10 \, \text{m/sec}^{-1}$ are required when the size reaches 1,000,000, and $14 \, \text{m/sec}^{-1}$ at 10,000,000. Yet the surface roughness of the city serves to reduce wind speeds and inhibit this ventilation: average wind speed may be reduced as much as 30% by the big city. In the larger cities over 10,000,000, the mean annual minimum temperature may be as much as 4°F higher than that of the surrounding rural periphery. This difference is much greater in summer than in winter.

The causes are twofold, both of which are seasonally dependent. (1) In summer, the tall buildings, pavement, and concrete of the city absorb and store large amounts of solar radiation, and less of this energy is used for evaporation than in the country because of the high runoff. The stored energy is released at night, warming the urban air. (2) In winter, manmade energy used for heat and light produces the warming, yet the blanket of emissions reduces incoming radiation by as much as 20%. If the BosWash megalopolis reaches a popu-

Table 7-4 *On-Average Effects of Urbanization on the Climate of Cities*

Element	Compared to rural environs
Contaminants	
Condensation nuclei	10 times more
Particulates	50 times more
Gaseous admixtures	5–25 times more
Radiation	
Total on horizontal surface	0–20% less
Ultraviolet, winter	30% less
Ultraviolet, summer	5% less
Sunshine duration	5–15% less
Cloudiness	
Clouds	5–10% more
Fog, winter	100% more
Fog, summer	30% more
Precipitation	
Amounts	5–15% more
Days with less than 5 mm	10% more
Snowfall, inner city	5–10% less
Snowfall, lee of city	10% more
Thunderstorms	10–15% more
Temperature	
Annual mean	0.5–3.0°C more
Winter minimums (average)	1–2°C more
Summer maximums	1–3°C more
Heating degree days	10% less
Relative Humidity	
Annual mean	6% less
Winter	2% less
Summer	8% less
Wind Speed	
Annual mean	20–30% less
Extreme gusts	10–20% less
Calm	5–20% more

Source: Landsberg 1981.

lation of 50–60 millions by the year 2000, it will be characterized by heat rejection of 65 cal/cm²/d. In winter, this is 50%, and in summer, 15%, of the heat received by solar radiation on a horizontal surface. In Manhattan, the heat produced by combustion alone in winter has been estimated to be two and one-half times the solar energy reaching the ground. This energy is trapped by the blanket of pollutants over the city, including particulates, water vapor, and carbon dioxide, and is reemitted downward to warm the ambient air.

In addition to the heat island, other climatic effects of urbanization – all increasing with city size – include greater cloudiness, fog, dust, and precipitation, but lower humidity. And as wind dissipates the heat island, a downwind urban heat plume is detectable in the atmosphere. Along this plume, there are increased precipitation, thunderstorm and hail probabilities. Beyond such regional-scale consequences, urban activities are a major source of CO_2 and of the fluorocarbons

that, in combination, may affect future global climates and sea levels.

Urbanization and Environment in the Years Ahead

The local- and regional-scale environmental effects of urbanization are all big-city, high-density, maximum-imperviousness consequences of million-plus, core-oriented, high-rise concentrations. Between 1975 and 2000, the number of million-plus cities is expected to more than double, from 190 to 440 (Table 7-2). Where they coalesce into larger agglomerations, the environmental effects converge at even broader regional scale – one graphic example of which is provided by a schematic illustration of the extent of air pollution in California (Fig. 7.12; Berry and Horton 1974: 83). But the regional distribution of large agglomerations is changing rapidly, suggesting a new locus for such regional-scale environmental effects. Urbanization is increasing most speedily in Latin America, Africa, and South Asia (Table 7-5), and it is there that the most rapid increases in the proportion of the population concentrated in million-plus cities are taking place (Fig. 7.13). Between 1950 and 1985, Europe and North America's share of the world's urban population dropped from 45% to 26%, even while the numbers in their cities grew from 325 to 500 million. In the rest of the world, the urban population jumped from 400 million to almost 1,600 million. During the next Kondratiev, much of the world can be expected to urbanize as completely as the more developed regions, and what this means is that the Third World will have large numbers of very large urban regions. At the end of the Great Depression, the world's more developed regions were barely 40% urbanized, but by the 1980s the percentages were in the 70s. Today, the world's less developed regions are approaching the 40% level, and their urban growth is still accelerating.

For the next half century, much of the world will be experiencing the process of population concentration that has

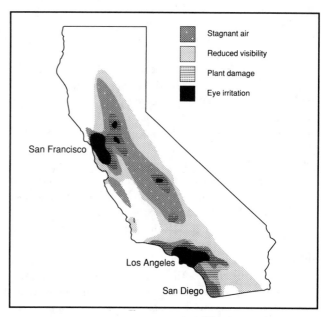

Figure 7.12 The extent of air pollution in California.

Table 7-5 *The World's Urban Population, 1950–1985 (in thousands)*

	1950 pop.	%	1960 pop.	%	1970 pop.	%	1975 pop.	%	1980 pop.	%	1985 pop.	%
World total	726,673	100	1,019,847	100	1,368,169	100	1,573,913	100	1,809,439	100	2,084,844	100
Percentage of total pop.	28.9		33.7		37.2		39.0		41.0		43.2	
Annual growth rate (%)			3.4		3.0		2.8		2.8		2.9	
Africa	32,434	4.5	50,416	4.9	80,644	5.9	103,832	6.6	134,951	7.5	174,829	8.4
Percentage of total pop.	14.8		18.4		22.8		25.6		28.8		32.1	
Annual growth rate (%)			4.5		4.8		5.2		5.4		5.3	
Latin America	67.465	9.3	106,520	10.4	162,075	11.8	197,250	12.5	238,283	13.2	285,274	13.7
Percentage of total pop.	41.2		49.5		57.3		61.2		64.7		67.8	
Annual growth rate (%)			4.7		4.3		4.0		3.9		3.7	
North America	106,018	14.6	133,280	13.1	159,493	11.7	170,167	10.8	181,433	10.0	194,871	9.3
Percentage of total pop.	63.8		67.1		70.5		72.0		73.7		75.4	
Annual growth rate (%)			2.3		1.8		1.3		1.3		1.4	
East Asia	112,638	15.5	199,855	19.6	276,808	20.2	322,530	20.5	371,199	20.5	425,010	20.4
Percentage of total pop.	16.7		24.5		28.2		30.3		32.7		35.3	
Annual growth rate (%)			5.9		3.3		3.1		2.9		2.7	
South Asia	112,507	15.5	158,717	15.6	234,924	17.2	286,228	18.2	352,827	19.5	437,409	21.0
Percentage of total pop.	15.9		18.3		21.2		22.8		24.8		27.2	
Annual growth rate (%)			3.5		4.0		4.0		4.3		4.4	
Europe	217,205	29.9	256,023	25.1	302,276	22.1	323,465	20.6	340,785	18.8	357,588	17.2
Percentage of total pop.	55.4		60.2		65.8		68.2		70.5		72.6	
Annual growth rate (%)			1.7		1.7		1.4		1.0		1.0	
Oceania	7,741	1.1	10,451	1.0	13,680	1.0	15,519	1.0	17,245	1.0	19,098	0.9
Percentage of total pop.	61.2		66.2		70.8		73.4		75.7		78.0	
Annual growth rate (%)			3.0		2.7		2.6		2.1		2.1	
USSR	70,765	9.7	104,589	10.3	138,270	10.1	154,923	9.8	172,715	9.5	190,765	9.2
Percentage of total pop.	39.3		48.8		56.7		60.9		64.8		68.2	
Annual growth rate (%)			4.0		2.8		2.3		2.2		2.0	

Source: United Nations 1980.

already ended in North America and western Europe. In the economically advanced regions, urbanization is not a stationary process, however; there is change in the nature of change, the environmental consequences of which are unclear. As metropolitan regions have rushed outward, urban densities and inner-city populations have dropped, leaving behind the most disadvantaged people in and around the former cores, inheriting the urban environments produced by earlier rounds of growth. Major reversals of patterns and reshaping of urban systems have been unfolding: what I have called a *process of counterurbanization* and what others have called *polarization reversal* or the *urban turnaround* (Ogden 1985; Richardson 1980; Vining and Kontuly 1978; Vining and Strauss 1977). Thus, in 1976 I wrote that "a turning point has been reached in the American experience. Counterurbanization has replaced urbanization as the dominant force shaping the nation's settlement patterns.... The process of counterurbanization has as its essence decreasing size, decreasing density, and decreasing heterogeneity: *counterurbanization is a process of population deconcentration; it implies a movement from a*

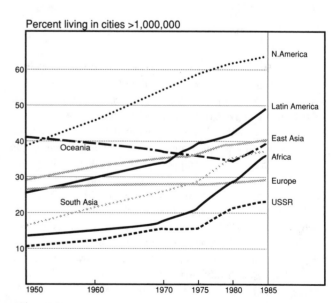

Figure 7.13 Increases in the percentage of urban population living in million-plus cities.

state of more concentration to a state of less concentration." Counterurbanization is occurring in most of the world's advanced economies, often helped along by planning policies designed to stem big-city growth, and in the socialist world, by attempts to create the "city of socialist man" (Berry 1981).

One explanation for the turnaround is the existence of urban disamenities: that premiums have to be paid to do business in larger urban agglomerations, where the social costs and environmental burdens of urban living are greater. On the one hand, larger urban areas have been places of greater productivity, but on the other, they have been the locus of growing disamenities. If the disamenities keep growing and technological change reduces the productivity advantages of agglomeration, the point will be reached where a turnaround will occur and growth will disperse, and as growth disperses, the disamenities should be ameliorated. Some have argued that what is emerging are *urban civilizations without cities*. New technologies are compressing time and space and accelerating change, lessening the need for face-to-face contact because of instantaneous electronic communications in the new age of the computer. Populations are therefore moving into high-amenity areas newly endowed with electronic access, reducing the local- and regional-scale pressures that result in environmental modification at those scales. A new kind of much more harmonious relationship with natural environments that are valued appears to be emerging in such civilizations.

This is, however, not the end of the story. Other forces are beginning to exert their influences: (1) the reemergence of external economies as primary locational factors; (2) the rise of flexible production systems; (3) as a consequence, the reagglomeration of production in new regions in which the settlement pattern is polycentric; (4) the connection of these polycentric urban networks into a global system or polycenter organized by a limited number of complexes of multinational headquarters. One way to characterize the resulting urban systems is as dynamic networks. No longer are vertical hierarchies arranged regionally into heartlands and hinterlands; instead, the "cores" are centers of creativity and entrepreneurial activity wherever they may be located, and are linked into transnational networks. The important decisions are made in some 500 major private corporations, whose headquarters are dispersed throughout 19 great urban regions. These regions, tightly interlinked, constitute the polycenter of the global urban network (Table 7-6 and Fig. 7.14). This polycenter controls networks of interdependent specialists, and wherever such networks have penetrated, the old models of neat urban hierarchies topped by big cities, of heartlands and hinterlands, and of metropolitan and nonmetropolitan spaces have vanished. Yet we do not know if the environmental effects of the new-form settlements will be regional-scale disruptions of the biosphere (California style), or if they will signal an amelioration of the worst of the environmental effects of the large, core-oriented metropolis.

Meanwhile, in the world periphery beyond the polycenter, there is a growing list of very large cities in which the process of population concentration accompanied by local- and regional-scale environmental modification is being repeated. In 1975, Chandler's list included 19 urban regions that already had exceeded 4 million in population (Table 7-7). Another 46 had exceeded 2 million. As the dispersed polycenter continues to evolve in the First World, it is in these massive urban agglomerations, peripheral to the main chanels of global interdependence, that the greatest modifications of the biosphere will occur, changing the regional environments within which a growing proportion of the world's population will live

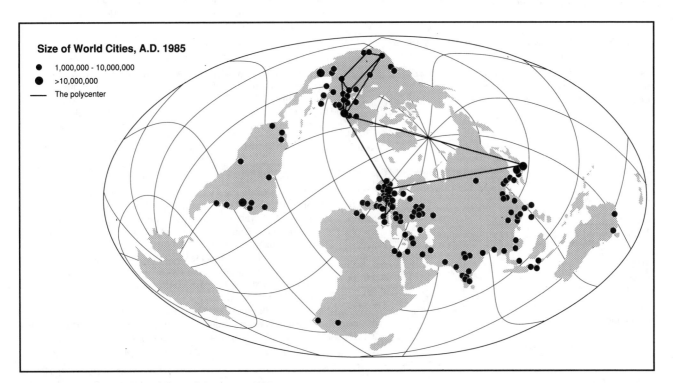

Figure 7.14 The polycenter and the periphery, A.D. 1985.

Table 7-6 *Nodes of the Global Polycenter*

Region (Urban complex)	Headquarters	Population
North America		
New York	90	17,100,000
Chicago	28	7,600,000
Los Angeles	22	8,900,000
San Francisco	15	4,400,000
Philadelphia-Wilmington	14	5,200,000
Dallas–Fort Worth	14	2,400,000
Houston	13	2,100,000
St. Louis	10	2,200,000
Detroit	9	4,800,000
Pittsburgh	9	2,000,000
Asia		
Tokyo	88	23,000,000
Osaka-Kobe	37	15,500,000
Seoul	9	6,800,000
Europe		
London	63	10,500,000
Paris	39	9,400,000
Ruhrgebiet	21	5,500,000
Frankfurt	13	1,600,000
Randstadt	9	2,000,000
Rome	4	3,600,000

marginal lives, pressed to the threshold of subsistence. The scale of Third World urban growth is such that even if First World environmental impacts are significantly reduced, the reductions will be swamped by the increases occurring elsewhere. It is from the Third World's economic growth and urban concentration that the most serious regional threats to the global environment will come.

Table 7-7 *Urban Regions outside the Global Polycenter with Populations Exceeding 4,000,000 in 1975*

Mexico City	11,300,000
Moscow	10,700,000
Sao Paulo	10,000,000
Buenos Aires	8,400,000
Cairo	8,400,000
Rio de Janeiro	8,300,000
Shanghai	8,000,000
Calcutta	7,800,000
Bombay	7,000,000
Manila	5,400,000
Jakarta	5,300,000
Peking	5,200,000
Tientsin	4,600,000
Karachi	4,400,000
Delhi	4,400,000
Bangkok	4,300,000
Leningrad	4,200,000
Tehran	4,300,000
Madrid	4,100,000

Source: Chandler 1987: 511.

Notes

1. The city sizes used in this chapter are those reported by Chandler 1987.

2. Chinese cities were built according to cosmological principles derived from Han Confucianism (Wheatley 1971). They were always walled cities, constructed according to a preconceived plan, in a regular and formalized pattern, an ecological symbolization of the cosmic order: first, as an *axis mundi* symbolizing the powerful centripetal forces in the universe; second, with the most important buildings arranged along a cardinally oriented ceremonial axis (the "celestial meridian writ small"; Wheatley 1971: 456); third, centered on a sacred enclave; fourth, walled in the form of a square; fifth, facing in the propitious southerly direction. The physical design was embedded in a cosmology that incorporated explicit views about the wholeness of humankind and nature (Eisenstadt and Shachar 1987: 140). In contrast to the emergent Western views of humans' dominion over nature that structured environmental attitudes as growing urban demands in Europe sparked both agricultural development and imperial expansion, Han Confucianism advanced ideas of the organic unity of humankind and nature, ineluctably and physically interdependent, with an order that had to be maintained by tradition and ritual.

3. The key elements of Japanese urban design also were determined by the Chinese urban model. At the core of the capital was the emperor's residence and the principal courts and temples, encircled by downwardly sloping gradients of status arranged with respect to a cardinally oriented square-grid design, reinforcing the fundamental principles of centrality and concentration, of the stability of social hierarchies, and of the unity of existence.

4. The overall pattern was one of the city-centered organization of economic activities along three dimensions:

1. A heartland-hinterland arrangement of industrial and resource regions linked by intermetropolitan flows.
2. A system of cities within each region, arranged in a hierarchy according to the functions performed by each.
3. Corresponding areas of urban influence or urban fields surrounding each of the cities in the system.

Within this framework, impulses of economic change and of environmental modification and exploitation were transmitted simultaneously along three planes:

1. Outward from heartland centers to those of the regional hinterlands on a national scale.
2. From each regional capital to centers of lower level in the hierarchy, in a pattern of "hierarchical diffusion" within each of the regions.
3. Outward from urban centers into their urban fields, radiating "spread effects" into the surrounding countryside.

The resulting spatial patterns were these:

1. The size and functions of a central city, the size of its urban field, and the spatial extent of development and environmental "spread effects" radiating outward from it were proportional.
2. Since impulses of economic change were transmitted in order from higher to lower centers in the urban hierarchy, continued innovation in large cities remained critical for extension of growth over the complete economic system.
3. The resulting spatial incidence of economic growth was a function of distance from the central city. Troughs of economic backwardness lay in the most inaccessible peripheries of the lowest-level centers in the hierarchy.
4. The growth potential of any area situated along an axis between two cities became a function of the intensity of interaction between them, which in turn was a function of their relative location and the quality of transportation arteries connecting them.

5. Similar ideas had been expressed by Adna Weber in 1899: "the 'rise of the suburbs' it is, which furnishes the solid basis of a hope that

the evils of city life, so far as they result from overcrowding, may in large part be removed. If concentration of population seems destined to continue, it will be a modified concentration which offers the advantages of both city and country life...a complete fusion of their different modes of life and combination of the advantages of both, such as no country in the world has ever seen." (Weber 1899: 475)

References

Aldridge, H. R. 1915. *The Case for Town Planning*. London: National Housing and Town Planning Council.

Berry, B. J. L. 1968. *Metropolitan Area Definition*. Washington, D.C.: U.S. Bureau of the Census.

———. 1976. *Urbanization and Counterurbanization*. Beverly Hills, CA: Sage Publishing Co.

———. 1977. *The Changing Shape of Metropolitan America*. Cambridge, MA: Ballinger Publishing Co.

———. 1981. *Comparative Urbanization*. Basingstoke, U.K.: Macmillan.

Berry, B. J. L., E. C. Conkling, and D. M. Ray. 1987. *Economic Geography: Resource Use, Locational Choices and Regional Specialization in the Global Economy*. Englewood Cliffs, NJ: Prentice-Hall.

Berry, B. J. L., and F. E. Horton. 1974. *Urban Environmental Management*. Englewood Cliffs, NJ: Prentice-Hall.

Borchert, J. A. 1967. American metropolitan evolution, *Geographical Review* 57 (1967): 301–22.

Bourneville Village Trust. 1941. *When We Build Again*. London: Allen and Unwin.

Braudel, F. 1984. *Civilization and Capitalism: 15th–18th Century*. Vol. III, *The Perspective of the World*. New York: Harper and Row.

Chandler, T. 1987. *Four Thousand Years of Urban Growth. An Historical Census*. Lewiston/Queenston: St. David's University Press.

DeVries, J. 1981. Patterns of urbanization in preindustrial Europe, 1500–1800. In *Patterns of European Urbanization since 1500*, ed. H. Schmal, 77–109. London: Croom Helm.

Eisenstadt, S. N., and A. Shachar. 1987. *Society, Culture and Urbanization*. Beverly Hills, CA: Sage Publishing Co.

Friedmann, J., and J. Miller. 1965. The urban field. *Journal of the American Institute of Planners* 31: 312–19.

Gelderen, J. van (alias J. Fedder). 1913. Springvloed beschouwingen over industriele ontwikeling en prijsbeweging. *De Nievwe Tijd* 18: 253–57, 445–64.

Gottman, J. 1961. *Megalopolis*. New York: The Twentieth Century Fund.

Hall, P. 1966. *The World Cities*. London: World University Press.

———. 1973. *The Containment of Urban England, or Megalopolis Denied*. London: Allen and Unwin.

Handlin, O., and J. Burchard, eds. 1963. *The Historian and the City*. Cambridge, MA: Harvard University Press.

Kondratiev, N. 1935. The long waves in economic life. *Review of Economic Statistics* 17: 101–15.

Landsberg, H. E. 1981. *The Urban Climate*. New York: Academic Press.

Leopold, L. B. 1968. *Hydrology for Urban Land Planning*. Washington, D.C.: U.S. Government Printing Office, G.P.O. Geological Survey Circular 554.

Ogden, P. E. 1985. Counterurbanization in France: the results of the 1982 population census. *Geography* 70: 24–35.

Richardson, H. W. 1980. Polarization reversal in developing countries. *Papers of the Regional Science Association*, 45: 67–85.

Schumpeter, J. 1934. *The Theory of Economic Development*. London: Cambridge University Press.

Tisdale, H. 1942. The process of urbanization. *Social Forces* 30: 311–16.

United Nations, Department of International Economic and Social Affairs, Population Division. 1980. *Urban, Rural, and City Population, 1950–2000*. Working paper ESA/P/PW.66 (June 1980).

U.S. Bureau of the Budget. 1967. *Standard Metropolitan Statistical Areas*. Washington, D.C.: U.S. G.P.O.

U.S. Bureau of the Census. Metropolitan districts, 1932. *Fifteenth Census of the United States, 1938*. Washington, D.C.: U.S. G.P.O.

Vining, D. R. Jr., and A. Strauss. 1977. A demonstration that the current deconcentration of population in the United States is a clean break with the past. *Environment and Planning* Ser. A, 9: 751–58.

———, and T. Kontuly. 1978. Population dispersal from major metropolitan regions: an international comparison. *International Regional Science Review* 3: 49–73.

———, and R. Pallone. 1982. Migration between core and peripheral regions: a description and tentative explanation of the patterns in 22 countries. *Geoforum* 13: 339–410.

Wallerstein, I. 1974. *The Modern World-System*. New York: Academic Press.

Webber, M. M. 1963. Order in diversity: community without propinquity. In *Cities and Space*, ed. L. Wingo, 23–56. Baltimore, MD: Johns Hopkins University Press.

Weber, A. F. 1899. *The Growth of Cities in the Nineteenth Century. A Study in Statistics*. New York: The Macmillan Co.

Wells, H. G. 1902. *Anticipations. The reaction of mechanical and scientific progress on human life and thought*. London: Harper and Row.

Wheatley, P. 1971. *The Pivot of the Four Quarters*. Chicago: Aldine.

Williamson, J. G. 1985. The urban transition during the first industrial revolution: England, 1776–1871. Paper No. 1146, April. Cambridge, MA: Harvard Institute for Economic Research, Discussion.

Wirth, L. 1938. Urbanism as a way of life. *American Journal of Sociology* 44: 1–24.

Wittfogel, K. 1957. *Oriental Despotism*. London: Oxford University Press.

Wolman, M. G. 1967. The cycle of sedimentation and erosion in urban river channels, *Geografiska Amaler* 49A: 285–95, 385.

Wrigley, E. A. 1987. *People, Cities and Wealth*. Oxford: Basil Blackwell.

8

Awareness of Human Impacts: Changing Attitudes and Emphases

DAVID LOWENTHAL

The acceleration of environmental transformations blinds us to their antiquity. Mankind has been altering the earth since before the dawn of history, albeit more slowly and less visibly in earlier times. Appalled by some adverse effects, many long ago blamed themselves or others even for natural or imaginary environmental change. It is one measure of contemporary concern about the consequences of impact that we are apt mistakenly to suppose that all such consciousness is new.

Nor are environmentalist successes wholly new, although today's widely publicized environmental protests foster the belief that the public has only now become alert and combatant (Ashby 1978: 44–45; 79–80). "Today it takes a brave factory manager to keep polluting in the face of community opinion," maintains a reporter, whereas "twenty years ago it took a brave citizen to stand up to a town's major employer for dumping chemicals into the creek" (Kuralt 1987). Yet pollution control in England dates back to 1388, and environmental sanitation and air pollution abatement acts in Britain and America to the mid-nineteenth century (Brimblecombe 1987: 90–112; Sinclair 1973: 175–79).

Early Transformation Beliefs: The Decay of Nature

Those who regard modern awareness of impact as unprecedented are apt to consider our predecessors as little aware of their environmental powers as of their environmental perils. "The idea that humans can change nature" is quite recent, supposes Ehrenfeld (1986a:168), but in fact the opposite is the case; many premoderns attributed environmental change more readily to human agency than to nature, God, or chance.

The roots of modern concern about environmental impact are properly traceable to eighteenth-century observations and nineteenth-century ecological insights. Yet analogous environmental fears had engaged previous epochs, when men were likewise seen as major agents of terrestrial change – notably for the worse. Such alterations were commonly ascribed to divine punishment for mortal misdeeds, as with Biblical accounts of the Flood.

The view that human evil engendered nature's decay permeated late-sixteenth and early-seventeenth-century European thought. In Luther's sacred history, Adam had initiated not only the Fall of man but the decay of nature, and subsequent sins induced further deterioration; some theologians thought global dissolution imminent. Scenes of monastic ruin heightened English awareness of decay:

> Heaven's just displeasure & our unjust ways
> Change nature's course, bring plagues dearth and decays.
> This turns our lands to Dust, the skies to Brass,
> Makes old kind blessings into curses pass.

"Man drew the curse upon the world, and crack't the whole frame with his fall." (Vaughan [1666; 1655] 1957: 679, 440). Decay thus predicated was confirmed by every falling leaf – and by geographical exploration, the telescope, and the microscope (Davies 1969; Harris 1949; Lowenthal 1985; 87–88, 136–37; Nicolson 1959: 100–104).

Were those who found man responsible for nature's decay preternaturally perceptive about human environmental impact? Quite to the contrary: they fantasized change, used spurious data to forecast degradation, and "explained" natural events as divinely ordained. Wanting to believe that sin caused decay, they massively misread the environmental evidence so as to chronicle a morally reprehensible history.

Many today remain prescientific catastrophists. Because the notion of a nature unresponsive to man's desires seems to them impious, intolerable, or incomprehensible, they view mankind as the prime agent in global history. Along with scientifically grounded environmental concerns, modern catastrophists retain antiscientific millenarian apprehensions. We inherit outworn environmental attitudes along with often worn-out environments.

Eighteenth- and Nineteenth-Century Hubris: Man over Nature

Early catastrophism for the most part gave way, however, to the cornucopian hubris of eighteenth- and nineteenth-century views about impact. Yet the earlier and later views shared one perspective: both viewed mankind as a potent environmental force. But the catastrophists saw that force as essentially destructive, the cornucopians as beneficial.

Apocalyptic doom had shaped the scrutiny of the pessimists; faith in progress through evolving science and technology guided the environmental observations of the optimists.

Human Impact Seen As Beneficial

Environmental optimists were entrepreneurial experts. Developers and technicians engaged in damming rivers, draining swamps, clearing forests, digging harbors, and domesticating and transplanting plants and animals built up detailed data on their terrestrial effects. Global exploration prompted comparisons of lands long cultivated with new worlds but recently or lightly settled. Improved instrumentation verified and quantified technology's accelerated impacts.

These impacts were seen in the main as decided improvements. The more profoundly nature was manipulated, the more fertile and productive it seemed to become. Increased productivity advanced civil order and happiness, sustaining the view that God had left nature raw and incomplete for mankind to perfect. As a token of man's dominion, subduing and transforming the wild became a hallmark of civilizing progress.

The classic statement was Buffon's. "The entire face of the earth today bears the stamp of the power of man," making the rude environment he had inherited "perfect and magnificent." Land won from moors, fens, and forests, reclaimed from marshes and seas, ordered and embellished and cared for, demonstrated both man's unique place in nature and his ability to improve it. "Wild nature is hideous and dying," felt Buffon, along with most eighteenth-century improvers; men alone made it "agreeable and living" (Glacken 1967: 668, 663).

The quintessential enactors of Buffon's scenario were American pioneers. They found the untouched environment repugnant, the forests "howling" and "dismal," the prairie a "trackless waste" to be "transformed into fruitful farms and flourishing cities." Seen through improvers' lenses, trees became lumber, prairies farms. As it was their mission "to cause the wilderness to bloom and fructify," Genesis 1:28 was invoked to "subjugate" the "enemy" – the wilderness. Pioneer goals transcended personal gain: they "broke the long chain of savage life" and replaced "primitive barbarism" with "civilization, liberty and law" to ensure a glorious American destiny. In the self-imposed mission to subdue the land the settler would proudly say that "*I* vanquished this wilderness and made the chaos pregnant with order and civilization." Even those who admired the splendors of the wild celebrated the civilizing impact; Walt Whitman's "Song of the Redwood Tree" bids farewell to the arboreal giant who "must abdicate his kingship so that man can build a grander future" (Carroll, P. N. 1969; Lowenthal 1982: 10–15; Nash 1967: 27–41).

Any adverse side-effects, such as excessive erosion and flooding, were thought easily put right, whether in the Old World or the New. Those who deplored overexploitation supposed environmental degradation limited and reparable. When a Fabre or a Surrell inveighed against the ignorance of Swiss herders or the greed of French peasants, they assumed that enlightened governments could soon effect environ-

mental reform – a managerial confidence that persisted among conservationists well into the 1950s.

Experience Circumscribes Optimism

It was in eighteenth- and early-nineteenth-century North America that fears about heedless exploitation most seriously clashed with pioneer optimism. What had recently seemed inexhaustible contrasted poignantly with the devastations of just a few decades. The engrossment of lands cultivated only lightly if ever before; widespread deforestation for fuel and timber, fencing and pasturage; the supplanting of wild animals by intensively grazing livestock; the transplantation of Old World agriculture, without the saving grace of regular manuring – all this patently depleted native flora and fauna, induced extremes of flooding and aridity, and hastened the erosion and exhaustion of lands less fertile, in any case, than they initially seemed. Plenty had bred waste; nature's abundance led to prodigality. Such men as Franklin and Bartram and Rush saw the American legacy diminished by their forebears' profligate husbandry (Cronon 1983: 116–48, 169–70; Glacken 1967: 690–98).

Man and Nature

By the mid-nineteenth century, "the signs of artificial improvement" everywhere commingled "with the tokens of improvident waste." A single generation had ravaged much of green New England: the conversion of "smiling meadows into broad wastes of shingle and gravel and pebbles, deserts in summer, and seas in autumn and spring [was] too striking to have escaped the attention of any observing person." Like George P. Marsh (1848: 3, 18–19), "every middle-aged man who revisits his birthplace after a few years of absence, looks upon another landscape."

These observations led to Marsh's classic warnings. The impact of deforestation and grazing on river regimes recounted by other eyewitnesses buttressed his own Vermont experience. Ancient denudation in Mediterranean landscapes that Marsh traversed in the 1850s offered ominous analogues. His magisterial *Man and Nature* ([1864] 1965) drew on observations from both hemispheres, along with historical sources and correspondence with French hydrologists, Swiss foresters, Italian engineers.

Man and Nature revolutionized environmental thought. It had been conventional wisdom that the earth made man; Marsh showed that man made the earth (1965: ix). Confuting the mystique of superabundant and inexhaustible resources, he demonstrated that human impacts were largely unintended, often harmful, and sometimes irreversible. Alike comprehensive and comprehensible, *Man and Nature* became a widely influential text (Lowenthal 1958: 267–70; Marsh 1965: xxi–xxiii; Thomas 1956: xxviii–xxx). Vivified by local examples, it adduced the causes of deforestation, river regime changes, avalanches, desertification, and wildlife extirpation from universal principles. It explained landscape change through social and technological forces familiar to every reader. And its reformist perspective lent hope: neither innate predisposition nor divine edict, in Marsh's view, compelled men to lay the earth waste; they did so only out of corrigible greed or ignorance. Those who saw the causal connections might mend their ways to restore the balance between forest and arable, nature and culture, mankind and other species.

Marsh stressed that timely understanding could reverse the ill effects of human impact. But accelerating degradation made imminent the need for reform. Return a quarter of the land to forest cover, curtail the indiscriminate slaughter of wildlife, inculcate environmental awareness, monitor future change, and almost all could yet be well.

Such exhortations seemed both compelling and practicable. Marsh saw men not as subject to nature but as self-willing surrogates for the divinity that had shaped the globe. Only by taming and improving the earth had men exchanged savagery for civilization, slavery for freedom, unremitting toil for contemplative reason. But progress was neither ordained nor certain; it required ceaseless stewardship.

Echoing Enlightenment activism, Marsh's views also presaged evolutionary perspectives. Men must not passively submit to nature but continually struggle against it. Man's transforming power embodied both the promise of well being and the threat of disaster. A fruitful and balanced globe had awaited the time when man's "Creator should call him forth to enter into possession." But men might either immeasurably improve or irreparably damage that legacy. Left to itself, a gradually changing natural fabric usually regained equilibrium; but "man is everywhere a disturbing agent. Wherever he plants his foot, the harmonies of nature are turned to discords.... The face of the earth is either laid bare or covered with a new and reluctant growth" (Marsh 1965: 36). And the contingent effects of deliberate alterations were still more damaging, for nature was "wholly impotent" to resist man's destructiveness.

Such damage did not, however, mean that men should desist from tampering with their environment. On the contrary, they must continue to defy natural forces. Science had "already virtually doubled the span of human life by multiplying our powers and abridging" the time needed to gain a livelihood. Man must continue to subjugate nature, for "wherever he fails to make himself her master, he can but be her slave" (Marsh 1860: 34, 56, 60–61; ([1864] 1965: xxv–xxvi).

Marsh felt a deep affinity with wild and untouched landscapes. But like many of his time, he admired nature's harmonies while deploring its amorality. "Visible nature is all plasticity and indifference," as William James (1896: 43) put it. "To such a harlot we owe no allegiance; with her ... we can establish no moral communion." James concurred with John Stuart Mill's ([1850–58] 1969: 400) argument that "conformity to nature has no connection whatever with right and wrong." Others thought it more wrong than right. Huxley and Spencer reprehended nature as ruthless, cruel, savage, wasteful, selfish; men must subdue it not only to improve their surroundings but also because wild nature was evil and vile.

The Darwinian paradigm reinforced the argument that nature was morally reprehensible. Instead of following nature, men must overcome "natural" instincts to avoid behaving like beasts; in effect, "man is the animal for whom it is natural to

be artificial" (Lucius Garvin, quoted in Rolston 1979: 20). Opposed to nature, red in tooth and claw, was the benign and harmonious state of human artifice (Rolston 1979: 8, 18–30; Sober 1986: 180–82).

Conservation as Resource Management

Marsh had emphasized that victory over nature required vigilant care for the global fabric. But few who applauded *Man and Nature* heeded its cautionary precepts. Focusing on productive resource management, conservationists generally ignored the unforeseen side-effects that Marsh had shown to be so devastating. Several generations continued to hold that mankind's great mission was to subdue and transform nature. Conservationists saw environmental impact as mainly benign; remedies for attendant injuries were to be sought in centralized control over selfish or foolish entrepreneurs. But they shared with most entrepreneurs a technocratic optimism that prevailed well into the twentieth century. Though the environment was ever more drastically altered, most changes still seemed improvements, and few doubted that technology would soon rectify any damage (Hays 1959: 189–98, 271–73).

Persuaded that the forces of nature vastly exceeded those of man, earth scientists from Lyell on shared that faith in progress. Whatever men did, they could not seriously harm nature. However far technology extended environmental impacts, man would remain only a minor geological force; the gravest manmade disasters meant only small and temporary setbacks in his progressive mastery of an infinitely resourceful earth (Gregory and Walling 1987: 3).

Myriad observations detailed mounting environmental damage. But these untoward effects, seldom widely publicized, were ignored by policymakers. Evidence of impact went unremarked because its scattered and abstruse sources were accessible only to specialists. Meanwhile progressivist thinkers went on believing that science could safely enlarge its power over nature, whereas environmental determinists left ultimate power still safely sheltered in nature's might (Glacken 1956: 81–88).

One measure of our present distance from such confidence is how crude Freud's 1929 (1946: 53–54) accolade to the conquest of nature now sounds:

We recognize that a country has attained a high state of civilization when we find ... everything in it that can be helpful in exploiting the earth for man's benefit and in protecting him against nature.... In such a country the course of rivers ... is regulated.... The soil is industriously cultivated; ... the mineral wealth is brought up assiduously from the depths; ... wild and dangerous animals have been exterminated.

Though most people would probably still share Freud's belief that technological impact is progressive and benign, such blithe neglect of its negative consequences is today scarcely conceivable.

Dust Bowl Doubts and Ecological Dialectics

Gloomier perspectives gained salience, and not only in North America, in the Depression and Dust Bowl decade of the 1930s. The equilibrium model of ecology, developed by Frederic Clements and others since the 1920s, helped explain a succession of environmental disasters (Sears 1935). The lesson was that technology did not improve nature but destroyed it. Nature was most fruitful where it was altered least. Left undisturbed, flora and fauna gradually attained maximum diversity and stability. But massive monoculture and extractive despoliation thwarted the culmination or shortened the duration of this beneficent climax. Meanwhile human population growth exhausted nonrenewable resources and endangered renewable ones (Worster 1977: 209–42).

These evils emanated only from so-called advanced cultures, however. Exempt from blame were hunters and gatherers and early agriculturalists, who supposedly respected nature's balance. Their environmental wisdom might help moderns to restore "natural" environments fit to live in and to hand on. In this view, instinctive ecological harmony made the savage noble.

Echoes of older ways of thought made the idea of climax equilibrium appealing. In the plenitude required by the classical Great Chain of Being, the loss of even one species might dismember the universe (Lovejoy [1936] 1960: 243; Rescher 1980: 118). Stability had been an eighteenth-century virtue; the climax concept echoed previous ideas of progress; diversity ennobled both nature and culture (Goudie 1986: 290–95). Steady states seemed consonant with older tendencies to perpetuate existing ways (Bates 1956: 1136–37). Most philosophers from Plato to the present have upheld the value of stasis: "everybody equated happiness with the absence of change and considered change, even change for the better, to be intolerable" (Munz 1985: 314). Homeostatic ecosystems that benefited their interrelated components deserved protection against unwitting intervention, unplanned growth, or defiant rejection of nature (Bellini 1986: 248; Rolston 1979: 14).

The steady-state, succession-to-climax model of ecology early became entrenched in social science. In the 1920s and 1930s, sociology borrowed Clementian concepts to lend it reputable rigor. Notions of stability, natural balance, and self-regulating equilibria permeated sociological language (Hawley 1968).

Within a generation this ecological mystique became a conservation precept, almost a religious tenet. Aldo Leopold's famous "Land Ethic" (1949: 224–25) – "A thing is right when it tends to preserve the integrity, stability, and beauty of the biotic community. It is wrong when it tends otherwise" – bade fair to become global gospel (Cowan 1966: 56; Flader 1978: 34–35, 270–71).

The virtues of stability and passive noninterference mirrored reformers' views about human nature, too. They invested nature with "ecological" qualities they believed should govern mankind: balance, integrity, order, harmony, stasis, diversity – all that is benign, caring, respectful, holistic (Birch and Cobb 1981: 273–74, 282–83; Evernden 1985a: 15–16). The ecological utopia remains a moral order. To "replace the chaos of a world torn by human greed and voraciousness with a well-ordered moral universe," we are adjured to limit our population, our technology, and our habits of consumption (Taylor 1986: 258).

Ecology itself, to be sure, had long since disowned much

of the Clementian paradigm. By the 1950s it was mainly nonecologists who extolled equilibrium states, maximum diversity and stability, and noninterference (Darling in Thomas 1956: 407–408; Egler in ibid.: 447, 940–41). Yet it would have been hard to gather from 1950s ecology texts that ecologists had abandoned these concepts (Glacken in ibid: 941). A generation on, the succession-to-climax model continues to dominate much biological thinking (Oldfield 1983: 248).

Much of today's environmental-impact literature deploys these outdated ecological perspectives. Nature is cast in the role of normative good, technological man as evil destroyer. This turns on its head the "ecological" perspective of Social Darwinians, who saw the conquest of nature as desirable and praiseworthy.

In sum, the concept of nature as an unfinished fabric to be perfected by human ingenuity gave way to the view that technology debased nature and endangered its beneficence. Environmental interference was anathematized, the wilderness venerated. In the state of nature envisioned by the Enlightenment, by Marsh, and by his technocratic successors, rational managers would cultivate an ever more artificial environment. In the state of nature sought by twentieth-century ecological reformers, human impact would dwindle until the environment recovered stability. By the end of the World War II, "ecology" had become a token of right thinking even in official environmental agencies (Hays 1987: 347; Mellanby 1988).

After Hiroshima

Man's Role in Changing the Face of the Earth

It was in this general climate, also profoundly marked by nuclear fears, that the memorable Wenner-Gren symposium at Princeton took stock of "what man had done and was doing to change his physical-biological environment on the earth" (Fejos 1956: viii). *Man's Role in Changing the Face of the Earth* was intended as a tribute and a successor to Marsh's *Man and Nature*, hailed for pioneering awareness of the risks entailed by heedless interference with nature.

In both tone and content, however, the symposium on balance displayed a remarkably low level of concern about human impacts. Sketching the history of awareness, Glacken and Thomas limned transitions from early ignorance to eighteenth-century hubris, to nineteenth-century fears about resource exhaustion and unwanted side-effects, to twentieth-century reforms felt sufficient to rectify abuses. Although technology had accelerated environmental change, most human impacts were now adjudged purposeful and beneficial, the heedless exploitation of the past giving way to rational, conservation-minded manipulation (Glacken 1956: 85–88; Thomas 1956: xxviii–xxxvii).

Most *Man's Role* participants themselves saw things in this benign light. Except for Boulding, Darling, Mumford, Sauer, and Sears, optimism prevailed. Such pessimism as did surface stemmed largely from ecological premises scored as outdated. Sears' alarm at human violations of living systems' "steady state" (1956: 472–73), Darling's diatribe against "climax-breaker" pastoralists (1956: 779–81), Sauer's fear that ethnocentric American technocrats "may be destroying wise and durable native systems of living with the land" (1956: 68) – these all reflected perspectives already abandoned by biologists and suspect among anthropologists. When Boulding expressed concern over interference with stable natural equilibria (447), Egler and Steinbach pooh-poohed his use of this obsolete concept: "ecologists should not be blamed for what is no longer ecology" (447; see Mellanby 1988).

Specters of global impact mainly elicited superficial, imprecise, or unconcerned responses. Curtis found acceptable the "running-down" of rain-forest ecosystems because "the improbability of the climax biotic community was too great to be sustained" (1956: 734–35). Seidenberg worried lest undue concern with stability might thwart creative innovation (1095); Darwin expressed gratitude that the Bomb was only deuterium, not hydrogen (1115); Tax mused over the psychological implications of prospective annihilation (1121); Mumford, invoking Teilhard de Chardin's noösphere, concluded that "only when love takes the lead will the earth, and life on earth, be safe again" (1956: 1152). Recalling what some of these men had said on other occasions, one wonders what cat got their tongues at Princeton.

Putting trust in impact management, many exhibited extreme complacency in the face of threats that now seem evident. Through technology and monitoring, Gutkind foresaw irresponsible expansion yielding to environmental controls (1956: 11, 27, 37). Michael Graham considered the world's oceans too immense to warrant concern about sullying or despoiling them (1956: 501–502). Citing Marsh out of context, Klimm found the environmental impact of ports and harbors almost universally beneficial; he could think of no harmful consequences (1956: 539). In global climatic patterns "man is incapable of making any significant change," asserted Thornthwaite; even on microclimates human impacts were so trivial "that special instruments are often required to detect them" (1956: 582) (presumably like those now used to detect ozone layer depletion). Noting the self-regenerating power of plant communities, E. H. Graham lauded a half-century's progress in biotic resource manipulation (1956: 690). Edgar Anderson took as given the aim "eventually to control the living world around us" (1956: 777). Applauding the use of nuclear fission products as tracers in atmospheric and marine research, Bugher regarded such wastes as wholly benign (1956: 847). Other than loss of stratigraphic data, McLaughlin saw no threat from the extraction of minerals (1956: 861).

Albrecht's initial alarm ("man is exploiting the earth that feeds him much as a parasite multiplies until it kills its host") gave way to confidence that wise management would rebuild battered soils (1956: 670–72). Fifty years of soil conservation, forestry, range and wildlife management, and agronomy satisfied E. H. Graham about the pace and depth of environmental reform; soil conservation was now restoring land as no previous generation would have thought possible (1110). Why worry about population growth or atomic explosions, scoffed Malin, since past fears of the consequences of science and technology had always come to naught (1127)? To most of those at *Man's Role*, environmental impact seemed a matter of major concern only to scientific ignoramuses or crackpots.

Levels of 1950s Concern

These views were not, however, truly representative of their time. Mid-1950s pessimism about impact was greater than that of the scholars at Princeton. Vivid fears of global annihilation had been unleashed by Hiroshima a decade earlier. Many condemned industrial society – America in particular – for exploitative greed and blind faith in technological progress (Siegfried 1955: 6–7). Any untoward environmental episode engendered fear and confusion – a fall of red dust in Baltimore was widely rumored to be radioactive fallout or the harbinger of a new Dust Bowl. If some welcomed artificial satellites as technological triumph, one congressman echoed many Americans in fearing "that we are too smart and that the world will be destroyed by the machines and weapons created by our own mind" (Short 1955).

Neo-Malthusian alarms were also more prevalent than *Man's Role* suggests. With Kingsley Davis warning that science could not forever compensate population growth in a finite world (1955:34) and David Brower predicting an ultimate limit "approaching faster than we thought" (1957: 5), reversion to barbarism seemed a minor peril for a globe with standing room only. Many feared that "tinkering with nature" through antibiotics, destroying "uneconomic" plant and animal species, introducing foreign predators, and prolonging human lifespans would unleash biological havoc.

Most warnings betrayed an animistic or primitivist outlook. As a well-known ruralist put it, China, Rome, Greece, Africa, and the Americas had all disregarded nature's warnings and suffered her revenge, for "nature always has the last word" (Collis 1950: 246). Others implied retrogression from some previous state of harmony. "Any attempt to master and dominate nature can only result in disaster"; until the "immemorial unity . . . between man and nature is once again an everyday conviction, we shall continue to race toward material and spiritual disaster" (Anson 1953–54). Both human error and nature's purpose were invoked against allowing "the taint of Man's World [to] infect Nature beyond the limit of forbearance" (Murray 1954: 142). Even an enthusiast for environmental engineering saw nature "taking her revenge" for man's heedless acts (Spilhaus 1956: 452).

Nuclear warfare aroused a host of fears. Biological chain reactions elicited concern (World Health Organization 1957: 683) along with fallout, radioactive waste disposal, and the effect of genetic mutations. Yet *Man's Role* virtually ignored nuclear issues. Given their public visibility, why were they thus scanted? "The general silence on this subject is strange, and our own silence is even stranger," reflected Mumford (1966: 723) at a later environmental colloquy. "That we have not said a word about the fact that the leaders in the Pentagon . . . may destroy the major habitats on the planet . . . is frightening." Perhaps the nuclear holocaust was too horrifying to confront. Mumford suspected repressed awareness of the threat to all life in "oversensitivity" about the extinction of this or that species. "In our concern with the whooping crane we are at once symbolizing and concealing a far deeper anxiety" – namely, the prospective total extermination of all species.

These apprehensions, although cushioned by lingering faith in science and technology, were widespread a generation ago. Their absence from *Man's Role* reveals an extraordinary disparity between expert and public opinion. Explicitly meant to enlighten the future, *Man's Role* envisaged no role for a concerned public, whose apprehensions the symposium nowhere touched upon. It was not people in general but "scholars in oncoming generations" that the book was meant to reach (Thomas 1956: xxii).

Recent Perception of Environmental Impacts

Public Participation

The prominence of public voices is one of the most striking changes in environmental impact since *Man's Role*. Public pressure has triggered environmental research, monitoring, national and local legislation, and international regulation. Environmental advocacy reflects three postwar developments, first Western, latterly global. Authoritative warnings of the limits of earth and the fragility of the biosphere have brought home these concerns to a wider public. Postwar Western affluence has led to demands for environmental quality even at the cost of productivity. And participatory experience leads people to take active roles in vital environmental matters. To the environmentally conscious public, environment is too important to be left to experts no longer seen as omniscient or incorruptible.

Relations between professionals and publics rapidly altered during the late 1950s and 1960s (Mikesell 1974: 8–11, 17–19). Up to then, aloofness was common: many scientists openly scorned the public as irrational, emotionally involved, hastily judgmental, fickle in its fears and enthusiasms. Some continue to belittle public fears and deride amateur views (Cohen 1984: 564; Mellanby 1988). But many scientists have responded to wider environmental concerns by applying research and technical innovation in order to monitor and contain impacts. At the same time, others work for economic and managerial interests to discount impact fears and discourage environmental reform. With impact issues intensely politicized and traditional objectivity eroded, scientists have willy-nilly become environmentally embattled (Amy 1987; Hays 1987).

Public activism, like impact control generally, displays differing tempos in various parts of the world. Experts and the public, rich and poor, urban and rural, America and Europe, capitalist and socialist states, the developed and the Third World exhibit disparate types and levels of concern. Only recently manifested in the wake of development fiascos, famine, and Bhopal-type catastrophes, the Asian and African environmental concerns noted in *Our Common Future* (1987) attest an awareness far more widespread than a decade earlier.

Consciousness of human impact is no continuously progressing saga, however. Unlike the gains of technology, awareness of their environmental effects is not cumulative. Alarms triggered by environmental crises dissipate as crises die away. Awareness of particular issues lasts only for a limited time even amidst general concern. Chernobyl dominated global consciousness for months, but news of most impact disasters endures for only a few weeks. Levels of concern rarely carry over from one crisis to the next.

Shifting public moods likewise shroud long-term trends in doubt. Did American concern peak with Earth Day in 1970? Does the subsequent falling off in media references truly reflect declining environmentalist support? We simply do not know. The steady growth of impact awareness and concern are articles of faith among many environmentalists (Nicholson 1987; *Our Common Future* 1987: 28; Strong 1980: 616; White, R. 1985: 306); each successive text finds "an unprecedented interest in the environmental future" (Goudie 1986: 295–96). But while some analysts see environmental concerns as impressively durable – a durability that Reaganite advocates of unrestricted growth disregarded to their cost in the early 1980s – others see them as momentary and superficial, still others as fluctuating with economic trends (Hays 1987: 491–512; Lake 1983; Mitchell 1984: 52–57). The partisanship of some pollsters exacerbates uncertainties about levels of concern and what they imply. Analysts who themselves favor environmental caution tend to discern broad-based public support for environmentalism. Analysts who prefer untrammeled growth perceive a low level of public concern, much of it irrationally based (Hays 1987: 317–18).

Conflicting views about underlying attitudes toward nature exemplify these doubts. On the one hand, nine Americans in ten polled in 1982 rejected the old "exemptionalist" view ("nature's bounty is infinite, humans are omnipotent") (Mitchell 1984: 58), and nineteen of twenty Pacific Northwesterners polled in 1973 agreed that "humans must live in harmony with nature in order to survive" (Hays 1987: 32–33). On the other hand, almost half of self-styled environmentalists held that mankind was created to rule over the rest of nature and that plants and animals existed primarily for human use (Dunlap and Van Liere 1978), and almost nine out of ten believed that "technology got us into environmental problems, but technology will get us out" (Cotgrove 1982: 31; Richard J. Bordon in Polunin 1980: 438).

Substantial majorities feel it wise to eliminate toxic pollution, protect endangered species, and limit economic growth in order to enhance environmental quality – but strong and steady support for these aims is scanty (Mitchell 1980: 3, 41; 1984: 56). The chasm between Green words and deeds is awesome: thus almost three of four Britons polled in 1982 were ready to insist on lead-free petrol even at extra cost, but hardly anyone six years later would take the least trouble to find it (Porritt and Winner 1988: 176). Only a tiny fraction of the millions in the National Audubon Society, the Royal Society for the Protection of Birds, or the various National Trusts actively back environmental reform. Green party votes of under 6% in West Germany in 1983 (8% in 1987) and 2.5% in Italy in 1987 were termed "stunning" and "amazing" victories (Porritt and Winner 1988: 214, 217; Spretnak and Capra 1985: 18).

The most potent public fears about impact are hard to convert into electoral policies. Although seven out of ten British voters agreed that party environmental stands would be important in how they voted, the 1987 General Election was "a distinctly un-green affair" (Porritt and Winner 1988: 62). "Unless God opens an ozone hole directly above the Palace of Westminster, or melts the polar ice-cap just enough to bring the Thames lapping round the chair-legs in the Members' Bar," concludes one analyst, "'Green' issues will never rank with the central concerns of British politics" (Malcolm 1989). Notwithstanding sustained alarm over global warming, the 20% backing British Greens gained in the 1989 European elections soon plummeted to below 10%.

The huge range of viewpoints and preferences now linked with environmental concerns makes views about impacts still more difficult to assess. Little can be concluded or even surmised about environmental awareness in Japan, when "environmental education" for most (70%) high-school teachers turns out to mean "teaching children to tidy their rooms and not drop litter" (Stewart-Smith 1987: 190). Not much can be forecast about American environmental policies on the basis of George Bush's prediction that he "will be a great conservation and environmental president [because] I plan to fish and hunt as much as I can" (in Dowd 1989: 3).

Yet the rapid spread and high visibility of environmentalist literature over the past four decades are undeniable. Sensationalism may have inflamed doom-mongering, but in the process many have learned to become environmentalists, and "there are almost no instances of people learning to become non- or anti-environmentalists" (Milbrath 1984: 80).

Above all, environmental impacts have increasingly come to seem global and interrelated, complex and unknowable, long-lasting and prospectively irreversible. None of these perspectives is wholly new – many echo Marsh's *Man and Nature*. But only since the 1950s have they come to dominate scientific apprehensions and public fears and to pervade and polarize environmental debate.

Global Awareness

Environmental transformations are more and more felt to involve the whole interrelated biosphere. "Think globally, act locally" is a Green movement motto. The most worrisome impacts – loss of biotic diversity, CO_2 buildup, ozone-layer depletion – are worldwide, not local, problems. As its title suggests, *Our Common Future* (1987) addresses global concerns that override local interests, even national institutions. Whether for acid rain or for wildlife protection, international collaboration is essential, and sociopolitical matters are no less critical than ecological ones (Aniansson 1986). "Our environmental problems today are multidisciplinary and transnational," as a Norwegian engineer says, "not mainly scientific or technological but political, economic, and cultural" (*Our Common Future* 1987: 342). Most world leaders now address the transcendent problem, identified by Boulding (1977: 289), that while the globe is being seen as a single ecosystem, it is far from becoming a single community (Carroll, J. E. 1988: 275–79).

Interconnectedness

A growing recognition that everything connects with everything else in an indivisible causal web (*World Resources 1986*: xiii) has generated awareness that the effects of human impact are interactive as well as global. Finding radioactive iodine from Hiroshima and Nagasaki in lichens in Lapland and Alaska proved that the world was one in peril; awareness of bioaccumulation mounted as America lurched from atomic testing fallout to Hopewell and Love Canal. No one now feels secure against such devastating interdependencies (Hays 1987: 172–73).

The interconnectedness of nature is a central tenet not only of radical environmentalism but also of mainstream science. A generation ago even scholars seldom drew such causal connections. Today it is tabloid routine to link population pressure with rain-forest depletion, acid rain with heavy runoff, excess CO_2 with climatic change. These linkages are fostered by the growing interrelatedness of the environmental sciences. Not that the disciplines that monitor human impacts all now contentedly chew the same ecological cud. Rivalries corrode vital collaboration; the neglect of proper precautions in pesticide use, for example, is blamed on the fragmentation of embattled disciplines. But environmental scientists are increasingly conscious that their mutual concerns demand the pooling of knowledge.

Uncertainty

Impact assessment is beset by uncertainty because the consequences of new technology always outrun our ability to monitor them. Since we are constitutionally "incapable of weighing their immediate, still more their ultimate consequences," as Marsh recognized long ago, we are bound to affect nature in ways that we cannot ascertain or assess. Some of these impacts are minuscule. But it is wrong to assume "a force to be insignificant because its measure is unknown, or even because no physical effect can now be traced to it" (Marsh [1864] 1965: 465).

During the subsequent century of managerial hubris, most conservationists forgot Marsh's maxim. But radiation and toxicity issues of the 1950s and 1960s revived doubts about scientific omniscience (Mitchell 1985: 6); growing pressures on the biosphere now seemed to presage literally incalculable damage, if only because many impacts operate too slowly to be apparent within a human lifespan. Reliable data on environmental impact typically came too little or too late for appropriate response, and each advance in environmental understanding raised more doubts than it resolved (*Our Common Future* 1987: 343; SCEP 1970: 126). Thus chemists improved their detections of levels of concentration by six orders of magnitude within a decade, but no comparable advance occurred in knowledge of toxicity; hence the health risks of the chemical traces measured with such precision remained unassessed (Rosen and Gretch 1987: 127).

The public meanwhile grew more fearful of dangers that mounted with time, yet could be detected only when precautions would be too late. Scientists were chastised for their inability to predict adverse environmental effects with speed, precision, and certainty (Hays 1987: 172–74). Above all, people found intolerable even remote possibilities of long-term, low-level exposure that might cause cancer or birth defects (Efron 1984; Wilkinson 1987: 34). Obsessive popular fears are held to have forced the United States Environmental Protection Agency to spend so much on human health that the broader environmental impacts of pesticide use were left virtually unstudied (Briggs 1987: 10). In the same way, some argue, unrealistic fears of radiation impede nuclear relief of far more hazardous CO_2 buildup from coal mining (Bodansky 1987).

What seems most fearsome is that impacts may become irreversible. Such fears are not exclusively ecological; they are also aroused by the mining of exhaustible minerals and the restoration of historic buildings and works of art. But substitutability mitigates the loss of inanimate substances – something else can be used in their place. By contrast, irreversible impacts put earth's ecosystems wholly at risk. Fear of extinguishing human life, perhaps all life, underlies current environmental awareness.

That fear originated with Marsh's memorable 1864 warning:

There are parts of Asia Minor, of Northern Africa, of Greece, and even of Alpine Europe, where the operation of causes set in action by man has brought the face of the earth to a desolation almost as complete as that of the moon; . . . known to have been covered with luxuriant woods, verdant pastures, and fertile meadows, they are now too far deteriorated to be reclaimable by man. . . . The earth is fast becoming an unfit home for its noblest inhabitant, and another era of equal human crime and human improvidence . . . would reduce it to such a condition of impoverished productiveness, of shattered surface, of climatic excess, as to threaten the depravation, barbarism, and perhaps even extinction of the species ([1864] 1965: 42–43).

Today's plight seems more parlous because it is less obvious. How much and what kinds of aerosol emission, when and where, would irretrievably open the ozone hole? How much can an ecosystem be depleted before becoming degraded to the point of no return? Slow bioaccumulation; the lengthy half-life of many radioactive disintegration products; the centuries-long ecosystem effects of species extinctions; the differential pace of biological, edaphic, and geological processes; the immeasurable acceleration of technological impact – all this generates alarm about consequences of unpredictable finality (Randall 1986: 86–87).

Economists seeking to distinguish reversible from irreversible effects assumed it was a "simply empirical matter" to tell which was which (Arrow and Fisher 1974: 318–19). But it is neither simple nor wholly empirical. Whether or not a process is irreversible is unknown at its inception and usually in doubt when preventive measures are applied. Precisely because ecological impacts are subtle, multiple, and often long-delayed, controls needed to safeguard reversibility are often under- or overestimated (Bishop 1978; Meadows et al. 1972: 72; Norton 1986: 119; Randall 1986: 101; SCEP 1970: 125–26).

Species extinction illustrates how such uncertainties arouse mistrust and foment exaggeration. The debate involves such diverse matters as the causes of Cretaceous and Pleistocene extinctions, current rain-forest depletion, how far present extinctions entail further losses, and the relative worth of endangered species. But the pace of prehistoric extinctions, current losses, ecosystem degradation, even the numbers of existing species are poorly known, if at all. And ignorance spawns speculative claims on both sides.

Those worried about the biosphere charge that accelerating extinctions may deplete one-fourth of the earth's genetic heritage within a century, setting in train irreversible losses of entire ecosystems; advocates of development term such alarms bogus. Unfortunately, both views are compatible with existing evidence. Neither the catastrophists' claim that species disappear before they are known to be threatened, nor their opponents' assertion that many more species were lost during prehistoric times, can be refuted; and the relevance of each assertion for impact predictions is also unclear.

Hence both sides exaggerate for effect. "Extinctions will increase dramatically; as many as 20% will be irretrievably lost if their habitats vanish" is a typical environmentalist claim (*Global 2000 Report* 1981). Cornucopians complain that this is "guesswork" based on shaky estimates. But nothing now known is inconsistent with that forecast, either. The absence of a "*prima facie* case for any expensive policy of safeguarding species" (Simon 1986: 62–63) does not make such a policy wrong or foolish, any more than what is known about extinction justifies the Greens to conclude that "the way most of us in the Western world now live poses a fundamental threat to the planet" (Jenkins 1988).

Numbers become tokens of faith. Economists disregard the intangible for the concrete, eschew qualitative for quantitative criteria, and ignore as "externalities" environmental variables that do not fit traditional cost-benefit analyses (Ehrenfeld 1986b: 42; Hays 1987: 405–409; Pearce 1976; Randall 1987: 416; Rosen and Gretch 1987: 141). Environmentalists deploy numbers that have "the power to frighten" (Simon and Wildavsky 1984: 181), such as the World Wildlife Fund's claim that "now we're destroying [plants'] principal habitat at the rate of *50 acres every minute*" and that "horrifyingly, some 25,000 of all flowering species are on the verge of extinction" (advertisement, *International Herald Tribune*, Jan. 2, 1989, p. 7). The emotive appeal of specific temporal goals galvanizes immediate action: "Before the end of the century we must accomplish basic change in our relations . . . with nature" (SCEP 1970: 12); "we have five years to make our choice for human survival or extinction" (Bellini 1986: 251). Issued to rivet public attention as cautionary uncertainties cannot do, such "imminence" statements are seldom carefully calculated.

The frequent invisibility of their cause also impels environmentalists to emotive specifics. Thus biologists most worried about ecosystem diversity in Madagascar harp on cute, exotic creatures like lemurs and loris (although they themselves may deplore such "vertebrate chauvinism"), otherwise the public will not hear them (Joyce 1986; Kellert 1986: 60–61). Focused outrage accomplishes more than reasoned argument. The SCEP (1970) report's public impact was negligible, but a sensationalist commentary, *Blueprint for Survival* (Goldsmith et al. 1972), engendered widespread response. Often only disaster achieves immediate remedial action; it took London's killer smog of 1952 to bring about Britain's Clean Air Act (Ashby 1978: 21–22; Sinclair 1973: 180).

Mistrust of environmental managers mounts when expert assurances prove false. The ozone layer issue is a case in point. Much as engineers at Three Mile Island customarily disregarded malfunction alarms because they went off so frequently, so ozone researchers blinded themselves to reality because they could not credit observations so much at odds with predicted stability. The "long-run dangers of ill-founded concerns about environmental dangers" and the costs of overreaction to them (Simon 1986; Solow 1988) are matched by the mortal risks of scientific optimists' ill-founded assurances that all is well.

Impact Attitudes and Advocacy

Polarization

A rancorous adversarial tone features current discussion of biosphere impact. When and why did this begin?

More than a century ago, Marsh castigated earth's despoilers for their heedless greed. But *Man and Nature* unleashed no embittered debate. No entrepreneur or industrialist, planter or hunter, refuted Marsh's accusations, defended the gutting of forests or the slaughter of wildlife as economically essential, or dismissed his ecological fears as hysterical.

Why were there no such rebuttals? First, Marsh couched his warnings in a framework of environmental improvement and economic progress; he disputed not the desirability of conquering nature but the bungling way it was being done. Second, no one took personal offense: notwithstanding Marsh's moralistic invective ("Joint-stock companies have no souls; their managers . . . no consciences" [(1864) 1965: 51n]), he inveighed more against mankind in general than against particular entrepreneurs. Third, Marsh's corrective measures – reafforestation, planting sand dunes, monitoring environmental impacts – seemed to entail no economic sacrifices or to require any draconian remedies. Self-interest underwrote most of his prescriptions. Fourth, no one in Marsh's day quarrelled with his emphasis on stewardship for the future, though few exploited resources in that spirit. Fifth, no media broadcast his warnings throughout the world or sought out reactions from likely malefactors. Finally, although Marsh's ecological admonitions were revolutionary, they elicited no sustained opposition because their underlying philosophy inspired broad agreement.

Subsequent impact concerns tended, however, to bifurcate into mutually exclusive economic and inspirational components. Americans worried about resource scarcity, like Gifford Pinchot, opted for centralized environmental management. Those concerned with environmental quality, like John Muir, focused mainly on wilderness areas that interfered relatively little with demands for resource use – although when they did clash, as at Hetch Hetchy, antagonists did not spare their vitriol. Only a small and generally disregarded minority expressed general doubts about exploitative technology (Fox 1985; Hays 1959; Nash 1967; 122–81).

Not even Dust Bowl calamities set conservationists sharply against entrepreneurial interests. It was the *past* that was blamed for that set of disasters – the blithe frontiersman's confidence that resources, however maltreated, could never be exhausted. Both industrial managers and conservationists assumed that these heedless and wasteful habits were over and done with. And successful corrective action – the soil

conservation reforms and shelter belts of the 1930s and 1940s – seemed to bear them out (Graham, E. H. 1956: 690; 1110). Global reformers like Fairfield Osborn (1948) and William Vogt (1948) were considered heretical because of their "lamentable lack of faith in man's ability to control his future with new technology" (Williams 1987: 230). Marsh's warnings were thought germane only to man's *past* impacts.

Polarization in earnest began with Rachel Carson's (1962) assault against interests responsible for pesticide use. *Silent Spring* condemns as much by tone as by content. Chapter titles – "Elixirs of Death," "Needless Havoc," "Beyond the Dreams of the Borgias," "Nature Fights Back" – bristle with confrontation. The book was irresistibly polemical. "How could intelligent beings seek to control a few unwanted species by a method that contaminated the entire environment?" A quarter-century of lethal disturbance had forged a "chain of evil." The "ruthless power" of special interests had launched an insane "crusade to create a chemically sterile, insect-free world." Confuting the "false assurances" of growth-merchants and the "arrogance" of applied entomology, Carson alerted millions to the poisoning of their environment. Nothing did more to awaken the world to the consequences of meddling with nature or to set the terms of subsequent debate.

Time magazine's charge that Carson's "emotional and inaccurate outburst may do harm by alarming the non-technical public" typified industrialists' reaction to *Silent Spring* (Evernden 1985b: 8).

The really hysterical reaction on the part of the chemical industries and so on was not really because "we can't sell so much DDT and our profits are going to fall." . . . The really scary thing was that she was questioning the whole attitude of industrial society toward the natural world. This was heresy and this had to be suppressed (Paul Brooks, 1972, in Briggs 1987: 6).

The manner as much as the matter of the environmentalist assault Carson initiated captured – and altered – public attention. For example, the revivalist, accusatory style of F. F. Darling's 1969 Reith lectures (1970) brought home to listeners their own complicity in the rape of nature (Chisholm 1972: xi–xiv, 39, 51–53; Cotgrove 1982: 8). Replacing the dispassionate tone of "conservation" and "wise use," Earth Day's emphasis on environmental quality, scarcity, spaceship earth, and endangered species popularized symbols that carried potent protective implications (Mitchell 1984: 67–68). The same emotive moralism still features environmentalism. Thus in the British media bulldozers/planners/speculators/juggernauts/pollution/big business consistently threaten the people/the community/a rare species/local beauty spot/unspoiled nature/the national heritage (Lowe and Goyder 1983: 76).

Global confrontation began with the limits-to-growth debate, *Models of Doom* (Cole et al. 1973), countering the Meadows' (1972) book on the U.N. Stockholm Conference on the Human Environment. Since then every minatory caution has elicited impassioned rebuttals that discredit evidence of impacts or discount deleterious effects. Prominent scholars trade accusations not only of shortsighted error but of willful perversion of reality. Incredulous catastrophists and cornucopians each rage at opponents who ignore or ridicule what seems to them evident (Cotgrove 1979). Thus Medawar assails the "rancorous criticism of science and technology by people who believe, and seem almost to hope, that the environment has deteriorated" too far to support human life (1984: 189–90). Holding that Paul Ehrlich's "morbidly fascinating" exaggerations and "dire threats [aim to] shock us so we don't apply the same critical faculties we do with less emotional statements," Julian Simon cited NAS President Philip Handler's warning that "the nations of the world may yet pay a dreadful price for the public behavior of scientists who depart from fact to indulge in hyperbole" (1981: 39–42). Ehrlich (1981: 48; 1982: 386) retorted that growth-at-any-cost cornucopians were as "moronic" and "incompetent" as flat-earthers and antievolutionists.

The bitterness of debate reflects the inconclusive and shifting nature of impact evidence. Vital concerns impossible to cost impede adjudications of environmental risks and benefits. Crusaders denounce their opponents as Cassandras or Pollyannas, frighten and confuse the public, and leave experts at loggerheads. "Everyone wants to be seen to be doing something" about the greenhouse effect, notes a science editorial. "As a result, there has been a plethora of 'our scientists say this' announcements. Not surprisingly, everyone's scientists say something slightly different" (*New Scientist* 1988).

Social and Political Cleavages

Another reason why environmental disputes are so impassioned is that they reflect differences more fundamental than those of risk assessment alone. Adversaries may disagree not merely about levels of impact but about the role and worth of science and technology, society and politics.

To be sure, few alarmed about environmental damage and deterioration wholly reject the tenets of industrial or capitalist society (Lowe and Goyder 1983: 27). Even the most environmentally concerned look to new technology against the ill effects of the old. Since the mid-1970s thousands of alternative ecology projects, assessed by the Green Party for their environmental compatibility, economical use of energy, and humane working conditions, have come into being in West Germany (Spretnak and Capra 1985: 88–89).

Most environmentalists differ with the established order less over the virtues of technology than in their rejection of productivity as good in itself. Many in affluent and leisured societies no longer accept the environmental costs of unrestricted production. Lifestyles of the 1960s and 1970s shifted from an ethos of accumulating wealth to one of enjoying it and of living lightly on the land (Hays 1987: 263–66, 540–41; Lowe and Goyder 1983: 25–26).

These preferences worry economists because they transgress traditional growth and consumerist tenets. But growing awareness of the costs of degradation have begun to alter industrialists' outlooks too; British Land Rover's 1987 loss of a substantial Swiss Army order because it could not meet Swiss air pollution control standards is not a unique episode (Porritt and Winner 1988: 141). Indeed, although American media persist in calling those concerned about impact pessimists and their opponents optimists, during the 1980s it was in fact "the environmentalists [who] were the purveyors of optimism about the possibilities of human achievement while the administrative and technical leaders were the constant bearers of bad news," remarks Hays (1987: 542). "The driving forces behind environmental [impulses] were hope and confidence and the possibilities of a better life; there was a constant search for the very latest in science and technology."

Whereas industrial managers now warn of the economic limits to what can be done to make the environment safe, pleasant, and healthy, environmentalists look to science to rectify impacts and construct a safer and sounder biosphere. Few of them query the legitimacy of technology, but only how it is applied and who controls it. Many innovations – the electronically integrated internal combustion engine, fluid-bed combustion, the photovoltaic cell – are now widely applied owing originally to environmentalist advocacy (Hays 1987: 364–65, 376–77, 528–29; Tom Burke 1977, in Lowe and Goyder 1983: 133).

Nonetheless, occupational roles still broadly reflect traditional polarization on impact. Cornucopians are typically engineers, managers, salesmen, industrial scientists – those at the heart of the productive system who consider growth a cardinal virtue. Catastrophists are typically teachers, social workers, artists, and others on the periphery of industrial society; occupationally shielded from direct engagement with the marketplace, they take longer-range environmental views. Among the latter, some conflate environmental fears with critiques of mainstream social institutions. Thus the environmental debate is not only about differing assessments of impacts but also about opposing social values (Cotgrove 1982; Cotgrove and Duff 1980: 340–44).

Some analysts regard apprehensions of biosphere impact as exclusively social in origin. In their view, fears of risk have no basis in environmental reality; they simply reflect the antipathy of peripheral "sectarians" toward "centralists" in power. Sectarians have a vested interest in bad news; threats of irreversible disaster bolster their belief that present institutions are doomed, that nature will punish technological hubris, materialist corruption, and vaulting ambition. As they see it, environmental health cannot be regained by reforming modern technology, only by eradicating it (Douglas and Wildavsky 1983; Inglehart 1977: 377–78; Lowenthal 1970).

That environmental fears have social correlates – even explanations – does not, however, prove them simply chimerical. "A thousand years ago, we were afraid of witches. Today, we are afraid of industrial and nuclear pollution." But the fears are not equally imaginary, adds Munz (1985: 47, 301–306). That original sin engendered environmental evils was, like belief in witchcraft, an article of faith inaccessible to rational argument or empirical falsification. Modern impact warnings may seem dogmatic but must ultimately rely on observations open to public scrutiny. Present-day fears about deranging nature have some roots in earlier fears, but unlike them they get confirmed or resolved by testable knowledge. Like their prescientific precursors, some today exploit environmental fears for apocalyptic or revolutionary goals. But that is not sufficient reason to discount those fears as bogus or unreal.

Differing creeds and attachments do nonetheless polarize impact debate. For a small but vocal environmentalist minority, science and technology are the problem, not the solution; only scrapping industrial society can prevent imminent, irreversible biosphere damage. Radical Greens mistrust science, abhor technology, reprobate the materialism of modern capitalism (and communism) and the hegemony of the marketplace. Considering addiction to economic growth incurable, these reformers demand nonexploitative, non-technological communities in harmony with nature (Norton 1986: 132; Porritt and Winner 1988: 11, 135).

The utopian (though not the Luddite) values of their agenda find allies in environmentalism at large and are mirrored in the tone and content of environmental politics. Green alliances bracket environmental concerns with every imaginable deficiency of mainstream society. In the United States they make common cause with antiracism, ecofeminism, and bioregionalism. Some British Greens assert that the "holocaust . . . engulfing our planet" requires sharply curtailing, if not dismantling, the industrialized economy (Binyon 1987; Shabecoff 1987).

These sweeping proscriptions reflect mounting alienation from mainstream institutions. More and more Americans doubt that "Public officials care what people like me think" (up from 30% in 1956 to 54% in 1974) or that "People like me have some say in what government does" (up from 20% to 59% since 1956); trends in Britain and elsewhere are similar (Cotgrove 1982: 77–79; Inglehart 1977: Table 11-1). Environmental reformers express increasing disillusion. Despite a few clear gains, three out of four polled in 1980 rated environmental threats as more serious than 20 years before and thought them likely to worsen.

This pessimism reflects the growing sophistication of those who oppose reform. The mere suggestion of prospective damage was sometimes enough to halt the production or control the emission of some noxious product in the United States during the 1960s. By the 1980s, industrialists had persuaded courts and regulatory agencies to require firm proof of damage before enjoining production. Assessments of risk undertaken beyond levels of precise knowledge now undermined scientists' credibility with industry and threatened their academic and governmental careers. Stigmatized by managerial opponents and stymied by lawyers who demand "yes" or "no" responses about uncertain levels of damage from varying degrees of contamination, fewer and fewer scientists stick their necks out as crusaders against asbestos or whatever (Hays 1987: 341, 351, 360–61, 412–13; Wilkinson 1987: 40, 42–43).

Finding producers often implacably hostile to environmental goals, the public has become more cynical about business influence in governmental controls (Hays 1987: 534, 580). Only one American in six thought industry could cope with the environmental problems it had engendered, and only one in three thought government could handle them (Hays 1987: 206). Everywhere people express doubts that existing institutions are willing or competent to set in train the needed reforms (*World Resources 1987*: 350, Table 26-4). Yet few thus disillusioned take remedial action; as in Germany, "de-spite their frequent complaints, people are in the habit of letting the monolithic agencies and institutions make decisions for them" (Spretnak and Capra 1985: 212).

At least since Malthus, many have seriously questioned whether science and technology enhance life. More and more now doubt it. The malign effects of progress loom larger not simply because they seem more noxious and dangerous, but because their attendant benefits are discounted in advance. And as new conquests of nature come at ever greater expense, mounting costs make it harder to resolve existing environmental problems and respond to new ones (Rescher 1980: 282). Even if its effects are reversible, the environmental crisis may be incurable. Institutions will become less, not more, able to contain impacts – especially when most people may be clinging for dear life to the messy technology of environmentally damaging production.

The social effects of this double disillusionment – that technological progress will make people happy; that saving miracles will continue to unfold – are as depressing as the physical anxieties they foreshadow. The failure of inflated expectations and of utopian reform and the loss of faith in progress induce despondency, impotence, and *après nous le deluge* escapism (Rescher 1980: 19, 24–28). Growth–antigrowth polarization, alarmist intensification of public fears, agenda for wholesale sociopolitical change now frequently accompany impact awareness, as does massive managerial denial that such impacts require control – or even that they exist. Public fears converge, however, with growing dismay among scientists. Like nuclear physicists in ban-the-bomb days, biologists turn crusaders for reform. Mainstream scholars who in the 1970s dismissed alarms about species extinction as extremist now term habitat destruction a threat "second only to thermonuclear war" (Callicott 1986; Lovejoy 1986; Norton 1986; Rensberger 1986).

Conclusion

Public awareness and fear outrun impact control. "The pessimism which is prevalent today," suggested Henry Tizard (1950: 109) a generation ago, "is due not so much to fundamental causes as to a greater availability of information." Today we dread both what we know and what remains unknown. A less self-confident scientific community is more pessimistic about technology's untoward side-effects. A series of major disasters whose risks were inadequately foreseen, the buildup of increasingly malign residues, contaminations that are invisible, unknowable, and unlimited in duration, induce a sense of vulnerability especially frightening because beyond remedy (Lifton 1986).

Heightened concern and environmental monitoring have increased public knowledge of impact and brought a few dramatic reforms – banning atmospheric nuclear testing to reduce strontium 90, banning DDT to revive food chains. Emission controls have made some gains. But numerous failures offset these successes, and risks from impacts newly perceived induce graver anxiety.

Most such concerns generate little more than band-aid remedies, however. The majority shun radical cures. When people "come to regard all wild living things as possessing inherent worth," predicts an ecological reformer (Taylor 1986: 223) "they will enact such laws as are needed to protect the good of those wild creatures." But few are that much concerned, save by animal rights' terrorism. And threats to basic livelihood make radical environmentalism increasingly unpalatable. People prefer to be gradually poisoned by industry than rapidly starved by the lack of it. A Green Coalition in Germany foundered when it seemed to express more concern about laboratory rats than about unemployed factory workers; almost a third of the German population now feel profoundly threatened by the Greens (Commoner 1987: 68–69; Porritt and Winner 1988: 15). Opting for economic gain over environmental caution, two out of three Americans favored the widescale deployment of genetically engineered bacteria (Louis Harris survey, in I. Anderson 1987).

Ecological awareness has, however, softened managerial bents toward growth. Environmental control is now so clearly fragile and worries about risk are so widespread that the most troglodyte industrialist could no longer celebrate mastery over nature as an unalloyed virtue. The loss of entrepreneurial hubris reflects the decline of the faith, pervasive from the Enlightenment through the World War II, that man's impacts were either benign or miniscule.

Technological confidence erodes for other reasons too. Today's entrepreneurs cannot avoid seeing how environmental impacts proliferate. In times past, pollution or degradation could be dismissed as local in character, confined in both scope and duration. But the scale of modern exploitation, the ubiquity of travel, and regulatory constraints bearing on entire watersheds, far-flung river systems, oceanwide contamination, the atmospheric range of acid rain bring home the global scale of environmental issues to anyone of influence. Entrepreneurs who once could cocoon themselves from environmental discomfort – and awareness – can do so no longer, however wealthy or privileged they may be.

Moreover, the moral fervor that once justified assaults on nature is now passé. The need to prove superiority has lost its force. Dogmas enthroning our position above nature have lost their sanction. They are replaced by ethical doctrines emphasizing kinship with other living things. Lynn White's (1967) ascription of ruthless Western exploitation to a Christian creed that enthroned man above the rest of creation has aroused intense debate (Passmore 1980; Bratton 1984; Fox 1985: 359–61; Hargrove 1986). But what is significant is not whether Scripture proves White's point; it is that both sides take for granted that the notion of conquest is deplorable. We may enjoy the benefits of technology's mastery of nature, but we no longer morally justify that mastery.

Dubious ecologically, dubious technologically, dubious even economically, the cornucopian view is now also morally bankrupt. No guiding certainties remain to buttress faith in progress. Self-interest still impels entrepreneurs and nationstates to outproduce their rivals. But awareness of impact may finally persuade them that even self-interest must weigh environmental concern against economic gain. Shorn of a moral credo, self-interest becomes amenable to rational adjudication.

Shorn of Scriptural authority, catastrophism too lacks its former apocalyptic fervor. Few who dwell on the evils they imagine have led to our present plight consciously espouse the views some impute to them – that they *want* humanity to perish, or that doomsday is certain because it is God's will; instead, they insist that we do something *now*, before it is too late – implying that doom *can* be averted.

The intensity of current debates nonetheless reflects differences more consciously and keenly articulated than at any time in the past. The industrial-military establishment, confident that it can cope with untoward impacts, remains for the most part environmentally untroubled. The public at large, increasingly desirous of safe and healthy environments, retains lingering but diminished faith that technology can secure these aims but is fast losing faith that government will secure them. The media, always feeding off environmental confrontation, evinces growing sympathy for environmental causes – strikingly signaled by *Time* magazine's advocacy, a quarter-century after attacking *Silent Spring*, of a Nobel prize for Rachel Carson (*Time* 1989: 37). On all these actors in the environmental scene impinge more and more activists, including scientists from many disciplines, who cry havoc at global transformations of unimaginable cost and risk to present and future generations.

Acknowledgments
I am grateful to Hugh Prince for gratifying encouragement; to Michael Bell, Bob Kates, and Andrew Warren for generous criticism; to David Bodansky, Robert Mitchell, Vaclav Smil, and Michael Williams for useful ammunition; to Martin Holdgate and Michael Watts for spotting major lacunae that alas remain unfilled; and, in the spirit of *Man's Role*, to George P. Marsh for insights still unsurpassed.

References
Albrecht, W. A. 1956. Physical, chemical, and biochemical changes in the soil community. In W. Thomas, ed. 1956, q.v., 648–73.

Amy, D. J. 1987. *The Politics of Environmental Mediation*. New York: Columbia University Press.

Anderson, E. 1956. Man as a maker of new plants and new plant communities. In W. Thomas, ed. 1956, q.v., 763–77.

Anderson, I. 1987. Activists damage outdoor gene test plot. *New Scientist* (June 4): 32.

Aniansson, B., ed. 1986. *Europe's Air – Europe's Environment*. Report of the Nordic Council of Ministers to the International Conference on Transboundary Air Pollution. Stockholm.

Anson, P. G. 1953–54. Review of G. H. T. Kimble, *The Way of the World. Landscape* 3: 2.

Arrow, K. J., and A. C. Fisher. 1974. Environmental preservation, uncertainty and irreversibility. *Quarterly Journal of Economics* 88: 312–19.

Ashby, E. 1978. *Reconciling Man with the Environment*. London: Oxford University Press.

Bates, M. 1956. Process. In W. Thomas, ed. 1956, q.v., 1136–40.

Bellini, J. 1986. *High Tech Holocaust*. Newton Abbott: David & Charles.

Binyon, M. 1987. Greens in search of votes and saved deposits. *The Times* (London) June 9: 6.

Birch, C., and J. E. Cobb, Jr. 1981. *The Liberation of Life*. Cambridge: Cambridge University Press.

Bishop, R. C. 1978. Endangered species and uncertainty: the economics of a safe minimum standard. *American Journal of Agricultural Economics* 60: 10–18.

Bodansky, D. 1987. Perspectives on radon and other radiation sources. *Physics and Society* 14(4) (October): 7–8.

Boulding, K. 1977. Commons and community: the idea of a public. In *Managing the Commons*, ed. G. Hardin and J. Baden, 280–94. San Francisco: Freeman.

Bratton, S. P. 1984. Christian ecotheology and the Old Testament. *Environmental Ethics* 6: 195–209.

Briggs, S. A. 1987. Rachel Carson: her vision and her legacy. In G. Marco et al., eds. 1987, q.v., 3–11.

Brimblecombe, P. 1987. *The Big Smoke: A History of Air Pollution in London Since Medieval Times*. London: Methuen.

Brower, D. E. 1957. Wilderness – conflict and conscience. *Sierra Club Bulletin* 42(6) (June): 1–12.

Bugher, J. C. 1956. Effects of fission material on air, soil, and living species. In W. Thomas, ed. 1956, q.v., 831–48.

Callicott, J. B. 1986. On the intrinsic value of nonhuman species. In B. Norton, ed. 1986, q.v., 138–72.

Carroll, J. E., ed. 1988. *International Environmental Diplomacy: The Management and Resolution of Transfrontier Environmental Problems*. Cambridge: Cambridge University Press.

Carroll, P. N. 1969. *Puritanism and the Wilderness: The Intellectual Significance of the New England Frontier, 1629–1700*. New York: Columbia University Press.

Carson, R. [1962] 1982. *Silent Spring*. Harmondsworth, Middlesex: Penguin.

Chisholm, A. 1972. *Philosophers of the Earth: Conversations with Ecologists*. London: Sidgwick & Jackson.

Cohen, B. L. 1984. Statement of dissent. In *The Resourceful Earth: A Response to Global 2000*, ed. J. L. Simon and H. Kahn, 564. Oxford: Blackwell.

Cole, H. S. D., C. Freeman, M. Jahoda, and K. L. R. Pavitt, eds. 1973. *Thinking about the Future: A Critique of Limits of Growth*. London: Chatto & Windus for Sussex University Press.

Collis, J. S. 1950. *The Triumph of the Tree*. London: Jonathan Cape.

Commoner, B. 1987. A reporter at large: the environment. *New Yorker* (June 15): 46–71.

Cotgrove, S. 1979. Catastrophe or cornucopia? *New Society* (March 22): 683–84.

———. 1982. *Catastrophe or Cornucopia: The Environment, Politics and the Future*. New York: John Wiley.

Cotgrove, S., and A. Duff. 1980. Environmentalism, middle-class radicalism and politics. *Sociological Review*. 28: 333–51.

Cowan, I. M. 1966. Management, response, and variety. In *Future Environments of North America: Transformation of a Continent*, ed. F. F. Darling and J. P. Milton, 55–65. Garden City, NY: The Natural History Press.

Cronon, W. 1983. *Changes in the Land: Indians, Colonists, and the Ecology of New England*. New York: Hill and Wang.

Curtis, J. T. 1956. The modification of mid-latitude grasslands and forests by man. In W. Thomas, ed. 1956. q.v., 721–36.

Darling, F. F. 1956. Man's ecological dominance through domesticated animals on wild land. In W. Thomas, ed. 1956, q.v., 778–87.

———. 1970. *Wilderness and Plenty*. The Reith Lectures 1969. London: British Broadcasting Corporation.

Davies, G. L. 1969. *The Earth in Decay: A History of British Geomorphology 1578–1878*. London: Macdonald.

Davis, K. 1955. The ideal size for our population. *New York Times Magazine* (May 1): 12ff, 34.

Douglas, M., and A. Wildavsky. 1983. *Risk and Culture: An Essay on The Selection of Technical and Environmental Dangers*. Berkeley: University of California Press.

Dowd, M. 1989. For Bush, sports comes with the job. *International Herald Tribune* (January 3): 1, 3.

Dunlap, R. E., and K. D. Van Liere. 1978. The "new environmental paradigm": a proposed measuring instrument and preliminary results. *Journal of Environmental Education* 9: 10–19.

Efron, E. 1984. *The Apocalyptics: Politics, Science, and the Big Cancer Lie*. New York: Simon and Schuster.

Ehrenfeld, D. 1986a. Life in the next millennium: who will be left in the earth's community? In *The Last Extinction*, ed. L. Kaufman and K. Mallory, 167–86. Cambridge, MA: MIT Press.

———. 1986b. Thirty million cheers for diversity. *New Scientist* (June 12): 38–43.

Ehrlich, P. R. 1981. An economist in Wonderland. *Social Science Quarterly* 62: 44–49.

———. 1982. That's right: you should check it for yourself. *Social Science Quarterly* 63: 385–87.

Evernden, N. 1985a. Constructing the natural: the darker side of the environmental movement. *North American Review* 270: 15–19.

———. 1985b. *The Natural Alien*. Toronto: University of Toronto Press.

Fejos, P. 1956. Foreword. In W. Thomas, ed. 1956, q.v., vii–viii.

Flader, S. L. 1978. *Thinking Like a Mountain: Aldo Leopold and the Evolution of an Ecological Attitude toward Deer, Wolves and Forests*. Lincoln: University of Nebraska Press, Bison Book.

Fox, S. 1985. *The American Conservation Movement: John Muir and His Legacy*. Madison: University of Wisconsin Press.

Freud, S. [1929] 1946. *Civilization and Its Discontents*. 3d ed. Translated by J. Riviere. London: Hogarth Press and the Institute of Psycho-analysis.

Glacken, C. J. 1956. Changing ideas of the habitable world. In W. Thomas, ed. 1956, q.v., 70–92.

———. 1967. *Traces on the Rhodian Shore: Nature and Culture in Western Thought from Ancient Times to the End of the Eighteenth Century*. Berkeley: University of California Press.

The Global 2000 Report to the President. 1981. Council on Environmental Quality. 3 vols. Washington, D. C.: USGPO.

Goldsmith, E., R. Allen, M. Allaby, J. Davoll, and S. Lawrence. 1972. *A Blueprint for Survival*. Boston: Houghton Mifflin.

Goudie, A. 1986. *The Human Impact on the Natural Environment*. 2d ed. Oxford: Basil Blackwell.

Graham, E. H. 1956. The re-creative power of plant communities. In W. Thomas, ed. 1956, q.v., 677–91.

Graham, M. 1956. Harvests of the seas. In W. Thomas, ed., 1956, q.v., 487–503.

Gregory, K. J., and D. E. Walling, eds. 1987. *Human Activity and Environmental Processes*. New York: John Wiley & Sons.

Gutkind, E. A. Our world from the air: conflict and adaptation. In W. Thomas, ed. 1956, q.v., 1–44.

Hargrove, E. C., ed. 1986. *Religion and Environmental Crisis*. Athens: University of Georgia Press.

Harris, V. 1949. *All Coherence Gone*. Chicago: University of Chicago Press.

Hawley, A. H. 1968. Human ecology. In *International Encyclopedia of the Social Sciences*. Vol. IV, ed. D. L. Sills, 328–35. New York: Macmillan/Free Press.

Hays, S. P. 1959. *Conservation and the Gospel of Efficiency: The Progressive Conservation Movement, 1890–1920*. Cambridge, MA: Harvard University Press.

———. 1987. *Beauty, Health, and Permanence: Environmental Politics in the United States, 1955–1985*. Cambridge: Cambridge University Press.

Inglehart, R. T. 1977. *The Silent Revolution: Changing Values and Polity Styles among Western Publics*. Princeton: Princeton University Press.

James, W. 1896. *The Will to Believe*. New York: Longmans, Green.

Jenkins, S. 1988. How Green are our politics? *Sunday Times* (London) (September 4): B1.

Joyce, C. 1986. Species are the spice of life. *New Scientist* (October 9): 20–21.

Kellert, S. R. 1986. Social and perceptual factors in the preservation of animal species. In B. Norton, ed., 1986, q.v., 50–73.

Klimm, L. E. 1956. Man's ports and channels. In W. Thomas, ed., 1956, q.v., 522–41.

Kuralt, C. 1987. Twenty years on the back roads of America. *International Herald Tribune* (June 18).

Lake, L. M. 1983. The environmental mandate: activists and the electorate. *Political Science Quarterly* 98: 215–33.

Leopold, A. 1949. The land ethic. In his *A Sand County Almanac and Sketches Here and There*, 201–26. New York: Oxford University Press.

Lifton, R. J. 1986. A fear that life is being extinguished. *International Herald Tribune* (May 20).

Lovejoy, A. O. [1936] 1960. *The Great Chain of Being: A Study of the History of an Idea*. New York: Harper Torchbook.

Lovejoy, T. 1986. Species leave the ark one by one. In B. Norton, ed., 1986, q.v., 13–27.

Lowe, P., and J. Goyder, 1983. *Environmental Groups in Politics*. London: Allen & Unwin.

Lowenthal, D. 1958. *George Perkins Marsh: Versatile Vermonter*. New York: Columbia University Press.

———. 1970. The environmental crusade: ideals and realities. *Landscape Architecture* 60: 290–96.

———. 1982. The pioneer landscape: an American dream. *Great Plains Quarterly* 2: 5–19.

———. 1985. *The Past is a Foreign Country*. Cambridge: Cambridge University Press.

Malcolm, N. 1989. Green thoughts in a blue shade. *Spectator* (January 6): 7.

Marco, G. J., R. M. Hollingworth, and W. Durham, eds. 1987. *Silent Spring Revisited*. Washington, D.C.: American Chemical Society.

Marsh, G. P. 1848. *Address delivered before the Agricultural Society of Rutland County, Sept. 30, 1847*. Rutland, Vt.

———. 1860. The study of nature. *Christian Examiner* 58: 33–62.

———. [1864] 1965. *Man and Nature; or, Physical Geography as Modified by Human Action*, ed. D. Lowenthal. Introduction, ix–xxix. The John Harvard Library. Cambridge, MA: Harvard University Press.

McLaughlin, D. H. 1956. Man's selective attack on ores and minerals. In W. Thomas, ed. 1956, q.v., 851–61.

Meadows, D. H., D. L. Meadows, J. Randers, and W. W. Behrens. 1972. *The Limits to Growth: A Report for the Club of Rome's Project on the Predicament of Mankind*. New York: Universal Books.

Medawar, P. 1984. *Pluto's Republic*. London: Oxford University Press.

Mellanby, K. 1988. Seal deaths. Letter in *The Times* (London) (September 2): 11.

Mikesell, M. W. 1974. Geography as the study of environment: an assessment of some old and new commitments. In *Perspectives on Environment*, ed. I. R. Manners and M. W. Mikesell, 1–23. Commission on College Geography Publication No. 13. Washington, D.C.: Association of American Geographers.

Milbrath, L. W. 1984. *Environmentalists: Vanguard for a New Society*. Albany: State University of New York.

Mill, J. S. [1850–58] 1969. Nature. In *The Collected Works*, vol. X. 373–402. Toronto: University of Toronto Press.

Mitchell, R. C. 1980. *Public Opinion on Environmental Issues: Results of a National Public Opinion Survey*. CEQ/DOE/EPA/USDA. Washington, D.C.: USGPO.

———. 1984. Public opinion and environmental politics in the 1970s and 1980s. In *Environmental Policy in the 1980s: Reagan's New Agenda*, ed. N. J. Vig and M. E. Kraft, 51–74. Washington, D.C.: Congressional Quarterly Press.

———. 1985. From conservation to environmental movement: the development of the modern environmental lobbies. Discussion Paper QE85-12. Washington, D.C.: Resources for the Future, Quality of the Environment Division.

Mumford, L. 1956. Prospect. In W. Thomas, ed., 1956, q.v., 1141–52.

———. 1966. Closing statement. In *Future Environments of North America*, ed. F. F. Darling and J. P. Milton, 718–29. Garden City, NY: Natural History Press.

Munz, P. 1985. *Our Knowledge of the Growth of Knowledge: Popper or Wittgenstein?* London: Routledge & Kegan Paul.

Murray, E. G. D. 1954. The place of nature in man's world. *American Scientist* 42: 130–35, 142.

Nash, R. 1967. *Wilderness and the American Mind*. New Haven, CT: Yale University Press.

New Scientist. 1988. The warmth of unity. (November 19): 17.

Nicholson, M. 1987. *The New Environmental Age*. Cambridge: Cambridge University Press.

Nicolson, M. H. 1959. *Mountain Gloom and Mountain Glory: The Development of the Aesthetics of the Infinite*. Ithaca, NY: Cornell University Press.

Norton, B. G., ed. 1986. *The Preservation of Species: The value of Biological Diversity*, On the inherent danger of undervaluing species, 110–37. Epilogue, 268–83. Princeton: Princeton University Press.

Oldfield, F. 1983. Man's impact on the environment: some recent perspectives. *Geography* 68: 245–56.

Osborn, F. 1948. *Our Plundered Planet*. Boston: Little, Brown.

Our Common Future. 1987. World Commission on Environment and Development. Oxford: Oxford University Press.

Passmore, J. 1980. *Man's Responsibility for Nature: Ecological Problems and Western Traditions*. 2nd ed. London: Duckworth.

Pearce, D. 1976. The limits of cost-benefit analysis as a guide to economic policy. *Kyklos* 29: 97–112.

Polunin, N., ed. 1980. *Growth Without Eco-Disasters? Proceedings of the 2d International Conference on the Environmental Future, Rekjavik*. New York: Macmillan.

Porritt, J., and D. Winner. 1988. *The Coming of the Greens*. London: Fontana.

Randall, A. 1986. Human preferences, economics, and the preservation of species. In B. Norton, ed., 1986, q.v., 79–109.

———. 1987. *Resource Economics*. 2d. ed. New York: John Wiley.

Rensberger, B. 1986. Mass extinctions worry experts. *International Herald Tribune* (September 30).

Rescher, N. 1980. *Unpopular Essays on Technological Progress*. Pittsburgh: University of Pittsburgh Press.

Rolston, H., III. 1979. Can and ought we to follow nature? *Environmental Ethics* 1: 7–30.

Rosen, J. D., and F. M. Gretch. 1987. Analytical chemistry of pesticides: evolution and impact. In G. J. Marco, et al., eds. 1987, q.v., 127–43.

Sauer, C. O. 1956. The agency of man on the earth. In W. Thomas, ed., 1956, q.v., 49–69.

SCEP 1970. *Man's Impact on the Global Environment*. Cambridge, MA: MIT Press.

Sears, P. B. 1935. *Deserts on the March*. Norman, OK: University of Oklahoma Press.

———. 1956. The processes of environmental change by man. In W. Thomas, ed., 1956, q.v., 471–84.

Shabecoff, P. 1987. Green party studied by activists. *International Herald Tribune* (July 7): 3.

Short, D. 1955. In *New York Times* (July 30): 9.

Siegfried, A. 1955. *America at Mid-Century*. New York: Harcourt, Brace.

Simon, J. L. 1981. Environmental disruption or environmental improvement? *Social Science Quarterly* 62: 30–43.

———. 1986. Disappearing species, deforestation and data. *New Scientist* (May 15): 60–63.

Simon, J. L., and A. Wildavsky. 1984. On species loss, the absence of data, and risks to humanity. In *The Resourceful Earth: A Response to Global 2000*, ed. J. L. Simon and H. Kahn, 171–83. Oxford: Blackwell.

Sinclair, T. C. 1973. Environmentalism: a la recherche du temps perdu – bien perdu? In H. S. D. Cole et al., eds., 1973, q.v., 175–91.

Sober, E. 1986. Philosophical problems for environmentalism. In B. Norton, ed., 1986, q.v., 173–94.

Solow, A. W. 1988. Greenhouse effect: hot air in lieu of evidence. *International Herald Tribune* (December 29): 4.

Spilhaus, A. 1956. Control of the world environment. *Geographical Review* 46: 451–59.

Spretnak, C., and F. Capra. 1985. *Green Politics*. London: Paladin/

Grafton.

Stewart-Smith, J. 1987. *In the Shadow of Fujisan: Japan and Its Wildlife*. New York: Viking.

Strong, M. F. 1980. The international community and the environment. In *Growth without Eco-Disasters?*, ed. N. Polunin, 613–25. New York: Macmillan.

Taylor, P. W. 1986. *Respect for Nature: A Theory of Environmental Ethics*. Princeton: Princeton University Press.

Thomas, W. L., Jr., ed. 1956. *Man's Role in Changing the Face of the Earth*. Wenner-Gren International Symposium, 1955. Introductory at xxi–xxviii. Chicago: University of Chicago Press.

Thornthwaite, C. W. 1956. Modification of rural microclimates. In W. Thomas, ed., 1956, q.v., 567–83.

Time. 1989. Planet of the year: endangered earth. (January 2): 9–47.

Tizard, H. 1950. Men against nature. In *Mid-Century: The Social Implications of Scientific Progress*, ed. J. E. Burchard, 107–16. Cambridge, MA: MIT Press.

Vaughan, H. [1656; 1666] 1957. Daphnis; Corruption. In *Works*, 676–80; 387–545. Oxford: Clarendon.

Vogt, W. 1948. *Road to Survival*. New York: William Sloane Associates.

White, L. Jr. 1967. The historic roots of our ecologic crisis. *Science* 155: 1203–07.

White, R. 1985. American environmental history: the development of a new historical field. *Pacific Historical Review* 54: 297–335.

Wilkinson, C. F. 1987. The science and politics of pesticides. In G. Marco et al., eds., 1956, q.v., 25–46.

Williams, M. 1987. Sauer and "Man's Role in Changing the Face of the Earth." *Geographical Review* 77: 218–31.

World Health Organization. 1957. In London diary, *New Statesman & Nation* (November 23): 683.

World Resources 1986. World Resources Institute and International Institute for Environmental Development. New York: Basic Books.

World Resources 1987. WRI and IIED. New York: Basic Books.

Worster, D. 1977. *Nature's Economy: A History of Ecological Ideas*. Cambridge: Cambridge University Press.

II

Transformations of the Global Environment

Editorial Introduction

The transformations in human society detailed in the previous section have brought with them a tremendous expansion in the human capacity to transform the physical environment, whether deliberately or inadvertently, and whether for better or worse. The nineteen papers in this section, the core of this volume, investigate the physical consequences of human actions as they have been registered on the biosphere. They trace the growth of the major human impacts on the environment as they have mounted in the past three centuries from acute local effects to potentially irreversible, global-scale – though still often regionally variable – transformations of unprecedented magnitude and rate.

The topics examined here were divided originally according to a distinction between the "faces" of the biosphere and the "flows" of energy and materials through these landscape compartments. The former were the focus of some of the classic volumes in whose path this one follows, from Marsh's *Man and Nature* to so relatively recent a work as *Man's Role in Changing the Face of the Earth*. Yet in the past few decades, the human impact on the great biogeochemical cycles of the global environment, foreseen by V. I. Vernadsky early in this century, has raised new concerns about the alteration of these key global flows. The essential unity of most faces and flows changes is now evident, and these papers are grouped here instead by common physical features. The topics they address range from single variables (for example, forests and carbon and sulfur flows) to broad sets of variables addressed as integrated realms of the biosphere (climate, marine environment, atmosphere).

A prime goal of the symposium and volume was to assemble the best global estimates of the magnitudes and chronologies of change that could be made on the basis of current knowledge. The extent to which this mandate could be fulfilled, as will be seen, varied across the range of subject matter. In the atmosphere, as Graedel and Crutzen point out (chap. 17), present-day monitoring and historical proxy data allow changes in some trace constituents, many of them unknown only a few decades ago, to be documented with an accuracy exceeding our ability to interpret their significance. When it comes to assessing our impact on the terrestrial biota, on the other hand, as Peters and Lovejoy note (chap. 20), the denominator in the ratio of extinctions, the number of species extant, varies in estimates from a few million to some thirty million. The numerator, the number of species actually lost, is also open to debate. As a rule, even where the present state of things can be assessed with confidence – and this is less common than one might think, as witness Williams' compilation of varying estimates of the present-day global extent of forests (chap. 11) – establishing past states as a benchmark for measuring change presents enormous difficulty. One way of proceeding, best illustrated in this section by Rozanov and colleagues and by L'vovich and White (chaps. 12 and 14), is to estimate the dimensions of typical regional situations and extrapolate to higher scales. The data, recording actual changes in all regions, that would ideally be drawn upon usually do not exist or have not been assembled. The need for better and more reliable information on the past and the present is a central lesson of these studies. So the global estimates presented here should be regarded as starting points for further refinement, as a challenge presented rather than a task completed.

Even a precise assessment of change may leave open the question of how much of the change was due to human action and how much was merely a reflection of natural processes. McDowell, Webb, and Bartlein (chap. 9) set the stage by documenting the considerable natural variation in climate, vegetation, and landforms over the past 20,000 years. Clearly such variation is still very much with us. As it is still only incompletely explained, let alone predicted, by emergent unifying theories, the problem of winnowing out the natural component from any supposed human-induced change remains a fundamental and sometimes a pervasive one. Some realms of investigation, to be sure, are freer than others of these worries. Few such problems occur in the interpretation of land use change and forest loss over the past three centuries. Other realms – notably climate, as Jäger and Barry (chap. 19) demonstrate – are particularly bedevilled by them. These problems are deepened by the interactive nature of some changes. Hilborn (chap. 21) notes that the collapse of marine fish stocks may reflect overharvesting, climatic or other natural shocks, or the coincidence of the two. Assessments of the importance of land-use change in raising flood heights can be equally controversial.

The size of past natural fluctuations also offers one benchmark for assessing the significance of human-induced change (once specified). The rates of change may offer another. Trajectories of change in many of these realms during the post-glacial epoch are presented in the introduction to the volume (see chap. 1). Only a few – notably the soils, forests, and biota central to the agricultural economy – were much affected by humankind in pre-modern times. Acceleration of human impact during the twentieth century and especially since World War II has been a common trend though not a universal one. The moderation in some impacts, such as global emissions of sulfur (chap. 24) and of some trace pollutants (chap. 26), reflects environmental management combined in some cases with the less deliberate effects of economic restructuring. But the global patterns are not uniform across the earth's surface. Examples of improvement, largely in the developed world, are more than matched by many of rapid deterioration in the developing countries.

The lands have always borne the most visible marks of human use. The unmistakable trend in global land use (chap. 10), for all its unevenness by time and place, has been the accelerating expansion of cropland at the expense of forest and rangeland. The total of arable land has expanded by some 450 percent in the past three centuries. The dynamic frontiers of agricultural expansion that Richards describes have at the same time often been ones of massive and rapid forest clearance (chap. 11). Other sources of impact such as cutting for timber and fuel have contributed to a net loss of more than six million km^2 of forest in the last three centuries. Today the major fault line separates most of the developed world, where rates of deforestation have peaked and are now declining or negative, from the Third World, particularly the tropics, where continued rapid clearing generates secondary shocks to the rich but fragile ecosystem. Changes in land use and land cover are further reflected in the underlying soils. The authors of chap. 12 detail the functions of soil in the global system and venture estimates of the net magnitude of human impact in the forms of erosion, salinization, desertification, and dehumification. A theme paralleling these place-bound impacts is that of sediment flows, or earth materials set in motion by human disturbance (chap. 13). These processes lend themselves poorly to global estimates, but the data marshalled make it clear that sediment flows, both those initiated and those increased by human action, have greatly accelerated. The coastal zone (chap. 16), where land meets water, is a fragile, high-energy, highly productive environment whose manifold resources have long attracted settlement. Such centuries-long impacts as pollution, wetland conversion, and sediment transfer have been magnified in recent times by the expansion of population and technical capacity.

So vital and versatile a resource as fresh water is subject to many forms of impact. Withdrawal has grown thirty-five-fold since the late seventeenth century. At the global level, irrigation, a highly consumptive use, is far and away the principal source of demand on the hydrologic cycle, followed by industrial and domestic-municipal uses. A century of large impoundments has done much to even out global surface flows, though not without many costs, while land-use change and urbanization exert more subtle effects (chap. 14). For a resource so confined in basins and aquifers, a regional/local focus forms a necessary complement to the global aggregates (chap. 15). Case studies from a variety of settings document shortages in supply and deterioration in quality, the pervasive problems of water-borne diseases in the developing world and the emergence of less well-understood health problems from chemical substances. Groundwater supplies are more vulnerable than surface ones to persistent, even irreversible problems of depletion and contamination. The magnitude of impact notwithstanding, some cause for optimisn exists in the prospects that use will become more sparing and efficient and that management will increasingly anticipate secondary problems and provide for solutions.

Though proverbially fluid and capable of acting as global systems, the oceans, atmosphere, and climate (chaps. 17–19) are no strangers to localized and regional impacts. The severest marine pollution is concentrated in coastal and estuarine waters and the greatest temperature enhancement in urban heat islands. The reactivity of many atmospheric contaminants, such as sulfur dioxide and tropospheric ozone, significantly restricts their spatial range. The possible impacts of substances stable enough to operate globally are especially troubling, however, be they plastics in the ocean or carbon dioxide and chlorofluorocarbons in the atmosphere. The recently discovered stratospheric ozone hole created over Antarctica by CFC releases represents a transformation of unprecedented scale if still of uncertain consequences. The global climate change expected to result from the accumulation of CO_2, CFCs, and other greenhouse gases is likely to be of profound significance to every realm of the earth's environment.

Global climate change, should it occur, would represent only the latest and largest human alteration in the habitat of the earth's flora and fauna. Habitat alteration, harvesting, pollution, and the introduction of non-native species have been what Peters and Lovejoy term "the four horsemen of development" responsible for substantial losses in biotic diversity that are likely to be multiplied many times over in the near future by processes, especially deforestation, now underway (chaps. 20–22). Endemic species, especially those of islands and the tropics, have been especially vulnerable among the terrestrial flora and fauna; anadromous fishes and marine mammals, among the inhabitants of the oceans. As the scale of human impact rises, though, so expands that of the populations at risk.

Once, locally severe disturbances in the chemical balance – around smelters, downstream of cities, in smoky industrial districts – were swamped by natural flows in the global aggregate. Now, the human input to the basic chemical flows of the biosphere is on the same scale as the natural (chaps. 23–27). As well as magnifying those flows that exist in nature – some many-fold, as in the case of metals and some radionuclides – human action has, through the chemical industry, created entirely new ones (chaps. 26–27). Among the major biogeochemical cycles, emissions of carbon (chap. 23) are of importance principally for their effects on climate. Those of sulfur, nitrogen, and phosphorus (chaps. 24–25), on the other hand, contribute to a wider range of processes, from the damage done by acid precipitation (sulfur and nitrogen), to the increased agricultural production made possible by artificial fertilizers and the water pollution and eutrophication worsened by agricultural and urban wastes (nitrogen and phosphorus). Concerns in all of these realms once focused on the wastes from point sources of production. They have broadened to include the ever-growing dissipative releases from consumption, which are far less readily managed and controlled.

The papers in this section are clear evidence of a major challenge. The last three centuries can be seen as the period over which humankind emerged from several million years as a minor actor on the planetary stage to assume the role of a major transformer of the biosphere. One billion people are now being added to the global population per decade, aggregate economic growth has more than quadrupled since 1950 with energy use growing comparably, and species loss is running at an estimated 100 per day. With today's growing though still far from adequate, knowledge of the earth system and our role in it comes a responsibility to reflect on and be accountable for our actions. The task of understanding global change, anticipating impacts, and keeping human activity in some harmony with the physical environment looms as a test that our species could easily fail. It can only be hoped that the next century will turn out to be the one in which humankind learns to manage its global and growing power to transform planet earth.

WILLIAM C. CLARK
JESSICA T. MATHEWS

9

Long-Term Environmental Change

PATRICIA F. McDOWELL   THOMPSON WEBB III   PATRICK J. BARTLEIN

The interrelated systems of climate, vegetation, and the physical landscape (landforms and soils) are both the major determinants of the human environment and the major subjects of human environmental exploitation. Even without human perturbations, these systems are highly dynamic, on time scales ranging from hours to millions of years. Each of these environmental systems changes naturally when influenced by external forcing factors and internal dynamics. Positive and negative feedbacks within these systems are common. Environmental systems exhibit complex behavior, because their responses to a particular type of stimulus can differ at different temporal or spatial scales.[1]

This environmental dynamism and complexity has long hampered attempts to develop some unifying theory to explain general patterns of long-term environmental change. Many early students of human impact ignored natural dynamics altogether; George Perkins Marsh attributed to nature an almost "unchanging permanence of form, outline, and proportion," and "a condition of equilibrium . . . which, without the action of man, would remain with little fluctuation for countless ages" (Marsh 1885: 26). In the 1955 predecessor of this conference (Thomas 1956), several authors discussed climatic and landscape change, but the emphasis was on description of the symptoms of environmental change and on review of new, potentially synthetic approaches to understanding long-term environmental change. Today, we use many synthetic approaches and unifying theories that were not foreseen in 1955. The emerging picture is at once more complex and more integrated than that of 1955.

Our predecessor at the 1955 symposium observed that "[i]n a conference on 'Man's Role in Changing the Face of the Earth,' a summary of environmental changes through forces independent of man appears to be an assignment to the voice of a loyal opposition" (Russell 1956: 453). Long-term environmental change, however, provides an important background to human transformation of the earth. Members of the genus *Homo* first appeared at the beginning of the Quaternary, and many cultural activities, such as agriculture, developed within the past 20,000 years during which the present interglacial environment and landscape became established. Natural environmental changes provide a scale for judging the magnitude and some of the possible effects of human impacts on the environment. Indeed, without a knowledge of natural change, the change due to human intervention cannot be specified.

The goals of this chapter are to describe how environmental systems have changed not only during the past 20,000 years[2], but also within the 1.8-million-year long Quaternary epoch, and to provide an overview of various emergent unifying theories of long-term environmental change. The most important of these is the astronomical theory of climatic change (Berger et al. 1984; Imbrie and Imbrie 1979; Milankovitch 1941), which states that variations in the earth's orbit and axial tilt cause variations in solar energy input to the earth's atmosphere and are the overriding pacemakers of the highly significant, long-term variations of global ice volume and monsoon intensity (Hays, Imbrie, and Shackleton 1976; Kutzbach 1981). The climatic dependence of vegetation, geomorphology, hydrology, and soils, at time scales of 100 to 100,000 years, makes an understanding of climate change key to obtaining a unifying theory for the dynamics of these systems. The environmental symptoms of these longer and shorter climatic cycles are many and widespread, affecting not only high-latitude glaciated regions, but also tropical and desert areas and the oceans.

To understand the changes of the past 20,000 years, we will examine system controls and responses at scales ranging from 100 to 1 million years. It is important to specify time (and space) scales when discussing environmental change, because (1) the scale of the system's response and recovery provides a perspective by which to gauge the magnitude of human and natural impacts, and (2) systems that are controls at one temporal or spatial scale may be dependent responding systems at another scale (Saltzman 1985). Chisholm (1980) recognized that the latter point also applies to social systems.

Climate: Scale, Control, and Response

Of the three environmental systems that we describe, we view climate and its variations as setting the pace for many of the variations in the other systems. We therefore describe the scales and types of climatic variations before discussing the associated vegetational and geomorphic changes.

Global Climatic Change at Different Time Scales

The earth's climate varies at time scales ranging from very short (severe weather phenomena, <1 hour) to extremely long (geological warming or cooling trends, 10 million years). Kutzbach (1976) suggested that climate variance is greatest at short time scales (days to 10 years) and at long time scales (10,000 to >100,000 years) and that it is fairly low at intermediate time scales. Climate variation at time scales of 1 month to 100 years is significant, however, because its scale is comparable to (or shorter than) those of social, political, and ecological adjustment processes such as national industrialization, national urbanization, and demographic change. Even though relatively small in magnitude, climatic variations at these intermediate scales, therefore, can have a disrupting effect on human subsistence (Clark 1985). They are also those most likely to be attributed incorrectly to human action.

From a long-term perspective, climatic and other environmental changes operating at time scales of 1,000 to 1 million years are likely to have a significant influence on human cultural and biological evolution (Huntley and Webb 1988). Furthermore, the physical landscape that humans occupy is largely the result of climatic, marine, and hydrologic processes operating at these time scales. The distribution of natural biotic resources varies significantly at these time scales. For these reasons, so-called long-term climatic changes, which we examine here, have great relevance for the human environment.

The spatial scales of short- and intermediate-term climatic variations were compiled by Clark (1985), and his scheme is extended here (Fig. 9.1). We have divided the temporal range of global climatic variations into five time-dependent systems, each of which includes processes and events occurring at various spatial scales. Within each system, smaller phenomena generally have shorter response times and operate over shorter periods. The positive slopes for the phenomena in each system reflect this trend. Our five systems include (1) weather phenomena, (2) quasi-biennial to short-term climatic fluctuations, (3) 100-to-1,000-year neoglacial variations, (4) the orbitally driven, glacial-interglacial and monsoon variations, and (5) the long-term, tectonically driven climatic variations over millions of years.

The general climatic pattern of the past 800,000 years and much of the Quaternary period is one of large-amplitude, glacial-interglacial cycles about 100,000 years long. These cycles involve maximum extension and retreat of large continental ice sheets. Superimposed on these long-term cycles are smaller amplitude fluctuations at several shorter time scales, including the long-term regular variations in monsoon intensity in the tropics. The longest of long-term climatic variations, such as the shift into the present glacial epoch, glacial-interglacial cycles, and stadial-interstadial cycles, affect the entire earth, although the effects are not necessarily synchronous or similar in magnitude and direction everywhere. At a somewhat shorter temporal scale are fluctuations such as the Little Ice Age – a period of expanded alpine glaciers, cooler temperatures, and expanded sea ice in North America, Europe, and the North Atlantic, about 600 to 100 years ago (Grove 1988; Lamb

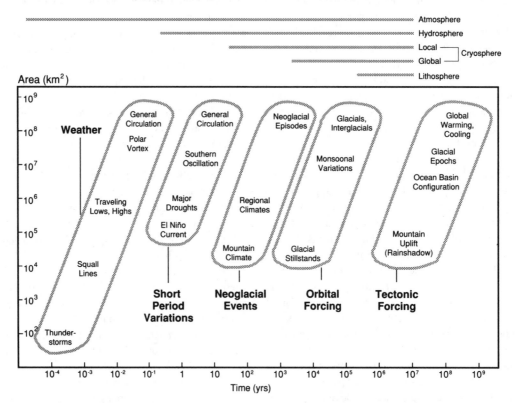

Figure 9.1 Spatial and temporal scales of variations in weather and climate. Short-term variations are limited primarily to the atmosphere, but longer-term variations involve progressively more earth systems. Each bubble encloses a group of related types of variations, in which the shorter-term, smaller-area features are part of the longer-term, larger-area features.

1982). This is the latest and best-documented in a series of episodes of alpine glacier expansion that have occurred during the past 12,000 years (Grove 1979). Outside the midlatitudes, climate fluctuations at a similar temporal and spatial scale probably also occurred in subtropical areas and in arid regions (e.g., Mehringer 1986; Street-Perrott 1981), but they are less well documented. These changes are subhemispheric, not global, in scale. Climatic variations of intermediate time scale include the historical warming that has taken place since the late 1800s, major droughts such as the North American Dust Bowl, and El Niño–Southern Oscillation (ENSO) events. The best studied and most regular intermediate-scale changes are weather and sea-surface variations associated with the ENSO. Formation of a warm, southerly-flowing current off Peru is called El Niño since it forms in December. The Southern Oscillation is a quasibiennial, east-west change in atmospheric pressure across the tropical Pacific. In western South America and the adjacent Pacific Ocean, these effects are always similar, but the effects in other regions can vary from one ENSO event to the next. At the smallest temporal and spatial scales are weather phenomena, including major storm systems.

Controls of Climatic Variations

Controls of long- and short-term climatic variation are not fully understood. Many possible controls exist (Kutzbach 1976; Mitchell 1976; Saltzman 1985), but their relative significance is unclear, and in general, the ultimate controls for many known patterns of climatic variation have not been identified. Major controls, including those external and those internal to the climate system, are listed in Table 9-1. Some of these controls operate very slowly (continental drift) or in a regular, predictable fashion (orbital variations), but many occur as sudden, random perturbations (volcanic activity, asteroid impact). The global climate system is complex, consisting of four major linked subsystems: atmosphere, oceans, biosphere, and cryosphere (and for changes of 10,000 to 100 million years, even variations in the lithosphere are involved). The linkages among the subsystems occur through the exchange of heat, and to a lesser extent, through the exchange of water vapor and CO_2. The atmosphere – the fastest-responding and most variable of these subsystems – is most directly responsible for climate conditions, but atmospheric conditions are partially dependent on the temperature and circulation patterns of the ocean surfaces and on the extent and height of major ice sheets (Kutzbach and Guetter 1986; Saltzman 1985). The oceans, and particularly the cryosphere, vary more slowly than the atmosphere, and therefore have a damping effect upon it. In addition, moisture, temperature, and albedo characteristics of the continental surfaces influence the atmosphere, at least on the short-term scale.

Numerous positive and negative feedbacks arise among these four subsystems, and some create resonances in climatic variation (Saltzman 1985). Feedbacks may be nonlinear, resulting in a distinctive pattern of climatic variation without any external cause, termed autovariation (Kutzbach 1976). At time scales shorter than 1,000 years, the regional climatic signal can be of high amplitude and noisy. This fact makes it difficult to extrapolate long-term trends in historical weather records (Bradley et al. 1987).

Climatic Variations during the Cenozoic: Geological Control

During the past 100 million years (since the late Cretaceous), the earth's climate has cooled (Lloyd 1984). This long-term trend is most likely related to the changing position of the continents (in particular, the shift of continental masses into higher latitudes), and accompanying changes of sea level, topography, and albedo, although changes in atmospheric composition – particularly CO_2 – may also be important (Barron and Washington 1984; Kerr 1984a).

Several key stages appear in the long-term cooling trend (extensive reviews are given by Lloyd [1984] and Crowley [1983]). Between 30 and 40 million years ago, Antarctica separated from Australia and South America, and thus thermally isolated Antarctica and initiated glaciation there. Continuous glaciation was established in Antarctica by 15 million years ago, initiating the current ice age (i.e., a period during which continental ice sheets are continuously present somewhere on the earth's surface). The Arctic Ocean became ice-covered by 5 million years ago, and continental glaciation in the Northern Hemisphere began 2.5 million years ago (Shackleton et al. 1984), ushering in the ice-age climates of the Quaternary. During this late-Cenozoic ice age, many glacial/interglacial episodes have occurred.

Climatic Variations during the Quaternary: The Astronomical Theory of Climatic Variations

Superimposed on the long-term trend are intervals of ice-sheet growth and decay, as well as regular fluctuations in the intensity of the tropical monsoons (Crowley, Short, Mengel, and North 1986; Kutzbach 1981; Prell and Kutzbach 1987). These range from stadial-interstadial or monsoon-intensity fluctuations lasting on the order of 20,000 years, to glacial-interglacial fluctuations every 100,000 years, to longer-term fluctuations several million years in duration (Miller, Fairbanks, and Mountain 1987). These variations result mainly from changes in the earth's orbital elements (Hays, Imbrie, and Shackleton 1976; Imbrie et al. 1984; Milankovitch 1941), with amplification from atmospheric chemistry (CO_2 content), land-sea contrast, ice cover, and resulting changes in albedo and sea level.

Three elements of the earth's orbit that vary systematically are the eccentricity of the earth's orbit around the sun, the obliquity of the earth's axis relative to the ecliptic, and the precession of the equinoxes relative to perihelion and aphelion (Fig. 9.2). These regular variations in orbital geometry control the amount and seasonal distribution of solar radiation intercepted at the top of the earth's atmosphere. For example, 10,000 years ago, the tilt of the earth's axis was about 24.2° (as opposed to the present 23.4°), and perihelion (time when the earth is closest to the sun) occurred in July (as opposed to January, at present). Consequently, the northern midlatitudes received about 8% more radiation in July than at present, and about 10% less in January (Fig. 9.3). The general circulation of the atmosphere and oceans must respond to such changes

Table 9-1 *Controls of long-term climatic variability*

Control	Effect	Status of control at time scales of (years) 10^7	10^5	10^3	$\leq 10^1$
External:					
Shift of continents to higher latitudes	– increased pole-equator temperature gradient – cooling of high latitudes	I	NA	NA	NA
Increased land area by tectonic processes	– increased albedo, cooling – increased monsoon intensity	I	NA	NA	NA
Changing orientation of ocean basins	– changes in circulation controls and monsoons	I	NA	NA	NA
Mountain-building and increased continental elevation	– changes in circulation controls, monsoon intensity, and albedo	I	I	NA	NA
Closing (tectonic and eustatic) of gateways between ocean basins: zonal gateways	– increased meridional transport of warm water – high-latitude warming – increased precipitation on high-latitude continents	I	I	NA	NA
meridional gateways	– isolation and cooling of high-latitude oceans				
Volcanic activity	– increased dust and SO_2 in atmosphere – increased back-scattering of solar radiation, cooling	X	X	I	I
Asteroid impact	– increased dust in atmosphere – increased back-scattering of solar radiation, cooling	I	I	I	I
Changes in the earth's orbital parameters: Increased eccentricity of orbit	– greater seasonality for one hemisphere	X	I	I	NA
Increased obliquity of axis	– greater seasonality for both hemispheres	X	I	I	NA
Precession of solstices to coincide with peri/aphelion	– greater seasonality for hemisphere with summer solstice at perihelion	X	I	I	NA
Internal:					
Decreased salinity of oceans	– surface stratification of oceans, decrease in heat storage	I	X	D	I
Growth of ice sheets	– increased albedo, cooling – shifts in circulation features	D	D	I	I
Growth of sea ice	– increased albedo, cooling – shifts in circulation features	D	D	I	D
Eustatic sea level fall	– increased albedo, cooling	D	D	I	I
Cooling of sea surface temperatures	– decreased transfer of water vapor to atmosphere, starvation of ice sheets	D	D	D	I
Change in terrestrial biomass	– changes in CO_2 in ocean and atmosphere	X	X	D	I
Change in aerosols	– warming or cooling, depending on aerosol height and composition	X	X	D	D

Note: I = independent; characteristic that operates independently of, and to some extent controls, climatic variation. D = dependent; characteristic that is determined by climatic conditions. X = indeterminate; characteristic that is too variable to be reconstructed at the time scale. NA = not applicable; characteristic that is not controlled by climate, or that varies too slowly to be significant. For brevity, most controls and corresponding effects are chosen to represent a shift toward glacial conditions. During a shift toward interglacial conditions, the direction of the controls and effects are reversed.

Eccentricity of the Orbit (a)

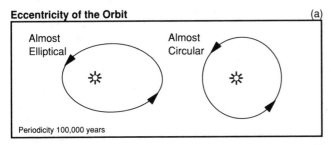

Almost Elliptical

Almost Circular

Periodicity 100,000 years

Obliquity of the Axis (b)

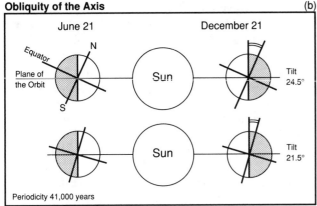

June 21

December 21

Equator

N

Plane of the Orbit

Sun

Sun

S

Tilt 24.5°

Tilt 21.5°

Periodicity 41,000 years

Precession of the Equinoxes (c)

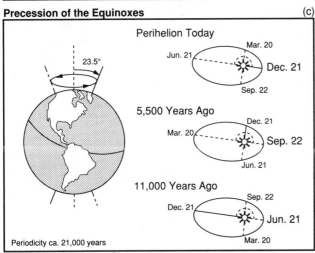

Perihelion Today

23.5°

Jun. 21

Mar. 20

Dec. 21

Sep. 22

5,500 Years Ago

Mar. 20

Dec. 21

Sep. 22

Jun. 21

11,000 Years Ago

Dec. 21

Sep. 22

Jun. 21

Mar. 20

Periodicity ca. 21,000 years

Figure 9.2 Orbital variations and their effects on long-term climatic change. (a) Eccentricity of the orbit. When the earth's orbit is nearly circular, solar radiation receipt on earth (summed over both Northern and Southern hemispheres) is nearly equal throughout the year, but as the orbit becomes more elliptical, intraannual variation in radiation receipt increases. (b) Obliquity of the earth's axis. Increased tilt of the earth's axis increases each hemisphere's difference between summer and winter solar input, and therefore enhances seasonality. (c) Precession of the equinoxes. Precession, which is due to "wobble" of the earth's axis (change in the orientation of the axis of rotation) causes differences in the degree of seasonality between the Northern and Southern hemispheres. When perihelion occurs near December 21, the Northern Hemisphere experiences reduced seasonality and the Southern Hemisphere experiences increased seasonality; when perihelion occurs near June 21, the reverse is true. Based on Imbrie and Imbrie 1979; Lowe and Walker 1984.

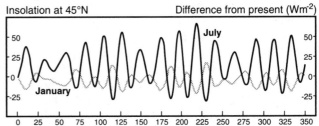

Insolation at 45°N

Difference from present (Wm^{-2})

July

January

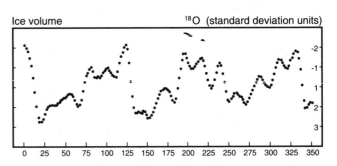

Ice volume

^{18}O (standard deviation units)

Figure 9.3 Insolation variation from the present-day level, at 45°N, and the composite oxygen isotope record from deep-sea cores. ^{18}O is expressed as standard deviations. The data are plotted so that interglacial conditions (less ice, warmer) plot at the top of the graph, and glacial conditions at the bottom. *Sources:* Berger 1978; Imbrie et al. 1984.

in energy input. The general circulation is maintained by the imbalance in energy received between high and low latitudes, and the atmosphere and ocean transport energy and moisture to redistribute the energy surplus of the tropics. Regional climatic conditions, in turn, are controlled by atmospheric circulation, which determines storm tracks and the movement of different air masses, and by the direct effects of the insolation changes on heating and evapotranspiration.

The signal of the orbital variations is clearly seen in the Quaternary climatic record reconstructed from deep-sea sediment cores, in particular the oxygen-isotope records from these cores (Broecker and van Donk 1970; Hays, Imbrie, and Shackleton 1976). The relative proportion of heavy (^{18}O) to light (^{16}O) oxygen isotopes in carbonate skeletons of plankton (which are preserved in deep-sea sediments) varies in response to long-term climatic variations, with heavy oxygen being relatively concentrated in the oceans during intervals when ice sheets are larger and oceans cooler. Continuous records of oxygen-isotope variations over the past 500,000 to 1 million years have been reconstructed from cores from all of the major ocean basins, including both high- and low-latitude sites (Fig. 9.3). These records present a remarkably coherent and detailed record of ice-age climatic variations, consisting of alternating cold and warm periods, with warm, relatively ice-free interglacial periods occurring every 100,000 years or so, and lasting about 10,000 years (Kukla and Matthews 1972).

Glacial periods are initiated by reduced winter-summer contrast (due to low obliquity and/or a precessional position such that perihelion coincides with an equinox). The resulting mild winters enhance the delivery of winter precipitation (snow) in the Northern Hemisphere high latitudes; the cool summers suppress snow melt in the same regions. The result is glacierization (Ruddiman and McIntyre 1981). Interglacial and interstadial periods are initiated by the opposite conditions: cold winters and warm summers. For example, the last deglaciation, 18,000 to 6,000 years ago, coincided with a precessional position (between 13,000 and 7,000 years ago) in which perihelion occurred during Northern Hemisphere summer. Northern Hemisphere summers were therefore generally warmer than those of today.

Climatic Variations during the Past 20,000 Years: Control by Surface Boundary Conditions and Insolation

During the past 20,000 years, climate has changed from the extreme of a glacial interval to an interglacial one (see Fig. 19.2 in Jäger and Barry, chap. 19, this volume). CLIMAP Project Members (1976; 1981) summarized the climate of the last glacial maximum, about 18,000 years ago. At this time, the ice sheets were close to their maximum extent, sea level was lower, and portions of the northern oceans were more than 10°C cooler than present.

During this time span, the ice sheets assumed the role of an independent variable in the climate system, because of their large thermal inertia. Similarly, the oceans, which on the Quaternary time scale warm and cool in response to the orbitally controlled insolation variations, changed rather slowly over this time period. Together with the insolation variations (Fig. 9.3), the ice sheets and oceans provided a set of changing boundary conditions during the past 20,000 years (Fig. 9.4). Kutzbach and Guetter (1986) used these changing boundary conditions to carry out a set of "natural experiments" with a climate simulation model. They used the National Center for Atmospheric Research Community Climate Model

(NCAR CCM) to simulate climate at 3,000-year intervals from 18,000 years ago to present. The NCAR CCM is a general circulation model and provides a simulated "snapshot" of regional and global climatic patterns consistent with a specified set of boundary conditions.

Geologic evidence supports two important results of these simulations: (1) the Laurentide ice sheet had a major impact on the atmospheric circulation of the Northern Hemisphere when it was large, and (2) the amplification of the seasonal cycle of insolation around 10,000 years ago resulted in strengthened monsoonal circulation and heating of the Northern Hemisphere continental interiors (COHMAP Members 1988). Both results are of some importance in understanding the impact of climatic variations on human activities during the past 10,000 years, because they contributed to regional climatic variations in Africa and Eurasia.

Between 9,000 and 6,000 years ago, lakes in the broad region extending across Africa north of the equator to the Indian subcontinent had water levels greater than either present or earlier times (Street-Perrott and Harrison 1985). These elevated levels were the result of greater effective moisture produced by the stronger monsoonal circulation that operated when Northern Hemisphere summer insolation was greater than at present. In North America (Bartlein and Webb 1985) and in Europe (Huntley and Prentice 1988), pollen evidence suggests that these regions were characterized by warmer summers 6,000 years ago than at present, again in response to elevated summertime insolation.

A striking feature of the maps of past climates (for example, Bartlein and Webb 1985, Fig. 9; CLIMAP Project Members 1981; Street-Perrott and Harrison 1985, Figs. 11 to 14; Wahl and Lawson 1970, Figs. 1 and 7) is that the spatial anomaly patterns (the differences between the past and present) are not uniform. Rather, the climatic changes vary spatially, which is a necessary result of the circulation changes in both the atmosphere and the ocean that occur in response to global-scale changes in boundary conditions (Fig. 9.4). The spatial patterns are strong enough that even though the global mean temperature 18,000 years ago may have been 4 to 6°C lower than it is today (Gates 1976; Kutzbach and Guetter 1986), some regions of the ocean had sea-surface temperatures higher than those today (CLIMAP Project Members 1976; 1981). The existence of spatial pattern in climate anomalies is a general feature of climatic variations at all time scales, and requires caution in the use of global climatic changes to predict changes in regional or local climates.

Climatic Variations on the Decadal-to-Millennial Time Scale: Sunspots, Volcanos, Carbon Dioxide, and Autovariations

Despite the greater abundance of paleoclimatic evidence and even instrumental data for the decadal-to-millennial time scale, the causes of the climatic variations that occur on this time scale are perhaps less well understood at present than are the causes of the longer-term variations. Several external factors, such as volcanic eruptions, may account for the observed record, but internal variations of the climate system itself (i.e., autovariation) also may be important on this time

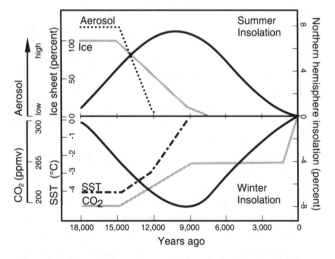

Figure 9.4 Changing boundary conditions during the past 18,000 years. Aerosol is a qualitative estimate of atmospheric aerosol and dust loading, ice is a reconstruction of global ice volume, SST is sea-surface temperature, and CO_2 is a qualitative estimate of concentration of carbon dioxide in the atmosphere. *Source:* Kutzbach and Guetter 1986.

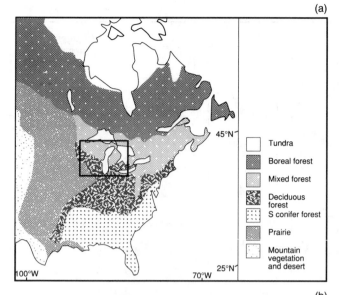

(a)

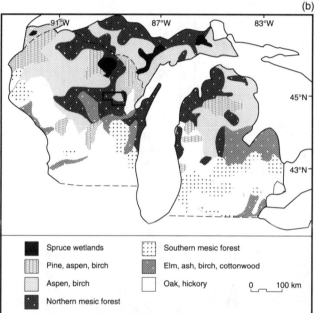

(b)

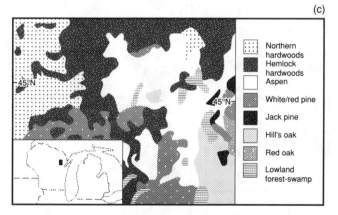

(c)

Figure 9.5 Modern vegetation patterns at decreasing spatial scales. (a) Generalized vegetation map for eastern North America. (b) Major forest types in Michigan and Wisconsin. Spruce wetlands, pine-aspen-birch, aspen-birch, and northern mesic forest are forest types within the larger mixed forest region of (a). Southern mesic forest, elm-ash-birch-cottonwood, and oak-hickory are forest types within the larger deciduous forest region. (c) Major forest types within the Menominee Indian Reservation (MIR) of northeastern

scale. Variations at this time scale may be controlled by volcanic eruptions (e.g., Bryson and Goodman 1980; Hammer, Clausen, and Dansgaard 1980; Porter 1981), by solar variability (in particular, sunspot frequency) (Harvey 1980; Labitzke and van Loon 1988; Stuiver 1980; van Loon and Labitzke 1988), or by combinations of these controls and variations in the concentration of CO_2 in the atmosphere (Hansen et al. 1981). Because a given climatic change might be attributable to several different causes, acting separately or interactively, short-term climatic variations may never be assigned to one specific cause. For instance, the extreme El Niño event of 1982 was accompanied by the eruption of the Mexican volcano El Chichón, and the resulting unusual weather patterns were induced by both "causes" (Schneider 1983).

During the past century, global, as well as hemispheric, mean temperatures have increased (Jones, Wigley, and Wright 1986; see Fig. 19.3 in Jäger and Barry, chap. 19 of this volume), but again, the pattern of temperature change is not spatially uniform (for example, Wahl and Lawson 1970, see Figs. 1, 7). Much concern has focused on this recent warming because of its possible linkage to the increase in the concentration of CO_2 and other trace gases in the atmosphere, which has resulted from human activities (MacCracken and Luther 1985). The global change in CO_2 concentration also will result in spatial patterns of change, but the nature of these patterns is still uncertain. It is ironic that as we are achieving a basic understanding of how the climate system works, the nature of the system itself is being fundamentally changed by human activity.

Vegetation: Scale, Control, and Response

Vegetational Change at Different Time and Space Scales

Vegetation is dynamic and varies on all time scales. It is responsive to several frequencies of climate variation as well as to variations in soils, grazing, fire-frequency, disease, disturbance, and human impact. The factors that appear to influence vegetation patterns vary according to the spatial extent and resolution of the data used. A zoom-lens view of the mapped patterns of modern vegetation at different spatial scales illustrates this point (Fig. 9.5). The 10 million km^2 of eastern North America contains seven major vegetation regions (called plant formations), each about 1 million km^2, ranging from tundra and boreal forest in the north to pine-oak forest in the south and prairie in the west. These are aligned along temperature and moisture gradients. The 300,000 km^2 of Wisconsin and Michigan contains seven forest types, each about 40,000 km^2 and differing between the north and south because of climate, but grouped into specific areas by soil-texture contrasts (fine-grained tills versus sandy out-

Wisconsin [outlined in (b)]. Within MIR, the northern mesic forest of (b) is subdivided into hemlock hardwoods and northern hardwoods. Part of the aspen forest is included in the aspen-birch type of (b), and the rest is included within the pine-aspen-birch type of (b). *Source:* Bradshaw and Webb 1985.

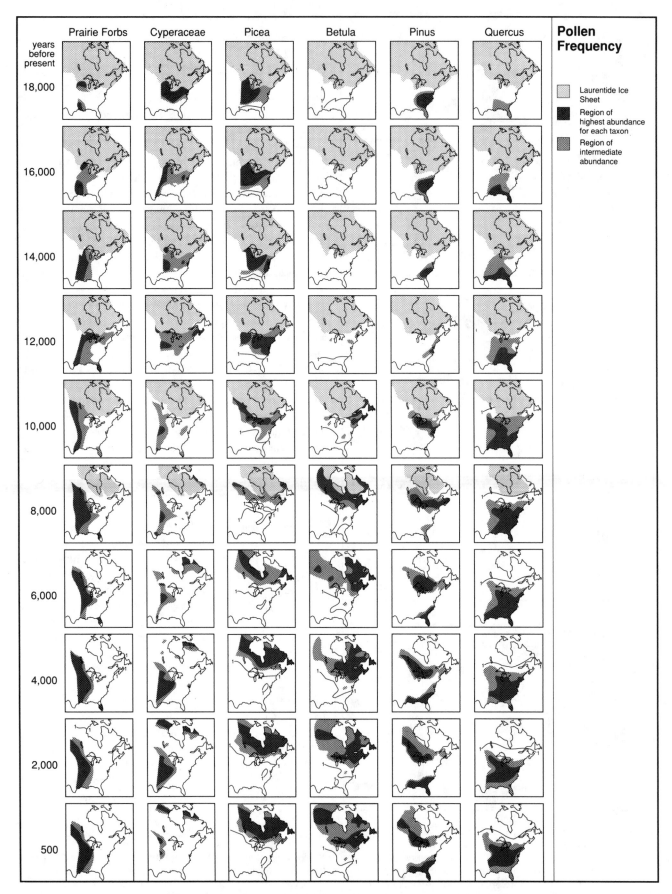

Figure 9.6 Maps with contours of equal pollen frequency for leafy herbs (forbs), sedge (Cyperaceae), spruce (*Picea*), birch (*Betula*), pine (*Pinus*), and oak (*Quercus*). For each taxon, the map series shows spatial changes at 2,000-year intervals from 18,000 years ago to present (500 years ago). Light-shaded areas indicate the Laurentide ice sheet. Dark-stippled areas are the region of highest abundance for each taxon. *Source:* Webb 1988.

wash and glaciolacustrine deposits). Within the 1,000 km² of Menominee County (in northeastern Wisconsin), the eight small forest-types of about 100 km² grow on soils of different texture and also in regions with different degrees of human or natural disturbance. Climate variation is minimal within the county. The southwest of Menominee County is an outwash plain supporting Hills oak and jack pine, the northern hardwoods grow on fine-textured soils, but the large area of aspen forest reflects disturbance by logging and fire. This series of vegetation maps shows how (1) spatial variations in macroclimate control the continental-scale patterns of plant formations, (2) soil variations control the location of forest types within a region, and (3) contrasts in soils and human disturbance control vegetation patterns within a county.

This scale dependence in the pattern and controls of the spatial variations in vegetation suggests that a scale dependence may also exist for the patterns and controls of temporal variations. Delcourt, Delcourt, and Webb (1983) published a preliminary time-space diagram for vegetation that resembles in form Fig. 9.1 and the standard textbook scale diagrams for atmospheric turbulence (e.g., Anthes et al. 1978) or oceanic circulation (Haury, McGowan, and Wiebe 1978). Recent studies of vegetational dynamics, however, suggest that certain modifications are needed in this vegetation diagram. Webb (1987) has used temporal sequences of pollen maps for the past 18,000 years (Fig. 9.6; see Huntley and Webb 1988, for a general review of methods and studies concerned with vegetation history) to illustrate the changing associations among several major plant taxa. Each taxon has had a unique trajectory, and therefore major plant formations and ecosystems have appeared and disappeared over this time span. Webb, Richard, and Mott (1983) showed similar types of variations for forest types in southern Quebec, and many pollen diagrams illustrate such variation in local to regional vegetation. These data provide evidence that individual plant formations and forest types have relatively short lifetimes.

Between 18,000 to 12,000 years ago, the patterns and spatial gradients of vegetation in eastern North America differed markedly from those of present (Fig. 9.6), with the modern patterns of spatial gradients appearing about 10,000 years ago. These modern patterns could emerge only after the ice sheet had shrunk below a critical size and after associated changes in atmospheric circulation had occurred (Kutzbach and Guetter 1986; Webb, Bartlein, and Kutzbach 1987). During the past 10,000 years, smaller but still significant changes have occurred, including a shift of the prairie/forest border, first to the east and then the west (Webb, Cushing, and Wright 1983). Comparisons of past climatic conditions reconstructed from pollen data and model simulations of past climates indicate that climate played a major role in producing the pattern and timing of vegetation changes during the past 18,000 years (Webb, Bartlein, and Kutzbach 1987).

Because plant taxa change independently of each other in space and time, taxon associations at all spatial scales have changed through time (Fig. 9.7). The different types of vegetational associations (from formations down to forest types in counties) all have specific sizes and lifetimes. So too do individual trees at 10 m² and 10 to 100 years (when younger than 10 years, trees are considered only seedlings or saplings),

as well as plant communities at the spatial scale at which two or more trees interact and directly compete. For the latter, the frequency of disturbance-induced succession sets their average lifetime. This series from individual trees up to large vegetation regions has a steep slope in Fig. 9.7, and the duration of the orbitally induced climate variations at periodicities of 10,000 to 100,000 years sets an upper temporal bound for these [ecological] units (Huntley and Webb 1988; Jacobson, Webb, and Grimm 1987).

The sequences from individual trees up to plant formations illustrate the spatial and temporal characteristics of vegetation phenomena that result from a variety of ecological controls. A comparable sequence can be constructed for taxonomic units that result from evolutionary processes (e.g., changes in gene frequency, extinction, and speciation). Estimates for the average temporal and spatial limits of various taxonomic units from individuals up to the level of class (e.g., Angiosperma or flowering plants) determine the slope on the log-log, time-space plot for these units (Fig. 9.7). The key observations are the time and space scales for individual trees, species, and the class of flowering plants. The last evolved 100 million years ago and today grow over much of the earth's land surface. Stanley (1985) and Tiffney (personal communication) estimate the average lifetime of species to be

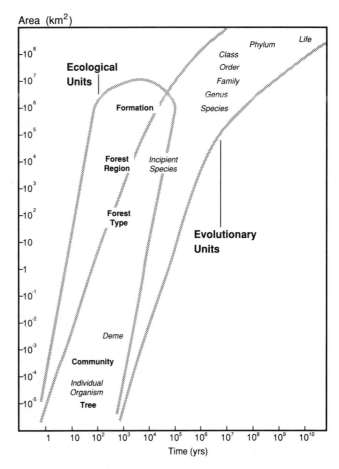

Figure 9.7 Spatial and temporal scales of biologic phenomena. The scales shown here apply to wind-pollinated trees and may not be appropriate for other organisms, such as microorganisms, for example. Evolutionary units are shown in italics, and ecological units are shown in boldface.

Table 9-2 *Controls of biological change, with emphasis on vegetation*

Control	Effect	Status of control at time scales of (years)			
		10^7	10^5	10^3	$\leq 10^1$
Plate tectonics					
continental drift	– divides (joins) continents – separates (joins) floras and faunas – moves continents from climates favorable to life to climates largely devoid of life	I	NA	NA	NA
mountain building	– creates barriers to migration, interaction – creates new habitats (rainshadows, deserts) – controls atmospheric circulation features	I	I	NA	NA
Catastrophic events*	– increased extinction rates or mass extinctions	I	NA	NA	NA
Climate					
orbital variations in seasonal insolation	– biomes and ecotones appear and disappear – taxa migrate – marine and terrestrial taxa change in range, area, and abundance	X	I	I	NA
neoglacial events (e.g., Younger Dryas, Little Ice Age)	– alpine glaciers advance and retreat – forest types change in composition – ecotones move short distances – alpine tree line fluctuates	X	X	I	NA
droughts (Sahel, Dust Bowl, ENSO)	– composition and dominance changes in biomes, communities – local extinctions – annual growth variations in trees	X	X	X	I
seasonal cycle	– birds and other animals migrate – phenological events (leafing out, flowering, etc.) – animals hibernate, perennials vernalize – leaf loss in the face of colder temperatures or dry seasons – plankton blooms (abundance variations) – cycle for annual plants or insects – waxing and waning of secondary tree growth	NA	NA	NA	I
diurnal cycle	– photosynthesis turned on and off – diurnal behavior in animals	NA	NA	NA	I
Soil					
soil development (profile differentiation)	– changes in soil fertility, tilth that alter biomass and composition of vegetation	X	I	I	NA
soil degradation (e.g., salinization, laterization)	– can limit diversity of plant taxa	X	I	I	I
Disturbance regimes					
disease	– selective death of most individuals of one or a few taxa throughout range of taxa	X	X	I	I
	– cyclic impact on abundance of individuals within a taxon	X	X	X	I
fire	– selection for or against certain taxa – initiates secondary succession	X	X	I	D
blowdowns	– initiate secondary succession	X	X	X	I
glacial fluctuations	– bulldoze vegetation or make land available for vegetation	X	I	I	NA

Table 9-2 (*cont.*)

Control	Effect	Status of control at time scales of (years)			
		10^7	10^5	10^3	$\leq 10^1$
human activities	– alteration or elimination of habitats	X	D	I	I
	– selective removal of taxa (trees, mammals, birds, smallpox)	X	D	I	I
	– extinctions on continents	X	D	I	NA
	– extinctions on islands	X	X	X	I
	– spread of exotic plants and animals	X	X	I	I
	– domestication	X	X	I	I

Note: I = independent; characteristic that operates independently of, and to some extent controls, biologic variation. D = dependent; characteristic that is determined by biologic conditions. X = indeterminate; characteristic that is too variable to be reconstructed at the time scale. NA = not applicable; characteristic that is not controlled by biologic conditions, or that varies too slowly to be significant.
* Catastrophic events (e.g., episodes of increased dustiness due to increased frequency of meteor impacts or explosive volcanism) are potentially regular features on the 10^7 to 10^8 time scale, and are unlikely for most periods shorter than 10^7 years. When they occur, their impact is greatest at time scales of 10^{-1} to 10^5 years.

1 to 10 million years, and the area of coverage for most species is within an order of magnitude of $100,000 \, \text{km}^2$. These genetic and taxonomic units plot along a less-steep slope on the log-log, time-space plot than do the vegetational units (Fig. 9.7). Taxonomic units tend to have a longer lifetime than vegetational units for a similar area of coverage. This difference in slope implies that species can survive the continuous appearance and disappearance of vegetational units (associations) at all spatial scales. Tectonically induced changes in climate, mountain barriers, and continent alignments are probably a key factor leading to extinctions and speciation, but meteorite impacts may be another key factor.

What the future holds, however, is difficult to tell. The predicted increased rate for CO_2-induced climatic change during the next century could significantly increase rates of species extinction. The ability of species to survive large past changes in climate depended in part on the rate of major climate change being slow enough that individual species could track the environmental conditions favorable for their growth (Webb 1986). A human-caused climate change in the next 100 years, equal in magnitude to past changes that previously took 1,000 to 10,000 years, may be too fast for certain taxa to adjust and may result in their extinction (Davis 1989). The location, size, and composition of various scales of vegetational regions will also change. These changes will alter the competitive relationships among taxa and thus influence the future course of evolution.

Controls of Vegetational Change

Certain aspects of vegetational change are closely linked to climatic change, but other processes can also be important, such as long-term geological processes, short-term fluctuations in weather, and various environmental disturbances (such as floods, volcanic eruptions, windstorms, and fires) (Table 9-2). One reason for plotting vegetational and taxonomic units on the log-log, space-time plots is to use the characteristic temporal and spatial scales of each unit to help in identifying the various physical and biological processes that act to control the unit. Mathematical theory for the general laws

governing ecological and evolutionary change is not as well advanced as the theory used by meteorologists to understand and model weather and climatic variations. Empirical studies are therefore valuable in helping to show the relative importance of various processes in determining key spatial and temporal variations in the biosphere (Delcourt, Delcourt, and Webb 1983; Webb, Bartlein, and Kutzbach 1987). A full understanding of cause and effect between biospheric and environmental phenomena is complicated because feedbacks and linkages in biological systems can blur the distinction between control and response and because processes that are controls of biological change at one time scale may be dependent on biological conditions at another time scale. For example, fire frequency is partly dependent (at short time scales and small spatial scales) on vegetation successional status for fuel buildup, but it is an independent control of vegetation patterns at intermediate time scales (Delcourt, Delcourt, and Webb 1983). Linkages and feedbacks in the vegetation cause soil conditions, fire regime, disease, micrometeorological conditions, and even human activities to vary as the biological system varies over time scales of <1 to 1,000 years. Our assignment of controls (Table 9-2) is therefore tentative, and we will welcome future research that improves on our summary.

Landscape Change: Scale, Control, and Response

Dynamics and Inheritance in the Physical Landscape
In contrast to elements of the climatic and vegetational systems, elements (individual landforms, soil bodies) within the physical landscape have long lifespans. A climatic regime is made up of numerous transient weather events. The lifespan of an individual tree is 10 to 1,000 years – generally shorter than the lifespan of the community of which it is a part. A cliff, glacial moraine, or river floodplain, on the other hand, may outlive the geomorphic regime under which it formed. An episode of landscape adjustment involving erosion of preexisting landforms and construction of new ones usually does not rework the entire older landscape; remnants of it

are preserved. The result is that most landscapes contain landform assemblages dating from several generations of landscape development.

Inherited elements in a landscape may have been formed by processes similar to those operating today, but some landscapes are polygenetic. In polygenetic landscapes, elements formed by a particular geomorphic process, such as wind erosion, may persist long after that process has ceased to operate on the landscape and another process has replaced it as the dominant process. The best-known examples of polygenetic landscapes are the midlatitude regions that were glaciated during the most recent ice age but now are completely free of glacial and even periglacial activity. In the midwestern and northeastern United States and in central and northern Europe, glacial landforms are being reshaped by weathering, soil development, slope erosion, mass movement, and fluvial activity, but present-day landscape characteristics such as slope, regolith depth (i.e., depth of loose surficial material over bedrock), and drainage patterns are mainly inherited features from glaciation.

Polygenetic landscapes are widespread, and they certainly are not limited to midlatitude glaciated regions. In deserts, relict elements from past humid phases, such as ancient river systems, old archaeological sites, fossil karst phenomena, strandlines of expanded lakes, and deep weathering profiles, have long been recognized (Goudie 1985; 1986). Relicts of past arid phases, such as stabilized fossil dune fields, are also present on desert margins in Africa (Grove and Warren 1968; Thomas and Goudie 1984) and Asia (Allchin, Goudie, and Hegde 1978). Modern coastlines are the result of (1) long-term, climatically controlled processes (postglacial eustatic and glacioeustatic sea-level rise), (2) types and rates of coastal erosional and depositional processes operating under present climate, and (3) inherited Quaternary landforms and deposits (such as shore platforms of former interglacials or beach ridges) (Hopley 1985). Present-day coastal features, including beaches, estuaries, lagoons, barrier islands, coastal dune sheets, and near-shore zones, all have developed since the last glacioeustatic sea-level minimum at about 18,000 years ago, at which time the ice sheets were at their maximum extent. Many have developed only within the past 5,000 years. Landscapes similar to today may have been present during the previous interglacial at about 125,000 years ago, when sea levels were at a maximum, but they were not necessarily at the same locations (Bloom 1983). Even in the humid tropics, long thought to be the most stable morphoclimatic zone, the physical landscape is polygenetic and many features are relict. For example, fluvial dissection occurred in the central Amazon Basin (Tricart 1985) and in Sierra Leone (Thomas and Thorp 1985) under dry conditions at about 20,000 to 12,500 years ago.

Past changes in environmental controls, therefore, have resulted not only in changes in rates of geomorphic activity, but also in shifts in dominant geomorphic process, for example, from glacial to fluvial processes or from eolian to fluvial processes. King (1980) pointed out that a shift in the dominant geomorphic process results in a landscape that is necessarily out of equilibrium with the current processes. The result is a

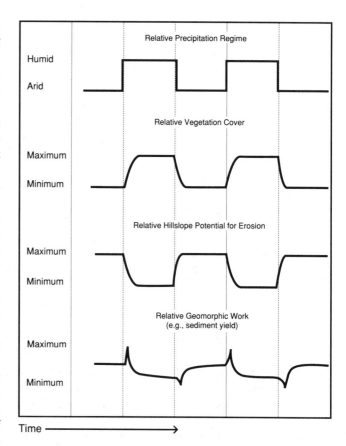

Figure 9.8 Suggested biogeomorphic responses to a series of climatic intervals with abrupt transitions. Curves apply to fluvial systems in midlatitude climates with 25–150 cm mean annual precipitation. Each humid or arid climatic period is several hundred to several thousand years long. Geomorphic work, integrating changes in the driving force of precipitation and the resisting force of vegetation cover, is concentrated at the times of change rather than throughout humid or arid periods. *Source:* Knox 1972.

period of intense geomorphic activity, in which reshaping of hillslopes and reworking of soil profiles occur, in addition to major changes in the sediment storage zones such as valley bottoms, etc. Even if climatic change does not result in a shift in the dominant process, it will change the rates of processes. The time of change in rates is a time of disequilibrium and increased geomorphic activity (Fig. 9.8).

Theories of Geomorphic Change

Long-term geomorphic change has no unifying theory equivalent to the astronomical theory for long-term climatic changes. In the late-nineteenth and early-twentieth centuries, W. M. Davis' (1899) theory of the geographical cycle served as a unifying theory. It was a theory of gradualism, with a cycle of landscape evolution being initiated by a regional fall in relative base level, followed by a long period of unidirectional landscape evolution and adjustment to the base level. By the 1960s, new attention to the physics of geomorphic processes and a growing body of empirical data on geomorphic processes (in short-term operation) led to abandonment of Davisian theory and a focus of attention on time-independent processes. Research on Quaternary geomorphic change has focused on regional studies, with climatic and/or base-level changes as the inferred causes. In the nineteenth century, endogenic forces (earth's internal forces, including tectonics and volcanism) were considered the most important external control of geomorphic processes, but today climate and adjustments internal to the geomorphic system are recognized as equally important. Most geomorphologists working at the Quaternary and historical time scales operate from a loosely defined paradigm consisting of concepts of thresholds, feedbacks, complex response, and episodic activity (Chorley, Schumm, and Sugden 1984: 1–42). Theories that specify how climate change affects geomorphic systems are not well developed or widely accepted (see Cooke and Reeves 1976: 1–23; Schumm and Parker 1973). In process studies, landscape units commonly are analyzed in a framework of a system budget, which divides the landscape into areas of sediment source, sediment transport, and sediment storage, linked by geomorphic processes.

The concepts of long-term geomorphic change have many similarities with those of long-term behavior of the climate system. Both systems are viewed as complex groups of linked subsystems, with multiple feedback links, both positive and negative. These feedback links, as in climatology, make it difficult to separate controls from responses. In river systems, for example, channel gradient is both a control (of sediment transport rates) and a response (to net aggradation or degradation). As in the climate system, responses are frequently nonlinear. Threshold response occurs when a continuous or gradually changing control process triggers a sudden change in geomorphic form or rate of process. Thresholds cause geomorphic activity to be episodic rather than steady through time, certainly on time scales up to 1,000 years. Threshold response also makes identification of a particular controlling factor difficult, because control and response do not necessarily occur closely in time.

Schumm (1973, 1980, 1981) called attention to the existence of intrinsic geomorphic thresholds – sudden changes in system behavior due to gradual morphological changes that are inherent in the system. For example, in arid watersheds, sediment delivered to the channel system tends to be stored there over the short term (10 to 1,000 years), leading to a steeper channel gradient and ultimately to gullying. The shift from an aggrading to an incising channel is typically abrupt in both space and time. This kind of change, with no obvious external trigger, can significantly affect the morphology of the system. Adjacent watersheds with similar geology, climate, and base level may have quite different morphologies at a certain time, because they stand in different positions in relation to their intrinsic geomorphic thresholds. Schumm and his students also developed the concept of complex response, and they documented experimental and empirical cases of it. Complex response refers to a series of oscillations in the direction of geomorphic change, in response to a single perturbation of the system. The best empirical example is that of Douglas Creek in western Colorado, which developed four cut-and-fill terraces in 80 years, in response to historical grazing disturbance (Womack and Schumm 1977). Davis (1976) documented a similar response to agricultural conversion of a midwestern United States watershed. Complex response

presents obvious problems for the identification of causes of geomorphic change and for prediction of geomorphic change.

Despite the complexity of geomorphic change suggested by this modern paradigm of geomorphic system behavior, consistent patterns of geomorphic behavior are evident for time scales ranging from 1,000 to 10,000 years. The effects of threshold response and complex response apparently are concentrated at time scales less than 1,000 years. In environments as diverse as Texas (Baker and Penteado-Orellana 1977), Wisconsin (McDowell 1983), and Poland (Kozarski 1983), episodes of river terracing attributed to climatic change have occurred at intervals of 2,000 to 10,000 years during the past 20,000 years. These episodes of landscape development lasting 1,000 to 5,000 years appear to be largely controlled by system response and adjustment to changes in climatic, eustatic, or tectonic conditions.

Physical Landscape Change at Different Time and Space Scales

Like climatic processes, geomorphic and pedologic processes operate over a large range of temporal and spatial scales (Fig. 9.9). The temporal and spatial scales of landscape features are related; large features change and persist over much longer time scales than do small features (Baker 1986).

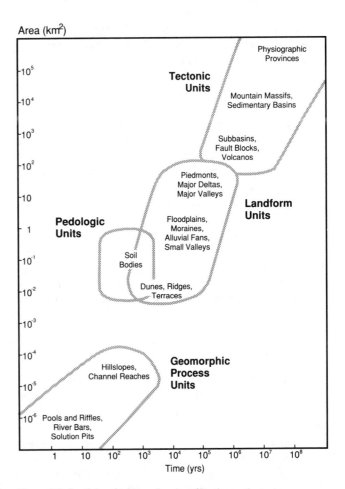

Figure 9.9 Spatial and temporal scales of landscape features. Bubbles enclose the typical time-space scales of each of the four types of landscape features. Some specific examples for each type are shown within the bubbles. Based partly on Baker 1986.

At the largest spatial scale are tectonic units, ranging from physiographic provinces to individual fault blocks. The dominant controls of landscape development at this scale are tectonic processes and denudation. This is the classical cyclic time scale of W. M. Davis. Development of plate tectonics theory has provided insight into the temporal variability of these processes. In tectonically stable regions, large segments of paleolandscapes may persist for 100 million years or longer, such as the Gondwana and post-Gondwana planation surfaces of the Southern Hemisphere (King 1983). In contrast, in tectonically active areas such as the Pacific Rim, some mountain ranges may be less than 1 million years old. In both cases, however, these features show significant changes only over 1,000 years or longer – much longer than the scale of human social and political adjustment processes.

Features of intermediate temporal and spatial scale are termed erosional-depositional units by Baker (1986). They include landforms deposited or eroded by the fluid geomorphic forces – running water, wind, waves, and glaciers – and by mass-movement processes. Causal explanations of intermediate-scale landscape features are complex, because three types of controlling factors (climate, tectonic control of base levels, and human impacts on hydrology and vegetation cover) can influence geomorphic and pedologic processes at this scale. These controls may operate individually or interactively. Intermediate-scale landscape features are most significant to human occupation of the environment, but they vary more slowly than do social and political adjustment processes.

Development of soil bodies is controlled primarily by climatic conditions (and the resultant vegetation cover) and by geomorphic processes that supply parent material and determine relief. Soils show significant variation at equivalent or slightly shorter time scales than the landforms on which they develop. Soil A horizons develop to a steady-state level of maturity in about 100 years, whereas argillic B horizons need at least 1,000 years to develop and do not reach a steady state for 100,000 years (Birkeland 1984).

Small geomorphic process units are not significant to human societies, but they may be significant to individual farms, families, and villages. Their variation at time scales of 1 to 1,000 years is controlled largely by climatic conditions and internal dynamics of, for example, the river system or weathering mantle.

Controls of Physical Landscape Change

Schumm and Lichty (1963) first pointed out that geomorphic characteristics that are dependent variables at one time scale may be independent variables at shorter time scales. Table 9-3 illustrates such functional changes in system variables, with an emphasis on denudation and fluvial geomorphic systems. The three decreasing spatial scales of fluvial geomorphic systems shown – physiographic province, drainage basin, and river channel – are examples of tectonic units, landform units, and geomorphic process units, respectively (from Fig. 9.9). Similar tables could be constructed for glacial, eolian, coastal, and mass-movement processes,

and for pedologic processes. At time scales most relevant to human activities – 10 to 1,000 years – climate and the shortest-scale manifestations of tectonic processes are the most important variables controlling landscape development. For example, movement on faults and earthquakes can effect minor reshaping of the landscape on time scales of 1,000 years, in regions that are tectonically active. More importantly, most regional landscapes are affected by climatic change at this time scale. At the spatial scale of a watershed, geology (lithology and structure) is the dominant variable controlling the physical landscape at 100,000 to 10 million years, but it is virtually unvarying at 1,000 years or less. Climate and its effects on hydrology, weathering, vegetation, and soil development are the most important landscape controls at 100 to 1,000 years. River channels – the smallest and most dynamic landform scale included in Table 9-3 – are truly human-scale and are significant features to social units such as farms, villages, and cities. For river channels, climate is the most important controlling variable at 1,000 years.

Glacial-interglacial cycles probably are the most effective type of climatic variations in reshaping landscapes in the high- and midlatitudes, dry subtropics, and perhaps even the humid tropics (where geomorphic history is poorly known at present). Midlatitude geomorphic conditions during full- and late-glacial times were characterized by glaciation, and outside the glacial limit by intensified fluvial activity (Schumm and Brakenridge 1987), periglacial processes (Péwé 1983), eolian activity (Osterkamp et al. 1987), and pluvial lakes (Smith and Street-Perrott 1983) – all absent or greatly reduced today. Eustatic sea level was about 100 to 120 m lower than at present, exposing extensive areas of continental shelves. The glacial-time landscapes of the high- and midlatitudes were in general geomorphically active, with intensified sediment transfer processes and diminished soil development, compared to Holocene landscapes, characterized by more geomorphic stability and intensified soil development.

In many regional geomorphic systems, such as the glaciated areas, areas of periglacial regime, and pluvial lakes region, the major shift in geomorphic regimes occurred rapidly at the end of full-glacial climatic conditions at about 12,000 to 10,000 years ago. In other geomorphic systems, the shift from full-glacial conditions to postglacial conditions was prolonged and complex. Coastlines, for example, retreated continuously as eustatic sea level rose between 18,000 and 6,000 years ago, and coastal landform assemblages were not established in their modern positions until 5,000 years ago or later (Bloom 1983; McDowell 1987).

The full-glacial to postglacial shift in geomorphic regimes generally was greater than changes during the last 10,000 years, but changes during the latter period have been significant, particularly in fluvial and eolian systems. Sand dune fields in the central and western United States have been reactivated intermittently during dry periods of the Holocene (Mehringer 1986; Osterkamp et al. 1987). In many river systems, the past 10,000 years have been characterized by alternating periods of fluvial stability and instability, of 500-to-2,000-years duration, caused primarily by climatic change (Knox 1983).

Table 9-3 *Controls of geomorphic processes*

Control	Effect	Status of control at time scales of (years)			
		10^7	10^5	10^3	$\leq 10^1$
Physiographic province:					
Megatectonic cycle	– rifting, sea-floor spreading, subduction, continental collision, orogeny	I	I	NA	NA
Tectono-eustasy	– base-level change	I	I	NA	NA
Neotectonic pulses	– uplift, subsidence, faulting	X	X	I	I
Earthquakes	– uplift, subsidence, faulting – mass movements – drainage changes	X	X	X	I
Climatic change	– glaciation – hydrologic cycle changes	X	I	I	I
Change in vegetation cover	– changes in rates of sediment yield and/or runoff	X	I	I	I
Glacio-isostasy	– base-level change	X	I	I	NA
Glacio-eustasy	– base-level change	X	X	I	NA
Drainage basin:					
Geology (lithology, structure)	– controls drainage pattern, slope morphology, sediment type	I	I	NA	NA
Climate	– influences type and rate of weathering, hydrologic regime, vegetation cover	X	I	I	I
Relief	– controls slope morphology, erosion potential	D	D	I	I
Vegetation cover	– changes in erosion rates	D	D	D	I
Human impacts	– changes in land cover, hydrologic system, erosion rates	X	D	I	I
Drainage network and morphology	– influences delivery of water and sediment	D	D	I	I
Hillslope morphology	– influences erosion rates, water delivery to channel, mass-movement rates	D	D	I	I
River channel:					
Geology	– influences valley slope, sediment type	I	I	NA	NA
Climate	– influences runoff into channel, vegetation	X	I	I	I
Vegetation	– influences bank stability, roughness	D	D	I	I
Human impacts	– dams, channel modifications, water diversions	X	D	I	I
Valley slope	– influences channel slope, channel pattern	D	D	D	I
Channel morphology (slope, sinuosity, shape, etc.)	– influences velocity, flooding regime, sediment transport	X	X	D	I

Note: I = independent; characteristic that operates independently of, and to some extent controls, geomorphic variation. D = dependent; characteristic that is determined by geomorphic conditions. X = indeterminate; characteristic that is too variable to be reconstructed at the time scale. NA = not applicable; characteristic that is not controlled by geomorphology, or that varies too slowly to be significant.

Human Impacts in the Context of Long-Term Environmental Change

Natural environmental changes provide a yardstick for judging the magnitude of human impacts on the environment. For example, the impact of European settlement on the North American pollen record between 1700 and today has been large in local areas (McAndrews 1988; Van Zant et al. 1979). Conversion of some areas of the eastern deciduous forest to an artificial savanna of cropland, pastureland, and woodlots was an event comparable in magnitude to climatic-induced vegetation changes over the past 6,000 years (Bernabo and Webb 1977). The human impact on the regional or national scale, however, appears less significant when compared to vegetation changes documented in the pollen records for the past 4,000 years.

Desertification of the Sahel is one of the most significant human environmental impacts of this century. Yet even this event is minor compared to lake-level fluctuations, river system changes, and vegetation changes that occurred during the past 10,000 years. Deforestation of the Amazon basin, in contrast, is similar in scale to natural vegetational variations during the past 10,000 years (Dickinson 1987).

Pollen records of human impact in Europe date back to Paleolithic times – about 300,000 years ago (West 1956). Impact at a regional scale dates from Mesolithic times (10,000 to 5,300 years ago) (Edwards and Ralston 1984; Simmons and Innes 1988), and many paleoecologists have interpreted the widespread synchronous (±500 years) decline in elm pollen abundance at 5,000 (radiocarbon) years ago as resulting from human activity (see discussion in Huntley and Birks 1983). Although disease rather than selective forest clearance might be the factor that killed the elms, human activities may have helped spread the disease. Pollen evidence of Neolithic agricultural activity is widespread in Europe after 5,000 years ago. Human impact in Europe before A.D. 1700 contrasts markedly with that in North America, where only nine out of over 300 radiocarbon-dated sites with pollen data record any evidence of human activity (McAndrews 1988).

The major controls of long-term change (1,000 to 10,000 years) in geomorphic systems are climatic change, sea level, and tectonic changes (Table 9-3). One important question is whether or not human impacts are significant compared to natural changes, at these time scales. Although good evidence exists for significant human impact on geomorphic systems during recent historic times, evidence of significant prehistoric human impact is less clear.

One of the best-studied examples of probable prehistoric human impact on geomorphic systems is the case of accelerated hillslope erosion and resulting valley alluviation in Greece and elsewhere in the Mediterranean region, in Classical (3,500 to 1,800 years ago) and post-Classical times. These alluvial episodes have been attributed to deforestation and intensive land use under Greek and Roman cultures (Butzer 1980), climatic change (Vita-Finzi 1969), and a combination of the two factors (Bintliff 1982). Evidence tends to support the hypothesis of human cause for erosion in the first and second millennia B.C. (2,000 to 4,000 years ago), but this evidence is fragmentary (Davidson 1980).

In central Europe, alluviation during and after the late Bronze Age has also been attributed to human impact through deforestation, expansion of agriculture, and grazing. Some significant alluvial episodes predate major human impact on vegetation cover and soils. Butzer (1980) argued, however, that after 3,500 years ago, fluvial adjustments took place in the context of human disturbance of the landscape and that the role of this disturbance in causing fluvial adjustments is not understood and is probably underestimated. Bell (1982) examined evidence from archaeological sites of erosion, alluviation, and colluviation in Britain and northwestern Europe. He concluded that times of geomorphic activity were asynchronous, suggesting that local factors, particularly prehistoric human land use, were the primary controls rather than climatic change.

Prehistoric arroyo-cutting in the valleys of the southwestern United States also has been cited as an example of early human impact on fluvial systems. Bryan (1954) suggested that during development of the Pueblo culture 1,500 to 600 years ago (A.D. 500–1350), the inhabitants practiced floodwater agriculture on unincised valley floors. He hypothesized that a combination of human impacts and drought decreased the watershed vegetation cover and that channel incision occurred at the end of the drought. Channel incision lowered water tables on the canyon floor, resulting in the decline of agriculture and abandonment of the pueblos. But more recent studies (Love 1979) have shown that arroyo incision did not follow pueblo settlement and that arroyo filling actually occurred toward the end of the pueblo occupation.

These examples suggest that the impact of prehistoric human activity on geomorphic systems, while real in some instances, was minor and highly localized. Human impacts since the Industrial Revolution, on the other hand, have been major and are well documented (Goudie 1986; Graf 1985; Knox 1977; Trimble 1974; Trimble and Lund 1982). In some local areas, these recent human impacts have resulted in alluviation or erosion, concentrated within a few decades, that is equal in magnitude to natural changes on the 1,000-year time scale.

Conclusions

An understanding of natural change in the human environment is essential to an understanding of human impacts. Because of the inherent dynamics of natural processes, it is difficult to identify with confidence many of the changes that may be due to human forces. Some transformations – deforestation, for instance – are easily identified as anthropogenic, but others – human impact on global climate, for instance – remain equivocal as long as natural processes of change and internal system dynamics are poorly understood. The study of natural changes, moreover, provides a means for assessing the relative significance of anthropogenic perturbations, as compared with natural variations. Our knowledge of the response of environmental systems to natural stimuli may also assist in predicting their response to human forces that are comparable in type, rate, and magnitude.

Climatic change is one of the most important controls of long-term change in the natural environment, and at some time scales it is the dominant control. An understanding of climatic variations is therefore basic to understanding and assessing environmental change. Our knowledge of climatic variations has advanced significantly in the past 30 years, but the picture remains complex. Numerous controls of long-term climatic change have been identified. These controls depend on the length and resolution of the time scale. Astronomical factors, which dominate at time scales of 1,000 to 100,000 years, are predictable, but climatic change is not yet predictable at shorter time scales.

Controls of temporal change in biological systems and in the physical landscape are also scale dependent. Climatic variations influence the variations in vegetation patterns and associations at periods greater than 1,000 years; at shorter time scales, other factors, including natural biological processes and human activities, become important. In some areas, for example Europe and parts of Asia, human activities have influenced the vegetation for thousands of years. Landform development is controlled by climatic and geologic factors at temporal scales greater than 1,000 years, and by internal processes, short-term climatic variation, and human actions at shorter time scales. The physical landscape has a longer "memory" than the climate system and the biosphere, and therefore major human impacts on the physical landscape may be more serious and long-lived than major human impacts on the atmosphere and biosphere. But many uncertainties still exist concerning the impacts of and recovery from current human actions, such as those affecting the vegetation in tropical regions and the atmospheric concentrations of greenhouse gases like carbon dioxide and methane.

Acknowledgments

This work was partially supported by grants NSF/ATM-8713981 and DOE FG02-85ER60304 (Webb) and NSF/ATM-8713980 (Bartlein). We thank K. Anderson, K. Wolter, K. Edwards, and I. C. Prentice for their input.

Notes

1. Our focus on climate, vegetation, and physical landscapes is not meant to imply that other systems vary insignificantly. Fluxes in marine biota (chap. 21) present one of many examples of other natural systems experiencing major changes.

2. Our summary draws heavily upon COHMAP, a Cooperative Holocene Mapping Project, which is an international paleoclimatic research group that has used data and simulation models to study the changes in climate, vegetation, lakes, and oceans that occurred during the past 20,000 years (COHMAP Members 1988; Kerr 1984b). Its main goals are to assemble global sets of paleoclimatic data, to calibrate these data in climatic terms, and to use these data to test the ability of global circulation models to simulate past climates (COHMAP Members 1988). COHMAP researchers have mapped and described the vegetation, surface oceans, and surface hydrological regimes of the past 20,000 years. COHMAP research follows the lead set by CLIMAP (Climate, Long-range Investigation, Mapping, and Prediction; CLIMAP Project Members 1976; 1981), which was a well-organized international interdisciplinary paleoclimatic research group that first mapped and modeled the full-glacial climate of 18,000 years ago (Gates 1976). We have used a summary of environmental changes and their causes assembled by the COHMAP group (COHMAP Members 1988) to review the major environmental changes of the past 20,000 years.

References

Allchin, B., A. Goudie, and K. Hegde. 1978. *The Prehistory and Palaeogeography of the Great Indian Desert*. London: Academic Press.

Anderson, P. M., and L. B. Brubaker. In *Global Climates for 6000 and 9000 Years Ago in the Perspective of Glacial/Interglacial Climatic Change*, ed. COHMAP Members. Minneapolis: University of Minnesota Press. (In press.)

Anthes, R. A., H. A. Panofsky, J. J. Cahir, and A. Rango. 1978. *The Atmosphere*, 2d. ed. Columbus, OH: Merrill.

Baker, V. R. 1986. Introduction: regional landforms analysis. In *Geomorphology from Space, a Global Overview of Regional Landforms*, ed. N. M. Short and R. W. Blair, Jr., 1–26. National Aeronautics and Space Administration, SP-486. Washington, D.C.: U.S. Government Printing Office.

Baker, V. R., and M. M. Penteado-Orellana. 1977. Adjustment to climatic change of the Colorado River in central Texas. *J. Geol.* 85: 395–422.

Barron, E. J., and W. M. Washington. 1984. The role of geographic variation in explaining paleoclimates, results from Cretaceous model sensitivity studies. *J. Geophys. Res.* 89: 1267–79.

Bartlein, P. J., and T. Webb III. 1985. Mean July temperature at 6,000 yr B.P. in eastern North America: regression equations for estimates from fossil-pollen data. In *Climatic Change in Canada 5: Critical Periods in the Quaternary Climatic History of Northern North America*, ed. C. R. Harrington. *Syllogeus* 55: 301–342.

Bell, M. 1982. The effects of land-use and climate on valley sedimentation. In *Climatic Change in Later Prehistory*, ed. A. Harding, 127–42. Edinburgh: Edinburgh University Press.

Benson, L., and R. S. Thompson. 1987. The physical record of lakes in the Great Basin. In *North America and Adjacent Oceans during the Last Deglaciation*. Vol. K-3, *The Geology of North America series*, ed. W. F. Ruddiman and H. E. Wright, Jr., 241–60. Boulder, CO: The Geological Society of America.

Berger, A. L. 1978. Long-term variations of caloric insolation resulting from the earth's orbital elements. *Quaternary Res.* 9: 139–67.

Berger, A., J. Imbrie, J. Hays, G. Kukla, and B. Saltzman. eds. 1984. *Milankovitch and Climate*. Dordrecht, Netherlands: Reidel.

Bernabo, J. C., and T. Webb III. 1977. Changing patterns in the Holocene pollen record from northeastern North America: a mapped summary. *Quaternary Res.* 8: 64–96.

Bintliff, J. L. 1982. Climatic change, archaeology, and Quaternary science in the eastern Mediterranean region. In *Climatic Change in Later Prehistory*, ed. A. Harding, 143–61. Edinburgh: Edinburgh University Press.

Birkeland, P. W. 1984. *Soils and Geomorphology*. New York: Oxford University Press.

Bloom, A. L. 1983. Sea level and coastal changes. In *Late-Quaternary Environments of the United States*. Vol. 2. *The Holocene*, ed. H. E. Wright, Jr., 42–51. Minneapolis: University of Minnesota Press.

Bradley, R. S., H. F. Diaz, J. K. Eischeid, P. D. Jones, P. M. Kelley, and C. M. Goodess. 1987. Precipitation fluctuations over Northern Hemisphere land areas since the mid-nineteenth century. *Science* 237: 171–75.

Bradshaw, R. H. W., and T. Webb III. 1985. Relationships between contemporary pollen and vegetation data from Wisconsin and Michigan, U.S.A. *Ecology* 66: 721–37.

Brakenridge, G. R. 1987. Fluvial systems in the Appalachians. In *Geomorphic Systems of North America*. Centennial Special Vol. 2, ed. W. L. Graf, 37–44. Boulder, CO: The Geological Society of America.

Broecker, W. S., and J. van Donk. 1970. Insolation changes, ice volume, and the O^{18} record in deep-sea cores. *Rev. Geophys. Space Phys.* 8: 169–98.

Bryan, K. 1954. The geology of Chaco Canyon, New Mexico, in relation to the life and remains of the historic peoples of Pueblo

Bonito. *Smithsonian Misc. Collections.* vol. 122, pub. 4141: 1–65.

Bryson, R. A., and B. M. Goodman. 1980. Volcanic activity and climatic changes. *Science 207*: 1041–44.

Butzer, K. W. 1980. Holocene alluvial sequences: problems of dating and correlation. In *Timescales in Geomorphology*, ed. R. A. Cullingford, D. A. Davidson, and J. Lewin, 131–42. Chichester, Great Britain: John Wiley and Sons, Ltd.

Chisholm, M. 1980. The wealth of nations. *Trans. Inst. Brit. Geog.*, n.s. 5: 255–76.

Chorley, R. J., S. A. Schumm, and D. E. Sugden. 1984. *Geomorphology*. London: Methuen.

Clark, W. C. 1985. Scales of climatic impact. *Clim. Change 7*: 5–27.

CLIMAP Project Members. 1976. The surface of the ice-age earth. *Science 191*: 1131–37.

CLIMAP Project Members. 1981. Seasonal reconstructions of the earth's surface at the last glacial maximum. *Geol. Soc. Amer. Map and Chart Series*, MC-36: 1–18.

COHMAP Members. 1988. Climatic changes of the last 18,000 years: Observations and model simulations. *Science 241*: 1043–52.

Cooke, R. U., and R. W. Reeves. 1976. *Arroyos and Environmental Change in the American South-west*. Oxford: Clarendon Press.

Crowley, T. J. 1983. The geologic record of climatic change. *Rev. Geophys. Space Phys. 21*: 828–77.

Crowley, T. J., D. A. Short, D. G. Mengel, and G. K. North. 1986. Role of seasonality in the evolution of climate during the last 100 million years. *Science 231*: 579–84.

Davidson, D. A. 1980. Erosion in Greece during the first and second millennia B.C. In *Timescales in Geomorphology*, ed. R. A. Cullingford, D. A. Davidson, and J. Lewin, 143–58. Chichester, Great Britain: John Wiley and Sons, Ltd.

Davis, M. B. 1976. Erosion rates and land-use history in Southern Michigan. *Env. Cons. 3*: 139–48.

———. 1989. Lags in vegetation response to greenhouse warming. *Clim. Change 15*: 75–82.

Davis, W. M. 1899. The geographical cycle. *Geog. J. 14*: 481–504.

Delcourt, H. R., P. A. Delcourt, and T. Webb III. 1983. Dynamic plant ecology: the spectrum of vegetational change in space and time. *Quat. Sci. Rev. 1*: 153–75.

Dickinson, R. E. ed, 1987. *The Geophysiology of Amazonia*. New York: John Wiley & Sons.

Edwards, K. J., and I. Ralston. 1984. Postglacial hunter-gatherers and vegetational history in Scotland. *Proc. Soc. Antiq. Scot. 114*: 15–34.

Gates, W. L. 1976. Modeling the ice-age climate. *Science 191*: 1138–44.

Gaudreau, D. C., and T. Webb III. 1985. Late-Quaternary pollen stratigraphy and isochrone maps for the northeastern United States. In *Pollen Records of Late-Quaternary North American Sediments*, ed. V. M. Bryant and R. G. Holloway, 247–80. Dallas, TX: American Association of Stratigraphic Palynologists.

Goudie, A. 1985. Themes in desert geomorphology. In *Geomorphology: Themes and Trends*, ed. A. Pitty, 56–71. Totowa, NJ: Barnes & Noble Books.

———. 1986. *Environmental Change*, 2d ed. Oxford: Clarendon Press.

Graf, W. L. 1985. The Colorado River, instability and basin management. *Resource Pub. in Geog.* No. 1984/2. Washington, D.C.: Association of American Geographers.

Grove, A. T., and A. Warren. 1968. Quaternary landforms and climate on the south side of the Sahara. *Geog. J. 134*: 194–208.

Grove, J. M. 1979. The glacial history of the Holocene. *Prog. Phys. Geog. 3*: 1–53.

———. 1988. *The Little Ice Age*. London: Methuen.

Hammer, C. U., H. B. Clausen, and W. Dansgaard. 1980. Greenland ice sheet evidence of post-glacial volcanism and its climatic impact. *Nature 288*: 230–35.

Hansen, J., D. Johnson, A. Lacis, S. Lebedeff, P. Lee, D. Rind, and G. Russell. 1981. Climatic impacts of increasing atmospheric CO_2. *Science 213*: 957–61.

Harvey, L. D. D. 1980. Solar variability as a contributing factor to Holocene climatic change. *Prog. Phys. Geogr. 4*: 487–530.

Haury, L. R., J. A. McGowan, and P. H. Wiebe. 1978. Patterns and processes in the time-space scales of plankton distributions. In *Spatial Patterns in Plankton Communities*, ed. J. H. Steele, 277–327. Proc. Nato Conference on Marine Biology, Erice, Italy, 1977. New York: Plenum Pub.

Hays, J. D., J. Imbrie, and N. Shackleton. 1976. Variations in the earth's orbit: pacemaker of the ice age. *Science 194*: 1121–32.

Hopley, D. 1985. Geomorphological development of modern coastlines: a review. In *Geomorphology: Themes and Trends*, ed. A. Pitty, 56–71. Totowa, NJ: Barnes & Noble Books.

Huntley, B. 1988. Glacial and Holocene vegetation history: Europe. In *Vegetation History*, ed. B. Huntley and T. Webb III, 341–83. Dordrecht, Netherlands: Kluwer Academic Publishers.

Huntley, B., and H. J. B. Birks. 1983. *An Atlas of Past and Present Pollen Maps for Europe: 0–13,000 Years Ago*. London: Cambridge University Press.

Huntley, B., and I. C. Prentice. 1988. July temperatures in Europe from pollen data 6,000 years before present. *Science 241*: 687–90.

Huntley, B., and T. Webb III. eds. 1988a. *Vegetation History*. Dordrecht, Netherlands: Kluwer Academic Publishers.

———. 1988b. Migration: species' response to climatic variations caused by changes in the earth's orbit. *J. Biogeog. 16*: 5–19.

Imbrie, J., J. D. Hays, D. G. Martinson, A. McIntyre, A. C. Mix, J. J. Morley, N. G. Pisias, W. L. Prell, and N. J. Shackleton. 1984. The orbital theory of Pleistocene climate: support from a revised chronology of the marine O^{18} record. In *Milankovitch and Climate*, ed. A. Berger, J. Imbrie, J. Hays, G. Kukla, and B. Saltzman, 269–305. Dordrecht, Netherlands: Reidel.

Imbrie, J., and K. P. Imbrie. 1979. *Ice Ages: Solving the Mystery*. Short Hills, NJ: Enslow Publ.

Jacobson, G. L., T. Webb III, and E. C. Grimm. 1987. Patterns and rates of vegetation change during the deglaciation of eastern North America. In *North America and Adjacent Oceans during the Last Deglaciation*. Vol. K-3, *The Geology of North America Series*, ed. W. F. Ruddiman and H. E. Wright, Jr., 277–88. Boulder, CO: The Geological Society of America.

Jones, P. D., T. M. L. Wigley, and P. B. Wright. 1986. Global temperature variations between 1861 and 1984. *Nature 322*: 430–34.

Kerr, R. A. 1984a. How to make a warm Cretaceous climate. *Science 223*: 677–78.

———. 1984b. Climate since the ice began to melt. *Science 226*: 326–27.

King, C. A. M. 1980. Thresholds in glacial geomorphology. In *Thresholds in Geomorphology*, ed. D. R. Coates and J. D. Vitek, 297–321. London: Allen & Unwin.

King, L. C. 1983. *Wandering Continents and Spreading Sea Floors on an Expanding Earth*. New York: Wiley-Interscience.

Knox, J. C. 1972. Valley alluviation in southwestern Wisconsin. *Ann. Assoc. Amer. Geog. 62*: 401–410.

———. 1977. Human impacts on Wisconsin stream channels. *Ann. Assoc. Amer. Geog. 67*: 323–42.

———. 1983. Responses of river systems to Holocene climates. In *Late-Quaternary Environments of the United States*. Vol. 2, *The Holocene*, ed. H. E. Wright Jr., 26–41. Minneapolis: University of Minnesota Press.

Kozarski, S. 1983. River channel changes in the middle reach of the Warta valley, Great Poland Lowland. *Quaternary Stud. Poland 4*: 159–69.

Kukla, G. J., and R. K. Matthews. 1972. When will the present interglacial end? *Science 178*: 190–91.

Kutzbach, J. E. 1976. The nature of climate and climatic variations. *Quaternary Res. 6*: 471–80.

———. 1981. Monsoon climate of the early Holocene: climate experiment with the earth's orbital parameters for 9,000 years ago. *Science 214*: 59–61.

Kutzbach, J. E., and P. J. Guetter. 1986. The influence of changing orbital patterns and surface boundary conditions on climate simulations for the past 18,000 years. *J. Atmos. Sci. 43*: 1726–59.

Kutzbach, J. E., and F. A. Street-Perrott. 1985. Milankovitch forcing of fluctuations in the level of tropical lakes from 18 to 0 kyr B.P. *Nature 317*: 130–34.

Labitzke, K., and H. van Loon. 1988. Associations between the 11-year solar cycle, the QBO and the atmosphere. Pt. I: the troposphere and stratosphere in the northern hemisphere in winter. *J. Atmos. Terr. Phys. 50*: 197–206.

Lamb, H. H. 1982. *Climate, History and the Modern World*. London: Methuen.

Lloyd, C. R. 1984. Pre-Pleistocene paleoclimates: the geological and paleontological evidence; modeling strategies, boundary conditions, and some preliminary results. *Adv. Geophys. 26*: 35–140.

Love, D. W. 1979. Quaternary fluvial geomorphic adjustments in Chaco Canyon, New Mexico. In *Adjustments of the Fluvial System*, ed. D. D. Rhodes and G. P. Williams, 277–308. Dubuque, IA: Kendall-Hunt Pub. Co.

Lowe, J. J., and M. J. C. Walker. 1984. *Reconstructing Quaternary Environments*. London: Longman.

MacCracken, M. C., and F. M. Luther. eds. 1985. Detecting the Climatic Effects of Increasing Carbon Dioxide. DOE/ER-0235. Washington, D.C.: U.S. Department of Energy.

Marsh, G. P. 1885. *The Earth As Modified by Human Action*. New York: Charles Scribner's Sons.

McAndrews, J. H. 1988. Human disturbance of North American forests and grasslands: the fossil pollen record. In *Vegetation History*, ed. B. Huntley and T. Webb III, 673–97. Dordrecht, Netherlands: Kluwer Academic Publishers.

McDowell, P. F. 1983. Evidence of stream response to Holocene climatic change in a small Wisconsin watershed. *Quaternary Res. 19*: 100–116.

———. 1987. Geomorphic processes in the Pacific Coast and mountain system of Oregon and Washington. In *Geomorphic Systems of North America*, Centennial Special Vol. 2, ed. W. L. Graf, 539–49. Boulder, CO: The Geological Society of America.

Mehringer, P. J., Jr. 1986. Prehistoric environments. In *Handbook of North American Indians*. Vol. 11, *Great Basin*, ed. W. L. D'Azevedo, 31–50. Washington, D. C.: Smithsonian Institution.

Milankovitch, M. 1941. *Kanon der Erdbestrahlung und Seine Anwendung auf das Eiszeitenproblem*. Special Publication 133. Belgrade: Royal Serbian Academy. (English translation published in 1969 by Israel Program for Scientific Translations.)

Miller, K. G., R. G. Fairbanks, and G. S. Mountain. 1987. Tertiary oxygen isotope synthesis, sea level history, and continental margin erosion. *Paleoceanog. 2*: 1–19.

Mitchell, J. M., Jr. 1976. An overview of climatic variability and its causal mechanisms. *Quaternary Res. 6*: 481–93.

Osterkamp, W. L., M. M. Fenton, T. C. Gustavson, R. F. Hadley, V. T. Holliday, R. B. Morrison, and T. J. Toy. 1987. Great Plains. In *Geomorphic Systems of North America*, Centennial Special Vol. 2, ed. W. L. Graf, 163–210. Boulder, CO: The Geological Society of America.

Péwé, T. L. 1983. The periglacial environment in North America during Wisconsin time. In *Late-Quaternary Environments of the United States*. Vol. 1, *The Late Pleistocene*, ed. S. C. Porter, 157–89. Minneapolis: University of Minnesota Press.

Porter, S. C. 1981. Recent glacier variations and volcanic eruptions. *Nature 291*: 139–42.

Prell, W. L., and J. E. Kutzbach. 1987. Monsoon variability over the past 150,000 years. *J. Geophys. Res. 92*: 8411–25.

Prentice, I. C. 1986. Vegetation responses to past climatic changes. *Vegetatio 67*: 131–41.

Ruddiman, W. F. 1985. Climate studies in ocean cores. In *Paleoclimate Analysis and Modeling*, ed. A. D. Hecht, 197–257. New York: John Wiley and Sons.

Ruddiman, W. F., and A. McIntyre. 1981. Oceanic mechanisms for amplification of the 23,000 year ice volume cycle. *Science 212*: 617–27.

Russell, R. J. 1956. Environmental change through forces independent of man. In *Man's Role in Changing the Face of the Earth*, ed. W. L. Thomas, Jr., 453–70. Chicago: University of Chicago Press.

Saltzman, B. 1985. Paleoclimatic modeling. In *Paleoclimate Analysis and Modeling*, ed. A. D. Hecht, 341–96. New York: John Wiley and Sons.

Sarntheim, M. 1978. Sand deserts during glacial maximum and climatic optimum. *Nature 272*: 43–46.

Schneider, S. H. 1983. Volcanic dust veils and climate: How clear is the connection? – An editorial. *Clim. Change 5*: 111–13.

Schumm, S. A. 1973. Geomorphic thresholds and complex response of drainage systems. In *Fluvial Geomorphology*, Proceedings Volume of the Fourth Annual Binghamton Geomorphology Symposium, Binghamton, N.Y., ed. M. Morisawa, 299–310. Binghamton, NY: Publications in Geomorphology, State University of New York.

———. 1980. Geomorphic thresholds: the concept and its applications. *Trans. Inst. Brit. Geog.*, n.s., 15: 485–515.

———. 1981. Some applications of the concept of geomorphic thresholds. In *Thresholds in Geomorphology*, ed. D. R. Coates and J. D. Vitek, 473–85. London: Allen & Unwin.

Schumm, S. A., and G. R. Brakenridge. 1987. River response. In *North America and Adjacent Oceans During the Last Deglaciation*. Vol. K-3, *The Geology of North America Series*, ed. W. F. Ruddiman and H. E. Wright, Jr., 221–40. Boulder, CO: The Geological Society of America.

Schumm, S. A., and R. W. Lichty. 1963. Time, space and causality in geomorphology. *Amer. J. Sci. 263*: 110–19.

Schumm, S. A., and R. S. Parker. 1973. Implications of complex response of drainage systems for Quaternary alluvial stratigraphy. *Nature 243*: 99–100.

Shackleton, N. J., J. Backman, H. Zimmerman, D. V. Kent, M. A. Hall, D. G. Roberts, D. Schnitker, J. G. Baldauf, A. Desprairies, R. Honrighausen, P. Huddlestun, J. B. Keene, A. J. Kaltenback, K. A. O. Krumsiek, A. C. Morton, J. W. Murray, and J. Westburg-Smith. 1984. Oxygen isotope calibration of the onset of ice-rafting and history of glaciation in the North Atlantic region. *Nature 307*: 620–23.

Shackleton, N. J., and N. G. Pisias. 1985. Atmospheric carbon dioxide, orbital forcing, and climate. In *The Carbon Cycle and Atmospheric CO$_2$: Natural Variations Archean to Present*, Geophysical Monograph, vol. 32, ed. E. T. Sundquist and W. S. Broecker, 303–317. Washington, D.C.: American Geophysical Union.

Simmons, I. G., and J. B. Innes. 1988. Late Quaternary vegetational history of the North York Moors, VIII–X. *J. Biogeog. 15*: 249–72.

Smith, G. I., and F. A. Street-Perrott. 1983. Pluvial lakes of the western United States. In *Late-Quaternary Environments of the United States*. Vol. 1, *The Late Pleistocene*, ed. S. C. Porter, 190–212. Minneapolis: University of Minnesota Press.

Stanley, S. M. 1985. Rates of evolution. *Paleobiol. 11*: 13–26.

Street-Perrott, F. A. 1981. Tropical paleoenvironments. *Prog. Phys. Geog. 5*: 157–85.

Street-Perrott, F. A., and S. P. Harrison. 1985. Lake levels and climate reconstruction. In *Paleoclimate Analysis and Modeling*, ed. A. D. Hecht, 291–340. New York: John Wiley and Sons.

Stuiver, M. 1980. Solar variability and climatic change during the current millennium. *Nature 286*: 868–71.

Thomas, D. S. G., and A. Goudie. 1984. Ancient ergs of the Southern Hemisphere. In *Late Cainozoic Palaeoclimates of the Southern Hemisphere*, ed. J. C. Vogel, 407–418. Rotterdam: Balkema.

Thomas, M. F., and M. B. Thorp. 1985. Environmental change and episodic etchplanation in the humid tropics of Sierra Leone. In *Environmental Change and Tropical Geomorphology*, ed. I. Douglas and T. Spencer, 239–67. London: Allen & Unwin.

Thomas, W. L., Jr. ed. 1956. *Man's Role in Changing the Face of the Earth*. Chicago: University of Chicago Press.

Tricart, J. 1985. Evidence of Upper Pleistocene dry climates in northern South America. In *Environmental Change and Tropical Geomorphology*, ed. I. Douglas and T. Spencer, 197–217. London: Allen & Unwin.

Trimble, S. W. 1974. *Man-induced Soil Erosion on the Southern Piedmont, 1700–1970*. Ankeny, IA: Soil Conservation Society of America.

Trimble, S. W., and S. W. Lund. 1982. Soil conservation and the reduction of erosion and sedimentation in the Coon Creek Basin, Wisconsin. U.S. Geol. Surv. Prof. Pap. No. 1234. Washington, D.C.: U.S. Government Printing Office.

van Loon, H., and K. Labitzke. 1988. Associations between the 11-year solar cycle, the QBO and the atmosphere. Pt. II: surface and 700mb in the northern hemisphere in winter. *J. Climate 1:* 905–20 (1988).

Van Zant, K. L., T. Webb III, G. M. Peterson, and R. G. Baker. 1979. Increased Cannabis/Humulus pollen, an indicator of European agriculture in Iowa. *Palynol. 3:* 229–33.

Vita-Finzi, C. 1969. *The Mediterranean Valleys*. Cambridge: Cambridge University Press.

Wahl, E. W., and T. L. Lawson. 1970. The climate of the mid-nineteenth-century United States compared to current normals. *Mon. Weath. Rev. 98:* 259–65.

Webb, T., III. 1986. Is vegetation in equilibrium with climate? How to interpret late-Quaternary pollen data. *Vegetatio 67:* 75–91.

———. 1987. The appearance and disappearance of major vegetational assemblages: long-term vegetational dynamics in eastern North America. *Vegetatio 69:* 177–87.

———. 1988. Eastern North America. In *Vegetation History*, ed. B. Huntley and T. Webb III, 385–414. Dordrecht, Netherlands: Kluwer Academic Pub.

Webb, T., III, E. J. Cushing, and H. E. Wright, Jr. 1983. Holocene changes in the vegetation of the Midwest. In *Late-Quaternary Environments of the United States*. Vol. 2, *The Holocene*, ed. H. E. Wright, Jr., 142–65. Minneapolis: University of Minnesota Press.

Webb, T., III, P. J. Richard, and R. J. Mott. 1983. A mapped history of Holocene vegetation in southern Quebec. *Syllogeus 49:* 273–336.

Webb, T., III, P. J. Bartlein, and J. E. Kutzbach. 1987. Climatic change in eastern North America during the past 18,000 years: comparison of pollen data with model results. In *North America and Adjacent Oceans during the Last Deglaciation*. Vol. K-3, *The Geology of North American Series*, ed. W. F. Ruddiman and H. E. Wright, Jr., 447–62. Boulder, CO: The Geological Society of America.

West, R. G. 1956. The Quaternary deposits at Hoxne, Suffolk. *Phil. Trans. R. Soc. London B 239:* 265–356.

Womack, W. R., and S. A. Schumm. 1977. Terraces of Douglas Creek, northwestern Colorado: an example of episodic erosion. *Geology 5:* 72–76.

Wright, H. E., Jr., J. C. Almendinger, and J. Gruger. 1985. Pollen diagram from the Nebraska Sandhills, and the age of the dunes. *Quaternary Res. 24:* 115–20.

10

Land Transformation

JOHN F. RICHARDS

The modern world has seen massive changes in its lands in the past few centuries. Forests, wetlands, savannas and grasslands, and deserts have altered profoundly in area and in composition. The area of human settlement and agriculture and the scale of timbering, mining, quarrying, and other land-using activities has grown enormously. If we compare the face of the land in 1500, 1700, or even 1850, with landscapes today, we find a much-altered realm in virtually every corner of the globe (Richards 1986). Over the same centuries, a tightening global economic order has pushed human production to unprecedented levels. Paced by advances in technology, we produce and move foodstuffs, clothing, and other goods and services throughout the world in an abundance that is startling. At the same time, soaring human needs and unequal distribution press ever-rising demands on the world economy. These two powerful secular trends are interlinked in a direct relationship: the reverse side of economic development has been intensified use and the depletion of the world's lands.

A modeled estimate of world changes in land use over the past three centuries calculates that the world's forests and woodlands diminished by 1.2 billion ha, or 19% of the 1700 total. Grasslands and pastures have declined by 560 million ha, or 8% of the 1700 estimate. Croplands brought into cultivation show a net increase of 1.2 billion ha, for a 466% increase in less than three centuries (see Table 10-1). The magnitude of the changes is clear.

Table 10-1 suggests that the pace of change is accelerating. Agricultural expansion and depletion of forests and grasslands was greater in absolute terms over the 30 years between 1950 and 1980 than in the 150 years elapsed between 1700 and 1850. World cropland grew by 331 million ha after World War II, in contrast to growth of 272 million ha in the eighteenth and early-nineteenth centuries in total. Withdrawals from the world's forests and grasslands followed the same proportions.

The rate of change has not been uniform across world regions. Instead, agricultural expansion, forest clearing, wetland drainage, irrigation of grasslands, expansion of human settlement, and similar processes have traced a spiraling arc that is determined, for the most part, by European political and economic control. Acreage of North American croplands – the product of New World settlement – grew early and rapidly, peaking in 1950. African agriculture developed later, with its most impressive growth arriving in the post-1920 period. Australia and New Zealand, the "Pacific developed countries," show a steady rise in cropland and commensurate depletion of the two other categories after 1850. Agricultural expansion is not the only measure of intensified land use for production, of course, but it is a potent indicator. Activities in timbering and the international timber trade, in mining, in urbanization, and in later years, the impact of industrialization, grow in tandem with agricultural expansion.

Finally, these figures mask at least one important trend. Over longer periods of time – from century to century – accruing investments in the land, despite occasional setbacks, raised the level of exploitation to new heights in Europe and other world regions. The standards for productive use of land – as with other standards for human productivity – have risen substantially over the past five centuries, so that rough grazing on untilled lands might have been considered perfectly appropriate usage of lands 10 km from a major city in the sixteenth century, but not today. Or, keeping a small woodlot might have been practicable in land the same distance from a city in the nineteenth century, but not in the late-twentieth century.

As productivity has increased, so has our domination of the land. Humans now plan and assign tasks to all categories of land. Intensification of land use is intensification of control. Formal classification systems – zoning – strictly regulate the uses to which any hectare of publicly or privately owned land may be put in virtually all countries of the world. Usage of topsoil, subsurface minerals, surface and subsurface water, even sunlight falling on that hectare, is regulated by various arms of the state. And it is the modern, centralizing state that has extended its control assiduously over every tract of land within its boundaries.

Greater productivity may include, as it has in the current century, lessened overt activity such as with some forms of preservation and conservation. That is, we now limit human intervention in territory freed from intrusive modes of pro-

Table 10-1 *Global land use, 1700–1980*

Regions	Vegetation types	Area (million ha)					Percentage changes from:				
		1700	1850	1920	1950	1980	1700 to 1850	1850 to 1920	1920 to 1950	1950 to 1980	1700 to 1980
Tropical Africa	Forests and woodlands	1358	1336	1275	1188	1074	−1.6%	−4.6%	−6.8%	−9.6%	−20.9%
	Grassland and pasture	1052	1061	1091	1130	1158	0.9%	2.8%	3.6%	2.5%	10.1%
	Croplands	44	57	88	136	222	29.5%	54.4%	54.5%	63.2%	404.5%
North Africa/ Middle East	Forests and woodlands	38	34	27	18	14	−10.5%	−20.6%	−33.3%	−22.2%	−63.2%
	Grassland and pasture	1123	1119	1112	1097	1060	−0.4%	−0.6%	−1.3%	−3.4%	−5.6%
	Croplands	20	27	43	66	107	35.0%	59.3%	53.5%	62.1%	435.0%
North America	Forests and woodlands	1016	971	944	939	942	−4.4%	−2.8%	−0.5%	0.3%	−7.3%
	Grassland and pasture	915	914	811	789	790	−0.1%	−11.3%	−2.7%	0.1%	−13.7%
	Croplands	3	50	179	206	203	1566.7%	258.0%	15.1%	−1.5%	6666.7%
Latin America	Forests and woodlands	1445	1420	1369	1273	1151	−1.7%	−3.6%	−7.0%	−9.6%	−20.3%
	Grassland and pasture	608	621	646	700	767	2.1%	4.0%	8.4%	9.6%	26.2%
	Croplands	7	18	45	87	142	157.1%	150.0%	93.3%	63.2%	1928.6%
China	Forests and woodlands	135	96	79	69	58	−28.9%	−17.7%	−12.7%	−15.9%	−57.0%
	Grassland and pasture	951	944	941	938	923	−0.7%	−0.3%	−0.3%	−1.6%	−2.9%
	Croplands	29	75	95	108	134	158.6%	26.7%	13.7%	24.1%	362.1%
South Asia	Forests and woodlands	335	317	289	251	180	−5.4%	−8.8%	−13.1%	−28.3%	−46.3%
	Grassland and pasture	189	189	190	190	187	0.0%	0.5%	0.0%	−1.6%	−1.1%
	Croplands	53	71	98	136	210	34.0%	38.0%	38.8%	54.4%	296.2%
Southeast Asia	Forests and woodlands	253	252	247	242	235	−0.4%	−2.0%	−2.0%	−2.9%	−7.1%
	Grassland and pasture	125	123	114	105	92	−1.6%	−7.3%	−7.9%	−12.4%	−26.4%
	Croplands	4	7	21	35	55	75.0%	200.0%	66.7%	57.1%	1275.0%
Europe	Forests and woodlands	230	205	200	199	212	−10.9%	−2.4%	−0.5%	6.5%	−7.8%
	Grassland and pasture	190	150	139	136	138	−21.1%	−7.3%	−2.2%	1.5%	−27.4%
	Croplands	67	132	147	152	137	97.0%	11.4%	3.4%	−9.9%	104.5%
USSR	Forests and woodlands	1138	1067	987	952	941	−6.2%	−7.5%	−3.5%	−1.2%	−17.3%
	Grassland and pasture	1068	1078	1074	1070	1065	0.9%	−0.4%	−0.4%	−0.5%	−0.3%
	Croplands	33	94	178	216	233	184.8%	89.4%	21.3%	7.9%	606.1%
Pacific developed countries	Forests and woodlands	267	267	261	258	246	0.0%	−2.2%	−1.1%	−4.7%	−7.9%
	Grassland and pasture	639	638	630	625	608	−0.2%	−1.3%	−0.8%	−2.7%	−4.9%
	Croplands	5	6	19	28	58	20.0%	216.7%	47.4%	107.1%	1060.0%
Total	Forests and woodlands	6215	5965	5678	5389	5053	−4.0%	−4.8%	−5.1%	−6.2%	−18.7%
	Grassland and pasture	6860	6837	6748	6780	6788	−0.3%	−1.3%	0.5%	0.1%	−1.0%
	Croplands	265	537	913	1170	1501	102.6%	70.0%	28.1%	28.3%	466.4%

Note: The estimates in this table for 1700 were drawn from R. A. Houghton et al., Changes in the Carbon Content of Terrestrial Biota and Soils Between 1860 and 1980: A Net Release of CO_2 to the Atmosphere, *Ecological Monographs* 53 (1983): 235–62, Table 1, 237. I have combined the areas for seven classes of woodland and shrubland for the forest and woodland figure and for five categories of grassland, shrub land, and pasture land for the grassland and pasture figure. These are estimated figures arrived at by assigning areas of natural vegetation to each world region and then reducing that vegetation by the assumed area of agriculture in 1700. The latter figure was calculated by estimating the extent of agriculture in each region on the basis of the population estimates in C. McEvedy and R. Jones, 1978 *Atlas of World Population History*. Middlesex, Eng: Penguin Books. The remaining values in the table are taken from World Resources Institute, 1987 *World Resources 1987*, Table 18.3 "Land Use, 1850–1980", 272. New York: Basic Books. R. A. Houghton and D. Skole supplied the modeled values for this table for the report. The sources for this table included "four sets of information: maps of natural vegetation, population size and growth data between 1700 and 1980, literature on historical land use and cover, and recent (post-1950) land-use data collected by the United Nations Food and Agriculture Organization (FAO)" (p. 273). The primary driving force in land conversion was presumed to be expansion of sedentary agriculture. Extension of agriculture drew land from natural ecosystems in direct proportion to its area. The model presumes change to be generally linear.

Despite its obvious limitations, this modeled estimate is the most plausible scenario of land use change that we possess on a global scale. Until much more detailed work is done aimed at quantifying changes in the land over time, world region by world region, we can do little more than this.

duction to meet human aesthetic needs for wilderness or intellectual needs for scientific data. These reserved lands are intensively controlled, but buffered against the usual forms of intervention.

Every hectare from the Arctic to the Antarctic is owned, demarcated, and controlled. Every hectare of land is subject to the formally recognized ownership and control of an individual, an organization, or a nation-state. Primeval wilderness – in the sense of untrodden forests or deserts – exists only in our collective imagination. In the late 1980s, the land and its wealth is subject to human management. The earth is now at our disposal.

A World View

To understand how and why human land use has changed in the modern era, we must dissect the social forces that have so tightly coupled land and economic growth. What are the forces that have propelled world economic development? Within this context how and why has our domination and control of the land risen so dramatically? These questions are meaningful only when understood in the context of long-term, half-millennium trends that have followed a spiraling trajectory to encompass the entire world.

This is no modest task. The difficulties of conceptualization and systematic data collection are formidable. In any society, at any time, human use of the land is regulated by one of the most complicated set of relationships entered into by human beings. The variety of ecological settings around the world and of human approaches to those ecological settings is vast indeed. Control and management of the land by no means rules out surprises. Intervention in the land confronts natural forces engaged in their own cycles of change. Planned actions, no matter how well-intentioned, have often had the most unexpected consequences. Nor should we overlook the longer-term effects of human action that do not show up immediately. Partly for these reasons, generalizations resting firmly upon a long-term global perspective have a unique value.

Despite these difficulties, a global perspective has a unique value. From this vantage point, underlying structures and processes are thrown into sharp relief. It is far easier at this scale to discern secular trends and major variables in the modern history of human interaction with the land. The modern conjuncture leaves us no alternative but to move to the largest social forces and to long-term trends in world history.

Underlying the long-term trend toward intensified land use is a central fact. Since the Age of Discovery, the most dynamic force in human history has been the steady growth of a sea-borne capitalist world economy centered on western Europe (Braudel 1984: 21–70). This core, or metropolitan region, has later stretched to North America, Russia, and Japan. In totting up the economic gains of the modern capitalist world economy, land and the stored energy within it is too often overlooked. Intensification of human land use – both conversion and extraction of natural resources – is an essential feature of the spiraling, ever-extending domain of the modern capitalist states and the modern world economy.

That dual model of land use evolved in the core nation-states of northwestern Europe has been imposed upon an ever-growing portion of the world's lands. At the heart of this model is the urge to make complementary use of lands at the center and those in the peripheral areas. Maximizing production in all categories of land use – arable, urban, woodland, and pasture – has uniformly characterized the domestic territories of England, France, the Low Countries, Germany, Italy, and Spain since the sixteenth century. Intensive land use at the center also relied upon resources extracted ruthlessly from lands in eastern Europe, the New World, and other dependent regions.

In its initial stages, land use in the European periphery responded to demands for commodity production – through monoculture and rapid extraction of timber, minerals, and other natural resources. Very few controls on the rate of usage or conservation were in effect.

Under close scrutiny, the pattern of intensifying land use in Europe betrays a common pattern focused upon the great cities. Urban demands for foodstuffs, energy, water, and other commodities drive land conversion and resource extraction in their immediate hinterlands. Rising populations and improved access enlarged each city's immediate hinterland. Highly intensive market-gardening pushed outward extensive grain farming and livestock raising in belts around most early modern European cities. We find therefore a center-periphery model replicated in the regions surrounding each city.

Over time, colonial or dependent states moved closer to the European model of intensive land use and control. Those patterns already in evidence in early modern Europe and its outliers persist through the centuries. Century after century they are imposed directly or diffused by imitation to the remaining parts of the globe. South and Southeast Asia, Australasia, Latin America, Africa, and other dependent regions were subjected first to heavy resource extraction and commodity production typical of the periphery. In time, indigenous core regions of intensive land use coalesced to form a new land-use hierarchy within each region. At this secondary or intermediary level, core regions directed extraction of resources from their own peripheries as new frontiers of settlement were opened. Thus, Calcutta, already responding to stimuli from London, directed the extraction of tea, timber, paddy rice, jute, and other commodities from eastern Bengal, Assam, and Orissa in the colonial period. At a still deeper level, subregional centers emerged in which the process of urban-dominated land use commenced. Dacca in Eastern Bengal and Gauhati in Assam directed the expansion of settlement, land clearing, timbering, and other exploitative activities in their hinterlands. At this and even lower levels, we can see arrays of smaller frontier regions and subregions merging one into the other. In this fashion, intensified control and productivity on the world's lands gained momentum in each succeeding century.

Virtually all human societies have experienced that dynamic form of changing land use referred to as a frontier. The frontier is that period and area in which a peripheral region is created or extended. We all are familiar with the transient frontier epoch during which time forests, grasslands, and even deserts are transformed into agricultural, pastoral, and urban landscapes of settlement and sedentary agriculture. Populations of diverse human "tribal" societies – hunter-gatherers, pastoralists, shifting cultivators – succumb to the urgent claims of pioneer settlers backed by the modernizing state. Populations of wild animals are displaced by domesticated draft and grazing animals or are exterminated altogether. Frontiers of settlement often were accompanied by extensive commercialized fur-gathering, timbering, and mining activity. Partly stimulated by external forces, partly generated by internal energies, one society after another has undergone episodes of frontier expansion.

Certainly the dominant theme in the history of the New World is that of European frontier expansion. Subduing indigenous peoples and wild animals; clearing forests; plowing grasslands; draining wetlands; extracting timber, minerals, and other commodities – these are the motifs of North American and South American history right up to the present. Similarly, the settlement frontier occupies a central position in the history of Australia and New Zealand, Russia, or South Africa. Not so well recognized are the settlement frontiers of Asia and nonsettler Africa. Chinese, Burmese, Bengali, Ghanaian settlers, among others, moved into forested regions in Asia and Africa throughout our period. Some groups were subject to European colonial control; many were not. Frontier expansion is a nearly universal human experience in the modern world.

Frontier expansion generally has followed irregular, rather than smooth, patterns of spatial diffusion. In each frontier episode, frontierspeople followed river valleys, grassland corridors, or other natural corridors to reach desirable lands, which they exploited first.

The initial process of penetration is accompanied by the creation of secondary and tertiary frontier zones, in which more intensive land conversion and use of resources occurs. It is these later episodes, during which secondary and tertiary frontiers proliferate, that speed intensified use in all regions.

Delineating the opening and closing of frontiers obviously depends upon defining scale. The global frontier is in its last decades after a five-century run. In Brazil and Indonesia, we contemplate the final episodes of the world settlement frontier in the last two decades of the twentieth century. At the level of the major world regions, frontier expansion has varied from three centuries or more in North America to as little as one and a half centuries in Australia and New Zealand. Larger regions within the continents have had more restricted frontier experience. Clearing and settlement of the American and Canadian Midwest required between 100 to 150 years. State and provincial-level frontiers in the United States and Canada lasted perhaps 50 to 80 years from opening to closure. Frontier episodes, when seen at the level of an individual county, might be as fleeting as two to three decades. The structural identity is manifest; the transient event is often difficult to measure unless we are very precise in our definitions.

Expanding settlement frontiers generally have heightened physical impacts on the land – more frequent traffic, more intrusive earth-moving or tilling, more thorough harvesting of plants and animals, larger-scale diversion, flooding, and drainage of water. It is the frequency, scale, and duration of these physical operations and their effects that are usually indexed in assessing the intensity of land use. But the true measure of intensity is not physical impact or even economic product, rather the extent to which land is controlled and managed.

Social Forces

The accelerating impulse toward mastery of the land and its resources has its origin in a complex set of interlinked causes: state power and organizational momentum, expanding economic demand expressed through increasingly integrated world markets, and population growth. Another variable – technological advance – facilitates, but does not drive, transformations in the land. It is the interaction between these variables that has shaped modern consumption of natural resources and uses of the land. To identify the dominant force for a particular episode or case study is often difficult. To assign primacy on a global scale is extremely speculative – at least at this stage of our knowledge of world environmental history. Nevertheless, state action repeatedly plays a primary role in exploitation of the world's lands. Governmental power, however, must be supported by growing market demands and rising populations. In the end, of course, it is the sum of millions of human decisions and the cumulative effect of countless days of human energy expended in daily labor that creates new conditions on the land.

Modern human societies have developed an ever-increasing capacity for collective action – especially in large-scale complex organizations. At the heart of this trend is the centralizing power, efficiency, and expanding spatial and social reach of the state and its dependent corporate entities. In the sixteenth century, technically superior, efficient state structures appeared in the Islamic world (the Safavids and Ottomans), in India (Moghul and contemporary Muslim Sultanates), and in China under the Ming. Building on expansive economies, long histories of administrative competence, and strong military prowess, the rulers of these states commanded impressive organizations of great depth and complexity. Nevertheless, in the intervening centuries, it has been the metropolitan nation-states of Europe and North America that have consolidated and expanded their corporate power most effectively. It is they who established maritime power, conquered territories, and defined new territorial, social, and legal entities around the world. It is they who honed their bureaucratic structures to unprecedented levels of efficiency and control. It is their subordinate corporate structures – private business firms, churches, voluntary agencies – that have added to this dynamic spurt in humanity's capacity for collective action.

Throughout the world, European colonial regimes imprinted state structures and corporate entities directly in their own images or inspired imitation by a process of diffusion. In extending their reach, metropolitan powers consistently have manipulated incentives and sanctions, altered land tenures, encouraged markets, and built public works to force greater productivity from the land. Behind every frontier and frontiersman lies the military power, legal institutions, and financial resources of the modernizing state.

Since 1500, a world market system has strengthened its grasp on local and regional economies, just as new state structures strengthened their grip on local polities. In the early modern period, Europe stabilized its resource base at home and expanded its reach by land along the Russian/Asian frontier, and more significantly, throughout the oceans of the world. Burgeoning trade and power fed on steadily increasing maritime capacities. Thus, Christian Europe, rather than Islamic or Sinic civilization, began the global trend of intensifying land use. This "Great Frontier" added real resources to the European economy (Jones 1981: 80–84).[1] The economies of western Europe tapped the mineral resources of Latin America for precious metals; the fisheries of the New World, for protein and oil; the boreal woods, for furs, timber and forest products; warm-weather lands in North America and the Indian Ocean, for plantation-grown sugar, indigo, cotton, and rice; and the temperate zone of North America, for grain, timber, and furs. These initial links required intensified use of land to meet production demands. As resource flows to Europe proved profitable and feasible, state and market demands grew. The expansive process of land transformation in the modern world began with the compressed social energy of western Europe.

Over the past 500 years, human numbers have moved upward. Prior to World War I, this increase was halting, but dramatic in the long-term. Thereafter we have seen steeply ascending populations in every world region. One informed estimate shows the following progression for world population (FAO 1981; McEvedy and Jones 1978: 342):

1500	425 millions
1700	600 millions
1850	1,200 millions
1920	2,000 millions
1980	4,430 millions

Global population had grown tenfold in just under 500 years, in a curve that began a steeper ascent in the early nineteenth century and has inclined upward more sharply after 1920. Numbers rising at these accelerating rates mean that the total stock of human capital – energy and intellect – has grown as well. As interregional linkages and contact tightened, surplus populations and labor reserves became more mobile. Surplus populations could migrate more readily to take advantage of frontier conditions when new lands opened up. At the same time, more people required more food and commodities from agriculture and natural resources. More people occupied greater space in enlarged urban areas. Rising human numbers in the modern world therefore contribute to changes in the land. Growing demand for food and commodities pushed the expansion of arable lands worldwide as well as the consumption of natural resources. Ready

availability of labor determined episodes of land-clearing, conversion, and degradation. On a global scale, within an increasingly interconnected global economy, population growth has been one of the primary forces pressing against the land. Certainly, the correlation between population growth and increased production on the land is robust and unmistakable (Boserup 1965).[2]

Another force for change is that of technological adaptation. Technology has not been a direct cause of intensified land use – at least from a global perspective. Technological change removes barriers, but does not drive intensified exploitation of land. Instead, social organization – the dynamic assembly and direction of human energy and intellect – seizes opportunities created by technical improvements. (Or, alternatively, societies mandate technical innovation as well as its configuration.) In the largest context, accumulating technical advances have been vital to the growth of an integrated international economic order. Improvements in transportation and communication obviously have had a critical importance. At a more focused context, technical improvements in industry have created a demand for natural resources and industrial crops. At its most direct, technology offers increasingly more efficient means to control and manipulate the landscape. Tools ranging from powered mechanical reapers to chain saws to herbicides have all made their mark on the land. All these complex and varied interactions must be considered in reviewing the role of technological change.

Technology's impact on land use was limited before the 1850s. Water, wind, gravity, and animal and human muscle were the principal sources of power. Wood was the dominant source of heat for domestic and industrial purposes. Fire was the most effective agent for land clearing. Communications moved at the speed of horseback or sailing ship. Despite these limits, human ingenuity – especially in Europe and North America – made incremental gains in technique by trial-and-error experimentation (Singer et al. 1958). Sailing ships advanced from the ungainly, small, but still seaworthy, galleon of the early sixteenth century to giant East Indiamen and warships of the European navies in the late eighteenth century. Canal- and road-building enabled goods, people, and messages to be carried at a new level of efficiency and speed. Water- and windmills became more and more efficient in grinding grain, pumping water, and sawing timber. Other gains, in optics, glassmaking, printing, and metallurgy were important for human productivity and had some implications for intensified land use – such as in use of the telescope for surveying and mapmaking.

The European Model: Early Modern Poland

The characteristic pattern of agricultural expansion in distant dependent areas emerged in eastern Europe as early as the sixteenth and seventeenth centuries. Poland and its adjacent regions responded to the economic strength of the highly developed countries of western Europe. Amsterdam, followed by London, was the urban center for the sea-borne imports of Baltic staples reaching western Europe. The demands pulsing outward from Amsterdam and London pressed to capacity producers in eastern Germany, Poland, Hungary, Scandinavia, and Russia. The strength of the sea link is reflected in the long-term magnitude and fixity of the Baltic trade. Between 1497 and 1660, ship entries and exits through the Sound averaged between 1,200 and 1,300 completed passages per annum, or a total of over 200,000 voyages for the 163-year period (Glamann 1971: 39). Over this period, cereals carried from the Baltic averaged 60,000 t per year.[3] This was, moreover, an ascending figure until the mid-seventeenth-century slump in trade. In effect, the grain fields of the east were a giant food-grain reserve for western Europe.

As is well recognized, the Polish nobility responded eagerly to opportunities for profit in the export grain trade. To ensure a steady labor supply at favorable wages, they resorted to subjugating the peasantry of the east into a revived manorial system. Only a harshly repressive system could hold peasants in a labor-scarce economy, as they saw an alternative in flight to a settler frontier to the east (Anderson 1974: 206–07). Another response to market incentives was to increase production.

It is virtually certain that prior to the mid-seventeenth-century slump, the newly galvanized estate owners in the east had enlarged their cultivated fields. In 1534, a diplomat employed by the court of Brussels reported that for the last quarter-century, the Polish and Prussian nobility had prospered from the export grain trade, but "before that, the Polish seigneurs had had no outlet for their grain and had left much land uncultivated" (Malowist 1959: 182–83) In order to produce the average annual grain export moving through the Sound in the period 1600 to 1650, Polish, Lithuanian, and Russian estate owners had to commit between 500,000 and 700,000 ha of land to tillage.[4] In the early 1500s, Polish landowners could have filled the export orders for rye by allocating 70,000 to 80,000 ha of land.[5] This was a tenfold increase in exports of grain and presumably a similar increase in cultivated area.

Timber, potash, pitch, and tar were another grouping of exports from the eastern lands. Like grain, these bulky products could be carried economically only by water: first down the river networks to Danzig and the other Baltic ports, and second, as bulk cargoes for timber ships sent from Amsterdam or London. Like grain, imported Baltic timber was a vital resource for the economies of the eastern seaboard. The navies and merchant marines of England, Holland, France, and Spain were dependent upon timber shipments from the Baltic forests. And, as with rye and wheat, the market demand for wood grew more and more insistent in the sixteenth and seventeenth centuries (Pounds 1979: 280). Quantities shipped increased steadily, as did prices.

Since the days of the Hanse trading towns, the Vistula river served as the main artery for timber rafted to the sea. Danzig (Gdansk) was a leading market for Baltic fir (*Pinus sylvestris*) (drawn from the forests of northern and central Poland) and Baltic oak (drawn from the deciduous forests as far as Galicia to the west and south). Riga was also a major timber port for Baltic fir (drawn from the forests of Livonia and later from Russian woodlands). Timber merchants, having obtained credits from their sources in Danzig or Riga each autumn, purchased stumpage rights from owners of timberlands in Poland and Russia. The latter were usually nobles, but might also be villages selling communal rights.

The proprietors mobilized timber cutters from among their tenants or from the village community itself. Several hundred woodcutters using axes felled selected trees and employed oxen or horses to drag sledges over the winter snow to the nearest stream. Prevailing timber prices imposed a limit of 20 miles (32 km) to either side of a stream. If snow depths were adequate, logging contractors assembled individual logs into great rafts of thousands of logs at the Vistula or its branches. After a several-month journey, the logs were sorted in ponds at the ports. Water-driven mills converted the logs into eight-inch-square timbers and into a sequence of smaller and narrow categories (planks, deals, and ultimately battens). Dutch, English, or French traders or factors purchased either unsawed logs or milled lumber under various graded categories. These they sent on the thousand-mile journey on timber ships that carried on average 300 "loads" of timber equivalent to 300 tons displacement (Albion 1926: 138–51).

The timber industry formed a nearly perfect fit with grain and cattle. Unlike the situation in France and Germany, Polish and Russian landlords held virtually untrammeled property rights in the woodlands on their estates. Some royal forest holdings existed, especially in Russia, but they were open for sales of timber also. Landed proprietors in Eastern Europe could use serfs and tenants in the winter, when labor requirements in cereal growing were minimal, to fell and ship timber. The timber trade was considerably less given to fluctuation than the grain trade. West European dockyards and building construction demanded uninterrupted supplies of wood and naval stores.

Two centuries of intensifying timbering bore predictable results. Early on, Danzig ceased to produce the best mast timber. Riga instead was the source for these impressive fir sticks, which ideally were an inch in diameter to every yard of length. Thus, the greatest masts for capital war ships had to be over 27 inches in diameter and 27 yards in length (Albion 1926: 28–29). Gigantic trees such as these were no longer available in the Polish forests, but had to come from Russia instead. By the early decades of the seventeenth century, if not before, timber contractors had to journey farther up the river system to find dense stands of timber for stumpage contracts. Agricultural expansion and timbering together degraded the forests of the Vistula basin and more generally those of southern and central Poland (Malowist 1960). Consequently, the timber trade declined in the southern Baltic and shifted to Riga and other northern ports, as well as to the west coast of Norway.

Maritime Dominance and Continental Frontiers, 1700–1850

During this period, a group of states dominated by Europeans or by colonists of European descent extended their boundaries and populations. Britain, France, Holland, Spain, and Portugal aggressively deployed their navies in the world's oceans. They used maritime power to establish a network of colonies controlled from the sea. As early as the 1730s and 1740s, the naval flotillas of western Europe patroled the world's seas unchallenged. No non-European navy could confront the massed firing power and maneuverability of these two- and three-decker frigates and ships of the line.

In large measure European maritime expansion rested on the strength of its trading companies holding trade monopolies by royal charter. By 1700, northern European companies moved enormous quantities of goods (or human beings, as in the slave trade) at a profit in the new world, Africa, and Asia. Each was firmly backed by central government sanction and support. Creation of these new links of administered or regulated trade (Fig. 10.1) spurred increased production in the export regions of Central America and the Caribbean, South and Southeast Asia, the Middle East and Africa. In order to trade profitably, each company evolved rationalized control centers composed of boards of directors, carrying out policymaking and control by committee; professional administrative staff; and mechanisms to control their traders, funds, and stock. The trading companies' impact on their trading partners was far from neutral. It is not accidental that two of the largest colonial domains, the British empire in India and the Dutch empire in Indonesia, grew out of the activities of the two East India companies. Dutch control of Java and Sri Lanka and British control of Bengal stimulated greater agrarian production in these colonies. French expansion was tied more directly to the state, without intervening structures. Everywhere dominant naval power spilled over into outright aggression on land.

The same period saw massive expansion along several continental settlement frontiers. Forest clearing and pioneer settlement began in earnest on the North American continent. Powerful demand from the British timber market reached across the Atlantic to stimulate timbering and a simultaneous settlement frontier in eastern Canada. Exploitation of the Canadian forests surged ahead with the near-closure of Baltic supplies of timber to Great Britain as a result of Napoleon's continental system. New Brunswick, for example, became a large-scale supplier of pine and hardwoods to the British timber markets by 1810 (Wynn 1981). In this new "timber colony," small-scale lumber operators obtained licenses from the Royal Surveyor to exploit crown-controlled tracts adjacent to rivers and streams. Each winter, parties of lumbermen founded camps, built roads, and dragged the logs to the rivers for the spring drives to the saw mills at the ports. Oxen, river transport, and water-driven saw mills sufficed to process the cut, and wind power moved the timber fleet across the Atlantic. By the 1840s New Brunswick was sending 200,000 t of timber across the Atlantic each year, as well as 160 million board feet of sawed lumber (Wynn 1981: 33). This annual assault on the forests certainly reduced the standing stock of the largely untouched New Brunswick forests. Lumbering also provided part-time supplemental employment for growing numbers of settlers. The population of New Brunswick grew from approximately 25,000 persons thinly scattered in the coastal regions in 1800 to 193,000 souls 50 years later. Cleared land increased tenfold, from 60,000 acres in 1800 to 640,000 acres in 1850.

Subject to similar forces, Czarist Russia pressed ahead with its own pioneering frontier to the east along the Great Russian Plain (chap. 33). And, China, under the Manchus, reached definitive limits in its own ecological frontier by the mid-1800s.

Internal Frontiers in China

Secure in its massive territory and its effectively centralized imperial system, the Ching Empire was largely impervious to external political forces. Only with the amphibious assaults of British gunboats in the Opium War of 1839 did Chinese defenses against foreign political domination crumble.

The new Manchu rulers of China carefully restored the state apparatus of the defeated Ming. The Ching Dynasty (1644–1911), from its origin to the mid-nineteenth century, was a formidable machine. The state recruited, disciplined, armed, and deployed a massive army. Literati, the scholar-gentry, chosen by ability through competitive examinations, presided over the structure at every level of the state.

The Ching state, in common with its predecessors, was especially strong in strategic economic planning to encourage sufficient food grain production and distribution. This involved major investment in waterworks, in grain transport and storage, and in incentives and controls from the country-side to the consumer (Chuan and Kraus 1975). Effective, shrewd state policies generally imposed peace and order while encouraging economic growth.

One palpable result of dynastic stability showed in the population figures. Casualties in the Manchu invasion and two extremely severe pandemics forced the total from 150 million in 1600 to 130 million in 1650 at the start of the dynasty. By 1700 this figure was up to 150 million again, and by 1850 the total had reached 215 million. Thus, population had more than doubled in the three centuries since 1500.[6]

The Manchus inherited from the previous regime a wide-span, powerful, flexible market structure, which linked urban markets with the rural economy. Merchants and traders had ample capital and expertise. Demand rose steadily. The use of paper money and commercial credit was well established. In the next two centuries, we find evidence of growing proliferation of market towns throughout the countryside. New merchant-organized putting-out systems enabled peasant households to spin and weave cotton for urban markets. As the pace of economic development quickened, so did the growth of the market structure (Elvin 1973: 268–84).

Under the early Ching Dynasty, Chinese rural society departed from the former manorial order with "serf-like tenants" to a more commercialized and fragmented system. Gradually the shape of rural society altered. Large landowners moved out of the countryside to become absentee holders of their lands. Tenants, rather than landlords, became effective managers of the land as they acquired permanent tenurial rights to the surface of the land (i.e., the right to occupy and cultivate without fear of expulsion). The landlords retained rights to the subsurface, or essentially residual control of the properties. In the new order that emerged, constraints against social mobility – either upward or downward – for cultivators

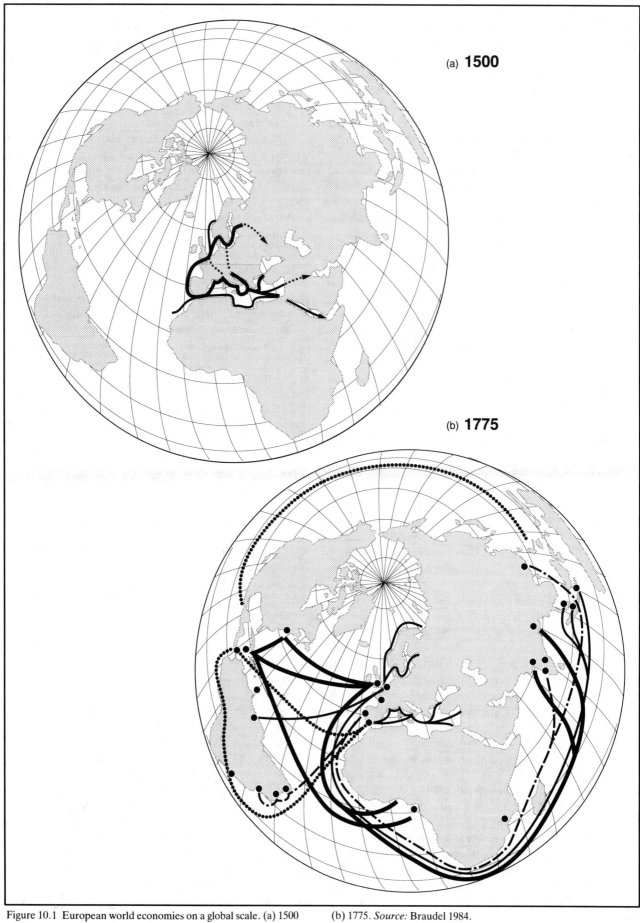

Figure 10.1 European world economies on a global scale. (a) 1500   (b) 1775. *Source:* Braudel 1984.

were loosened. The new system repaid intensive working of the land by ambitious small holders (Elvin 1973: 255–58).

Despite its size and autonomy, the Chinese empire began to respond to the emerging world economy. In 1685, the Manchu emperor opened Chinese ports to foreign trade in a reversal of Ming maritime policy. This coincided with the discovery of the delights of tea as a stimulant in western Europe. First the Dutch, and later the English, East India Companies moved to supply the new demand. By 1706, imports of tea into London alone had reached 100,000 pounds (Furber 1976: 127). They continued to climb thereafter. Early in the century, Canton also began to import Indian opium in ever-increasing quantities (Richards 1981a). From the 1770s onward, Canton also imported growing quantities of raw cotton from western India, as the British encouraged this trade (through Bombay) to offset the cost of Chinese tea (Guha 1972: 3).

The constellation of forces – state, market and human numbers – drove impressive agricultural expansion in Manchu China. Cultivated area in the empire enlarged from 33 (±7) million ha in 1600 under the Ming to 63 (±7) million ha in 1766, or nearly double after 120 years of Manchu rule. Over the next century, cultivated area grew more slowly, to 81 (±3) million ha in 1873 (Perkins 1969: 16). Expansion of arable land on this scale resulted from steady migration under frontier conditions by hundreds of thousands of settlers who reclaimed and resettled lands abandoned in northern China since the Mongol incursions. Later these settlers pushed the settlement frontier into previously uncultivated lands (Perkins 1969: 25).

Ching success in encouraging renewed productivity on the land is most apparent in the provinces of southern China. Government officials made a sustained effort to increase population, cultivation, and tax revenues in opening an internal frontier within the underutilized lands south of the Yangtze.

The history of Hunan Province under Ching rule illustrates this point. In the sixteenth and early seventeenth centuries, Hunan remained a sparsely-settled frontier region with abundant land (Perdue 1987). The population (between 5 and 6 million) was divided between the majority Han Chinese, primarily peasant-farmers, and the indigenous Miao and Tuijia peoples of the hills. The area of permanent cultivation was about 1.8 million ha, or only 6% of the total land area in Hunan.[7] In the mountain areas the Han peasant-farmers grew rice, sorghum, millets, and pearl barley as dry-land crops. In the fertile alluvial plains of Hunan's lake and four river basins, they grew single-crop paddy rice under irrigation. The Miao and Tuijia engaged in shifting cultivation in the mountains to grow millets, sorghum, and beans. Both groups resorted to hunting, fishing, and gathering for supplemental income. But the Manchu invasion and a series of local rebellions devastated the nascent economy of the province in the mid-seventeenth century. During the first decades of Manchu rule, Hunan had just begun to recover from the heavy mortality and land abandonment.

From 1700 to 1800, Hunan's prosperity recovered and forged strongly ahead. The province was subject to two basic forces: "a strong administration encouraging agricultural

settlement and land clearance, and a wave of new immigrants to occupy the newly cleared land" (Perdue 1987). Under Zhao Shenqiao, imperial governor between 1703 and 1710, the regime took firm charge of restoring Hunan's productivity. He and his successors offered migrants tax exemptions and loans of seed, tools, and even draft animals to clear land.

Given these incentives, great numbers of migrants seized upon the new economic opportunities opening in Hunan. It did not take long for the province's population to soar. At its height under the Ming in the 1580s, Hunan was home to 5 to 6 million people. When the first accurate official count was taken in 1776, the provincial total had reached 14.9 million.

Simply by marking off land with bamboo markers and paying tax on it settlers could claim homesteads. After 3 years of cultivation, the settlers received permanent tenure with full ownership rights. Chinese customary land law, when actively backed by the state, effectively secured private property rights in land. By 1724, Ching records show that the amount of registered, cultivated land had doubled in 40 years and was now at the highest rate of the Ming (about 1.8 million ha).[8]

Pressure to increase cultivation hit the mountain lands and their inhabitants hardest. Despite official attempts to protect the hill-dwellers from encroachment, the Miao tribal groups lost heavily. Widespread adoption of New World crops – maize, tobacco, sweet potatoes – added considerably to the productive potential of upland farming. As a result, Han cultivators moved higher into the hills, cleared more upland forests, and squeezed the Miao and other tribals toward a refuge area in the northwestern corner of Hunan. In 1766, the official tax rolls showed a total of 3.2 million ha under cultivation in the province, for close to a doubling of arable land.

Throughout the eighteenth century, Hunan's agriculture became more intensive and commercialized. Annual cropping in the hills replaced shifting cultivation. Various types of forest products and wild game and fish became less abundant and more expensive. Cultivable land values climbed steadily.

By the early nineteenth century, scholar gentry in Hunan, as well as more ordinary inhabitants, were fully conscious of some of the effects of agricultural expansion. Land scarcity had become apparent in climbing prices, land disputes, and division of holdings. Firewood had become scarce and expensive. Bamboo and forest fibers were hard to find. Land clearance on the mountains had resulted in frequent, dangerous, earth slides as flash floods grew more frequent and massive. Soil erosion had begun to bite into the productivity of upland fields. The signs of extreme land degradation were at hand.

Maritime Domination and the World Economy, 1850–1930

After victory in the Napoleonic wars, Britain's Royal Navy gradually imposed unprecedented control and security over the world's sea routes. Admiralty charts compiled painstakingly over the nineteenth century added another dimension to the security of mariners. Britain and other imperial rulers built a network of colonial port cities – Calcutta, Bombay, Madras, Capetown, Jakarta, and Hong Kong, among others – to serve as nodes in the global political and economic system. Each empire invested heavily in ports and harbors (dredging, breakwaters, lighthouses) and warehousing and other facilities at these gateways around the world.

It was the arrival of steam-powered transportation of goods, mail and people, and electrically transmitted information by wire and cable that created a truly integrated new world economic order. The period of transition was relatively rapid. Steam-powered riverboats and ocean vessels started to supplant sailing vessels as early as the 1820s, and by 1840 there were scheduled steam services across the Atlantic.[9] Construction of the Suez Canal speeded steam services from Europe to Asia by 1869, and in fact the Canal was a crucial link in the emerging global network. Construction of a global railway network began in earnest in the 1850s. By 1913, world railways totaled 1.1 million km (Hastings 1972 and Latham 1978: 22). In the same period, telegraph wires accompanied newly laid railway tracks. With the refinement of telegraphy and transoceanic cables, information could travel faster than goods or people for the first time. Orders, money transfers, and prices flowed over the wires and cables to reach a new level of commercial integration. The enormous investment in capital, machinery, and labor required to construct and maintain this worldwide system made its own demands on the land. The railways were especially voracious in their appetite for coal and timber.[10] By 1870, all elements of the system were in place.

London became the hub of a global market system with a vast spatial reach, startling technical efficiency, and upwardly moving demands for goods and commodities (with only occasional lapses in the latter). The efficiency and accessibility of credit facilities, reliable money supplies, insurance, commodity storage, communication, and transportation were without precedent in human history. Transaction costs declined. For example, after the opening of the Suez Canal, freight rates from Burma to the United Kingdom dropped from 60 shillings per ton to 22 and 6 pence in 1913 (Latham 1978: 193). Similar declines occurred on other sea lanes. Commodities and industrial products edged toward a uniform band of world prices.

The nineteenth century was the great age of commodity demand and consequent changes in land uses (Tucker and Richards 1983). Around the world agriculturalists grew dozens of crops for cash sale and export. Coal and other minerals flowed into the world supply-demand mechanism. Everywhere timber became a commercial item – relatively cheap in frontier areas to be sure, but a marketable commodity. Industrial products flowed outward: firearms, machine tools, cotton textiles, railway rolling stock – all found markets. Although the terms of trade were tilted unequally in favor of Britain and the other industrialized metropolitan societies of Europe and North America, commodity flows and industrialized goods did not conform strictly to the classical pattern. Some industrial development occurred in dependent colonies. Metropolitan areas also produced staples. The global market was taking on an existence and vitality essentially independent of either individual or collective actions by Britain or other states of the world.

New global linkages stimulated the most extensive burst of land clearing and conversion yet experienced in human history. The modeled calculations for land use change shown in Table 10-1 reveal an increase in the world's croplands of 376 million ha, or a 70% increase over seven decades. Another estimate for land areas converted to regular cropping is even higher. Between 1860 and 1919, the cropped area increased by 432 million ha (see Table 10-2). Agriculture expanding at this rate was the most significant and visible form of land transformation. All types of ecosystems around the world felt the pressure of the human drive for production on the land.

Individual crops and markets displayed distinctive configurations in region after region. The strengthened world economy nurtured several forms of large-scale, capitalist agriculture within divergent ecological settings: permanent bush and tree crops in the tropics, grazing animals in temperate semiarid grasslands, wheat in both zones, and wet rice production by peasant smallholders on river deltas in the tropics. Each sector mobilized capital, migrant labor, and entrepreneurial energy to transform the land.

The nineteenth and early twentieth centuries were the high point for large plantations in Asia and Latin America, less so in sub-Saharan Africa (Grigg 1974: 235–38). Successful operation of sugar and cotton plantations in the Caribbean and the North American mainland had generated a fund of experience and confidence. European owners and managers mobilized migrant labor to clear jungle lands in order to grow rubber, cacao, tea, coffee, bananas, or other bush or tree crops. These large, European-owned and run, specialized industrial entities were clearly a product of the late-nineteenth-century world economy. Land use by plantations included that cleared for their principal crops, for fuel and processing needs, and for food crops to feed their laborers. Rubber in Malaysia, tea in India, bananas in Central America, coffee in Brazil – all comandeered vast tracts of forest land for the new world market (Grigg 1974: 210–40).

The late-nineteenth-century economic closure had a substantial impact on zones of long-standing plantation agriculture as well. Thus, in Cuba's Oriente Province, long-isolated and relatively undeveloped, sugar became the province's primary cash crop only after 1860. The big boom in sugar came after 1900, as a direct result of the U.S. military occupation of the island. Completion of a railway into the eastern end of the island by 1902 provided the impetus for a new burst of investment in sugar by individual U.S. investors and by United Fruit Company. In Oriente Province in 1899, cane totaled 28,700 ha, but 20 years later the new sugar plantations occupied 200,000 ha. The new lands were planted at the expense of Oriente's mahogany forests (Hoernel 1976).

Ranching, or "commercial grazing," is a product of European conquest and the nineteenth-century international economic order (Grigg 1974: 241–45). The demand for beef, mutton, and wool in Europe and North America stimulated the growth of export-focused pastoral systems in areas of European settlement. The major ranching areas included

Table 10-2 *Land areas converted into regular cropping (10^6 ha)*

World region	First period (1860–1919)		Second period (1920–1978)	
	To crops	From crops	To crops	From crops
Africa	15.9	—	90.5	—
North America	163.7	2.5	27.9	29.4
Central America and the Caribbean	4.5	—	18.8	0.4
South America	35.4	—	65.0	—
Middle East	8.0	—	31.1	—
South Asia	49.9	—	66.7	—
Southeast Asia	18.2	—	39.0	—
East Asia	15.6	0.2	14.5	8.4
Europe (excluding Soviet Europe)	26.6	6.0	13.8	12.7
USSR	88.0	—	62.9	—
Australia/New Zealand	15.1	—	40.0	—
TOTAL	440.9	8.7	470.2	50.9
Net area	432.2		419.3	

western North America; the grasslands of Brazil, Uruguay, Argentina, and Venezuela; the South African veldt; and the grasslands of New Zealand and Australia. Reduced freight rates and refrigerated rail and steamer services by the 1880s, and new techniques for meat-canning boosted the potential for European ranchers around the world. With intense demand and dwindling costs of transportation, ranchers could profitably place large herds on huge tracts of semiarid land. Tiny numbers of ranch hands displaced nomadic pastoralists and their herds in some areas. Elsewhere, cattle and sheep displaced unmanaged wildlife such as buffalo, zebras, and kangaroos, in a massive population shift in the world's grasslands (Richards 1986).

Ranching in general has been a frontier activity. As new fodder crops have dispersed, such as alfalfa, true ranching has been pushed to the margin. Intensive mixed farming and stock raising eventually prevailed in the more humid zones. By the early twentieth century, however, ranching remained the most productive means to crop unirrigated semiarid grasslands in many parts of the world.

Steeply escalating urban demand for foodstuffs in the eastern United States and western Europe was the stimulus to large-scale wheat growing. The western United States and Canada, Argentina, Australia, and Russia brought large areas of wood and grassland under cultivation. By 1930, these five countries had 78.2 million ha of land under wheat in large estates or farms. Most of these hectares were new lands unplowed before the mid-nineteenth century. State public lands policies and market demand for wheat, reapers and other powered machinery, and above all placement of the world rail and steamer network drove the international wheat economy. The world's plains and steppes underwent a massive alteration in a very short time (Grigg 1974: 259–64).

The booming global market in foodgrains had its impact on rice production in Asia. In the river deltas of South and Southeast Asia, individual peasant cultivators were pioneers in the struggle to convert wetland forests into wet rice zones.

After British conquest in 1852, Burmese pioneer-cultivators, encouraged by new export markets for rice, cleared the forested wetlands of the Irrawaddy Delta to construct rice paddies. With peace, order, credit, and water control guaranteed by the colonial state, these pioneers enlarged the wet rice area from 441,000 ha in 1855 to 4 million ha in 1930. The vast forest of the Delta disappeared (Grigg 1974: 103; Adas 1983). The Mekong Delta in Vietnam, the Chao Phraya Delta in Thailand, and the Ganges-Brahmaputra Delta in Bengal saw similar frontier clearing and development of their forested wetlands for rice. Only the Sundarbans mangrove forest areas in the Bengal Delta remained partially intact, thanks to forestry policies of the government of India. In this case the Forest Department argued successfully for wood production as a vital resource that should not be sacrificed for greater foodgrain production (Richards and Flint, forthcoming).

Population Pressures and Five-Year Plans, 1930–1988

Frontier expansion generated by new commodity markets halted suddenly in 1930. The world depression sent agricultural prices tumbling, and sharply curtailed the cultivated area worldwide. Over the next decade, economic recovery was slow and partial. But World War II, with its frenzied need for food and industrial crops, expanded arable land to new levels in those areas left untouched by wartime devastation. Forested areas succumbed to the heavy wartime use of timber, or to outright destruction from battle.

In the postwar decades, a new political order emerged as one colony after another gained its independence. Newly independent regimes in Asia and Africa, determined to wring the utmost from their rural sectors, invested heavily in state-run programs of agricultural intensification. Irrigation projects on an enormous scale spread into the world's grasslands and deserts. Newly unleashed popular demands for access to reserved forests and pervasive illegal use of these state resources seriously degraded lands long since secured by the professional foresters.

Over these years, the international transportation system was reinforced by the triumph of petroleum, electricity, and the internal combustion engine. More efficient diesel engines replaced coal-fired steam engines in locomotives and steamships. Mass-produced automobiles and trucks hauled goods and people over flexible networks of paved roads. By the 1950s, superhighways offered deadly competition to railways for all but the bulkiest cargoes. Finally, the growing predominance of air carriage gave new speed and efficiency to the movement of goods. More than any single technological change, the motor vehicle placed the state and the market directly beside even the most isolated farmer. Every kilometer added to the world's road system has thereby increased human access to land. Ease of access has put us at the end point in our long struggle to control the world's lands.

The international economic order assumed a more complex pattern in the interwar period. New York began to challenge London as the dominant financial center. After World War II, New York, Tokyo, and London formed the axes of a more powerful world market-system. The global market in the twentieth century has become so pervasive that every human society is subject to its demands. Simultaneously market demand has pressed human control over the land toward ever-increasing intensity.

The long-term trend toward intensified land use has continued. By one estimate, world cultivated area grew by 588 million ha over the 60 years since 1920. Another calculation, shown in Table 10-2, is 419 million for the net increase in arable land. Whether the high or low figure is accepted, it suggests that arable land continued to grow at a rate equivalent to or higher than that for the previous 60-year period (1860–1920). New settler frontiers did open up after World War II: in Nepal's terai zone, in Brazil's Amazonian forests, in Indonesia's targeted areas for transmigration. Vast areas of North America consist still of forest lands grown up in the past century on abandoned farmlands. Nevertheless, the expansion of arable land in this period has come increasingly from marginal lands found in the interstices of settled areas.

The amount of culturable land that can be squeezed out from densely settled rural areas is surprising. In Pakistan, northern India, and Bangladesh, every conceivable hectare of scrub, pasture, or fallow has been a candidate for more intensive use. An intensive study of a 1.6-million-km^2 area in these three countries (183 administrative districts) over the past century shows expansion of arable land. Between 1930 and 1970, total cultivated area grew from 45.1% of the total land area (65.9 million ha) to 55.3% (86 million ha), for an increase of 20 million ha. A considerable proportion of this expansion was driven by new irrigation projects that converted semiarid lands to grain cultivation. But much of this increase was due to an assault on "waste" lands that had laced already densely settled agricultural areas in the subcontinent. Forage areas formerly used by nomadic graziers came under the plow. Scrub woodland fell to the clearing ax of peasant cultivators – woodland that had earlier separated villages on the plains. The result has been a new measure of human crowding in the north Indian countryside (Richards et al. 1985).

As the South Asian example suggests, by midcentury steeply rising populations in the less-developed countries of the world have consumed proportionately more of their agricultural and natural resource production at home. In the aftermath of World War II, postcolonial states have experienced a more direct form of human pressure on limited lands. Formerly expansive frontiers of settlement have narrowed and closed. The result has been the spread of squatter-settlement, extreme degradation of forest and grassland resources, and a myriad of other land impacts due to human crowding (Richards and Tucker 1988). State policies in less-developed countries have responded to loudly articulated human needs by increasing efforts at massive development in the countryside. In the current phase of world history, human subsistence needs confront the imperatives of prudent land use for long-term sustainability. The frontiers have turned in upon themselves.

Taxonomies and Territoriality

In reviewing the spiraling effect of the new world political and economic order, we must not overlook the power of an imposed cultural artifact. New expressions of territoriality were an essential tool in the struggle to dominate the land. Aggrandizing European states, in particular, bounded, demarcated, and denoted land and its physical features throughout the modern world. This process was an important aspect of the Western appropriation and ownership of subject peoples and culture. European notions of territoriality found expression within the context of a new world taxonomy. Early modern Europe began to name the world, and in so doing, to appropriate the world as object. In a vast, still ongoing taxonomical exercise, Western explorers, administrators, and scientists (among others) identified and classified the world's animals, fish, plants, minerals, soils, geologic formations, and indigenous peoples. The impetus for this effort was partly intellectual, partly utilitarian. How could these enormous possessions best be deployed and consumed?

Botanists, zoologists, and ichthyologists used Linnaean classification to denote plant, animal, and fish species on every continent. Geologists and pedologists classified minerals and soils. Colonial administrators, who later formally became ethnologists and demographers, classified and ranked their subject peoples. Linguists classified languages and dialects. Specimens collected in botanical gardens, zoos, and museums of the great capitals of Europe buttressed taxonomy. The rich mosaic of local taxonomies eroded and disappeared. New universal systems largely ignored the textured taxonomies and understandings of tribals, agriculturalists, and indigenous peoples everywhere. An abstract, uniform taxonomy shaped a rigid intellectual grid – a utilitarian structure over the globe.

Brockway (1979) stresses the role of botanical gardens as one form of metropolitan institution devoted to gathering systematic data on the world's flora. She argues that from the eighteenth century on, the search for economically valuable plants forced the pace of scientific research. These efforts had considerable impact on land use in South and Southeast Asia for the cultivation of cinchona and rubber. Research at Kew provided the technical means to establish commercial sisal cultivation in British East Africa to rival that of Yucatan.

Within this larger enterprise, the new conquerors paid special attention to demarcating and locating territory and its physical features as a means of power and domination. Territoriality in this context is somewhat broader than property, jurisdiction, or sovereignty. As Robert Sack defines it: "territoriality is intimately related to how people use the land, how they organize themselves in space, and how they give meaning to place" (Sack 1986: 2). Control of territory implies classification by area, communication by means of boundary markers, and controlled access to the demarcated area (Sack 1986: 28).

In his extended theoretical discussion, Sack points out that modern societies have employed territoriality to further centralization, hierarchy, and bureaucracy; to mold human activities; and to reify dominant power. Perhaps most significantly for our purposes, territoriality can be used to empty space, to demarcate an area that is unused and capable of being filled. In other words, the use to which land is devoted can be altered and rearranged. The new world order made frequent use of the idea of a "socially emptiable place" (Sack 1986: 33). Whatever the numbers of human and animal inhabitants, or the vegetation, soils, and natural features, the new rulers could define an area as devoid of socially valuable use. This cleared space was then available for a new, more productive use.

The new masters made sweeping use of this device for the relatively sparsely inhabited lands of the New World and the antipodes. Bold assignments of unknown territory by papal bulls and royal charters were the first step in clearing space for European settlement in the New World (Sack 1986: 131–38). Thereafter, colonial surveyors and mapmakers fixed the location of natural features and human settlement. They set precise boundaries for the new colonies and their internal administrative units. As they did so, the indigenous native peoples of North America were cleared conceptually from the land by defining them as savage and barbarous.

Nowhere was the Western urge to mark, bound, and identify objects more firmly displayed than in mapmaking and surveying. From about 1700, refinement of the Mercator projection permitted accurate depiction of latitude and longitude for marine charts. By the latter decades of the eighteenth century, the basic techniques of geodesic and cadastral surveying were understood and employed. Cartographers could identify any point on land by reference to the fixed position of the stars in a global spatial grid. The latter reached a new level of abstraction. It was a product of the Western concern with defining space – an artifact of European culture. In Paul Bohannon's (1963: 102) vivid analysis:

It is obvious that the grid must be completely rigid. To achieve precision, it is defined astrally, with overtly assigned relationships to quite arbitrary points on the earth's surface. It is specifically not defined terrestrially by earthly landmarks, except as such land marks have been located astrally. The Western map, like the Polynesian, was created by sea-farers. Thus, culturally, land – whatever else it may also be – is a measurable entity divisible into thing-like "parcels" by means of mathematical and technical processes of surveying and cartography. This complex notion of "land," with its accompanying technology, is an absolute essential to the Western system of land-tenure.

Once stabilized, state boundaries defined the territorial competence of the central authority. Within this domain, central governments or their colonial subordinate regimes imposed precise internal administrative bounds at two, or even three or more, nested levels of jurisdiction. Whether established upon preexisting "natural" regions or newly established spatial grids, the state claimed and gradually exerted coercive powers at each level.

In defining its nested administrative hierarchy, the state simultaneously defined landed property and terms of ownership. It appropriated some lands as reserved or public lands, with the state as owner. Ownership of the land remaining was left to private hands. Legal tenures depended upon two actions by the state: (1) recorded spatial bounds and location by recognized survey, and (2) state registration of ownership. Thereafter, continued ownership and secure tenure over each parcel of land relied upon regular payment of taxes, if required. With these requirements met, both private and public owners held full territorial competence over each registered parcel of land. That is, tenure-holders, whether individual or corporate, possessed absolute ownership and untrammeled rights of use and development, subject only to overarching land legislation by the state. One of the most striking examples of the enduring impact of gridded land surveys and tenures tailored to these surveys can be seen from the air in the American Midwest (Johnson 1976).

In general, European land tenures were based on the quiritary rights of Roman law, which had been revived in early modern Europe. As Anderson (1974: 25) comments, "The great distinguishing mark of Roman civil law had been its conception of absolute and unconditional private property." This system provided for nearly absolute ownership rights.[11] Each owner could freely sell, give, or bequeath his or her property. Each owner could freely mortgage his or her landed domain. Other than requirements for registration, title validation, and a review of tax obligations, the owner was free to dispose of owned property. Having done so, the state guaranteed title and possession. Of course, the owner's competence and control ended abruptly at the bounds of his or her landholding, no matter how tiny or large. And, for that matter, so did responsibility to the larger society. Short of defaulting on taxes or criminal activity, the landowner was secure in his or her domain.

The autonomy of owners in the Western gridded system contrasted sharply with the flexible, permeable, and layered rights found in other localized tenures around the world. By and large these more flexible systems held land in what now often is referred to as common property systems. Common property resources by definition (1) are open to individual use, but not individual possession, (2) have a number of users who hold rights of use, and (3) are controlled by the collectivity of users who act to exclude outsiders (Blaikie and Brookfield 1987: 186). The enclosure movements in western Europe in the seventeenth and eighteenth centuries were but the opening episode in a worldwide process. Either private property owners or the state have appropriated virtually all those lands under this form of control.

As states imposed new forms of territoriality on lands formerly held by shifting cultivators, hunters-gatherers, or pastoralists, their lands became either public lands or private property. In either event, they ceased to be common property resources. Later, commons long fixed by tradition within areas of sedentary agriculture around the world have come under assault by market forces and more rigid definitions of tenurial rights. Under new pressures from the world economy, old rules have lost their efficacy and shared resources have vanished.

These changes have not been cost-free. The landscapes created by such groups by and large tended to be sustainable over extended periods. On the whole, their environmental impact was restrained. The local taxonomies and ecological wisdom of these groups largely have disappeared. Modern land use has put an end to a rich source of human understanding about varied ecological systems as well, as depleting the number of such systems. Moreover, in the context of an encroaching world economy, the decline of common property generally has been a harbinger for land degradation.

Radical security and autonomy on the one hand, and limited responsibility and free rights of alienation and mortgage on the other, created a mechanism that encouraged productive use of this asset. When coupled with intensifying world market-forces and the support of a strong state, landowners under this form of tenure consistently tried to maximize their returns and productivity from their domains. Population growth added its incentive for aggressive investment in more intensive land use. As supplies of "waste" land diminished, land prices, rents, and opportunities for profit increased. Just as the state exercised autonomy within its borders and tried to maximize its returns, so also did the individual or corporate landowner. The result was twofold: first, conversion of lands to more intensely managed agricultural use, to industrial pursuits, or in human settlement; and second, the exploitation and eventual impoverishment of the resources of the land – whether animals, plants, water or soil.[12]

Conclusion: Long-Term Trends

In concluding, let us return to the notion of the frontier. Depending upon the scale of one's definition, scores to hundreds of agricultural-settlement frontiers have opened and closed over the past five centuries. Rarely receding, these many frontier episodes signaled victory for intensified exploitation of the land. Human energy, economic stimuli, and state policies propelled these settler frontiers. Without surplus population, no frontier can exist. Without funding and outlets for produce, settlers cannot live. Without the ability of human beings to create communities and to organize themselves for self-sufficiency, frontiers would not be possible. But above all, it is the state that has created and sustained settler frontiers by appropriating "empty" tracts as public lands. These lands are surveyed, allocated, and titled to pioneers and their backers or to state agencies.

Extension of the frontier is an extension of the political order – of power. Clearing and settlement provide new lands to rule and tax. Frontier expansion offers access to formerly uncontrolled forests, arid lands, hill areas, or marshes that hitherto harbored bandits, rebels, and smugglers or defiant aborigines. The centralizing state deploys military force to subdue hostility from tribal peoples. It builds roads, canals, and railways for access to new lands. It constructs irrigation facilities in arid zones: embankments in coastal deltas. It ensures that credit and markets for frontier produce are made secure. It offers bounties on wild predators. These measures generally have succeeded.

In stressing the singular importance of the modern state in shaping frontiers, we should not overlook the dynamic quality of the frontier experience. Frontier life is marked by an absence of limits. Frontier populations of all types see endless possibilities for land, wealth, and prosperity. For a time, at least, the frontier frees them from the confines of more settled societies. As a result, frontiers draw upon new reservoirs of human energy and spirit. Access to almost-free resources – wood, water, wild game – reinforces this buoyancy and optimism. New, more egalitarian organizations emerge to transform the land and defend the new settlements. The frontier takes on a strenuous life of its own, which melds human energy, capital, and the ordered framework imposed by the state into a new, unfolding society.

When settler frontiers close, resources are no longer abundant and cheap. Societies become more hierarchical, more rigid. The state appropriates active powers of intervention and management over new lands by determining appropriate uses. Those lands not taken up by settlers become public lands subject to control by the state and its dependent agencies. The exhilaration of frontier life gives way to political order and new territoriality. Over time, unless the state falters, this control is extended. Agricultural practices and forest and game management diverge from slowly changing, discrete customs of localities toward widely accepted beliefs and policies common to the nation-state and increasingly to the world.

Landscapes have always changed over time, but we sense, somewhat uneasily, that the processes now at work are more powerfully focused and possibly irreversible. As we have opened one frontier after another and moved on, throughout the world we have imposed a new degree of domination on the land. We have thereby raised human productivity. At what price? Is the reverse of rising production, degradation and biotic impoverishment?

Degradation is the twin face of intensified land use. A recent study has defined land degradation as a decline in intrinsic quality or the capability to produce for human needs (Blaikie and Brookfield 1987: 6–7). By this definition, the world's lands have been upgraded, not degraded, in the modern world. The process of intensified use and intrusive management has occurred at an accelerating rate in the modern world. Societies and individual land managers have invested heavily in improving the productive capacity of the land. The useful product obtained from the world's lands every year is far greater at present than it was three centuries ago. By definition this implies rising capacity in the world's lands.

From another perspective – that of productive capacity in the longer term – human land use remains exploitative. The pattern of sequential frontier expansion has done little to encourage systematic investment in sustained productivity on the land. It is likely that worldwide capital investment in the land is less than the demands put upon it. Leaching of soil nutrients, soil erosion, loss of watershed capacity, are only a few of the many aspects of land degradation found in virtually every country of the world. Certainly careful management in any mode of land use can prevent declining capacity. Here and there, one can point to various productive uses of the land that are sustainable, but not many. When we examine it closely, we may find that the capital investment in these areas depends upon extraction of resources on other lands, which are being degraded in another mode of exploitation.

Degradation is the most difficult global trend to isolate and analyze. The problem of accurate measurement is acute – even for such a seemingly straightforward process as soil erosion. Defining natural versus social causes of degradation is a knotty and sometimes virtually unsolvable problem in individual cases (Blaikie and Brookfield 1987). Natural forces do degrade land all the time; they also increase its capacity for human use. Changing technologies and needs can change the qualities of land required. Measuring the on-site and off-site effects of exploitation is difficult. Land in some areas may be extremely sensitive to human interference; land in other areas may be far less sensitive. Some lands and ecosystems may be resilient; others much less so. Our present assumption is that generally tropical lands are much more sensitive and less resilient than those in the temperate zones, for example. Whether this assumption will stand is not yet certain. Despite these complexities, the long-term world trend in land use is a cascading loss in capacity (i.e., degradation) in every broad category of land use.

The strength of this spiraling worldwide process of land transformation is evident. Stacked arrays of settlement frontiers have mobilized human energies and increased our domination over new lands. The unremitting twin drives for domination and production, embodied in the ever-more efficient state, fostered these frontiers and consumed the resources of the land. We have not comprehended fully the degree to which human society has relied upon landed resources to undergird economic development. Those untouched lands and new frontiers are fast dwindling, but the social forces that have driven frontier expansion have abated little, if at all. Our states, markets, and peoples search for, but will no longer find, new frontier lands.

Notes

1. Jones (1981) refers to Walter Prescott Webb's notion of the Great Frontier for Europe before 1700, in which a vast domain of new lands in effect reduced the man-land ratio of Europe: in 1500, 26.7 persons per square mile, to 6.5 in 1750. Table 4.1: 83.

2. Boserup (1965: 11) has argued more strongly that heightened population density is "the independent variable which . . . is a major factor determining agricultural production." In her more recent study (Boserup 1981), she has directly established "a quantitative relation-

ship between an area's population density and its predominating food supply system." In this line of analysis, population growth should be the most important and probably the defining causal variable for intensification on the land.

3. This figure is based on the work of several historians making estimates of shipments based on the medieval unit of measurement, the last. Jeannin (1960: 49) argues that the actual weight of a last varied by the commodity carried. After assessing the evidence, he suggests that a last of wheat at this period was 2.2 metric tons, or 31 hectoliters. I have used this conversion to figure the metric tons from the figures given by Glamann.

4. This area figure is based on the average annual Sound total shipping of 68,500 lasts. The average yield for rye in eastern Europe is assumed to have been 1:4. Average seeding was 1.5 hectoliters per ha, for a total return of 6 hectoliters of grain. Net available for shipping to market was therefore 4.5 hectoliters per ha of grain cultivation. Jeannin (1960: 49) supplies a conversion of 2,200 kilograms = 1 last = 31 hectoliters in early-seventeenth-century Baltic trade. Therefore the 68,500 lasts = 2,123,500 hectoliters of grain, which required 471,888 ha to produce. At a minimal rate of wastage and spoilage of 10–20% during the river transit and warehousing, the total area required would be between 519,000 and 566,000 ha. If the average yield ever dropped to 3.5 – which is not at all unlikely – the requisite hectarage for export would have shot up to 691,000 ha. The average seed input of 1.5 taken from Braudel argues that "as today, between one and two hectoliters of corn were sown per hectare" (Braudel, 1973: 79). Braudel summarizes van Bath's yield estimates for eastern Europe at 4.1 between 1550 and 1820. But he also (ibid.: 80) cites Leonid Zykowski, whose general average for Poland in the sixteenth to eighteenth centuries shows that two-thirds of the harvests were normal, with very low yields of 2 to 4.

5. Based on the calculations made above for shipments of 6,000 to 10,000 lasts of grain. See Malowist (1959: 184).

6. McEvedy and Jones (1978: 170–73), relying on calculations made by Ping-ti Ho (1959).

7. Calculated from figures given by Perdue (1987: 50, Table 4) for 1582, the date of the last reliable Ming survey of cultivated land. Conversion from mou to hectares is at 16.28.

8. Perkins (1969: 234–36). Ching officials were required only to meet a quota for registered land that was equal to the highest level reached by Ming land surveys. The imperial government avoided a stringent land survey in Hunan to encourage expansion and land clearing, rather than discourage it by exacting rigorous land taxes.

9. Singer et al. (1958: 594). The East India Company employed two iron steam-tugs to pull accommodation boats up the Ganges on a regular basis as early as 1834. See Bernstein (1960: 80–117); also Latham (1978: 26).

10. Olson (1971: 12) reproduces official U.S. Government calculations to show that obtaining 89 million replacement and new cross ties consumed 188,000 ha of timber in an average year. Timber for bridges, buildings, and other needs cleared a similar area each year (ibid.).

11. The evolved system of land tenures in Ming Dynasty China offered virtually the same flexibility and protection of property rights as did those in western Europe. Since China was not colonized, the legal system with its indigenous tenures did not change until 1950, with the successful revolution that ushered in the People's Republic of China.

12. This interpretation is consistent with the arguments advanced by North and Thomas (1970; 1973). North and Thomas, who are economic historians, come at the argument from the opposite direction. They see effective private property rights in land and other property as the mechanism by which "efficient economic organization" could develop in the West. Security and unconfined control of property led to a cycle of enhanced productivity. Thus, if this argument is followed to its conclusion, incentives to use the lands of the world efficiently

increased with the European mode of territoriality and, more specifically, with new land tenures.

References

Adas, M. 1983. Colonization, commercial agriculture, and the destruction of the deltaic rainforests of British Burma in the late nineteenth century. In *Global Deforestation and the Nineteenth-Century World Economy*, ed. R. P. Tucker and J. F. Richards. Durham, NC: Duke University Press.

Albion, R. G. 1926. *Forests and Sea Power*. Cambridge, MA: Harvard University Press.

Anderson, P. 1974. *Lineages of the Absolutist State*. London: New Left Books.

Bernstein, H. T. 1960. *Steamboats on the Ganges*. Calcutta: Orient Longmans.

Blaikie, P., and H. C. Brookfield. 1987. *Land Degradation and Society*. London: Methuen.

Bohannon, P. 1963. "Land," "tenure," and "land-tenure." In *African Agrarian Systems*, ed. D. Biebuyck, 101–115. Oxford: Oxford University Press.

Boserup, E. 1965. *The Conditions of Agricultural Growth*. Chicago: Aldine Publishing.

———. 1981. *Population and Technological Change: A Study of Long-Term Trends*. Chicago: University of Chicago Press.

Braudel, F. 1973. *Capitalism and Material Life, 1400–1800*. Translated by M. Kochan. New York: Harper and Row.

———. 1984. *Civilization and Capitalism, 15th–18th Century*. Vol. III, *The Perspective of the World* (English translation). New York: Harper and Row.

Brockway, L. H. 1979. *Science and Colonial Expansion: The Role of the British Royal Botanic Gardens*. New York: The Academic Press.

Chuan, H.-S., and R. A. Kraus. 1975. *Mid-Ching Rice Markets and Trade: An Essay in Price History*. Cambridge, MA: Harvard University Press.

FAO 1981. *FAO Production Yearbook 1980*. Rome: FAO.

Furber, H. 1976. *Rival Empires of Trade in the Orient, 1600–1800*. Minneapolis: University of Minnesota Press.

Glamann, K. 1971. European trade, 1500–1700. In *Fontana Economic History of Europe*. Vol. II, *The Sixteenth and Seventeenth Centuries*, ed. C. M. Cipolla, 427–526. London: Fontana.

Grigg, D. B. 1974. *The Agricultural Systems of the World*. Cambridge: Cambridge University Press.

Guha, A. 1972. Raw cotton of western India: 1750–1850. *The Indian Economic and Social History Review 9*.

Hastings, P. 1972. *Railroads: An International History*. New York: Praeger.

Hoernel, R. B. 1976. Sugar and social change in Oriente, Cuba, 1898–1946. *Journal of Latin American Studies 8*: 215–49.

Jeannin, M. P. 1960. Le tonnage des navires utilisés dans la Baltique de 1550 à 1640 d'après les sources prussiennes. In *Le Navire et l'economie maritime du nord de l'Europe du moyen-age au XVIIIe siècle*, ed. M. Mollat. Paris: S.E.V.P.E.N.

Johnson, H. B. 1976. *Order upon the Land*. New York: Oxford University Press.

Jones, E. L. 1981. *The European Miracle*. Cambridge: Cambridge University Press.

Latham, J. H. 1978. *The International Economy and the Undeveloped World 1865–1914*. London: Croom Helm.

Malowist, M. 1959. The economic and social development of the Baltic countries from the fifteenth to the seventeenth centuries. *The Economic History Review*, 2d ser., 12: 177–89.

———. 1960. L'approvsionnement des ports de la Baltique en produits forestiers pour les constructions navales aux XVe et XVIe siècles. In *Le Navire et l'Economie Maritime du Nord de l'Europe du Moyen-Age au XVIIIe siècle*, ed. M. Mollat, 25–43. Paris: S.E.V.P.E.N., 25–43.

McEvedy, C., and Jones, R. 1978. *Atlas of World Population History*. London: Penguin Books.

North, D., and R. P. Thomas. 1970. An economic theory of the growth of the western world. *The Economic History Review*, 2d ser., 23: 1–17.

Olson, S. 1971. *The Depletion Myth: A History of Railroad Use of Timber*. Cambridge, MA: Harvard University Press.

Perdue, P. C. 1987. *Exhausting the Earth: State and Peasant in Hunan, 1500–1850*. Cambridge, MA: Harvard University Press.

Perkins, D. H. 1969. *Agriculture Development in China, 1368–1968*. Chicago: Aldine.

Pounds, N. G. 1979. *An Historical Geography of Europe, 1500–1840*. Cambridge: Cambridge University Press.

———. 1985. *An Historical Geography of Europe, 1800–1914*. Cambridge: Cambridge University Press.

Richards, J. F. 1981a. The Indian empire and peasant production of opium. *Modern Asian Studies 15*: 59–82.

———. 1981b. Mughal state finance and the premodern world economy. *Comparative Studies in Society and History 23*: 285–308.

———. 1986. World environmental history and economic development. In *Sustainable Development of the Biosphere*, ed. W. C. Clark and R. E. Munn, 53–71. Cambridge: Cambridge University Press.

Richards, J. F., and E. P. Flint. The expanding cultivation frontier in the Sundarbans. (In press.)

Richards, J. F., E. S. Haynes, and J. R. Hagen. 1985. Changes in the land and human productivity in northern India, 1870–1970. *Agricultural History 59*: 524–47.

Sack, R. D. 1986. *Human Territoriality: Its Theory and History*. Cambridge: Cambridge University Press.

Singer, C., E. J. Holmyard, A. R. Hall, T. S. Williams. 1958. *A History of Technology*. Vol. 4, *The Industrial Revolution c. 1750 to 1850*. Oxford: Clarendon Press.

Tucker, R., and J. F. Richards. 1983. *Global Deforestation and the Nineteenth-Century World Economy*. Durham, NC: Duke University Press.

Wynn G. 1981. *Timber Colony*. Toronto: University of Toronto Press.

11

Forests

MICHAEL WILLIAMS

Measuring Deforestation

Perhaps the most important factor that has altered the face of the earth in many parts of the world is the clearing of the forests. The forest has been subject to a sustained and steady attack by humankind throughout the centuries. Consequently, the effort to use and subdue the forest has been a constant theme in the transformation of the earth, in many societies, in many lands, at most times.

The forest is one of the great inherited resources of the earth. It provides wood for construction, for shelter, and for making tools; it provides fuel to keep warm, to cook food, and to smelt metals; above all, the forest when cleared provides land for food production. As the world's population has grown, the forest has been either converted or modified. If modified, once-dense stands of closed forest have been replaced by more open or depauperate stands of secondary species that yet further thinning has changed into a savanna of open grasslands – the whole process frequently being a prelude to clearing for agriculture. What humans do not clear by ax or fire, livestock can eliminate.

Whereas clearing has slowed down and even been reversed to regeneration in the developed world during this century (for example, approximately $20 \times 10^6 \, \text{km}^2$ of forest in 1900 compared to $21 \times 10^6 \, \text{km}^2$ in 1985), it has accelerated in the developing world, so that the forest there has perhaps halved since the beginning of the century. Just as the topic of the destruction of "the woods" and the consequences of that were a matter of concern in George Perkins Marsh's *Man and Nature* (1864) over 120 years ago, so they are again today, when the scale and intensity of change are far greater than perhaps at any other time.

Crucial to a discussion of deforestation is the calculation of how much forest has been cleared. But the task is not an easy one. Even today, with all the modern aids of land use censuses and satellite imagery, there is no unequivocal inventory of contemporary woodland (Allen and Barnes 1985). If this calculation is a problem now, how much more difficult for past ages. A contributory factor to our uncertainty has been the attitude to clearing. It has been regarded as an incidental byproduct of agricultural expansion and timber exploitation. As such, deforestation has been regarded as part of the "natural" process of development and only rarely has been commented on, let alone been recorded. In nearly all cultures, it is the first step on the ladder upward out of a simple gathering, hunting, and herding economy toward a more sophisticated sedentary farming economy with wider horizons and greater prosperity. In addition, the "virtue" of clearing, compounded by the image of the heroic struggle of "Man against nature," has seemed so self-evident as to cause little comment and beg no apology.

Matthews (1983) estimated that the preagricultural closed forest once covered $46.28 \times 10^6 \, \text{km}^2$ of the globe, and woodland, some $15.23 \times 10^6 \, \text{km}^2$ – these estimates being reduced to $39.27 \times 10^6 \, \text{km}^2$ and $13.10 \times 10^6 \, \text{km}^2$, respectively, by the latter years of this century. The differences of $7.01 \times 10^6 \, \text{km}^2$ of forest and $2.13 \times 10^6 \, \text{km}^2$ of woodland are difficult to account for with any great degree of accuracy. No overall synthesis of reliable data is at hand. One could leave it at that, except that some pieces of evidence do exist (and these can be assembled, as in Table 11-1) that show the area of forest possibly affected by clearing and modification from before 1650 to the present. The data for five of the major world regions (mainly the newly settled parts of the world) can be assembled with some degree of accuracy, but the three oldest-settled continents (Europe, Asia, and Africa) present many difficulties. The best that can be done is to indicate the magnitude of likely change that could be expected to occur, based on the possible size of the population at the time (itself an estimate based on Durand 1967; 1977) and assigning a fifth of a hectare of permanently cleared land to each person, on the assumption that new cultivated land would be most likely to be taken out of the productive forested areas. These figures are shown as high (H) and low (L) estimates in Table 11-1.

There is much guesswork in Table 11-1, and it must be treated with caution and refined constantly, as much of it is subjective. Nevertheless, the overall total of $7.4 \times 10^6 \, \text{km}^2$, based on the low estimate, or $8 \times 10^6 \, \text{km}^2$, based on the high estimate, goes some considerable way to accounting for the estimated decrease of $9.14 \times 10^6 \, \text{km}^2$ calculated by Matthews on other evidence. We simply cannot be more accurate than

Table 11-1 *Estimated area cleared (×000 km²)*

Region or country		Pre-1650	1650–1749	1750–1849	1850–1978	Total high estimate	Total low estimate
North America		6	80	380	641	1,107	1,107
Central America	H	18				288	
	L	12	30	40	200		282
Latin America	H	18				925	
	L	12	100	170	637		919
Oceania	H	6	6	6		380	
	L	2	4		362		374
USSR	H	70	180	270	575	1,095	
	L	42	130	250			997
Europe	H	204	66	146		497	
	L	176	54	186	81		497
Asia	H	974	216	596		3,006	
	L	640	176	606	1,220		2,642
Africa	H	226	80	−16		759	
	L	96	24	42	469		631
Total highest		1,522	758	1,592	4,185	8,057	
Total lowest		986	598	1,680	4,185		7,449

that, particularly as we know that land affected by conversion is not necessarily converted permanently; it can revert to forest, as so often happened in Europe during the Plague, population decrease, and economic recession (Jäger 1951). Nevertheless, the general magnitude and the trend of the estimates in Table 11-1 correspond to other internal evidence of change. Bearing in mind the overall picture of change, perhaps the best solution is that suggested by Richards (1986): to erect a framework for synthesis, and then to concentrate on particular forests that have been affected at different times in an attempt to use whatever evidence is available. In this way, the transformation of the earth through the conversion of the forest will be made clearer, and some tentative assessment of the impact can be made.

A Framework for Synthesis: European Expansion, 1600–1850

The causes and progress of deforestation can be found in world economic development – (1) in the emergence of an integrated world economy from the late fifteenth century onward, when the spiraling expansion of Europe led to a redistribution of people, plants, and technologies, all of which altered existing arrangements either though the colonization of new lands (Barraclough 1978) or (2) through the reorientation of the economies of old lands. The net result was that world isolation was dissolved, and the integration of a world economy through European trade and imperialism began to emerge (Wallerstein 1974; 1980). By the early seventeenth century, the unifying legacy of European expansion on the forest lands of the world was beginning to emerge more clearly through a multiplicity of interconnected factors.

First, the familiar temperate forest environment of North America and of central and Asiatic Russia proved to be a tempting stage for the reenactment of the great European forest colonizations of the early Middle Ages. In North America, from the St. Lawrence River to the Savannah River, British and French refugee and adventurer immigrant groups were clearing woodland to create farms. In Europe, energetic colonists were emigrating in all directions from the growing state of Moscovy with imperial and some ecclesiastical backing. They moved into the forest/steppe ecotone to the south and into the southern margins of the coniferous forests to the east, so that by 1630 European settlers were nearly 1,000 miles east of the Urals. Europe's colonists had shifted their frontiers of deforestation beyond the old boundaries of the continent (Barraclough 1978).

Second, parts of the tropical and subtropical forests were altered radically by the purposeful introduction of new crops and new methods of exploitation. European trade had moved away from its medieval preoccupation with small quantities of high-value luxury goods such as spices, perfumes, and fine cloths, to a mass trade of bulky commodities for a growing and increasingly affluent population, such as tea from India and China, coffee from Brazil, sugar from the Caribbean, and cotton from Asia and North America. This trade was made possible by the improvement in ocean transport and the building of more ships through access to New World and Scandinavian timber and naval stores (pitch, tar, and turpentine). The production in bulk of the new commodities was achieved through a new system of exploitation. Plantations and other forms of monoculture maximized and concentrated output in areas of specialization. The labor was supplied by slaves (part of the new economic system) and later by indentured laborers, and the whole was made possible by chartered, joint-stock companies, which concentrated investment, spread risks, and combined the tasks of settlement, conquest, investment, and defense. The emergence of reliable banking and credit arrangements, which undoubtedly facilitated trade, cannot be ignored.

The concentration of these products was possible because plants had been moved around by European trade. For example, sugar cane had been introduced into Brazil and the Caribbean from Southeast Asia in the sixteenth century. Similarly, bananas and coffee had been moved to the New World. In reverse, America provided tobacco and cotton (in its commercial form), to say nothing of the high-yielding food crops such as potatoes and maize (Curtis 1956). Goats, sheep, cattle, and horses came from the Old World to the New (and later to Australia and New Zealand), with devastating effect on the local vegetation stability (Clark 1949; 1956). In brief, the European-led biological invasion of the tropical world made just as much impact on the forests as did the more well-known European population invasion of the temperate world (Crosby 1986).

Whilst some of these exchanges could be detrimental to the host country, many were beneficial to the imperial country. A significant minority of Europeans now had a better and more varied diet than hitherto, and many had more food than formerly, because, for example, potatoes had a yield per hectare of four times that of wheat, and high-yielding maize replaced sorghum and millet in much of Mediterranean Europe (Harlan 1976). This overall better nutrition, in conjunction with many other factors, including increased spending power, may have been one of the reasons that the previously slow but steady increase of population suddenly started on a new and upwardly sloping curve after the middle of the eighteenth century, at the beginning of the Industrial Revolution. Whether the onset of European expansion was a consequence or a contributing factor to this new upward expansion is difficult to say, but the net result was that the most important factor in increasing global deforestation had been set in motion, that is, the spread of agriculture for crops and livestock to feed ever-increasing numbers of people.

Therefore, as we look at the global impacts on the forest at different times and for different places, we will need to be aware of the new energies and innovations released by the aggressive and predatory outreach of Europe and its peoples, which form a framework for synthesis of change in the forest. At nearly every stage, and certainly at every place, the forest supplied the new ground for the invasion, expansion, and transformation, and the raw materials and fuel for settlement – and it suffered accordingly.

Regional Impacts, 1650–1849

Europe

Before the great outward movement from the continent, Europeans had colonized vigorously and cleared their own forests during the Middle Ages. The evidence of place-names, settlement types, and documents testifies to a concerted attack on the forests of the continent (Darby 1956). The surge of clearing had more or less spent itself by 1300, when the Plague, possibly deteriorating climate, and certainly, economic recession resulted in a period of stagnation and even abandonment of clearings (Jäger 1951). Yet, during the early sixteenth century, economic life experienced a resurgence, population rose from approximately 71 million in 1600 to approximately 200 million by 1800 (Durand 1977; Russell 1985), and the forests were under attack again.

The attack was twofold: (1) a slowly expanding population needed more food, and nibbled away at the edges of the forest to create arable land and pasture, and (2) expanding industrial and mining activity, to say nothing of ship construction, created new demands on the remaining areas.

In peninsular and insular Europe (e.g., Italy, Spain, Portugal, the British Isles, Denmark, Holland), about only 5–10% of the land was forested (USDA 1873). Immense inroads were made in the forests for wood-getting and charcoal-making for a growing iron-smelting industry and other industrial processes, such as soap, glass, tin, lead, copper, and salt-making. As early as 1548, there was a commission of inquiry into the diminution of the forests of the Weald in southeast England by iron-making, and it was not until a substitute fuel could be found to smelt iron (as happened with the discovery of coke in 1709) that the impact on the forests lessened (Darby 1951; 1956; Cleere and Crossley 1985). Above all, however, it was the prodigious demands of shipbuilding (both merchant and naval) and the need for large timbers, masts, and "naval stores" (pitch, tar, and turpentine) that prompted Britain, in particular, to cultivate trade with Sweden and Russia and its North American colonies to obtain these strategic supplies essential for mastery of the world's oceans and the pursuit of trade (Albion 1926; Pollitt 1971; Williams 1988). John Evelyn's famous work *Sylva or Discourse on Trees* (1664), the first treatise on trees and forestry, was a response to these needs, which contrary to his advocacy, were not met from increased home production but from further expansion overseas and exploitation of, for example, the white pine forests of Maine and New Brunswick, the longleaf forests of the Carolinas, the teak forests of the Malabar coast of India and Burma, and the cedar forests of New South Wales. To some degree or other, the other states of the West had a similar experience, especially Spain.

Somewhat intermediate between these overseas-oriented nations of the West and the more inward, land-looking nations of the East were France and the states that make up the modern Germanies and Austria. Both had up to one-quarter of their land in forests, both experienced depredations from iron- and metal-smelting (in, for example, the upland areas of the Massif Central, the Vosges, the Rhenish uplands [particularly near the Ruhr], and the uplands of the Erzgebirge and Tyrol), and both had gradually expanding farming populations that colonized the land (Darby 1956). France, in addition, had similar problems to Britain of naval supplies (Corvol 1987).

In contrast, in the East lay the vast forested areas of continental central Europe, which were between one- and two-thirds forest covered. The intricacies of the changing galaxy of middle, eastern, and Balkan European states make it difficult to discern what was happening there, but in the more stable political system of Russia, events can be summarized more easily. Persistent and relentless peasant clearing in the heartland of Russia in the mixed-forest zone of oak, pine, aspen, and birch (situated roughly in the triangular area between Petrograd, Moscow, and Kiev, south of the coniferous taiga and north of the open steppe) took a great leap during the sixteenth and seventeenth centuries, when the previous slash-and-burn agriculture was abandoned for a more sedentary and intensive three-field farming system. Tsvetkov (French 1963; 1983) calculated that in 12 of the 16 provinces of this mixed-forest zone, the woodland was reduced by 47,000 km² between 1696 and 1796, so that instead of 60.6% of the land being forested, only 53.0% was: the arable land increased proportionately. The clearing continued unabated throughout the rest of the nineteenth century, so that a further 97,000 km² were cleared by 1914, and the amount of forested land had fallen to 37.4% in the 12 provinces. Overall, in the 48 provinces in European Russia, 67,000 km² were cleared from the end of the seventeenth to the beginning of the twentieth century (French 1983).

The Eastern Seaboard of North America

The creation of a "settler empire" (Meinig 1969) of over 2 million people on the eastern seaboard of North America left an indelible imprint on the forest. Initially the impact was not great, because European settlers learned to use the clearings of the previous Amerindian inhabitants. We can never be sure of the true extent of Amerindian clearing, but many of the estimated 12 million pre-Columbian Amerindians of North America (Dobyns 1966; Jacobs 1974) must have lived in the forest. Certainly, the frequent references by European explorers and settlers to "meadows," "fields," "openings," "flats," and "savannas" leave little doubt that clearing and thinning of the forest by repeated firing was extensive (for reviews see Day 1953; Martin 1973; Maxwell 1910). Russell (1976) identifies upwards of 50 major settlements in New England that had been located in "open areas already cultivated or at least cleared", and this was common elsewhere. John Strachey's comment in 1620 on Hampton, Virginia that there was "enough already prepared to receive corne and viniards of two or three thousand acres" (Strachey [1620] (1849)) was conclusive and not uncommon.

As the flow of migrants became greater, farm-making soon occurred everywhere in the forests. In the north, a hectare or so would be cleared annually, mainly by clear-cutting, or less commonly by girdling, and crops were cultivated in mounds between the stumps, which were removed later. Stock were left to roam and graze in the surrounding forest, and were rounded up at least annually. Eventually, the farmer would have cleared between 12 to 16 ha, which was enough to achieve self-sufficiency, with a small surplus besides. In the South, commercially oriented plantation agriculture with slave labor replaced the pioneer family farmer. As an essential part of the newly emerging international trade, tobacco and cotton were cultivated. But because cotton, and particularly tobacco, were heavy consumers of soil nutrients and even caused soil toxicity, and because no manure was put back into the soil, yields soon declined drastically, and the planter moved on to clear fresh forest land after an interval of 10 to 20 years. Consequently, they rarely thought it worth grubbing up the stumps, and the field would be abandoned to weeds and soon regenerate to pine forest. This continual clearing and shifting on was worthwhile, as tobacco yielded high returns and new forest land was abundant and cheap to buy.

Backward extrapolations of later data of the amount of improved land in predominantly forested counties suggest that 100,000 km² of forest must have been cleared in order to support the population by the time of the American Revolution. During the ensuing 70 years, up to the midpoint of the nineteenth century, clearing continued on the eastern seaboard, but as the trans-Appalachian population grew to about 10×10^6 with the settlement of states such as Ohio, Indiana, Illinois, Kentucky, Tennessee, and even the forested eastern portions of Iowa, Missouri, and Arkansas, the pace accelerated. A further 360,000 km² were felled throughout the country between 1780 and 1850 (Williams 1983; 1989).

Although the destruction and removal of the forest for agriculture have been emphasized, it should not be forgotten that timber was also a resource of the highest value for housing, fencing, and fuel, and for making furniture and implements. In addition, if the farmer was fortunate enough to have access to a nearby market for selling wood, potash or pearlash, and tannin, turpentine, pitch, and even lumber, then the value of the forest increased as he made cash that could be used to hire labor to offset the heavy task of clearing. To take just one of these other uses of the forest: the average farmer probably spent between one-eighth and one-fifth of his working life chopping, splitting, stacking, and hauling fuelwood (Gates 1972). With an annual consumption somewhere between 70 and 80 m³ for a rural household and even more for a large farm (Crèvecoeur [1770] (1925); Reynolds and Pierson 1942), the destruction of the forest was enormous. Great as it was, however, it was mere prelude to what was to come as the trickle of Europeans became a flood and the native-born population grew rapidly.

Brazil

The forests of Brazil are among the most extensive in the world. In addition to the well-known Amazonian rainforest, there was once a vast (approximately 780,000 km²) subtropical rainforest that stretched along the Atlantic coast from Recife (Pernambuco) in the north nearly to Porto Allegre in the south, through the states of Pernambuco, Alagôas, Sergipe, Espirito Santo, Rio de Janeiro, and large portions of the eastern thirds of Bahia, Minas Gerais, and São Paulo (daFonseca 1985). It was a closed forest with a rich variety of species with tropical hardwood trees (ironwood and brazilwood), entwined with lianas and epiphytes, and on the coastal-facing escarpments, it closely resembled the larger Amazonian rainforest to the northwest.

In pre-Columbian and early European times, aboriginal swidden cultivation (consisting of slash-and-burn clearing and the growing of mainly manioc, but also some corn, squash, beans, peppers, and peanuts) was widespread. It was the intensification of these traditional agricultural practices through European "invasion" that had the greatest effect on the forest, rather than sugar growing.

European contact became more intensive after 1600, and the local native population that had survived disease was killed, driven out, or enslaved and replaced in the coastal area by a mixed mestizo population that adopted the aboriginal agricultural regime (Galeano 1973). The swidden was

Table 11-2 *Global land areas converted to regular cropping, 1880, 1920, 1978 (× 10,000 km²)*

	Area cropped			Net change		
	1860	1920	1978	1860–1919	1920–1978	1860–1978
Developed regions						
Canada/U.S.	760	2,372	2,357	1,612	−15	1,596
Europe	1,200	1,406	1,417	206	11	217
USSR	810	1,690	2,319	880	629	1,509
Oceania	40	191	591	151	400	551
	2,810	5,659	6,684	2,849	1,025	3,874
Developing regions						
Africa	630	799	1,694	159	905	1,064
Asia	2,110	3,025	4,454	915	1,429	2,344
Latin America	170	571	1,405	399	834	1,233
	2,910	4,395	7,553	1,473	3,168	4,694
World total	5,720	10,054	14,237	4,322	4,193	8,515

Sources: Richards 1986; FAO Production Yearbook 1979.

intensified by the introduction of a number of European innovations, such as iron axes and machetes, and the introduction of pigs. Whereas the aboriginals might have cut and burned about 1 ha per family per annum, the Europeanized mestizo destroyed 3 ha or more. Forest did not regenerate under such widespread burning and was reduced to grass and ferns. Once fertility decreased, the farmers shifted on into the abundant forest, and the old degenerate areas were grazed by cattle (Dean 1983). As in most pioneer forested areas, the cleared land was valued more highly than the forested land, and because the system was condoned, it spread. Consequently, white and mestizo swidden agriculture was the first step in the establishment of export-oriented plantation crops.

Although intermittent logging of the valuable hardwoods caused some local destruction, it was little compared to the impact of gold and diamond mining. In 1690, the discovery of gold in Minas Gerais and scattered pockets of gold and diamonds elsewhere led to a further inflow of migrants and more forest destruction, so that possibly 20,000 km² were felled. The food and the fuel needed for the new economy left great swathes throughout the forest; farms and cattle ranches were formed. Dean (1983) estimates that another 25,000 km² were cleared for planting manioc, corn, and rice, with larger areas (perhaps 50,000 km²) for ranches, making a total of 95,000 km² in the 100-year life of the mineral workings. Further gold findings in Matto Grosso and Goias caused another influx of migrants, and they were supported by food grown on newly cleared lands on the coast, especially around São Paulo.

By the mid-eighteenth century, another export crop, sugar, was putting pressure on the forest. Sugar arrived in Brazil in 1531, and cultivation was mainly in the north in the states of Pernambuco, Alagôas, and Sergipe, with minor concentrations around Rio de Janeiro and the Campos region. Primary forest was always favored for sugar growing, and slaves supplied the labor to fell it and to harvest the cane.

Demands on the forest were not confined to clearing the land for cultivation alone, as extreme heat was required to crystallize the juice, and vast areas were cut for wood fuel. Sternberg (1968) notes that the so-called Zona da Mata, or Forest Zone around Pernambuco, is forest in name only, having been denuded of trees by centuries of sugar cultivation and cutting for fuel for sugar factories.

Global Economy

From the opening decades of the nineteenth century, and certainly from about 1860 onward, the pace of forest exploitation and change began to quicken. All the changes, modifications, and forces associated with the phrase Industrial Revolution diffused beyond the confines of a tiny portion of northwest Europe and were released on the wider world. New forms of energy, new materials, and new systems of transport and organization transformed the earth. Broadly speaking, the reasons for change in the forests were threefold:

(1) A greater integration of the world economy and trade occurred as the last pieces of land were absorbed economically, if not politically, into the world system focused on Europe, with the United States as a subsidiary but increasingly important center (Wallerstein 1974; 1980). The extension of railroads and the increase of shipping (specifically steam) brought standards of regularity, speed, and cheapness to goods and passenger traffic hitherto unknown. Transport efficiency was coupled with massive overseas investment (Christopher 1985; Davis and Huttenback 1987) organized by a reliable financial and banking service, backed up by efficient administrative and business organizations.

(2) A growing and spreading world population, in its search for food, caused more land to be brought into cultivation. World population started its new upward and accelerating trajectory, rising from $1,171 \times 10^6$ in 1850 to $2,515 \times 10^6$ in 1950, to double again to 5×10^9 in 1987 (World Bank 1985). Concomitant with this growth was the spread of people;

Table 11-3 *Global Areas of Different Ecosystems Converted to Cropping, 1860–1978 (× 000 km²)*

	Forests	Woodlands	Savannas	Grasslands	Swamps	Deserts	Total
Developed regions							
Canada/U.S.	511	130	107	849	—	?	1,597
Europe	78	03	18	84	34	—	217
USSR	439	136	17	884	—	32	1,509
Oceania	239	123	133	51	—	05	551
	1,267	392	275	1,868	34	37	3,874
Developing regions							
Africa	180	289	239	325	—	31	1,064
Asia	592	628	500	374	177	73	2,344
Latin America	384	253	161	401	01	31	1,233
	1,156	1,170	900	1,100	178	135	4,641
World total	2,423	1,562	1,175	2,968	212	172	8,515

Source: Revelle 1984, based on Richards, Olson, and Rotty 1983.

Note: In Richards (1986), the conversions were revised as per Table 11-1, and the overall adjustment of 70,000 km² was assigned to forest ecosystems in this table by this author, as many of the adjustments concerned forest regrowth.

about 60×10^6 left Europe between 1850 and 1950, primarily for the Americas, but also for Australia, New Zealand, and southern Africa (Trewartha 1969).

The total amount of land in regular cropping in 1860 was 5.7×10^6 km² (Richards 1986). During the succeeding 60 years to 1919, an additional 4.3×10^6 km² net were added to this amount, and a further 4.1×10^6 km² from 1920 to 1978 (Table 11-2), so that the world's arable land increased by 8.5×10^6 km², to become nearly three times the extent it had been in 1860. It is possible to calculate roughly the areas of the different major natural ecosystems that were affected by the transformation of land to agriculture (Table 11-3). Approximately 2.4×10^6 km² of the forest and 1.5×10^6 km² of woodland, or 46.9% of the total area, affected were converted to agricultural land. In addition, a further 1.1×10^6 km² of savanna were also cleared. Thus, in the space of only 118 years, 3.9×10^6 km² of forest and woodland were eliminated and replaced by crops, or an average of nearly 34,000 km² per annum.

But this must be only a part of the story, as there were other impacts: for example, domestic and industrial fuel-getting; cutting roads and railroad rights of way; commercial timber-getting and intensification for pastoral purposes (particularly in Australia and Latin America); the intensification and shortening of bush fallows as shifting cultivators were pushed into more restricted areas by the advancing tide of sedentary cultivators; and the knock-on effect on the pastoralists beyond, who grazed savanna and sparse woodlands more intensively as their room to maneuver was reduced also. It is impossible to put a precise figure to the amount of forest converted or modified as a result of these processes, but a variety of evidence suggests that it cannot have been less than about half the area affected by the expansion of cultivation, i.e., 17,000 km². But as some of the disturbance was modification only, then perhaps only half (e.g., 8,000 km²) of that 17,000 km² was converted totally to other uses, and half

was modified, making a total of 42,000 km² converted and 8,000 km² modified per annum between 1860 and 1978. We cannot be more accurate than that.

(3) Within the forests themselves, methods of exploitation changed as invention and demand fed off each other in an ever-upward spiral of production. Many of the inventions originated or at least saw their greatest development in the United States (Davis 1983), which witnessed probably the greatest commercial demand on forests of any country at this time.

The actual cutting of the trees changed little from previous centuries. Improved cross-cut saws were adopted for felling by 1870, and prototypes of mobile chain saws appeared as early as 1927, but it was not until 1947 that the mechanism was perfected, and then the modern single-handed assault on the forests of the world began.

Whereas most agriculturalists burned their felled trees, or at best, selected a few for constructional purposes or sale, the commercial lumbermen took all the millable timber possible in order to maximize returns and reduce costs, and they left behind their trash, which often became the fuel for devastating forest fires. Therefore, improvements in cutting were of less significance than improvements in the transport of logs which were bulky, cumbersome, and of relatively low value per unit weight (Rector 1953). The movement from forest to mill, where the low-value product was broken down into a high-value and more-handleable product (timber), was cheapened and speeded up by a variety of means. Water transport was cheapest, and therefore "log-driving" or log rafting expanded. Logging railroads appeared during the 1860s and were adopted rapidly; stationary steam engines that hauled in, or "yarded" logs by cables, were common after the 1880s; and high-lead logging in difficult terrain (as in the Pacific Northwest) was developed at the turn of the century. Finally, tractors and bulldozers, together with powerful articulated trucks – all of which displayed great versatility and had little need of permanent capital works or large work forces – began to appear in the forests in the years following World War I, and were universal after about 1945.

The increasing volume and movement of logs had to be matched by a greater cutting capacity at the mills. Steam power – not common until after 1870 – boosted production, as it meant regular running of saws unaffected by river flow, and 24-hour running. Production rose several hundredfold, as the water-powered, single-up-and-down saws were replaced by steam-powered circular saws, then by gangs of circular saws, and after the 1880s by band saws that moved even faster and could cope with the largest of logs. By the latter 1920s, electricity was replacing steam (Van Tassel and Bluestone 1940). Each invention accelerated the production of lumber, which meant that more lumber had to be found for the mill and that larger areas of forest were cleared more quickly than ever before.

The economic and social organization of the industry changed radically too. Heavy investment in steam plants and permanent railroads necessitated a steady supply of timber and the means for moving it. The systematic cutting of large areas replaced the felling of individual trees. Ownership (or at least access) to large tracts of land became essential in order to ensure an even flow of raw material. Concentration of ownership was aided by the rapid evolution of joint stock companies and monopolies aided by trade associations, by specialized labor living in specialized settlements, and by a concern for greater efficiency, the elimination of waste, greater competition, tight contractual controls based on the time element, and the mass production of a standardized end-product. The shift in technology, energy consumption, and organization in the lumber industry between the mid-nineteenth and mid-twentieth centuries mirrored changes in the rest of the industrialized society. The forests of the world were drawn into this new nexus of production and consumption; few escaped it.

Regional Impacts, 1850–1950

North America

The processes of forest clearing already described continued with little change until the beginning of the twentieth century (Williams 1989). Clear-cutting took an average of 50 mandays per hectare, whereas girdling took 33.5 mandays, but as so many tasks were deferred with girdling, such as disposing of the tree trunks, both methods were eventually about as time-consuming. Both left stumps, which if they did not rot, had to be grubbed, axed, and hauled out by oxen, which added another 25 to 30 mandays per hectare (Primack 1962). In theory, therefore, it was possible to clear 4 ha/yr, but because of the other tasks during pioneering, usually little more than 2 ha were cleared. This rate did not change until the 1880s (when dynamite to blast out stumps was introduced), and then again during the 1920s (with tractors, trucks, and bulldozers), and later still, with mobile mechanical saws. For the majority of farmers, the task of clearing was not one of a few years, but of at least a generation.

Table 11-4 *Improved/cleared land in farms in forested and nonforested counties, United States, 1850–1909 ($\times$ 000 km^2)*

Year	Forested	Nonforested
Before 1850	460	—
1850–59	161	37
1860–69	79	79
1870–79	200	197
1880–89	116	234
1890–99	125	166
1900–09	91	209
Total	1,232	922

Source: Primack 1962.

If the would-be farmer could save money or even sell some of the fuelwood and timber, then he could hire itinerant clearers or "set-up men" for $25 to $30 per hectare. Alternatively, if he had enough capital, he could take the advice of the old forest hands and "pay a little more for land *lately* cleared." It was evident that there were many mobile "farm-makers" who moved on once a profit could be made from selling their "improvements" to the next wave of settlers.

The amount of forest converted can be estimated by calculating the area of "improved" land created out of the predominantly forested areas, with adjustments for reversion. Thus, 460,000 km^2 had been improved/cleared by 1850, in the eastern half of the country (Table 11-4). Despite the attraction of the easier-to-convert prairie lands, a massive 200,000 km^2 were converted in the decade after the Civil War, and it was not until after 1910 that farm abandonment and forest reversion in New England first, and then throughout the East, reduced significantly the net amount taken out of forest. Nevertheless, even then, conversion still stood at about 96,000 km^2/yr. It was, as one Ohio pioneer farmer said, "a war on the woods."

Although Americans were immune to the destruction going on around them, foreign travelers were not. Thus, Basil Hall (1829), a British artist and writer, sketched (Fig. 11.1) and commented on the scenes he encountered in western New York.

The trees are cut over at a height of three or four feet from the ground and the stumps are left for many years till the roots rot; the edge of the forest, opened for the first time to the light of the sun looks cold and raw; – the ground rugged and ill-dressed ... as if nothing could ever be made to spring from it. The houses which are made of logs, lie scattered about at long intervals; while the snake fences constructed of split trees, placed in a zig-zag form, disfigure the landscape.

With slight variation here and there, the sketch and the description were a vignette and epitome of agricultural deforestation that could be applied to almost anywhere in the temperate world, at any time.

Although fuelwood-cutting probably consumed more timber than any other use to which the forest had been put, its impact was less one of conversion and more one of modification and thinning (Reynolds and Pierson 1942). Fuel was

Figure 11.1 Newly cleared land in America. *Source:* Hall 1829.

the incidental byproduct of agricultural clearing and, to a lesser extent, of logging. Only where mineral deposits and large towns impinged on the forests or where specific routeways concentrated steam locomotives or boats (as along the Ohio and Mississippi) were exorbitant demands made on them.

Locally, charcoal iron-making caused destruction and modification, especially as the use of charcoal lingered on until this century because of the abundance of wood, and also because it made a good all-purpose iron for frontier conditions, with positive qualities of toughness, heat resistance, and malleability (Schallenburg 1975). In 1856, there were 560 iron furnaces, of which 439, or 78%, were still charcoal-fueled, and these furnaces were concentrated in the Hanging Rock district of Ohio, the Allegheny Valley northeast of Pittsburgh, and the Juniata Valley in south-central Pennsylvania. If every 1,000 t of iron produced needed 60 ha of woodland, then the total charcoal-iron production between 1855 and 1910 (24.1×10^6 t) would have consumed about 14,400 km² of woodland, or about a third less if a 25-year rotation were employed. Impressive as that is, it is placed in perspective by comparing it to the amount of woodland cleared for agriculture during the same period: a mere 1.2%. But because destruction was noticeable locally and because industry and the railroad were "alien" intruders into the forest, whereas agriculture was "normal" and laudable, iron-making and the locomotive were portrayed as the great destroyers of the forest. Nationally, they were mere pin pricks (Williams 1982).

Over and above all of the industrial and mechanical needs and impacts on the forest was the demand for domestic fuelwood. In 1879, it was calculated to amount to 95.5% of a total of 40.2×10^6 m³ cut for fuel. But we know little about its cutting and marketing, as they are the combination of millions of individual unrelated actions and are submerged in the grander topic of agricultural clearing (Cole 1970). Nevertheless, the conclusion must be that fuelwood-getting exceeded by far all other demands on the forest (lumber included) until 1880, and was a significant drain, even until the 1930s.

In comparison, lumbering underwent a revolution during the late nineteenth and early twentieth centuries as it adapted, invented, and even led the way in using the technology and human organization of the Industrial Revolution; barely a year went by without some new invention or device being tried out with success in the forest. Between 1850 and 1920, the lumber industry consistently outstripped almost all other forms of manufacturing by value, and large firms like Weyerhaeuser rivaled the capital investment and profits of Carnegie in steel and Rockefeller in oil.

The scramble for profits meant a ruthless exploitation of the timber stand, and the "cut-out-and-get-out" mentality prevailed as the lumbermen tried to feed the insatiable public demand for lumber products, which rose steadily from 1840 to reach a peak of 107.3×10^6 m³ per annum in 1920. One by one, each of the regions of production peaked and then declined as the lumber industry moved westward to new forest stands. The normal expectation was that lumbering was the first step in the exploitation of the land and that the cleared ground would be taken up and improved by farmers. In many cases this happened, but in vast areas it did not. Across the northern portions of the Great Lakes states, deserts of stumpland were created in areas with a marginal growing season and poor, glacially derived soils. In the South there were even larger, but scattered stumpland areas, too remote from services and markets to support farming, and/or on poor soils. In the Pacific Northwest were many areas of steep slopes, strewn with the massive stumps of the redwoods and Douglas fir, in a climate too wet for normal agriculture.

By 1920, it was estimated that there were 127,000 km^2 of stumpland in the Great Lakes states (Black and Gray 1925), 346,000 km^2 in the South, and about 29,000 km^2 in the North-west – some of which had been taken up for farming (U.S. Forest Service 1920).

The cut-overs did not regenerate because exploitive lumbering had stripped them of young trees and even topsoil, and the trash left on the ground from the lumbering operations was fuel for frequent forest fires. Putting aside the spectacular fires that devastated thousands of square kilometers in the Great Lakes states during the 1880s and 1890s, the problem built up steadily, so that during the 1910s an annual average of 34,000 km^2 were burned throughout the country – much of it in the cutovers. This figure rose to 96,000 km^2 during the 1920s, and a phenomenal 158,000 km^2 per annum during the 1930s. Not until it was recognized that most of these once-timber lands could not be farmed, but had to revert to growing what they produced best – trees – were they going to be reclaimed to be a part of the living forest.

Brazil

By the early 1830s, coffee had begun to pass sugar as the main money earner in Brazil and remained the principal export commodity until 1964, reaching its apogee in 1925, when it accounted for three-quarters of the country's export earnings. The crop had been introduced into Amazonia from East Africa in 1727, but spread only slowly. By the 1770s, it was being cultivated in the hills around Rio de Janeiro, from where cultivation spread over the Serro do Mar and into the Paraibo du Sul Valley and the surrounding São Paulo highlands, and by the 1840s the coffee *fazendas* extended into, and meant the destruction of, the extensive tropical coastal forests of Minas Gerais and adjacent portions of Espirito Santo (Dean 1983; Dickerson 1982; James 1932). Open savanna was avoided in favor of heavily forested ridges, and unless ground could be found that already had been cleared for sugar cultivation or thinned through fuel gathering for the sugar mills, then the forest was cleared by ax and fire. The coffee bushes were planted up and down steep hillsides in order to facilitate the drainage of cold air, as the crop was sensitive to frost. The net result was devastating soil erosion, which hastened abandonment and migration. Although the bushes could yield for many decades if looked after, they were usually neglected, as in the time-honored Brazilian tradition it was easier to shift on to more forest land, clear it, and plant again rather than fertilize and cultivate carefully. This movement was encouraged by the widespread belief that the coffee bush needed the soils of the newly cleared forest in order to thrive (Dean 1976; Stein 1957). Thus, the forest was felled in a restless cycle as the coffee frontier moved continuously inland.

The construction of the Santos–São Paulo railway over the obstacle of the Serro do Mar in 1867 allowed a new wave of exploitation to be unleashed in the interior uplands, and the railroads fanned out from Campinas in all directions to southern Minas Gerais and the Paulista west from 1860 to 1885. The realization of the inherent fertility of the decomposed basaltic-derived red soils, or *terra roxa*, encouraged the massive expansion of the *fazenda* frontier toward Ribeirô Prêto between 1885 and 1900, but further depletion of even these soils and further expansion meant yet further migration west onto the interfluves of the many rivers flowing roughly northwestward toward the Paraná River (Monbeig 1952).

The creation and extension of the coffee *fazendas* was founded originally on slave labor (see e.g., Dean 1976; Stein 1957), but with the construction of the railroad in 1867, major social and economic changes were unleashed, which led to the crumbling of the old regime. Slavery was abolished in 1888, and the influx of over half a million subsidized Italian, Spanish, and Portuguese migrants – their movement greatly facilitated by the railways – replaced the slaves, and ensured more clearing for growing food and to supply the burgeoning cities of the unpland. The railroads were crucial in the further destruction of the forests, not only as a means of importing the migrants and exporting the coffee beans through the new port of Santos, but also because they encouraged further extensive and wasteful clearing of virgin forest along the track. There were 6,000 km of line by 1900 and a total of approximately 12,000 km by 1929 (Monbeig 1952). In addition, the railroad, as elsewhere in the world, consumed vast quantities of timber for fuel and ties, and facilitated the movement of fuelwood and food to the growing cities of the region, and thus was instrumental in causing further cycles of destruction.

Coffee cultivation was dynamic, mobile, and wasteful (Dean 1983). About 4,000 km^2 of forest had been destroyed by the end of the century, which is almost exactly the area of coffee cultivation. If the area of land in coffee is used as a surrogate measure for the area of forest destroyed, then at least 7,980 km^2 would have been cleared by 1920, and 140,000 km^2 by 1931.

South of São Paulo in the states of Paraná, Santa Catarina, and Rio Grande do Sul lay some 250,000 km^2 of temperate forest of Paraná pine, or *Araucaria augustiflora*, which were widely spaced (approximately 25 to 60 trees/ha), straight-grained, thick conifers. This once-extensive forest was reduced to a mere 445 km^2 in 1980, by immigrant European and Japanese farmers who established small, independent, intensive, and highly mechanized holdings of temperate crops (Heinsdjik, Soares, and Houfe 1962; Maack 1953). The forest was slashed and burned, the fires often getting out of hand in the inflammable pine – such as in 1963, when over 20,000 km^2 were destroyed (Lowden 1965; Sternberg 1968). By 1980, 128,000 km^2 were farmed, the overwhelming proportion from former forest land. In addition to the pioneer clearing, a thriving lumber industry flourished to garner this straight-grained and easily worked pine for construction purposes. The growth of local towns and of more distant markets such as Montevideo and particularly Buenos Aires (from 750,000 in 1893 to 4 million by 1940) led to massive destruction (McNeill 1983). Over 17.7 × 10^6 t of logs have been exported.

Finally, the recent expansion of coffee cultivation south from São Paulo has mopped up about another 10,000 km^2 of Paraná pine forest, where it abutted and merged with the tropical rainforest of São Paulo (Nicholls 1969).

The impact of industrial and domestic fuel rivaled that of agricultural clearing, particularly in the highly industrialized and urbanized state of São Paulo (Dean 1987). Approximately three-quarters of its 250,000 km^2 (i.e., 180,000 km^2) were forested originally. Of this, about 40,000 km^2 had been converted to ranches and agriculture, of which coffee constituted over half the land use by the 1930s. At the same time, industrial and domestic uses were eating into the forest reserves at an alarming rate. For example, domestic fuel use averaged about 2.4 m^3/capita/annum, and each ton of pig iron produced consumed 12 m^3 of charcoal, iron production being almost totally charcoal-based until 1940 (Baer 1969). Thus, if the primary forest yielded a minimum of 400 m^3 of woodfuel/ha, then every 1,000 people caused the destruction of a little less than 6 ha, and every 1,000 t of pig iron, about 30 ha of primary forest per annum. These figures could be doubled if *copoeira*, or cutover regenerating a depauperate forest, was being used. In these calculations, many of the drains on the forests are omitted (for example, breweries, bakeries, sugar refineries, and all the other primary processing plants that relied on woodfuel). The railroads alone were using 3.9 × 10^6 m^3 of woodfuel in 1949, the yield of 97.5 km^2 of primary forest.

By 1950, industrial and domestic demand probably had reached its peak, 20 × 10^6 m^3 being used in industry and transport, and 18 × 10^6 m^3 in domestic hearths (Dean 1987). If these figures are correct, this would have meant felling 950 km^2 of primary forest, or 1,900 km^2 of *copoeira*, annually to satisfy the demand. Against these calculations of destruction, one must remember that the forest does grow back, but only up to a point, as the existence of vast areas of *copoeira* shows. Increasingly, in the years since 1950, it is the substitutes like coke, diesel oil, bottled gas, and hydroelectricity that have reduced consumption and ameliorated the rate of destruction. All that we know for certain is that by 1970, only 20,000 km^2 of the primary forest remained out of the original area of 180,000 km^2. The bulk of the Brazilian Atlantic coast subtropical forest in this state had disappeared.

South and Southeast Asia

The purposeful alteration of the forest by overseas immigrants as in Brazil, the United States, and Australia had almost no counterpart in South and Southeast Asia. Nevertheless, the countries of this part of the world, which for so long had kept the European immigrant and influence at arm's length, succumbed slowly during the early nineteenth century to the powerful envelopment and linkage of the world market. Rates of economic change accelerated as each step of conquest or suzerainty brought stability with peace and orderly administration, and foreign and local entrepreneurs seized opportunities to make profits.

The bulk of the area of British administration in present-day Pakistan, Bangladesh, and northern India, but with the exception of Burma and Malaysia, started with a dense rural population already engaged in intensive, sedentary agriculture. By 1880, there were already 187.7 × 10^6 people in these territories, a population that was poised to expand rapidly to 310 × 10^6 by 1950 and then take a sudden upward-sweeping curve to more than double to 625.2 × 10^6 by 1980. During the late nineteenth century, government revenue and land tenure policies, the extension of railways, massive irri-

Table 11-5 *Changing land use, south and southeast Asia, 1880, 1950, 1980 (× 000 km^2)*

	1880	1950	1980
Arable			
South Asia	716	971	1,103
Southeast Asia	41	121	150
	757	1,092	1,253
Forest			
South Asia	362	257	203
Southeast Asia	526	418	339
	888	675	542
Interrupted forest			
South Asia	340	284	239
Southeast Asia	242	236	247
	582	520	486
Other			
South Asia	1,400	1,306	1,274
Southeast Asia	203	237	276
	1,603	1,544	1,550
Total area			
South Asia	2,818	2,818	2,818
Southeast Asia	1,012	1,012	1,022
	3,831	3,831	3,831

Source: Richards et al. 1987.
Note: Other land uses include grassland and shrub complexes, deserts, mountain, tundra, swamp, settlements, and standing water.

gation works, the establishment of regular steamship sailings, and the opening of the Suez Canal in 1869 – all coalesced to make it worthwhile for the small proprietors to produce for a wider world market cash crops such as oilseed, wheat, indigo, tea, and particularly cotton (especially after the interruption of North American supplies with the Civil War in 1860–65). There was a sevenfold increase in British-Indian trade between 1869 and 1929.

Consequently, there was a steady expansion of arable land, with a consequent decline of forest lands and interrupted woods (basically long fallows and thinned woods) (Richards et al. 1987). Imperceptibly, all land was coming into use, being converted into arable or being modified by grazing and fuelwood-getting. Throughout the region, arable land increased from 757,000 km^2 in 1880 to 1 × 10^6 km^2 in 1950, and then on to 1.2 × 10^6 km^2 in 1980 (Table 11-5 and Fig. 11.2). Nearly all of this increased arable land came out of forest, which decreased from 888,000 km^2 in 1880 to 675,000 km^2 in 1950, with a major downward trend to 542,000 km^2 by 1980. Interrupted or sparse woodlands also have been destroyed, but not to the same extent – declining from 582,000 km^2 in 1880 to 526,000 km^2 in 1950 to 486,000 km^2 in 1980. It should be borne in mind, however, that partially cleared forest may become sparse and interrupted woodland, which may, therefore, increase in size as the forest decreases. All other

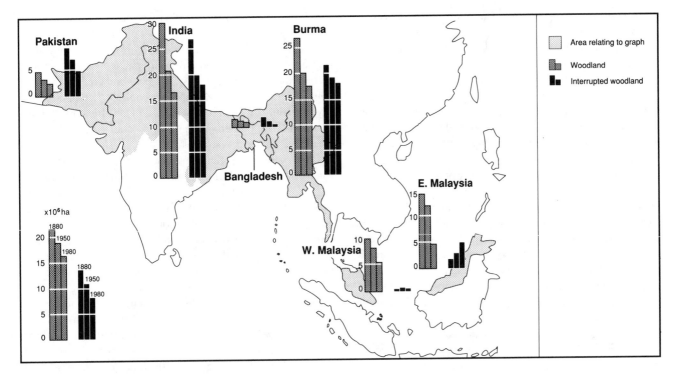

Figure 11.2 Changes in woodland and interrupted woodland in South and Southeast Asia, 1880, 1950, and 1980. *Source:* Richards et al. 1987.

lands have declined from $1.6 \times 10^6\,\mathrm{km}^2$ in 1880 to $1.5 \times 10^6\,\mathrm{km}^2$ 100 years later.

The local and regional story of the steady loss of over $213,000\,\mathrm{km}^2$ of forest and $62,000\,\mathrm{km}^2$ of interrupted woodland between 1880 and 1950 is scarcely known, as the expansion of arable usually went unnoticed and unrecorded as part of the improvement of agriculture and the expansion of cash cropping. It was considered the most natural thing in the world to British officials, who felt they should strive to improve the lot of the subject people. A number of studies have attempted to trace the shifts in land use (Richards, Hagen and Haynes 1985; Richards and McAlpin 1983; Tucker 1982; 1983), but the best-documented change is that of Lower Burma, largely because it was a purposeful change over a short period of time which caused a dramatic transformation in the landscape.

Initially, British interest in Burma revolved around the extraction of teak and ironwood (first in coastal Arakan and Tenassarim, and later inland along the Sittang and Salween rivers) for ship construction and the maintenance of global naval supremacy. Finally the *kanazo* (*Heritiera fomes*) forests of the deltaic Lower Burma were annexed in 1852, and Burma became part of the British Empire in 1886. The official British quest to acquire timber for naval construction culminated in a progressive policy of conservation of the monsoon forest in highland Upper Burma. But the opposite was true of deltaic Lower Burma, where government officials pursued a deliberate policy of clearing forest and mangrove for cultivation and food supply for the larger empire (Adas 1983). At midcentury, between 35,000 and $40,000\,\mathrm{km}^2$ of land were under *kanazo* forest in the lower delta basin. The *kanazo* was a tree taller than 45 m that grew on drier land

away from the rivers, which were fringed with mangrove swamp forest. No more than about $3,200\,\mathrm{km}^2$ were in cultivation at this time, but the region was regarded as ideal for growing rice that would produce revenue and alleviate the periodic famines of neighboring India. The colonial regime introduced a system of land tenure and taxation that would attract pioneering peasant migrant cultivators to clear the land and plant paddy rice. Canals, embankments, roads, railways, and mills were built, and steamship routes established. As a consequence, the population of the delta area rose from 1.5 million in 1852 to over 4 million in the early 1900s, and it became one of the main rice-exporting regions of the world.

By the early 1920s, only several hundred hectares of *kanazo* forest were left standing in Lower Burma. Over Burma as a whole, $65,000\,\mathrm{km}^2$ of forest and $24,000\,\mathrm{km}^2$ of interrupted forest had been destroyed by 1950. In a phrase reminiscent of the de Tocqueville description of pioneering in North America over 100 years before, Grant said, "The sound of the pioneer's ax is heard daily as the forests are cleared to prepare for the rice crop" (Grant 1932). The transformation of the earth in this part of the world was being completed rapidly.

Since 1950, the expansion of cultivation throughout the region has been the result of the sheer pressure of population, as hungry, small-scale proprietors desperately need land to grow food to eat.

Global Concern, 1950 Onward

Although deforestation has occurred for as long as humankind has been on earth, it is only during the last few decades or so that the world has been concerned about the rate and extent of the process. The cause of this concern is broadly twofold.

First, in many of the countries of the developing (largely tropical) world, population numbers have almost doubled between 1950 and 1980, so that whatever economic gains have been made since independence have been negligible or even swallowed up. Consequently, pressures on the forest have increased as they became one of the last sources of new land for the extension of arable and pasture, for fuelwood for heating and cooking and even for industry, and as a source of hard currency from exported logs and wood chips.

Second, in the countries of the developed world (largely temperate in location), unbridled economic growth was checked with the oil-price crisis of the early 1970s and the subsequent recession, which coincided with a mounting concern over the environmental consequences of development, growth, and exploitation of natural resources. For the first time (perhaps because of space exploration and imagery), many people became aware of the finite resource base of the earth. Much of the concern over forest depletion has been articulated by people in countries that are least concerned directly, and who, ironically, already long ago reaped the economic benefits of the exploitation of their own rich forest resources. Nevertheless, the cause for concern seems real enough.

Changes in technology also have had an enormous effect on forest exploitation. The chain saw, the truck, and the tractor have enabled even the most inaccessible areas to be logged, almost single-handed. In addition, the invention of a host of chemical and manufacturing processes has given us, for example, chip board, particle board, masonite, and laminated timbers. Add to these uses the ever-growing demand for pulp for fibers and for paper and packing, and forests that would before have never been cut on account of their inaccessibility, poor-quality stands, and low yields are now exploited so thoroughly that at times little vegetation is left for the natural processes of regeneration to take place. In short, all trees have a commercial value and all trees can be harvested.

The consequences of this rapid and extensive deforestation are manifold (Eden 1978). In addition to the diminution of timber for construction and heating purposes, species are disappearing at an alarming rate, and the loss may well equal the predicted 20% of all existing species by 2000 (Myers 1980a; 1985). Soils, particularly many of those of the tropical areas, are unsuitable for agriculture, and once opened up to the sunlight and direct impact of the rain, become degraded irreversibly through laterization, oxidization, and erosion (Sanchez et al. 1982; Tosi and Voertman 1964; 1975). The beneficial effects of forests in regulating water flows and preventing soil erosion are diminished (Daniel and Kulasingam 1974; Salati and Vose 1984), thus raising the likelihood of severe flooding and the siltation of reservoirs and dams. In the background lies the ever-present specter of long-term climatic change, as diminished biomass may be decreasing the absorption of carbon dioxide, causing global heating, possibly rising sea levels from a melting ice cap, and certainly a lessening of the moderating effect on local climates (Brown

and Lugo 1980; Houghton 1986; Prance 1986; Woodwell et al. 1983).

In addition, the decrease in the forest area is pushing shifting cultivation into more marginal lands, with either increased risks of erosion on steep slopes and greater flooding downstream as in the Himalayas (Cool 1980; Gupta 1981; Myers 1986), or greater desertification on drier margins as pastoralists are pushed out in turn into drier grasslands, as in the Sahel. In the forests that are left, the shortening of the shifting cycle means that the vegetation does not have the chance to reestablish itself, and so it becomes impoverished (e.g., Gomez-Pompa, Vasquez-Yanes, and Guevara 1972). The problem in many developing countries is largely one of a conflict between the utilization of an inherited property resource regarded as a common good and the expropriation and overexploitation of that resource by a mass of people. In nearly every case, the agricultural base undergoes further degradation and diminishes as a means of alleviating poverty.

Debate about the magnitude of change and the extent of the forest being cleared is common (Allen and Barnes 1985; Fearnside 1982; Lugo and Brown 1982; Melillo et al. 1985; Molofsky, Hall, and Myers et al. 1986; Myers 1982; Sedjo and Clawson 1983), but all agree that the forest is being destroyed on a large scale, and the balance of opinion seems to be that the rate is accelerating. Disagreement arises largely from differences in the reliability and appropriateness of underlying assumptions in the various studies – for example, the definition of the forested area, the role of shifting agriculture in causing permanent conversion or disturbance and modification, the fate of fallow lands, the rate of regeneration, the absence of a reliable base figure against which to measure change, and the aggregating of individual country figures to achieve a world total.

The main sources and some of their characteristics are summarized in Table 11-6. In the light of this varied evidence, ranging as it does from 73,000 km² to 200,000 km² per annum, it is difficult to be dogmatic about the rates of deforestation, although a rate of about 110 to 113,000 km²/yr seems increasingly to be accepted with the possibility of approximately 45,000 km² being modified (Houghton et al. 1985). In a detailed analysis of the estimates of the annual rates of change calculated from the FAO Yearbook 1979 (FAO 1980), the FAO/UNEP study (FAO/UNEP 1982a, b, and c), and Myers (1980b), Allen and Barnes (1985: 167–68) concluded that three sources showed that "on average, deforestation is occurring at rates of less than 1% of forest area per year . . . or 1–2% of the forest area per year in Africa, Latin America, and Asia." But there the comparability ends. Although broad agreement exists of the magnitude of rates of deforestation for a number of countries, great disagreement remains over others. For example, the Philippines has rates of −2.2%, −1.2%, and −1.25% in the FAO Yearbook, the FAO/UNEP study, and Myers, respectively. Not until a uniform, systematic, and objective measure (perhaps such as LANDSAT imagery) is employed over large areas and long periods of time (Grainger 1984; Tucker et al. 1986; Williams and Miller 1979; Woodwell et al. 1986), can we be sure of the true

Table 11-6 *Estimates of deforestation in tropical lands, 1978–1986 (× 000 km²)*

Year/author	Definition	Change/year		Percentage
1978 Saouma	n.a.	120		
1978 Barney	n.a.	200		2
1979 Lanly and Clement	n.a.	73		
1980 Barney and *Global 2000*	n.a.	180–200		?
1980 U.S. Interagency Task Force	Decline in closed forest cover	100–200		1–2
1980 Myers (1980b and 1984)	Transformation of primary closed forest to any other formation	pasture fuelwood agriculture	20 25 $\underline{160}$ 205*	2+
1980 FAO Production Yearbook (1979)	Loss of forest land (1968–78)	ca. 111		0.53
1982 FAO/UNEP (1982a, b, c)	Loss of any kind of forest	Closed Open	72 $\underline{39}$ 111	0.60
1985 International Task Force	Cleared for other uses	Closed Open	75 $\underline{38}$ 113	0.58
1986 FAO Production Yearbook (1985)	Loss of forest land (1974–84)	117		0.61

Note: All figures and definitions are as quoted in the various publications.

n.a.: not available.

* Based on a reinterpretation of Myers in Houghton et al. 1985.

magnitude of change. The work of Morain and Klankamsorn (1978) on clearing in Thailand between 1973 and 1976 is one of the few examples that exist. Of one thing we can be certain, however: identical evidence can be interpreted in either a pessimistic or an optimistic light. Both terms are loaded, and in both cases their proponents undoubtedly would rather be labeled as realistic. Nevertheless, bleak scenarios are painted by some (e.g., Barney 1980; Caufield 1985; Eckholm 1976; 1982; Myers 1980b; 1983; 1984), whereas others feel that abundance will prevail if forests are managed correctly (e.g., Castle 1982; Clawson 1981; Sedjo and Clawson 1984; Simon 1981).

Regional Impacts: 1950 – Onward

Clearing for Cattle: Central America

In the roughly 550,000 km² of Central America that lie between the central valley of Mexico and the Pacific coasts of Colombia and Ecuador, probably 500,000 km² were covered by dry and moist forests at the time of first European contact in the early sixteenth century. Successive waves of export-oriented monoculture cropping such as sugar, dyes, and the culling of selected timbers during the colonial era, coffee after about 1830, bananas after the 1890s, and cotton after the 1940s – all coupled with sustained population growth – have reduced the original forest cover of this fertile and productive region significantly by the immediate post–World War II period. Extensive public health programs for the elimination of malaria in the coastal areas and other pandemic diseases led to an unprecedented population growth, which topped 3.5% during the early 1960s and has rarely dropped below 2.5%/year since, with consequent pressure on the remaining

forested areas as a source of land for growing food (Myers and Tucker 1987).

With a population in the region of now over 30×10^6, landlessness and poverty are common, but the pressure on the remaining forest has been augmented drastically by another wave of export-oriented cropping; that is, the conversion of vast areas to pastures for cattle ranching for beef (Parsons 1976). The market for the rather poor-quality beef produced on these pastures is mainly the United States, where high per capita consumption of beef, rising prices, and the growth of the "fast food" industry and the pet trade led to the search for new low-cost sources of meat. Clearing was no problem with bulldozers and tractors, and the ability to convert areas to pasture is possible because of the particular social and economic structure of most of the Central American republics, in which a few individual hacienda proprietors own and control a disproportionately large area of land and can therefore respond positively and quickly to market profits (Guess 1979; Myers 1981; Myers and Tucker 1987; Nations and Komer 1982; Shane 1986).

From the late 1950s onward, the area of pasture land and the number of beef cattle have more than doubled (De Walt 1983; Guess 1979; Place 1985), and although a slightly downward trend on exports is now discernible, the so-called hamburger connection (Myers 1981) is still present and is but the latest manifestation of the consequences for the forests of the tropical world of the purchasing power and lifestyle of the developed world.

The exact amount of forest left is not clear. Myers and Tucker (1987) put it at "about 200,000 km²", whereas Nations and Komer (1983) are more precise and calculate that a mere 126,050 km² of "undegraded forest" remained by mid-1983

Table 11-7 *Remaining lowland and lower montane tropical rainforests and annual rate of loss, Central America, mid-1983*

Country	Undegraded rainforest (× km²)	Current rate of loss per year (km²)	Major threats
Nicaragua	27,000	1,000	Cattle ranching
Guatemala	25,700	600	Colonization, cattle ranching
Panama	21,500	500	Cattle ranching, logging
Honduras	19,300	700	Cattle ranching, colonization
Costa Rica	15,400	600	Cattle ranching
Belize	9,750	32	Colonization
Mexico	7,400	600	Cattle ranching, colonization
El Salvador	0	0	(Deforested)
Totals:	126,050	4,032	

Source: Nations and Komer 1982.

(Table 11-7) and that the rate of loss was 4,032 km²/yr. (Fig. 11.3). Certainly, the denudation has been so severe that accelerated runoff and accompanying erosion from the bare hills of Panama has meant that the Canal is in danger of being clogged, with larger vessels already being diverted around South America. Paradoxically, the high-level locks are starved of water to refill them after they have been lowered to allow ships to pass through (Alvarado 1985; Robinson 1985).

Clearing for Colonists: Amazonia

The 5×10^6 km² of lowland tropical rainforest of Amazonia occupies only 61% of the vast Amazon river basin. Nevertheless, it is this tranquil forest that is currently undergoing dramatic changes, and is the focus of world interest and concern over the potentially irreversible nature of the change

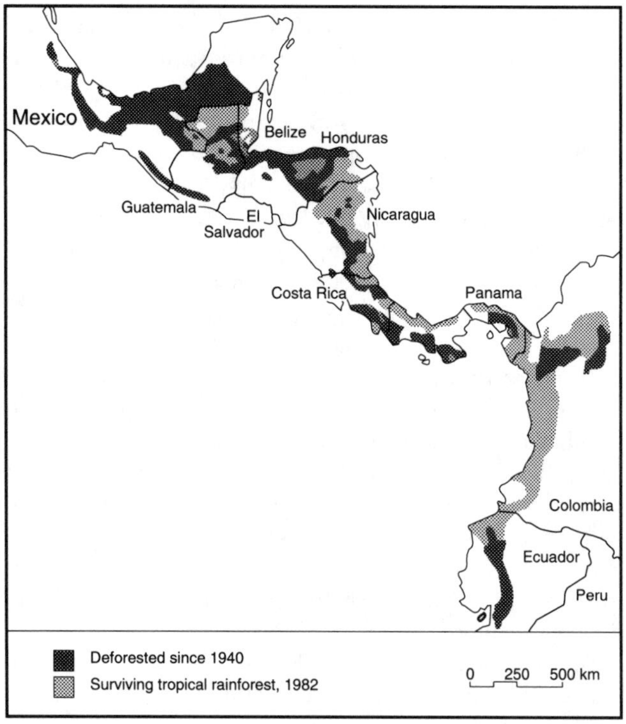

Figure 11.3 Forest clearing in Central America, 1940 to 1982. *Source:* Nations and Komer 1982.

(Barbira-Scazzocchio 1980; Denevan 1973; Fearnside 1979; 1986; Goodland and Irwin 1975; Moran 1982). Since the late 1950s, the Brazilian government has constructed a number of major highways across the forested region, such as the Belém-Brasilia highway during the 1950s, the 5500-km-long Transamazonia highway (BR-230) during the 1970s, and the BR-364 through Rondônia state in 1967. Currently a northern-perimeter highway (BR-210) also is being constructed (Goodland and Bookman 1977; Moran 1983; Smith 1981).

The highways act as spearheads of spontaneous penetration and exploitation. Over 2 million people moved into the vicinity of the Belém-Brasilia Highway in a decade, as well as many large ranching companies, and roughly equal numbers are now strung out along the Transamazonian and other highways. The expectation that 70% of migrants would come from the drought-prone Northeast has not materialized – only a mere 30% have. Far more have come voluntarily from the former coffee and food-crop lands in Paraná, São Paulo, and other southern states, where mechanization of soya bean and wheat cultivation, and the cultivation of vast sugar-cane plantations for alcohol production drove out former sharecroppers and small landowners (Fearnside 1985). In contrast to these spontaneous movements, there is direct colonization with a high degree of government intervention, finance, and control. The government designs and constructs feeder roads, plans towns and services, selects migrants, and controls land subdivisions. The Independent Colonization Project (PIC) at Altimira on the Transamazonian Highway was one such settlement (Moran 1983; Smith 1981), and the Rondônia colonization scheme initiated by INCRA (Brazilian National Institute for Colonization and Agrarian Reform) was another.

In Rondônia and northern Mato Grosso, Highway BR-364, paved and completed in 1984, runs roughly parallel at about 200 km from the Bolivian border for some 1,000 km, from Porto Velho in the northwest to Cuiabá in the southeast. Along the line of the highway, particularly in Rondônia, roads are constructed at right angles into the forest for up to 80 km. The land is subdivided into 100-ha (500 m × 1000 m) lots, each with a road frontage. Clearing starts at the road side and slowly penetrates into the forest as the colonist settler clears more land in order to maintain or increase agricultural production and to reach soil not yet depleted of nutrients (Furley 1980; Mueller 1980; Tucker et al. 1986). Although the colonists use the shifting agriculturalists' practice of axing, slashing, and burning the primary vegetation, there the similarity ends. They do not adopt long cycles of shifting, which would allow the first-cleared land to revert to secondary growth, nor do they diversify their crops, which consequently are stricken often by disease.

Everywhere in Amazonia, cattle ranching dominates the newly cleared landscape, even in government-initiated and backed schemes to promote small holders and perennial crops, as in Rondônia. In time, however, even cropland becomes pasture for a variety of economic, social, and institutional reasons, of which beef production is a very low priority. The cost of fertilizer is such that ranchers do not improve pastures but extend them (Fearnside 1985; Furley and Leite 1986).

Outside Brazilian national territory, but still within the rainforest, is the Marginal Forest Highway, which stretches from Caracas in Venezuela in the north to Santa Cruz in Bolivia in the south, via Colombia, Ecuador, and Peru. This highway has been constructed piecemeal over decades, but is now more or less complete. Together with its feeder roads, its existence has encouraged (1) massive migration from the poverty-stricken areas of the Andean region, and (2) the clearing of 45,000 km^2 of low forest by 1974 and 72,000 km^2 by 1987 (chap. 29). The population of the Peruvian Amazonian provinces alone has risen from about 400,000 in 1940 to 2.2 million in 1985 (Bromley 1972; Crist and Nissly 1973; Eidt 1962; Hegen 1966; Hiraoka and Yamamoto 1980; Kirby 1978, Stewart 1968).

But how much of the Amazonian forest has disappeared? Lovejoy (1985) concludes that official estimates, derived from satellite imagery, of only 77,000 km^2 (1.55%) cleared of the legal Amazon (which totals 4.9×10^6 km^2) are probably underestimated by at least a half. Fearnside suggests that clearing shows exponential tendencies that lead in a short time to an explosive expansion of clearing. Certainly the case of the recent paving of Highway BR-364 in Rondônia (area 244,000 km^2) seems to have unleashed an amazing attack on the forest. From less than 10,000 indigenous Indians and few rubber-gatherers in 1960, the population has risen to over 500,000 in 1984 as migrants flow in from the south. Logging companies follow in their wake (World Bank 1981a). Using satellite evidence, various teams of workers have concluded that the amount of land converted from forest to nonforest has risen from 1,217 km^2 to 4,185 km^2 between 1975 and 1978 (Fearnside 1982) to 7,600 km^2 in 1980 (Fearnside 1984) to 11,400 km^2 in 1982 (Tucker, Holben, and Goff 1984; Woodwell et al. 1986), to 27,658 km^2 in 1987, and perhaps as much as 86,000 km^2 are being disturbed to some degree (Malingreau and Tucker 1987). Destruction in the neighboring states of Acre and Mato Grosso reached 5,300 km^2 and 56,500 km^2, respectively, by 1987, and looks to be going along the same path of wholesale conversion as Rondônia. Such increases are tending toward the exponential, as Fearnside feared (Fearnside 1982), and suggest that with conversion running at a rate of perhaps as much as 20,000 km^2/yr (Leopoldo and Salati 1987), we will see the demise of one of the last great

forests on earth by the early years of the next century (Goodland and Irwin 1975).

Clearing for Products of the Forest

Clearing to create land in order to grow more food is an obvious drain on the forest. But it is not the only one. About

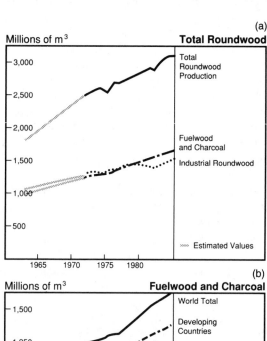

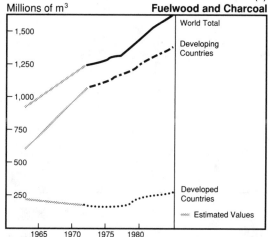

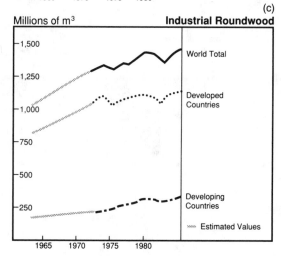

Figure 11.4 (a) Total roundwood production, 1963–1985. (b) Fuelwood and charcoal production, 1963–1985. (c) Industrial roundwood production, 1963–1985. *Source:* FAO 1986.

$3.2 \times 10^9 \, m^3$ of roundwood was harvested from the forests in 1985, a massive increase from the $1.8 \times 10^9 \, m^3$ harvested just over 20 years before (Fig. 11.4). The quantity of industrial roundwood and of fuel and charcoal produced was roughly equal for most of this period (Figs. 11.4b and 11.4c), but after 1980, fuelwood represented an ever-increasing proportion. At present, 53% of all wood harvested is used to generate energy (FAO 1986) primarily for cooking and keeping warm in the countries of the developing world.

Fuelwood   On average, $0.45 \, m^3$ of wood are consumed per person per annum in the developing world, and more than 90% of *total* energy requirements are supplied by wood in some countries. It is estimated that some 2 billion people rely on wood to make their food palatable and to provide basic comfort, and if fuelwood is not available, they turn to valuable crop and animal wastes because their low incomes do not allow the purchase of alternative fuels such as kerosene. Demand will not slacken, but will increase in line with the expected increase in population. Already it has risen from $634 \times 10^6 \, m^3$ in 1940 to $1,274 \times 10^6 \, m^3$ and $1,663 \times 10^6 \, m^3$ in 1985 (Arnold and Jogma 1978; Cecelski, Dunkerley, and Ramsey 1979; Earl 1975; FAO 1983; 1986).

The dearth of fuelwood supplies is widespread (see Fig. 11.5). Countries with chronic shortages include, for example, Andean Peru, Bolivia, Chile, Haiti (Lewis and Coffey 1985), upland Turkey, most of India, Afghanistan, Pakistan, Bangladesh, and particularly Nepal. But the sub-saharan part of the African continent has received the most attention because of its high dependency on wood for total energy requirements (90% compared to 42% for Asia, and 30% for Latin America) (Dunkerly and Ramsey 1983) and because of the intricate and tragic relationship of fuelwood cutting, deforestation, desertification, declining fertility on dung-

starved fields, and famine. Average annual fuelwood consumption in Africa is estimated conservatively to be about $0.6 \, m^3$ in urban households and about $0.8 \, m^3$ in rural households. So essential is fuelwood that it consumes 20% to 40% of cash income of urban households and costs more than the food that is being cooked.

Nearly everywhere in western and sub-saharan Africa, fuelwood consumption is outstripping the mean annual increase in the stock of trees by between 30% and 200% (Table 11-8) (Anderson and Fishwick 1984; Club du Sahel 1978). For example, Niger consumed $4.1 \times 10^6 \, m^3$ of fuelwood in 1980, but the tree stock increment was only $1.4 \times 10^6 \, m^3$, leaving a deficit of $2.7 \times 10^6 \, m^3$, and this does not include other uses such as construction timber and fencing. With a population growing currently at 2.77% from a base of 5.6 million in 1981, Niger will have 8.8 million people in the year 2000, and consequently, a proportionately greater demand on its dwindling wood resources (Thomson 1983). Gross figures can be mis-

Table 11-8 *Africa: fuel consumption compared to net annual growth of tree stocks around 1985 ($\times 100 \, m^3/yr$)*

	Net supply annual	Annual consumption	Difference
Mauritania	97	963	−866
Senegal (1981)	7,200	4,600	+2,600
Niger (1980)	1,400	4,100	−2,700
Sahel (1980)	17,000	22,000	−5,000
Northern Nigeria	13,500	23,300	−9,800
Ethiopia (1982)	13,600	34,000	−20,400
Sudan (1980)	44,400	75,800	−31,400

Source: Anderson and Fishwick 1984.

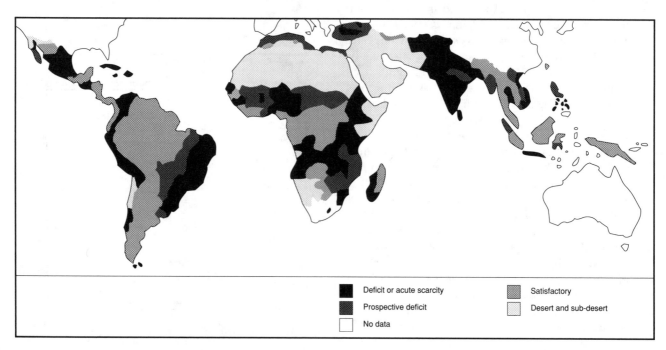

Deficit or acute scarcity
Prospective deficit
No data
Satisfactory
Desert and sub-desert

Figure 11.5 Fuelwood deficits. *Source:* FAO 1983.

leading, as they hide sharp regional contrasts within countries. For example, Kano state in northern Nigeria has an overall consumption that is five times higher than that of supply, which will lead to outright timber depletion within decades, whereas the rest of Nigeria has a surplus.

Localized deficiencies are serious. Wood is scarce around Kinshasha in Zaire, Brazzaville in the Congo Republic (Gibert 1978), and Nairobi in Kenya. There is virtually no wood for between 50 and 100 km around Niamey, the capital of Niger (Delwaulle and Roederer 1973); and around Ouagadougou, the capital of Burkina Faso, the average haul for wood is 54 km. A similar swathe of land cleared of all woody fiber, though of smaller proportions, surrounds all towns and villages (Eckholm 1975; 1976). So scarce is the fuelwood that from 100 to 300 days a year can be spent by women and children in the search and transport of wood – a situation well documented for Nepal (FAO 1983).

In total, it is estimated that perhaps as much as $1{,}408 \times 10^6$ m^3 of wood are burned annually in the developing countries (Fig. 11.4), which could be translated into about 65,000 km^2 of open woodland. In addition, about 300 to 400×10^6 t of animal dung are burned in India alone – enough to depress the grain harvest by 20×10^6 t. Worldwide, 1.5 billion of the 2 billion people dependent on fuelwood for normal household needs are cutting at a greater rate than replacement, and certainly 100 million of these people simply do not have enough wood and have had to change diet, whereas the rest are in a "deficient situation," a figure that could rise to 450 million by the year 2000 (FAO 1983; 1986).

Environmentally, the consequences of depletion are disastrous. In semiarid regions, erosion and declining yields are triggered into complete ecosystem destruction with drought, and land abandonment and famine result. In more humid regions with steep slopes such as the Central American highlands, the Andes, and the Himalayas, watersheds become unprotected and massive erosion and run-off occurs so that the combined effect of excessive water and the silt it carries causes flooding further downstream.

Industrial wood In contrast to the increase in fuelwood production during the past few years, the production of industrial wood products, such as timber, panels, and paper, has risen slowly, from 1.0×10^9 m^3 in 1963, and leveling off after 1973, to about 1.5×10^9 m^3 in 1985 (Fig. 11.4c).

The pattern of world trade is complex, and Table 11-9 is a momentary glimpse of a constantly shifting pattern, as areas of deficit and surplus attempt to satisfy the needs of each other. Nor is the pattern unidirectional. Many importing countries, for example the United States, are also exporters because of the desire to obtain different types of wood for different purposes. Exports are predominantly from the softwood coniferous forests of the temperate and therefore developed world, (for example, Canada, Sweden, Finland, Norway, the USSR, the United States, and West Germany), which account for 60% of world exports. But increasingly, countries such as Malaysia, Indonesia, and Brazil are becoming major exporters. The importers are again in the developed world (for example, all western Europe, Japan, China, and

Table 11-9 *Export and import of forest products, 1985 (million US$)*

Country	Exports	Imports	Net trade
Canada	11,221	980	10,241
Sweden	4,930	557	4,373
Finland	4,604	298	4,306
USSR	2,726	889	1,837
Malaysia	1,703	226	1,477
Indonesia	1,189	208	981
Austria	1,311	620	691
Brazil	801	148	653
Norway	808	432	376
Belgium-Luxembourg	1,091	1,221	−130
Hong Kong	78	539	−461
Denmark	186	885	−721
Netherlands	863	1,872	−1,009
France	1,578	3,014	−1,436
China	440	1,894	−1,454
Italy	720	2,653	−1,933
West Germany	2,885	5,064	−2,179
United Kingdom	704	5,123	−4,419
Japan	771	5,872	−5,101
United States	5,335	10,551	−5,216

Source: FAO (1986). *Yearbook of forest products, 1984–85*

surprisingly, the United States), which altogether account for 76% of the trade by value.

Cutting and exports on the scale just outlined is acceptable if the forests are managed carefully for some sort of sustained yield, but in countries such as Indonesia or Brazil, where no such programs of management exist, the long-term impact on their fragile forest resources can be disastrous.

The Forest Now

Because of the disparate sources and measures, the obvious gaps and uncertainties in the evidence, and the fluctuating rates of change, it is difficult to come to a definitive conclusion about the extent of the forest now. Moreover, forests are not static, but living entities; they regenerate and grow in favorable environments, and degenerate and die in unfavorable conditions. They can be replanted as well as removed, managed as well as neglected, and their productivity hindered or encouraged.

Deforestation and reforestation

At present, the world's forests cover about 40×10^6 km^2, having covered as little as 38.4×10^6 km^2 in 1953 and as much as 41.5×10^6 km^2 in 1976 – a fluctuation of 3.1×10^6 km^2 to be sure, but not the downward trend one might have thought (see Allen and Barnes 1985 for estimates, 1971–1980). At present, forest and woodland stands at 40.9×10^6 km^2, which is still nearly three times the area of land in cultivation (FAO 1986). Surprisingly too, the forests of the developed countries of the temperate world (including China) show a slow but steady net increase due to forest reversion, as marginal land is abandoned and agricultural production is concentrated in more favorable areas and as active replanting programs are instituted. As an example of reversion, we know that 171,000 km² of land reverted to forest in the United States between 1910 and 1959, and possibly another 68,000 km² between 1959 and 1979, although the process has reversed in the past decade. Elsewhere reforestation has been the dominant process. In China, between 10 and 30,000 km² have been planted annually since 1965, increasing the forest area by 130,000 km². A similar picture of massive planting is true of the USSR, where annual reforestation amounted to 45,000 km² in 1980. Other large amounts are recorded for the United States (18,000 km²), Canada (7,200 km²), and for most of the countries of western Europe and Japan (FAO/ECE 1985).

The other side of the picture is the decline of forested areas, most of which is occurring in the developing tropical world. About 56,000 km² per annum is cleared in tropical America, 37,000 km² in tropical Africa, and 20,000 km² in Asia (FAO 1982). Locally, deforestation can be severe, as in Central America, West and Sahelian Africa, and Southeast Asia. In other countries, such as Brazil, the amount of forest cut is enormous, but because of the size of the country, the pressures are not yet so obvious.

The distribution of gains and losses can be seen by looking at Fig. 11.6, which shows the distribution of annual percentage change between 1974 and 1984. Much of the credence we put on the distribution depends on the accuracy of the FAO statistics on which it is based, and they have been open to criticism. Nevertheless, some of the biggest surprises are in those countries in which we have less reason to be suspicious of the statistics and for which exists independent corroborative evidence – for example, the significant increase of 14,000 km² in India (+0.21%) or 19,700 km² in China (+1.71%), and the remarkable decrease of 214,000 km² in Australia (−1.64%) and 254,000 km² in the United States (−1.64%). The case of the United States is instructive, as it highlights the fact that the dynamics of land use are far greater than the usually reported net changes. Although approximately 239,000 km² of farmland reverted to forest between 1910 and 1979, the total forested area between 1940 and 1982 has declined from 2.43 × 10⁶ km² to 2.29 × 10⁶ km² – a difference of 140,000 km² – as new farmland areas have been cleared in response to high agricultural prices and as large tracts of forests have been taken over for urban and industrial uses (U.S. Council for Environmental Quality 1986). The onslaught of humankind on the forests of the world has not abated; it is just vastly more complicated than we thought.

Management

By the early 1960s, it was estimated that 9.7×10^6 km² of the world's forests (23%) were managed in some way or another, particularly with regard to logging practice, replanting, and regeneration, or some form of sustained yield requirement (FAO 1966: 66). By the early 1980s, the situation had changed little in global terms, for although the percentage of managed forest went up in the developed world to 86%, it declined in the developing world.

By far the greatest area of managed forest is in the USSR $(7.9 \times 10^6$ km²$)$, followed by Europe and the United States

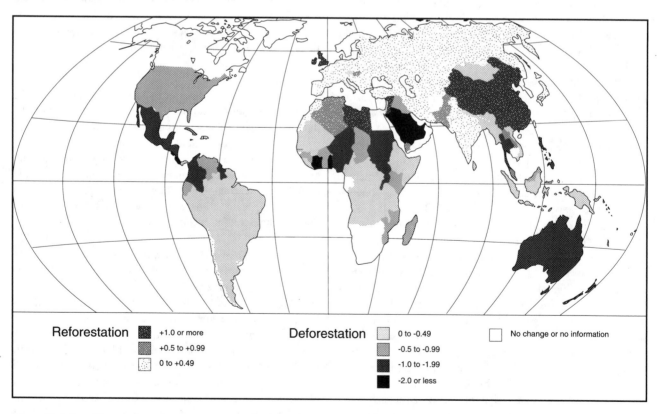

Reforestation
- +1.0 or more
- +0.5 to +0.99
- 0 to +0.49

Deforestation
- 0 to -0.49
- -0.5 to -0.99
- -1.0 to -1.99
- -2.0 or less

No change or no information

Figure 11.6 Annual percentage change in forest and woodland area, 1974–1984. *Source:* FAO 1986.

Table 11-10 *Management of closed forests (× 000 km²)*

Region	Total area of closed forests	Area under management plans			
		1963	(%)	1983	(%)
Developed regions					
USSR	7,916	3,000	(38)	7,916	(100)
United States	1,953	844	(43)	1,024	(52)
Europe	1,455	930	(64)	835	(58)
	11,324	4,774	(42)	9,775	(86)
Developing regions					
Tropical Asia	3,055	374	(12)	398	(13)
Tropical Africa	2,166	106	(5)	17	(0.8)
Tropical Latin America	5,678	15	(−)	0	(−)
Central America	1,109	9	(1)	5	(−)
	12,008	504	(4)	420	(3)
	23,332	5,278	(23)	10,195	(47)

Source: WRI/IIED 1986.

(see Table 11-10). In the developing world, the management picture is dismal, with barely 1% of Africa's forests, 13% of Asia's, and none of Latin America's being managed. Only in Ghana, Uganda, Sudan, and Kenya in Africa; Burma, Malaysia, Bangladesh, Pakistan, and India in Asia; and Nicaragua, Cuba, and Trinidad and Tobago in Central America are any significant areas managed. Many plans for management in the future have been drafted, but few are implemented. The economic necessity of providing exports for hard currencies and of allowing land settlement for expanding populations, and the belief in the age-old idea that any form of land use other than forest is more productive, as well as a basic lack of silvicultural knowledge – all mitigate against the careful husbanding of the forest resource. Needless to say, in developing countries the protection of the forest for the preservation of wildlife, biota, or for watershed management, is rarely attempted.

Productivity

The productivity of the world's forests is as much a function of management as it is of areal extent and the growth potential of specific bioclimes. Nevertheless, management is more complex than logging practice alone. A host of issues must be considered, such as fire, disease, pollution, and purposeful management action, such as tree improvement and breeding.

Fire prevention was probably the first and most obvious way of maintaining productivity, and consequently, more effort went into this aspect of forestry at an early stage than anything else, particularly in the temperate forests of the Northern Hemisphere. Biological diseases, such as insect infestation, fungi, and other disease organisms, always have been present in the forests, and the experience of Dutch elm disease in Europe and North America between 1960 and 1980, chestnut blight in the United States in the early twentieth

century, and the devastation of the red spruce forests of North America between 1870 and 1880 are too well known to be ignored. But these sporadic biotic and associated climatic disasters of the past now pale into insignificance against the actual and potential damage from airborne chemical pollution (Earthscan 1985). The evidence is now incontrovertible that ozone, acid rain, and possibly heavy metals and other pollutants from automobiles and industrial processes are producing forest death, or *Waldsterben*, in over a dozen species of broadleaf and particularly coniferous trees (Schütt and Cowling 1985). Trees become stunted and mortality is accelerated. The problem is particularly acute in central and eastern Europe and at high elevations in the eastern United States. In West Germany the march of *Waldsterben* has been mapped and logged carefully; it rose from 5,620 km² in 1982 to 25,400 km² in 1983 to 36,980 km² in 1984, from 8% to 50% of all forests in that country. It is estimated that about 70,000 km² are affected in West Germany, Czechoslovakia, Poland, Yugoslavia, East Germany, Switzerland, and western USSR (Earthscan 1985). In the San Bernardino Mountains of California, Ponderosa and Jeffrey pine are being damaged or killed, as are loblolly and shortleaf and pitch pine in the piedmont states such as Alabama, Georgia, and the Carolinas.

The causes are imperfectly understood, the pollutants responsible varying from tree to tree in a forest, from place to place on the globe and change over time. The complexity of exact diagnosis, and hence cure, is great. It may be that unless positive steps are taken to curb gaseous emissions into the atmosphere in the future, *Waldsterben* could be as great a threat to the continued existence of the forests of the temperate, developed world as land clearing and fuelwood extraction are to the forests of the tropical developing world.

Finally, in the face of the human-induced changes, applied genetics or tree breeding will become increasingly important in the future. Selection and experimentation have long been resorted to in order to exploit a tree's favorable genetic endowment, but now seed collection and various sorts of improvements, such as root cutting, tissue culture, lopping, and even bioengineering and cell culture to propagate numerous clones from a successful single tree hold the key to more disease- and environmentally resistant trees, and to the extension of their range into other parts of the world – as already has been seen with the extension of various types of eucalyptus.

It is possible that the forests illustrate more clearly than anything else how the flows of the earth, be they migration, trade, or atmospheric circulation, interact with the face of the earth.

References

Adas, M., 1983. Colonization, commercial agriculture, and the destruction of the deltaic rainforests of British Burma in the late nineteenth century. In *Global Deforestation and the Nineteenth-Century World Economy*, ed. R. P. Tucker and J. F. Richards. Durham, NC: Duke University Press.

Albion, R. G. 1926. *Forests and Sea-power*. Cambridge, MA: Harvard University Press.

Allen, J. C., and D. F. Barnes. 1985. The causes of deforestation in developing countries. *Annals, Association of American Geographers* 75: 163–84.

Alvarado, L. A. 1985. *Sedimentation in the Madden Reservoir of the Panama Canal Watershed*. Balboa, Panama: Panama Canal Commission.

Anderson, D., and R. Fishwick. 1984. *Fuelwood Consumption and Deforestation in African Countries*. World Bank Staff Working Paper No. 704. Washington, D.C.: World Bank.

Arnold, J. E. M., and J. Jogma. 1978. Fuelwood and charcoal in developing countries. *Unasylva 29*: 2–9.

Baer, W. 1969. *The Development of the Brazilian Steel Industry*. Nashville, TN: Vanderbilt University Press.

Barbira-Scazzocchio, F., ed. 1980. *Land, People and Planning in Contemporary Amazonia*. Occasional Publication 3. Cambridge, England: Cambridge University Centre for Latin American Studies.

Barney, G. O., ed. 1980. *Global 2000 Report to the President. Entering the Twenty-first Century*. Vol. 2: Technical Report. Report prepared by the Council of Environmental Quality and the Department of State. Washington, D.C.: GPO.

Barney, J. 1978. *The Nature of the Deforestation Problem – Trends and Policy Implications*, 25–34. Proceedings of U.S. Strategy Conference on Tropical Deforestation, June 12–14, 1979. Washington, D.C.: U.S. Department of State and U.S. Agency for International Development.

Barraclough, G., ed. 1978. *The Times Atlas of World History*. London: Times Books.

Barrie, W. D. 1970. *The Growth and Control of World Population*. London: Weidenfeld & Nicholson.

Billington, J. H. 1966. *The Icon and the Axe: An Interpretative History of Russian Culture*. London: Weidenfeld & Nicholson.

Black, J. D., and L. C. Gray. 1925. *Land Settlement and Colonization in the Great Lakes States*. U.S. Department of Agriculture Bulletin No. 1295. Washington, D.C.: GPO.

Bromley, R. J. 1972. Agricultural colonization in the upper Amazon basin. *Tijdschrift voor Economische en Sociale Geografie 63*: 278–94.

Brown, S., and A. E. Lugo. 1980. Preliminary estimate of the storage of organic carbon in tropical forest ecosystems. In *The Role of Tropical Forests in the World Carbon Cycle*, ed. S. Brown, A. E. Lugo, and B. Liegel. Washington, D.C.: Department of Energy.

Castle, E. 1982. Resource adequacy, global development and international relations. Paper to Annual Meeting of American Association for the Advancement of Science, January. Washington, D.C.

Caufield, C. 1985. *In the Rainforest*. London: Heinemann.

Cecelski, E., J. Dunkerley, and W. Ramsey. 1979. *Household Energy and the Poor in the Third World*. Baltimore: Resources for the Future.

Christopher, A. G. 1985. Patterns of British overseas investment in land, 1885–1913. *Transactions, Institute of British Geographers* n.s. 10: 452–67.

Clark, A. H. 1949. *The Invasion of New Zealand by People, Plants and Animals: the South Island*. New Brunswick, NJ: Rutgers University Press.

———. 1956. The impact of exotic invasions on the remaining New World mid-latitude grasslands. In *Man's Role in Changing the Face of the Earth*, ed. W. L. Thomas. Chicago: University of Chicago Press.

Clawson, M. 1981. Entering the 21st century: the Global 2000 report to the President. *Resources 66*: 19–21.

Cleere, H., and D. Crossley. 1985. *The Iron Industry of the Weald*. Leicester: Leicester University Press.

Club du Sahel 1978. Energy in the development strategy of the Sahel situation – perspectives – recommendations. Paris, France: Club du Sahel.

Cole, A. H. 1970. The mystery of fuelwood marketing in the United States. *Business History Review 44*: 339–59.

Cool, J. C. 1980. *Stability and Survival – the Himalayan Challenge*. New York: Ford Foundation.

Corvol, A. 1987. *L'homme aux bois: histoire des relations de l'homme et de la forêt, XVIIᵉ–XXᵉ siecle*. Paris: Fayard.

Crévecoeur, J. H. St. John [1770] 1925. *Sketches of Eighteenth-Century America*, ed. H. Bodkin. New York: Yale University Press.

Crist, R. E., and M. C. Nissly. 1973. East from Andes. *University of Florida Social Sciences Monograph*, No. 50. Gainesville, FL: University of Florida Press.

Crosby, A. W. 1986. *Ecological Imperialism: The Biological Expansion of Europe, 900–1900*. New York: Cambridge University Press.

Curtis, J. T. 1956. The modification of midlatitude grasslands and forests by man. In *Man's Role in Changing the Face of the Earth*, ed. W. L. Thomas. Chicago: University of Chicago Press.

Daniel, J. G., and A. Kulasingam. 1974. Problems arising from large-scale forest clearing for agricultural use – the Malaysian experience. *Malaysian Forester 37*: 152–60.

Darby, H. C. 1951. The clearing of the English woodlands. *Geography 36*: 71–83.

———. 1956. The clearing of woodland in Europe. In *Man's Role in Changing the Face of the Earth*, ed. W. L. Thomas. Chicago: University of Chicago Press.

Davis, L. E., and R. A. Huttenback. 1987. *Mammon and the Pursuit of Empire: The Political Economy of British Imperialism, 1860–1912*. Cambridge: Cambridge University Press.

Davis, R. C., ed. 1983. *Encyclopedia of American Forest and Conservation History*. 2 Vols. New York: Macmillan Publishing Company. (See in particular entries under logging technology and tools, log transport and lumber production).

Day, G. M. 1953. The Indian as an ecological factor in the northeastern forest. *Ecology 34*: 329–46.

Dean, W. 1976. *Rio Claro: A Brazilian Plantation System, 1820–1920*. Stanford, CA: Stanford University Press.

———. 1983. Deforestation in southeastern Brazil. In *Global Deforestation in the Nineteenth-century World Economy*, ed. R. P. Tucker and J. F. Richards. Durham, NC: Duke University Press.

———. 1987. *Firewood in Paulista Industrialization and Urbanization, 1900–1980*. Unpublished manuscript given to Conference of American Environmental History Society/Forest History Society Conference. Duke University, NC, April.

Delwaulle, J. C., and J. Roederer. 1973. Firewood at Niamey. *Bois et Forêts des Tropiques 152*: 55–60.

Denevan, W. M. 1973. Development and the imminent demise of the Amazon rainforest. *Professional Geographer 25*: 130–35.

De Walt, B. R. 1983. The cattle are eating the forest. *Bulletin of the Atomic Scientists 39*: 18–23.

Dickenson, J. 1982. *Brazil*. In *The World's Landscapes series*. London and New York: Longman.

Dinsdale, E. 1965. Spatial patterns and technical change: the lumber industry in northern New York. *Economic Geography 41*: 252–74.

Dobyns, H. F. 1966. Estimating aboriginal America population: an appraisal of techniques with a new hemispheric estimate. *Current Anthropology 7*: 395–416.

Dunkerley, J., and W. Ramsey. 1983. *Analysis of Energy Prospects and Problems of Developing Countries*. Washington, D.C.: Resources for the Future.

Durand, J. D. 1967. The modern expansion of world population. *Proceedings, American Philosophical Society 111*: 133–93.

———. 1977. Historical estimates of world population: an evaluation. *Population and Development Review 3*: 253–96.

Earl, D. E. 1975. *Forest Energy and Economic Development*. Oxford: Clarendon Press.

Earthscan 1985. *Earthscan Press Briefing*. Doc. No. 41. London: Earthscan.

Eckholm, E. 1975. *The Other Energy Crisis: Firewood*. Paper No. 1. Washington, D.C.: Worldwatch Institute.

———. 1976. *Losing Ground: Environmental Stress and World Food Prospects*. Worldwatch Institute, with the support and cooperation of the United Nations Environment Program. New

York: W. W. Norton & Company.

———. 1982. *Down to Earth: Environment and Human Needs*. New York: W. W. Norton & Company for the International Institute for Environment and Development.

Eden, M. J. 1978. Ecology and land development: the case of Amazonian rainforest. *Transactions, Institute of British Geographers* n.s. 3: 444–63.

Eidt, R. C. 1962. Pioneer settlement in eastern Peru. *Annals of Association of American Geographers* 52: 255–78.

Evelyn, J. 1664. *Sylva: or a Discourse on Forest Trees and the Propagation of Timber in His Majesty's Dominions, As Directed at the Royal Society. 15th October, 1662*. London.

FAO 1966. Wood: world trends and prospects. *Unasylva 20*: 60–92.

———. 1980. *Production Yearbook, 1979*. Vol. 33. Rome: FAO.

———. 1982. *Tropical Forest Resources*. Forestry Paper No. 30. Rome: FAO.

———. 1983. *Wood for Energy*. Forest Topics Report No. 1. Rome: FAO.

———. 1986. *Yearbook of Forest Products, 1974–1985*. Rome: FAO.

———. 1986. *Production Yearbook, 1985*. Vol. 39. Rome: FAO.

FAO and Economic Commission for Europe (FAO/ECE) 1985. *Forest Resources, 1980*. Rome: FAO/ECE.

FAO and United Nations Environmental Program (FAO/UNEP) 1982a. Proyecto de evaluacion de los recursos forestales tropicales – (en el marco de SIMUVIMA) – los recursos forestales de la America tropical. Primera parte: Sintesis regional. Prepared by J. P. Lanly. Rome: FAO.

FAO and United Nations Environmental Program 1982b. Tropical forest resources assessment project – (in the framework of GEMS) – forest resources of tropical Africa. Part I: Regional synthesis. Prepared by J. P. Lanly and Y. S. Rao. Rome: FAO.

FAO and United Nations Environmental Program 1982c. Tropical forests resources assessment project – (in the framework of GEMS) – forest resources of tropical Asia. Part I: Regional synthesis. Prepared by J. P. Lanly & Y. S. Rao. Rome: FAO.

Fearnside, P. M. 1979. The development of the Amazon rain forest: priority problems for the formulation of guidelines. *Interciencia 4*: 338–42.

———. 1982. Deforestation in the Brazilian Amazon: how fast is it occurring? *Ambio 7*: 82–88.

———. 1984. A floresta vai acabar? *Ciencia Hoje 2*: 42–52.

———. 1985. *Agriculture in Amazonia*. In *Amazonia*, ed. G. T. Prance and T. E. Lovejoy. Oxford: Pergamon Press.

———. 1986. *Human Carrying Capacity of the Brazilian Rainforest*. New York: Columbia University Press.

daFonseca, G. A. B. 1985. The vanishing Brazilian Atlantic forest. *Biological Conservation 34*: 17–34.

French, R. A. 1963. The making of the Russian landscape. *Advancement of Science 20*: 44–56.

———. 1983. Russians and the forest. In *Studies in Russian Historical Geography*, ed. J. H. Bater and R. A. French. Vol. 1. London: Academic Press.

Furley, P. A. 1980. Development planning in Rondônia based on naturally renewable resource surveys. In *Land, People, and Planning in Contemporary Amazonia*, ed. F. Barbira-Scazzocchio. Occasional Publication No. 3. Cambridge, England: Cambridge University Centre for Latin American Studies.

Furley, P. A., and L. L. Leite. 1986. Land development in the Brazilian Amazon with particular reference to Rondônia and the Ouro Preto Colonization Project. In *Change in the Amazon Basin: the Frontier after a Decade of Colonization*, ed. J. Hemming. Manchester: Manchester University Press.

Galeano, E. H. 1973. *The Open Veins of Latin America: Five Centuries of the Pillage of the Continent*. New York: MRP.

Gates, P. W. 1972. Problems of agricultural history, 1790–1840. *Agricultural History 46*: 33–51.

Gibert, G. 1978. La ravitaillement de Brazzaville en bois de chauffage (the supply of firewood to Brazzaville). *Bois et Forêts des Tro-*

piques 182: 19–36.

Gomez-Pompa, A. C., C. Vasquez-Yanes, and S. Guevara. 1972. The tropical rainforest: a nonrenewable resource. *Science 177* (4051): 762–65.

Goodland, R., and J. Bookman. 1977. Can Amazonia survive its highways? *Ecologist 7*: 376–80.

Goodland, R. J. A., and H. S. Irwin. 1975. *Amazon Jungle: Green Hell to Red Desert?* Amsterdam: Elsevier.

Grainger, A. 1984. Quantifying changes in forest cover in the humid tropics: overcoming current limitations. *Journal of World Forest Resource Management 1*: 3–63.

Grant, J. W. 1932. *The Rice Crops of Burma*. Rangoon: Supd't, Government Printing and Stationery.

Guess, G. 1979. Pasture expansion, forestry and development contradictions: the case of Costa Rica. *Studies in Comparative International Development 14*: 42–55.

Gupta, R. K. 1981. Impact of human influences on the vegetation of the western Himalaya. *Vegetation 37*: 111–18.

Hall, B. 1829. *Forty Etchings from Sketches Made with the Camera Lucida in North America, in 1827 and 1828*. Edinburgh: Cadell & Company.

Harlan, J. R. 1976. The plants and animals that nourish man. *Scientific American 235*, 5 (Sept.): 88–97.

Hegen, E. E. 1966. *Highways in the Upper Amazon Basin: Pioneer Lands in Southern Colombia, Ecuador, and Northern Peru*. Latin American Monographs, 2d ser., No. 2. Gainesville, FL: University of Florida Press.

Heinsdjik, D. R., O. Soares, and H. Haufe. 1960. The future of Brazilian pine forests. *Proceedings, Fifth World Forestry Congress 1*: 669–73.

Hiraoka, M., and S. Yamamoto. 1980. Agricultural development in Upper Amazon of Ecuador. *Geographical Review 52*: 423–45.

Houghton, R. A. 1986. Estimating changes in the carbon content of terrestial ecosystems from historical data. In *The Changing Carbon Cycle: A Global Analysis*, ed. J. R. Trabalk and D. E. Reichle. New York: Springer-Verlag.

Houghton, R. A., R. D. Boone, J. M. Melillo, C. A. Palm, G. M. Woodwell, N. Myers, B. Moore III, and D. L. Skole. 1985. Net flux of carbon dioxide from the tropical forests in 1980. *Nature 316* (6029): 617–20.

International Task Force 1985. *Tropical Forests: a Call for Action*. Report of an international task force convened by the World Resources Institute, The World Bank and the United Nations Development Programme, 3 parts. Washington, D.C.: World Resources Institute.

Jacobs, W. R. 1974. The tip of the iceberg: pre-Columbian Indian demography and some implications for revisionism. *William & Mary Quarterly 31*: 123–33.

Jäger, H. 1951. *Die Entwicklung der Kulturlandschaft im Kreise Hofgeismar*. Gottingen Geographische Abhandlungen, No. 8. Gottingen: Hans Mortensen.

James, P. E. 1932. The coffee lands of southeastern Brazil. *Geographical Review 22*: 225–43.

Kirby, J. M. 1978. Colombian land-use changes and the settlement of the Oriente. *Pacific Viewpoint 19*: 1–25.

Lanly, J. P., and J. Clement. 1979. *Present and Future Forest and Plantation Areas in the Tropics*. Rome: FAO.

Leopoldo, P. R., and E. Salati. 1987. Estimative do desmatamento na Amazonia Brasileira, 1986. Unpublished.

Lewis, L. A., and W. J. Coffey. 1985. The continuing deforestation of Haiti. *Ambio 14*: 158–60.

Lovejoy, T. E. 1985. Amazonia, people and today. In *Amazonia*, ed. G. T. Prance and T. E. Lovejoy. Oxford: Pergamon Press.

Lowden, M. S. 1965. Fire crisis in Brazil. *American Forests 71*: 42–44, 46.

Lower, A. G. M. 1973. *Great Britain's Woodyard, British America and the Timber Trade 1763–1867*. Montreal: McGill-Queens University Press.

Lugo, A. E., and S. Brown. 1982. Conversion of tropical rainforests:

a critique. *InterSciencia 7*: 89–93.

Maack, R. 1953. Devastacao das matas do Paraná e sua Solucao. *Rev. Cons. Nac. Econ. 13*: 22–32.

Malingreau, J. P., and C. J. Tucker. 1987. The contribution of AVHRR data for measuring and understanding global processes: large-scale deforestation in the Amazon Basin. INGARSS, May 1987. Ann Arbor, MI.

Marsh, G. P. [1864] 1965. *Man and Nature; or, Physical Geography As Modified by Human Action*, reissued, with introduction by D. Lowenthal. Cambridge, MA: Belknap Press of Harvard University Press.

Martin, C. 1973. Fire and forest structures in the aboriginal eastern forest. *The Indian Historian 6*: 38–42.

Matthews, E. 1983. Global vegetation and land use. *Journal of Climate and Applied Meteorology 22*: 474–87.

Maxwell, H. 1910. The use and abuse of the forests by the Virginia Indians. *William & Mary College Quarterly 19*: 73–104.

McNeill, J. R. 1983. The decline and precipitous fall of *Araucaria Angustifolia* in southern Brazil, 1900–1983. Unpublished manuscript given to Conference on World Deforestation. April. Duke University, NC.

Meinig, D. W. A macrogeography of Western imperialism: Some morphologies of moving frontiers of political control. In F. Gale and G. H. Lawton, eds., *Settlement and Encounter: Geographical Studies Presented to Sir Grenfell Price*. Melbourne: Oxford University Press, 1969, 213–40.

Melillo, J. M., R. A. Palm, G. M. Houghton, G. M. Woodwell, and N. Myers. 1985. A comparison of recent estimates of disturbance in tropical forests. *Environmental Conservation 12*: 37–40.

Molofsky, J., C. A. S. Hall, and N. Myers. 1986. *A Comparison of Tropical Forest Surveys*. Washington, D.C.: U.S. Department of Energy.

Monbeig, P. 1952. *Pionniers et planteurs de São Paulo*. Paris: Librairie Armand Colin.

Morain, S. A., and B. Klankamsorn. 1978. Forest mapping and inventory techniques through visual analysis of LANDSAT imagery: examples from Thailand, 417–26. *Proceedings, 12th International Symposium on Remote Sensing of Environment; Manslay.*

Moran, E. F. 1982. Ecological, anthropological and agronomic research in the Amazon basin. *Latin American Studies 17*: 3–41.

———. 1983. Government-directed settlement in the 1970s: an assessment of Transamazon highway colonization. In *The Dilemma of Amazonian Development*, ed. E. F. Moran. Boulder, CO: Westview Press.

Mueller, C. 1980. Frontier-based agricultural expansion: the case of Rondônia. In *Land, People, and Planning in Contemporary Amazonia*, ed. F. Barbira-Scazzocchio. Occasional Publication No. 3. Cambridge, England: Cambridge University Center of Latin American Studies.

Mumford, L. 1931. *Technics and Civilization*. New York: Harcourt Brace & Company.

Myers, N. 1980a. *The Sinking Ark*. Oxford: Pergamon Press.

———. 1980b. *Conversion of Tropical Moist Forests*. Report prepared for the Committee on Research Priorities on Tropical Biology of the Nature Research Council. Washington, D.C.: National Academy of Sciences.

———. 1981. The hamburger connection: how Central America's forests become North America's hamburgers. *Ambio 10*: 3–8.

———. 1982. Response to the Lugo-Brown critique of "Conversion of tropical moist forests." *Interciencia 7*: 358–60.

———. 1983. Tropical moist forest. Overexploitation and underutilization? *Forest Ecology & Management 6*: 59–79.

———. 1984. *The Primary Source: Tropical Forests and Our Future*. New York: W. W. Norton & Company.

———. 1985. Tropical deforestation and species extinction: the latest news. *Futures 17*: 451–63.

———. 1986. Environmental repercussions of deforestation in the Himalayas. *Journal of World Forest Resource Management 2*:

63–72.

Myers, N., and R. Tucker. 1987. Deforestation in Central America: Spanish legacy and North American consumers. *Environmental Review 11*: 55–71.

Nations, J. D., and D. I. Komer, 1982. Indians, immigrants and beef exports: deforestation in Central America. *Cultural Survival Quarterly 6*: 8–12.

———. 1983. Central America's tropical rainforests: positive steps for survival. *Ambio 12* (5): 232–38.

Nicholls, W. 1969. The agricultural frontier in modern Brazilian history. The state of Paraná, 1920–1965. In *Cultural Change in Brazil*. Midwest Association for Latin American Studies. Muncie, Ind.: Ball State University.

Parsons, J. J. 1976. Forest to pasture: development or destruction? *Revista Biologica Tropicale 24*: 121–38.

Place, S. 1985. Export beef production and development contradictions in Costa Rica. *Tijdschrift voor Economische en Sociale Geografie 76*: 288–97.

Pollitt, R. L. 1971. Wooden walls: English seapower and the world's forests. *Forest History 15*: 7–15.

Prance, G. T. ed. 1986. *Tropical Rain Forests and the World Atmosphere*. (AAAS selected symposium 101). Boulder, CO: Westview Press.

Primack, M. 1962. Land clearing under nineteenth-century techniques: some preliminary calculations. *Journal of Economic History 22*: 485–86.

Rector, W. G. 1953. *Log Transportation in the Lake States Lumber Industry, 1840–1918*. Glendale, CA: Arthur H. Clark Company.

Revelle, R. 1984. The effects of population growth on renewable resources. In *Population, Resources, Environment, and Development*. International Conference on Population, 1983. Department of International Economic & Social Affairs. Population Studies 90: 223–40. New York: United Nations.

Reynolds, R. V., and A. H. Pierson. 1942. *Fuelwood Used in the United States, 1630–1930*. USDA Circular No. 641. Washington, D.C.: GPO.

Richards, J. F. 1986. World environmental history and economic development. In *Sustainable Development of the Biosphere*, ed. W. C. Clark and R. E. Munn. Cambridge: Cambridge University Press.

Richards, J. F., J. R. Hagen, and E. S. Haynes. 1985. Changing land use in Bihar, Punjab, and Haryana, 1850–1970. *Modern Asian Studies 19*: 699–732.

Richards, J. F., E. S. Haynes, J. R. Hagen, E. P. Flint, J. Arlinghaus, J. B. Dillon, and A. L. Reber. 1987. Changing land use in Pakistan, Northern India, Bangladesh, Burma, Malaysia, and Brunei, 1880–1980. MS Report to U.S. Department of Energy.

Richards, J. R., and M. B. McAlpin. 1983. Cotton cultivating and land clearing in the Bombay Decca and Kannatak, 1818–1920. In *Global Deforestation and the Nineteenth-Century World Economy*, ed. R. P. Tucker and J. F. Richards. Durham, NC: Duke University Press.

Richards, J. F., J. S. Olson, and R. M. Rotty, 1983. *Development of a Data Base for Carbon Dioxide Release Resulting from Conversion of Land to Agricultural Uses*. Oak Ridge, TN: Institute of Energy Analysis.

Robinson, F. H. 1985. *A Report on the Panama Canal Rainforests*. Balboa, Panama: Panama Canal Commission.

Russell, H. S. 1976. *A Long, Deep Furrow: Three Centuries of Farming in New England*. Hanover, NH and London: University Press of New England.

Russell, J. C. 1985. Late ancient and medieval population. *Transactions, American Philosophical Society*, n.s. 48.

Salati, E., and P. B. Vose, 1984. Amazon Brazil: a system in equilibrium. *Science 225* (4658): 129–37.

Sanchez, P. A., D. E. Bandy, J. H. Villachica, and J. J. Nicholaides. 1982. Amazon basin soils: management for continuous crop production. *Science 216*: 821–27.

Saouma, E. 1978. Keynote address to Eighth World Forestry Congress. October. Jakarta, Indonesia.

Schallenburg, R. H. 1975. Evolution, adaption and survival: the very slow death of the American charcoal iron industry. *Annals of Science 32*: 341–58.

Schlüter, O. 1959. *Atlas Ostliches Mitteleuropa*, plate 10. Belefeld: Velhagen & Klasing.

Schütt, P., and E. Cowling. 1985. Waldsterben – a general decline of forests in Central Europe: symptoms, development, and possible causes. *Plant Disease 69*: 448–58.

Sedjo, R. A., and M. Clawson. 1983. Tropical deforestation: how serious? *Journal of Forestry 81*: 792–94.

———. 1984. Global forests. In *The Resourceful Earth: A Response to Global 2000*, ed. J. L. Simon and H. Kahn. Oxford: Basil Blackwell.

Shane, D. R. 1986. *Hoofprints on the Forest: Cattle Ranching and the Destruction of Latin America's Tropical Forests*. Philadelphia: Institute for the Study of Human Relations.

Simon, J. 1981. *The Ultimate Resource*. Princeton, NJ: Princeton University Press.

Smith, N. J. H. 1981. *Rainfall Corridors: The Transamazon Colonization Scheme*. Berkeley, CA: University of California Press.

Stein, S. J. 1957. *Vassouras: A Brazilian Coffee Country, 1850–1900*. Cambridge, MA: Harvard University Press.

Sternberg, H. O. 1968. Man and environmental change in South America. In *Biogeography and ecology in South America*, ed. E. J. Fittkau, J. Illies, H. Klinge, G. H. Schwabe, and H. Sioli. The Hague: W. Junk.

Stewart, N. R. 1968. Some problems in the development of agricultural colonization in the Andean Oriente. *Professional Geographer 20*: 33–38.

Strachey, J. 1849. *The historie of Travails into Virginia Britannia* (1620). Reprinted in London: Hakylut Society Publication 6.

Tardin, A. T., D. C. L. Lee, R. J. R. Santos, O. R. de Assis, M. P. Barbosa, M. T. Moreira, M. T. Pereira, and C. P. Filho. 1980. *Subprojecto desmatamento Convenio IBDF/CNP-INPE*. Instituto de Pesquisas Espaciais, Sao Jose dos Campos, Brazil.

Thomson, J. T. 1983. Deforestation and desertification in twentieth-century arid Sahelian Africa. Paper given to Conference on "The world economy and world forests in the twentieth century." April. Durham, NC.

Tosi, J. A., and R. F. Voertman. 1964. Some environmental factors in the economic development of the tropics. *Economic Geography 40*: 189–205.

———. 1975. Making the best use of the tropics. *Unasylva 27*: 269–83.

Trewartha, G. T. 1969. *A Geography of Population: World Patterns*. New York: Wiley.

Tucker, R. P. 1982. The forests of the water Himalayas: the legacy of British Colonial Administration. *Journal of Forest History 26* (3): 112–23.

———. 1983. The British Colonial System and the forest of the western Himalayas. In *Global Deforestation and the Nineteenth-Century World Economy*, ed. R. P. Tucker and J. F. Richards, eds. Durham, NC: Duke University Press.

Tucker, C. J. B., B. N. Holben, and T. E. Goff. 1984. Intensive forest clearing in Rondonia, Brazil, as detected by satellite remote sensing. *Remote Sensing Environment 15*: 225–61.

Tucker, C. J., J. R. G. Townshend, T. E. Goff, and B. N. Holben. 1986. Continental and global scale remote sensing of land cover. In *The Changing Carbon Cycle: A Global Analysis*, ed. J. R. Trabalka and D. E. Reichle. New York: Springer-Verlag.

U.S. Council on Environmental Quality. 1980. *Global 2000 Report to the President*. Washington, D.C.: GPO.

———. 1986. *Sixteenth Annual Report*. Washington, D.C.: GPO.

U.S. Department of Agriculture 1873. *Annual Report 1872*. Washington, D.C.: GPO.

U.S. Forest Service 1920. *Timber Depletion, Lumber Prices, Lumber Exports, and Concentration of Ownership* (Capper Report). U.S. Congress, Senate. 66th Congress, 2d Session. Report on Senate Resolution 311. Washington, D.C.: GPO.

U.S. Interagency Taskforce on Tropical Forests 1980. *The World's Tropical Forests: A Policy Strategy and Program for the United States. Report to the President*. Department of State Publication 9117. Washington, D.C.: GPO.

Van Tassel, A. J., and D. W. Bluestone. 1940. *Mechanization in the Lumber Industry: A Study in Technology in Relation to Resources and Employment Opportunity*. National Research Project Report No. M-5. Philadephia: Philadelphia Works Projects Administration.

Wallerstein, I. 1974. *The Modern World System*. New York: Academic Press.

———. 1980. *The Modern World System II*. New York: Academic Press.

Williams, D. L., and L. D. Miller, 1979. *Monitoring Forest Canopy Alteration around the World with Digital Analysis of LANDSAT Imagery*. Greenbelt, MD: NASA.

Williams, M. 1982. The clearing of the United States forests: the pivotal years, 1810–1860. *Journal of Historical Geography 8*: 12–28.

———. 1983. Ohio: microcosm of agricultural clearing in the Midwest. In *Global Deforestation in the Nineteenth-Century World Economy*, ed. R. P. Tucker and J. F. Richards. Durham, NC: Duke University Press.

———. 1989. *Americans and their Forests: A Historical Geography*. New York: Cambridge University Press.

Woodwell, G. M., J. E. Hobbie, R. A. Houghton, J. M. Melillo, B. Moore, B. J. Peterson, and G. R. Shaver. 1983. Global deforestation: contribution to atmospheric carbon dioxide. *Science 222* (4628): 1081–84.

Woodwell, G. M., R. A. Houghton, T. A. Stone, and A. B. Park, 1986. Changes in the area of forests in Rondonia, Amazon basin, measured by satellite imagery. In *The Changing Carbon Cycle: A Global Analysis*, ed. J. R. Trabalka and D. E. Reichle. New York: Springer-Verlag.

World Bank, 1981. *Brazil. Integrated Development of the Northwest Frontier*. Latin America and the Caribbean Office. Washington, D.C.: The World Bank.

———. 1985. *World Development Report, 1984*. New York/London: Oxford University Press.

World Resources Institute and International Institute for Environment and Development (WRI/IIED) 1986. *World Resources 1986*. New York: Basic Books.

12

Soils

BORIS G. ROZANOV   VIKTOR TARGULIAN   D. S. ORLOV

This study attempts an assessment of the global changes in soil wrought by human action over the past 300 years. This task is by no means simple for a number of reasons. Order must be made of the great variability in soils across the earth, and distinctions must be made between natural and anthropogenic soil changes at varying space and time scales – past and current changes, global and local changes – and between reversible and irreversible changes, again at varying scales. Moreover, because of the woeful gaps in the data, both spatial and temporal, and the paucity of work of this kind, a global assessment requires generalization of a high order.

A full analysis can be achieved only through a step-by-step approximation procedure, *bearing in mind the extreme scarcity and unreliability of the existing global and even local quantitative data*. Many of the "data," especially at the global scale, are a product of estimation and not the result of actual measurement. Estimates typically are produced by the application of a "constant" of change to general soil types and groups, and as a result, they can vary greatly with a change in the constant used. At the present stage of our efforts, it is impossible to avoid the controversy that is inherent in providing global estimates and generalizations. Our effort, however, provides an initial, if rudimentary, assessment, and points to the areas in which future research is especially needed, including the development of estimation methods.

Soil As a Subsystem of the Biosphere

Soil is not only a productive layer of the earth's surface; it is a "natural" body with regular structure and specialized features, a subsystem within the ecosystem or geosystem. The soil cover, or pedosphere, is a zone of interaction at the elusive boundary of the biosphere and geosphere. It is not only a simple friable layer and a stock of plant nutrients at the land surface, but also a specific membrane, regularly differentiated in space and depth, that regulates biosphere-geosphere interactions. The pedosphere is a part of the lithosphere, and is also penetrated and saturated with elements of all of the other geospheres: gases, water, solutions, and micro-, meso-, and macrobiota. Both soil as a natural body and the pedosphere as a surface geomembrane are systems with their own

laws of development, evolution, stability, and behavior, which constitute a very complicated set of direct and indirect links with surface processes, both natural and anthropogenic.

Soil Formation

Soil is formed and developed as a structure of dynamic equilibrium with a firm framework in the upper lithosphere as a result of continuous ($n \times 10^2 - n \times 10^5$ yr) atmospheric, hydrospheric, biologic, and geologic processes. In a narrow and precise sense, soil formation is a result of accumulation *in situ*, at specific points, of solid-phase products of the continuous functioning of the biosphere. In a broader sense, soil formation occurs in combination with lithogenesis, as in the case of fluvigenic, eolian, and volcanically transported sediments. Soil may show radical changes from the original attributes of parent rocks, accumulate fertility, and become a component of the environment for living organisms. It is a powerful regulator of further functioning of ecosystems, as well as affecting many flows of matter and energy on the land surface. Thus, soils are simultaneously products of the functioning of the biosphere and the upper lithosphere, and necessary components and regulators of the operation of the entire terrestrial surface system. In light of these considerations, the study of soil change must involve the changes in the solid-phase framework of the soil body, accumulating the products of and changes in the functioning of the soil as a multiple-phase system with a set of current biospheric processes.

Studies of these attributes of soils and the estimates that will result are considered by some soil scientists to be of top priority. The data that have been accumulated in this direction are rather fragmented, controversial, and often unreliable. As a result, it is virtually impossible to undertake such a program in detail at this time, although the general structure for such a program is offered. In addition, we suggest certain trends in soil change under the impress of human action over the past 300 years, recognizing that the overall changes in the pedosphere have also been affected by natural factors. As a rough approximation, we assume that the largest part of the pedosphere is in a state of quasi-equilibrium with the environment; that is, it is either in a state of gradual evolution synchronous with the natural evolution of climate, topography, and biota, or in a state of reversible fluctuations adequate to short- and medium-term fluctuations of climate and other factors.

Soil Functions in the Global System

Our assessment of the global soil changes induced by human action begins with the functions served by soil in the geosystem and particularly in the biosphere. The first and the main function is to support life. During soil formation, minerals essential to organisms are concentrated in the available forms of chemical compounds. Soil provides the primary producers of terrestrial ecosystems with a steady supply of minerals, nutrients, and water. It is a home for plant roots and is inhabited by a multitude of small animals and microorganisms.

The second important soil function is the maintenance of sustainable interaction between the great geological and the small biological turnovers of substances on the earth's surface. It is through the soil that biogeochemical cycles of elements, including the crucial ones of carbon, nitrogen, and oxygen, are performed.

The third function of soil lies in the regulation of the chemical composition of the atmosphere and hydrosphere. Due to its porosity (up to 60% of its volume) and its dense population of soil organisms, soil constantly is exchanging different gases with the lower atmosphere; it absorbs oxygen and evolves carbon dioxide. What is known as "soil respiration" supports, together with the direct photosynthesis and respiration of organisms, the stable composition of near-surface air. Soil also absorbs or evolves such gases as methane, ammonia, hydrogen sulfide, carbohydrates, nitrogen oxides, and various organic gaseous compounds. Because of its physicochemical exchange capacity and its specific hydrophysical features, soil selectively discharges water-soluble chemical compounds or ions into surface and underground water flows, thus affecting the hydrochemical state of the continents and the coastal areas of the oceans.

The fourth soil function is the regulation, along with climatic regulators, of biospheric processes, particularly the density and productivity of organisms on the earth's surface. Soil properties in a given climate limit the activity of particular plant and animal species.

The fifth and final function is the accumulation of active organic matter, or soil humus, and the energy bound to it, at the earth's surface. Organic matter, especially in the warmer and more humid environments, is quickly destroyed and mineralized soon after the death of an organism. A certain part of it is transferred into the soil humus and preserved.

These functions of soil vary greatly under human impacts, which can be either intentional or unintentional, and direct or indirect. Soil functions in the future may be divided between those of soil as a "natural" or physical body and soil as a geomembrane, analogous in some ways to a biomembrane, which regulates interactions between the internal and external earth spheres. While soil science has accumulated a relatively large body of knowledge in regard to the former division, the latter is in its infancy of study and understanding. The very concept of soil as a geomembrane needs definition and development. It would seem useful to include within the concept the capacities to reflect, absorb, or admit selectively and to transform substances and energy flows between the internal and external earth spheres.

Specific to human needs, soil is a vital resource, critical to food production and to forestry and important to settlement in general. These roles are so well known that they need not be reiterated here; more important to this discussion are the impacts upon soil of these and other human uses.

Human Impacts

In the analysis of human or anthropotechnogenic impacts (henceforth referred to as ATIs) and corresponding soil changes, a sequence of types may be identified. Here we identify five types, ranging from the slightest to the strongest impacts.

In the *first type*, human action has changed certain unstable components of the environment, while the basic structure of the whole ecosystem remains unchanged. Regions that display this ATI tend to be the most ecologically hostile to, and typically the most remote from, human settlement, such as the arctic and subarctic tundra, and some mountain forests, swamps, and the like; and they comprise about 39% of the land area of the earth. Certain slight and relatively "harmless" anthropogenic changes in atmospheric and hydrospheric components of these ecosystems have taken place, as have some consequent changes in soil functioning (including the results of pollution and acid rain), but not yet in the soil body.

In the *second type*, human-induced changes have occurred in the biota, while changing the soil only marginally. These ATIs are found in rangelands, pastures, and meadows, comprising about 20% of the global land area. Certain naturallike processes of soil evolution, usually of degradation, can occur following changes in biota, such as soil erosion, dehumification, loss of structure, and compacting. These processes may be combined with the changes characteristic of the first type of ATI. It must be recognized that radical changes in biota can have significant impacts on rangelands and that the impacts of any class of changes vary by broad climatic zones (such as tropical versus midlatitude grasslands).

The *third type* is the most important for humankind. This is the ATIs affecting arable land, comprising about 10% of the global land area and occupying the most productive soils of the pedosphere. In this type, soils are exposed particularly to highly complex and diversified impacts and changes.

The *fourth type* takes place in ecogeosystems that have been severely damaged or destroyed by human activity up to the state of sterility. In such landscapes, the structure of the entire ecosystem and soil body is destroyed, and the principal remaining processes are abiotic or almost abiotic, in some cases resulting in bare rock outcrops, badlands, shifting sands, and desert pavements. The extent of the total global area thus affected in the history of humankind is a highly speculative and controversial matter. Some authors (Dobrovolsky and Urusevskaja 1984; Kovda 1981; Ryabchikov 1972) believe that much of the area of such landscapes, perhaps 7% of the world's land, is of anthropogenic origin. Other scholars would find this figure excessive and claim that relatively little of the land now entirely unusable for productive activity has been rendered so by human action.

The *fifth type*, which occupies about 6% of the earth's land surface, involves landscapes also radically changed, but for productive human uses, such as settlement, roads, and reservoirs. Such withdrawals are necessary, as human populations require land on which to live, but they often have been excessive and irrational.

The last two types of lands affected by anthropogenic processes up to the extent of almost total loss of their original productivity make about 13% of the world's land. This constitutes an area larger than that of the present arable land. Remembering that these estimates are controversial, we suggest that large fractions of the world land surface have been damaged in such major ways as to be basically useless for agriculture (crops and livestock), constituting an area about the size of Africa. The effects of these impacts are illustrated in the following world estimates: (1) about 15 million km^2 of land (nearly 10% of the global land area, and larger than Antarctica) are under permanent cultivation at present; (2) about 20 million km^2 (an area larger than South America) of formerly productive land were irreversibly lost, whether transformed into badlands and deserts or covered with water, buildings, or asphalt pavements in the past 10,000 years of agricultural civilization; (3) about only 10 million km^2 (approximately the area of Europe) of land suitable for agriculture remain as an arable land reserve of human development, being scattered in small patches throughout the continents and occupying more or less larger areas in savannas and forests of Africa and South America; and (4) today's annual irreversible loss of productive land amounts to 60 to 70,000 km^2 (the area of Sierra Leone), a rate 30 to 35 times higher than the average historical losses for the 10,000-year period.

It is necessary to emphasize that all of these ATIs are closely interconnected in space and time, and may be combined with one another in various ways, producing unexpected synergistic and emergent effects. ATIs in reality, moreover, are much more complicated than this rather simplified typology would suggest. In general, it may be said that the nature of the pedosphere itself tends to produce a so-called lump or patchwork pattern, one of extremely high lateral heterogeneity of the soil cover at all levels and scales. This natural diversity has been significantly overlain for more than 10,000 years, and with particular intensity for the past 300 with very complex ATIs that change sharply and rapidly in type, strength, and depth over time and space. For the pedosphere as a whole, consequently, it would be virtually impossible to distinguish one principal or leading tendency of change over the past three centuries. *What can be positively stated is that within this period, the total area and quality of productive soils available for human and biotic use has decreased at an accelerating speed.* In all other respects, we see a multitude of varying soil changes produced by the diversity of the pedosphere. Both the natural soil geography and the geography of ATIs must be considered in order to obtain the resulting geography of soil changes.

Method and Classification

The complexity and the heterogeneity of the world's soil cover, coupled with those of the rates, areas, and directions of anthropotechnogenic impacts, make it impossible to distinguish any consistent soil change at a global scale. There is, rather, a multitude of soil changes across the face of the earth. What is needed is a global-scale classification of: (1) natural geosystems and soil systems experiencing ATIs; (2) major ATIs as factors in soil change; and (3) historical sequences of ATIs within the general chronology of human impact on soils. The next step would be to establish a matrix of these three classifications as a means of systematizing knowledge for spatial and temporal analysis.

As examples, the following combinations of the three-part matrix might be considered:

1. geosystems in which neither structure nor function has been changed substantially by ATIs, the system existing and evolving primarily in its "natural" course.
2. geosystems in which the biotic and all underground layers are preserved in the natural state, but the surface layers, as atmosphere and hydrosphere, are changed or are changing in concentrations of gases or solutions, that is, slight contamination. Usually these changes occur due to brief, relatively simple, and weak or slight ATIs. The functioning of the systems is affected, but without alteration to the structure of the geosystems, including their biota and soils.
3. geosystems in which the above-ground biotic layer has been altered by strong direct or weaker indirect ATIs, such as forest cutting, pastoral use, or chemical change in atmospheric or hydrospheric components, but in which the major underground layers (the soil and the crust of weathering) have been altered only slightly, if at all. Several cases should be distinguished here. The biotic changes may be such that they do not exceed the "thresholds of sensitivity" of the soil and the crust of weathering and do not affect the basic soil-forming processes. For instance, changes may occur in the composition of a forest or a grass-stand without major impacts on biological turnover or the plant-roots layer. In these cases, soils do not reflect the biotic changes and are sustainable on account of a low sensitivity and/or an ability to process a new environmental signal to support the existing structure. In another set of circumstances, the biotic changes are substantial, but are transmitted into the underground layers only gradually and after substantial delay of varying duration. In such cases, a new, naturallike evolution of soils (and probably of crusts of weathering) begins, proceeding in accordance with physical laws under the influence of changes in the above-ground tiers of a system. The lengthier the duration of the impact, the more and deeper are the changes in the most conservative underground tiers of a geosystem – the soil and the weathering interface.
4. geosystems in which the deeper layers also experience direct ATIs. Here distinctions must be drawn regarding the strength, nature, depth, and rate of the impacts.

Various types of erosional-denudational ATIs, operating

through different naturelike mechanisms (aeolic, fluvic, cryosolifluctional, landsliding) are of particular importance within the last type of geosystem. Whereas in some classes of ATIs, certain transformations occur in the underground tier with preservation of the main substance of the tier, soil erosion leads to the partial or complete physical destruction of the structure and substance of the underground tier. The loss of the fine soil is irreversible and irretrievable on the human time scale. For this reason, it is important to assess the losses of fine soil components and the changes in the structure of the soil and crust. Two criteria in assessing erosion must be considered. The first is an estimation of the total amount of fine soils already lost and being lost annually in relation to its total reserve in a geosystem. Special attention needs to be given to the proportions of elements potentially useful for biota, and nonuseful because of such physical and chemical features such as hardness, nonpermeability, salinity, and toxicity. The second is an estimation of the work accomplished by erosion in changing the horizontal structure of the underground tier.

It is possible to construct a sequence of geosystems changed by erosion of underground tiers on the basis of the second criterion, depending on the horizon that has been lost or brought to the surface into contract with biotic and other aboveground tiers. Erosion may proceed within the bio-accumulative horizons, and middle or lower parts of the same have been brought to the surface; eluvial horizons are at the surface; subsoil middle or lower horizons are at the surface (clay-illuvial, alfehumus-illuvial, metamorphic, saline, alkaline, compacted, and so on); the whole soil is removed and various horizons of the crust of weathering or different layers of the underlying loose or hard rocks are at the surface. In all of these cases, which are usually designated as ones of slightly to strongly eroded soils, substantially new natural-anthropogenic bodies or underground tiers of geosystems appear whose properties are determined by combinations of the inherited horizon or horizons of the original soil or crust of weathering with young, usually weakly advanced soil formation or weathering. Depending on the horizon of the natural underground tier on which this new process develops, it may diverge to different degrees from the "pure" model of soil formation and weathering on the original parent rock. A complicated mosaic of soil cover occurs in these conditions, even in stable environments, generated by varying depths and rates of anthropotechnogenic erosion processes.

In order to forecast the consequences of ATIs, it is important to assess the total stock and the stratigraphy of the fine soil in the underground tier of geosystems. A number of classes may be distinguished:

1. shallow (up to 1 m), stony, fine soil thicknesses, underlain by rocks. These are either young Holocenic soils, duricrusts, or very old and strongly eroded soils. Exposed to human activity, they may disappear quickly from the surface, leaving behind rock outcrops in any climate within the human time scale. This ecological catastrophe occurs because the rate of weathering at these surfaces is so low that natural soil formation is extremely slow. The regime of exogenic processes often changes radically at these surfaces after the elimination of fine soil cover. Instead of producing fine materials, these surfaces generate stony material that moves rapidly along the slope. The reproduction of soil on such rocky surfaces is possible only if the fine soil is "imported" from elsewhere and deposited in conjunction with slope terracing.

2. thick (up to 5–10 m) cover of loose and homogeneous sediments with well-developed soils. Loesses and deep sands are the examples of this kind. In this case, even complete soil erosion does not lead to catastrophe, although the loss of soil humus, structure, and stock of nutrients is serious. Even if the friable underlying layers are exposed, however, soil rehabilitation is possible in principle, even within centuries or decades while cultivating. Agricultural management can increase sharply the rate of rehabilitation of productive soil cover on such materials.

3. thicknesses of friable sedimentary rocks, fully developed profiles of soil and crusts of weathering, which are sharply stratified into different layers and horizons, varying in their usefulness for the biota. In this case, erosion and denudation may play different positive or negative roles, depending on the circumstances. Examples are cases in which:

(a) the sedimentary thickness contains a "comforting" upper horizon, within which the soil is developed, underlain by one that is toxic or unfavorable for the biota (e.g., too compact, structureless, gleyic, or saline). Erosion brings to the surface this "discomforting" layer, in which soil formation is possible, but follows a different process and produces much less productive soil.

(b) the soil profile consists of contrasting horizons, with upper-structured, organic-rich, porous ones over compacted ones of clay-illuvial, gleyic, cemented, weakly permeable, rich in free aluminum or soluble salts, silica-iron-calcaire-gypsum pans. Soil erosion eliminates the upper comforting horizons and brings the discomforting ones to the surface. This creates many problems for their cultivation and requires the application of extensive technology.

(c) the upper soil horizons are represented by the most-weathered heavy clay, which is impoverished with total and available bases and does not contain a reserve of weatherable minerals, whereas the lower horizons of soil may be rich in mineral resources, including calcium, magnesium potassium, and phosphorus. Erosion exposes these richer and usually more favorable layers. This is sometimes the case in the humid tropics. On the whole, erosion in such cases may improve the potential fertility of the substratum and does not represent an ecological catastrophe, as long as it is contained within the fine soil horizons of the crust and is not permitted to reach deeper rocky layers, initiating gully erosion and leading to the formation of badlands.

These examples provide a general outline of a sequence of

geosystem changes by different tiers. In the analysis of general soil change, this sequence should be overlain by those of the types of ATIs, which would be differentiated on the bases of their substance, intensity of impact, duration, and depth of action, as well as by the sequence of types of natural geosystems and the corresponding soil sequence. Then the three-dimensional matrix can be constructed: natural background, character of the impact, character of change. This matrix subsequently should be expanded to include the fourth dimension of historical evolution of ATIs, specifying the duration and sequence of the impacts.

In considering single ATIs or those that are repeated regularly in time without changes in substance, depth, or strength, the distinction between reversible and irreversible changes is a useful one. Reversible changes occur when, following the impact, physical processes are able to return the system to its original state within a time frame acceptable for human activity. Irreversible changes take place when the rehabilitation structure and functioning of the system is at best only partial. Two outcomes are possible in the case of irreversible change. The physical processes may take a different direction, as in desertification after forest destruction in the forest-steppe zone; or the restoration processes may be so slow that rehabilitation is impossible or impractical on a human time scale, although possible in terms of soil-geological time.

In this connection, it is important to know and classify the features of geosystems and soils by the time spans characteristically involved in their formation and rehabilitation, even by so general a division as between the rapidly and slowly formed. It is also important to understand which of the soil features are formed and reproduced in the contemporary natural setting and which are "relict" features inherited from past conditions of soil formation. It is evident that when the latter are destroyed or changed by ATIs, they will disappear forever. If these relict properties are harmful for present-day land use, their disappearance is desirable and manageable, if there are no ecological side-effects. But if they are useful, then their loss is serious because restoration may be impossible. Thus, for the purposes of analysis, all soil properties should be divided into the reproducible and the inherited nonreproducible.

Where soils are affected by multiple ATIs, the history and evolution of human impact requires scrutiny because of the complexities involved. Analysis of this kind first should consider how ATIs have been recorded in soils. Several possible situations exist. ATIs of differing type, strength, depth, and duration may be recorded in the same soil layers, and the changes overlie each other. ATIs may cause the total or partial destruction of the soil profile by erosion, destroying the traces of previous ATIs together with the destroyed horizons, while the new ATIs act upon the newly exposed deeper horizons. Or, ATIs act at the background of the increasing soil thickness, which is induced by different natural or anthropogenic processes as in cases of siltation or alluvial or sand deposition; different by time, ATIs are recorded in different horizons of the growing soil-lithological column.

The second aspect of analysis should address the time sequence of ATIs. More recent ATIs, by their intensity and depth of impact, may surpass earlier ones, erasing their results in the soil body. Or the earlier ATIs may have introduced irreversible changes, such that the later ATIs are unable to erase the impacts of the former, and, indeed, may be predetermined by them to a considerable degree. Cases exist in which soils are exposed to natural processes of rehabilitation, but the legacy of the ATIs steers the direction of development and the pattern of soil formation away from those that would be expected had the ATIs not occurred.

The main difficulty in the use of these methods for the analysis of global soil change lies in the time element, particularly in specifying the changes that have transpired over the history of human civilization (10,000 years), during the era of European colonization, industrial development, and market-oriented agriculture (the past 300 years), or within the demographic explosion, scientific-technical revolution, and postcolonial development of the past half-century. The development of the three-dimensional matrix compared with a cartographic model of land-use history should provide some revealing insights. More accurate assessment of the quantitative characteristics of change will require detailed studies at varying scales in key areas representing a diversified variety of existing geosystems.

Application of the Method

As noted, the proposed comprehensive approach cannot be implemented at a global scale because of the unavailability of the data. At this time, we can attempt to provide only a very general picture of human-induced global soil change as a trial approximation. This picture will necessarily be more qualitative than quantitative in its basis.

There are, of course, well-known examples of the phenomena of soil degradation, including transformation estimates, that have been generated in recent monographs (Brown 1984; Rozanov 1984; Clark and Munn 1986). A large number of familiar examples come to mind: the Dust Bowl of the 1930s in the United States; water erosion in eastern Nigeria, Tanzania, Lesotho, Ethiopia, India, and Nepal; the salinization of irrigated lands in Iran, Iraq, Pakistan, and Egypt; and pasture degradation in the Sahel and Australia. But focusing upon these cases, even using more accurate data and spatial extrapolations, would provide little progress toward the creation of a reliable global picture of the kind sought in this volume. Therefore, we attempt a cursory use of portions of the three-dimensional matrix as described and consider the applicability of this method to several concrete examples. It must be remembered that, to our knowledge, no one has attempted a 300-year global estimation of human-induced soil change.

The global classification of "natural" geosystems can be made, using, for example, the data and method of Rozov and Stroganova (1979) in a somewhat reorganized form. Five great "latitudinal," or radiational, belts are recognized, each with distinctive radiation balances (Table 12-1). Each of these can be further segmented according to coefficients of atmospheric moisture and the character of the topography. Atmospheric moisture coefficient can be taken as that pro-

Table 12-1 *Global radiation belts*

Symbol/Type	Sum of temperatures above 10°C (C°)	Average annual temperature (C°)	Radiation balance (kcal/cm²/yr)
T – tropical	>8,000	>20	>75
ST – subtropical	4,000–8,000	13–20	50–75
SB – subboreal	2,200–4,000	7–13	35–50
B – boreal	1,000–2,200	1–7	22–35
P – polar	<1,000	<0	11–22

posed by Ivanov (1941), which is a ratio between annual precipitation and potential evaporation. Arid (a = coefficient < 0.3), semiarid (s = 0.3–0.6), and semihumid and humid (h > 0.6) sectors are identified here. Topographically, we recognize the main types of relief as plains and lowlands (p) and mountains and high plateaux (m). The global pattern is illustrated by Fig. 12.1, showing the radiation belts and moisture sectors of the world.

Each spatial unit – in this case, global sectors – can be characterized by a specific combination of principal soil and land-use types (Tables 12-2 and 12-3). Presently, soils can be assessed only by sector, although we are working toward more detailed assessments. Land-uses can be distinguished as follows: rain-fed agricultural lands, including plantations (A); irrigated lands (I); pastures and grazing lands (R); forests and woodlands (F); and other lands (directly used or not), including sands, rock outcrops, badlands, water reservoirs, lands under settlement, and roads (O). The varying global estimates of land-use types (Table 12-2) reflect the uncertain nature of statistical information – a problem to be considered in all global surveys.

Table 12-2 *Global areas of principal types of land uses*

Land-use types	Areal estimates (10⁴ km²) by Rozov and Stroganova (1979)	FAO production yearbook 1969–71	1980
A – agriculture (rain-fed) + I – irrigation	1,442	1,413	1,452
R – pasture and grazing	3,057	3,126	3,116
F – forests	4,060	4,209	4,093
O – other*	4,608	4,325	4,412
Total*	13,239	13,073	13,073

* Does not include ice cover and inland waters.

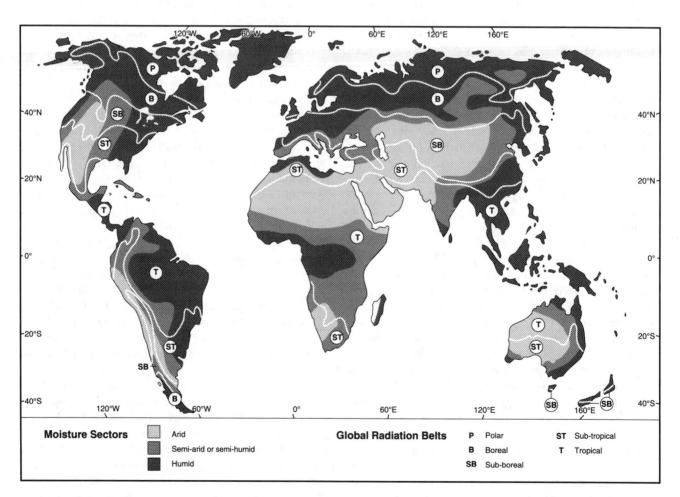

Figure 12.1 Global radiation belts and moisture sectors.

Table 12-3 *Land-uses associated with major environmental/soil regions*

| Environmental regions | Dominant soils* | Area of land-uses (10^4 km^2) | | | | | | Present CLU** |
		A	I	R	F	O	Total	
T		360	62	1,407	1,720	2,080	5,269	0.07
Tp		303	62	1,275	1,508	1,761	4,909	0.07
Tm		57	—	132	212	319	720	0.08
Th	ferralsols, nitrosols,	188	—	440	1,330	630	2,588	0.07
Thp	acrisols, plinthosols	161	—	408	1,160	500	2,229	0.07
Thm		27	—	32	170	130	359	0.08
Ts	vertisols, oxic	162	60	570	390	560	1,742	0.13
Tsp	cambisols, ferric	132	60	480	348	440	1,460	0.13
Tsm	lixisols	30	—	90	42	120	282	0.11
Ta	regosols, arenosols	10	2	397	—	890	1,299	0.01
Tap	leptosols, calcisols	10	2	387	—	821	1,220	0.01
Tam		—	—	10	—	69	79	0.00
ST		320	110	620	570	960	2,580	0.17
STp		216	110	413	326	758	1,823	0.19
STm		104	—	207	244	202	757	0.14
STh	nitosols, lixisols,	130	—	50	340	140	660	0.20
SThp	acrisols, alisols	102	—	40	170	58	370	0.27
SThm		28	—	10	170	82	290	0.11
STs	chromic cambisols,	160	60	270	210	160	860	0.22
STsp	calcaric cambisols,	98	60	150	148	100	556	0.23
STsm	vertisols	62	—	120	62	60	304	0.19
STa	calcisols, arenosols,	30	50	300	20	660	1,060	0.07
STap	regosols	16	50	223	8	600	897	0.07
STam		14	—	77	12	70	163	0.08
SB		412	48	570	300	850	2,180	0.21
SBp		351	48	386	138	530	1,453	0.26
SBm		61	—	184	162	320	727	0.08
SBh	cambisols, luvisols	200	—	60	260	80	600	0.30
SBhp		145	—	37	120	60	362	0.40
SBhm		55	—	23	140	20	238	0.23
SBs	chernozems,	212	38	250	40	250	790	0.31
SBsp	kastanozems, solonetz	206	38	186	18	180	628	0.38
SBsm		6	—	64	22	70	162	0.04
SBa	calcisols, regosols,	—	10	260	—	520	790	0.01
SBap	arenosols, solonchaks	—	10	163	—	290	463	0.02
SBam		—	—	97	—	230	327	0.00
B		130	—	190	1,440	620	2,380	0.05
Bp		123	—	153	979	308	1,563	0.09
Bm		7	—	37	461	312	817	0.01
Bh	podzoluvisols, podzols,	130	—	140	870	400	1,540	0.08
Bhp	histosols	123	—	108	719	215	1,165	0.10
Bhm		7	—	32	151	185	375	0.02
Bs	gelic, cambisols	—	—	50	570	220	840	0.00
Bsp		—	—	45	260	93	398	0.00
Bsm		—	—	5	310	127	442	0.00
P	gelic gleysols, histosols,	—	—	270	30	270	570	0.00
Pp	leptosols	—	—	235	30	201	466	0.00

Table 12-3 (*cont.*)

Environmental regions	Dominant soils*	Area of land-uses (10^4 km^2)						Present CLU**
		A	I	R	F	O	Total	
Pm		—	—	35	—	69	104	0.00
Ice cover		—	—	—	—	1,390	1,390	0.00
Inland water surface		—	—	—	—	200	200	0.00
Total land		1,222	220	3,057	4,060	6,270	14,829	0.10

* FAO soil classification.

** Coefficient of land utilization = ratio between arable land and the total area.

Note: For explanation of codes for environmental regions and land-use types see p. 208.

The combination of these criteria provides the first facet of the three-dimensional matrix (Table 12-3). To obtain the next facet of the matrix, it is necessary to classify ATIs. For a first approximation, the main soil-degradation processes associated with different ATIs are used; subsequently, it should be possible to classify ATIs themselves. The principal soil-degradation processes we consider are wind erosion or deflation; water erosion; soil salinization and alkalinization; waterlogging; physical degradation, including compacting, surface crusting, and siltation; destruction, including excavation and the creation of pavements; and chemical contamination. It is also necessary to take into account the degree of soil degradation, which can be estimated for each process by using common an index from soil science: slight, moderate, and strong. Each grade of the index, of course, has a distinct quantitative range for each of the processes.

Finally, the third facet of the matrix involves the history of ATIs. At this time, we distinguish three time scales connected with the major phases of the development of ATIs in the history of human civilization: the past 10,000 years; the past 300 years; and the past 50 years. The impacts of ATIs on the global soil cover, while not yet calculable with any certainty, can be suggested by the following examples.

Losses Due to Irrigation

Estimates are available for the development of irrigated agriculture (Table 12-4). In 1984, out of 2,200,000 km^2 of irrigated land, 1,550,000–1,600,000 km^2 were in the developing countries (mainly in Asia), about 200,000 km^2 were

Table 12-4 *The growth of global irrigated agriculture*

Date (A.D.)	Area (10^3 km^2)
1800	80
1900	480
1949	920
1959	1,490
1980	2,000
1981	2,130
1984	2,200

Sources: FAO 1984; Szabolcs 1984.

in the USSR, and nearly 250,000 km^2 in the United States. Approximately 50% of the total irrigated land is affected to varying degrees of secondary salinization. Up to 10,000 km^2 of irrigated land are lost annually because of salinization – a loss that is balanced by the reclamation of new lands. This process of loss and compensation has continued throughout the history of irrigation. The losses have not been exactly proportional to the reclamation of new lands, but have increased progressively with the reclamation of lands of lower quality, as in the movement of irrigated agriculture from alluvial floodplains onto higher river terraces.

From 1700 to 1984, the global area of irrigated land increased from 50,000 to 2,200,000 km^2, while at the same time, some 500,000 km^2 were abandoned as a result of secondary salinization. It follows that within the past 300 years, nearly 2,650,000 km^2 have been brought into irrigated agriculture, out of which about 1,600,000 were affected by secondary salinization, including 500,000 affected catastrophically up to the point of destruction. To these soil losses should be added others induced by waterlogging and salinization of nonirrigated lands along the canals and reservoirs; desertification in the lower reaches of rivers caused by water uptake for irrigation in the middle and upper reaches and by saline drainage into the river (e.g., the deltas of the Amudarja, Syrdarja, Colorado, Ganges, and Indus rivers); and inundation, waterlogging, and salinization of land in places of discharge or storage of saline waters (e.g., Sarykamysh Lake). These losses add 500,000 km^2 to the total.

Therefore, we estimate the total soil loss within the past three centuries due to irrigation to be 1,000,000 km^2 of land destroyed, plus 1,100,000 km^2 of land with diminished productivity due to salinization. These losses are concentrated in sectors Tsp, STsp, STap, and SBsp, in which the main irrigated lands of the world are located and which comprise an area about the size of South Australia or Mauritania. We must emphasize, however, the possible error in the data from which these estimates are derived, even for a technology as important as irrigation.

Losses Due to Desertification

The present state of the vulnerable soil cover in the arid regions of the world is a source of serious concern due to the global progress of desertification. We have, unfortunately, no

Table 12-5 *Environmental regions and land uses affected by soil-degradation processes of desertification on arid plains of the world*

Environmental regions	Land uses	Percentage of total area affected by soil-degradation processes									Total (%)
		Wind erosion			Water erosion			Salinization and alkalinization			
		Sl	M	St	Sl	M	St	Sl	M	St	
Tsp	A	10	5	5	10	10	25	—	—	—	65
	I	—	—	—	10	—	—	15	10	5	40
	R	30	10	10	20	15	15	—	—	—	100
Tap	A	40	30	20	10	—	—	—	—	—	100
	I	—	—	—	10	—	—	30	20	20	80
	R	20	30	50	—	—	—	—	—	—	100
STsp	A	15	10	5	15	10	5	—	—	—	60
	I	—	—	—	20	—	—	20	10	10	60
	R	30	15	5	20	15	5	—	—	—	90
STap	A	20	15	10	—	—	5	—	—	—	50
	I	—	—	—	20	—	—	20	10	10	60
	R	55	30	10	—	—	5	—	—	—	100
SBsp	A	15	10	5	15	10	5	—	—	—	60
	I	—	—	—	10	—	—	20	15	5	50
	R	30	20	10	15	10	5	—	—	—	90
SBap	A	20	15	10	—	—	5	—	—	—	50
	I	—	—	—	20	—	—	20	10	10	60
	R	55	30	10	—	—	5	—	—	—	100
Bsp	A	—	—	—	—	—	—	—	—	—	—
	I	—	—	—	—	—	—	—	—	—	—
	R	—	—	—	5	—	—	—	—	—	5

Source: Rozanov 1986.

Note: For explanation of codes for environmental regions see p. 208. Other codes: Sl = slight; M = moderate; St = strong.

reliable data on the state of land resources in the arid regions of any country. Our estimates of the areas affected in some way are derived from figures drawn from analysis of numerous publications (e.g., Dregne 1983; Kovda 1977; Mabbutt 1985; Rapp 1987; Stiles 1987) and spatially extrapolated (Table 12-5). We suggest a +/− 25% error factor for these estimates, but they constitute the best obtainable until land survey results from space-based technology can be acquired and interpreted. Damage by various degrees is estimated to have taken place on 570,000–950,000 km^2 of the earth's land surface.

Losses and Degradation in Areas of Rain-fed Agriculture

For this category, it is possible only to provide a qualitative global picture. It is well known that the main regions of expansion of world agriculture in the past 300 years include the chernozemic steppes, plains, and prairies of eastern Europe (Russia), western Siberia (the past 100 years), Manchuria, North America, Argentina, Australia, and New Zealand. At present, these are the principal wheat- and maize-producing regions of the world. In addition, arid lands were also re-claimed for natural or improved pastures. The typical process of loss for these regions involves the conversion of arable land into the category of "other lands," whether settlement features or badlands, and the cultivation of forest and pasture lands to compensate for the loss. Estimates of the degradation of these soils are available from numerous publications, but they are highly inaccurate at a global scale. It is evident that erosion on much of this land is serious, particularly considering its important role in meeting the food needs of the world.

Losses in the Humusphere

The organic substance of soils is humus, and the "humusphere" tends to associated with the upper, humus-rich horizons of the pedosphere. Its content and its composition and the properties of its components react quickly and adequately to an environmental change, whether natural or anthropogenic. Humus is a complex but well-organized system with certain ratios of components conditioned by biothermodynamic causes. The most general regularity of humus is that the higher the thermodynamic and biochemical resistivity of a substance or group of substances, the greater its share in humus composition. At the same time, the ratio of the groups of different resistivity depends on the level of soil biological activity; the content of most labile and easily decomposed compounds is lower in soils with high biological activity, whereas in soils with decreased biological activity, the share of such substances in humus is higher. This first rule of soil humus state can be formulated in another way: the direction of the humification process is conditioned by selection of the most stable substances, under a given thermodynamical environment, and their compounds with mineral components. The second rule states that the depth of humification, or the extent of transformation of organic substances of plant residues into humus acids, depends on the speed of the humification process, which is proportional to the soil biological activity.

These two rules (others follow) allow us to analyze the changes that have occurred in the humusphere within the past several centuries, and are still occurring, as a result of anthropogenic impacts. The system of humus substances is transformed by the change of the conditions of humus substances into an equilibrium with the new conditions. These relations provide a solution to the problem of explaining changes in soil properties observed for a certain time and place, and make it possible to reconstruct and predict the humus state of soils under known tendencies of agricultural or other anthropogenic impact.

In nature, the transformation of humus proceeds rather slowly, save in the tropics, and marked changes require many decades or centuries, save in extreme situations. Anthropogenic impact induces sharp changes of ecological equilibrium, followed by deep and rapid reconstruction of soil organic profiles. The cultivation of "pristine" lands, at least in the majority of cases, historically was accompanied by a considerable decrease of humus content because of increased mineralization and decreased plant residues. Direct observations indicate that the humus stock may be lowered 30–50% in newly cultivated lands within one to two decades. It has been shown at a number of sites that the humus content in cultivated fields was lower by 20–30% on average than in climax forest or meadow soils. At the same time, it would be erroneous to regard this process of mineralization and loss of organic material as permanent. Numerous experimental data show that the content and composition of soil humus can be maintained indefinitely under the proper agricultural management.

This evidence corresponds fully to the general theory of humification: the stability of factors of humification provides for the stability of humus content, stock, and composition. Consequently, the changes in soil properties are conditioned mainly by overall changes in agricultural technology.

The rate of change in humus content and stock varies substantially, depending on the character of the process. The data in this regard are rather contradictory. Under midlatitude conditions, however, only small fractions of a percent may be accumulated within a year. With the formation of a "mature" soil profile, the rate of humus accumulation gradually decreases, and at the climax stage, the processes of new humus formation come into an equilibrium with the processes of

mineralization. As a result, the maximum level of humus accumulation for a given set of soil-ecological conditions will be reached in tens and hundreds of years. Substantially different rates are characteristic of "pristine" lands brought under cultivation. In these cases, the rate of humus mineralization will be higher by an order than the rate of humus formation, and, as mentioned, the humus stock may come down by 20–35–50% within a few years. These figures are even larger in the humid tropics.

The human-induced changes in soil organic matter are related not only to the content and stock, but also to the qualitative composition of the matter as well, primarily to its group and fractional composition. These changes are not simple; the same agricultural technology often induces contrary effects depending on the situation in which it is applied.

The group composition of soil humus is conveniently characterized by the ratio of humic and fulvic acid content, the Cha : Cfa ratio. This figure, designating the type of humus or the degree of "humateness," usually increases when human impact on the soil is accompanied by growth of the quantity of organic substances introduced, such as plant residues or organic manures, by growth of soil biological activity, by optimization of soil pH and hydrothermical regime, by provision of soil microorganisms with energy and nutrients, and by growth of seasonal and secular length of the humification process. Hence, the changes in the direction of humification will differ, depending on the ecological conditions of humus formation over comparable time scales.

The second important indicator of humus change is the fractional composition or the distribution of humus substances by their forms of bonds with the mineral components. This indicator changes in time and space more simply than the humus group composition. The ratio of different fractions of humic and fulvic acids in both cultivated and uncultivated soils is a function of pH and the mineralization of soil solution and groundwater. In calcareous and gypsic soils, particularly at higher pH, the humic acids saturated with calcium are dominant. The liming of acid soils and gypsum application to alkali soils will have similar effects. Application of acid mineral fertilizers without prior liming will induce a reverse process of loss of calcium humates and their transformation into free acids or heteropolar-complex salts with iron and aluminum cations. Thus, the extent of a change of humus fractional composition depends directly on the intensity and rates of soil liming, gypsum and mineral fertilizer application, and irrigation with fresh or mineralized water.

For a general assessment of changes in humus fractional composition, it is possible to use the ratio between the second fraction of humus substances (sum of humic and fulvic acids saturated with calcium) and their first fraction (sum of humic and fulvic acids, free or bound with free sesquioxides). This indicator reveals even early changes in humus composition under relatively recent ATIs.

All changes in soil humus within recent centuries are ecologically conditioned; the direction and extent of the changes depend on the concrete conditions and the rates and character of the anthropogenic impact. There cannot be a uniform scheme applicable to all regions and systems of agriculture. In

Table 12-6 *Assumptions for estimates of global changes in the humusphere*

Criteria	Previous to major ATIs	Subsequent to major ATIs	
		Cultivated soils ($15 \times 10^6 \, \text{km}^2$)	Anthropogenic badlands ($20 \times 10^6 \, \text{km}^2$)
Average thickness (humus layer)	0.5 m	0.5 m	0.1 m
Average density (humus layer)	1.3 g/cm^3	1.2 g/cm^3	1.4 g/cm^3
Average organic carbon content	2.0%	1.5%	0.25%
Average stock of organic carbon	13,000 t/km^2	12,000 t/km^2	350 t/km^2
Total stock of organic carbon in humusphere	1,700,000 million t (1.7×10^{18} g)	180,000 million t (1.8×10^{17} g)	7,000 million t (7.0×10^{15} g)

Note 1: See Kovda 1970; Grigorieva 1980.
Note 2: Present total stock of organic carbon in humusphere = 1,432,000 million t (1.4×10^{18} g)
Note 3: Organic carbon lost from humusphere from the Neolithic to present = 268,000 million t (2.68×10^{17} g)
— involving anthropogenic badlands = 253,000 million t (2.53×10^{17} g)
— involving existing cultivated lands = 15,000 million t (0.15×10^{17} g)

order to estimate the loss of organic matter as a result of ATIs on the humusphere, it is necessary to derive calculations on the basis of the world soil map in accordance with the general principles already stated. At present, we can construct only a very approximate global picture founded upon several basic assumptions (Table 12-6).

The calculations show that within the history of agricultural civilization, the following quantities of organic carbon were lost from the humusphere of the planet: from the anthropogenic badlands, 253,000 million t; from the existing cultivated land, 15,000 million t; totaling 268,000 million t. Placing these figures into broad time scales used, the losses are estimated as: within the past 10,000 years, 253,000 million t; within the past 300 years, 90,000 million t; within the past 50 years, 38,000 million t.

Therefore, the total losses of organic carbon from the humusphere of the earth, within the history of agricultural civilization, and the accompanying formation of anthropogenic badlands and of contemporary cultivated lands, comprise 268,000 million t, or 15.8% of its original stock. These estimates, again, should be regarded only as approximations that indicate the general trend of the process.

These figures could be interpreted in terms of rates of "dehumification" during the times under consideration. If within the past 10,000 years, the loss of humus occurred at an average rate of 25.3 million t/yr, then within the past 300 years, it accelerated to 300 million t/yr, and within the past 50 years, it became as high as 760 million t/yr. By any time scale, the process appears to have accelerated logarithmically, and this situation should be regarded as ecologically dangerous.

Concluding Remarks

It is understandable that the analysis that has been given of the present state of the world's soil cover and of its changes under the impact of ATIs in various time scales, particularly the past 300 years, represents only a first approximation. This caution noted, we estimate that human activity has altered the fundamental condition of soils throughout the world, albeit with regional variations. The magnitude and spatial scale of the transformation may rival or exceed those associated with deforestation (chap. 11) and atmospheric pollution. Indeed, we estimate that the amount of lands severely damaged or rendered useless for agriculture exceeds the area that is currently cultivated. Other forms of transformation also have been important and are escalating, such as dehumification.

It is curious that so little research of this kind has been undertaken that a standard method of analysis does not exist. For this reason, it has been necessary to propose such a method here. The analysis and estimates that follow from it obviously can be improved through compilation and use of the appropriate soil maps and statistical data by countries and continents. The global picture that will be drawn in the future should be not only more accurate, but, equally important, should also show more detail by types of natural geographic situation, ATIs, and time scales. This will make it more operation-oriented – useful not only for the prognosis of future global or regional soil changes, but also for the management of these changes.

References

Brown, L. R., ed. 1984. *State of the World. 1984: A Worldwatch Institute Report on Progress Toward a Sustainable Society.* New York: W. W. Norton.

Clark, W. C., and R. E. Munn, eds. 1986. *Sustainable Develpment of the Biosphere.* Cambridge: Cambridge University Press.

Dobrovolsky, G. V., and I. S. Urusevskaja. 1984. *Soil Geography.* Moscow: Moscow University Press. (In Russian.)

Dregne, H. 1983. *Desertification of Arid Lands.* Harwood: Chur.

FAO. 1981. *Production Yearbook, 1980.* Rome: Food and Agriculture Organization, United Nations.

———. 1984. *Production Yearbook, 1983.* Rome: Food and Agriculture Organization, United Nations.

Grigorieva, T. V. 1980. Turnover of the main elements of the biosphere. In *Turnover of Substances in Nature and Its Change by Economic Activity of Man*, ed. A. M. Ryabchikov. Moscow: Moscow University Press. (In Russian.)

Ivanov, B. G. 1941. Moisture zones of the earth. *Izvestia Academii*

Nauk SSSR, ser. Geogr. and geophys. 3: 8–26.

Kovda, V. A. 1970. Soil science and the productivity of the biosphere. *Vestnik Academii Nauk SSSR* 6: 8–13. (In Russian.)

———. 1977. *Aridization of Land and Drought Control*. Moscow: Nauka. (In Russian.)

———. 1981. *Soil Cover: Its Improvement, Use, and Protection*. Moscow: Nauka. (In Russian.)

Mabbutt, J. A. 1985. Desertification of the world's rangelands. *Desertification Control Bulletin*, UNEP, Nairobi, 12: 5–11.

Rapp, A. 1987. Desertification. In *Human Activity and Environmental Process*, ed. K. J. Gregory and D. E. Walling, 425–43. London: John Wiley and Sons.

Rozanov, B. G. 1984. *Bases of the Environmental Science*. Moscow: Moscow University Press. (In Russian.)

———. 1986. Land Resources of the Arid Belt of the USSR, Their Rational Use and Conservation. *Problemy Osvoenia Pustyn 5*: 22–28. (In Russian.)

Rosov, N. N., and M. N. Stroganova. 1979. *Soil Cover of the World*. Moscow: Moscow University Press.

Ryabchikov, A. M. 1972. *Structure and Dynamics of the Geosphere, Its Natural Evolution and Change By Man*. Moscow: Moscow University Press. (In Russian.)

Stiles, D. N. 1987. Camel vs. cattle pastoralism: stopping desert spread. *Desertification Control Bulletin*, UNEP, Nairobi, 14: 15–21.

Szabolcs, I. 1984. *Impact of Irrigation on Soil and Water Salinity: Failure Due to Salinization*. Budapest: Research Institute for Soil Science and Agricultural Chemistry.

13

Sediment Transfer and Siltation

IAN DOUGLAS

The dynamics of the earth surface and the lives of all people and organisms depend on flows of energy, water, and materials. These flows are profoundly modified by people to sustain both urban and rural life. The act of gathering food or fuel is a transfer of chemicals and energy. In terms of materials flows, these people-made transfers have to be compared with the geochemical circulations involved in rock weathering, erosion, transportation, and sediment deposition.

Erosion is a natural process which, although often imperceptible, can be quite extreme, even in areas remote from any disturbance by people. High, natural erosion rates occur in wet, mountain environments from the humid tropics to cool, temperate latitudes, particularly where heavy rains fall on weak, poorly consolidated rocks such as the greywackes of the west coast of the South Island of New Zealand and in the mountains of Taiwan and Japan (Aniya 1985). Some of the world's highest estimated erosion rates are for rivers draining young, tectonically active mountain regions in humid tropical and temperate regions (Table 13-1). In such areas, landsliding, often triggered by earthquakes, and stream-bank erosion and channel adjustment leave abundant spreads of debris in valley floors, which are swept downstream by runoff from major storms.

Outside these steep, tectonically active areas, natural erosion rates may be high where easily eroded, dispersable rocks occur. Despite the conventional wisdom that in tropical areas the danger of soil erosion from runoff and rain is negligible wherever dense evergreen forest is present (FAO 1978), in those places where geological conditions provide outcrops of easily erodible material, such as the mudstones and shales of the Chert-Spilite and Kuamut formations of Borneo, landslipping, bank, and channel-bed erosion often supply large quantities of mud, sand, and gravel to rivers in dense tropical forest devoid of any human disturbance. Unfortunately, the absence of permanent monitoring stations in such undisturbed areas makes it difficult to quantify natural erosion rates.

Many estimates of present-day fluvial sediment and solute loads (Table 13-2; Fig. 13.1) include both natural and people-accelerated erosion. Few estimates truly reflect the rates of erosion likely to have operated through geologic time

(Douglas 1967). Many do not include all the erosion caused by human activity, as much eroded sediment is redeposited after a short movement downslope or downwind. In a simplified way, three spatial scales of sediment transfer may be envisaged (Fig. 13.2). Many soil particles are detached and carried downslope only to be held and trapped by a plant, tree, or other obstacle a little further downslope. Such retention on the hillslope leads to the buildup of colluvial deposits. The sediment reaching the valley floor may not be completely removed by the river, but may be redistributed as alluvial floodplain deposits. That sediment carried downstream may be redeposited again on another part of the floodplain or in managed rivers in reservoirs. Much of the sediment now being carried by rivers is derived from the erosion of channel banks in alluvial floodplain material.

The records of fluvial sediment loads are in the form of either the quantity of material carried past a given point on a river or the rate of deposition in a lake, reservoir, or ocean basin. Few river sediment records extend over more than a decade. All such records exhibit considerable variation from year to year (Fig. 13.3) and reveal the role of extreme events such as hurricanes (Table 13-3a). The material carried past a downstream point on a river may have been supplied to the channel upstream some years before and have been stored in the system (Table 13-3b). In many environments, over half the annual sediment load may be carried in only a few days (Table 13-3c), indicating the importance of detailed monitoring if reliable estimates of total fluvial material transfer are to be obtained. Such factors make it difficult to describe the changes in sediment transfer over the past 300 years accurately.

Lake and reservoir sediments offer an alternative, provided that accurate dating can be obtained. The recent growth of lake-catchment studies (Oldfield 1977; Petts and Foster 1985) has provided good data for several areas (Fig. 13.4). The effects of agricultural change, especially continuous cropping, hedgerow removal, subsoil drainage, and higher stocking densities, in accelerating topsoil removal, are well shown in the records of small lakes in the English midlands (Fig. 13.4, records 6 and 7).

Table 13-1 *Estimated erosion rates for mountainous areas*

River	Catchment runoff area (km²)	(mm/y)	Percentage natural vegetation	Suspended sediment yield (t/km²y⁻¹)	Source
New Guinea					
Ok Tedi	420	5,695	95	4,300–7,400	Pickup, Huggins, and Warner 1981
Aure	4,360	2,220	95	10,500	"
Fly at Kiunga	6,300	5,360	95	650–875	"
Asia					
Ching	5,700			7,150	Holeman 1968
Lo	26,000			7,300	"
Kosi	62,000			2,750	"
Amahata, Japan	97			4,900	Aniya 1985
Mt. Usu, Japan	0.21*			340,000	Chinen and Kadomura 1986
New Zealand					
Western Alps, South Island				15,000	Whitehouse 1983
Italy					
Torrente Idice	397			2,400	Ciccacci et al. 1981
Fiume Trebbia	226			1,520	Ciccacci et al. 1981
Taiwan					
Choshui	3,000	2,000		22,000	Milliman and Meade 1983
Kaoping	3,000	3,000		13,000	"
Tsengwen	1,000	2,000		28,000	"

* Rate of erosion of fresh volcanic material in the first few years after eruption.

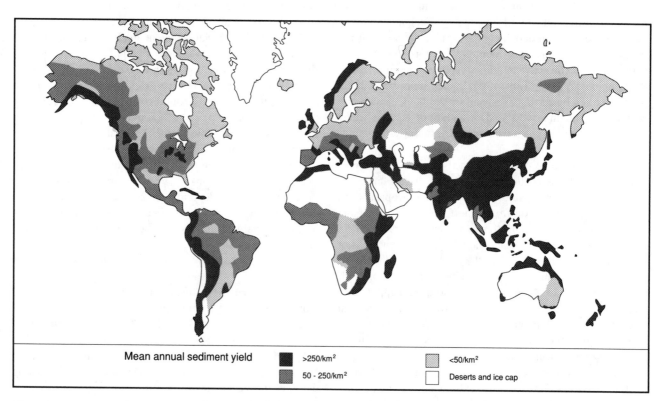

Figure 13.1 A tentative map of global variations in sediment yield.
Source: Walling and Webb 1983.

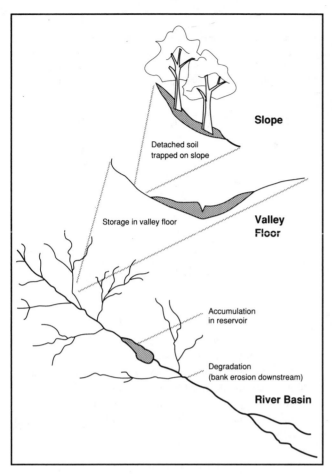

Figure 13.2 Spatial cases of sediment transfer emphasizing localities in which eroded sediment may be detained or trapped within a fluvial system.

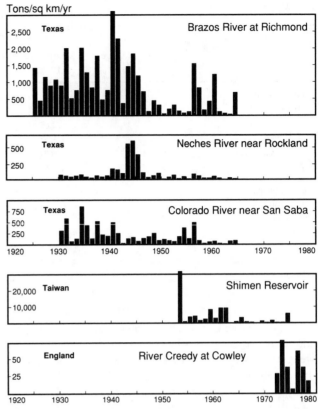

Figure 13.3 Annual fluvial sediment yields for five river systems. *Sources:* (Texas rivers) Adey and Cook 1964; Cook 1967; 1970; Mirabel 1974; (Shimen Reservoir) Shimen Reservoir Commission 1975; Stout, Bentz, and Ingram 1961; (River Creedy) Webb and Walling 1982.

Table 13-2 *Sediment and dissolved loads of major rivers*

River	Mean discharge ($10^3 m^3 s^{-1}$)	Drainage area ($10^3 km^2$)	Mean sediment load (10^6 t/yr)	Mean dissolved load (10^6 t/yr)	% of total load carried in solution
Africa					
Congo	39.2	4,000	43	47	52
Zambezi	7.1	1,340	20	15	43
Niger	6.1	1,125	40	10	20
Orange	2.9	1,000	17	12	41
Nile	2.8	3,000	0	17	100
Asia					
Ganges-Brahmaputra	19.3	1,480	1,670	151	8
Mekong	18.3	795	160	59	27
Yenisei	17.2	2,600	13	73	83
Lena	16.3	2,430	12	85	88
Huang He	1.5	752	1,080	—	—
Indus	6.7	950	100	65	39
Choshui (Taiwan)	0.14	3	66	—	—
Australia & New Guinea					
Murray-Darling	0.7	1,070	30	9	23
Purari	2.44	31	80	—	—
Europe					
Volga	8.4	1,350	26	77	77
Danube	6.4	85	19	60	76
Dnieper	1.6	500	1	11	91

Table 13-2 *(cont.)*

River	Mean discharge ($10^3 m^3 s^{-1}$)	Drainage area ($10^3 km^2$)	Mean sediment load ($10^6 t/yr$)	Mean dissolved load ($10^6 t/yr$)	Percentage of total load carried in solution
North America					
Mississippi	18.4	3,267	210	131	38
St. Lawrence	10.7	125	4	54	93
Mackenzie	9.6	1,800	100	70	41
Columbia	8.0	670	8	35	81
Yukon	6.2	770	60	34	36
South America					
Amazon	175	6,300	900	290	24
Orinoco	30	950	225	50	18
Paraná	18	2,800	112	56	33
Magdalena	7.5	240	220	28	11

Sources: Knighton 1984, Meybeck 1976, Milliman and Meade 1983.

In Australia and the United States, the impact of agricultural expansion is shown by high late-nineteenth- and early-twentieth-century sediment yields, followed by reduced yields after better practices and soil conservation works had been established (Fig. 13.4, records 1, 2, and 3).

Deliberate trapping of sediment for land reclamation and soil conservation not only reduces the amount lost to rivers, but also yields a valuable agricultural resource. In examining the present state of the global sediment budget as affected by human action, the prehistoric and historic phases of acceleration of sediment transfer are considered first, followed next by examination of artificial sedimentation and then by assessment of the human modification of river, wind, and coastal erosion.

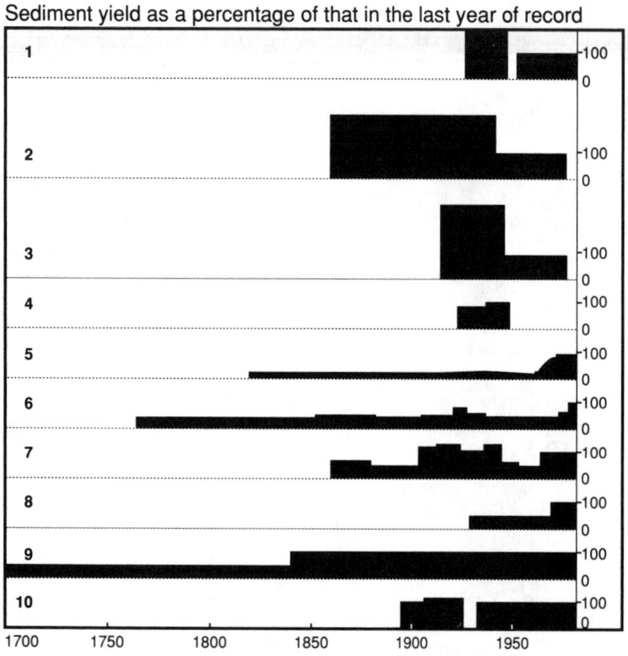

Prehistoric and Preindustrial Transformation of the Landscape and Increased Erosion

The process of modifying river-catchment areas goes back into prehistory, with the use of fire as a local management tool by the original people of most continents. The native tribes of the east coast of North America used fire to create the parklike aspect of the eastern forests described by early European travelers. In California, the chapparal was adapted to fires, caused both by lightning and by Indians who burned off the chapparal to encourage new growth to provide better browse for deer. The extent of the grassland areas of the Great Plains was partly a result of burning the grass either in the course of buffalo hunting or in providing new grass that would be attractive to grazing buffalo (Kidwell 1985). The Australian aborigines used fire to manipulate the extent of the dense rain forests of northeast Queensland, with pollen analysis revealing a people-induced vegetation change to sclerophyll (eucalypt) forest after 10,000 B.P., when no apparent climatic deterioration had occurred (Kershaw 1976). The role of such burning in causing erosion is not clear, but modern studies of the consequences of bush and wildfires suggest that much sediment is washed away by heavy rains before ground cover can be reestablished.

The introduction of agriculture, deforestation, and pastoralism to part of upland western Europe promoted major changes in soil character, particularly an increase in acid, podzol conditions associated with the development of peat bogs. Forest clearance by fire was at least a contributing factor, if not the prime cause, of the development of peat bogs or blanket mires, which coincides with the decline of

Sediment yield as a percentage of that in the last year of record

Figure 13.4 Sediment-yield reconstructions based on lake and reservoir sediment records. *Locations and sources(* (1) Burrinjuck Reservoir, N.S.W., Australia: Wasson et al. 1987; (2) Coon Creek, Wisconsin: Trimble 1976; (3) Piedmont province, Maryland: Costa 1975; (4) Lake Decatur, Illinois: Brown, Stall, and DeTurk 1947; (5) Loch Grammoch, Scotland: Battarbee et al. 1985; (6) Seeswood Pool, England: Dearing and Foster 1987; (7) Merevale catchment, England: Foster et al. 1985; (8) Coombs Brook, England: Stott 1987; (9) Llangorse Lake, Wales: Jones, Benson-Evans, and Chambers 1985; (10) Montepulciano Lake, Italy: Basile and Dragoni 1987.

Table 13-3 *Examples of the irregularity of fluvial sediment transport*

a. *The role of exceptional years in the mean rate of annual sediment discharge of streams draining to the Atlantic coast of the United States*

River	Time period	Mean annual sediment discharge 10^3 t	Percentage of suspended sediment discharged in:		
			1% of time	5% of time	10% of time
Delaware River at Trenton, NJ	(a) 30 years, 1950–1979	680	49	76	85
	(b) as above excluding 1955 (the years of hurricanes Connie and Diane)	631	44	74	84
Juniata River at Newport, PA	(a) 28 years, 1952–1979	255	44	75	85
	(b) as above excluding 1972 (the year of Hurricane Agnes)	229	41	72	83

Source: Meade 1982.

b. *Yearly changes in channel storage of sediment on a Californian coastal river*

		Total load (1,000 million t)					
Water year	Percentage of normal runoff	Carmel at Robles	Tributary input	Bank erosion	Total inputs	Carmel at Carmel	Balance (in channel and storage change)
1980	167	50.7	14	831	896	432	+464
1981	43	1.8	1.4	negl.	3.1	44.7	−416
1982	166	26.5	14	91.2	132	317	−185
1983	413	220	65	699	985	1620	−639
1984	73	37.2	3.3	negl.	40.5	82.1	− 41.6
1985	20	0.48	0.4	negl.	0.84	12.0	− 11.1
1986	120	44.1	7.7	48.1	99.9	298	−198
Total 1980–1986		381	105	1670	2160	2810	−653

Source: Matthews and Kondolf 1987.

c. *Proportion of annual sediment discharge carried in one day on the Waikele Stream at Waipahu, Oahu, Hawaii*

Water year	Total annual load, tons	Maximum daily load, tons	Percentage of annual load carried in one day
1977–78	3,428.89	574	16.7
1978–79	38,211.01	31,800	83.2
1979–80	53,622.52	14,700	27.4
1980–81	3,268.67	498	15.2
1981–82	92,732.27	32,900	35.5
1982–83	5,673.72	1,880	33.1
1983–84	1,445.16	635	43.9

Source: U.S. Geological Survey Water Data Reports HI-78-1, 79-1, 80-1, 81-1, 82-1, 83-1 and 84-1.

elm in the pollen record (5,300–5,100 B.P.) (Moore 1975). The basal layers of marginal peat bogs in the southern Pennines of England contain evidence of the use of fire to clear vegetation, such as sootlike particles, charred plant fragments, and lumps of charcoal (Tallis 1975). These fires not only exposed soil to mechanical erosion, but also may have released readily soluble salts containing nutrients, thereby adding to soil degradation (Dimbleby 1974). During this upland clearance, by Neolithic and Bronze Age peoples approximately 5,300–2,500 B.P., soil disturbance was high, and alluviation occurred in nearby valleys.

Massive ground-cover changes were produced by the spread of agriculture and the intensive use of land by the great agrarian civilizations. It is unclear if the severest episodes of soil erosion coincided with the peak of agricultural activity or with the lack of maintenance of soil conservation works following the breakdown of agricultural systems, for either sociopolitical or climatic and environmental reasons. The siltation behind Roman dams in North Africa suggests that erosion occurred after agricultural development, but two other series of events are equally possible. Sedimentation could have been deliberately encouraged to ensure a deeper soil in a small area in which soil moisture retention would be much greater, or in which gradual pressure on the vegetation of catchment areas (especially in the search for fuelwood) could have led to less protection of the soil, with washing of silt into dams and irrigation systems during heavy storms.

Certainly, the advent of Berber and Arab pastoralists in North Africa led to further depletion of the vegetation cover and the later general alluviation of Mediterranean valleys, when climates became more humid (Judson 1968a; Vita-Finzi 1969). Quantifying rates of erosion during and after the early and classical civilizations of the Near East and Mediterranean is not as easy. Although the possible period of silt accumulation may be known, it is more difficult to tell if the debris was moved in a few large, rare events or if it accumulated steadily over decades and centuries. All that is known now about earth-surface processes and sedimentation suggests that the rare events may be the prime cause. This fact then raises the question: Were the classical agricultural systems under stress when a major event occurred – either through long drought, through social disruption, or through disease of crops or people?

Not all severe erosion in classical times can be explained by an extreme-event theory. Gradual soil-deterioration processes, such as salinization (today important in the Indus and Colorado valleys), were significant in the past. Salt probably played a major role in the deterioration of agriculture in Mesopotamia, and since then has been a cause of loss of ground cover and soil erosion in many arid, semiarid, and Mediterranean countries.

Before A.D. 1000, agricultural expansion led to widespread forest destruction from latitude 60°N to 40°S. Clear signs of widespread human activity after 6,200 years B.P. are detectable from the pollen record in Sumatra (Maloney 1985), with similar evidence from other parts of tropical Asia. In Europe, good climatic conditions at various times since A.D. 1000 seem to have favored the expansion of agriculture into marginal areas. However, both economic difficulties and climatic cooling caused stress at different times, leading to degradation of the marginal lands, especially where wind action affected light, sandy soils in France, Germany, and adjacent countries during the fourteenth and fifteenth centuries and again in the eighteenth century.

Industrialization, Minerals, Materials and Food Transfers over the past 300 Years

Under the small-scale agricultural civilizations, and even under those as great as the Romans, Chinese, and Incas, water control, sediment, and food transfers were essentially local. The large-scale regional and intercontinental movement of raw materials, food, and manufactured goods did not begin really until after the great age of European ocean exploration and the establishment of the colonial trading empires in the seventeenth and eighteenth centuries. It remained small until the steam age of the mid-nineteenth century.

The great acceleration in the transfer of earth-surface materials began with the rapid growth of population from the beginning of the nineteenth century. With the construction of the first industrial canals in the eighteenth century, an age of colossal earthworks started, involving the movement of huge quantities of soil and rock from cuttings to embankments.

Coupled with an immense expansion of quarrying and mining, this new industrial age moved minerals, rocks, and soils on an unprecedented scale.

Urban centers of population over 100,000 grew by 76% from 1800 to 1850, outstripping the 29% increase in world population at the time and necessarily involving great quantities of building supplies and raw materials for trade and industry. Mine waste dumps, clay and gravel pits, quarries and urban rubbish dumps became new landforms around the great industrial cities. At the same time, the trade that fired the growth in markets for the products of cities like Manchester, Lille, Liège, and Pittsburgh led to the degradation of vegetation in distant tropical lands.

At the end of the eighteenth century, large-scale sugar plantations had begun to encroach inland into the rain forests of southeastern Brazil. By 1830, the expansion of coffee plantations had surpassed that of sugar, and was intensified with the ending of slavery in 1880. The general belief that coffee grew well only in virgin soil led to more extensive and sustained forest clearance than was probably necessary. In Asia, the colonial encouragement of export rice economies led to an increase in harvest from 700,000 t/y in 1860 to 4,200,000 t/y in 1914 in the Irrawaddy, Chao Phya, and Mekong deltas (Tucker and Richards 1985). When deltaic land was unavailable, adjacent lowland forest was removed. Similar clearing took place in the Western Ghats in the Bombay hinterland in India, where only designated government forest reserves retained any of the original rain forest.

This beginning of the globally interdependent, deliberate transfer of materials started the hectic phase of transformation of the earth's surface that has since accelerated as the world's urban populations expanded further. By the 1860s, the consequences of these transfers began to pose serious problems in and around major cities. In Manchester, navigation on the River Irwell became more and more difficult because of the shoals of gravel and cinders built up from the waste ashes from domestic and factory fires, which had been thrown into the river for decades. Channel cross-sections drawn up by a Royal Commission on the Pollution of Rivers in 1870 show that half of the river channel had been filled with cinders and that the capacity for floodwaters was greatly reduced. This steady deterioration of British rivers led to the famous 1910 Royal Commission 20/30 standard for sewage effluents to rivers, 20 mg/l BOD and 30 mg/l maximum for suspended sediment.

Deterioration of rivers was accompanied by the atmospheric pollution, long considered essentially a local phenomenon, which reached its peak in the severe Donora, Liège, and London smog episodes of the 1950s. Now it is realized that this smoke and sulfur dioxide pollution led to a massive transcontinental transfer of chemicals, which have affected forests and lakes hundreds of kilometers from pollutant sources. More locally, acid rain is likely to have contributed to the erosion of blanket peats on the moorlands of northwest Europe, especially in the Pennines and the Ardennes.

The machinery produced in the industrial cities in turn had its effect on agriculture. Not only was demand growing for food, but also new methods of broad-acre farming, to grow more at lower cost. By the 1930s, soil erosion had begun to be a major problem in the great wheatlands of North America, Argentina, and Australia. In the United States, the Soil Conservation Service noted an annual loss of 3,600 million t of soil in the 1930s, 2,700 million t of which came from cropland (Troeh, Hobbs, and Donahue 1980). Severe dust storms occurred, such as that of May 12, 1934, in the panhandles of Texas and Oklahoma, southeastern Colorado, and southwestern Kansas, which carried dust 2,500 km to New York City and Washington, D.C. and several hundred kilometers out to sea, shifting an estimated 185 million t of soil.

At the same time, the expanding mining industry began to have severe erosive impacts. Late-nineteenth- and early-twentieth-century tin mining in peninsular Malaysia, for example, led to many instances of valley aggradation, the most severe being that which forced the relocation of the entire town of Kuala Kubu in northern Selangor. Elsewhere mine tailings and smelter fumes denuded vegetation, creating the type of barren, eroded landscape found around Queenstown, Tasmania. Some mining, such as the "gold rushes" of the second half of the nineteenth century, lasted only two or three decades but left continuing soil-erosion and chemical-contamination problems.

Rates of expansion of mineral extraction vary through time. A doubling of world coal production in two decades 1860–1880 (from 200 to 400 million t) was followed by faster increases, up to almost 1,500 million t by 1914. However, world production of over 2,000 million t was not reached until 1960, after which it accelerated to 2,700 million t in 1980. Such expansion is accompanied by shifts on the places of production. Coal production in many early industrial countries has declined, but it has expanded in the southern continents, particularly in South America, Africa, and Australia. Even in old mining areas, such as Britain, the form of coal mining has altered. Open-cut, or strip, mining has become more widespread.

Above all, the continuing growth of the urban population, the expansion of the built-up area of cities, accelerated the volume of flows in the global resource transfer system. Between 1900 and 1950, when the world population grew by 49%, the urban population grew by 254% – with the highest urban growth rates in Asia (a 444% increase) and Africa (a 629% increase). The proportion of the world's people living in cities still is increasing in every continent, but particularly in Asia and Africa (Table 13-4). The urban population of Indonesia, which accounted for 22% of the total in 1980, will make up 40% of the total in the year 2000. Concomitant with urban growth is increased per capita consumption of earth materials. The annual coal consumption in Britain was about 0.5 t per capita in 1700, 1 t per capita in 1800, and 6 t per capita in 1900. Power consumption in the United States rose from just over 3 kW per capita per year in 1900 to about 12 kW in 1980.

This urban expansion requires vast areas of land. About 15,000 km^2 of Indian rural land were consumed by cities between 1955 and 1985, with another 10,000 km^2 expected to be used by the year 2000. The consumption of rock, sand, and gravel to manufacture cement and concrete is enormous. In

Table 13-4 *Actual and estimated percentage of total population in urban areas*

Area	(urban as % of total)			
	1950	1980	2000	2025
Oceania	61.3	71.8	73.1	78.4
North America	63.9	73.8	78.0	85.8
USSR	39.3	63.2	74.3	83.4
Europe	55.9	71.1	79.0	85.9
Latin America	41.1	65.3	76.6	84.2
Africa	14.8	23.7	42.4	58.3
East Asia	17.8	28.0	34.2	51.2
South Asia	16.1	25.4	36.8	55.3

Source: United Nations, Department of Industrial, Economic, and Social Affairs 1985.

1961, world cement production was 383.5 million t but by 1982 it had risen to 892.1 million t – an increase of 267% (Fig. 13.5). But in newly industrializing countries and in the big nations of low latitudes, the expansion of production was far greater (Table 13-5). If most of this cement was used to make concrete, even greater quantities of sand and gravel or of crushed rock must have been involved, creating new depressions in the landscape and removing hills. As Sham Sani (1984) has noted around Kuala Lumpur, rock crushing is a major source of atmospheric particulates that represent an addition to the total transfer of sediment as a direct consequence of urban growth.

These demands for construction material are but part of the picture of the transformation of the earth's surface by removal, transportation, and deposition of materials. The sheer quantities of material involved in excavation, embankment, and landfill operations during civil-engineering works are great; for example, 2.5 million t had been removed for the diversion shipping channel during the construction of the Thames barrier in London. If these volumes are seen as part of a global sediment budget – either natural or people-accelerated – transfers of sediment must be compared with

Table 13-5 *World cement production growth*

Area	1982 production as % of 1961 production	National production as % of world total	
		1961	1982
World	267		
Republic of Korea	3,420	0.1	2.0
China	1,744	2.4	10.5
Taiwan	889	0.5	1.5
Mexico	713	0.8	2.0
Brazil	539	1.4	2.8
Japan	341	7.4	9.4
India	272	2.5	2.5
USSR	244	15.3	13.9
U.K.	90	4.3	1.5

Source: Bureau of Mines Staff 1984.

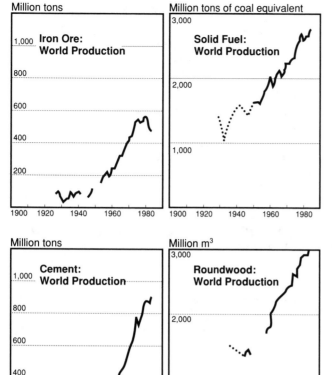

Figure 13.5 Growth in world production of iron ore, solid fuel, cement, and roundwood.

purposeful, artificial extraction and with landfill operations. Lest it be thought that all transfers of sediment and material are potentially deleterious or harmful, it is important to recall that much deposition of material by people is beneficial to human well-being. A large part of the world's population depends on land reclaimed and protected by controlled sedimentation processes for food production.

Artificial Sedimentation

Waste Disposal and Landfill Deposition of waste materials, tipping of mining spoil, disposal of power-station fly-ash, and the reclamation of land from the sea are all people-made forms of sedimentation, which, in many cases, are beneficial in human terms. Some of the building materials for the greater London area come from gravel pits along the Thames Valley in Oxfordshire and others from brick pits in Bedfordshire. The pits are reused as dumping grounds for solid wastes, wheat now being grown on former gravel pits filled with London's rubbish near Didcot, Oxfordshire. Many authorities, such as the Greater Manchester Waste Disposal Authority, have to transfer large volumes of material by rail or road to sites outside their area, Manchester depositing 0.7 million t out of a total of 1.18 million t of waste produced per year in old quarries and pits beyond its own boundaries. Still, 0.42 million t are dumped within the Authority's area,

where much of the Mersey floodplain has been raised by such sanitary landfill, providing flood protection in many areas. Similar policies were adopted in San Bernardino County, California, where waste was used to construct a 430-m levee along the Santa Anna River. The compacted landfill is 76 m wide at the base and 10.7 m high, with 4 : 1 side slopes, and it has been capped with concrete to withstand erosion during floods.

Coastal and estuarine landfill has proceeded for centuries, creating new areas for industry, commerce, and residential development. Great airports, such as La Guardia in New York, Changi in Singapore, and Kai Tak in Hong Kong (Fig.

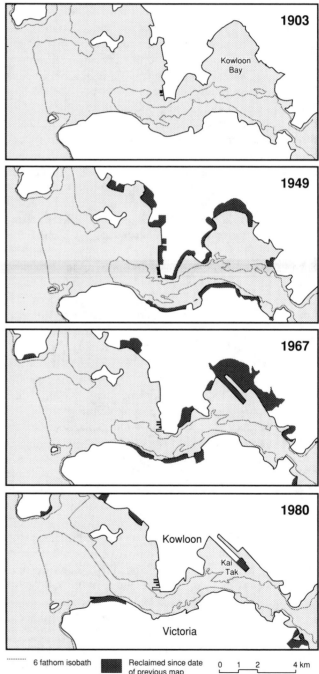

Figure 13.6 Changes in the coastline of Hong Kong harbor due to land reclamation, 1903–1980.

13.6) are built on filled areas, and many ports, such as Southampton in England, Marseille in France, and Singapore have the majority of their installations on reclaimed, filled coastal land. Such sanitary landfill has eliminated many areas of estuarine wetland to create valuable coastal real estate, such as the canal estates of Florida and Queensland.

Although many benefits accrue from such landfill operations, disadvantages also occur. The filling of swamps, estuarine wetlands, or floodplains may adversely affect flood conditions, especially when high river discharges coincide with coastal storm surges. Flood control is essentially a space-allocation problem. If the natural overflow areas, such as back swamps and marshes, are no longer available for flood storage, the space needed to accommodate floodwaters can be obtained only by raising flood heights. This in turn puts occupiers at a greater risk of inundation than before. Many immigrants within Australia and the United States move from temperate cities to subtropical coastal canal estates, only to be surprised at the cyclones and hurricanes that cause domestic flooding around their new homes.

Mining Waste Mineral extraction creates large volumes of spoil, which were traditionally dumped to form mounds on the ground surface, creating such notorious landforms as the "Wigan Alps" of greater Manchester. Since 1950, many countries have reclaimed these spoil heaps, often redesigning the landscape, reorganizing the drainage system, and re-establishing vegetation. In some cases, the spoil can be used for building material manufacture, but often it merely is bulldozed into new forms, as happened with the Wigan Alps, which have been landscaped into a country park. Spoil heaps occupied 131 km² of England in 1974, 43 of them associated

largely with China-clay working in the Southwest (Kivell 1984), but since then much reclamation has occurred, more in the coal mining and industrial areas than in china-clay areas.

Power-Station Fuel Ash By 1979, the annual output of pulverized fuel ash (PFA) from the coalfield power stations of England and Wales was of the order of 10.5 million t (Coughlan 1979), but much of it is used as a consistent load-bearing hill and as a lightweight aggregate. Most of the 4 million t not so used went to 4 km² of disused clay pits at Peterborough and Gale Common, Yorkshire, where a 50-m-high mound has been landscaped as part of the reclamation of an area affected by waterlogging following mining subsidence.

In 1969, the electricity industry in the United States produced over 30 million t of PFA from burning bituminous coal and lignite – only about 20% of it finding any use (Berry and Horton 1974). The annual quantity to be dumped is now probably in excess of 32×10^6 t. The estimated annual ash production by the Liddell power station in New South Wales is 0.9 million t. The newer Bayswater power station is likely to produce 45 million t of ash during its lifetime (Day 1986), some of which can be used to fill open-cast coal workings.

Reclamation of Land from the Sea Although the deposition of urban and industrial waste is a direct, people-made sedimentation process, much sedimentation occurs by deliberate or accidental modification of natural systems. Reclamation of land from the sea is probably the most deliberate modification (Table 13-6). Areas of salt marsh usually are enclosed by banks, which are often built of material dragged from the marsh. The banks not only serve to trap fine sediment within

Table 13-6 *Land reclamation from the sea*

Country	Locality	Area (km²)	Dates	Sources
Europe				
Northwest Europe	Overall figure	5,900	1200–1967	Smith 1967
Netherlands	Total	6,925	1200–2000	
	Zuider Zee	2,250	1930–1975	Knights 1979
	Waddensee	1,600	Since thirteenth century	"
Germany	Ems, Weser, Elbe estuaries and Schleswig-Holstein	120	Since 1900	Cole and Knights 1979
United Kingdom	Wash	310	Since eleventh century	Cole and Knights 1979
	Romney Marsh	200	Since first century	Coates 1985
France	Loire estuary, Brittany	370	Since sixteenth century	Musset 1958
Italy	Maremma	630	Since 1951	Houston 1964
Spain	Guadalquivir delta	1,362	Since 1948	Houston 1964
Asia				
China	Yangtse delta (east Shanghai)	240	721–1936	Cressey 1936
	Chongming Island	266	Since 1949	Ren et al. 1985
America				
United States	Sacramento – San Joaquin delta, California	600	Since mid-nineteenth century	Cole and Knights 1979
	Florida coastal swamps and estuaries	240	Since European settlement	Encyclopaedia Britannica

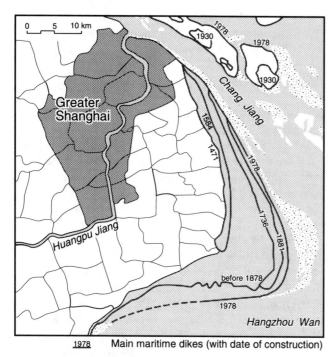

1978   Main maritime dikes (with date of construction)

Figure 13.7 Land reclamation in the Chang Jiang (Yangtse River) estuary. (Early data after Cressey 1936.)

their confines, but also may lead to accelerated accretion on their seaward side, creating more reclaimable land, but possibly also leading to interference with drainage or shipping channels (Kestner 1979).

Construction of sea dikes in the Yangtse delta from A.D. 721 led to the growth of the foreshore east of Yangtse cape 9.5 km out to sea up to 1878 (Cressey 1936). By encouraging artificial sedimentation and by moving large quantities of material to construct dikes, some 240 km² have been reclaimed from the sea between the mouth of the Huang Po River and Hangchow Bay (Fig. 13.7). The famous Fangong embankment, built between A.D. 960 and A.D. 1279 for coastal protection, is now 50 to 60 km from the sea. Chinese reclamation works with nature, encouraging and directing natural sedimentation processes. The 1,083-km² Chongming Island in the Yangtse estuary developed as a shoal in the sixteenth century, but since 1949 some 266 km² have been added to it by land reclamation (Ren et al. 1985).

In prehistoric times, the Dutch or their Flemish forefathers began building mounds known as terpen, on which to place their dwellings. Some 1,500 terpen, 0.01 to 0.1 km² in area, can still be recognized in the Netherlands, with others in Flanders (Smith 1967). When these terpen were linked together by dikes, the possibility of permanently excluding the sea arose. However, the medieval peat diggings in the coastal swamps, as in the Norfolk marshes in England (now occupied by the Broads), and the marshes of the Loire estuary in France, merely served to increase the waterlogged areas. Most of the reclamation of these areas began in the seventeenth century, and since then, 5,090 km² in the Netherlands (IDG 1979) and some 370 km² in Brittany (Musset 1958) have been converted to agricultural land.

Gradual reclamation for urban expansion proceeds even

in difficult environments such as Hong Kong (Fig. 13.6). Dredging of the sea bed for fill material often returns material deposited under past climatic conditions to the land. Care has to be taken that such operations do not lead to coastal erosion elsewhere.

Soil Conservation   Efforts to impede or to draw benefit from sediment transfer processes extend back to the early history of agriculture around the Mediterranean. In the northern Negev desert, where annual rainfall averages 75 mm to 100 mm, sedentary agriculture was made possible by ingenious water-harvesting techniques. Runoff collected from the rocky upper parts of the hillslopes was directed into cultivated fields that occupied the valley floors. Soil erosion on the steep slopes was beneficial to this system because it encouraged rapid runoff into the colluvium of the valley floor and also helped to sustain the supply of sediment and nutrients to the cultivated area (De Ploey and Yair 1985; Yair 1983). Roman agriculture in North Africa, especially Tripolitania and Cyrenaica, was similarly dependent on managing water and trapping sediment in valley floors. Low dams built across valley floors impeded sediment transfer and helped to sustain the high productivity of olives and other crops required by the colonial administration.

Terracing of steep slopes has long been used to reduce erosion and increase crop production on steep slopes in environments from the semiarid to the humid tropical (Sheng 1977). Experiments at the Suide Soil and Water Conservation Experimental Station of the Huang Ho Conservatory Commission suggest that beach terracing can reduce runoff by 90% to 100% (Jiang et al. 1981). By a series of soil-conservation measures including afforestation, check dams, and terracing, 1,480 million t of sediment were retained in the 30,217-km² Wuding Valley in the loess plateau of northern Shaanxi in a 22-year period – equivalent to an annual retention of 2,226 t/km². Deliberate control of sedimentation in this highly erodible area tops 30% to 40% of the annual sediment load of almost 7000 t/km². Such figures, admittedly from one demonstration area, indicate the way in which artificial sedimentation can alter fluvial sediment yields.

Many areas of the United States and Australia had periods of severe soil erosion as forests were converted to agricultural land in the eighteenth and nineteenth centuries (Davis 1975). These relatively high erosion rates were followed by soil-conservation measures and better practices, which led to falls in sediment transfer, as shown in the records for the Burrinjuck Reservoir, Australia; Coon Creek, Wisconsin; and the Maryland Piedmont (Fig. 4, records 1, 2 and 3, respectively). Coon Creek was one of the first demonstration areas for the U.S. Soil Conservation Service, and the record indicates the success of the work undertaken.

Reservoir Sedimentation   Not all artificial sedimentation is beneficial. The trapping of sediment in reservoirs is usually an inevitable, but unwanted, byproduct of water-storage schemes. Almost 2,000 million t of sediment accumulate each year in the reservoirs of the United States (Zachar 1982). If a reservoir is poorly sited in an area of high-sediment yields, its life may be short – restricted to ten years or so. However, many well-planned and well-sited reservoirs will take more than 1,000 years to fill.

In the past 100 years, some 135 weirs and dams were built in New South Wales. Of these, 94 were small-town water-supply reservoirs, 15 of which have sedimentation problems with capacities reduced from 25% to 100% (Morse and Outhet 1986). Overall, sedimentation of town water-supply reservoirs in New South Wales represents a cost of $A3.7 million per year. Sedimentation of reservoirs in the United States costs about U.S. $50 million a year in lost capacity in 1960. Similar problems with town water supplies occur in many areas. Lake Decatur in Illinois (Fig. 13.4, record 4) lost 26.2% of its storage capacity by sedimentation between its completion (in 1922) and 1946. Most of the incoming sediment came from sheet erosion, primarily from corn and soybean fields with slopes of 2% to 15% (Brown, Stall, and Delurk 1947). Generally, the smaller the reservoir, the faster the rate of silting and the shorter its serviceable life.

The larger, irrigation reservoirs of southeastern Australia are filling at a far slower rate, most of the sediment removed in the upper parts of their catchments being trapped within the catchment on footslopes and alluvial fans or in swamps and floodplains (Wasson et al. 1984). In semiarid areas, reservoir sedimentation may be more rapid. In Algeria, some large reservoirs became choked with sediments after 20 years, whereas others had a serviceable lives of 50 years (Zachar 1982). The Shah-Banou Farah reservoir in northern Iran, opened in 1961, lost 2.4% of its capacity annually, and the Imagi Reservoir in Kenya had its storage area reduced by 0.8% each year (Table 13-7). In the wetter area of northern Thailand, the large Bhumipol reservoir initially lost 1.5% of its capacity annually, but the rate subsequently slowed, so that useful life of the reservoir may be 600 years, compared with only another 15 years for the Kisongo Dam in Tanzania. Infilling rates in these tropical areas are four to twenty times those in temperate areas of moderate or low relief in the United States or Britain (Table 13-7). Even in England, moorland reservoirs in Northumberland and Yorkshire receive ten times the sediment yield of the Cropston Reservoir in the Midlands.

Reservoir sedimentation may be reduced, releasing the sediment from reservoirs to increase soil fertility, improve soil properties, and convert barren lands to farmland. In China, some reservoirs are operated to store water when inflow is clear, but to discharge sediment-laden water, especially in the Huang He catchment during the months of July and August (Chang et al. 1977). In this way the rate of sediment accumulation was reduced from 10.75 million t each year from 1959 to 1961, to 2 million t each year from 1962 to 1973.

People-Modified Erosion Processes

River Erosion; Sediment Yield   The magnitude of erosion by rainfall and running water is difficult to express in a meaningful manner. Considerable errors may arise if records are short or if inappropriate estimation procedures are used (Walling 1977; 1979). Most measures express erosion as a volume, or weight, of material removed per unit area, and the measurements from which they are derived may be based on a small experimental plot, a hillslope, or a small catchment at a major river basin. Whatever the area supplying the sediment to a collection point, however, the volume measured represents the *net* result of all the processes that have been going on upstream. The measures do not indicate the sources of the sediment, the total volume of material detached, or the amount deposited between source areas and measurement point. On rivers, the sediment passing a measurement station may not reflect present-day erosion at all, but will be derived from erosion of river banks that may contain material deposited on the valley floor during some past phase of a different climate or during a phase of brutal land clearance, such as the removal of the forests by pioneer European settlers in North America or Australia (Douglas 1981).

Some data to indicate the scale of modification of erosion rates by people over the past 300 years are available, especially from areas in which forests have been removed (Table 13-8). Much of the extra erosion caused by human activity comes from specific localities such as forest roads, cultivated fields, construction sites, and spoil banks (Table 13-9). Llyn Peris, a lake of glacial origin in Snowdonia, Wales, received sediment at a rate of less than 5 t/km^{2}y^{-1} from its catchment prior to 1820. During the nineteenth century, sediment transfer increased mainly due to slate quarrying immediately adjacent

Table 13-7 *Reservoir filling rates*

Reservoir	Catchment area (km^2)	Sediment inflow (t km^2/y^{-1})	Source
Shah-Banou Farah, northern Iran		1,900	Khodjeini and Mohammed 1973
Kisongo, Tanzania 1960–69	9.3	1,115	Murray-Rust 1972
" " 1970–71		1,600	" "
Imagi, Kenya		1,505	Christiansson 1979
Roma catchment, Lesotho	0.5	810	Chakela 1980
Bhumipol, Thailand	26,400	1,250	Chitchob and Cowley 1973
Lake Decatur, Illinois, United States	2,346	112	Brown, Stall, and DeTurk 1947
Catcleugh, Northumberland, United Kingdom		285	Douglas 1970
Strines, Yorkshire, United Kingdom		317	"
Cropston, Leicestershire, United Kingdom		30	"

Table 13-8 *Increases in sediment yield due to human activity*

Situation	Magnitude of increase	Source
In large rivers, generally	3.5 times	Dedkov and Mozzherin 1984
In small rivers, generally	8	" "
Forest clearance, Cameron Highlands, Malaysia	5	Shallow 1956
From erosion of forest roads, Idaho	200–500	Megahan 1975
Forest clearance, South Island, New Zealand	up to 100	Whitehouse 1983
Coon Creek, Wisconsin 1870–1930	10	Trimble and Lund 1982
Cultivation on forest land, Java	2	Douglas 1981
Trinidad	9	"
Ivory Coast	18	"
Tanzania	5	"
Urbanization in rainforest area, Malaysia	20	"

to the lake. In the twentieth century, rates increased to $20 \ t/km^2y^{-1}$ in the 1920s and over $50 \ t/km^2y^{-1}$ in the 1960s due to a combination of overgrazing, trampling, and construction work (Petts and Foster 1985). In Llangorse Lake (Fig. 13.4, record 9) and also in Wales, agriculture had affected sediment transfer for 2,650 years prior to 1830, but thereafter more marginal hill land was put into cultivation to supply the expanding industrial towns and cities of Britain, causing a fourfold increase in sediment input. Historical records and lake-sediment studies reveal a similar story of agricultural intensification affecting Lake Torestorpso in southern Sweden, sediment transfer reaching a peak as plowed-land expansion coincided with the historically highest sheep population in the catchment area at about 1850 (Petts and Foster 1985).

Historical records such as these show that the pattern and volume of sediment transfer vary from locality to locality. If maximum pressure on the land coincides with an exceptional extreme climatic event, then soil loss may be severe. If the pressure is in a climatically relatively calm period, the sediment transfer may not be increased greatly. The records for the Texas rivers (Fig. 13.3) show generally low sediment yields from 1947 to 1957, but it is not clear whether these reflect rainfall and runoff conditions or the trapping of sediment in newly constructed reservoirs upstream. The difference between the yields of the Neches River and those of the Brazos and Colorado rivers in the 1930s indicates the wide spatial variability in one state and emphasizes the difficulty of

Table 13-9 *Examples of erosion rates influenced by human activity*

Environment	t/km^2y^{-1}
Cultivated land with slope over 5%	1,000–5,000
(exceptional values up to	25,000)
Long-overgrazed mountainous area, Argentine	2,560
Fire-affected chaparral rangeland, Arizona	8,308
Unreclaimed strip-mine spoil banks, Kentucky	10,425
Urban construction sites	1,614–22,640

Source: After Jansson 1982.

making regional, let alone global, statements about the trend of people-modified sediment transfers over the past 300 years.

However, human activity also increases the frequency of mass movements, which in turn increase river-sediment loads. Two hundred years ago, forests covered more than 70% of the Liusha basin in western Sichuan, China, and mudflows occurred about once in 10 years in some 15 mudflow gullies. By 1968, the population had increased fivefold and the forest cover was reduced to 17% of the area, with mudflows now occurring several times a year in up to 42 mudflow-generating gullies (Du Ronghuan and C. Bifan 1985). Clearance of forests in the South Island of New Zealand increased landslide densities from 0.5–1 per km^2 to 12–30 per km^2 and slope denudation rates from 100 to 1,100–400 $m^3/km^2/y$ (Williams 1980).

Sediment supplied from the slopes does not always enter the river, and much entering the river is stored in the floodplain and valley floor. The net output to the ocean may be only a small part of the total sediment transfer within a drainage basin. Of $0.02 \ km^3$ of material eroded since 1700 off the upland soils of a 155-km^2 drainage basin in the Maryland Piedmont in the United States, 34% was removed by the river, 14% has been stored in the floodplains of the basin, and over half – 52% – has been held in colluvium and sheetwash deposits and at the junctions of headwater tributaries (Costa 1975). In the driftless area of Wisconsin, the 1930s saw sediment accumulated in alluvial deposits at almost 3,000 $t/km^2/y$, but only 160 $t/km^2/y$ left the basin, 95% of the eroded soil being retained. Following soil conservation measures, the supply from the slopes is now less than the amount removed by rivers, the difference being made up by removal from valley deposition (Trimble 1983). Elsewhere, as indicated earlier, reservoirs trap sediment; further erosion may occur downstream of reservoirs and much material is deposited in coastal estuaries, salt marshes, mangrove swamps, and deltas (Meade 1982). During all these phases of removal, transportation, deposition, and remobilization, elements are removed from solid particles and are added to the total solute loads of streams. However, solute loads do not reflect merely erosion within the catchment area, but include atmospheric inputs, volcanic eruptions, and chemical elements added by human activity. Possibly 15% of the worldwide dissolved load is derived from the atmosphere, and 12% from human activity (Meybeck 1979), but the effects on particular rivers vary greatly. Some 85% of the dissolved load of the Rio Tete, an Amazon tributary 1,700 km inland from the Atlantic, is derived from the atmosphere (Gibbs 1970), whereas the bulk of the solutes in many urban streams is derived from pollutant discharges.

Both sediment and solute loads may be reduced by land and waste-water treatment. The efficiency of soil-conservation measures is well documented (Trimble 1983). The decrease in sediment yield to the Shimen Reservoir, Taiwan (Fig. 13.3) since 1963 is largely due to the construction of check dams upstream and erosion-control works on the steep, unstable shale and sandstone slopes of the typhoon-affected catchment area. Afforestation is not always as effective in reducing sediment yields, conversion of moorland pasture to pine forest in Britain actually leading to increased sediment discharges (Newson 1979). Construction of drainage ditches leads to increases in sediment yields from highly erodible soils beneath British pine plantations, as in the Macclesfield Forest (Fig. 13.4, record 8). Plowing of land prior to afforestation has led to tenfold increases in sediment transfer into some southern Scottish lakes (Fig. 13.4, record 5). Removal of pollutants from waste discharges may be only an alteration to the location and pathway of material transfers. For example, treatment of municipal sewage wastes may lead to discharge of clean water to rivers but have a residual sludge which has to be dumped, often into coastal waters.

Human Impact on the Chemical Elements Carried by Some Major Rivers If nineteenth-century estimates of fluvial solute loads are compared with modern calculations, the loads of some rivers, such as the Danube (Table 13-10), show pronounced increases, which may be a result of urban and

Table 13-10 *Nineteenth- and twentieth-century estimates of fluvial solute loads*

	Total load (million t/y)	
River	Russell 1898	Meybeck 1976
Danube	22.97	60.38
Nile	17.29	17.40
Mississippi	115.9	130.68
Rhone	8.45	18.24

industrial dicharges of chemical elements in waste waters. In other areas, the sodium chloride loads of rivers have increased as a result of the mobilization of salt through agricultural operations, as on the rivers Murray in Australia, Indus in Pakistan, and Colorado in the United States. The salt load of the River Murray increases from 0.14 million t/yr at Albury to 1.4 million t/yr at Morgan, South Australia, with at least 0.41 million t/yr of that increase being due to human activity. Chloride concentrations at Morgan have increased by an average of 1.4% per year since 1940 (Peck, Thomas, and Williamson 1983).

Industrial and urban activity have also increased major solute loads significantly. Mining effluent plays a major part in this process, with acid mine drainage affecting streams in many coal-mining areas, such as the Appalachians of the United States. However, one of the most marked increases has been in the chloride load of the Rhine (Table 13-11), largely due to waste discharge from potash mines (Van Haaren 1963). Meybeck (1979) attributes increases in major solute contents of rivers to urban and industrial activity, calculating that some 450 million t/yr of dissolved matter are carried to the oceans as a direct result of waste discharges.

Table 13-11 *Temporal changes in the solute loads of major rivers*

(a) *Mean Concentrations* (mg/l)

	Ca		Na		K		Cl		SO$_4$	
River	ca.1900	ca.1970	ca.1900	ca.1970	ca.1900	ca.1970	ca.1900	ca.1970	ca.1900	ca.1970
Mississippi	34	39	11	17	2.8	2.8	10.3	19.3	25.5	50.3
St. Lawrence	30	50	5.5	12.6	1.35	1.35	7.5	27.5	14	29.4
Rhine	50	100	5	120	5	8.5	20	133	35	96
Seine	74	97	7.3	39.7	2.2	6.9	7.5	4	21.8	75
Oder and Vistula	42	65	3.8	44	2.1	17.4	4.9	6.1	18.5	58

(b) *Increase in total land (million t/y) and increase in load (waste discharge) per inhabitant (kg/yr)*

	Ca		Na		K		Cl		SO$_4$	
River	Increase	Per capita	Increase	Per capita	Increase	Per capita	Increase	Per capita	Increase	Per capita
Mississippi	2.3	34	3.5	52	0	0	5.2	77	14.5	215
St. Lawrence	2.1	90	1.45	65	0	0	4.15	185	3.2	143
Rhine	3.5	86	8	200	0.24	6	5.5	137	4.15	103
Seine	0.15	10	0.25	16	0.04	2.5	0.27	18	0.42	28
Oder and Vistula	1.1	34	2.0	62	0.77	24	2.8	87	1.95	61

Source: After Meybeck 1979.

Some heavy metals, especially copper, molybdenum, bromine, antimony, lead, and zinc, occur in river waters in much greater quantities than would be expected from natural weathering and sediment and solute transfer processes (Martin and Meybeck 1979). Not all the increased abundance of these elements in rivers can be attributed to industrial activity, but at least some of it is. Many specific cases of heavy-metal pollution highlight the importance of these transfers. Sediments from the Elbe River in and upstream of the German port of Hamburg have concentrations of mercury that exceed natural background values by 8 to 85 times (Table 13-12). The scale of increases in the fluxes of heavy metals may be gauged from estimates that the amount of mercury carried to the oceans by rivers has increased by four times; that of cadmium released by mining compared to the natural flux, by thirty times; and that of lead in the open ocean, by three to five times (Ehrlich et al. 1977).

Wind erosion   Natural movements of dust on a global scale reflect the transport of material out of the world's deserts into the oceans and across the continents. About 500 million t of wind-blown dust are lifted from the continental surfaces each year – primarily from the great deserts (McCauley et al. 1981). Falls of Saharan dust in the countries of northwest Europe occur about once every seven to eight years (Pitty 1968; Goudie 1978), while dust from the Chinese deserts regularly reaches Beijing (Liu et al. 1981) and is occasionally carried to northern Alaska (Rahn, Borys, and Shaw 1981).

On the other hand, transport of dust on a continental scale is often associated with the blowing of fine particles from cultivated fields. The blowing of soil from the plains of parts of Texas, New Mexico, Colorado, Oklahoma, and Kansas in the 1930s seriously damaged 28,000 km² in the heart of the affected zone (Lockeretz 1978). Although the terrible people- and climate-induced erosion of the 1930s Dust Bowl was never supposed to happen again, wind erosion remains a

problem, albeit less severe, in this area. More land in the Great Plains was damaged annually by wind in the 1950s than in the 1930s, although the earlier dust storms were more spectacular. In February 1977, strong winds in the first winter storm to hit the drought-stricken high plains eroded plowed fields locally to depths exceeding 1 m, depositing the eroded material in locate sheets from several to more than 100 cm thick, extending several kilometers downward of the source areas and blowouts (McCauley et al. 1981). The dust was swept across the southern states out into the Atlantic, thereby adding to the sedimentary record of the ocean floors.

This people-enhanced wind erosion from cultivated fields often involved the remobilization of ancient aeolian deposits that had accumulated under previous climatic conditions. Many areas of Quaternary loess in mid- to high latitudes or of former desert dunes in lower latitudes become unstable when the vegetation is removed and cultivation commenced. Some areas, such as the Great Plains of the United States, had not become completely stable before European settlement. During 21 five-year droughts in the 748 years before 1950, windstorms carried dust from areas in which vegetation had died. However, clearance of vegetation and plowing aggravated the situation. Now wind erosion removes 907 million t of soil a year from the United States, mainly in exceptional storms, such as that of February 1977, which removed as much as 1,100 t/km² from parts of eastern Colorado (McCauley et al. 1981). Dust deposition rates vary greatly; in Tempe, Arizona, dust accumulates at a rate of 54 t/km² y⁻¹ as a result of dust storms (haboobs) bring material mainly from cultivated, desert areas and dry stream courses within 50 to 200 km of Tempe, (Péwé et al. 1981). Harmattan dust is deposited at Kano, Nigeria at a rate of 99 t/km² y⁻¹, where it adds beneficial phosphorous and potassium to local soils (Wilke et al. 1984).

Remobilization of physical wind-blown material and loess is common in areas close to such sources, as in China and Iceland, but it is also significant in once-forested agricultural regions in Europe. In Britain, the danger of wind erosion when the surface soil is dry, particularly in flat areas with few windbreaks such as the Fens, is widely recognized by many farmers (Observer 1967). Accounts of such erosion in the vales of Pickering and York (Brade-Birks 1944; Briggs and France 1982; Radley and Simms 1967), parts of the West Midlands (Fullen 1985; Reed 1979), south Lancashire (Wilson and Cooke 1980), Nottinghamshire (Stamp 1948; Wilkinson, Broughton, and Parker-Sutton 1969), Lincolnshire (Robinson 1968), and the Fenland and Breckland areas of East Anglia (Brade-Birks 1944) point to four conditions favoring wind erosion: (1) the paucity of binding materials (clay or humus) in the surface soil; (2) the paucity of rain, with consequent drying of the surface soil; (3) level topographic surfaces devoid of windbreaks; and (4) wind of sufficient velocity (about 14 m/s in the Fens and 12 m/s in Shropshire) (Douglas 1970).

Blowing of soil occurs in many parts of continental Europe. The well-sorted sands of agricultural areas of Denmark and southern Sweden are particularly prone to wind erosion (Mattsson 1984; Moller 1985). Since 1539, Danish govern-

Table 13-12 *Heavy-metal concentrations in sediments from the Elbe River and its tributaries near Hamburg: enrichment in relation to background values*

Element	Background	Range of concentrations (mg/l) Minimum	Maximum	Range of enrichment of four highly polluted sites compared to background
Zinc	94	136	2,717	4.1–29
Copper	16	16	529	3.1–34
Chromium	59	5	369	1.0–6.3
Lead	30	33	110	3.1–37
Arsenic	10	8	183	1.1–19
Nickel	21	19	89	0.9–4.2
Cobalt	8	7.2	23.7	1.1–3.1
Calcium	0.4	0.3	19.4	4.5–56
Mercury	0.2	0.4	17.0	8.0–85

Source: After Lichtfuss and Brummer 1981.

ments have sought to curtail sand drift, but present farming practices, with large, carefully cultivated and rolled fields that are bare in spring, contribute to soil erosion (Moller 1986). Although the total area of the USSR potentially affected by wind erosion is unknown, about 35,000 km^2 of the Ukraine, approximately 20% of the arable and pasture land of that republic, are at risk from deflation (Silvestrov 1971). Dust storms that affected the southern and southwestern parts of European Russia in the spring of 1960 damaged 4,000 km^2 of newly sown crops. In eastern Georgia in 1953, deflation caused the loss of 1,450 km^2 of crops.

Wind erosion is not divorced from water erosion. Frequently, wind-blown deposits are degraded by raindrop splash and water runoff, whereas fluvial deposits, especially from floodwaters, may be deflated by wind. In the Kairouan area of Tunisia, the great floods of 1969 deposited material that has produced 200 km^2 of shifting dunes. Polymer soil stabilizers are needed to assist dune stabilization by planting vegetation (De Kesel and De Vleeschauwer 1981).

Coastal Erosion   Coastal change is a spatially differentiated pattern of erosion and accretion. Land is lost in some places and gained in others. Some eroded sediment is transferred out to the sea floors, but other sediment is delivered to the coastlines by the discharge of rivers. For many stretches of coastline, a series of natural compartments with their own sediment budgets may be recognized. The southern Californian coast may be divided into four discrete sedimentation cells, each containing a complete cycle of littoral transport and sedimentation. Rivers are the principal sources of sediments for the cells, and the chief sinks are the series of submarine canyons, which bisect the continental shelf and intercept the sand as it moves southward along the coast (Komar 1983). Any discussion of coastal erosion ought to be in this sediment budget framework, examining the destination of the eroded sediment and the sources of replenishment. Beaches and cliffs offer somewhat different situations, but the erosion of both depends on wave action and may be drastically affected by storm surges. When Hurricane Frederic hit the sandy barrier Dauphin Island, Alabama in 1979, the shoreline retreated an average of about 25 m both on the Gulf and Sound sides, reducing the width of the island by about 10% (Nummedal 1983). On the north shore of Long Island, New York, a hurricane in 1944 cut back the cliff at Shoreham 12 m in one day (Sunamura 1983). A low cliff in East Anglia, England, was driven back more than 30 m overnight during the 1953 North Sea storm surge (King 1980).

The exposure and nature of coastlines affects their resistance to erosion (Table 13-12), but many coastal landforms reflect the delicate balance of their sediment budget. Reduction or augmentation of the sediment supply may lead to considerable changes in erosion or deposition. At Hallsands, south Devon, England, about 0.5 million m^3 of shingle were removed for building materials between 1897 and 1902 from the foreshore of a micaschist cliff. As a result, the whole beach was lowered by 3.6 m, and rapid cliff erosion followed, ruining the fishing village (Sunamura 1983). The dumping in 1963 of some 2.9 million m^3 of mud, sand and pebbles dredged from Oceanside

Harbor, California, on beaches south of the San Luis Rey River led to severe erosion during storms. Waves lifted pebbles as much as 6 m in the air, throwing them against nearby buildings and using them to undermine the beach road (Kuhn and Shepard 1983). Harbor construction frequently disrupts coastal sediment budgets, often leading to accumulation of sand where it is unwanted and producing severe erosion of tourist beaches, which have to be replenished at great cost, as on the Belgian coast near Zeebrugge (Douglas 1971).

The exploitation of the coastline and nearshore environment as a resource, for transportation, aggregates, industry, residential development, and recreation, has profound impacts on aquatic and wetland ecosystems. Coastal sediment budgets are modified drastically by these human activities, with severe off-site impacts. Delta progradation may be accelerated by land reclamation, as in the Wanqingsha and Denglongsha areas of the Zhujiang (Pearl River) deltas of China, which are now advancing at 63.6 and 121.7 m/y, respectively, compared with an average rate of around 15 m/y in previous centuries (Huang 1987). Reduction of sediment yield, on the other hand, may cause drastic coastal erosion. While Holeman (1968) estimated the sediment discharge of the Nile to be 111 million t/y, Milliam and Meade (1983) argued that since the closing of the Aswan High Dam, the Nile transports virtually no sediment to the sea (Table 13-2). The 245-km-long Nile Delta coastline, no longer augmented by Nile sediment, is now subject to aggravated erosion (Table 13-13), some 1.8 km^2/y being lost from the Damiette and Rosette promontories (Paskoff 1981). Erosion has been a problem in this area for a long time, but it is now worsened by subsidence due to groundwater abstraction and to lack of replenishment. Modification of the transfer of water to benefit irrigation and power generation has led to an unwanted change in the sediment budget, with deposition in the reservoir and erosion of the delta.

Coastal protection works may actually aggravate erosion, as near Bournemouth, England. Harbor works often produce deposition on one side and erosion on the other. Breakwaters at Lagos Harbor, Victoria Island, Nigeria have accelerated the natural erosion rate from a tolerable 2–4 m/y to a disastrous and worrying 20 m/y (Chidi 1987). So great is the variation in these effects from place to place, and at any given site, through time as a result of extreme events, that it is difficult to estimate the net global effect of coastal changes caused directly or indirectly by people. However, they are most severe where coastlines are most modified, and such places are usually where coastal population densities are greatest. Sand replenishment to make up for the losses caused by human action is a common remedy from Lagos to Zeebrugge to Santa Barbara. It is a sediment transfer that will have to be repeated again and again, however, as the beaches are pounded relentlessly by the waves, which drag away material to be carried down the coast by longshore drift.

Conclusion

When the volumes of the deliberate, people-made transfers of material are compared with some of the people-

Table 13-13 *Rates of coastal erosion*

Catergory or locality	Long-term rate (m/y)	Maximum rate in extreme event	Source
Global orders of magnitude			
Granitic rocks	0.001		Sunamura 1983
Limestone	0.001–0.01		"
Flysch and shale	0.01		
Chalk and Tertiary sedimentary rocks	0.1–1		"
Quaternary deposits	1–10	12	"
Unconsolidated volcanic ejecta	10	140	"
Quaternary deposits			
Wolin Island, Poland	0.81		Kostrzewski and Zwolinski 1987
Holderness, England			
Volcanic islands			
Krakatoa, Indonesia	33		Sunamura 1987
Surtsey, Iceland	25–38		
Nishinoshima, Japan	80		
Barrier islands			
Chandleur islands, Louisiana	2–12	30	Kahn and Dolan 1985
Mid-Atlantic coast, U.S.			Dolan and Lins 1987
General U.S. rates			
Atlantic coast	0.8	(loss) 24.6 to 25.5 (gain)	Dolan, Hayden, and May 1983
Gulf Coast	1.8	(loss) 8.8 to 15.3 (gain)	
Pacific coast	0.0	(loss) 5.0 to 10.0 (gain)	
Nile delta			
Rosette Point	60		Paskoff 1981
Damiette Point	30–40		"

affected fluvial sediment loads (Table 13-14), the similarities of the orders of magnitude of both deliberate and inadvertent transfers is apparent. Clearly, both sets of figures fail to tell the whole story. Much sediment eroded on hillslopes merely accumulates at the base of the slopes or in valley floors and is not evacuated by major rivers. In some places, the volume of such locally moved material may be several times the net load exported by major rivers. Equally, the figures for mineral production do not take into account the overburden, waste products, and mining residues involved in the mineral-extraction process.

Comparison of the historic trends of growth in resource exploitation, as indicated by cement, iron ore, solid fuel, and roundwood production (Fig. 13.5) with historic trends in sediment transfer (Figs. 13.3 and 13.4) reveals an exponential growth in the deliberate transfer of materials, with threefold to tenfold increases since the 1920s, but only a slight increase in the sediment yields of some rivers. At present the deliberate and accidental transfer of materials by people's activities is of approximately the same order of magnitude (Table 13-15). The deliberate transfer accelerates the accidental transfer. Both transfers are episodic, but the deliberate transfer is increasing more rapidly. Long recognized as a major geological agent, human action will soon account for most of the transfer of earth-surface materials. The scale of this human action is illustrated by the area of the United States disturbed for bituminous coal mining from 1930 to 1971, a total of

$5,880 \text{ km}^2$, or approximately twice the area of the Grand Duchy of Luxembourg. With growing world population, the loss of land to agricultural uses for fuel, for mineral and construction-material extraction, and for residential development may soon become a factor limiting the

Table 13-14 *Comparison of mineral production and fluvial sediment yields*

Process	Million tons per year
World lime production, 1982	112
Mean annual sediment yield of the Mackenzie River	100
World phosphate rock production, 1982	122
Mean annual sediment yield of the Red River	130
World salt production, 1982	169
Mean annual sediment yield of the Mekong River	160
World iron-ore production, 1982	795
Mean annual sediment yield of the Amazon River	900
World bituminuous coal production, 1982	2,718
Mean annual sediment yield of the Ganges, Brahmaputra, and Yangtse rivers	2,750

Sources: Mineral production: Bureau of Mines Staff 1984; and sediment yields: Milliman and Meade 1983.

Table 13-15 *Global sediment transfer estimates*

	Date	Million tons per year	Source
Transfers by natural processes			
Average denudation rate for the ice-free land surface	1983	33,127*	Saunders and Young 1983
Loss of topsoil	1984	25,700	Brown 1984
River sediment yield to the oceans (a)	1968	24,000	Judson 1968b
(b)	1968	18,300	Holeman 1968
(c)	1983	13,505	Milliman and Meade 1983
Yield of dissolved matter to the oceans	1976	3,250	Meybeck 1976
People-made transfers			
Total mineral production			
(a) nonmetallic minerals	1982	6,339[†]	Bureau of Mines Staff, 1984
(b) metals	1982	926	" " " "
(c) oil and natural gas	1984	4,255	World Resources Institute 1986
U.S. production of nonmetallic construction materials	1972	1,875[‡]	Ehrlich et al. 1977
Total cereal production	1984	1,780	World Resources Institute 1986
Total grain exports	1984	153	" " " "
Total carbon dioxide emissions from anthropogenic sources	1984	153	" " " "
Total fluvial solute load from anthropogenic sources	1979	450	Meybeck 1979

* Based on the authors' statement that average denudation rates for all climates are $10-1,000 \, m^3/km^2y^{-1}$.

[†] Does not include the amount of overburden and mine waste involved in mineral production, and neglects sand and gravel and similar, but includes 892 million t of cement.

[‡] Includes approximately 100×10^6 t of cement production.

choice of energy-generation techniques. At present the deliberate transfers reflect economic and political conditions, the accidental, more closely climatic extremes. However downturns in economic activity lead to stress in land management and aggravation of the work of natural processes. In times of recession, environmental issues take a back seat.

Some areas suffer a relatively short period of sediment removal and then are stabilized by careful management, as the U.S. Soil Conservation Service demonstration area at Coon Creek, Wisconsin has shown (Trimble 1983). In other circumstances, a change in land use is the cause of temporary instability, as during land development for urban construction (Douglas 1985; Wolman 1967). Nevertheless, the overwhelming impression is that transfer of materials is changing the face of the earth at a faster rate than that at which the world's population is growing.

Sediment transfer may be deliberate or the accidental by-product of some other form of resource use or land management. Many successful techniques to minimize the detrimental effects of erosion and sedimentation are available but often all that the technology can do is to transfer the problem to another location. If waste cannot be disposed of on land, it may be dumped at sea. Retention of sediment upstream may lead to further erosion downstream. Further transformation of the global geochemical budget is inevitable, but many of the present problems of erosion and sedimentation could be reduced by careful land management and better choice of alternative sources of energy and strategies for water use.

References

Adey, E. A., and H. M. Cook. 1964. Suspended-sediment load of Texas streams. Compilation Report October 1959–September 1961. *Texas Water Commission Bulletin 6410.*

Aniya, M. 1985. Contemporary erosion rate by landsliding in Amahata River basin, Japan. *Zeitschrift fur Geomorphologie NF 29:* 301–14.

Basile, G. F., and W. Dragoni. 1987. Geomorphology and erosion of the southern Chiana Valley, Italy. In *International Geomorphology 1986.* Part I, ed. V. Gardiner, 843–52. Chichester: Wiley.

Battarbee, R. W., P. G. Appelby, K. Odell, and R. J. Flower. 1985. [210]Pb dating of Scottish lake sediments, afforestation and accelerated soil erosion. *Earth Surface Processes and Landforms 10:* 137–42.

Berry, B. J. L., and F. E. Horton. 1974. *Urban Environmental Management: Planning for Pollution Control.* Englewood Cliffs, NJ: Prentice-Hall.

Brade-Birks, S. G. 1944. *Good Soil.* London: English Universities Press.

Briggs, D. J., and J. France. 1982. Mapping soil erosion by wind for regional planning. *Journal of Environmental Management 15:* 159–68.

Brown, C. B., J. B. Stall, and E. E. DeTurk. 1947. The causes and effects of sedimentation in Lake Decatur. *Illinois State Water Survey Bulletin 37.*

Brown, L. R. 1984. The global loss of topsoil. *Journal of Soil and Water Conservation 39* (3): 162–65.

Bureau of Mines Staff. 1984. *Minerals Yearbook 1982.* Washington, D.C.: U.S. Department of the Interior.

Chakela, Q. K. 1980. Reservoir sedimentation within Roma Valley and Maliele catchments in Lesotho. *Geografiska Annaler 62A:* 157–69.

Chang Hao, Hsia Mai-Ting, Chen Shih-Chi, Li Chen-Wu, Hsia Heng-Pin, Chiang Nai-Sen, and Lin Pin-Wen 1977. Regulation of sediments in some medium-sized and small reservoirs on the heavily silt-laden streams in China. *Scientia Sinica* 20: 89–105.

Chidi, I. A. 1987. Harbor-development-related erosion at Victoria Island, Lagos. In *International Geomorphology 1986,* Part I, ed. V. Gardiner, 165–81. Chichester: Wiley.

Chinen, T., and H. Kadomura. 1986. Posteruption sediment budget of a small catchment on Mt. Usu, Hokkaido. *Zeitschrift fur Geomorphologie NF Suppl-Bd 60:* 217–31.

Chitchob, S., and J. E. Cowley. 1973. Bhumibol reservoir-sediment status after eight years of operation. *International Association for Hydraulic Research International Symposium on River Bangkok 1*: 35–45.

Ciccacci, S., P. Fredi, E. Lupia Palmieri, and F. Pugliese. 1981. Contributo dell'analisi geomorfica quantitativa alla valutazione dell'entita dell'erosione nai bacini fluviali. *Bolletino Societa Geologica Italiana 99*: 455–516.

Coates, D. R. 1985. *Geology and Society*. New York: Prentice-Hall.

Cole, G., and B. Knights. 1979. An introduction to estuarine and coastal land reclamation and waste storage. In *Estuarine and Coastal Land Reclamation and Water Storage*, ed. B. Knights and A. J. Phillips, 3–20. Farmborough: Saxon House.

Cook, H. M. 1967. Suspended-sediment load of Texas streams. Compilation Report October 1959–September 1961. *Texas Water Development Board Report 45*.

———. 1970. Suspended-sediment load of Texas streams. Compilation Report October 1963–September 1965. *Texas Water Development Board Report 106*.

Costa, J. E. 1975. Effects of agriculture on erosion and sedimentation in the Piedmont province, Maryland. *Geological Society of America Bulletin 86*: 1281–86.

Coughlan, J. 1979. Aspects for reclamation in Southampton Water. In *Estuarine and Coastal Land Reclamation and Water Storage*, ed. B. Knights and A. J. Phillips, 99–124. Farmborough: Saxon House.

Cressey, G. B. 1936. The Fengshien landscape: A fragment of the Yangtse Delta. *Geographical Review 26*: 396–413.

Davis, M. B. 1975. Erosion rates and land use history in southern Michigan. *Environmental Conservation 3*: 139–48.

Day, D. G. 1986. *Water and Coal*. Canberra: Center for Resource and Environmental Studies, Australian National University.

Dearing, J. A., and I. D. L. Foster. 1987. Limnic sediments used to reconstruct sediment yields and sources in the English midlands since 1765. In *International Geomorphology 1986*. Part I, ed. V. Gardiner, 853–68. Chichester: Wiley.

Dedkov, A. P., and V. I. Mozzherin. 1984. *Erosion and Sediment Yield on the Earth*. Kazan: Kazan University Press. (In Russian.)

De Kesel, M., and D. De Vleeschauwer. 1981. Sand dune fixation in Tunisia by means of polyurea polyalkylene oxide (Uresol). In *Tropical Agricultural Hydrology*, ed. R. Lal and E. W. Russell, 273–81. Chichester: Wiley.

De Ploey, J., and A. Yair. 1985. Promoted erosion and controlled colluviation: A proposal concerning land management and landscape evolution. *Catena 12*: 105–110.

Dimbleby, G. W. 1974. The legacy of prehistoric man. In *Conservation in Practice*, ed. A. Warren and F. B. Goldsmith, 279–89. London: Wiley.

Dolan, R., B. Hayden, and S. May. 1983. Erosion of the U.S. shorelines. In *CRC Handbook of Coastal Processes and Erosion*, ed. P. D. Komar, 285–99. Boca Raton, FL: CRC Press.

Dolan, R., and H. Lins. 1987. Beaches and barrier islands. *Scientific American 257* (1): 52–59.

Douglas, I. 1967. Man, vegetation, and the sediment yields of rivers. *Nature 215*: 925–28.

———. 1970. Sediment yields from forested and agricultural lands. In *The Role of Water in Agriculture*, ed. J. A. Taylor, 57–88. Oxford: Pergamon.

———. 1971. Dynamic equilibrium in applied geomorphology – two case studies. *Earth Science Journal 5*: 29–35.

———. 1981. Soil conservation measures in river basin planning. In *River Basin Planning: Theory and Practice*, ed. S. K. Saha and C. J. Barrow, 49–73. Chichester: Wiley.

———. 1985. Urban sedimentology. *Progress in Physical Geography 9*: 255–80.

Du Ronghuan, and C. Bifan. 1985. Distribution of mudflows and landslides and examples against them in China.

Ehrlich, P. R., A. H. Ehrlich, and J. P. Holdren. 1977. *Ecosci-ence: Population, Resources, Environment*. San Francisco: W.H. Freeman.

FAO. 1978. The state of natural resources and the human environment for food and agriculture. *The State of Food and Agriculture 1977*. FAO Agriculture Series 8, 3-1-3-65.

Foster, I. D. L., J. A. Dearing, A. Simpson, A. D. Carter, and P. G. Appleby. 1985. Lake catchment based studies of erosion and denudation in the Merevale catchment, Warwickshire. *Earth Surface Processes and Landforms 10*: 45–68.

Fullen, M. A. 1985. Wind erosion of arable soils in east Shropshire (England) during spring 1983. *Catena 12*: 111–20.

Gibbs, R. J. 1970. Mechanisms controlling world water chemistry. *Science 170*: 1088–90.

Goudie, A. S. 1978. Dust storms and their geomorphological implications. *Journal of Arid Environments 2*: 105–12.

Holeman, J. N. 1968. Sediment yield of major rivers of the world. *Water Resources Research 4*: 737–47.

Houston, J. M. 1964. *The Western Mediterranean World*. London: Longman.

Huang Zhenguo, Li Pingri, Zhang Zhonqying, and Li Konghong. 1987. The geomorphological evolution of the Zhujiang delta. In *International Geomorphology 1986*. Part I, ed. V. Gardiner, 989–97. Chichester: Wiley.

IDG. 1979. Information and Documentation Centre for the Geography of the Netherlands. *Compact Geography of the Netherlands*. Utrecht: IDG.

Jansson, M. B. 1982. *Land Erosion by Water in Different Climates* (UNGI Rapport No. 57). Uppsala: Department of Physical Geography, Uppsala University.

Jiang Dequi, Qi Leidi, and Tan Jieshang. 1981. Soil erosion and conservation in the Wuding River Valley, China. In *Soil Conservation: Problems and Prospects*, ed. R. P. C. Morgan, 461–79. Chichester: Wiley.

Jones, R., K. Benson-Evans, and F. M. Chambers. 1985. Human influence on sedimentation in Llangorse Lake, Wales. *Earth Surface Processes and Landforms 10*: 227–36.

Judson 1968a. Erosion rates near Rome, Italy. *Science 160*: 1444–46.

———. 1968b. Erosion of the land. *American Scientist 56*: 356–71.

Kahn, J. H., and R. Dolan. 1985. Longhsore bars and shoreline erosion along the Chandeleur Islands, Louisiana. *Zeitschrift fur Geomorphologie NF 29*: 89–97.

Kershaw, A. P. 1976. A late Pleistocene and Holocene pollen diagram from Lynch's Crater, north eastern Queensland, Australia. *New Phytologist 77*: 469–98.

Kestner, F. J. T. 1979. Loose boundary hydraulics and land reclamation. In *Estuarine and Coastal Land Reclamation and Water Storage*, ed. B. Knights and A.J. Phillips, 23–47. Farmborough: Saxon House.

Khodjeini, V., and A. Mohammed. 1973. Etude de l'engravement et de l'envasement de la retenue du barrage de Shah-Banou Farah. *International Association for Hydraulic Research International Symposium on River Mechanics Bangkok 1*: 23–34.

Kidwell, C. S. 1985. Science and ethnoscience: Native American world views as a factor in the development of native technologies. In *Environmental History: Current Issues in Comparative Perspective*, ed. K. E. Bailes, 277–87. Lanham and London: University Press of America.

King, C. A. M. 1980. *Physical Geography*. Oxford: Blackwell.

Kivell, P. T. 1984. Environmental management through derelict land reclamation. In *Environmental Management: British and Hungarian Case Studies* (Studies in Geography in Hungary 16), ed. P. A. Compton and M. Pecsi, 75–90. Budapest: Akademiai Kiado.

Knighton, A. D. 1984. *Fluvial Forms and Processes*. London: Edward Arnold.

Knights, B. 1979. Reclamation in the Netherlands. In *Estuarine and Coastal Land Reclamation and Water Storage*, ed. B. Knights and A. J. Phillips, 209–33. Farmborough: Saxon House.

Komar, P. D. 1983. Beach processes and erosion – An introduction. In *CRC Handbook of Coastal Processes and Erosion*, ed. P. D. Komar, 1–20. Boca Raton, FL: CRC Press.

Kostrzewski, A., and Z. Zwolinski, 1987. Operation and morphologic effects of present-day morphogenetic processes modeling the cliffed coast of Wolin Island, NW Poland. In *International Geomorphology 1986*. Part I, ed. V. Gardiner, 1231–52. Chichester: Wiley.

Kuhn, G. G., and F. P. Shepard. 1983. Beach processes and sea cliff erosion in San Diego County, California. In *CRC Handbook of Coastal Processes and Erosion*, ed. P. D. Komar, 267–84. Boca Raton, FL: CRC Press.

Lichtfuss, R., and G. Brummer. 1981. Naturlicher Gehalt und anthropogene Anreicherung von Schwermetallen in den Sedimenten von Elbe, Eider, Trace, und Schwentine. *Catena 8*: 251–64.

Liu Tungsheng, Gu Xiongfei, An Zhisheng, and Fan Yongxiang. 1981. The dust fall in Beijing, China on April 18, 1980. *Geological Society of America Special Paper 186*, 149–57.

Lockeretz, W. 1978. The lessons of the dust bowl. *American Scientist 66*: 560–71.

Maloney, B. K. 1985. Man's impact on the rainforests of West Malaysia. *Journal of Biogeography 12*: 537–58.

Martin, J.-M., and M. Meybeck. 1979. Elemental mass-balance of material carried by major world rivers. *Marine Chemistry 7*: 173–206.

Matthews, W. V. G., and G. M. Kondolf. 1987. Changes in sediment storage over time in a coastal Californian river. *International Association of Hydrological Sciences Publication 165*: 413–14.

Mattsson, J. O. 1984. Erosionsprobleme i Svergie. I Vinderosionsproblem med sarskild hansyn till de skanska odlingsomradena. *Kungliga Soogs-och Lantbruksabademiens Tidskrift 123 (5–6)*: 371–81.

McCauley, J. F., C. S. Breed, M. J. Crolier, and D. J. Mackinson. 1981. The U.S. dust storm of February 1977, 123–47. *Geological Society of America Special Paper 186*.

Meade, R. H. 1982. Sources, sinks, and storage of river sediment in the Atlantic drainage of the United States. *Journal of Geology 90*: 235–52.

Megahan, W. F. 1975. Sedimentation in relation to logging activities in the mountains of central Idaho. In *Present and Prospective Technology for Predicting Sediment Yields and Sources*. ARS-S-40, 74–82. U.S. Department of Agriculture: Agricultural Research Service.

Meybeck, M. 1976. Total mineral dissolved transport by world major rivers. *Hydrological Sciences Bulletin 21*: 265–84.

———. 1979. Concentrations des eaux fluviales en elements majeurs et apports en solution aux oceans. *Revue de geologie dynamique et geographie physique 21*: 215–46.

Milliman, J. D., and R. H. Meade. 1983. World-wide delivery of river sediment to the ocean. *Journal of Geology 91*: 1–21.

Mirabel, J. 1974. Suspended-sediment load of Texas streams. Compilation Report October 1965–September 1971. *Texas Water Development Board Report 184*.

Moller, J. T. 1985. Soil and sand-drift in Denmark. *GeoSkrifter 22*.

———. 1986. Soil degradation in a north European region. In *Desertification in Europe*, ed. R. Fantechi and N. S. Margaris, 214–30. Dordrecht: Reidel.

Moore, P. D. 1975. Origin of blanket mires. *Nature 256*: 267–69.

Morse, R. J., and D. N. Outhet. 1986. Sediment management on a total catchment basis. *Journal of Soil Conservation New South Wales 42*: 11–14.

Murray-Rust, D. H. 1972. Soil erosion and reservoir sedimentation in a grazing area west of Arusha, northern Tanzania. *Geografiska Annaler 54A*: 325–43.

Musset, R. 1958. *La Bretagne*. Paris: Armand Colin.

Newson, M. D. 1979. The results of ten years' experimental study on Plynlimon, Mid-Wales, and their importance for the water industry. *Journal of the Institution of Water Engineers and Scientists 33*: 321–33.

Nummedal, D. 1983. Barrier islands. In *CRC Handbook of Coastal Processes and Erosion*, ed. P. D. Komar, 77–121. Boca Raton, FL: CRC Press,

Observer, The. 1967. Farmers' Dust Bowl fears. January 29, 1967.

Oldfield, F. 1977. Lakes and their drainage basins as units of sediment-based ecological study. *Progress in Physical Geography 1*: 460–501.

Paskoff, R. 1981. *L'erosion des cotes*. Paris: Presses Universitaires de France.

Peck, A. J., J. F., Thomas, and J. R. Williamson. 1983. *Salinity Issues: Effects of Man on Salinity in Australia* (Water 2000: Consultants Report 8). Canberra: Australian Government Publishing Service.

Petts, G., and I. Foster. 1985. *Rivers and Landscapes*. London: Arnold.

Pewe, T. L., E. A. Pewe, R. H. Pewe, A. Journaux, and R. M. Slatt. 1981. Desert dust: characteristics and rates of deposition in central Arizona, USA. *Geological Society of America Special Paper 186*: 169–90.

Pickup, G., R. J. Huggins, and R. F. Warner. 1981. Erosion and sediment yield in Fly River drainage basins, Papua New Guinea. *International Association Hydrological Sciences Publication 132*: 438–56.

Pitty, A. F. 1968. Particle size of the Saharan dust which fell in Britain in July 1968. *Nature 220*: 364–65.

Radley, J., and C. Simms. 1967. Wind erosion in East Yorkshire. *Nature 216*: 19–22.

Rahn, K. A., R. D. Borys, and G. E. Shaw. 1981. Asian desert dust over Alaska: anatomy of an Arctic haze episode. *Geological Society of America Special Paper 186*: 37–70.

Reed, A. H. 1979. Accelerated erosion of arable soils in the United Kingdom by rainfall and runoff. *Outlook on Agriculture 10*: 41–48.

Ren Mei'E, Yang Renzhang, and Bao Haosheng. 1985. *An Outline of China's Physical Geography*. Beijing: Foreign Language Press.

Robinson, D. N. 1968. Soil erosion by wind in Lincolnshire, March 1968. *East Midland Geographer 4*: 351–62.

Russell, I. C. 1898. *River Development As Illustrated by the Rivers of North America*. London: John Murray.

Saunders, I., and A. Young. 1983. Rates of surface processes on slopes, slope retreat, and denudation. *Earth Surface Processes and Landforms 8*: 473–501.

Shallow, P. G. D. 1956. River flow in the Cameron Highlands. *Hydroelectric Board Technical Memorandum 3*.

Sham Sani. 1984. Inadvertent atmospheric modifications through urbanization in the Kuala Lumpur area. In *Urbanization and Ecodevelopment with Special Reference to Kuala Lumpur* (Institut Pengajian Tinggi Prosiding Seminar PRO 2), ed. Yip Yat Hoong and Low Kwai Sim, 155–69. Kuala Lumpur: Universiti Malaya.

Sheng, T. C. 1977. Protection of cultivated slopes – terracing, steep slopes in humid regions. *FAO Conservation Guide 1*: 147–69.

Shimen Reservoir Authority. 1975. *Shimen Reservoir Catchment Management Work Report*. Taipei: The Authority. (In Chinese.)

Silvestrov, S. I. 1971. Efforts to combat the process of erosion and deflation of agricultural land. In *Natural Resources of the Soviet Union: Their Use and Renewal*, ed. I. P. Gerasimov, D. L. Armand, and K. M. Yefron, 161–83. San Francisco: Freeman.

Smith, C. T. 1967. *An Historical Geography of Western Europe before 1800*. London: Longman.

Stamp, L. D. 1948. *The Land of Britain: Its Use and Misuse*. London: Longman.

Stott, A. P. 1987. Medium-term effects of afforestation on sediment dynamics in a water-supply catchment: A mineral magnetic interpretation of reservoir deposits in the Macclesfield forest,

N. W. England. *Earth Surface Processes and Landforms 12*: 619–30.

Stout, I. M., L. C. Bentz, and H. W. Ingram (compilers). 1961. Silt load of Texas streams: a compilation report June 1889–September 1959. *Texas Board of Water Engineers Bulletin, 6108.*

Sunamura, T. 1983. Processes of sea cliff and platform erosion. In *CRC Handbook of Coastal Processes and Erosion*, ed. P. D. Komar, 233–65. Boca Raton, FL: CRC Press.

———. 1987. Coastal cliff erosion in Nii-jima Island, Japan: Present, past and future – an application of mathematical model. In *International Geomorphology 1986*. Part I, ed. V. Gardiner, 1199–1212. Chichester: Wiley.

Tallis, J. H. 1975. Tree remains in southern Pennine peats. *Nature 256*: 483–84.

Trimble, S. W. 1976. Sedimentation in Coon Creek Valley, Wisconsin. *Proceedings, Third Federal Interagency Sedimentation Conference*, 5: 100–112.

———. 1983. A sediment budget for Coon Creek Basin in the driftless area, Wisconsin, 1853–1977. *American Journal of Science 283*: 454–74.

Trimble, S. W., and S. W. Lund. 1982. Soil conservation in the Coon Creek Basin, Wisconsin. *Journal of Soil and Water Conservation 37*: 355–56.

Troeh, F. R., J. A. Hobbs, and R. L. Donahue. 1980. *Soil and Water Conservation for Productivity and Environmental Protection.* Englewood Cliffs, NJ: Prentice-Hall.

Tucker, R., and J. F. Richards. 1985. The global economy and forest clearance in the nineteenth century. In *Environmental History: Critical Issues in Comparative Perspective*, ed. K. E. Bailes, 577–85. Lanham and London: University Press of America.

United Nations. Department of Industrial, Economic, and Social Affairs. 1985. *World Population Prospects: Estimates and Projections as Assessed in 1982* (Population Studies No. 86). New York: United Nations.

Van Haaren, F. W. J. 1963. The River Rhine as a source of drinking water. *Proceedings of the Society for Water Treatment and Examination 12*: 177–96.

Vita-Finzi, C. 1969. *The Mediterranean Valleys: Geological Changes in Historical Times.* Cambridge: Cambridge University Press.

Walling, D. E. 1977. Assessing the accuracy of suspended-sediment rating curves for a small basin. *Water Resources Research 13*: 531–38.

———. 1979. Reliability considerations in the evaluation and analysis of river loads. *Zeitschrift fur Geomorphologie NF Supp-Bd 29*: 29–42.

Walling, D. E., and B. W. Webb. 1983. Patterns of sediment yield. In *Background to Palaeohydrology*, ed. K. J. Gregory, 69–100. Chichester: Wiley.

Wasson, R. J., R. L. Clark, I. R. Willett, J. Waters, B. L. Cambell, and D. N. Outhet. 1984. Erosion history from sedimentation in Burrinjuck Reservoir, N. S. W. *Proceedings Drainage Basin and Sedimentation Conference, University of Newcastle, Australia.*

Wasson, R. J., R. L. Clark, P. M. Nanninga, and J. Water. 1987. ^{210}Pb as a chronometer and tracer, Burrinjuck Reservoir, Australia. *Earth Surface Processes and Landforms 12*: 399–414.

Webb, B. W., and D. E. Walling. 1982. The magnitude and frequency characteristics of fluvial transport in a Devon drainage basin and some geomorphological implications. *Catena 9*: 9–24.

White, B. M., B. J. Duke, and W. L. O. Jimoh. 1984. Mineralogy and chemistry of Harmattan dust in northern Nigeria. *Catena 11*: 91–96.

Whitehouse, I. E. 1983. Erosion in the eastern South Island high country – a changing perspective. *Tussock Grasslands and Mountain Lands Institute Review 42*: 3–23.

Wilkinson, B., W. Broughton, and J. Parker-Sutton. 1969. Survey of wind erosion on sandy soils in the East Midlands. *Experimental Husbandry 18*: 53–59.

Williams, P. W. 1980. From forest to suburb: The hydrological impact on man in New Zealand. In *The Land Our Future: Essays on Land Use and Conservation in New Zealand*, ed. A. G. Anderson, 103–24. Auckland: Longman Paul/New Zealand Geographical Society Inc.

Wilson, S. J., and R. U. Cooke. 1980. Wind erosion. In *Soil Erosion*, ed. M. J. Kirkby and R. P. C. Morgan, 217–51. Chichester: Wiley.

Wolman, M. G. 1967. A cycle of sedimentation and erosion in urban river channels. *Geografiska Annaler 49A*: 385–95.

World Resources Institute. 1986. *World Resources 1986: An Assessment of the Resource Base That Supports the Global Economy.* New York: Basic Books.

Yair, A. 1983. Hillslope hydrology, water harvesting, and areal distribution of some ancient agricultural systems in the northern Negev Desert. *Journal of Arid Environments 6*: 283–301.

Zachar, D. 1982. *Soil Erosion.* (Development in Soil Science 10). Amsterdam: Elsevier.

14

Use and Transformation of Terrestrial Water Systems

MARK I. L'VOVICH   GILBERT F. WHITE   with the collaboration of
A. V. BELYAEV   JANUSZ KINDLER   N. I. KORONKEVIC
TERENCE R. LEE   G. V. VOROPAEV

In the years since the beginning of the Industrial Revolution, the distribution of fresh water on the face of the earth has changed as a result of direct human efforts to manage water and also as a consequence of alterations in urban and rural land use influencing the flow and storage of water (Fig. 14.1). The principal direct actions were in manipulating stream channels, damming watercourses, draining wetlands, transferring water to urban and industrial consumers, extracting groundwater, and of greatest human consequence, irrigating agricultural lands. Chief among the indirect actions were the spread of cities, the plowing of grasslands, and the felling of forests. Thereby, the hydrologic cycle and associated ecosystems were disturbed in the search for enhanced agricultural and industrial production and urban amenities.

Determining the full nature of those transformations is handicapped by lack of statistics as to the human activities and waterflows, and also by imprecise understanding of how natural systems have been affected. Even where transformation processes are moderately well recognized, it is difficult to quantify them for large areas. One relatively accurate set of data, covering the land surfaces of the globe and permitting estimates of conditions prevailing in the seventeenth century, is the water balance analysis summed up by L'vovich in 1963, 1974 (English edition in 1979) and 1986.* While necessarily generalized as to the situation in local areas, those estimates offer a rough basis for comparing the approximate magnitude of transformations that have occurred over time and from place to place. We would like to have made the analysis in terms of clusters of river basins, but this was not practicable. We chose to provide global estimates by continents rather than to describe a few areas in detail. The case studies in chap. 15 illustrate certain of the situations and trends noted here. We do not examine changes in water quality and flow regimen that are mentioned in that chapter. We note, however, that perturbations in the water cycle often produce detrimental effects on quality rather than quantity, and we stress the rapidly growing proportion of stream flow that is affected by contamination.

We begin our review of changes in fresh-water location and use by briefly reviewing the world terrestrial hydrologic resource and river runoff in 1965. We then outline the spread of navigation channels, and also appraise the less comprehensive evidence as to changes in four types of land drainage, in flood management, and in groundwater aquifers. We next estimate the ways in which water balances and associated ecosystems have been modified by the construction of reservoirs and by withdrawals for irrigation, municipal, industrial, and livestock supply. This enables us to arrive at a calculation of the 300-year increases in runoff and consumptive water use. The influences of urbanization and of changes in soil moisture through farming and forestry are reviewed, and a final estimate is made of underground runoff, surface runoff, total river runoff, and evaporation for 1980 by comparison with 1680. We conclude with a series of observations on the interrelation of population, social organization, technology, and environmental conditions as they help explain the enormous changes in the past and as they possibly point the way toward promoting a more harmonious future.

World Fresh-water Resources

Information on the present use and anthropogenic transformation of world resources of fresh water permits description only in approximate terms. There are no completely comparable worldwide statistics on use, and to obtain a retrospective picture it is necessary to use fragmental initial data, expert estimations, and indirect evidence. For example, calculations of domestic and municipal water withdrawal may be made from data on size of population and prevailing techniques of water supply and withdrawal. The withdrawal of water by irrigated agriculture clearly accounts for the overwhelming proportion of all water resources use, but to determine the specific volumes we employ relatively reliable data on area currently irrigated and only very approximate data on the amount of water withdrawn and used consumptively for that purpose in different areas: estimates of earlier use require inference as to the relation of irrigation to population and agricultural land within similar climate zones.

The confidence level for estimates of changes in water regime depends on their character. Calculation of some direct

---

* This chapter contains two separate references: one for English, French, and German words; the second for Russian words.

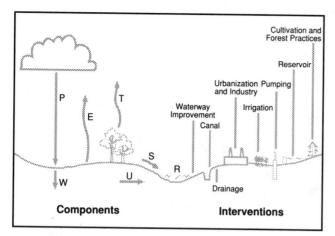

Figure 14.1 Major components and human interventions in the hydrologic cycle. The six components of the water balance are shown on the left, and evapotranspiration is divided between evaporation (E) and transpiration (T). The interventions embrace both direct and indirect activities and are shown on the right. P = precipitation, R = runoff, U = underground (stable) runoff to rivers, or base flow, S = surface runoff, W = soil moisture.

interventions, such as construction of large reservoirs, may be relatively reliable. Much more complicated is evaluation of indirect impacts on the water cycle, for instance, those resulting from nonirrigated agricultural practices. Notwithstanding these difficulties, it now seems practicable to use recent hydrologic and geographic research to venture estimates of water resources for those continental regions whose hydrology has not been studied (L'vovich 1945, 1974). This involves considerable parts of developing countries.[1]

We have been obliged to assume a conditional stability and to eliminate descriptions of natural fluctuations from year to

year during the period of 300 years. The estimates are for mean annual conditions.

The forerunners of the methods that provide modern knowledge of water resources of the world's continents, individual countries, and regions appeared at the beginning of our 300-year period. In subsequent years, a general view of the water cycle as atmospheric precipitation equaling the sum of evaporation and river runoff was elaborated and refined. By the middle of the twentieth century, a six-component method represented a new stage in water balance studies (Fig. 14.1). It interprets the process of water cycle in a broader and deeper framework:

$$P = U + S + E; \quad R = U + S; \quad W = P - S; \quad W = U + E$$

At first, this method was used for studying and evaluating the anthropogenic transformation of water balance, and, later on, for making global water-balance maps (L'vovich 1974, 1979 in English; Dreier 1969, 1978; Karasik 1970, 1974; Chernogaeva 1971; Nikolaeva and Chernogaeva 1977).

Those maps are constructed by interpolating relationships of climatic, vegetation, and soil factors within geographic zones. (The theoretical aspect has been analyzed by Belyaev 1978.) The six-component method requires the estimation of runoff hydrographs based on daily data that in many areas are either not collected or not published. By using zonal relationships, estimates of those parameters may be made for such areas. Details of the computational theory and practice are to be found in L'vovich 1979.

The maps of water-balance elements published in *World Water Resources and Their Future* (L'vovich, in Russian, 1974; in Polish and English, 1979) included anthropogenic impacts on the water balance up to 1965. Those data sub-

Table 14-1 *Estimated constituents of river runoff and anthropogenic change, 1680–1980 (km³/yr)*

Continents	Total river runoff (R)			Base flow (U)			Surface runoff (S)			Atmospheric precipitation on continents (P)	Evaporation from land (E)	
	1680	Anthropogenic change	1980	1680	Anthropogenic change	1980	1680	Anthropogenic change	1980		1680	1980
Europe	3,240	−200	3,040	980	+210	1,190	2,260	−410	1,850	7,165	3,925	4,125
Asia	14,550	−1,740	12,810	3,630	+50	3,680	10,920	−1,790	9,130	32,140	18,140	19,880
Africa	4,320	−140	4,180	1,250	+450	1,700	3,075	−595	2,480	20,780	16,450	16,600
North America	6,200	−320	5,880	1,180	+1,170	2,350	5,020	−1,490	3,530	13,910	7,710	8,030
South America	10,420	−60	10,360	3,650	+260	3,910	6,770	−320	6,450	29,355	18,940	18,995
Australia and Oceania	1,970	−10	1,960	450	+40	496	1,520	−50	1,470	6,405	4,435	4,445
World	40,700	−2,470*	38,230	11,140	+2,180†	13,320	29,560	−4,650‡	24,910	110,305	69,605	72,075

* Consumptive use of fresh-water resources.

† (+) = increase of the resources of stable runoff due to regulation by reservoirs – transfer in time from the periods abundant in water (flood) to low-water periods, when rivers are mainly replenished from the underground basins, and not an absolute increase.

‡ Including 2,500 km³/yr consumptive use, and 2,200 km³/yr from the runoff regulated by reservoirs.

Note: In this table, the estimated runoff for 1680 is modified to account for changes estimated to have occurred as a result of withdrawals for irrigation, domestic, industrial, and livestock uses, and of urbanization. It does not include estimates of changes due to altered soil and vegetation conditions.

sequently were revised to take account of changes to 1985. Table 14-1 presents an estimate of actual river runoff (R) by continents in the mid-1960s. It distributes that runoff between the underground, or base, flow (U) and the surface runoff (S). The resulting totals differ somewhat from estimates prepared for the period 1970–1980 by other research groups.[2] Altogether, about 20 separate computations have been made of global river runoff. The spread in estimates resulting from these computations suggests that the figures we present, as well as the underlying data, should be regarded as subject to further refinement and correction as better data are obtained and relationships are better understood. Taking account of differences in time period, areas covered, and modes of calculation, the data in Fig. 14.2 are believed to be reasonably consistent internally, and do not differ from other major estimates in ways that indicate gross distortion from reality.

More than one-half of total runoff is from the Asian and South American land masses. It has not been practicable to compute the water balance for subdivisions of the continents, although approximate estimates are available with the help of maps for 128 countries of the world. The proportions of runoff to atmospheric precipitation and of base flow to total runoff provide rough indicators of the extent to which flows are influenced over short periods by variations in precipitation, and reflect losses from evaporation, transpiration, and other consumptive uses.

The estimates of river runoff should be supplemented by two other sets of data to yield a global perspective on total resources of fresh water. They would be incomplete without taking account of ice and water runoff from polar glaciers. Krenke (1987) estimated water runoff from melting of ice and snow in Greenland to amount to 240 km³/yr. Contributions from calving ice are considered to be 237 km³/yr (Kotlyakov and Krenke 1980), making total input of water and ice from glacial covers of the arctic region about 477 km³/yr. As for the Antarctic area, nearly all water reaching the sea is in the form of ice and comprises 2,400 km³/yr (Kotlyakov, Losev, and Loseva 1977). Liquid runoff in the Antarctic, as calculated by Krenke, accounts for only 15 km³/yr. These data introduce important additions to estimates of magnitude of water and ice runoff from polar glaciers. They also change perceptions of runoff patterns from the Antarctic glaciers: only 0.6% of that runoff is liquid, and 99.4% is in the form of ice.

Direct underground runoff into oceans by paths other than rivers also is a second important source of fresh-water resource that is now used in a few cases, and represents great potentialities. Studies of these elements of the water cycle give the following figures, in km³/yr (Zektser, Dzhamalov, and Meskheteli 1984): Europe, 167; Asia, 328; Africa, 236; North America, 344; South America and Oceania, 385; Australia, 938; World, 2,398.

Taking into account all three major sources, contemporary world fresh-water flows amount to approximately:

River runoff, including anthropogenic transformations in 1965:	38,830 km³/yr
Water and ice runoff from polar glaciers:	2,900 km³/yr
Direct underground runoff into oceans:	2,400 km³/yr
Total:	44,130 km³/yr

Within this broad framework of fresh water in its global forms and flows, we move to a review of principal changes in water on the face of the earth. These changes have been described in a number of ways, including Falkenmark's diagram of crucial points in the water cycle (1986). From this

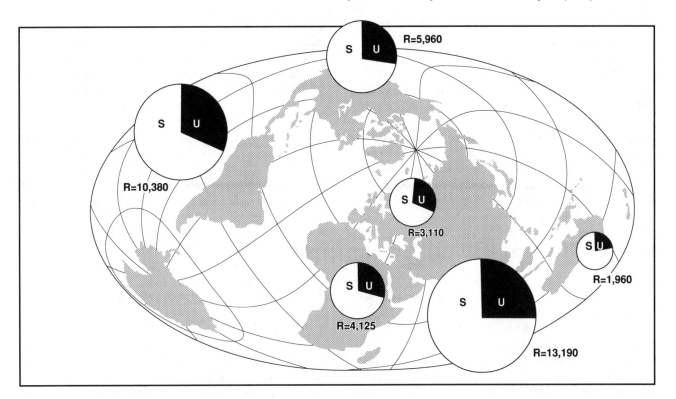

Figure 14.2 Estimated world river runoff, 1985 (km³/yr).

review we conclude with a summary estimate of the magnitude of anthropogenic alterations since 1680. The specific processes of change have been discussed in a number of scientific reviews such as those of L'vovich (1986) and Hirsch et al. (forthcoming).

During the past 50 years, the working definition of usable fresh water changed as a result of two types of technological developments. Processes for desalting sea water became increasingly economical, so that in a number of very dry areas, as in the Persian Gulf, it was feasible to convert seawater for domestic use. Parallel to desalting, means were developed to use salty water for cooling of industrial operations, and also to apply it successfully to specially bred crops, such as rice, with careful control of application and drainage.

In estimating the period 1980–1985 to earlier periods, the assumptions carry the possibility of deviation from the true conditions prevailing at the time. The farther back the estimates are extended, the greater the probability of error. The probability can be expressed as our judgment as to the range of years over which the estimate might apply, as follows:

Century	Confidence Band in Years
17th	20–30
18th	10–15
19th	5–10
20th	2–4

This suggests, for example, that an estimate for 1980 should be interpreted as being possibly valid for any year between 1976 and 1984, and that an estimate for 1800 should be interpreted as being possibly valid for any year between 1790 and 1810. The effects of human activities in much of the early period may have been minor by comparison with natural variations.

Direct Alterations

Inland Waterways

The earliest extensive human modifications of fresh water on the face of the earth were for transport and irrigation. The improvement of waterways for navigation involved a wide variety of measures, including deepening, bank revetments, simple flash locks, ponds, inclines, and canals. Most of those works had relatively minor effects on water flow and aquatic ecosystems, except to the extent they required water storage or diverted flows outside their natural watersheds or reduced the channel length.

By the end of the seventeenth century, many earlier Roman and Babylonian projects had fallen into disuse, but a few large canal projects and a number of smaller improvements of streams were in operation (Encyclopedia Britannica 1986). They included the Grand and Sian-Huang Ho canals in China, a network of canals in the Low Countries, the Naviglio Grande in Italy, the Loire-Seine and Languedoc canals in France, and the Spree-Oder Canal in Germany, with a total length of about 1,430 km (Fig. 14.3). Small canals were in use in the basin of Mexico. Canal building accelerated in France, Germany, and the Low Countries, and took hold in Britain and Russia during the eighteenth century.

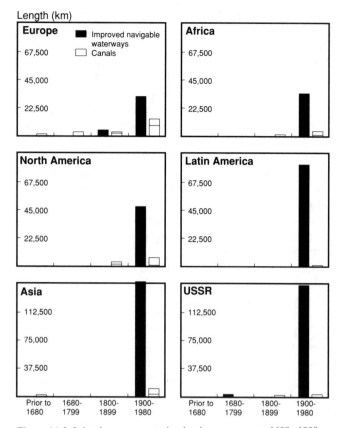

Length (km)

Figure 14.3 Inland waterway navigation improvements, 1680–1980. The length of improved waterways includes channels that have been deepened, widened, or straightened in some degree to promote waterborne transportation.

By the early nineteenth century, the main components of the European waterway systems had been completed. Canal building and river improvement in the United States was prominent throughout the nineteenth century, although there, as in Europe, railroad competition forced the abandonment of numerous smaller waterways after midcentury. During the same time, a few very large waterways for ocean vessels were undertaken: the Suez, Kiel, and Panama canals, completed, respectively, in 1869, 1884, and 1914.

In most parts of the industrialized world, canal construction amounting to over 20,000 km had ended by the early 1900s, but a few new projects were undertaken thereafter, and channel improvements continued to assure navigation on larger systems such as the Danube, Rhine, Yangtze, Ganges, and Mississippi rivers. The major extensions were a part of new reservoir construction such as on the Tennessee, Dneiper-Don-Volga, and Danube rivers.

In 1985, the length of navigable waterways exceeded 500,000 km. The pattern of modified river courses had been set, and few major changes were in prospect.

The Role of Reservoirs

In the last quarter of the nineteenth century, reservoirs began to play an important role in water economy by transforming the water regime of rivers and by creating new water surfaces. They now are one of the main anthropogenic impacts on water. Their geographic and social role was not

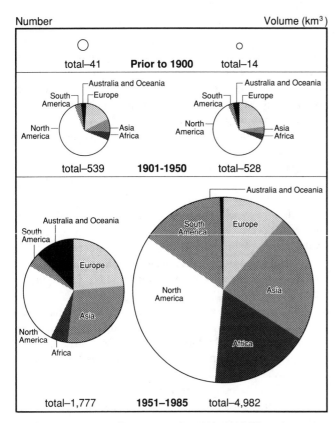

Figure 14.4 Volume of large reservoirs, 1900–1985. The volumes, totaled by continent, are for all reservoirs with a storage volume of 100 million m³ or more.

poses of either navigation, irrigation, hydroelectric power generation, or municipal water supply. At that period attention turned to construction for multiple purposes, often planned for river basins as units, and construction was expanded to include flood control by either storage or detention, pollution abatement, wildlife conservation, or recreation purposes (White 1957; United Nations 1970). The great burst in building of large dams was accompanied in subsequent years by concern for the environmental effects of the new water bodies and the alteration in downstream flows. A series of scientific inquiries into those consequences took shape, and have continued into recent years, with studies of the physical and biological consequences for ecosystems and of the effects on populations and economies (Ackermann et al. 1973; ICOLD 1973; Petts 1985; SCOPE 1972).

In addition to the flooding of reservoir land, for most dams the major immediate impact was in alteration of flow downstream – whether by storage to increase low flows or to curb high flows – and this was accompanied by few or many among a large array of other changes. Those other impacts include: physical changes in evaporation, groundwater seepage, channel and bank scouring, sediment transport and deposition, mineral quality, and soil moisture; biological changes in lake, river, and estuary biota and flora; and social changes in human population location, health, and economy (Voropaev and Avakian 1986). Because of the immense diversity in reservoir size, operation schedule, and environment, it is difficult to generalize about the resulting combination of effects, but it is practicable to estimate the magnitude on a continental scale of the alterations in downstream flow and in reservoir evaporation.

Figure 14.5 gives very rough estimates of the water-regulating efficiency of large reservoirs for which data are available. As shown, the total maximum volume reaches approximately 5,500 km³, while that portion actively used in the regulation of river runoff is 3,500 km³, which makes it possible to increase stable runoff by about 30%. In arriving at this figure, we make the highly simplified assumption that the useful volume of a reservoir is filled once a year, a condition applying chiefly to rivers that are characterized by one yearly spring wave of floods or by floods coming closely one after another. Where the interflood periods are prolonged, it may be possible to empty the useful volume and replenish it several times a year, depending on the reservoir capacity and on a number of natural, constructional, and economic circumstances. For that reason, we consider our estimates of the influence of reservoirs on the regime of rivers to be conservative.

The largest degree of runoff regulation, using the above calculation, is in North America, and the smallest in South America and Australia with Oceania. In Europe, Asia, and Africa, the increase of efficiency ranges between 26% and 36%. In the USSR, the increase of the stable river runoff with the help of reservoirs reaches 54%. Obviously, these figures do not imply an absolute increase of fresh-water resources; water is reserved from periods of abundant supply for periods when the supply is deficient.

The most direct physical effect of permanent or seasonal

limited to regulation of river runoff: new impoundment areas were created that differed radically from the riverine ecosystems, as well as from natural lakes, in their environmental consequences.

The history of water reservoirs over several thousand years is concisely presented by Voropaev and Avakian (1986), but large reservoirs began to be significant only in the second half of the nineteenth century (see Fig. 14.4).

After 1951, three times as many reservoirs with volumes of more than 100 million m³ were created as in all previous years. Their total volume was nine times as great. Their maximum water surface now is estimated at about 590,000 km². Some larger reservoirs constructed before that time had been destroyed, as in Sri Lanka, while thousands of small reservoirs, many with mill wheels, were created on small drainage areas. Voropaev and Avakian estimate the aggregate volume of such small impoundments to be only 4.5% of the total world volume of reservoir storage. This is within the accuracy limits of the regulating capacity of the large ones. The surface area of the smaller units nevertheless is important in comparison to total agricultural land in their respective river valleys, and we have estimates of the extent of small reservoir development in selected countries, but cannot venture a global total. For areas in which reservoirs are numerous, the most promising sites usually were developed first, and the mean size of storage, accordingly, declined thereafter.

Until the 1930s, the central concern with dam and reservoir design was in river-flow regulation, primarily for single pur-

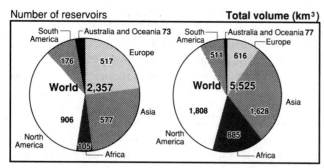

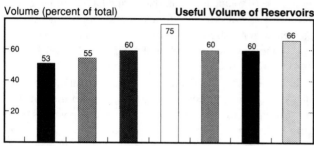

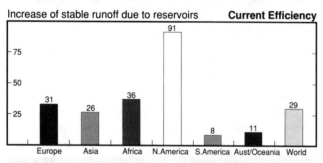

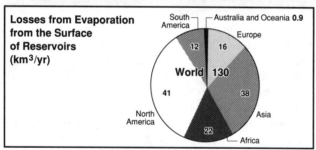

Figure 14.5 Estimated regulation of river and evaporation by reservoirs of over 100 million m³ capacity, 1985.

for evaporation from large reservoirs comprise about 130 km³. This is less than 4% of the regulated volume of runoff, but in extreme arid climates, it may be very important, as at Lake Nasser behind the High Aswan Dam where annual evaporation losses amount to as much as 11% of lake volume. No general estimates are available for seepage losses not compensated by increased stable flow downstream, as at Lake Powell on the Colorado River. Nor is there general information on sedimentation, groundwater, and broader ecosystem and social effects.

Hydropower

Inasmuch as hydroelectric generation is mainly connected with surface-water storage, it has large significance for water management as well as for environmental quality. It has stimulated water development for other purposes, and poses major questions as to environmentally sound energy production.

Water wheels as sources of mechanical energy had been used in many countries before 1680, and their proliferation was associated with the Industrial Revolution in Europe. The first steps in the construction of hydropower plants were made in the 1870s and 1880s.

With the development of technology for electricity generation and transmission, the design and construction of water storage and diversion works was significantly affected in several ways. The sale of electric power provided a new, strong incentive for water storage. Those works could be located at a distance that progressively lengthened from the centers of electricity consumption. The revenues from sale of electric power made it possible through a variety of cost-allocation arrangements to fund components of storage projects, such as flood control, that did not readily yield monetary returns. The availability of relatively cheap electric power enabled new water-pumping and conveyance projects to be developed for irrigation, domestic, and industrial purposes. Industry became less dependent upon riverside location.

In addition, hydropower offered the technical opportunity to generate electricity without the degrading effects of mineral extraction and air and water pollution associated with coal- and oil-fueled plants, and without the radiation hazard and waste generation of nuclear plants. It thus became an attractive alternative, where economically feasible, to those sources of electricity, At the same time, reservoirs increasingly were recognized as generating major alterations in the areas flooded as well as in downstream aquatic ecosystems.

In 1984, the proved capacity of all hydropower plants in the world was estimated to be 542 million Kw, or 23% of the capacity of all electric power plants (Fig. 14.6). In 1970, the capacity of the world hydropower plants had been almost half (290 million Kw), or 24%, of the capacity of all plants. Beginning in the late nineteenth century and up to the 1970s, hydro's share of total energy capacity increased. In recent decades, it has more or less stabilized, but not uniformly in all the continents. For instance, in North America the ratio of hydropower plants to total energy-generating capacity decreased, in Europe and Asia it decreased slowly, while in South America it rapidly increased.

storage is in the loss of land resources. The economic impact depends upon the utility of inundated areas in relation to the use of neighboring territory. Excluding surfaces of contributing lake and river waters, the maximum surface areas of all the large reservoirs when full comprises about 390,000 km² (Voropaev and Avakian 1986). This area is comparable with the area of France, or 0.3% of the continents. At a global scale, inundation of that magnitude provides about 9 km³ of stable runoff for each 1,000 km² of land inundated.

Evaporation losses from reservoir surfaces are taken to be equal to potential evaporation minus the evaporation from soil (E) prior to the filling of the reservoir, using mean figures for E for each climatic zone. In our estimates, the surfaces of affluent lakes and rivers also have been deducted from the total area of reservoirs. The results show that annual losses

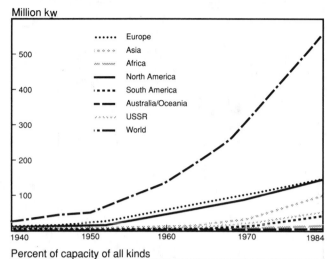

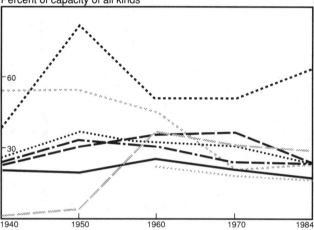

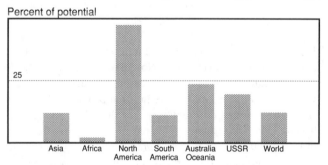

Figure 14.6 World hydropower potential and developed capacity, and proportion of total electricity-generating capacity, 1940–1984.

By 1985, it was estimated that of the theoretical capacity of the world's rivers to generate hydroelectric power, neglecting economic criteria, about 20% had been developed (Hubbert 1974, for potential).

Transbasin Diversions

Early in the twentieth century a number of engineering projects were undertaken to transfer water from one river basin to another (Golubev and Biswas 1985). Chiefly near the watersheds in which water was available to divert into an adjoining basin with more urgent uses for irrigation, municipal, or electrical-generation purposes, the transfers were for the most part small in size. A few, such as the diversions from the upper Colorado basin to the upper Missouri basin or from the lower Colorado basin to the southern California coastal area,

had significant effects on the basins of origin, as did the California State Water Plan. Several canals in the USSR annually divert in total more than $60 \, km^3$ of water resources. In addition to changing runoff in each basin, they alter the conditions of aquatic life.

By the late 1970s, there had been enough experience with a few of the transfer projects, and proposals to initiate much larger projects were sufficiently advanced to stimulate more intensive appraisal of the social and environmental consequences of such enterprises, as reported in Golubev and Biswas. The proposed new transfers were of huge proportions: the North American Water Power Alliance in Canada and the United States; the north-south river diversions in the USSR; and the south-north transfer in China. None of them had been initiated by 1987, and planning for those in the United States and the USSR had been suspended, and the discussions relating to them mark a new, more critical stage in thinking about manipulation of water resources on a continental scale.

Aquifer Depletion

Although the water balance estimates attempt to take into account the movement and storage of underground water that contributes to the base flow of streams, they do not deal with the modifications that have been made in the volumes of water stored in deeper aquifers and that are withdrawn only by pumping. The volume of such pumping has been included in the estimated annual withdrawals for domestic, municipal, industrial, power, and irrigation uses, but there is no readily available set of data to indicate their magnitude and depletion rates on a continental scale.

Current calculations of the fresh-water resources of the world suggest that of some 64 million km^3 of undergound water, perhaps 4 million km^3 are in a zone of active exchange with the surface (L'vovich 1979). As a result of advances in the technology of well drilling and pumps, and in response to relatively low costs of diesel and electric power for pumping, exploitation of the more accessible aquifers increased rapidly after the 1930s. To the extent that it exceeded natural recharge (for many deeper aquifers there is no recharge), the balance was altered, reserves were depleted, and in extreme cases of rapid depletion, as at Osaka and Houston, ground subsidence resulted.

Lacking comprehensive data on these massive alterations of the past four decades, it is practicable to note only a selection of instances of aquifer depletion, as reported by the United Nations (1975, 1982, 1986a) and the U.S. Geological Survey (1983), to indicate the extent and rapidity of the changes under way. In some areas, such as in certain sectors of the Danube and Rhine valleys, artificial recharge and demand management are maintaining the aquifer. In others, the capacity to maintain a stable resource is threatened by delay in instituting corrective measures, as in the Ghazin plain in Iran, and the Lathi aquifer in Rajasthan. In still others, the pace of continued depletion is steady: in High Plains of the United States during the 1980s, 19% of the area underlain by the aquifer system reported water-level declines of more than 3 m.

Floodplains

As a result of reservoir detention, channel straightening and deepening, and levees, the surfaces of the earth subject to inundation by peak river flows were reduced over very wide areas beginning in the late nineteenth century and continuing into the midtwentieth century. Some of this restriction in lands reached by floods was incidental to navigation, irrigation, and drainage improvements (polders are noted in a later section), and some was undertaken explicitly to reduce damage hazard in urban areas or to permit more stable agriculture in rural areas. As with most efforts at flood control, there is rarely complete assurance that the area protected will be free of inundation by the maximum possible flood, but much of it may be protected from all but very rare, and then catastrophic, events.

In terms of mean annual flood damage, in contrast to areas subject to inundation, the reductions in floodplain were accompanied in many areas by increases in potential losses from catastrophic events, as well as by more intense occupation of unprotected areas, so that losses continued to mount in a number of countries, including the United States and Japan, where flood-control measures were undertaken.

One effect of the reduction in flood hazard, beyond the changes in damages from the more frequent floods, was the alteration of ecosystems that were dependent upon periodic scouring or inundation and sediment deposits. Another effect was encouragement and support of more intensive agriculture in areas previously subject to damaging inundation.

Irrigated Agriculture

At the end of the seventeenth century, the world's irrigated areas comprised a little over 2% of their present extent and were mainly concentrated in southern, eastern, and central Asia, as well as between the Tigris and Euphrates rivers. Irrigation was widespread in the delta and valley of the Nile in Africa, and on scattered and very modest scales, in the south of Europe and in North and South America.

During the eighteenth and nineteenth centuries, the world's irrigated areas increased on an average of not more than 2% a year. Much of the growth occurred in North America, where, during the nineteenth century, there was an almost tenfold increase. By this time North America was next only to Asia in farming area reached by canals (Fig. 14.7).

With the second half of the twentieth century, a qualitatively new stage in the development of irrigation began. In that period, the mean annual growth of irrigated areas increased two- or threefold, and was particularly striking in Europe and America. The limits of irrigated agriculture were pushed to the north; in regions with favorable temperature conditions, it increasingly was practiced year-round (for instance, when rice is planted as seedlings), and was used as a supplemental means to raise yields.

By 1985, the area of the world's irrigated lands was estimated to be as follows (in thousands of km^2): Europe, 170; Asia, 1,790; Africa, 90; North America, 275; South America, 67; Australia and Oceania, 17; world, 2,509. These data are of a tentative character: different sources estimate the total figure as ranging from 2,198 thousand km^2 (FAO Production

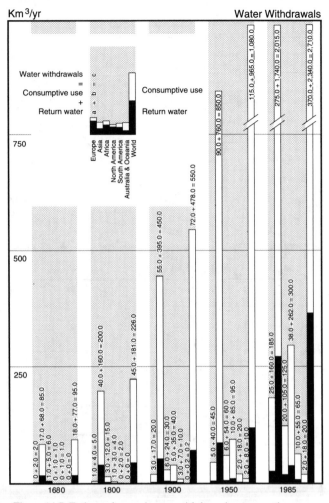

Figure 14.7 Estimated annual water withdrawal, consumptive use, and return flow for irrigation, 1680–1985.

1986) to 4,580 thousand km^2 (Framji and Mahajan, 1969). Another source (Zonn and Nosenko 1981) gives 2,640 thousand km^2. There are several reasons for such differences. Systematic statistics are lacking in some countries. Irrigated lands are classified differently: two or three harvests on one hectare may be considered to be one or two or three hectares of irrigated land. Under some conditions, one sowing is done with irrigation, and another without it, when the latter period is sufficiently humid. Sometimes the whole growing period during a wet year has abundant precipitation and there is no need of irrigation during that season. In some countries, the irrigated area is counted as land that could be reached by water when projected works are completed and in operation. In certain countries, lands are counted even when abandoned because of water logging or salinization. We have chosen conservative estimates of the lands actually affected, and working back from the present, have calculated the volumes of water withdrawn, transpired, or evaporated in irrigation activities.

It should be underlined that it is the return water that carries salts and other pollutants, and that it may empty into streams whose dilution capacity has been reduced by diversion. Where such drainage is inadequate, water logging occurs, and where the application of water is insufficient to leach the soil, salinization or alkalinization follows. The total area of soils whose productivity now is impaired as a result of deficient drainage or leaching is in doubt. The rates of deterioration are known in only scattered areas, and range from slight impairment to complete abandonment of cultivation, but they are substantial, and should be considered along with gains from new irrigation. In recent decades, due to extensive application of fertilizers, pesticides, fungicides, and herbicides, the return waters have become more and more dangerous for the natural environment.

Although irrigation projects have been completely abandoned in a few areas, the more common situation is either partial abandonment or decreased productivity; data are not available to quantify the respective proportions. Thus, it has been conventional wisdom in parts of the eastern Mediterranean and southwest Asian regions to argue that irrigated-land productivity has been declining at about the same rate as new lands are brought into production.

In preparing Fig. 14.7, the world consumptive use of water for irrigation was estimated separately for three irrigated cultures in appropriate climatic provinces: rice, other grain crops, and cotton and other technical cultures. Norms of water use for each culture are taken from available sources (L'vovich 1986). In regions of extensive irrigation, return water makes up between 20% and 30% or even more of the total water intake. In regions with more limited water resources, an economical application of water predominates, and so smaller estimates of return waters are given.

Drainage

Four different types of alteration of the water cycle result from wholesale elimination of wetlands by drainage. The first is the drainage of natural bogs and boggy lands, whose thickness sometimes reaches several meters, mainly in the humid forest zone. The second is the drainage of low-lying areas of grasslands to permit their cultivation. Third is the drainage and protection of coastal lands, or polders, otherwise subject to inundation from high tides and storm surges. The fourth is the disposal of excess water from irrigated fields, a measure in some places essential to developing an irrigation project, and in virtually all areas essential to preventing the long-term destruction of irrigated lands by water logging, salinization, or alkalinization.

There is no comprehensive set of data for drained lands comparable to irrigated lands, partly because drainage is a requisite for continued productive cultivation of most irrigated

lands, and may or may not be reported in those statistics.

The areas shown as drained in Fig. 14.8 include the information available as to the first, second, and fourth categories. While incomplete, it reflects high concentrations of drainage works in irrigated areas in the forest and peat lands of temperate zones.

The polder lands of the world are areas of highly intensive treatment that otherwise would be periodically flooded or waterlogged, and may total something over 7,000 km^2. With areas in hundred thousand hectares shown in parentheses, they are located for the most part in the Netherlands (2,000), Bangladesh (1,360), United Kingdom (900), Romania (741), West Germany (440), Poland (180), Thailand (176), and Guinea Bissau (100). Where located near dense urban populations, they are the base for sophisticated market gardening, as in the Netherlands, but they also provide a major segment of grain production in Bangladesh. Although the Netherlands polders were underway in the sixteenth century, the major expansion began in the period from 1930 to 1960. For all classes of drained lands, the pace of development was 1–2% annually in recent years.

For many years it was believed that the drainage of these low areas would alter the water balance and runoff regimes of downstream rivers. It now is recognized that in a natural state, a large proportion of this water evaporates and that, when these low areas are drained, the evaporation may decrease and the increase in runoff lower in their basins is significant for only a few years (Ivanov 1975). The long-term consequences of drainage for water balance, thus, are relatively modest, whereas their effects on ecosystems and agricultural productivity are massive.

Other Water Supply and Withdrawal

Beginning in the nineteenth century, the diverse and complicated types of water use were characterized not only by rapid growth of withdrawals for domestic and industrial purposes, but also by the appearance of waste waters. Improved methods of water withdrawal and cheaper energy sources promoted an increasing intake of water per unit of population served. Methods for treating or preventing the waste in water not consumed did not grow proportionately.

Domestic and Municipal Water Supply

The actual withdrawal for domestic purposes ranges from 10–20 to 200–500 l. per day per person. These parameters greatly vary in space and have a tendency to increase in time. For households without piped supply, where water must be carried each day, the daily per capita withdrawal rarely exceeds 20 l., and little water returns to streams. This is the case for about 60% of the present world population. In 1687, only an insignificant part of the world population used piped water.

During the nineteenth century, Europe and North America probably experienced a threefold increase in the volume of water withdrawn for domestic municipal needs, and this kind of use enlarged its share in total water withdrawal (Fig. 14.9). By the twentieth century, especially in its second half, the accelerated rates of population growth accompanied by

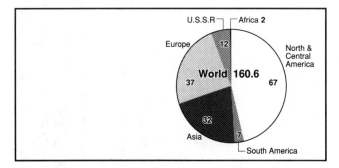

Figure 14.8 Estimated area of drained lands in thousands of km^2, 1985. Numbers are rounded.

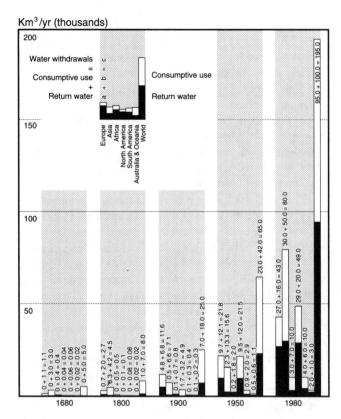

Figure 14.9 Estimated annual water withdrawal, consumptive use, and waste water for domestic-municipal uses, 1680–1980.

began to be transported to irrigated fields, as in Berlin. The amounts of waste water per unit of urban area were considerable, reaching between 60,000 and 80,000 m³ hectares/year and more. As a result, the level of the underground water rose in some places and pollution threatened water supply.

From the 1920s onward, industrial municipalities began to consider a variety of waste treatment, ranging from simple removal of solids through activated sludge treatment to complete recycling, and by the 1960s, the annual investment in treatment plants had become substantial. We have no accurate global data on the extent or degree of treatment or its effect on the receiving waters. We can be confident, however, of the approximate volume of waste water returned to streams, and that much of it has not been treated.

Water Supply in Industry and Power Production

Withdrawal for industry and power production occupies the leading place after irrigation, and in 1980 was estimated at about 700 km³ (Fig. 14.10). The withdrawals involve water for transport, cooling, and processing within manufacturing plants, and cooling for thermal power stations.

The first industrial enterprises – textile mills – appeared in

the advancement of water-supply technology for extracting groundwater, lifting water, and piping it, promoted a rapid rise in the amount of water used for those purposes. During the past 300 years, the domestic-municipal use of water increased almost 40-fold. At present it comprises about 200 km³.

Until the midnineteenth century, over half of the domestic withdrawal was in Asia, corresponding to the large population of that continent. By the beginning of the twentieth century, Europe and North America accounted for two-thirds of the world use. At present, developing countries, due to a considerable growth of population, approach this level of withdrawal and in the near future will surpass it.

With the construction of municipal and piped systems of water supply, waste waters appeared as significant features of water use. On the eve of the twentieth century, the annual volume of return water comprised 7 km³, out of a total water intake of 25 km³. At present, it is almost 100 km³. Early in the 300-year period, the volume of all municipal waste water was minute and was significant chiefly in a few cities (London, Moscow, Paris, and Rome). Regular sewerage systems were scarce; the majority of citizens dumped all their wastes directly into the street gutters that occasionally carried storm drainage. In Chinese cities, domestic waste commonly was carried to the fields. During the second half of the nineteenth century, sewers began to appear in many cities. As long as the burden of waste was small in relation to the assimilative capacity of the receiving stream or lake, the effects on aquatic ecosystems were minor. During the mid-1800s, recognition that unsanitary conditions fostered disease encouraged improvement in sanitary facilities. In a number of cases, waste waters

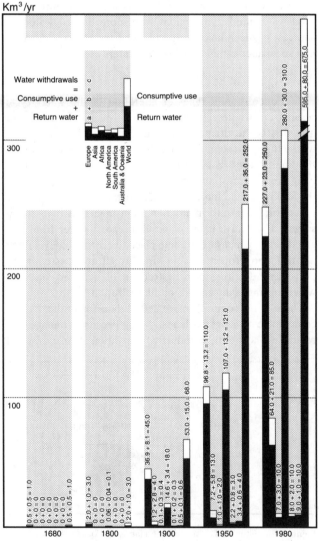

Figure 14.10 Estimated annual water withdrawal, consumptive use, and return water for industrial and power production, 1680–1980.

the second half of the sixteenth century – first in England, and then in other, mainly European, countries as the Industrial Revolution advanced. Until the early nineteenth century, manual labor and mechanical power predominated at these enterprises, and they consumed little water. With the growth of industrial and energy production, the volumes of water used for those purposes considerably increased. This was primarily true of Europe and the United States, which together by the beginning of the nineteenth century accounted for about 95% of the world industrial-power intake of water. At that time, the industry of Europe used 2.5 times as much water as the United States and Canada, but in the twentieth century the picture reversed. In the first half of the twentieth century, the consumption of water by the North American industrial complex increased by more than six times, and then by another three times during the subsequent 35 years. Industrial and power water use in Europe increased fivefold 1900–1980. Increased water consumption was due, in part, to the development of large thermal electricity generating plants, which placed a new demand on water for cooling. Approximately half of all industrial withdrawals are now for cooling water that is returned, heated, to rivers.

In Europe and North America, there is lively interest in measures of economic, technologic, and ecologic character, such as water-demand management, industrial-processing improvements, and closed cycles of water supply, which would reduce water intake. In the near future, however, a considerable increase of the industrial and power water intake, and consequently of waste water, should be expected in developing countries.

At present, the volume of used, polluted waters returned to rivers by industry reaches 600 km³ a year, comprising 88% of the total water intake by these sectors of the economy.

Water Supply for Livestock

Using FAO data on current numbers and distribution of livestock, and information on water requirements, we have estimated the numbers and water needs of domestic animals for earlier years (FAO 1981, 1986). Numbers of human population, relations of cattle population to pasture areas, and human requirements for animal proteins were taken into account.

This rough assessment suggests that water withdrawal for domestic livestock increased 20-fold and has reached a magnitude of 60 km³/yr. Roughly one-sixth of this water is returned to rivers by overground or underground flow. The volume is not large by comparison with other uses, but the high organic content of the waste water (one average head of the more than 1 billion cattle produces 10 times more waste than one average human) means that as the numbers mount, there are problems of deteriorating quality of domestic supplies. Depending upon management practice, household energy sources, and local conditions, the wastes can be either beneficial or detrimental to the environment.

Withdrawals for All Uses

From 1687 to 1987, the total amount of water withdrawn for all needs has increased probably 35-fold. At present, it is over 3,600 km³ (Fig. 14.11). The rate of increase was the

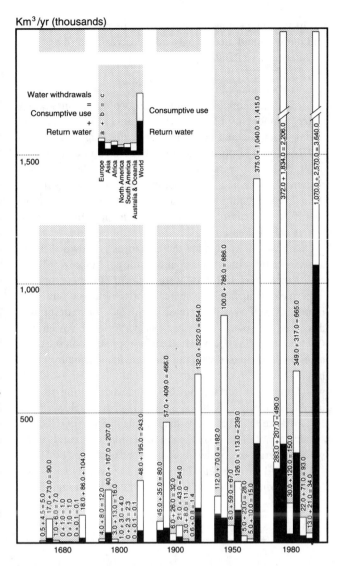

Figure 14.11 Estimated total water withdrawn, consumed, and returned for all purposes, 1680–1980.

greatest after 1950, and in volume equaled all gains prior to that period. This tendency appears on all the continents. In Europe, North America, and Australia the acceleration in rate had begun to be felt in the nineteenth century.

Although irrigation is the principal consumer, its share decreased during the past three centuries from 90% to 75%. In industry and energy production, mainly in Europe, water use began to expand on the eve of the nineteenth century. Increasing at a very high rate, by 1890 it was 2.5 times as great as domestic-municipal withdrawal, and by 1980 it reached almost 20% of total water withdrawal. The share of domestic-municipal withdrawal changed little and comprised about 5%, while water used by livestock decreased to 2%.

Reviewing the principal features of water use, two changes stand out: a very rapid growth of consumptive use since the middle of this century, and rapid buildup of huge amounts of waste water.

Indirect Alterations

The two principal indirect alterations in the distribution of water were from urbanization and from transformations in management practices in farms and forests. These alterations led in various degrees to changes in stream-flow magnitude and duration and, accordingly, to the occurrence of water in channels and wetlands.

Urbanization

The development of cities had two major impacts on water components of the environment: (1) by sewers and drains, domestic and industrial wastes that might have been widely deposited on the soil were channeled into rivers and other bodies of water in volumes noted in the preceding section; (2) by increasing the number of impermeable surfaces through constructing roads and roofs of buildings, the surface runoff was increased, and the replenishment of underground waters was decreased.

One basis for calculating these changes is provided by an analysis of the water balance in the cities of Moscow, Minsk, and Kursk. Relationships were found between extent of impermeable surface and increase of the surface and total runoff, as well as with decrease of the base or underground discharge (L'vovich and Chernogaeva 1978; L'vovich and Chernyshev 1983). Elements of the water balance in the three cities were compared with the same elements in nearby river basins having predominantly rural land use (Fig. 14.12). It was found that surface runoff, particularly during storms, increases sharply with the expansion of impermeable surfaces. For instance, in Moscow, within the ring of Sadovoye Koltso, surface runoff is 260% of that in comparable rural areas, while underground water replenishment decreases by 50%.

Increased surface runoff from urban areas may carry pollution beyond city limits. In the seventeenth and eighteenth centuries, many cities were poorly cleaned, and so a heavy shower could be a benefit for the population of the city, but the pollution of the nearest river could be considerable and unfavorable.

On the world scale, tremendous differences exist in city structures, and we have made very conservative estimates. Using available data on city populations, we have ventured estimates of river runoff for the period 1800–1950 for the total population of the world, and since 1950 for individual continents.

In 1800, the population of cities of the world comprised 29,000,000 persons, or only 3% of the total population, and the volume of storm runoff was not great, but the pollution in the immediate urban area was probably much higher than at present. By mid-1986, the urban population of the world, estimated to be 2,200,000,000 people, including industrial enterprises and roads, occupied an area of about 1,200,000 to 1,400,000 km². Assuming that the impermeable surface within this territory comprises 25% of the total and, using the relationships just noted, the transformation of all three elements of river runoff is estimated to be that in Fig. 14.13. Surface runoff in the aggregated cities of the world may have increased by as much as 163 km³/yr, and the total runoff by 137 km³/yr, while replenishment of the underground waters decreased by 26 km³/yr. These volumes are large for individ-

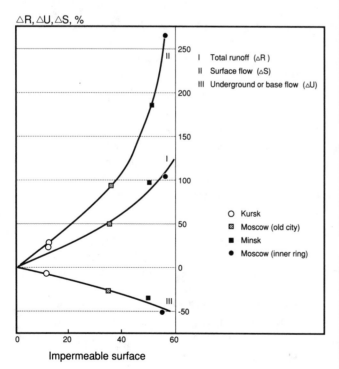

Figure 14.12 Changes in water balance under the influence of urbanization in three cities and adjacent rural lands. (I = total runoff (ΔR); II = surface flow (ΔS); III = underground or base flow (ΔU).)

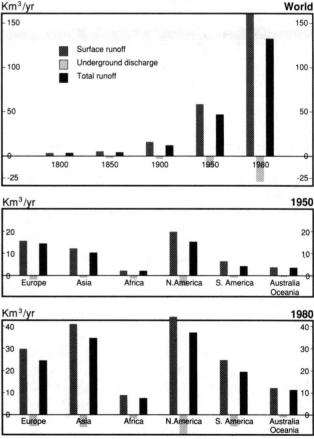

Figure 14.13 Estimated change of runoff under the influence of urbanization in the world, 1800–1980. World figures are totaled from 1800 to 1950, and are subdivided by continents for 1950 and 1980.

ual urban areas but appear small when merged with flows for entire basins.

Land and Vegetation Transformations of Water

In hydrology there long predominated the climatological assumption that "rivers are the product of climate" (Voeikov 1884). But it gradually became common knowledge that soil is an intermediary between the atmosphere and the hydrosphere and that practically all the hydrological phenomena on land are considerably influenced by soil and vegetation conditions (L'vovich 1963).[3]

The precise impacts of soil-vegetation changes on water balance and fresh-water regime are associated with a great number of complex diverse factors that need to be modeled as well as to be tested with experimental studies, and we have not attempted to summarize or generalize from the many studies. Probably the first such experiment was made in 1892 by Dokuchaev in the Kamennaya (Stone) Steppe of the Voronezh region. In 1950, one of the authors of this paper resumed those experimental studies, but on a broader scale, including study of the impact on the water balance and river runoff of some cultivation practices, of forest belts, of irrigation, and of the ratio between transpiration and evaporation in the Kamennaya Steppe and in the region of the city of Kursk.

These findings illustrate the problems of generalization and also permit quantitative estimates of the virgin steppe's water balance approximately as it was in the ninth and tenth centuries, and suggest the influence on water balance of different agricultural technologies used in the past 100 years (Fig. 14.14). Under the conditions of a virgin steppe where plowing had not been practiced, the total river runoff was much lower,

and grassy and forest vegetation consumed much more water for transpiration than became the case on early plowed lands. Underground runoff in the virgin state of lands was 60% as high as at the beginning of the twentieth century. Beginning with the 1930s and especially in the 1950s, the changes in agrotechnical methods led to a considerable increase of soil moisture, surface runoff decreased, and a significant replenishment occurred for underground waters.

We have ventured a very general approximation of the influence of cultivation in order to suggest the magnitude of alterations involved. For this purpose, we use a relationship of water consumption by plants (total evaporation during the growing season) with primary biological productivity

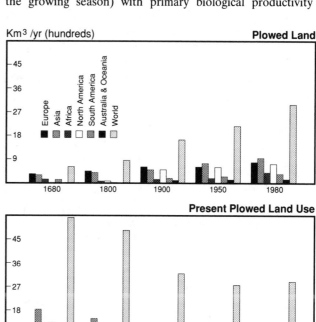

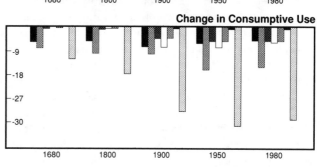

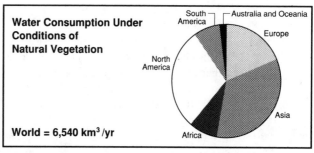

Figure 14.15 Estimated changes in water consumption on cultivated lands, 1680–1980.

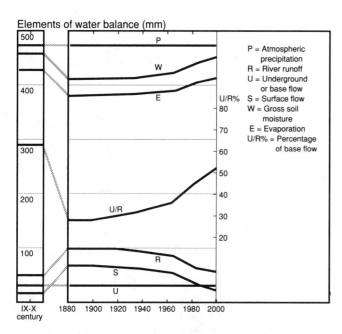

Figure 14.14 Changes in water balance in a forest-steppe area under the influence of plowing and different technical practices. P = atmospheric precipitation; R = river runoff; U = underground or base flow; S = surface flow; W = gross soil moisture; E = evaporation; U/R% = percentage of base flow.

(including roots and the whole above-ground biomass) and with grain yields.[3] The results are presented in Fig. 14.15. Such calculations are highly tentative, and we have not allowed for those possible impacts in estimating total anthropogenic changes in runoff.

Transformed World Water Resources

The scales of the changes described in preceding sections for the period 1687–1987 were somewhat systematically associated with population growth and with technological and social developments. Table 14-1 compares the estimates of the state of water resources in 1982–1984 with what is estimated to have been the situation in the latter part of the seventeenth century.[2] The weights of anthropogenic transformations are shown with signs to indicate increases or decreases. In addition, the table includes data on world precipitation and evaporation, and makes the broad assumption that the decrease in runoff is offset by increased evaporation from the continents.

Here we allow for a regulating function of reservoirs that accumulate high flows and feed rivers in dry seasons. Some reservoirs with over-year regulation provide water for low-water periods following years of accumulation. Accordingly, the natural total and surface runoff are assumed to be 5% and 10% higher than 1965, while the natural underground runoff is taken to be 6% lower.

Any such alteration in stream-flow volume and fluctuation would, of course, make itself felt in channel form, sediment transport, and the configuration and groundwater tables of deltas. These are to be noted in most alluvial stream systems.

We should emphasize that Table 14-1 is an attempt to reconstruct the natural runoff, which in its initial, unchanged form has been preserved in only a few regions of the world. It takes into account only those anthropogenic changes that concern the channel runoff: consumptive use or regulation by reservoirs. As for influences conditioned by change in soil permeability, only the factor of urbanization is calculated. The impact of nonirrigated agriculture and forest management has been studied insufficiently to permit global generalization, although it clearly is of major importance in some drainage areas.

The withdrawal of water per capita increased about fourfold from 1687 to 1987, and the rate of increase accelerated. This raises a basic question as to whether or not these rates can be expected to be reduced in the years immediately ahead. Does the historical record provide any reasonable basis for believing the looming crisis in water quality may be averted?

As represented in Fig. 14.16a, the rates of increase in water withdrawal and of consumptive use of water accelerated after 1900 and still further after 1950. The volume of river runoff polluted to some degree by waste waters climbed more rapidly (Fig. 14.16b). It would be misleading to extrapolate these trends into the distant future: the rates of growth in industrial use have been declining, and there is widespread interest in making more efficient use of water in agriculture as well as in industry and households (Falkenmark 1986). More-

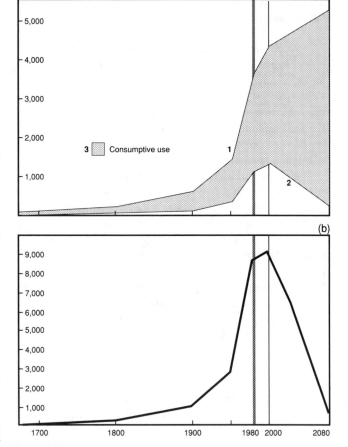

Figure 14.16 The chronology of water consumption for 400 years. Chart (a) shows (1) water intake from all sources; (2) waste water returned to streams, and (3) consumptive use. Chart (b) shows the volume of river runoff polluted by waste water. Both charts present projections of all four parameters from 1680 to 2000 and from 2000 to 2080, assuming drastic measures are adopted to reduce waste-water discharge.

over, the global hydrology is itself changing (Eagleson 1985). A reasonable goal would be to eliminate the discharge of troublesome pollutants in most streams in the long run. Although moves in that direction have been strong only in the past three decades, they have commanded earnest attention. Emphasis would shift from a strategy of trying to cope with waste by treating or diluting effluents to a strategy of avoiding the production of waste by changing processes or material use and by employing natural processes of decontamination in soils and organisms. Although some colleagues consider us hopelessly sanguine, we suggest that if a combination of waste reduction, waste treatment, and water-use efficiency were achieved while population and industrial production continue to expand at conservatively projected rates, the course of water consumption and waste-water production might be as shown in Fig. 14.16a. New development and necessary retrofitting of obsolete systems need not repeat the techniques of the early twentieth century. The experience of the past century indicates that it is technically possible and perhaps socially practicable to reverse those earlier trends. If a healthy human environment is to be achieved, it is essential to do so.

Past and Future

From this review we draw a few observations.

First, the major alterations in the distribution of water on the face of the earth from 1687 to 1987 have resulted from the withdrawal of water for irrigation and, to a lesser degree, for domestic, municipal, and industrial purposes; from the impoundment of streams; and from land-management practices and the drainage of wetlands and constriction of flood flows. These activities have modified both river runoff and evaporation, and the volumes and waste loads of waters returned to rivers after use. The amounts of groundwater have been reduced by altered soil conditions – rural and urban – and by depletion of aquifers. In the train of impoundments and withdrawals, stream channels and sediment loads have changed. Although the first extensive alterations in stream systems, beginning in the sixteenth century, for navigation and power purposes created a network of waterways and diversion dams, they did not modify stream flows greatly.

Second, the consequences for biological systems of these physical changes are less readily quantified, but they include principally the creation of many large reservoirs with their distinctive aquatic environments, the disruption of riverine ecosystems in which water flows have changed, the wholesale conversion of terrestrial ecosystems on more than $250,000 \text{ km}^2$ of arid lands subject to irrigation and more than $150,000 \text{ km}^2$ of wetlands subject to drainage and flood protection, the stabilization of processes along regulated watercourses, and mounting loads of inorganic and organic contaminants in streams.

Third, in human terms, the major effects of these physical and biological transformations are to be found in enhanced internal waterway transportation, electric-power production, relatively potable water for city populations, water for industrial processing and cooling, agricultural production from irrigated and poldered land, reduced flood hazard in some areas and enlarged hazard in others, recreation on reservoirs, contamination of streams and aquifers, reduced lengths of wild rivers, and a variety of other environmental disturbances. Their development supported economic growth in many instances, and also had environmental drawbacks. We have not attempted to appraise the social costs and benefits of these diverse modifications, but we do point out a few of their implications for the future of the globe.

Fourth, a number of the major changes during the 300 years were associated with technological innovation. Earth-moving equipment, steel, and concrete made possible the large dams, drainage works, and water-distribution systems. Electricity became the base for hydropower construction and dispersed economic location. Well drilling and pump improvements opened up wider and deeper segments of the hydrosphere for exploitation. Plastics expanded the opportunities for water delivery in city and field. Pesticides and herbicides expanded the short-term production from irrigated land. It is notable that in these developments the measures to cope with negative environmental effects usually followed the innovations after a period of decades. Thus, drainage typically followed irrigation in a considerable proportion of agricultural lands, fish ladders came along after high dams, waste treat-

ment lagged behind water-purification devices, floodplain management received attention after levee and dam construction flourished, and water-efficiency measures in irrigation succeeded emphasis on water storage.

Fifth, the location and rates of applications of new technology were strongly influenced in a variety of ways by prevailing political systems, and we do not attempt to analyze them. During the period of very rapid expansion of water management beginning in the late nineteenth century, three systems were powerful. At first, the colonial powers guided and stimulated new technologies in the Indian subcontinent and the eastern Mediterranean. Later, the United Nations family of technical and financial assistance agencies played a major part in the spread of water management in South America and Africa, based in part on the experience in North America and Europe. The great bursts of large-scale changes in land treatment and water storage in the USSR and China were associated with new, centrally planned governments.

Sixth, the past quarter-century was distinguished by a lively expansion of knowledge about the physical, biological, and social consequences of water management and by concerns to appraise them in integrated fashion, taking account of all viable alternatives before undertaking major water investments. While this concern was reflected only rarely in coherent action, it permeated much of the planning and decisions of recent years, and it fueled the increasing emphasis expressed by cohorts of the environmental movement on evaluation of environmental implications of water development.

Last, considering the evolution of water-management measures in recent years, as reflected in Fig. 14.16, no more urgent problem seems to emerge than the question of how present and prospective management can be oriented to cope in practical ways with the rising volume of polluted waste water from factory and field. To do so will require a reorientation of approaches taken to the management of water on the land. While the volume withdrawn has increased, so, too, has the variety and mix of organic and inorganic contaminants. There can be little satisfaction in reviewing the numbers of cubic kilometers of water that remain to be withdrawn from surface or ground sources in many basins if their quality is so degraded as to render them useless or harmful. The problem is to avoid ways of generating the contaminants where the water is first used or, failing that, to treat the waste suitably where it is first generated, taking full advantage of the capacities of soil and aquatic systems to reduce or handle waste products. The emphasis would then turn to circular rather than linear systems of handling water, just as water in nature is a cycle that regenerates its quality.

We stress that water-management measures should be based on principles that aim at preventing further deterioration in quality and at reducing present contamination. To achieve this will require persistent hydroecological assessment before repair, retrofitting, and new construction are undertaken.

Further Observations

In the full manuscript to be published by Clark University there are further observations by Terence Lee and

Janucz Kindler. There are also more detailed explanations of methods of making the estimates and of the development of thinking about the world water balance.

Acknowledgments
Supplemental materials have been provided by Terence Lee and V. A. Sharapov.

Jeffrey D. Colby served as research assistant in compiling materials other than on water use and water balance.

We are grateful to the following for reviews of the preliminary draft: Malin Falkenmark, Genady Golubev, Robert M. Hirsch, Robert Cameron Mitchell, Samuel J. Ratick, and M. Gordon Wolman.

Notes

1. The first map of world river runoff was compiled in 1940 and published in 1945, when over half of the dry land of the earth had not been hydrologically studied. In 1974, a series of detailed water-balance maps of the world came out with more satisfactory information on the daily river runoff. Discharge records were still available for only about half of the dry land. Interpolation relationships, obtained on a theoretical basis, permitted a positive resolution of the problem of missing data (L'vovich 1945, 1974).

2. It should be noted that the estimates of world water balance published in 1974 and 1986 differ from several others that have been prepared in recent years by other investigators, principally Baumgartner and Reichel (1975), and by Shiklomanov (1979) and colleagues in the State Hydrological Institute, Leningrad. To indicate the extent to which the estimates differ, we compare the findings for the three estimates, by continent, for river flow in the period 1970–1980.

	Average stream flow (km³/yr)				
	Baumgartner and Reichel	Shiklomanov	L'vovich (1974, 1986)		
Continent	(1974: 66)	(1979: 278)	R	U	S
Europe	2,800	3,210	3,110	1,065	2,045
Asia	12,200	14,410	13,190	3,410	9,780
Africa	3,400	4,570	4,225	1,465	2,760
North America	5,900	8,200	5,960	1,740	4,220
South America	11,100	11,760	10,380	3,740	6,640
Australasia and Oceania	2,400	2,300	1,965	465	1,500
Total	39,700	44,540	38,830	11,885	26,945

Baumgartner and Reichel. The world water balance. By the three-component method.

Shiklomanov. Anthropogenic changes in water flow. By the three-component method.

L'vovich. By the six-component method. When account is taken of runoff of ice and water from polar glaciers and of direct underground runoff into oceans, the total is 44,130.

3. The specific consumption of water with the total biomass was determined by comparing data on biological productivity of natural vegetation (including forest and grassy vegetation) from the world map of Bazilevich and Rodin (1967) with the ratio of evaporation and potential evaporation for different regions of the world continents as defined by Zubenok (1976). The resulting relationship is consistent with the outcome of corresponding experiments and calculations for a number of regions (Bulavko and Loginova, 1975; and others), including agricultural ones. These served as ground for constructing the interdependencies of the total specific evaporation and grain yields. (On the average, for grain crops the relation of grain yields to the total biomass ranges within the limits of about one-third.) Water use per unit of product decreases with the growth of biomass. At the same time, with the growth of biomass, the total evaporation increases or remains the same, if evaporation is equal to potential evaporation. This is characteristic of a well-developed vegetation cover under conditions of sufficient soil moisture. It should be noted that with equal biological productivity of plants and duration of the growing season, the total use of water by different plant species generally is of the same order (Alpat'ev 1969).

Considerable difficulties arise in trying to get information on the land use and yields of different crops for previous years. We used FAO and experiment station sources (sometimes controversial), and also devised indirect methods of assessment (by number of human population, per capita needs for agricultural products, primarily in grain, and by analogs). It was impossible to make calculations for all principal crops. So we estimated grain crops (without rice), assuming that under conditions of nonirrigated agriculture, grain crops may be sufficiently representative of total water consumption of agricultural plants. Areas of plowed lands, yields, and water consumption were calculated by these means.

References (English, French, and German)

Ackermann, W. C., G. F. White, and E. B. Worthington. 1973. *Man-Made Lakes: Their Problems and Environmental Effects.* Washington, D.C.: American Geophysical Union.

Alley, W. M., and J. E. Vennhuis. 1983. Effective impervious area in urban runoff modeling. *ASCE Journal of Hydraulic Engineering 109*: 313–19.

Baumgartner, A., and E. Reichel. 1975. *The World Water Balance.* Amsterdam: Elsevier Scientific Publishing.

Berghaus, H. 1837. *Zäder-und Völkerkunde*, Vol. II.

Berner, E. K., and R. A. Berner. 1987. *The Global Water Cycle: Geochemistry and Environment.* Englewood Cliffs, NJ: Prentice-Hall.

Biswas, A. K. 1970. *History of Hydrology.* Amsterdam: Elsevier.

Calvert, R. 1963. *Inland Waterways of Europe.* London: Allen & Unwin.

Chi, Ch'ao-Ting. 1963. *Key Economic Areas in Chinese History* (reprint). New York: Paragon Book Reprint Corp.

Eagleson, P. S. 1985. *The Emergence of Global-Scale Hydrology.* Fourth Kisiel Memorial Lecture. Tucson, AZ: University of Arizona, Department of Hydrology and Water Resources.

Encyclopedia Britannica. 1986 ed. Canal.

Falkenmark, M. 1986. Fresh water – time for a modified approach. *Ambio 15*: 192–200.

Falkenmark, M., A. K. Biswas, H. Hori, T. Ishibashi, and G. Koracs. 1987. Water-related limitations to local development. *Ambio 16*: 191–200.

FAO. 1981. *Production Yearbook, 1980.* Rome: FAO.

———. 1986. *Production Yearbook, 1985.* Rome: FAO.

FAO/UNESCO. 1973. *Irrigation, Drainage and Salinity: An International Source Book.* London: Hutchinson & Co.

Flynn, P. J. 1891. *Irrigation Canals and Other Irrigation Works.* San Francisco: George Spaulding & Co.

Framji, K. K., and I. K. Mahajan. 1969. *Irrigation and Drainage in the World: A Global Review.* Vols. I and II. International Commission on Irrigation and Drainage. New Delhi: Caxton Press Private Ltd.

Framji, J. K., B. C. Garg, and S. D. L. Luthra. 1981. *Irrigation and Drainage in the World: A Global Review.* 3 vol. International Commission on Irrigation and Drainage. Delhi: The Central Electric Press.

Geophysics Study Committee. 1982. *Scientific Basis of Water-Resource Management.* Washington, D.C.: National Academy Press.

Golubev, G. N., and A. K. Biswas, eds. 1985. *Large-Scale Water Transfers: Emerging Environmental and Social Experiences.* Oxford: Tycooly.

Gulhati, N. D. 1955. *Irrigation in the World: A Global Review.* International Commission on Irrigation and Drainage. New Delhi: IASH.

Hirsch, R. M., J. F. Walker, J. C. Day, and R. Kallio. 1987. The influence of man on hydrologic systems. (Forthcoming.)

Howe, C. W., J. L. Carroll, A. P. Hurter Jr., W. J. Leininger, S. G. Ramsey, N. L. Schwartz, E. Silberburg, R. M. Steinberg. 1969. *Inland Waterway Transportation.* Baltimore: Johns Hopkins University Press.

Hubbert, M. K. 1974. World potential and developed water power capacity. *Water Resources Bulletin 10* (2).

International Association for Scientific Hydrology. 1970. *Symposium on World Water Balance.*

International Institute for Environment and Development and World Resources Institute. 1987. *World Resources 1987.* New York: Basic Books.

International Institute for Land Reclamation and Improvement. 1983. *Polders of the World: Final Report.* Wageningen, The Netherlands: ILRI.

Jeans, S. J. 1890. *Waterways and Water Transport in Different Countries.* New York: E. & F. M. Spon.

Keller, H. 1906. Abfluss und Verdunstung in Mitteleuropa. *Jahrbuch für die Gewässerkunde Noddeutschlands,* Bd. 1, No. 4.

Keller, Reiner. 1962. *Gewässer und Wasserhaushalt des Festlandes.* Leipzig.

———. 1979. *Hydrologischer Atlas der Bundesrepublik Deutschland.*

Klige, R. K. 1985. Variations in Global Water Exchange. Moscow: Nauka. (In Russian.)

Langbein, W. B. 1959. *Water Yield and Reservoir Storage in the United States.* Washington, D.C.: U.S. Geological Survey Circular 409.

———. 1982. *Dams, Reservoirs and Withdrawals for Water Supply – Historic Trends.* Washington, D.C.: U.S. Geological Survey Open File Report 82–256.

L'vovich, M. I. 1979. *World Water Resources and Their Future.* Chelsea, MI: Litho Crafters. (Translated by American Geophysical Union; translation edited by R. L. Nace.)

Mariotte, E. 1686. *Traité du mouvement des eaux et des fluides.* Publié par les soins de M. de la Hire, Paris.

Mather, J. R. 1984. *Water Resources Distribution, Use, and Management.* New York: John Wiley & Sons.

Miller, D. H. 1977. *Water at the Surface of the Earth.* New York: Academic Press.

Pardé, M. 1925. *Le Régime du Rhone.* Lyon.

———. 1961. Sur la puissance des crues en diverses parties du monde. *Geographica Zaragoza,* numero monografico.

Penk, A. 1896. Untersuchuingen über Verdunstung und Abfluss von grossen Landflächen. *Geogr. Abhandlungen 5* (5): 000–000.

Perrault, P. 1674. *De l'origine des fontaines.* Paris.

Petts, G. 1984. *Impounded Rivers.* Chichester: John Wiley & Sons.

Rangeley, W. R. 1985. *Irrigation and Drainage in the World.* Washington, D.C.: World Resources Institute, International Institute for Environment and Development.

Repetto, R. 1985. *The Global Possible: Resources, Development, and the New Century.* New Haven, CT: Yale University Press.

Schreiber, P. 1904. Über die Beziehung zwischen dem Niederschlag und der Wasserführung der Flüsse in Mitteleuropa. *Meteor. Zeitschift.*

Scientific Committee on Problems of the Environment. 1972. *Man-Made Lakes As Modified Ecosystems.* Paris: SCOPE.

Shalhevet, J. J. Kamburov, and K. K. Framji, eds. 1976. *Irrigation and Salinity: A World-Wide Survey.* New Delhi: Caxton Press, Ltd.

Tanner, H. S. 1970. *Canals and Railroads of the United States.* New York: Augustus M. Kelley.

Turner, R. M. 1974. *Quantitative and Historical Evidence of Vegetation Changes along the Upper Gila River, Arizona.* Washington, D.C.: U.S. Geological Survey Professional Paper 655–H.

UNESCO. 1978. *World Water Balance and Water Resources of the Earth.* Paris.

UNESCO/WMO/IASH. 1974. *Three Centuries of Scientific Hydrology, 1674–1974.* Paris.

United Nations. 1951. *Statistical Yearbook, 1952.* New York.

———. 1970. *Statistical Yearbook, 1962.* New York.

———. 1975. *Groundwater Storage and Artificial Recharge.* Natural Resources/Water Series No. 2. New York.

———. 1982. *Groundwater in the Eastern Mediterranean and Western Asia.* Natural Resources/Water Series No. 9. New York.

———. 1985. *The Water Resources of Latin America and the Caribbean and Their Utilization.* Santiago.

———. 1986a. *Groundwater in Continental Asia (Central, Eastern, Southern, Southeastern Asia).* Natural Resources/Water Series No. 15. New York.

———. 1986b. *1983/84 Statistical Yearbook.* New York.

U.S. Geological Survey. 1983. *National Water Summary 1983 – Hydrologic Events and Issues.* Water Supply Paper 2250. Washington, D.C.: USGS.

U.S. Office of Technology Assessment. 1985. *Wetlands: Their Use and Regulation.* Washington, D.C.: OTA.

USSR National Committee for the International Hydrologic Decade. 1974. *World Water Balance and Water Resources of the Earth.* Leningrad.

van der Leeden, F. 1975. *Water Resources of the World: Selected Statistics.* Port Washington, NY: Water Information Center.

Vermeer, E. B. 1977. *Water Conservancy and Irrigation in China.* The Netherlands: Leiden University Press.

Vernon-Harcourt, L. F. 1896. *Rivers and Canals.* Vol. II, Canals. Oxford: Clarendon Press.

Wex, G. 1873. Über die Wasserabnahme in den-Quellen, Flüssen und Strömen. *Zeitschrift d. Öster. Ing. u. Arch. Vereins.*

White, G. F. 1957. A perspective of river basin development. *Law and Contemporary Problems 22* (2): 157–84.

Zonn, I. S., and P. P. Nosenko. Modern level of and prospects for improvement of land reclamation in the world. *ICID Bulletin 31* (3): 73–78.

References (Russian)

Agupov, A. V. 1960. Normy stoka i kolebaniia vodonosnosti rek Zapadnoi Sibiri. *Kolebaniia i izmeneniia rechnovo stoka.* Moskva.

Alpat'ev, A. M. 1969. *Blagooboroti v prirode i ikh preobrazovanie.* Leningrad: Gidrometeoizdat.

Apollov, B. A. 1957. *Uchenie o rekakh.* Moskva: Izd. Moskovskovo Universiteta.

Avakian, A. B., V. A. Sharapov, V. P. Saltapkin and M. Fortunatov. 1979. *Vodokhranilishcha mira.* Moskva.

Bazilevich, N. A., and L. E. Rodin. 1967. "Kartoskhemy produktivnosti i biologicheskovo krugovorota glavneishikh tipov rastitel'nosti sushi Zemli." *Izv. VGO,* vol. 99, No. 3.

Belyaev, A. V. 1978. "Metod sostavleniia kart élementov vodnovo balansa na osnove zonal'nykh kompleksnykh zavisimostei." *Izvestiya AN SSSR, ser. geogr.*

Berg, E. V. 1955. Svedeniia o vesennikh polovod'iakh na rekakh Volge i Oke v raione g. Gor'kovo v XVIII i XIX stoletiiakh. *Uchenye zapiski LGU, ser. geogr.* No. 10.

———. 1956. O vysote vesennevo polovod'ia p. Volgi u g. Gor'kovo. *Vestnik LGU,* No. 6.

Bolt, B., 1981. *Zemletriaseniia.* Moskva.

Bruk, S. I. 1986. *Naselenie mira. Étnodemograficheskii spravochnik.* Moskva: Nauka.

Bulavko, A. G., and N. I. Loginova. 1975. "Osnovy kompleksnoi otsenki dinamiki ispareniia sel'skokhoziaistvennykh kul'tur pri intensifikatsii zemledeliia." *Trudy IV Vcesoiuzn. gidrol. c"ezda,* 337–44. Leningrad: Gidrometeoizdat.

Chernogaeva, G. M. 1971. *Vodnyi balans Evropy.* Moskva.

Davydov, L. K. 1953. *Gidrografiya SSSR*. Part I. Leningrad.

Davydov, L. K. 1955. *Gidrografiya SSSR*. Part II. Leningrad.

Dokuchaev, V. V. 1892. *Nashi stepi prezhde i teper'*. Sankt Peterburg.

Dreier, N. N. 1969. Raspredeleniye élementov vodnovo balansa territorii SSSR. *Vodnoi Balans SSSR i evo preobrazovaniye*. Moskva.

———. 1978. *Vodnyi balans Severnoi Ameriki*. Moskva.

Fedoseev, I. A. 1975. *Istoriia izucheniia osnovnykh problem gidrosfery*. Moskva.

Geints, E. A. 1898. *Ob osadkakh, kolichestve snega i ob isparenii na raznykh basseinakh Evropeiskoi Rossii*. Sankt Peterburg.

Glushkov, V. G. 1961. *Voprosy teorii i metody gidrologicheskikh issledovanii*. Izd. AN SSSR. Moskva.

Ivanov, K. E. 1975. *Vodoobmen v. bolotnykh landshaftakh*. Leningrad.

Karasik, G. Ia. 1970. *Vodnyi balans Afriki*. Moscow.

———. 1974. *Vodnyi balans Iuzhnoi Ameriki.*, Moscow.

Koronkevich, N. I. 1973. *Preobrazovanie vodnovo balansa*. Moskva.

———. 1986. Polistrukturnyi analiz v issledovanii vodnovo balansa territorii. *Izv. AN SSSR, ser. geogr.* 3: 16–27.

Kotlyakov, V. M. 1977. *Gory, l'dy i gipotezy*. Leningrad.

Kotlyakov, V. M. and A. N. Krenke. 1980. Rol' nazemnovo oledeneniia v vodnoledovom balanse Arktiki. *Izv. AN SSSR, ser. geogr.* 6: 11–21.

Kotlyakov, V. M., K. N. Losev, and I. A. Loseva. 1977. Lednikovyi balans Antarktiky. *Izv. AN SSSR, ser. geogr.* 1.

Krenke, A. N. 1987. Sovremennye ledniki i klimat. *Vzaimodeistvie oledeneniia s atmosferoi i okeanom*, 6–33. Moskva: Nauka.

Kupriianov, V. V. 1977. *Gidrologicheskie aspekty urbanizatsii*. Leningrad.

Kvitsinskii, L. I. 1986. O predskazaniiakh kolebaniia urovnei vody i glubin farvatera na rekakh. *III s''ezd russkikh deyatelei po vodnym nutyam*. Part I. Sankt Peterburg.

L'vovich, M. I. 1945. *Élementy rezhima rek zemnovo shara*. Moskva-Sverdlovsk.

L'vovich, M. I. 1950. O metode raschetov izmenenii pitaniia rek podzemnymi vodami. Metodika raschetov ozhidaemykh izmenenii rezhima rek pod vliianiem osushchestvleniia plana lesonasazhdenii. *Doklady AN SSSR*, vol. 75, Nos. 1, 2.

L'vovich, M. I. 1963. *Chelovek i vody. Preobrazovanie vodnovo balansa i rechnovo stoka*. Moskva.

L'vovich, M. I. ed. 1969. *Vodnyi balans SSSR i evo preobrazovanie*. Moskva: Nauka.

L'vovich, M. I., and N. N. Dreier. 1964. Raspredelenie Élementov vodnovo balansa (na territorii SSSR). *Fiziko-geograficheskii Atlas mira*, plate 250. Moskva.

L'vovich, M. I., and G. M. Chernogaeva. 1978. Izmenenie vodnovo balansa territorii pod vliianiem urbanizatsii. *Problemy gidrologii*. Moskva.

L'vovich, M. I., and A. G. Georgiadi. 1983a. Geograficheskii printsip raschetov maksimal'novo vesennovo stoka. *Izv. AN SSSR, ser. geogr.* 4.

L'vovich, M. I., and E. P. Chernyshev. 1983b. Zakonomernosti

vodnovo balansa i veshchestvennovo obmena v usloviiakh goroda. *Izv. AH SSSR, ser. geogr.* 3.

Mirovoi vodnyi balans i vodnye resursy Zemli. 1974. Leningrad: Gidrometeoizdat.

Nazarov, G. V. 1970. *Zonal'nye osobennosti vodopronitsaemosti pochv SSSR*. Leningrad: LGU.

———. 1981. *Gidrologicheskaia rol' pochvy*. Leningrad: Nauka.

Nikolaeva, G. M., and G. M. Chernogaeva. 1977. *Vodnyi balans Azii*. Moskva.

Ol'dekop, É. 1911. *Ob isparenii c poverkhnosti rechnykh basseinov*. Iur''ev.

Oppokov, E. V. 1916. O vodonosnosti v svyazi s atmosfernymi osadkami i drugimi faktorami stoka. *Zapiski Russkovo geograficheskovo obshchestva po obshchei geografii*, vol. XLVII.

Oroshenie i osushenie v stranakh mira. 1974. Moskva: Kolos.

Plotiny i zemletriaseniia. 1982. Tr. konferentsii v Londone, Oct. 1–2, 1980. Referativnyi zhurnal. Geofizika. Fizika Zemli. Svodnovo toma. No. 7. Moskva.

Polyakov, B. V. 1938. Issledovanie prichin umen'sheniya stoka v Zavolzh''e. Sb. *Nizhnevolgoproekta*. No. 8. Moscow-Leningrad.

Shiklomanov, I. A. 1979. *Antrpogennye izmeneniia vodnosti rek*. Leningrad.

———. 1986. Dinamika vodopotrebleniia i vodoobespechennosti v mire. *Vodnye resursy* 6: 119–39.

Shvets, G. I. 1972. *Vydaiushchiesia iavleniia na yugo-zapade SSSR*. Leningrad.

Urlanisa, B. Ts., and V. A. Borisova, eds. 1984. *Narodonaselenie stran mira*. Moskva: Financy i statistika.

Velikanov, M. A. 1948. *Gidrologiia Sushi*. Leningrad.

Voeikov, A. I. 1884. *Klimaty zemnovo shara v osobennosti Rossii*. Sankt Peterburg.

———. 1894. Vozdeistviye cheloveka na prirodu. *Zemlevedenie*. vol. 1, Nos. 2, 4.

Voropaev, G. V., and A. B. Avakian, eds. 1986. *Vodokhranilishcha i ikh vozdeistviye na okruzhaiushchuiu sredu*. Moskva: Nauka.

Zaikov, B. D. 1938. Karta srednevo mnogoletnevo stoka Evropy. *Tr. Gos. Gidrologicheskovo Instituta*, No. 6.

———. 1946. Srednii stok i evo raspredelenie v godu na territorii SSSR. *Tr. nauchno-iccled. ychrezhd. GUGMC SSSR*, Ser. IV, No. 24.

———. 1954. *Vysokie polovod'ia i pavodki na rekakh SSSR za istoricheskoe vremya*. Leningrad.

Zaikov, B. D. and S. Iu. Belikov. 1937. Srednii mnogoletnii stok SSSR. *Tr. Gos. Gidrologicheskovo Instituta*, No. 2. Moskva-Leningrad.

Zektser, I. S. 1977. *Zakonomernosti formirovaniia podzemnovo stoka i nauchnometodicheskie osnovy evo izucheniia*. Moskva.

Zektser, I. S., R. G. Dzhamalov, and A. V. Meskheteli. 1984. *Podzemnyi vodoobmen sushi i moria*. Leningrad.

Zonn, I. S., and I. A. Nosenko. 1981. Sovremennyi uroven' i perspektivy melioratsii zemel' v stranakh mira. *Gidrotekhnika i melioratsiia*, 1.

Zubenok, L. I. 1976. *Isparenie na kontinentakh*. Leningrad.

15

Water Quality and Flows

HARRY E. SCHWARZ   JACQUE EMEL   WILLIAM J. DICKENS   PETER ROGERS
JOHN THOMPSON

Water circulates from the ocean through the air to land masses, where it precipitates, evaporates, is transpired by plants, is used and consumed by humans and other animals, percolates into the ground, and flows back to the ocean, above and below ground. Over 70% of the earth's surface is covered with water; another 4%, by polar ice. Clearly, the earth is a water planet, yet what we know about water on a global scale is quite small. Measuring the exact amount of water in the ocean basins and underground is very difficult. Both types of estimates are made by multiplying average depths by areas, and the resulting uncertainties are great. Global water-quality monitoring has begun only recently, and again, we are confronted with considerable baseline uncertainty. Ascertaining the impacts of humans on the hydrologic system is vastly complicated by these uncertainties.

We assume that global water quantity is finite and has not changed significantly since the dawn of civilization (ranges of estimates of water fluxes and reservoirs are shown in Table 15-1). Yet the quantity of fresh water available to humankind has varied considerably over space and time. Climatological factors, such as the El Niño Southern Oscillation, have played a significant role in these variations. In recent history, however, regional and local changes in the quantity, quality, and spatial and temporal distribution of fresh-water resources have also resulted from human manipulation of the environment. Diversions, impoundments, irrigation works, reservoirs, wells, deforestation, crop production, and other alterations of the landscape have created changes in the circulatory patterns of water. Human activities have directly and indirectly altered the qualities of fresh-water resources, and in some areas reduced their quantities.

Nevertheless, the effect of human activity on the totality of global water resources is minimal. Fresh water comprises less than 1% of the global water volume. Of that volume, groundwater is by far the largest quantity; rivers and fresh-water lakes constitute about 1% of the world's fresh-water resources (Table 15-1). Apart from groundwater reservoirs, the bulk of fresh water is concentrated in large lakes, notably Lake Baikal in Asia, the Great Lakes in North America, and the lakes in eastern Africa. Only about $1,700\,km^3$ of fresh water is present in rivers and streams, and of course the temporal variation of this amount is considerable. Of these river systems, most of those with the greatest annual discharge to the world oceans traverse relatively unpopulated, unindustrialized terrains.[1]

Focus of the Study

Although a global history of the impact of human activities on fresh-water resources is clearly needed, reconstructing such a history is no small task. During the past few decades, much of the debate regarding water-resource management has taken place without historical insight. Scientists and policymakers alike have focused their attention on present states and future trends, giving cursory notice to the long-term historical conditions. As a result, a major problem with assessing the performance of recent pollution-control programs is the absence or nonuniformity of historical data. Global fresh-water-quality monitoring began in 1979 (see, for example, International Institute for Environment and Development and The World Resources Institute [1987]), and the International Lake Environment Committee was established in 1986 to collect data on 50 to 80 important lakes to promote rational management. Information trends on water quality and availability that could illustrate human impacts must therefore be based on studies of selected rivers and aquifers with historically severe water-quality or depletion problems. Even these investigations, however, have been discontinuous in time for all but a few rivers (Smith, Alexander, and Wolman 1987). Monitoring data exist for a number of locations (albeit only within recent decades), yet the differences in methods generally preclude the use of these data for comprehensive assessments.

Establishment of a three-century historical trend for global fresh-water resources can be based only on an understanding of the general process of human effects on water and on inferences drawn from the knowledge of specific river basins and aquifer characteristics and the human activities affecting them. As differences in climatic, geologic, geomorphic, and geochemical characteristics will alter human impacts, only very broad generalizations are possible.

Table 15-1 *Water reservoirs and fluxes*

	Values (km³)	Range of values in recent literature (km³)
Reservoirs:		
Ocean	1,350,000,000	$1.32-1.37 \times 10^9$
Atmosphere	13,000	10,500– 14,000
Land:		
Rivers	1,700	1,020– 2,120
Fresh-water lakes	100,000	30,000–150,000
Inland seas, saline	105,000	85,400–125,000
Soil moisture	70,000	16,500–150,000
Groundwater	8,200,000	$7-330 \times 10^6$
Ice caps/glaciers	27,500,000	$16.5-29.2 \times 10^6$
Biota	1,100	1,000– 50,000
Flux:		
Evaporation	496,000	446,000–557,000
Ocean	425,000	383,000–505,000
Land	71,000	63,000– 73,000
Precipitation	496,000	446,000–577,000
Ocean	385,000	320,000–458,000
Land	111,000	99,000–119,000
Runoff to oceans	39,700	33,500– 47,000
Streams	27,000	27,000– 45,000
Ground feed	12,000	0– 12,000
Glacial ice	2,500	1,700– 4,500

Source: Speidel and Agnew 1982.

The process of human modification of the fresh-water resources begins with the driving variables – human population and the living standard of this population. Humans directly affect water through the production of human wastes and through their water needs for biologic and hygienic purposes. The far greater effect, especially in the last two centuries, has been through the activities related to an improving living standard, the effects of industry, and large-scale agriculture. These secondary driving variables have, in many localities and regions, most of all affected water quality and to a lesser extent water quantity. Where these activities have damaged water resources to the point of being detrimental to the users or their activities, either the consequences have been accepted and the specific water uses abandoned, or action has been taken to change, or at least reduce, the damaging effects by applying water-control technologies. Thus a number of stages in the human-water relationship could be postulated that have occurred at different times in different continents, regions, and specific river basins:

1. Humans consumed, stored, and diverted water and used it to carry away wastes without regard to health or ecological consequences, which were considered inconsequential.
2. Health effects, property damage, and social impacts were clearly visible, but accepted as unavoidable or escaped by those who could through position or wealth.
3. Water-management technology was applied to eliminate, or at least reduce, the deleterious effects, but often with spotty results and sometimes unanticipated consequences.

Developments to fill perceived need, such as irrigation or flood control, belong in this stage. During early applications of these techniques, damaging impacts often occurred and were not mitigated.

4. In this final stage, human knowledge is applied to anticipate effects and to avoid, or at least mitigate, possible deleterious effects before their occurrence.

Stages can occur simultaneously in any one region, and stages can be skipped.

In the following sections of this chapter, we use two types of case studies to characterize these stages. First, we present an overview of the relationships among human action, water quality, and health, to show how quality and health have changed through time. Second, we present a number of illustrative examples of fresh-water systems that indicate the range and diversity of long-term human impacts. In the final section, we offer some very cautious speculations drawn from the foregoing sections on the historical trends in human impacts upon global fresh-water resources.

Humans, Water, and Health

The relationship between water resources and health has occupied a position of special significance throughout human history. For while water has always been an absolute necessity of life, it has also been a bearer of disease and death. The water-health relationship is a complex affair that includes both positive and negative aspects; it is one that is tied intimately to the larger, often conflicting relationship between economic development and the natural environment. Thus, over the past three centuries, the major transforming activities of humankind – population growth and urbanization, agricultural development and the expansion of arable land, industrial development and the rise of the modern world economy, and the production and consumption of energy (i.e., fossil fuels and hydroelectricity) – have directly and indirectly affected water quality and availability, which, in turn, have had a profound effect on human health.

There are two fundamental connections between development and health. The first is characterized by infectious, water-related diseases such as cholera, diarrhea, malaria, onchocerciasis, schistosomiasis, and typhoid. This pattern of infectious water-related diseases has dominated the water-health cycle throughout human history. Promoted by inadequate sanitation, the diseases were prevalent little more than a century ago in the countries that now comprise the developed world. Enteric diseases transmitted by fecal-contaminated drinking water, such as typhoid and cholera, were widespread in Europe and North America during the late nineteenth and early twentieth centuries, and ranked among the leading causes of death and illness. These represent the second stage of human intervention.

Many of the major urban centers of the day suffered through severe epidemic cholera outbreaks during the nineteenth-century pandemics. A revolution in sanitary science and public health occurred in those countries beginning in the latter half of the nineteenth century, effectively decreasing the incidence of infectious diseases. Improvements in public water supplies and sewerage, heralding the third stage of human intervention, contributed to a marked increase in average life expectancies in those countries and have, for all practical purposes, eliminated endemic and epidemic water-related diseases from those regions (McKeown, Brown, and Record 1972).

In the developing countries, the negative relationship between water and health is still characterized by infectious water-related diseases such as cholera, diarrhea, malaria, onchocerciasis, schistosomiasis, and typhoid. At present, approximately one-quarter of the world's people lack access to safe drinking water and sanitary excreta disposal (WHO 1985, 1986a, 1986b; WRI 1987). Often exacerbated by poor nutrition, diarrheal diseases are endemic throughout the developing world and are the primary cause of infant mortality and a direct contributor to the relatively low life-expectancy levels found there (UN Population Division 1984). The lack of potable water and basic sanitation, combined with the development of water projects that provide the basic ecological conditions for the proliferation of bacterial, helminthic, protozoal, and viral water-related diseases result in the infestation and debilitation of millions of persons in the tropics and subtropics.

Recent evidence suggests that many developing countries are repeating or are on the verge of repeating Western history. It has been shown, for instance, that there is a similarity in the historical decline in enteric diseases in the United States and in a sample of 51 developing countries if the time scale is adjusted (Fig. 15.1) (Cvjetanovic 1975). The decline in these diseases in the United States closely paralleled the establishment of adequate water supplies and excreta disposal facilities and, it should be noted, improved overall standards of living. Correlations were particularly strong for communities drawing their water supplies from unprotected sources with measurable declines following, first, filtration and then chlorination of

Table 15-2 *Principal infectious diseases in relation to water supply*

Disease	Frequency	Severity	Persons infected (millions)	Controllable with water and sanitation improvements (percentage)
Water-borne or water-washed diseases:				
Cholera	+	+++	N.A.	90
Diarrhea	+++	+++	500	50
Typhoid	++	+++	N.A.	80
Water-based diseases:				
Guinea worm	++	++	N.A.	100
Schistosomiasis	++	++	200	60
Vector-borne, water-related diseases:				
Malaria	+++	+++	300	N.A.
Filariasis	++	++	250	N.A.
Onchoceriasis	++	++	30	20
Trypanosomiasis	+	+++	N.A.	80
Water-hygiene diseases:				
Roundworm	+++	+	650	40
Hookworm	+++	+	450	N.A.

Sources: Chandler 1984; McJunkin 1982; Bradley 1977.

their water supplies (NAS 1977). It has been estimated that the provision of sanitary water supplies would reduce the incidence of diarrheal diseases by half, that of cholera by 90%, of typhoid fever by 80%, and of schistosomiasis by 60% (Table 15-2).

The second connection between development and health had its beginning in the Industrial Revolution, which witnessed the emergence of noninfectious, degenerative, water-related diseases. This pattern did not become significant until after the 1880s, when epidemiological and public-health practices led, sometimes dramatically, to the control and prevention of communicable, water-related diseases in the rapidly industrializing countries.

The connection between water and chronic, noninfectious diseases, such as cancer and heart diseases, is still not well understood. Research has shown that the roles of most water contaminants have not yet been sufficiently investigated to give reasonable assurance as to whether or not they will have any lasting or profound impact on human health (Cannon and Hopps 1971; Dugan 1972; OECD 1982; Rise 1985). This holds true, for instance, for most of the potential carcinogens that are of such great concern at present, but for which epidemiological and toxicological evidence is sparse and inconclusive (NAS 1977, 1980a, 1980b, 1981, 1982). Over the past century, only a few relatively simple water-related problems have been documented sufficiently to permit accurate evaluation of dose-response relationships. Thus, the question of which constituents may be hazardous in drinking water or at concentrations encountered in practice remains highly speculative and controversial (Arrhenius 1977; Forstner and

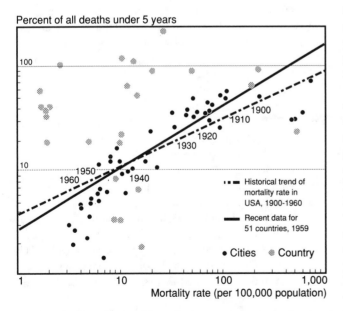

Percent of all deaths under 5 years

Figure 15.1 Historical trend of U.S. mortality rate for gastroenteric disease compared to 1959 data for 51 countries. *Source:* Cvjetanovic 1975.

Whitmann 1981; Nriagu 1984). It should be noted, however, that the emergence of chronic, noninfectious diseases has led to a shift in emphasis among health agents in developed countries from water availability and disposal of human wastes, the primary factors in the control of infectious, water-related diseases, to a focus on chemical and radiological water pollution, its monitoring and control.

Despite the development and application of sophisticated technologies to monitor and control bioaccumulation of water pollutants, it is becoming increasingly difficult to identify their impacts on the environment and on human health because of the sheer number of chemicals produced and the multiplicity of their respective applications. Since World War II, for example, the worldwide production of organic chemicals has increased almost 3,600% (UNEP 1986). The Organization for Economic Cooperation and Development (1984) has estimated that there are now 80,000 organic and inorganic chemicals in commercial production, with another 1,000 to 2,000 new ones appearing on the market each year. Because of the relatively recent appearances of many synthetic chemicals, it is likely that their impacts on water quality and human health will not be known for some time.

From the foregoing, it can be seen that contamination of water resources has been primarily the result of human intervention in natural biochemical cycles, the creation of the basic conditions for the multiplication of breeding places for water-related diseases, and the release of human-made chemicals into the hydrosphere. At the same time, however, great strides have been made in public-health education; water supply and management; sanitation; water and waste-water treatment; and water-pollution monitoring, control, and abatement – especially over the past 50 years – which have played an integral role in improving the general health and well-being of a substantial number of the world's people, thus representing both the second and third stages of human intervention.

Specific Examples of Human Influence on Water

As previously stated, we have elected to use five case studies to illustrate the types of local and regional impacts humans can have on fresh-water resources. The cases we present reflect the intensive study these systems have received because of historical importance, scholarly interest, record-keeping, and location. We were unable to select a water system from each continent because records and studies do not exist on that basis. By looking at two river systems in relatively dry climates, however – the Colorado River in North America and the Nile in Africa – we see some effects of intensive development in both a relatively industrialized and a relatively unindustrialized setting. The Thames River illustrates the historical development of industrial use and waste-disposal problems in a relatively moderate climate. This case in particular illustrates the rise and decline of infectious disease from human use of river systems. The Ganges, the product of a monsoon climate, is exemplary of long-time settlement with relatively slow industrial and agricultural development. The one groundwater case, the High Plains Aquifer in the mid-western United States, shows the effects of intensive de-velopment of a large aquifer system for that most consumptive use of water, irrigation.

The Colorado River

Despite the Colorado's relatively low flow, it is the most politicized, litigated, and fought-over river in the United States, and perhaps the world. Draining $631,960\,km^2$ of largely semiarid and arid land, the Colorado is an important water source for seven states of the United States and portions of northwestern Mexico (Fig. 15.2).[2] Major uses of the Colorado's waters include irrigation, municipal supply, energy production, and recreation. Other uses commonly associated with large river systems like navigation and waste disposal have played a very small part in the river's history. From a virtually unexplored system prior to John Wesley Powell's famous float trip in 1869, the river has experienced many human impacts in its role as a source of water for over 15 million people, many industries, and about 1.2 million ha of irrigated agriculture in the United States (Table 15-3).

Flows Despite its vast watershed and artery of tributaries, the Colorado does not discharge a large volume of water. Its estimated average annual virgin flow of about $18.5\,km^3$ is approximately 1/30th that of the Mekong, 1/18th that of the St. Lawrence, and 1/15th that of the Indus – all of which have comparable drainage areas. Average precipitation for the entire basin is only 38 cm/yr, and nearly 90% of that evaporates before reaching the river channel (Hundley 1966).

Measured historical annual flows on the Colorado River range from a low of $2.47\,km^3$/yr to over $25.9\,km^3$/yr.[3] Figure 15.3 shows estimates of the range of flows from 1896 to 1975. The white blocks on top of the bar graph show depletion, indicating its increase from 1896 to 1975. The sharp difference between 1962 and 1963 through 1965 was caused by the filling of Glen Canyon Dam. In total, some 30 reservoirs exist on the tributaries and mainstem of the river basin, providing an aggregate capacity of $89.7\,km^3$ (five times the average annual flow) (National Academy of Sciences 1968). Flow during water year 1984 was $24.8\,km^3$, the largest annual volume since 1917. The estimated recurrence interval for this annual volume is 100 years (U.S. Geological Survey 1985).

For the past 52 years, flooding in the lower reaches of the Colorado River has been controlled by Hoover Dam. This dam has encouraged development close to the river's edge, a situation that has invited flood damage. During the spring of 1983, significant flood damage occurred because reservoirs in the Colorado River Storage Project entered the water year at nearly full capacity for the first time since the completion of the Glen Canyon Dam in 1963, and then intercepted the high spring flows (U.S. Geological Survey 1984a). In 1984, higher-than-average releases from all major reservoirs within the basin caused continued minor flooding in some downstream areas that had been flooded in 1983. Because flood storage space was made available by the sequence of operations throughout the 1984 water year, thus enabling the Colorado River Storage Project to accommodate the largest annual volume of runoff since 1917, flood damage was minor except

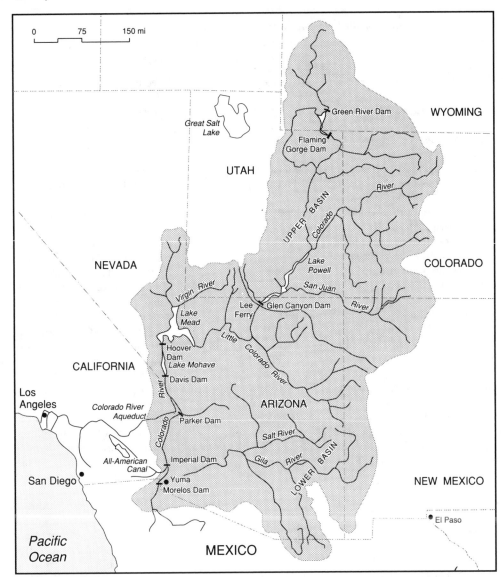

Figure 15.2 Colorado River basin.

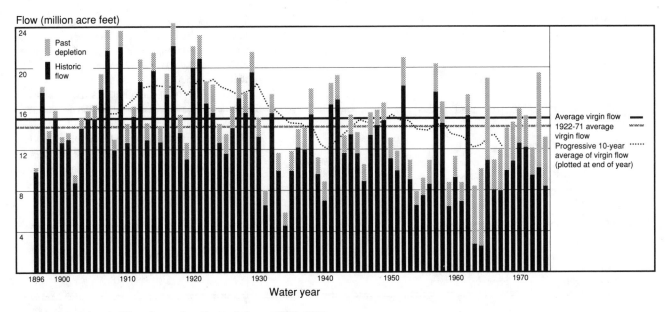

Figure 15.3 Colorado River flow at Lee Ferry, Arizona, 1896–1975.
(1 acre-foot = 1,234 m³.) *Source:* U.S. Bureau of Reclamation 1983.

Table 15-3 *Human actions and effects on the Colorado River*

Action	Dates	Effect
Anasazi Indians built water-supply system near Chaco Canyon.	A.D. 600–A.D. 1200	Effect on river system is insignificant.
Hohokam Indians built canal system off the Salt and Gila rivers.	?–A.D. 1450	Effect is insignificant.
Irrigation diversion works were constructed near Fort Bridge, Wyoming.	1850s	Minimal alteration of flow pattern.
Mormons constructed irrigation canals in Utah.	Midnineteenth century	Minimal alteration of flow pattern.
Water from Colorado River was diverted via Alamo Canal, Mexico, to Imperial Valley in California.	1901	Minimal alteration of flow pattern.
First upper-basin project financed with government assistance, the Uncompaghre Project, was begun.	1902	Minimal alteration of flow pattern.
Yuma Valley Irrigation Project, the first lower-basin Bureau of Reclamation irrigation development project, was authorized; first water delivered 1912.	1904	Provided water to irrigate nearly 24,280 ha (60,000 acres) of land in Arizona and California. Seasonal alteration of flows to Colorado River.
California Development Company cut canal from river to Imperial Valley.	1905	Floods destroyed canal banks, and entire river poured into Salton Sink, creating the Salton Sea.
Construction was completed on Roosevelt Dam.	1911	Significantly reduced the flow in the Salt River, a tributary of the Colorado.
Construction of Hoover Dam was completed (active reservoir storage of 27.2 mm acre-feet).	1935	Sediment discharge below dam was reduced significantly; water discharge was reduced through diversion and evaporation.
Imperial Dam (diversion structure for Imperial and Coachella) was completed.	1938	Water discharge to Colorado River was reduced.
Delivery of water from Imperial Dam via All-American Canal to Yuma and Imperial valleys was begun.	1940	The canal system provided a supply of irrigation water to over 202,350 ha (500,000 acres) outside of the Colorado River basin.
Water began flowing 242 miles from Colorado River to California's southern coast through Colorado River Aqueduct.	1940	Approximately 1.48 km^3 (1.2 million acre-feet) of water from the Colorado River was exported from the basin by Metropolitan Water District of Southern California in the early 1980s prior to construction of the Central Arizona Project.
Morelos Dam was completed.	1950	Served as diversion point for Mexican allocation of 1.85 km^3 (1.5 million acre-feet) per year, as established by the 1944 Treaty.
Drainage waters from wells in Wellton-Mohawk Irrigation Project were discharged into Colorado River.	1961	Salinity of waters delivered to Mexico increased significantly.
Glen Canyon Dam was completed.	1964	Allowed upper basin to meter carefully deliveries to lower basin. Historic flows through the Grand Canyon varied from almost nothing to more than $5,660 \text{ m}^3/\text{s}$ ($200,000 \text{ ft}^3/\text{s}$). With impoundment, they have varied between 283 and $991 \text{ m}^3/\text{s}$ ($1,000–35,000 \text{ ft}^3/\text{s}$) (from 1963–1981).
Colorado–Big Thompson Project was constructed.	1965	Largest upper-basin transbasin diversion in project; supplied Denver and the eastern slope of Colorado with water from the Colorado River. Diversions in 1980 were approximately 0.32 km^3 (260,000 acre-feet). Other projects on the Colorado and its tributaries – Gunnison, Eagle, and Yampa rivers – supplied an estimated $0.31 \text{ km}^3/\text{yr}$ (250,000 acre-feet) as of 1980.
Minute No. 242 to U.S.–Mexico treaty was adopted.	1973	Agreement to deliver about $1.68 \text{ km}^3/\text{yr}$ (1,360,000 acre-feet) at Morelos Dam, with annual average salinity of no more than $115 \text{ mg/l} + 30 \text{ mg/l}$.
Central Arizona Project was completed, a delivery system to Phoenix	1986	Reduced California's depletion of river waters.

in some areas adjacent to uncontrolled streams in the up-stream part of the basin (U.S. Geological Survey 1985).

Quality Changes The Colorado River is not subjected to the waste disposal problems that plague rivers supporting large municipal and industrial enterprises. Due to the largely agricultural use of the river's waters, the scarcity of vegetation in the semiarid lower reaches of the river, and the geological terrain through which the river flows, the major water-quality problems are silt and salinity.

SEDIMENT. The Colorado River is one of the biggest silt carriers in the world. It carries five times that of the Rio Grande, ten times that of the Nile, and seventeen times that of the Mississippi (Hundley 1966). In 1917, before construction of any large dams, 500,000 t of sediment a day passed Yuma in the river water (Hundley 1966). The sediment so colored the river that the Spanish explorer Garces named it Colorado, Spanish for ruddy (National Academy of Sciences 1968).

According to the U.S. Geological Survey (1985), the Colorado River delivered an average of 125–150 million t of suspended sediment per year to the delta at the Gulf of California prior to 1930. Following the completion of Hoover Dam in 1935, the sediment discharge decreased to 100,000 t annually (Fig. 15.4). Water discharge to the Gulf declined more slowly due to depletions from irrigation and municipal uses (Fig. 15.4), but sediment discharge declined abruptly due to the filling of Lake Mead behind Hoover Dam during the years 1934 to 1938. This situation on the Colorado is analogous to the Nile, which used to discharge 100 million t of sediment annually to its delta on the Mediterranean; the Colorado now discharges neither sediment nor water to the sea (U.S. Geological Survey 1985).

SALINITY. Salinity is the major water-quality problem of the Colorado River. Approximately one-half of the salinity is attributable to natural sources; the other half is caused by irrigation, reservoir evaporation, river-basin exports, and municipal and industrial use (U.S. Bureau of Reclamation 1983). Salinity generally increases from the headwaters to the mouth. Measured as dissolved-solids concentration, salinity averaged less than 50 mg/l. at the headwaters to about 850 mg/l. at Imperial Dam in the early 1980s (U.S. Geological Survey 1985).

Salinity levels at the northern border between Mexico and the United States rose to a high of 2,700 mg/l. in 1961 – nearly three and a half times the normal salt content of the water (Hundley 1966). The major source of the additional salt was irrigation return flow from the Wellton-Mohawk Irrigation and Drainage District, which was being dumped into the Colorado upstream. This became an international problem because of Mexico's dependence on and legal right to Colorado River water. High concentration at the boundary between the United States and Mexico prevailed until the agreement of August 30, 1973, whereby the United States was to bring about a "permanent and definitive solution" through a multimillion-dollar project including a water-desalinization plant above Morelos Dam (Minute No. 242 of the International Boundary and Water Commission, United States, and Mexico). By 1979, the average salinity of the river water at the northerly international boundary was approximately 750 mg/l. (International Boundary and Water Commission 1979). This reduction was largely due to the extension of a drain from Wellton-Mohawk Irrigation and Drainage District to the Santa Clara Slough in 1977, which disposed of the return flow waters from the district apart from the river flow, the increased pumpage of lower-salinity groundwater to meet the U.S. requirement to Mexico, and the reduction of irrigated area within the Wellton-Mohawk Irrigation and Drainage District. The desalinization plant, as originally envisioned, has not been completed.

A recent statistical analysis of trends in dissolved-solids concentrations in the Colorado basin undertaken by the U.S. Geological Survey (1985) showed that concentrations at 20 of the 26 stations have decreased between 1965 and 1983. The report suggests that reservoir storage and operation, changes in irrigation practices, retirement of farmland, well plugging, and variations in natural runoff may be responsible for the decreasing trends.

Summary The Colorado River is one of the most heavily used and controversial rivers in the United States, if not the world. Legally allocated between American states and Mexico at a time when flows appeared higher than those estimated in recent years, the river waters have escaped becoming the subject of even more controversy only because the upper-basin states have yet to demand their full allocation. Problems of intense dependence on supply and problems of salinity have fostered numerous acts of legislatures, court decisions, and administrative actions – not to mention expenditures in the billions of dollars. Whether the existing civilization supported by the river will go the way of many that have relied upon the rivers of arid lands is a question that most who have familiarized themselves with the Colorado have asked at one

Water discharge (millions of acre-feet/yr)

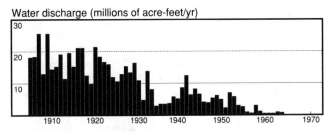

Suspended-sediment discharge (millions of tons/yr)

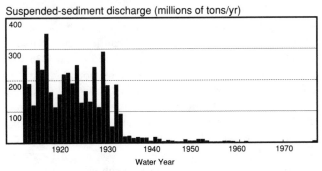

Water Year

Figure 15.4 Historical sediment and water discharge of the Colorado River. *Source:* U.S. Geological Survey 1985.

time or another. For now, the tamed river will flow on, providing sustenance and beauty to those who share its bounty.

Fitting the Colorado River into our taxonomy of the four stages of human intervention, the Colorado is a special case of stage three. Here technologic intervention in the river-flow regime was precipitated not by a deterioration of the river, but by perceived needs to utilize the river in the twentieth century. Technological intervention also occurred to displace saline wastewater away from the river.

The Thames River

The Thames River rises in the southwestern end of the Cotswold hills and flows in an easterly direction through Oxford and Central London to the North Sea. The total length of the river is 348 km, and the drainage area is 13,800 km², roughly rectangular in shape, with maximum elevations of 300 m. Daily air temperatures are, on average, 5°C in winter and 15°C in summer. Average rainfall varies over the basin from 535 mm to 890 mm.

The Thames basin supports agriculture, industry, and commerce, and has a major port and a population of 11.6 million, 60% of whom live in greater London. Agriculture accounts for 65% of land use, mainly in the upper basin and the western part of the lower basin. The remainder of the lower basin is heavily urbanized.

Flows Records of flows on the Thames River have been kept continually since 1883. For previous periods, only random information is available. There are references to floods in A.D. 9 and A.D. 48, in 1382, 1555, 1774, 1809, 1821, 1823, 1852, 1853, 1877, and 1894. Although severe in terms of levels, the flood flows, other than in 1894, were probably not very large. Evidence suggests that the high levels were influenced by poor channel conditions and inadequate weir structures. During the flood of 1894, maximum flow at Teddington reached 92 million m³/day. More floods occurred in 1915, 1929, 1947, 1968, and 1974. The flood of 1947 was the second-largest flow on record, with 61.7 million m³/day recorded at Teddington. While this flood was generally about 15 cm lower than the flood of 1894, at six Thames weir sites the stage was a little higher. This was attributable to increased development on the floodplain and to debris brought down by the flood. The mean flow over Teddington weir is 5.8 million m³/day.

The available data show clearly that construction and other human activities have changed flood stages on the Thames. The construction of weirs and dams by the mill owners and the structures built to facilitate navigation are probably the earliest works of major importance. The replacement of flash locks by the more familiar pound locks began as early as 1635. The Thames Conservancy, created in 1857, began a program of lock and weir reconstruction after 1870 to accommodate the increasing pleasure traffic. Since 1950, a weir-improvement program to replace Victorian-era lift gates with radial gates has aimed at achieving higher hydraulic efficiencies.

Water Quality There is evidence that, as early as the fourteenth century, attempts were being made to restrict the use of the river as a sewer. In 1357, King Edward III reported

that "dung and other filth had accumulated in diverse places upon banks of the river and fumes and other abominable stenches arose therefrom." In 1388, an act of Parliament was passed requiring that waterways be kept clear and that all refuse be carried away to an appointed place before it became a nuisance. Nevertheless, for several centuries there was little control over the river. Navigation interests were dominant, and by the eighteenth century commercial traffic on the Thames had become very important.

From 1581, waterworks were installed, drawing water directly from the Thames downstream of Teddington. During the first half of the nineteenth century, however, the tidal section of the river suffered a dramatic deterioration in quality. There were three main reasons for this: (1) the increase of population in London; (2) the expansion of the industrial revolution; and (3) the invention of the water closet. The population of London doubled between 1700 and 1820 to 1.25 million, by 1851 it rose to 2.75 million, and by 1880 it was 4.75 million. These increases led to the generation of more wastes and an increased pollution load to the Tideway. The growing number of industrial premises in London discharged polluting wastes to the Tideway. The worst – from chemical and gas manufacture – were phenols and ammonia, which are very toxic to aquatic life and have high oxygen demands.

The development that had the greatest impact on the quality of the river was the increasing use of water closets, patented in 1775. They were connected to cesspools, which either overflowed into town drains or were connected directly to watercourses. The first Metropolitan Commission of Sewers was set up in 1847 to improve domestic drainage. Legislation was passed requiring all new properties to have water closets and making it mandatory to connect cesspools to sewers. This had a disastrous effect, causing the entire contents of water closets to be discharged to the Thames, via what were, in fact, surface water sewers. The river, which during the 1830s could no longer support migratory fish, became so polluted that, by 1850, no fish of any kind could survive in the lower Thames.

Between 1831 and 1871, London suffered a series of cholera epidemics; in 1849 more than 18,000 people died, and in 1854 nearly 20,000 died. A clear connection was identified between the disease and polluted water supplies. The Thames was polluted to the extent that it could not scour itself clean, and this led to a period of intensive legislative, administrative, and engineering activity.[4]

The improvement in river quality achieved during the late nineteenth century was, unfortunately, short lived. From about 1920, the river became so polluted that fish and marine life could not survive in the metropolitan river from Tilbury to Fulham, a distance of 57 km. Between 1880 and 1930, the population of London and the resulting polluting load of effluents from the works at Beckton and Crossness increased rapidly. Around 1915, the capacity of the river to accept the polluting loads seems to have been exceeded, and it was no longer able to provide the dilution and dissolved oxygen required. The condition of the river was also affected by World War II, mainly as a result of bomb damage to sewers and sewage works throughout London. Effluents from power stations contributed to the deterioration; the heated discharges caused temperature increases in the estuary and led to an accelerated consumption of oxygen. Another factor was the widespread use of nonbiodegradable synthetic detergents. They produced persistent foams, causing unsightly river conditions and interfering with the transfer of oxygen from the atmosphere through the air-water interface. The use of these "hard" detergents was effectively reduced by 1965, as they were replaced by biodegradable, "soft" products that could be broken down during sewage treatment.

By the 1950s, the river was in an appalling state, with long stretches devoid of oxygen. In 1951, the government set up a committee under the chairmanship of Professor Pippard to report on the effects of effluents discharged to the tidal Thames. The report recommended that a dissolved oxygen concentration of not less than 10% saturation should be maintained at all times, to prevent the river from becoming offensive. To achieve this, it was essential that the effluents from Beckton and Crossness be improved. The London County Council, which had replaced the Metropolitan Board of Works, embarked on a major program of rebuilding and extending the sewage treatment works. The scheme took over 20 years to complete, during which time the Greater London Council, and since 1974 the Thames Water Authority, carried through the project, which, at 1984 prices, cost some £200 million.

At the same time, Sewage Treatment Drainage Boards were established with the aim of improving water quality upstream of the Tideway. Due to the reduction in the natural river flow in certain stretches, however, it has to be admitted that the consequences were, in some cases, detrimental.

Between 1951 and 1961, the contribution of industry to the pollution load in the Thames Tideway was reduced from 9% to 3% of the total, and from 1968 the Port of London Authority, formed in 1908, was given legal powers to control discharges to the Tideway. This was done by issuing Consents based on effective oxygen loads, i.e., the amount of oxygen consumed from the river by the effluent.

The sewage works at Crossness were improved into a full treatment facility in 1964 and, in 1976, commissioning was completed of the full treatment works at Beckton. Since that time, following an almost 90% reduction in the polluting load, the river has consistently met the Pippard standard of 10% dissolved oxygen at all times and places in the estuary. The results of this work are effectively demonstrated by the gradual return of fish and marine life to the river.[5] The number of different fish species found in the estuary increased from three in 1964 to seventy-five in 1974, and now more than 100 species have been recorded. In 1974, the first salmon recorded in the Thames for 140 years was recovered from the intake screens at West Thurrock power station.

Summary

The foregoing sections of this paper show clearly the effect of human habitation on the river. Construction of engineering works for navigation and water supply has only a slight effect on the river, causing an increase in flood heights at certain places. The changes in water quality, however, have been dramatic. Figure 15.5 shows a graph of dissolved

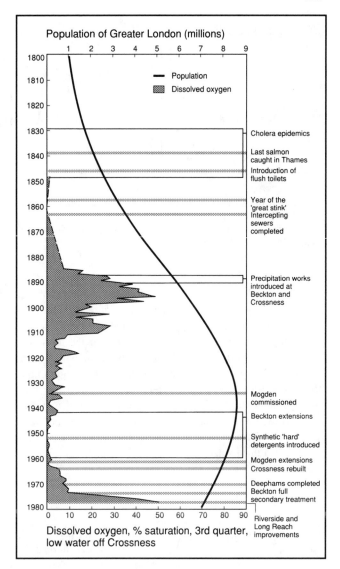

Figure 15.5 Effects of improvements in sewage treatment in oxygen levels in the Tideway.

oxygen and the population of greater London since 1800. Three sections of the graph are particularly telling. In the period from about 1800 to 1860, incidental data show the gradual deterioration of water quality, a result of increased population and the discharge of effluents to the river. Then, after about 1885, in spite of a continuing increase of population, water quality improved dramatically, in terms of dissolved oxygen concentration. This was achieved through human action in the form of better sewers and treatment. Following that period, further growth in population and the growth of industry again destroyed the quality of the river (Figs. 15.5 and 15.6) – a condition that continued through both world wars and into the 1960s.[6] Concentrated action in the form of complete sewage treatment, coupled with some decline in population and a reduction in the polluting load from industrial wastes, again restored the river's health. Achieved through the integrated management of the waters of the Thames, this situation is likely to be permanent.

Dissolved oxygen (% saturation)   Length (km)

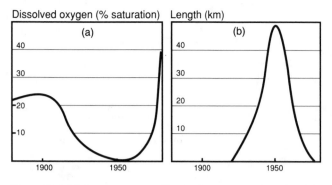

Figure 15.6 (a) Average autumn dissolved oxygen concentrations in the tidal Thames River. (b) Length of the tidal Thames River with dissolved oxygen concentrations below 5% of saturation. *Source:* Wood 1982.

The ups and downs of water quality show that advance can be followed by regression. Through the eighteenth and nineteenth centuries, until 1885, the Thames was in the second stage of human intervention. Significant damage to human health and property occurred, caused by the activities of the population. The end of the nineteenth and the beginning of the twentieth century clearly put the river into the third improvement stage. The period of the world wars and their aftermaths, however, caused regression to the second stage. Only toward the end of the twentieth century did progress return, and third-stage, and now fourth-stage, intervention is becoming the norm.

The Ganges River

Night wheels on, while the sands of the Ganges tip the scales of time.   Dante, Purgatorio 2.4–6

Five of the great rivers of the world rise from the watershed of one mountain in the Himalayas. Fed from the waters of Lake

Manasarovar at the foot of Mount Kailas, the Karnali and the Brahmaputra rivers flow south and east to meet up with the Ganges River before reaching the Bay of Bengal 3,060 km away. The Indus and the Sutlej rivers flow westward to meet on the Punjab plains and flow into the Arabian Sea 2,900 km in the opposite direction. The descent of these five great rivers through the gorges of the Himalayas is the stuff that myths are made from. For the inhabitants of the plains south of the Himalayan mountain wall, the Ganges, usually referred to as *Ganga*, is their mother, the provider of their livelihood along the banks of the river. Figure 15.7 presents a time line of the river's development.[7]

The river basin (Fig. 15.8) is bounded by the Himalayas in the north and by the Vindhyas in the south. Of a total basin area of more than $1,060,000\,km^2$, $861,000\,km^2$ are in India, $140,800\,km^2$ are in Nepal, and $67,000\,km^2$ are in Bangladesh (Chaturvedi and Rogers 1985). The basin area in India is 26.3% of that country's total area.

There are seven important tributaries from the north and six from the south. Figures for the average flows of the rivers can be misleading for two reasons: first, the flows are highly seasonal due to the monsoon, and second, the flows are highly variable from year to year. Figure 15.9 shows the average annual hydrograph, based on monthly flows, for the Ganges River at the Farakka barrage on the Bangladesh border. In this figure are reconstructed hydrographs for the years 1850, 1900, and 1980. The enormous range between the monsoon flows and the winter flows is apparent.

Flows   Irrigation on a large scale began as early as the seventeenth and nineteenth centuries, and accelerated up to and including the twentieth. Thus, large amounts of flow were taken from the river and consumed. Figure 15.9 presents, next to today's annual hydrograph, hydrographs estimated from the change in irrigated area for 1850 and 1900. The enormous effects of human intervention, especially in the low-flow season, are clearly shown.

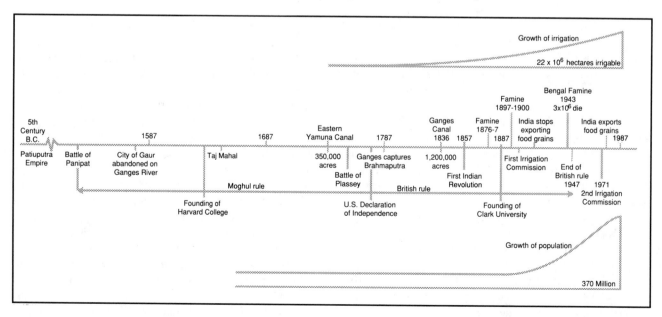

Figure 15.7 Time line for the development of the Ganges River.

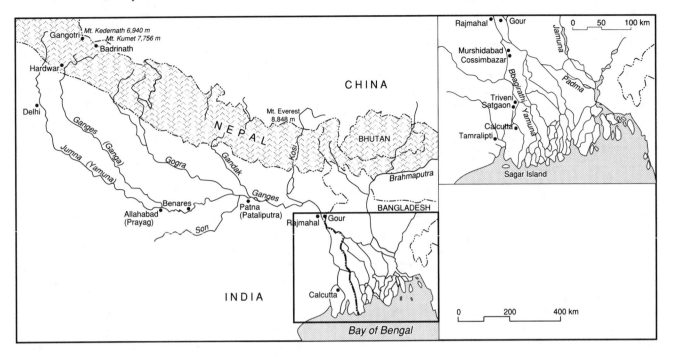

Figure 15.8 The route of the Ganges River from the mountains to the sea. *Source:* Darian 1978.

Water Quality

SILTATION. The clearing of the primeval forests was the first obvious impact of human settlements in this region. No doubt the forest clearing had a major impact on the local fauna and flora. In addition, the clearing over a short time of such large tracts of land must have had a large impact on the local and the regional climate. It is not clear that the sediment load of the river would have been significantly affected by this deforestation. It was only much later, in our own era, that massive upland deforestation with its potential for increasing sediment yields came about.

There is a large popular literature that assumes that since the upland soils are eroding quickly, the sediment load in the rivers must also show a similar rapid rise (see Eckholm 1976). The actual data on this are poor, but van der Leeden (1975) lists the Ganges River as second only to the Yellow River in China in terms of total suspended sediment. Rogers (1977) reviewed the historical data for the Kosi River, an important northern tributary of the Ganges, and concluded that despite large deforestation in the Nepali parts of the Kosi watershed, the sediment loads in the river had not increased significantly from 1949 to 1960. This makes sense from a scientific point of view, since the Himalayas are relatively new mountains and the erosion/deposition process has not yet stabilized. As a result, the rivers are already carrying the maximum amount of sediment that they can carry, and any more material will remain in the upland reaches of the river until sometime in the distant future when the river will be able to carry this material away. Recall that the thick layer of sediment that constitutes the present Ganges plains was carried down from the Himalayas long before humankind was able to affect significantly the sediment yields upstream.

POLLUTION. With the growth of large cities along the river, serious public health problems arose due to the handling and disposal of human and industrial wastes. The traditional dilution factors (1 ft^3/sec per 1,000 of contributing population) are quite acceptable except for periods of extreme low flow (March and April), when the carrying capacity of the river

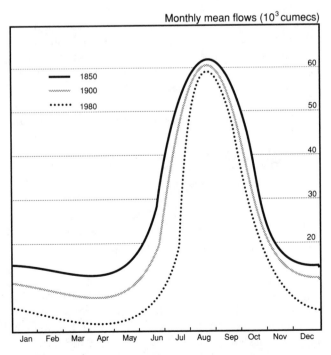

Monthly mean flows (10^3 cumecs)

1850
1900
1980

Figure 15.9 Mean monthly hydrograph of the Ganges River and reconstructed hydrographs for 1850, 1900 and 1980. Flows are in thousand m^3/sec.

could drop as low as that of 70 million of population equivalents. Of course, the travel times in the river are such that few reaches have tributary populations that large during the low-flow seasons. Even so, in some reaches biological-oxygen-demand concentrations varying between 5.3 ppm in winter and 16 ppm in summer have been observed (reported in Sinha 1986) and fecal coliform levels of over 1,900 per 100 ml. have been reported in the lower Ganges in Bangladesh (World Resources Institute 1987). Since only a very small fraction of the total basin population is sewered and contributes wastes directly to the river system, these measurements are quite high and do not bode well for the near future, when an increasing percentage of the population will be sewered. Fortunately the works of Sinha (1986) and others do not reveal large concentrations of toxic chemicals (in particular, pesticides, which are used in increasingly heavier doses) in the water or the sediments. Excess nutrients may, however, become a problem as the rate of chemical-fertilizer application increases. For example, Sinha reports a more than 10% per year increase in the use of nitrogen in the Patna region from 1977 to 1982.

Diseases that are associated with water and sanitation, such as cholera, could well have been transmitted from location to location because of the wide trade connections that grew up along the river. Even today, the seasonal rise in cholera cases in Bangladesh can be partially attributed to the transfer of the cholera vibrio by the monsoon floods from upstream regions.

One major health hazard that is often attributed to human intervention in the water cycle is malaria. As early as the 1830s, government officials in the Ganges basin were aware of the strong correlation with waterlogging and flooding due to poor irrigation management, or design, even without undersanding the epidemiology of malaria. Klein (1983) recounts how the introduction of improperly designed irrigation works into areas that previously had had malaria caused a major flare-up in the mortality due to malaria. He argues that the authorities ignored the health effects in their rush to promote irrigation projects. Other writers, such as Buckley (1880), tell of important officials who were aware of the environmental consequences of economic development and who were willing to take actions to protect the environment and public health. It was well known, for example, that the governor general of India at the time, Lord Ellenborough, was concerned about environmental decay and disease brought about by irrigation projects, and he strongly opposed the proposed Ganges Canal. In 1843, he set up a canal committee composed of engineers and medical doctors to review the project. This committee carried out its work conscientiously and made a series of suggestions to Cautley, the canal builder. Cautley accepted all of the Committee's recommendations, even though they led to a 50% increase in the cost of the project.

The major environmental problems currently faced by the Ganges waters stem from the increasing affluence of the population as well as the direct demands placed on the water resources. The population of the basin in 1987 was approximately 370 million, up from 260 million in 1971. By the year 2000, as many as 490 million people may be living in the basin. This is twice the population of the United States, living in approximately one-quarter of the U.S. land area. Under such conditions, one would expect that, in addition to the reduced flows from consumption by agriculture, the major environmental impacts would be those of toxic industrial chemicals, municipal pollution, and nonpoint source contamination due to agricultural chemicals. All of these impacts would of course be greatly exacerbated if the irrigation diversions follow current plans.

Summary   From this cursory review of the historical and current situation, we can conclude that despite continual settlement for almost 4,000 years, humans have not yet caused irreparable damage to one of the world's most valued ecosystems. To be sure, the ecosystem is radically different from what it would have been if humans had not settled in the area. We can also conclude that the most serious impacts are likely to be those of the near future (within 30 years), when the inhabitants will enjoy much higher material standards of living, which will stress the absorptive capacity of the environment. Thus the Ganges is in – and has been for more than 300 years – the second stage of human intervention.

The Nile River

The Nile River, the world's longest river, is far from the world's largest. Its annual volume is only about one-fifth that of the Zaire and about 60% of that of the Mississippi. Draining 3,348,900 km^2, its flow is dominated by runoff from the Ethiopian highlands, and is characterized by great variations within each year. The ratios of high and low average daily flows are 2 to 1 for the White Nile, 48 to 1 for the Blue Nile, and 9 to 1 for the main stem at Aswan.

This river is the life blood of Egypt and the Sudan, and has been utilized, and therefore, affected by human action for thousands of years. The large effects on the river are, however, of relatively recent origin. Two actions, the building of large storage reservoirs on tributaries and on the main stem, and the development of large-scale irrigation, have had impacts on water quality and temporal distribution.

The Jebel Aulia Dam, built in 1937, the low Aswan Dam (1933), and the dams at Roseries (1966), Sennar (1926), and Kashm el Girba (1966) were all constructed to provide seasonal storage, by holding wet-season flows for the next dry season. The High Dam at Aswan, completed in 1971, is an attempt to eliminate the differences in water availability between wet and dry years. Although none of these structures fulfills its role completely, in all years the distribution of seasonal flows is affected and differences between wet and dry years are reduced. Figure 15.10 is a schematic of the Nile River works.

Flows   Large irrigation projects in the Sudan built during the period of Anglo-Egyptian rule and since are the second major incursion into the hydrologic regime of the Nile. Irrigation in the Sudan has grown to cover an area of 19,019 km^2. The water requirements of these irrigated areas add up to 45,629 million m^3/yr. As almost all this water is lost from the river through evapotranspiration, it represents a significant re-

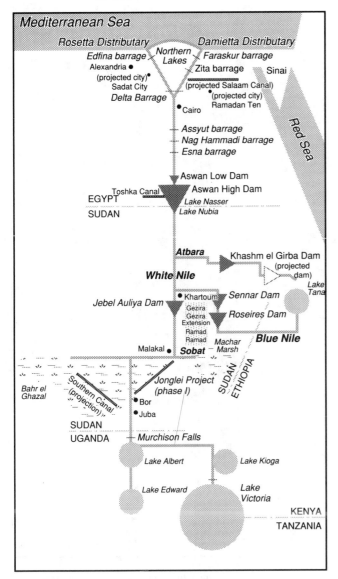

Figure 15.10 Schematic of the Nile River works.

duction in volume available at the Sudan-Egyptian border of about 15% of the annual flow.

Water Quality The storage reservoirs had, however, an additional effect. The Nile River carries a very high sediment load from the Blue Nile and the other tributaries originating in the Ethiopian highlands. The reservoirs are efficient silt traps (the Kashm el Girba Reservoir operates at only 40% capacity after 20 years) and have reduced significantly the silt load in the river. While this could be seen as an improvement in water quality, it has had disastrous effects on the land and people in the lower basin. Lowered silt deposition during floods on the agricultural overbank areas has reduced fertility. Bank erosion has increased in many areas. In addition, the reduced silt load has caused large changes in the morphology of the delta and the productivity of the eastern Mediterranean.

Summary Human action has affected the Nile River for at least 2000 years. Yet major changes in the natural flow regime and in the water quality are a product of the twentieth century. The consequences, whatever they may be, of development for irrigation, the change in the flood regime on the delta farmers, the ecological changes, and the growing pollution from the burgeoning city of Cairo have not as yet spurred major action for mitigation. Thus the Nile is, and has been for the past 300 years, in the second stage of human intervention.

The High Plains (Ogallala) Aquifer

Our final case considers one of the great underground water resources in North Ameria – the High Plains Aquifer. Depletion of water in storage has been the major impact on this resource. The High Plains Aquifer has received more attention in the past two decades than any other aquifer in the United States and perhaps the world. As it underlies nearly 453,250 km^2 and serves as a water source for the irrigation of more than 5 million ha of farmland (20% of the irrigated acreage in the United States), the aquifer is certainly worthy of national, state, and even international focus. In many places, the aquifer is being mined at what many consider a rapid rate. This depletion raises controversies of national import over the fate of communities dependent upon the aquifer.

The High Plains area overlying the aquifer system is characterized by flat to gently rolling terrain that regionally slopes upward from east to west. The climate may be generally characterized as a middle-latitude, dry, continental climate. Annual precipitation is less than 51 cm over most of the area, although in eastern Nebraska and the central Kansas area, it averages as high as 71 cm.

The High Plains Aquifer is, regionally, a water-table aquifer, consisting mostly of near-surface sand and gravel deposits.[8] The maximum saturated thickness is about 305 m, and the average thickness 61 m. Figure 15.11 shows the saturated thickness of the aquifer in 1980.

Recharge to the aquifer is fairly scant because evapotranspiration potential is much greater than precipitation. Stream-bed recharge and recharge through sandy soils does occur in some areas of the High Plains; the long-term average annual recharge, however, probably ranges around 1 cm (U.S. Geological Survey 1984b).

Impacts of Human Use The major impact on the aquifer from human activities is the reduction of water in storage and the consequent decline in the water-table elevation. Figure 15.12 shows the estimated water-level change from predevelopment to 1980. The reason for this change in storage is the irrigation that began in the high plains in the late nineteenth century. Windmills were the first source of power for development of groundwater, but large-scale development did not occur until inexpensive energy became available for turbine pumps in the 1940s. Coupled with technological advances in well-drilling and pumping plants, the demand for irrigation generated by the Dust Bowl years of the 1930s encouraged large increases in irrigated area.

Beginning in the southern high plains of Texas and New Mexico, irrigation has spread throughout most of the high

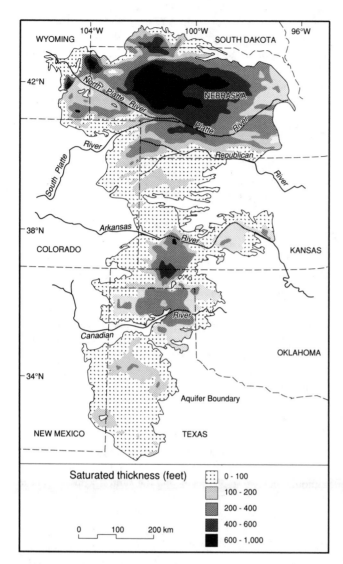

Figure 15.11 Saturated thickness of the High Plains Aquifer in 1980.
Source: U.S. Geological Survey 1984b.

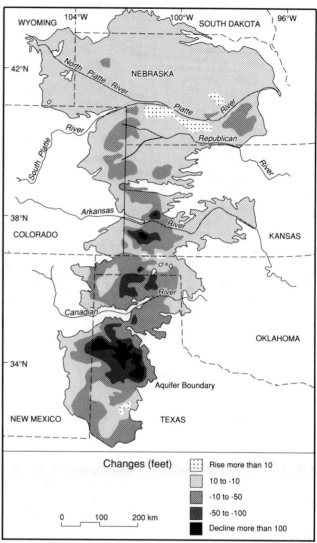

Figure 15.12 Predevelopment to 1980 water-level changes in the High Plains Aquifer (modified from Luckey and others 1981).
Source: U.S. Geological Survey 1984b.

plains. Center-pivot irrigation systems have enabled large areas of land to be irrigated that were previously unsuitable (U.S. Geological Survey 1983). During 1978, some 170,000 wells in the high plains pumped an estimated 19 km^3 of water to irrigate 5,261,000 ha (U.S. Geological Survey 1984b).

Because of the depletion of saturated thickness and increased pumping costs relative to prices received by farmers for their crops, some farmers in western Kansas, western Texas, eastern Colorado, and perhaps other areas have reverted to dry-land farming. Unfortunately, data are not readily available to quantify the extent of this change in irrigated area and groundwater pumping. Poor market conditions have also reduced groundwater pumpage in recent years. As a result of these two factors, groundwater levels have stabilized or risen in some areas of the high plains.

The quality of water in the High Plains Aquifer generally is suitable for irrigation but, in many places, the water does not meet U.S. Environmental Protection Agency drinking-water regulations. According to the U.S. Geological Survey (1984b),

hazardous concentrations of dissolved solids and sodium occur naturally, but along major streams, irrigation practices have greatly concentrated dissolved constituents. Nonpoint-nitrate contamination from agricultural sources occurs in several areas of Nebraska and possibly other states (U.S. Geological Survey 1985). Pesticide contamination and pollution from development of oil and gas wells are problems in some areas of the High Plains as well.

Summary The High Plains Aquifer is one of the most extensive and important interstate aquifers in the United States. About 95% of all water pumped from the aquifer is used for irrigation. For several years, the economic health of the High Plains region overlying the aquifer has been in question because the aquifer is being mined. Water-supply change over time has been the overwhelming issue with regard to this water source, with water quality relegated to a distant second. Changes in the world agricultural economy, decreased well yields (due to depletion), and increased relative pumping costs have engendered reductions in the pumpage levels of the 1960s and 1970s. In the development of a nonrenewable resource such as the Ogallala, however, there is no future but exhaustion. It is only the time period of use that may be lengthened or shortened.

The High Plains Aquifer is in the third stage of intervention over much of its extent. Several states have established authority for centralized or decentralized control of depletion rates. Generally, these efforts do not reduce the rate of depletion but prevent it from increasing. Federal and state regulations of pesticide and fertilizer use are attempts to reduce future water-quality deterioration.

Conclusions

Over the past 300 years, the impacts of humans on hydrologic flow regimes have been regionally and locally significant, albeit insignificant on a global scale. Developments in agriculture, manufacturing, mining, and other activities have produced demand for temporally and spatially reliable water resources. As a result, water has been diverted, mined, stored, treated, transferred between basins, allocated between nations, and otherwise managed by numerous institutions. These same developments in human activities, in addition to population growth and the concurrent need for waste disposal, have contributed to a deterioration of water quality in those rivers affected by development on or near them. Reduced virgin flows and increased return flows from irrigated lands in river basins supporting large irrigated areas (for example, the Colorado, the Ganges, and the Nile rivers) have caused increases in salinity and polluted the waters with fertilizers and pesticides. Use of river systems for industrial and municipal waste disposal has created a variety of health hazards ranging from infectious diseases to cancer (for example, the Thames and the Ganges rivers). Storage projects on the Nile

and Colorado rivers have greatly reduced sediment discharge to their sea outlets, to some extent improving water quality, but at the same time, drastically altering the preexisting ecology. A particularly noteworthy impact has been the irreversible depletion of groundwater from aquifers, as exemplified by the High Plains Aquifer.

Nevertheless, many of the water-related problems suffered by humankind have been mitigated by intervention in hydrologic regimes. Some amount of flooding has been controlled, certainly, on the Colorado, the Thames, the Nile, and the Ganges (although one might argue that Bangladesh suffers more catastrophic flooding now than it did prior to India's dam building); water is available for producing large quantities of food and fiber due to storage capacity and groundwater development; and water-quality treatment and waste-disposal programs have reduced much of the infectious disease and biological debilitation that accompanies early stages of economic development.

As described in the "Focus of Study," intervention in hydrologic-flow regimes has taken four general forms over the past 300 years, leading from minor effects, to activities with little regard for health-related and other ecological consequences, to restoration, and finally to the planning of activities with no or minimal impacts. These stages (following the consequential escalation of disease, property damage, and ecological deterioration) have – through developments in the physical, natural, and social sciences, greater understanding of our interventions, expanded technologies for treatment, planning, and institutional management, and growth in capital and institutions for financing – achieved reversals and improvements in deleterious patterns of use. Of course, we are well aware that the advanced stages and even the first ones have not occurred in every hydrologic regime. We are also keenly aware that new problems of a perhaps

Table 15-4 *Stages of human intervention on the waters of the world*

Continent	Eighteenth century	Nineteenth century	Twentieth century
Africa	No impacts on regional scale	First stage – probably only minor local impacts	Second stage in some major basins
Asia	First and second stages – concentration of local population and irrigation	Second stage – large impacts from locally dense population and irrigation	Second stage continuing
Australia	No effects	First stage – probably only local impacts	Third and probably fourth stage, with planning for compatible development
Europe	Second stage – health effects are the major impacts	Mostly second stage, due to increasing population and the Industrial Revolution. Third-stage improvements near the end of the century	Third stage throughout the periods around the world wars; fourth stage strongly indicated
North America	First stage – limited local impacts	Second stage – population and industrial growth – little recovery in the last years	Third stage throughout; fourth stage initiated in many areas
South America	No significant impacts on a regional scale	Second stage in some areas, no impacts in others	Second stage in many large areas; some third stage near urban centers

more insidious, delayed-effect nature have arisen in the past two decades. Clearly, human interventions or impacts have been and will continue to be a mixed assortment of negative and positive effects – exemplifying a diversity of values, a waxing and waning of scientific understanding, and an ever-shifting degree of local and regional economic health. The case studies that have been included in this chapter attest to this.

Using the experience from the case studies and our general knowledge of world geography, and making major assumptions, we have assembled a tentative estimate of the stages of human intervention throughout the globe. Table 15-4 presents this summary.

Notes

1. The world's two largest rivers in terms of discharge to the ocean, the Amazon and the Congo, together constitute almost 15% of the total runoff to the ocean (Speidel and Agnew 1982).

2. The Colorado River rises high in the glaciers of the Wind River Range in Wyoming and in the Rocky Mountains and San Juan Mountains of Colorado. From the true start of the river system at the Continental Divide, the Colorado drops 4,270 m in its 2,700-km course to the flat, burning sands of its delta at the Gulf of California, an embayment of the Pacific Ocean (Fradkin 1981). Along its course, the river flows through mountain wilderness of the high country, spectacular canyonlands of naked rock (the most dramatic being the titanic rift in the Kaibab Plateau, the Grand Canyon), and hot, low deserts.

3. Considerable controversy exists as to the actual virgin and average flows, despite the fact that the Colorado is one of only 25 rivers in the world for which records go back more than 60 years (National Academy of Sciences 1968). Estimates range from 13.6 km^3 to 11.2 km^3/yr, with the lower estimates being the most recent. A National Academy of Sciences report (1968) on the river suggested several explanations for the uncertainty as to the Colorado River's average flow: the river may be experiencing a long-period fluctuation and the average may rise again, there may exist a long-term downward trend in flow, an error may exist in the reported stream flows, depletions may be underestimated, and changes in the ecology of the basin may have increased evapotranspiration and reduced stream-flow. The disturbing consequences of this uncertainty are manifest in the legal problems of allocation and regulation between the states and between the United States and Mexico.

4. The need for an effective body to control drainage in the capital became increasingly evident and in 1855 the Government set up the Metropolitan Board of Works. The Board's chief engineer, Sir Joseph Bazalgette, recommended the interception of the sewage, which was running directly into the river. Some 160 km of sewers were constructed, and the sewage was conveyed to storage tanks downstream of the metropolis, to be discharged at ebb tide. The construction of the outfalls, completed in 1864, appears to have been immediately successful in improving the quality of the river in the center of London. The nuisance now was moved downstream to the lower river. In 1884, the condition of the river at Barking and Crossness was described as "extremely foul," and the report of the Royal Commission on Metropolitan Sewage was issued, recommending that the solid matter should be separated from the sewage. In 1887, lime precipitation was introduced; the effluent continued to be discharged directly from the works, but from 1889 the solid matter was dumped in the outer estuary, 111 km below London Bridge, by a fleet of six sludge vessels.

5. Fundamental to any program of water-quality management is the provision of adequate means of controlling and monitoring quality. Regulation of discharges represents the most practicable means of controlling river-water quality, and this is done by issuing "Consents

to Discharge." Consents stipulate the maximum quantity that may be discharged in a given period and the maximum concentrations for various substances.

6. Figure 15.6 was provided by the authors (Jickells et al.) of Chapter 18 (Marine Environment).

7. In all likelihood hunting and gathering populations started to be replaced by shifting cultivators about 10,000 years ago in the Ganges basin (Gadgil 1985). Settled agriculture probably spilled over into the basin from the nearby Harappan culture in the Indus Basin by 2500 B.C.. The invasion of the area by the Aryan, or Vedic, tribes in the twelfth century B.C. ushered in a period of rapid deforestation of the virgin woodlands of the Ganges basin. By the year 487 B.C. (the year of the Buddha's death), there was a flourishing empire centered on Patiliputra (now Patna), which dominated the entire Ganges basin. Trade flourished as far afield as Java and Ceylon.

As transportation uses of the river began to decline at the end of the nineteenth century, irrigation became the predominant use of the river. Early during the Moghul period (1620–1757), large irrigation diversion works were carried out in the vicinity of Delhi and Agra. In the early nineteenth century, the British turned their attention to stabilizing control of needed export crops. This led, at first, to the remodeling of the Moghul canals on the tract of land between the main stem of the Ganges and its major tributary, the Yamuna. In 1838, for example, they repaired and remodeled the Eastern Yamuna Canal, originally built by Mohammed Shah in the 1740s. The repaired canal irrigated some 141,600 ha. In 1836, Sir Proby T. Cautley commenced work on the Ganges Canal, which was completed in 1854 at a cost of 2,155,997 pounds sterling (one-half the cost of constructing the Taj Mahal). Irrigating 487,700 ha using 3,580 km of canals and distributories, this was the largest irrigation canal completed in the world at that time, and even today remains one of the largest. The canal diverted almost all of the low-flow season flow out of the Ganges at Hardawar.

Since that time many more irrigation projects have been developed in the Ganges basin from both surface and groundwater sources. Chaturvedi and Rogers (1985) estimated that 22 million ha are irrigable by existing developments. Of these, surface-water diversions account for two-thirds and groundwater for one-third.

Many of the storages on the tributary streams are multipurpose projects, producing hydropower and providing some flood mitigation, as well as municipal and industrial water supplies. Large floods and droughts have been measured only since the 1870s. These events are closely correlated with the summer monsoon and have led to major famines and great loss of life. For example, the massive crop failure and famine of 1876–77 led to recommendations for more irrigation by the Famine Commission of 1880. No action was taken. The two great famines of 1897–98 and 1899–1900 led to the formation of the Irrigation Commission in 1901 and a renewed emphasis on irrigation both within the Ganges basin and outside of it. The last great famine in the basin was the 1943 famine in Bengal, when an estimated 3 million people perished.

8. Geologically, the Aquifer consists of hydraulically connected geologic units of late Tertiary or Quaternary age. The upper Tertiary rocks include part of the Brule formation, Arikaree group, and Ogallala formation. Quaternary deposits consist of alluvial, dune-sand, and valley-fill deposits. The Ogallala formation is the principal geologic unit in the High Plains Aquifer and underlies an area of about 347,060 km^3. Thought to have been formed from braided stream deposition, the aquifer is a sequence of clays, silts, sands, and gravels carried eastward from the Rocky Mountains (U.S. Geological Survey 1984b).

References

Arrhenius, E. 1977. Health effects of multipurpose use of water. *Ambio 6* (1): 59–62.

Bradley, D. J. 1977. Health aspects of water supplies in tropical countries. In *Water, Wastes, and Health in Hot Climates*, ed.

R. Feachem, M. McGarry, and D. Mara, 3–17. London: John Wiley and Sons.

Buckley, R. B. 1880. *The Irrigation Works of India and Their Financial Results*. London: W. H. Allen and Co.

Cannon, H. L., and H. C. Hopps, eds. 1971. *Environmental Geochemistry in Health and Disease*. American Association for the Advancement of Science Symposium, Dallas, Texas, December 1968. The Geological Society of America Memoir 123. Boulder, CO: The Geological Society of America.

Chandler, W. U. 1984. *Improving World Health: A Least-Cost Strategy*. Worldwatch Paper No. 59. Washington, D.C.: Worldwatch Institute.

Chaturvedi, M., and P. Rogers. 1985. *Water Resources Systems Planning: Some Case Studies for India*. Bangalore: Indian Academy of Sciences.

Cvjetanovic, B. 1975. Epidemiology and control of water- and food-borne infections. In *The Theory and Practice of Public Health*, ed. W. Hobson, 216–31. London: Oxford University Press.

Darian, S. G. 1978. *The Ganges in Myth and History*. Honolulu, HI: The University Press of the University of Hawaii.

Dubos, R. 1968. *Man Adapting*. Silliman Milestone in Science. New Haven, CT: Yale University Press.

Dugan, P. R. 1972. *Biochemical Ecology of Water Pollution*. New York and London: Plenum Press.

Eckholm, E. 1976. *Losing Ground: Environmental Stress and World Food Prospects*. New York: Norton.

Förstner, U., and G. T. W. Whitmann. 1981. *Metal Pollution in the Aquatic Environment*. Berlin: Springer-Verlag.

Fradkin, P. L. 1981. *A River No More*. Tucson, AZ: University of Arizona Press.

Gadgil, M. 1985. Towards an ecological history of India. *Economic and Political Weekly* 20, Nos. 45, 46, and 47, Special Number November, 1909–18.

Ganguli, G. 1938. *Trends of Agriculture and Population in the Ganges Valley*. London: Methuen.

Hundley, N., Jr. 1966. *Dividing the Waters*. Berkeley and Los Angeles: University of California Press.

———. 1975. *Water and the West*. Berkeley and Los Angeles: University of California Press.

Hurst, H. E. 1957. *The Nile Basin 1957*. rev. ed. London: Constable Publishers.

International Boundary and Water Commission, United States and Mexico. 1979. *Flow of the Colorado River and Other Western Boundary Streams and Related Data*. El Paso, TX: IBWC.

International Institute for Environmental and Development and World Resources Institute. 1987. *World Resources 1987*. New York: Basic Books.

Kandl, H. 1968. Die Entwicklung der Donau Regulierung in Osterreich. *Osterreichische Wasserwirtschaft*, Jahrgang 21, Heft 12. Wien.

Klein, I. 1983. Irrigation, Environmental Decay and Disease in British India. Mimeo. Washington, D.C.: Department of History: The American University.

Mahajan, J. 1984. *The Ganga Trail*. New Delhi: Clarion Books.

McJunkin, F. E. 1982. *Water and Human Health*. Report prepared by National Demonstration Water Project for the U.S. Agency for International Development. Washington, D.C.: U.S. Agency for International Development.

McKeown, T., R. G. Brown, and R. G. Record. 1972. An interpretation of the modern rise of population in Europe. *Population Studies* 26: 345–82.

Meyers, C. J. 1966. The Colorado River. *Stanford Law Review* 19: 1–75.

National Academy of Sciences Safe Drinking Water Committee. 1977, 1980a, 1980b, 1981, 1982. *Drinking Water and Health*. 5 vols. Washington, D.C.: National Academy of Sciences – National Research Council.

National Academy of Sciences. 1968. *Alternatives in Water Management*. Washington, D.C.: National Academy Press.

Nriagu, J. O., ed. 1984. *Changing Metal Cycles and Human Health*.

Report on the Dahlen Workshop on Changing Metal Cycles and Human Health, Berlin, March 20–25, 1983. Berlin: Springer-Verlag.

Organization for Economic Cooperation and Development. 1982. *Control Policies for Specific Water Pollutants*. Paris: OECD.

———. 1984. Environment and Economics. Background Papers, Vol. 1. Paris: OECD.

Rao, K. L. 1975. *India's Water Wealth*. New Delhi: Orient Longman.

Rise, R. G., ed. 1985. *Safe Drinking Water: The Impact of Chemicals on a Limited Resource*. Drinking Water Research Foundation. Chelsea, MI: Lewis Publications.

Rogers, P. 1977. Environmental Consequences of Development Projects: A Proposed Case Study of the Kosi Project. Mimeo. Cambridge, MA: Harvard University.

———. 1983. Irrigation and economic development: Some lessons from India. In *Issues in Third World Development*, ed. K. C. Note and R. K. Sampath, 347–90. Boulder, CO: Westview Press.

Rosen, G. 1958. *A History of Public Health*. MD Monographs on Medical Theory No. 1. New York: MD Publications.

Sedgwick, W. T. 1908. *Principles of Sanitary Science and the Public Health with Special Reference to the Causation and Prevention of Infectious Diseases*. London: Macmillan.

Simmons, M. 1979. Water Resource of the Colorado River Basin (unpublished). Report No. 79–178 ENR, Congressional Research Service.

Sinha, U. K. 1986. *Ganga Pollution and Health Hazard*. New Delhi: Inter-India Publication.

Smith, R. A., R. B. Alexander, and M. G. Wolman. 1987. Water-quality trends in the nation's rivers. *Science* 235: 1607–15.

Speidel, D. H., and A. F. Agnew. 1982. *The Natural Geochemistry of Our Environment*. Boulder, CO: Westview Press.

Spink, W. W. 1978. *Infectious Diseases: Prevention and Treatment in the Nineteenth and Twentieth Centuries*. Minneapolis, MN: University of Minnesota Press.

United Nations. 1978. *Water Development and Management: Proceedings of the United Nations Water Conference*. Mar del Plata, Argentina, 1977. Oxford: Pergamon Press.

United Nations Environment Program. 1986. *The State of the Environment: Environment and Health*. Nairobi: UNEP.

United Nations Population Division. 1984. *World Population Prospects: Estimates and Projections As Assessed in 1984*. New York: United Nations.

U.S. Bureau of Reclamation. 1983. *Colorado River Improvement Program, Status Report, January 1983*. Denver: U.S. Bureau of Reclamation, Colorado River Quality Office.

U.S. Geological Survey. 1983. *Estimating 1980 Groundwater Pumpage for Irrigation on the High Plains in Parts of Colorado, Kansas, Nebraska, New Mexico, South Dakota, Texas, and Wyoming*. U.S.G.S. Water-Resources Investigations 83–4123. Washington, D.C.: Government Printing Office.

———. 1984a. *National Water Summary 1983 – Hydrologic Events and Issues*. U.S.G.S. Water-Supply Paper 2250. Washington, D.C.: Government Printing Office.

———. 1984b. *Geohydrology of the High Plains Aquifer in Parts of Colorado, Kansas, Nebraska, New Mexico, Oklahoma, South Dakota, Texas, and Wyoming*. U.S.G.S. Professional Paper 1400-B. Washington, D.C.: Government Printing Office.

———. 1985. *National Water Summary 1984 – Hydrologic Events, Selected Water-Quality Trends and GroundWater Resources*. U.S.G.S. Water-Supply Paper 2275. Washington, D.C.: Government Printing Office.

Van der Leeden, F. 1975. *Water Resources of the World*. Port Washington, NY: Water Information Center.

Waterbury, J. 1979. *Hydropolitics of the Nile Valley*. New York: Syracuse University Press.

Wilson, H. M. 1903. *Irrigation in India*. U.S. Geological Survey Water Supply and Irrigation Paper No. 87. Washington, D.C.: U.S. Department of the Interior.

Winslow, C.-E. A. 1980. *The Conquest of Epidemic Disease: A Chapter in the History of Ideas*. Madison, WI: University of Wisconsin Press.

Wolman, A., and A. E. Gorman. 1939. Water-borne outbreaks in the United States and Canada. *Journal of the American Water Works Association 31*: 225–373.

Wood, L. B. 1982. *The Restoration of the Tidal Thames*. Bristol: Adam Higher Ltd.

World Health Organization. 1983. *World Health Statistics 1983*. Geneva: WHO.

———. 1985. *World Health Statistics 1985*. Geneva: WHO.

———. 1986a. *The International Drinking Water Supply and Sanitation Decade: Review of Regional and Global Data (as of December 31, 1983)*. Geneva: WHO.

———. 1986b. *World Health Statistics 1986*. Geneva: WHO.

World Resources Institute. 1987. *World Resources 1987*. New York: Basic Books.

16

The Coastal Zone

H. JESSE WALKER

Although most present-day uses and modifications of the coastal zone had their origin in the distant past, the intensity of human impact on coastal resources increased dramatically during the Industrial Revolution. The exploitation of both mineral and biotic resources, the construction of harbors, the reclamation of coastal marshes and mudflats, and even the use of beaches for recreation, were known to the ancients.

Despite the fact that the coastal zone, no matter the definition used,[1] is a narrow band relative to other land- or seascapes, physical change along it generally has gone unrecorded throughout much of history. It was accepted that shoreline position and coastal character change and that human adjustment is necessary.

Because of the dynamic character of the natural processes acting upon the coast (whether they be oceanographic, terrestrial, atmospheric, or biotic) and because humans often have responded in an equally dramatic way, it is difficult to distinguish between those changes that should be credited (or debited) to nature and those to humans. In many (if not most) instances, either may aggravate the other. Typhoon surges are often countered by building seawalls, and seawalls are likely to enhance wave reflection and increase the rate of erosion of adjacent beaches. Cause and effect are difficult, often impossible, to separate.

Difficulty in quantifying coastal change stems from four facts: (1) the world's coastal zone consists of a number of relatively distinct forms; (2) it is affected by almost all natural processes and human endeavors; (3) those records that have been kept by the inhabitants of the 141 (out of 171) coastal nations (Bair 1988) are highly varied in type, length, and accuracy, making comparability nearly impossible; and (4) only recently have there been attempts at establishing worldwide comparisons. During the 1980s, for example, preliminary assessments of beach erosion (Bird 1985), sea-level variation (Pirazzoli 1986), and artificialization (Walker 1988) were published.

The Coastal Stage

The *sine qua non* of the so-called coastal stage are its interfaces – those between land and water, land and air, and water and air (Fig. 16.1). Possibly the most important division within the coastal zone is that between water and land. This interface may be virtually linear, as along cliff coasts, or it may be spread across a wide extent, as in low-lying coasts with high tidal ranges. In some places, as for example in salt marshes, mangrove swamps, estuaries, and lagoons, it may be indistinct. This demarcation band has been roughly calculated to be about 4.4×10^5 km long (Inman and Brush 1973) in its generalized outline and at least 10^6 km long when all shoreline indentations are used in the measurement (Bird and Schwartz 1985).[2]

The potential of this zone from the standpoint of human food supply is implied in the statement by Hedgpeth (1976) that "the ultimate region of the sea is . . . the narrow fringe where the sea impinges on the land," a fringe he calls "the living edge." This edge, which was so important biotically to pre–Industrial Revolution peoples (Fig. 16.2), has only recently again become appreciated (especially its coastal

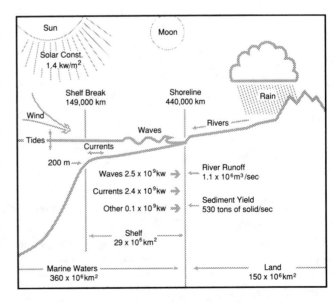

Figure 16.1 The coastal zone and its energy sources. After Inman and Brush 1973.

Figure 16.2 "How to catch fish": an engraved print of a painting by John White made ca. 1586. *Source:* Lorant 1946.

marshes, estuaries, and lagoons) for its role in the productivity of desirable marine biota.

Plate Tectonics, Drainage Basins, and Sediment Supply

On a global basis, the structure and configuration of coasts are dominated by plate tectonics. The movements of the earth's plates – so slow that only recently have they been measured (Kerr 1985) – are responsible for the major coastal forms. Along the leading edges of the moving plates deep ocean trenches, narrow continental shelves, mountains, and rugged islands dominate and form what Inman and Nordstrom (1971) have labeled collision coasts (Fig. 16.3). This type of coast is present along virtually the entire shoreline that borders the Pacific Ocean and is characterized by volcanic and earthquake activity.

Coasts that are embedded within plates tend to be tectonically passive, although they vary somewhat in physical expression. Amero-embedded coasts, best exampled by the east coast of North America, are low-lying and have extensive beaches and wide continental shelves. Afro-embedded coasts, usually somewhat more rugged, are often backed by hills or plateaus.

Marginal seacoasts, separated from the oceans by island arcs, are bordered by shallow seas and are highly varied in relief. The coast of the People's Republic of China, with its alternating headlands and deltaic plains, is a good example.

In addition to determining the gross form of most of the

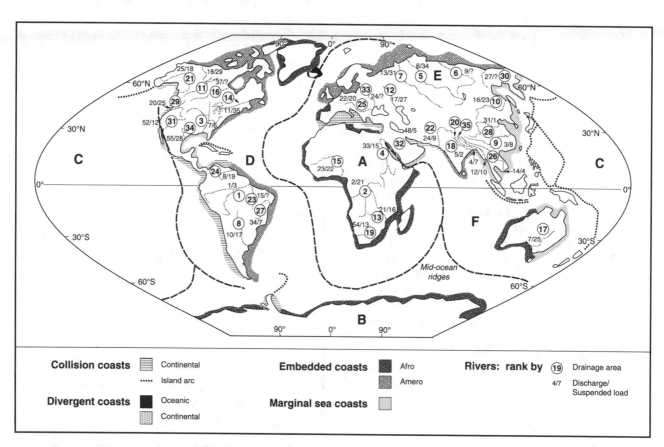

Figure 16.3 Distribution of coastal types and drainage systems. Modified from Davies 1977; Emery 1969; Inman and Nordstrom 1971; and Walker 1975.

earth's coasts, plate tectonics is also largely responsible for the size and lithology of drainage basins, and even exerts some control on their climate and vegetation. Thus, plate tectonics, even if indirectly, is responsible for the amount and type of sediment carried to the oceans (Walker 1975).

Along collision-type coasts, where gradients are steep and drainage distances short, textures are usually coarse, with sand dominating. Along embedded coasts, where river gradients are gentle and distances long, sediment usually has a fine texture and often is rich in organic matter.

Shifting Sea Level and Still-Stand

The juncture between land and sea is constantly in flux. Daily, seasonal, and sporadic fluctuations because of tides, waves, storm surges, and atmospheric pressure changes, among others, are locally significant, and in some locations must be measured in meters. Such fluctuations, no matter their extremes, vary around a base level that itself changes with time (Mörner 1986).

During the period of time humans have occupied the earth, a perturbing hydrologic cycle has been responsible for alternately storing ice on and dissipating it from the continents. The concomitant lowering and raising of sea level within a range of about 200 m formed shorelines that are now stranded both above and below present-day sea level. The most recent major rise, which began about 18,000 years ago, continued at rates of 0.6 to 1.5 m/100 yr until about 5,000 years ago (Carr 1972), when glacially controlled sea level stabilized.

As sea level rose, deep estuaries were formed and the world's coastline lengthened. Although estuarine filling began with the initiation of sea-level rise, fill probably did not begin to dominate until about the time still-stand was attained. Subsequently many estuaries have been "over filled" and converted into deltas that extend seaward (e.g., the Mississippi River). Others are still in the process of filling, as exemplified by the Persian Gulf and Mobile Bay in the United States, which is now only one-fourth the size it was 5,000 years ago.

During sea-level rise, former coastal plains were overridden, and their sand and gravel deposits reworked. This rich source of sand made possible the creation and maintenance of extensive beaches and dunes during most of the past 5,000 years. With a nearly stable sea level, however, offshore sand deposits available for natural renourishment are being depleted, primarily by loss offshore, but also to some extent inland by wind. Beaches are increasingly dependent upon rivers for new sand supplies. The present-day reduction in beach size along much of the coastline of the world, although aggravated by human activity, is largely a natural consequence of still-stand.

Process and Form

Although the gross character of the coast stems from the long-term tectonic activity that is associated with plate movement, many of the details are the result of numerous physical, chemical, and biotic processes that have been operative both subaerially and subaqueously since the sea reached its present level. In some instances, the actual position of the shoreline has changed little. Along most coasts, however, shoreline position has changed greatly – advancing with aggradation and uplift, retreating with erosion and subsidence.

Coastal Processes. Probaby the most important coastal processes are those associated with moving water in nearshore environments, especially waves.

Three distinct forces (astronomical, impulsive, and meteorological) act upon water to generate waves (Weggel 1972). Astronomical forces are responsible for the tides that influence the size of the band over which other processes operate and which are very important to the growth patterns of numerous biota. Impulsive forces – those caused by earthquakes, volcanic eruptions, and landslides – although relatively rare and basically random, produce waves such as the dangerous tsunami. Waves produced by meteorological forces (i.e., sea, swell, and storm waves) are especially important from the standpoint of coastal modification. They, along with the currents they generate, serve as erosional, transportational, and depositional agents.

The frequency, type, and origin of waves vary sufficiently uniformly along coastlines to permit the identification of specific wave environments. Storm-wave environments (high energy) are found mainly along midlatitude coasts, whereas swell-wave environments (low energy) tend to be common in lower latitudes (Davies 1977).

Wind, which is responsible for the generation of the bulk of the waves that do most of the work along the coast, is also significant directly as an erosional, transportational, and depositional agent. Wind-formed dunes, many of them stabilized today, border some shorelines in nearly all coastal environments.

Although usually less important than wave action, chemical and biological processes dominate along some coastal sectors. Gases, elements, and minerals in solution, and organic and inorganic particles within the water column, air, and bottom sediments may all be chemically active. Chemical weathering and chemical precipitation are major modifiers and producers of coastal forms.

In addition, $CaCO_3$, SiO_2, and other compounds in seawater make possible the formation of reefs by such animals as hermatypic corals, vermetid gastropods, polychaete worms, oysters, and such plants as calcareous algae (Jablonski 1982). Higher types of vegetation, especially mangroves (low latitudes) and salt-marsh grasses (higher latitudes), trap sediment, provide organic matter, and aid in stabilizing shorelines.

Coastal Forms. From the standpoint of human utilization, the type of landform that is present along the coastline is especially important. Forms range from hard rock cliffs devoid of sediment to rapidly accreting deltas. The number of forms in between includes beaches and barriers, lagoons and estuaries, dunes, and coral reefs, among others.

Cliffy coasts, which occupy about half of the world's coastline, consist of those that are composed of "hard" rock, "soft" rock (also referred to as earth cliffs), and ice (along some 5% of the world's coastline). Hard-rock cliffs tend to be stable, and unless there are coves or bays present, their "value" is mainly the result of "their exhilarating scenery and wildlife" (Goldsmith 1977). In contrast, both earth and ice cliffs are usually unstable, undergoing erosion, with frequent landsliding in the former and calving with iceberg formation in the latter.

Beaches, which have been defined in a variety of ways (Davis 1982), are the most dynamic of shore-zone types. Composed of unconsolidated sediments, beaches range greatly in length, width, composition, and texture. Their existence depends on materials derived from inland, offshore, along-shore, and biotic sources. Recent studies have shown that "about 20% of the world's coast is sandy and backed by beach ridges, dunes, or other sandy depositional terrain" (Bird 1985). Some 70% of these beaches (equal to 14% of the total length of the world's coastline) is being eroded whereas less than one-seventh that length is prograding (Bird 1985).

Barrier beaches, which extend along 10–15% of the world's coast (Fisher 1982), are especially common (with a total length of about 5,000 km) along the Atlantic and Gulf coasts of the United States. Barrier beaches may extend out from land masses in the form of spits or be completely separate in the form of islands. Most barrier beaches are backed by dunes and many have back swamps facing the enclosed lagoon. Because of tidal inlets, barrier beaches on a worldwide basis are isolated. However, once connected by bridges and roads to population centers, they become prime recreational territory.

Coastal dunes, present on all continents including Ant-arctica, are one of the most common forms along many coastlines. Dependent on wind and an adequate supply of sand, dunes, like beaches, are being lost. After still-stand was reached, dunes, which had been migrating inland during sea-level rise, began to stabilize. In contrast, those near the shore served as sources of sand during storm surges. Coastal dunes today are viewed as major storage areas for beach sand and as a natural defense for back-barrier areas (Leatherman 1979), and in many locations attempts are being made to stabilize them (Fig. 16.4).

Six thousand years ago, deltas, which now occupy about 1.5% of the world's coastline, were few in number. Their size and configuration depend not only on the sediment delivered to the sea, but also on its redistribution by waves and currents. Deltas include many subenvironments such as levees, barriers, beaches, lakes, marshes, and mudflats.

In the United States, some 80–90% of the Atlantic and Gulf coasts and 10–20% of the Pacific coast are bordered by estuaries and lagoons (Emery 1967). Estuaries, which were formed as sea level rose, developed best where coastal plains were wide. When valley systems were drowned (as in the Chesapeake Bay system), very irregular shorelines were produced. Originally estuaries were open-mouthed. However, with sedimentation, many have been separated from the sea by barriers. Although the barrier shoreline is essentially straight, the original drowned mainland shoreline often remains serrated. The water body that develops between the

Figure 16.4 Construction on and protection of sand dunes along the Atlantic coast of Virginia, United States. Photo by H. J. Walker.

barrier and the mainland is a typical lagoon. Usually shallow, lagoons are connected with the sea by inlets and are maintained by some combination of river inflow and ebb and flow of tidal water. Lagoons tend to fill with sediment and are rapidly converted into marshes and mudflats. Although estuaries and lagoons have greatly decreased in extent, they nonetheless remain one of the most important of coastal types.

Coral reefs have a more restricted distribution than any of the physically created forms just discussed. Their presence and form depend on the growth restrictions of the reef builders, as well as on the more general physical processes. Water temperature, salinity, turbidity, depth, and circulation are all important (Guilcher 1988).

Mangrove swamps and salt marshes are also organic coastal types. Mangroves (with as many as 50 species of woody plants) are tropical and subtropical in locale, whereas salt marshes are found most commonly along mid- and high-latitude coasts. Both usually occur in association with bays, estuaries, lagoons, and other areas without strong wave action. These wetlands are especially important as nursery grounds for marine life and are highly productive systems. Occupying only about 0.4% of the world's area, wetlands account for 2.3% of the world's net productivity (Long and Mason 1983).

Coastal Utilization and Modification prior to the Industrial Revolution

Just when ancestral humans first began to utilize coastal resources is unknown. If Sauer (1962), who believed that "the path of our evolution turned aside from the common primate course by going to the sea," and Russell (1974), who with a slightly different tack, considered that "seacoasts localized many of man's activities when he acquired hominid characteristics," are correct, it was several million years ago.

One of the major advantages of the shore zone to humans was as an ecologic niche where there was no major competition from other primates, or for that matter, even from other mammals (Walker 1981b). Resources were theirs for the taking, and movement along the coast was relatively easy. By the end of the Pleistocene, partly because of the land bridges that existed during low sea stands, much of the usable coastal zone was occupied.

During the rise in sea level that accompanied the waning of the continental glaciers, humans were gradually (albeit unknowingly) forced upslope on what is now the continental shelf. Even at its maximum rate, the sea probably never rose more than about 25 cm per generation. Archaeological excavations of what is now a headland cave in Greece not only gave evidence that there was continuous occupation between 20,000 and 5,000 B.P., but also that there was a gradual increase in the proportion of marine resources utilized, at least until 8,000 B.P., when goats (domesticated) as well as wheat and barley began to dominate (Jacobsen 1976).

During the late Holocene, as sea level was approaching its still-stand position, agriculture and animal husbandry were becoming increasingly important, and may be credited with the first reversal in the trend of slowly increasing coastal population, at least in the eastern Mediterranean area. It is possibly a trend that was typical with the first agriculturists in other areas as well.

Agriculture, even if it did not originate in floodplains or deltas, soon spread to them. Along with that spread came direct modification through the construction of canals for irrigation and drainage and levees for flood control (van Aart 1974). These structures apparently aided in the build-up (reclamation?) of surrounding wetlands and slowed deltaic extension. In Mesopotamia, for example, during periods when canal systems were neglected, coastal extension was more rapid than during those periods when cultivation was extensive (Davis 1956).

Agriculture led to the development of permanent settlements, and with them came occupational specialization, social and political organization, commercial development, and over-water contact (Walker 1981b).

Many of the earliest ports were established, as they still are, where there was natural protection from the vagaries of the sea. In parts of the Mediterranean Sea (especially in Greece and Turkey), small protected bays are numerous and served well as harbors. At many of them, however, additional security was insured through the construction of breakwaters across seaward openings.

The Hanseatic League, formed in the thirteenth century, was a major factor in expanding trade by sea and increasing the number of coastal ports. In northern Europe, however, ports were usually river-oriented, a possibility not available along most Mediterranean coasts because of topography. Normally, these river-port cities were positioned on the sides of rivers with the best and most spacious terraces. Expansion to the opposite sides of the rivers was a nineteenth-century phenomenon. Today, most of the large river ports in Europe are descended from those founded during Hanse times (Karmon 1980).

The major differences between the ports built before the Industrial Revolution and its early stages and those of today are that the former often had poor connection with their hinterland, had minimal facilities for ship-handling (Fig. 16.5), often had harbors that were shallow (even for the shallow-draft vessels of the day), were dredged rarely, and had minimal breakwaters, which required frequent repair.

The Industrial and Technological Revolutions

During the days of exploration that straddled the beginning of the Industrial Revolution, most coastlines were outlined even though, as Penrose (1967) wrote, "a fair coastal survey was the sole result – nothing more." Nonetheless, these coastal surveys often included the mapping (and naming) of bays, straits, peninsulas, and even such smaller features as tidal inlets that led to "safe havens" for their small vessels.

Davis (1974) suggested that these early voyages were the beginning of the conversion of the world into a "migratory network dominated by a single group of technologically advanced and culturally similar states." Thus, the exploratory period provided the basic information needed for settlement along these "new" coastlines.

Although most coastal uses and types of modification existed before the Industrial Revolution, there have been

Figure 16.5 The port of Messina, Italy, ca. 1700. *Source:* Van der Aa 1963.

major changes since then in the extent, intensity, and efficiency of involvement. Nonetheless, there are some new – or essentially new – impacts. For example, although coastal winds were used in energy production, the utilization of coastal waters in power production – whether it be the use of tides for electrical generation or the use of water as a coolant in generating plants – is relatively new. From the standpoint of the world's coastline, however, it is the basic uses that have been with humans since at least 7,000 years ago that are still dominant: the use of coastal environments for their resources, the use of harbors and the development of ports, reclamation, and protection from the sea.

Selected Coastal Environments and Their Resources

Virtually every aspect of the coastal zone, whether it be space, climate, beauty, animal or plant life, minerals, or water, must be considered a resource. Thus, everything humans do in the coastal zone (and many of the things they do outside it) alters the resource base. Although there are a few case studies detailing impacts on some coastal resources,

those data needed to form a worldwide assessment are lacking.

Estuaries. During preindustrial times, fishing and navigation dominated the use of estuaries (Siry 1984). Although these two activities remain important, with the Industrial Revolution the shorelines of estuaries became prime locations for development, which in turn affected estuarine biota.

The uses of estuaries are numerous, and include the mining of sand, shell, oil, gas, and chemicals; recreation; electricity generation; and fishing, among others (National Research Council 1983).

Major reasons for the location of fisheries in estuaries are their convenience and large supplies of fish. In the United States, some 70% of commercial fish and 65% of recreational fish come from estuaries (National Research Council 1983). The unique characteristics of estuaries, such as changing salinities and temperatures within limits, a plentiful supply of nutrients, favorable bottom sediments, and protected waters, help insure high productivity.

Impacts today are great – so great that Haedrich (1983) wrote that "the affairs of estuarine fishes are closely intertwined with the affairs of men." Fishing itself, when heavy and selective, affects abundance and composition within estuaries. Other activities may be even more critical.

Activities in watershed areas (which began in the Old World several millennia ago) that affect estuaries include those that change the amount, seasonal distribution, and composition of the fresh water flowing into them. Within estuaries themselves, thermal pollution, disturbance of circulation patterns by dredging and construction, and the addition of industrial and other chemicals will generally adversely affect estuarine biota (Cronin 1967).

Coral Reefs. Many of the world's hermatypic coral reefs, which have been "heralded as the most diverse, most highly organized, and aesthetically the most pleasing of all ecosystems" (Odum and Copeland 1974), were occupied at the time of their discovery by Europeans. Although their utilization was relatively intense by native populations, they were not under serious stress. Subsequent to the introduction of Western culture and technology, many human-induced changes have occurred. Guilcher (1988) considers that the "vigor and even the existence of coral reefs have been threatened by man [and] on a world scale, the general opinion is . . . that reefs and their environment have deteriorated."

Human impact on coral reefs occurs in many ways (Table 16-1). Some reefs, such as the extensive fringing reefs in the Solomon Islands and the Red Sea, have generally escaped serious impact except locally. Reef mining has supplied much of the construction material for buildings, roads, and even airport runways. The use of dynamite in mining, as well as for reef fishing (a technique introduced during World War II), has been common, but mining also is done by simply breaking off coral heads with crowbars for use in lime kilns (Walker 1962). Somewhat more destructive has been the use of dredges both for reef materials, as in Tahiti where 36 sites were being mined in 1985 (Guilcher 1988) and for deepening channels, as in Jeddah, Saudi Arabia (Fig. 14.6). Inland mining (as for tin in Thailand), various types of agriculture (especially sugar cane), and urban expansion aid in the destruction of reefs by causing the introduction into the sea of fine sediments, which smother the growing corals.

Agriculture, industry, and population growth affect coral reefs by polluting the waters with fertilizers, pesticides, other chemicals, sewage, and even fresh water, which changes critical salinities. In the Hawaiian Islands, and especially on Oahu, these pollutants (including thermal effluents from power plants) have resulted in wholesale death to many corals.

Coral-reef destruction increased drastically with the development of tropical-island tourism and with the demand for corals, tropical fish, and other reef organisms (Brown 1986). Intrusions onto reefs, even the dropping of cruise-boat anchors and the dragging of fish nets across growing corals, have changed coral-reef ecologies. For example, the taking of the giant triton (*Charonia tritonis*) from the Great Barrier Reef and around Mauritius is believed to have allowed outbreaks of the Crown of Thorns (*Acanthaster planci*), which kills corals (Guilcher 1988). Because of such destruction, many countries have now placed restrictions on collecting specimens and some have established marine parks within their coral-reef areas.

Coastal Wetlands. The word "wetlands" in the term coastal wetlands is so new that it "cannot be found in the 1948 list of words and phrases of Mencken's *American Language . . .* although in excess of thirty meanings of the word 'swamp' can be found" (Walker 1973), nor can it be found in the Glossary published by the U.S. Army Coastal Engineering Research Center (CERC 1977). It has evolved in response to the recognition that the terms swamp and marsh are not the wastelands they were believed to be during recent history.

Coastal wetlands, especially areas of mangroves and salt marshes, occupy most low-lying coasts across nearly the entire latitudinal extent of the world's coastline. This low-lying character makes them relatively easy for human encroachment, especially with modern technology, including insecticides. During most of the time since the Industrial Revolution began, wetland drainage was thought to represent progress.

Mangrove swamps, which dominate the coastlines between 25°N and 25°S, with extensions to 32°N and 40°S, have

Table 16-1 *Coral reef stresses in the Pacific*

Cause	A*	B	C	Cause	A	B	C
Siltation	2[†]	1–2	1	Collecting			
Destructive fishing				Corals	2	1	0
Blasting	2	1	0	Shells	2	1	1
Breaking coral heads	1	1	0	Pollutants			
Trawling	1	0	0	Oil	1	1	0
Poisons	1–2	0	0	Industrial effluents	1	1	1
Overfishing	1–2	2	1–2	Domestic sewage	1–2	1–2	1
Building materials	2	0	0	Agricultural wastes	1	1	1
Tourism	2	1	1	Construction activities	1	1	1

Source: Adapted from Pacific Science Association 1988.

* A – Southeast Asia, B – Central Polynesia and Western Melanesia including New Caledonia, C – Hawaii.

[†] O – no problem, 1 – minor problem, 2 – major problem.

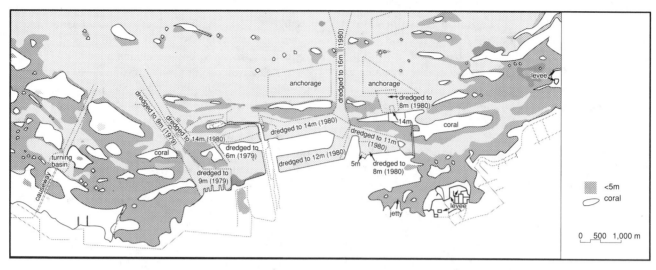

Figure 16.6 Map of harbor at Jeddah, Saudi Arabia, 1981, showing dredged channels in coral and fill. *Source:* Red Sea-Saudi Arabia-MĪNĀ' JIDDAH; Defense Mapping Agency: Washington, D.C.

become increasingly affected since World War II. The uses of mangroves and the swamps they form are numerous. Probably most mangrove species are used in some way, but it is the wholesale clearance of swamps in order to make wood chips for the pulp industry and obtaining the area needed for agriculture, aquaculture, solar salt ponds, and housing space that have caused major losses (Snedaker 1978). Some swamp areas have been destroyed through the diversion of the fresh water needed to maintain healthy stands (Walsh 1977).

The indirect uses of mangrove swamps have proven to be even more important than direct uses – a fact that has only recently begun to be realized. Mercer and Hamilton (1984) note that:

Mangrove ecosystems constitute a reservoir, refuge, feeding ground, and nursery for many useful and unusual plants and animals. Through the export of decomposable organic matter . . . into adjacent coastal waters, mangroves provide an important nutrient input and primary energy source . . .

The importance of mangroves in fisheries has been documented by Snedaker (1978), who writes that the "majority (upward of 90%) of marine species in a region are predictably found in mangrove estuaries during one or more periods in their life cycle."

Maritime salt marshes occur in a narrow band along mid- and high-latitude coasts, and although rare, they also are present in some tropical locations. Of the total $3.5 \times 10^6 \, \text{km}^2$ classified as marsh and marsh-ridden lands on earth, only a small percent is salt marsh (Bulvako 1971). It is far more important to man than its small total area would suggest because, like mangrove swamps, it serves as nursery and growing grounds for many of the most utilized of fin- and shellfish. Most nontropical estuaries, lagoons, and bays are bordered by salt marshes.

Salt marshes have been used for grazing and haymaking, although in recent decades, these uses are increasingly uneconomical (Beeftink 1977). Of much lesser importance,

except locally, than grazing or haying were the uses of marsh grasses for thatch and packing material (Queen 1977).

As with mangroves and other coastal wetlands, large areas of salt marsh have been reclaimed and others have been reduced in size by pollution from both land and sea, by canal cutting (which is often associated with petroleum exploration and production [Fig. 16-7]), mosquito control, and trapping (by saltwater intrusion, by reduction of sediment contribution from inland through the damming of rivers and the use of

Figure 16.7 Louisiana marsh illustrating disruption of marsh surface by dredged canals, spoil banks, and marsh buggy trails. Picture taken during the laying of pipeline leading from LOOP (Louisiana Offshore Oil Pipeline) inland. Photo by D. Davis.

contour plowing and other soil-conservation practices, and even by species changes). When these human-induced changes are compounded by a rising sea level, marsh reduction can be extreme. In Louisiana, over $100\,km^2$ of coastal wetlands are being lost each year (Gagliano 1981).

Some species changes have been intentional, as for example the introduction of *Spartina townsendii* to numerous salt marshes. Because its reproductive rate is high, it crowds out other species and spreads rapidly. Selective grazing by different animals is responsible for species changes as well.

Harbors, Ports, and Cities

The close relationship between harbors, ports, and human settlements has been present ever since humans took to the sea and came back to the place from which they started. Water conveyance early became the easiest and most economical way of transporting people and goods, and the shoreline became an attractive place to establish cities. Usually, they were built in bays, estuaries, lagoons, and rivers. With large rivers, ports were often established at some distance from the ocean. A modern example is New Orleans, Louisiana (second only to Rotterdam in tonnage shipped), which is over $150\,km$ from the Gulf of Mexico by river. Although not a coastal city per se, its effectiveness is achieved by the fact that it has deep-water access both down and up river.[3]

As emphasized during "The Coastal Zone Workshop" held in Woods Hole, Massachusetts in 1972, "man's place in the coastal zone developed primarily from ocean commerce and the need for a transfer point to inland distribution systems" (Ketchum 1972).

Whereas port cities were only occasionally among the largest cities during pre–Industrial Revolution days, they gradually came to dominate in proportion as the industrial age progressed (Table 16-2). In 1500, only four out of the top ten, and ten of the top forty cities were coastal ports. By 1800, the numbers had increased to eight of the first ten, and twenty of the top forty, or just a doubling in amounts during that 300-year period. Since about 1900, proportions have remained at about 70% (Chandler 1977).

The growth rates of coastal cities continue to be larger than those at inland locations. Meyer-Arendt (1983) examined the growth rates of the 548 port cities with populations of over 100,000. He found that 67.5% grew at a more rapid rate than their country's average during the 1960s and 1970s and that coastal cities with the most rapid growth rates were located in developing countries. In the United States, although only 28% of the Country's 243 Standard Metropolitan Statistical Areas (SMSAs) are coastal, they contain 55% of the nation's population (Walker 1981b) (Fig. 16.8).

As in pre–Industrial Revolution days, technological development furthered the development of ports. The invention of steam engines enhanced industrial production, the demand for raw materials, and the development of transportation facilities. The coming of railroads provided competition to shipping by sea, but at the same time provided more rapid transfer of goods and raw materials to and from ports.

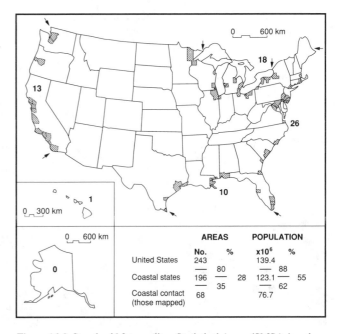

	AREAS		POPULATION	
	No.	%	x10⁶	%
United States	243		139.4	
		80		88
Coastal states	196	28	123.1	55
		35		62
Coastal contact (those mapped)	68		76.7	

Figure 16.8 Standard Metropolitan Statistical Areas (SMSAs) and the coast of the United States. After Walker 1981b.

Table 16-2 *World's largest port cities as percent of world's largest cities*

	Number of largest cities					
	10 port cities		20 port cities		40 port cities	
Date	(Number)	(Percentage)	(Number)	(Percentage)	(Number)	(Percentage)
1500	4	40	8	40	10	25
1600	4	40	8	40	14	35
1700	5	50	12	60	18	45
1800	8	80	14	70	20	50
1900	7	70	16	80	26	65
1925	7	70	15	75	28	70
1950	7	70	14	70	28	70
1970	7	70	13	65	28	70

Source: Adapted from data in Chandler 1977.

Even by the time the Industrial Revolution began, ports and harbors were outdated. This condition was exacerbated by the addition of great numbers of deep-draft steamships capable of carrying large cargoes. A solution to the problem of space was met temporarily by the construction of docks, an innovation that had been introduced in the eighteenth century. They were relatively easy to construct in estuaries, in which most ports were located in the industrialized countries. The sediment of the estuaries was easy to excavate, and it served as material to be used in raising the adjacent ground for port facilities, a procedure that has been used around the world subsequently. Presteamship ports were relatively small, and port areas usually were surrounded landward by city structures. Therefore, area needed for expansion often was obtained by reclaiming the shallow estuarine waters that bordered the waterfront. In other areas, especially the Mediterranean, artificial harbors had to be made. Breakwaters were constructed out from and parallel to the shore enclosing large areas of water. Excavation within these artificial bays produced sand, gravel, and rock, which was used to create land to support new port facilities.

It has been customary throughout history to build ports near population centers – small ports for fishing villages (Fig. 16.9), large ones near industrial centers and cities. Another trend has developed recently, however, a trend best exemplified in Japan. That country's decision to decentralize, including the transfer of some of its industry to remote locations, has led to the development of large new harbors.

Instead of being constructed into the sea, these new harbors are being dredged out of large dune fields, as at Kashima, 80 km northeast of Tokyo on the open Pacific shore (Walker and Mossa 1986). The construction has involved the excavation of wide channels to depths of 19 m and distances of 8 km into the dune ridges and swales, (i.e., of a size to accommodate vessels of 200,000 t).

The environmental impact of ports is related to the type of structures, channel configuration, and operations used. Floating systems have relatively little effect. Structures on pilings, those necessitating fill, and those built on the bottom, however, will modify currents and sediment distribution and may induce erosion or deposition, necessitating protective structures or dredging.

Impoundment

"Voltaire said that God created the world, but that the Dutch created Holland" (Volker 1982). The conversion of wetlands into agricultural fields goes back a few thousand years and was being practiced on all continents save Australia and Antarctica when the Industrial Revolution began.

Although reclamation is the term most commonly applied to this process, it generally connotes conversion of wetlands or shallow water bodies into land that can be cultivated or used as bases for urban and industrial development. However, also a part of this general concept is the conversion to water bodies for aqua- or maricultural pursuits. In both instances

Figure 16.9 Typical open-coast fishing-boat harbor in Japan. Photo by H. J. Walker.

impoundment in necessary, to keep either undesired water out or desired water in.

One of the most famous of impoundment types is the polder, a word of Dutch origin. It refers to a reclaimed area that has a high, but controllable, water table (Volker 1982). Empoldering has been carried out in most types of low-lying coastal areas, including deltas, estuaries, lagoons, bays, marshes, swamps, and tidal flats, and in most climates.

Tidal flats, with their usually fine sediments, are one of the most desirable of coastal types for conversion to agricultural land. As accretion raises and expands a tidal flat, dikes and levees are built to enclose its upper parts. In many areas, the initial dikes are constructed so that sediment will be trapped inside them during river flooding and high tides. In addition, sediment trapping is enhanced by planting water vegetation (such as *Cyperus malaccensis*), which also contributes organic matter to the developing soil (Fig. 16.10). At Ai Nan, near the mouth of the west distributary in the Zhujiang Delta, this method was used during the 1980s to aid in the reclamation of a 51-km² area (Walker 1980b). It is only one of the most recent projects that has been undertaken during the past 6,000 years in this delta (Fig. 16.11). Within it, there are 1,490 km² of reclaimed lands, whereas in the whole of the

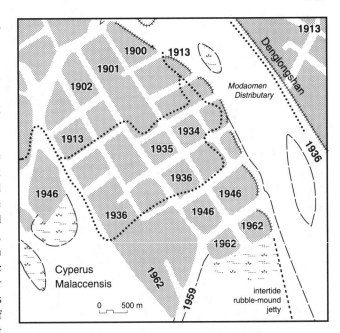

Figure 16.10 Modern reclamation of a 20-km² area in the Zhujiang Delta, China, illustrating an intertidal jetty and plantings of *Cyperus malaccensis*.

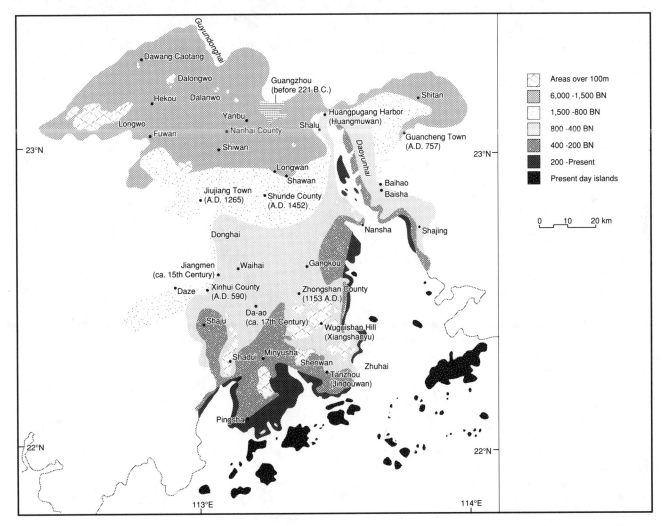

Figure 16.11 The historic development of the Zhujiang Delta, China. Many of the locations have names that refer to shoreline characteristics and, because the date of their founding is known, give indications of the sequence of deltaic advance and reclamation.

Figure 16.12 Dike connecting two islands across tidal mudflat and marsh in western South Korea. Photo by H. J. Walker.

Guangdong Province of south China, there are 2,625 km² (Zhao 1988).

Agricultural reclamation in most of the rest of Asia has also had a long history. The high tidal ranges and extensive mudflats of west Korea lend themselves well to impounding (Fig. 16.12). Since World War II, over 500 km² of mudflats have been reclaimed in South Korea (Park 1988), and plans for further reclamation call for an additional area of 7,270 km² by 2001. According to Park (1988), the tidal flats of South Korea have remained about the same size "in spite of extensive reclamation over a long period of time because new tidal flats reform in front of the dikes whenever tidal flats are newly reclaimed". Today, nearly all of Korea's reclamation is confined to tidal flats because most of the coastal marshlands had been reclaimed previously. Nearly as impressive has been the reclamation of coastal areas in Japan (Fig. 16.13).

Probably the largest empoldered region in the world is the delta of the Ganges and Brahmaputra rivers, where an area of at least 30,000 km² is involved. "The polders here consist of many small units, all encircled by *bunds*, forming an archipelago of embanked islands" (Volker 1982). Because of the dangers from storm surges to about two-thirds of this reclaimed area, the Bangladesh government in the 1970s built mounds called *kilas* (similar to the *terpen* of the early marsh-dwellers in the Netherlands).

In Europe, empoldered areas include the Netherlands (Fig. 16.14), with some 14,000 km² (over 40% of the coun-

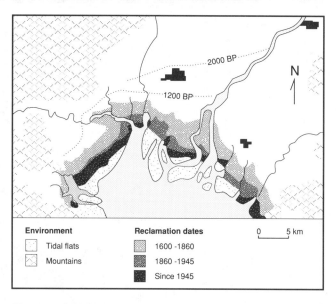

Figure 16.13 Shoreline positions and reclamation dates in Ariake Bay, Japan. After Koike 1988.

try); the other low countries; England (where over 300 km² of The Wash has been reclaimed); the Soviet Union; the Mediterranean countries; and Romania among others. In South America, parts of the deltas of the Orinoco, the Paranà, and the Rio Magdalena rivers, as well as tidal areas in

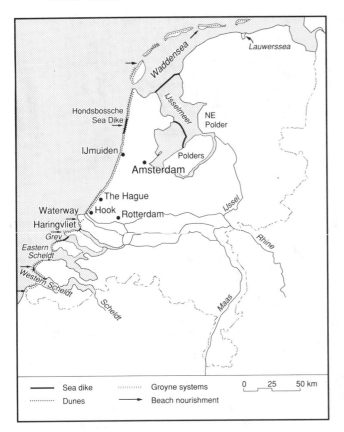

Figure 16.14 The Netherlands, illustrating polderization and shoreline shortening. After Terwindt, Kohsiek, and Visser 1988.

Romans, as Marsh ([1874], 1970) wrote, "not only stocked natural but constructed artificial ponds, of both fresh and saltwater, and cut off bays for this purpose."

Most of the polderized area of the Orient today contains large tracts of aquacultural ponds. It is a very diverse practice and includes the growth of finfish, shellfish (Fig. 16.15), and seaweed (Fig. 16.16) for food, and the production of nonfood items such as pearls, pharmaceuticals, and industrial products (Conklin and Hartman 1982).

Impoundment for solar salt production (Fig. 16.17), at least in its most primitive form, predates agriculture. Salt production, at one time or another, has been a major occupation in most coastal countries, and in some of them solar salt pans represented the most common coastal modification. Today, in many countries (Japan, France, and Italy, for

Figure 16.15 The manufacture of platelets for use in oyster cultivation in the shallow bay water of the Zhujiang Delta. Photo by H. J. Walker.

Venezuela, Guyana, and Suriname, are reclaimed. Over 80% of the Sacramento–San Joaquin Delta (with an original area of about 3,500 km^2), some of the Mississippi River Delta, and marshes and mudflats along most other coastal states in the United States, have been converted for agriculture. In Canada 350 years ago, the French began reclamation in the Bay of Fundy, following the practices they brought with them from the high-tidal-range areas of France. In Africa, polders have not been developed to the extent elsewhere, although the Nile Delta (with 1,530 km^2 of polders) and the Niger Delta are exceptions.

Volker (1982), while noting that empoldered land probably represents only about 2% of the total 14 million km^2 of cultivated land in the world, states that it "forms part of the most intensively used, most productive, and most densely populated part of the world's cultivated area [and that] it is also the most expensive, the most risky, and the most difficult part in terms of reclamation, operation, and maintenance."

Whereas reclamation for agriculture involves by far the bulk of the world's reclaimed area, other uses are gaining in importance. The conversion of wetlands for aquaculture and mariculture is receiving major emphasis in many parts of the world and especially in the Orient. Its expansion in the Americas, in Africa, and in Europe is slower than in Asia, but still of major importance.

Although aquaculture may not be as old as agriculture, it was a well-established practice long before the Christian era. In 500 B.C., a Chinese book was devoted to aquaculture. The

Figure 16.16 The collection of cultivated seaweed in the coastal waters of northeast Japan. Photo by H. J. Walker.

Figure 16.17 Solar salt pans on the west coast of France. Photo by H. J. Walker.

example), the expense of producing salt by solar evaporation is resulting in the abandonment of former salt pans. In Japan, where the solar-salt industry has nearly disappeared, salt pans have been converted into aquacultural ponds. In contrast, in China and Korea, salt operations are still extensive.

Another major development, mainly as a result of the continuing rapid increase in industry, commerce, and population, is the conversion of nearshore wetland areas into industrial, transportational, and residential sites.

Much of this expansion is economically and topographically dictated because expansion seaward adjacent to large coastal cities is often more expeditious than it would be landward. Thus, many of the world's lagoons, estuaries, and bays have been reduced in size by landfill and their adjacent marshes reclaimed. Venice, Amsterdam, Boston, and Buenos Aires are examples of cities that are located on reclaimed marshes. Amsterdam and Venice are relatively unique in that they continue to have water as a primary element in their form (Konvitz 1978).

Although the reclamation of nearshore zones for industry in Japan began about the turn of the century, it was not until the middle of the 1950s that it became dominant. As the result of an infill rate of about 10 km²/yr between 1960 and 1980 (Fig. 16.18), Tokyo Bay has been reduced in area by about 20% (Koike 1988). These new lands in Tokyo Bay stand three to four m above sea level. Within the city proper, however, about 1 million people live below the zero-meter

line. It is an area that has suffered extreme subsidence, not unlike many other reclaimed areas.

In Louisiana, it has been estimated that a total of 3,500 km² of the coastal zone has been completely impounded, and possibly another 1,000 km² partially impounded. Of this total, 1,050 km² have been reclaimed for urban and industrial purposes, including the city of New Orleans (Day et al. 1986). These impoundments represent the conversion of marsh and swamp land, whereas that of Tokyo Bay was mainly bay water, the marshes having been reclaimed in earlier times.

One of the newest reclamation techniques is the creation of new islands offshore. Islands built in the Arctic Ocean in order to support petroleum production, and islands (or peninsulas) built to serve as air fields (as in Japan, Hong Kong [Fig. 16.19], and Hawaii) are two of the most recent examples.

A type of impoundment that has limited distribution at the present time is the damming of straits or bays for the purpose of creating fresh-water reservoirs. In Hong Kong, two such reservoirs have converted over 25 km of seashore into a fresh-water shoreline and have a capacity of nearly 600 million m³. If, as predicted in 1977 at the First United Nations Conference on Water, water shortage will replace energy at the top of the world's crisis list by the year 2000, this type of coastal modification should prove increasingly important (Walker 1980a).

Impoundment inland, through the recent damming of rivers and streams, has resulted in major changes along many

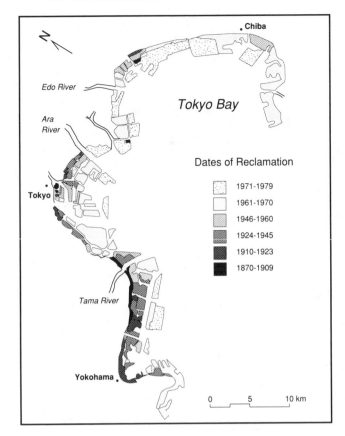

Figure 16.18 Reclamation in Tokyo Bay since 1870. After Koike 1988.

dredging, and pipeline emplacement all usually have major impacts on hydrologic and ecologic regimes.

Engineering and Coastal Modification

At the time humans built the first breakwater to protect their ships or the first dike to keep out unwanted water or keep in needed water, they became coastal engineers in the practical sense of the term.

From the simple stone breakwaters of the ancient Mediterranean cultures and the earthen bunds of Asia, the materials used and forms created have increased greatly in type and complexity. Today, artificial structures can be found along nearly all types of coastline, the major exception being those coasts dominated by glaciers.

Structures and Materials. The types of structures and materials used in coastal modification depend on a variety of considerations, including economics, politics, law, cultural heritage, aesthetics, technology, availability of materials, and the nature of the perceived problem. Most structures are designed to improve navigation (especially breakwaters and jetties) or control coastal erosion (seawalls, groins, and some types of breakwaters). Horikawa (1978) considered beach erosion as "one of the largest world problems from the perspective of land preservation."

Structures may form an interface between land and sea, they may be constructed at some angle to the shoreline, or they may be placed offshore more or less parallel to it. Land/sea interface structures are a varied group and include seawalls, dikes, levees (often restricted to estuarine and riverine banks), embankments, revetments, and bulkheads (CERC 1977). Although functions overlap within this group, it is the seawall, revetment, and bulkhead that are primarily used as antierosion devices.

Those structures that run more or less normal to the shoreline include jetties, groins, piers, and drainage pipes. Jetties are constructed at the mouths of rivers to prevent drift from entering the channel to be protected and to serve as a training wall for rivers. Groins, on the other hand, often are constructed in sufficient numbers to warrant designation as "groin fields" (Fig. 16.20).

Structures placed offshore serve mainly as breakwaters. Although historically their use was mainly for port protection, recently they have become increasingly popular for beach protection and restoration and have come to be referred to as offshore, or detached, breakwaters.

Structures, which are basically static, (although a degree of flexibility or permeability is added to some of them) are built with the idea of permanence. In recent years, however, geomorphically compatible dynamic approaches have become important. As Nordstrom and Allen (1980) point out, they are distinguished from structural methods in that "their forms are allowed to be freely worked by waves, currents, winds, or biological processes. Included are direct renourishment of beaches, dune construction, establishment of offshore deposits for replenishment by natural processes, and the planting of grasses. In Miami Beach, Florida, between 1976 and 1980, over 10 million m³ of sand were added to 17 km of beach,

coastlines because of sediment and nutrient starvation. The Nile River, before the Aswan High Dam was constructed, transported 140×10^6 t of silt to the Mediterranean Sea annually. The Dam's trapping of silt led not only to increased deltaic erosion, but also to a reduction in the fish catch, a reduction that extended past Egypt to Israel and Lebanon (Ben-Tuvia 1983). Along the southern coast of California, the damming of all major streams aggravated beach erosion. Some of the loss was temporarily compensated for by using sediment dredged from the many small boat harbors that dot the southern California shoreline.

Impoundment, thus, has been a major way in which humans have modified low-lying coastal areas. It has reduced drastically the size of some of the world's mudflats, marshes, estuaries, lagoons, and bays. Most projects have shortened the coastline through the construction of dikes between islands and across the mouths of bays and estuaries. Further, they have altered the biological component of the former environment by both substitution (intentional and unintentional) and elimination. Some of the major results of impoundment are subsidence, compaction because of sediment accumulation, oxidation of peats when drained, and consolidation accompanying dewatering (Walker et al. 1987), as well as the biological changes that necessarily accompany it.

Impounding within coastal regions may be incidental to many other activities. Fill for roads, spoil banks made in canal

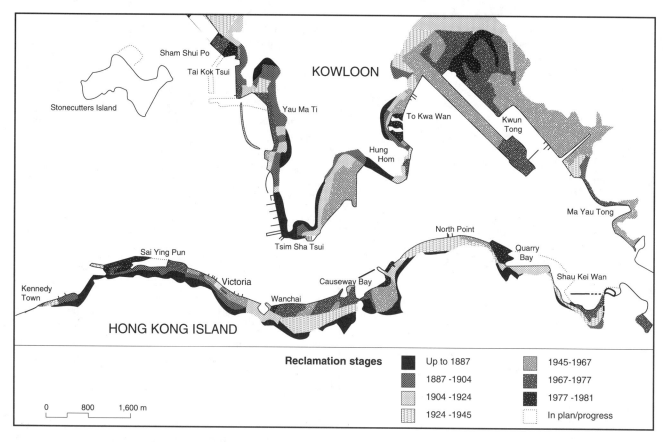

Figure 16.19 Sequential reclamation in Hong Kong, with an airport built on fill. After So 1988.

Figure 16.20 Japanese shoreline, illustrating the use of armor units to provide shore protection for seawall and groin field, which has been unsuccessful in trapping sediment. Photo by H. J. Walker.

widening it on the average by 90 m (National Research Council 1987).

Effect of Artificial Structures on the Shore Zone. The reason for adding a structure in the first place is to initiate a change in the coastal environment or to attempt to preserve some aspect of it (whether natural or artificial). Commonly, it is to reduce wave action, but in the process, both material and form are changed, usually drastically. These three factors are so closely linked that a change in one inevitably results in changes in the others (Bruun 1985).

The major processes modified by seawalls are related to waves and currents, and in turn, to erosion and sediment transport and deposition. Seawalls are frequently constructed on retreating shores, and their presence often enhances the erosion they were intended to stop. Wave energy is reflected back and down rather than being spread over a sloping shore, and erosion and deepening usually follow. Deepening, in turn, leads to larger waves and increased overtopping (Fig. 16.21).

Seawalls also change the character of sediment-drift alongshore. In some locations (for example, along the Gagra section of the Black Sea coast), "oblique surf waves striking the wall" develop a fast current that "carries with it a mass of sediment [that] greatly exceeds that on beach sections without walls" (Zenkovich 1973). Along cliffy coasts, seawalls are responsible for major nearshore and longshore changes. Possibly the most important effect is the reduction of the amount of sediment that normally is supplied to downdrift locations and, in turn, is responsible for the reduction and even elimination of downdrift beaches. Seawalls (as well as houses and other structures) often separate inland dunes from their source region and lead to dune decay.

Groins, jetties, and other nonparallel structures also change the morphology of the coast (Fig. 16.22). Instead of straightening and often shortening the shoreline, however, these nonparallel structures lengthen and compartmentalize it. Depending on the length of individual groins and the spacing between them, shoreline lengths are usually more than doubled (Walker 1984). The trapping of sediment on the updrift side of the structure usually results in starvation and erosion of downdrift locations, which frequently leads to the addition of new structures. This process may be continued downdrift many kilometers, only to be discontinued when a natural headland is reached or where erosion protection is not considered sufficiently important.

If jetties and groins are sufficiently long, longshore drift will be directed seaward far enough to be temporarily and even permanently lost, especially if it is transferred into a submarine canyon. At Port Hueneme, California, after current-deflecting jetties were constructed, sand was deflected into Hueneme submarine canyon, and beach erosion occurred. Subsequently, a system for piping the sand trapped north of the jetties to the eroded area south of them was installed (Sanders 1966).

Groin fields, most commonly found along shores where tourism is important (Italy, Japan, the United States), frequently serve their primary purpose, even though it is usually at the expense of sacrificing beaches in downdrift locations.

Offshore, or detached, breakwaters "alter waves through reflection, refraction, diffraction and energy dissipation, creating a wave shadow to the lee of the structures" (Walker 1981a). When sand is present in the system, which is one of the major reasons for using detached breakwaters along recreational shores, deposition between the structures and the beach often ties the two together, forming what are called

Figure 16.21 Seawall damaged by overtopping waves, now being protected by armor blocks in Japan. Photo by H. J. Walker.

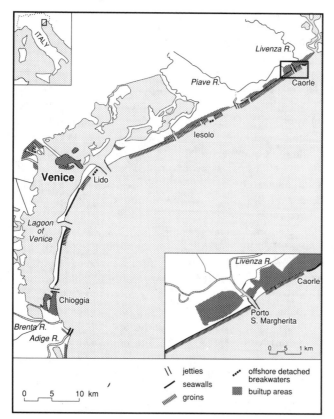

Figure 16.22 The shoreline of the Venice area, Italy, showing a variety of artificial structures. After Cencini and Varani 1988.

tombolos. Wong (1988) wrote that in Singapore "breakwaters act as headlands between which seaward concave bays could be formed."

Although a major objective of beach nourishment is the avoidance of the problems associated with hard structures, the addition of materials from offshore or inland does alter beach composition and size (the most often desired objective). Often dredging (especially when offshore sources are utilized) is the main method of sand acquisition. Dredging not only disturbs the bottom, but also increases turbidity, causes flocculation, and disturbs biota.

Distribution of Artificial Structures. Although most coastlines of the world are still structure-free, the proportion is

decreasing. However, in recent years pressure from some groups (including coastal scientists in a few countries) has resulted in a reduction of the rate at which fixed structures are being added to the shoreline, and in a few instances, has even been responsible for the removal of some that were already in place.

Fixed structures are unevenly distributed around the world's coastline. Generally, they are most common along the coasts of industrial countries both of the East and West. A worldwide figure has yet to be calculated, although some data are available from a few countries (Walker 1988). Total lengths range from near zero to nearly 100 on a percentage scale (Table 16-3). Even though fewer data for numbers and lengths of individual types of structures exist, some detailed listings have been published and some generalizations can be made.

Jetties, for example, are especially common in countries in which rivers, estuaries, and lagoons are important in navigation. Most water entrances to the sea are jettied along some coasts as, for example, in Rhode Island and New Jersey, US, and in New South Wales, Australia. Jetties are one of the most common structures to be found in developing coastal countries.

Groins and detached breakwaters tend to be numerous along recreational coasts, although there are many exceptions (Fig. 16.20). These two types of antierosion forms are very numerous in Italy, where the number of tourists seeking recreational beaches has increased many fold since the 1970s (Fig. 16.23) and in Japan (a country that is coast-oriented). By 1982, the Japanese had constructed 3,202 km of dikes and seawalls, 10,012 groins and jetties, and 2,843 detached breakwaters, in addition to over 4,000 harbors.

Unusual and Extreme Events and Coastal Protection

Most of the foregoing discussion has been devoted to those coastal modifications that might be considered responses to average conditions within specific coastal environments. However, extreme natural events such as hurricanes (typhoons) and tsunamis have prompted the construction of special structures along some coasts. There are also those changes in coastal environments that have been caused, or at least aggravated, by human action, such as subsidence and pollution. Lastly, the potentials for future impacts on coasts

Table 16-3 *Percent of coastline bordered by artificial structures for selected coastal sectors*

Region	Percentage	Region	Percentage	Region	Percentage
Iceland	<2	Italy	13	Lake Erie, U.S.	61
Sweden	7	Kuwait	29	Alaska, U.S.	<1
Finland	<2	Sierra Leone	<1	Oregon, U.S.	6
Belgium	85	South Africa	9	California, U.S.	9
Scotland	8	South Korea	21	S. Carolina, U.S.	39
England	38	Japan	51	Barbados	22
Ireland	<5	Victoria, Canada	4	Montserrat	3
Portugal	7	Lake Erie, Canada	21	Brazil	1

Source: Various chapters in Walker 1988.

Figure 16.23 Detached breakwaters, protecting beach that fronts tourist hotels along the Adriatic Sea, Italy. Photo by H. J. Walker.

exist because of the possibility of directly modifying shorelines by the use of nuclear energy and because of the indirect influence on sea level through changing temperatures of the atmosphere.

Hurricanes and Tsunamis

Among the most damaging of natural phenomena to coastal structures are hurricanes and tsunamis. On a worldwide basis, they are quite limited in distribution. However, some of the most-developed coasts are affected at irregular intervals. Many shorelines in hurricane-prone areas are now protected by seawalls, some of which are over 12 m high (Fig. 16.24). In locations in which the surrounding region is low-lying (as for example, New Orleans, Louisiana), dikes usually are constructed so that they encircle the area of concern.

Tsunamis, or seismic sea waves, which are associated with earthquakes, cause surges along coasts that reach more than 10 m in some locations. The Hawaiian Islands experienced 41 damaging tsunamis in a 142-year period (Bretschneider 1982). Because of damage at Hilo, Hawaii from several tsunamis, a decision was made to establish a structure-free waterfront area. Normally, however, tsunami protection has been attempted by constructing high seawalls, often at some distance from the shoreline. In Japan, in some tsunami-prone bays along the northeast coast, bay entrance gates have been built with the objective of intercepting the wave before it deepens in the inner parts of the bay.

Subsidence

Subsidence is a natural process that can be initiated or aggravated by human endeavors and, as Jones (1986) notes, is a relatively recent geomorphological phenomenon. When it

occurs along the shoreline, it increases the danger of flooding. Today, partly because of subsidence, many populated areas (such as New Orleans, Louisiana, and Tokyo, Japan) are below sea level and are protected from flooding by seawalls, levees, dikes, and pumps.

Artificially caused subsidence can result from groundwater, liquid petroleum, and gas withdrawal and from surface loading through the impoundment of water, the construction of buildings, and the establishment of land fill. The withdrawal of fluids and gas is the most important. Groundwater withdrawal was responsible for subsidence in Tokyo (4.6 m), Osaka (3 m), and Nagoya (mostly for eel cultivation), Japan, and in Houston-Galveston, Texas (2.75 m). Oil and gas extraction was accompanied by subsidence in Lake Maracaibo (3.9 m), Venezuela, and in Long Beach, California (8.8 m), among many other coastal locations (Jones 1986).

The subsidence history in Tokyo is an excellent example of how the activities of humans affect the trend in coastal processes. Subsidence was first measured in Tokyo in 1924 in response to a 1923 earthquake. Subsequent measurements showed that the rate of compaction was increased by the weight of structures, by traffic, and by the pumping of water. With the increased industrial use of water prior to and during World War II, subsidence increased, but, with the destruction of these industries through bombing, subsidence rates decreased, only to increase again after industrial demands for water were renewed in the 1950s. Because of this increased rate of subsidence, the Japanese government decided to begin controls on groundwater withdrawal in 1961. These controls have been successful, and measurements subsequent to 1965 have shown declining rates of subsidence (Inaba et al. 1970).

Surface loading in deltas was caused by the increased sediment discharge that followed upriver deforestation, grazing,

Figure 16.24 High concrete seawall, designed to provide protection from typhoon surges along the east coast of Honshu, Japan. Photo by H. J. Walker.

and agriculture in many parts of the world. However, today many of these same deltas are being eroded because dams upstream have reduced sediment discharge, often even below the levels present prior to deforestation.

Another common cause of subsidence is shrinkage after reclamation. In the Netherlands, the Zuider Zee was dammed in 1932, creating an area of 1,660 km². The 4-m-thick, soft, water-logged bottom sediments shrank and compacted after drainage to amounts up to 1.5 m. The amount of such subsidence is critical to the determination of the design of drainage systems and pumping stations (de Glopper 1970).

Pollution

Coastal waters have served as a dump from the earliest times, but until recently, were little affected by such usage. With the substitution of modern means of transportation for nonpolluting sails and oars, with the growth of industrial and urban centers, and with the development of herbicides, insecticides, fertilizers, and plastic, pollution has increased. Contamination of coastal waters usually stresses the fish, wildlife, and vegetation occupying them, and in extreme cases causes their elimination.

Although oil enters the coastal system from catastrophic accidents, more than 90% of the total "enters the marine environment through mundane . . . sources. Chronic contamination comes from small amounts of oil released on a continuing basis – in sewage effluents, storm-water runoff in urban centers, discharges from oil refineries, [and] intentional discharges" (Howarth 1981).

Sewage is basically a pollutant, although in certain quantities it can have beneficial effects. Coates (1981) writes that 2% of the discharge of all of the world's rivers that reaches the oceans is sewage effluent. Some 7% of all of the solids in rivers is of human production. The extent of pollution is such that "there are few unpolluted estuaries left for study, and most of these are comparatively small" (Ketchum 1983).

One of the most conspicuous pollutants is the trash that finds its way onto the shore. Along many beaches of the world, it represents a new type of material, and requires periodic cleanups. Among these, human waste materials, plastics, and styrofoam dominate. In one Texas beach cleanup, 171,479 pieces of debris were collected, with plastic items representing 56% of the total (O'Hara et al. 1987).

Occasionally fill is for the purpose of dispensing unwanted material such as garbage, rubble, and tailings. This dumping results in progradation of the shoreline and has similar effects on the shoreline as coastal structures. On the coast of the Atacama Desert, Chile, between 1938 and 1975, tailings from mining were dumped into the sea at a rate of 4.4 million m³/yr, about 60% of which remained in the bay. Coastal progradation averaged about 25 m/yr between 1958 and 1975 (R. Paskoff, personal correspondence). Similar progradations have occurred in Denmark, on Corsica, and in Lake Michigan, United States.

Thermal pollution, created when waste heat is transferred from generating plants to coastal waters, affects many of the properties of the water and, in turn, the life forms. The frequency of such transfer of heat is suggested by the fact that one-third of the power plants of the United States are located along estuaries.

Atmospheric Temperature and Sea-level Change and Potential Human Response

Within the past few decades, the increase of CO_2 and other gases in the atmosphere has been documented (Kerr 1988). This increase has served as the basis for projecting potential temperature increase (the so-called greenhouse warming) and in turn, for predicting a rise in sea level. The U.S. National Academy of Sciences, reported that a global warming of 3–4°C over the next century would likely cause a global sea-level rise of about 70 cm (Revelle 1983) – an amount that approaches the magnitude of those rises experienced 8,000 to 18,000 years ago. Other estimates have sea-level rise over the next 100 years ranging from a low of 36 cm to a high of over 200 cm (Titus 1987).

Although 70 cm represents one estimate of eustatic rise, the changes along particular shorelines will vary greatly from that number, depending on local rates of uplift, subsidence, and compaction.

The implications of such changes are critical from the standpoint of coastal modification, especially protection of coastal structures. The advance of the sea inland with a 70-cm rise would be negligible on a cliff but might have to be measured in kilometers along low-lying coastal areas. Although most seawalls and other interface structures are built so that a water level rise of 50 cm or so by itself might not overtop them, the margin of safety would be drastically reduced, and storm waves would inundate many presently protected areas. Such rises in level would also change the position of the interface between the fresh and brackish waters of estuaries, lagoons, and bays, as well as the composition and size of marsh and mangrove areas.

Dwellers of low-lying coastal areas can counter such changes in sea level in four basic ways: (1) to armor the shoreline; (2) to use fill to raise land levels; (3) to retreat to higher levels, and (4) to "Venice-ize."

Armoring the shore with protective structures is the practice that has been used most often to date. When already in place, enlarging and raising the structures on an incremental basis will likely be used. The shore character will change, toe

Figure 16.25 Artificial structures and resultant modification on processes, materials, and forms at Morro Bay, California. Photo by Spence Air Photos in 1947, provided by A. Orme.

erosion rates will increase, beaches will disappear, and armor blocks will be needed.

The raising of the area to be protected by fill is a practice that has been used extensively in reclamation. It also has been used to raise cities. Buildings in Galveston, Texas were jacked up, and as much as five m of fill placed beneath them in response to the flooding that accompanied a devastating hurricane in 1900. The new elevated city was provided further protection with the construction of a seawall (National Research Council 1987). It is probable that massive fill operations in already-established cities are not economically or structurally feasible. However, waterfront reclamation projects, such as in Singapore (Wong 1988), can be built to heights anticipatory of a sea-level rise.

Set back or retreat, as used at Hilo, Hawaii, for tsunami protection, is a third possibility. By anticipating the amount of water encroachment, existing structures can be set back and new ones established in safe zones. Sections of the Mississippi coast adopted the buffer-zone idea after shore-front structures were destroyed by a hurricane in 1969. The states of Maine and North Carolina have adopted the idea of gradual retreat (National Research Council 1987).

As Konvitz (1978) noted, Amsterdam and Venice were constructed to capitalize on the use of canals within their urban areas. A shift by low-lying coastal cities from a land-oriented to a water-oriented base would require major adjustments and would probably be unpopular on a large scale. On a small scale, the creation of Venice-type communities in the form of marinas and residential canal subdivisions already is popular within coastal recreational communities.

Conclusions and a Look toward the Future

Technological skills insofar as the coastal zone is concerned began when humans first used tools in the acquisition of food from the shore. Today, instead of only taking the resources that the coast offers, they have developed extensive agricultural and aquacultural complexes; worldwide coastal transportational facilities; industrial, commercial, and residential centers; and coastal recreational areas. In the process, they have modified coastal materials, processes, and forms (Fig. 16.25); have advanced the shoreline in places and initiated or aggravated retreat in others; and have altered its biotic component through the destruction of some species and the addition of others. Many of these changes have been intentional; others have not been.

Although the end of such change is not yet in sight, it is now beginning to be realized that the coastal zone and its resources are limited in extent and quantity, and are being destroyed or altered at alarming rates. The "discovery" that coastal wetlands serve as nursery grounds for many of the ocean's fishes has resulted in a changing attitude toward their use in a few countries. Nonetheless, on a worldwide basis, their conversion for more traditional purposes (as a perceived sign of progress) is increasing. Another example is the change in approach in dealing with coastal erosion. Whereas fixed structures have long been considered the way to combat erosion, recently new approaches such as renourishment and accommodating coastal retreat by retreating with it have been increasingly adopted. Such options are likely to grow in appeal with time, especially if the anticipated rapid rate of rise in sea level materializes.

Notes

1. The terms shore, coast, shoreline, coastline, littoral zone, and coastal zone have been variously defined, and many are often used interchangeably. In this essay, the terms shore, shoreline, and shore zone are generally used to indicate those zones directly affected by waves and tides, whereas the terms coast and coastal zone are used in a broader context and, in some instances, they even include all of the coastal plain and continental shelf. It is hoped that the precise meaning is clear by the context in which the term is used.

2. Actual variation for specific coastlines may be much greater; e.g., the U.S. National Ocean Survey (1981) states that the general shoreline length of the state of Alaska is 10,693 km, whereas it lists the tidal shoreline length as 54,600 km, or more than five times as much.

3. Humans have a penchant for adjusting their activities to short-term-average environmental limits. In the case of the Mississippi River, the ship and barge traffic is adjusted to certain river stages. In 1988, a severe drought brought river levels and discharge to record lows. Barges became grounded, and dredging could not keep channels open. Low discharge allowed the salt-water wedge to penetrate upstream, affecting fresh-water intakes that service both domestic and industrial demands. In response, the U.S. Army Corps of Engineers constructed an underwater sill 500 m long to within 15 m of the water surface in the river south of New Orleans in order to slow the advance of salt water upstream. Although the low water was disadvantageous from the standpoint of shipping and water supply, it proved to be beneficial to oystermen. The reduction of silt-laden water into oyster-growing bays prompted the removal of a quarantine on oyster harvesting.

References

Bair, F. E. 1988. *Countries of the World*. Detroit: Gale Research Co.

Beeftink, W. G. 1977. Salt-marshes. In *The Coastline*, ed. R. S. K. Barnes, 93–121. London: John Wiley & Sons.

Ben-Tuvia, A. 1983. The Mediterranean Sea, B. biological aspects. In *Estuaries and Enclosed Seas*, ed. B. H. Ketchum, 239–51. Amsterdam: Elsevier Scientific Publishing Company.

Bird, E. C. F. 1985. *Coastline Changes: A Global Review*. New York: John Wiley & Sons.

Bird, E. C. F., and M. L. Schwartz. 1985. *The World's Coastline*. New York: Van Nostrand Reinhold Company.

Bretschneider, C. L. 1982. Tsunamis. In *The Encyclopedia of Beaches and Coastal Environments*, ed. M. L. Schwartz, 843–46. Stroudsburg: Hutchinson Ross Publishing Company.

Brown, B. E., ed. 1986. *Human-Induced Damage to Coral Reefs*. Reports in Marine Science, 40. Paris: UNESCO.

Bruun, P. 1985. *Design and Construction of Mounds for Breakwaters and Coastal Protection*. Amsterdam: Elsevier Science Publishers.

Bulvako, A. G. 1971. The hydrology of marshes and marsh-ridden lands. *Nature and Resources VII(1)*: 12–15.

Carr, A. P. 1972. Tide marks on the sands of time. *Geographical Magazine 54*: 207–211.

Cencini, C., and L. Varani. 1988. Italy. In *Artificial Structures and Shorelines*, ed. H. J. Walker, 193–206. Dordrecht. Kluwer Academic Publishers.

CERC (Coastal Engineering Research Center). 1977. *Shore Protection Manual*. Fort Belvoir: U.S. Army Corps of Engineers.

Chandler, T. 1977. The forty largest cities: a statistical note. *Historical Geography 7(182)*: 21–23.

Coates, D. R. 1981. *Environmental Geology*. New York: John Wiley & Sons.

Conklin, D. E., and M. C. Hartman. 1982. Aquaculture. In *The*

Encyclopedia of Beaches and Coastal Environments, ed. M. L. Schwartz, 48–49. Stroudsburg: Hutchinson Ross Publishing Company.

Cronin, L. E. 1967. The role of man in estuarine processes. In *Estuaries*, ed. G. H. Lauff, 667–89. Washington, D.C.: American Association for the Advancement of Science.

Davies, J. L. 1977. *Geographical Variation in Coastal Development*. London: Longman.

Davis, J. H. 1956. Influences of man upon coast lines. In *Man's Role in Changing the Face of the Earth*, ed. W. L. Thomas, Jr., 504–521. Chicago: The University of Chicago Press.

Davis, K. 1974. The migrations of human populations. *Scientific American 231(3)*: 93–105.

Davis, R. A., Jr. 1982. Beach. In *The Encyclopedia of Beaches and Coastal Environments*, ed. M. L. Schwartz, 140–41. Stroudsburg: Hutchinson Ross Publishing Company.

Day, J. W., R. Costanza, K. Teague, N. Taylor, G. P. Kemp, P. H. Day, and R. E. Becker. 1986. *Wetland Impoundment: A Global Survey for Comparison with the Louisiana Coastal Zone*. Baton Rouge, LA: Coastal Ecology Institute, Louisiana State University.

de Glopper, R. J. 1970. Shrinkage of subaqueous sediments of Lake Ijssel (The Netherlands) after reclamation. In *Land Subsidence, 192–201*. Paris: UNESCO.

Emery, K. O. 1967. Estuaries and lagoons in relation to continental shelves. In *Estuaries*, ed. G. H. Lauff. Publication No. 83, 9–11. Washington, D.C.: American Association for the Advancement of Science.

———. 1969. The continental shelves. *Scientific American 221*: 106–123.

Fisher, J. J. 1982. Barrier islands. In *The Encyclopedia of Beaches and Coastal Environments*, ed. M. L. Schwartz, 124–33. Stroudsburg: Hutchinson Ross Publishing Company.

Gagliano, S. M. 1981. *Special Report on Marsh Deterioration and Land Loss in the Deltaic Plain of Coastal Louisiana*. Baton Rouge, LA: Coastal Environments, Inc.

Goldsmith, F. B. 1977. Rocky cliffs. In *The Coastline*, ed. R. S. K. Barnes, 237–51. London: John Wiley & Sons.

Guilcher, A. 1988. *Coral Reef Geomorphology*. New York: John Wiley & Sons.

Haedrich, R. L. 1983. Estuarine fishes. In *Estuaries and Enclosed Seas*, ed. B. H. Ketchum, 183–207. Amsterdam: Elsevier Scientific Publishing Company.

Hedgpeth, J. W. 1976. The living edge. In *Coastal Research*, ed. H. J. Walker. Geoscience and Man. Vol. XIV, 17–51. Baton Rouge, LA: Louisiana State University.

Horikawa, K. 1978. *Coastal Engineering*. New York: Wiley and Sons.

Howarth, R. W. 1981. Oil and fish: can they coexist? In *Coast Alert*, ed. T. C. Jackson and D. Reische, 49–72. San Francisco: Friends of the Earth.

Inaba, Y., I. Abe, S. Iwasaki, S. Aoki, T. Endo, and K. Kaido. 1970. Reviews of land subsidence researches in Tokyo. In *Land Subsidence 87–98*. Paris: UNESCO.

Inman, D. L., and B. M. Brush. 1973. The coastal challenge. *Science 181*: 20–32.

Inman, D. L., and C. Nordstrom. 1971. On the tectonic and morphologic classification of coasts. *Journal of Geology 79*: 1–21.

Jablonski, D. 1982. Reefs, noncoral. In *The Encyclopedia of Beaches and Coastal Environments*, ed. M. L. Schwartz, 679–81. Stroudsburg: Hutchinson Ross Publishing Company.

Jacobsen, T. 1976. 17,000 years of Greek prehistory. *Scientific American 234(6)*: 76–87.

Jones, D. K. C. 1986. Subsidence. In *A Handbook of Engineering Geomorphology*, ed. P. G. Fookes and P. R. Vaughan, 284–97. New York: Chapman and Hall.

Karmon, Y. 1980. *Ports around the World*. New York: Crown Publishing, Inc.

Kerr, R. A. 1985. Continental drift nearing certain detection. *Science 229*: 953–55.

———. 1988. Is the greenhouse here? *Science 239*: 559–61.

Ketchum, B. H. 1972. *The Water's Edge*. Cambridge, MA: MIT Press.

———. 1983. Estuarine characteristics. In *Estuaries and Enclosed Seas*, ed. B. H. Ketchum, 1–14. Amsterdam: Elsevier Scientific Publishing Company.

Koike, K. 1988. Japan. In *Artificial Structures and Shorelines*, ed. H. J. Walker, 317–30. Dordrecht: Kluwer Academic Publishers.

Konvitz, J. W. 1978. *Cities and the Sea*. Baltimore, MD: The Johns Hopkins University Press.

Leatherman, S. P. 1979. *Barrier Island Handbook*. College Park, MD: University of Maryland.

Long, S. P., and C. F. Mason, 1983. *Saltmarsh Ecology*. Glasgow: Blackie & Son Limited.

Lorant, S. 1946. *The New World: The First Pictures of America*. New York: Duell, Sloan & Pearce.

Marsh, G. P. [1874] 1970. *The Earth As Modified by Human Action*. New York: Arno Press Inc.

Mercer, D. E., and L. S. Hamilton, 1984. Mangrove ecosystems: some economic and natural benefits. *Nature and Resources 20(2)*: 14–19.

Meyer-Arendt, K. 1983. *Recent Urbanization Rates among World Coastal Cities of over 100,000 Inhabitants*. Unpublished manuscript.

Mörner, N-A. 1986. The concept of eustasy: a redefinition. *Journal of Coastal Research*, Special Issue, *1*: 49–51.

National Research Council. 1983. *Fundamental Research on Estuaries: The Importance of an Interdisciplinary Approach*. Washington, D.C.: National Academy Press.

———. 1987. *Responding to Changes in Sea Level: Engineering Implications*. Washington, D.C.: National Academy Press.

Nordstrom, K. F., and J. R. Allen. 1980. Geomorphically compatible solutions to beach erosion. *Zeitschrift für Geomorphologie*, Supplement, *34*: 142–54.

Odum, H. T., and B. J. Copeland. 1974. A functional classification of the coastal systems of the United States. In *Coastal Ecological Systems of the United States*, Vol. I, ed. H. T. Odum, B. J. Copeland, and E. A. McMahan, 5–84. Washington D.C.: The Conservation Foundation.

O'Hara, K., L. Maraniss, J. Deichmann, J. Perry, and R. Bierce. 1987. *1986 Texas Coastal Cleanup*. Austin, TX: Center for Environmental Education.

Pacific Science Association. 1988. *Information Bulletin*.

Park, D. W. 1988. Korea – South. In *Artificial Structures and Shorelines*, ed. H. J. Walker, 311–16. Dordrecht: Kluwer Academic Publishers.

Penrose, B. 1967. *Travel and Discovery in the Renaissance*. Cambridge, MA: Harvard University Press.

Pirazzoli, P. A. 1986. Secular trends of relative sea-level (RSL) changes indicated by tide-gauge records. *Journal of Coastal Research*, Special Issue *1*: 1–26.

Queen, W. H. 1977. Human uses of salt marshes. In *Wet Coastal Ecosystems*, ed. V. J. Chapman, 363–68. New York: Elsevier Scientific Publishing Company.

Revelle, R. 1983. Probable future changes in sea level resulting from increased atmospheric carbon dioxide. In *Changing Climate*, 433–47. Washington, D.C.: National Academy Press.

Russell, R. J. 1974. Coastal features. *Encyclopedia Britannica*. 15th ed. *(4)*: 795–802.

Sanders, N. 1966. Port Hueneme, California. *Association of Pacific Coast Geographers Yearbook 28*: 119–34.

Sauer, C. O. 1962. Seashore-primitive home of man. *Proceedings American Philosophical Society 106*: 41–47.

Siry, J. V. 1984. *Marshes of the Ocean Shore: Development of an Ecological Ethic*. College Station, TX: Texas A & M University Press.

Snedaker, S. C. 1978. Mangroves: their value and perpetuation. *Nature and Resources 14(3)*: 6–13.

So, C. L. 1988. Hong Kong. In *Artificial Structures and Shorelines*, ed. H. J. Walker, 369–382. Dordrecht: Kluwer Academic Publishers.

Terwindt, J. H. J., L. H. M. Kohsiek, and J. Visser. 1988. The Netherlands. In *Artificial Structures and Shorelines*, ed. H. J. Walker, 103–114. Dordrecht: Kluwer Academic Publishers.

Titus, J. G. 1987. The greenhouse effect, rising sea level, and societies' response. In *Sea Surface Studies*, ed. R. N. Devoy, 499–509. London: Croom Helm.

U.S. National Ocean Survey. 1981. *United States Coast Pilot*. Washington, D.C.: NOAA, U.S. Department of Commerce.

van Aart, R. 1974. Drainage and land reclamation in the Lower Mesopotamian Plain. *Nature and Resources 10(2)*: 11–17.

van der Aa, P. 1963. *Europäische Städte-Ansichten Um 1700*. Hamburg: Harry v. Hofmann Verlag.

Volker, A. 1982. Polders: an ancient approach to land reclamation. *Nature and Resources 18(4)*: 2–13.

Walker, H. J. 1962. Coral and the lime industry of Mauritius. *The Geographical Review 52(3)*: 325–36.

———. 1975. Coastal morphology. *Soil Science 119*: 3–19.

———. 1980a. Reservoirs from the sea: Hong Kong's answer to its water supply demands. *Scientific Bulletin 5(1)*: 19–25.

———. 1980b. The Pearl River Delta. *Scientific Bulletin 5(2)*: 1–6.

———. 1981a. Man and shoreline modification. In *Coastal Dynamics and Scientific Sites*, ed. E. C. F. Bird and K. Koike, 55–90. Tokyo: Komazawa University.

———. 1981b. The peopling of the coast. In *The Environment: Chinese and American Views*, ed. L. J. C. Ma and A. G. Noble, 91–105. London: Methuen.

———. 1984. Man's impact on shorelines and nearshore environments: a geomorphological perspective. In *Geoforum 15(3)*: 395–417.

———, ed. 1988. *Artificial Structures and Shorelines*. Dordrecht: Kluwer Academic Publishers.

Walker, H. J., J. M. Coleman, H. H. Roberts, and R. S. Tye. 1987. Wetland loss in Louisiana. *Geografiska Annaler, 69(1)*: 189–200.

Walker, H. J., and J. Mossa. 1986. Human modification of the shoreline in Japan. *Physical Geography 7*: 116–39.

Walker, R. A. 1973. Wetlands preservation and management on Chesapeake Bay: The role of science in natural resource policy. *Coastal Zone Management Journal 1(1)*: 75–101.

Walsh, G. E. 1977. Exploitation of mangal. In *Wet Coastal Ecosystems*, ed. V. J. Chapman, 347–62. New York: Elsevier Scientific Publishing Company.

Weggel, J. R. 1972. Water motion and process of sediment entrainment. In *Shelf Sediment Transport*, ed. D. J. P. Swift, D. B. Duane, and O. H. Pilkey, 1–20. Dowden, Stroudsburg: Hutchinson & Ross Publishing Company.

Wong, P. P. 1988. Singapore. In *Artificial Structures and Shorelines*, ed. H. J. Walker, 383–92. Dordrecht: Kluwer Academic Publishers.

Zenkovich, V. P. 1973. Geomorphological problems of protecting the Caucasian Black Sea coast. *The Geographical Journal 139*: 460–66.

Zhao, H. 1988. The People's Republic of China – South. In *Artificial Structures and Shorelines*, ed. H. J. Walker, 355–68. Dordrecht: Kluwer Academic Publishers.

17

Atmospheric Trace Constituents

T. E. GRAEDEL   P. J. CRUTZEN

Except while visiting the most polluted cities during periods of atmospheric stagnation, it is easy to regard the atmosphere as pristine. Reports of declining air quality are easily ignored in the face of crystal skies and fresh air. It is therefore important to address such questions as:

1. How long have changes in the atmosphere been occurring?
2. How widespread are the changes?
3. How well is the atmosphere understood?
4. What will be the consequences of the changes that can be detected?

In this chapter, we begin to answer some of these questions, realizing that full answers may be crucial to the sustainable development of the planet.

More than 99.9% of the molecules comprising the earth's contemporary atmosphere are nitrogen (N_2), oxygen (O_2), or one of the chemically inert, noble gases (largely argon). These species have been present at near-constant levels throughout the human presence in the biosphere. The remaining atmospheric constituents, comprising less than 0.1% of the atmospheric molecules, are of surprising diversity and importance and are capable of influencing or controlling a number of crucial atmospheric processes. Carbon dioxide, which is the chemical feedstock for the photosynthesis of organic matter, is also an important factor in the earth's radiation balance. It is chemically unreactive in the troposphere (the lowest portion of the atmosphere), and is currently present at an average concentration of about 340 ppm by volume. The most abundant of the reactive gases is methane, which comprises less than 2 ppm of the tropospheric gas. Other reactive species are still less prevalent; the combined concentration of all of the reactive trace constituents in the lower atmosphere seldom totals 10 ppm, yet these rather rare components are crucial to radiation, climate, and global habitability.

Atmospheric Chemical Fluctuations

At the time of World War II, barely two dozen different chemical species were known to be present in the earth's atmosphere. A decade later, as scientists began investigating the chemical and biological implications of atmospheric composition, that number was still less than 100. Today, nearly 3,000 species have been identified, and are presented in detailed tables and cross-reference listings in a recent book (Graedel, Hawkins, and Claxton 1986).

Although the occurrence of these compounds in the troposphere is of pedagogical interest, the impact produced by them depends not on their occurrence, but on their concentrations, their reactivity, the products of their reactions, and their effects on atmospheric photochemistry – that is, on the chemistry resulting from the interaction of sunlight with trace atmospheric species. It turns out that the species concentrations vary greatly because of source distributions, atmospheric mixing, and chemical lifetimes. For example, consider hydrogen sulfide (H_2S). Concentrations over salt marshes, a major source, can be in the 1-to-10-ppb (parts per billion) range, but are usually lower. In locations such as grasslands or mountains, 0.1-to-1-ppb levels of H_2S are seen sometimes, but levels of a few parts per trillion (ppt) are more common Urban areas generally have H_2S concentrations of 0.1–1 ppb as a consequence of petroleum refining or sewage treatment. This measured variation of concentrations from place to place demonstrates (1) that H_2S is quite reactive, since its concentrations show wide variations in the troposphere and decrease away from the source regions, and (2) that no significant upper atmospheric sources exist, since in the free troposphere (i.e., the troposphere above the surface boundary layer), the concentrations are much lower than those near the ground.

In contrast to the concentration behavior for H_2S, that for carbonyl sulfide (COS) (another ubiquitous sulfur gas) is everywhere uniform at a level of 0.6 ppb. This behavior indicates that COS has widely dispersed sources and that its atmospheric lifetime is very long, so that it has become very well mixed. A third type of behavior is indicated by sulfur dioxide (SO_2), which has a very strong urban source and spatially diffuse and relatively weak natural sources. The result is that the SO_2 concentration in urban regions can be very high and elsewhere quite low, generally in the range of 10–100 ppt.

In addition to concentration variations from one type of

region to another, variations occur as well in air over regions with similar characteristics, in part because of the locations within the region of major sources of trace species, but especially because of the diffusion and dispersion produced by motions of air parcels. A particularly nice demonstration of such variations was provided by a gas-filter radiometer experiment aboard one of the flights of the U.S. Space Shuttle (Reichle et al. 1982). The radiometer looks down upon the earth from space and makes a determination of the carbon monoxide concentrations averaged throughout the middle troposphere (about 6-km altitude). A sample result is shown in Fig. 17.1. The ground track of the spacecraft, when compared with the data, shows strong peaks in carbon monoxide concentrations over western South America and just south of Cyprus. Carbon monoxide concentrations differ significantly over the oceans, the values over the Atlantic being noticeably higher than those over the Indian Ocean. Clearly, the variations are sufficiently large that general assessments only can be regarded as providing some perspective on typical transient concentrations, rather than giving definite values for a specific location.

Variations in atmospheric quality are greatest within and between urban areas, since most anthropogenic emissions to the atmosphere occur there. As with the subcontinent distance scale discussed earlier, this point is perhaps best made by example. A convenient data set for that purpose is that of the Global Environmental Monitoring System (GEMS), established by the World Health Organization. At present, fourteen countries have contributed data to the program, which has concentrated on sulfur dioxide and suspended particulate matter. Comparisons of trace atmospheric species among cities require that data be collected over the long term

and with substantial completeness of measurements at several sites within each city. For cities meeting these criteria, GEMS has averaged the data over the period 1976–1980. The results for sulfur dioxide are shown in Fig. 17.2. They indicate that the concentration of a single trace gas can differ by a factor of as much as 20 between different urban areas, even when long-term averages are used.

The fluctuations just described are consequences of the natural variations of the atmosphere, the discontinuous forcing of meteorology, chemical reactivity, and the distributions and strengths of emissions of various trace species into the atmosphere. These factors cannot be separated easily in such a complex system. To begin to do so, one must understand something about atmospheric transformations and techniques of measurement, as well as the observed chemical patterns. Only in the last two decades have atmospheric scientists had a fundamental understanding of some of these processes.

The Background Chemistry of the Atmosphere

The Troposphere

In the early part of this century, ground-based measurements (Goetz, Meetham, and Dobson 1934; Strutt 1918) and in-situ balloon-borne observations (Regener and Regener 1934) made it apparent that most of the atmosphere's ozone is located in the stratosphere, the peak concentration occurring at altitudes between 20 and 30 km. For a long time, it was believed that tropospheric ozone (the troposphere consists of the lowest 16–20 km of the atmosphere) originated from the stratosphere and that most of it was destroyed by contact with the earth's surface. In the mid-1940s, however, it became obvious that tropospheric production of ozone was taking place. After heavy injury to vegetable crops had occurred repeatedly in the Los Angeles area, it was shown by Haagen-Smit (1952) that the plant damage could be produced by ozone, which was known to be a prominent constituent of "photochemical smog" (Haagen-Smit and Fox 1956). The overall reaction mechanism was identified as:

$$NMHC + NO_x + h\nu \rightarrow O_3 + \text{other products}$$

where NMHC denotes various reactive nonmethane hydrocarbons, NO_x is NO plus NO_2, and $h\nu$ is solar radiation of wavelengths less than about 400 nanometers (10^{-9} m or nm). Ozone formation by this mechanism is possible because solar radiation of wavelengths between about 300 and 400 nm can reach the earth's surface and dissociate NO_2 into NO and O. The recombination of O with O_2 produces O_3.

Another fundamental aspect of the atmosphere's reactivity was discovered by Levy (1971; 1972), who pointed out that ozone photolysis at wavelengths shorter than about 310 nm leads to the production of the hydroxyl radical (HO·, a molecular fragment) through the reactions:

$$O_3 + h\nu(\lambda \leq 310\,\text{nm}) \rightarrow O(^1D) + O_2 \qquad (1)$$

$$O(^1D) + H_2O \rightarrow 2HO· \qquad (2)$$

(The centered dot is chemical notation for an unpaired electron, a structure that renders the constituent highly reactive,

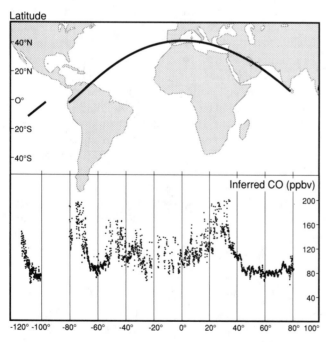

Figure 17.1 Inferred middle-tropospheric carbon monoxide mixing ratio and corresponding ground track from the MAPS (measurement of air pollution from satellites) experiment on the flight of the NASA Space Shuttle, November 13, 1981. Source: Reichle et al. 1982.

SO$_2$ concentration (ppb)

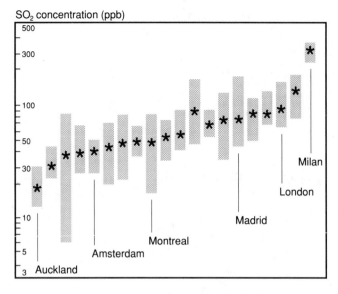

Figure 17.2 Annual mean concentrations of sulfur dioxide in urban areas around the world for the period 1976–1980. The bars indicate the range of annual averages at individual sites in each city, and the asterisks indicate the composite averages. The full list of urban areas and the original version of the diagram are in Bennett et al. 1985.

and the O(^{1}D) notation refers to a specific excited state of the oxygen atom.) This was a crucial hypothesis, since it was known that the hydroxyl radical was capable of reacting with a very large number of molecules, far more effectively than O$_3$. (The major atmospheric constituent O$_2$ does not react with any of the primary emitted compounds.) Levy (1971) also proposed that a chain reaction leading to increased hydroxyl production could occur via the formation of formaldehyde (HCHO) in the methane (CH$_4$) oxidation cycle. McConnell, McElroy, and Wofsy (1971) and Wofsy, McConnell, and McElroy (1972) then suggested that atmospheric CO concentrations in the "background" air were mainly governed by the reactions

$$CH_4 + HO \cdot \rightarrow \cdots \rightarrow CO \quad \text{(several steps)} \qquad (3)$$

$$CO + HO \cdot \rightarrow H \cdot + CO_2 \qquad (4)$$

Because carbon monoxide concentrations are much more variable than those of methane, however, especially in the northern hemisphere, it was clear that a variety of natural and anthropogenic processes must make additional important contributions to the atmospheric carbon monoxide cycle.

In 1973, Crutzen demonstrated that ozone can be both produced and destroyed by the methane and carbon monoxide oxidation cycles in the atmosphere, depending on the concentration of nitric oxide (NO). For instance, the carbon monoxide oxidation can proceed through reactions that produce ozone in the presence of the catalyst molecules NO and NO$_2$:

$$CO + HO \cdot \rightarrow H \cdot + CO_2 \qquad (4)$$

$$H \cdot + O_2 + M \rightarrow HO_2 \cdot + M \qquad (5)$$

$$HO_2 \cdot + NO \rightarrow HO \cdot + NO_2 \qquad (6)$$

$$NO_2 + h\nu(\lambda \leq 400\,nm) \rightarrow NO + O \qquad (7)$$

$$O + O_2 + M \rightarrow O_3 + M \qquad (8)$$

$$\text{Net: } CO + 2O_2 \rightarrow CO_2 + O_3$$

where M refers to any molecule which carries away excess energy, usually either N$_2$ or O$_2$. Alternatively, if NO$_x$ concentrations are low, the result of the chemical reactions is to destroy O$_3$:

$$CO + HO \cdot \rightarrow H \cdot + CO_2 \qquad (4)$$

$$H \cdot + O_2 + M \rightarrow HO_2 \cdot + M \qquad (5)$$

$$HO_2 \cdot + O_3 \rightarrow HO \cdot + 2O_2 \qquad (9)$$

$$\text{Net: } CO + O_3 \rightarrow CO_2 + O_2$$

Because the rate coefficient for reaction (6) is about 4,000 times faster than that for reaction (9), the ozone-producing carbon monoxide oxidation branch is more important than the ozone destruction branch in the case of NO to O$_3$ concentration ratios exceeding 1 : 4,000, i.e., for NO volume-mixing ratios larger than about $5 - 10 \times 10^{-12}$ (5–10 ppt) in the lower troposphere. Although this may appear to be a very low minimum mixing ratio, because of the very short lifetimes of NO and NO$_2$, there are large portions of the unpolluted atmosphere with concentrations currently below this critical point.

Similar but more complex reaction cycles also take place during the atmospheric oxidation of the hydrocarbon gases, with methane being the most important example in extensive portions of the atmosphere, especially in remote marine environments. Methane is sufficiently abundant, in fact, that its oxidation, in addition to that of CO, plays a large role in the tropospheric ozone and hydroxyl radical balances. Again the availability of NO determines the results. To briefly summarize the detailed reaction sequences, the oxidation of one methane molecule to carbon monoxide and then to carbon dioxide yields (Crutzen 1987):

1. In NO-poor environments: a net loss of 3.5 odd hydrogen (HO· and HO$_2$·) radicals and 1.7 ozone molecules.
2. In NO-rich environments: a net gain of 0.5 odd hydrogen radicals and 3.7 ozone molecules.

These results are very important for the photochemistry of the "background" troposphere, because NO and CH$_4$ emissions to the atmosphere are now strongly influenced by anthropogenic activities and because CH$_4$ and CO are the principal reaction partners of HO·.

For the future, it is important to realize that the potential for ozone formation in the troposphere is large and is limited only by the availability of NO and NO$_2$ as catalysts. It can be estimated roughly that if all worldwide hydrocarbon and carbon monoxide emissions would result in ozone formation, then the tropospheric ozone concentration could be more than ten times larger than that produced by the principal preindustrial source for tropospheric ozone, downward transport from the stratosphere (Crutzen 1987).

The Stratosphere

Ozone (O_3) in the stratosphere is produced by the photodissociation of molecular oxygen by solar ultraviolet radiation. This process produces two oxygen atoms, each of which combines with molecular oxygen:

$$O_2 + h\nu(\lambda \leq 240 \, nm) \rightarrow O + O \qquad (10)$$

$$2[O + O_2 + M \rightarrow O_3 + M] \qquad (8)$$

$$\text{Net: } 3O_2 \rightarrow 2O_3$$

Because most oxygen in the atmosphere is present as O_2, it is clear that there must be processes that reconvert most of the O_3 into O_2. The initial proposal by Chapman (1930) was that this mainly occurred through the reaction sequence:

$$O_3 + h\nu(\lambda \leq 1,140 \, nm) \rightarrow O + O_2 \qquad (11)$$

$$O + O_3 \rightarrow 2O_2 \qquad (12)$$

$$\text{Net: } 2O_3 \rightarrow 3O_2$$

For about 40 years, it was generally accepted that this sequence explained the cycle of stratospheric ozone. However, research over the past two decades has shown that several minor constituents play an essential role in stratospheric ozone destruction due to catalytic reaction cycles that may be summarized as:

$$X + O_3 \rightarrow XO + O_2 \qquad (13)$$

$$O_3 + h\nu \rightarrow O + O_2 \qquad (11)$$

$$O + XO \rightarrow X + O_2 \qquad (14)$$

$$\text{Net: } 2O_3 \rightarrow 3O_2$$

In this reaction set, X and XO are atoms or molecules that catalyze the conversion of O_3 to O_2. In the natural stratosphere, the most important catalysts are the oxides of nitrogen NO and NO_2 (Crutzen 1970). They in turn are formed through the oxidation of nitrous oxide (N_2O), which is produced at the earth's surface mainly by natural microbiological denitrification or nitrification processes on land and in the oceans. In particular, the tropical-forest ecosystem can be a large source of N_2O. At present, agricultural activities (e.g., the use of nitrogen fertilizers) and fossil-fuel and biomass burning are a substantial fraction (≈ 30–40%) of the natural N_2O emissions. This fraction seems likely to increase in the future.

The industrial production and emission of several fully halogenated organic compounds (CFCs, i.e., organic compounds in which all hydrogen atoms are replaced by a combination of chlorine, fluorine, or bromine atoms), which are not broken down in the troposphere by reactions with the hydroxyl radical or any other potential oxidizing constituent, cause strong increases in the stratospheric CFC compounds (currently about 5–6% annually). Of particular importance for the stratospheric ozone layer are the chemically very stable gases $CFCl_3$ and CF_2Cl_2. Over time, these gases are transported upward from the earth's surface to the stratosphere. At an altitude of about 25 km, the available solar radiation is energetic enough to destroy the CFCs, releasing chlorine

atoms ($Cl\cdot$) and chlorine monoxide ($ClO\cdot$) molecules, which are even more powerful ozone-destroying catalysts than are NO and NO_2. Consequently (according to computer-model calculations), the steady increase of CFCs is expected to lead to substantial reductions in ozone concentrations in the stratosphere above about 25 km. For lower altitudes, the same model calculations indicate the possibility of increased ozone concentrations due to a variety of causes, including the more efficient penetration of solar radiation as a consequence of the reduced upper-ozone levels and complex chemical interactions among the reactive radical gases. However, as we will note, an unanticipated problem, not predicted by the models, has developed in the springtime in the Antarctic during the past 10 years: the so-called ozone hole.

Atmospheric Chemical Measurements

Overview

At first thought, it seems almost inconceivable that we could say very much about the trace species concentrations of atmospheres much older than the 20 years or so during which modern analytical instruments have been developed and used. It turns out, however, that there exist at least four techniques that have the potential for the determination of historic air quality:

1. If a sample of ancient air has been preserved in some way, it can be analyzed by modern analytical techniques. The best examples of such preserved samples are air bubbles in polar or glacial ice cores.

2. Analytical chemistry as a discipline is well over 100 years old, and in some cases data exist from detailed atmospheric-measurements programs of a century ago. These data can be used today if the measurement technique is reproduced and the response certified. In the case of modern atmospheric measurements, extremely careful analyses and calibrations produce highly accurate results for the trace constituents of both gases and liquids.

3. Interactions occur between atmospheric constituents and the surfaces with which they come into contact. If these interactions are understood, and if the interacting surfaces preserve the signature of the interaction, the surfaces might be useful for establishing past atmospheric characteristics.

4. For all but the most reactive species, the atmospheric concentrations that are measured can be related to the emission fluxes from various sources. Modern source/concentration relationships can (perhaps with the help of a computer model) provide information on trace constituents in past atmospheres, provided that historical data related to emission fluxes are known or can be estimated.

Ice Core Chemistry: An Introduction

On several areas of the earth temperatures seldom or never exceed the freezing point of water: Antarctica, Greenland, and some mountain glaciers. Each year's snow in these areas gradually changes to ice and becomes part of the ice mass on which it fell. The process generally incorporates small bubbles of air, which are then retained within the ice matrix. Any atmospheric particles that have fallen onto the ice are incorporated along with the snow. The prospect thus exists for examining the chemistry of the trapped gases, the frozen precipitation, and the incorporated particles.

The use of ice cores to study the chemistry of ancient atmospheres is a development only of the past decade or so. The technique is to locate an appropriate ice mass, drill a core in such a way that the sample is retrieved in a chemically uncontaminated state, and return the core in the frozen state to the laboratory for study. The measurement of soluble species frozen into the ice is made by slicing off a section of the ice corresponding to the desired age period, melting it under ultraclean conditions, and analyzing the resulting solution. If gas concentrations are to be measured, the ice sample is placed in a vacuum chamber and either melted or cracked; the gases are then analyzed by gas chromatographic or spectrometric methods.

Ice-core techniques are particularly appropriate for species that are relatively unreactive, such as methane or carbon dioxide, because the possible complication of reactive loss during or after freezing is minimized. Species of this type are long-lived and well-mixed in the atmosphere, so the ice sample provides an approximate average of global atmospheric concentrations.

Trace Gas Analysis: An Introduction

The first analytical measurements of an atmospheric trace gas were those made for carbon dioxide and ozone in the late nineteenth century. Other forms of "wet chemistry" have been used for a variety of atmospheric gases, particularly in the 1950s and 1960s. In almost all cases, the techniques suffer from insufficient sensitivity to the low gas concentrations common in the atmosphere, and from being subject to interferences from gases other than those whose concentrations were determined. Few instruments of this type remain in use today.

An alternative technique for the detection and measurement of trace atmospheric gases is that of the analysis of spectroscopic data. As sunlight passes through the atmosphere, the gases in the air absorb radiation at specific wavelengths. The amount of absorption is a function of the molecular properties and the abundances of the different gases. Thus, it is possible to identify and determine the concentrations of atmospheric trace gases by examining the absorption lines in solar spectra. Mostly for astronomical purposes, solar spectra have been recorded for nearly a century, and many of these old spectra are now being analyzed.

Modern techniques for trace-gas analysis generally involve the capture of a sample of air, followed by an analytical procedure based on the physical and/or chemical properties of the specific gas to be studied. The modern techniques are much more sensitive than their classical analogs and much less prone to interferences from other atmospheric species. As a result, the data accumulated over the past decade are generally of much higher quality than those of the past, and reveal much lower levels of trace atmospheric species.

Precipitation Chemistry: An Introduction

Performing a chemical analysis on precipitation is a two-step process. The first step is to acquire an uncontaminated sample of the precipitation, a process much more difficult than might be supposed. In the case of rain, samples can be gotten by rainfall sampling in a relatively straightforward fashion, provided carefully cleaned and acid-washed plasticware or similar containers are used. Fog is much more difficult to collect, but several advances in experiment design in the past few years now have provided numerous fog-water samples. In the case of dew, the sample is collected from runoff on large Teflon surfaces, sometimes backed by cooling coils.

Once the precipitation sample is collected, analyses of several types generally are performed. The ions in the sample, including Cl^-, NO_3^-, SO_4^{2-}, Na^+, NH_4^+, and K^+, are quantified by ion chromatography or a similar liquid-phase technique. Atomic-absorption spectroscopy is used to determine concentrations of metals, including lead, cadmium, iron, copper, manganese, and nickel. Detailed organic analyses may utilize mass spectroscopy, chromatography, or a variety of liquid-phase techniques.

Possible Surrogates for Atmospheric Species Concentrations

It is common for atmospheric chemists to wish to know the historic concentrations of a particular species in a particular location, and to find that suitable measurements have not been made. In these cases, it is sometimes possible to use other information to infer the concentrations of the atmospheric species of interest. Listed below are examples of such approaches.

1. In many regions of the world, and throughout the centuries, sulfur dioxide has been emitted almost entirely by the combustion of coal. Since coal traditionally has been an important item of commerce and industry, records of its use are available. As a result, the magnitude of coal use, combined with information on the typical sulfur content of the coal, can be used with a computer model of atmospheric dispersion and flow patterns to estimate sulfur dioxide concentrations (Brimblecombe 1977).

2. Atmospheric visibility, or lack thereof, is directly related to the concentrations of small particles. It is possible, therefore, to use records of visibility to infer changes in the atmospheric small-particle concentration (Husar et al. 1981).

3. One of the earliest indications of photochemical smog in the Los Angeles basin was the high rate of cracking of rubber products, especially automobile tires (Yocom and McCaldin 1968). Taking advantage of this characteristic, Los Angeles officials developed a monitoring technique in which bent strips of rubber of precise formulation were exposed to the atmosphere, and the depths of cracks that resulted were used to estimate the smog content of the atmosphere.

4. Materials exposed to the atmosphere are in a continuous state of deterioration, although the deterioration time

scales for different materials show enormous variation. Among the most easily observed examples of such deterioration is the decay of stone monuments: statues, tombstones, and the like; the effects are due largely to the action of dissolved sulfur dioxide (Amoroso and Fassina 1983). Because monuments are often described, sketched, and photographed, they offer great promise for retrospective surrogate analyses of trace atmospheric species. The decay history of stone monuments provides perhaps the best potential for productive collaboration between historians and atmospheric scientists.

5. Copper roofing, originally a salmon-pink color, eventually acquires a greenish-blue patina highly enriched in copper sulfate compounds (Graedel 1987). Particularly in Europe, where copper roofs and bronze statuary are common, where records are often detailed, and where major atmospheric changes have occurred over the past century, efforts to relate patination to atmospheric sulfur dioxide concentrations are likely to be fruitful in providing inferential information on historical atmospheric sulfur concentrations.

6. The atmospheric sulfidation of silver has been recognized for a long time and remains a problem today, being demonstrated to layperson and scientist alike by the tarnishing of electrical equipment, jewelry, artifacts, and household silverware (Franey, Kammlott, and Graedel 1985). If the relationship between tarnishing rate and corrosive species concentrations can be established, the phenomenon may serve as a historical H_2S–COS detector.

7. Damage to agricultural crops was one of the earliest effects of air pollution to be recognized (EPA 1978). The concentration thresholds at which damage begins to occur are about 30 ppb for ozone (Reich and Amundson 1985; Tonneijck 1986) and less than 35 ppb for peroxyacetyl nitrate (EPA 1978). The extensive recent research on the "forest dieback" problem may produce sufficient methodology to make this surrogate technique suitable for wide use.

Historical Air Chemistry: Global Scale, Troposphere

Carbon Dioxide

For no atmospheric species has more effort been expended, nor more results obtained, than on deriving the historical concentration patterns of carbon dioxide (CO_2). The data resulting from these efforts are described and illustrated by Houghton and Skole (chap. 23). It is of interest here, however, to comment briefly on the measurement techniques and the overall results of those studies.

Most estimates of historic atmospheric carbon dioxide concentrations have been derived from ice-core analyses, which generally give values of 280–290 ppm for samples from the midnineteenth century and earlier (Neftel et al. 1985; Pearman et al. 1986). Some exciting new ice-core analyses have shown substantial variability of atmospheric CO_2 over millennia, with low values of about 180–200 ppmv during ice ages and 260–280 ppmv during interglacials (Barnola et al. 1987; Neftel et al. 1985). Currently, atmospheric carbon dioxide is present in remote air at concentrations of about 340 ppm. The increase

in atmospheric carbon dioxide since the beginning of the nineteenth century has been due to a variety of worldwide, and accelerating, human activities. Until about 1950, the total release of carbon dioxide was mainly due to the oxidation of organic matter which is facilitated by the tilling of agricultural soils. Currently, the largest net source of carbon dioxide to the atmosphere comes from fossil-fuel combustion. Tropical deforestation also contributes to the atmospheric carbon dioxide increase. These findings are of special concern in connection with the rapid perturbations that are inflicted on the earth's chemical and radiation balance by the accumulation of various industrial products in the atmosphere.

Carbon Monoxide

Carbon monoxide (CO) is emitted into the atmosphere largely as a result of the atmospheric oxidation of methane and other alkanes, oxidation of organics emitted by vegetation, and the incomplete combustion of fossil fuels and biomass. Since its lifetime is relatively short (a few months) and its land-based sources discontinuously spread all over the world, its concentrations vary substantially with time at any one location and from location to location; thus it is extremely difficult to observe a small systematic increase without frequent measurements spanning a relatively long period of time. Nonetheless, two sets of data seem to establish clearly an upward trend in carbon monoxide.

The first data set was collected in three urban New Jersey locations between 1968 and 1977. Studying the minima in these data as a function of time to look for changes in background carbon monoxide, Graedel and McRae (1980) first detected the possible increase. Later, detailed gas-chromatographic studies (Khalil and Rasmussen 1984) at a Pacific coast site between 1979 and 1983 confirmed the increase. Carbon monoxide concentration increases, averaging 0.5–4%/yr between 1950 and 1977 have now been seen at midlatitudes in the Northern Hemisphere, based on optical total column measurements taken on the Jungfraujoch Mountain in Switzerland (Rinsland and Levine 1985). Increases in tropospheric carbon monoxide concentrations of about 2%/yr have been confirmed for the winter months in the Northern Hemisphere by Dianov-Klokov and Yurganov (1981), but no long-term changes were observed during the summer. Data by Seiler (personal communication) for Cape Town, South Africa do not yet show a clear, systematic long-term increase in carbon monoxide concentrations. The carbon monoxide increase seems, therefore, to be concentrated mainly in the northern midlatitudes, as would be expected for a gas with an atmospheric lifetime of only a few months, if the increase is due to industrial activities.

Methane

Methane (CH_4) enters the atmosphere from a wide variety of sources, some natural and some anthropogenic. The combined source strengths are such that methane is the most abundant reactive atmospheric gas, with current typical concentrations in remote areas of about 1.65 ppm. Bingemer and Crutzen (1987) have attempted to quantify the various source strengths. Their compilation suggests significant roles in the atmospheric methane cycle for fossil-fuel combustion, biomass burning, ruminants, landfills, and crop production. As a result of the many and expanding human influences on methane emissions, one may expect that the atmospheric concentrations of methane will continue to increase over the next several decades.

The possibility of an increasing trend in atmospheric methane was first suggested by Graedel and McRae in 1980. Since that time, extensive and carefully calibrated measurements all over the world have confirmed that suggestion. Rasmussen and Khalil (1984) and Blake and Rowland (1986) described the recent measurements in detail and demonstrated that the rate of increase in global methane concentrations is approximately 1% per year. Over a longer time period, measurements of methane in samples recovered from Antarctic ice cores show that atmospheric methane concentrations have approximately doubled since 1750 (Fig. 17.3).

A direct consequence of the increasing methane concentration is an increased trapping of outgoing infrared radiation emitted by the earth. The calculated contribution to the greenhouse effect is about 0.04°C per decade. When this is added to the direct contributions to the greenhouse effect produced by other trace species, the result equals or exceeds the warming effect expected from carbon dioxide alone (Ramanathan et al. 1985). As already discussed, a second consequence is the major role played by methane in the HO· budget, a role similar to that for carbon monoxide. Thirdly, methane strongly affects the stratospheric H_2O budget and ozone photochemistry.

Nitrous Oxide

Nitrous oxide (N_2O) is a natural product of bacterial activity in ocean waters and soils but is also produced by biomass combustion. Its historic concentrations in an ice core from Antarctica have recently been examined; the result is shown in Fig. 17.4. The data from the ice core for relatively modern periods agree with modern measurements (e.g., Weiss 1981). A linear regression of the whole record shows that concentrations have increased by 8% over the past 300 years. The current trend of 0.2–0.3%/yr is much higher, however. Nitrous oxide averaged 285 ppb between 1700 and 1800, compared with modern Southern Hemisphere values of about 310 ppb.

Chlorofluorocarbons

Chlorofluorocarbons (CFCs), that is, compounds containing carbon, chlorine, fluorine, and possibly hydrogen, are used extensively as refrigerants, blowing agents, and aerosol propellants as a consequence of their chemical inertness and low toxicity. The vast majority (including those most chemically inert) are wholly anthropogenic in origin. They have no natural sinks in the troposphere, but eventually migrate to the stratosphere, where they encounter high-energy radiation, which fragments them and inaugurates a series of chemical chains that destroy stratospheric ozone (see below). $CFCl_3$, CF_2Cl_2, and $C_2F_3Cl_3$ also play important roles as greenhouse gases; at current concentrations, their impact on the estimated global greenhouse effect is as much as 20% that of CO_2, in spite of concentrations about a million times lower.

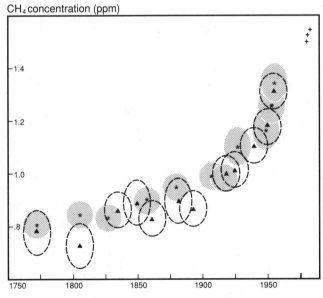

Figure 17.3 Historical record of atmospheric methane concentration based on measurements of air trapped in an ice core from Antarctica. Stars with solid ellipses represent results obtained from melt extraction, and triangles with dashed ellipses represent results from dry extraction. The plus signs indicate modern measurements in atmospheric air. The vertical semiaxes of the ellipses indicate the estimated precision, and the horizontal semiaxes the duration of the gas enclosure process. Source: Stauffer et al. 1985.

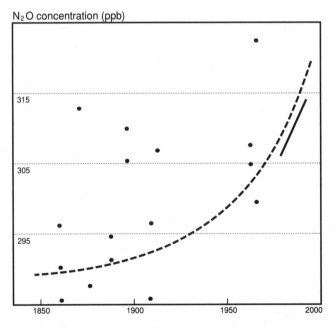

Figure 17.4 Historical record of atmospheric nitrous oxide concentration based on measurements of air trapped in an ice core from Law Dome, Antarctica. The solid line indicates modern tropospheric measurements. The dashed line is a global tropospheric average concentration from a model incorporating constant noncombustion and growing combustion sources of nitrous oxide. Source: Pearman et al. 1986.

Despite stagnating release rates, the concentrations of many of the CFCs are known to be increasing (Prinn et al. 1983; World Meteorological Organization 1985). Such behavior indicates that the release rates are still larger at present than are the photochemical breakdown rates in the stratosphere. Examples of the increases are shown in Fig. 17.5 for $CFCl_3$ and CF_2Cl_2. In each case, the increase is about 5%/yr on a worldwide basis.

Hydrogen Ion (H^+)

As has been noted, snow and ice cores collected from glaciers provide an opportunity to determine the chemistry of previously deposited precipitation and hence allow the production of reliable historic data bases for areas remote from local anthropogenic influences. An example of such a study is that made on an ice core from a site in south Greenland (Hammer, Clausen, and Dansgaard 1980). The location and meteorology of this site and the time scale over which the precipitation is accumulated render the data much more representative of global than of local conditions. The published record extends backward in time some 1,500 years, although we reproduce in Fig. 17.6 only that portion dating from 1700. This data record and others like it indicate that the acidity of high-latitude ice cores is greatly influenced by volcanic eruptions, particularly eruptions at high latitudes, but also by anthropogenic emissions.

Sulfate Ion (SO_4^{2-})

Anion concentrations as a function of depth (and thus of year) have been performed on several ice cores, notably those from Greenland (e.g., Mayewski et al. 1986). Of interest for the present discussion are the data for "excess sulfate" in Fig. 17.7. The value for excess sulfate (referred to hereafter simply as sulfate) is derived by subtracting the portion of sulfate due to sea salt from the total, to give the component that is largely volcanic or anthropogenic in origin.

Changes in the ice-core sulfate record can be separated into the following approximate groupings: 1870–1900, relatively constant; 1900–1910, sharply increasing; 1910–1940, relatively constant; 1940–1960, generally increasing; 1960–1968, sharply increasing; and 1968–1984, relatively constant. Abrupt changes in sulfate such as the one between 1900 and 1910 probably represent volcanic input of sulfate. The mean sulfate from 1968 to 1984 is 85 µg/kg. This work and that of others demonstrates that the sulfate deposition in south Greenland precipitation now is approximately three times what it was at the turn of the century. In addition, the data document the estimated increase of global anthropogenic sulfur since 1940.

Nitrate Ion (NO_3^-)

Precipitation nitrate is also analyzed in ice cores from the glaciers of Greenland and elsewhere. In the case of Greenland, the sources of nitrate are thought to include anthropogenic activities such as fossil-fuel and biomass burning and unknown natural sources, primarily of biogenic origin.

Changes in trend in the nitrate record of the south Greenland ice core (Fig. 17.7) indicate a relative constancy in value from 1869 to 1955, followed by a period of general increase from 1955 to 1975, and an intensified increase from 1975 to 1984. The magnitude of the increase is in good agreement with the results from other ice cores and with North American emission estimates for NO and NO_2.

Chloride Ion (Cl^-)

Chloride in ice cores has known sources from the marine environment and from volcanos, together with the possibility of anthropogenic sources. The influence of the marine source can be estimated by studying the ratio of chloride to sodium in the ice. For the south Greenland ice-core data shown in Fig. 17.7, no significant trend is identifiable in the chloride concentrations for the period 1869 to 1984.

Total Particulate Matter

Historical concentrations of atmospheric aerosols are available from a number of high-latitude ice cores (e.g., De Angelis, Barkov, and Petrov 1987). As with the ice-core data on acidity, the aerosol data are heavily influenced by volcanic eruptions, but the total aerosol loading does not show a significant anthropogenic influence. The same is not true of some of the trace metals in the aerosol, however. A particularly striking example is that of lead, whose ice-core concentrations have increased at least tenfold in the past century (Ng and Patterson 1981). This increase is attributed to industrial production of lead and its subsequent use, particularly as an additive for gasoline.

Historical Air Chemistry: Local and Regional Scales

On the local or regional scale, appropriate historical samples of air generally are not available. As a consequence, it is necessary to look for surrogate data or to restrict oneself to the relatively recent measurements that are extant. Thus far, at least, surrogate approaches have been most useful in western Europe and in North America, although some modest

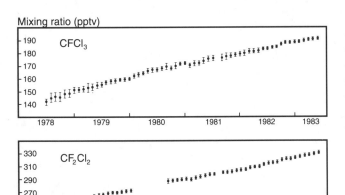

Figure 17.5 Monthly means and standard deviations for five years of $CFCl_3$ data at Cape Grim, Tasmania, 1978–1983. The trends from other sites around the world are similar. Similar data for CF_2Cl_2. Source: Cunnold et al. 1986.

surrogate analyses have been made for other geographical areas (e.g., Darmstadter et al. 1987). Analytical measurements also are quite sparse; only for a few locations in Europe (and nowhere else) are data available for before and shortly after 1900. Modern analytical measurements were begun in North America in the late 1950s and perfected during the 1960s and 1970s. Only since the late 1970s have air-quality data from sites around the world become widely available.

In the following paragraphs, we present a selection of the past and present air-quality data for local and regional distance scales. The examples illustrate both analytical and surrogate assessments and show instances of both deleterious and ameliorative trends in the constitution of the atmosphere.

Europe

Paris, Northern Europe (O_3; 1880–1905). By the middle of the nineteenth century, it had been clearly demonstrated that ozone was a normal constituent of atmospheric air (e.g., Andrews 1856). This had already been proposed in 1845 by Schoenbein, who also introduced an "ozonometer," consisting of iodized starch paper, which was used extensively at many sites throughout the world. The interest in ozone measurements was especially stimulated by Schoenbein's discussion of the possible role of ozone as a disinfectant against epidemic disease. It is unfortunate that the many data on tropospheric ozone that were taken with the Schoenbein test paper are of little value, because the method is unspecific and even dependent on meteorological factors such as wind speed and atmospheric humidity.

Although efforts continue to derive useful information from the old data, there is probably only one long series of measurements that may be taken as representative of ground-level ozone concentrations during the past century, namely those made by A. Levy and coworkers at the Montsouris Observatory in Paris between 1876 and 1907 (Levy 1907). The quality of these observations has been ascertained recently by Volz and Kley (1988), and the data indicate two to four times lower average concentrations than are presently measured at comparable sites in western Europe. During photochemical "smog" episodes, about ten times as much ozone may occur.

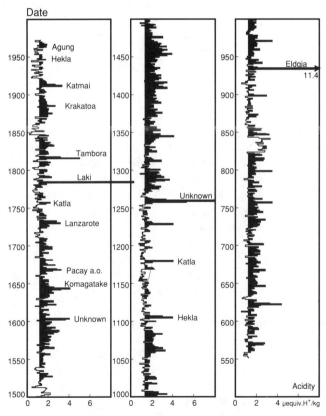

Figure 17.6 Mean acidity of annual layers from A.D. 553 to A.D. 1972 in an ice core from central Greenland. Acidities about the background, $1.2 \pm 0.1 \mu eq\ H^+$ per kg ice, are due to fallout of volcanic acids, mainly H_2SO_4, from eruptions north of 20°S. The ice core is dated with an uncertainty of ± 1 year in the past 900 years, increasing to ± 3 years at A.D. 553. This precision makes possible the identification of several large eruptions known from historic sources, and the accurate dating of the Icelandic Eldgja eruption shortly after the settlement that was completed A.D. 930. Source: Hammer, Clausen, and Dansgaard 1980.

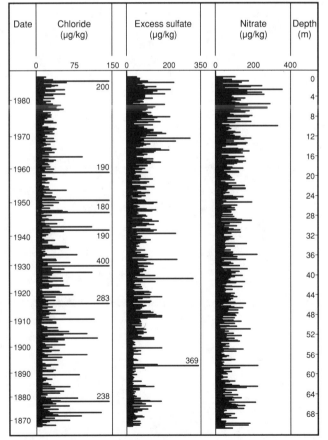

Figure 17.7 Chloride, excess sulfate, and nitrate time series from a south Greenland ice core, 1869–1984. Chloride and excess sulfate values that are off-scale appear as numbers. The time scale is compressed to accommodate annual layer compaction with depth. Excess sulfate is the value given by subtracting sea-salt-related sulfate from total sulfate. Source: Mayewski et al. 1986.

Belgium, Netherlands, England (NH$_4^+$, NO$_3^-$; 1853–1980). Historical data for nitrate and ammonium ions in precipitation began to be collected in 1853 in England, and several decades later on the European continent. The data are shown in Fig. 17.8. It is readily apparent that the deposition of nitrate ion to the ground has increased strongly throughout the duration of the record (by a factor of about four), while the increase in the amount of deposited ammonium ion has been smaller in a relative sense. These results are approximately consistent with the flux of oxides of nitrogen thought to have been released during the century 1880–1980 from combustion processes in the western European region (Brimblecombe and Stedman 1982). During the same period, the sources of deposited ammonium ion, which consist largely of soil emissions and livestock husbandry, have increased significantly as well, but the deposition data do not appear to reflect fully this change in source strength.

Coal Use As a Surrogate for SO$_2$ and Total Particulate Matter: London, 1700–1950

Not only has London been a major city for many centuries, but its citizens have diligently documented their history over that period. As a result, modern measurements of air quality sometimes may be related to historical descriptions, particularly in the case of species present in concentrations high enough to cause obvious and significant effects on the population. Using such concepts as a starting point, Brimblecombe (1977) has produced estimates of concentrations of sulfur dioxide and total particulate matter (TPM) in London for the period 1500–1950. The latter half of that period is of interest in the present study, and some of Brimblecombe's results are discussed here.

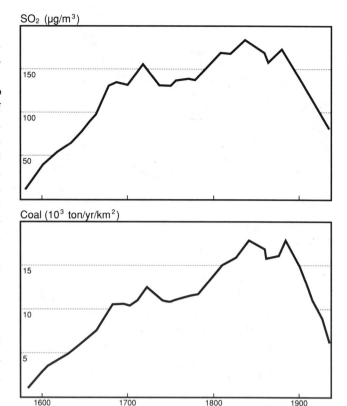

Figure 17.9 Decadal mean sulfur dioxide concentrations in London air. Source: Brimblecombe 1977.

Adopting a technique similar to that used for New York City (see below), coal use in London has been related to atmospheric levels of sulfur dioxide (Fig. 17.9). The sulfur dioxide concentrations show features that reflect population changes and industrial development. During the period 1700–1900, the urban radius expanded from about 3 km to about 15 km, while the use of coal per unit area remained stable. This resulted in gradual increases in sulfur dioxide concentrations throughout most of the period. At the start of the twentieth century, importation of coal with lower sulfur content and a gradual decrease in the use of coal for the heating of private residences gradually reduced atmospheric sulfur dioxide. Similar results were obtained for TPM.

North America

Hubbard Brook, NH (SO$_4^{2-}$, NO$_3^-$, pH; 1964–1985). At Hubbard Brook, NH, there exists the longest continuous, scientifically rigorous record of precipitation ion concentrations in the United States, from 1964 to the present time (National Research Council 1986). The Hubbard Brook concentrations have been extended further back in time with the use of a computer model linked to the emission fluxes of species of interest. Fay, Golomb, and Kumar (1986) thus report trends in precipitation ions sulfate and nitrate for the period 1900–1980. Their results are shown in Fig. 17.10.

Historical Hubbard Brook values for sulfate appear on the top panel of Fig. 17.10. They mirror in some sense the pattern of New York City SO$_2$ in that they reflect the large sulfur

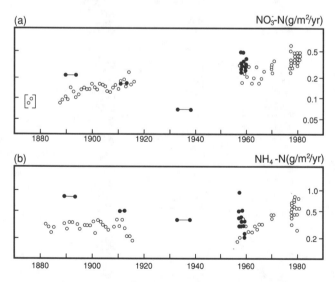

Figure 17.8 Trends in the amount of nitrate (a) and ammonium (b) ion brought down annually in Belgium, England, and the Netherlands. Dark circles joined with a bar indicate precipitation weighted annual means and the periods over which they are averaged. The open circles indicate English data, the filled circles indicate data from the western European continent. The two bracketed points in the nitrate graph are displaced 20 years from 1855 and 1856.

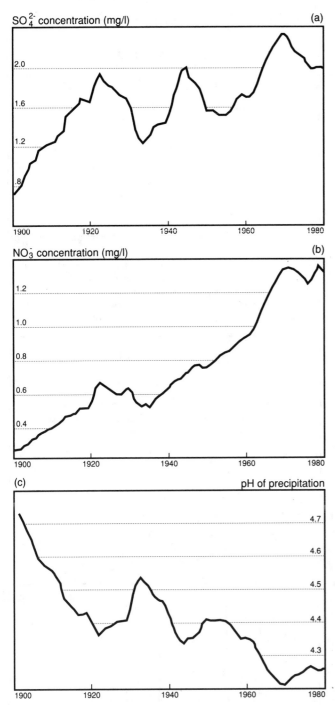

SO$_4^{2-}$ concentration (mg/l) (a)

NO$_3^-$ concentration (mg/l) (b)

(c) pH of precipitation

Figure 17.10 Estimated concentrations of (a) sulfate, (b) nitrate, and (c) acidity in Hubbard Brook, New Hampshire. Source: Fay, Golomb, and Kumar 1986.

increase in high-temperature combustion of fossil fuels in power plants and in automobiles.

The precipitation pH is related to both the sulfate and nitrate concentrations, and is shown for the 1900–1980 period in the bottom panel of Fig. 17.10. The figure shows a reasonably steady decrease in pH throughout the period, interrupted chiefly by the depression years of the mid-1930s. Since about 1970, the pH has become much more stable, perhaps as a consequence of the increasing limitations being placed on emissions to the atmosphere.

Los Angeles (NO$_x$, NMHC, O$_3$; 1955–1985). Photochemical smog was first recognized as a consequence of automotive and other emissions into the atmosphere in Los Angeles, and observations of several atmospheric trace species in the Los Angeles basin date from the mid-1950s. Much of the earliest data has been summarized by Merz, Painter, and Ryason (1972), the later data by Trijonis et al. (1978), and the most recent data by EPA (1985). Kuntasal and Chang (1987) have recently summarized the data for the period 1968–1984. For carbon monoxide, the data show a definite downward trend, consistent with vehicular emission control measures (Fig. 17.11). Basin-wide ambient hydrocarbons, NO$_x$, and O$_3$ show downward trends as well (Fig. 17.12).

Coal Use As a Surrogate for SO$_2$: New York City, 1880–1980

Sulfur dioxide concentrations have been measured in New York City since the 1940s, but it was not until the late 1950s that regular monitoring programs were put into effect. Although detection techniques have been changed from time to time, the program continues to the present day. This set of data can be augmented by studies of sulfur dioxide emissions prior to the period of measurement. It happens that sulfur dioxide is emitted within the region almost entirely by the combustion of coal. Since coal has traditionally been an im-

emissions during the 1920s, the 1940s, and the 1960s, and the decrease during the years of the Great Depression. The marked decrease in SO$_2$ concentrations that has occurred since about 1960 is not mimicked by the SO$_4^{2-}$ data, however, and this is evidence for the nonlinear atmospheric chemical effects on the conversion of sulfur dioxide to sulfate ion in precipitation.

Nitrate ion concentrations are shown in the center panel of Fig. 17.10. The near-monotonic increase is substantially different from that for SO$_4^{2-}$, since it reflects the gradual

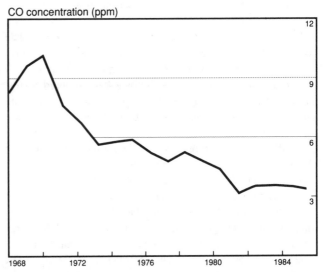

CO concentration (ppm)

Figure 17.11 Trend for nine-station, third-quarter, daily maximum hour carbon monoxide concentrations in the South Coast Air Basin, California, 1968–1985. Source: Kuntasal and Chang 1987.

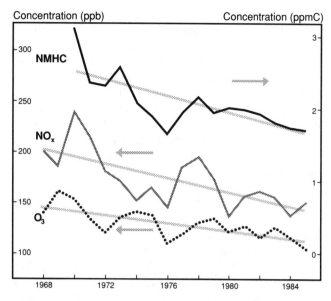

Figure 17.12 Linearized trends of nine-station, third-quarter, daily maximum hour averages for NMHC, NO$_x$, and O$_3$ in the South Coast Air Basin, California. The observational data are also shown. Source: Kuntasal and Chang 1987.

portant item of commerce and industry, records of its use are available. As a result, the magnitude of coal use, combined with information on the typical sulfur content of the coal, can be used with a computer model of atmospheric dispersion and flow patterns to estimate sulfur dioxide concentrations.

Figure 17.13 shows the results of such an exercise. For the period from 1958 onward, the results of the computer model have been compared with measurements, so that the approximate validity of the computer approach has been established. The concentration patterns seen in the data turn out to reflect the Industrial Revolution in the New York City metropolitan area, with SO$_2$ peaks during World Wars I and II, declines following the wars and during the economically depressed period of the 1930s, and a decrease to an annual average concentration of about 20 ppb following the imposition of air pollution-control legislation in the period around 1970.

The Entire United States (Many Species; 1972–1983). The concentrations of a number of atmospheric trace species have been monitored regularly for more than a decade at state or federally supervised locations throughout the United States. The information from these sites has been collected and summarized on a national basis since 1975 and is presented in a form in which typical concentrations, their ranges throughout the differing monitoring sites, and their long-term trends can be seen readily. The "boxplot" technique that is used is shown in Fig. 17.14, where the 5th, 10th, and 25th percentiles of the data depict the "cleaner" monitoring sites, the 75th, 90th, and 95th percentiles depict the "dirtier" sites, and the median and average describe the "typical" sites. Although both the average and median characterize typical behavior, the median has the advantage of not being affected by a few extremely high or low observations.

The U.S. urban concentrations of sulfur dioxide over the past decade are shown in Fig. 17.15. As noted earlier, the

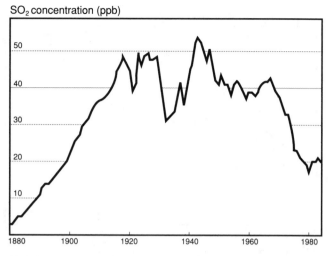

Figure 17.13 Sulfur dioxide concentration determinations for New York City. For 1880–1980, the data are from the estimates of Husar and Patterson 1985. For 1981–84, the data were measured by the New York Department of Environmental Conservation at the representative monitoring site nearest the Statue of Liberty.

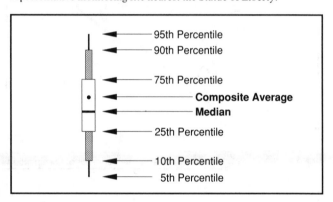

Figure 17.14 The plotting convention used for boxplots in subsequent figures for U.S. air-quality trends. Source: EPA 1985.

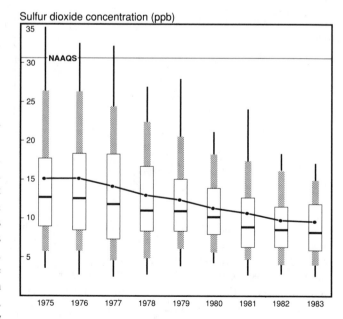

Figure 17.15 Boxplot comparisons of trends in annual mean sulfur dioxide concentrations at 286 sites, 1975–1983. On this figure and others of its type, NAAQS indicates the U.S. national ambient (i.e., outdoor) air-quality standard for this species. Source: EPA 1985.

emission of sulfur dioxide is dominated by fossil-fuel combustion, with industrial activity, motor vehicles, and other sources being much less important. As increased controls and cleaner fuels have been used over the past decade, sulfur dioxide concentrations have decreased steadily, and continued improvement is expected over the next decade. As of 1983, the typical annual mean concentration of U.S. urban sulfur dioxide was about 9 ppb.

Boxplots of annual mean nitrogen dioxide concentrations are given in Fig. 17.16. For the upper percentiles, they show a concentration increase from 1975–1979, followed by a decrease from 1979–1983. This behavior mirrors the trend in total NO_x emissions, which increased slightly in the late 1970s, decreased slightly in the early 1980s, and now is relatively stable. The trend is less evident in the mean values of the annual concentrations, and disappears entirely from the lower percentiles of the data. Most sites have annual mean concentrations of nitrogen dioxide in the range of 20–30 ppb and all are below the national ambient air-quality standard of 53 ppb.

As is the case for Los Angeles, the composite data for the United States show a decrease over the past decade in carbon monoxide concentrations and a slight downward trend for O_3. Significant decreases have occurred in the concentrations of total suspended particulates. Perhaps the most dramatic evidence for improvement in an air-quality component as a result of legislation is that for airborne lead in urban areas in the United States. Figure 17.17 shows the ambient lead data for the past decade. The substantial reductions in leaded gasoline use that have occurred during this period (EPA 1985) correlate well with the sharply decreasing atmospheric lead concentrations. As of 1983, the mean lead level was about $3 \mu g/m^3$.

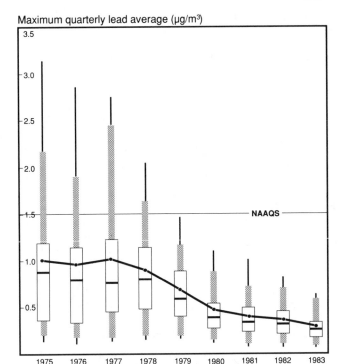

Figure 17.17 Boxplot comparisons of trends in maximum quarterly lead levels at 61 sites, 1975–1983. Source: EPA 1985.

Historical Air Chemistry: Global Scale, Stratosphere

Model calculations based on current knowledge of stratospheric photochemical processes estimate that only small changes in total stratospheric ozone should have occurred up to the present time. For the future, the calculated ozone changes depend strongly on emission scenarios for various gases, including the chlorofluorocarbons, methane, nitrous oxide, and carbon dioxide.

There are recent indications, however, that present calculations of ozone depletion are unreliable due to insufficient scientific knowledge. Totally unexpected, very large ozone depletions increasing to about 50% over the past decade have been observed above Antarctica during September and October of each year. The discovery of this "ozone hole" was made by researchers of the British Antarctic Survey (Farman, Gardiner, and Shanklin 1985; see Fig. 17.18). The major question at the moment concerns the cause of the ozone depletion. Some researchers had concentrated on atmospheric dynamics as the likely cause, perhaps as a result of slower poleward transport of air from lower latitudes or the development of an upward-moving circulation cell of tropospheric (ozone-poor) air. As a consequence of recent detailed observation in Antarctica, it is now clear, however, that the observed ozone depletions are caused by chemical reactions in which CFC-derived chlorine atoms and chlorine monoxide radicals play an essential role.

A sequence of chemical processes is responsible for the formation of the ozone hole. One important contributing factor (Crutzen and Arnold 1986; Toon et al. 1986) is that in the particularly cold lower stratosphere (with temperatures below about $-75°C$), most of the normally present oxides of nitrogen are frozen out, together with water vapor, forming

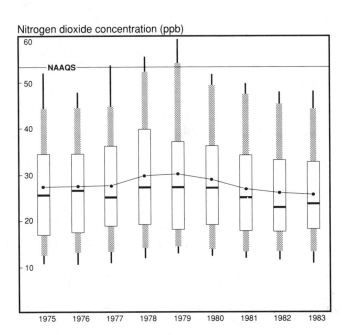

Figure 17.16 Boxplot comparisons of trends in annual mean nitrogen dioxide concentrations at 177 sites, 1975–1983. Source: EPA 1985.

Total ozone (matm cm)

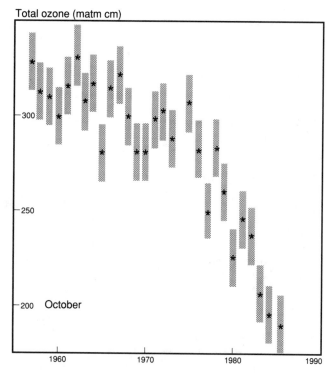

Figure 17.18 Monthly means of total ozone (represented by stars) at Halley Bay, Antarctica for October of the years 1957–1985. The vertical bars indicate one standard deviation in the data. Sources: Farman, Gardiner, and Shanklin 1985; Gardiner and Shanklin 1986. Data for 1986 and 1987 (not shown) follow the sharp downward trend of recent years, each year's values being lower than in any previous year.

trihydrate ($HNO_3 \cdot 3H_2O$) particles. The formation of particles in the lower stratosphere under cold conditions has indeed been observed regularly from satellites. These so-called polar stratospheric clouds were previously thought to consist mostly of pure ice particles.

The removal of the oxides of nitrogen from the gas phase in the cold lower stratosphere and chemical reactions on the particles (Molina et al. 1987; Tolbert et al. 1987) produce a tremendous activating effect on the chlorine chemistry, such that large amounts of ClO molecules are produced from HCl. This sets up a particularly important catalytic cycle, which destroys ozone:

$$ClO + ClO + M \rightarrow Cl_2O_2 + M \qquad (15)$$

$$Cl_2O_2 + h\nu \rightarrow 2Cl + O_2 \qquad (16)$$

$$2(Cl + O_3 \rightarrow ClO + O_2) \qquad (17)$$

$$\text{Net: } 2O_3 \rightarrow 3O_2$$

It currently seems likely that the input of long-lived CFC compounds can explain the observed rapid ozone depletions occurring in the Antarctic lower stratosphere during the Austral springtime. Because the stratospheric abundance of inorganic chlorine gases is increasing currently by about 5%/yr, it follows from the above chemical mechanisms (which depend on the square of the ClO concentration) that ozone destruction will accelerate further in the future.

Recent observations are in favor of the chemical theories

that are presented above. Unusually large reactive chlorine oxide (OClO) concentrations have been measured in the lower stratosphere during the recent measurements campaign in Antarctica (Solomon et al. 1987). It has also been observed that low temperatures are correlated with low concentrations of ozone, HCl, and nitric acid (HNO_3) concentrations, and with high ClO concentrations, in agreement with the proposed chemical mechanisms (Farmer et al. 1987).

The assessment of changes in the stratosphere is still at a preliminary stage. A recent evaluation of total ozone observations indicates that ozone depletion is also occurring at middle to high latitudes during the winter to early spring months in the Northern Hemisphere (Ozone Trends Panel 1988). Fortunately, the depletion in the Northern Hemisphere is about ten times smaller than that over Antarctica. The important realization, however, is that a very substantial change has occurred in the earth's atmospheric system in a very short time, that the change was not predicted, that its consequences are not yet fully understood, and that atmospheric scientists cannot exclude the possibility of other drastic changes taking place as humanity continues to place large stresses upon a poorly understood environmental system.

Interactions and Predictions

In addition to its intrinsic historical value, the information presented in the previous pages is of use in the definition and development of models designed to predict the atmospheres of the future. This chapter is not the place to describe in detail the results of such exercises. It is worth noting, however, that a shortcoming of many of them is that they have been excessively limited in scope. It has been common for a study to focus only on a narrowly defined spatial regime or on a restricted time scale. Still more limiting has been the tendency to assess impacts and sources of those impacts in isolation – stratospheric ozone this week, acid rain or forest decline next week, and so forth. Such an approach inevitably cannot select the proper solution, for the incredibly intertwined environmental system has a way of reflecting actions taken in one region or regime in different and unexpected ways elsewhere. The proper course – and one that is completely consistent with the goal of the present volume – is to consider simultaneously the impacts of a specific action on air, water, soil, climate, and so forth, so that decisions reflect as comprehensive a scope of assessment as possible. Such an approach will be difficult and has not yet been accomplished to any degree; a possible model is a study limited to atmospheric impacts, but broadly based within that scope restriction (Darmstadter et al. 1987; Graedel 1988).

Human activities do not only change the chemical composition of the global environment, but through the accumulation of several long-lived trace gases and their effect on the earth's thermal radiation budget, climate can also be affected, as discussed by Jäger and Barry (chap. 19). Currently several important greenhouse gases, including carbon dioxide, methane, and the chlorofluorocarbons, are increasing at significant-to-large rates. Only recently have we become aware of the fact that these greenhouse gases add as much warmth to the planetary system as carbon dioxide. However, within the next two decades, the expected temperature changes are so substantial (about 0.8°C in 20 years) that many scientists are now calling attention to this issue. The global environmental consequences include a sea-level rise of 0.2–0.4 m over the next century, together with important regional effects.

Due to the increasing atmospheric concentrations of the greenhouse gases, not only surface temperatures but also middle-atmospheric temperatures are expected to change. Especially in the stratosphere, the major changes that are envisaged to occur in the ozone distribution will lead to a substantial cooling (several tens of degrees) above about 30 km. At lower altitudes, the future situation is less predictable and is dependent on the detailed fate of ozone. The future constitution of the lower stratosphere may be of great importance, because of its controlling effect on the height of the tropopause (the troposphere-stratosphere boundary). The latter probably plays an important role in the radiation budget and dynamics of the troposphere (e.g., the intensity of convective storms). Another important feedback from the troposphere to the stratosphere may occur because tropopause temperatures, especially in the tropics, regulate the water-vapor content of the stratosphere. This in its turn may feed back on stratospheric chemistry and ozone and temperature distributions and dynamics in ways that currently are not understood and cannot be quantified due to lack of scientific knowledge.

Finally, it is important to realize that future climatic changes will almost certainly lead to changes – probably increases – in emissions of biogenic trace gases to the atmosphere. Of particular importance may be the high-latitude regions of the Northern Hemisphere, which are expected to experience the largest temperature increases of all the regions on the earth. Because much organic carbon is buried there in peat lands, tundra lands, and beneath permafrost, it will be of the greatest importance to follow what this can imply for future increases in the emissions, especially for such gases as carbon dioxide and methane (Carbon Dioxide Assessment Committee 1983).

Discussion and Summary

The data that have been presented in this paper demonstrate that preserved samples of ancient atmospheres and historical atmospheric measurements provide a surprisingly detailed picture of the concentrations and trends of a number of the atmosphere's trace constituents. On the global scale, and in some cases on smaller spatial scales, a typical trend is one of gradual concentration increases from the dates of the earliest reliable measurements until the present century. Within the past several decades, the rate of increase for many constituents has increased rapidly.

In contrast to this general pattern, examples have been shown of improvements in regional-scale air quality in response to significant changes in emission fluxes. A good example is the decrease in the levels of lead in atmospheric particulate matter in the United States as a result of the very large decrease in the use of leaded gasoline. In other cases, such as the decrease in U.S. sulfur dioxide levels produced by the use of fossil fuels with low sulfur content, the continuation of vigorous emission restrictions in the face of changing fuel supplies and prices may be difficult. In many areas throughout the world, the available economic resources may be insufficient to permit constraints to industry sufficient to maintain satisfactory atmospheric quality.

Although human action clearly is changing the chemistry of the atmosphere, that chemistry has always been subject to modification by the earth's biosphere, in ways only dimly appreciated at present. Strong interactions exist among the planet's plants and animals, its temperature, its cloudiness, and its trace atmospheric constituents (Lovelock 1979). It is important to make the point that modifications of the atmosphere as a result of human action may result in quite vigorous and unexpected responses on the part of the earth's plant life. The recent and dramatic decrease in ozone concentrations over the Antarctic during the Austral spring has demonstrated that the atmosphere can be extremely sensitive to what seem to be quite small perturbations and that the time scale for the manifestation of chemical changes in the atmosphere can be much more rapid than had been supposed. While good evidence exists that local air quality can be improved by strong action, the same may not be true of events on a global scale for which the scientific understanding is so much poorer and the time constants so much longer.

This somewhat discouraging picture can perhaps be balanced by the knowledge that many people and institutions are now aware that their actions concerning the atmosphere have consequences on a global as well as a local scale. The best evidence of this concern is the recent international agreement to control the release of the chlorofluorocarbons to 50% of current rates by the end of the century. Although not sufficient, this agreement marks the beginning of global political actions taken in favor of the environment. Discussions have begun as well on international agreements on the rates of release of other greenhouse-active trace gases, including CO_2, CH_4, and N_2O. With proper attention being given to the concerns about the atmosphere's stability, perhaps the chemical surprises that have already been seen and the new ones that will inevitably occur can be kept within sustainable limits.

References

Amoroso, G. G., and V. Fassina. 1983. *Stone Decay and Conservation.* Elsevier: Amsterdam.

Andrews, T. 1856. On the constitution and properties of ozone. *Phil. Trans. Roy. Soc.* 6: 1–13.

Barnola, J. M., D. Raynaud, Y. S. Korotkevich, and C. Lorius. 1987. Vostok ice core provides 160,000–year record of atmospheric CO_2. *Nature* 329: 408–14.

Bennett, B. G., J. G. Kretzschmar, G. G. Aklund, and H. W. deKoning. 1985. Urban air pollution worldwide. *Environ. Sci. Technol.* 19: 298–304.

Bingemer, H. G., and P. J. Crutzen. 1987. The production of methane from solid wastes. *J. Geophys. Res.* 92: 2181–87.

Blake, D. R., and F. S. Rowland. 1986. Worldwide increase in tropospheric methane, 1978–1983. *J. Atmos. Chem.* 4: 43–62.

Brimblecombe, P. 1977. London air pollution, 1500–1900. *Atmos. Environ.* 11: 1157–62.

Brimblecombe, P., and D. H. Stedman. 1982. Historical evidence for a dramatic increase in the nitrate component of acid rain. *Nature* 298: 460–62.

Carbon Dioxide Assessment Committee. 1983. *Changing Climate.* Washington, D.C.: National Academy Press.

Chapman, S. 1930. A theory of upper-atmospheric ozone. *Mem. Roy. Meteor. Soc.* 3: 103–25.

Crutzen, P. J. 1970. The influence of nitrogen oxides on the atmospheric ozone content. *Quart. J. Roy. Meteorol. Soc.* 96: 320–25.

———. 1973. A discussion of the chemistry of some minor constituents in the stratosphere and troposphere. *Pure Appl. Geophys.* 106–108: 1385–99.

———. 1987. The role of the tropics in atmospheric chemistry. In *Geophysiology in Amazonia*, ed. R. E. Dickinson, 107–30. Chichester–New York: Wiley.

Crutzen, P. J., and F. Arnold. 1986. Nitric acid cloud formation in the cold Antarctic stratosphere: a major cause for the springtime "ozone hole", *Nature* 324: 651–55.

Cunnold, D. M., R. G. Prinn, R. A. Rasmussen, P. G. Simmonds, F. N. Alyea, C. A. Cardelino, A. J. Crawford, P. J. Fraser, and R. D. Rosen. 1986. Atmospheric lifetime and annual release estimates for $CFCl_3$ and CF_2Cl_2 from five years of ALE data. *J. Geophys. Res.* 91: 10797–817.

Darmstadter, J., L. W. Ayres, R. U. Ayres, W. C. Clark, P. Crosson, P. J. Crutzen, T. E. Graedel, R. McGill, J. F. Richards, and J. A. Tarr. 1987. *Impacts of World Development on Selected Characteristics of the Atmosphere: An Integrative Approach.* Washington, D.C.: Resources for the Future.

De Angelis, M., N. I. Barkov, and V. N. Petrov. 1987. Aerosol concentrations over the last climatic cycle (160 kyr) from an Antarctic ice core. *Nature* 325: 318–21.

de Zafra, R. L., M. Jaramillo, A. Parrish, P. Solomon, B. Connor, and J. Burnett. 1987. Observations of abnormally high concentrations of chlorine monoxide at low altitudes in the Antarctic spring atmosphere. I. Diurnal variations. *Nature* 328: 408–10.

Dianov-Klokov, V. I., and L. N. Yurganov. 1981. A spectroscopic study of the global space-time distribution of atmospheric CO. *Tellus* 33: 262–73.

Environmental Protection Agency. 1978. *Air Quality Criteria for Ozone and Other Photochemical Oxidants.* Report EPA-600/8-78-004. Washington, D.C.

———. 1985. *National Air Quality and Emission Trends Report, 1983.* Report EPA-450/4-84-029. Research Triangle Park, NC.

Farman, J. C., B. G. Gardiner, and J. D. Shanklin. 1985. Large losses of total ozone in Antarctica reveal seasonal ClO_x/NO_x interaction. *Nature* 315: 207–10.

Farmer, C. B., G. C. Toon, P. W. Shaper, J.-F. Blavier, and L. L. Lowes. 1987. Ground-based measurements of the Antarctic atmosphere during the 1986 spring season. I. Stratospheric trace gases. *Nature* 329: 126–30.

Fay, J. A., D. Golomb, and S. Kumar. 1986. Modeling of the 1900–1980 trend of precipitation acidity at Hubbard Brook, New Hampshire. *Atmos. Environ.* 20: 1825–28.

Franey, J. P., G. W. Kammlott, and T. E. Graedel. 1985. The corrosion of silver by atmospheric sulfurous gases. *Corros. Sci.* 25: 133–43.

Gardiner, B. G., and J. D. Shanklin. 1986. Recent measurements of Antarctic ozone depletion. *Geophys. Res. Lett.* 13: 1199–1201.

Goetz, F. W. P., A. R. Meetham, and G. M. B. Dobson. 1934. The vertical distribution of ozone in the atmosphere. *Proc. Roy. Soc. (London)* A145: 416–46.

Graedel, T. E. 1987. Copper patinas formed in the atmosphere. III. A semiquantitative assessment of rates and constraints in the greater New York metropolitan area. *Corros. Sci.* 27: 741–69.

———. 1988. Regional environmental forces: a paradigm for assessment and prediction. In *Energy: Production, Consumption, and Consequences.* Washington, D.C.: National Academy Press.

Graedel, T. E., and J. E. McRae. 1980. On the possible increase of the atmospheric methane and carbon monoxide concentrations during the last decade. *Geophys. Res. Lett.* 7: 977–79.

Graedel, T. E., D. T. Hawkins, and L. D. Claxton. 1986. *Atmospheric Chemical Compounds: Sources, Occurrence, and Bioassay.* Orlando, FL: Academic Press.

Haagen-Smit, A. J. 1952. Chemistry and physiology of Los Angeles smog. *Ind. Eng. Chem.* 44: 1342.

Haagen-Smit, A. J., and M. M. Fox. 1956. Ozone formation in photochemical oxidation of organic substances. *Ind. Eng. Chem.* 48: 1484.

Hammer, C. U., H. B. Clausen, and W. Dansgaard. 1980. Greenland ice sheet evidence of postglacial volcanism and its climatic impact. *Nature* 288: 230–35.

Husar, R., and D. Patterson. 1985. *SO₂ Concentration Estimates for New York City, 1880–1980.* Final Contract Report 68-02-3746, Ctr. for Air Pollution Impact and Trend Analysis, Washington University. St. Louis, MO.

Husar, R. B., J. M. Holloway, D. E. Patterson, and W. E. Wilson. 1981. Spatial and temporal pattern of eastern U.S. haziness: A summary. *Atmos. Environ.* 15: 1919–28.

Khalil, M. A. K., and R. A. Rasmussen. 1984. Carbon monoxide in the earth's atmosphere: increasing trend. *Science* 224: 54–56.

Kuntasal, G., and T. Y. Chang. 1987. Trends and relationships of O_3, NO_x and HC in the South Coast Air Basin of California. *J. Air Pollut. Contr. Assoc.* 37: 1158–63.

Levy, A. 1907. Analyse de l'air atmosphérique-ozone. *Ann. d'Observatoire Municipal de Montsouris* 8: 141–43.

Levy, H., II. 1971. Normal atmosphere: Large radical and formaldehyde concentrations predicted. *Science* 173: 141–43.

———. 1972. Photochemistry of the lower troposphere. *Planet. Space Sci.* 20: 919–35.

Lovelock, J. E. 1979. *Gaia: A New Look at Life on Earth.* Oxford and New York: Oxford University Press.

Mayewski, P. A., W. B. Lyons, M. J. Spencer, M. Twickler, W. Dansgaard, B. Koci, C. I. Davidson, and R. E. Honrath. 1986. Sulfate and nitrate concentrations from a south Greenland ice core. *Science* 232: 975–77.

McConnell, J. C., M. B. McElroy, and S. C. Wofsy. 1971. Natural sources of atmospheric CO. *Nature* 233: 187–88.

Merz, P. H., L. J. Painter, and P. R. Ryason. 1972. Aerometric data analysis – Time series analysis and forecast and an atmospheric smog diagram. *Atmos. Environ.* 6: 319–42.

Molina M. J., T.-L. Tso, L. T. Molina, and F. C.-Y. Wang. 1987. Antarctic stratospheric chemistry of chlorine nitrate, hydrogen chloride, and ice: release of active chlorine. *Science* 238: 1253–57.

National Research Council. 1986. *Acid Deposition: Long-Term Trends.* Washington, D.C.: National Academy Press.

Neftel, A., E. Moor, H. Oeschger, and B. Stauffer. 1985. Evidence from polar ice cores for the increase in atmospheric CO_2 in the past two centuries. *Nature* 315: 45–47.

Ng, A., and C. Patterson. 1981. Natural concentrations of lead in ancient Arctic and Antarctic ice. *Geochim. Cosmochim. Acta* 45: 2109–21.

Ozone Trends Panel. 1988. *Trends in Atmospheric Ozone.* Washington, D.C.: National Academy of Sciences. (In preparation.)

Pearman, G. I., D. Etheridge, F. de Silva, and P. J. Fraser. 1986. Evidence of changing concentrations of atmospheric CO_2, N_2O, and CH_4 from air bubbles in Antarctic ice. *Nature* 320: 248–50.

Prinn, R. G., R. A. Rasmussen, P. G. Simmonds, F. N. Alyea, D. M. Cunnold, B. C. Lane, C. A. Cardelino, and A. J. Crawford. 1983. The atmospheric lifetime experiment. 5. Results for CH_3CCl_3 based on three years of data. *J. Geophys. Res.* 88: 8415–26.

Ramanathan, V., R. J. Cicerone, H. B. Singh, and J. T. Kiehl. 1985. Trace gas trends and their potential role in climate change. *J. Geophys. Res.* 90: 5547–66.

Rasmussen, R. A., and M. A. K. Khalil. 1984. Atmospheric methane in the recent and ancient atmospheres: concentrations, trends, and interhemispheric gradient. *J. Geophys. Res.* 89: 11599–605.

Regener, E., and V. H. Regener. 1934. Aufnahmen des ultravioletten Sonnenspektrums in der Stratosphare und vertikale Ozonverteilung. *Phys. Z.* 35: 788–93.

Reich, P. B., and R. G. Amundson. 1985. Ambient levels of ozone reduce net photosynthesis in tree and crop species. *Science* 230: 566–70.

Reichle, H. G., Jr., S. M. Beck, R. E. Haynes, W. D. Hesketh, J. A. Holland, W. D. Hypes, H. D. Orr III, R. T. Sherill, H. A. Wallio, J. C. Casas, M. S. Saylor, and B. B. Gormsen. 1982. Carbon monoxide measurements in the troposphere. *Science* 218: 1024–26.

Rinsland, C. P., and J. S. Levine. 1985. Free tropospheric carbon monoxide concentrations in 1950 and 1951 deduced from infrared total column amount measurements. *Nature* 318: 250–54.

Schoenbein, Ch.F. 1845. Einige Bemerkungen uber die Anwesenheit des Ozons in der atmospharischen Luft und die Rolle welche dieser bei langsamen Oxydationen spielen durfte. *Ann. Phys. Chim. (Poggendorf)* 65: 161–72.

Solomon, S., G. H. Mount, R. W. Sanders, and A. L. Schmeltekopf. 1987. Visible spectroscopy at McMurdo Station, Antarctica. 2. Observations of OClO. *J. Geophys. Res.* 92: 8329–38.

Stauffer, B., G. Fischer, A. Neftel, and H. Oeschger. 1985. Increase of atmospheric methane recorded in Antarctic ice core. *Science* 229: 1386–88.

Strutt, R. J. 1918. Ultraviolet transparency of the lower atmosphere and its relative poverty in ozone. *Proc Roy. Soc. (London)* A94: 260–68.

Tolbert, M. A., M. J. Rossi, R. Malhotra, and D. M. Golden. 1987. Reaction of chlorine nitrate with hydrogen chloride and water at Antarctic stratospheric temperatures. *Science* 238: 1258–60.

Tonneijck, A. E. G. 1986. Effecten van ozon op vegetatie, paper presented at Proc. Symp. Ozon: Fysische en Chemische Veranderingen in de Atmosfeer en de Gevolgen, Ede, Netherlands, Nov. 13–14.

Toon, O. B., P. Hamill, R. P. Turco, and J. Pinto. 1986. Condensation of HNO₃ and HCl in the winter polar stratosphere. *Geophys. Res. Lett.* 13: 1284–87.

Trijonis, J., T. Peng, G. McRae, and L. Lees. 1978. Oxidant and precursor trends in the metropolitan Los Angeles region. *Atmos. Environ.* 12: 1413–20.

Volz, A., and D. Kley. 1988. Evaluation of the Montsouris series of ozone measurements made in the nineteenth century. *Nature* 332: 240–42.

Weiss, R. W. 1981. The temporal and spatial distribution of tropospheric nitrous oxide. *J. Geophys. Res.* 86: 7185–95.

Wofsy, S. C., J. C. McConnell, and M. B. McEiroy. 1972. Atmospheric CH₄, CO, and CO₂. *J. Geophys. Res.* 77: 4477–93.

World Meteorological Organization. 1985. *Atmospheric Ozone 1985.* Global Ozone Research and Monitoring Project–Report No. 16, Vol. 1.

Yocom, J. E., and R. O. McCaldin. 1968. Effects of air pollution on materials and the economy. In *Air Pollution*, ed. A. C. Stern. 2d ed., Vol. I, 617–54. New York: Academic Press.

18

Marine Environment

TIMOTHY D. JICKELLS   ROY CARPENTER   PETER S. LISS

When nonspecialists consider human-made changes in ocean chemistry, two apparently contradictory thoughts may cross their minds. The first is the observation of ocean explorers, such as Thor Heyerdahl, of lumps of tar, flotsam and jetsam, and other products of human society thousands of kilometers from inhabited land. An alternative, vaguer feeling is that given the vastness of the oceans (more than 1,000 billion billion liters of water!), how can man have significantly polluted them? It is the statement and evaluation of this conundrum in scientific terms that is, in essence, the aim of this chapter. We will not make any judgment of the significance to present and future societies of confirmed changes in ocean chemical composition. Our goal is to establish to what extent such changes have occurred and, if so, for which substances and in which parts of the system. We will also consider whether or not recent efforts to reduce human discharges of potentially harmful chemicals are having the desired reductions in concentrations.

The approach we will adopt is to evaluate possible chemical changes in seawater composition, due to changing inputs of a few types or classes of chemicals. This means that changes in physical, biological, and geological processes will not be covered explicitly. They certainly cannot be ignored, however, since the redistribution of chemical inputs around and within the system involves physical mixing processes, interactions with sediments, and biological transformations. The last can involve uptake of dissolved substances in surface waters by plankton, which, at the end of their lifecycle, will die and sink rather rapidly into the deeper parts of the water column, or breakdown/degradation of the substances themselves by organisms.

The chemicals to be examined in the chapter are examples of (1) those that were essentially absent from the system before human beings started to influence it and (2) natural substances whose rate of cycling through the oceans has been enhanced by anthropogenic activities. Histories of the human use of many of these chemicals are provided elsewhere in the chapters on carbon, sulfur, nitrogen, trace pollutants, and ionizing radiation. Synthetic organic chemicals that we will look at include the polychlorinated biphenyls (PCBs) (a widely used class of industrial chemicals), the pesticide DDT and other agricultural chemicals, and the chlorofluorocarbon group of compounds used as aerosol propellants and refrigerants. Polycyclic aromatic hydrocarbons (PAHs) are a range of compounds examined here that arise from incomplete combustion processes. They arise not only from human activities but also by the natural process of burning of forest and scrub. We shall consider hydrocarbons from oil that enter the marine environment from natural seeps as well as shipping and other anthropogenic activities. Another natural chemical whose input to the oceans has been enhanced by humans is carbon dioxide, but it is discussed in (chap. 23). Most of the radionuclides we examine are mostly anthropogenic, with the exception of carbon-14, whose oceanic inventory humans have managed to increase by only a few percent. We also look at human-made litter found at sea.

Two further classes of substances discussed in the chapter are trace metals, which, as their name implies, exist at low concentrations in seawater; and the plant-nutrient elements phosphorus, nitrogen, and silicon. Both classes are natural, but have had their rates of input increased by humans – in the case of trace metals, by various industrial and automotive activities; and for the nutrients, by inflow of agricultural fertilizers, detergents, and sewage.

Probably the most important reason for selecting these substances for study was the availability of data on their ocean concentrations and how they may have changed in the recent past. We also chose chemicals that had low or zero concentrations in seawater before major industrialization occurred, in the hope that increments due to human activities would be more readily discernible. Further, many of the substances considered here are biologically important, so that any major increase in their concentrations in the oceans might have a potentially deleterious effect on marine life.

The chapter is structured in the following way. The next section briefly discusses how human-made or human-influenced chemicals reach the oceans and react therein. Then follows a description of the methodology of how recent temporal changes in seawater composition may be identified. After this follow three major sections, in which the behavior of some or all of the substances identified earlier are described in three marine environments taken as examples. They are (1) the open oceans, (2) the coastal seas of northwestern Europe, and (3) the coastal seas of the Pacific Northwest of the United States. The latter two areas were selected in part for the intensity with which they have been studied, but also because they have different hydrography and patterns of human settlement and development. The chapter finishes with some thoughts on the present and likely future chemical state of the marine environment.

Sources, Sinks and Internal Processing of Chemicals in the Oceans

The main input routes for chemicals entering the oceans are rivers, the atmosphere, submarine volcanic activity, glaciers, and finally direct dumping by humans. In this chapter, concerned with human-induced changes, we will ignore submarine volcanic inputs and glacial inputs, since humans have not yet managed to alter significantly the chemistry of these sources.

Rivers are an important conduit for the transport of both natural and human-made chemicals to the oceans. In pristine conditions, dissolved and particulate loads of rivers are determined by the rates at which weathering and erosional processes operate. Human activities have increased these rates in some areas, leading to increased amounts of natural products being carried seaward. These processes of increased erosion are discussed in chap. 13. In addition, industrial, urban, and agricultural developments bring some new synthetic chemicals into rivers and lakes.

Estimation of the fraction of this riverborne material that actually enters the oceans is remarkably difficult. First, individual rivers show wide variations in flow and chemical composition day to day as well as seasonally. Second, differences in dissolved and particulate loads between rivers from different areas are large. However, given sufficient observations, it is possible to make some tentative estimates of the total global seaward flux of some substances in rivers (UNESCO 1987). Third, before entering the open oceans, the substances first must pass through estuarine and coastal zones, which are often effective at trapping riverine particulate material, at least in the short term, and are also sites at which dissolved and solid phases can interact strongly. Such processes substantially decrease the reliability of estimated inputs of riverborne materials to the oceans.

Terrestrial material entering the oceans by the atmospheric route can be in the form of a gas or solid particulate material (together called dry deposition); alternatively, it can be as dissolved or particulate matter in rain (wet deposition). The material will be both natural and from human-made or human-enhanced sources. Until recently, less attention has been paid to estimating atmospheric inputs to the oceans than those from rivers. This is because of the difficulty of measuring atmospheric deposition to the oceans and then correcting this for material recycled from the oceans to the atmosphere and then deposited. Recently, sufficient data have become available to allow preliminary estimates of the relative importance of riverine and atmospheric inputs to the ocean (GESAMP 1989).

The general pattern that emerges is that riverine inputs tend to be the dominant source in inshore waters close to estuaries. The further out into the open oceans one goes, the greater the significance of the atmospheric route.

The final important source of materials to the marine environment is deliberate dumping of industrial and urban wastes. Although in the past, some limited dumping has been done in the open oceans, it now is regulated by international convention. Most current sea dumping is in coastal waters, which are subject to national or regional jurisdiction. Since emplacement is purposeful in terms of both location and type of material dumped, estimation of this source of marine pollution is significantly easier than for the river and atmospheric routes discussed earlier.

The ultimate sink for all material entering the marine environment from any of the routes described is coastal, shelf, and oceanic sediments, at least on the time scale of hundreds of years with which this book is concerned. Quantification of the sedimentary sink at any location can in principle be done by the chemical analysis of sediment cores as a function of depth (time) down the core. In the next section, we point out some limitations of this approach.

After chemicals arrive in the oceans, irrespective of their route of entry, they are subject to mixing processes and to chemical and biological transformations. For coastal inputs, the mixing will be both longshore and offshore under the action of waves, tides, and currents. The degree of vertical stratification of the water will determine the depth to which the coastal inputs are mixed. Quite often the degree of tidal stirring is sufficient to ensure rapid (a matter of days) mixing right to the bottom. By contrast, in many open-ocean situations, a strong pycnocline (rapid increase in density at one to several hundred meters depth) greatly inhibits vertical mixing, so that material entering tends to spread horizontally much more readily than it can mix vertically across the pycnocline, although the time scales of even this mixing are still decades. Exceptions are the limited areas at high latitudes in the North Atlantic Ocean and around Antarctica, where surface water sinks to great depths, forming the bottom waters of the oceans. In these cases, pollutants can bypass the pycnocline barrier and directly enter the deep circulation in a matter of a few years.

In addition to vertical and horizontal mixing, chemical and especially biological processes can greatly enhance the rate at which material is circulated within the oceans, and in particular the speed at which it can be carried from surface water to the sediments. For example, phytoplankton growing in the surface oceans take up a variety of dissolved species (for example, plant-nutrient elements and trace metals) and incorporate them into their structure. When they die, the phytoplankton are no longer buoyant, and sink out of the surface layers and into the deep water. This sinking debris can also adsorb chemicals from the seawater. The filter-feeding activities of zooplankton tend to aggregate smaller food particles into larger ones, which when voided as faecal matter, sink much more rapidly into deeper waters. This sinking of biogenic particles (which may also include inorganic solids held together in an organic matrix) is a much more rapid means by which material can reach the deep sea than by water movements. For example, such particles can reach the seabed in months to years, whereas the circulation time for surface water and its dissolved constituents to reach the abyss is much longer – of the order of tens to hundreds of years. Further, being particulate, the biogenic remains will readily sediment and become part of the very long-term sedimentary reservoir. It should be noted that only a small fraction of the material removed from the surface water by organisms actually reaches the bottom and sediments out; much of it dissolves and returns to the water during its passage downward.

Chemicals that are very reactive and are thus quickly removed to the sediments have short residence times (Broecker and Peng 1982) in the oceans ($<10^3$ yr), in contrast to unreactive ones, whose calculated residence times can be up to tens of millions of years.

The key point is that oceanic chemical distributions are the result of a complex set of interactions of chemical, biological, geological, and physical processes, with a variety of feedback loops. These interactions cause natural variations in chemical concentrations in time and space, which can be hard to separate from human-induced changes in inputs. For further information on the relevant aspects of marine chemistry, refer to the textbooks by Broecker and Peng (1982) and Riley and Chester (1971).

Methods for Determining Changes in Ocean-Water Chemistry over Hundreds of Years

Direct Determination of Temporal Changes in Ocean-Water Samples

Concentrations of trace chemicals in seawater can be highly variable in both space and time, making it hard to obtain truly representative samples of ocean-water-column chemical composition. For example, pronounced changes in trace-chemical concentrations occur due to seasonal changes in most coastal zones. Such seasonal changes, plus longer-period changes due to natural fluctuations, such as El Niño conditions in the equatorial Pacific, and the nonsteady-state nature of oceanographic processes, will always make it hard to separate the natural and the anthropogenic components of any changes noted in ocean-water composition. Furthermore, a lack of reliable data sets spanning more than a few tens of years hinders attempts to describe temporal changes in ocean chemistry.

Data on dissolved water-column concentrations of "reactive phosphate" (P) and oxygen (O_2) go back to the late 1920s, and in some cases even earlier – much further than for other chemicals. This is because reasonably reliable methods for their analyses were available then and because problems of contamination during collection and analysis are less severe than for most trace chemicals. Most data for combined nitrogen (N) until the mid-1970s accounted for only nitrate plus nitrite. Only since then have reliable techniques been developed to measure the low concentrations of ammonia, urea, amino acids, and other reduced nitrogen compounds. Dissolved silicate (Si) measurements have been possible for some decades, but silica is of lesser concern since it rarely limits plankton growth in the sea and is not much mobilized by man.

The effects of inputs of trace metals on seawater chemistry have been the subject of extensive recent study. Prior to 1970, deficiencies in analytical facilities and inadequate control of contamination during sampling and analysis at the very low trace-metal concentrations (10^{-6} to 10^{-9} g/l) found in the oceans led to reporting of trace-metal data that now appear to overestimate true values. Recent reviews of trace metals in ocean waters are available in the following references: Bruland 1983; Burton and Statham 1982; Salomons and Forstner 1984; Wong et al. 1983.

It is now apparent that many trace elements are involved in the biological cycling of material in the oceans. For example, cadmium and zinc have oceanic profiles that co-vary with phosphate and silicate, respectively, suggesting biological cycling of these elements and resulting in differences in concentration between various oceans. This rapid biological removal results in very low concentrations of these elements in, and very rapid removal from, surface ocean waters, making it very difficult to detect any anthropogenic impact on surface concentrations. In deep ocean waters, the relatively large reservoirs of these elements serve to mask any increases in concentration that may have occurred over the past 100 or so years as a result of increases in inputs. Thus for all elements for which biological cycling has been suggested to be important (including nickel, copper, zinc, arsenic, selenium, silver, cadmium, antimony, as well as nitrogen, phosphorus, and silicon), direct measurements of seawater concentrations are of limited value in describing human effects on the oceans.

Analytical sensitivity for measurement of chlorinated hydrocarbons in environmental samples became adequate only during the 1970s. Unlike the naturally occurring trace metals, in the absence of contamination during collection or other analytical errors, there should be no background concentrations of synthetic chlorinated hydrocarbons in samples prior to their large-scale commercial production around 1940.

In summary, our ability to collect and reliably determine trace chemicals in seawater samples without contaminating the sample during collection, storage, and workup has improved greatly over the past two decades. Thus reliable time series of dissolved constituents other than nutrients and oxygen do not go back farther in time than 1970. Our skills at detecting trace amounts of chemicals in seawater are now far ahead of our ability to determine whether or not the minute concentrations actually are available to marine organisms or are having any harmful effects on them.

Analyses of Materials that May Record Prior Changes in Ocean Chemistry

Biological Materials. Scleractinian corals are the dominant reef-building corals, which grow in shallow depths in warm waters bounded roughly by 30°N and 30°S latitudes. They have 2-to-15-mm-wide annual growth bands, which are often sufficiently regular to allow precise dating by just counting the number of bands inward from the surface. Concentrations of several trace elements in the bands are proportional to concentrations in waters in which the coral grew, so analyses of the bands can allow determination of changes in ocean-water chemistry during recent decades for several chemicals, such as lead, cadmium, plutonium and [14]C (Druffel 1981; Shen and Boyle 1987; Shen, Boyle, and Lea et al. 1987).

Bivalve molluscs, such as mussels and oysters, are found around most coasts of the world. These filter-feeding organisms live 2 to 4 years, and concentrations of contaminants in their tissues reflect a short-term balance between uptake of both dissolved and particulate substances and excretion, or breakdown, rates. Molluscs accumulate a number of heavy metals, transuranic radionuclides, petroleum hydrocarbons, and synthetic chlorinated hydrocarbons to several orders of magnitude higher concentrations than in the surrounding waters. They thus provide a large initial concentration step, which allows scientists to circumvent the need to sample large volumes of seawater without contamination. Molluscs also have little or no capability to degrade most of the potentially harmful organic compounds.

For these reasons, molluscs were proposed as sentinel organisms to monitor temporal and spatial changes in contaminant concentrations in coastal zones. The U.S. National Mussel Watch Program began in 1976 (Goldberg et al. 1983). It includes yearly sampling of molluscs from over 60 sites around the U.S. coast. Results of the first three years of data have been summarized (Farrington et al. 1983b). Broman and Ganning (1985) used *Mytilus edulis* and *Macoma baltica* to monitor diffuse oil pollution in the northern Baltic.

Sedimentary Phases.   Determinations of vertical-concentration profiles of chemical contaminants in dated sediment horizons have been used widely to try to reconstruct the extent of past changes in chemical composition of ocean waters. Concentrations on sediment particles are expected to be roughly proportional to concentrations in waters from which they accumulated. One obtains from sediment profiles not absolute concentrations, but a sense of when and by roughly how much water concentrations might have changed. The time frame often is based on measurements of the natural radionuclide ^{210}Pb, although this approach has its limitation (Carpenter, Peterson, and Bennett 1985).

The approach works best for fine-grained, coastal anoxic sediments that accumulate at rates of several millimeters per year. Fig. 18.1 shows in such cases how the history of lead discharges to the Mississippi estuary has been preserved in sediments.

Even when cores of fine-grained materials can be properly collected and dated, interpretation of profiles in sediment chemical concentrations in terms of changes in chemistry of overlying waters is complicated by several factors. The natural background concentrations of certain metals like copper in detrital aluminosilicate phases that dominate coastal sediments tend to mask changes in metal inputs from overlying waters. Some metals may dissolve at depth in sediments due to changes in pH and redox potential caused by organic matter decomposition, and they may migrate vertically from the layer in which they were deposited. Decreases with depth in concentrations of certain organic contaminants may indicate destruction of the organics rather than indicate changes with time in concentrations arriving at the sediment-water interface.

Finally, determination of temporal changes in contaminants in surface coastal sediments by analyses of sediments collected sequentially over a several-year period is limited by the mixing of surface sediments by the activities of benthic organisms, tides, currents, and storms. We can use cores to look at changes over the past few hundred years with temporal resolutions of a few years, but as we go further back in time, the temporal resolution becomes hundreds, thousands, and ultimately millions of years.

Analysis of Archived Samples
Collections of seawaters, organisms, and sediments began in earnest with the *HMS Challenger* cruise from 1872 to 1876 to the Atlantic, Pacific, and Southern oceans. Since then, oceanographic institutions and museums have collected and archived large numbers of samples. Unfortunately, prior to the 1970s, the specimens were not collected and preserved using the clean techniques now recognized as mandatory to avoid chemical contamination during sampling, or gain or loss during subsequent storage.

Conclusion
Thus while several methods are available to determine changes in ocean chemistry, all have drawbacks, and it is often necessary to apply several to reach unambiguous conclusions.

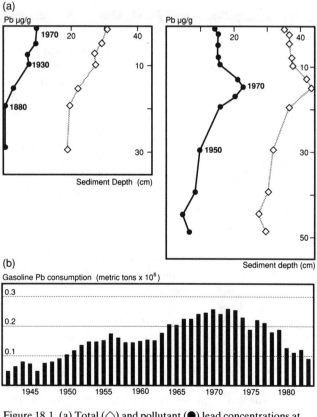

Figure 18.1 (a) Total ($\diamond$) and pollutant ($\bullet$) lead concentrations at various depths in sediment cores off the Mississippi River estuary. Estimated dates of deposition are marked. (b) Annual consumption of lead in gasoline additives in the United States. Source: Trefry et al. 1985.

Changes in Open-Ocean Composition

The oceans cover more than 70% of the globe, but because human beings can live only on the fringes or sail briefly over them, human impact is limited compared to that on terrestrial environments. Furthermore, the size of the open oceans gives them an enormous dilution capacity. Humankind has had a significant effect, however, on the oceanic distribution of some substances, particularly in the North Atlantic (Farrington, Vandermeulan, and Cook 1983a), and we shall focus on them here. These changes affect three groups of chemicals. The first are those that are entirely (or overwhelmingly) human-made, such as synthetic organic chemicals and artificial radionuclides. The very existence of most of these substances in the oceans is evidence of human impact. Second, some contaminants float and hence are not diluted in the conventional fashion, such as litter and tar balls. Finally, a group of contaminants exists for which human impact is so large relative to natural inputs and that have sufficiently short oceanic residence times that an effect can be seen. Lead is the best example of this group.

Synthetic Organic Contaminants

High-molecular-weight halocarbons include such human-made persistent and toxic groups of chemicals as the DDT pesticides and polychlorinated biphenyl (PCB) compounds, which have been used widely in a series of industrial applications (Tanabe 1988; chap. 26). These compounds can be concentrated in fats and along food chains, thus posing a particular threat to top predators with large fat reserves, such as marine mammals.

Both groups of compounds were first produced commercially in the period 1920–1940, with production increasing to the late 1960s. The realization of the toxicity of these compounds then led to a rapid decline in production and usage. Since the sources to the environment of these volatile compounds were atmospheric (spraying of the pesticides, incineration of the PCBs), it is reasonable to surmise that they reached the oceans soon after, and in amounts approximately proportional to, their production. The efficiency of atmospheric transport has led to the worldwide contamination of the oceans with these substances. Concentrations in mid-northern latitudes are several times those in the Southern Hemisphere, because of proximity to source regions and the latitudinal patterns of winds (Atlas and Giam 1986), as illustrated by the distribution of these compounds in seals from various locations (Fig. 18.2, and Clurg 1984).

Following measures to reduce the discharge of these compounds to the environment, declines in concentrations have been reported. Burns, Villeneuve, and Fowler (1985) demonstrated a three- to fourteenfold decline in PCB concentrations in several marine environmental compartments in the Mediterranean over a five-year period. A likely explanation for such rapid rates of decline is rapid transport to the deep sea in faecal pellets (Knap, Binkley, and Deuser 1986). Addison et al. (1984) reported a two- to fivefold decline in DDT residues in seals from Nova Scotia, and Falandysz and Szefer (1984) also reported relatively rapid declines in DDT levels in marine birds in the Baltic. Both groups reported less

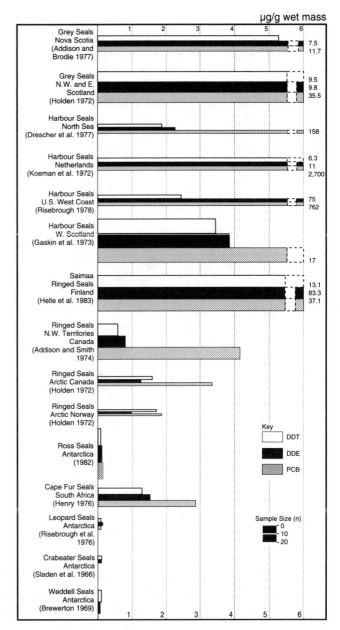

Figure 18.2 A comparison of some chlorinated hydrocarbon concentrations in seal blubber from various locations. Bar width denotes sample size. Adapted from Clurg 1984.

rapid declines in PCB concentrations, probably reflecting continued diffuse inputs of the compounds (Tanabe 1988). In general, PCB and DDT concentrations in tissues (Fig. 18.2) are comparable. Total DDT production was greater than PCB production, and environmental discharges of DDT were probably greater because DDT was discharged directly to the environment by spraying. Thus comparable DDT and PCB concentrations in biota must reflect the slower environment degradation and greater biotic uptake of PCBs. Within the marine environment, the coastal sediments may continue to act as a source of these compounds to benthic organisms for many years (Young, McDermott-Ehrlich, and Heesen 1977; Smokler, Young, and Gard 1979; Tanabe 1988).

Low-molecular-weight chlorofluorocarbons (CFCs) appear to pose no threat to the marine environment, in contrast to their effect on stratospheric ozone. However, they do provide another unique tracer of human impact on the oceans. Because they enter the oceans via gas exchange and then remain dissolved in ocean waters, their oceanic distribution is different from that of the high-molecular-weight halocarbons, which are more particle-reactive. Passage of the low-molecular-weight halocarbons into the deep ocean is slower and governed by rates of water mass mixing. By 1981, these compounds had penetrated the interior of the North Atlantic Ocean (Weiss et al. 1985).

Artificial Radionuclides

Several long-lived radionuclides were introduced into the oceans by the atmospheric testing of atomic weapons in the 1950s and 1960s (see chap. 27). Of particular interest are the isotopes of hydrogen (tritium), with a half life ($t_{1/2}$) of 12.3 years, cesium (^{137}Cs, $t_{1/2}33y$), carbon (^{14}C, $t_{1/2}5650y$), strontium (^{90}Sr, $t_{1/2}28y$), and plutonium (^{239}Pu, $t_{1/2}24,100y$; ^{240}Pu, $t_{1/2}6,580y$). Additional ^{137}Cs has reached the oceans via discharges from the Windscale Reprocessing Plant (see later) and the accident at the Chernobyl nuclear reactor. Except for ^{14}C, the human-made emissions of these nuclides greatly exceed any natural background. For ^{14}C bomb nuclides, only in surface waters is there a significant enhancement of activity over natural levels (Fig. 18.3).

The atmospheric testing of nuclear weapons and the subsequent injection of radionuclides to the upper atmosphere resulted in widespread dispersion of the nuclides across the globe, and very good records of the fallout of several isotopes are available (Fig. 18.4). For several of these isotopes the historic pattern of concentrations in surface ocean waters is preserved in coral skeletons (Fig. 18.4). The records preserved in the coral skeletons broadly reproduce the deposition history. However, the record is smoothed somewhat by mixing with deep water, which reduces the peaks and continues the signal after the cessation of testing. Radionuclides such as tritium and ^{137}Cs dissolve in seawater and are subsequently rather unreactive. They therefore enter the deep oceans in association with mixing of water masses and, like the CFCs,

are only slowly transported to the ocean interior (Fig. 18.5). By contrast, ^{14}C, ^{90}Sr, and Pu isotopes become involved in biogeochemical cycles and are rapidly transported to the ocean interior (e.g., Bowen et al. 1980).

The accident at the Chernobyl nuclear power plant in April 1986 released a substantial quantity of radioactive material into the environment. Because of the lower temperatures involved in the emissions, the majority of the deposition occurred over Europe, and global dispersion was much less efficient than for the bomb-testing nuclides. All the studies in the Mediterranean, Black, and North seas indicated rapid transport of particle-reactive radionuclides (e.g., cerium and ruthenium) through the upper ocean, while isotopes with a low particle reactivity (e.g., cesium) remained in surface waters (Buesseler et al. 1987; Fowler et al. 1987; Kempe and Nies 1987; Kempe et al. 1987).

Tar Balls and Litter

Tar balls range in size from millimeters to many centimeters. They have been reported on beaches since the 1930s, but the writing of Thor Heyerdahl drew particular attention to the problem of tar and litter on the oceans (Butler 1975; Jeffrey 1980). Any oil discharged at sea can produce tar by a process of evaporation of all the volatile compounds, but the major source is believed to be chronic discharges of ballast water from ships (Butler 1975; Jeffrey 1980; NAS 1985; Payne and Phillips 1985). Thus, it seems likely that tar pollution began in the 1920s, as large-scale transport of oil began.

The biological effects of tar pollution are uncertain, though the encrustation of tar balls with organisms suggests that tar is not particularly toxic, as might be expected, since the most toxic volatile fraction of oil is lost prior to tar-ball formation. Tar has been found in fish stomachs (Horn, Teal, and Backus 1970) and throughout the free-floating oceanic *Sargassum* community (Morris et al. 1976b).

Estimation of the concentration of tar on the oceans is complicated by difficulties of sampling the patchy distribution, which arises from small-scale, ocean-circulation patterns

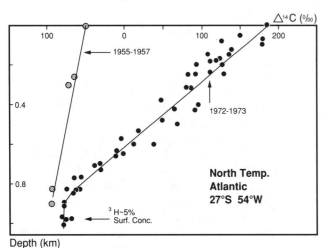

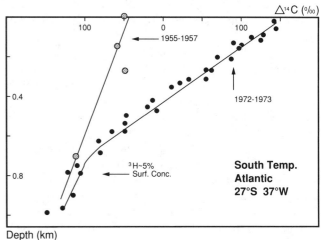

Figure 18.3 Vertical profiles of ^{14}C in the north and south Atlantic Ocean in 1955–1957 and 1972–1973. Source: Broecker and Peng 1982.

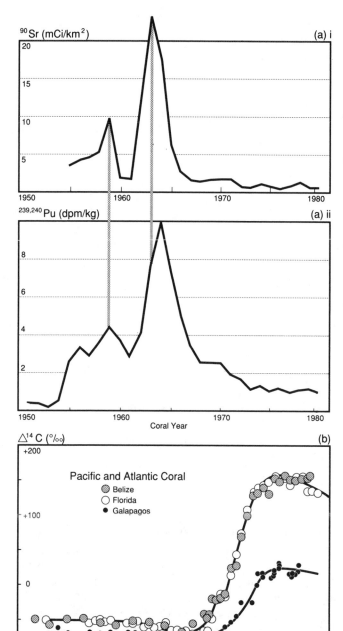

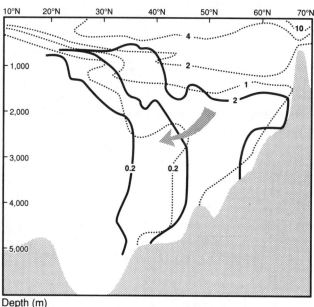

Figure 18.4 (a) Comparison of (i) ⁹⁰Sr deposition at New York City and (ii) ²³⁹,²⁴⁰Pu in year bands from corals near St. Croix, West Indies. Source: Benninger and Dodge 1986. (b) Changes in ¹⁴C in year bands from Pacific and Atlantic corals. Source: Druffel 1981.

been proposed. The relatively short lifetime of tar balls implies that a rapid decline should follow reductions in inputs. Such reductions have occurred due to political problems (e.g., closure of the Suez Canal), the rapid increase in oil price in the 1970s, economic recession in the 1980s, and pollution-control measures. The net result of these changes appears to have been a decline in tar pollution in many areas in recent years (Smith and Knap 1985; Holdway 1986).

Litter is another obvious contaminant of the oceans because much of it floats. The composition and distribution of marine litter indicates that it arises mainly from dumping at sea and loss of cargo (Colton, Knapp, and Burns 1974; Cundall 1973; Dixon and Dixon 1981; Merrell 1984; Vauk and Shrey 1987; Wolfe 1987). It has been estimated that more than 6 million tons of litter are dumped at sea every year by merchant shipping alone (NAS 1975), including more than half a million plastic containers every day (Horsman 1982). Connor and O'Dell (1988) suggest that 700 miles of fishing net may be lost in the North Pacific every year. It is clear that the amounts of material discarded are very large, and international laws designed to ban garbage dumping have yet to come into effect (Connor and O'Dell, 1988). We have no direct historical record of the problem of marine litter, and it has certainly existed since seafaring began. However, the large increase in shipping activity this century and the introduction of plastic packaging and fishing gear in recent times have probably made the main problem of recent origin.

Litter has been observed systematically at sea (Dixon and Dixon 1983; Morris 1980a, b; Venrick et al. 1973), and plastic debris is clearly dominant. Quantitative sampling with nets has emphasized the importance of small (<5 mm) plastic granules (Carpenter and Smith 1972; Morris 1980b; Shaw 1977; Shaw and Mapes 1979; Wong, Green, and Cretney 1974), which are probably industrial plastic precursors lost at sea or discharged to coastal waters. Concentrations of these

Figure 18.5 Concentration of tritium in the North Atlantic 1972⋯⋯ and 1981——. Source: Crane and Liss 1985.

(Morris 1971; Butler 1975; Jeffrey 1980). Despite these uncertainties, a compilation of available literature does show a clear pattern (Table 18.1), with high concentrations in oceanic gyres, in which floating debris accumulates due to low wind stresses, and near major oil transportation routes (Mediterranean Sea, Sargasso Sea, western Pacific Ocean).

Morris et al. (1976a) estimated a residence time for tar on the surface of the oceans of months to a few years. Removal mechanisms have not been fully elucidated, although bacterial degradation, disintegration, sinking after biological colonization, and incorporation into zooplankton faecal pellets have

Table 18-1 *Estimated pelagic tar concentration in various oceanic regions*

Location	Reported tar concentration (mg/m^2)	Reference
Mediterranean	5–37	1, 2, 3
Sargasso Sea	10	2
Western Atlantic	6	4
Eastern Atlantic	1–16	1, 4, 5
Equatorial Atlantic	0.03–0.1	1, 5
Grand Banks off Newfoundland	0–0.1	6
Caribbean	0.05–1	5, 7
Kuroshio Current (W. Pacific)	1–10	8, 12
Northwest Pacific	0.4	8
Northeast Pacific	0.03	8
Gulf of Alaska	0.003	9
Central Southern Pacific	0.0003–0.03	3, 8
Indian Ocean	0.01	3
East Indies	0.08	3
Gulf of Aden	2.5	3
Cape of Good Hope	0.02–2.8	10
Southern Ocean	0	11

1. Horn, Teal, and Backus et al. (1970)
2. Morris et al. (1976a)
3. Holdway (1986)
4. Sleeter et al. (1973)
5. Sleeter, Morris, and Butler (1974)
6. Levy (1983)
7. van Vleet et al. (1983)
8. Wong, Green, and Cretney (1976)
9. Shaw (1977)
10. Eagle, Green, and Williams (1979)
11. Gregory, Kirk, and Mabin (1984)
12. Suzuki and Matsuzaki (1983)

granules are similar in central-ocean gyres of the North and South Atlantic and North Pacific (Carpenter and Smith 1972; Morris 1980b; Wong et al. 1974), although lower in high-latitude areas of the Pacific (Gregory et al. 1984; Shaw 1977). This distribution reflects source regions and a tendency to accumulate in areas of low wind stresses, such as ocean gyres. Because plastics float and are designed for long life, they are bound to be persistent on the oceans, and few obvious removal routes exist for the materials, apart from beaching. Day and Shaw (1987) report increases in concentrations from 1976 to 1985.

The effects of this litter are not well known, but the entanglement of fish, birds, and marine mammals in litter has been reported (Anon 1971; Bonner and Cann 1982; Connor and O'Dell 1988; Dixon and Dixon 1981; Laist 1987; NAS 1975; Merrell 1984; Weisskopf 1988) and has been suggested as a reason for the decline in at least one population of seals (Fowler 1987). Furthermore, plastic debris is found in the stomachs of fish and seabirds, even from remote areas (Carpenter et al. 1972; Furness 1985a, b; Hays and Cormons 1974; Parslow and Jefferies 1972; van Franeker 1985).

Trace Metals

An assessment of the changes human beings have wrought on trace-metal concentrations in and fluxes through the oceans is complicated by the existence of substantial, natural background concentrations in the oceans and biogeochemical cycles that control concentrations to varying extents. Thus, while it is clear that for some metals human inputs to the global environment exceed natural inputs (Mackenzie, Lantzy, and Paterson 1979; chap. 26 in this volume), it is difficult in many cases to see clear evidence of changes in oceanic concentrations. Coral skeleton records suggest that human beings have increased concentrations of cadmium in surface waters of the North Atlantic over the past 100 years (Shen et al. 1987) and possibly the fluxes of cadmium, copper, nickel, and zinc through the water column of the Sargasso Sea (Jickells, Church, and Deuser 1987).

The clearest case of changes in oceanic distribution resulting from human impact is that of lead, because of its low natural abundance, short oceanic residence time, and massive human-made mobilization, with direct emission to the atmosphere allowing efficient dispersal. The primary source of lead to the oceans in prehistoric times was fluvial, but now it is anthropogenic emissions to the atmosphere from cars and metal-smelting operations (Patterson and Settle 1987; chap. 26 in this volume). Because these activities currently are centered in North America, Europe, and Southeast Asia, there is a strong regional variability in the inputs and oceanic distribution, with highest concentrations nearest to sources (Buat-Menard 1986). These changes are recent, as shown by lead concentrations in coral skeletons (Fig. 18.6; Dodge and Gilbert

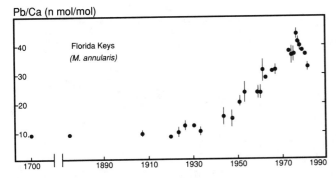

Figure 18.6 Lead concentrations in dated year bands from a coral collected off Florida. Source: Shen and Boyle 1987.

1984; Shen and Boyle 1987). The pattern of stable lead isotopes in samples can be diagnostic of source regions. For example, in water masses in the northeast Pacific, Asian sources of lead dominate surface waters, North American sources dominate in mid-depth water, and Asian sources dominate in deep water (Flegal et al. 1986). Recent pollution-control legislation has reduced emissions of lead, and the effects of this reduction have been seen in surface waters of the North Atlantic in less than 10 years (Boyle et al. 1986; Shen and Boyle 1987).

The effects of these changes in trace-metal concentrations on biological systems in the oceans are unknown, but evidence that small changes in iron (Martin and Fitzwater 1988) and copper concentrations (Knauer and Martin 1983) could affect primary production rates in oceanic waters demands that any changes in trace-metal levels be viewed with concern.

Changes in Chemistry of Coastal Seas of Northwest Europe

Nutrients and Oxygen

The extent of temporal changes in nutrient concentrations are of concern, because additions of nutrients via rivers, discharges from sewage-treatment plants, industries, or nonpoint sources such as runoff from fertilized farmlands, tend to stimulate growth of plankton in surface waters, or eutrophication (see chap. 25). Plankton tend to sink into deeper waters after their death, where they decay and consume dissolved oxygen. Organic matter in certain types of discharge (notably sewage) may also consume significant amounts of oxygen. Most biota have difficulty surviving when oxygen concentrations drop to around 10% of saturation, and the onset of sulphate reduction and hydrogen sulfide production when oxygen is exhausted causes macrofauna to move or die. We will therefore consider changes in nutrients and oxygen together.

The effects of anthropogenic additions of nutrients have been seen most clearly in relatively shallow, coastal seas such as the Baltic, which have restricted water circulation and relatively low natural inputs via in-flowing seawaters. Open ocean waters and coasts more open to vigorous exchange of waters from the open seas, such as Puget Sound (see next section), have as yet shown no changes in nutrients or oxygen, even though they have received substantial amounts of sewage and fertilizer runoff.

The story of the Thames estuary in the United Kingdom (see chap. 15) provides an excellent example of sewage-related problems that arise as a large conurbation (in this case London) develops around a sheltered waterway (Wood 1982). A similar story of gross sewage pollution resulting in major oxygen deficiency in estuaries can be told for many estuaries around the world (e.g., Clyde estuary in Scotland, Mackay, Taylor, and Henderson 1978; and the Chesapeake Bay in the United States, Officer et al. 1984). In all these cases, several common threads appear. Firstly, while sewage is a source of many persistent contaminants (e.g., trace metals, organochlorines, nutrients), in a confined water course, its primary pollutant effect will be via oxygen consumption, with a direct and detrimental effect on the biology. Secondly, sewage pollution is not a recent phenomena, but is exacerbated by the sewage systems that greatly improve public health. Thirdly, given the financial and political resources, the situation can be remedied over periods of decades or less.

The relatively shallow and semienclosed North Sea receives the discharges of several major rivers draining the European continent. Van Bennekom and Salomon (1980) have documented the increase, by a factor of five or more, in nitrate, ammonia, and phosphate concentrations in the largest river, the Rhine, during the past century as a result of increases in population, industrialization, and agricultural activity.

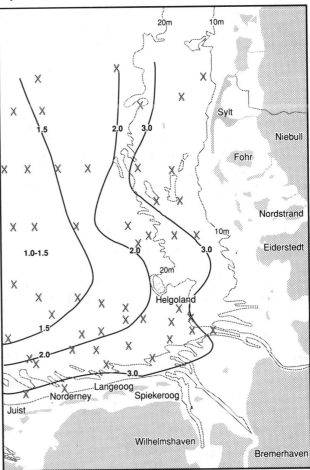

Figure 18.7 Factor of increase for the phosphate concentration of surface waters of the southern North Sea, 1936–1978. Source: Weichert 1986.

Figure 18.7 shows how the ratio of phosphate concentrations in 1978 to those in 1936 changed from 3–4 near the German-Dutch coasts to 1.0 further offshore to the west and north. This is because the Rhine plume tends to flow north and east along the Dutch/German/Danish coasts and because of a major influx of open ocean water from around the north of Scotland and down the eastern coast of the United Kingdom. The concentration of dissolved silica changes much less between 1936 and 1978, because it is not a major component of either sewages or fertilizers. Further evidence for the eutrophication of Dutch coastal waters is reviewed by Postma (1985). Lancelot et al. (1987) suggest that eutrophication has helped cause increased frequency of occurrence, intensity, and duration of major blooms of the nuisance *Phaeocystis* algae in the southern bight of the North Sea. Layers of foam and mucus from these flagellates can occasionally cover beaches with 1-to-2-m-thick layers of foam. The gas dimethyl sulphide, produced by *Phaeocystis* and released to the atmosphere where it oxidizes to sulphur dioxide and other products, may well contribute significantly to the acidity of rain over Europe (Turner et al. 1988).

Water temperature, salinity, and concentrations of phosphate, silicate, nitrate, and oxygen have been monitored since 1954 at a relatively open station in the Irish Sea (Fig. 18.8) by scientists at the Port Erin Laboratory (Slinn and Eastham 1984). Seasonal fluctuations occur in dissolved nutrient concentrations, with winter concentration maxima from January to March, followed by decreases due to incorporation into phytoplankton. The winter maximum in phosphate increased from about 0.5 µmol in 1960 to 0.8 µmol in 1977. This increase is likely the result of increased discharges of phosphorus from sewage and agriculture. In contrast, the winter maximum in dissolved silicate remained at 6.4–6.6 µmol throughout the 27 years. The mean winter maximum in dissolved nitrate was 5.7 µmol for 1960–1969 and 7.0 µmol for 1972–1981, although this difference may not be statistically significant. By contrast, in the waters of the English Channel, open to exchange with the North Atlantic, no changes clearly linked to human activities can be seen (Southward 1980).

The Baltic is a relatively small, shallow, and semienclosed sea or basin surrounded by a number of heavily populated and industrialized nations, which have discharged wastes into it for centuries. Water circulation in it is sluggish due to the

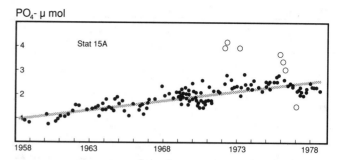

Figure 18.9 Increase in phosphate concentrations at 100-m depth in Gotland Deep. Source: Nehring 1981.

presence of several sills. The Baltic is actually a series of several interconnecting subseas, which are almost separate hydrologic units (Falkenmark 1986).

Natural nutrient inputs in in-flowing seawater are relatively low due to their removal in the basins through which open ocean waters pass before reaching the inner Baltic. Riverine discharges of fresh water to the Baltic may have been reduced in recent decades, leading to less frequent flushing of deeper waters (Fonselius 1969). For a combination of these reasons, human discharges of nutrients via rivers and directly into the Baltic coastal zone have led to increased nutrient concentrations in deep and surface waters of some parts of the Baltic, and to decreased oxygen concentrations in deeper waters. These changes have been documented by long-time series of data on concentrations of phosphate, nitrate, and oxygen produced primarily by the dedicated efforts of Fonselius and colleagues in Sweden.

Nehring, Schultz, and Kaiser (1984) summarized evidence that nutrient concentrations in Baltic surface waters have increased in recent years. For example, Fig. 18.9 shows increases of factors of 2–3 in phosphate concentrations in deeper waters of the Gotland Deep during the period of the records. However, long-term trends in nutrient concentrations are not uniform in all the Baltic basins, and there are regional variations.

Figure 18.10 shows that concentrations of dissolved oxygen in deep or bottom waters of several Baltic basins have decreased from a few ml/l around 1900 to ≤1 ml/l in 1975. Deeper waters of several Baltic basins may periodically even become anoxic, due to natural oscillations in production of oxygen-demanding organic matter and in timing of deep-water renewals. Incidences of anoxia appear more frequently in recent years in deep waters of the Gotland Deep, presumably due to a combination of the anthropogenic factors mentioned earlier (Fonselius 1986). Concurrent with the increased periods of anoxia in deep waters are increased concentrations of dissolved ammonia, the thermodynamically stable form of combined nitrogen under such conditions, and a disappearance of the thermodynamically unstable nitrate, while dissolved silicate concentrations have not changed noticeably in the same time frame.

Radionuclides

The Chernobyl accident in late April 1986 released a number of radionuclides to the air, a fraction of which deposited directly into coastal seas of Europe. Activities of

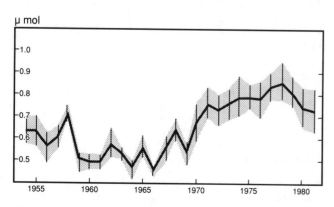

Figure 18.8 Changes in dissolved phosphorus concentrations at Port Erin, Irish Sea. Source: Slinn and Eastham 1984.

^{137}Cs in air in parts of the United Kingdom later in 1986 were as high as activities during 1963–1964, years of peak fallout of nuclear-weapons test debris (Cambray et al. 1987). The rapid transport to deep waters of some of the more particle-reactive elements in this fallout has been reported (Kempe and Nies 1987; Kempe et al. 1987). Plutonium activities in cores from the Baltic taken prior to the Chernobyl accident are relatively low and show subsurface peaks at shallow depths in the sediments (Fig. 18.11a). The subsurface peaks are attributed to peaks in air fallout of weapons tests debris in 1963–1964, which have not been obliterated by biological or physical mixing of surface deposits. Plutonium is believed to be immobile in sediments once deposited (Beasley, Carpenter, and Jennings 1982; Sholkovitz and Mann 1984, and references therein).

The Sellafield (formerly Windscale) nuclear-fuel reprocessing plant located on the Irish Sea coast of the United Kingdom (Fig. 18.12) has discharged since 1955 via pipeline relatively large amounts of many artificial radionuclides to

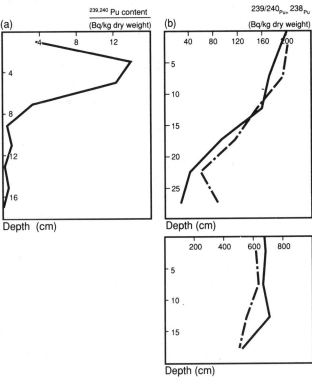

Figure 18.11 Vertical distribution of ^{239,240}Pu in sediment cores from (a) the Baltic and (b) the Irish Sea off Sellafield. Sources: (a) Niemisto and Voipio 1981; (b) Kershaw et al. 1983.

the adjacent ocean. The activities and fates of the long-lived radionuclides of plutonium and ^{137}Cs have been of particular concern. The discharged plutonium tends to accumulate in muddy sediments close to the outfall (Aston, Assinder, and Kelly 1985; Kershaw et al. 1984), whereas the more soluble ^{137}Cs is transported much greater distances by ocean currents. In contrast to the Baltic results, plutonium activity profiles at two Irish Sea sites off Sellafield show substantially higher activities, much deeper depths of penetration into the sediments, and no subsurface maximum (Fig. 18.11b). The sediments of the Irish Sea are extensively bioturbated, with mixing down to 55 cm evident in profiles of ^{14}C activity (Kershaw 1986). Thus, although the fine-grained, muddy sediments off Sellafield are an important sink for the discharged plutonium, the extensive bioturbation obliterates most of the historical record of plutonium discharges.

Since 1969, Sellafield discharges of ^{137}Cs have been an even more important source of this nuclide to the high-latitude North Atlantic than global fallout. Fig. 18.12 shows that in 1971, ^{137}Cs activities in waters of the Irish and North seas and the English Channel were dominated by inputs from fallout and from the French nuclear-fuel reprocessing plant at La Hague. By 1973, however, the Sellafield discharges dominated.

The ratios of ^{137}Cs to ^{90}Sr activities in Sellafield discharges have varied with time, but have been consistently several times greater than the worldwide fallout ratio of 1.45 (Livingston, Bowen, and Kupferman 1982). Both ^{137}Cs and ^{90}Sr have strong chemical tendencies to remain in solution in seawater and to travel along with the water mass. The relatively large ^{137}Cs discharges through the 1970s, combined with their

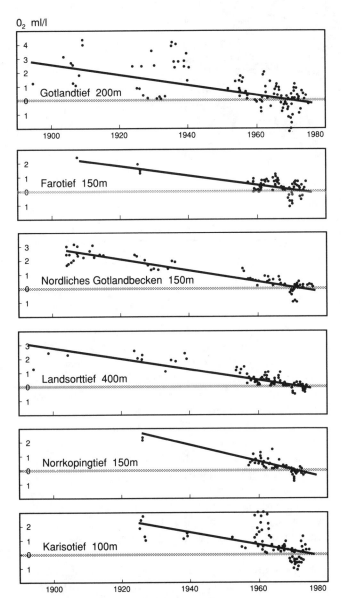

Figure 18.10 Decreases in oxygen content of the bottom waters in several areas of the Baltic. Source: Fonselius 1981.

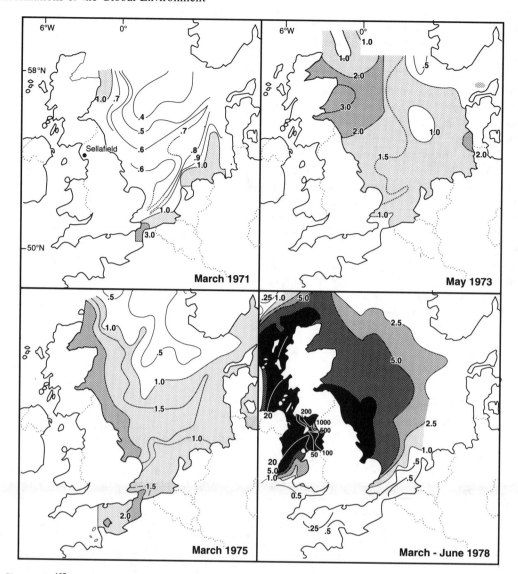

Figure 18.12 Changes in ^{137}Cs activity in seawater around the British Isles from 1971 (dominated by global fallout) to 1978 (dominated by Windscale/Sellafield discharges). Source: MAFF 1981.

distinctive ^{137}Cs/^{90}Sr ratios, gave waters affected by the Sella-field discharges a unique radionuclide signature. Measure-ments of ^{137}Cs, ^{134}Cs, ^{90}Sr, and ^{99}Tc seawater activities have been skillfully exploited to trace the flow of Sellafield-labeled waters from the Irish Sea around the north of Scotland, along the Norwegian coast, and even into the Arctic Ocean (Fig. 18.13, Aarkrog et al. 1987; Dahlgaard et al. 1986; Livingston 1988; and references therein).

Trace Metals

We know of no time-series data on dissolved trace-metal concentrations in any northwestern European Sea.

However, the available spatial results do indicate sig-nificant contamination of coastal North Sea regions (Jones and Jefferies 1983; Nolting 1986), with concentrations high along the southern North Sea coasts in areas influenced by major rivers, although the plumes of individual rivers are not always evident. Dilution and active removal modify the inputs

of dissolved metals as they are transported into the North Sea. Dissolved lead concentrations in North Sea waters remain remarkably low even though there are major inputs from rivers and the atmosphere, because scavenging and removal to underlying sediments is so rapid (Brugmann et al. 1985). The rapid attenuation of metal inputs during the transition from fresh water to seawater has also been noted for lead in the Mississippi estuary (Trefry et al. 1985).

Another source of metal contamination in the coastal marine areas is dumping of dredge spoil or sewage sludge. The impact of this practice varies with the hydrography of the receiving site and the solubility of the contaminants. In some areas, rapid water movements distribute and dilute the con-taminants and any resulting harmful effects over a very wide area (Carmody, Pearce, and Yasso 1973). In others, the contaminants are concentrated in a single site (Mackay, Halcrow, and Thornton 1972), where the effects can be dramatic over a limited area.

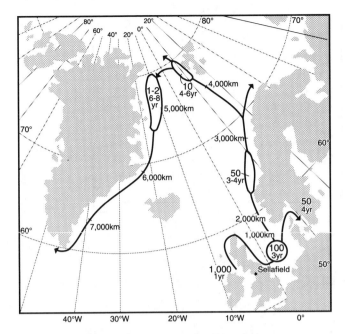

Figure 18.13 Relative concentrations (Bq^{137}Cs/m^3) and approximate transit times for ^{137}Cs in North Altantic. Source: Dahlgaard et al. 1986.

Erlenkeuser, Suess, and Willkomm (1974) reported that certain heavy metals increase in concentration toward surface layers in sediments from the western Baltic. At two sites that had relatively high accumulation rates of fine-grained sediments and little reworking of deposited material, cadmium, lead, zinc, and copper concentrations in surface sediments were 7, 4, 3, and 2 times, respectively, those at the bottoms of cores, whereas concentrations of iron, manganese, nickel, and cobalt remained unchanged. The increases were attributed to increasing inputs of residues from fossil fuels.

Changes since the nineteenth century in heavy-metal concentrations in dated sediment cores from the Baltic and from a Norwegian fjord are shown in Fig. 18.14. Certain metal concentrations began to increase as far back as around 1900, but the largest increases began around 1930. Concentrations of several metals show hints of lower values in sediments deposited in the Baltic since about 1970 (Fig. 18.14), but appear to still increase until the 1972 sampling data in the Norwegian fjord. The extent of increases varies from place to place and from one metal to another, as does whether or not concentrations have stabilized in most recently deposited layers. The leveling-off and decreases in concentrations are perhaps due to a variety of discharge-reduction measures instituted in recent decades in the countries of northwestern Europe. Note, however, the uncertainties in recognizing small changes due to human actions on top of the natural concentrations and fluctuations in them for these metals.

Langston (1986) reported changes in mercury and lead concentrations in several species of organisms collected from the Mersey estuary in the western United Kingdom between 1980 and 1984. Concentrations of both mercury and lead in organisms decreased by factors of 2 to 3 over this period (Fig. 18.15). The progressive reductions occurred in response to

efforts to reduce industrial inputs of these metals to the Mersey system.

Antifouling boat paints contain high concentrations of metals designed to prevent algal growth on boats and structures. Over time these metals are lost to the marine environment. Copper has been used extensively as an antifouling agent, and in many environments where other contaminant inputs are small (e.g., Bermuda, the Florida Keys), this input can be the major source of copper to the area (Jickells et al. 1986; Trefry et al. 1983). Recently organo-tin has become a preferred antifouling agent. However, it has now become apparent that the organo-tin paints give rise to increased organo-tin concentrations in the water column (Cleary and Stebbing 1985; Hall et al. 1987) and in tissues of some organisms (Bryan et al. 1986). The effects of this tissue burden of organo-tin appears to be deleterious. For example, it can seriously interfere with reproduction of *Nucella lapillus*, resulting in rapid and substantial declines in numbers (Bryan et al. 1986). Such paints are now being regulated in several countries (Goldberg 1986).

Chlorinated Hydrocarbons of the DDT and PCB Families

Temporal, global, and regional trends in the use of chlorinated hydrocarbons are described by Brown, Kasperson, and Raymond (chap. 26). Production of DDT reached maximum levels in 1964–1965, whereas PCB production peaked in 1968–1970. Marked declines in production followed the maxima. Figure 18.16 shows changes with time in concentrations of PCBs and total DDT (i.e., DDT and its breakdown products) in sediment cores from the Baltic Sea dating back to the beginning of this century (Niemisto and Voipio 1981). Total DDT concentrations show clear subsurface maxima in concentrations in horizons dated as deposited around 1960, with decreases in more recently deposited layers at three sites, and constant concentrations at another. PCB concentrations show subsurface maxima in horizons dated as late 1960s in two sites, and continual increases at the other two sites. Recognition of temporal trends of these families of synthetic compounds is easier than for stable metals, because they have no naturally occurring background concentrations, their degradation rate in sediments is slow relative to accumulation rates, and surface sediment mixing appears minor at these sites, so some record of time history of inputs is preserved. Olsson and Reutergardh (1986) have demonstrated a decline in the concentrations of chlorinated organics from 1969 to 1984 in herring muscle tissue taken from three different parts of the Baltic. Herring younger than four years were chosen as indicator organisms, since such young herring are believed to stay in the region where sampled, and concentrations of DDT and PCBs in them are not believed to vary greatly due to age, size, or sex, but primarily with fat content.

Total DDT concentrations in the herring from all areas and for both spring and fall collections decreased during the study period. Relative amounts of parent DDT declined, while amounts of the metabolites, mainly DDE, increased. This aging of the DDT compounds occurred, along with the decrease in total concentrations. PCB concentrations in herring

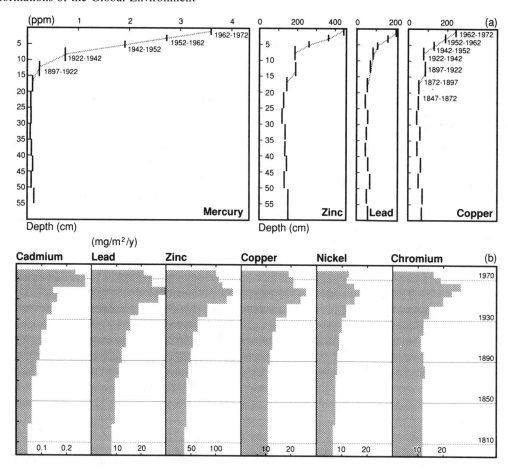

Figure 18.14 (a) Depth profile of mercury, zinc, lead, and copper in a dated sediment core from Sorfjord, Norway. Source: Skei 1981. (b) Variations in metal accumulation rates through time from dated concentration profiles in the Baltic. Source: Larsen and Madsen 1986.

from two of the three areas also decreased, but to a smaller extent than the DDT family concentrations. PCB concentrations in herring from the Bothnian Sea remained steady, for unknown reasons. Several previous studies (reference in Olsson and Reutergardh 1986) have reported decreasing total DDT levels in Baltic fish, with smaller decreases in or unchanged PCB levels.

Eggs of fish-eating guillemot birds (*Uria algae*) were collected from a rock island in the central part of the Baltic and analyzed for chlorinated hydrocarbons (Olsson and Reutergardh 1986). The guillemots feed to a large extent on herring, which as adults may migrate over vast areas of the central Baltic. The birds remain in the Baltic all year and catch fish from many different herring groups, thus integrating variations in DDT/PCB burdens due to different fish-migration routes. These properties make their eggs a good biological material for studying trends of concentrations of persistent chlorinated organics. The annual samples of guillemot eggs showed clear and significant decreases in amounts of DDE and PCBs (Fig. 18.17). (Only DDE was found in the eggs – all DDT had been metabolized to DDE.)

The lowered worldwide consumption of DDT, which started in the mid-to-late 1960s, rather than local reductions in discharges from nations around the Baltic, is believed to explain the simultaneous decrease of DDT family concentrations observed in all biotypes and in both fresh-water and marine locations. The results imply a time lag of 5 to 7 years between reduction in production and reduction in DDT environmental concentrations for a region like the Baltic.

Unlike DDT, PCB compounds were in widespread use in Sweden and around the Baltic until restrictions in PCB use were begun in the early 1970s. In the Baltic organisms, amounts of PCBs were constant until the mid 1970s, suggesting that PCB pollution of the Baltic continued longer than DDT pollution. The fact that material collected from the southern Bothnian Sea showed no PCB reductions through 1984 implies that inputs to this region continued (Olsson and Reutergardh 1986). If the U.S. PCB production figures (chap. 26) are representative of worldwide consumption, one finds a 5-to-7 year delay between reduction of production and decreased PCB concentrations in Baltic organisms.

Falandysz and Szefer (1984) reported concentrations of

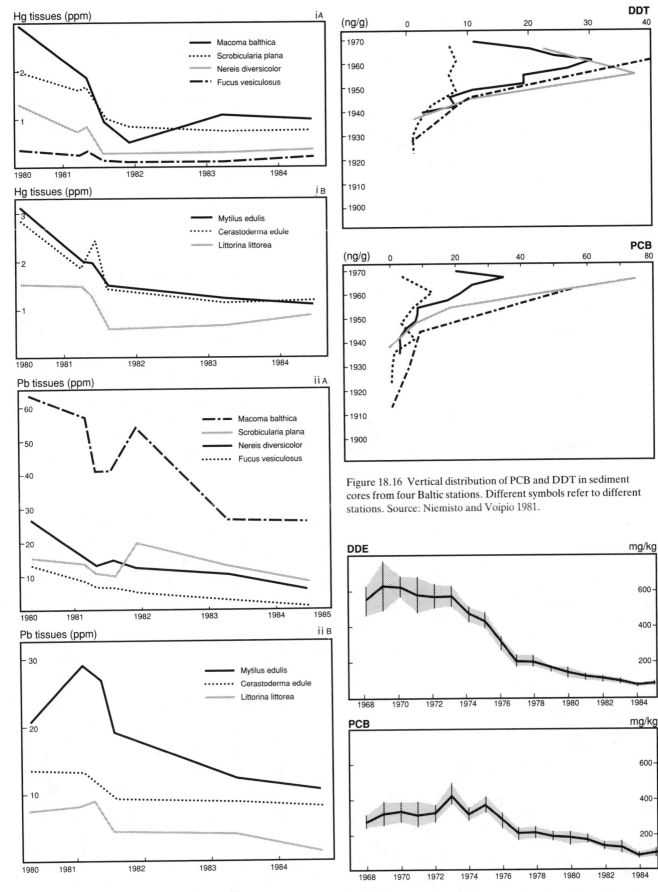

Figure 18.15 Temporal changes in (i) mercury and (ii) lead content of biota at two sites (A and B) in Mersey estuary, United Kingdom. Source: Langston 1986.

Figure 18.16 Vertical distribution of PCB and DDT in sediment cores from four Baltic stations. Different symbols refer to different stations. Source: Niemisto and Voipio 1981.

Figure 18.17 Levels of DDE and PCB in guillemot eggs from the Baltic. Vertical bars are 95% confidence intervals. Source: Olsson and Reutergardh 1986.

chlorinated hydrocarbons in fish-eating birds collected during wintering in Gdansk Bay, Poland. Auks, which probably stay the whole year in the Baltic area, contained twice the levels of PCBs as mergansers, and 5 to 6 times more PCBs than grebes and divers, birds that move out to the more open sea after the breeding season.

We know of no similar studies of temporal trends of DDTs and PCB concentrations in other northwestern European seas. The trends just described for Baltic organisms, however, agree with those observed in seal tissues from Nova Scotia (Addison et al. 1984; and chap. 26 of this volume). A decline in DDT group residues following discharge reductions was also noted in brown pelicans off the southern California coast and in northern anchovies, their major food fish (Anderson et al. 1975).

Changes in Chemistry of Coastal Seas of the Northwestern United States

Changes in seawater chemistry along the open coast of Washington state and in the semienclosed waters of Puget Sound in the northwestern United States have some interesting similarities and differences to changes in the coastal seas of northwest Europe.

Nutrients and Oxygen

Nutrient discharges from the population of about 1 million people living around Puget Sound have entered the Sound in increasing amounts since the 1950s, after varying degrees of treatment. The largest single-point source since 1967 has been effluent from a primary sewage treatment plant in Seattle (PSWQA 1986). This plant was built to collect most of the sewage from the Seattle urban area, which had previously flowed untreated into Lake Washington and had caused severe eutrophication problems. The plant was to give it primary treatment and to discharge it to the Sound instead. In addition, increasing amounts of sewage nutrients and viruses have entered the Sound from nonpoint sources, including the numerous pleasure boats on the Sound and wastes from livestock on farms and dairies bordering creeks and streams that flow into the coastal zone.

Puget Sound is separated from the open North Pacific by the 160-km long Strait of Juan de Fuca and has three sills that restrict deep-water circulation. At first glance, its situation may look similar to the Baltic Sea. However, in contrast to the Baltic, central Puget Sound data show no discernable change in concentrations of phosphate or O_2 between 1934 and 1973 (Duxbury 1975). Why is this?

The glacially carved system of fjords making up Puget Sound is relatively deep (mostly deeper than 200 m), and experiences strong tidal exchange of waters twice each day. Thus, the wastes entering Puget Sound are more effectively diluted and dispersed than in most coastal seas. The inflowing seawater is from 200 to 300 m deep in the north Pacific, and brings with it relatively high concentrations of nutrients, which are not significantly reduced during the water's short residence time in the Strait of Juan de Fuca. Because of the high normal nutrient inputs, sewage discharges from the growing but still relatively small population add small amounts to nutrients already entering the system. Thus, eutrophication has not been a serious problem in central Puget Sound, although other potentially toxic chemicals within the sewage are of more environmental concern.

Concentrations of oxygen, phosphate, nitrate, plus nitrite and silicate in waters of the Washington shelf and slope north of the Columbia River have not detectably changed since 1961 (Carpenter 1987). Smith, Alexander, and Wolman (1987) and Carpenter (1987) have suggested that the riverine fluxes of nitrate and phosphate to the area have changed little between 1966 and 1981.

Fossil Hydrocarbons

Aliphatic and polycyclic aromatic hydrocarbons (PAH) may enter the ocean in a variety of ways: the most spectacular inputs are spills from wrecked tankers and blowouts of oil-production platforms. Less widely recognized, but persistent and extremely important, are deliberate discharges of oily ballast-waters of tankers, and urban discharges from street runoff, sewage-treatment plants, etc. – either directly into the ocean or indirectly via rivers (NAS 1985). The importance of hydrocarbon inputs via urban discharges has been especially well-documented for the Puget Sound region (Barrick 1982). Changes in aliphatic and PAH concentrations and fluxes due to human discharges must be sought above background concentrations and fluxes due to natural inputs, including forest fires, coal erosion, and crude-oil seeps (Barrick et al. 1980). Chemical and microbial alterations that occur after introduction of a set of fossil hydrocarbons to the ocean can significantly modify the original composition and complicate efforts to identify a particular source. The rate of change depends upon several factors, including water temperature, redox potential, and hydrocarbon phase associations.

Changes with time in inputs of fossil hydrocarbons such as the PAHs, which are only very slowly degraded after deposition, have been deduced from profiles of PAH concentrations in sediment cores whose accumulation rates were determined from profiles of radionuclides (Barrick and Prahl 1987; Bates, Hamilton, and Kline 1984; Gschwend and Hites 1981; Muller, Grimmer, and Boehnke 1977; Pavoni, Sfrisco, and Marcomini 1987; Prahl and Carpenter 1979; 1984; and references therein).

A subsurface maximum in concentrations in layers deposited around 1950–1960 is a feature common to PAH profiles from such widespread areas as lakes in Germany and the northeastern United States, a Rhode Island estuary, Puget Sound, and the lagoon of Venice. Reductions in PAH concentrations in sediments deposited since about 1960 are attributed to reductions in PAH inputs to the environment resulting from improvements in air-pollution emission-control technology and in combustion efficiency, and a shift from coal to natural gas as a fossil-fuel energy source. Fig. 18.18 illustrates the subsurface concentration maximum for one combustion-derived PAH, fluoranthene, at several Puget Sound locations. Note that the maximum is not equally pronounced at all locations – most likely due to input differences and to mixing of surface sediments, which tend to obscure changes in inputs (Carpenter, Peterson, and Bennett 1985).

Fluoranthene concentration µg/g OC

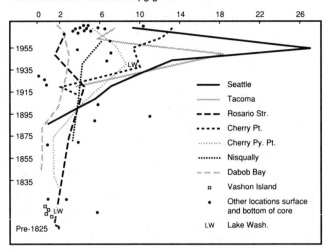

Figure 18.18 Depth profiles of fluoranthene in dated sediment cores from Puget Sound, United States. Source: Barrick and Prahl 1987.

We believe that it is important to note this recent reduction in amounts of combustion-derived PAH fluxing through the air and euphotic zones of aquatic reservoirs and accumulating in underlying sediments. A return to greater reliance on coal combustion as an energy source would in all likelihood lead to increased environmental fluxes of these potentially harmful compounds, even given the more efficient combustion technologies developed since 1960. This likely increase should be considered in evaluating the environmental impacts of this and alternative-energy generation schemes.

Trace Metals

Several studies have determined trace-metal concentration profiles in ^{210}Pb-dated sediments from Puget Sound to elucidate changes in metal concentrations during the past century. Arsenic concentrations in sediments of a bay several kilometers downwind of a large smelter began to increase after the smelter began operating in 1890, with a time lag due to mixing of surface sediments (Carpenter and Peterson 1989; Carpenter, Peterson, and Jahnke 1978; Crecelius, Bothner, and Carpenter 1975). Arsenic concentrations had increased about ten times by the time the smelter ceased operations in 1986. Bothner et al. (1980) determined how rapidly mercury-concentration profiles in sediments near a chloralkali plant decreased after the mercury discharge was essentially eliminated. The contaminant mercury burden decreased, with an apparent half-life of 2 to 3 years. In oxic sediments, natural physical resuspension and removal of contaminated particles caused the mercury loss. In anoxic sediments, mercury losses were by diffusion of soluble mercury from sediments.

Central Puget Sound surface sediments have 10 to 12 times higher concentrations of silver, 5 to 6 times higher concentrations of lead and mercury, and 2 times higher concentrations of copper than concentrations in sediments deposited over 100 years ago (Bloom and Crecelius 1987) (Fig. 18.19). In some areas of central Puget Sound, sediment accumulation rates and mixing depths are so great that the depth of contaminated sediments is over 200 cm. Subsurface concentration

maxima observed for lead, mercury, and possibly silver (but not copper and cadmium) (Fig. 18.19) probably result from reductions in contaminant discharges to the Sound since about 1960.

Artificial Radionuclides

Establishment of plutonium-production reactors at the Hanford Nuclear Reservation adjacent to the Columbia River in Washington state during the period 1943–45 resulted in the discharge of cooling waters that contained a mixture of radionuclides to the Columbia River. From the end of World War II until late 1971, the most important source of artificial radioactivity to the ocean off Oregon and Washington was the Hanford-derived nuclides in the Columbia River plume. The original reactors were unique in that Columbia River water was used as the primary coolant in a single-pass, flow-through system, and radionuclides were formed by neutron activation of elements in the river water. The suite of artificial nuclides discharged into the Pacific from Hanford was thus quite different from the suite discharged from the Sellafield nuclear-fuel reprocessing facility into the Irish Sea.

The Hanford-derived radionuclides also served as unique and valuable tags for studies of dispersion of the river plume into the North Pacific, and of rates and mechanisms of complex processes. [65]Zn ($t_{1/2}$, 245d) was the predominant gamma-emitting artificial isotope that reached the ocean and was probably the biologically most important of the Hanford nuclides in the marine environment.

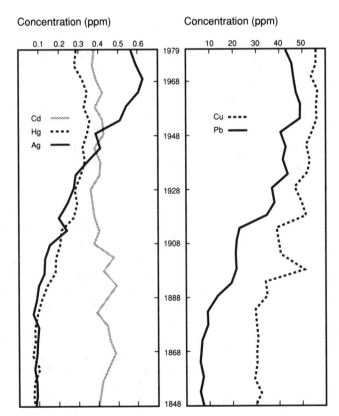

Figure 18.19 Depth profiles of Ag, Cd, Hg, Pb, and Cu in dated, fine-grained sediment cores from Puget Sound, United States. Source: Bloom and Crecelius 1987.

The operation of the plutonium-production reactors at Hanford was phased out from January 1965 to February 1971. The shutdown of the last such reactor eliminated the source of practically all Hanford-derived artificial nuclides to the Columbia and its plume. A rapid decline in ^{65}Zn activity in mussels and several other kinds of organisms along the Washington coast followed (Pearcy and Vanderploeg 1973). The Columbia River received as much as 300,000 Ci/yr of artificial radioactivity in the mid-1960s, but by 1978 the residual artificial nuclide activity in riverine sediments had declined greatly, to the point that natural radioactivity of U, Th, Ra, and K isotopes exceeded that of artificial isotopes by nearly an order of magnitude (Beasley and Jennings 1984).

Analyses of sediment between Hanford and the Columbia River mouth showed that the reactors added only relatively small amounts of Pu and Am to the river and coastal ocean, above amounts due to global fallout of nuclear-weapons debris (Beasley and Jennings 1984). This conclusion is supported by measurements of Pu and Am in mussels collected from 1976 to 1978 as part of the U.S. National Mussel Watch Program (Goldberg et al. 1983). Pu and Am activities in mussels from the Washington coast were not exceptionally high compared to activities in mussels from other West Coast sites. Activities of Pu and Am in mussels from the Washington coast changed little between 1976 and 1978, probably because the major source of these fallout-derived nuclides was from well-mixed, up-welling seawaters.

The lack of Hanford-related increases in plutonium activities off the Washington coast contrasts markedly with the situation in Irish Sea sediments, where discharges from the Sellafield nuclear-fuel reprocessing plant have introduced much more Pu than global fallout. Although not appreciably enhanced by plutonium discharges from Hanford, Washington shelf and slope sediment inventories of plutonium and ^{210}Pb are 5 to 14 times greater than inventories of the same isotopes in sediments from most coastal zones, other than off Sellafield, and greater than inventories possible from air fallout alone at this latitude. The elevated plutonium concentrations are the result of several natural processes collectively called "boundary scavenging" (Bacon, Spencer, and Brewer 1976; Carpenter et al. 1987).

Conclusions

In drawing together conclusions from this review of human impact on the marine environment, several clear features appear. One is the contrast between open oceans and regional seas. The physical and chemical environment of the open oceans have not been greatly affected by events over the past 300 years, principally because of their large diluting capacity. Careful investigation in the open oceans can detect the presence of several classes of anthropogenic substances, such as synthetic organic chemicals and radioactive isotopes derived from nuclear explosions or energy programs. For other substances that occur naturally but for which humans have changed the rates of transport through the global water/atmosphere system, however, it is difficult to find clear evidence of changes in the ocean, with the exception of lead.

This is in part due to the vast, complex, natural-cycling processes in the oceans. The volume of the oceans and long residence time of compounds within them, while it offers a vast diluting capacity, does imply that any contamination will be removed only very slowly. Material that floats and is therefore not diluted, such as tar balls and litter, can be shown to have increased in amount and to have changed in character over the past 300 years.

In contrast to the open oceans, regional seas close to large population centers show clear evidence of increasing concentrations of several substances over the past 100 or so years. These increases are almost certainly linked to human activities. Such increases are more apparent in coastal areas, which are closer to sources and have less dilution capacity. However, the hydrography of coastal areas is variable and complex, and this plays a crucial role in determining the magnitude of human impact, as illustrated by our comparison of the northwest coasts of Europe and North America. We noted for coastal seas of both northern Europe and the northwestern United States examples of certain chemical contaminants whose concentrations have decreased in the last few years. The decreases probably result, at least partially, from the control measures and reductions in contaminant discharges instituted in recent decades. It is important to understand that human actions (or lack of them) can still make noticeable differences to contaminant concentrations in the coastal zone, with time lags of perhaps a decade.

We have considered here only changes in concentrations of chemicals, without directly considering the biological effects of such changes. The positive identification of adverse effects on the marine environment as a result of human activities is very difficult to establish. Changes in phytoplankton species in the North Sea, for example, may be the result of increased nutrient concentrations, but the effects, if any, of these changes on the remainder of the ecosystem are unknown. There appears to be evidence of damage to several marine species from entanglement in litter and from the use of tributyl tin antifouling paints. On a larger scale, the evidence of increasing areas of low-oxygen concentrations in estuaries and coastal seas represents a major cause for concern.

Our ability to assess the state of the marine environment has been severely constrained by a lack of information on the concentrations of substances of concern in the oceans a few hundred years ago. This problem leads us to the conclusion that scientists must adequately and accurately describe the current state of the marine environment to provide a baseline against which future changes can be assessed. In order to distinguish between natural and manmade changes, it is essential that we monitor the marine environment over long periods of time. Very few long-term time-series of ocean measurements exist, yet they provide very important evidence of the complexity of natural cycles in the seas. These time-series require long-term commitments of time and money, with little expectation of short-term returns, and they are regularly under threat of funding termination. If this happens, then it is likely that our successors will still be in difficulty when asked to describe long-term human impact on the marine environment.

Acknowledgments

Much of the preparation of this chapter was done while one of us (R. C.) was on sabbatical in the School of Environmental Sciences, University of East Anglia. We are especially grateful for the skill and patient secretarial assistance of Rosie Cullington during the many revisions of this chapter and to Philip Judge for drawing the figures. We wish to thank the many scientists who have helped us by sending preprints and correcting our own misunderstandings, particularly S. Fonselius. We thank the "Earth As Transformed..." committee for inviting us to write this chapter, for supporting one of us (T. J.) in attending the Earth As Transformed by Human Action Conference, and for their patience while we completed the written text. This is contribution number 1790 from the University of Washington, School of Oceanography.

References

Aarkrog, A., S. Boelskifte, H. Dahlgaard, S. Duniec, L. Hallstadius, E. Holm, and J. N. Smith. 1987. Technetium-99 and Cesium-134 as long-distance tracers in Arctic waters. *Est. Coastal Shelf Sci.* 24: 637–47.

Addison, R. F., P. F. Brodle, M. E. Zinck, and D. E. Sargeant. 1984. DDT has declined more than PCBs in eastern Canadian seals during the 1970s. *Environ. Sci. Technol.* 18: 935–37.

Anderson, D. A., J. R. Jehl, R. W. Risebrough, L. A. Woods, L. R. Deweese, and W. G. Edgecomb. 1975. Brown pelicans: improved reproduction off the southern California coast. *Science* 190: 806–08.

Anon. 1971. Elastic band pollution. *Mar. Pollut. Bull.* 2: 165.

Aston, S. R., D. J. Assinder, and M. Kelly. 1985. Plutonium in intertidal coastal and estuarine sediments in the northern Irish Sea. *Est. Coastal Shelf Sci.* 20: 761–71.

Atlas, E., and C. S. Giam. 1986. Sea-air exchange of high-molecular-weight synthetic organic compounds. In *The Role of Air-Sea Exchange in Geochemical Cycling*, ed. P. Buat-Menard, 295–329. Dordrecht, Holland: D. Reidel Co.

Bacon, M. P., D. W. Spencer, and P. G. Brewer. 1976. $^{210}Pb/^{226}Ra$ and $^{210}Po/^{210}Pb$ disequilibria in seawater and suspended particulate matter. *Earth Planet. Sci. Lett.* 32: 277–96.

Barrick, R. C. 1982. Flux of aliphatic and polycyclic aromatic hydrocarbons to central Puget Sound from Seattle (Westpoint) primary sewage effluent. *Environ. Sci. Technol.* 16: 682–92.

Barrick, R. C., J. I. Hedges, and M. L. Peterson. 1980. Hydrocarbon geochemistry of the Puget Sound region – I. Sedimentary acyclic hydrocarbons. *Geochim. Cosmochim. Acta* 44: 1349–62.

Barrick, R. C., and F. G. Prahl. 1987. Hydrocarbon geochemistry of the Puget Sound region – III. Polynuclear aromatic hydrocarbons in sediments. *Est. Coastal Shelf Sci.* 25: 175–91.

Bates, T. S., S. E. Hamilton, and J. D. Cline. 1984. Vertical transport and sedimentation of hydrocarbons in the central main basin of Puget Sound, WA. *Environ. Sci. Technol.* 18: 299–305.

Beasley, T. M., R. Carpenter, and C. D. Jennings. 1982. Plutonium, ^{241}Am, and ^{137}Cs ratio, inventories and profiles in Washington and Oregon continental-shelf sediments. *Geochim. Cosmochim. Acta* 46: 1931–46.

Beasley, T. M., and C. D. Jennings. 1984. Inventories of $^{239,240}Pu$, ^{241}Am, ^{139}Cs, and ^{60}Co in Columbia River sediments from Hanford to the Columbia River estuary. *Environ. Sci. Technol.* 18: 207–212.

Benninger, L. K., and R. E. Dodge. 1986. Fallout plutonium and natural radionuclides in annual bands of the coral *Montastrea annularis*, St. Croix, U.S. Virgin Islands. *Geochim. Cosmochim. Acta* 50: 2785–97.

Bloom, N. S., and E. A. Crecelius. 1987. Distribution of silver, mercury, lead, copper, and cadmium in central Puget Sound sediments. *Mar. Chem.* 21: 377–90.

Bonner, W. N., and T. S. Cann. 1982. Neck collars on fur seals, *Artocephalus gazella*, at South Georgia. *Bull. Br. Antarct. Survey* 57: 73–77.

Bothner, M. H., R. A. Jahnke, M. L. Peterson, and R. Carpenter. 1980. Rate of mercury loss from contaminated estuarine sediments. *Geochim. Cosmochim. Acta* 44: 273–85.

Bowen, V. T., V. E. Noshkin, H. D. Livingston, and H. L. Volchok. 1980. Fallout radionuclides in the Pacific Ocean: Vertical and horizontal distributions, largely from GEOSECS stations. *Earth Planet. Sci. Lett.* 49: 411–34.

Boyle, E. A., S. D. Chapnick, G. T. Shen, and M. P. Bacon. 1986. Temporal variability of lead in the western North Atlantic ocean. *J. Geophys. Res.* 91: 8573–935.

Broecker, W. S., and T. H. Peng. 1982. *Tracers in the Sea.* Palisades, NY: Lamont-Doherty Geological Observatory.

Broman, D., and B. Ganning. 1985. Bivalve molluscs (Mytilus edulis and Macoma baltica) for monitoring diffuse oil pollution in a northern Baltic archipelago. *Ambio* 14: 23–28.

Brugmann, L., L-G. Danielson, B. Magnusson, and S. Westerlund. 1985. Lead in the North Sea and the northeast Atlantic Ocean. *Mar. Chem.* 16: 47–60.

Bruland, K. W. 1983. Trace elements in seawater. In *Chemical Oceanography*, Vol. 8, ed. J. P. Riley and R. Chester, 157–220. New York: Academic Press.

Bryan, G. W., P. E. Gibbs, L. G. Hummerstone, and G. R. Burt. 1986. The decline of the gastropod *Nucella lapillus* around southwest England: evidence for the effect of tributyltins from antifouling paints. *J. Mar. Biol. Ass. U.K.* 66: 611–40.

Buat-Menard, P. 1986. Air-to-sea transfer of anthropogenic trace metals. In *The Role of Air-Sea Exchange in Geochemical Cycling*, ed. P. Buat-Menard, 477–529. Dordrecht: Reidel.

Buesseler, K. O., H. D. Livingston, S. Honko, B. J. Hay, S. J. Manganini, E. Degens, V. Ittekkot, E. Izdar, and T. Konuk. 1987. Chernobyl radionuclides in a Black Sea sediment trap. *Nature* 329: 825–28.

Burns, K. A., J. P. Villeneuve, and S. W. Fowler. 1985. Fluxes and residence times of hydrocarbons in the coastal Mediterranean – how important are the biota? *Est. Coastal Shelf Sci.* 20: 313–30.

Burton, J. D., and P. J. Statham. 1982. Occurrence, distribution, and chemical speciation of some minor dissolved constituents in ocean waters. In *Environmental Chemistry*, Vol. 2, ed. H. J. M. Bowen, 234–65. Specialist Periodical Report, Royal Society of Chemistry, London.

Butler, J. N. 1975. Pelagic tar. *Sci. Amer. 232(6)*: 90–97.

Cambray, R. S., P. A. Cawse, J. A. Garland, J. A. B. Gibson, P. Johnson, G. N. J. Lewis, D. Newton, L. Salmon, and B. O. Wade. 1987. Observations on radioactivity from the Chernobyl accident. *Nuclear Energy 26*: 77–101.

Carmody, D. J., J. B. Pearce, and W. E. Yasso. 1973. Trace metals in sediments of New York Bight. *Mar. Pollut. Bull.* 4: 132–35.

Carpenter, E. J., and K. L. Smith. 1972. Plastics on the Sargasso Sea surface. *Science* 175: 1240–41.

Carpenter, E. J., S. J. Anderson, G. R. Harvey, H. P. Miklas, and B. R. Peck. 1972. Polystyrene spherules in coastal waters. *Science* 178: 749–50.

Carpenter, R. 1987. Has man altered the cycling of nutrients and organic C on the Washington continental shelf and slope? *Deep-Sea Res.* 34: 881–96.

Carpenter, R., M. L. Peterson, and R. A. Jahnke. 1978. Sources, sinks, and cycling of arsenic in the Puget Sound region. In *Estuarine Interactions*, ed. M. L. Wiley, 459–80. New York: Academic Press.

Carpenter, R., M. L. Peterson, and J. T. Bennett. 1985. ^{210}Pb-derived sediment accumulation and mixing rates for the greater Puget Sound region. *Mar. Geol.* 64: 291–312.

Carpenter, R., T. M. Beasley, D. Zahnle, and B. L. K. Somayajulu. 1987. Cycling of fallout (Pu, ^{241}Am, ^{137}Cs) and natural (U, Th, ^{210}Pb) radionuclides in Washington continental slope sediments. *Geochim. Cosmochim. Acta* 51: 1897–921.

Carpenter, R., and M. L. Peterson. 1989. Chemical cycling in Washington's coastal zone. In *Coastal Oceanography of Washington and Oregon*, ed. B. M. Hickey and M. R. Landry. New York: Elsevier Science.

Cleary, J. J., and A. R. D. Stebbing. 1985. Organotin and total tin in coastal waters of southwest England. *Mar. Pollut. Bull. 16*: 350–55.

Clurg, T. P. 1984. Trace metals and chlorinated hydrocarbons in Ross Seals from Antarctica. *Mar. Pollut. Bull. 15*: 384–89.

Colton, J. B., F. D. Knapp, and B. R. Burns. 1974. Plastic particles in surface waters of the northwestern Atlantic. *Science 185*: 491–97.

Connor, D. K., and R. O'Dell. 1988. The tightening net of marine plastics pollution: Strategies for intervention. *Environment 30*: 16–36.

Crane, A., and P. Liss. 1985. Carbon dioxide, climate, and the sea. *New Scientist*, November 21, 50–54.

Crecelius, E. A., M. H. Bothner, and R. Carpenter. 1975. Geochemistries of arsenic, antimony, mercury, and related elements in sediments of Puget Sound. *Envir. Sci. Technol. 9*: 325–33.

Cundall, A. M. 1973. Plastic materials accumulating in Narragansett Bay. *Mar. Pollut. Bull. 4*: 187–88.

Dahlgaard, H., A. Aarkrog, L. Hallstadius, E. Holm, and J. Rioseco. 1986. Radiocesium transport from the Irish Sea via the North Sea and the Norwegian Coastal Current to East Greenland. *Rapp. P.-v. Reun. Cons. Int. Explor. Mer. 186*: 70–79.

Day, R. H., and D. G. Shaw. 1987. Patterns in the abundance of pelagic plastic and tar in the North Pacific Ocean, 1976–1985. *Mar. Pollut. Bull. 18*: 311–16.

Dixon, T. R., and T. J. Dixon. 1981. Marine litter surveillance. *Mar. Pollut. Bull. 12*: 289–95.

———. 1983. Marine litter distribution and composition in the North Sea. *Mar. Pollut. Bull. 14*: 145–48.

Dodge, R. E., and T. R. Gilbert. 1984. Chronology of lead pollution contained in banded coral skeletons. *Mar. Biol. 82*: 9–13.

Druffel, E. M. 1981. Radiocarbons in annual coral rings from the eastern tropical Pacific Ocean. *Geophys. Res. Lett. 8*: 59–62.

Duxbury, A. C. 1975. Orthophosphate and dissolved oxygen in Puget Sound. *Limnol. Oceanogr. 20*: 270–74.

Eagle, G. A., A. Green, and J. Williams. 1979. Tar ball concentrations in the ocean around the Cape of Good Hope before and after a major oil spill. *Mar. Pollut. Bull. 10*: 321–25.

Erlenkeuser, H., E. Suess, and H. Willkomm. 1974. Industrialization affects heavy-metal and carbon-isotope concentrations in recent Baltic Sea sediments. *Geochim. Cosmochim. Acta 38*: 823–42.

Falandysz, J., and P. Szefer. 1984. Chlorinated hydrocarbons in fish-eating birds wintering in the Gdansk Bay 1981–82 and 1982–83. *Mar. Poll. Bull. 15*: 298–301.

Falkenmark, M. 1986. Hydrology of the Baltic Sea area: temporal fluctuations in water balance. *Ambio 15*: 97–102.

Farrington, J. W., J. H. Vandermeulan, and D. G. Cook, eds. 1983a. Proceedings of the Conference on Pollution in the North Atlantic Ocean. *Can. J. Fish. Aquat. Sci. 40* (Suppl. 2): 1–362.

Farrington, J. W., E. D. Goldberg, R. W. Risebrough, J. H. Martin, and V. T. Bowen. 1983b. U.S. Mussel Watch 1976–1978: an overview of the trace-metal, DDE, PCB, hydrocarbon, and artificial radionuclide data. *Environ. Sci. Technol. 17*: 490–96.

Flegal, A. R., K. Itoh, C. C. Patterson, and C. S. Wong. 1986. Vertical profile of lead isotopic compositions in the northeast Pacific. *Nature 321*: 689–90.

Fonselius, S. H. 1969. *Hydrographic Report 23*. Sweden: Fisheries Board.

———. 1981. Oxygen and hydrogen sulfide conditions in the Baltic Sea. *Mar. Poll. Bull. 12*: 187–94.

———. 1986. On long-term variations of dissolved oxygen in the deep water of the Baltic Sea. In *Baltic Sea Monitoring Symposium*. Tallinn, USSR: Helsinki Commission.

Fowler, C. W. 1987. Marine debris and northern fur seals: a case study. *Mar. Pollut. Bull. 18*: 326–35.

Fowler, S. W., P. Buat-Menard, Y. Yokoyama, S. Ballestra, E. Holm, and H. V. Nguyen. 1987. Rapid removal of Chernobyl fallout from Mediterranean surface waters by biological activity. *Nature 329*: 56–58.

Furness, R. W. 1985. A plastic particle pollution: accumulation by Procellariform seabirds at Scottish colonies. *Mar. Pollut. Bull. 16*: 103–106.

———. 1985b. Ingestion of plastic particles by seabirds at Gough Island, South Atlantic Ocean. *Envir. Pollut. 38A*: 261–72.

GESAMP. 1989. Land to ocean transport of contaminants: comparison of riverine and atmospheric fluxes. Annex IIC Report on the State of the Marine Environment.

Goldberg, E. D. 1986. TBT: an environmental dilemma. *Environment 28*: 17–20, 42–44.

Goldberg, E. D., M. Koide, V. Hodge, A. R. Flegal, and J. Martin. 1983. U.S. Mussel Watch: 1977–1978 results on trace metals and radionuclides. *Est. Coast. Shelf Sci. 16*: 69–93.

Gregory, M. R., R. M. Kirk, and M. C. G. Mabin. 1984. Pelagic tar, oil, plastics, and other litter in surface waters of the New Zealand sector of the southern ocean, and on Ross Dependency shores. *N. Z. Antarct. Rec. 6*: 12–28.

Gschwend, P. M., and R. A. Hites. 1981. Fluxes of Polycyclic aromatic hydrocarbons to marine and lacustrine sediments in the northeastern United States. *Geochim. Cosmochim. Acta 45*: 2359–68.

Hall, L. W., M. J. Lenkevich, W. S. Hall, A. E. Pinkney, and S. J. Bushong. 1987. Evaluation of butyltin compounds in Maryland waters of Chesapeake Bay. *Mar. Pollut. Bull. 18*: 78–83.

Hays, H., and G. Cormons. 1974. Plastic pellets found in tern pellets on coastal beaches and at factory sites. *Mar. Pollut. Bull. 5*: 44–46.

Holdway, P. 1986. A circumnavigational survey of marine tar. *Mar. Pollut. Bull. 17*: 374–77.

Horn, M. H., J. M. Teal, and R. H. Backus. 1970. Petroleum lumps on the surface of the sea. *Science 168*: 245–46.

Horsman, P. V. 1982. The amount of garbage pollution from merchant ships. *Mar. Pollut. Bull. 13*: 167–69.

Jeffrey, L. 1980. Petroleum residues in the marine environment. In *Marine Environmental Pollution*. Vol. 1, *Hydrocarbons*, ed. R. A. Geyer, 163–79. New York: Elsevier.

Jickells, T. D., A. H. Knap, and S. R. Smith, 1986. Trace-metal and nutrient fluxes through the Bermuda in-shore waters. *Rapp. P-v Reus. Cons. Int. Explor. Mar.*: 251–62.

Jickells, T. D., T. M. Church, and W. G. Deuser. 1987. A comparison of atmospheric inputs and deep-ocean particle fluxes for the Sargasso Sea. *Global Biogeochemical Cycles 1*: 117–30.

Jones, P. G. W., and D. F. Jefferies. 1983. The distribution of selected trace metals in the United Kingdom shelf waters and the North Atlantic. In *Proceedings of the Conference on Pollution in the North Atlantic Ocean*, ed. J. W. Farrington, J. H. Vandermeulen, and D. G. Cook, 124–31. *Can. J. Fish. Aquat. Sci. 40* (Suppl. 2).

Kempe, S., and H. Nies. 1987. Chernobyl nuclide record from a North Sea sediment trap. *Nature 329*: 828–31.

Kempe, S., V. Ittekkot, H. Nies, E. T. Degens, K. O. Buesseler, H. Livingston, S. Honjo, B. J. Hay, S. Manganini, E. Izdar, and T. Konuk. 1987. Comparison of Chernobyl nuclide deposition in the Black Sea and in the North Sea. In *Particle Flux in the Ocean*. Vol. 62, ed. Mitteil. Geol. Pal. Inst., Univ. Hamburg, E. T. Degens, E. Izdar, and S. Honjo, 165–78.

Kershaw, P. J. 1986. Radiocarbon dating of Irish Sea sediments. *Est. Coastal Shelf Sci. 23*: 295–303.

Kershaw, P. J., D. J. Swift, R. J. Pentreath, and M. B. Lovett. 1983. Plutonium redistribution by biological activity in Irish Sea sediments. *Nature 306*: 774–75.

Kershaw, P. J., D. J. Swift, R. J. Pentreath, and M. B. Lovett. 1984. The incorporation of plutonium, americium, and curium into the Irish seabed by biological activity. *Sci. Total Environ. 40*: 61–68.

Knap, A. H., K. S. Binkley, and W. G. Deuser. 1986. Synthetic organic chemicals in the deep Sargasso Sea. *Nature 319*: 572–75.

Knauer, G. A., and J. H. Martin. 1983. Trace elements and primary production: problems, effects and solutions. In *Trace Metals in Seawater*, ed. C. S. Wong, E. Boyle, K. W. Bruland, J. D. Burton, and E. D. Goldberg, 825–40. New York: Plenum Press.

Laist, D. W. 1987. Overview of the biological effects of lost and discarded plastic debris in the marine environment *Mar. Pollut. Bull. 18*: 319–26.

Lancelot, C., G. Billen, A. Sournia, T. Weisse, F. Colijn, M. J. W. Veldhuis, A. Davies, and P. Wassman. 1987. Phaeocystis blooms and nutrient enrichment in the continental coastal zones of the North Sea. *Ambio 16*: 38–46.

Langston, W. J. 1986. Metals in sediments and benthic organisms in the Mersey estuary. *Est. Coastal Shelf Sci. 23*: 239–61.

Larsen, B., and P. P. Madsen. 1986. Heavy-metal budgets for selected Danish sea areas. *Rapp. P.-V. Reun. Cons. Int. Eplor. Mer. 186*: 244–50.

Levy, E. M. 1983. Baseline levels of volatile hydrocarbons and petroleum residues in the waters and sediments of the Grand Banks. In *Proceedings of the Conference on Pollution in the North Atlantic Ocean*, ed. J. W. Farrington, J. H. Vandermeulen, and D. G. Cook. *Can. J. Fish. Aquat. Sci. 40* (suppl. 2): 1–362.

Livingston, H. D. 1988. The use of Cs and Sr isotopes as tracers in the Arctic and Mediterranean seas. *Phil. Trans. R. Soc. Lond. A 325*: 161–76.

Livingston, H. D., V. T. Bowen, and S. L. Kupferman. 1982. Radionuclides from Windscale discharges II: their dispersion in Scottish and Norwegian coastal circulation. *J. Mar. Res. 40*: 1227–50.

Mackay, D. W., W. Halcrow, I. Thornton. 1972. Sludge dumping in the Firth of Clyde. *Mar. Pollut. Bull. 3*: 7–10.

Mackay, D. W., W. K. Taylor, and A. R. Henderson. 1978. The recovery of the polluted Clyde estuary. *Proc. Royal Soc. Edinburgh 76B*: 135–52.

Mackenzie, F. T., R. J. Lantzy, and V. Peterson. 1979. Global trace metal cycles and predictions. *Math. Geol. 11*: 99–142.

MAFF. 1981. *Atlas of the Seas Around the British Isles*. London: Ministry of Agriculture, Fisheries, and Food.

Martin, J. H., and S. E. Fitzwater. 1988. Iron deficiency limits phytoplankton growth in the northeast Pacific subarctic. *Nature 331*: 341–43.

Merrell, T. R. 1984. A decade of change in nets and plastic litter from fisheries off Alaska. *Mar. Pollut. Bull. 15*: 378–84.

Morris, B. F. 1971. Petroleum: Tar quantities floating in the northwestern Atlantic taken with a new quantitative neuston net. *Science 173*: 430–32.

Morris, B. F., J. N. Butler, T. D. Sleeter, and J. Cadwallader. 1976a. Transfer of particulate hydrocarbon material from the ocean surface to the water column. In *Marine Pollutant Transfer*, ed. H. L. Windom and R. A. Duce, 213–34. Lexington, MA: Lexington Books.

Morris, B. F., J. Cadwallader, J. Geiselman, and J. N. Butler. 1976b. Transfer of petroleum and biogenic hydrocarbons in the Sargassum Community. In *Marine Pollutant Transfer*, ed. H. L. Windom and R. A. Duce, 235–59. Lexington, MA: Lexington Books.

Morris, R. J. 1980a. Floating plastic debris in the Mediterranean. *Mar. Pollut. Bull. 11*: 125.

———. 1980b. Plastic debris in the surface waters of the South Atlantic. *Mar. Pollut. Bull. 11*: 164–66.

Muller, G., G. Grimmer, and H. Boehnke. 1977. Sedimentary record of heavy metals and polycyclic aromatic hydrocarbons in Lake Constance. *Naturwissenschaffen 64*: 427–31.

NAS. 1975. Assessing potential ocean pollutants. A report of the Study Panel on Assessing Potential Ocean Pollutants to the Ocean Affairs Board, Commission on Natural Resources, National Research Council. Washington, D.C.: National Academy of Sciences.

———. 1985. *Oil in the Sea: Inputs, Fates and Effects*. Washington, D.C.: National Academy of Sciences, National Academy Press.

Nehring, D. 1981. Phosphorus in the Baltic Sea. *Mar. Pollut. Bull. 12*: 194–98.

Nehring, D., S. Schultz, and W. Kaiser. 1984. *Rapp. P-V. Reun. Cons. Int. Explor. Mer 183*: 193–203.

Niemisto, L., and A. Voipio. 1981. Notes on the sediment studies in the Finnish pollution research in the Baltic Sea. *Rapp. P-V. Reun. Cons. Int. Explor. Mer. 181*: 87–92.

Nolting, R. F. 1986. Copper, zinc, cadmium, nickel, iron, and manganese in the Southern Bight of the North Sea. *Mar. Pollut. Bull. 17*: 113–17.

Officer, C. B., R. B. Biggs, T. J. Taft, L. E. Cronin, M. A. Tyler, and W. R. Boynton. 1984. Chesapeake Bay anoxia – origins, development, and significance. *Science 223*: 22–27.

Olsson, M., and L. Reutegardh. 1986. DDT and PCB pollution trends in the Swedish aquatic environment. *Ambio 15*: 103–109.

Parslow, J. L. F., and D. J. Jefferies. 1972. Elastic thread pollution of puffins. *Mar. Pollut. Bull. 3*: 43–45.

Patterson, C. C., and D. M. Settle. 1987. Review of data on eolian fluxes of industrial and natural lead to the lands and seas in remote regions on a global scale. *Mar. Chem. 22*: 137–62.

Pavoni, B., A. Sfriso, and A. Marcomini. 1987. Concentration and flux profiles of PCBs, DDTs, and PAHs in a dated sediment core from the lagoon of Venice. *Mar. Chem. 21*: 25–36.

Payne, J. R., and C. R. Phillips. 1985. *Petroleum spills in the marine environment*. New York: Lewis Publishers Inc.

Pearcy, W. G., and H. A. Vanderploeg. 1973. Radioecology of benthic fish off Oregon. In *Radioactive Contamination of the Marine Environment*, Proceedings of a symposium in Seattle, WA, July 1972. Vienna: IAEA.

Postma, H. 1985. Eutrophication of Dutch coastal waters. *Neth. J. Zoology 35*: 348–59.

Prahl, F. G., and R. Carpenter. 1979. The role of zooplankton fecal pellets in the sedimentation of polycyclic aromatic hydrocarbons in Dabob Bay, Washington. *Geochim. Cosmochim. Acta 43*: 1959–72.

———. 1984. Hydrocarbons in Washington coastal sediments. *Est. Coastal Shelf Sci. 18*: 703–20.

PSWQA. 1986. *State of the Sound, 1986*. Report, Puget Sound Water Quality Authority, Seattle, WA.

Riley, J. P., and R. Chester. 1971. *Introduction to Marine Chemistry*. London: Academic Press.

Salomons, W., and U. Forstner. 1984. *Metals in the Hydrocycle*, Berlin: Springer-Verlag.

Shaw, D. G. 1977. Pelagic tar and plastic in the Gulf of Alaska and Bering Sea, 1975. *Sci. Total Envir. 8*: 13–20.

Shaw, D. G., and G. A. Mapes. 1979. Surface circulation and the distribution of pelagic tar and plastic. *Mar. Pollut. Bull. 10*: 160–62.

Shen, G. T., and E. A. Boyle. 1987. Lead in corals: reconstruction of historical industrial fluxes to the surface ocean. *Earth Planet. Sci. Lett. 82*: 289–304.

Shen, G. T., E. A. Boyle, and D. W. Lea. 1987. Cadmium in corals: chronicles of historic upwelling and industrial fallout. *Nature 328*: 794–96.

Sholkovitz, E. R., and D. R. Mann. 1984. The pore water geochemistry of ^{239,240}Pu and ^{137}Cs in sediments of Buzzards Bay, Massachusetts. *Geochim. Cosmochim. Acta 48*: 1107–14.

Skei, J. 1981. Dispersal and retention of pollutants in Norwegian fjords. *Rapp. P-V. Reun. Cons. Int. Explor. Mer. 181*: 78–86.

Sleeter, T. D., B. F. Morris, and J. N. Butler. 1973. Quantitative sampling of pelagic tar in the North Atlantic. *Deep-Sea Res. 21*: 773–75.

———. 1974. Pelagic tar in the Caribbean and equatorial Atlantic. *Deep-Sea Res. 23*: 467–74.

Slinn, D. J., and J. F. Eastham. 1984. Routine hydrographic observations in the Irish Sea off Port Erin, Isle of Man, during 1972–1981 inclusive. *Ann. Biol. 38*: 42–44.

Smith, R. A., R. B. Alexander, and M. G. Wolman. 1987. Water-quality trends in the nation's rivers. *Science 235*: 1607–15.

Smith, S. R., and A. H. Knap. 1985. Significant decrease in the amount of tar stranding on Bermuda. *Mar. Pollut. Bull. 16*: 19–21.

Smokler, P. E., D. R. Young, and K. L. Gard. 1979. DDT in marine fish following termination of dominant California input: 1970–77. *Mar. Pollut. Bull. 10*: 331–34.

Southward, A. J. 1980. The Western English Channel – an inconstant ecosystem? *Nature 285*: 361–66.

Suzuki, Y., and Matsuzaki 1983. Tar ball distribution and dynamics of surface waters in the western North Pacific. *Oceanogr. Mag. 33*: 19–26.

Tanabe, S. 1988. PCB problems in the future: foresight from current knowledge. *Environ. Pollut. 50*: 5–28.

Trefry, J. H., M. Sadoughi, M. D. Sullivan, J. S. Steward, and S. Barber. 1983. Trace metals in the Indiana River Lagoon, Florida: The copper story. *Florida Scientist 46*: 415–27.

Trefry, J. H., S. Metz, R. P. Trocine, and T. A. Nelsen. 1985. A decline in lead transport by the Mississippi River. *Science 230*: 439–41.

Turner, S. M., G. Malin, P. S. Liss, D. S. Harbour, and P. M. Holligan. 1988. The seasonal variation of dimethyl sulfide and dimethylsulfoniopropionate concentrations in near-shore waters. *Limnol. Oceanogr. 33*: 364–75.

UNESCO. 1987. Land/sea boundary flux of contaminants: contributions from rivers. GESAMP Reports and Studies No. 32.

Vauk, G. J. M., and E. Schrey. 1987. Litter pollution from ships in the German Bight. *Mar. Pollut. Bull. 18*: 316–19.

Venrick, E. L., T. W. Backman, W. C. Bartram, C. J. Platt, M. S. Thornhill, and R. E. Yates. 1973. Manmade objects on the surface of the central North Pacific Ocean. *Nature 241*: 271.

van Bennekom, A. J., and W. Salomon. 1980. Pathways of nutrients and organic matter from land to ocean through rivers. In *River Inputs to Ocean Systems*, ed. J. M. Martin, J. D. Burton, and D. Eisma, 33–51. Lanham, MD: UNESCO/SCOR.

van Franeker, J. A. 1985. Plastic ingestion in the North Atlantic Fulmar. *Mar. Pollut. Bull. 16*: 367–69.

van Vleet, E. S., W. M. Sackett, F. F. Weber, Jr., and S. B. Reinhardt. 1983. Input of pelagic tar into the northwest Atlantic from the Gulf Loop Current: chemical characterization and its relation to weathered DXTOC-1 Oil. In *Proceedings of the Conference on Pollution in the North Atlantic Ocean*, ed. J. W. Farrington, J. H. Vandermeulen, and D. G. Cook. *Can. J. Fish. Aquat. Sci. 40* (suppl. 2): 1–362.

Weichert, G. 1986. Nutrients in the German Bight, a trend analysis. *Deutsche Hydrographiscle Zeitung 39*: 197–206.

Weiss, R. F., J. C. Bullister, R. H. Gammon, and M. J. Warner. 1985. Atmospheric chlorofluoromethanes in the deep equatorial Atlantic. *Nature 314*: 608–610.

Weisskopf, M. 1988. Plastic reaps a grim harvest in oceans of the World. *Smithsonian 18*: 58–67.

Wolfe, D. A., ed. 1987. *Plastics in the Sea*, selected papers from the Sixth International Ocean Disposal Symposium. *Mar. Pollut. Bull. 18* (6B).

Wong, C. S., D. R. Green, and W. J. Cretney. 1974. Quantitative tar and plastic waste distribution in the Pacific Ocean. *Nature 247*: 30–32.

Wong, C. S., D. R. Green, and W. J. Cretney. 1976. Distribution and source of tar on the Pacific Ocean. *Mar. Pollut. Bull. 7*: 102–106.

Wong, C. S., E. Boyle, K. W. Bruland, J. D. Burton, and E. D. Goldberg. 1983. *Trace Metals in Seawater*. New York: Plenum Press.

Wood, L. B. 1982. *The Restoration of the Tidal Thames*. Bristol, U.K.: Adam Higher Ltd.

Young, D. R., D. McDermott-Ehrlich, and T. C. Heesen. 1977. Sediments as sources of DDT and PCB. *Mar. Pollut. Bull. 11*: 254–57.

19

Climate

JILL JÄGER   ROGER G. BARRY

The boundaries between what is called "weather" and what is called "climate" are difficult to draw. In fact, climate statistics are obtained by averaging weather data over a period that is long compared to the time limit over which the behavior of the atmosphere can be predicted locally (of the order of two weeks). Climate statistics can thus be obtained by averaging data (e.g., for January, for the winter, or for the year) over a number of years. Thirty years of data are usually used to define "normals." However, since climate is continually changing, there are no fixed normals and the statistics always depend on the averaging period.

Climate processes involve what can be termed the "slow physics" of the atmosphere and its interactions with the oceans, land surfaces and their vegetation, and snow and ice cover. The complexity of the interactions makes it difficult, if not sometimes impossible, to unravel causes and effects of climate variations. Thus, as will be described in more detail later, changes of the characteristics of the land surface (for example, as a result of deforestation or desertification) can lead to changes in the amount of solar radiation absorbed at the earth's surface in the affected region. In turn, this may produce changes of surface temperature and possibly of one or more climatic variables in other regions also, as a result of responses in the atmosphere.

Variations of Climate

Any general discussion of the impact of human activities on climate must begin with a short description of observed natural fluctuations of climate. Direct and indirect observations of climatic variables, such as temperature, precipitation, and pressure, show that the climatic state varies on all time and space scales. Figure 19.1 shows the geographic distributions of major climatic variables observed in recent years.

During at least the past 1 million years, a series of eight glacial/interglacial cycles has occurred. These were driven by changes in the earth's orbit around the sun, amplified by feedbacks within the climatic system. Figure 19.2 shows how the global climate is understood to have varied during the past 20,000 years, based on a variety of evidence. The earth is

at present in an interglacial period that began about 10,000 years ago. At the maximum of the last glacial period (about 18,000 years ago) ice sheets covered large areas of North America and Europe, for instance, and the global temperature was several degrees lower than that of today. The period between 10,000 years ago and the present is known as the Holocene. The early Holocene (9,000 to 6,000 years B.P.) was a time of possibly global and certainly regional warmth compared with today and was characterized by moist conditions in the present tropical desert areas. During the Holocene, many minor warming and cooling episodes occurred on the 100-year time scale. Over the past 2,000 years, the most widespread changes observed in the climate record are those associated with the Medieval Warm Epoch and the Little Ice Age. The former may have been restricted to the North Atlantic Basin, whereas the Little Ice Age seems to have been more nearly global (Wigley, Jones, and Kelly 1986). For the period after A.D. 1850, it is possible to make reasonably accurate quantitative estimates of climatic changes on the basis of observed data. Temperature is the best-documented variable, and in recent years a number of studies have been made of hemispheric and global temperature changes during the past 100 years. Figure 19.3 shows the global mean-temperature curve derived by Wigley et al. (1986) using data from the land areas of both hemispheres and measurements of temperature from the ocean areas. This curve shows a warming until about 1940, a cooling until the mid-1960s, and a warming since around 1970. The overall result is a global surface-temperature increase of the order of 0.5°C in the past 100 years. In order to understand which climatic variations are natural and which are due to human activities, it is necessary to look at the basic mechanisms of climatic change.

Basic Mechanisms of Climatic Change

The Climate System

The climate system consists of five interacting subsystems: atmosphere, ocean, cryosphere (ice and snow), biomass, and land. Numerous processes, such as evaporation

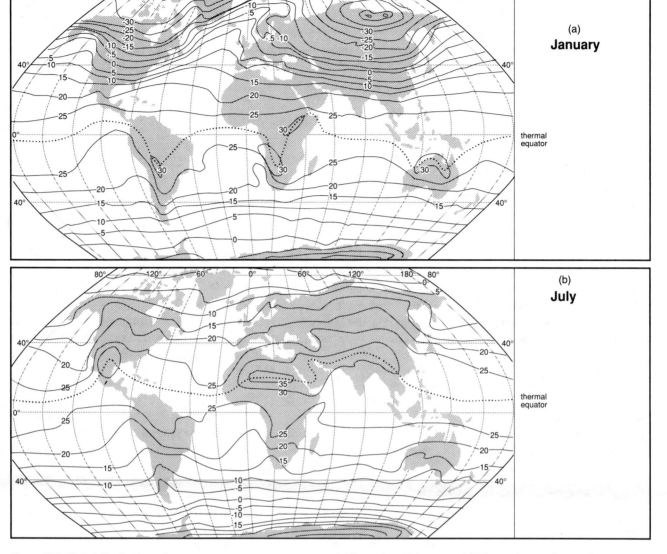

Figure 19.1 Global distributions of average temperature at sea level in (a) January and (b) July; and of precipitation (mm) for (c) December–February and (d) June–August. Source: Barry and Chorley 1987, after Möller.

and heat exchange, link these components (Fig. 19.4). Because of all of the interactions, the total climate system is very complex, and changes in one part of the system can lead to changes in another part.

Natural Causes of Climatic Changes

The causes of natural climatic changes can be divided into external and internal causes. *External* changes of global climate are forced by processes that change the flows of radiative energy within the system. Dickinson (1986) lists possible reasons for change as:

1. a change of solar output or a change in the geometry of the earth's orbit around the sun;
2. a change in the fraction of incoming energy at the top of the atmosphere that is absorbed by the surface or the atmosphere;
3. a change of the amount of net outgoing energy at the top of the atmosphere;
4. a change of the amount of heat stored by the deep ocean.

Changes from (2) and (3) could result from:

(a) changes in the fluxes of radiation as a result of changing atmospheric composition;
(b) changes of atmospheric transmissivity as a result of volcanic or anthropogenic aerosols or variations of cloudiness;
(c) changes in the amount of radiation reflected by the earth's surface;
(d) changes in the amount of long-wave radiation emitted by the surface and/or absorbed by water in the atmosphere.

Internal changes are manifested as feedbacks between the climatic variables in the atmospheric, water, and ice subsystems. For example, there is a feedback between the atmosphere and ice, as illustrated in Fig. 19.5. Many feedback loops within the climate system have been identified (Hansen and Takahashi 1984; Schneider and Dickinson 1974). The interactions between many feedback processes acting simultaneously, however, are not completely known.

Human Sources of Climatic Change

Interest in the possible effects of human activities on climate has increased dramatically in the past 20 years. Fol-

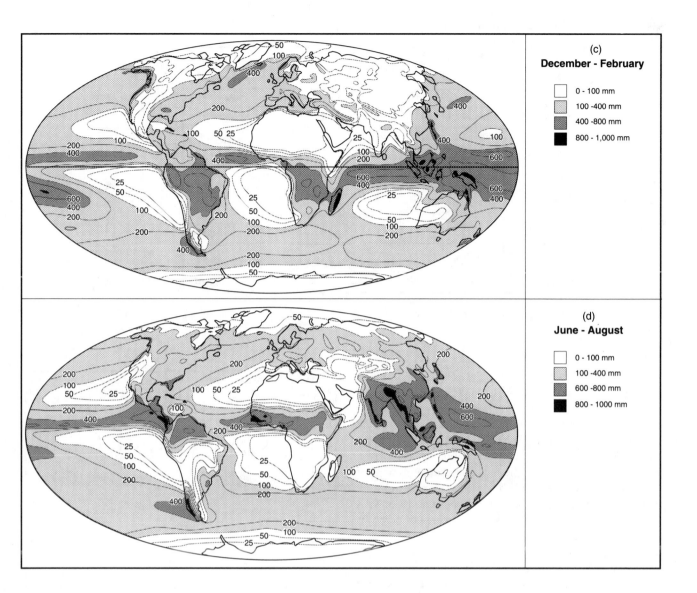

(c)
December - February

☐ 0 - 100 mm
▨ 100 -400 mm
▨ 400 -800 mm
■ 800 - 1,000 mm

(d)
June - August

☐ 0 - 100 mm
▨ 100 -400 mm
▨ 600 -800 mm
■ 800 - 1000 mm

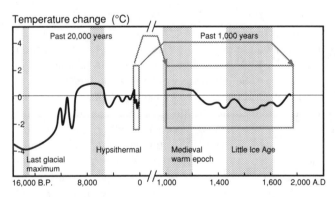

Figure 19.2 Schematic representation of the temperature changes during the past 20,000 years. Source: Jäger 1983.

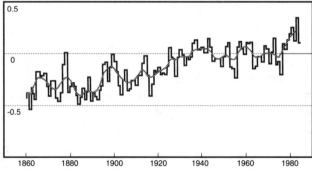

Figure 19.3 Global mean annual surface temperature changes. Smooth curve shows 10-year Gaussian filtered values. Source: Wigley, Jones, and Kelly 1986.

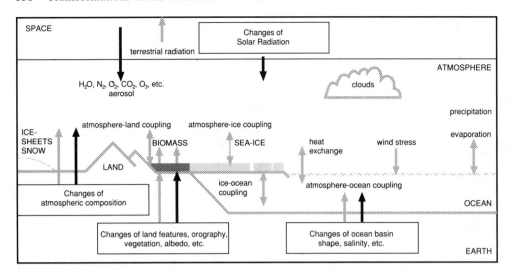

Figure 19.4 The climate system. Source: World Meteorological Organization 1975.

lowing the 1970 Study of Critical Environmental Problems (SCEP), the Study of Man's Impact on Climate (SMIC) was carried out in 1971 (SMIC 1971). This study provided an authoritative assessment of the state of understanding of the possible impacts of man's activities on regional and global climate. Since SMIC, considerable attention has been given to the effects on climate of the increasing concentrations of atmospheric trace gases, especially carbon dioxide, released by human activities (e.g., Clark 1982; Bolin et al. 1986; NAS 1983). Other studies have considered the effects of deforestation (e.g., Dickinson 1987; Gornitz 1985), and the general effects on climate of a number of human activities have been reviewed in several studies (e.g., Bach, Pankrath, and Kellogg 1979; Bach, Pankrath and Williams 1980; Jäger 1983; Kellogg 1978; Schneider and Londer 1984).

Changes in Atmospheric Composition: The Greenhouse Gases
A number of atmospheric trace gases, referred to as greenhouse gases, have received considerable attention because their concentrations have been observed to be increasing and because some of them have a so-called greenhouse effect, leading to a warming of the earth's surface.

The greenhouse effect can be explained by considering the annual and global average radiative energy budget of the earth-atmosphere system (Ramanathan et al. 1986). Figure

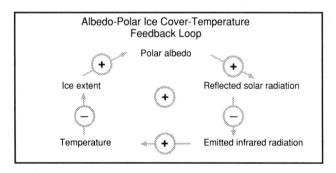

Figure 19.5 Albedo – polar ice cover – temperature feedback loop. Source: Jäger 1983.

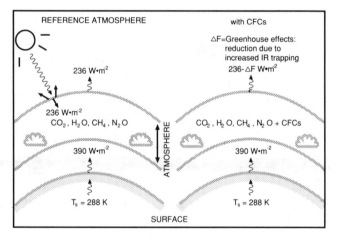

Figure 19.6 Global energy balance and the greenhouse effect. Source: Ramanathan et al. 1986.

19.6 shows the amounts of incoming solar radiation, reflected solar radiation, and outgoing infrared (long-wave) radiation at the top of the atmosphere as measured by satellites. The surface-atmosphere system emits roughly 236 Wm^{-2} to space, which balances the absorbed solar radiation. At a surface temperature of 288K, the long-wave emission by the surface is about 390 Wm^{-2}; the difference ($\sim$154 Wm^{-2}) between this and the outgoing infrared radiation at the top of the atmosphere is referred to as the greenhouse effect (Ramanathan et al. 1986). The most important atmospheric constituents that contribute to the greenhouse effect are H_2O, CO_2, and clouds, which together contribute about 90% of the total effect observed today. Ozone, CH_4, and N_2O contribute much of the remaining 10%. When the concentration of one of these radiatively active gases increases, the net effect, as a result of changes in the amounts of long-wave energy absorbed and emitted, is a warming of the lower atmosphere and the earth's surface.

As discussed by Ramanathan et al. (1986), gases can influence climate through a number of processes.

1. Radiatively active gases (e.g., CO_2 and H_2O) enhance the greenhouse effect.
2. Chemically active gases (e.g., CO and NO) can alter concentrations of radiatively active gases (e.g., CH_4 and O_3) by chemical interactions (see chap. 17).
3. Radiatively and chemically active gases can influence both the greenhouse effect and the concentrations of trace gases (e.g., CH_4 oxidation in the lower atmosphere can lead to increased tropospheric ozone, which has a greenhouse effect).
4. Ozone change and stratosphere-troposphere radiative interactions can occur.
5. Radiative-chemical interactions can take place because of the strong temperature dependence of the interaction rates of various chain reactions in the stratosphere that ultimately govern the stratospheric ozone concentration.
6. Interactions that involve large-scale motions (dynamics) in the stratosphere can occur.
7. Climate-chemistry interactions can take place – the greenhouse warming of the surface causes an enhancement of the evaporation of moisture from land and oceans, leading to an increase of tropospheric water content. This increase can lead to changes of the concentrations of other atmospheric trace gases.

The sources and observed trends of the concentrations of the atmospheric trace gases are summarized in chaps. 17 and 23.

Changes in Atmospheric Composition: Aerosols. Aerosols are particles of smoke, dust, and sea spray that are larger than molecular size. Bolle, Seiler, and Bolin (1986) distinguish among five major aerosol types:

1. coarse mechanically produced mineral dust,
2. coarse oceanic sea-salt particles,
3. fine, directly produced soot,
4. fine- and medium-sized products of gas-to-particle conversion,
5. volcanic ash of varying composition.

The range of radiative characteristics of aerosols is reasonably well known from measurements and theoretical analysis (Deepak and Gerber 1984). Nonabsorbing aerosols increase the albedo (reflectivity) of the atmosphere and reduce the amount of solar radiation that reaches the surface. Aerosols that absorb short-wave energy effectively heat the atmosphere and cool the underlying surface. Aerosols that absorb and emit infrared radiation have the effect that while energy is withdrawn from the upper troposphere, the greenhouse effect near the surface is increased. The net effect depends on the ratio of the absorption coefficients for short-wave and long-wave radiation and on the albedo of the underlying surface and the altitude of the aerosol layer. Most tropospheric aerosols are confined to the planetary boundary layer. Because the temperature in this layer is close to that of the earth's surface, the aerosols do not have a large impact on outgoing radiation fluxes. As a result of the short-wave radiative properties of the aerosols, more incoming solar radiation is absorbed at the ground, and the heating due to this additional

absorption partly compensates for the infrared cooling at the top of the planetary boundary layer.

In addition to the direct effects of aerosols on the radiation balance, aerosols can also affect cloud optical properties. Aerosols located within a water droplet or ice cyrstal can alter the radiative properties of the cloud. Aerosols can also serve as condensation or freezing nuclei and can influence the size and concentrations of droplets or ice crystals, which in turn govern the radiative properties of the clouds (Twomey, Piepgrass, and Wolfe 1984).

Several difficulties exist in assessing the climatic effects of aerosols added to the atmosphere as a result of human activities. First, the residence time of the aerosols in the atmosphere is short. Therefore, the global and temporal distribution is quite variable. Second, the radiative characteristics of atmospheric aerosols vary significantly in space and time, depending on the sources. Table 19-1 shows the major sources of aerosols, together with some estimates of their magnitude.

Bolle et al. (1986) emphasize that although we know that local and regional changes of aerosol concentration have occurred, it is not certain if there have been global changes as a result of human activities.

Long-distance transport of tropospheric aerosols has been observed. The transport of Saharan dust over the Atlantic Ocean has been traced in satellite pictures as far as the Caribbean and Europe, and dust from Texas deserts has been traced to Europe (e.g., Carlson and Benjamin 1980; Deepak and Gerber 1984; Joseph and Wolfson 1975). Aerosol particles have been collected in winter in the North Polar region that clearly come from automobile and diesel exhaust and indus-

Table 19-1 *Estimated relative rates for aerosol-production processes (%)*

Processes	a	b	c	d
Sulfates (from H_2S and SO_2, gas-to-particle conversion, including volcanic and manmade)	35	27–15	29–18	41–37
Ammonium salts	—	8–10	9–12	41–37
Sea-salt spray	33	31–11	33–14	23–27
Soil and rock debris	16	10–19	11–23	14–16
Organic volatiles from plants, forest fires, agricultural burnings, hydrocarbons from natural decay	6	9–17	9–12	
Volcanic dust	2	3–6	3–7	7–1
Nitrates (from NO)	6	9–18	3–2	3
Human-made particulates (heating, industry, engine exhausts)	2	3–6	3–8	3–4

Source: Work by Peterson and Judge (a), SMIC (b), Twomey (c), and Dittberner (d), cited in Bolle et al. 1986.

trial operations at middle latitudes (Rosen, Novakov, and Bodhaine 1981; Stonehouse 1986).

Ramanathan et al. (1986) conclude that the aerosol-climate problem is so complicated that, even after decades of research, it is still difficult to make any general statements about the net effects of aerosols in general. Some direct effects of aerosols resulting from human activities are discussed in a later section.
Changes in Atmospheric Composition: Water Vapor. An additional factor that must be taken into account with regard to the impact of trace gases on climate is the water-vapor content of the atmosphere. Calculations suggest that a warming as a result of greenhouse-gas increases would result in an increase in tropospheric water-vapor content. The increase in water vapor would vary according to latitude and altitude, ranging from 5% to 15% in the low altitudes to as much as 50% in polar regions. This water-vapor feedback would amplify the surface warming by about 50% to 80%. Observations made in recent years at a number of meteorological stations suggest that the tropospheric water-vapor content is increasing (Flohn 1986).

The Effects of Heat Release. The effects of heat released during human activity depend on the rate of heat release and the area over which it is added. Large rates of heat release in localized areas can increase convection and even lead to increased vorticity, whereas more moderate rates of heat release over a larger area lead to increases of temperature such as those observed for urban areas. When averaged over the globe, the amount of heat released by human activities is a small fraction of the solar radiation absorbed at the earth's surface. The following values, taken from Munn and Machta (1979), compare the heat releases from human activities with other energy sources.

Global average solar radiation at the outer edge of the atmosphere	$305 \, \mathrm{Wm}^{-2}$
Global average solar radiation absorbed at the earth's surface	$160 \, \mathrm{Wm}^{-2}$
1970 energy use distributed evenly over the globe	$0.016 \, \mathrm{Wm}^{-2}$
1970 energy use distributed evenly over the continents	$0.054 \, \mathrm{Wm}^{-2}$
Annual global energy flow from the earth's interior	$0.06 \, \mathrm{Wm}^{-2}$
Heat from major U.S. cities: summer	$20{-}40 \, \mathrm{Wm}^{-2}$
winter	$70{-}210 \, \mathrm{Wm}^{-2}$

These figures show that on a global average, the use of energy is 10^{-4} of the solar energy absorbed at the earth's surface. However, at individual places on the earth's surface, the heat release due to human activities is of the same order of magnitude as the absorbed solar energy. One of the main observed consequences of this is the warming of urban areas, discussed in more detail in a later section.

The Effects of Changes in the Characteristics of the Land Surface. There are basically three ways in which changes in the characteristics of the land surface can influence the climate. First, the albedo or reflectivity of the surface can be changed,

and this changes the amount of solar energy absorbed at the surface. Second, the roughness of the surface can be changed, and this affects the transfers of energy, moisture, and momentum into the atmosphere. Third, the surface wetness can be changed, affecting the evaporation from the surface. Human activities that lead to such changes include deforestation for agricultural purposes or for energy use, urbanization, irrigation, and creation of artificial lakes.

As an example of the effects of land use changes on the albedo, the average albedo of a number of vegetation types is shown in Table 19-2. Sagan, Toon, and Pollack (1979) have estimated the geographic area altered over the past few millennia and in the past 25 years by desertification, salinization, temperate deforestation, tropical deforestation, and urbanization. Further, they estimated the changes in global albedo caused by the land-use modifications. This work was updated by Henderson-Sellers and Wilson (1983) and the results are shown in Table 19-3. Henderson-Sellers and Wilson conclude that the leading causes of global albedo change are desertification and deforestation of tropical regions. They also point out that all changes except for irrigation, dam-building, and urbanization produce an increase in the earth's albedo and a cooling of the planet. Sagan et al. (1979) suggest that during the past several thousand years, the earth's temperature could have been depressed by about 1K, primarily because of desertification, but Henderson-Sellers and Wilson calculated a smaller albedo effect, with only a 0.1K cooling.

By changing the surface roughness, human activities alter the frictional characteristics of the earth's surface and thus influence the speed of local winds, the amount of turbulence, and the transfer of momentum between the earth's surface and the atmosphere. For example, Baumgartner and Kirchner (1980) list the roughness parameters of various surface types: forest 100–300 cm; grass 5 cm; crops 30 cm; bare land 0.1–1 cm. This roughness parameter is used to incorporate the effects of surface roughness in equations calculating the fluxes of energy and momentum from the earth's surface into the atmosphere. Knowledge of the effect of forest barriers on winds has been utilized in the construction of windbreaks to protect crops and soil.

Changes of surface hydrological characteristics can occur as a result of deforestation, irrigation, reservoir construction, and wetland drainage, for example. Studies in Amazonia have shown that in areas in which vegetation cover is reduced, the relative humidity is reduced and the temperature is raised. About 50% of the precipitation in the Amazon region returns to the atmosphere as water vapor through evapotranspiration, which depends on the forest cover. Of the solar radiation absorbed by the forest surface in the Amazon Basin, about half of the energy is returned to the atmosphere as latent heat and about half as sensible heat. Salati (1987) concludes that changing the land use to permanent agricultural systems leads to months with a greater water deficit and higher temperatures.

Measurements

Basically two different types of data can be used to reconstruct climatic history: (1) observations made with meteoro-

Table 19-2 *Albedo of natural vegetation*

Vegetation type	Winter	Spring	Summer	Fall	Annual average
Tropical evergreen rainforest	11	11	11	11	11
Tropical evergreen rainforest	13	13	13	13	13*
Tropical evergreen seasonal forest	11	11	11	11	11
Tropical evergreen seasonal forest	13	13	13	13	13
Xeromorphic forest/woodland	28	32	28	28	29
Evergreen sclerophyllous woodland	15	13	12	13	13.3
Tropical drought-deciduous woodland	20	18	17	18	18.3
Xeromorphic (dwarf) shrubland	28	32	28	28	29
Tall/medium/short grassland with 10–40% woody tree cover	14	15	17	15	15.3
Tall/medium/short grassland with <10% woody tree cover	14	15	16	14	14.8
Tall/medium/short grassland with shrub cover	16	18	25	20	19.8
Tall grassland, no woody cover	17	17	20	17	17.8
Medium grassland, no woody cover	16	20	20	18	18.5
Desert	30	30	30	30	30

Source: Gornitz 1985.
* Oguntoyinbo 1970; Pinker et al. 1980.

Table 19-3 *Global albedo changes due to anthropogenic modifications (in past 30 years).*

Process	Land type change	Surface albedo change (wavelength integrated)	Change in area, over 30 years, relative to earth's surface area	Cloud cover/ insolation factors	Fractional change in system albedo over 30 years
Deforestation of tropical forest	(1) forest ⟶ savannah (maximum*)	0.09	0.00647	0.5/1.2	(1) 4.59×10^{-4}
	(2) forest ⟶ clearings (minimum[†])	0.03			(2) 1.53×10^{-4}
Deforestation of temperate forests	forest ⟶ field, pasture	0.05	small	0.5/0.8	small
Dam-building	field ⟶ water	−0.14	0.00059	0.25/1	-0.68×10^{-4}
Salinization	field ⟶ saline field	0.06	0.000074	0.25/1	0.64×10^{-4}
Irrigation of arid land	desert soil ⟶ field	−0.17	0.00072	0/1	-1.19×10^{-4}
Urbanization	field, pasture ⟶ urban	−0.05	0.00059	0.5/0	-0.23×10^{-4}
	forest ⟶ urban	~0.0	0.00059	0.5/1	~0.0
Desertification	scrub/shrub ⟶ desert soil	0.12	(a)[‡] 0.00318	0/1	(a) 3.81×10^{-4}
	protected exclosure	0.05	(b)[‡] 0.00159	0/1	(b) 1.91×10^{-4}
			(c)[‡] 0.00318	0/1	(c) 1.59×10^{-4}
			(d)[‡] 0.00159	0/1	(d) 0.79×10^{-4}

Source: Henderson-Sellers and Wilson 1983.
* Total surface albedo change: maximum effect of tropical deforestation: (a) 6.35×10^{-4}, (b) 4.45×10^{-4}, (c) 4.13×10^{-4}, (d) 3.33×10^{-4}.
† Total surface albedo change: minimum effect of tropical deforestation: (a) 3.29×10^{-4}, (b) 1.39×10^{-4}, (c) 1.07×10^{-4}, (d) 0.27×10^{-4}.
‡ (a) and (c) are U.N. estimates, and (b) and (d) allow for 50% recovery.

logical instruments and diary records of weather phenomena such as snowfalls, frosts, floods, or droughts; and (2) so-called proxy records of climate, such as tree rings, pollen preserved in peat deposits and lake sediments, ocean-floor deposits of foraminifera, and ice cores. Ice cores provide a suite of information on air temperature, volcanic events, atmospheric composition (CO_2, CH_4, trace metals, aerosols), and snow accumulation.

Detailed descriptions of proxy climate data are given by Lamb (1977) and Bradley (1985). The possibilities of using many of these types of record have barely been exploited.

Each record must first be calibrated or processed to provide an estimate of the climate. For example, the elevation of an ancient coral reef is a record of a previous sea-level, but before it can be used for palaeoclimatic purposes, the effect of local crustal movements must be removed. The width of tree rings is known to reflect the joint influence of several ecological factors, and multivariate statistical analyses are used to obtain estimates of selected variables such as temperature and precipitation. Because no proxy source yields as long and continuous a record as would be desired and because the quality of data varies considerably from site to site, a coherent picture of past climate requires assembly of data from different periods and with different sampling intervals (NAS 1975). After proxy data have been processed, an absolute chronology must be established in order to date specific features in the climatic record. The most accurate dating techniques are those used in tree-ring analysis and ice-core analysis, from which dates accurate to within a year may be determined over several thousand years under favorable conditions. Annually layered lake sediments (or varves) also provide dating accuracy to within several years over several thousand years. Dating using radiocarbon is possible with an accuracy of 5% of the true age for about 40,000 years.

The instrumentally recorded climatic data bases have been described in detail by Bradley and Jones (1985). For the temperature record, Bradley and Jones point out that the first reliable thermometers were not developed until the mid-eighteenth century, and only careful analyses have been able to extend records further back (e.g., Manley 1974 compiled a record of central England temperature starting in 1659). Most analyses of observed surface-air temperature have used essentially the same data source: *World Weather Records*. These records have been supplemented with additional data from published and manuscript material in meteorological archives. Jones et al. (1986) have assessed the effects of two main sources of possible error (errors in individual station records, and changes in spatial coverage), and conclude that the Northern Hemisphere temperature series is probably reliable on a year-to-year basis after 1875. In contrast to the land-based data, it is more difficult to obtain a strictly homogeneous time series of ship-based data due to changes in instrumentation and problems related to instrument exposure. Jones, Wigley, and Wright (1986) have compiled a series of land- and ocean-based temperature records to produce a record of globally averaged temperature changes for the period 1861–1984.

Precipitation and surface-pressure data sets are comparable in length to those for temperature. Upper-air analyses, which show changes in the troposphere and stratosphere, are available only since 1950. Bradley and Jones (1985) have also discussed these data bases with respect to their errors, homogeneity, and potential significance in evaluating the climatic effect of increasing CO_2 concentrations. Even though long records do exist, the analysis of long-term fluctuations in precipitation amount is more difficult than the analysis of, say, surface-air temperature. Precipitation is a discontinuous process, and areal averaging of precipitation data is difficult because of sparsity of station coverage and the effects of orography. There are also more difficulties in measuring precipitation amount accurately, especially snowfall.

Climatic Changes due to Human Activities: the Global Scale

Human activities could change the climate on a global scale in two basic ways. First, large-scale regional changes could induce downstream, hemispheric, or even global effects as a result of "teleconnections." Second, a uniform change in the global atmospheric composition (e.g., trace-gas concentration) could be accompanied by changes of the globally averaged temperatures and associated changes of climate ¿ all scales.

The idea of teleconnections can be illustrated by looking at the anomalies of the atmospheric circulation associated with anomalies of the sea-surface temperature in certain tropical ocean areas. For example, a localized winter warming of the ocean waters off the coast of Peru, referred to as El Niño, spreads into the central and eastern Pacific Ocean every two to seven years, associated with changes in wind regime and pressure centers across the Pacific Ocean. Major episodes, such as that which occurred during 1982/1983, are associated with massive displacements of the rainfall regions in the tropics, and the related atmospheric circulation anomalies extend far into the extratropics, where they are associated with unusual wintertime conditions over regions as far apart as the United States and New Zealand (Ramage 1986; WCP 1987). Similarly, it is conceivable that regional-scale changes of the surface characteristics, as a result of, say, deforestation, could affect the surface energy balance to such an extent that the general atmospheric circulation is modified, and related changes of variables such as temperature and rainfall may then occur in other regions, as well as in the one in which the human activities first played a major role. Such teleconnections related to large-scale changes of the earth's surface characteristics have not been observed, but it is possible that they have occurred and remain undetected because the causes of regional climatic changes are complex and not completely understood. The energy-balance change and areas involved are possibly smaller than those associated with natural sea-surface temperature anomalies, but this remains to be investigated thoroughly. In any case, numerical models of the atmospheric circulation have shown that such teleconnections and downstream effects are possible (e.g., Henderson-Sellers 1987).

Global climatic changes can also result from global-scale activities, such as the addition of trace gases to the atmosphere. These emissions are not distributed uniformly over the globe, but the gases are relatively quickly distributed by the atmospheric circulation. The increased concentrations of the so-called greenhouse gases lead, as has been shown, to a warming of the earth's surface and lower troposphere.

Trace Gases

Using information about recent trends of greenhouse-gas concentrations, Ramanathan et al. (1986) have computed the global mean greenhouse forcing for decadal increases in trace-gas abundances (Fig. 19.7). This figure suggests that the nongreenhouse gases now add to the greenhouse effect by an amount at least comparable to the effect of CO_2. The greenhouse-gas changes between 1850 and 1980 are computed to have given rise to an equilibrium surface-air temperature change of about 0.9K, with CO_2 contributing about 0.6K. As a result of detailed considerations of the radiative characteristics of the relevant trace gases, in particular their absorption features, the changes of heating rate due to trace-gas increases can be calculated accurately. Greater uncertainties arise, however, in estimating the change of global mean surface temperature resulting from the change in the heating

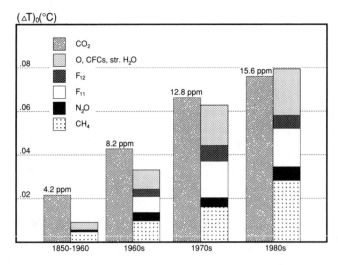

Figure 19.7 Decadal additions to global mean greenhouse forcing of the climate system. The temperature change on the ordinate is the computed temperature change at equilibrium for the estimated decadal increases in trace-gas abundances with no climate feedbacks included. Source: Ramanathan et al. 1986.

rate, because a number of feedback processes can increase or decrease the change in heating rate. The change of surface-air temperature as a result of changes of trace-gas concentration has been computed by a large number of models of the climate system. For a doubling of the atmospheric CO_2 concentration (or equivalent changes of other trace-gas concentrations), models compute an increase of the global mean surface temperature of 1.3K to 4.2K. Dickinson (1986) argues that the global average equilibrium warming for a doubling of the CO_2 concentration would lie between 1.5K and 5.5K, and probably between 2.5K and 4.5K. The report of the NAS (1983) suggested that the temperature increase would be 3 ± 1.5K. Model results also suggest that the warming would be greatly enhanced in high latitudes, and there is some evidence of midlatitude, midcontinent summer drying (Dickinson 1986). Such regional climatic changes, however, are not modeled with great reliability at present.

Most studies of the response of the climate to increases of trace-gas concentrations have considered the changes of the equilibrium climate of the earth resulting from an abrupt increase of the trace-gas concentration. More recent work has focused on the transient response of climate to both abrupt and realistic increases of trace-gas concentration. The actual response of the climate lags behind the equilibrium response because of the thermal inertia of the ocean. Ramanathan et al. (1986) calculate that the Northern Hemisphere surface-air temperature should have increased by 1.3K between 1850 and 1980 as a result of the increase of CO_2 concentration from 270 ppmv to 338 ppmv. In fact, the observed temperature increase is about 0.5K. The discrepancy does not necessarily mean that the calculations are wrong, since they are based on the assumption that the climate system comes into equilibrium with the trace-gas increase. In fact, the ocean-surface mixed layer takes a few decades to equilibrate with the atmospheric temperatures. Taking the oceanic inertia into account, Wigley et al. (1985) calculate that the transient warming to date due to CO_2 and other trace-gas increases should be in the range

0.3K to 1.1K, which is in agreement with the observed temperature change (see Fig. 19.3), but does not necessarily prove that the observed temperature changes during the past 100 years are a result of changes of concentrations of atmospheric trace gases. These calculations also ignore other possible factors that may have affected global temperature (solar output and volcanic and other aerosols).

Clouds

During the Study of Critical Environmental Problems, Machta and Carpenter (1971) reported observations of changes in the amount of high clouds. Figure 19.8 shows the annual average high-cloud cover at six stations in the United States for occasions when no low or middle clouds were present. The dashed lines show roughly the increase of jet traffic in the United States since 1958. The curves show an increase in high cloudiness since 1965. The SMIC (1971) report points out that the coincidence of more high clouds with increased commercial jet flights suggests a causal relation but that two points must be noted. First, there was nothing unique about 1965 in aircraft operations. Second, an analysis of middle-cloud cover during times with no low clouds indicated a marked decrease at five of the six stations shown in Fig. 19.8. Therefore, the SMIC authors suggested that the increase of high clouds after 1964 could have natural origins.

Henderson-Sellers (1986a; 1986b) has analyzed cloud-cover records for western Europe and North America and has examined the cloud-cover differences between a cold period (1901–1920) and a warm period (1934–1953). The observations of cloud cover are generally given in tenths of sky cover. For Europe, she finds that cloud cover generally increased from the cold period to the warm period, except in the central European region (Germany, France, and some parts of Spain), in which there was a tendency for decreasing cloud amounts as warming occurred. Similarly for the United States, cloud amount increased over almost all of the area considered in all seasons. Figure 19.9 compares the Northern Hemisphere mean surface-air temperature variations since 1900 with the United States mean annual cloud amount, calculated by averaging the observations from 77 stations. Assuming that at least part of the observed surface-temperature increase is a result of the increasing concentrations of atmospheric trace gases due to human activities, it is possible that the observed increase in total cloud amount is also related to human activities.

Climatic Changes due to Human Activities: the Regional Scale

In the cases in which human activities have altered large areas of the earth's surface, some evidence of regional-scale climatic alteration exists. This section discusses the changes resulting from three widespread processes: overgrazing, deforestation, and pollution (arctic haze).

The Effects of Overgrazing

Bryson and Baerreis (1967) suggested that overgrazing was the cause of the expansion of the Rajasthan Desert of India. The argument went as follows. Several thousand years

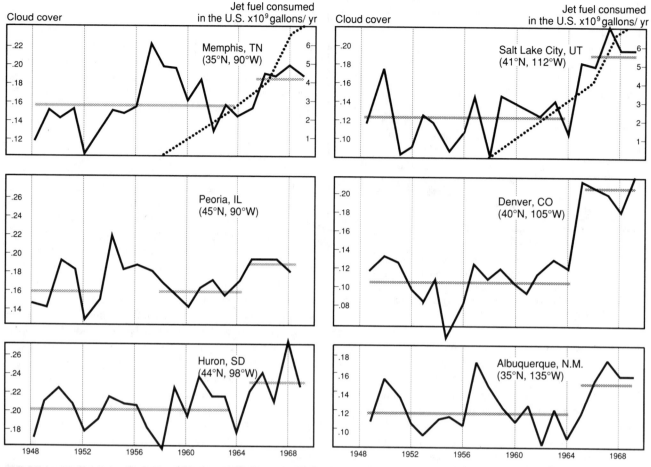

Figure 19.8 Average annual high-cloud cover with no low or middle clouds for six observing stations in the U.S. Source: Machta and Carpenter 1971.

ago this region was the site of the Indus Valley (Harappan) civilization. At that time, the climate was arid, but not as dry as today. The present-day aridity is caused by subsidence in the atmosphere, and Bryson and Baerreis proposed that this aridity is augmented by radiative cooling of suspended dust, the presence of which is caused by sparsity of vegetation as a result of overgrazing. In areas protected from grazing, the grass is observed to grow rapidly, thus confirming that the sparsity of vegetation is a result of overgrazing. Sagan et al. (1979) pointed out that although it is clear that the Rajasthan Desert has expanded over the millennia and that overgrazing has contributed to growth, the role of dust in creating the desert is still being debated. Harshvardhan and Cess (1978) made calculations that suggested that the radiative cooling due to dust is less important than Bryson believed. Hare's (1983) review and synthesis of observational and modeling studies indicates that increases of albedo due to overgrazing or unwise cultivation in arid areas cause increased subsidence, thereby suppressing precipitation. Over geological time scales, however, deserts have varied in extent and shifted latitudinally.

Sagan et al. (1979) also believed that human influences have played a major role in desertification. They mentioned evidence of ancient farming villages now covered by desert,

demonstrating that the water balance was once more favorable. They suggested that humans have been living in the Sahara and modifying it extensively by fire and by grazing activities for many thousands of years. Longer-term changes in moisture balance due to natural climatic variations are demonstrated, however, by the documented fluctuations of tropical lake levels since the maximum recorded in early Holocene times, approximately 8,000 B. P. (Street-Perrott and Harrison 1984). Sagan et al. (1979) concluded that although most damage in arid lands is due to overgrazing or deforestation, another problem is salinization by irrigation projects. They gave the example of Iraq, where 20% to 30% of the country's potential farmland has in this way been converted to deserts.

Otterman (1977) also suggested that domestic animals may have contributed to the desertification in much of the Middle East and the Fertile Crescent. Overgrazing has also been suggested as one of the factors in the protracted Sahel drought. Rainfall in this sub-Saharan region of Africa during the early 1970s was generally far below the long-term average for several years running, and there was considerable loss of livestock and crops. After a brief respite, severe conditions resumed, and rainfall in the Sahelian zone in 1981 through 1984 was less than in the early 1970s (Nicholson 1985). Glantz (1977) suggested that the intervention by Western countries

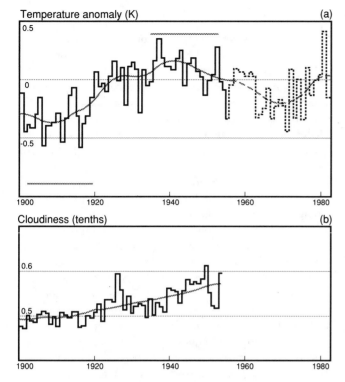

Temperature anomaly (K)   (a)

Cloudiness (tenths)   (b)

Figure 19.9 (a) Northern Hemisphere mean surface temperature variation (K) since 1900 shown as anomalies for 1946–1960 reference period. (b) U.S. mean annual cloud amount for 77 stations averaged for the period 1900–1954. Both curves show 20-year filtered values. Source: Henderson-Sellers 1986b.

with inappropriate technology made the impacts of the drought worse. He pointed out that foreign aid had financed the digging of wells, which upset the established nomadic way of life that was adapted to periodic droughts. In the Sahel, the wells encouraged nomads to increase the size of the herds beyond the long-term carrying capacity of the land and to stay in areas close to the wells. The herds overgrazed these areas and depleted and trampled the available vegetation.

The Effects of Deforestation

The clearing of forests for agricultural purposes has been practiced for hundreds of years. Schneider and Londer (1984) note that the consequences of forest clearing were also observed almost 500 years ago in the biography of Christopher Columbus; they cite the following description of the explorer's 1494 departure for the Caribbean island of Jamaica:

The sky, air, and climate were just the same as in other places; every afternoon there was a rain squall that lasted for about an hour. The admiral writes that he attributes this to the great forests of that land; he knew from experience that formerly this also occurred in the Canary, Madeira, and Azore islands, but since the removal of forests that once covered those islands they do not have so much mist and rain as before.

In the tropics, slash-and-burn agriculture has long been used to clear the land. According to Sagan et al. (1979), some 40% of the African equatorial forests have been converted to savanna over the past few thousand years, and half of the remaining forest has been altered. In recent years, the effects

of shifting cultivation have been overtaken by the wholesale removal of vast tracts of forests for highway development, large-scale cattle ranching, and small-scale farming colonization (Fearnside 1982; 1987). The loss of tropical forest as a result of shifting cultivation, new permanent agriculture, cattle grazing, logging, and fuelwood demand is imprecisely documented, but is estimated to be 9–24.5 million ha/yr (Henderson-Sellers 1987). Some of this range can be explained by differences of definition: some researchers look at degraded forests, whereas others look at areas in which the forest is completely removed. Differences also exist in the definition of current land use and the method for calculating deforestation rate (Henderson-Sellers 1987). Therefore, any attempt to assess rates of deforestation is based on unreliable data (see also chaps 10, 11, and 23).

Sagan et al. (1979) estimated that $7 \times 10^6 \, km^2$ of tropical forest have been removed as a result of human activities. This is 5% of the continental surface area and about 50% of the present tropical forest area. The same authors pointed out that the differences between the microclimates of tropical forests and of denuded areas are immense. The removal of the forest causes the daily ground temperature variation to be greater, and drastically alters the hydrological conditions.

In the Mediterranean area and in China, early civilizations destroyed the temperate forests. The forests of North America and Europe have been reduced mainly during the past 1,000 years (especially the past 500 years), although some reforestation is occurring (see chap. 11). The SMIC (1971) report estimated that during the past 1,000 years $1.5–2 \times 10^7 \, km^2$ of temperate forests have been converted to arable land and grassland. Sagan et al. (1979), however, pointed out that this is 10% to 15% of the earth's continental surface area and comparable to the total area now in temperate grassland and nontropical cultivated land. They used a more conservative estimate of $8 \times 10^6 \, km^2$, assuming that the present extent of temperate evergreen and deciduous forest is 60% of the original forest area.

Sagan et al. (1979) suggested that a link existed between the extensive deforestation in North America and Europe and the Little Ice Age (see Fig. 19.3). Their statistics indicate substantial reduction of forests in Europe and North America during the nineteenth-century industrialization. They proposed a physical mechanism for the relationship between deforestation and the climatic cooling. They pointed out that the albedo of snow-covered deciduous and coniferous forests is generally less than that of snow-covered farmland (0.2–0.5) and suggested that since the winter albedo of forest land is generally 0.2–0.3, deforestation nearly doubles the albedo in winter. Such a large change in albedo over an area as extensive as Europe would affect regional winter climate and perhaps the climate over a significant fraction of the globe. On the other hand, the authors pointed out that the Little Ice Age has other possible causes, including changes in volcanic activity and solar activity, which also had observed variations during the same period. Moreover, the expansion of European glaciers, which serves to define the primary characteristic of the Little Ice Age, was probably caused primarily by cooler summers.

Gornitz (1985) has examined the albedo change resulting from human modification of the vegetation during the past century in western Africa. The historical vegetation changes were digitized on a 1° × 1° grid map based on a literature survey of government censuses, forestry and agricultural reports, and other sources. Land-cover modification was found to have occurred as a result of clearing of the natural vegetation for agriculture, grazing, logging, and degradation of marginal semiarid to arid ecosystems by excessive grazing or cultivation. Forest surveys for western Africa showed a clearance of about 56% of the forest zone. Gornitz finds that the change in albedo corresponding to the land-use modification is relatively small, amounting to an increase of about 0.4% regionally over the past 100 years, and 0.5% since agriculture began.

The effect of large-scale changes in albedo on the atmospheric circulation have been studied using numerical models of the climate system. These studies began when scientists were attempting to explain the origins of the Sahel drought. Charney (1975) proposed a biogeophysical feedback mechanism to explain the drought. He argued that a reduction of the vegetation cover (initially as a result of overgrazing) would increase the albedo in the Sahel region and that this would lead to an increase in atmospheric sinking motion, giving additional drying, which would perpetuate the arid conditions. To test this hypothesis, Charney, Stone, and Quirk (1975) used the model of the atmospheric circulation developed at the Goddard Institute of Space Studies to compare the atmospheric circulation simulated when the albedo in the Sahel area was 0.14 and when it was 0.35. A decrease of precipitation and convective cloud cover was reported as a response to the increased albedo. A further series of numerical-model experiments made by Charney et al. (1977) took better account of the interaction between surface hydrological processes, albedo changes, and the atmospheric circulation. Further tests of Charney's idea subsequently have been made using a number of different models (see reviews by Jäger 1983 and Henderson-Sellers 1987).

Potter et al. (1975) used a numerical model of the climate system to assess the impact of changing surface albedo from 0.07 to 0.25 in a fraction of the tropical zone. They showed that in the simulations performed, precipitation decreased in the deforested zone (5°N–5°S). Wilson (1984) analyzed the sensitivity of a numerical climate model to land-use changes throughout the tropics. In the deforestation experiment, both moisture capacity and surface albedo were changed from values appropriate to forest conditions to those appropriate for grassland vegetation cover. The model was found to be sensitive to the prescribed changes at a regional scale.

In summarizing the results of such model experiments, Henderson-Sellers (1987) points out that changes in surface hydrology are at least as important as changes in the surface albedo and that the results are sensitive to the assumptions made in the models and the information on land surface that is used. The assumed vegetation changes appear to cause local meteorological perturbations, but whether or not further changes in other regions occur is debatable.

Arctic Haze

The best-documented aerosol disturbances in the troposphere are arctic haze (Leighton 1983; Stonehouse 1986), Saharan dust (Fouquart et al. 1984), and urban aerosols (Galindo 1984). Arctic haze contains large amounts of anthropogenic components, such as carbon soot and sulfuric acid, and has a substantial impact on springtime solar heating rates. Under clear-sky conditions, the haze layer can enhance the heating rate by as much as 50% (Porch and MacCracken 1982).

Arctic-haze concentrations are greatest between December and April because south-north air-mass movements are stronger and more frequent at this time and because the pollutants are less readily removed due to the low cloudiness and stability of the arctic atmosphere (Barrie 1986). The increased absorption of solar radiation by haze layers may augment atmospheric heating rates by 0.15K to 0.25K/day. Over highly reflective ice surfaces, the absorbed solar radiation increases in the atmosphere and decreases at the surface, whereas the reverse occurs over water surfaces (Valero and Ackerman 1986). In addition, soot deposition reduces the albedo of the snowpack and can thereby accelerate the rate of snowmelt (Clarke and Noone 1985). Observations from an ice cap in Ellesmere Island suggest a marked post-1950 increase in arctic air pollution (Barrie 1985); the arctic can no longer be regarded as having a pristine atmospheric environment.

Climatic Changes due to Human Activities: Local Scales

Changes due to Power Plants

Energy conversion, whether it involves coal to electricity at a power plant or electricity to light in a home, releases heat to the environment. In the case of power plants, conversion efficiencies are much less than 100%. In efficient, fossil-fuel-fired, steam-electric plants, only about 40% of the heat produced by combustion is converted to electricity; about 45% of the heat is discharged to cooling water, and the remaining 15% is lost in the plant, up the stack and in the ash.

Most of the heat that is not converted to electricity in a power plant must be removed from the power plant by a cooling system. Several types of cooling system are in use (Bach 1979; Bhumralkar and Williams 1980). The most frequently observed climatic change near power plants is due to condensation forming low stratus clouds or fog in the plumes from cooling ponds and towers. Hanna (1974) found that ground fog occurs within 200 m of the Oak Ridge mechanical-draft cooling towers 40% of the time and that a stratus cloud extends several kilometers downwind on naturally rainy or foggy days. There are only a few reports of precipitation enhancement in the vicinity of power plants (Hanna 1978). Kramer et al. (1976) reported that during the winter of 1975–1976, snowfall was observed from plumes of large, natural-draft cooling towers. Similarly, snowfalls downwind of cooling towers have been reported by Culkowski (1962) and Ott (1976). On the other hand, Martin (1974) reported a study of local weather records near a 2 GW (e) power station with eight natural-draft cooling towers. For the four years of operation of the power station, he concluded that emissions had not affected the values of total rainfall, hours of bright sunshine, or incidence of morning fog recorded by stations at distances of 4 km or more from the power plant. Landsberg (1977) suggested that the small difference in precipitation due to emissions from present-day power plants is significant only during special situations with short time and space scales.

A further effect of power plants is the concentration of vorticity by large buoyant plumes. Observations of local vortices have been reported (Hanna 1978), and small water-spouts have been observed over a cooling pond (Everett and Zerbe 1977). Hanna and Gifford (1975) summarized the effects of power plants on local meteorological conditions by pointing out that the maximum amount of electrical power currently generated at a single power station is about 3 GW (e) and that the atmospheric effects of current heat-dissipa-tion rates are not serious problems. They concluded that fog formation and drift deposition are generally localized and that although more cumulus clouds are observed, no signifi-cant changes in rainfall in areas of study have been detected.

Rural Areas

Modification of the local climate has been brought about by human activities in areas in which shelter belts have been planted. Knowledge of the effect of forest barriers on winds has been utilized in the construction of windbreaks to protect crops and soil, as in the Great Plains of North America, the USSR, the Rhone Valley in Germany, and northern Hokkaido in Japan. It has been found that the denser the obstruction, the greater the shelter immediately behind it, although downwind the extent of its effect is reduced by lee turbulence set up by the barrier (Barry and Chorley 1987). Figure 19.10 shows the influence of shelter

Table 19-4 *Energy Consumption Density (ECD) and average net radiation for certain urban-industrial areas*

Urban-industrial area	Area (km²)	ECD (W/m²)	Average net radiation (W/m²)
Nordrhein-Westphalen	34,039	4.2	50
Same, industrial area only	10,296	10.2	51
West Berlin	234[a]	21.3	57
Moscow	878	127.0	42
Sheffield, England (1952)	48[a]	19.0	46
Hamburg, West Germany	747	12.6	55
Cincinnati, OH	200[a]	26.0	99
Los Angeles County, CA	10,000	7.5	108
Los Angeles, CA	3,500[a]	21.0	108
New York, Manhattan	59	117.0	93
Fairbanks, AL	37	18.5	18

Source: SMIC 1971.
[a] Building area only.

belts on wind-velocity distributions. The maximum protection is produced by a break with about 40% penetrability.

The Urban Climate

One of the noted characteristics of urban areas is the heat island. The generally higher urban temperatures are a result of the following factors (Barry and Chorley 1987):

1. changes in the radiation balance due to atmospheric composition,
2. changes in the radiation balance due to albedo, heat con-ductivity, and thermal capacity of urban surface materials,
3. release of heat due to human activities,
4. reduction of heat diffusion due to changes in airflow patterns as a result of urban surface roughness,
5. reduction in thermal energy required for evaporation and evapotranspiration due to the surface character, rapid drainage, and generally lower wind speeds of urban areas.

The urban heat island is, therefore, not just due to the heat release from energy conversion and use. In some high-latitude, densely populated, or industrialized cities, however, the anthropogenic heat release plays a major role. This is illus-trated in Table 19-4, which compares the energy consumption density in several American and European urban-industrial areas with the average net radiation. On a local scale (up to 10^3 km²), the artificial energy flux density has the same order of magnitude as the next radiation. When the values are examined on a seasonal basis, it is seen that in the cold season the anthropogenic heat release may well dominate as the energy source, whereas in summer it may be insignificant in comparison with the net radiation balance (Oke 1974). Computations confirm that during winter in high latitudes, a major part of the heat island can be accounted for by anthro-pogenic heat release (e.g., Leahey and Friend 1971; Oke and East 1971).

The urban heat island effect recently has been observed

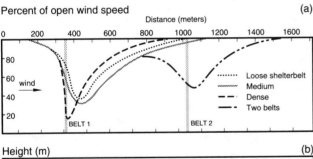

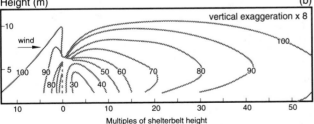

Figure 19.10 The influence of shelter belts on wind-velocity distributions (expressed as percentages of the velocity in the open). (a) The effects of one shelter belt of three different densities and of two back-coupled, medium-dense shelter belts. (b) The detailed effects of one half-solid shelter belt. Source: Barry and Chorley 1987.

Table 19-5 *Maximum heat island effect of eleven metropolitan areas*

	Maximum heat-island effect (urban-rural temperature) (°C)	Population[a] (× 10⁶)
Louisville, KY (SDF)	6.5	0.89
Baltimore, MD (BAL)	5.2	2.14
Washington, D.C. (DCA)	5.2	3.02
Cincinnati, OH (CVG)	5.1	1.38
Indianapolis, IN (IND)	4.5	1.14
Dayton, OH (DAY)	4.5	0.84
St. Louis, MO (STL)	4.4	2.37
Richmond, VA (RIC)	3.8	0.57
Columbus, OH (CMH)	3.3	1.07
Kansas City, MO (MCI)	3.2	1.30
Petersburg, VA —	2.6	0.04

Source: Matson et al. 1978.

[a] 1974 metropolitan populations based on U.S. Census Standard Metropolitan Statistical Areas (SMSAs) as defined in the 1970 census.

using satellite imagery. Matson et al. (1978) showed that on July 28, 1977, an unusually cloud-free, night-time, thermal infrared image of the midwestern and northeastern United States enabled detection of more than 50 urban heat islands. Analysis of digital data from the satellite for selected cities showed the maximum urban-rural temperature differences listed in Table 19-5.

The effect of air pollution in the urban environment is to reduce the transmissivity of the atmosphere compared with that of nearby rural areas. For example, during the period 1960–1969, the atmospheric transmissivity over Detroit, Michigan averaged 9% less than that for nearby areas, and reached 25% less under calm conditions (Barry and Chorley 1987).

The urban climate is influenced to a large extent by the character and density of the urban surface. As a result of the urban thermal processes, the urban temperatures generally are higher than those of the surrounding rural areas. The urban areas can have minimum temperatures that are 5–6°C higher in the early hours of calm, clear nights in large cities. For the period 1931–1960, the center of London had a mean annual temperature of 11.0°C, compared with 10.3°C in the suburbs and 9.6°C in the surrounding countryside (Chandler 1965). Calculations for London for the 1950s indicated that domestic fuel combustion gave rise to a 0.6°C warming in the city in winter, accounting for one-third to one-half of the average city heat excess compared with surrounding rural areas.

The heat island is most obvious when the wind speed is less than 5–6 m/s, and is especially noticeable on calm nights during summer and early autumn (Barry and Chorley 1987). The effects on minimum temperatures are especially significant. Cologne, West Germany, for example, has an average of 34% fewer days with minima below 0°C and Basel has 25% fewer. Kew (London) has an average of some 72 more days with frost-free screen temperatures than rural Wisley.

Urban areas affect both the speed and the direction of airflow. The aerodynamic roughness of urban areas is larger by some 0.5–4.0 m than in rural areas, and the city therefore produces more frictional drag (Brazel 1987). Generally, when the prevailing wind is light, the winds tend to accelerate in urban areas because of strong rural atmospheric stability and the increased turbulence over the warmer, rougher city surface. When the wind is strong, it is generally decelerated in urban areas due to greater frictional effects of the city (Brazel 1987). Differences in wind direction between urban and rural areas also result from frictional effects. In addition, diurnal patterns of urban air circulations, analogous to the sea-breeze circulation, have been observed.

Many studies have shown that precipitation can be increased up to 30% in and/or downwind of large, urban areas. Detailed investigations in the Metropolitan Meteorological Experiment (METROMEX) in St. Louis, Missouri, have provided estimates of the urban effects on precipitation (Ackerman et al 1978; Changnon 1981). Results indicated that the maximum urban effect on precipitation occurs in summer, because of the dominance of convection. The reasons for summer increase of precipitation include the orographic and turbulence effects of buildings, the increased density of condensation nuclei, and thermal convection. The anomalies of summer rainfall, rate of heavy rains, hail frequency, and thunderstorm frequency downwind of St. Louis are shown in Fig. 19.11. Huff and Changnon (1986) have looked at the urban influences on rainfall in other seasons and find maximum alterations in precipitation northeast of St. Louis of 14% in spring, 5% in winter, and 7% in fall, when averaged over the 40-year sampling period. In addition, they found 5–10% less

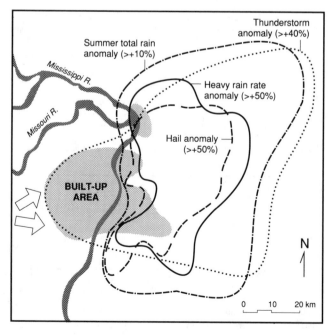

Figure 19.11 Anomalies of summer rainfall, rate of heavy rains, hail frequency, and thunderstorm frequency downwind of the St. Louis metropolitan area. Arrows show the prevailing motion of summer rain systems. Source: Barry and Chorley 1987 after Changnon.

Table 19-6 *Climate alterations produced by cities*

Element	Compared to rural environs
Contaminants	
Condensation nuclei	10 times more
Particulates	10 times more
Gaseous admixtures	5–25 times more
Radiation	
Total on horizontal surface	0–20% less
Ultraviolet, winter	30% less
Ultraviolet, summer	5% less
Sunshine duration	5–15% less
Cloudiness	
Clouds	5–10% more
Fog, winter	100% more
Fog, summer	30% more
Precipitation	
Amounts	5–15% more
Days with less than 5 mm	10% more
Snowfall, inner city	5–10% less
Snowfall, lee of city	10% more
Thunderstorms	10–15% more
Temperature	
Annual mean	0.5–30°C more
Winter minimums (average)	1–2°C more
Summer maximums	1–3°C more
Heating degree days	10% less
Relative humidity	
Annual mean	6% less
Winter	2% less
Summer	8% less
Wind speed	
Annual mean	20–30% less
Extreme gusts	10–20% less
Calm	5–20% more

Source: Landsberg 1981.

snowfall over the city than over adjacent rural areas. European and North American cities apparently record 6–7% more days with rain per year than their surrounding regions, giving 5–10% increases in urban precipitation. The main changes in the hydrology of urban areas are: peak flow is increased; total runoff is increased; water quality is lowered (Mather 1978).

A summary of the climatic alterations produced by cities is given in Table 19-6. All of these effects have been discussed in detail by Landsberg (1981). Urban climates are dominated by the geometry and composition of the built-up surfaces and by the effects of human activities in the urban area, especially the release of energy. In addition, the composition of the urban atmosphere is modified, and pollution domes and plumes are produced around urban areas if the vertical temperature structure and wind speed are appropriate. As a result of the urban influences, the heat island develops and an increase of rainfall downwind of the urban area often has been noted.

Conclusion

This chapter shows that human activities can alter the climate through a number of mechanisms. In particular, the climate can be affected by changes in atmospheric composition, by heat added to the earth-atmosphere system, and by changes of the characteristics of the earth's surface. Numerous examples exist of changes of microclimate as a result of human activities. The provision of shelter (housing) and the protection of agricultural land by the use of shelter belts alter climates on the small scale. On a somewhat larger scale, the changes of climate due to urbanization are well documented, even in terms of the temporal developments in some cases. On a regional scale, human activities have the potential to influence the climate – especially in the cases of deforestation, desertification, and irrigation. The regional-scale changes, however, are not proven, and there is a need for more careful observation and analysis. On the global scale, it is possible that changes in atmospheric composition as a result of human activities are changing the climate, but again, there is as yet no unequivocal proof. Improved documentation, including more comprehensive comparisons of observations and climate theory, could provide firmer evidence of regional-scale climatic changes resulting from human activities. Such questions are the focus of new multidisciplinary programs on global change, especially the proposed International Geosphere-Biosphere Program.

References

Ackerman, B. S., S. A. Changnon, G. Dzurisin, D. L. Gatz, R. C. Grosh, S. D. Hilberg, F. A. Huff, J. W. Mansell, H. T. Ochs, M. E. Peden, P. T. Schickedanz, R. G. Semonin, and J. L. Vogel. 1978. *Summary of METROMEX*. Vol. 2, Causes of precipitation anomalies. Bulletin 63, Illinois State Water Survey, Urbana, IL.

Bacastow, R., and C. D. Keeling. 1981. Atmospheric carbon dioxide concentration and the observed airborne fraction. In *Carbon Cycle Modeling*, ed. B. Bolin. SCOPE 16. Chichester: Wiley.

Bach, W. 1979. Waste heat and climatic change. In *Perspectives on Energy and the Environment*, ed. L. Theodore, A. J. Buonicore, and E. J. Rolinski. West Palm Beach, Fl: CRC Press.

Bach, W., J. Pankrath, and W. W. Kellogg, eds. 1979. *Man's Impact on Climate*. Amsterdam: Elsevier.

Bach, W., J. Pankrath, and J. Williams, ed. 1980. *Interactions of Energy and Climate*. Dordrecht, Holland: Reidel.

Barrie, L. A. 1985. Twentieth-century trends in arctic air pollution revealed by conductivity and acidity observations in snow and ice in the Canadian high arctic. *Atmos. Environ.* 19: 1995–2010.

———. 1986. Arctic air chemistry: An overview. In *Arctic Air Pollution*, ed. B. Stonehouse, 5–23. Cambridge: Cambridge University Press.

Barry, R. G., and R. J. Chorley. 1987. *Atmosphere, Weather and Climate*, 5th ed. London: Methuen.

Baumgartner, A., and M. Kirchner. 1980. Impacts due to deforestation. In *Interactions of Energy and Climate*, ed. W. Bach, J. Pankrath, and J. Williams. Dordrecht, Holland: Reidel.

Bhumralkar, C., and J. Williams. 1980. *Atmospheric Effects of Waste-Heat Discharge*. New York: Marcel Dekker.

Bolin, B. 1986. How much CO_2 will remain in the atmosphere? In *The Greenhouse Effect, Climatic Change and Ecosystems*, ed. B. Bolin, B. Döös, J. Jäger, and R. A. Warrick. Chichester: Wiley.

Bolin, B., B. Döös, J. Jäger, and R. A. Warrick, ed. 1986. *The Greenhouse Effect, Climatic Change and Ecosystems*. SCOPE 29. Chichester: Wiley.

Bolle, H. J., W. Seiler, and B. Bolin. 1986. Other greenhouse gases and aerosols. In *The Greenhouse Effect, Climatic Change and Ecosystems*, ed. B. Bolin, B. Döös, J. Jäger, and R. A. Warrick. SCOPE 29. Chichester: Wiley.

Bradley, R. S. 1985. *Quaternary Paleoclimatology*. Boston: Allen and Unwin.

Bradley, R. S., and P. D. Jones. 1985. Data bases for isolating the effects of the increasing carbon dioxide concentration. In *Detecting the Climatic Effects of Increasing Carbon Dioxide*, ed. M. C. MacCracken and F. M. Luther, 29–54. DOE/ER-0235. Washington, D.C.: U.S. Department of Energy.

Brazel, A. J. 1987. Urban climatology. In *The Encyclopedia of Climatology*, ed. J. E. Oliver and R. W. Fairbridge, 889–901. New York: Van Nostrand Reinhold Co.

Bryson, R. A., and D. A. Baerreis. 1967. Possibility of major climatic modifications and their implications: northwest India, a case for study. *Bull. Amer. Meteor. Soc.* 48: 136–42.

Carlson, T. N., and S. G. Benjamin. 1980. Radiative heating rates for Saharan dust. *J. Atmos. Sci.* 37: 193–213.

Chandler, T. J. 1965. *The Climate of London*. London: Hutchinson.

Changnon, S. A., Jr. 1981. METROMEX: a review and summary. *Meteorol. Monogr.* 40: 1–181.

Charney, J. G. 1975. Dynamics of desert and drought in the Sahel. *Quart. J. Roy. Meteor. Soc.* 101: 193–202.

Charney, J. G., P. H. Stone, and W. J. Quirk. 1975. Drought in the Sahara: A biogeophysical feedback mechanism. *Science* 187: 434–35.

Charney, J. G., W. J. Quick, S.-H. Chow, and J. Kornfield. 1977. A comparative study of the effects of albedo changes and drought in semiarid regions. *J. Atmos. Sci.* 34: 1366–85.

Clarke, A. D., and J. Noone. 1985. Measurements of soot aerosol in arctic snow. *Atmos. Environ.* 19: 2045–54.

Clark, W. C. 1982. *Carbon Dioxide Review 1982*. Oxford: Oxford University Press.

CMA. 1982. World production and release of chlorofluorocarbons 11 and 12 through 1981. Report of the Fluorocarbon Program Panel, Chemical Manufacturing Association.

Culkowski, W. M. 1962. An anomalous snow at Oak Ridge, Tennessee. *Mon. Wea. Rev.* 90: 194–96.

Deepak, A., and H. E. Gerber. 1984. *Aerosols and Their Climate Effects*. Hampton, VA: A. Deepak Publ.

Dickinson, R. E. 1986. How will climate change? In *The Greenhouse Effect, Climatic Change and Ecosystems*, ed. B. Bolin, B. Döös, J. Jäger, and R. A. Warrick. SCOPE 29. Chichester: Wiley.

———, ed. 1987. *The Geophysiology of Amazonia*. Chichester: Wiley.

Everett, R. G., and G. A. Zerbe. 1977. Winter field program at the Dresden cooling ponds. ANL 76-88. Part IV. *Radiol. Environ. Res. Div. Ann. Report*: 108–113.

Fearnside, P. M. 1982. Deforestation in the Brazilian Amazon: How fast is it occurring? *Interciencia* 7: 82–88.

———. 1987. Causes of deforestation in the Brazilian Amazon. In *The Geophysiology of Amazonia*, ed. R. E. Dickinson, 37–61. Chichester: Wiley.

Flohn, H. 1986. Warm phases in climatic history and changes of the CO_2 concentration. Paper presented at the Meeting on Mankind and Climate, Evang. Academy, Loccum, F. R. Germany, Oct. 24–26, 1986.

Fouquart, Y., B. Bonnel, G. Brogniez, A. Cerf, M. Chaovi, L. Smith, and J. C. Vanhoutte. 1984. Size distribution and optical properties of Saharan aerosols during Eclats. In *Aerosols and Their Climatic Effects*, ed. A. Deepak and H. E. Gerber. Hampton, VA: A. Deepak Publ.

Galindo, I. 1984. Anthropogenic aerosols and their regional scale climate effects. In *Aerosols and Their Climatic Effects*, ed. A. Deepak and H. E. Gerber. Hampton, VA: A. Deepak Publ.

Gornitz, V. 1985. A survey of anthropogenic vegetation changes in West Africa during the last century – climatic implications. *Climatic Change* 7: 285–326.

Glantz, M. 1977. Nine fallacies of a natural disaster: the case of the Sahel. *Climatic Change* 1: 69–84.

Hanna, S. R. 1974. Fog and drift deposition from evaporative cooling towers. *Nuclear Safety* 15: 190–96.

———. 1978. Effects of power production on climate. American Meteorological Society Conference on Climate and Energy: Climatological Aspects and Industrial Operations, May 8–12, Asheville, NC.

Hanna, S. R., and F. Gifford. 1975. Meteorological effects of energy dissipation of large power parks. *Bull. Amer. Meteor. Soc.* 56: 1069–76.

Hansen, J. E., and T. Takahashi, ed. 1984. *Climate Processes and Climate Sensitivity*. Geophysical Monograph 29. American Geophysical Union, Washington, D.C.

Hare, F. K. 1983. Climate and desertification. WMO-WCP-44. World Meteorological Organization, Geneva.

Harshvardhan and R. D. Cess. 1978. Effect of tropospheric aerosols upon atmospheric infrared cooling rates. *J. Quant. Spectrosc. Radiat. Trans.* 19: 621–32.

Henderson-Sellers, A. 1986a. Cloud changes in a warmer Europe. *Climatic Change* 8: 25–52.

———. 1986b. Increasing cloud in a warming world. *Climatic Change* 9: 267–310.

———. 1987. Effects of changes in land use on climate in the humid tropics. In *The Geophysiology of Amazonia*, ed. R. E. Dickinson, 463–93. Chichester: Wiley.

Henderson-Sellers, A., and A. Wilson. 1983. Surface albedo data for climate modeling. *Rev. Geophys. Space Phys.* 21: 1743–48.

Huff, F. A., and S. A. Changnon. 1986. Potential urban effects on precipitation in the winter and transition seasons at St. Louis, Missouri. *J. Clim. Appl. Meteor.* 25: 1887–1907.

Jäger, J. 1983. *Climate and Energy Systems*. Chichester: Wiley.

Jones, P. D., S. C. B. Raper, R. S. Bradley, H. F. Diaz, P. M. Kelley, and T. M. L. Wigley. 1986. Northern Hemisphere surface air temperature variations 1851–1984. *J. Clim. Appl. Meteor.* 25: 1213–30.

Jones, P. D., T. M. L. Wigley, and P. B. Wright. 1986. Global temperature variations between 1861 and 1984. *Nature* 322:430–34.

Joseph, J. H., and N. Wolfson. 1975. The ratio of absorption to backscatter of solar radiation during Khamsin conditions and effects on the radiation balance. *J. Appl. Meteor.* 14: 1389–96.

Kellogg, W. W. 1978. Effects of human activities on global climate. WMO Tech. Note No. 156, WMO No. 486, World Meteorological Organization, Geneva.

Kramer, M. L., D. E. Seymour, M. E. Smith, R. W. Reeves, and T. T. Frankenberg. 1976. Snowfall observations from natural draft cooling tower plumes. *Science* 193: 1239–41.

Lamb, H. H. 1977: *Climate – Present, Past, and Future*. Vol. 2, Climatic History and the Future. London: Methuen.

Landsberg, H. E. 1977. Rainfall variations around a thermal power station. *Atmos. Environ.* 11: 565.

———. 1981. *The Urban Climate*. New York: Academic Press.

Leahey, D. M., and J. P. Friend. 1971. A method of predicting the depth of the mixing layer over an urban heat island with application to New York City. *J. Appl. Meteor.* 10: 1162–73.

Leighton, H. 1983. Influence of arctic haze on the solar radiation budget. *Atmos. Environ.* 17: 2065–68.

Machta, L., and T. Carpenter. 1971. Trends in high cloudiness at Denver and Salt Lake City. In *Man's Impact on the Climate*, ed. W. H. Mathews, W. W. Kellogg, and G. D. Robinson. Cambridge, MA: MIT Press.

Manley, G. 1974. Central England temperatures: monthly means, 1659 to 1973. *Quart. J. Roy. Meteor. Soc.* 100: 389–405.

Martin, A. 1974. The influence of a power station on climate – a study of local weather records. *Atmos. Environ.* 8: 419–24.

Mather, J. R. *The Climatic Water Budget in Environmental Analysis*. Lexington, MA: Lexington Books.

Matson, M., E. P. McClain, D. F. McGinnis, Jr., and J. A. Pritchard. 1978. Satellite detection of urban heat islands. *Mon. Wea. Rev.* 106: 1725–34.

Munn, R. E., and L. Machta. 1979: Human activities that affect climate Proceedings of the World Climate Conference, WMO Publication No. 357. World Meteorological Organization, Geneva.

NAS. 1975. *Understanding Climatic Change*. Washington, D.C.: U.S. National Academy of Sciences, National Academy Press.

———. 1983. *Changing Climate*. Report of the Carbon Dioxide Assessment Committee. Washington, D.C.: National Academy Press.

Nicholson, S. 1985. Subsaharan rainfall, 1981–1984. *J. Clim. Appl. Meteor.* 24: 1388–91.

NRC. 1983. *Global Tropospheric Chemistry: A Plan for Action*. Washington, D.C.: National Academy Press.

Oke, T. R. 1974. Review of urban climatology, 1968–1973. WMO Tech. Note No. 134. World Meteorological Organization, Geneva.

Oke, T. R., and C. East. 1971. The urban boundary layer in Montreal. *Bound. Layer Meteor.* 1: 411–37.

Ott, R. E. 1976. Locally heavy snow downwind from cooling towers. NOAA Technical Memo, NWSER-62, WSFO, Charleston, WV.

Otterman, J. 1977. Anthropogenic impact on the albedo of the earth. *Climatic Change* 1: 137–55.

Porch, W. M., and M. C. MacCracken. 1982. Parametric study to the effects of arctic soot on solar radiation. *Atmos. Environ.* 16: 1365–71.

Potter, G. L., H. W. Ellsaesser, M. C. MacCracken, and F. M. Luther. 1975. Possible climatic impact of tropical deforestation. *Nature* 258: 697–98.

Ramanathan, V., L. B. Callis, Jr., R. D. Cess, J. E. Hansen, I. S. A. Isaken, W. R. Kuhn, A. Lacis, F. M. Luther, J. D. Mahlman, R. A. Reck, and M. E. Schlesinger. 1986. Trace gas effects on climate. In *Atmospheric Ozone, 1985*. Vol. III, WMO global Ozone Research and Monitoring Project. Report No. 16. World Meteorological Organization, Geneva.

Ramage, C. S. 1986. El Niño. *Sci. Amer.* 254: 76–83.

Rosen, H., T. Novakov, and B. A. Bodhaine. 1981. Soot in the Arctic. *Atmos. Environ.* 15: 1371–74.

Sagan, C., O. B. Toon, and J. B. Pollack. 1979. Anthropogenic albedo changes and the earth's climate. *Science* 206: 1363–68.

Salati, E. 1987. The forest and the hydrological cycle. In *The Geophysiology of Amazonia*, ed. R. E. Dickinson, 273–96. Chichester: Wiley.

Schneider, S. H., and R. E. Dickinson. 1974. Climate modeling. *Rev. Geophys. Space Phys.* 12: 447–93.

Schneider, S. H., and R. Londer. 1984. *The Coevolution of Climate and Life*. San Francisco: Sierra Club Books.

SMIC. 1971. *Inadvertent Climate Modification*. Report of the Study of Man's Impact on Climate. Cambridge, MA: MIT Press.

Stonehouse, B., ed. 1986. *Arctic Air Pollution*. Cambridge: Cambridge University Press.

Street-Perrott, F. A., and S. P. Harrison. 1984. Temporal variations in lake levels since 30,000 B.P. – An index of the global hydrological cycle. In *Climate Processes and Climate Sensitivity*, ed. J. E. Hansen and T. Takahashi, 118–29. Washington, D.C.: Am. Geophys. Union.

Twomey, S. A., M. Piepgrass, and T. L. Wolfe. 1984. An assessment of the impact of pollution on global albedo. *Tellus* 36B: 356–66.

Valero, F. P., and T. P. Ackerman. 1986. Arctic haze and the radiation balance. In *Arctic Air Pollution*, ed. B. Stonehouse. Cambridge: Cambridge University Press.

WCP. 1987. *The Global Climate System, Autumn 1984–Spring 1986*. CSMR84/86. World Meteorological Organization, Geneva.

Weiss, R. F. 1981. The temporal and spatial distribution of tropospheric nitrous oxide. *J. Geophys. Res.* 86: 7185–95.

Wigley, T. M. L., J. K. Angell, and P. D. Jones. 1985. Analysis of the temperature record. In *Detecting the Climatic Effects of Increasing Carbon Dioxide*, ed. M. C. MacCracken and F. M. Lutter, 55–90. U.S. Department of Energy, Carbon Dioxide Research Division, Washington, D.C.

Wigley, T. M. L., P. D. Jones, and P. M. Kelly. 1986. Empirical climate studies. In *The Greenhouse Effect, Climatic Change and Ecosystems*, ed. B. Bolin. SCOPE 29. Chichester: Wiley.

Wilson, M. F. 1984. Construction and use of land surface information in a general circulation climate model. Ph.D. thesis. University of Liverpool, Liverpool, England.

World Meteorological Organization. 1975. *The Physical Basis of Climate and Climate Modeling*. GARP Publ. Series No. 16. World Meteorological Organization, Geneva.

20

Terrestrial Fauna

ROBERT L. PETERS   THOMAS E. LOVEJOY

The past 300 years have seen a continuation and amplification of processes that began with the advent of efficient tool technology and that speeded up dramatically with the development of agriculture: increasing human populations, armed with increasingly efficient technology, have converted more and more natural ecosystems to human use.

These conversions have included the largely complete destruction of some ecosystem types, such as the American tall grass prairie, and the creation of some new ones, such as the wheat fields of Kansas or the irrigated lawns of Tucson. The tall grass prairies are now farms – with concomitant displacement of most of the large mammal species that once roamed them – and most of the habitat of the endangered Houston toad (*Bufo houstonensis*) has become the city of Houston (Potter et al. 1984).

The toll has been large in the number of species that have become extinct. Moreover, the anthropogenic processes that caused these extinctions are becoming ever greater, as the number of people and their need for resources become greater. According to best guesses, the number of extinctions is expected to continue rising rapidly, possibly reaching 20% of all species by the year 2000 (Lovejoy 1980). Estimates for the New World tropics based on projected deforestation rates predict that 15% of plant species and 12% of bird species may be extinct by the year 2000 (Simberloff 1986). Projections on into the twenty-first century, given continuing deforestation, are that 66% of plant species and 69% of Amazon birds will be lost (Simberloff 1986). And this estimate makes the sanguine assumption that conservation areas will remain undegraded and able to provide habitat appropriate for the original plants and birds.

The forces that are causing this impoverishment are the four horsemen of development: habitat destruction, harvesting, introduced species, and pollution. Although local or temporary increases in species diversity may occur because of habitat disturbance, on a global scale these anthropogenic forces decrease diversity. Disturbance often selects for species that represent early successional stages, that are opportunistic colonizers, and that do well in disturbed habitats – the "weed" species.

Conversely, selection is against those requiring a mature, stable community or those requiring large blocks of habitat. Thus, the Bornean ironwood (*Eusideroxylon zwageri*), a valuable timber tree of Indonesian forest, does not regenerate well after clearcutting, leaving a forest substantially composed of secondary, "weedy" species (Kartawinata et al. 1981); species of *Proechimys*, the dominant nocturnal rodents of some undisturbed Brazilian forests, completely disappear from isolated forest fragments (Lovejoy et al. 1986); and a North American river, such as the Colorado, obstructed and chilled by dam construction, rapidly loses its native migratory fish, such as the squawfish (*Ptychocheilus lucius*) and humpbacked chub (*Gila cypha*), which have evolved in response to warm, turbid water (Rose and Hamill 1988).

Introduced species, released from natural competitors, predators, and parasites, take advantage of such changes, although they may also establish themselves in previously undisturbed habitats. In California, nearly 1,000 alien higher-plant species have established themselves since 1750 (IGBP 1986). Introduced animals, such as rats, domestic cats, and livestock, have caused extinctions and reductions in plant and animal species around the world.

For some groups of animals, particularly large ungulates, mammalian carnivores, and birds, hunting has caused reduction or extinction regardless of whether habitat remained. One report found that approximately as many bird and mammal species have been lost worldwide due to hunting as to habitat destruction or the introduction of species (Nilson 1986). The South African bluebuck (*Hippotragus leucophaeus*) and quagga (*Equus quagga*) were hunted to extinction in the nineteenth century, well before habitat loss was a problem (Smithers 1983).

The various direct causes of population reduction usually act in synergy (Myers 1987). For example, clearing of vegetation can make animals more vulnerable to hunting pressure. Further, because of the intricately interlocking nature of ecosystems, direct anthropogenic perturbations cause more subtle secondary effects through what Myers (1987) has called "cascades" of species interaction. Although specific examples may be difficult to demonstrate unequivocally because of their subtle nature, secondary effects are pervasive, particularly in the tropics, in which a high degree of coevolution has occurred (Lovejoy et al. 1986). For example, it has been suggested that on the island of Mauritius, the tambalocoque tree (*Sideroxylon grandiflorum*) has had very poor reproductive success since the dodo bird (*Raphus cucullatus*), which prepared the seeds for germination in its gut, became extinct 300 years ago (Temple 1977, 1979, 1984); and Janzen (1986) believes that the present distribution of the guanacaste tree (*Enterolobium cyclocarpum*) in Central America reflects a range retraction following the late-Pleistocene extinction of its large mammalian seed dispersers and a subsequent re-expansion following the introduction of the horse by the Spanish.

These interlocking relationships and the special dependence that animals have upon the plant life essential to habitat mean that human-induced changes in animal distributions cannot be discussed without also discussing changes in the plant communities upon which the animals depend. The barren lands of the Middle East, overgrazed for centuries, do not support the forest species that once lived there. The spotted owl (*Strix occidentale*), center of a struggle between conservationists and the logging industry, cannot survive in the American Northwest without the old-growth conifer forests upon which it depends (Dawson et al. 1986).

Because of this interrelation, the following discussion will in large part take the approach of discussing how human activities have affected terrestrial animals by changing the plant communities upon which they depend.

Patterns of Diversity and Extinction

Each type of species or biological community is found in only certain places, in which temperature, solar radiation, precipitation, wind exposure, soil type, water chemistry, and coexisting species, among other conditions, are suitable. Thus calcicolous plants, such as the British horseshoe vetch (*Hippocrepis comosa*), are found only in calcareous soils (Seddon 1971). This variability of distribution is the rule, and "unevenness of spatial distribution is as basic a characteristic of living organisms as locomotion or respiration" (Cox and Moore 1985).

Biogeographical variability is distributed on a number of scales: on a global scale, differences in temperature determine that tropical biomes are very different from those found at higher latitudes, whereas locally, a north-facing slope may have different species of plants than a south-facing slope because of differences in the amount of sunlight received. At the microhabitat level, the top of a tree represents a different habitat from the trunk, and different species of, for example, harvest spiders (Order Opilones) will be found at different heights on trees (Cox and Moore 1985).

Species do not, of course, live everywhere that conditions are suitable for them because of limitations on dispersal. Oceans, for example, restrict the dispersal of most land organisms. The present distribution of a species, then, is a product of both its evolutionary and its environmental history: Its distribution is determined by location of evolution, the amount of time it has had to disperse, the barriers it has had

to disperse, the ways in which other species have restricted or facilitated its expansion, and the types of habitat in which it can survive.

Although a few species, such as the plantain (*Plantago major*), are common and cosmopolitan, being found on all continents except Antarctica (Cox and Moore 1985), most others are geographically restricted. In the tropical forests, for example, a high proportion of species are endemics, meaning that they are restricted to a single locality or habitat type. Endemism may occur for ecological reasons, such as narrow habitat specialization, or for historical reasons. Often endemics are "relict" populations – remnants of original wider populations, geographically reduced by, for example, climate change or human activities.

Species may be particularly susceptible to extinction if they exist in low abundances, either because they have been reduced by, say, hunting or competition with introduced species or because they naturally occur in low abundances (e.g., Fig. 20.1), as do many top predators. Also, species that are geographically restricted are at higher risk, an extreme case being local endemics, which are restricted to a single or a few localities.

Some areas are "hotspots" of endemism, and degradation of habitat in such places can threaten many species at once. A single act of agricultural clearing, for example, occurred on the top of Centinela, an Andean foothill in western Ecuador, and caused the extinction of at least 38 plant species found only on this 20-km² ridgetop (Gentry 1986).

Such rapid extirpations of a complete community are not as common as those due to piece-meal, gradual transformation, which breaks the habitat into increasingly numerous and small fragments (Fig. 20.2). Within such recently created fragments, populations of many species die out, some shortly after a fragment is isolated, others after time (Harris 1984;

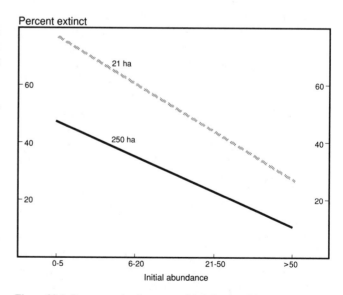

Figure 20.1 Percent extinction among birds having different initial levels of abundance in two Brazilian woodlots, one of 21 ha, the other of 250 ha. Abundance values are numbers of individuals detected per 100 observer hours. Risk of extinction decreases with population density. Source: Terborgh and Winter 1980, based on data of Willis 1980.

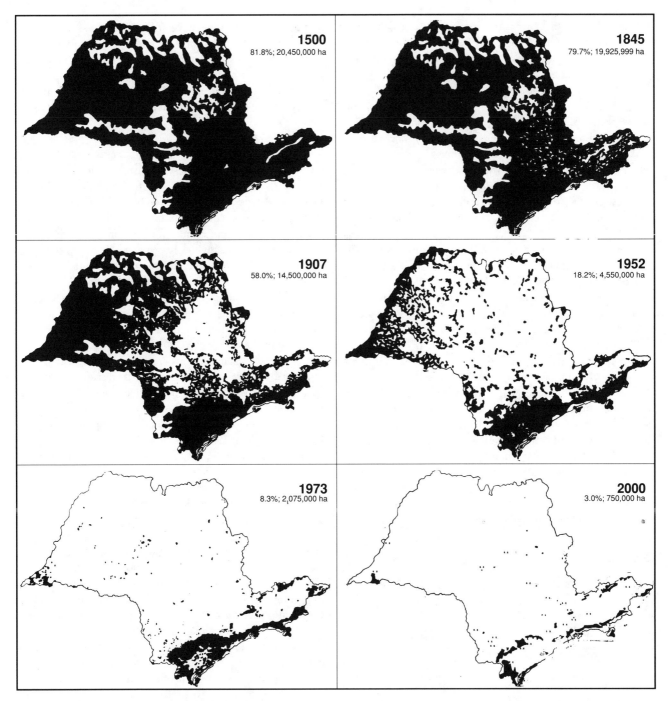

Figure 20.2 Depletion of the forest area in São Paulo State, Brazil.
Source: Oedekoven 1980.

Lovejoy et al. 1986). The remaining habitat may lack resources necessary to sustain a species at all, or the remaining population may be so small that it gradually becomes extinct through environmental accident, such as a forest fire, or because of genetic problems created by low population size.

The numbers of endemic and rare species, and biological diversity in general, are not evenly distributed over the earth. The tropical forests are astoundingly more species-rich than other terrestrial biomes: at least twice – and perhaps 10 times – as many species are in the tropics as in temperate biomes (Erwin 1982, 1983; Raven 1986). The situation with regard to

endemics also is confused by poor knowledge about tropical species, but it has been concluded that at least for plants, local endemics (species known only from a local area) are more common in the tropics than in the temperate regions. This concentration of species numbers and endemism in the tropics means that more species are lost in the tropics per unit area of habitat degradation than in the temperate regions (Gentry 1986).

As the range of estimates suggests, current knowledge about the number of species on earth is very poor. Approximately 1.7 million species have been named and classified, less than half of these from the species-rich tropics (Raven 1986). The temperate regions, surpassingly well-known compared with the tropics, are estimated to have somewhere around 1.5 million species, but of even this fauna, E. O. Wilson has said, "If you went anywhere in the United States and scooped up a handful of dirt, you would find unidentified species of nematodes or other organisms" (personal communication).

A conservative estimate for the tropics, based upon an estimate that there are approximately twice as many birds, mammals, and plants in the tropics as in temperate regions, would suggest a tropical total of 3 million and a world total of around 5 million (Raven 1986). However, the whole question has been opened wide by the recent discovery that tropical rainforests may be much richer in insects, primarily beetles, than previously imagined, and some have revised world estimates to upward of 30 million (Erwin 1982, 1983).

We are even more adrift when it comes to monitoring extinctions. For vertebrates we have a relatively good grasp. We know, for example, that the rate of bird extinctions has been rising rapidly since 1600 (Fig. 20.3). But for invertebrates and nonanimal species, only rough guesses exist. Certainly hundreds of thousands and probably millions of species will be lost during the next 20 years. Estimates depend on assumptions about deforestation rates and the total number of species in the deforested regions. Even for larger vertebrates, low in number and comparatively well-studied, conservation status is poorly known. Diamond (1987), a tropical bird expert, has pointed out the inadequacy of monitoring and listing of endangered birds with the example of the Solomon Islands, for which the *ICUN Red Data Book* lists only a single extinct bird and no endangered birds. There are, however, an

additional 11 species that have not been observed by scientists since the 1950s and that may be endangered or extinct.

An increase in systematic activity to strengthen knowledge of species' distributions and taxonomic relationships would provide information necessary for conservation, as well as for purely scientific and practical needs (Lovejoy et al. 1989).

Island Fauna

Even though islands make up relatively little of the earth's land surface, they deserve disproportionate attention because they may be seen as microcosms illuminating the degree and types of degradative change that tend to occur more gradually on continents, but that are happening nonetheless. First, because islands are small in area compared to continents, human activities have been able to degrade large portions of their ecosystems very rapidly. One hundred square miles of deforestation may diminish a continental ecosystem little, but it could destroy an island forest type entirely. Similarly, pollution, hunting, and introduced species can rapidly have great impact on the relatively small populations of individual island species.

Additionally, island species are generally considered to be intrinsically more extinction-prone than continental ones because they have evolved in relative isolation from other biotas, and thus often have few defenses against introduced competitors, predators, and diseases (Carlquist 1974, 1985; Mueller-Dombois 1981a). Again, this susceptibility to deleterious effects of colonizing species is found on continents as well – witness the effects of introduced Dutch elm disease (*Ceratostomella ulmi*) and the chestnut blight (*Endothia parasitica*) in the United States – but the effect tends to be more severe and readily observed on islands.

Because of the special vulnerability of island species, at least 75% of vertebrate extinctions to data have occurred among island fauna (Table 20-1; Diamond 1984; Nilson 1986). However, the increasing scale of human-caused degradation is putting continental biota at greater risk, and mainland vertebrate species threatened with extinction now outnumber island species by more than 2 to 1 (Nilson 1986).

Because of the special vulnerability of island fauna, their overwhelming representation in lists of endangered fauna, and the warning they provide about the increasingly jeopardized continental faunas, we present a detailed study of Hawaii, a mid-sized (6,429-km^2) group of islands 4,000 km from the nearest continental mass.

Hawaii

The Hawaiian islands, like other isolated oceanic islands, have evolved unique flora and fauna. The Hawaiian islands are more than 700 km from their nearest island neighbor and have over the last few million years developed entire communities of endemic species (Mueller-Dombois 1981a). Almost 100% of the native insects, 98% of the birds, 93% of the flowering plants, and 65% of the ferns are endemic (Holing 1987; Mueller-Dombois 1981a; Simon et al. 1984).

For Hawaii and many other tropical islands, there is increasing paleontological evidence that extensive habitat alteration and extinction caused by indigenous peoples predated

Number of bird species becoming extinct

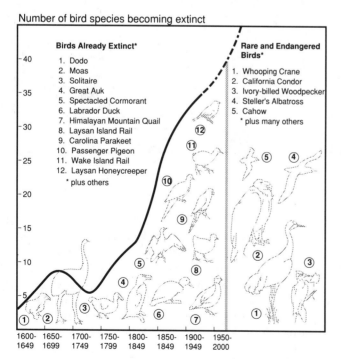

Figure 20.3 Rising rate of bird extinctions. The number of extinctions occurring in each 50-year period since 1600 has risen steadily. Source: Nilson 1986, based on various sources.

Table 20-1 *Species and subspecies of mammals and birds extinct since 1600.*

Location	Mammals	Birds
Continents		
Africa	11 (10/1)[*]	0
Asia	11 (9/2)	6
Australia	22 (0/22)	0
Europe	7 (6/1)	0
North America	22 (17/5)	8
South America	0	2
Total	73 (42/31)	16
Pelagic	1 (1/0)	0
Islands		
Continental		
Africa	0	2
Asia	4 (4/0)	0
Australia	0	2
North America	4 (3/1)	3
Oceanic		
Pacific Ocean		
Galapagos	4 (0/4)	0
Baja California islands	0	8
Hawaii	0	24
New Zealand	0	16
Chatham	absent	5
Lord Howe	0	8
Norfolk	absent	6
Cebu (Philippines)	0	11
Bonin, Ryukyu	0	10
Other	0	21
Indian Ocean		
Madagascar	1 (0/1)	2
Christmas	3 (0/3)	0
Mascarenes	0	14
Seychelles	0	2
Atlantic Ocean		
West Indies	22 (0/22)	15
Other	1 (0/1)	5
Mediterranean	2 (0/2)	1
Total, all islands	41 (7/34)	155
Total, all locations	115 (50/65)	171

Sources: Mammal data are from Goodwin and Goodwin 1973, except that two extinct named races of deer from remote Pacific islands are assumed to represent populations introduced by man and are omitted. Bird data are from King 1985. This table is reproduced in its entirety from Diamond 1984.

[*] ( ) = number of large mammal taxa (>44 kg)/number of small taxa.

Note: This tabulation omits numerous island birds believed to have become extinct after 1600 but known only from recently reported subfossil bones (e.g., Olson and James 1984; Steadman and Olson 1985; see also our discussion of Hawaii in the text).

European colonization (Captain Cook arrived in Hawaii in 1778) (Olson and James 1984). The Polynesians extensively cleared the lowlands for cultivation, and they introduced exotic species, including rats, dogs, pigs, and jungle fowl. During this pre-European period, at least 53% of the known total of 82 Hawaiian birds became extinct (Olson and James 1984). Losses include species of geese (although one specie remains), ibis, owls, crows, a sea eagle, a hawk, a honey eater, and at least 15 Hawaiian finches (Drepanidini), and Olson and James (1984) point out that undoubtedly subfossils of many other vanished species remain to be found.

With the arrival of Europeans, Hawaii received many new species that had negative effects on native biota: rooting by feral hogs damages native vegetation, prevents regeneration of young plants, and facilitates the spread of nonnative plants, such as the grass *Holcus lanatus* (Ralph and Maxwell 1984; Spatz and Mueller-Dombois, 1975). Two endemic forest dominants, the koa (*Acacia koa*) and mamane (*Sophora chrysophylla*), are not regenerating successfully due to grazing by cattle and feral goats (Mueller-Dombois 1981b; Spatz and Mueller-Dombois 1973). Predators such as cats, rats, and the small Indian mongoose (*Herpestes auropunctatus*) decrease the number of native birds and insects.

Additionally, it has been estimated that the seed plants in Hawaii include 4,987 introduced species and varieties, compared with only 2,744 native species (cited in Mueller-Dombois 1981a). Over 2,000 species of insects and 200 other arthropods are known to have been introduced (Howarth 1985), compared with a known native arthropod fauna of more than 6,000 (Gagné and Christensen 1985).

Wide areas have been cleared of native vegetation, and introduced plant species have moved into disturbed areas "blanketing wide areas cleared of forest for grazing and invading native forests" (Mueller-Dombois 1981a). The coastal lowlands, after years of agricultural use and urban development, contain little native vegetation, dominant species now including the introduced mesquite (*Prosopis pallida*) (Mueller-Dombois 1981b). Even more remote sites that have been disturbed by animals, roads, or other causes may be largely free of native plants. For example, 74% of the plants growing alongside roads near the Mauna Loa volcano, on the island of Hawaii, were of introduced species, whereas native species were dominant on adjacent, recent-lava-flow substrate (Wester and Juvik 1983). Exotic birds seem to be associated with exotic vegetation (Mueller-Dombois et al. 1981).

The result of these more recent changes has been the loss of at least 23 species of birds and 177 species of native plants since 1778 (TNC 1987). An additional 30 species of birds and 680 species of plants are listed as endangered. Although the taxonomic and conservation status of invertebrates is poorly known compared with vertebrates, it is known that the native insects are generally coevolved with endemic plants (Mueller-Dombois 1981a) and appear to be restricted to them, showing little ability to use introduced species. Loss of native plant cover is therefore likely to be associated with decreases in population size and extinctions of native insects. Many of the Hawaiian tree snails of the Family Achatinellidae are threatened by a predatory snail, *Euglandina rosea*, introduced from Florida in 1957 to prey on the introduced giant African snail, *Achatina fulica*, itself an introduced agricultural pest (Mueller-Dombois 1981a).

According to an evaluation by the Hawaiian chapter of The Nature Conservancy, disruption of the remaining native ecosystems is still increasing. For example, introduced ungulates have spread "so rapidly in the past two decades that today only the summits of west Maui and a single peak on Molokai still can be called ungulate-free" (TNC 1987). Habitats and populations of most endemic bird species continue to decline (Mueller-Dombois 1981a).

Other Islands

Other tropical islands have suffered much the same fate as Hawaii. First Polynesian and then European colonists altered habitat, introduced species, increased the rate of fire, and hunted vulnerable endemic animals unadapted to predators. In New Zealand, which was colonized by Maoris around 1,000 years ago, more than 34 species of birds were exterminated, including various species of moa (Trotter and McCulloch 1984). On the Chatham islands off the coast of South Island, New Zealand, at least 19 bird species, both large and small, also disappeared following colonization by Maoris (Cassels 1984; Diamond 1984), and a number of other islands today show suspiciously sparse avifauna (Cassels 1984). Steadman and Olson (1985) have hypothesized that the extinction of native birds throughout the Pacific was so complete that what remains today is only a glimpse of what once existed. They suggest that "before human contact, one or more flightless rails probably occurred on nearly every island in the Pacific, but almost all such populations are extinct today."

That the early Pacific island extinctions affected both large and small species, including those on Hawaii, suggests that hunting, habitat destruction, and the invasion of commensal species all played a part. Olson and James (1984) point out that the small song birds were unlikely to have disappeared through hunting pressure and suggest that clearing of lowland forest was responsible for their loss.

On Madagascar, also peopled some thousand years ago, the disappearances appear to be limited to large species, including many species of giant lemurs, flightless birds, and land tortoises (Dewar 1984). There is good evidence that people were responsible, and the taxa extirpated suggest hunting as the primary cause.

In general, the biota of these islands has continued to be degraded during the European period. New Zealand, for example, has lost five species and six subspecies of birds since 1800 (King 1984).

Continental Fauna

Continental regions have been relatively resilient to habitat degradation and species loss compared to islands, in the ways detailed next. This said, they are nonetheless finite in their capabilities to withstand environmental insults, and the number of insults, and hence extinctions, on continents is rising rapidly. Growing human populations and expanding economies throughout the world are creating pressures that threaten to overwhelm some continental ecosystems. The Brazilian Atlantic forest, home to thousands of endemic species, is nearly all gone. Worldwide, tropical forests – home to most of the earth's diversity – are being cut at a rate exceeding 74,000 km²/yr (Lanly 1982). In the Mediterranean, where some large mammals and birds have survived the

destruction of the past, many of those that remain have disturbingly small populations (see below).

Generally, where the environment is most suitable for people or where historical settlement patterns have created high densities or a long period of sustained use, ecosystems have experienced heavy degradation. Such regions of first settlement and high density are the Brazilian Atlantic coast, the eastern United States, and the Mediterranean region.

As a single example of what happens when human populations outstrip the carrying capacity of the land, consider the Sahel, the 500-km-wide strip lying along the southern border of the Sahara Desert. Drought and human ecological abuse, including tremendous deforestation (in excess of 1% annually between 1950 and 1975; see in Le Houérou and Gillet 1986), overgrazing, and fires have combined with hunting to extirpate virtually all large mammals outside of game refuges.

Many continental species originally had larger ranges than island species, so that even with considerable range reduction, some populations have survived. For example, the range of the grizzly bear (*Ursus arctos horribilis*) originally covered Alaska, all of western Canada and the United States, and much of northern Mexico. Although extirpated from almost all the United States and Mexico, it continues to do well in Alaska and portions of Canada (Fig. 20.4; Servheen 1985). The presence of such refugia has in some cases allowed widespread reestablishment of previously rare species, such as the wild turkey (*Meleagris gallopavo*; Hewitt 1967), after persecution stopped or habitat recovered. Most species, however, once their numbers are reduced, have remained rare.

In addition, continental terrestrial species – with the exception of Australia – evolved along with many placental mam-

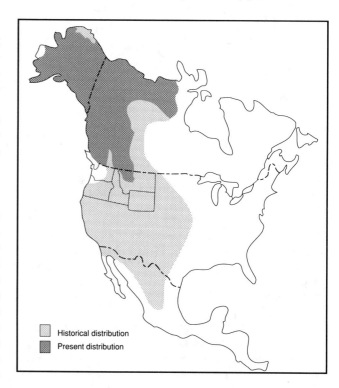

Figure 20.4 Historic and present range of grizzly bear (*Ursus Arctos horribilis*). Source: Servheen 1985.

malian predators, and thus have been relatively resilient to new introductions. In Australia, for unknown reasons, few swift, mammalian carnivores evolved (only five modern species), and the impact of introduced predators on small mammals has been severe (Diamond 1984).

Continental fresh-water faunas throughout the world also have been damaged by introduced predators and competitors – many of the fresh-water ecosystems may be thought of as islands of water, whether they be lakes or isolated rivers, and the fauna is analogously vulnerable. In the North American southwest, at least 20 fish taxa have become extinct in the twentieth century, primarily through combined effects of exotic fishes and habitat destruction (Meffe 1990). Endangered fishes include the Colorado squawfish (*Ptychocheilus lucius*) and three other fishes native to the Colorado River basin, jeopardized in large part because of dam construction (Kaeding, Burdick, and McAda 1985). These fishes had evolved to cope with very fast, warm, turbid water, and the construction of dams changed the water to cold and clear, allowing the introduction of trout and preventing migration.

Finally, continental species often have had a longer history of coevolution with people, so that gradual adaptation to humans' damaging technologies and commensal species has been possible. Martin (1984) proposes that at least some of the variation observed in timing and degree of extinction in different areas may be explained by people who arrived at different times and who had developed different levels of "weaponry," including tools, fire, and commensal species. In cases in which first contact with humans occurred before the full arsenal had developed, some coadaptation would have occurred, and extinction waves would not have been as rapid or severe. Intrinsic characteristics of the continental fauna, as for island fauna, also would have been important. For example, continental fauna may have been more vulnerable if there was a previous absence of fast-moving predators or if the climate was conducive to human-set fires.

The following continental examples have been chosen to illustrate differing patterns of human density, duration of occupation, and intrinsic ecologies. Among them, North America has the lowest population density (approximately 26 people per km^2) and the shortest duration of occupancy (with settlement mostly having occurred within the past 200 years). Great Britain, although actually a collection of islands, was connected to Europe during the last ice age and has a fauna that is a somewhat depauperate extension of the European. Moreover, its large size originally supported populations of even the most range-demanding species. Britain has had some degree of habitat destruction for the past 3,000 to 4,000 years, although most lowland forests remained in place at least until A.D. 500. By the Middle Ages, extensive clearing had occurred. Its present population density is high (some 230 people per km^2). The Mediterranean, with a drier climate than Britain and much of the United States, represents a history of intensive use beginning at least 8,000 years ago, and demonstrates the most extensive degradation. Mediterranean population densities vary by country but are high (189 people per km^2 for Italy, 75 per km^2 for Greece, and 258 per km^2 for Lebanon). The Atlantic forest region of Brazil, the most densely settled portion of the country, has a density of approximately 66 people per km^2.

Survey of these examples shows that prolonged use by dense populations is generally associated with destruction of the ecosystems and loss of fauna. Where people are, animals generally are not.

North America

At the time of European settlement, North America teemed with animal life. (See Cronon 1983, for a careful discussion of early European observations.) Even though the Amerindians supported themselves in large part by hunting, they had less impact on prey species than did the later activities of Europeans. The Amerindians, however, did undoubtedly affect abundances of particular species, in part through frequent burning, which removed shrubs from forests and created clearings, thus increasing the abundances of edge- and second-growth-dependent species, such as deer (Cronon 1983). There is also the strong though still controversial possibility that ancestors of these Indians were responsible for the Pleistocene extinction of many species of American megafauna (see in Martin and Klein 1984), including the mastodon, the woolly mammoth, and the native species of wild horse.

Initial impacts by Europeans were primarily through hunting. Hunters had largely extirpated deer from southern New England by the late 1700s, along with elk (*Cervus canadensis*), bear (*Ursus americanus*), and lynx (*Lynx canadensis*) (Cronon 1983). Wild turkey (*Meleagris gallopavo*) became extinct in Massachusetts in 1851, in South Dakota in 1875, and in Michigan in 1897 (Hewitt 1967), although it has been reintroduced widely in this century.

As European populations grew, the forests were cleared, prairies were plowed, and hunting pressure increased. In the eastern United States, millions of acres were logged and abandoned by the early twentieth century (Shands and Healy 1977), although much has now regrown to forest. As happened previously in Europe, marshes were drained, rivers dammed, and prairies plowed. Today, for example, only some 10% of the area originally covered by bluestem prairie remains (Klopatek et al. 1979), and much is in degraded condition. Klopatek et al. (1979) list over 50 native vegetation types, including southern floodplain forest, grama buffalo grass, and oak-hickory forest, that have lost more than 20% of their precolonization extent.

Despite a precedent-setting system of national parks and reserves, degradation of habitat continues both within and outside of protected areas. For example, the U.S. Fish and Wildlife Service estimates that over 11 million acres of palustrine wetlands were destroyed, largely for farmland and urban development, between the mid-1950s and mid-1970s (Conservation Foundation 1984). Rangelands continue to be degraded by excessive stocking rates, and as of 1980, 54% of rangeland in the contiguous 48 states was considered to be in poor or very poor condition (U.S. Forest Service 1980). Rangeland degradation is worst in the southwestern states, which share not only arid climate and prolonged grazing seasons, but also a long history – 400 years – of use.

In the words of the U.S. Forest Service, "any downward departure from good condition will usually have a negative effect upon the supply," meaning that carrying capacity for both stock and wildlife is reduced. Overgrazing of its habitat by cattle caused the disappearance of the masked bobwhite quail (*Colinus virginianus ridgwayi*) from its northern range in Arizona by the 1930's, although a remnant population of less than 300 birds survives north of Hermosillo in Mexico (King 1981; Drabelle 1985).

In a number of cases, grazing has been shown to decrease bird, mammal, and insect species diversity, although densities of individual species may increase (Risser et al. 1981). Where introduced grass species replace native grasses (the case throughout much of the southwest), similar diversity decreases may occur. A study comparing native grassland with nearby areas planted with Lehmann and Boer lovegrass (*Eragrostis lehmanniana* and *E. curvula*) showed much higher bird, insect, and mammal diversity in the native grasslands (Bock et al. 1986).

Regenerated forest cover is now extensive in the eastern United States, and throughout the United States 295 million ha (31% of the total U.S. area) were forest in 1977 (U.S. Forest Service 1980). This recovery benefited many forest species that do well in young forests and plantations. However, detrimental changes in forest cover continue as a result of logging and clearing for agriculture and ranching. From 1970 to 1980, the southwestern United States lost hundreds of thousands of acres of pinyon-juniper ecosystem to ranching (U.S. Forest Service 1980). Continued logging of old-growth forest, a required habitat for many species, threatens some species, such as the red-cockaded woodpecker (*Picoides borealis*) – once widespread in the southern United States and now reduced to between 4,500 and 10,000 individuals (Jackson 1987). Establishment of plantation forests on already-deforested land may take pressure off remaining native forests in the United States and elsewhere.

National parks and wildlife refuges have been increasingly disturbed by higher levels of use within reserves and increased development surrounding them (Norris and Lenhart 1987; Conservation Foundation 1985). Kesterson National Wildlife Refuge, experiencing malformed waterfowl due to selenium contamination, is only one of 78 National Wildlife Refuges that the U.S. Fish and Wildlife Service identified as having potential contamination problems (U.S. Fish and Wildlife Service 1986a).

The overall result of habitat destruction, hunting pressure, and, to a lesser extent, effects of exotic species and pollutants has been dramatic decreases in populations of many species. Figure 20.5 shows the nearly complete replacement of native ungulates on western ranges by domestic stock (Wagner 1978). Original abundances of North American species can be estimated only by assumptions of potential densities in suitable habitat or through contemporary descriptions. Original numbers of passenger pigeons have been estimated as high as 5 billion, pronghorn antelope at 40 million west of the Mississippi River, and buffalo from 30 to 60 million (Kimball and Johnson 1978). Many species not considered endangered survive with only small fractions of their original numbers.

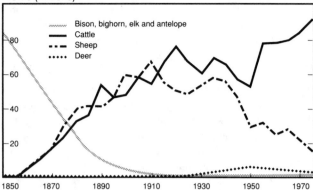

AUMs (millions)

Figure 20.5 Conjectured forage demand of wild and domestic ungulates on rangelands of 11 western states. Units are Animal Unit Months (AUMs), a standard measure of range utilization. AUMs may be taken as roughly proportional to biomass. Source: Wagner 1978.

U.S. migratory song birds have been declining substantially. Reasons probably include fragmentation of forest habitat in the United States and massive clearing of winter-forest habitat in Latin America (see Wallace 1986 for an overview).

Endangered U.S. species, as of 1986, included 49 mammals, 81 birds, 26 reptiles, 8 amphibians, 68 fishes, 8 snails, 23 clams, 4 crustaceans, and 13 insects (U.S. Fish and Wildlife Service 1986b). Of them, nearly all the mammals, fishes, snails, clams, crustaceans, and insects are continental species. More than half the birds and approximately half the reptiles and amphibians are endemic to Hawaii or other islands under U.S. jurisdiction (U.S. Fish and Wildlife Service 1987).

The number of species officially listed underestimates the problem considerably. Because of administrative bottlenecks, a large backlog of species is proposed for listing that is not included in these totals; in 1984, 876 invertebrates and 363 vertebrates were identified for listing by the Fish and Wildlife Service (Defenders of Wildlife 1984).

The British Isles

Britain's land area is 243,977 km² – enough to have originally sustained large populations of ungulates and large predators, such as bears and wolves. However, a long history of dense human settlement (232 people per km² in 1986) has resulted in great changes in the landscape. Little of Britain is wilderness now, and dramatic changes in flora and fauna have occurred.

England once was dominated by expansive oak forests, which now largely are gone (Kirby 1987). With them were lost large mammals unable to survive the effects of hunting and habitat conversion, including the aurochs (*Bos primigenius*), wolf (*Canis lupus*), wild boar (*Sus scrofa*), brown bear (*Ursus arctos*), and beaver (*Castor fiber*) (Corbet 1974). Conversely, the rabbit (*Oryctolagus cuniculus*), probably introduced from Europe by the Romans (Sheail 1984), flourished as England was converted from forest to grazing and agricultural land.

As of 1978, this conversion had removed nearly 14 million

ha of Britain's original 16 million ha of forest habitat – less than 10% remains (Locke 1970; Perry 1978). None is virgin forest; all has been cut over at one time or another (Grainger 1981). As early as the thirteenth century, agricultural clearing and a demand for construction timber necessitated the importation of timber from Scandinavia (Perry 1978), and by the time of the Industrial Revolution, when wood fueled the ship-building and iron-smelting industries, almost no oak remained in England (Grainger 1981). At the same time, England's rise as a major textile producer demanded larger flocks of sheep than ever before, and a growing human population also required more cattle and pigs. Once cut, even if left untilled, forest areas often were unable to regenerate because of grazing pressure. By the 1940s, 50% of England and Wales was in "permanent" grassland (Sitwell 1984).

The forest that remains is often changed in character from the original oak-dominant forests. From an original 35 native species of British trees, the number has been increased to 1700 by introductions (Grainger 1981). The most dramatic examples of these introductions have been the widespread plantations of exotic conifers – the Douglas fir (*Pseudotsuga menziesii*) and the Sitka spruce (*Picea sitchensis*) of North America (Grainger 1981).

Such changes in species composition and physical structure of the forest are well known to affect faunal composition. Structurally simpler forests, or forests with few plant species, such as even-aged plantation stands, sustain fewer bird species (e.g., MacArthur, MacArthur, and Preer 1962), as has been demonstrated for breeding birds in Scotland (See Fig. 20.6; Moss 1978). A change from deciduous to evergreen trees also brings change to the species of birds present (Fuller 1982). Among insects, many species of beetle are dependent on

mature trees or dead wood, and have declined in number as England has become a land of younger forests (Hammond 1974). Diversity of plant-eating insects is also influenced by the number of plant species present, as many of them tend to be specific in their dietary requirements, and native trees generally support more species than introduced ones (Southwood 1961).

Among higher vertebrates, species that have survived in the new landscape are often smaller forest species that could make do with reduced islands of habitat. Of the huntable species, small nocturnal representatives, such as the pine marten (*Martes martes*) and the polecat (*Mustela putorius*), have fared better than the large diurnal ones. Species adapted to the open, such as badgers (*Meles meles*) and foxes (*Vulpes vulpes*), have expanded habitat, and foxes remain common in suburban environments.

The practice of planting hedgerows of trees and other vegetation, mandated by the Enclosure Acts between 1750 and 1845 (Perry 1978), created additional forest "edge" habitat. Many woodland birds, 20 butterfly species, other insects, and almost one-half of Britain's mammals can live in hedgerows (Sitwell 1984). Recent destruction of hedgerows at a rate of 4,000 miles per year (Terrasson and Tendron 1981) has caused population declines in species dependent upon them, as seen by a drop in the number of partridges (*Perdix perdix*) (Perry 1978) and Brown hairstreak butterflies (*Thecla betulae*) (Heath 1974).

The grasslands created by forest clearing have themselves been degraded by overgrazing. Selection against palatable plants has caused hundreds of thousands of acres of grazing land to become dominated by carcinogenic bracken fern (*Pteridium aquilinum*) (Grainger 1981; Taylor 1986). Changes in grassland management caused the extinction of the Mazarine Blue butterfly (*Cyanaris semiargus* Rott), which was dependent on red clover (Heath 1974).

Conversion of native heathlands (predominantly heather, *Calluna vulgaris*) to agricultural use has caused declines in the numbers of Dartford warblers (*Sylvia undata*), sand lizards (*Lacerta agilis*), smooth snakes (*Coronella austriaca*), and at least 20 species of butterflies (Ford 1982; Prestt, Cooke, and Corbett 1974; Ravenscroft 1987).

Continued drainage and filling of wetlands and bogs has decreased populations of birds and aquatic mammals, such as otters (*Lutra lutra*) (Perry 1978), and declines have been observed among the butterflies (Heath 1974), Diptera (Smith 1974), and Coleoptera (Hammond 1974). Threatened amphibians include the Natterjack toad (*Bufo calamita*) (Prestt et al. 1974) and the crested newt (*Triton cristatus*) (FFPS 1986a; Prestt et al. 1974). In all, 2 out of 6 United Kingdom amphibians (33%) and 18 of 37 fish species (49%) are considered threatened (Table 20-2).

Introduced species are widespread. Because Britain's flora and fauna were originally depauperate, as a result of glacial extinction, compared with those of the European continent, many European species were introduced successfully, including 14 currently established mammals (Corbet 1974), edible snails (genus *Helix*), and others. The brown rat (*Rattus norvegicus*), introduced around 1728 (Lever 1985), has had

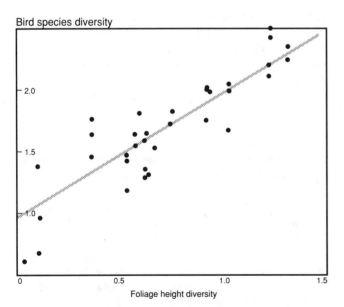

Bird species diversity

Figure 20.6 The relationship between the complexity of woodland structure and the complexity of breeding-bird communities in 34 Scottish woods. Foliage-height diversity is a measure of the distribution of foliage between selected height intervals; bird-species diversity measures breeding-bird diversity. Source: Fuller 1982, redrawn from Moss 1978.

Table 20-2 *Threatened species in selected Mediterranean and other OECD countries (early 1980s)*

Country	Mammals	Birds	Reptiles	Amphibians	Fishes
Mediterranean Countries					
France	58(57)*	155(58)	19(39)	18(53)	20(27)
Italy	13(13)	60(14)	24(52)	13(46)	70(14)
Spain†	53(53)	142(37)	20(41)	18(78)	12(9)
European Non-Mediterranean Countries					
Austria	38(46)	121(60)	X‡	X	54(59)
Denmark	14(29)	41(22)	0(0)	3(21)	17(10)
Finland	21(34)	15(7)	1(20)	0(0)	4(7)
West Germany	44(47)	98(22)	9(75)	11(58)	40(23)
Hungary	14(X)	83(X)	4(X)	1(X)	2(X)
Netherlands	29(48)	85(33)	6(86)	10(67)	11(22)
Norway	10(14)	28(10)	1(20)	1(20)	X
United Kingdom	26(51)	51(26)	2(33)	2(33)	18(49)
North America					
Canada	6(6)	10(2)	2(6)	2(4)	15(2)
United States	35(8)	69(6)	25(7)	8(4)	44(2)
Oceania					
Australia	40(13)	36(5)	8(1)	6(4)	X
New Zealand	14(21)	16(6)	7(19)	X	3(0)

Sources: Adapted from table published by World Resources Institute 1987, based primarily upon data from the Organization for Economic Cooperation and Development (OECD), OECD Environmental Data Compendium 1985 (Paris 1985).

* Numbers given are total number of threatened species in each taxon. Numbers in parentheses are the threatened species expressed as a percentage of the total number of species known to exist in a particular country.

† Data for Spain refer to peninsular Spain and the Baleares only.

‡ Estimates not available. "Threatened" refers to the sum of the number of species in both "endangered" and "vulnerable" categories, which are roughly analogous to U.S. "endangered" and "threatened" categories, respectively.

negative effects on some bird populations, including Manx shearwaters (*Puffinus puffinus*) on Lundy Island in the Bristol Channel (Lever 1985). Other exotics include a now widely established dwarf Asian deer, the muntjac (*Muntiacus reevesi*) and a locally established Tasmanian wallaby (*Macropus rufogriseus*). Podloucky (1986) reviews literature showing correlations between U.K. amphibian declines and stocking and introduction of fish, including the introduced North American sunfish (*Lepomis gibbosus*), which prey on larvae of frogs and toads.

Although introduced rabbits may have been detrimental to some native species by hindering forest regeneration, they have benefited others that require closely cropped vegetation. The widespread death of rabbits due to myxomatosis in the 1950s is thought to have contributed to the extinction of the large blue butterfly, *Maculinea arion*, which required short vegetation for survival (IUCN 1983).

Numbers of many species of larger animals have been reduced through human control. With firearms reaching widespread use in the early seventeenth century, hunting became more efficient (Perry 1978), and by the mid-nineteenth century the survival of larger woodland fauna depended upon the tolerance of landowners. Predatory birds and mammals were controlled heavily (some to the point of extinction) to protect stock and game populations. The last wolf (*Canis lupus*) was killed in 1743, the last goshawk (*Accipiter gentilis*) in 1850,

the last wildcat (*Felis catus*) by 1870, and the last white-tailed sea eagle (*Haliaetus albicilla*) disappeared in 1918, although better protection has caused predatory bird numbers to rise since the last century (Sharrock 1974). As in the United States, pesticides have been implicated in reductions of predatory birds, which receive concentrated doses at the top of the food chain. In England, Dieldrin has been implicated in drops in golden eagle (*Aquila chrysaetos*) numbers (Sitwell 1984).

The Mediterranean Region

For this discussion we will use the term Mediterranean somewhat loosely, to describe the lands surrounding the Mediterranean Sea – including some, like Portugal, that do not border on the Mediterranean, but that support Mediterranean-type vegetation (in DiCastri and Mooney 1973).

The Mediterranean region is an example of extreme degradation of natural plant and animal communities, accompanying centuries of intense human use. The once ubiquitous evergreen-oak forest is largely gone (Pignatti 1983). Agriculture, forest cutting, fire, and domestic animals have permanently changed most landscapes to unnatural plant and animal communities. Portugal is reported to contain no virgin forests or other natural ecosystems, and disruption in Portugal and elsewhere has been of such long duration that it is difficult to determine which plants are natural or introduced, or what the original vegetation was like (Kardell, Steen, and Fabiao 1986; Thirgood 1981). Throughout the Mediterranean region, degradation of forested areas has been so extreme – with changes in soils, water regimes, and loss of seed sources – that even if an area is protected, regeneration of original vegetation often will not occur. Land originally in forest, for example, now ends regeneration with shrubs only (Gigon 1978, cited in Pignatti 1983).

Habitat conversion began in the Middle East at least 7,000 B.C., as indicated by excavated villages and harvesting tools (Zohary 1983). Significant faunal displacement was occurring by 6000 B.C., as the bones of wild animals in kitchen refuse heaps were replaced by bones of domestic sheep (Jacobsen 1976). By the classical period, beginning in the fourth and fifth centuries B.C., use of timber for charcoal, fuel, and ship- and building-construction had begun to reduce forests throughout the Mediterranean region, beginning in the more densely settled and drier southern and eastern portions of the basin. The result was drying up of streams, increasing local temperatures, and erosion. "Forest gave way to maquis, a dense evergreen thicket, and this in turn to garigue, a sparse growth of spiny and often aromatic low shrubs.... Further destruction can produce landscapes as bare as any steppe, a condition seen on countless Mediterranean hillsides today" (Hughes and Thirgood 1982).

Destruction of the Mediterranean forests, including those of Spain and Italy, was largely completed during the medieval period. Attenborough (1987) details the economic and demographic processes responsible. The raising of Merino sheep in Spain and Italy during the fifteenth and sixteenth centuries, a process that was highly profitable and dominated by the aristocracy, resulted in the clearing of remaining forests to create pasture – by 1526 there were 3½ million Merino sheep in Spain. Demands for timber for shipbuilding contributed to the removal of mature trees, and by the late sixteenth century, the Mediterranean basin, except for inaccessible regions, had been stripped of trees.

In the modern technological period, taken by Pignatti (1983) to begin in 1869, modern monocultural agriculture, including the use of pesticides and synthetic fertilizers, began. Additional dramatic population increases (now more than 300 million people live in the countries of the Mediterranean basin [Henry 1977]) intensified all these uses.

Regeneration of natural forests has been prevented by unrelenting grazing and fire. Trees that remain are largely in managed forests, where many are coppiced regularly to provide wood for charcoal and fodder (Pignatti 1983). In the 4-million-km^2 Mediterranean arid zone, including southeastern Spain, Morocco, Algeria, Syria, and Israel, tree cutting for fuel alone may denude 14% of the remaining forest cover per year (Le Houérou 1977).

Fire and grazing have dramatically changed species composition. There are widespread antipyric communities, in which species of plants susceptible to fire have been replaced by resistant ones, such as succulents (e.g., *Anabasis hausknechtii* in southwestern Iran) or those that regenerate from roots. Similarly, grazing pressure has caused replacement of palatable plants by unpalatable or thorned species over "enormous

areas" of grazed lands (Zohary 1983). In some cases, these antipastoral plants are exotics, such as the American prickly pears and the Australian eucalyptus (Pignatti 1983; Zohary 1983).

The result of these effects has been the extinction of thousands of species of plants (Zohary 1983). The disturbance and extinctions among the plant communities (loss of habitat) has caused reduction in the ranges of native animals. Even by the first century B.C., Virgil observed, "as trees were felled, the birds had no place to nest" (in Hughes and Thirgood 1982), an observation backed up by modern workers who find that transformation of forests to unforested vegetation causes substantial loss of bird diversity (Cody 1986). In Morocco, when Cody studied the few remaining hectares of cedar forest in the Jbel Ayachi of the High Atlas Mountains, he could not find nine of the bird species that are "typical of this habitat" (1986).

The status of the vertebrate fauna is relatively well known, and much of it is threatened (see Table 20-2). In Spain, for example, which has high populations of large mammals and birds compared with many other countries, 37% of its birds are threatened with extinction within its national boundaries (a species might be unthreatened elsewhere), 53% of its mammals threatened, 41% of reptiles, and 45% of amphibians (OECD 1985).

Mediterranean predatory birds have been so reduced through hunting, pesticide poisoning, and habitat loss that a special conference was convened by the International Council for Bird Preservation in 1982 (Newton and Chancellor 1985). In Spain, as of 1975, 17 species had shown significant declines during the preceding few years, and four of them had fewer than 250 pairs left (Garzon 1977).

Finally, with respect to birds, it has been estimated that hundreds of millions of migratory birds are killed annually by market hunters in the Mediterranean, as they travel between Europe and Africa – including some 3 million in Malta alone (Verheugt 1986).

Among reptiles, a partial list of threatened species found in the Mediterranean includes the spur-thighed tortoise (*Testudo graeca graeca*), Hermann's tortoise (*Testudo hermanni*), the Egyptian tortoise (*Testudo Kleinmanni*), and the Nile crocodile (*Crocodylus niloticus*) (IUCN 1982). Hermann's tortoise in France was originally widespread throughout the Mediterranean parts of the country, where it lived in coastal dunes and sheltered lowland areas. This natural habitat was converted to agricultural use over past centuries, but the tortoise survived where peasants used upland regions for nonintensive garden plots and olive terraces, which artificially created the types of open, sunny sites the tortoise needed for nesting. Now, however, abandonment of this agriculture threatens the tortoise with extinction unless encroaching brush and trees are intentionally cleared (FFPS 1986b).

Relatively few Mediterranean mammals have yet become entirely extinct, in part due to their large historic ranges. However, many survive with only much reduced populations in remote areas. As elsewhere, large, huntable species are particularly at risk. For example, the U.S. Endangered Species List includes seven species of gazelle from North Africa and the Arabian Pennisula (U.S. Fish and Wildlife Service 1987). In the arid regions, increasing desertification and usurpation of existing water by humans and stock threatens many mammals, including Israel's otter (*Lutra lutra*), which has dwindled in the past century to approximately 100 adults, in large part because its aquatic habitat has been pumped out for irrigation (Yom-Tov 1986).

Invertebrates as a group are poorly known (IUCN 1983). However, given the dramatic prehistoric and historic habitat conversions that are documented for the region, including the loss of thousands of plant species (Zohary 1983), it is likely that many invertebrate extinctions have also occurred, even though few have been noted. Indeed, Pyle, Bentzien, and Opler (1981) have stated that the known extent of invertebrate extinctions and endangerment undoubtedly represents only a fraction of the total. A study by the Council of Europe estimated that in Europe as a whole (Mediterranean and non-Mediterranean countries), 20% of butterfly species are threatened with extinction, as much as 35% of dragonfly species are endangered, and perhaps 10% of insect species are threatened overall (reported in Speight 1985).

Brazil: Atlantic Forest

As with the areas previously discussed, the regions of Brazil with the highest human densities over the greatest period of time show extensive degradation of plant and animal communities. For Brazil, this means the Atlantic forest region, in which both Rio de Janeiro and São Paulo are located. Atlantic coastal forest includes both tropical moist evergreen forest, semideciduous moist forest in areas of lesser rainfall, and areas of Paraná pine (*Araucaria angustifolia*) (da Fonseca 1985). In its primeval state, the Atlantic forest complex contained some of the richest, tallest, and most endemic-rich forests on earth (Mittermeier et al. 1982). Prior to 1500, this forest stretched in a strip 3,700 km long and up to 100 km deep along the Atlantic coast (McNeill 1986), for a total area of some 1,000,000 km^2 (Mittermeier, personal communication).

In 1500, Pedro Álvares Cabral landed on the Brazilian coast, off course on the way to India, and opened the way to centuries of intense utilization. As McNeill (1986) describes, in the seventeenth century extensive clearing took place for sugar-cane production, which required freshly cleared soils for maximum production and wood for processing. It was a migratory agriculture, constantly in need of new land. Late seventeenth century gold strikes in Minas Gerais increased the population and created new land demands. In the eighteenth and nineteenth centuries coffee production, again dependent upon freshly cleared land, increased dramatically, destroying large areas in São Paulo state. With export agriculture moved food crops and stock-raising. The introduction of European ungulates, which created unaccustomed grazing and browsing pressure, helped to prevent any reestablishment of the native forests. In the late nineteenth century railroads made the remaining coastal regions accessible, opening northern Paraná, most of São Paulo state, and southern Minas Gerais to agriculture. In the past 30 years, the rate of forest clearance has increased tremendously, due to expansion of agricultural monocultures and industry, including steel

mills in need of charcoal (da Fonseca 1985). Now, 43% of the Brazilian population (some 61 million people) is located in this 11% of the country's land (da Fonseca 1985).

The result is that only small, fragmented remnants of this forest are left – less than 7% in any condition, with perhaps less than 1% undisturbed (da Fonseca 1985; Mittermeier et al. 1982). No large stands of the Paraná pine forest are left, although they originally covered 200,000 km^2 (McNeill 1986).

The forest originally held a wealth of endemic species in various taxa: birds, reptiles, and mammals (see da Fonseca 1985 for references). Endemic species originally comprised 40% of all small, nonflying mammals and 53.5% of tree species (da Fonseca, personal communication). The best example, however, is that of the primates, 80% of whom are found only in this region (15 of 21 known species and subspecies; Mittermeier 1986). These primates include 10 endemic marmosets of the genus *Callithrix*, 3 of the genus *Leontopithecus* (lion tamarins), 3 subspecies of *Callicebus personatus* (the masked titi money), and the largest New World monkey, *Brachyteles arachnoides* (the muriqui). Thirteen of them are already endangered. The primary reason for their decrease, as for forest primates throughout the world, is forest destruction, with significant reduction from hunting as well (Mittermeier 1986). As for many huntable species, including the larger birds in Puerto Rico (Brash 1987), forest destruction not only decreases range and fragments populations, but it brings hunters into proximity with remnant populations.

The muriqui once had a range throughout much of southeastern Brazil and an original population of perhaps 400,000 (Aguirre 1971, cited in Mittermeier 1986). It is now reduced to a known population of 240 individuals, scattered in 10 widely separate sites (Mittermeier 1986). Publicizing its endangerment has led to promising conservation efforts in Brazil.

Mittermeier, expert in the primate fauna of the region, says (Mittermeier 1982), "the Atlantic forests and their fauna must be considered among the most endangered forest ecosystems on earth." This is in part because the Atlantic forest, although initially widespread, had the misfortune to exist in a relatively narrow band along the coast, which was the first area of Brazil to be settled and remains the most heavily exploited region. In the eastern United States, by comparison, the species found in the coastal zone largely were spread throughout the interior of the continent as well. Even given this peculiarity of distribution, the situation in the Atlantic forest remains a preview of the future for many of the tropical moist forests throughout the world, including parts of the Brazilian Amazon, where new waves of settlement and clearing are occurring. Rondônia State, in the Brazilian Amazon, for example, was being cleared at 0.43% per year between 1975 and 1978, and in the municipality of Cacoal, the cleared area increased from 2,150 ha in 1975 to 66,960 ha in 1978 (in Fearnside 1982).

The Continuing and Increasing Threat

Although this analysis has been largely historical, the implications for the future are clear. The same forces of population, development, and human colonization of previously undisturbed habitat are continuing and even increasing. The United Nations projects a doubling of world population by the year 2100 (WRI 1987). With growing population will come irresistible pressure to expand crop and grazing lands. In countries in which the standard of living goes up, per capita impact on the environment also can be expected to rise. For example, the industrial nations, which contain 30% of the world's population, consume 88% of its industrial wood, and per capita consumption of paper is 25 times higher than in the developing countries (Grainger 1981). With increased human mobility will come increased numbers of importations – willful and accidental – of exotic species.

Our case studies have focused on only a few regions of the world, but we have attempted to make them exemplary. The same lessons can be drawn elsewhere. It has been variously projected that much of Africa and Asia will be deforested within the next 20 years (Myers 1980; Lanly 1982). Wildlife trade is threatening many species of vertebrates and plants throughout all regions of the world. Traffic-U.S. estimates the world total in wildlife trade to be at least $5 billion per year (Hemley, personal communication). Some areas, notably northern regions of Europe and North America, are in much better shape than others, given that climatic conditions there keep human densities low. Nonetheless, human impacts are rising even there, as witness recent struggles over whether to open arctic refuge lands to mineral and oil exploration (Frazier 1987). In Antarctica, exploitation of biological resources, such as fish and krill, is increasing, and two species of finfish have been harvested to dangerously low levels (Pyle, personal communication; Quigg 1983).

The effects of rapidly increasing human expansion are being felt even on the protected areas of the world – the last bastions. Even in the United States, a country with a tenth of the population density of many, the national parks are losing species and experiencing habitat degradation from excessive numbers of people and their activities, both inside the parks and around the boundaries (Conservation Foundation 1985; Newmark 1986). In the developing world, protected areas are often that in name only. Different social attitudes and inadequate budgets for enforcement, management, and education prevent adequate protection for the environments within. How to make protected areas functional is now one of the major concerns of the world conservation community. Increasingly, plans are focusing on incorporating local peoples into regional plans, often involving sustained utilization of the natural resources within the protected areas. Projects based upon this premise are generally too few in number to assess the viability of the overall strategy, but many conservationists feel that nurturing local concern and economic involvement is our best hope (IUCN et al. 1980).

In addition to these local human effects, our collective activities have now reached such a scale that regional and global processes are being changed. Acid rain is causing widespread forest death and is poisoning waters in industrialized countries and their neighbors. Extensive forest clearing, as is occurring in the Amazon basin, may be enough to change regional rainfall patterns. It is estimated that the moist tropical forest contributes significantly to regional rainfall by evapotranspiration – perhaps up to 48% in the Amazon

basin – and it is possible that extensive clearing of tropical forests could affect climatic conditions enough to prevent normal patterns of regeneration after clearing or damage to the remaining forest (Salati et al. 1986). Lovejoy et al. (1986) have demonstrated that forest remnants are very sensitive to reductions in local humidity, showing "marked changes" in woody plant communities and thus on their dependent animals.

On a global level, anthropogenic changes in atmospheric chemistry are occurring as fossil-fuel use, industry, and agriculture put large quantities of carbon dioxide, chlorofluorocarbons, and methane into the atmosphere. Ozone depletion, which increases the amount of ultraviolet light penetrating the atmosphere, has already been observed. That carbon dioxide elevations will affect plant communities by changing photosynthetic efficiencies is accepted (Lemon 1983), and there is a consensus among most atmospheric scientists that the observed and projected increases in carbon dioxide and other greenhouse gases will cause global warming on an ecologically significant scale (NRC 1983; WMO 1986). With global warming would come major changes in rainfall patterns and in soil and water chemistry.

The effects of global warming on faunal communities, both directly and secondarily through vegetation changes, are likely to be profound. Large changes in species' potential ranges are likely, on the order of hundreds of kilometers in the temperate regions, and more in the Arctic (Peters and Darling 1985). The result would be changes in composition of biological communities and probably many more extinctions than already are expected, based on consideration of human encroachment alone.

Conclusions

The preceding examples leave us with some general conclusions:

1. In general, the risk of habitat degradation and extinction increases with the length of human occupation and human density, moderated by other factors, such as climate, native-ecosystem characteristics, and human-use patterns. Thus, Britain has experienced greater habitat modification than North America.

2. The human impact will be affected by characteristics of the particular human culture, for example, the prevalence of timbering, agriculture, or stock-raising. Each land-use type changes conditions to favor some species and to select against others. Changing land-use over time will change the mixes of species in a particular area.

3. Preindustrialized cultures, including those of Polynesia and Madagascar, brought about extensive extinctions of many animals, including many birds and lemurs.

4. Intrinsic characteristics of the ecosystems and species initially present will help determine impact. For example, island faunas tend to be more immediately susceptible to anthropogenic extinction than continental fauna.

5. Historically, island species have suffered the most extinctions, relative to area.

6. Introduced species, including wild predators, plants, and domestic animals, remain one of the greatest extinction

threats, particularly on islands and in fresh-water systems.

7. Fresh-water ecosystems are analogous to islands in their isolation and fragility, and they also have suffered many extinctions.

8. Little is known about the conservation status of many taxa, particularly the "lower" ones. Even high-visibility species, such as the grizzly bear (*Ursus arctos horribilis*), are often too poorly known to enable humans to make sound conservation plans. Further, we do not even know how many species exist to within an order of magnitude.

9. The continents are experiencing a new massive wave of habitat degradation and concomitant extinction as human populations and associated development continue to climb.

10. The greatest number of extinctions is occurring in the tropics. The tropical forests have at very minimum twice the number of species found in the temperate regions, and they are being cleared at a rate in excess of 74,000 km^2 per year.

11. The level of human impact is now transcending local effects. Both large-scale forest clearing and the production of a wide variety of pollutants are likely to poison wide areas (e.g., with acid rain) and to cause ecologically significant changes in precipitation and temperature on both regional and global levels.

12. Increasing commitments to various fields of conservation biology, including systematic surveys and restoration ecology, hold the key to slowing the loss of species.

Acknowledgments

The authors would like to thank Timothy Werner and Martha Hays-Cooper for valuable assistance in research and production of the manuscript. Support was granted by World Wildlife Fund.

References

Attenborough, D. 1987. *The First Eden: The Mediterranean World and Man*. Boston: Little, Brown, and Co.

Bock, C. E., J. H. Bock, K. L. Jepson, and J. C. Ortega. 1986. Ecological effects of planting African lovegrasses in Arizona. *National Geographic Research* 2(4): 456–63.

Brash, A. R. 1987. The history of avian extinction and forest conversion on Puerto Rico. *Biological Conservation* 39: 97–111.

Carlquist, S. 1974. *Island Biology*. New York: Columbia University Press.

———. 1985. *Hawaii: A Natural History: Geology, Climate, Native Flora and Fauna above the Shoreline*. Honolulu: Pacific Tropical Botanical Garden.

Cassels, R. 1984. The role of prehistoric man in the faunal extinctions of New Zealand and other Pacific islands. In *Quaternary Extinctions: A Prehistoric Revolution*, ed. P. S. Martin and R. G. Klein, 741–67. Tucson, AZ: University of Arizona Press.

Cody, M. L. 1986. Diversity, rarity, and conservation in Mediterranean-climate regions. In *Conservation Biology: The Science of Scarcity and Diversity*, ed. M. E. Soulé, 122–52. Sunderland, MA: Sinauer Associates.

Conservation Foundation. 1984. *State of the Environment: An Assessment at Mid-decade*. Washington, D.C.: The Conservation Foundation.

Conservation Foundation. 1985. *National Parks for a New Generation: Vision, Realities, Prospects*. Washington, D.C.: The Conservation Foundation.

Corbet, G. B. 1974. The distribution of mammals in historic times. In *The Changing Flora and Fauna of Britain*, ed. D. L. Hawksworth, 179–202. New York: Academic Press.

Cox, C. B., and P. D. Moore. 1985. *Biogeography: An Ecological and Evolutionary Approach*. Boston: Blackwell Scientific Pub.

Cronon, W. 1983. *Changes in the Land: Indians, Colonists, and the Ecology of New England*. New York: Hill and Wang.

da Fonseca, G. A. B. 1985. The vanishing Brazilian Atlantic forest. *Biological Conservation* 34: 17–34.

Dawson, W. R., J. D. Ligon, J. R. Murphy, J. P. Myers, D. Simberloff, and J. Verner. 1986. *Report of the Advisory Panel on the Spotted Owl: Audubon Conservation Report No. 7*. New York: National Audubon Society.

Defenders of Wildlife. 1984. *Saving Endangered Species: A Report and Plan for Action*. Washington, D.C.: Defenders of Wildlife.

Dewar, R. E. 1984. Extinctions in Madagascar: The loss of the subfossil fauna. In *Quaternary Extinctions: A Prehistoric Revolution*, ed. P. S. Martin and R. G. Klein, 574–93. Tucson, AZ: University of Arizona Press.

di Castri, F., and H. A. Mooney. 1973. *Mediterranean-Type Ecosystems: Origins and Structure*. New York: Springer-Verlag.

Diamond, J. M. 1984. Historic extinctions: A Rosetta Stone for understanding prehistoric extinctions. In *Quaternary Extinctions: A Prehistoric Revolution*, ed. P. S. Martin and R. G. Klein, 824–62. Tucson, AZ: University of Arizona Press.

———. 1987. Extant unless proven extinct? Or, extinct unless proven extant? *Conservation Biology* 1: 77–79.

Drabelle, D. 1985. The National Wildlife Refuge System. In *Audubon Wildlife Report, 1985*, ed. R. L. Di Silvestro, 151–79. New York: National Audubon Society.

Elton, C. S. 1972. *The Ecology of Invasions by Animals and Plants*. London: Chapman and Hall Ltd.

Erwin, T. L. 1982. Tropical forests: their richness in Coleoptera and other arthropod species. *Coleopterists Bulletin* 36: 74–75.

———. 1983. Beetles and other insects of tropical forest canopies at Manaus, Brazil, sampled by insecticidal fogging. In *Tropical Rain Forest Ecology and Management*, ed. T. C. Whitmore and A. C. Chadwick, 59–75. Oxford: Blackwell Scientific Pub.

Fauna and Flora Preservation Society (FFPS). 1986a. Great crested newts, decline and crisis. *Herpetofauna News* 5 (August): 3.

———. 1986b. Management program started for French tortoise habitat. *Herpetofauna News* 4 (May): 3–4.

Fearnside, P. M. 1982. Deforestation in the Brazilian Amazon: how fast is it coming? *Interciencia* 7 (2): 82–88.

Ford, M. J. 1982. *The Changing Climate: Responses of the Natural Fauna and Flora*. London: George Allen and Unwin.

Frazier, D. 1987. On the edge of the Arctic. *National Parks* 61 (11–12): 18–23.

Fuller, R. J. 1982. *Bird Habitats in Britain*. Calton, England: T. & A. D. Poyser.

Gagné, W. C., and C. C. Christensen. 1985. Conservation status of native terrestrial invertebrates in Hawaii. In *Hawaii's Terrestrial Ecosystems: Preservation and Management*, ed. C. P. Stone and J. M. Scott, 105–26. Honolulu: University of Hawaii.

Garzon, J. 1977. Birds of prey in Spain, the present situation. In *World Conference on Birds of Prey: Report of Proceedings, Vienna, 1975*, ed. R. D. Chancellor, 159–70. Cambridge: International Council for Bird Preservation.

Gentry, A. H. 1986. Endemism in tropical versus temperate plant communities. In *Conservation Biology: The Science of Scarcity and Diversity*, ed. M. E. Soulé, 153–81. Sunderland, MA: Sinauer Associates.

Grainger, A. 1981. Reforesting Britain. *The Ecologist* 11 (2): 56–81.

Hammond, P. M. 1974. Changes in the British Coleopterous fauna. In *The Changing Flora and Fauna of Britain*, ed. D. L. Hawksworth, 323–69. New York: Academic Press.

Harris, L. D. 1984. *The Fragmented Forest: Island Biogeography and the Preservation of Biotic Diversity*. Chicago: University of Chicago Press.

Heath, J. 1974. A century of change in the lepidoptera. In *The Changing Flora and Fauna of Britain*, ed. D. L. Hawksworth, 275–92. New York: Academic Press.

Henry, P. 1977. The Mediterranean: a threatened microcosm. *Ambio* 6(6): 300–307.

Hewitt, O. H. 1967. *The Wild Turkey and Its Management*. Washington, D.C.: The Wildlife Society.

Holing, D. 1987. Hawaii: the Eden of endemism. *The Nature Conservancy News* 37 (1): 6–13.

Howarth, F. G. 1985. Impacts of alien land arthropods and mollusks on native plants and animals in Hawaii. In *Hawaii's Terrestrial Ecosystems: Preservation and Management*, ed. C. P. Stone and J. M. Scott, 149–79. Honolulu: University of Hawaii.

Hughes, J. D., and J. V. Thirgood. 1982. Deforestation in ancient Greece and Rome: A cause of collapse? *The Ecologist* 12(5): 196–208.

International Geosphere-Biosphere Program (IGBP). 1986. *Global Change in the Geosphere-Biosphere: Initial Priorities for an IGBP*. Washington, D.C.: National Research Council, National Academy of Sciences.

International Union for the Conservation of Nature (IUCN). 1982. *The IUCN Amphibia–Reptilia Red Data Book, Part 1: Testudines, Crocodylia, Rhynchocephalia*. Gland, Switzerland: IUCN.

———. 1983. *The Invertebrate Red Data Book*. Gland, Switzerland: IUCN.

International Union for the Conservation of Nature (IUCN), United Nations Environment Program (UNEP), and World Wildlife Fund (WWF). 1980. *World Conservation Strategy: Living Resource Conservation for Sustainable Development*. Gland. Switzerland: IUCN.

Jackson, J. A. 1987. The red-cockaded woodpecker. In *Audubon Wildlife Report, 1987*, ed. R. L. Di Silvestro, 479–93. New York: National Audubon Society.

Jacobsen, T. W. 1976. 17,000 years of Greek prehistory. *Scientific American* 234 (6): 76–87.

Janzen, D. H. 1986. *Guanacaste National Park: Tropical Ecological and Cultural Restoration*. San José, Costa Rica: Editorial Universidad Estatal A Distancia.

Kaeding, L. R., B. D. Burdick, and C. W. McAda. 1985. *A Study of the Endangered Fishes of the Upper Colorado River*. Grand Junction, CO: Fish and Wildlife Service, Colorado River Fishery Project.

Kardell, L., E. Steen, and A. Fabião. 1986. Eucalyptus in Portugal – a threat or a promise? *Ambio* 15 (1): 6–13.

Kartawinata, K., S. Adisoemarto, S. Riswam, and A. P. Vayda. 1981. The impact of man on a tropical forest in Indonesia. *Ambio* 10 (2–3): 115–19.

Kimball, T. L., and R. E. Johnson. 1978. The richness of American wildlife. In *Wildlife in America*, ed. H. P. Brokaw, 3–17. Council on Environmental Quality. Washington, D.C.: Government Printing Office.

King, C. 1984. *Immigrant Killers: Introduced Predators and the Conservation of Birds in New Zealand*. Auckland: Oxford University Press.

King, W. B. 1981. *Endangered Birds of the World: The ICBP Bird Red Data Book*. Washington: Smithsonian Institution Press.

———. 1985. Island birds: Will the future repeat the past? In *Conservation of Island Birds: Case Studies for the Management of Threatened Island Species*, ed. P. J. Moors, 3–15. ICBP Technical Pub. No. 3. Cambridge: International Council for Bird Preservation.

Kirby, K. J. 1987. Exploitation to integration: the changing relationship between forest management and nature conservation in Britain. *Acta Ecologica/Ecol. Gener.* 8(2): 219–25.

Klopatek, J. M., R. J. Olson, C. J. Emerson, and J. L. Joness. 1979. Land-use conflicts with natural vegetation in the United States. *Environmental Conservation* 6(3): 191–99.

Lanly, J. 1982. *Tropical Forest Resources*. Rome: FAO.

Le Houérou, H. N. 1977. Man and desertization in the Mediterranean region. *Ambio* 6(6): 363–65.

Le Houérou, H. N., and H. Gillet. 1986. Conservation versus desertization in African arid lands. In *Conservation Biology: The Science of Diversity and Scarcity*, ed. M. E. Soulé, 444–61. Sunderland, MA: Sinauer Associates.

Lemon, E. R. 1983. *CO_2 and Plants: The Response of Plants to Rising Levels of Atmospheric Carbon Dioxide*. Washington, D.C.: American Association for the Advancement of Science.

Lever, C. 1985. *Naturalized Mammals of the World*. New York: Longman.

Locke, G. M. L. 1970. *Census of Woodlands 1965–67*. London: Forestry Commission.

Lovejoy, T. E. 1980. A projection of species extinctions. In *The Global 2000 Report to the President: Entering the Twenty-First Century*, 328–31. Council on Environmental Quality and the Department of State. Washington, D.C.: Government Printing Office.

Lovejoy, T. E., R. O. Bierregaard, Jr., A. B. Rylands, J. R. Malcolm, C. E. Quintela, L. H. Harper, K. S. Brown, Jr., A. H. Powell, G. V. N. Powell, H. O. R. Schubart, and M. B. Hays. 1986. Edge and other effects of isolation on Amazon forest fragments. In *Conservation Biology: The Science of Scarcity and Diversity*, ed. M. E. Soulé, 256–85. Sunderland, MA: Sinauer Associates.

Lovejoy, T. E., C. Black, R. Hoffman, P. Humphrey, D. H. Janzen, K. C. Kim. C. Myers, R. Patrick, P. H. Raven, and E. O. Wilson. 1990. Systematics and conservation: the needs. (In preparation.)

MacArthur, R. H., J. W. MacArthur, and J. Preer. 1962. On bird species diversity. II. Prediction of bird census from habitat measurement. *American Naturalist* 96: 167–74.

Martin, P. S. 1984. Prehistoric overkill: The global model. In *Quaternary Extinctions: A Prehistoric Revolution*, ed. P. S. Martin and R. G. Klein, 354–403. Tucson, AZ: University of Arizona Press.

Martin, P. S., and R. G. Klein, ed. 1984. *Quaternary Extinctions: A Prehistoric Revolution*. Tucson, AZ: University of Arizona Press.

McNeill, J. R. 1986. Agriculture, forests, and ecological history: Brazil, 1500–1984. *Environmental Review*, summer, 123–33.

Meffe, G. K. Fish utilization of springs and cienegas in the arid Southwest. In *Freshwater Wetlands and Wildlife: Perspectives on Natural, Managed, and Degraded Ecosystems*, ed. R. R. Sharitz and J. W. Gibbons, 475–485. Office of Scientific and Technical Information. Oak Ridge, TN: U.S. Department of Energy.

Mittermeier, R. A. 1986. Primate conservation priorities in the Neotropical region. In *Primates: The Road to Self-sustaining Populations*, ed. K. Benirschke, 221–40. New York: Springer-Verlag.

Mittermeier, R. A., A. F. Coimbra-Filho, I. D. Constable, A. B. Rylands, and C. Valle. 1982. Conservation of primates in the Atlantic forest regions of eastern Brazil. *Int. Zoo. Yearbook* 22: 2–17.

Moss. D. 1978. Diversity of woodland song-bird populations. *J. An. Ecol.* 47: 521–27.

Mueller-Dombois, D. 1981a. Some bioenvironmental conditions and the general design of IBP research in Hawaii. In *Island Ecosystems: Biological Organization in Selected Hawaiian Communities*, ed. D. Mueller-Dombois, K. W. Bridges, and H. L. Carson, 3–32. Stroudsburg, PA: Hutchinson Ross.

———. 1981b. Understanding Hawaiian forest ecosystems: the key to biological conservation. In *Island Ecosystems: Biological Organization in Selected Hawaiian Communities*, ed. D. Mueller-Dombois, K. W. Bridges, and H. L. Carson, 502–19. Stroudsburg, PA: Hutchinson Ross.

Mueller-Dombois, D., G. Spatz, S. Conant, P. Q. Tomich, F. J. Radovsky, J. M. Tenorio, W. Gagné, B. M. Brennan, W. C. Mitchell, D. Springer, G. A. Samuelson, J. L. Gressitt, W. A. Steffan, Y. K. Paik, K. C. Sung, D. E. Hardy, M. D. Delfinado,

D. Fujii, M. S. Doty, L. J. Watson, M. F. Stoner, and G. E. Baker. 1981. Altitudinal distribution of organisms along an island mountain transect. In *Island Ecosystems: Biological Organization in Selected Hawaiian Communities*, ed. D. Mueller-Dombois, K. W. Bridges, and H. L. Carson, 77–180. Stroudsburg, PA: Hutchinson Ross.

Myers, N. 1980. *The Conversion of Tropical Moist Forests*. Washington, D.C.: National Academy of Sciences.

———. 1987. The extinction spasm impending: synergisms at work. *Conservation Biology* 1 (1): 14–21.

National Research Council (NRC). 1983. *Changing Climate*. Washington, D.C.: National Academy Press.

Newmark, W. D. 1986. *Mammalian Richness, Colonization, and Extinction in Western North American National Parks*. Unpublished Ph.D. dissertation. University of Michigan.

Newton, I., and R. Chancellor. 1985. Editors' preface. In *Conservation Studies on Raptors*, ed. I. Newton and R. Chancellor, xi–xii. Cambridge: International Council for Bird Preservation.

Nilson, G. 1986. *The Endangered Species Handbook*. Washington, D.C.: Animal Welfare Institute.

Norris, R., and C. Lenhart. 1987. The national wildlife refuge system. In *Audubon Wildlife Report: 1987*, ed. R. L. Di Silvestro, 239–62. Orlando, FL: Academic Press.

Oedekoven, K. 1980. The vanishing forest. *Environ. Pol. Law* 6 (4): 184–85.

Olson, S. L., and H. F. James. 1984. The role of Polynesians in the extinction of the avifauna of the Hawaiian Islands. In *Quaternary Extinctions: A Prehistoric Revolution*, ed. P. S. Martin and R. G. Klein, 768–80. Tucson, AZ: University of Arizona Press.

Organization for Economic Cooperation and Development (OECD). 1985. *OECD Environmental Data Compendium 1985*. Paris: OECD.

Perry, R. 1978. *Wildlife in Britain and Ireland*. London: Croom Helm.

Peters, R. L., and J. D. Darling. 1985. The greenhouse effect and nature reserves. *Bioscience* 35: 707–17.

Pignatti, S. 1983. Human impact in the vegetation of the Mediterranean basin. In *Geobotany 5: Man's Impact on Vegetation*, ed. W. Holzner, M. J. A. Werger, and I. Ikusima, 151–61. London: Dr. W. Junk.

Podloucky, R. 1986. Some implications for fishrearing for amphibians. *Herpetofauna News* 4 (May): 6.

Potter, F. E., L. Brown, W. McClure, N. Scott, and R. Thomas. 1984. *Houston Toad Recovery Plan*. Albuquerque, NM: U.S. Fish and Wildlife Service.

Prestt, I., A. S. Cooke, and K. F. Corbett. 1974. British amphibians and reptiles. In *The Changing Flora and Fauna of Britain*, ed. D. L. Hawksworth, 229–54. New York: Academic Press.

Pyle, R. M., M. Bentzien, and P. Opler. 1981. Insect conservation. *Ann. Rev. Ent.* 26: 233–58.

Quigg, P. W. 1983. *A Pole Apart: The Emerging Issue of Antarctica*. New York: McGraw-Hill.

Ralph, C. J., and B. D. Maxwell. 1984. Relative effects of human and feral hog disturbance on a wet forest in Hawaii. *Biol. Cons.* 30: 291–303.

Raven, P. H. 1986. *We're Killing Our World*. Keynote address, American Association for the Advancement of Science, Chicago, February 14, 1986. Unpublished.

Ravenscroft, N. 1987. Vanishing blues and frantic ants. *BBC Wildlife*. 5(9): 466–68

Risser, P. G., E. C. Birney, H. D. Blocker, S. W. May, W. J. Parton, and J. A. Wiens. 1981. *The True Prairie Ecosystem*. Stroudsburg, PA: Hutchinson Ross.

Rose, S., and J. Hamill. 1988. Help is on the way for rare fishes of the Upper Colorado River Basin. *Endangered Spec. Tech. Bull.* 13 (3): 1, 6–7.

Salati, E., P. B. Vose, and T. E. Lovejoy. 1986. Amazon rainfall, potential effects of deforestation, and plans for future research.

In *Tropical Rain Forests and the World Atmosphere*, ed. G. T. Prance, 61–74. Boulder, CO: Westview Press.

Seddon, B. 1971. *Introduction to Biogeography*. New York: Harper and Row.

Servheen, C. 1985. The grizzly bear. In *Audubon Wildlife Report, 1985*, ed. R. L. Di Silvestro, 401–15. New York: National Audubon Society.

Shands, W. E., and R. G. Healy. 1977. *The Lands Nobody Wanted*. Washington, D.C.: The Conservation Foundation.

Sharrock, J. T. R. 1974. The changing status of breeding birds in Britain and Ireland. In *The Changing Flora and Fauna of Britain*, ed. D. L. Hawksworth, 203–20. New York: Academic Press.

Sheail, J. 1984. The rabbit. *Biologist* 31 (3): 135–40.

Simberloff, D. 1986. Are we on the verge of a mass extinction in tropical rainforests? In *Dynamics of Extinction*, ed. D. K. Elliott, 165–80. New York: Wiley.

Simon, C. M., W. C. Gagné, F. G. Howarth, and F. J. Radovsky. 1984. Hawaii: a natural entomological laboratory. *Bull. Ent. Soc. Amer.* 30 (3): 8–17.

Sitwell, N. 1984. *The Shell Guide to Britain's Threatened Wildlife*. London: William Collins & Sons Limited.

Smith, K. G. V. 1974. Changes in the British Dipterous fauna. In *The Changing Flora and Fauna of Britain*, ed. D. L. Hawksworth, 371–91. New York: Academic Press.

Smithers, R. H. N. 1983. *The Mammals of the Southern African Subregion*. Pretoria: University of Pretoria.

Southwood, T. R. E. 1961. The number of species of insect associated with various trees. *J. An. Ecol.* 30: 1–8.

Spatz, G., and D. Mueller-Dombois. 1973. The influence of feral goats on koa tree reproduction in Hawaii Volcanoes National Park. *Ecology* 54: 870–76.

———. 1975. Succession pattern after pig-digging in grassland communities on Mauna Loa, Hawaii. *Phytocoenologia* 3: 346–73.

Speight, M. C. D. 1985. European insects. *Naturopa* 49: 4–6.

Steadman, D. W., and S. L. Olson. 1985. Bird remains from an archaeological site on Henderson Island, South Pacific: Man-caused extinctions on an "uninhabited" island. *Proc. Nat. Acad. Sci.* 82: 6191–95.

Taylor, J. A. 1986. The bracken problem: A local hazard and global issue. In *Bracken: Ecology, Land Use and Control Technology*, ed. R. T. Smith and J. A. Taylor, 21–42. Park Ridge, NJ: The Parthenon Pub. Group.

Temple, S. A. 1977. Plant-animal mutualism: coevolution with dodo leads to near-extinction of plant. *Science* 197: 885–86.

———. 1979. Reply to letter to editor. *Science* 203: 1364.

———. 1984. Reply to letter to editor. *Animal Kingdom* 87 (1): 7–8.

Terborgh, J., and B. Winter. 1980. Some causes of extinction. In *Conservation Biology: An Evolutionary-Ecological Perspective*, ed. M. E. Soulé and B. A. Wilcox, 119–133. Sunderland, MA: Sinauer.

Terrasson, F., and G. Tendron. 1981. The case for hedgerows. *The Ecologist* 11: 210–21.

The Nature Conservancy (TNC). 1987. Unpublished Hawaii state overview.

Thirgood, J. V. 1981. *Man and the Mediterranean Forest: A History of Resource Depletion*. New York: Academic Press.

Trotter, M. M., and B. McCulloch. 1984. Moas, men, and middens. In *Quaternary Extinctions: A Prehistoric Revolution*, ed. P. S. Martin and R. G. Klein, 708–27. Tucson, AZ: University of Arizona Press.

U.S. Fish and Wildlife Service. 1986a. Division of refuge management. *Preliminary Survey of Concern on National Wildlife Issues*. Washington, D.C.: U.S. Department of the Interior.

———. 1986b. Endangered species program. *End. Spec. Tech. Bull.* 11 (7): 12.

———. 1987. Republication of the lists of endangered and threatened species. *Code of Federal Regulations* (CFR) 50, part 17: 1–24.

U.S. Forest Service (USFS). 1980. *An Assessment of the Forest and Range Land Situation in the United States*. Washington, D.C.: Department of Agriculture.

Verheugt, W. 1986. Education. *Naturopa* 54: 28–29.

Wagner, F. H. 1978. Livestock grazing and the livestock industry. In *Wildlife and America*, ed. H. P. Brokaw, 121–45. Council on Environmental Quality. Washington, D.C.: Government Printing Office.

Wallace, J. 1986. Where have all the songbirds gone? *Sierra* 71 (2): 44–47.

Wester, L., and J. O. Juvik. 1983. Roadside plant communities on Mauna Loa, Hawaii. *J. Biogeog.* 10: 307–16.

Willis, E. O. 1980. Species reduction in remanescant woodlots in southern Brazil. In *Acta XVII Congressus Internationalis Ornithologici*, Vol. 2, ed. R. Nohring, 783–86. Berlin:

World Meteorological Organization (WMO). 1986. *Report of the International Conference on Assessment of the Role of Carbon Dioxide and of Other Greenhouse Gases in Climate Variations and Associated Impacts*. WMO Publication No. 661. Villach, Austria: WMO.

World Resources Institute (WRI). 1987. *World Resources 1987: An Assessment of the Resource Base That Supports the Global Economy*. Washington, D.C.: World Resources Institute.

Yom-Tov, Y. 1986. Otters between extinction and survival. *Israel – Land and Nature* 11 (4): 167–69.

Zohary, M. 1983. Man and vegetation in the Middle East. In *Man's Impact on Vegetation: Geobotany* 5, ed. W. Holzner, M. J. A. Werger, and I. Ikusima, 287–95. London: Dr. W. Junk.

21

Marine Biota

RAY HILBORN

Most of the earth's surface is covered by the oceans, and most of the animal biomass of the world lives in the seas. About 10% of protein consumed by humans comes from marine animals (Bell 1978), although this figure differs greatly from country to country. In many countries, the animals of the sea provide almost all the animal protein eaten.

What impact has human activity had on the animal biota of the seas? Are the oceans dramatically changed from their condition of 300 years ago, and if so, what has humanity done to cause this change? While I will attempt to answer these questions, the task is doubly difficult because marine animals are not counted easily. Geographers can look at historical maps and records of land use to determine human impacts upon soils, forests, and plains, and zoologists can often estimate the abundance of terrestrial animals with some reliability. Marine animals, particularly fishes, are difficult to find, and even when they are easily captured, the problem of determining numbers remains. When a fish stock is no longer easy to catch, is it because all the fish are gone, have moved elsewhere, or have learned to avoid fishermen? In most of the analysis presented here, I rely on catch histories to determine human impact on marine animals, but I do recognize the weaknesses in this approach. In a few instances, estimates of actual abundance are available. Specific problems for each group discussed will be considered in the appropriate sections.

A second problem in determining human impact on marine animals is the high level of variation. Many marine animals have short life cycles, often 2 to 5 years, and the numbers in a population may easily double or halve from year to year. Combine this with what are now thought to be naturally caused, longer-term (decades or half-century) fluctuations, and even when a substantial change in a fish species or community can be documented, how can it be determined if human action was the cause? We will find that this problem permeates our analysis and will consider it in some detail later on.

The animals in the ocean behave according to normal ecological principles; animals low on the food chain are more abundant than animals high on the food chain. Thus small planktivorous fishes are far more abundant than large piscivorous fishes. The fishes toward the top of the food chain are preferred for human consumption. Indeed, the price per pound is almost directly related to the species' place on the food chain (and therefore its abundance). Tuna, salmon, and large groundfish are expensive, whereas sardines and herring are much cheaper and more abundant. Even more abundant in the seas are the invertebrates and the zooplankton.

This chapter is confined to human impact on the fish and mammals of the oceans, including the anadromous fishes, which lay their eggs in fresh water but spend part of their lives in the seas. Certainly these groups have been the most strongly affected. With some isolated exceptions (lobster, crab, abalone), human impact on the invertebrates of the seas has probably been slight, and it is difficult to document.

Figure 21.1 shows the recent trends in catch of marine animals since 1800. Although the total catches in the twentieth century are far larger than those of the preceding centuries, documentation of earlier fisheries shows that human impact on some species was quite significant many centuries ago, too.

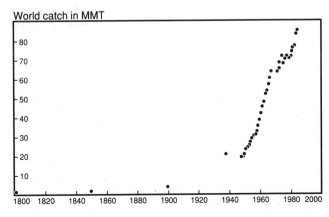

World catch in MMT

Figure 21.1 Historical trends in the catch from the seas. Data from 1938 to the present are from FAO Yearbook of Fisheries statistics. Estimates from 1800, 1850, and 1900 are from Moiseev 1969.

Anadromous Fishes

Anadromous fishes spawn in fresh water and spend some part of their lives in the oceans. By far the best known are the Atlantic and the Pacific salmon, but this group also includes eels, sturgeon, and the shad, among others. Anadromous fishes have been much more affected by humanity than have marine fishes; their dependence upon fresh-water habitat brings them into far more intimate contact with agricultural and industrial activity, and their presence in rivers and streams makes them more vulnerable to harvesting than fish who remain in the sea.

In the following analysis I confine myself to the history of the many species of salmon: they are the most important anadromous species throughout much of the world and certainly the best studied.

Trends in Abundance

Atlantic Salmon. The Atlantic salmon (*Salmo salar*) once ranged from Spain to Norway in Europe (including all of the Baltic countries), and from New England to Labrador. Over their entire range the fish were generally quite abundant in streams and rivers. The earliest recorded documentation in England (according to Netboy 1968) is from the Venerable Bede, writing in the early eighth century A.D. In most of Europe, harvesting salmon was a lordly prerogative throughout most of the Middle Ages, and continued to be so in France until the Revolution. During the Revolution in France, fishing was open to all, and considerable overharvesting is thought to have taken place (Netboy 1968). The long-term threat to salmon in France, however, as elsewhere in Europe, came with the advent of industrialization, when habitat began to be lost to dams, stream blockages, and pollution.

One of the better documented examples is the River Tweed in Scotland, where catches at the beginning of the nineteenth century were over 100,000 fish per year, but declined to less than 20,000 per year by the second half of that century. Catch records are shown in Fig. 21.2. Throughout Europe, the trend in salmon numbers has been closely related to the intensity of development. The stocks in Spain and France are extremely

small remnants of the original populations; generally, English, Welsh, and Scottish rivers have suffered a bit less, whereas in Sweden and Ireland things are better, and in Norway salmon actually appear to have increased in the last century.

Institutional mechanisms have proved to be important modifiers of industrial impact. In Spain, where government authority was quite weak on the local scale, stream blockage and poaching were poorly controlled, whereas on some English streams, particularly the Wye, strong local authorities were established to protect the fish, and current stocks are quite healthy in comparison to similar rivers without such regulatory bodies.

The story is similar in North America. In New England, where industrialization was early and rapid, salmon were almost completely eliminated, whereas in Canada, particularly in Labrador and Newfoundland, there has been little loss of riverine habitat, and the principal human impact has been excess harvesting in the last few decades.

Pacific Salmon. Six species of Pacific salmon are found from California to Alaska in North America, and from Japan to northern Russia in Asia. The principal human impact has been through harvesting, and this within the past 100 years. Only in the lower 48 states of the United States and in Japan has habitat loss (primarily due to impassable dams) been a serious factor. In Canada, Alaska, and the USSR, the rivers remain reasonably untouched.

Figure 21.3a and b shows Pacific salmon catch for Canada and the United States and for Japan and the USSR since 1920. Prior to about 1850, most salmon catch was for local consumption and probably had little impact on the stocks. It was also poorly documented. Modern canning methods led to the great development of the Pacific salmon fisheries, and

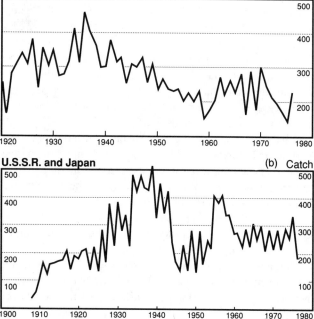

Figure 21.3 Catch histories in metric tons of Pacific salmon from (a) Canada and the United States, (b) USSR and Japan. Source: I.N.P.F.C. 1979.

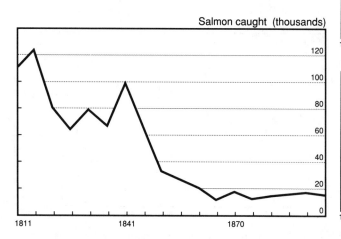

Figure 21.2 Catch of salmon from the River Tweed, Scotland in the nineteenth century. Source: Netboy 1968.

the catch histories reflect this. As with other fisheries, the catch histories, particularly in the early stages of exploitation, will reflect fishing effort rather than abundance of the stocks. In almost all areas, however, the stocks were undoubtedly heavily fished by 1930, and probably beginning to be overfished.

Causes of Change

Human actions that have changed the abundance of anadromous species are, in order of importance, habitat modification, harvesting, pollution, displacement by cultivated species, and introductions. Habitat modification, particularly loss of fresh-water habitat, and harvesting are the dominant factors.

Habitat Modification. The greatest threat to plants and animals is loss of habitat. Populations can recover from overharvesting, and disease and predators can be overcome in various ways, but once the habitat is gone, the populations cannot come back. Habitat loss and degradation are the dominant factors in the decline of the Atlantic salmon populations in Europe outside of Norway, of all species of salmon in the continental United States, and of Pacific salmon in Japan. There are many ways to degrade habitat including siltation of spawning gravel, water diversions, and loss of gravel for other uses. But the major agent has been construction of dams and weirs that make large regions of a watershed inaccessible to upstream migration.

The advent of industrial development marked the beginning of large-scale habitat loss. Weirs were constructed for mills of various forms, water was diverted for industrial use, and salmon had fewer and fewer places to reproduce. Table 21-1 shows the status of the major salmon rivers in England in 1868. By that time, roughly half of the area formerly available to salmon had been closed by weirs. Substantial loss of habitat had taken place well before 1868. According to various sources, the last salmon was caught in the Thames River in either the 1820s or 1833. A commission investigating the disappearance of salmon concluded that the major causes were disposal of sewage, discharges from gasworks, poisonous drainage from mines, overfishing, blockage by weirs, and navigation by steamers.

The deterioration of the salmon resource was severe enough to prompt legislative action in both England and France by the 1860s. A law was promulgated in France in 1865 to require builders of weirs to provide ladders for fish passage. The salmon fisheries act of 1861 in England was intended to protect the fish from further overfishing and to control weirs.

The American experience was similar but more catastrophic. The largest river in New England, the Connecticut, was almost untouched as late as 1790, but in 1798 the Upper Locks and Canal Company built a large dam at Hadley Falls. By 1814, salmon had almost disappeared from the Connecticut River. The destruction of New England waterways proceeded apace with industrial development, reaching Maine by the end of the nineteenth century. Although over 70,000 kg of salmon were landed commercially each year between 1873 and 1889, by 1925 salmon were found in only two rivers in Maine, and since 1950 the total catch has been less than 900 kg per year.

Industrial development and habitat loss came later to the western United States and to Canada. The Pacific salmon resources of the Northwest were almost untouched until the late nineteenth century, and major habitat loss began only with large-scale hydroelectric projects. Although rivers throughout California, Oregon, and Washington have been dammed extensively, the Columbia is the largest and best known. The completion of the Grand Coulee Dam in the late 1930s closed thousands of miles of the upper Columbia watershed (including all of the Canadian portion of the Columbia)

Table 21-1 *Status of English salmon rivers in 1868*

River	Length (miles)	Area of catchment basin (sq. miles)	Area still accessible (sq. miles)	Area closed by weirs (sq. miles)	Area closed by pollution (sq. miles)
Severn	178	4,437	2,037	2,400	0
Dee	93	850	400	450	0
Wye	148	1,655	880	775	0
Wear (Durham)	70	455	35	0	420
Tees	95	744	444	300	0
Ribble	61	501	251	250	0
Mersey	68	1,760	0	0	1,706
Don (Yorkshire)	68	721	0	0	802
Aire and Calder	134	802			
Ouse	59				
Swale	71	1,905	700	1,205	0
Wharfe	75				
Ure and Nidd	61				
Derwent	72	928	360	568	0
Trent	167	3,543	1,500	2,043	0
Total	1420	18,301	6,607	7,991	2,928

Source: Netboy 1968, Table 12.

to salmon forever. While fish ladders have been provided at most subsequent dams on the Columbia system, each dam has eliminated miles of spawning rivers and impedes downstream movement of juveniles. A generally accepted figure is that 10% of downstream-migrating salmon are killed in the passage through each dam-reservoir complex. Since most salmon spawning grounds have between 5 and 10 dams between them and the ocean, this additional mortality alone is responsible for substantial loss of fish.

Harvesting.   Harvesting is the second major threat to salmon populations. Prior to about 1800, salmon were quite abundant throughout their range, abundant enough to be considered a poor man's food, and there is little evidence that harvesting had reduced their abundance. Coincident with industrialization came a breakdown in traditional authority and lordly regulation of salmon harvests. This was most pronounced during the French Revolution, when the overthrow of the monarchy led to public access to salmon netting and rapid depletion of many rivers. Similar but less dramatic increases in harvesting took place throughout most of Europe. As mentioned earlier, the salmon of the Thames River had disappeared early in the nineteenth century, with overfishing cited as a major cause.

Salmon, being large fish in relatively small rivers, are extremely vulnerable to fishing of all kinds, and in the absence of regulations, are rapidly eliminated. Even when laws regulate commercial and sport fishing, poaching often prevents a depleted stock from recovering. The Atlantic salmon resources of New England and of Europe south of the Baltic were greatly reduced by land-based fishing and by habitat loss. The salmon resources of Sweden, Norway, and eastern Canada, and most Pacific salmon stocks did not suffer from such overharvesting, simply because human population densities were so much lower and therefore the local demand for fresh fish was not sufficient to deplete the stocks.

Commercial canning changed this. While runs of Atlantic salmon in Europe and North America were counted in the thousands, the Pacific salmon runs on the Columbia, Fraser, and Alaskan rivers numbered in the tens of millions. Large-scale commercial exploitation began late in the nineteenth century on almost all major salmon rivers in western North America, and as early as 1902 the British Columbia Commissioner of Fisheries (Babcock 1902) was concerned with overexploitation. The vulnerability of salmon in fresh-water streams has perhaps also proved their salvation in some systems, because salmon were among the first fishes to be recognized as being overexploited. Many early commentators noticed that the numbers returning to the rivers were far fewer than before, and remarked that unless sufficient fish were allowed to reach their spawning grounds, the runs could not maintain themselves. The history of salmon-fisheries management in the twentieth century has been one of fisheries biologists and conservationists trying to provide large numbers of fish on the spawning grounds, and commercial packing companies and fishermen trying to catch as many fish as possible.

Pollution.   Pollution of rivers, streams, and lakes undoubtedly has been a major factor in the decline of Atlantic salmon, although one quite difficult to document. The disappearance of salmon from the Thames River, discussed in the previous section, was blamed on, among other causes, sewage releases and mine tailings flowing into the river. It is quite difficult, unfortunately, to document the effects of pollution. While we can measure catches and record stream blockages by weirs, only the most dramatic and catastrophic fish kills by pollutants are recorded. Thus, while pollution has undoubtedly altered the productivity of many salmon streams, it is almost impossible to describe the extent of its effects.

Displacement by Cultivated Species.   A recent and growing impact on salmon has been replacement of natural species and stocks by cultivated stocks, primarily those produced in hatcheries. Attempts have been made to rear salmon through their early lives in hatcheries since the late nineteenth century, but since 1960 the techniques have become much more successful, and hatchery programs are now widespread in Japan and on the west coast of the United States and Canada. Figure 21.4 shows estimated total returns of one of the most cultivated species, chinook salmon, from the Columbia River, giving estimated hatchery and natural components. Most of the current catch now comes from hatcheries, and the natural stock is being replaced.

There is a question of cause and effect. Is the development of large hatchery programs causing the diminution of the natural stocks, or are hatcheries simply our response to a dwindling natural resource?

The initial motivation for most of the hatchery programs has been to compensate for loss due to dams or other uses. Indeed, on the Columbia River system, the power authorities are required to build hatcheries to compensate for the losses they cause. A second reason for the construction of hatcheries, especially in Canada, has been to rebuild stocks depleted by overfishing or by habitat damage from logging. A final motive has been the desire to make use of some rivers that were "underutilized," as in the case of the Babine Lake spawning

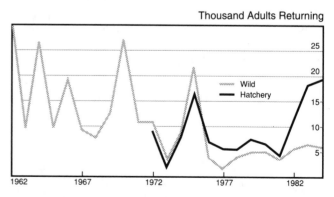

Figure 21.4 Catch of chinook salmon, showing contribution of natural and hatchery reared stocks. The black line represents wild stocks and the gray line represents hatchery stocks. Source: Raymond 1988.

channels in northern British Columbia, where a large lake appeared to be underutilized by sockeye salmon because of insufficient spawning rivers. The Canadian Department of Fisheries and Oceans built several miles of artificial rivers to provide spawning grounds for fish, which could then use Babine Lake in their first two years of life.

Despite the good intentions behind most of these projects, they have led to a decline in the natural stocks by stimulating the profitability of the fisheries in the area. When hatchery-produced fish return to spawn, fishermen come to fish them, and in the process the natural fish are fished harder and disappear faster. On the Babine system, for instance, the total number of sockeye salmon returning to their natural rivers is less than half of what it was when the artificial propagation system began. Fisheries managers are only now beginning to understand this interaction between artificial and natural production and to regulate the fisheries accordingly.

The largest replacement of natural by hatchery stocks has been in Japan, where almost all production now comes from hatcheries. The loss of the wild stocks was due to habitat loss, pollution, and overfishing, however, and the development of the hatchery stocks is not thought to have been a major cause of loss of the original wild stocks.

Introductions of Species.   Salmon are among the few marine fishes that have been successfully introduced around the world. Introductions of chinook salmon to New Zealand took place at the beginning of this century, and coho salmon have recently been introduced to southern Chile. So far, neither of these introductions has produced large-scale runs, and the returns are quite small compared to the introduction of many fresh-water species around the world.

The one introduction of salmon that has had a great impact is that of several species of Pacific salmon to the Great Lakes. This introduction, primarily of coho, but also of chinook and pink salmon, has been wildly successful (from the perspective of the advocates), and the Great Lakes now support one of the most valuable sport fisheries in the world, with several million fish caught each year. Most of these fish are produced in hatcheries, although some wild spawning and rearing does take place. Salmon have essentially replaced lake trout as the dominant predators in the Great Lakes system.

Summary

Human activities have had a great impact on the various types of salmon. Industrialization, at least as practiced in the nineteenth century, was quite incompatible with the use of rivers and streams by salmon, which disappeared from Europe and North America as factories and mills sprang up. The dominant mechanism for change in Atlantic salmon was initially habitat loss, pollution, and fresh-water fishing, whereas for both the surviving stocks of Atlantic salmon and the Pacific salmon in the twentieth century it has been ocean-based fishing. Where the habitat has been retained in a suitable condition, however, declines can be reversed by prudent management practice, and in many places salmon populations are now increasing.

Marine Mammals

Of all the major groups of animals found in the seas, large whales have suffered most from human activities.[1] The history of whaling is one of repeated discovery and depletion of new stocks, with the whaling fleets becoming wider ranging and more efficient, so that today most whale stocks are reduced to a small fraction of their size of 500 years ago.

Although whales have been hunted for thousands of years, the development of modern whaling is thought to have begun in the eleventh or twelfth centuries with the Basques, who hunted right whales in the Bay of Biscay. Right whales were so named because they were slow-moving and did not sink when killed, and thus were the "right" whales to attack. By the thirteenth century, the Basques had depleted the local stocks close to their fishing ports, and the whalers were forced to move farther from home in search of new stocks of whales. Technological innovations by the fifteenth century enabled these whalers to catch and process the whales at sea, which inaugurated modern pelagic whaling. Other nations, notably Holland and England, adopted the Basque fishing techniques, and by the seventeenth century, right whales were scarce throughout the North Atlantic.

Greenland Bowhead Whale Fishery

The Greenland bowhead whale fishery was the next major whale fishery to be discovered. This fishery is traditionally divided into two stocks, the Spitsbergen stock, which is found east of Greenland, and the West Greenland, or Davis Strait, stock, found west of Greenland. According to Nansen (1924) and Tomilin (1967), these stocks were discrete. The Greenland whale fishery began in 1610 near Spitsbergen as a British fishery, but the Basques, Dutch, and Danes quickly joined in.

The Dutch soon dominated, fishing from land stations on Jan Mayen and Spitsbergen. By 1670, the catch was greatly reduced, and the only profitable form of fishing was from boats in the ice around Spitsbergen and between Spitsbergen and East Greenland. Between 1690 and 1710, the catches were so poor that the Dutch whalers looked farther afield, and found unexploited stocks in the Davis Strait. Despite the longer travel distances and subsequent higher costs, the Davis Strait fishery grew rapidly, and by early in the eighteenth century it was the most important one. Fishing in the Spitsbergen area had been quite poor between 1725 and 1735, and almost all whaling took place on the West Greenland stock. In 1735, however, catches in the Spitsbergen stock rose (apparently due to better ice conditions), while catch rates in the West Greenland fishery had been poor, and much of the fleet moved back to the Spitsbergen stock. Figure 21.5 shows the history of the Dutch Greenland whale fleet.

The next major change in the Greenland whale fishery was the decline of the Dutch fleet and the emergence of the British as the dominant power. This was due to a combination of factors, including the blockade of continental ports from 1795 to 1813 and the emergence of much more aggressive fishing masters from several English ports (De Jong 1983). According to Scoresby (1820), an English whaler, the Dutch

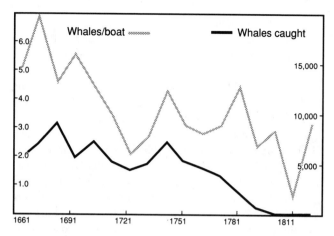

Figure 21.5 The history of total catch and whales caught per voyage from the Dutch fishery for the Greenland whale from 1660 until 1812. The gray line represents whales per boat (left-hand scale) and the black line represents total catch (right-hand scale). Data from De Jong 1983.

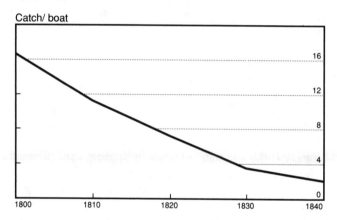

Figure 21.6 Catch per boat of Greenland whales for ships sailing from Peterhead, Scotland. Data from Gray 1932, reprinted in De Jong 1983.

and many English captains had become lazy and were content to catch two or three whales on a voyage. By contrast, this new breed of English masters, aided by some strengthening of their ships against ice, were not satisfied with a voyage until their vessel could hold no more whales.

Whale stocks declined further. First the Spitsbergen stock was depleted to an unprofitable level. Then the fleet went back to the Davis Strait and pursued the stock to the limits of the vessels' ranges. By the mid-nineteenth century, these stocks were considered to be on the brink of extinction. Figure 21.6 ([Gray 1932] De Jong 1983) shows the average number of whales processed per voyage from ships of Peterhead, Scotland. As whales became scarce, vessels either converted to other whale stocks elsewhere in the world or became sealers. Some whaling voyages did continue, however, and according to De Jong, the last two British whaleships returned empty from Baffin Bay to Dundee in 1913.

The Greenland whale fishery is the first well-documented example of sequential exploitation and depletion of whale stocks. The widely accepted history of this fishery is that

harvesting almost exterminated these two stocks of bowhead whales. Vibe (1967) has challenged this view and has asserted that the changes in catch and abundance were possibly caused by changes in ice patterns, which affect both the access of the whales to their feeding areas and the access of the whalers to the whales. Vibe directed his criticism at Nansen (1924), the established reference on the traditional view of this fishery. Jonsgård (1972) supported Nansen against Vibe's criticisms, and in general the view of hunting as the driving force in the decline of the Greenland bowhead whale stocks is widely supported.

American Sperm Whale Fishery

The American sperm whale fishery began in the port of Nantucket, Massachusetts, where six small sloops were engaged in deep-sea whaling by 1715. The demand for sperm-whale oil by candlemakers and the collapse of the Davis Strait bowhead fishery about 1750 led to a major increase in the sperm-whale fishery, and until prior to the American War of Independence, the fishery produced at least 45,000 barrels of sperm oil annually. In this early stage of the fishery, all whaling took place in the Atlantic Ocean. In 1789, the first whalers entered the Pacific, in 1818 the whaling grounds in the central Pacific were discovered, in 1820 the Japanese ground was opened, and in 1823 the whaling grounds around the Seychelles were found. Figure 21.7 shows the major sperm-whaling grounds, giving the years of their first utilization.

In the nineteenth century, Britain, France, Germany, Holland, Australia, Chile, and New Zealand took part in this fishery, although the United States was at all times dominant. Figure 21.8 shows the history of sperm-whale catches from 1800 to 1970 by decades (Best 1983). Again, the history of this fishery is one of sequential depletion of stocks and the fleet moving on to the next fishery. Detailed time series of catch by each region are not available, but the importance of different whaling grounds is evident (Table 21-2). Interestingly, the North Atlantic, where this fishery began

Table 21-2 *Catch distribution of sperm whales in the eighteenth and nineteenth centuries*

Region	Whales killed	
	Number	Percentage
North Atlantic	7,113	19.3
North Pacific	8,791	23.8
Southwest Atlantic	1,977	5.4
Southeast Atlantic	3,157	8.6
Southwest Indian	2,528	6.8
Central Indian	704	1.9
Southeast Indian	2,015	5.5
East Australian	908	2.5
New Zealand	3,399	9.2
Central Pacific	2,899	7.9
Southeast Pacific	3,417	9.3
Total	36,908	

Source: Best 1983.

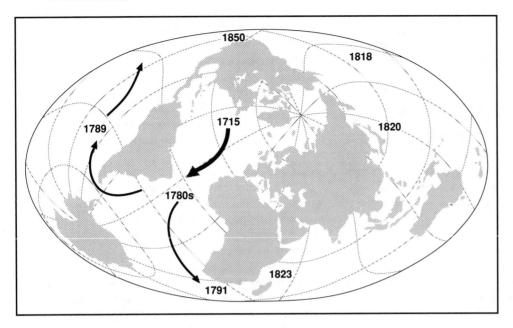

Figure 21.7 Major sperm-whaling grounds of the nineteenth century and their year of discovery.

and remained for its first 70 years, provided about only 12% of the total catch.

The cause of the decline of this fishery in the second half of the nineteenth century is discussed extensively by Best (1983). There are two schools of thought. (1) Kugler (1981) emphasized a reduced demand for whale-oil products, primarily due to the advent of alternatives to whale oil for lighting, with a contributing factor being the severe loss of shipping due to the American Civil War. (2) The second school argues that the decline in the sperm-whale fishery was due to depletion of the population. Schuster (1972) showed that oil production per trip declined from 1820 to 1849, and he concluded that depletion of the whale stocks (vulnerable to nineteenth-century technology) was the major cause.

Even if we accept that catches were smaller due to a scarcity of whales as the nineteenth century progressed, this may have been due to changing behavior of whales, so that the actual numbers were not depleted as much as the catch rates would indicate. Indeed, the advent of steam whaling and harpoons in the twentieth century brought sperm-whale catches to nearly five times the level found during the peak of the nineteenth century. Best (1983) concludes that we really cannot determine how severe an impact the nineteenth-century sperm-whale fishery had on the total abundance of the stock, although estimates presented in Scarff (1977) are that even today sperm-whale stocks in oceans other than the Atlantic may be still at least half of their size prior to commercial whaling.

California Gray Whales

The California gray whale fishery has perhaps the shortest, most concise history of all. The whales bear their young in lagoons on the coast of Mexico, and are extremely vulnerable during this period. The largest of these nursery areas was discovered in 1851 by Charles Scammon (Scarff 1977), and by 1890 the gray whale fishery was dead and the

species was believed to be extinct. Fortunately this was not true, and some individuals survived. Under total protection, this species has increased in the last 100 years and is now thought to be approaching its virgin population size.

Arctic Bowhead Fishery

The Arctic bowhead whale stocks of Greenland, which were severely depleted by the mid-nineteenth century, were two of the three major bowhead stocks of the world. The third stock, found in the Bering Straits and in the western Arctic Ocean, was not discovered by commercial whalers until 1848, when Captain Thomas Roys sailed into the Bering Strait and discovered a valuable virgin stock (Bockstoce and Botkin 1983). By 1852, more than 200 whaling ships operated in the Bering Strait. This fishery was so intense that the catches by 1854 were poor enough to cause the fleet to move to the Okhotsk Sea, which was also rapidly depleted. Here is a clearly documented case, on a rather small spatial scale, of the easily accessible whales rapidly being fished down, with effort then moving into the less accessible and more dangerous

Catch (thousands)

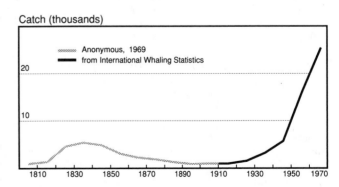

Figure 21.8 Catch of sperm whales by decade, 1800–1970. Source: Best 1983.

regions, until by 1914 the fishery had almost totally collapsed. Current estimates are that the Arctic bowhead stock is at less than 10% of its virgin size, despite over 50 years without major commercial fishing.

We cannot say if the whales consisted of discrete stocks or if the changing distribution of catch simply reflects the fleet increasingly intercepting the whales farther and farther north, with the whales learning to avoid sailing vessels. Regardless of the details of the whales' biology, there is no doubt that the commercial fishery for bowheads in the Bering Strait severely depleted the population. Bockstoce and Botkin (1983) estimate that whereas the original population size was approximately 30,000, it is now about 3,000.

Antarctic Whale Fishery

By 1900, whaling was a dead or dying industry throughout the world. The bowhead whales in the western and eastern Arctic Ocean were nearly extinct, sperm whales were increasingly difficult to catch and unprofitable, California gray whales were thought to be extinct, and petroleum and electricity had eliminated the traditional market for whale products. Few people would have thought that the next four decades would see more whales captured than the combined previous 700 years of commercial exploitation.

Three technical innovations revived the whale industry: (1) the use of steam-powered catcher boats, which allowed whalers to chase species of whales, particularly blue, fin, humpback, and sei whales, that swam too fast for rowed catcher boats; (2) the development of explosive harpoons, which killed whales on impact; and (3) the use of pumps, which inflated whales and kept them afloat until processing.

These techniques had been developed as early as 1868 (Scarff 1977), and used in the North Atlantic on the relatively small populations of blue and fin whales there. These North Atlantic stocks were rapidly depleted in sequence. For instance, Scarff gives figures for the catch of these species off Iceland: 8 in 1883, 1,300 in 1902, and 54 in 1915.

When the first Antarctic whaling station was established on South Georgia Island, the world's largest whaling ground was opened, and by 1914 Norway alone had 60 whaling companies, 22 shore stations, and 145 catcher boats operating in the Antarctic (Scarff 1977). World War I caused a slight drop in the catch, while World War II led to a near-total cessation in Antarctic whaling.

Early Antarctic whaling concentrated on humpback whales, moved on to blue whales, then fin whales, and finally in its last years concentrated on sei and sperm whales. The most easily captured or more desirable species were fished down, and the boats then moved on to the less-preferred species.

Conclusions

Humankind has had a stunning impact on the whale populations of the world. Table 21-3 shows the current estimates of whale population sizes and estimates of the current sizes as percentages of the virgin size. The large, valuable, and easily harvested species (bowhead, right, gray, humpback, and blue) suffered reductions to a small fraction of their initial abundance through commercial fishing. The smaller and less-valuable species have been less affected.

The pattern has been the same: discovery of a new resource or a technical innovation that makes exploitation practical, reduction of the abundance to levels that are not commercially profitable, and decline of the industry until a new stock is discovered or technology makes an unprofitable stock profitable. This pattern was repeated over a long time, moving from right whales in the eastern Atlantic, to bowheads in the North Atlantic, to sperm whales in the Atlantic, then around the world to bowheads in the western Arctic, and finally to the Antarctic whale stocks. Each fishery saw a similar pattern of sequential depletion, spatially in the Basque right whale fisheries and in the bowhead and sperm whale fisheries, and by species in the Antarctic fishery.

Factors other than harvesting may have been important in some places and times. Vibe's (1967) suggestion that much of the variation in the Greenland bowhead fishery was caused by climatic change reminds us that it is perhaps too easy to ascribe all the changes to harvesting. While it is unlikely that we will be able to reconstruct the actual numbers of whales alive in each year in each stock, we can say with some confidence that, generally, harvesting has been the dominant factor in whale populations.

We are now in a position to estimate the abundance of

Table 21-3 *Current estimates of whale population sizes in thousands of whales and percentages of initial populations*

Species	Southern Hemisphere	North Pacific	North Atlantic
Bowhead	Not present	1–2? (10%?)	<0.1 (1%?)
Right	3–4 (<10%)	0.3–0.4 (unknown)	<0.2? (unknown)
Gray	Not present	11–12 (~100%)	Not present
Humpback	2–3 (3%)	2 (unknown)	<1.5 (70%)
Blue	7–8 (4%)	1.5–2 (30–40%)	< 1 (10%)
Fin	80 (20%)	14–19 (40%)	>31 (unknown)
Sei	50–55 (33%)	21–23 (~50%)	>2 (unknown)
Bryde's	>10 (90%)	20–30 (~100%)	Unknown
Minke	120–200 (80%)	Unknown	>10 (unknown)
Sperm (males)	128 (50%)	74 (41%)	38 (unknown)
Sperm (females)	295 (90%)	103 (82%)	Both sexes

Source: Scarff 1977, Table 2.

many whale populations, and since commercial whaling is almost nonexistent, we could wait until the stocks recover to their "virgin" size to determine how severe human impact has been. Unfortunately, there is no guarantee that stocks will ever recover to their virgin size, since many substocks may have been eliminated and those species may never return to cover all their former range. This is an unknown factor that will probably be impossible to assess. Experience with seals and otters – other marine mammals that were severely depleted and have now started recovery – is that local populations may expand quite rapidly, but it is much more difficult to get the species to recover over their entire former range.

Marine Fishes

Most of the animal protein in the oceans that is harvested for human consumption comes from marine fishes. While the biomass of zooplankton and invertebrates in the seas is near boundless, the human preference is for fish. Despite their high value and sometimes localized importance, anadromous fishes and marine mammals constitute a very small proportion of the world's catch. As discussed earlier, marine fish are one of the major sources of protein for humankind, and in many developing countries are the dominant source of animal food. In addition to being the target of most human exploitation in the oceans, fish are also at the top end of the food chain, and thus among the species most vulnerable to toxic substances and other forms of marine pollution. Thus, an understanding of human impact on marine fishes, in the past and present, is of great importance for many of the 5 billion people alive in the world today.

Prior to World War II, it was generally considered that human activities, and fishing in particular, had only a minor effect on fish populations. Technology was thought to be reasonably inefficient, and the major fluctuations that occurred in fish abundance were thought to be environmentally induced. The dramatic recovery of North Sea fish stocks during World War II and subsequent work on population dynamics during the 1950s led to a major reassessment in the scientific community, and by the 1960s and 1970s, fishing was widely regarded as potentially destructive of fish populations. The dramatic declines of many fish stocks, often directly attributable to heavy fishing pressure, reinforced this view. This led to the widespread conviction that when fish stocks were low, the solution was to reduce the fishing effort. There are hundreds of well-documented cases of fish abundance declining as fishing pressure increased. One of the most thorough collections of the response of fish stocks to fishing can be found in the papers in Gulland (1977).

In the past 10 years there has again been a major reassessment, which recognizes the importance of climatic change and natural variation in fish stocks. Many declines that were previously ascribed to fishing are now felt to be environmentally induced. It is therefore more difficult to determine exactly the nature and mechanism of human impact.

Patterns in Fish Abundance

Although one may be able to determine the number of square kilometers of farmland or tropical forest from surveys and from air and satellite photography – and such things change rather slowly from year to year – determining the abundance of marine fish populations is altogether different. First, the fish are hard to count because they live in the oceans and they exhibit a great deal of short-term variability in numbers. We are therefore reduced to estimating abundance, usually from commercial fish landings, and we have to deal with numbers that may change over orders of magnitude within a few years.

Caddy and Gulland (1983) have described four types of behavior of fish populations: steady state, cyclical, irregular, and spasmodic. Traditional fisheries theory, as taught in almost all textbooks, assumes that if a fish stock is not harvested, it will return to and fluctuate around an equilibrium level. If the stock is harvested, the population size will be reduced, but some level of sustainable yield can be obtained from the stock. These stocks are called steady state. Cyclical stocks exhibit quite regular cycles in abundance, with periods of high abundance regularly followed by periods of low abundance. Other, irregular stocks will occasionally have one or two very strong year classes, which produce temporarily large population sizes. Finally, spasmodic stocks exhibit quite different population levels, occurring perhaps at high densities for several or dozens of years, then mysteriously dropping to low densities for some time, and then perhaps going back to high densities. Figure 21.9 shows examples of all four types of behavior. It will be easiest to detect human impact on steady-state stocks, and quite difficult to detect such impacts on irregular or spasmodic stocks.

European Herring. The history of the northern European herring fishery, as described in Cushing (1982), illustrates the intensity of both natural variation and human effects. There appears to be an alternation in herring fisheries between the western Baltic (Sweden) and the Atlantic coast of Norway. Table 21-4 shows comments on the relative success of fisheries in southern Sweden (Ljungman's comments in Cushing 1982) and Boeck's information on the Norwegian fishery (from Cushing 1982). The Swedish fishery has a history of periods of good harvests interspersed with periods of poor harvests. Good and bad periods were approximately one-half century in duration. Times of poor harvest in Sweden were often periods of good harvest in Norway.

Prior to the twentieth century, there is no reason to believe that harvesting had a significant effect on the herring stocks. Fishing technology was extremely limited and catches were small compared to current catches from the same stocks. The variability seen in Table 21-4 is therefore almost certainly natural, and as Cushing argues, probably climatically induced.

Figure 21.10 shows the past 200 years of such catches, with Bohuslän being the dominant Swedish fishery. Note again how the Swedish fishery has come and gone, whereas the western Norway fishery grew dramatically in the twentieth century, until by 1960 it was so large that the stock was almost fished to extinction. Conventional fisheries analysis indicates that the western Norway fishery reduced the stock to a few percent of its virgin biomass, so that a total ban on fishing was introduced and the stock has gradually recovered during the

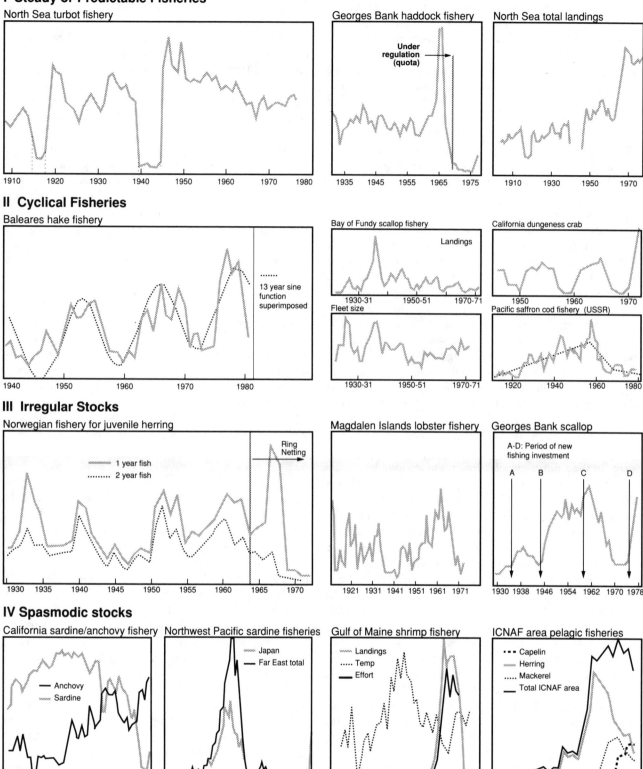

Figure 21.9 Four types of stock dynamics, illustrating that sustainable equilibria are often not possible. Source: Caddy and Gulland 1983.

Table 21-4 *History of the Swedish and Norwegian herring fisheries according to Ljungman and Boeck.*

Ljungman's periods of Bohuslän fisheries (years)	Ljungman's comments	Boeck's dates of Norwegian fisheries
971–1026	good fisheries at least during the	
1027–1082	reign of Olav the Saint.	
1083–1138	Commercial growth of	
1139–1194	Konungahalla; probably good fisheries.	
1195–1250	Colonization of islands; covenents. Probably good fisheries.	
1251–1306	No good fisheries at beginning and middle, but probably good toward the end.	
1307–1362	Particularly good fisheries at least during the last 30 years of the century.	
1363–1418	No good fisheries.	
1419–1474	Good fisheries at least during midcentury.	
1475–1530	No good fisheries.	1500–1568 low abundance
1531–1586	Particularly good fisheries in 1556–1587.	
1587–1642	No good fisheries.	1600–1648
1643–1698	Good fisheries at least between 1660 and 1680.	
1699–1754	No especially good fisheries until 1747–1781.	1700–1784 variable
1755–1810	Rich fisheries 1748–1808.	
1811–1866	No good fisheries.	1818–1870
1867–1922	Rich fishery began in 1877	1896 (or 1910) to 1967

Source: Cushing 1982.

past 20 years. Another interpretation, however, is that such fluctuations are quite natural and would have occurred without the fishery. Human impacts are sometimes difficult to distinguish from natural ones.

California Sardine.   The California sardine fishery was made famous by John Steinbeck; Cannery Row was established to process the valuable catches of California sardines in the first half of this century. The fishery began on a commercial scale early in this century, and by the 1930s was yielding over 60,000 t/yr. By 1950, the fishery was almost completely gone. California sardine are now rare, and there is no directed

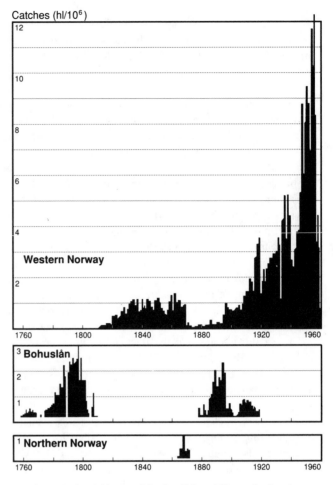

Figure 21.10 Catch history of the Swedish and Norwegian herring fisheries for the past 200 years. Source: Cushing 1982.

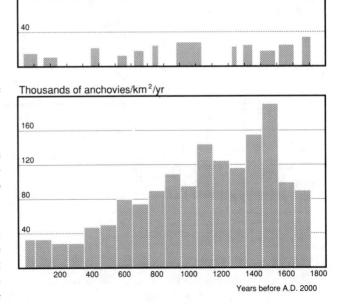

Figure 21.11 A 2,000-year history of major fish species in the Santa Barbara basin off of California. Source: Soutar and Isaacs 1969.

commercial fishery. This used to be considered a classic example of severe overfishing. The stock failed to recover through the 1950s and the 1960s, despite low fishing pressure; however, and it was suspected that some long-term change in the ecosystem had taken place because anchovy, which had formerly been quite rare, were now highly abundant. Some have suggested that fishing had caused a switch in the dominant species of this ecosystem and that it might be difficult to switch the system back to its former condition, with sardines abundant and anchovy rare.

Soutar (1967) discovered that in certain basins of sea bottom, the anaerobic muds preserve fish scales in layers, much like glacial cores, and that long-term patterns of abundance can be determined. This method has provided a 2,000-year history of the four major species or species groups in the area of the former California sardine fishery (Fig. 21.11). The highly valuable sardine shows irregular patterns of abundance, with decades of almost total absence occurring quite regularly. Anchovy show a more regular pattern, with a downward trend continuing for approximately the past 1,500 years.

These data indicate that the fluctuations in the catch of California sardine are quite likely to be natural and not anthropogenic. Indeed, given this evidence, it is possible that fishing has had no detectable impact on the California sardine.

South African Pilchard. A second time series is available from anaerobic sediments off Namibia, in a fishery for anchovy and pilchards. Figure 21.12 shows an estimated 100-year history (Shackleton 1987), with a distinct downward trend in the abundance of both species, including some major fluctuations along the way. For the past 30 years, pilchards have been intensely fished by purse seiners, who are now subject to catch restrictions due to concerns about overfishing. As in the case of the California sardine, however, it is quite difficult to

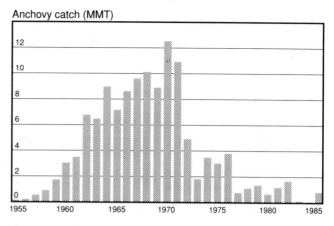

Figure 21.13 Catch history of the Peruvian anchoveta. Source: FAO Yearbook of Fisheries Statistics 1952–85.

determine the importance of fishing against the background of natural variability.

Peruvian Anchoveta. In the 1960s, the Peruvian anchoveta was the most important fishery in the world, providing nearly 10,000,000 t of animal protein – approximately 30% of the total fisheries catch in the world. Figure 21.13 shows the catch history. Just prior to 1972, the fishery was so intense that few fish were older than 2 years, and many biologists expressed concern about the danger of overfishing. The 1972 El Niño caused a reduction in recruitment and subsequent intense exploitation on the reduced stock. In the years immediately after 1972, the fishery continued and the stock was further reduced. By the late 1970s, the stock had fallen to as low as 1 million t, and directed commercial fishing was abandoned.

The most widely accepted explanation for the history of Peruvian anchoveta is that without fishing, short-term climatic changes such as El Niño caused short-term fluctuations in abundance, but when combined with intense fishing pressures, El Niño events produced a collapse of the anchoveta stock (Cushing 1982).

De Vries and Pearcy (1982) studied cores of anaerobic sediments off Peru from the past 16,000 years. They found major changes that they associated with glacial cycles. Again, it is quite difficult to determine the importance of harvesting relative to background natural variability. Yet it is almost equally difficult to believe that harvesting 50% or more of a population each year will not affect it!

Harvesting Power and Fleet Mobility

Of the three major groups discussed in this chapter, anadromous fishes, marine mammals and marine fishes, the last are clearly the least affected by human activities. Only in the past half-century have we had the technical capability to harvest truly large numbers of fish, to produce toxic substances in sufficient volume to begin to pollute the ocean, or potentially to alter world climate enough to affect fish populations. Of these three mechanisms, only the first, harvesting, appears to have had any major effect on marine fishes as yet.

The existing fishing fleets of the world have the capacity to deplete severely most of the important fish resources of

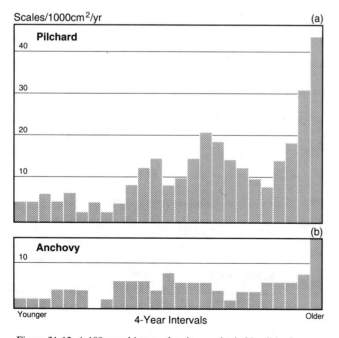

Figure 21.12 A 100-year history of major species in Namibia. Source: Shackleton 1987. (a) pilchard; (b) anchovy.

the world: the recent extension of national fisheries jurisdictions to 200 miles (320 km) was largely in response to the
threats posed by the harvesting capacity of the world's fishing
vessels. The development of large factory trawlers for bottom
fish and of large purse seine vessels for schooling fish, such
as anchoveta, sardines, herring, and tuna, severely endangers most major fish stocks around the world. It is little
wonder, therefore, that essentially all fisheries subject to
factory trawling or large-scale purse seining are regulated
now.

It is not only the great capacity of today's fishing fleets that
is so potentially damaging; the world's fisheries now are
linked intimately through the great mobility of the industrial
fishing fleets. The French purse seine fleet that operated in
West Africa in 1984 was fishing in the Indian Ocean in 1985.
The Japanese, Russian, and Polish factory trawlers are able
to go anywhere in the world within months, provided that
they can obtain permission to fish. Prior to the declaration of
200-mile fishing zones, these fishing fleets behaved much like
the whaling fleets of the previous century. The Russian trawl
fleet might spend two years fishing the groundfish on the
Grand Banks of Newfoundland, and then once these stocks
were reduced, move on to another resource somewhere else
in the world.

The economics of fishing vessels facilitated such mobility.
Following the collapse of the California sardine fishery in the
1950s, many purse seine vessels and fish-reduction plants sat
idle in California. These vessels were either paid for, or the
costs were "sunk"; this was capital equipment waiting for a
use. The depletion of the California sardine provided the
necessary precursor for a rapid development of the Peruvian
anchoveta, simply by freeing up vessels and reduction plants,
which could be moved quickly into a new location with little
opportunity cost.

An additional level of connection exists. The collapse of
the Peruvian anchoveta fishery greatly reduced the supply of
fish meal used as animal feed, particularly for chickens. This
is thought to have contributed significantly to a great escalation
in feed prices and consumer prices in the subsequent years.

Discussion

Detecting Change

Changes in the animal biota of the seas are probably
the most difficult to detect of all the areas considered in this
volume. The ocean is not an easy place to work: ships are
expensive to operate, much of the ocean is far from land, and
even within the seas the depths make finding and counting
animals a challenge. It is not surprising, therefore, that of the
groups considered in this essay, we can best document changes
in marine mammals, which must rise to the surface to breathe
and which often reproduce on or close to land. These attributes also make them most vulnerable to harvesting and
therefore more likely to have been affected by human activity.
Anadromous fishes are also easier to count and more vulnerable to harvest because they return to fresh water to spawn.

Marine fishes, which often live in the deep ocean, are the
most difficult to count. In practice, the only species that are

documented are those that are heavily exploited: the commercial fishery exerts enough effort steaming around the
oceans chasing after them that we feel we can tell when their
abundance has changed. This, by necessity, limits us to considering a small portion of the fishes of the world and
primarily for the last century. With the exception of the
anaerobic sediment cores described earlier, most detectable
change in fish populations has been in major industrial fisheries
of the past century. The Scandinavian herring stocks discussed in an earlier section would appear to be another
example, although one could argue that the changes in abundance as they appeared to fishermen reflected a shifting residence pattern of the fish rather than true changing abundance.

There is little doubt that many high-value and vulnerable
marine animals such as abalone and lobsters have been affected by fishing. Certainly we often know that we harvested
most of what was there.

Are Changes Human-induced?

Once we have some confidence that the abundance of
marine animals has changed, we still must determine if the
change is natural or if it is caused by human activity. Such a
determination would have been much easier 15 years ago,
when the long-term natural variation in many fish stocks was
not recognized. Now, I must reluctantly say that there are few
examples of changes in marine fishes that we can very confidently attribute to human activities.

In my correspondence for the preparation of this paper,
Dr. Tim Wyatt, who coordinated a recent international symposium on long-term changes in marine fish populations,
remarked that no one at the conference had even considered
human effects. I believe that this is partially due to the
prevailing views during the 1960s and 1970s, during which
time most people ascribed all change in fish populations to
fishing. Now the pendulum has swung back toward a view
more sympathetic to natural causes of variation.

The problem is highlighted by the dilemma of the International Pacific Halibut Commission (IPHC), a joint Canadian-
U.S. agency that studies and regulates the fishery for Pacific
halibut in U.S. and Canadian waters. The IPHC has one of
the best data series on a fishery available in the world: the
stock has been under IPHC management for over 50 years
and has seen wide changes in catch and fishing effort. In
short, it has a better chance of understanding the changes in
the stock than almost any other group. Yet even today, the
IPHC must admit that it cannot distinguish between two
hypotheses: (1) that the changes that have been observed
have been caused by fishing, or (2) that the changes are due
to systematic changes in the oceans that affect recruitment.

Spatial and Temporal Connectedness

Human impact on marine animals has been great, and
although it may be most easily documented in anadromous
fishes and marine mammals, many marine fishes have probably been reduced by fishing. Although habitat loss has been
a key agent of change in anadromous fishes, harvesting is the
major human activity affecting marine mammals, anadromous
fishes, and marine fishes alike. The mobility of fishing vessels

adds a distinctive dimension to understanding human impact on marine animals. We have seen a recurrent pattern in marine mammals, marine fishes, and anadromous fishes: a technology is developed that can economically exploit a population; the local stock is depleted; and the fishing vessels move farther afield, sequentially depleting stocks as the fleets move farther and farther from their original base. The pattern was first seen in the spread of Basque whaling technology and has continued unabated in whaling. Fur seal populations, too, were sequentially depleted. As new rookeries were found, the seals were taken. The large factory ship trawl fleets and the large purse seine fleets have acted in a similar fashion on marine fishes in the twentieth century. Anadromous fishes have been less affected by such spatial spreading of fishing fleets, because they are often shore based, but the high-seas salmon fishing in the Pacific and off Iceland exhibits similar characteristics.

We have also seen sequential depletion of different species in the same area: the more valuable and more vulnerable whale species were the first taken in the Antarctic; when they were gone, the whalers moved on to the smaller whales in the same seas. A similar pattern was found in salmon fisheries. The high-value sockeye and chinook stocks were taken first, with the lower-value pink salmon being the last to see heavy exploitation.

The capital dynamics of these fisheries cannot be ignored: after a whaling fleet or a herring purse seine fleet has been built, the costs are "sunk" and the fleet will keep fishing as long as it can meet its operating costs. Today's presence of large factory trawling and purse seine fleets guarantees that any desirable resources that are found will be fished if pol-

itically possible. The mobility of today's fleets means that a crushing fishing pressure can appear anywhere in the world on very short notice.

Ecosystem Level Changes

The discussion thus far has concentrated on species-by-species changes, yet many fisheries take many species from a community and do cause substantial changes in the community structure. A typical example is that of tropical multispecies trawl fisheries, in which often hundreds of different species are taken. The normal pattern is for the high-valued, large, and long-lived species to be depleted first, and for the fishery then to catch smaller, shorter-lived, and less-valuable species. The total biomass yield of the fishery may remain constant, but the species composition changes, as does the value of the catch. Figure 21.14 shows the relative abundance of different trophic groups before and after the development of a major mixed-species fishery in the Gulf of Thailand.

The Antarctic whale fishery of the twentieth century greatly reduced the abundance of the large baleen whales, which feed on krill. It is widely felt that the other krill-eating species, particularly seals, responded to this opportunity and increased in abundance.

The collapse of the California sardine was followed by a major increase in anchovy, and the collapse of the Peruvian anchoveta, by an increase in sardines. If these collapses were due to fishing, then human actions have caused remarkable ecosystem changes in these communities.

Conclusions

Human activities have substantially reduced the abundance of many high-value and vulnerable species, particularly whales, fur seals, and most species of salmon. Habitat loss and pollution of fresh water have had a great effect on many anadromous fishes, but by far the major agent of human activity has been harvesting. Impacts on whales began as early as the thirteenth century, and impacts accelerated in the eighteenth and nineteenth centuries, with truly massive depletions of most large species taking place in the twentieth century. Anadromous fishes were primarily affected by industrialization as it occurred in Europe and North America, although fishing pressure became significant in Europe in the early nineteenth century, and in North America and Asia in the twentieth century.

Marine fishes are more difficult to count and are now known to undergo extremely large natural variations on long time scales. Many marine fishes have been fished quite hard and are generally thought to be overfished. Yet given the difficulty in estimating abundance and the natural variability of these species, it is quite difficult to document large scale human-induced changes in marine fishes.

Although pollution and land-use changes have had major consequences for anadromous fishes in fresh water, except in extremely small and discrete locations, pollution of the seas cannot at this time be documented as affecting marine fish stocks in a major way.

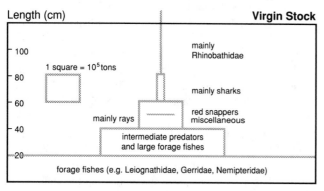

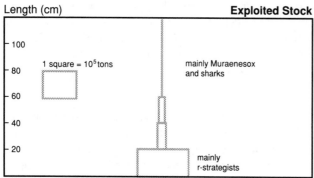

Figure 21.14 Size distribution of the virgin and exploited stocks in the Gulf of Thailand. Source: Pauley 1979.

Notes

1. Fur seals and sea otters have also been greatly affected by human exploitation. Due to limitations, however, their history is omitted from this chapter.

References

Babcock, J. P. 1902. Report of the Commissioner of Fisheries of British Columbia. Canadian Government Report.

Bell, F. W. 1978. *Food from the Sea*. Boulder, CO: Westview Press, Inc.

Best, P. B. 1983. Sperm whale stock assessments and the relevance of historical whaling records. *Rep. Int. Whal. Commn.* (Spec. Iss. 5): 41–55.

Bockstoce, J. R., and D. B. Botkin. 1983. The historical status and reduction of the western Arctic bowhead whale (*Balaena mysticetus*) population by the pelagic whaling industry, 1848–1914. *Rep. Int. Whal. Commn.* (Spec. Iss. 5): 107–141.

Caddy, J. F., and J. A. Gulland. 1983. Historical patterns of fish stocks. *Mar. Pol.* 7: 267–78.

Cushing, D. 1982. *Climate and Fisheries*. London: Academic Press.

De Jong, C. 1983. The hunt of the Greenland whale: a short history and statistical sources. *Rep. Int. Whal. Commn.* (Spec. Iss. 5): 83–106.

De Vries, T. J. and W. G. Pearcy. 1982. Fish debris in sediments of the upwelling zone off central Peru; a late Quaternary record. *Deep-Sea Res.* 28: 87–109.

Food and Agriculture Organization of the United Nations (FAO). 1952–1985. *Yearbook of Fisheries Statistics*. Rome, Italy.

Glantz, M. H. 1979. Science, politics, and economics of the Peruvian anchoveta fishery. *Mar. Pol.* 3: 201–210.

Gray, R. W. 1932. Peterhead sealers and whalers, a contribution to the history of the whaling industry. *Scotti. Nat.*: 197–200.

Gulland, J. A., ed. 1977. *Fish Population Dynamics*. London: John Wiley & Sons.

International North Pacific Fisheries Commission (INPFC). 1979. Historical catch statistics for salmon of the North Pacific Ocean. Bulletin 39. Vancouver, Canada.

Jonsgård, A. 1972. Biologiske Problemer i Tilknytning til Hvalfangsregulering: Nansen Minneforelesning 8 Oktober 1971. The Norwegian Academy of Science and Letters. Universitetsforlaget, Oslo.

Kugler, R. C. 1981. Historical records of American sperm whaling. *FAO Fish. Ser. No. 5*, 3: 321–26.

Moiseev, P. A. [1969] 1971. *The Living Resources of the World Ocean*. (Trans. from Russian.) Jerusalem: Israeli Program for Scientific Translations.

Nansen, F. 1924. *Hunting and Adventures in the Arctic*. Kristiania.

Netboy, A. 1968. *The Atlantic Salmon: a Vanishing Species*. Boston: Houghton Mifflin Co.

———. 1980. *The Columbia River Salmon and Steelhead Trout: Their Fight for Survival*. Seattle, WA: University of Washington Press.

Pauley, D. 1979. Theory and management of tropical multispecies stocks: a review, with emphasis on the Southeast Asian demersal fisheries. ICLARM Studies and Reviews No. 1. International Center for Living Aquatic Resources Management, Manila.

Raymond, H. L. 1988. Effects of hydroelectric development and fisheries enhancement on spring and summer chinook salmon and steelhead in the Columbia River basin. *N. Am. J. Fish. Mgmt.* 8: 1–24.

Scarff, J. E. 1977. The international management of whales, dolphins, and porpoises: an interdisciplinary assessment. *Ecol. Law Quart.* 6: 323–426 (part 1), 571–638 (part 2).

Schuster, G. W. 1972. Productivity and the decline of American sperm whaling. *Env. Affairs* 2: 345–357.

Scoresby, W., Jr. 1820. *An Account of the Arctic Regions, with a History and Description of the Northern Whale Fishery*. 2 vols. Edinburgh: A. Constable & Co.

Shackleton, L. Y. 1987. A comparative study of fossil fish scales from three upwelling regions. *S. Af. J. Mar. Sci* 5: 1–8.

Soutar, A. 1967. The accumulation of fish debris in certain California coastal sediments. *Calif. Coop. Ocean. Fish. Invest. Rept.*, 11: 136–139.

Soutar, A., and J. D. Isaacs. 1969. A history of fish populations inferred from fish scales in anaerobic sediments off California. *Calif. Mar. Res. Comm.* CalCOFI, 13: 63–70.

Tomilin, A. G. 1967. *Mammals of the USSR and Adjacent Countries: Cetacea*. Jerusalem: Israel Program for Scientific Translations.

Vibe, C. 1967. Arctic Animals in Relation to Climatic Fluctuations, Meddelelser om Grönland, Copenhagen: The Danish Zoogeographical Investigations in Greenland.

22

Flora

GHILLEAN T. PRANCE

Plants are basic to all life on earth, and therefore it is certainly important that they be discussed in a volume devoted to the history of environmental transformation. We have become aware both of the importance of plants as primary producers through the process of photosynthesis and of the severe threat of extinction to many – perhaps more than 15% – of the world's plant species. Plants are essential for life because they are the organisms that take in the energy of the sun through photosynthesis in their green leaves, and they convert the atmospheric gas carbon dioxide and the water from the soil into sugars. They begin the food chains that sustain all life. Plants are ultimately the source of all our food, but they are also the source of countless other products upon which human life depends for clothing, shelter, warmth, medicines, and much else. The status of the diversity of plant species that comprise the world's flora should be of prime interest to all concerned citizens.

The current estimate of the number of species of flowering plants in the world is between 250,000 and 300,000. Although we use a relatively small percentage of the plant species of the world today, a much greater number is likely to have potential uses. A recent study of South American Indians (Prance et al. 1987) quantified the percentage of tree species in species-diverse rainforest that are used by various tribes of Indians. On sample hectare plots, the percentage of tree species that was useful to each tribe was calculated. The results were: Chacobo 78.7%, Ka'apor 76.8%, Tembé 61.3%, and Panare 48.6%. A similar study by Balée (personal communication) with the Arawete Indians showed that they used 100% of the trees and woody vines on a sample hectare. These studies would indicate that a very large proportion of the plant species of the world are likely to prove useful for human purposes. If we consider the total world flora and the way in which it is used by indigenous peoples, it is likely that at least 50% of all plant species will prove useful in some direct way. Of course, many of the others have such indirect uses as maintaining the habitat for useful species and providing for the feeding of useful animals.

The estimates for species that fall into the three categories of the International Union for the Conservation of Nature and Natural Resources (IUCN) of extinct, endangered, or vulnerable is on the order of 25,000; that is, 10% of the plant species of the world are threatened with extinction. (See Table 22-1 for data from some areas.) This figure is backed up by the statistics for many of the northern temperate countries, for which lists of threatened and endangered species have been compiled (see Davis et al. 1986 for details). Whether it is in the United States, the USSR, or western European countries, the threatened plant species lists always contain near 10% of the total flora. We have no way to estimate such figures accurately for many of the species-diverse, tropical-rainforest countries. Since deforestation is proceeding at such a rapid rate in these countries, however, the number of threatened species certainly exceeds 10%. It is, therefore, reasonable to conclude that today about 15% of all plant species are threatened with extinction.

This figure is a huge leap from the statistics of 300 years ago, or of the time of George Perkins Marsh's *Man and Nature* (1864). In 1700, very few extinctions of plants were caused by humans – perhaps a few in the Mediterranean region and in North Africa and a few oceanic islands to which goats had been introduced. Almost all extinction was through natural causes. After the Industrial Revolution began, however, the human factor became important, and the extinction rate began to accelerate. By 1860, pollution had begun, and such pollution-sensitive plants as lichens began to decline in numbers. Writing in this period, Marsh gave details of the agriculture and deforestation that was destroying the natural vegetation of America and Britain, but he stated (1864: 70) that species were not being lost: "Lamentable as are the evils produced by the too general felling of the woods in the Old World, I believe it does not satisfactorily appear that any species of native forest tree has yet been extirpated by man on the eastern continent. The roots, stumps, trunks, and foliage found in bogs are recognized as belonging to still-extant species."

In the temperate regions today, this still may be generally true of trees, but it is certainly not the case for herbaceous plants. In the tropics and on many islands, a large number of species of trees are rapidly approaching extinction.

Table 22-1 *Plant species threatened in selected countries or regions with Red Data Books*

Country/region	Species	Rare and threatened taxa	Extinct taxa since 1700	Endangered taxa
Australia	25,000	1,716	117	215
Europe	11,300	1,927	20	117
New Zealand	2,000	186	4	42
South Africa	23,000	2,122	39	107
USSR	21,100	653	~20	~160
United States (Continental)	20,000	2,050	90	?
Worldwide*	250,000	25,000	5,050	15,000†

Source: Davis et al. 1986.

* Estimated from various sources.

† Includes 4,000 species from Pacific coastal Ecuador and 3,000 from Atlantic coastal Brazil.

For a good summary of the current situation of plant species endangerment on a country-by-country basis around the world, consult David and colleagues (1986). In addition to containing details of each country and of various island groups, this book contains the most up-to-date lists of references and data about the existence of *Red Data Books* and other important references to the plants of each political unit treated.

The Causes of Plant Extinction

The past 150 years have seen an industrial and population expansion that was inconceivable 300 years ago. The burgeoning human population and the demand for consumer products and for land to grow food has completely altered the picture. Marsh was certainly well aware of loss of natural habitat to agriculture, forestry, and urban development in the mid-nineteenth century, but this loss has increased at such a rate that today extinction is happening at an unprecedented rate.

Another aspect that concerned Marsh was the effect of introduced species replacing native ones through both deliberate introduction of useful plants and accidental introduction of weeds. He cited (1864: 68) the case of the aquatic species of alga *Anacharis absinastrum*: "A water plant not much inclined to spread in its native American habitat has found its way into English rivers, and extended itself to such a degree as to form a serious obstruction to the flow of the current, and even to navigation." This process has been repeated hundreds of times around the world. The text for *Anacharis* could apply equally well to the more recent invaders of English waterways, the Canadian pondweed (*Elodea canadensis*), and to the Australian waterway invader *Crassula helmsii* (see Pain 1987). In the tropics, the water hyacinth (*Eichhornia crassipes*) has had an identical history. This South American species was introduced into Louisiana for a flora-horticultural exhibition in 1864, the year in which Marsh's book was published, and it has become a huge weed problem in Florida and the gulf states. It is equally troublesome in Africa, where it is a threat to other life in the lake behind the Kariba Dam, and in India it has also become a noxious weed of lakes and rivers. Water hyacinth is no major problem in its native Amazonia, where it is controlled by predators. When introduced to other areas, it grows profusely because of the absence of its natural predators.

Marsh was fully aware of the many ways in which plant species were carried around the world. An amusing example that he cited is of the Russian troops who, in 1814, accidentally brought weed seeds in the stuffing of saddles from the banks of the Dnieper River to the valley of the Rhine!

Today methods of seed transport may have changed, but there is no cessation of plant transport by human action. A well-known example is the introduction of the prickly pear cactus (*Opuntia*) to Australia as a natural fencing material. It adapted so well to the Australian climate that it has become one of the biggest weed problems and has replaced much of the native flora.

One of the saddest cases of colonization, and a symbol of much species loss, is that of Imperata grass, or alangalang (*Imperata cylindrica*), which has replaced much of the tropical rainforests of Java, Indonesia, and other areas of the Far East. Imperata grows so aggressively in deforested areas that it prevents the regeneration of forest or indeed of any other flora. By obstructing the regeneration process, and since it is not a useful pasture grass, Imperata is the cause of much species loss.

It is easy to document the effect of deforestation or the invasion of alien species of plants, but it is much harder to show the effect on the flora of human-induced climate changes. The greenhouse effect is no longer controversial, and there is no doubt that world climate is warming, and will warm – perhaps as much as 3°C in the next 50 years. This will change climate distribution and hence the distribution of plant species. The problem is that the current climate changes are far more rapid than those of natural cycles, leaving too short a time for plants to adapt. The small amount of natural habitat also means that plants can migrate to fewer places, in following the type of climate to which they are adapted.

The other feature of the atmosphere that seriously affects plants is pollution. Plants are being harmed by acid rain, heavy-metal (especially lead) accumulations, and many other pollutants. Some of the plants most sensitive to pollutants are the lichens, species that have disappeared from the trunks of trees of many cities.

The IUCN *Red Data Book* (Lucas and Synge 1978) lists 22 causes of threats to the 250 species of plants that were included as a sample of the threatened and endangered plant species of the world. Although some of these effects are of comparatively recent origin, others have been going on through much of human history and have merely accelerated in recent years. Some of these categories that have threatened plant species the most over the past 150 years are included in the discussion that follows.

The most important of all causes of change in the world's flora, deforestation, is not discussed in any detail in this chapter because it is treated in chap. 11 in this volume. The gravest cause for concern about the plant species of the world, however, is deforestation of tropical rainforest. The statistics of forest loss for recent years are alarming. In 1987, a total of 204,000 km^2 of Brazil was seen to be burning in satellite images – some of the area primary forest and some the reburning of already-cleared areas. In 1988, the figure was 248,000 km^2 (Setzer 1988). On August 27, 1987, a satellite passing over southern Amazonia picked up 6,803 individual points of fire, and the plots show a huge plane of smoke rising to the upper atmosphere (see Malingreau and Tucker 1988). Deforestation is by no means confined to Brazil, and is the single most alarming change to the world's flora. This is not just because of the species that are eliminated in the felled areas, but also because of the climate changes that deforestation may be causing on a worldwide basis. The loss of tropical rainforest is a serious problem in many other countries, for example in Indonesia, where the transmigration project has caused great loss of forest (Whitten 1987) and the current estimate of deforestation is 9,000 km^2 per year (see also chaps. 11 and 30).

Browsing and Overgrazing

Humankind domesticated animals early in its existence, and as greater mobility was achieved, so animals have been transported outside their native regions and the habitats to which they were adapted. Goats have been particularly devastating to vegetation, but cattle, pigs, and sheep also share the blame for the loss of plant species. For example, many plants of the arid regions of Ethiopia and Somalia have disappeared because of overgrazing by domestic animals, particularly goats, that are agile and can reach the branches of many of the low, tortuous trees. The yeheb nut (*Cordeuxia edulis*) is a bush that produces a useful, edible nut. It now is regarded as an endangered species because browsing goats are fond of yeheb leaves, especially those of the young seedlings. Therefore the bushes do not stand a chance of regeneration. The elimination of this and other species of the region has been a gradual process over many years (see Bally 1966). A similar case is that of a close relative of the olive (*Olea laperrinei*) from Algeria, Niger, and Sudan. Maire (1933) reported that the Touary people cut the branches for cattle fodder. The tragedy is that even some of these economically important species are succumbing to overgrazing.

Many islands show dramatic examples of the effects of overgrazing. The Galapagos Islands are plagued by goats that were introduced by the early seafarers as a source of food. Islands with goats have dramatically poorer vegetation than those without goats. Goats have been eradicated from a few of the smaller islands, and the vegetation is beginning to recover. The reason for the endangerment of the Cretan carline thistle (*Carlina diae*) is interesting. Although its habitat, Dia Island, is a reserve, the plant is threatened from overgrazing by the Cretan ibex (*Capra aeyagrus cretensis*), which was introduced to the reserve because the ibex itself was threatened.

St. Helena is a good example of an island on which introduced goats have devastated the native flora. Goats were introduced there in 1513, and within 75 years there were herds that stretched for 2 km. The endemic-rich flora was devastated long before botanists began to discover what was left. The St. Helena redwood (*Trochetia erythroxylon*) was reduced to a single tree in the wild. Fortunately, it survived in gardens, because it is a beautiful tree. The Royal Botanic Gardens Kew has propagated the St. Helena redwood and has material ready for reintroduction to the island. At least 10 St. Helena endemics are already extinct, however, and another 15 species are severely endangered from almost 500 years of inhabitation by goats.

Clearing of Vegetation for Agricultural Crops

The amount of land used for agriculture around the world has increased dramatically over the past 150 years because of the demands for food by a rapidly increasing world population. Gentry (1977) documented the felling of the last of the forest on a ridge in the western coastal region of Ecuador. In that region, where deforestation for agriculture is almost total, many species have become extinct. A close relative of the avocado, the coaba tree (*Caryodaphnopsis theobromifolia*), which was described botanically only in 1977, survives in the small Río Palenque Reserve. Only about 12 trees remain in the reserve. They are the total population of this once-important timber tree.

Morojeya darianii, the big-leaf palm of Madagascar, was chosen by the Species Survival Committee of IUCN to be one of the 12 critically endangered species highlighted at its 1988 General Assembly in Costa Rica. This species was discovered only in 1982 and is confined to a single swamp in the northeastern part of the island. It is threatened because half of its swamp habitat has been cleared for an unsuccessful rice plantation. This huge-leaved palm has been reduced in numbers also because of the edible leaf apex that furnished heart-of-palm.

Restio acockii is a rare plant of the plains north of Cape Town, South Africa, which have long been heavily farmed. It was thought to be extinct for over 40 years, until a small, highly endangered population was discovered.

Examples of the effect of the increase of agricultural land on rare plants abound from all over the world. In Puerto Rico, only 7 trees of palo de nigue (*Cornata obovata*) remain. On April 7, 1988, this species was finally listed under the U.S. Endangered Species Act. This tree has become so rare because of the widespread deforestation over the island for both agriculture and residences.

The Logging Industry

The logging industry is certainly causing the loss of species in tropical rainforest areas, especially in Indonesia (chap. 30). Like many of the other causes of species loss, logging has increased over the past 150 years as the demand for timber has increased. The difference between now and 150 years ago is that logging has been transferred gradually from the north temperate regions to the tropics, where the species-diverse forest with much local endemism is considerably more prone to species loss.

Logging has tended to be species-specific rather than general, leading to the gradual elimination of some of the most useful of all timber species. These species are also those that have been cut for the longest time. Islands, where the quantities of any one resource tend to be limited, have been particularly susceptible to the loss of timber species.

Bois de prune blanc (*Drypetes caustica*) was the source of an excellent hard timber on Mauritius and Reunion islands in the Indian Ocean. This tree was soon reduced in numbers and was thought to be extinct on Mauritius for over 120 years, until two trees were rediscovered in the 1970s. On Reunion, only 12 trees remain. Since this species is dioecious, with male and female flowers on separate trees, there is little likelihood of long-term survival from such a small population.

The sandalo tree (*Santalum fernandezianum*) was one of the sandalwoods with a pleasantly scented valuable wood that grew on Juan Fernandez Island in the South Pacific. It was abundant there in 1624, but by the time of Marsh's book (1864), it had become extremely rare. It was last seen by the Swedish botanist Karl Skottsberg in 1908, but was already extinct when he revisited the "Robinson Crusoe" islands in 1916. The entire stock of this wonderful wood had been cut and shipped to Chile and Peru. Since the islands were also plagued by forest goats, the regeneration of young seedlings to replace the felled sandalo trees was impossible.

The sorva (*Couma utilis*) was a common tree throughout the Amazon forest. It is the source of a white latex that is extracted for use by the chewing-gum industry. The fruits are also edible. To extract the latex, the tree is felled by the latex gatherers, unlike the rubber tree, which is tapped. Gatherers have had to go progressively further and further into the remotest part of the Amazon forest to find sorva trees. They are one of the many tropical forest trees that are being mined out of the forest, rather than being managed. Another is the South American rosewood (*Aniba rosaeodora*), which is cut to extract its essential oil, linalol.

Hydroelectric Dams

During this century, as energy demands have increased, a large number of hydro-electric dams have been constructed. The earlier builders paid little attention to the species of animals and plants growing in the areas to be flooded. In the tropics today there is still no consideration of biological loss. For example, the Balbina hydroelectric dam north of the city of Manaus in the Brazilian Amazon was completed in 1987 and is flooding much of a center of plant endemism. It is probable that species extinction is occurring today as the lake is filling from the Uatamã River.

The case of the Dickey-Lincoln hydroelectric project of the U.S. Army Corps of Engineers on the St. John River in Maine is quite different. The area to be flooded would have eliminated 13 of the known 18 colonies of the rare special Furbish's lousewort (*Pedicularis furbishiae*). The construction of the dam has been held up because this lousewort is listed as an endangered species under the Endangered Species Act of 1973.

Collecting

People have collected plants over the ages for many purposes. As with logging and other causes of species loss discussed above, often some of the most useful or interesting species are depleted by collection.

The Spanish mugwort (*Artemisia granatensis*) is now an extremely rare plant of the Sierra Nevada in Spain. The leaves have been collected for many generations to make the popular artemisia tea and to flavor alcoholic drinks. As the plant became rarer and harder to find, its market value increased far beyond the normal inflation. In 1942, a kilogram was worth 3,500 pesetas. The efforts of local universities to reestablish this plant are constantly hampered by the industry of the collectors.

The plant groups that have suffered the worst from collecting are the orchids and the cacti. Both of these plant families have a large number of fanciers who build up large species collections, and both families have a large number of local and very rare species that are not spared by the collectors. The collection of cacti and orchids increased dramatically over this century, but is now more under control because of the CITES (Convention on International Trade in Endangered Species of Fauna and Flora) treaty.

The small cactus *Ancistrocactus tobuschii* is a collector's item because of its rarity. It is known in only three counties in Texas, and its population is being reduced by illegal collecting. The case of this *Ancistrocactus* is typical of many other cacti of the deserts of the western United States and adjacent Mexico.

Insectivorous plants are another group of plants that are threatened by overcollecting. The green pitcher plant (*Sarracenia oreophila*) has been so much sought after by horticulturalists and plant collectors that now it is critically endangered. It, like several other pitcher plants (for example, the mountain sweet pitcher plant *Sarracenia rubra*, subspecies *jonesii*), is rare because of the combination of overcollecting, drainage of swamps, and conversion of land to agriculture and grazing. The green pitcher plant is found today only in a small area of northeastern Alabama and in a single locality in Georgia.

Loss of Interactive Organisms

Today many plants are threatened because the animals upon which they depend have become rare or extinct. One of the best-known examples is that of the tambalocque tree in Mauritius, of which only 6 trees remain. It has been unable to reproduce for the past 300 years – since the dodo became extinct – because that fruit-eating bird prepared the fruit for germination in its gizzard. The Galapagos tomato (*Lycopersicon cheesmanii*) does not germinate unless the seeds have passed through the gut of a giant tortoise. Plants are intimately linked with animals for their seed dispersal and pollination, and over the last century the populations of many animals upon which plants depend have been severely reduced, so that the plants with which they interact are also threatened.

In the same way that introduced plants can take over and eliminate native plants, introduced animals can displace the animals upon which plants depend. One of the best-known cases began in 1954, when 19 queens of the Africanized honey bee escaped from a laboratory in São Paulo, Brazil. These bees are more aggressive than and replace native bees, which are good pollinators. In some cases, the African bee does not pollinate the flowers from which it has driven the pollinator.

These bees have migrated at a rate of about 200 km/yr and are now as far north as Mexico.

The Introduction of Aggressive Colonizer Plants

The danger of transplanting a useful species of plant to a new area is that in the absence of its natural predators it will out-compete the native flora. I have already cited the case of *Opuntia* in Australia. That continent country has been the victim of many invader plants and animals, since it has such a high level of endemism in the flora (estimated at 80% in *Flora of Australia*, 1981). It is estimated that 117 Australian plant taxa have become extinct and that another 1,931 from a total flora of 25,000 are threatened or endangered (see Davis et al. 1986). The latest invader on the Australian scene is a Central American sensitive plant, *Mimosa pigra* (see Lonsdale and Braithwaite 1988). This large shrub literally took over the floodplains of the Adelaide River during the 1970s. It is believed to have been introduced as a curiosity to Darwin Botanic Gardens, from whence it has spread throughout northern Australia, severely affecting the native species of animals and plants. Today the Australians are doing much research in Mexico to discover a suitable predator for *Mimosa pigra*. The introduction of one of its natural pests is the most likely way of controlling the aggressive mimosa.

South Africa is another region in which invasive plants have endangered the native species. For example, the Proteaceous plant *Serruria ciliata* is endangered and is reduced to three small relict populations, mainly because it has been replaced by the leguminous invaders *Acacia saligna*, *A. pycnantha*, and *A. cyclops* – all from Australia. These species of *Acacia* were introduced into South Africa for their tannin-rich bark and for sand-binding. Australia has both suffered from and produced invasive plants for other countries.

Another well-known invasive species in Florida and the Bahamas is the Brazilian pepper tree (*Schinus terebinthifolius*), which was introduced as an ornamental shade tree. It is also an unpopular arrival because it causes allergies in many people, giving them severe dermatitis and respiratory problems. It also intoxicates some of the native species of birds, and harbors the black scale insects of citrus. There is good reason for the strict control of plant introductions from one region to another!

Conclusions

The examples given here – only a few of the many that could be cited – show that the trends that influenced the world's flora that were pointed out by Marsh in 1864 have continued. All the factors that Marsh recognized, such as deforestation, the introduction of alien species, and the drainage of swamps, have become increasingly threatening problems to plant species, and many other newer threats exist. Problems of browsing and overgrazing by goats and cattle are ancient, but they continue to become more serious as time passes and as population increases. The deforestation of the tropics (see chaps. 11, 29, 30) is now reaching unprecendented rates and has become a much more serious threat, not only directly to species that are felled, but to all species through climatic change and the breakdown of the web of interaction that links species together. The planet is losing its plant genetic resources at an unprecedented rate, which should be a cause for growing concern. We must not allow the pressures of poverty and development to destroy the very resources that can offer solutions to the problems.

References

Bally, P. R. O. 1966. Enquiry into the occurrence of the yeheb nut (*Cordeuxia edulias* Hemsl.) in the Horn of Africa. *Candollea* 21: 3–11.

Davis, S. D., S. J. M. Droop, P. Grejerson, L. Henson, C. L. Leon, J. L. Villa-Lobos, H. Synge, and J. Zantouska. 1986. *Plants In Danger: What Do We Know?* Gland, Switzerland: IUCN.

1981 *Flora of Australia*. vol. 1. Canberra: Australian Government Printing Service.

Genty, A. H. 1977. Endangered plant species and habitats of Ecuador and Amazonian Peru. In *Extinction Is Forever*, ed. G. T. Prance and T. S. Elias, 136–49. New York: New York Botanical Garden.

Lonsdale, M., and R. Braithwaite. 1988. The shrub that conquered the bush. *New Sci.*, Oct 15: 52–55.

Lucas, G. L., and H. Synge. 1978. *The IUCN Plant Red Data Book*. Morges, Switzerland: IUCN.

Maire, R. 1933. Etudes sur la Flore et la Végétation du Sahara Central I.II. *Mém. Soc. Hist. nat. Afr. N.* 3: 166–68.

Malingreau, J.-P., and C. J. Tucker. 1988. Large-scale deforestation in the southeastern Amazon Basin of Brazil. *Ambio* 17: 49–55.

Marsh, G. P. 1864. *Man and Nature; Or The Earth As Modified by Human Action*. New York: Charles Scribner.

Pain, S. 1987. Australian invader. *New Sci.* 1570: 26.

Prance, G. T., W. Balée, B. M. Boom, and R. L. Carneiro. 1987. Quantitative ethnobotany and the case for conservation of Amazonia. *Conserv. Biol.* 1: 296–310.

Setzer, A. 1988. Quoted in *Veja*, Sept. 21: 74–78.

Whitten, A. J. 1987. Indonesia's transmigration program and its role in the loss of tropical rain forest. *Conserv. Biol.* 1: 239–46.

23

Carbon

R. A. HOUGHTON   DAVID L. SKOLE

Carbon is the key element for life. In its reduced form, it comprises 45% to 50% of the mass of plants and animals on a dry weight basis (water removed). In its oxidized form, it is one of the most critical elements in the atmosphere for determining the temperature and the climate of the earth.

The importance of carbon is largely this chemical flexibility – its existence in both reduced and oxidized states. Carbon accounts for about only 0.27% of the mass of elements in the earth's crust (Kempe 1979). The chemical bonds between carbon, oxygen, and hydrogen in organic matter are formed by green plants using the energy of the sun in the process of photosynthesis. The chemical reaction is as follows:

$$6CO_2 + 6H_2O \rightarrow C_6H_{12}O_6 + 6O_2 \qquad (1)$$

This chemical equation indicates that six molecules of carbon dioxide (CO_2) (carbon in a chemically oxidized form) and six molecules of water (H_2O) yield one molecule of organic matter ($C_6H_{12}O_6$) (carbon in a chemically reduced form) and six molecules of oxygen (O_2). The reaction requires the energy of the sun and stores some of this solar energy in the chemical bonds of the organic matter formed. Cellulose, carbohydrates, protein, and fats are all forms of organic matter, or reduced carbon. All embody energy and all are derived ultimately from photosynthesis.

Reaction (1) also goes in the opposite direction during the oxidation of organic matter. Oxidation occurs during the two, seemingly dissimilar but chemically identical, processes of respiration and combustion. During oxidation, the chemical energy stored in organic matter is released. Respiration is the life process that yields energy from organic matter, energy required for growth and maintenance. All living organisms oxidize organic matter; only plants and some microbes are capable of reducing carbon.

The common sources of energy used by industrial societies today are another form of organic matter. Coal, oil, and natural gas are the residuals of organic matter formed millions of years ago by green plants. The material escaped oxidation, became buried in the earth, and over time was transformed to what we call fossil fuels. The energy stored in the chemical bonds of these fossil fuels is released during combustion, just as the energy stored in carbohydrates, proteins, and fats is released during respiration.

The difference between the two processes of oxidation is related to the age of the organic matter and the rates of cycling of carbon on the earth. When young organic matter is oxidized, the total amount of carbon in the actively exchanging system is unchanged. It is merely redistributed among the reservoirs of the system – the atmosphere, the land, and the oceans. When fossil fuels are oxidized, however, the carbon dioxide released represents a net addition of carbon to the actively exchanging system (this short-term system operates from periods of years to centuries). The fossil carbon is in a longer-term system (millions of years), and the processes that govern the behavior of the long-term system (sedimentation, weathering, vulcanism, sea-floor spreading) are different from those that govern the behavior of the short-term system. In discussions focusing on the past 300 years, it is the short-term system that is of interest.

Carbon occurs in the hydrosphere, or oceans, as well as in the atmosphere and in the biota. The world's oceans hold about 50 times more carbon than the atmosphere and 18 times more than terrestrial ecosystems – most of this oceanic carbon is in the dissolved inorganic form, bicarbonate. On the time scale of hundreds to thousands of years, the oceans play the major role in determining the concentration of carbon dioxide in the atmosphere, but in the short term, the terrestrial biota is equally important. Because of the large amount of carbon in the oceans, shifts in the abundance of carbon among these three reservoirs (atmosphere, terrestrial ecosystems, oceans) will have a much greater significance for the terrestrial biota and for the atmosphere than they will for the oceans. The oceans have been relatively unaffected by shifts in the distribution of carbon in recent centuries.

In this discussion of the changes in the global distribution of carbon between 1700 and the present, we first describe the reservoirs and fluxes of carbon for the earth today. We next address the releases of carbon to the atmosphere that have resulted from human uses of land and energy. These changes have affected the distribution of carbon in the atmosphere, the oceans, and the terrestrial ecosystems. We address the changes in each reservoir over the past 300 years and, finally, offer some prospects for the future.

Several reviews of the global carbon cycle have appeared in recent years. For more information than can be conveyed in a chapter of this length, refer to the comprehensive summaries edited by Bolin (1981), Bolin et al. (1979), Bolin et al. (1986), Clark (1982), NRC (1983), Sundquist and Broecker (1985), Trabalka (1985), Trabalka and Reichle (1986), and Woodwell (1984).

The Contemporary Global Carbon Cycle

Reservoirs

The contemporary global carbon cycle is shown in simplified form in Fig. 23.1. The four major reservoirs are the atmosphere, the oceans, the reserves of fossil fuels, and the terrestrial ecosystems, including the biota and the soils. All of the reservoirs except the deep ocean are drawn to scale; the deep ocean would appear four times larger if drawn to the same scale. The size of the atmospheric reservoir of carbon relative to the other reservoirs makes it clear that the atmosphere is subject to large changes.

The carbon in the atmosphere occurs almost entirely as carbon dioxide, the well-known greenhouse gas that is more transparent to the sun's energy entering the earth's atmosphere than it is to the reradiated heat energy leaving the earth. Higher concentrations of carbon dioxide in the atmosphere cause a warmer earth; lower concentrations, a cooler one. The concentration of carbon dioxide in the atmosphere during the last glacial period was about half the concentration that exists during the interglacial maximum of today (see chap. 9).

Carbon dioxide exists in the atmosphere in very small concentrations. The concentration was about 345 parts per million (ppm) in 1985. The gas is chemically stable and has an average residence time in the atmosphere of about 5 years before it enters the oceans or the terrestrial biota.

Other trace gases containing carbon (Table 23-1) occur at lower atmospheric concentrations than carbon dioxide, but are important because they modify the chemical and/or the radiative properties of the earth's atmosphere (see chaps. 17 and 19). Methane (CH_4) is present at about 1.7 ppm, two

orders of magnitude more dilute than carbon dioxide. Methane is a reduced form of carbon, is much less stable than carbon dioxide, and has an average residence time in the atmosphere of 5 to 10 years. Carbon monoxide (CO), another oxidized form of carbon, has an atmospheric residence time of only a few months. Its low concentration (about 0.1 ppm) and its short residence time are results of its chemical reactivity with OH radicals. Carbon monoxide is not a greenhouse gas, but its chemical reactivity affects the abundances of ozone and methane and, thereby, the earth's radiative balance. The nonmethane hydrocarbons, another unstable form of carbon in the atmosphere, are present in even smaller concentrations. The oxidation of these biogenic trace gases is believed to be a major source of atmospheric carbon monoxide, and hence, they also affect the abundances of atmospheric ozone and methane.

Approximately the same amount of carbon (560 Pg) (1 Pg = 1 petagram = 1×10^{15} g = 1 billion metric tons) is contained in the living vegetation of terrestrial ecosystems as in the atmosphere (735 Pg). The soils of the earth are estimated to contain 1,400 to 1,700 Pg of carbon, two to three times the amount in the living biota. The carbon in terrestrial ecosystems is organic carbon in a reduced form. Approximately 45% to 50% of organic matter is carbon; the fraction varies little. Organic carbon exists in many forms, including living leaves and roots, animals, microbes, wood, decaying leaves, and soil humus. The turnover of these materials varies from less than one year to more than 1,000 years. In terms of carbon, the world's terrestrial biota is almost entirely vegetation; animals account for less than 0.1% of the carbon in living organisms. Most terrestrial carbon is stored in the vegetation and soils of the world's forests (Table 23-2). Forests cover about 30% of the land surface and hold about 75% of the live organic carbon. When soils are included in the inventory, forests hold almost half of the carbon of the world's terrestrial ecosystems. The soils of woodlands, grasslands, tundra, wetlands, and agricultural lands store most of the rest of the terrestrial organic carbon.

The amount of carbon in the surface ocean (about 600 Pg currently) is similar to the amount in the atmosphere. The amount in the intermediate and deep waters is about 60 times this amount. Because, at equilibrium, the concentration of carbon dioxide in air is the same as in the oceans, the oceans control the atmospheric concentration of carbon dioxide. The equilibrium may require hundreds of years to reach, however, because the rate of circulation of oceanic waters is slow. The dramatic increase in atmospheric carbon dioxide over the past 30 years demonstrates the extent of the present disequilibrium (see following).

The carbon in the oceans, as in the atmosphere, is mostly inorganic carbon in the oxidized state. The ocean's chemistry is such that less than 1% of this carbon is dissolved carbon dioxide. More than 97% exists in the form of the bicarbonate ion (HCO_3^-) and the rest as carbonate ion (CO_3^{2-}). The three forms are in chemical equilibrium. About 1,000 Pg of carbon in the oceans (out of the total of more than 36,000 Pg) is dissolved organic carbon. Carbon in living organisms amounts to less than 2 Pg in the sea, in comparison to about

Table 23-1 *Major forms of carbon in the atmosphere*

Gas reference	Chemical formula	Concentration in 1985 (ppm)	Total amount (Pg C)*
Carbon dioxide, Schnell 1986	CO_2	345	730
Methane, Khalil and Rasmussen 1987	CH_4	1.7	3
Carbon monoxide, Ramanathan et al. 1985	CO	0.09	0.2

* Pg = petagram (1 petagram = 1×10^{15} g = 1 billion metric tons).

Table 23-2 *Estimates of the areas of major types of vegetation, the mass of carbon in vegetation and soils, and the net primary productivity of terrestrial ecosystems*

Ecosystem	Area (10^8 ha)	Carbon in vegetation (Pg)	Net primary productivity (Pg C/yr)	Carbon in soil (Pg)
Tropical wet and moist forest	10.4	156.0	8.3	138.7
Tropical dry forest	7.7	49.7	4.8	45.8
Temperate forest	9.2	73.3	6.0	104.3
Boreal forest	15.0	143.0	6.4	181.9
Tropical woodland and savanna	24.6	48.8	11.1	129.6
Temperate steppe	15.1	43.8	4.9	149.3
Desert	18.2	5.9	1.4	84.0
Tundra	11.0	9.0	1.4	191.8
Wetland	2.9	7.8	3.8	202.4
Cultivated land	15.9	21.5	12.1	167.5
Rock and ice	15.2	0.0	0.0	0.0
Global total	145.2	558.8	60.2	1,395.3

Source: Adapted from Olson, Watts, and Allison 1983 and Post et al. 1982.

560 Pg on land. The mass of animal life in the oceans is almost the same as on land, however, pointing to the very different trophic structures in the two environments. The ocean's plants are microscopic. They have a high productivity, but the production of plant material does not accumulate; it is either grazed or decomposed almost immediately. In contrast, terrestrial plants accumulate large amounts of carbon in long-lasting structures (trees).

The amount of carbon stored in recoverable reserves of coal, oil, and gas is estimated to be about 5,000 Pg, larger than any other reservoir except the deep sea, and about ten times the carbon content of the atmosphere. Until 100 to 150 years ago, this reservoir of carbon was not a significant part of the short-term cycle of carbon.

The Natural Flows of Carbon

Each year the atmosphere exchanges 90 Pg to 120 Pg of carbon with terrestrial ecosystems and about the same amount with the surface ocean (Fig. 23.1). The exchanges with terrestrial systems are biotic flows of carbon (equation 1). Terrestrial photosynthesis withdraws on the order of 100 Pg of carbon from the atmosphere annually in the production of organic matter. About half of this photosynthesis occurs in the tropics, in which the conditions are generally favorable for growth and in which a large proportion of the earth's land area exists (Table 23-2). At least half of this photosynthetic production is respired by the plants themselves, and the rest is consumed by animals or is respired by decomposer organisms in the soil. This transfer of plant material to the consumer and decomposer communities is represented by the arrow from vegetation to soil in Fig. 23.1 (60 Pg of carbon per year).

The annual rate of photosynthesis in the world oceans is estimated to be about 50 Pg of carbon (Martin et al. 1987). Marine photosynthesis is not shown in Fig. 23.1 because the chemical properties of carbon dioxide in seawater are such that little of the carbon involved in either photosynthesis or respiration in the sea is exchanged with the atmosphere. On the time scale of 100 years, however, marine photosynthesis is very important in controlling the carbon dioxide concentration of the atmosphere. Marine photosynthesis and the sinking of organic matter out of the surface water are estimated to keep the concentration of carbon dioxide in air about 30% of what it would be in their absence.

The gross fluxes of carbon between the surface ocean and the atmosphere each year are largely the result of physico-chemical processes. The rate of transfer of carbon dioxide across the sea surface is estimated to be between 90 Pg and 100 Pg of carbon per year. The flux is in both directions. The gross flows of carbon between the surface ocean and the intermediate and deep ocean are estimated to be between 30 Pg and 40 Pg per year (Bolin 1983; Keeling 1983).

Net Fluxes of Carbon Introduced by Human Activities

Changes in the fluxes of carbon over the past 300 years as a result of agricultural and industrial activities will be addressed in more detail below. In 1980, the net release of carbon dioxide to the atmosphere from these activities was about 7 Pg of carbon. 5.1 Pg were released through the combustion of fossil fuels; another 0.1 Pg was released in the production of cement; and about 1.8 Pg of carbon (range of 0.4 Pg to 2.5 Pg) were released to the atmosphere as a result of changes in land use. Changes in land use either release carbon to or withdraw it from the atmosphere. Releases occur when forests are replaced with agricultural crops because the mass of carbon per unit area of forest is 20 to 100 times greater than that of croplands. The carbon in trees is released to the atmosphere when the wood is oxidized through burning

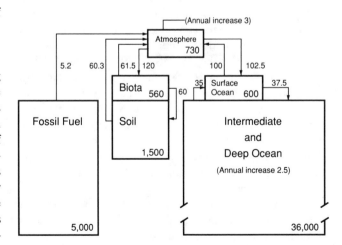

Figure 23.1 The major reservoirs and flows of carbon for the globe in about 1980. Data from Bolin 1983, Houghton et al. 1987, and Keeling 1983.

or decay. Some of the organic matter of soils is also oxidized following disturbance or cultivation and contributes to the net release of carbon. Carbon is withdrawn from the atmosphere when agricultural land is abandoned and allowed to return to forest. Over the past 300 years, the net flux has been from land to the atmosphere as the area of forests has been reduced.

Of the 7 Pg of carbon released to the atmosphere in 1980, about 3 Pg remained in the atmosphere and about 3 Pg were absorbed by the oceans. Given the current state of knowledge, the flows do not appear to balance. More carbon is estimated to have been released to the atmosphere than is accumulating in the oceans and the atmosphere. The apparent imbalance is the result of incomplete understanding; the carbon cycle in nature is indeed balanced. The imbalance is the result of errors of measurement, errors introduced in the simplifications of models, and errors resulting from the failure to account for all of the processes that may have changed as a result of increased human activities.

Mobilization of Carbon As a Result of Human Activities

Changes in Land Use

As just described, changes in the use of land affect the amount of carbon stored in vegetation and in soils and, hence, affect the distribution of carbon between land and the atmosphere. Although some changes in land use increase the carbon stored on land, the trend over the past 300 years has been to reduce the area of forests (see chap. 11), increase the area of agricultural lands (see chap. 10), and, therefore, reduce the amount of carbon on land.

The history of the net flux of carbon between terrestrial ecosystems and the atmosphere has been calculated using two different approaches. One approach is based on historical records of land-use change and on ecological data pertaining to the changes in vegetation and soil that accompany land use change. The other approach is based on ratios of carbon isotopes contained in tree rings or on the concentrations of carbon dioxide in bubbles of air trapped in glacial ice.

The first method to be discussed here is that based on ecological data and historical records of land use. The amount of carbon released to the atmosphere or accumulated on land depends not only on the magnitude and types of changes in land use, but also on the amounts of carbon held in different ecosystems. For example, the conversion of grasslands to pastures causes a smaller release of carbon to the atmosphere than the conversion of forests to pastures. The net release or accumulation also depends on the time lags introduced by the rates of decay of organic matter, the rates of oxidation of wood products, and the rates of regrowth of forests following harvest or following abandonment of agricultural land. Calculation of the net terrestrial flux of carbon requires knowledge of these rates in different ecosystems under different types of land use. Because there are several important forms of land use and many types of ecosystems in different parts of the world and because short-term variations in the magnitude of the flux are important, computation of the annual flux requires a computer model.

Few attempts have been made to calculate the net flux of carbon to the atmosphere over the past 100 to 300 years as a result of land-use change. What estimates there are range between 62 Pg and 180 Pg for the 120-year period 1860 to 1980 (Table 23-3). The lower estimate is probably an underestimate of the total flux, because the estimate was calculated from changes in the area of croplands only. The analysis did not consider changes in the area of pastures and other processes that reduce the carbon stocks on land – processes such as logging and shifting cultivation that generally replace primary forests with smaller-statured, secondary forests. The higher estimate of 180 Pg is probably an overestimate. It was based on early studies suggesting a contemporary net annual flux of 1.8 Pg to 4.7 Pg of carbon from terrestrial ecosystems to the atmosphere (Houghton et al. 1983). More recent estimates of the contemporary flux range from 0.4 Pg/yr to 2.5 Pg/yr (Detwiler and Hall 1988; Houghton et al. 1987). The total net flux over the 120-year period is therefore also probably lower than the early estimates by Houghton et al. (1983). For this chapter, we incorporated revised estimates of land-use change and carbon stocks into the analysis and calculated a new estimate of flux: our best estimate for the total net flux between 1850 and 1985 is 120 Pg carbon. Between 1700 and 1895, the net flux was about 170 Pg (Table 23-3).

The second method for calculation of the net biotic flux has yielded estimates for the 100- to 150-year flux that are similar to those obtained from analyses of land-use change (Table 23-3). The second method is based on records of past atmospheric concentrations of carbon dioxide or past atmospheric isotopic ratios of carbon. Analysis of $^{13}C/^{12}C$ ratios in tree rings was the first application of this method. The ^{13}C isotope of carbon is slightly heavier than the ^{12}C isotope and is discriminated against during photosynthesis. Thus trees have

Table 23-3 *Estimates of the net release of carbon from terrestrial ecosystems over the past 100 to 300 years*

Net release (Pg of C)	Interval	Method	Reference
62	1860–1978	Changes in cultivated area	Richards et al. 1983
180	1860–1980	Changes in land use	Houghton et al. 1983
110	1850–1980	Changes in land use	This study
170	1700–1985	" "	" "
150	1600–1975	Deconvolution of isotopic ratios in tree rings	Stuiver et al. 1984
40	1860–1975	" "	" "
145	1800–1980	" "	Peng 1985
90–150	1775–1980	Deconvolution of CO_2 concentrations in ice cores	Siegenthaler and Oeschger 1987

a lighter isotopic ratio (−22 ppt to −27 ppt) than does air (−7 ppt) (ratios are expressed in relation to a standard). The burning of forests therefore releases a disproportionate share of the lighter isotope, reducing the isotopic ratio of $^{13}C/^{12}C$ in air and, presumably, in tree rings laid down in the following years' growth. Unfortunately, the trends in isotopic ratios vary among the trees sampled, and it has become clear that the isotopic ratio of carbon in tree rings is determined not only by the ratio of the carbon isotopes in the atmosphere, but also by environmental conditions such as temperature and soil moisture that affect the physiology and metabolism of the plant (Francey and Farquhar 1982; Stuiver and Braziunas 1987).

Both carbon dioxide concentrations and $^{13}C/^{12}C$ ratios of past atmospheres can also be determined from the analysis of air trapped in bubbles of glacial ice (Neftel et al. 1985; Raynaud and Barnola 1985). Analyses of this air have established that the preindustrial concentrations of carbon dioxide were about 275 (±10) ppm. Analyses of the variations in concentrations of carbon dioxide over the past centuries suggest a biotic flux of 90 Pg to 150 Pg of carbon for the period 1775 to 1980 (Siegenthaler and Oeschger 1987) (Table 23-3).

Analyses of the biotic flux of carbon dioxide based on land-use change and based on concentrations of carbon dioxide in ice cores yield estimates that are similar (Table 23-3). The agreement is misleading, however, because the historical patterns of the release differ according to the two approaches (Fig. 23.2). The net flux of carbon dioxide calculated from changes in land use has been generally increasing over the past century. The approach based on the carbon dioxide concentrations in air trapped in glacial ice suggests, on the contrary, that the largest releases were near the turn of the century and that since 1940 the net releases of carbon have been small.

The difference between the two results may be due to errors in either or both of the approaches. On the other hand,

the difference could be real, because the two methods do not consider the same processes. The first approach calculates the net flux of carbon from changes in land use alone; ecosystems not directly modified by human activity are assumed neither to accumulate nor to release carbon. The second approach calculates the discrepancy between the history of carbon dioxide concentrations in the atmosphere, on the one hand, and the history of carbon dioxide releases from fossil fuels, on the other. This discrepancy identifies periods during which emissions from fossil fuels were not large enough to yield the observed atmospheric concentrations and periods during which the carbon dioxide released from fossil fuel must have accumulated somewhere other than the atmosphere. Generally, the discrepancy is assumed to define the net flux of carbon from terrestrial ecosystems, but it could result from variations in the uptake of carbon dioxide by the world's oceans or from some other process not included in the global carbon models used for the analyses.

Assuming that the estimated flux is indeed from terrestrial systems, the difference between the estimate from ice cores and that from land-use change could be due to the flux of carbon to or from terrestrial ecosystems not directly disturbed by land use. Ecosystems not directly cut or cleared could be accumulating or releasing carbon in response to small variations in climate, to increased concentrations of carbon dioxide in air, to increased availability of nitrogen or other nutrients from fertilizers or burning of fossil fuels, or to increased levels of toxins in air and soil resulting from industrialization. These possibilities will be discussed in more detail below. They are not considered in the land-use analyses.

The reasons for the different results of the two methods are not presently known. In the discussions that follow, we consider only those changes in terrestrial carbon that are thought to have occurred in association with changes in the use of land.

Combustion of Fossil Fuels

The major fossil fuels are coal, oil, and gas. The carbon dioxide released annually from the combustion of these fuels is calculated from records of fuel production published by the United Nations (Marland and Rotty 1984). The calculated emissions are thought to be known within 6% since 1950 (Rotty and Marland 1986), and within 20% for the years between 1860 and 1950 (Keeling 1973).

The annual release of carbon dioxide from combustion of fossil fuels, globally, since 1860 is shown in Fig. 23.3. The rate of combustion generally has increased exponentially, although one can recognize interruptions in the trend by the two world wars and by the increase in oil prices during the 1970s. Despite the price increases, the use of fossil fuels and the annual emission of carbon dioxide to the atmosphere increased each year until 1980. From 1980 through 1983, the annual emissions decreased each year, but the downward trend was temporary. Starting in 1984, the annual emissions increased again, such that by 1985 they were similar to 1979, and by 1986 they were the highest on record (WRI/IIED 1988). The annual emission of carbon from combustion of all fossil fuels was 5.5 Pg in 1986 (WRI/IIED 1988). Between

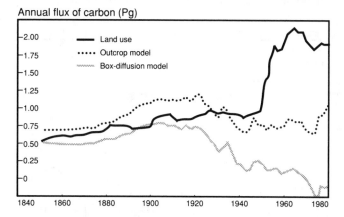

Annual flux of carbon (Pg)

Figure 23.2 Three estimates of the historic releases of carbon from terrestrial ecosystems (in Pg/yr of carbon). The solid line is based on an analysis of land-use change (this study). The dotted and gray lines are based on modeling analyses using as input the carbon dioxide concentrations in bubbles of air trapped in glacial ice (Siegenthaler and Oeschger 1987). The ocean models used in the analyses were the box-diffusion model (gray line) and the outcrop model (dotted line).

Table 23-4 *Recent growth rates in the production of different fossil and wood fuels*

Type of fossil fuel	1950–1973 (%/yr)	1973–1983 (%/yr)
Coal	1.7	2.6
Oil	7.1	1.0
Gas	8.1	3.2
Total fossil fuels	4.5	1.9
Fuelwood and charcoal	1.1	2.4

Source: From Rotty and Marland 1986; FAO 1985.

1860 and 1985, the total emission of carbon to the atmosphere from fossil fuels is estimated to have been about 190 Pg. Half of these emissions occurred after 1965.

The proportions of coal, oil, and gas production have changed through time. Coal was the major contributor to atmospheric carbon dioxide until 1968, at which time the production of oil first exceeded that of coal. Use of both oil and gas was growing rapidly until 1973. After 1973, their relative rates of growth were reduced dramatically, whereas that of coal increased (Table 23-4) (Rotty and Marland 1986).

The relative contributions of different world regions to the annual emissions of fossil-fuel carbon has also changed. In 1925, the United States, western Europe, Japan, and Australia were responsible for about 88% of the world's fossil-fuel carbon dioxide emissions (Darmstadter 1971). By 1950, the fraction contributed by these countries had decreased to 71%, and by 1980, to 48% (Rotty and Marland 1986). The annual rate of growth in the use of fossil fuels in these countries varied between 0.5% and 1.4% in the 1970s. In contrast, the annual rate of growth in the use of fossil fuels in the developing nations remained at 6.3%/yr during this period. The share of the world's total fossil fuel used by the developing countries has grown from 6% in 1925, to 10% in 1950, to about 20% in 1980. By 2020, the developing world is projected to consume annually about 60% of the world's fossil fuels (Goldemberg et al. 1985). They may soon be the major source of both fossil fuel and biotic carbon dioxide to the atmosphere.

Net Emissions

The net annual fluxes of carbon to the atmosphere from terrestrial ecosystems and from fossil fuels are shown in Fig. 23.3. The estimates of the net flux from land before 1800 are generally less reliable because such early estimates of land-use change are less available (see chap. 10). On the other hand, there were no worldwide economic or cultural developments in the eighteenth century that would have caused changes in land use of the magnitude that began in the nineteenth century and accelerated to the present day. The net annual biotic flux of carbon to the atmosphere before 1800 was probably less than 0.5 Pg and probably less than 1 Pg until 1950. The combined annual biotic and fossil-fuel sources first exceeded 1 Pg/yr at about the start of the twentieth century. It was not until the middle of this century that the

annual emission of carbon from combustion of fossil fuels exceeded the net biotic flux. Since then the fossil-fuel contribution has predominated, although both fluxes have accelerated in recent decades with the intensification of industrial activity and the expansion of agricultural area. The contemporary net flux is 6 Pg to 8 Pg of carbon per year, 5.5 Pg from fossil fuels and 0.4 Pg to 2.5 Pg from biotic sources.

Although the industrial flows of carbon now dominate the net biotic flows, the gross natural flows of carbon still greatly exceed the anthropogenic flows. The natural flows of carbon in terrestrial photosynthesis and respiration are about 100 Pg annually, as are the gross flows between oceans and atmosphere (Fig. 23.1). The proportions of industrial and natural flows for carbon are very different from the proportions for other materials (see chap. 24 through 27).

Figure 23.3 shows no substitution of fossil fuels for wood fuels. One reason that the switch does not appear is that it occurred in different regions of the world at different times. It has not yet occurred in many of the developing nations. In Africa and South Asia, for example, fuelwood still accounts for upward of 80% of total fuel use. Worldwide, the production of fuelwood and charcoal was about 1.5 billion m^3 in 1980 (FAO 1985), corresponding to an annual net release of carbon of about 0.5 Pg, about 10% of the fossil-fuel emissions that year. The substitution of fossil fuels for wood has begun in many tropical countries, but the increased price of oil has slowed the substitution. The relative rate of growth in the production of fuelwood and charcoal, for example, was greater between 1973 and 1980 than the relative growth rate in the production of fossil fuels (Table 23-4). Changes in the price of oil since 1983 may have changed these trends again.

Other reasons explain why the increases in fossil-fuel emissions were not accompanied by decreasing biotic emissions. Perhaps the most important is that the major releases of biotic carbon result not from use of wood fuels, but from the oxidation of vegetation and soils associated with the expansion of cultivated land. The harvest of forests for fuelwood is less important because the release of carbon to the atmosphere

Annual flux of carbon (Pg)

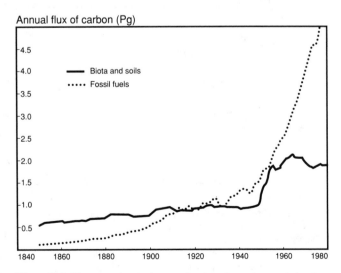

Figure 23.3 The annual net releases of carbon from changes in land use (solid line) and the annual emissions of carbon from combustion of fossil fuels (dotted line) between 1850 and 1980.

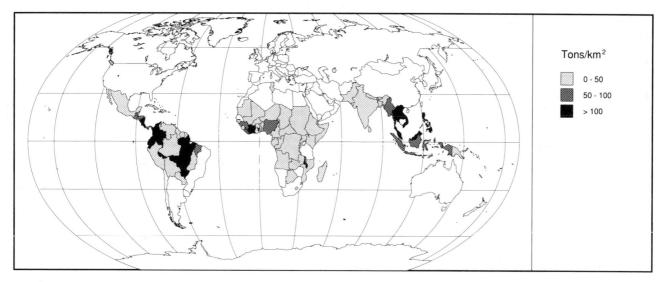

Figure 23.4 Geographic distribution of the net flux of carbon from terrestrial ecosystems to the atmosphere in 1980 as a result of deforestation and agricultural expansion. Source: Houghton et al. 1987.

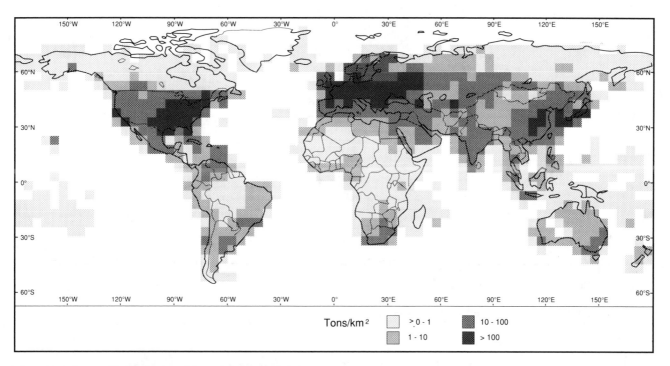

Figure 23.5 Geographic distribution of the emissions of carbon from combustion of fossil fuels in 1980. Source: Marland, Rotty, and Treat 1985.

from fuelwood is likely to be balanced by the storage of carbon in regrowing forests. The balance will occur only as long as the forests harvested for fuelwood are allowed to regrow, however. If the gathering of fuelwood leads to permanent deforestation, the process will result in a net release of carbon to the atmosphere.

It is interesting to compare the historical flows of biotic and fossil carbon in different regions. The most obvious difference is that between the lands of the middle latitudes and those of the tropics. In 1980, the net release of carbon from deforestation was almost entirely from the tropics (Fig. 23.4), whereas the emissions of carbon dioxide from fossil fuels were almost entirely from outside the tropics (Fig. 23.5).

The highest biotic releases of carbon were not always from tropical countries. Figure 23.6 shows that the net release of biotic carbon from the tropics is a relatively recent phenomenon. The largest current releases – from tropical America, Africa, and Asia – did not begin until about 1950. In the nineteenth century, the major regions of the biotic flux were of two kinds: the industrialized regions – North America,

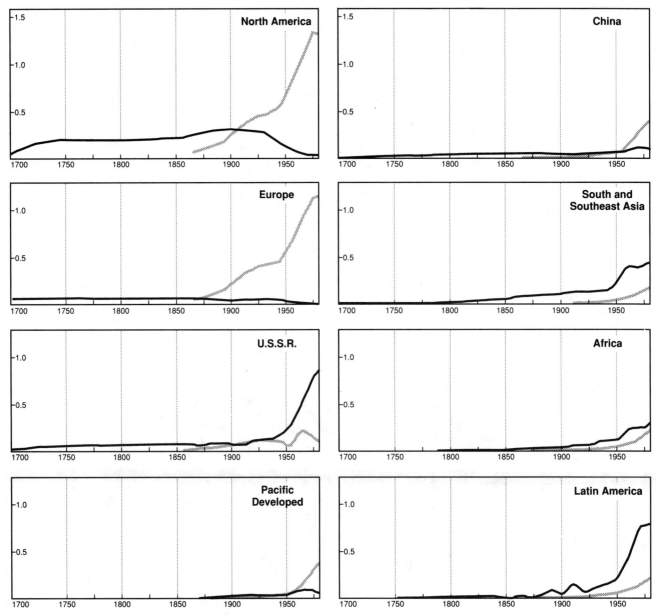

Figure 23.6 The annual releases of carbon to the atmosphere from changes in land use (dashed line before 1800, solid line after 1800) and from combustion of fossil fuels (dotted line) for major regions of the world.

Europe, and the Soviet Union – and those regions that have longest held the greatest densities of people – South Asia and China.

In an analysis of the emissions of carbon over the past 300 years, it is of interest to consider those trends that run counter to the trend of acceleration. The leveling off of the use of fossil fuels, globally, in the first half of the 1980s, and the absolute reduction in their use in North America, Europe, Japan, and Australia, have already been mentioned. Another counter trend of longer duration is the reduction in the net biotic release of carbon from North America, Europe, South Asia, and from the Pacific developed countries – Australia, New Zealand, Japan, and the Koreas. Even though a multitude of explanations exist for these reductions, the reductions seem to have occurred through choice. That is, most of these

regions still have forests remaining; the reduction in the release of biotic carbon, or the reduction in deforestation, was not due to having run out of forests. Whether the same reversal will occur in tropical regions remains to be seen.

Histories of Carbon

The Atmosphere

The concentration of carbon dioxide in the atmosphere has varied over most of the earth's history in the absence of human activity. Recent analyses of carbon dioxide in the bubbles of air trapped in glacial ice from Vostoc, Antarctica, show that the concentrations vary with global temperature. Over the past 160,000 years, the concentration of carbon dioxide varied from about 180 ppm during glacial periods to about 280 ppm during interglacial periods (Fig. 23.7). The concentration of carbon dioxide increases as global temperature rises and decreases as temperature falls. The coupling is evidence for the greenhouse effect of carbon dioxide, first advanced almost a century ago by the Swedish climatologist Arrenhius (1896). The glacial-interglacial difference of 100 ppm corresponds to a temperature difference of about 10°C in Antarctica.

Between the end of the last glaciation (about 10,000 years ago) and A.D. 1700, the concentration of carbon dioxide in the atmosphere seems to have remained fairly constant at 275 ppm to 285 ppm (Neftel et al. 1985). Since 1700, the concentration of carbon dioxide has increased from about 280 ppm to about 350 ppm in 1989, an increase of 25%. This increase is believed to have been due, first, to the widespread replacement of forests with cleared land and, second, to the emission of carbon dioxide to the atmosphere from the combustion of fossil fuels.

The concentrations of carbon dioxide in air were estimated or measured by a variety of techniques. The concentration of carbon dioxide in air is, according to textbooks, 0.03%. If 0.03% were the accuracy of measurement today, there would still be no evidence for its increase. Carbon dioxide in air is measured today to within one tenth of a part per million by volume (ppmv), or 0.00001%.

Numerous measurements of atmospheric carbon dioxide concentrations were made in the nineteenth century (Fraser, Elliott, and Waterman 1986), and Callendar (1938) estimated that the amount of carbon dioxide had increased by 6% between 1900 and 1935. Because of geographical and seasonal variations in the concentrations of carbon dioxide, however, no reliable measure of the rate of increase was possible until after 1957, at which time the first continuous monitoring of carbon dioxide was begun at Mauna Loa, Hawaii, and at the South Pole (Keeling et al. 1976a; 1976b). The measurements of the concentration of carbon dioxide in air made before 1957 had neither the continuous record nor the precision and accuracy required to show the increase.

In 1958, the average concentration of carbon dioxide in air at Mauna Loa was about 315 ppm; in 1989, it was about 350 ppm (Fig. 23.7), an average rate of increase of about 1 ppm per year. The rate of increase has itself been increasing, however, such that the annual increase in recent years has been about 1.5 ppm (Komhyr et al. 1985).

The most striking feature of Fig. 23.7, besides the steady increase in the concentration of carbon dioxide since 1957, is the regular saw-tooth pattern. This pattern repeats itself annually. The cause of the oscillation is believed to be the metabolism of temperate and boreal terrestrial ecosystems (Houghton 1987b). The highest concentrations occur at the end of each winter, following the season in which respiration has exceeded photosynthesis and caused a net release of carbon dioxide to the atmosphere. The lowest concentrations occur at the end of each summer, following the season in which photosynthesis has exceeded respiration and has drawn carbon dioxide out of the atmosphere. The latitudinal variability in the amplitude of this oscillation supports the dominant role of terrestrial metabolism: the highest amplitudes (up to about 16 ppmv) are in the Northern Hemisphere, with the largest land area. The phase of the amplitude is reversed in the Southern Hemisphere, corresponding to seasonal metabolism there.

The atmosphere is completely mixed in about a year, so that any monitoring station free of local contamination will show approximately the same year-to-year increase in carbon dioxide. Today more than 20 monitoring stations exist worldwide. They generally show the same year-to-year increase but

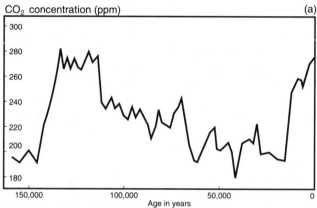

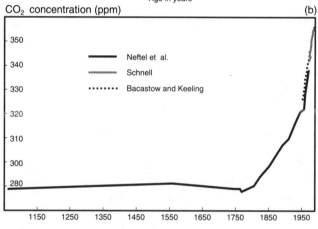

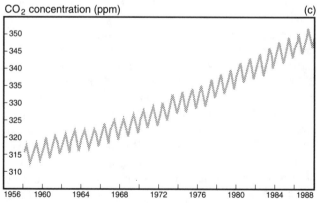

Figure 23.7 Records of the concentration of atmospheric carbon dioxide. (a) The past 160,000 years as obtained from the Vostoc ice core, Antarctica. Source: Barnola et al. 1987. (b) The past 1,000 years as obtained from the Siple Station ice core, Antarctica. Sources: Bacastow and Keeling 1981; Neftel et al. 1985; Schnell 1986. (c) Continuous measurements in the atmosphere at Mauna Loa, Hawaii, from 1958 to 1987. Sources: Bacastow and Keeling 1981; Schnell 1986.

vary with respect to absolute concentration, seasonal variability, and other characteristics useful for investigating the global circulation of carbon.

The best evidence for the concentration of atmospheric carbon dioxide before 1957 comes from measurements of carbon dioxide in bubbles of air trapped in glacial ice. Ice cores from Greenland and Antarctica show that the pre-industrial concentration was between 275 ppm and 285 ppm (Neftel et al. 1985; Raynaud and Barnola 1985) (Fig. 23.7). The increase between 1700 and 1985, therefore, has been about 70 ppm (or 25%), equivalent to about 150 Pg of carbon.

The increase in the concentration of methane in the atmosphere has been more than 100% in the past 100 years, from background levels of less than 0.8 ppm to a value in 1984 of about 1.6 ppm (Khalil and Rasmussen 1987; see also chap. 17). The pattern of the increase is similar to that of carbon dioxide, with annual increases of 1.5 ppbv (parts per billion by volume) between 1700 and 1900, accelerating to 17 ppbv per year during the past decade. Before 1700, no apparent trend was discernible in the concentration as far back as 10,000 years.

Methane is released from anaerobic environments (environments with very low oxygen concentrations), such as the sediments of marshes, peatlands, and rice paddies, and the guts of cattle and termites. The major sources of the increased methane are uncertain, but are thought to include the expansion of paddy rice, the increase in the world's population of cattle, and the warming of high-latitude wetland ecosystems. Raising the temperature of peatlands stimulates anaerobic as well as aerobic respiration and may have increased the release of both methane and carbon dioxide during the past century.

Atmospheric methane budgets are more difficult to construct than carbon dioxide budgets because increased concentrations of methane occur not only from increased releases from the earth's surface but also from decreased destruction (by OH radicals) in the atmosphere itself. The increase in atmospheric methane has been more significant for the greenhouse effect than for the carbon budget. The doubling of methane since 1700 has contributed less than 1 ppm, in comparison to the carbon dioxide increase of 70 ppm. On the other hand, methane is, molecule for molecule, 20 times more effective than carbon dioxide as a greenhouse gas.

The Oceans

Direct measurement of changes in the amount of carbon contained in the world's oceans has not been possible for two reasons: (1) the oceans are not mixed as rapidly as the atmosphere, so that spatial heterogeneity is large; and (2) the background concentration of dissolved carbon in seawater is large relative to the change, so that measurement of the change requires very accurate methods, which have not existed until the past few years. Most estimates of the uptake of terrestrial and fossil-fuel carbon dioxide by the oceans have, therefore, been with models.

Most oceanic models include the chemistry of carbon in seawater, the air-sea exchanges of carbon dioxide, and oceanic circulation. Reviews and comparisons of ocean models have been published by Bacastow and Bjorkstrom (1981), Killough and Emanuel (1981), and Bjorkstrom (1986). Broecker et al. (1979) reviewed the parameters used in the models, the data on which the parameters are based, and the sensitivity of the modeled results to these parameters.

The world's oceans contain about 60 times more carbon than either the atmosphere or the world's terrestrial vegetation. Thus, at equilibrium, the ocean might be expected to have absorbed about 60 times more of the released carbon than the atmosphere, or 98% of total emissions. Seawater is strongly buffered with respect to carbon dioxide, however, such that the percentage change in the concentration of total dissolved carbon dioxide (CO_2 + HCO_3^- + CO_3^{2-}) is about ten times less than the percentage change in the partial pressure of carbon dioxide alone. Because the partial pressure of carbon dioxide in the oceans is what determines the equilibrium with atmospheric carbon dioxide, the oceans are expected to hold about 86% of the total emissions when the equilibrium is reached (Broecker et al. 1979). As of 1980, the oceans are thought to have absorbed only about 40% of the emissions (20% to 47%, depending on the model used: Bolin 1986). Clearly, other mechanisms are slowing the oceanic absorption of carbon dioxide.

The two other mechanisms are (1) the transfer of carbon dioxide across the air-sea interface, and (2) the mixing of water masses within the sea (Broecker et al. 1979). The rate of transfer of carbon dioxide across the sea surface has been estimated by two different methods.

The first method is based on the fact that the transfer rate of naturally produced carbon-14 into the oceans should balance the decay of carbon-14 within the oceans. Both the production rate and the inventory of carbon-14 in the oceans are known, and the rate of transfer estimated by this method is about 100 Pg per year (Fig. 23.1).

The second method is based on the amount of radon gas in the surface ocean. Radon gas is generated by the decay of radon-226. The concentration of the parent radon-226 and its half-life allow calculation of the expected radon-gas concentration in the surface water. The observed concentration is about 70% of expected, so 30% of the radon must be transferred to the atmosphere during its mean lifetime of six days. Correcting for differences in the diffusivity of radon and carbon dioxide allows an estimation of the transfer rate for carbon dioxide. The transfer rates given by the carbon-14 method and by the radon method agree within about 10%. The rate of transfer of carbon dioxide across the air-sea interface is believed to have reduced the oceanic absorption of carbon dioxide by about 10% (Broecker et al. 1979).

The more important process in slowing the oceanic uptake of carbon dioxide is the rate of vertical mixing. The mixing of ocean waters has been modeled in several ways. One of the first models of the global carbon cycle (Craig 1957) recognized that the ocean was not homogeneous, but could be thought of as two layers – a surface layer, which was in contact with the atmosphere, and a larger deep layer, which could accumulate carbon only in exchange with the surface layer. This two-box ocean has since been included in a number of models (Bacastow and Keeling 1973; Keeling 1979).

Another version of this one-dimensional ocean consists of a shallow surface ocean and a deep ocean comprised of many boxes, stacked vertically, which exchange carbon with those boxes immediately above or below (Oeschger et al. 1975). This type of model is commonly referred to as the box-diffusion model. The vertical diffusivity that sets the rates of exchange between the layers is based on measured profiles of natural carbon-14, bomb-produced carbon-14, bomb-produced tritium, and other tracers. The profiles of these tracers were obtained during two extensive oceanographic surveys, one called GEOSECS (Geochemical Ocean Sections, carried out between 1972 and 1978) and the other called TTO (Transient Tracers in the Ocean, carried out in 1981). Both surveys measured profiles of carbon, oxygen, radioisotopes, and other tracers along transects in the Atlantic and Pacific oceans. The differences between the profiles of the two dates have been used to calculate directly the penetration of anthropogenic carbon dioxide into the oceans (e.g., Chen 1982, described below).

A modification of the box-diffusion model includes the addition of a layer of deep water in contact with the atmosphere in the polar regions (the polar outcrop model) (Siegenthaler 1983). Several other attempts have been made to model more than a one-dimensional ocean (Bolin et al. 1983; Broecker, Peng, and Engh 1980; Sarmiento 1986). In general these two- and three-dimensional models of oceanic circulation have not changed estimates of how much fossil-fuel and terrestrial carbon the oceans are absorbing.

The exception to the use of models is the calculation of carbon absorption based on the oceanic distribution of total carbon dioxide, oxygen, and alkalinity (Brewer 1978; Chen 1982; Chen and Drake 1986; Chen and Millero 1979). The approach is based on changes that occur in the chemistry of seawater as it ages. Certain regions of the ocean, such as the North Atlantic and the Weddell Sea off Antarctica, are the major sources of deep water for all the oceans. The surface waters in these regions are cold and, therefore, dense. As they sink and spread to other parts of the deep and intermediate ocean, their chemistry changes. The organic matter present in surface waters decays, increasing the concentration of carbon dioxide and various nutrients, and decreasing the concentration of oxygen. The surface waters also contain calcium carbonate, the hard parts of marine organisms. It too decays with age, increasing the alkalinity of the water (see chap. 18). From a knowledge of the concentrations of carbon dioxide, oxygen, and alkalinity throughout the oceans, it is theoretically possible to calculate the increased abundance of carbon in the ocean as a result of the increased concentration in the atmosphere (Fig. 23.8).

The approach is based on the assumption that the surface waters were in equilibrium with the atmosphere when they sank, or, at least, that the extent of disequilibrium is known. The approach is sensitive to seasonal variation in the carbon dioxide concentration in these surface waters. Most of the sinking occurs during winter, and, because of the logistical problems in sampling these regions in winter, almost no measurements have been made during winter. The data that exist, however, yield an estimate for oceanic uptake of carbon

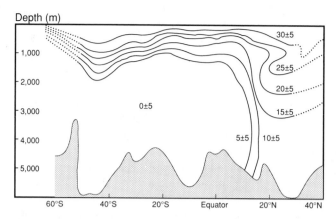

Figure 23.8 The distribution of anthropogenic carbon dioxide (μmol/kg) in the western Atlantic Ocean. After Chen 1982.

that is greater by this approach (Chen and Drake 1986) than by the more commonly used models, cited earlier. The approach is controversial (Broecker et al. 1985).

Further research may revise the estimates of oceanic uptake. For convenience, the ocean models have assumed the carbon cycle to be in steady state prior to the start of the Industrial Revolution. Evidence from the concentrations of carbon dioxide in ice cores, however, shows that no such steady state existed, although it is unlikely that departures from steady state will help to resolve the largest inconsistencies in the carbon balance – those inconsistencies centered around 1980.

Three other recent observations illustrate the types of surprises that may require reappraisal of the way the oceans have been modeled.

One surprise was the observation, based on measurements of the partial pressure of CO_2 in surface waters (Tans et al. 1990), that the oceans are currently absorbing less carbon than estimated by models. If the analysis is correct, terrestrial ecosystems and not the oceans must have accumulated much of the carbon released over the last decades (see below).

The second surprise was the observation that the alkalinity of tropical waters may have increased in recent years (Keeling et al. 1987). The period of observation is short, but if the observed increase in alkalinity has occurred in surface waters elsewhere, the uptake of carbon dioxide by the oceans has been larger than estimated by models. Alkalinity has generally been assumed to be constant.

The third surprise came from the development of a new technique for measuring the dissolved organic carbon (DOC) in seawater (Sugimura and Suzuki 1988). Use of this technique revealed concentrations of DOC much higher than previously measured. The new findings require a revision of the way organic carbon is thought to cycle in the sea, and these findings may have consequences for the modeled uptake of carbon by the world's oceans.

The Terrestrial Biota

The 300-year history of the mobilization of biotic carbon by humans has been described here. The most dramatic change has been the reduction in the area occupied by forests and other natural ecosystems, and their replacement by agricultural systems. This transformation began long before 1700, but the rates and the total change in the biotic carbon reservoir are poorly known. One estimate is that the live vegetation of terrestrial ecosystems held about 800 Pg of carbon before human modification of the landscape (Olson 1985). The estimate is based on the distribution of natural vegetation in the mid-Holocene (6,000 years B.P.). The date of 6,000 B.P. is thought to provide the best estimate of a pre-disturbance biomass for a climate similar to today's. Before 6,000 B.P., differences in climate were probably more important than human activities in affecting the storage of carbon on land. The mass of carbon in live vegetation in the early Miocene (20 million years ago), for example, was perhaps twice the mass of the mid-Holocene, or as much as 1,550 Pg of carbon (Olson 1985). Although there had already been some reduction in biomass by 6,000 B.P. as a result of shifting cultivation in limited areas of Africa, India, China, and Europe, there may also have been some increases in biomass since then as a result of small changes in climate.

According to Olson's (1985) estimate and our analyses, human activities have reduced the carbon in live vegetation from about 800 Pg in 6,000 B.P., to about 700 Pg in 1700, to 560 Pg in 1985. More than half of the loss in the past 6,000 years has occurred in the past 150 years. If the contribution from the oxidation of soil organic carbon has always been approximately the 15% calculated between 1850 and 1985, the reduction in terrestrial carbon caused by human activity has been 170 Pg since 1700 (Table 23-3) and about 275 Pg (about 15%) since the beginning of settled agriculture.

The rate of transformation of forests to cleared lands has accelerated over time. It is probably higher now than ever before. In 1980, the rate of deforestation of both closed and open forests in the tropics was about 110,000 km^2/yr (Lanly 1982), and the rate of loss of carbon from the forests of the earth was 0.4 to 2.5 Pg that year. Only one comprehensive survey of the world's tropical forests has been conducted since 1980 (Myers 1989), and the rates of deforestation are about 90% higher currently than they were in 1980. They are two to four times higher in the Brazilian states of Rondônia, Pará, and Mato Grosso, where data from satellites have been used to measure changes in the area of forests (Malingreau and Tucker 1988; Setzer and Pereira 1988; Woodwell et al. 1987).

All of the changes in the distribution of carbon discussed here have been direct changes resulting from land use. In this section of the chapter, we deal with another aspect of the transformation of terrestrial ecosystems: changes in the carbon content of systems not directly cleared by humans. Direct observation of such change is fragmentary and anecdotal; there are many examples but no quantitative estimates for the globe. The kinds of changes that might be expected depend on factors thought to have changed over this period in history. There are at least four such factors: the increased concentration of carbon dioxide in air, increased mobilization of nutrients, increased mobilization of toxins, and a gradual warming of the earth's surface.

The increase in the concentration of carbon dioxide over the past centuries is thought by many to have increased the storage of carbon on land. Based on the short-term response of annual plants, seedlings, and crops to elevated levels of carbon dioxide, there is reason to believe that plants have grown larger or faster as the concentration of carbon dioxide in the atmosphere has increased (Lemon 1983; Strain and Cure 1985). There is no unequivocal evidence of such an increased growth in natural ecosystems, and it is unclear whether the growth response found in annual crops applies to natural systems, whether it applies to periods longer than a growing season, and whether any enhanced growth that has occurred has increased the amount of carbon held in ecosystems.

One observation that has been interpreted to indicate a trend of increased photosynthesis is the increase in amplitude of the winter-summer oscillation of carbon dioxide concentrations (Bacastow et al. 1985; Cleveland, Freeny, and Graedel 1983; Pearman and Hyson 1981). Increased photosynthesis is not the same as increased storage of carbon, however, so the increased seasonal amplitude does not necessarily mean that terrestrial ecosystems have accumulated carbon. The increasing amplitude is also consistent with an increased winter respiration associated with warmer winters (Houghton 1987a), and, thus, the change in the seasonal amplitude of carbon dioxide concentrations could mean a decreased rather than an increased storage of carbon on land. The increasing amplitude is interesting, but its significance is not yet clear.

A trend of increasing widths in the growth rings of bristle-cone pine in the mountains of the southwestern United States has been attributed to the increasing concentration of atmospheric carbon dioxide (LaMarche et al. 1984), but recorded changes in precipitation at these locations can also explain the trend (Stockton, in Gates 1985).

In the only experiment yet to have been carried out on an intact ecosystem, the net uptake of carbon dioxide by tundra was positively correlated with the concentration of carbon dioxide within enclosures (Hilbert, Prudhomme, and Oechel 1987). The results suggest that increased concentrations of carbon dioxide have enhanced the growth of plants in a natural ecosystem. On the other hand, the gross uptake of carbon dioxide (photosynthesis) was unchanged by the level of carbon dioxide in the enclosure. The investigators could not determine if the greater uptake of carbon under elevated concentrations was due to decreased respiration of the ecosystem or to errors in measurement of the ecosystem's carbon balance. Subsequent analyses have shown an increased storage of carbon on the experimental sites (Oechel 1988), but the effect seems to have lasted only three to five years, or until some other factor became limiting to the growth of plants and the storage of carbon in the system. The results suggest that a response to elevated levels of carbon dioxide will be limited.

The reason that natural ecosystems are thought not to have accumulated carbon in response to increasing concentrations of atmospheric carbon dioxide is that environmental factors other than carbon dioxide generally limit production in systems neither fertilized with chemicals nor irrigated. Recent evidence, however – again from annual crops – suggests that plants may respond to elevated levels of carbon dioxide even though they are stressed by other factors, such as water, light, and temperature (Cure 1985).

The recent observation that the density of stomata on tree leaves has decreased over the past 100 years in an inverse relationship to the rise in carbon dioxide concentrations suggests that plants have responded to the increased carbon dioxide (Woodward 1987). Stomata are openings on the surfaces of leaves. The size of the openings is controlled by cells on the leaf. The stomata must be open to allow carbon dioxide to enter the leaf for photosynthesis; they can be closed by surrounding cells to prevent the loss of water. If the concentration of carbon dioxide in the atmosphere increases, plants can obtain the same amount of carbon and lose less water by reducing the time the stomata are open or by reducing the number of stomata. The observed decrease in the density of stomata suggests that plants have become less water stressed over the past 100 years. The lower density of stomata implies a more rapid uptake of carbon dioxide and shorter time for water to be lost from the leaf. It is not clear from this observation, however, that plants have fixed more carbon or have grown larger or that terrestrial ecosystems have stored more carbon as a result.

The response of plants to elevated carbon dioxide is less clear when nutrients are limiting growth. Nitrogen and phosphorus are often the critical nutrients. The ratios of carbon to nitrogen (C/N) and of carbon to phosphorus (C/P) are surprisingly constant in living tissues of all kinds. These same ratios in the emissions from fossil fuels, however, are very different; fossil fuels contain many fewer atoms of nitrogen and phosphorus per atom of carbon than living tissues require. Thus, the release of carbon to the atmosphere may have had no effect on the storage of carbon on land unless the availability of nitrogen and phosphorus has also increased. The mobilization of nitrogen and phosphorus is important to the mobilization of carbon. The global cycles of carbon, nitrogen, and phosphorus are linked (Bolin and Cook 1983).

Because the past 300 years have seen increased mobilization of nitrogen, phosphorus, and other nutrients, the ratios of the elements mobilized may correspond more to the ratios in living systems than the ratios in fossil fuels suggest. An analysis by Peterson and Melillo (1985) indicates that the increased storage of carbon on land as a result of increased mobilization of nitrogen and phosphorus was probably no higher than 0.2 Pg per year in 1980, an amount equal to 10% to 20% of the decreased storage due to changes in land use.

As mentioned before, increased widths of growth rings in trees may indicate that more carbon is stored on land now than in the past. Many analyses of tree rings, however, show trends of decreasing widths. The causes of the decrease are controversial, but the link to air pollution is a strong one, especially in the forests of central and northern Europe and in the northeastern United States and Canada (McLaughlin et al. 1987; Prinz 1987).

The last environmental change to be considered here is the gradual global warming of 0.5°C to 0.7°C that has occurred irregularly since about 1880 (Hansen and Lebedeff 1987; Jones et al. 1986) (see chap. 19). In general, as temperatures rise, rates of respiration increase more than rates of photosynthesis (Schleser 1982; Woodwell 1983). Thus, the global warming may have caused a net reduction in the amount of carbon stored in terrestrial ecosystems. It may have contributed to the observed increases in both carbon dioxide and methane.

Although all four of the environmental changes discussed here could have changed the amount of carbon stored in terrestrial ecosystems over the past 300 years, no direct evidence exists that any of them has yet been significant on a global basis. Their net effect has presumably been small relative to the reduction in terrestrial carbon that has occurred as a result of changes in forest area.

Summary and Prospects for the Future

The distribution of carbon on earth has shifted in the past 300 years so that the amount of carbon in the atmosphere has increased by 150 Pg (25%), the amount stored in the vegetation and soils of the earth has decreased by 170 Pg (about 7%), the amount originally held in the fossil-fuel reserves has been reduced by 190 Pg (about 4%), and the amount in the oceans has increased by 210 Pg (less than 1%) (Fig. 23.9). The largest relative changes have been in the atmosphere and in the world's terrestrial vegetation, 25% and 20%, respectively. The changes appear small relative to the sizes of the reservoirs. On the other hand, 50% of the carbon of the reservoirs. On the other hand, 50% of the carbon mobilized over the past 300 years has been mobilized in the past 30 to 40 years (Fig. 23.3). For the biotic carbon alone, the time by which half the mobilization had occurred was

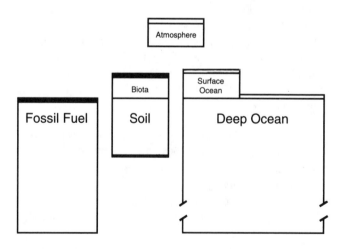

Figure 23.9 Relative changes in the major reservoirs of carbon between 1700 and 1985. Black indicates a loss of carbon; grey indicates a net accumulation of carbon.

$$F + B = A + S \ (Pg\,C)$$
$$190 + 170 = 150 + 210.$$

(F = fossil fuels, B = terrestrial ecosystems, A = atmosphere, S = oceans).

early in the twentieth century; for fossil-fuel emissions, the date was close to 1965.

Exceptions to this general acceleration in the rates of emission of fossil-fuel and biotic carbon were mentioned in an earlier section. The net biotic flux has declined to zero in the industrialized regions of the world. The reason for the decline has generally been the stabilization of, or even reduction in, agricultural area, reflecting both the increased yields of crops and, more recently, the increased supply of food from other regions of the world. It should be clear that the current balance of reforestation and deforestation in these regions could change in the future. Forests could be cleared again, as they were earlier in history, or their areas could be expanded. Similarly, the current biotic flux of carbon from deforestation in the tropics could either increase or decrease. It could also reverse direction and flow from the atmosphere onto land if reforestation were to replace deforestation.

The other exception to an accelerating increase in atmospheric carbon was the reduction in global emissions of fossil-fuel carbon that took place between 1979 and 1983, largely from reduced fossil-fuel consumption in the United States, western Europe, Japan, and Australia. These reductions were of short duration. Whether or not they will continue depends not only on the price of oil, but also on the willingness of the global community to continue emitting carbon dioxide to the atmosphere in the face of climatic change. The recent international agreement (the Montreal Protocol) to limit the production of chlorofluorocarbons, which endanger the earth's ozone shield, suggests that multilateral agreements with respect to carbon dioxide emissions may also be possible. Such agreements will have to require the industrialized countries to reduce consumption of fossil fuels and will have to guarantee the developing countries the opportunity for increased standards of living.

In the absence of such an agreement, the concentration of atmospheric carbon dioxide will continue to increase. The radiative properties of carbon dioxide and methane and the correlation between their atmospheric concentrations and global temperature in the past (Genthon et al. 1987; Lorius et al. 1988; Raynaud et al. 1988) make it clear that both gases are intimately coupled to the climate of the earth. They and most other recognized feedbacks are thought to be positive, that is, to amplify climatic change (Kellogg 1983; Lashof 1989). In the midlatitude forests, for example, the projected rate of warming could exceed the rates of migration of tree species (Bennett 1986), leading to a mortality of forests not matched by simultaneous regrowth. The decomposition of the dead material would further enhance the rate of global warming.

There is an urgent need to stabilize the atmospheric concentration of carbon dioxide and to prevent the politically destabilizing effects of climatic change. The ingredients of such a stabilization, including a reduction in the use of fossil fuels, a cessation of deforestation, and a substantial expansion of reforestation (Houghton and Woodwell 1989), are not only possible but good, for a number of reasons quite apart from limiting the extent of or reducing the rate of climatic change.

References

Arrhenius, S. 1896. On the influence of carbonic acid in the air upon the temperature of the ground. *Phil. Mag. J. Sci.* 41: 237–76.

Bacastow, R. B., and A. Bjorkstrom. 1981. Comparison of ocean models for the carbon cycle. In *Carbon Cycle Modeling*, ed. B. Bolin, 29–79. Scope 16. New York: John Wiley & Sons.

Bacastow, R., and C. D. Keeling. 1973. Atmospheric carbon dioxide and radiocarbon in the natural carbon cycle. II. Changes from A.D. 1700 to 2070 as deduced from a geochemical model. In *Carbon and the Biosphere*, ed. G. M. Woodwell and E. V. Pecan, 86–135. U.S. Atomic Energy Commission, Symposium Series 30. Springfield, VA: National Technical Information Service.

Bacastow, R. B., and C. D. Keeling. 1981. Atmospheric carbon dioxide concentration and the observed airborne fraction. In *Carbon Cycle Modeling*, ed. B. Bolin, 103–112. SCOPE 16. New York: John Wiley and Sons.

Bacastow, R. B., C. D. Keeling, and T. P. Whorf. 1985. Seasonal amplitude increase in atmospheric CO_2 concentration at Mauna Loa, Hawaii, 1959–1982. *Jour. Geophys. Res.* 90: 10, 529–10, 540.

Barnola, J. M., D. Raynaud, Y. S. Korotkevich, and C. Lorius. 1987. Vostoc ice core provides 160,000-year record of atmospheric CO_2. *Nature* 329: 408–414.

Bennett, K. D. 1986. The rate of spread and population increase of forest trees during the postglacial. *Phil. Trans. Roy. Soc. Lond.* B 314: 523–31.

Bjorkstrom, A. 1986. One-dimensional and two-dimensional ocean models for predicting the distribution of CO_2 between the ocean and the atmosphere. In *The Changing Carbon Cycle. A Global Analysis*, ed. J. R. Tralbalka and D. E. Reichle, 258–78. New York: Springer-Verlag.

Bolin, B., ed. 1981. *Carbon Cycle Modeling*. Scope 16. New York: John Wiley & Sons.

———. 1983. The carbon cycle. In *The Major Biogeochemical Cycles and Their Interactions*, ed. B. Bolin and R. B. Cook, 41–45. Scope 21. New York: John Wiley & Sons.

———. 1986. How much CO_2 will remain in the atmosphere? In *The Greenhouse Effect, Climatic Change, and Ecosystems*, ed. B. Bolin, B. R. Doos, J. Jager, and R. A. Warrick, 93–155. Chichester: John Wiley & Sons.

Bolin, B., and R. B. Cook, ed. 1983. *The Major Biogeochemical Cycles and Their Interactions*. SCOPE 21. New York: John Wiley & Sons.

Bolin, B., E. T. Degens, S. Kempe, and P. Ketner, ed. 1979. *The Global Carbon Cycle*. Scope 13. New York: John Wiley & Sons.

Bolin, B., A. Bjorkstrom, K. Holem, and B. Moore. 1983. The simultaneous use of tracers for ocean circulation studies. *Tellus* 35B: 206–236.

Bolin, B., B. R. Doos, J. Jager, and R. A. Warrick. 1986. *The Greenhouse Effect, Climatic Change, and Ecosystems*. SCOPE 29. New York: John Wiley & Sons.

Brewer, P. G. 1978. Direct observation of the oceanic CO_2 increase. *Geophys. Res. Lett.* 5: 997–1000.

Broecker, W. S., T. Takahashi, H. H. Simpson, and T.-H. Peng. 1979. Fate of fossil-fuel carbon dioxide and the global carbon budget. *Science* 206: 409–418.

Broecker, W. S., T.-H. Peng, and R. Engh. 1980. Modeling the carbon system. *Radiocarbon* 22: 565–98.

Broecker, W. S., T. Takahashi, and T.-H. Peng. 1985. Reconstruction of past atmospheric CO_2 contents from the chemistry of the contemporary ocean: an evaluation. TR020. Washington, D.C.: U.S. Department of Energy.

Callendar, G. S. 1938. The artificial production of carbon dioxide and its influence on temperature. *Quart. J. Roy. Meteor. Soc.* 64: 223–40.

Chen, C.-T. 1982. On the distribution of anthropogenic CO_2 in the Atlantic and Southern oceans. *Deep-Sea Res.* 29: 563–80.

Chen, C.-T. A., and E. T. Drake. 1986. Carbon dioxide increase in the atmosphere and oceans and possible effects on climate. *Ann. Rev. Earth Planet. Sci.* 14: 201–235.

Chen, C.-T. A., and F. J. Millero. 1979. Gradual increase of oceanic CO_2. *Nature* 277: 305–307.

Clark, W. C., ed. 1982. *Carbon Dioxide Review: 1982*. Oxford: Oxford University Press.

Cleveland, W. S., A. F. Freeny, and T. E. Graedel. 1983. The seasonal component of atmospheric CO_2: information from new approaches to the decomposition of seasonal time series. *J. Geophys. Res.* 88: 10, 934–10, 946.

Craig, H. 1957. The natural distribution of radiocarbon and the exchange time of carbon dioxide between atmosphere and sea. *Tellus* 9: 1–17.

Cure, J. D. 1985. Carbon dioxide doubling responses: a crop survey. In *Direct Effects of Increasing Carbon Dioxide on Vegetation*, ed. B. R. Strain and J. D. Cure, 99–116. DOE/ER-0238. Washington, D.C.: U.S. Department of Energy.

Darmstadter, J. 1971. *Energy in the World Economy: A Statistical Review of Trends in Output, Trade, and Consumption since 1925*. Baltimore, MD: Johns Hopkins Press.

Detwiler, R. P., and C. A. S. Hall. 1988. Tropical forests and the global carbon cycle. *Science* 239: 42–47.

Food and Agriculture Organization (FAO). 1985. *1983 Yearbook of Forest Products*. Rome: FAO.

Francey, R. J., and G. D. Farquhar. 1982. An explanation of $^{13}C/^{12}C$ variations in tree rings. *Nature* 297: 28–31.

Fraser, P. J., W. P. Elliott, and L. S. Waterman. 1986. (editors). In *The Changing Carbon Cycle. A Global Analysis* ed. J. R. Trabalka and D. E. Reichle, 66–88. New York: Springer-Verlag.

Gates, D. M. 1985. Global biospheric response to increasing atmospheric carbon dioxide concentrations. In *Direct Effects of Increasing Carbon Dioxide on Vegetation*, ed. B. R. Strain and J. D. Cure, 171–84. DOE/ER-0238. Washington, D.C.: U.S. Department of Energy.

Genthon, C., J. M. Barnola, D. Raynaud, C. Lorius, J. Jouzel, N. I. Barkov, Y. S. Korotkevich, and V. M. Kotlyakov. 1987. Vostok ice core: climatic response to CO_2 and orbital forcing changes over the last climatic cycle. *Nature* 329: 414–18.

Goldemberg, J., T. B. Johansson, A. K. N. Reddy, and R. H. Williams. 1985. An end-use oriented global energy strategy. *Ann. Rev. Energy* 10: 613–88.

Hansen, J., and S. Lebedeff. 1987. Global trends of measured surface air temperature. *J. Geophys. Res.* 92D: 13, 345–13, 372.

Hilbert, T., I. Prudhomme, and W. C. Oechel. 1987. Response of Tussock tundra to elevated carbon dioxide regimes: analysis of ecosystem CO_2 flux through nonlinear modeling. *Oecologia* 72: 466–72.

Houghton, R. A. 1987a. Biotic changes consistent with the increased seasonal amplitude of atmospheric CO_2 concentrations. *J. Geophys. Res.* 92: 4223–30.

———. 1987b. Terrestrial metabolism and atmospheric CO_2 concentrations. *BioSci.* 37: 672–78.

Houghton, R. A., and G. M. Woodwell. 1989. Global climatic change. *Sci. Amer.* 4: 36–44.

Houghton, R. A., J. E. Hobbie, J. M. Melillo, B. Moore, B. J. Peterson, G. R. Shaver, and G. M. Woodwell. 1983. Changes in the carbon content of terrestrial biota and soils between 1860 and 1980: A net release of CO_2 to the atmosphere. *Ecol. Mono.* 53: 235–62.

Houghton, R. A., R. D. Boone, J. R. Fruci, J. E. Hobbie, J. M. Melillo, C. A. Palm, B. J. Peterson, G. R. Shaver, G. M. Woodwell, B. Moore, D. L. Skole, and N. Myers. 1987. The flux of carbon from terrestrial ecosystems to the atmosphere in 1980 due to changes in land use: geographic distribution of the global flux. *Tellus* 39B: 122–39.

Jones, P. D., S. C. B. Raper, R. S. Bradley, H. F. Diaz, P. M. Kelly, and T. M. L. Wigley. 1986. Northern Hemisphere surface air temperature variations: 1851–1984. *J. Clim. Appl. Meteorol.* 25: 161–79.

Keeling, C. D. 1973. Industrial production of carbon dioxide from fossil fuels and limestone. *Tellus* 25: 174–98.

———. 1979. The Suess effect: $^{13}Carbon–^{14}carbon$ interrelations. *Environ. Intern.* 2: 229–300.

———. 1983. The carbon cycle: what we know and could know from atmospheric, biospheric, and oceanic observations. Pages II.3–II.62. In *Proceedings: Carbon Dioxide Research Conference: Carbon Dioxide, Science, and Consensus*, II.3–II.62. CONF-820970. Washington, D.C.: U.S. Department of Energy.

Keeling, C. D., R. B. Bacastow, A. E. Bainbridge, C. A. Ekdahl, Jr., P. R. Guenther, L. S. Waterman, and J. F. S. Chin. 1976a. Atmospheric carbon dioxide variations at Mauna Loa Observatory, Hawaii. *Tellus* 28: 538–51.

Keeling, C. D., J. A. Adams, Jr., C. A. Ekdahl, Jr., and P. R. Guenther. 1976b. Atmospheric carbon dioxide variations at the South Pole. *Tellus* 28: 552–64.

Keeling, C. D., P. R. Guenther, T. J. Leuker, and S. C. Piper. 1987. Interannual variations in the carbon chemistry of surface seawater: possible increases in inorganic carbon and alkalinity. *EOS* 68: 1691 (abstract).

Kellogg, W. W. 1983. Feedback mechanisms in the climate system affecting future levels of carbon dioxide. *J. Geophys. Res.* 88C: 1263–69.

Kempe, S. 1979. Carbon in the rock cycle. In *The Global Carbon Cycle*, ed. B. Bolin, E. T. Degens, S. Kempe, and P. Ketner, 343–77. Scope 13. New York: John Wiley & Sons.

Khalil, M. A. K., and R. A. Rasmussen. 1987. Atmospheric methane: trends over the last 10,000 years. *Atmos. Environ.* 21: 2445–52.

Killough, G. G., and W. R. Emanuel. 1981. A comparison of several models of carbon turnover in the ocean with respect to their distributions of transit time and age, and responses to atmospheric CO_2 and ^{14}C. *Tellus* 33: 274–90.

Komhyr, W. D., R. H. Gammon, T. B. Harris, L. S. Waterman, T. J. Conway, W. R. Taylor, and K. W. Thoning. 1985. Global atmospheric CO_2 distribution and variations from 1968–1982. NOAA/GMCC CO_2 flask sample data. *J. Geophys. Res.* 90: 5567–96.

LaMarche, V. C., D. A. Graybill, H. C. Fritts, and M. R. Rose. 1984. Increasing atmospheric carbon dioxide: tree-ring evidence for growth enhancement in natural vegetation. *Science* 225: 1019–21.

Lanly, J.-P. 1982. *Tropical Forest Resources*. FAO Forestry Paper 30. Rome: FAO.

Lashof, D. A. 1989. The dynamic greenhouse: feedback processes that may influence future concentrations of atmospheric trace gases. *Climatic Change* 14: 213–42.

Lemon, E. R., ed. 1983. *CO_2 and Plants: The Response of Plants to Rising Levels of Atmospheric Carbon Dioxide*. Boulder, CO: Westview Press.

Lorius, C., N. I. Barkov, J. Jouzel, Y. S. Korotkevich, V. M. Kotlyakov, and D. Raynaud. 1988. Antarctic ice core: CO_2 and climatic change over the last climatic cycle. *EOS* 69: 681, 683, 684.

Malingreau, J. P., and C. J. Tucker. 1988. Large-scale deforestation in the southeastern Amazon basin of Brazil. *Ambio* 17: 49–55.

Marland, G., and R. M. Rotty. 1984. Carbon dioxide emissions from fossil fuels: a procedure for estimation and results for 1950–1982. *Tellus* 36B: 232–61.

Marland, G., R. M. Rotty, and N. L. Treat. 1985. CO_2 from fossil-fuel burning: global distribution of emissions. *Tellus* 37B: 243–58.

Martin, J. H., G. A. Knauer, D. M. Karl, and W. W. Broenkow. 1987. VERTEX: Carbon cycling in the northeast Pacific. *Deep-Sea Res.* 34: 267–85.

McLaughlin, S. B., D. J. Downing, T. J. Blasing, E. R. Cook, and H. S. Adams. 1987. An analysis of climate and competition as contributors to decline of red spruce in high-elevation Appalachian forests of the eastern United States. *Oecologia* 72: 487–501.

Myers, N. 1989. Deforestation rates in tropical forests and their climatic implications. London: Friends of the Earth.

National Research Council (NRC). 1983. *Changing Climate*. Washington, D.C.: National Academy Press.

Neftel, A., E. Moor, H. Oeschger, and B. Stauffer. 1985. Evidence from polar ice cores for the increase in atmospheric CO_2 in the past two centuries. *Nature* 315: 45–47.

Oechel, W. C. 1988. Homeostatic adjustments of ecosystem CO_2 flux to elevated atmospheric CO_2: feedback patterns and controls. Paper presented at a conference, Interaction of the Global Carbon and Climate Systems, Scripps Institution of Oceanography, San Diego, California.

Oeschger, H., U. Siegenthaler, U. Schotterer, and A. Gugelmann. 1975. A box-diffusion model to study the carbon dioxide exchange in nature. *Tellus* 27: 168–92.

Olson, J. S. 1985. Cenozoic fluctuations in biotic parts of the global carbon cycle. In *The Carbon Cycle and Atmospheric CO₂: Natural Variations Archean to Present*, ed. E. T. Sundquist and W. S. Broecker, 377–96. Geophysical Monograph 32. Washington, D.C.: American Geophysical Union.

Olson, J. S., J. A. Watts, and L. J. Allison. 1983. Carbon in live vegetation of major world ecosystems. TR004. Washington, D.C.: U.S. Department of Energy.

Pearman, G. I., and P. Hyson. 1981. The annual variation of atmospheric CO_2 concentration observed in the Northern Hemisphere. *J. Geophys. Res.* 86: 9839–43.

Peng, T.-H. 1985. Atmospheric CO_2 variations based on the tree-ring ^{13}C record. In *The Carbon Cycle and Atmospheric CO₂: Natural Variations Archean to Present*, ed. E. T. Sundquist and W. S. Broecker, 123–31. Geophysical Monograph 32. Washington, D.C.: American Geophysical Union.

Peterson, B. J., and J. M. Melillo. 1985. The potential storage of carbon by eutrophication of the biosphere. *Tellus* 37B: 117–27.

Post, W. M., W. R. Emanuel, P. J. Zinke, and A. G. Stangenberger. 1982. Soil carbon pools and world life zones. *Nature* 298: 156–59.

Prinz, B. 1987. Causes of forest damage in Europe. *Environment* 29: 11–15, 32–37.

Ramanathan V., R. J. Cicerone, H. B. Singh, and J. T. Kiehl. 1985. Trace-gas trends and their potential role in climatic change. *J. Geophys. Res.* 90: 5547–66.

Raynaud, D., and J. M. Barnola. 1985. An Antarctic ice core reveals atmospheric CO_2 variations over the past few centuries. *Nature* 315: 309–311.

Raynaud, D., J. Chappellaz, J. M. Barnola, Y. S. Korotkevich, and C. Lorius. 1988. Climatic and CH_4 cycle implications of glacial-interglacial CH_4 change in the Vostoc ice core. *Nature* 333: 655–57.

Richards, J. F., J. S. Olson, and R. M. Rotty. 1983. Development of a data base for carbon dioxide releases resulting from conversion of land to agricultural uses. ORAU/IEA-82-10(M), ORNL/TM-8801. Oak Ridge, TN: Oak Ridge National Laboratory.

Rotty, R. M., and G. Marland. 1986. Fossil-fuel combustion: recent amounts, patterns, and trends of CO_2. In *The Changing Carbon Cycle. A Global Analysis*, ed. J. R. Trabalka and D. E. Reichle, 474–90. New York: Springer-Verlag.

Sarmiento, J. L. 1986. Three-dimensional ocean models for predicting the distribution of CO_2 between the ocean and atmosphere. In

The Changing Carbon Cycle. A Global Analysis, ed. J. R. Trabalka and D. E. Reichle, 279–94. New York: Springer-Verlag.

Schleser, G. H. 1982. The response of CO_2 evolution from soils to global temperature changes. *Z. Naturforsch. A.* 37: 2037/1–2037/5.

Schnell, R. C., ed. 1986. *Summary Report 1985. Geophysical Monitoring for Climatic Change, No. 14*. Boulder, CO: GMCC, NOAA.

Setzer, A. W., and M. C. Pereira. 1988. Amazon biomass burnings in 1987 and their tropospheric emissions. Unpublished manuscript.

Siegenthaler, U. 1983. Uptake of excess CO_2 by an outcrop-diffusion model of the ocean. *J. Geophys. Res.* 88 (C6): 3599–608.

Siegenthaler, U., and H. Oeschger. 1987. Biospheric CO_2 emissions during the past 200 years reconstructed by deconvolution of ice core data. *Tellus* 39B: 140–54.

Strain, B. R., and J. D. Cure, eds. 1985. *Direct Effects on Increasing Carbon Dioxide on Vegetation*. DOE/ER-0238. Washington, D.C.: U.S. Department of Energy.

Stuiver, M., and T. F. Braziunas. 1987. Tree cellulose $^{13}C/^{12}C$ isotope ratios and climatic change. *Nature* 328: 58–60.

Stuiver, M., R. L. Burk, and P. D. Quay. 1984. $^{13}C/^{12}C$ ratios in tree rings and the transfer of biospheric carbon to the atmosphere. *J. Geophys. Res.* 89D: 11731–48.

Sugimura, Y., and Y. Suzuki. 1988. A high-temperature catalytic oxidation method for the determination of nonvolatile dissolved organic carbon in seawater by direct injection of a liquid sample. *Mar. Chem.* 24: 105–131.

Sundquist, E. T., and W. S. Broecker, ed. 1985. *The Carbon Cycle and Atmospheric CO₂: Natural Variations Archean to Present*. Geophysical Monograph 32. Washington, D.C.: American Geophysical Union.

Tans, P. P., I. Y. Fung, and T. Takahashi. 1990. Observational constraints on the global atmospheric CO_2 budget. *Science* 247: 1431–38.

Trabalka, J. R., ed. 1985. *Atmospheric Carbon Dioxide and the Global Carbon Cycle*. DOE/ER-0239. Washington, D.C.: U.S. Department of Energy.

Trabalka, J. R., and D. E. Reichle, ed. 1986. *The Changing Carbon Cycle. A Global Analysis*. New York: Springer-Verlag.

Woodward, F. I. 1987. Stomatal numbers are sensitive to increases in CO_2 from preindustrial levels. *Nature* 327: 617–18.

Woodwell, G. M. 1983. Biotic effects on the concentration of atmospheric carbon dioxide: a review and projection. In *Changing Climate*, 216–41. Washington, D.C.: National Academy Press.

———, ed. 1984. *The Role of Terrestrial Vegetation in the Global Carbon Cycle: Measurement by Remote Sensing*. Scope 23. New York: John Wiley & Sons.

Woodwell, G. M., R. A. Houghton, T. A. Stone, R. F. Nelson, and W. Kovalick. 1987. Deforestation in the tropics: new measurements in the Amazon basin using Landsat and NOAA Advanced Very High Resolution Radiometer Imagery. *J. Geophys. Res.* 92: 2157–63.

World Resources Institute (WRI) and International Institute for Environment and Development (IIED). 1988. *World Resources 1988–89*. New York: Basic Books, Inc.

24

Sulfur

RUDOLF B. HUSAR   JANJA DJUKIC HUSAR

Sulfur, along with carbon, nitrogen, phosphorus, and water, is a key substance of life on earth. When sulfur arises from combustion of fuels or mineral processing, it causes air and water pollution. When it is deposited onto agricultural land, it is called fertilizer or nutrient. It is not just a matter of semantics, but of fact that sulfur compounds can be damaging to one part of the ecosystem and beneficial to another.

This chapter summarizes the flow of sulfur through the environment using a mass balance framework. In particular, we wish to compare the human-induced sulfur flows to the natural flows in air, land, and water.

Sulfur in the Four Spheres: Atmosphere, Hydrosphere, Lithosphere, and Biosphere

Sulfur compounds on earth are distributed among four major environmental compartments, or conceptual spheres: atmosphere, hydrosphere, lithosphere, and biosphere. Although this compartmentalization of nature is rather arbitrary, it serves to organize our existing knowledge on the distribution and flow of sulfur. A schematic representation of the four environmental compartments and their interrelationships is shown in Fig. 24.1. The circles represent the spheres and the curved arrows, the flow pathways of sulfur. In the diagram, circles and curved arrows are used instead of boxes and straight-line connections to emphasize the close, dynamic, inseparable, organic coupling among the environmental compartments; if one compartment or linkage changes, all other compartments respond.

In this conceptual frame, every sphere has a two-way linkage to every other sphere, including itself. The two-way linkage signifies that matter may flow from one compartment to another in both directions; the two-way transfer within a given compartment indicates movement of the substance from one physical location to another without changing the sphere. Since matter cannot be created or destroyed, the questions we seek to answer are the location and chemical form of the substance at any given time.

The atmosphere is best envisioned as a transport-conveyer compartment that moves substances from the atmospheric sources to the receptors. Its storage capacity for sulfur is small

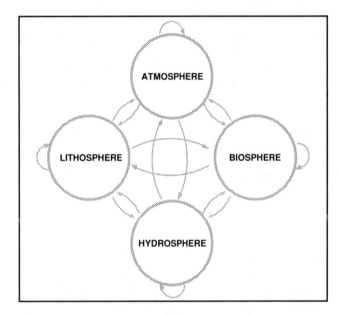

Figure 24.1 The four environmental spheres.

compared to the other spheres, but it has an immense capability for spatially redistributing sulfur, on the order of 1,000 km from its emission source.

The biosphere is the thin shell of organic matter on the earth surface. It occupies the least volume of all of the spheres, but it is the heart, or the chemical pump, of the natural sulfur flow through nature. Through chemical reduction, the sulfur compounds are volatilized by the biota, and the sulfur cycle is maintained.

The lithosphere is the solid shell of inorganic material at the surface of the earth. It is composed of soil particles and of the underlying rocks to a 50-km depth. The soil layer is also referred to as the pedosphere. Most of the sulfur interaction is with the soil, which itself is a mixture of inorganic and organic solid matter, air, water, and microorganisms. Within the soil, biochemical reactions by microorganisms are responsible for most of the chemical changes to sulfur. For our purposes, soil and rock are mainly storage compartments for sulfur.

The hydrosphere may be envisioned as two compartments: a conveyor (river system) that (1) collects the substances within the watershed and (2) delivers them to the second hydrologic compartment, the oceans.

Multimedia budgeting is not new. So far there have been two general approaches: global steady-state budgets, and small, "calibrated," watershed studies of multimedia sulfur flow. Our objective is to bridge the spatial gap between these two geographically extreme approaches. In the following, we wish to maintain a closed-system approach that is characteristic of global budgets, i.e., treating all environmental compartments of nature. At the same time, we wish to retain sufficient spatial and temporal resolution so that the budgeting scheme includes the key processes and a dynamic structure.

A close analogy exists between our perception of sulfur flow through nature and the materials flow through a chemical plant, say, a refinery: it is made of storage vessels, reaction vessels, as well as conveyors, pipes, valves, pumps, and a control mechanism that monitors and regulates the ever-changing flow through the plant. This naive, engineering analogy for the flow of matter through nature should not be taken too seriously, because human beings will never be able to, nor should they, control completely the flow of substances as the chemical engineer controls the refinery. The fact is, however, that human beings through manifold activities have changed the natural circulation of many substances. In most cases, the result of human intervention in nature's affairs has been to increase the natural flows, most notably by the mining and combustion of fossil fuels. In many ways, however, human beings have also reduced the natural flows, e.g., by virtually eliminating forest fires compared to preindustrial times.

The removal of carbon, sulfur, nitrogen, and crustal material from the long-term reservoir (mining) is continued for two purposes: (1) to "produce" energy from the fossil fuels, and (2) to use the extracted minerals for the production of disposable or "permanent" objects for human use. The production of energy refers to the release of sulfur, by combustion, and subsequent chemical and physical treatment. Hence, an overwhelming fraction of the human-induced releases to the atmosphere occur in fossil-fuel combustion and metal smelting.

The major elements released to the atmosphere during fossil-fuel combustion – carbon, sulfur, and nitrogen – are generally considered nature-friendly. Each of these elements had had a sizable flow (circulation) rate through nature well before the arrival of human beings on the global scene. Fossil-fuel combustion has enhanced significantly the flow of carbon, sulfur, and nitrogen compared to the preindustrial or natural flow rates. The possible environmental problems are caused not by their toxicity, but rather by the sheer quantities involved. Finding out the tolerance range can be aided substantially by accounting for the natural and human-made flow of these compounds. Specifically, the question we need to explore is: what is human-induced circulation compared to the natural biogeochemical flow? Undoubtedly, the perturbed geochemical flow has caused changes in the chemistry of atmosphere, land, water, and biota.

Whether the environmental and biological consequences of the changing chemical balance are considered beneficial or harmful is beyond our consideration here.

After these introductory remarks, one section reviews the flows and changes resulting from natural and human sources; the next examines the atmospheric segment of the flow in more detail; and a third discusses the relevant hydrological data.

Sulfur Flows and Pools – The Contemporary Picture

The Global Sulfur Cycle and Pools

The global sulfur cycle has been under investigation for several decades. (Eriksson 1960; Freney, Ivanov, and Rodhe 1983; Friend 1973; Granat et al. 1976; Robinson and Robbins 1968; Ryaboshapko 1983.) A summary graph from Granat et al. 1976, shown in Fig. 24.2, illustrates the main component of the global sulfur cycle between air, land, and the oceans. The main preindustrial sources to the atmosphere were volcanic emissions (3 Tg S/yr) and volatile biogenic sulfur emissions from land (3 Tg S/yr) and from the oceans (34 Tg S/yr), totaling 61 Tg S/yr. (1 Tg = 1 teragram = 10^{12} g.) Granat et al. (1976) also estimated that the preindustrial sulfur runoff through the world's rivers was 60 Tg S/yr, mostly due to weathering of rocks and soils. The estimated human contribution to the atmospheric emissions in the early 1970s was 65 Tg S/yr.

The utility of such global views is that they show that the global fluxes of sulfur induced by humans and those from nature are of comparable magnitude. Human perturbation of

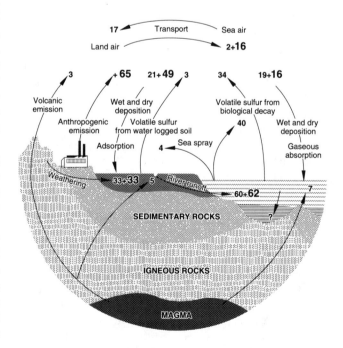

Figure 24.2 The global sulfur cycle in Tg S/yr. Small type denotes the estimated natural/preindustrial contribution, and the bold figures represent estimates for the anthropogenic contribution. Source: Granat et al. 1976.

Table 24-1 *Major sulfur reservoirs.*

Reservoir	
Atmosphere	Tg S
Troposphere	
Sulfate in aerosols	0.7
Sulfur dioxide	0.5
Carbonyl sulfide	2.3
Other reduced sulfur gases	0.8
Total in troposphere	4.3
Stratosphere	0.5
	4.8
Hydrosphere	
Ocean water	1.3×10^9
	1.3×10^9
Lithosphere	
Continental and subcontinental	
Sedimentary	5.2×10^9
Granite	7.8×10^9
Basalt	8.8×10^9
Oceanic	
Sedimentary (layer I)	0.3×10^9
Tholeitic and olivine basalt (layer II)	0.6×10^9
Layer III	1.6×10^9
	24.3×10^9
Pedosphere	
Soil	2.6×10^5
Soil organic matter	1.1×10^4
Land plants	760
	2.7×10^5

Source: Freney et al. 1983

the global sulfur cycle, however, is concentrated over the industrialized parts of the world, which constitute a small fraction of the earth's surface area. Hence, over those regions the human-induced sulfur flow exceeds the natural flows by a wide margin. A major purpose of this chapter is to illustrate the spatial and temporal pattern of the human-induced sulfur flow.

Table 24–1 summarizes the current information on distribution of sulfur between the various spheres. The bulk of sulfur is contained in the lithosphere (24×10^9 Tg S), moderate amounts occur in the pedosphere, and only small amounts (4.6 Tg S) are found in the atmosphere at any one time.

Within the lithosphere, most of the sulfur occurs in rocks of the present continents and subcontinents (22×10^9 Tg S), and the major forms are metal sulfides and sulfates. The maximum concentration of reduced sulfur is found in argillaceous rocks of platform areas (0.4% S), and the minimum

concentration occurs in effusive rocks (0.04% S). The amount of sulfate sulfur varies from fractions of 1% in humic pelagic formations to solid sulfate layers in evaporites.

In the pedosphere, the bulk of the sulfur occurs in organic compounds in soil and in living plants (1.210^4 Tg S), whereas in the ocean, inorganic sulfate predominates. Carbonyl sulfide appears to be the dominant form of sulfur in the atmosphere (Freney et al. 1983.)

Natural Sulfur Mobilization

Natural sulfur mobilization processes involve rock and soil weathering as enhanced by the water cycle, volcanic emissions, the release of volatile sulfur by biota, and the distribution of sea spray by the atmosphere.

Weathering of soils and rocks constitutes a major sulfur source to rivers (Bischoff, Paterson, and MacKenzie 1982). When atmospheric water is deposited onto the surface, sulfide and sulfate minerals release the sulfate ion to the hydrosphere. Based on the examination of the sulfur runoff from the major rivers of the world, Husar and Husar (1985) concluded that the global weathering rate should range between 40 and 80 Tg S/yr. This estimate is consistent with that of Granat et al. (1976) – 60 Tg S/yr.

Gaseous, reduced sulfur compounds are formed by biological reduction of sulfates during decomposition processes. Estimates of the oceanic and the continental biogenic sulfur flow into the atmosphere vary from 3.3–30 Tg S/yr (Bolin and Charlson 1976; Varhelyi and Gravenhorst 1981) to 280 Tg S/yr (Eriksson 1963). Most recent data indicate the values of less than 30 Tg S/yr, emitted mostly over the oceans. The geographic pattern of zones of high biological activity is depicted in Fig. 24.3 (Ryaboshapko 1983). It includes both equatorial and arctic coastal marine territories.

The estimates for global volcanic emissions to the atmosphere range between 1 Tg S/yr (Kellogg et al. 1972) and 10 Tg S/yr (Davey 1978). We tend to support estimates of Granat et al. (1976) of about 3 Tg S/yr.

The natural flow of sea-salt sulfur is an elusive quantity, since most of the salt originates in deposits over the oceans. According to Granat et al. (1976), only about 4 Tg/yr of sea-salt sulfur is deposited over land.

Human-induced Sulfur Emissions to the Atmosphere

The human-induced sulfur mobilization that is emitted to the atmosphere is responsible for much of the concern related to sulfur, because it contributes to acid rain and other effects. Atmospheric sulfur emissions are highly nonuniform over the continents (Fig. 24.4). The Northern Hemisphere is responsible for over 90% of the global sulfur emissions, as depicted in the emission density maps of the continents. Europe, due to its high emission rate and small size, has an emission density of 3.3 g S/m²/yr, followed by North America (0.8 g S/m²/yr) and Asia (0.7 g S/m²/yr). Within these continents, the emissions are concentrated over industrialized subregions.

The spatial distribution of sulfur emissions in North America is shown in more detail in Fig. 24.5, which illustrates that the emission density over the Ohio River Valley exceeds

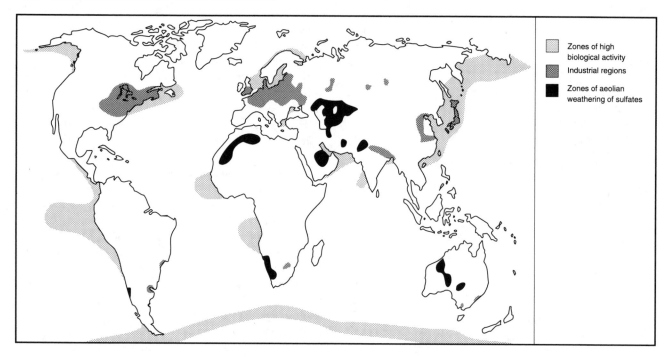

Figure 24.3 Characteristic zones of the world. According to
Ryaboshapko 1983.

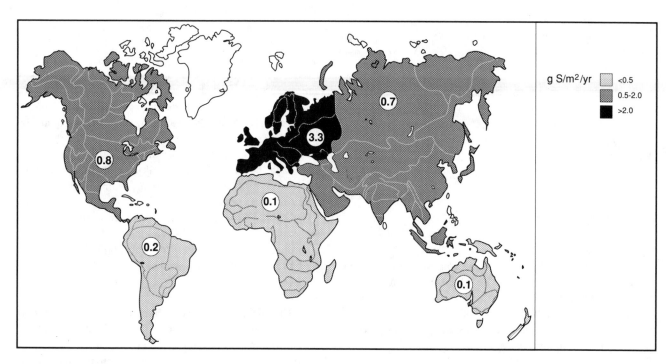

Figure 24.4 Sulfur emission density of the continents. Source:
Authors' calculations.

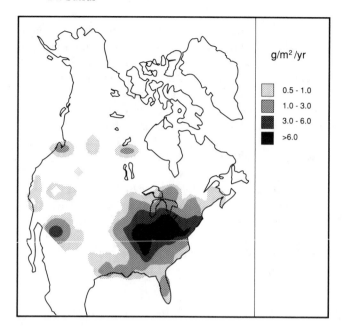

Figure 24.5 Sulfur emission density for North America, 1977–78.
Source: Authors' calculations.

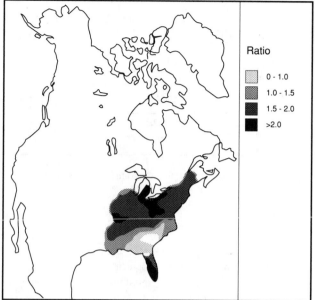

Figure 24.7 Ratio of the river sulfur runoff density to total
atmospheric sulfur plus fertilizer sulfur deposition. Source: Authors'
calculations.

6 g S/m²/yr. The eastern U.S. average is about 3.4 g S/m²/yr,
comparable to the emission density of Europe.

Multimedia Budget for the Eastern United States

This section illustrates the multimedia flow of sulfur
over the eastern United States by examining the geographic
pattern of each budget component (Husar and Husar, 1985).
This will illustrate the major flow and budget components on
a spatial scale that is relevant to effects such as acid rain.

The sulfur dry deposition from the atmosphere has been
estimated from a regional air-pollution model. The average

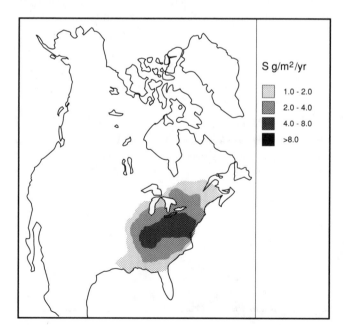

Figure 24.6 The sum of dry and wet human-made sulfur deposition
(g S/m²yr) for the eastern United States (total atmospheric sulfur
deposition) for 1978. Source: Authors' calculations.

dry deposition of the eastern United States has been
estimated to be 1.4 g S/m²/yr. The wet deposition as monitored
by several precipitation chemistry networks and the resulting
wet deposition from anthropogenic sources was estimated to
be 0.7 g S/m²/yr.

The sum of the dry and wet human-induced sulfur deposition
from the atmosphere for the eastern United States is shown
in Fig. 24.6. In the Ohio River region, the total deposition
exceeds 4 g S/m²/yr and the average in the eastern United
States is about 2.1 g S/m²/yr.

The map of sulfur runoff density shows that over the upper
Ohio River region the sulfur runoff exceeds 10 g S/m²/yr,
whereas over the coastal plains of South Carolina, Georgia,
and Alabama the runoff is less than 1 g S/m²/yr. Over the
eastern United States the river runoff averages 4.8 g S/m²/yr.
The ratio of river sulfur runoff to the sum of atmospheric
sulfur deposition and fertilizer use is shown in Fig. 24.7.
When the ratio is 1, the atmospheric and fertilizer input to the
region is equal to the sulfur output through the rivers. For the
southeastern plains, North and South Carolina, Alabama,
and Georgia, this ratio is <1, i.e., the river runoff over the
coastal plains is less than the atmospheric and fertilizer input.
On the other hand, for the industrialized Ohio River region,
this ratio is >1, where the runoff exceeds the atmospheric and
fertilizer use by a factor of 2. Thus, in the Ohio River region,
there are additional sources of river sulfur, beyond atmospheric deposition and fertilizer use, whereas in the southeastern plains, the land is a sink for atmospheric and fertilizer
sulfur.

This analysis clearly indicates that the multimedia budget
of sulfur needs to be treated on a spatial scale that is roughly
comparable to the spatial scale of the natural variations.
Nevertheless, it is useful to assemble a sulfur-flow diagram
that characterizes the average of the eastern United States

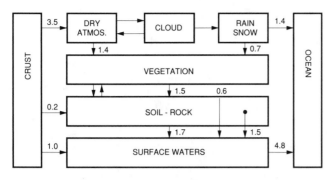

Figure 24.8 Multimedia sulfur flow diagram for the eastern United States (g S/m²yr). Source: Author' calculations.

(Fig. 24.8). The units of flow rate are given in g S/m²/yr, averaged over the area of the eastern United States (2.5 × 10¹² m²). The density of sulfur emissions to the atmosphere is 3.5 g S/m²/yr; fertilizer use is 0.2 g S/m²/yr; and the average mine runoff is estimated at 1.0 g S/m²/yr (by difference). The atmospheric emission rate (3.5 g S/m²/yr) is distributed as follows: 1.4 g S/m²/yr dry-deposited over land, 0.7 g S/m²/yr wet-deposited over land, and 1.4 g S/m²/yr exported out of the region. Terrestrial vegetation thus receives 2.1 g S/m²/yr from the atmosphere, mostly through dry deposition. The vegetation sulfur is partly transmitted to the soil (1.5 g S/m²/yr), and a fraction (0.6 g S/m²/yr) directly to the surface waters. The soil compartment thus receives 0.2 g S/m²/yr from fertilizers, 1.5 g S/m²/yr transmitted through vegetation. The soil release to the surface water is then estimated as 3.2 g S/m²/yr, which includes 1.5 g S/m²/yr released from soil-rocks by weathering. The total input to surface waters is 3.8 g S/m²/yr from the soil and vegetation (sewage) and 1.0 g S/m²/yr from mine drainage, i.e., 4.8 g S/m²/yr. The latter is the measured sulfur runoff value.

The flow of sulfur through the environment of the eastern United States is dominated by fuel-combustion emissions to the atmosphere. Over the Great Lakes and over the Ohio River valley, mine drainage and sewage input is comparable to the atmospheric input. In the coastal plains of the southeastern United States, in which mine drainage and sewage are insignificant, there is actually a loss of sulfur in the soil-vegetation. The subregional differences in the multimedia sulfur budget dictates that for future studies the spatial resolution of such budgeting be reduced to 100–200 km or less. The preceding constitutes a mass flow budget that is consistent with the available data. For many linkages, however, no data were assembled at this time.

Histories of Sulfur Mobilization by Human Action

The human-induced mobilization of sulfur falls into three major categories: (1) mining and combustion of fossil fuels, (2) mining and processing of sulfur-containing ores, and (3) agricultural movement. The total fuel combustion, smelting, and mined sulfur was estimated to be 148 Tg S/yr in 1984.

Fuel Combustion and Metal Smelting.   Fossil-fuel production is the most important category of human-made sources, and it amounts to about 120 Tg S/yr (Fig. 24.9). Coal contains most of the sulfur, followed by oil and natural gas. Smelting of metals, including copper, zinc, and lead, is another significant source of sulfur mobilization, amounting to about 13 Tg S/yr. Historically, coal combustion contributed most of the the sulfur mobilization. More recently, however, sulfur mined in crude-oil products also became significant.

It is worth noting that the sharp rise of the sulfur mobilization that began in the 1950s came to a halt by the mid-1970s. The leveling of sulfur mobilization is caused mainly by the reduced flow of oil products.

Sulfur Mining.   Sulfur is mined either as elemental sulfur or from sulfur-containing ores. Currently, the global mined-sulfur production is estimated at 24 Tg S/yr. The historical trend of global sulfur mobilization due to mining is included

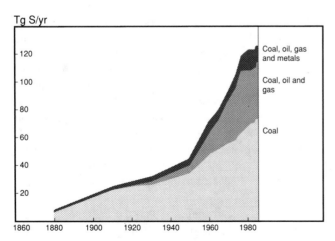

Figure 24.9 Sulfur flow from fuels and smelting. Data from United Nations 1986; and U.S. Bureau of Mines Mineral Yearbooks 1933–1985.

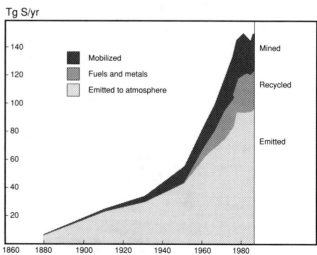

Figure 24.10 World industrial sulfur mobilization. Data from United Nations 1986; and U.S. Bureau of Mines Mineral Yearbooks 1933–1985.

in Fig. 24.10 and shows a leveling-off during the decade 1975–1985.

Agriculture, Land Use, and Fires. Vegetation contains sulfur, and agricultural activities mobilize sulfur through the movement of crops. Similarly, transport of forest products contributes to the sulfur mobilization. Major changes in land use also tend to influence the sulfur flow. Human beings have also influenced (reduced) the occurrence of forest fires and hence the natural biomass.

According to the U.S. Statistical Abstracts, the 1978 production of farm products in the United States was only about 350 million tons. About one-third, or 100 million tons, was exported to other countries. If we take the crop sulfur content to be 0.3% by weight, 1 million tons of sulfur were removed from the land by agricultural products. Much of this removal occurred over the fertile midwestern farmland. Following more detailed analysis, Beaton et al. (1974) estimated that Americans are removing about 4 million tons of sulfur per year by way of field or forage crops. Hence, this sulfur flow by ground transportation of crops, from the producers to the consumers, constitutes a significant soil-depletion rate of these nutrients.

Regrettably, we are not in position to assemble the global sulfur flow rates due to agriculture, land use, and fires. Hence, they are omitted from the following discussions.

Atmospheric Emission Trends. A substantial fraction of the sulfur that is mobilized by humans is emitted into the atmosphere as a waste product of fuel combustion and metal smelting. This fraction is responsible for major environmental effects, including acid rain, regional haze, and materials damage to buildings and paints. For these reasons, much of the impetus for the study of the sulfur cycle is driven by the effects of sulfur as it passes through the atmosphere.

The trend of the total human-induced sulfur flow (Fig. 24.10) is used to estimate the atmospheric emissions. It is assumed that all the mined sulfur is transformed to solid or liquid chemicals and that it is not vaporized to the atmosphere. A fraction of sulfur contained in natural gas, in crude oil, and in copper, zinc, and lead ores is extracted during the refining process and is referred to here as recycled sulfur. In 1984, this fraction was about 30 Tg S. It is here assumed that this fraction is not emitted to the atmosphere. Hence, the recycled sulfur is mobilized from the geological reservoir by mining, but it is not emitted to the atmosphere, being used instead for agricultural and industrial purposes.

The fraction of fuel and metal-ore sulfur that is not recycled is assumed to be emitted to the atmosphere. In 1984, the global human-induced sulfur emissions to the atmosphere were estimated to be 90 Tg S, or 60% of the total mobilized sulfur.

It is encouraging to observe that the global atmospheric sulfur emissions have remained essentially constant for the past decade. This constancy is evidently the consequence of reduced oil consumption and increased recycling as part of fuel and metal-refining processes.

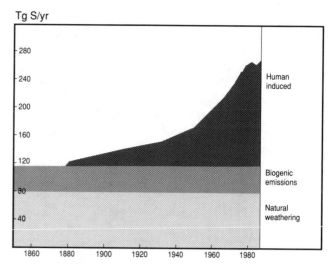

Figure 24.11 Global natural and human-induced sulfur mobilization.

Comparison of Natural and Human-Induced Flows. The global flow of sulfur induced by natural processes and human action is displayed in Fig. 24.11. The natural mobilization is dominated by weathering and by biogenic emissions. These rates were assumed to be invariant over the past 150 years, which may be a rather poor assumption. The human-induced sulfur flow increased gradually until the 1950s, followed by a sharp rise until the mid-1970s, and remaining roughly constant since then. Hence, on the global scale, the current sulfur flow from human actions exceeds the natural flow. Over the industrialized regions of Europe and North America the human-induced flow may be 5 to 10 times the natural flow.

It is also worth considering a few estimates of sulfur flow rates arising from simple "back-of-the-envelope" calculations.

Suppose that we pile the U.S. coal consumption over the past century (amounting to 500 million t/yr) into a single mountain. It would occupy 25 km^3, i.e., a pyramid with a base area of 6 × 6 km and 2 km high.

Spread over the entire eastern half of the United States a layer of coal would be about 1 cm thick. From a geophysical weathering perspective, this means that currently about 150 g S/m^2/yr of crustal mineral material "goes up in smoke," considering coal consumption only in the eastern United States. For comparison, the natural weathering of the earth's surface minerals carried to the oceans in rivers is about 20 g/m^2/yr. Thus, humanity, as a geological redistributor of the earth's crustal material, exceeds nature by an order of magnitude over the eastern United States.

Over the past 100 years, the emission density average over eastern North America was about 100–200 g S/m^2/100 yr. Most of that sulfur returns to the ground somewhere over eastern North America, resulting in an average sulfur flow of 100 g S/m^2/100 yr. For comparison, the total sulfur content of parent soils is 3–30 g S/m^2.

It is also instructive to consider the sulfur flow from a biological perspective: the U.S. average daily per capita emission rate to the atmosphere is roughly 200 g sulfur

$(400 \, \text{g} \, SO_2)$. This amount is comparable in weight to the daily per capita food consumption. The U.S. human-made sulfur-emission rate is about $15 \times 10^{12} \, \text{g} \, S/\text{yr}$ ($15 \, \text{Tg} \, S/\text{yr}$). Suppose that we distribute these emissions uniformly over $8 \times 10^{12} \, \text{m}^2$ of contiguous U.S. territory. We arrive at an average emission density of $2 \, \text{g} \, S/\text{m}^2/\text{yr}$, which is comparable to the density of sulfur contained and removed yearly by agricultural products, such as corn and wheat, from cultivated agricultural land.

Water is continuously recycled near the earth's surface by evaporation, condensation, and runoff. That is, it flows in rivers from the lithosphere to the hydrosphere, and it returns to rewash the land by way of the atmosphere. All water-soluble elements are certain to track the water cycle at least partway from land to sea. In the biosphere, at least three elements besides those of water fall in this mobile class – carbon, nitrogen, and sulfur. Among airborne sulfur compounds are SO_2 and H_2S. It is interesting that when sulfur is recycled, its valance changes: it is generally more reduced in the biosphere than it is in the geosphere. Both the atmosphere and the hydrosphere constitute an oxidizing environment, whereas the biosphere tends to reduce these compounds. In fact, it is the chemical reduction, or hydrogenation, that makes sulfur volatile. In the absence of the biosphere, all sulfur compounds ultimately would be washed to the oceans and remain there.

It is fortunate that the sulfur transported with the water can be monitored easily at two points in the cycle: (1) in the precipitation of water as it reaches the earth's suface from the atmosphere, and (2) in river runoffs as the surface waters enter the ocean. The sulfur flow through river runoff was discussed in this section; the sulfur in precipitation is treated in the atmospheric section.

Historical Changes in Sulfur Flows: Atmosphere

The current global pattern of atmospheric sulfur can be reconstructed from measurements of ambient concentrations and precipitation chemistry, but historical data of atmospheric sulfur compounds covering the past 100 years do not exist. Nevertheless, the role of human activities in changing the sulfur flow pattern can be estimated from spatial analysis of the current chemical climate. It can be argued that measurements at remote locations in the Northern Hemisphere and much of the data from the Southern Hemisphere represent the preindustrial or natural sulfur flow. The excess flow rates measured at industrial hot spots then represent the human-induced flow. This section utilizes this approach to infer the magnitude of human sulfur-flow enhancement through the atmosphere.

The atmosphere disperses the sulfur over large geographic areas, whereas the river system collects the sulfur over the watersheds. The specific processes that are involved include atmospheric dispersion with the winds, wet deposition through precipitation, dry deposition through gaseous absorption.

Atmospheric Transport

The atmosphere transports sulfur from the source to the receptor. For sulfur compounds, this atmospheric redistri-bution occurs over a 500–1,000-km region surrounding each source, which corresponds to an atmospheric residence time of 2 to 4 days.

Wet and Dry Deposition

Sulfur is removed from the atmosphere by wet deposition (rain, snow, fog), following the path of the water cycle, and by dry deposition (i.e., absorption, adsorption, and settling to the earth surface).

It is our current thinking that on a regional scale, most of the gaseous sulfur is absorbed or adsorbed by vegetation, and only a minor fraction is taken up directly from the atmosphere by soil and by continental surface waters.

The rate of wet deposition of sulfur can be obtained directly from measurements. Motivated by increasing concern about acid rain, several major rain-chemistry monitoring networks have been made operational over Europe and North America.

The continental-scale, wet-deposition patterns for North America are shown in Fig. 24.12. The highest sulfate deposition rate and concentration in precipitation occurs in the region surrounding the eastern Great Lakes. The sulfate wet deposition there exceeds $1 \, \text{g} \, S/\text{m}^2/\text{yr}$. For the region east of the Mississippi River and south of the James Bay (defining here eastern North America, ENA, area $5.8 \times 10^{12} \, \text{m}^2$), the sulfate wet deposition is about $0.63 \, \text{g} \, S/\text{m}^2/\text{yr}$. The lowest sulfate deposition rate, about $0.1 \, \text{g} \, S/\text{m}^2/\text{yr}$, is measured in northwestern Canada and the southwestern United States. Both of these regions have less than $0.5 \, \text{m}/\text{yr}$ of rainfall. The weighted average sulfate concentration in precipitation ranges between $15 \, \mu\text{eqv/l}$. (in remote U.S. and Canadian regions) and about $70 \, \mu\text{eqv/l}$. in the vicinity of the Great Lakes. Hence, although the average regional deposition rate varies tenfold over the continent, the average precipitation sulfate concentration increases only fivefold from remote regions to industrial regions.

It is also instructive to compare the measured wet-deposition pattern and rates to the emission field of human-made sulfur over the eastern United States (Fig. 24.5). The average emission density over the eastern United States is $3.5 \, \text{g} \, S/\text{m}^2/\text{yr}$, whereas the average wet deposition over the same region is $0.73 \, \text{g} \, S/\text{m}^2/\text{yr}$, (i.e., about 20% of the known human-emissions). If we further assume that the natural sources contribute to wet deposition on the average $0.07 \, \text{g} \, S/\text{m}^2/\text{yr}$, (Husar and Holloway 1982), the measured wet deposition of sulfur amounts to less than 20% of the human-made sulfur. The remaining 80% of the human-made sulfur is then either dry-deposited as SO_2 or $SO_4^=$ or is exported from the region by the prevailing winds. This leads one to conclude that human-made sulfur deposition over the eastern United States is 5 to 10 times that of the natural deposition.

Export to the Oceans

In spite of the uncertainties associated with the spatial-temporal coverage, the sampling and analytical procedures, and the interpretation of the wet-deposition data, it is most gratifying that such a continental-scale data base currently exists for North America and Europe. Prudent use of such a

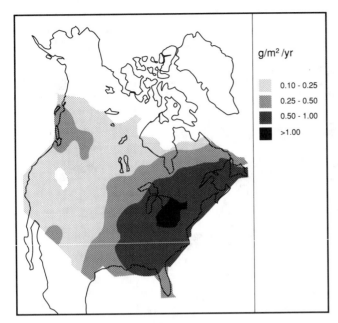 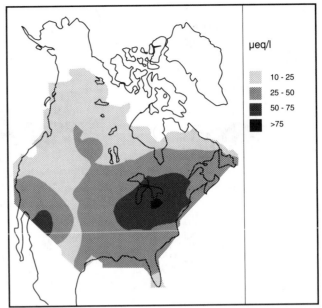

Figure 24.12 (a) Sulfur wet deposition (g S/m²/yr) and (b) concentration (μeq/l.) for 1977–1980 as monitored by the precipitation chemistry networks.

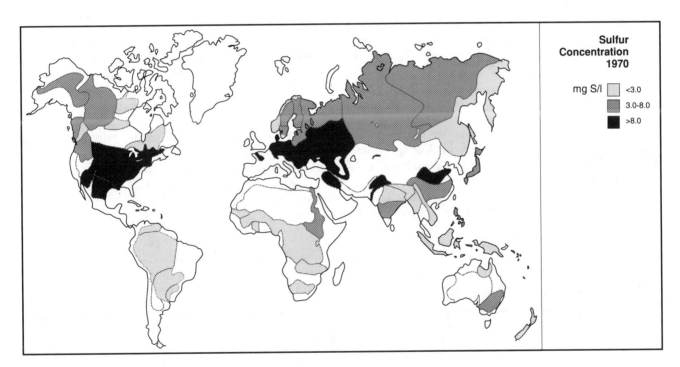

Figure 24.13 Sulfur concentration in the world rivers around 1970.

data base undoubtedly will provide us with a much-improved understanding of the flow of sulfur through the environment.

Historical Changes in Sulfur Flows: Hydrosphere

Rivers are the links between the atmosphere, the soil, and the oceans. Atmospheric precipitation is the principal source of water that makes up the lakes and rivers of the earth's surface. The chemical content of river water reflects the precipitation composition, physical and chemical weathering processes, industrial and residential waste water, and organisms' activity in the soils and rivers.

The chemical form of sulfur that occurs in surface waters is predominantly in the form of sulfates ($SO_4^=$). The sulfate ion is chemically stable in most of the environments to which natural waters are subjected.

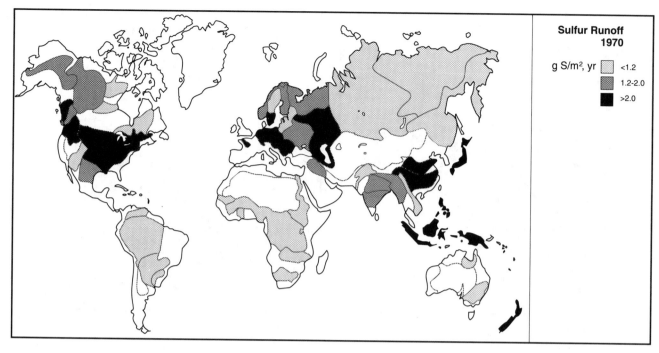

Figure 24.14 Sulfur runoff in the world rivers around 1970.

World River Runoff

Following the pioneering work of Livingstone (1963), there is a reasonable understanding of mean composition of major world rivers (Alekin and Brazhnikova 1968; Meybeck 1979).

As part of a continuing multimedia budgeting work, Husar and Husar (1985) have recently reexamined the data on the sulfur runoff in major rivers of the world (Figs. 24.13 and 24.14). Their primary goal was to examine the riverborne flow of minerals over regions of the world that are weakly influenced by people. In the Northern Hemisphere, such regions should include the eastern Siberian rivers in Asia and the arctic rivers in North America. They found that the major rivers of the world carry about $130 \; 10^{12} \, g \, S/yr$ ($105 \, Tg \, S/yr$ in the Northern Hemisphere and $25 \, Tg \, S/yr$ in the Southern Hemisphere) into the oceans. By comparison, the global anthropogenic sulfur emissions have been estimated to be $79 \, Tg \, S/yr$, out of which $72 \, Tg \, S/yr$ are emitted in the Northern Hemisphere, whereas only $7 \, Tg \, S/yr$ are emitted in the Southern Hemisphere (Varhelyi 1985).

A density map of sulfur river runoffs for the world is given in Fig. 24.14. It is evident that the sulfur river runoff is highest in the industrially influenced regions of North America and Europe, where it exceeds $1.75 \, g \, S/m^2/yr$. The major rivers in South America, Africa, and Australia show a sulfur runoff of less than $1 \, g \, S/m^2/yr$. Notably high sulfur runoffs are reported for the island countries of Japan, Indonesia, New Guinea, and New Zealand. Inspection of the chlorine runoff shows that these high sulfur runoffs are not attributable to sea salt. As a global average, the sulfur runoff is on the order of $1 \, g \, S/m^2/yr$.

For our purposes, the most interesting results are those for the arctic rivers of North America: the Yukon, McKenzie, and Nelson rivers, which show a runoff of $1 - 1.75 \, g \, S/m^2/yr$.

In particular, the basins of McKenzie and Nelson rivers are within the Canadian Shield, which has a geologic structure similar to that of the northeastern United States and southeastern Canada. A puzzling question arises: what is the source of high sulfur runoff in this region of North America? Preliminary simulation modeling for atmospheric long-range transport of human-made sulfur over North America suggests that atmospheric deposition from human-made, North American sources are unimportant for the Yukon, McKenzie, and Nelson drainage basins.

A limited historical data set for river sulfur concentrations is available for a few rivers in Europe and North America, as shown in Figs. 24.15, 24.16, and 24.17. The trend of sulfur

Sulfur concentration (mg/l)

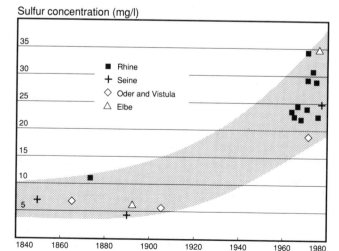

Figure 24.15 Trends in sulfur concentration in European rivers: Rhine ($\blacksquare$), Seine ($+$), Oder and Vistula ($\diamond$), and Elbe ($\triangle$). Sources: Meybeck 1979; Paces 1982; Steele 1980.

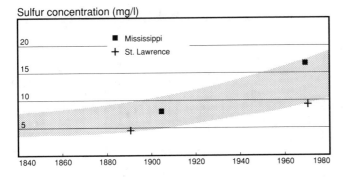

Sulfur concentration (mg/l)

Figure 24.16 Trend of sulfur concentration in North American rivers: St Lawrence (+) and Mississippi (■). Source: Meybeck 1979.

concentration in European rivers (Fig. 24.15) shows about a four-fold increase since the turn of the century. The sulfur concentration in the Rhine, Seine, Oder, Vistula, and Elbe rivers ranged between 5 mg/l. and 10 mg/l., before this century. By the 1970s, the concentration range had increased to 20–35 mg/l.

In North America, the sparse data for the Mississippi and St. Lawrence rivers show only slight increases in sulfur concentration. Both of these rivers are somewhat removed from the main industrial regions centered around the Ohio River Valley. The map of sulfur concentration for these rivers for the turn of this century is given in Fig. 24.17. It is evident that, with the exception of the Rhine River, these early concentration data are comparable to the values measured in the rivers over the remote regions.

The historical river sulfur concentration data show an increase in European rivers that is a factor of about 3 compared to a factor of 1.5 in the major North American rivers. This would indicate that the sulfur flow due to human

action in Europe is perturbed more significantly then in eastern North America, which is consistent with the observations (Fig. 24.4) that the current sulfur emission density for Europe significantly exceeds that in eastern North America.

Regional River Runoff

Budgets of sulfur, nitrogen, and other nutrients also have been investigated for small experimental watersheds in North America and Europe. The flow of ions has been investigated through the forest canopy (Horntvedt et al. 1980), soil (Seip and Freedman 1980), small watersheds such as Hubbard Brook, New Hampshire. (Likens et al. 1977), southern Swedish lakes (Environment 1982), and small streams in eastern Kentucky (Dyer and Curtis 1977) to assess the relationship of atmospheric deposition and surface-water concentration or effect of strip mining on first-order streams. However, these studies are very few and cover only small geographical areas. Thus such results cannot be easily extrapolated to a regional scale.

For the United States, a spatially extensive and long-term data base exists on the chemical composition of surface waters. These data are available from the U.S. Geological Survey (U.S.G.S) on magnetic tapes. In what follows we present a small subset of this rich data base. (Husar and Husar 1985).

For the purposes of establishing a sulfur budget over regional scales, we have chosen 52 rivers in the eastern United States with moderate watersheds ranging from 600 km² to 45,000 km². These watersheds are sufficiently large to integrate the small-scale runoff variability but sufficiently small to yield the spatial runoff pattern for different parts of the United States.

The 52 eastern U.S. rivers were selected because they have

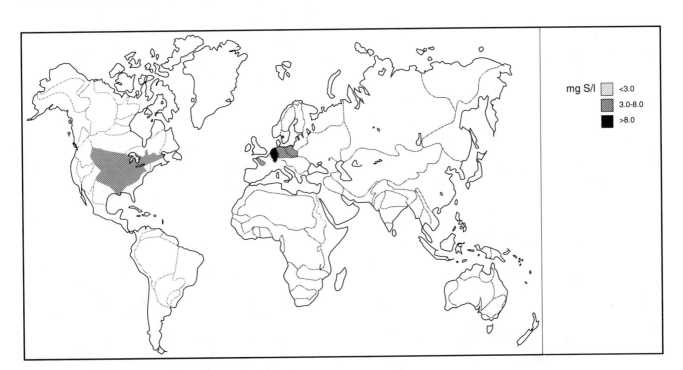

Figure 24.17 Sulfur concentration of European and North American rivers, 1846–1906.

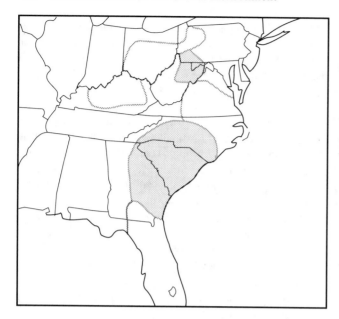

Figure 24.18 Watersheds of the rivers in the Pennsylvania–West Virginia mining district and over the coastal plains of the eastern United States.

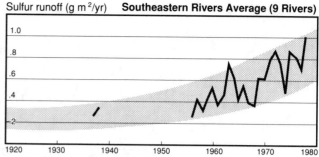

Figure 24.20 Trend of average sulfur runoff in nine rivers of the coastal plains in the eastern United States.

sulfur compounds to the concentration trends in rivers through a physicochemical model. Nevertheless, it is comforting to observe the consistency of these trend data.

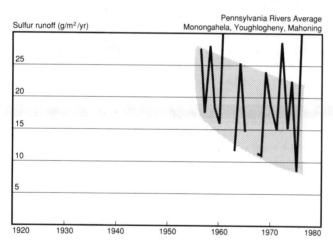

Figure 24.19 Trend of sulfur runoff in the Monongahela, Youghiogheny, and Mahoning rivers of the Pennsylvania–West Virginia mining district.

reasonable long water data records for trend analysis. In the following, we present the sulfur runoff trends for two subregions of the eastern United States, one located in the coal-mining districts of Pennsylvania and West Virginia, and another in the coastal plains of North Carolina, South Carolina, and Georgia (Fig. 24.18).

Data from three rivers in the coal-mining district show very high sulfur runoff (over $20\,\mathrm{g\,S/m^2/yr.}$) That region shows a decline between 1955 and 1975 (Fig. 24.19). Detailed analysis of the sulfur-emission data for that region shows a similar decline during this time period.

The trend data for the southeastern coastal rivers show that the sulfur runoff is only about $0.5\,\mathrm{g\,S/m^2/yr.}$ Also they show an increase of sulfur runoff of a factor of about 2 since the 1930's (Fig. 24.20). This again is consistent with the sulfur-emission and deposition trends in that region.

At present it is not possible to link the emission pattern of

References

Alekin, J. D., and L. V. Braznikova. 1968. Dissolved matter discharge and mechanical and chemical erosion. *Assoc. Int. Hydrol. Sci. 78*, 35–41.

Beaton, J. D., D. W. Bixby, S. L. Tisdale, and J. S. Platou. 1974. Fertilizer sulfur, status and potential in the U.S. *Tech. Bull. No. 21.* Washington, D.C., and London: The Sulfur Institute.

Bischoff, W. D., V. L. Paterson, and F. T. MacKenzie. 1982. Geochemical mass balance for sulfur and nitrogen-bearing acid components for eastern United States. In *Geological Aspects of Acid Deposition*, Acid Precipitation Series, vol 7, ed. O. P. Bricker, 1–21. London: Butterworth.

Bolin, B., and R. J. Charlson. 1976. The role of the tropospheric sulfur cycle in the short-wave radiative climate of the earth. *Ambio 5*, 47–54.

Davey, T. R. A. 1978. Anthropogenic balance for Australia. In *Production and Chemical Engineering*, Sydney, Australia:

Dyer, K. L., and W. R. Curtis. 1977. Effects of strip mining on water quality in small streams in eastern Kentucky, 1967–1975. Washington, D.C.: *NSDA Forest Service Res. Pap. NF-372.*

Electric Power Research Institute. 1984. *The Integral Lake Watershed Acidification Study.* Vol. 4, *Summary of Major Results*, R. A. Goldstein and S. A. Gherini, ed. EA-3221, 1109–15. Research Project.

Environment 1982 Committee. 1982. Acidification today and tomorrow. A Swedish study prepared for the 1982 Stockholm Conference on the Acidification of the Environment, June, Stockholm.

Eriksson, E. 1960. The yearly circulation of chloride and sulfur in nature: meteorological, geochemical and pedological implication. *Tellus 12*, 63–109.

———. 1963. The yearly circulation of sulfur in nature. *J. Geophys. Res. 68*, 4001–4008.

Freney, J. R., M. V. Ivanov, and H. Rodhe. 1983. The sulfur cycle. In *The Major Biogeochemical Cycles and Their Interactions*, ed. B. Bolin and R. B. Cook. Scientific Committee on Problems of the Environment (SCOPE). New York: John Wiley & Sons.

Friend, J. P. 1973. The global sulfur cycle. In *Chemistry of the Lower Atmosphere*, ed. S. I. Rasool. New York: Plenum.

Galloway, J. N., and D. M. Whelpdale. 1980. An atmospheric sulfur budget for eastern North America. *Atmos. Environment 14*, 409–417.

Granat, L., H. Rodhe, and R. O. Hallberg. 1976. The global sulfur cycle. In *Nitrogen, Phosphorus, and Sulfur–Global Cycles*, ed. B. H. Svensson and R. Soderlund. Scientific Committee on Problems of the Environment (SCOPE). New York: John Wiley & Sons.

Horntvedt, R., G. J. Dollar, and E. Joranger. 1980. Effects of acid precipitation on soil and forest. Atmosphere-vegetation interactions. In *Ecological Impact of Acid Precipitation*, ed. C. Drablos and A. Tollan, 192–93. SNSF project, Acid Precipitation – Effects on Forests and Fish. Oslo, Norway.

Husar, R. B., and J. M. Holloway. 1982. Sulfur and nitrogen over North America. In *Ecological Effects of Acid Deposition*, 95–115. National Swedish Environment Protection Board, Rpt. PM 1636. Stockholm.

Husar, R. B., and J. D. Husar. 1985. Regional river sulfur runoff. *J. Geophys. Res. 90*, 1115–25.

Husar, J. D., and R. B. Husar. 1985. Sulfur flow through air, land, and water over eastern United States. Presented at the Hudson River Conference on Acidification and Anadromous Fish of Atlantic Estuaries, October 15–18. West Point, NY.

Husar, R. B., and D. E. Patterson. 1985. Monte Carlo simulation of regional air pollution: transport dynamics. Submitted for publication.

Kellogg, W. W., R. D. Cadle, E. R. Allen, A. L. Lazarus, and E. A. Martell. 1972. The sulfur cycle. *Science 175*, 587–96.

Likens, G. E., J. H. Borman, R. S. Pierce, J. S. Eaton, and N. M. Johnson. 1977. *Biogeochemistry of a Forested Ecosystem*. New York: Springer-Verlag.

Livingstone, D. A. 1963. Chemical composition of rivers and lakes. *U.S. Geol. Surv. Prof. Pap. 44-G.*

Meybeck, M. M. 1979. Major elements contents of river waters and dissolved inputs to the oceans. *Rev. Geol. Dyn. Geogr. Phys. 21*, 215–6. (In French.)

Paces, T. 1982. Natural and anthropogenic flux of major elements from Central Europe. *Ambio 11*, 206–208.

Robinson, E., and R. C. Robbins. 1968. Sources, abundances, and fate of gaseous atmospheric pollutants. *Final Report, Proj. PR-6755.* Stanford Research Institute, Stanford, CA.

Ryaboshapko, A. G. 1983. *The Atmospheric Sulfur Cycle.* In *The Global Biogeochemical Sulfur Cycle*, ed. M. V. Ivanov, and J. R. Freney. Scientific Committee on Problems of the Environment (SCOPE). New York: John Wiley & Sons.

Seip, H. M. and B. Freedman. 1980. *Effects of Acid Precipitation on Soils. Rapporteurs Reports.* In *Effects of Acid Precipitation on Terrestrial Ecosystems*, ed. T. C. Hutchinson and M. Havas. New York and London: Plenum Press.

Steele, T. D. 1980. Computation of major solute concentrations and loads in German rivers using regression analysis. *Catena 7*, 111–24.

United Nations Statistical Yearbook 1983/84. 1986. New York: United Nations.

U.S. Bureau of Mines Mineral Yearbooks, 1933–1985. Washington, D.C.: U.S. Bureau of Mines.

United States – Canada Memorandum of Intent (MOI). 1983. Memorandum of intent on transboundary air pollution. Work group I. Impact assessment. Final Report. Washington, D.C.: U.S. Bureau of Mines.

United States Geological Survey, Water Data (tapes)

Varhelyi, G. 1985. Continental and global sulfur budgets, 1. Anthropogenic SO_2 emissions. *Atmos. Environment 19*, 1029–40.

Varhelyi, G., and G. Gravenhorst. 1981. An attempt to estimate biogenic sulfur emission into the atmosphere. *Idojaras 85*, 126–33.

25

Nitrogen and Phosphorus

VACLAV SMIL

Appreciation of the importance of nitrogen and phosphorus in perpetuation of life on the earth led fairly rapidly to rising human interference in their biospheric cycles. Before the middle of the nineteenth century, Dumas' lectures on elemental cycling delivered at the Ecole de Médicine in Paris outlined the interdependent fluxes of common nonmetallic elements with admirable clarity, and Liebig's elucidation of limiting nutrients set the course for nutritional management of crop farming. The stage was set for an exponential rise of anthropogenic intervention in the soil content of the two macronutrients and hence in their subsequent biospheric conversions and losses.

Although life requires close linkage of the two elements, many dissimilarities concerning their biospheric flows require separate treatment of human-induced changes. Most notably, phosphorus – unlike carbon, nitrogen, and sulfur – is not a doubly mobile element (i.e., it does not move to any significant extent through the atmosphere, but just through waters), and hence no atmospheric consequences result from its increased anthropogenic inputs.

Perhaps no less important is the relative simplicity of phosphorus releases to the environment: only fertilization and concentrated (that is, mostly urban) wastes are currently or potentially worrisome. In contrast, anthropogenic nitrogen compounds enter the environment on large scales, not only as fertilizers and organic wastes, but also from stationary and mobile combustion of both biomass and fossil fuels. Complexities of the nitrogen cycle open up more routes for undesirable escape to the environment.

This century has seen anthropogenic inputs of nitrogen and phosphorus increasing by two orders of magnitude, so that their fluxes are now significant fractions of natural flows. Considering the magnitude of these interventions, it may be surprising to see that the negative environmental effects have been relatively subdued. More importantly, prospects are excellent for substantial efficiency gains in the future use of nitrogen and phosphorus. With stabilized populations and improved environmental management, there is a solid hope that in the long run the necessity of continued human inter-vention in the flows of nitrogen and phosphorus can be made compatible with the security of the global environment.

Nitrogen

Life is basically a matter of carbonaceous compounds in wet tissues, but the quantity of carbon (45% of dry biomass) needs the quality of nitrogen for both autotrophic and heterotrophic prosperity. This relatively rare element – in the biosphere, carbon is about 100 times more abundant – is involved in just about every vital transformation of living matter, owing to its critical presence in amino acids, nucleic acids, enzymes, and chlorophyll. Nitrogen is the nutrient responsible for the vigorous vegetative growth and for the deep green color of the leaves, as well as for the size and protein content of cereal grains, the staples of humankind.

Unfortunately, its transfer to plants is not an easy affair, especially when considering that every leaf sways amidst a gaseous mixture composed, by volume, of 78% of nitrogen. Only three atmospheric processes are able to energize conversion of N_2 to NO_x: falling meteoroids, ozonization, and direct ionization of air by lightning.

But these high-energy phenomena fix only a fraction of available nitrogen, and most of its natural assimilable supplies come from the activities of bacteria and cyanobacteria capable of splitting N_2 at ambient temperature and pressure. This biotic fixation supplies the bulk of metabolizable nitrogen and limits photosynthesis in general and food production in particular.

Farming is thus fundamentally dependent on assuring adequate nitrogen inputs. Intensification of inputs through organic recycling and planting of nitrogen-fixing legumes has been practiced for millennia. A much more effective intervention emerged only with the synthesis of NH_3 in 1913, although its practical consequences – an era of intensive fertilization – came only with the post–World War II decades of global economic growth.

The story of human interference in biospheric nitrogen flows is greatly complicated by the inevitable and relatively rapid losses of useful nitrogen compounds from soils, owing

Table 25–1 *Major global reservoirs of nitrogen*

Reservoir		Estimated totals (Pg N)
Igneous rocks		$14–57 \times 10^6$
Atmosphere	N_2	3,800
	N_2O	1.8
	NO_x	0.0006
Hydrosphere	N_2, NO_3^-, organic N	20,000
Soils	NO_3^-, NH_4^+, organic N	100–760
Phytomass	terrestrial	7.5–10
	marine	300–500
Zoomass		200–370
Anthropomass		0.006

The values are from more than a dozen sources compiled by Rosswall 1983 and Smil 1985.

to incessant and complex global fluxes of the nutrient. Its easy double mobility – through the air and through the waters – assures the intensive and worldwide cycling that is a source of unwelcome economic losses and environmental concerns, yet is also the prerequisite of the element's perpetual biospheric availability.

Nitrogen Pools and Flows – The Contemporary Global Picture

Unlike carbon or sulfur, nitrogen does not have a large ocean storage, but this situation has not precluded substantial exchanges involving the whole biosphere; and the existence of four interacting nitrogen pools in the soils and waters (organic nitrogen, ammonia, nitrite, nitrate) and six in the atmosphere (N_2, NH_3, N_2O, NO, NO_2, and NO^{3-}) makes for a large number of vigorous fluxes. Especially notable is the number of pathways that the element can follow in escaping the place or the form of its human field application: nitrification, leaching, erosion, volatilization, denitrification, or immobilization. Deeper appreciation of the study of nitrogen cycling can be had by consulting, among others, Burns and Hardy 1975; Delwiche 1977; Rosswall 1983; Smil 1985; and Soderlund and Svensson 1976. Here are presented just the essentials.

By far the largest nitrogen reservoir is in igneous rocks beyond the reach of biospheric flows (Table 25–1). Consequently, only a fraction of 1% of lithospheric nitrogen can participate in global cycling. Compared to the lithosphere, the hydrosphere is a minuscule reservoir. The atmosphere contains 3.8×10^{21} g of nitrogen – virtually all of it as stable N_2, but the relatively small quantities of other nitrogen species provide very active links with the biota, land, and ocean. Soil nitrogen is stored largely in organic matter; ammoniacal nitrogen is second in importance. Published totals of global storage range from 175 Pg to 760 Pg, but an estimate based on actually measured concentrations can end up with less than 100 Pg. The typical range for temperate soils is between 2,500 kg N/ha and 6,000 kg N/ha (Stevenson 1982).

Biomass stores nitrogen in highly variable quantities. Leguminous plants average up to 3% nitrogen, cereal grains have just 1–2% nitrogen, and stemwood contains a mere

0.03–0.2% nitrogen in temperate and 0.5–0.7% nitrogen in tropical species. Assuming an average of 0.75% nitrogen and a total phytomass store of at least 1 Eg of dry weight results in the total storage of 7.5 Pg, and more liberal but still quite plausible assumptions may raise the sum to around 10 Pg N.

The zoomass pool was put at 200–280 Tg nitrogen, and anthropomass – with 5 billion people, mean weight of 50 kg, and average protein content of 15% of live weight – contains just 6 Tg nitrogen. Yet it is for the maintenance and expansion of this minuscule reservoir (a mere 1.5×10^{-9} of atmosphere's nitrogen stores) that we synthesize more than ten times as much nitrogen in ammonia plants and noticeably influence just about every major biospheric flow of the nutrient.

All principal flows are summarized in Table 25–2. As was already noted, nitrogen fixation by high-energy atmospheric processes is much surpassed by biotic fixation. Biotic reduction of atmospheric N_2 to NH_3 is done enzymatically by at least 25 free-living or symbiotic bacterial genera (with heterotrophic aerobes with symbiotic *Rhizobium* being by far the most prominent), 15 genera of symbiotic actinomycetes (*Frankia* being the leading genus), and 60 genera of cyanobacteria (most commonly, heterocystous filamentous forms led by *Anabaena*).

Although the information on biotic fixation has reached truly enormous dimensions – as readily attested by such reviews as Burns and Hardy 1975, Dixon and Wheeler 1986, Newton and Orme-Johnson 1980, Vincent 1982 – our quantitative knowledge of the key rates is surprisingly inadequate.

The most regrettable fact is that we still do not have a solid appreciation of nitrogen fixation done by symbiotic rhizobia (La Rue and Patterson 1981). Almost all published figures for major leguminous crops have at least a threefold range, with five- or sixfold differences not uncommon.

Table 25–2 *Major fluxes of the global biospheric nitrogen cycle*

Flux		Estimated range (Tg N)
Atmospheric fixation		1–30
Biotic fixation	terrestrial	44–200
	marine	1–130
Anthropogenic fixation	(1985)	90
Fossil-fuel combustion	NO_x	10–35
	NH_3	5–10
Phytomass burning		10–200
Biogenic NO_x releases		20–230
Denitrification	terrestrial	40–390
	marine	40–330
Volatilization		30–250
Atmospheric deposition	NH_3/NH_4^+	80–240
	NO_x	30–120
	organic N	10–100
River runoff		10–40

The ranges are rounded estimates published in 12 different sources between 1970 and 1983 and summarized in Rosswall 1983 and Smil 1985.

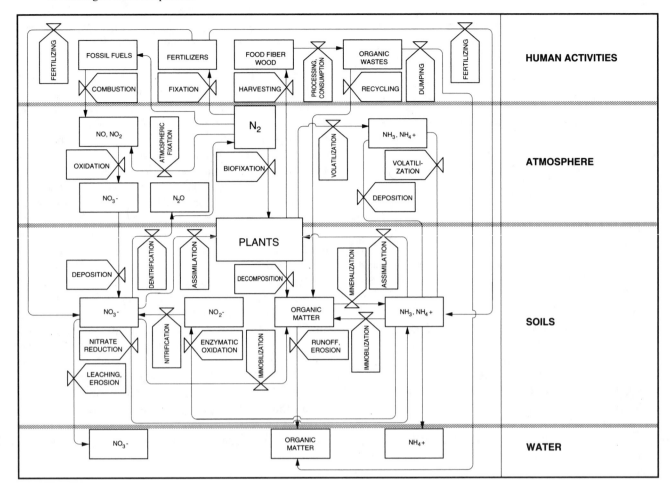

Figure 25.1 Principal reservoirs and flows in global nitrogen cycle.
Values for most of the storages and fluxes can be found in Tables 25-1
and 25-2.

Similar uncertainties prevail in quantifying denitrification
(the process opposite to fixation and hence the principal
closing arm of the nitrogen cycle). Denitrification is a stepwise reduction of nitrates to nitrogen oxides and ultimately to
N_2. Information on the total denitrification fluxes is so
uncertain that losses of soil nitrogen ascribed to this process
range from 15% to more than 50%. The range of uncertainty
is no smaller for ammonia volatilization, the other important
return of soil nitrogen to the atmosphere. Figure 25.1
summarizes all important reservoirs and flows of biospheric
nitrogen, including those originating in human interventions
whose extent can be appraised with greater accuracy than the
magnitude of biogenic flows.

Nitrogen Fluxes in Agriculture

Traditional farming had to rely on photosynthesis to
renew the fertility of fields and pastures. Basically only two
choices existed: (1) legumes could be used through inter-
cropping, rotation, or plowing under as a green manure; (2)
crop phytomass could be recycled either directly by incorporating often copious crop residues or indirectly in animal
and human wastes. By the eighteenth century, these practices
reached their greatest extent and highest intensity in parts of

East Asia and western Europe, and locally (the Kanto Plain
of Japan, the delta of the Yangtze River in China, and the
Netherlands) they were able to produce impressive yields:
over 1.5 t/ha of wheat, and more than 2 t/ha of rice.

But even the most assiduous manuring could not cover the
requirements of modern, high-yielding crops. USDA's (1978)
detailed estimates for the United States show the theoretical
total of manurial nitrogen to be equivalent to about 20% of
the nutrient applied in synthetic fertilizers. With higher
nitrogen losses from manures, the real share may be closer to
15%. Although leguminous rotations remain desirable, their
extent is limited by marketing and diet considerations, and
hence the practical options still fix far less nitrogen than
necessary. Modern agriculture is thus inextricably dependent
on a steady flux of synthetic fertilizers.

Before the synthesis of NH_3 only a few options (largely unsatisfactory) existed for nitrogen fertilization besides legumes
and organic recycling. Large deposits of Chilean nitrates
(mostly $NaNO_3$) were discovered in 1809 and became the
nineteenth century's most important source of inorganic
nitrogen, supplemented by the recovery of ammonium sulfate
from coking ovens. Guano was a highly concentrated organic
nitrogen fertilizer, and as such it was rapidly mined and

Chemical fertilizer N

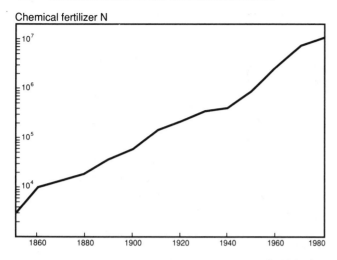

Figure 25.2 History of nitrogen fertilizer applications in the United States between 1840 and 1980. Source: Smil 1985.

eagerly bought. Thanks to the rainless climate off the Peruvian coast, thick (up to 200 m) deposits of guano on the Chincha Islands contained fertilizing ingredients, all of which were soluble, and 10 Tg (1 Tg = 10^{12} g) of the fertilizer were shipped to Europe and North America between the 1840s and 1870s (Wines 1985).

The marginal importance of all of these sources is shown by the U.S. utilization totals: a mere 3 Gg N (1 Gg = 1 gigagram = 10^9 g) in 1850, and still less than 60 Gg N by the end of the nineteenth century (Fig. 25.2). The German cyanamide process introduced in 1898 was a commercial possibility, but its high energy requirements and its need for large amounts of coke to react with CaO were not suited for easy diffusion. The oxidation of nitrogen to NO in an electrical arc introduced shortly afterward was another possibility, but one open only to those with access to cheap hydroelectricity.

Only the commercialization of Haber-Bosch synthesis opened up the era of vigorous fertilization – but not immediately. The process was first tested in 1913, but the first fertilizer plants were put into operation only in the early

Synthesis of fertilizer N (million tons)

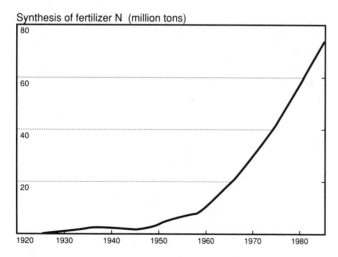

Figure 25.3 Exponential rise of global synthesis of nitrogenous fertilizers between 1920 and 1985. Assembled from a variety of historical statistics and from FAO 1986.

1920s. Then the global economic slowdown and World War II postponed the onset of large-scale demand until the early 1950s.

The global production trend has been exponential, with the level of 1 Tg N/yr passed in the early 1930s, 10 Tg N/yr in the late 1950s, 50 Tg N/yr in 1976, and 75 Tg N/yr in 1985 (Fig. 25.3). Cumulative 1925–1985 output of synthetic fertilizer nitrogen was just over 1 Pg (about 1.07 billion t), half of it since 1976. Total synthetic ammonia output has been about 15–20% higher: currently about 80% of the compound is used as a fertilizer, and the remainder goes as a feedstock into a variety of chemical processes. In 1985, average worldwide applications per hectare of arable land (including permanent crops) were about 46 kg N, with continental means ranging from just 10 kg N/ha in Africa to about 110 kg N/ha in Europe (FAO 1986).

Intensity of cultivation – both in terms of yields and multicropping – is closely linked to the nutrient consumption. Canada, the USSR, and the United States – extensive producers all – use only 25 kg, 45 kg, and 55 kg N/ha, respectively, whereas the French mean is about 125 kg, the Chinese 135 kg, the Japanese 145 kg, and the Egyptian 295 kg N/ha. During the 1970s construction of many new ammonia plants throughout the poorer countries helped to narrow the gap between applications in industrialized countries and in Asian, African, and Latin American agrarian societies. The wealthier countries' mean average consumption is now nearly 60 kg N/ha; the Third World's average, close to 40 kg N/ha.

Virtually all of this nitrogen is fixed in the way replicating the original Haber-Bosch synthesis: obviously, there have been many modifications and huge efficiency improvements, but the principle remains. Natural gas is now the major feedstock, and the synthesis of NH_3 in the most efficient large plants requires less than 35 MJ/kg N, compared to pre-World War II values in excess of 100 MJ/kg N, and anhydrous ammonia containing 82% nitrogen has increasingly become the fertilizer of choice (Smil 1985).

Ammonia is a gas under normal pressure, and special equipment is needed to store and handle it and to inject it into the soil. The next best choice in terms of nutritional density is urea, with 45% nitrogen. As urea is a stable solid, it can be easily bagged and spread by hand in small fields: not surprisingly, it has become the preferred fertilizer throughout rice-growing Asia.

Other nitrogen fertilizers with important application shares include ammonium nitrate (with 35% nitrogen the second most concentrated solid compound), nitrogen solutions, and a large variety of compound materials ranging from just nitrogen-phosphorus combinations to nitrogen-phosphorus-potassium with micronutrients. Extensive fertilization testing failed to establish any differences among gases, solids, and solutions as nitrogen sources for crops, which means that market shares of ammonia and urea, with their energy cost and hence their prices per unit of nitrogen lower than other fertilizers, will be increasing. Differences exist, however, in environmental impacts: nitrate fertilizers are leached more easily than ammoniacal compounds.

Aggregate removal of nitrogen in global farm crops can be estimated fairly well for cereals, tubers, and sugar crops: in the mid-1980s, it amounted to at least 45 Tg N, with two-thirds accounted for by the three largest grain crops – wheat, rice, and corn. For legumes it is easy to make an approximate calculation of incorporated nitrogen, but which portion of this storage has not been covered by self-fertilization, that is by symbiotic fixation, is rather uncertain. Should at least 10% of legume nitrogen come from the soil and should vegetables, fruits, and plantation crops remove no more than 4 Tg N, then the worldwide total would be no less than 50 Tg N, and it may be easily 10–15% higher.

These totals would represent 65–75% of global applications of synthetic nitrogen. This number, however, in no way indicates comfortable margins in replacing the removed nutrient, as the losses of fertilizer nitrogen through denitrification, volatilization, leaching, and runoff frequently can add up to more than half of the applied total. To evaluate global losses with satisfactory reliability is impossible, owing to the enormous variability of soil nitrogen removal rates. The ranges, for example, suggested by the Fertilizer Institute (1976) for potential losses of applied nitrogen are: denitrification 5–35%, erosion 0–20%, leaching 0–20%, immobilization 10–40%.

Nitrogen Fluxes from Combustion

Global emissions of nitrogen from the combustion of fossil fuels not only represent a much smaller nitrogen flux than crop fertilization, but also add up to a transfer smaller than the agricultural nitrogen losses. Their spatial concentration rather than their total magnitude is of the greatest environmental importance. These emissions are concentrated overwhelmingly in the temperate latitudes of the Northern Hemisphere. They are one of the major causes of photochemical smog in many large urban areas (see chap. 17). Nitrates arising from their atmospheric oxidation are a principal cause of acid deposition extending hundreds of kilometers downwind from the source areas (see chap. 24).

Owing to substantial differences of NO_x emission factors for large power plants, small industrial boilers, and household heating, as well as for coal, refined fuels, and natural gases, a reasonably accurate global estimate of these gaseous releases requires disaggregations by major users and fuels. A summary of such an exercise for the early 1980s (Smil 1985) shows the worldwide flux of 40 Tg NO_x/yr. Assuming these emissions to be largely NO, the total annual flux from stationary fossil-fueled combustion would be nearly 20 Tg N, with 95% released in the Northern Hemisphere. Burning of coal also releases ammonia: 15–25% of the total fuel nitrogen is liberated as NH_3. The compound is recovered during coking, however, and with this adjustment, the global NH_3 emissions from coal are now close to 10 Tg N/yr.

Mobile sources are a smaller but even more concentrated source of NO_x. Progressively stricter controls have been put in place since the late 1960s in the United States and since the early 1970s in Japan, but these controls have not been followed universally. Actual emission factors for passenger cars thus range from less than 0.5 g NO_x/km for well-controlled vehicles to over 2 g NO_x/km for the uncontrolled ones. Current worldwide passenger-car emissions add up to at least 6 Tg N/yr, and heavy vehicles and planes add another 2 Tg N.

To complete the account, chemical and other industries (portland cement, coking) contribute at least 2 Tg N/yr, and combustion of wood and crop residues and recurrent burning of vegetation in shifting farming release about 5 Tg N/yr. Global emissions of NO_x from all anthropogenic sources – about 35 Tg N – are then a significant addition to the biogenic NO_x releases, variously estimated to be 20–90 Tg N. But this biogenic flux is so uncertain that no clear comparison of relative contributions is possible.

As important as the relatively large anthropogenic NO_x flux is its recent rate of increase. As shown in Fig. 25.4, between 1950 and 1970 the rise of global NO_x emissions was steeply exponential, a result of a larger share of fossil fuels burned in electricity generation and of rapid increases of car ownership throughout the industrialized world. The recent leveling-off and decline of emissions, most impressive in Japan, follows mainly the introduction of mandatory automotive controls. Large NO_x releases in many locales (for example, the northeastern United States and parts of western Europe) have contributed heavily to acid deposition, and this realization forced a reevaluation of an earlier simplistic understanding of acid rain as an overwhelmingly SO_2-generated phenomenon.

Nitrogen in the Environment

Widespread fertilization and concentrated combustion introducing anthropogenic nitrogen compounds into the environment may be responsible for changes ranging from localized, acute life-threatening hazards (such as infant methemoglobinemia) to global, uncertain long-term degradations (such as N_2O-aided reduction of stratospheric O_3). The scope of concerns is enormous, and in order to appreciate

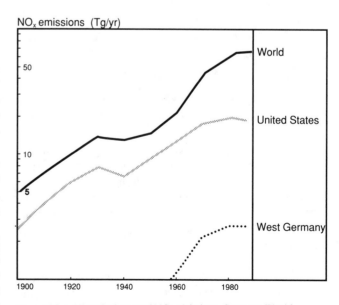

Figure 25.4 Historical rates of NO_x emissions. Sources: World Resources Report 1986 and author's calculations.

the potential complications and to manage the effects, the entry routes of anthropogenic nitrogen must first be understood. With combustion, the entry is obvious; with fertilization, the leakage of nitrogen from soil can take one of four routes: denitrification, volatilization, leaching, or erosion.

Without denitrification there would be no nitrogen cycle, indeed no biosphere as we know it: the process returns nitrogen to the air and makes it available at all locations to flow again through the plants. Denitrification is a stepwise process not always carried to N_2. Sometimes N_2O is released instead; its shares in emissions from fertilized soils appear to average around 5%, but the fluxes are highly variable. Estimates for 40 different agroecosystems show losses ranging from just 1 kg N/ha/yr to almost 200 kg N/ha/yr (Frissel and Kolenbrander 1977).

Increased use of nitrogen fertilizers, as well as extensive plantings of pasture legumes, should be expected to release more N_2O. Although this intensified flux is obviously still too small to have any direct ecosystemic or health effects, it may be a contributor to reductions of stratospheric O_3 (see chap. 17). These concerns attracted much attention during the 1970s (Delwiche 1981), but the only solid evidence consists of measurements of tropospheric background N_2O concentrations of five remote sites since 1977, showing annual increases of about one ppbv (about 0.33%/year), or doubling in 212 years (Schnell 1986). As a source of the gas, oceans may be at least two times, but perhaps as much as four times, larger than fertilizers. Biomass and fossil-fuel combustion may be an equally large source.

The other airborne nitrogen loss, volatilization of NH_3 from synthetic and organic fertilizers, is a common and frequently rather large flux, lowering the utilization efficiency of ammoniacal compounds and manures, but without adverse large-scale environmental impacts. Typical losses for surface-applied fertilizers are 5–20%, but proper incorporation into soils and adjustments of their pH can keep the losses tolerably low.

And so it is the waterborne fluxes of agricultural nitrogen, leaching, and erosion that immediately have been most worrisome. Leaching losses are almost exclusively as soluble nitrates, with the rates dependent on the kind, quantity, and placement of fertilizer, the water-holding capacity of soils, precipitation, and plant uptake. Ammonium fertilizers, now increasingly dominant worldwide, are relatively leach-proof owing to the ready adsorption of NH^{4+} ions on clay particles and humus.

Typical leaching losses rise with the applications from 10% for inputs below 150 kg N ha to 20% for very heavy fertilization, but generalizing here is no easier than about denitrification. Similarly, erosion losses are highly variable. W. E. Larson, F. J. Pierce, and R. H. Dowdy (1983) calculated annual nitrogen losses from U.S. cropland at 9.49 Tg N, or nearly the same amount as is annually applied in synthetic fertilizers.

Leached and eroded anthropogenic nitrogen in waters became one of the greatest environmental concerns of the late 1960s and the early 1970s. Most prominently, Commoner (1971) attempted to show that intensive fertilization, rather than urban sewage, in the corn belt led to an "appreciable rise" in average aquatic nitrate concentrations. Commoner's conclusion: the nitrogen cycle is seriously out of balance, and major corrective action is imperative.

Yet critical reevaluation of Commoner's arguments, most notably Aldrich's (1980) comprehensive review, exposed them as greatly exaggerated. Four decades of measurements of nitrate levels in American streams have showed no dramatic increases; with the exception of the Santa Ana River in California, only three among many hundreds of readings at 88 stations over a period of 43 years exceeded 3 mg/l., and only four rivers had clear upward NO^{3-} trends. Similarly, Kolenbrander (1972) found that in the Netherlands during a 40-year period, only one-third of the country's waterworks recorded marginally higher nitrate levels in spite of a huge increase (about 150 kg N/ha) in fertilization.

As for groundwaters, Rajagopal and Talcott's (1983) review of nitrates in Iowa groundwater is revealing: some of the world's most intensive fertilization appears to have had no undesirable effect on the quality of properly tapped drinking water. The Royal Society Study Group Staff (1984) found nitrate levels exceeding allowable limits in many localities in heavily fertilized England – yet no methemoglobinemia cases were recorded in the country.

Nitrate fertilization of surface water has also turned out to be less worrisome than some believed. Aquatic biologists argued for years about the relative importance of nitrogen and phosphorus in eutrophication. But by the late 1960s, the debate had been resolved, and phosphorus was identified as by far the most frequent growth-limiting nutrient, with nitrogen limiting only in shallow eutrophic lakes with loadings in excess of 2–3 g N/cm^2. Moreover, it is the uncontrolled, but reliably controllable, release of urban waste nitrogen, rather than the much more difficult-to-limit leaching and erosion, that is the largest source of aquatic nitrogen; the same is true about phosphorus.

Phosphorus

Considering its qualitative indispensability, nitrogen is a rather rare biospheric constituent. Phosphorus is rarer still: it is not, obviously, a part of carbohydrates storing the bulk of the planetary biomass, but it is also absent in nitrogen-rich protein. And yet neither complex sugars nor proteins can be made without it, as their synthesis is powered by energy released by the phosphate bond reversibly moving between adenosine diphosphate (ADP) and triphosphate (ATP).

Although about 45% of the standing phytomass of tropical rain forests, the largest repositories of global biomass, is carbon and at least 0.5% nitrogen, phosphorus makes up only about 0.03%. But vertebrate heterotrophs, whose muscles contain about 0.2% phosphorus, carry much more of the element in their skeletons. In an average adult, tricalcium phosphate makes up about 60% of noncellular bone structure and 70% of teeth. Our total bodily stores average nearly 3.5 kg of $Ca_5(PO_4)_3OH$, or 650 g P. We eat every day about 1.5 g of phosphorus, mostly in foods of animal origin, and excrete 98% of it as $NaNH_4HPO_4$ into sewage.

Although phosphorus does not have the ubiquity of carbon

or the frequent presence of nitrogen, phosphorus-containing compounds abound in industrial civilization (Emsley and Hall 1976; Toy 1976). For most of them, the starting point is the wet-acid process, which, through hydrogenation of phosphate rock – most commonly $Ca_5(PO_4)_3F$ – produces phosphoric acid. Fertilizers are the principal end-product of the wet process H_3PO_4. The bulk of the high-grade acid has been going into the synthesis of sodium tripolyphosphate ($Na_5P_3O_{10}$), used widely as an industrial deflocculant (to keep suspensions fine and mobile) and until the mid-1970s as the principal builder of detergents. Other relatively large phosphorus uses are in such diverse products as animal feeds, insecticides, metal surface and flameproofing treatments, matches, and oil additives.

Increasing rates of introduction of synthetic phosphorus compounds since the mid-19th century (the beginning of commercial production of phosphatic fertilizers) have greatly accelerated several key flows of biospheric phosphorus. Unlike carbon, nitrogen, and sulfur, phosphorus is not volatile and is not a part of any stable gaseous compound, and hence its biospheric flows have no significant atmospheric link from ocean to land. Even on a civilizational timescale (10^3 years), the grand phosphorus "cycle" is just a one-way flow with interruptions as terrestrial phosphorus is moving into the ocean.

On a geological time scale, the primary inorganic phosphate flows move in lockstep with slowly spreading sea-floors as oceanic phosphate deposits, aggraded by erosion and river transport, are returned to the land by tectonic uplift and the circle closes after 10^7–10^9 years. In contrast, the two secondary organic phosphorus flows work very promptly, with closures accomplished mostly in 10^{-1}–10^0 years. One is land-based, moving the nutrient from soils to plants and then making parts of decomposed plant and heterotrophic wastes again available for autotrophic production; the other is water-based, circulating phosphates between sediments and aquatic biota.

We can do nothing to change the timing of the tectonic return of phosphates to land. But mining of the phosphate rock and intensifying rates of phosphorus fertilization, as well as the conversion of forests and grasslands to cropfields, have accelerated the seaward flux of the element previously determined only by natural weathering and erosion. Consequently, I will focus on biospheric phosphorus in three ways: first looking at its noncycling global flows, and then concentrating on fertilization and on phosphorus in waters.

Phosphorus Pools and Flows – The Current Global Picture

Compared to the abundance of comprehensive evaluations of the nitrogen cycle, systematic quantifications of phosphorus reservoirs and fluxes have been rare. Stumm (1973) offered a basic set of five storage and six flux values, Delwiche and Likens (1977) summarized the principal storages and fluxes, Holland (1978) and Wollast (1981) quantified the oceanic segment of phosphorus flows, and Pierrou (1976) and Richey (1983) compiled fairly exhaustive records embrac-

ing all major biospheric compartments. As might be expected, substantial discrepancies exist.

Disregarding now largely exhausted guano deposits, currently mineable phosphate rocks are overwhelmingly in sedimentary marine ores (nearly nine-tenths of the global reserves), and the rest largely in igneous apatites (Lehr 1980; Sheldon 1982). The two leading producers, the United States and Morocco, mine marine carbonates containing 13.8–14.6% P. The spatial inequity of these deposits is astonishing: ten of the world's most populous poor nations with more than 50% of the global population and with enormous fertilization needs have a mere 5% of all high-quality reserves and extract just over 8% of worldwide tonnage.

Estimates of currently workable reserves vary, but the total is no less than 20 Pg, and known resources add up to a further 90 Pg (Cathcart 1980). Other resource estimates are as high as 300 Pg with 70 Pg of reserves. Annual production of phosphate rock in the mid-1980s was about 150 Tg (about 20 Tg P), with 80% going into fertilizers. In 1985, the actual annual production of phosphatic fertilizers was 16 Tg P, and consumption reached 15 Tg P (FAO 1986).

Assuming an average of 0.05% of inorganic phosphorus in the top 50 cm of soil and 13×10^9 ha of land area, the total reservoir would be about 40 Pg, or roughly 3 t P/ha. Organic phosphorus is well correlated with organic nitrogen, and with their average ratio at 1/12 and with at least 6 t organic N/ha, the global phosphorus storage would be about 6.5 Pg (500 kg P/ha), and total soil phosphorus reservoir would add up to nearly 50 Pg, or almost 4 t P/ha. Published estimates of seaward transport in rivers vary widely: for dissolved and particulate phosphorus, the range is 0.44–3.7 Tg, and a review of available measurements in major rivers favors the value of about 2 Tg (Holland 1978). Estimates of global erosion load carried by rivers add up to as little as 3.8 Pg/yr and as much as 58 Pg/yr. A total of about 10 Pg and a mean phosphorus sediment content of 0.12% would give about 12 Tg of solid phosphorus load, for a total of 14 Tg P moved by the rivers.

Larson et al. (1983) prepared a careful estimate of soil: erosion losses in the United States, showing an annual removal of 1.7 Tg of available phosphorus. Simply prorated to the global continent mass, this would give a total of about 24 Tg – but the U.S. flux obviously is much higher than the global mean. The best conclusion: 14–18 Tg P are moved each year oceanward by water. Values for phosphorus in ocean water are 80–128 Pg, and so 100 Pg may be a good approximation. Oceanic fluxes are highly uncertain, but their quantification is not as important to our inquiry. Vertical mixing may be circulating 50–70 Tg P/yr (Walsh 1984).

Some parts of the terrestrial phytomass contain relatively high shares of phosphorus. Most cereal grains and leguminous seeds have in excess of 0.3%, but phosphorus shares are low in forests. Even a liberal average of 0.2% phosphorus results in global accumulation of no more than 2,000 Tg P. A good estimate of phosphorus uptake in terrestrial phytomass can be made by using an average carbon/phosphorus ratio of 500 with the annual production of 100 Pg C, for a yearly total of 200 Tg P.

Transfers to soil must approximately balance the uptake:

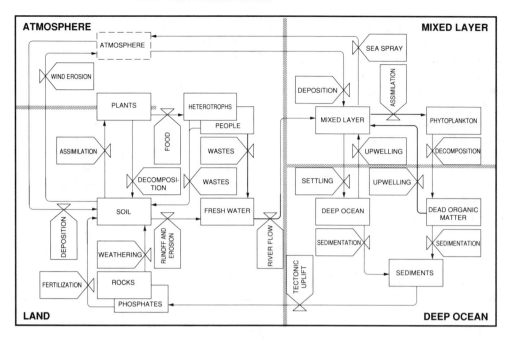

Figure 25.5 Principal reservoirs and flows of phosphorous compounds. Most of the corresponding values can be found in Table 25-3.

Table 25–3 *Global reservoirs and fluxes of phosphorus*

Reservoir		Storage (Tg P)
Phosphorus rock	resources	110,000–300,000
	reserves	20,000–70,000
Soil		40,000–160,000
Ocean	(dissolved P)	80,000–128,000
Phytomass		1,000–2,600
Zoomass		25
Anthropomass		2.5

Flux		Flows (Tg P/yr)
River transport		14–18
Phosphate rock mining	(1985)	20
Fertilizer applications	(1985)	15
Uptake by biota	terrestrial	200
	marine	600–1,000
Detritus	terrestrial	200
	marine	2–10
Vertical ocean mixing		50–70

These storage and flux estimates have been assembled from various sources by Richey (1983) or have come from the derivations described in the text.

the annual total is then also about 200 Tg P. Total global zoomass adds up to no more than 10 Pg, and with an average of 0.25% P, it would store about 25 Tg P. Anthropomass, with 5 billion people – average weight of 50 kg per capita and mean content of 1% – stores about 2.5 Tg P, or about a tenth of all heterotrophic mass. Principal biospheric reservoirs and fluxes of phosphorus are summarized in Fig. 25.5, and the ranges of estimated values are assembled in Table 15-3: the importance of human intervention in phosphorus flows is un-

mistakable, and the single largest interference is moving the nutrient from phosphate rocks to farm soils.

Phosphorus in Agriculture

Typical harvests now remove (in grains and straws) 15–35 kg P/ha of cereals, 15–25 kg P/ha in leguminous and root crops, and 5–15 kg P/ha in vegetables and fruits. Total phosphorus content of global crop production in the mid-1980s (including the harvested residues but excluding forages) was about 11.5 Tg. No combination of natural inputs could supply this amount of the nutrient: as with nitrogen, phosphorus fertilization is a critical civilizational practice whose growth is reversible only with cessation of global population increases and, in the industrialized countries, with a radical shift toward less meaty diets.

Before the introduction of phosphorus fertilizers derived from phosphate rocks, the extent of human intervention in agricultural phosphorus flows was very limited. For example, phosphorus requirements of a common eighteenth-century wheat harvest of 1.5 t/ha, removing about 8 kg P/ha in grain and straw, could be provided by mineralization of organic phosphorus in the soil (minimum of 3 kg P/ha) and by application of about 8–10 t/ha of livestock manure (containing most likely 8–12 kg P, including about 2 kg P from the harvested wheat straw used as bedding and feed).

Detailed appraisals for the United States show that recycled manures supply no more than 20% of actual phosphorus crop requirements (USDA 1978). Global estimates yield a similarly low share (Smil 1983). Total annual worldwide output of solid livestock wastes is now about 1.8 billion t, of which about one-third is actually recycled to fields. With an average of 0.5% P in the waste solids, this would amount to roughly 3 Tg P – compared to the total

Mining of phosphate rock (million tons)

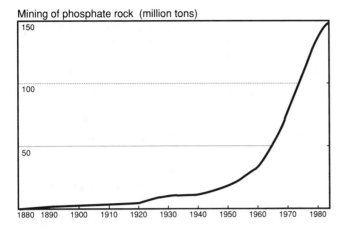

Figure 25.6 Global mining of phosphate rock. Data from Sauchelli 1965 and FAO 1986.

annual crop uptake of at least 11.5 Tg P, and hence an actual application need of some 18 Tg (assuming 65% utilization efficiency).

Search for more concentrated sources of phosphorus led to the treatment of phosphate rocks by diluted H_2SO_4, a practice pioneered by Sir John Bennett Lawes, Earl of Rothamsted. His experiments started in the early 1840s; by 1862 he had a continuous production line of 100 Mg ordinary superphosphate (OSP) a day, and by the 1870s the technique was spreading in Europe and the United States. Depending on the rock, the product contained 7–10.3% P (8.7% standard), an order of magnitude above phosphorus-rich organic wastes and more than the other new phosphorus fertilizer of the 1870s, with basic slag available as a by-product of smelting phosphatic iron ores, which contained 2–6.5% P. Consequently, phosphate rock mining took off.

The first commercial undertaking started in 1847 in Suffolk, followed in 1851 by apatite extraction in Norway, and in 1856 by rapidly expanding French operations, surpassed in the 1890s by American mining. Ever since, the United States has been by far the world's largest producer of phosphate rock. Two of the world's largest three producers were added between the world wars. Huge Moroccan deposits were identified in 1914, and their extraction commenced in 1921. The Soviets opened their high-grade apatite mines in the Khibini tundra of Kola Peninsula in 1930 and the Kazakhstan phosphate beds in 1937. The only sizable discoveries after World War II came in China and Jordan.

As shown in Fig. 25.6, between 1880 and 1985, extraction of phosphate rock increased exponentially, passing the 1 Tg/year mark in 1890, 10 Tg/year in the early 1920s, and 100 Tg/year in the mid-1970s. As with all cases of exponential growth, the long initial stage before reaching the J-bend added up to only a modest total: between 1850 and 1950 the cumulative transfer equaled only about two years of recent additions. During the 130 years of commercial phosphorus fertilization, the earth's soils received about 250 Tg P, or an equivalent of some 5% of arable soils' total phosphorus content.

The inevitable consequence of these large transfers is the intensification and acceleration of phosphorus cycling between farm soils and plants and the higher flux of the applied nutrient from soils to waters. Extensive land-use changes favoring higher erosion rates have further intensified the oceanward flux. The overall effect can be quantified roughly as follows.

Rivers unaffected by intensive farming and by large-volume dumping of wastes carry 30–300 µg P/l. If 100 µg P/l. would have been the prefertilization, presewage mean of the eighteenth century, the dissolved phosphorus P would have amounted to less than 4 Tg P/yr. Natural denudation of 1 m of lithosphere per 35,000 years would generate sediments carrying about 6 Tg P/yr. Therefore, the total preindustrial oceanward transfer could have been as low as 10 Tg P/yr – and the human activities would have been responsible for a 40–80% increase of this flux.

Another way to check the magnitude of this anthropogenic intervention is by estimating the effect of land-use changes. Assuming that between 1850 and 1980 the conversions of forests and grasslands to cropfields and settlements affected roughly 1 billion ha of land and were accompanied by average increase of 0.4 kg P/ha (from 0.1 to 0.5 kg P/ha in solution), the increment adds up to nearly 0.5 Tg P.

If the erosion in that land would have increased fourfold (from 1.5 to 6 t/ha) and if the average phosphorus concentration in sediments is taken as 0.075%, then the accelerated erosive transfer would be about 3.5 Tg, and the total intensification of land runoff would equal some 4 Tg P/yr, the total in excellent agreement with the differently derived estimates in the preceding paragraph. Settling on a well-rounded average, I would conclude that between 1850 and 1980 human actions have intensified global waterborne phosphorus flux by at least 50%.

The mean global annual application is now about 10 kg P/ha of arable land, with continental averages ranging from less than 3 kg/ha for Africa to over 25 kg/ha in Europe, and the highest national rates around 70 kg/ha. The fate of fertilizer phosphorus after application has been among a few key preoccupations of soil science for more than a century (Khasawneh, Sample, and Kamprath, 1980). Compared to nitrogen, the nutrient is relatively insoluble and hence immobile, and the plants had to evolve the ability to absorb it from extremely dilute solutions and to concentrate it 10^2–10^3-times to satisfy their growth needs.

But it is the complexity of chemical reactions in soils and the ensuing question of nutrient availability that have dominated the interest in phosphorus behavior. What portion of the nutrient is irreversibly fixed in the soil soon after the application and how much remains in forms utilizable by succeeding crops? The traditional, and once widely accepted, view of phosphorus fixation was that the major part of applied phosphorus was rather quickly tied up by the soil, piling up in unavailable forms. According to this view, phosphorus fertilization was largely a costly exercise in mass transfer of the element from phosphate rocks to insoluble soil compounds: mining it in Florida or Morocco, spending a good deal of energy to produce fertilizers (18–32 MJ/kg P, depending on the final product), and then having most of the nutrient irreversibly incorporated in the farm soils.

In practical terms, this misconception led to irrational use of fertilizers: worldwide N/P ratio was as low as 1.6 immediately after the World War II, and it passed 2.0 only in 1955; by 1970 it was about 3.5, and now it is over 4.5. Clearly, the efficiency of phosphorus utilization in most agroecosystems is not as dismal as implied by the traditional view of speedy and massive fixation. Retention of fertilizer phosphorus should be seen as a continuous process involving precipitation, chemisorption, and adsorption, and producing a large variety of products, many of which are initially metastable (Sample, Super, and Panoz, 1980).

Karlovsky's (1981) evaluation found that most of the agroecosystems had phosphorus utilization efficiencies of 70–90%. Karlovsky also calculated an approximate global average of phosphorus utilization in field cropping as 80%. I have prepared a more detailed global calculation for 1985 showing crop uptake of at least 11.5 Tg P, fertilizer applications of 12 Tg (80% of the total, the remainder going into permanent plantations, pastures, and forests), and organic recycling (animal wastes and crop residues) of 4 Tg. This would imply phosphorus utilization efficiency of about 70% (11.5/16).

Clearly, human intervention in global phosphorus flows cannot be seen as a largely helpless question of "digging out phosphorus at one place and storing it in the soil at another" (Tinker 1977). Utilization of the applied and the recycled phosphorus by crops is at least as efficient as that of the other two macronutrients. Problems with phosphorus in waters have not resulted from excessive fertilization or inferior nutrient utilization. Rather they are the consequence of the extraordinarily sensitive phytoplanktonic response to the presence of the available nutrient in water. Even so, fertilization is only of secondary importance in this response, as phosphorus from wastes is almost always dominant in the eutrophication process.

The total mass of wastes is small in absolute global terms. Assuming an addition of 4 billion people, the additional flux compared to the preindustrial era would be about 2 Tg P/yr, but most of it continues to be deposited on soils; even if one-half would be dumped into waters, the increment would be about 1 Tg P/yr. But since the introduction of urban sewage and the rapid growth of cities, its concentrated nature, combined with the sensitive response of aquatic autotrophs to phosphorus enrichment, has been the cause of eutrophication.

Phosphorus in Waters

Enrichment of waters with phosphorus supplies the nutrient whose naturally limited concentrations are the greatest obstacle to profuse growth of aquatic plants. Inadvertent fertilization of ponds, lakes, estuaries and, to a much lesser extent, running waters, creates eutrophic conditions and results in profuse algal growths, whose presence and decay has a variety of undesirable consequences ranging from aesthetic offenses to economic losses.

As Schindler (1985) stresses, there appears to be no mechanism in freshwater ecosystems allowing adjustments in the phosphorus cycle to maintain appropriate nutrient ratios (C106/N16/P1 for typical algae growth). But once phosphorus is added, nitrogen and carbon cycling will respond promptly. Moreover, phosphorus-driven increase in production is not easily toxified, and hence even wastes with relatively high heavy-metal levels can be an effective source of phosphorus. Consequently, in an overwhelming majority of cases, the availability of phosphorus stimulates complex ecosystemic mobilization of other nutrients to secure the proportions preferred by the plants, and the primary aquatic productivity is directly proportional to the supply of the element.

Concerns about eutrophication became prominent during the late 1960s, and they were much accentuated owing to the prevailing intensity of scientific and public interest in environmental pollution. Complexities of eutrophication have been the subject of numerous major publications between Vollenweider's (1968) pioneering study and recent surveys (Brock 1985; Stumm 1985).

Reliable long-term documentation of increased aquatic phosphorus loading is rare, but the trends in industrialized countries have been obvious. First occurred a century of slow increase, starting with the introduction of urban sewage and phosphorus-fertilization after 1840 in western Europe and North America and lasting until the 1940s, when came the introduction of phosphate detergents and rapid increases of agricultural phosphorus applications. This resulted in exponentially growing phosphorus inputs until the early 1970s. Since then a moderation of fertilization growth rates combined with lower phosphorus inflow in urban wastes ended the spell of exponential increases; phosphorus concentrations in the Thames and Rhine rivers document these trends (Fig. 25.7).

The contribution of various sources to increased aquatic phosphorus loading cannot be quantified with confidence, even for small ecosystems. Fertilization produces by far the highest areal loading, on the order of 10^1 kg P/ha: 10 kg P/ha is actually the current global average, and 20–30 kg P/ha can be taken as the most common range for intensively farmed areas. Typically, no more than 2–3% of the applied fertilizer will be leached (extremes of 1–5%), which translates to a mere 0.2–0.6 kg P/ha. Losses from fertilized pastures will

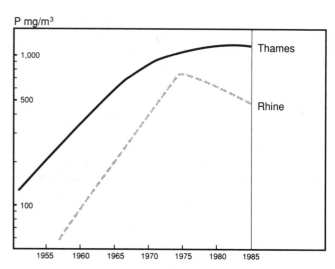

Figure 25.7 History of phosphate levels in the Thames and Rhine rivers. Data from Stumm 1973 and World Resources Report 1986.

rarely be over 0.3 kg and are commonly below 0.2 kg P/ha. Leaching rates from managed intensive forest plantings are lower still: even with applications of more than 200 kg P/ha in intensive short-rotation coniferous plantations, the escape amounted to less than 0.1%, or below 0.2 kg P/ha/yr. In less intensively managed forests, the losses will be well below 0.1 kg P/ha.

Generation of animal wastes is highly variable. The worldwide total of 9 Tg P prorated over 4.4×10^9 ha of crop-fields and pastures results in a mean rate of about 2 kg P/ha. In areas of high cattle density, however, with up to three heads/ha of pasture, the annual deposition of manurial phosphorus may be as high as 12 kg/ha, and large feedlots holding thousands of animals are highly concentrated sources of waste phosphorus, with generation densities easily in the order of 10^2 kg P/ha.

With washout rates of no more than 3%, animal wastes would thus add typically 0.05–0.2 kg P/ha of agricultural land so that the global mean of total farmland (croplands and pastures) phosphorus exports would be as low as 0.25 kg P/ha and the levels characterizing intensively farmed regions would be largely 0.4–0.8 kg P/ha. In an overwhelming majority of cases, these contributions will be surpassed by production of human and industrial wastes.

With an average daily excretion of 1.5 g P per capita production of human wastes preindustrial societies added no more than about 3 kg P/ha, and in many regions most of these wastes were recycled rather than simply dumped. Urban wastes, produced with even higher densities, were an eagerly sought fertilizer. With rapid urbanization and widespread introduction of sewers after 1840, the bulk of human waste generation has shifted into a relatively small number of large and often highly concentrated sources that use water as the easiest, most convenient sink. Current country-wide generation rates in Egypt or Japan are as high as 9 kg P/ha of cultivated and settled land. In the United States, the mean is only 0.6 kg, and the global average about 2 kg P/ha. In most cities with populations over 1 million people, the rates are an order of magnitude higher, that is 50–100 kg P/ha of urban area. In Shanghai proper, where 6 million people live on 158 km², the rate is about 210 kg P/ha!

All of these rates refer only to human wastes, whereas urban sewage contains additional phosphorus from a variety of domestic and industrial sources. Among these contributions synthetic detergents have received most attention. They were first sold in 1933 but made major market inroads only after World War II. In the United States, they captured over 50% of cleaners' sales by 1953 and passed the 75% mark a decade later. Sodium pyrophosphate or polyphosphate, low-cost compounds highly effective in binding dissolved metal ions and in supporting emulsification, were thus entering sewage in ever larger quantities, and in North American urban areas they contributed as much as 35% of all dumped phosphorus.

The combination of human wastes, detergents, and releases from industrial uses in urban sewage added up to at least 0.9 kg P per capita each year, in some instances up to 1.6 kg. The value of 1.3 kg P per capita each year was often suggested

as typical. These values translate into 80–150 (typical level, about 120) kg P/ha for most large Western urban areas in which at least 80–85% of all wastes are sewered.

As most of this sewage used to receive no treatment or was only inadequately controlled, contributions of agricultural runoff in any basin containing large urbanized populations will shrink to secondary proportions. The approximate global breakdown of farming and municipal phosphorus exports per unit area of farmed and settled land is 15% versus 85%.

During the 1960s and 1970s, in the United States waste-water shares accounted for 84% of the total phosphorus input in the Potomac River, 73% in the Hudson River, 72% in the Lake Erie basin, 69% in the Chesapeake Bay, and 60% in the San Joaquin delta (Jaworski 1981). Obviously, the most effective way to reduce phosphorus loading of waters is to control urban wastes. However, even the less important sources exporting relatively small amounts of phosphorus can cause eutrophication of those standing water bodies that are shallow and have long hydraulic residence times. Vollenweider (1976) expressed this proneness to eutrophication by relating total phosphorus loading (g P/m²/yr) to the quotient of mean depth (m) and hydraulic residence time (Fig. 25.8).

A simple example illustrates the importance of environmental factors. Typical fertilized farmland exports of 0.5 kg P/ha mean that a mere 200 ppb of phosphorus in solution will be washed away by 25-cm runoff (easily a summer mean in western Europe or eastern North America). A 2-ha, 3-m-deep lake draining 20 ha of such farmland, with inflow of 2 m³/min, will be oligotrophic; with 1 m³/min, it may be mesotrophic; with 0.5 m³/min, clearly eutrophic. The extremely low threshold of algal response to phosphorus enrichment makes it thus impossible to control eutrophication of some water bodies without abstaining from fertilization, that is, in practice, without returning the cropland to permanent pasture or forest.

In contrast, estuaries of the Tyne and the Thames rivers, whose phosphorus loadings are perhaps the highest recorded

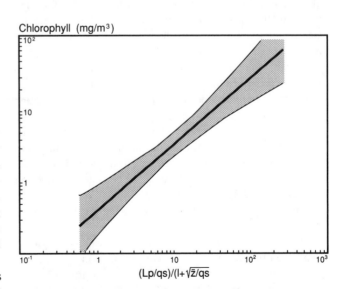

Figure 25.8 Relationship between phosphorus loading, mean water body depth, and hydraulic residence time. Source: Vollenweider 1976.

worldwide (as much as 190 and 110 g P/m²/yr, respectively), have no major algal blooms, owing to their short retention time. Moreover, primary production in estuaries is more likely to be nitrogen-limited, and the reduction of phosphorus in urban washes can lead to relatively rapid shifts from hypertrophic to eutrophic or from eutrophic to mesotrophic conditions with an outlook for further improvement. Changes in the Chesapeake Bay since the late 1970s are an excellent example of these possibilities (Lung 1986).

Managing the Interferences

Historically, the first control technique involving nitrogen releases was simple sedimentation of wastewater. This primary purification removes merely a portion of particulate organic matter (and so less than 20% of total nitrogen). Currently, the best available method to control nitrogen levels is biological nitrification-denitrification, a sequence that first converts the more offensive organic and NH_3-N into NO_3-N and then returns it to the atmosphere as N_2. When well run, 95% of total nitrogen is stripped from the treated wastewater (De Renzo 1978).

Proper fertilization and good agronomic practices can lower nitrogen losses by appreciable margins. The most obvious ones concern the timing of application and the placement of fertilizers: delaying the major application until some time after planting and incorporating the fertilizer into the soil are always the two most effective measures. A variety of soil-conservation practices ranging from contour and strip cropping to no-till farming cuts down the erosion losses. And legume-grain rotations can greatly economize the application rates. Good seedbed preparation, timely sowing, sufficient moisture, and good pest-control management are all manageable agronomic factors whose neglect may lead to huge cumulative nitrogen fertilizer losses.

Karlovsky's (1981) calculations of fertilizer efficiency show that nearly all of the studied agroecosystems have nitrogen efficiencies in excess of 50%, and my detailed evaluation for all American cropland indicates an overall nitrogen efficiency of about 60%. These are not inferior values, but they can be clearly improved to make the human intervention in the soil nitrogen cycle more acceptable.

Considerable progress already has been made in controlling NO_x emissions from two of the largest sources – gasoline-fueled passenger cars and large, thermal electricity-generating stations. Successful control techniques for vehicular NO_x include either modifications of the combustion process or treatment of exhaust gases. As shown by the recent Japanese efforts, the first approach, including lean carburetion, secondary air injection, and exhaust-gas recirculation, can bring impressive reductions of NO_x emissions, and the strict Japanese standards can be met by relying on these adjustments alone.

In contrast, the American automakers decided to augment these controls with catalytic converters and commercial installations of the three-way catalysis, controlling CO, hydrocarbons, and NO_x, started in 1981. These efforts lowered the emissions from their precontrol levels of 2.5 g NO_x/km to around 0.5 g, whereas the best of Japanese techniques can achieve as little as 0.13 g NO_x/km. Values well below 0.25 g should be generally achievable by the year 2000.

Control of NO_x from large stationary sources also relies on modifications of combustion, with the efforts aimed at lowering flame temperature, excess air, and residence time of fuel and air in the furnace chamber, and thus reducing formation of high-temperature NO_x. Maximum reductions of NO_x emissions have been approximately 50% for coal-fired units and as much as 90% for natural-gas furnaces. The latest designs raise the performance in coal-fired units up to 85%, that is emissions of around 150 ppm NO_x, but controlling to below 100 ppm would require expensive, and now still experimental, flue-gas treatment.

The diversity of anthropogenic nitrogen sources requires a multitude of controls ranging from efforts to reduce release rates to minimization of conversion losses to techniques for near-complete removal of the nutrient. Effective approaches now exist to manage all undesirable flows – except for denitrification, which is, of course, absolutely necessary, but whose stepwise reactions we would always prefer to end in N_2 rather than partially in N_2O in order to minimize potential risks that this oxide may give to stratospheric O_3.

Massive intervention in the biospheric nitrogen cycle through fertilizing has no practical alternatives in the world of growing populations and expanding meat production. Although our quantitative knowledge of nitrogen flows in agroecosystems remains unsatisfactory (Rosswall and Paustian 1984), enough is known to make human intervention compatible with both permanent cropping and minimization

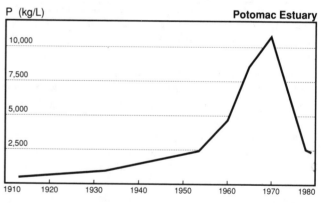

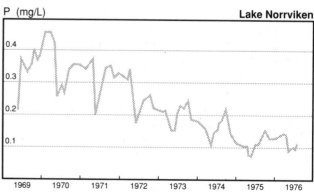

Figure 25.9 Trends of phosphate levels in Lake Norrviken (Sweden) and in the Chesapeake Bay. Data from Schindler 1973 and Jaworski 1981.

of undesirable environmental change. Although both extensive and intensive, human interference in the nitrogen cycle is manageable with relative ease and without excessive cost. Fortunately, a similar conclusion applies to our intervention in the flows of biospheric phosphorus.

Restoration of waters with excessive phosphorus loading is a practical possibility, and the reduction of phosphorus inputs is the most effective measure. Since the early 1970s, this reduction has been achieved largely by restricting or banning the use of phosphorus-containing detergents and by the removal of phosphorus from wastewaters. As illustrated by the examples of Lake Norrviken in Sweden and the Chesapeake Bay, such measures have rapid positive effects (Fig. 25.9). Simple settling removes only 5–10%, secondary treatment with trickling filters captures 10–20%, and activated sludge, 15–40%. The best control is achieved with chemically simple precipitation of phosphorus in insoluble salts after the addition of metals, either as $FePO_4$ (when using $FeCl_3$ or $FeCl_2$), or $AlPO_4$ (after adding $Al_2(SO_4)_3$), or $Ca_5(PO_4)_3OH$ (after treatment with lime) (De Renzo 1978).

Taking a typical American wastewater volume of 40 l. per person per day, the capital cost of phosphorus-removal facilities added to water-treatment plants would be most likely (in 1987 dollars) \$1.50–4.50 per person, and the cost of chemicals to precipitate phosphorus from wastewater would be 0.75–1.5¢ per person per day, or about \$2.75–5.50 per person per year.

The earlier concerns about bleak phosphorus recovery prospects owing to the permanent recycling of sedimentary phosphorus in lakes with hypolimnetic anoxia proved misplaced. Internal phosphorus cycling is sensitive to external inputs: phosphorus return from anoxic sediments declines fast after the outside inflow is eliminated. Lowering of lake phosphorus concentration also can be attempted by two internal measures: namely, by increasing phosphorus export by diversion of hypolimnic water with its high phosphorus levels, and by prolonging phosphorus retention through higher sedimentation or lowered redissolution (Gachter and Imboden 1985). Artificial mixing to destroy stratification and hypolimnetic oxygenation are other possibilities.

Encouraging results have been documented within less than a decade of reduced phosphorus loadings. In North America, the U.S. Federal Water Pollution Control Act Amendments and U.S.-Canadian Water Quality Agreement restricted all point sources discharging more than 3,800 m³/day to concentrations of less than 1 mg P/l, in 1972 in the Lake Erie and Ontario basins, and in 1978 to the entire Great Lakes basin. By 1980, Lake Ontario showed a substantial response in terms of spring phosphorus levels and less polluted sections of the lakes – such as Huron's Saginaw Bay with total phosphorus loading declining by 55% between 1974 and 1980 – had large chlorophyll concentrations drops and substantial decrease in threshold odor in the municipal water (Bierman et al. 1984).

In comparison with much larger, incomparably more mobile and much more difficult-to-control biospheric fluxes of nitrogen, anthropogenic phosphorus mobilization has considerably smaller environmental consequences, which are also much easier to manage. Utilization of fertilizer phosphorus is as high as or higher than that of other nutrients, and the element's low mobility prevents its widespread environmental diffusion.

As the element is not doubly mobile, its environmental effects are not worldwide, and its presence in some waters is the only worrisome flux. Eutrophication is a natural process, and the normal prospect for lakes is to disappear. Human intervention is thus quite along the expected evolutionary lines – but the much accelerated rate of change is seen as unacceptable. Compared to natural eutrophication, high phosphorus loadings may increase a lake's aging rate by up to two orders of magnitude. Control of phosphorus-rich wastes in urban sewage is only a marginal addition to proper water-treatment facilities, however, and eutrophication has, in a great majority of cases, a ready technical fix.

References

Aldrich, S. R. 1980. *Nitrogen in Relation to Food, Environment, and Energy*. Urbana-Champaign, IL: University of Illinois Press.

Bierman, V. J., D. M. Dolan, and R. Kasprzyk. 1984. Retrospective analysis of the response of Saginaw Bay, Lake Huron, to reductions in phosphorus loadings. *Environmental Science and Technology* 18:23–31.

Brock, T. D. 1985. *Eutrophic Lake*. New York: Springer-Verlag.

Burns, R. C., and R. W. F. Hardy. 1975. *Nitrogen Fixation in Bacteria and Higher Plants*. Berlin: Springer-Verlag.

Cathcart, J. B. 1980. World phosphate reserves and resources. In F. E. Khasawneh et al., eds., op. cit., 1–18.

Commoner, B. 1971. *The Closing Circle*. New York: Knopf.

Delwiche, C. C. 1977. Energy relations in the global nitrogen cycle. *Ambio* 6:106–111.

———, ed. 1981. *Denitrification, Nitrification, and Atmospheric Nitrous Oxide*. New York: John Wiley.

Delwiche, C. C., and G. E. Likens. 1977. Biological response to fossil-fuel combustion products. In: *Global Chemical Cycles and Their Alteration by Man*, ed. W. Stumm, 61–72. Dahlem Konferenzen, Berlin.

De Renzo, D. J., ed. 1978. *Nitrogen Control and Phosphorus Removal in Sewage Treatment*. Noyes Data Corporation, Park Ridge, NJ.

Dixon, R. O. D., and C. T. Wheeler. 1986. *Nitrogen Fixation in Plants*. London: Chapman and Hall.

Emsley, J., and D. Hall. 1976. *The Chemistry of Phosphorus*. London: Harper & Row.

Fertilizer Institute. 1976. *The Fertilizer Handbook*. Washington, D.C.: Fertilizer Institute.

Food and Agriculture Organization. 1986. *1985 Fertilizer Yearbook*. Rome: FAO.

Frissel, M. J., and G. J. Kolenbrander. 1977. The nutrient balances. *Agro-Ecosystems* 4: 277–92.

Gachter, R., and M. Imboden. 1985. Lake restoration. In: W. Stumm, ed., op. cit., 365–88.

Holland, H. D. 1978. *The Chemistry of the Atmosphere and Oceans*. New York: John Wiley & Sons.

Jaworski, N. A. 1981. Sources of nutrients and the scale of eutrophication problems in estuaries. In B. J. Neilson and L. E. Cronin, eds., op. cit., 83–110.

Karlovsky, J. 1981. Cycling of nutrients and their utilization by plants in agricultural ecosystems. *Agro-Ecosystems* 2:127–44.

Khasawneh, F. E., E. C. Sample, and E. J. Kamprath, eds. 1980. *The Role of Phosphorus in Agriculture*. Madison, WI: American Society of Agronomy.

Kolenbrander, G. J. 1972. Does leaching of fertilizers affect the quality of groundwater at the waterworks? *Stikstof* 15:8–15.

Larson, W. E. et al. 1983. The threat of soil erosion to long-term crop production. *Science* 219:458–65.

La Rue, T. A., and T. G. Patterson. 1981. How much nitrogen do legumes fix?: *Advances in Agronomy* 34:15–30.

Lehr, J. R. 1980. Phosphate raw materials and fertilizers. In F. E. Khasawneh et al., eds., op. cit., 81–120.

Lung, W. S. 1986. Phosphorus loads to the Chesapeake Bay: a perspective. *Journal WPCF* 58:749–56.

Neilson, B. J., and L. E. Cronin, eds. 1981. *Estuaries and Nutrients.* Clifton, NJ: Humana Press.

Newton, W. E., and W. H. Orme-Johnson, eds. 1980. *Nitrogen Fixation.* Baltimore, MD: University Park Press.

Pierrou, U. 1976. The global phosphorus cycle. *Ecological Bulletin* 22:75–88.

Rajagopal, R., and R. L. Talcott. 1983. Patterns in groundwater quality. *Environmental Management* 7:465–74.

Richey, J. E. 1983. The phosphorus cycle. In *The Major Biogeochemical Cycles and Their Interactions*, ed. B. Bolin and R. B. Cook, 51–56. New York: Wiley.

Rosswall, T. 1983. The nitrogen cycle. In *The Major Biogeochemical Cycles and Their Interactions*, ed. B. Bolin and R. B. Cook, 41–50. New York: Wiley.

Rosswall, T., and K. Paustian. 1984. Cycling of nitrogen in modern agricultural systems. *Plant and Soil* 76:3–21.

Royal Society Study Group Staff. 1984. *Nitrogen Cycle of the United Kingdom.* London: Royal Society.

Sample, E. C., R. L. Super, and G. J. Ranoz, 1980. Reactions of phosphate fertilizers in soils. In F. E. Khasawneh et al., eds., op. cit., 263–310.

Sauchelli, V. 1965. *Phosphorus in Agriculture.* New York: Reinhold.

Schindler, D. W. 1985. The coupling of elemental cycles by organisms. In W. Stumm, ed., op. cit., 225–50.

Schnell, R. C., ed. 1986. *Geophysical Monitoring for Climatic Change.* No. 14. Boulder, CO: U.S. Data Center.

Sheldon, R. 1982. Phosphate rock. *Scientific American* 246(6):45–51.

Smil, V. 1983. *Biomass Energies.* New York: Plenum Press.

——. 1985. *Carbon-Nitrogen-Sulfur Human Interference in Grand Biospheric Cycles.* New York: Plenum Press.

Soderlund, R., and B. H. Svensson. 1976. The global nitrogen cycle. *Ecological Bulletin* 22:23–73.

Stevenson, F. J., ed. 1982. *Nitrogen in Agricultural Soils.* Madison, WI: American Society of Agronomy.

Stumm, W. 1973. The acceleration of the hydrogeochemical cycling of phosphorus. *Water Research* 7:131–44.

——, ed. 1985. *Chemical Processes in Lakes.* New York: John Wiley & Sons.

Tinker, P. B. 1977. Economy and chemistry of phosphorus. *Nature* 270:103–104.

Toy, A. D. F. 1976. *Phosphorus Chemistry in Everyday Life.* Washington, D.C.: American Chemical Society.

U.S. Department of Agriculture 1978. *Improving Soils with Organic Wastes.* Washington, D.C.: U.S. Department of Agriculture, Organization for Economic Cooperation and Development.

Vincent, J. M., ed. 1982. *Nitrogen Fixation in Legumes.* New York: Academic Press.

Vollenweider, R. A. 1968. *Scientific Fundamentals of the Eutrophication of Lakes and Flowing Waters with Particular Reference to Nitrogen and Phosphorus As Factors of Eutrophication* Paris: OECD.

——. 1976. Advances in defining critical loading levels of phosphorus in lake eutrophication. *Mem. Ist. Ital. Idrobiol.* 33:53–83.

Walsh, J. J. 1984. The role of ocean biota in accelerated ecological cycles: a temporal view. *Bio Science* 34:499–507.

Wines, R. A. 1985. *Fertilizer in America.* Philadelphia: Temple University Press.

Wollast, R. 1981. Interactions between major biogeochemical cycles in marine ecosystems. In *Some Perspectives of the Major Biogeochemical Cycles*, ed. G. E. Likens, 125–42. Chichester: John Wiley.

World Resources Report. 1986. *World Resources 1986.* New York: Basic Books.

Appendix A *List of chemical formulas of nitrogen and phosphorus compounds*

N	nitrogen
N_2	dinitrogen (molecular N)
NO_x	nitrogen oxides (NO and NO_2)
NO	nitric oxide
NO_2	nitrogen dioxide
N_2O	nitrous oxide
NH_3	ammonia
NH_4^+	ammonium cation
HNO_3	nitric acid
NO_3^-	nitrate anion
P	phosphorus
H_3PO_4	phosphoric acid
$Ca_5(PO_4)_3F$	apatite
$NaNH_4HPO_4$	ammonium phosphate
$Na_5P_3O_{10}$	sodium tripolyphosphate
$AlPO_4$	aluminum phosphate
$FePO_4$	iron phosphate

26

Trace Pollutants

HALINA SZEJNWALD BROWN   ROGER E. KASPERSON   SUSAN SWEDIS RAYMOND

For purposes of this analysis, we define trace pollutants as *the undesired contaminants present in an environmental medium at concentrations ranging from less than a part per billion to parts per million*. Even with this definition, the potential list of agents is virtually unlimited. To bound the task and to focus on those trace pollutants with the greatest potential contribution to global transformation during the past 300 years, we limit our analysis to agents generated by the large-scale human activities of metal mining and utilization and organic chemical manufacturing and use (Fig. 26.1). These activities, in addition to energy generation (whose effects are discussed elsewhere in this volume), in our view carry the greatest potential for human action to transform the long-term global configuration of trace pollutants.

The relationship among these broadly defined human activities and the generation of pollutants is not unique, we hasten to note. A particular environmental pollutant usually originates from multiple activities, and conversely, any one activity commonly generates multiple pollutants. The multiplicity of causal relationships between human activities and the trace pollutants calls for multiple data bases and diverse analytic tools. Our data base draws upon the results of environmental monitoring as well as production, consumption, and emission

Spatial

	Local *Short-lived*	Global *Short-lived*
Temporal	Local *Persistent*	Global *Persistent*

Figure 26.2 Patterns in environmental fate of trace pollutants.

information. Each source has its limitations, and typically the data are fraught with gaps and inconsistencies.

The patterns of environmental movement and accumulation in environmental compartments and biota can be characterized in many ways. We have chosen to focus on two that are central themes of this symposium – the spatial and the temporal. Thus, we group the trace pollutants broadly into (1) locally concentrated and globally diffuse and (2) short-lived and persistent. Conceptually, the possible combination of these characteristics suggests a simple two-by-two matrix (Fig. 26.2).

The two sets of variables – spatial and temporal – are not independent. For instance, one would expect pollutants with short residence times in the environment to have mostly localized effects, and conversely, the persistent pollutants certainly to have a greater potential for global distribution and global effects. We should expect, therefore, most trace pollutants to cluster in the two diagonally located quadrangles – the upper left and the lower right.

The structuring of the analysis points to certain research questions. For trace pollutants with global/persistent effects, geographic shifts in the centers of production may be less important than cumulative worldwide production trends. For trace pollutants with local/short-lived effects, the reverse is true. For the pollutants with the other two combinations of effects, both types of data may be equally important. Within the limits of this analysis, we assess what is known about the

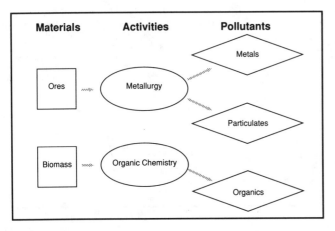

Figure 26.1 Relationship between industrial activities and environmental releases.

temporal and geographic patterns of these pollutants in the environment, and their effects on humans, ecosystems, and the planet Earth generally.

Mining and Use of Heavy Metals

World production of most metals has grown rapidly during the past 300 years (Fig. 26.3). Not only have production volumes increased exponentially, but the number of metals produced in large quantities has multiplied over time. This growth in total quantities and in the variety of metals produced has been linked in part to the demands of the electronics and space industries and to military uses (Huisken 1975; Nriagu 1980).

Both natural and human activities introduce trace metals into the environment. Anthropogenic sources include production-related activities such as mining, smelting, energy generation, manufacturing, and agriculture; and consumption-related activities such as use, wear, and disposal of consumer and commercial products. Among the production-related activities, the high-temperature processes are significant contributors to metal pollution, mainly through direct emissions of fine particles and gases into the ambient air. Activity-specific, high-temperature emissions are listed in Table 26-1 for a select group of heavy metals. The relative contributions of the individual activities differ among metals.

As shown in Table 26-1, the bulk of the arsenic and cadmium emissions comes from metal smelters, whereas selenium is primarily contributed by coal combustion. Lead is introduced mostly by combustion of leaded gasoline. Finally, environmental mercury is introduced by a mixture of technologic activities, with energy generation responsible for approximately 50% of the total. Combining the emissions from coal, wood, and petroleum combustion (excluding lead) also shows that, with the exception of selenium, energy generation by direct combustion of wood and fossil fuels contributes only a small part of total anthropogenic loading of heavy metals into the environment and that most of it originates from other activities, as graphically illustrated for arsenic, cadmium, lead, and mercury in Fig. 26.4. Table 26-1 also shows that the contribution from natural sources is an order of magnitude smaller than that from high-temperature industrial activities, and most likely represents only a very small fraction of the total anthropogenic loading.

In addition to the production-related processes, the normal use and wear of consumer and commercial products are an important source of these releases. According to Tarr and Ayres (chap. 38), the dissipative consumption includes: weathering of paints and pigments (silver, arsenic, chromium, cadmium, copper, mercury, lead, and zinc); incineration of discarded pharmaceuticals (silver, arsenic, chromium, and zinc), batteries (mercury, cadmium), electronic tubes (mercury), plastics (zinc), and photographic film (silver); wear and weathering of electroplated surfaces (cadmium), leather (chromium), plastics (zinc); and decomposition or combustion of treated wood (arsenic, chromium, copper). Whereas ambient air is the principal initial target of metal emissions from some of these processes, such as incineration of discarded materials and combustion of treated wood, it is the

soil and surface waters that receive the bulk of the emissions from dissipative consumption, mainly via surface runoff and sewage-treatment plants.

The relative contributions of consumption-related and production-related emissions to the total environmental loading of metals, either in the United States or worldwide, are largely unknown. In the United States, the environmental agencies traditionally have focused their attention on emissions from industrial and energy-generating sources into the air and surface waters, such as those listed in Table 26-1. More recently, discharges into soil and groundwater from agricultural activities and landfills have also become of concern. The inventories thus collected over the years provide information primarily on emissions from these activities and ignore the ubiquitous, highly diverse, and dissipated sources of metals associated with weathering and wear of myriads of consumer products. Comparison of the 1983 worldwide production of lead and mercury (Fig. 26.3), with their respective annual emissions from mining, smelting, and industrial processes combined (Table 26-1), shows that, at least for these two metals, most of the mass present in consumer and commercial products is not accounted for by emission inventories such as that shown in Table 26-1. Their ultimate environmental fate is not known. Tarr and Ayres (chap. 38) argue that a significant fraction of that unaccounted mass of material is mobilized and introduced into the environment through consumption-related processes. That these processes may in some areas be the primary source of trace-metal pollution is illustrated by Tarr and Ayres for several metals in the Hudson-Raritan basin.

Clearly, the contribution from dissipative consumption will vary with the industrial and agricultural traditions of a region, population density, technological development, wealth, and other variables. Therefore, although the data for metal emis-

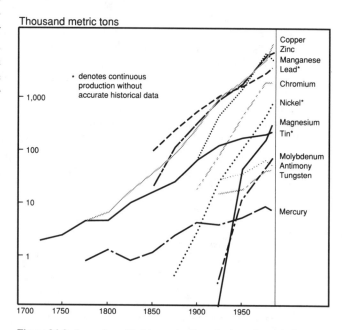

Figure 26.3 Annual worldwide production of selected metals from 1700 to 1983. Data from Schmitz 1979 and Minerals Yearbook 1984.

Table 26-1 *Global annual average contributions of trace elements from natural and anthropogenic high-temperature processes (1983)*

		Arsenic	Cadmium	Lead	Selenium	Mercury
				(thousands of metric tons)		
Natural						
Dust		0.24	0.25	10	0.3	0.03
Volcanoes		7	0.5	6.4	0.1	0.03
Forest fires		0.16	0.01	0.05		0.1
Vegetation		0.26	0.2	1.6		
Sea salt		0.14	0.002	0.1		0.003
	Total	7.8	0.96	18.6	0.4	0.16
Anthropogenic						
Mining		—	—	8.1	0.005	—
Smelting of nonferrous metals		15.2	5.3	77.2	0.28	0.29
Iron production		4.3	0.1	50.0	0.01	0.45
Other industrial activities		—	0.04	7.2	0.05	—
Waste incineration		0.4	1.4	9.0	—	—
Phosphorus fertilizer production		2.6	0.2	—	—	—
Coal combustion		0.5	0.05	13.9	0.68	0.63
Wood combustion		0.5	0.2	1.0	—	—
Petroleum combustion		—	—	273.0*	0.06	0.27
	Total	23.6	7.3	449	1.1	1.8

Source: Nriagu and Davidson 1986.

*Lead is introduced into the environment primarily from combustion of leaded gasoline. Since this may be considered a secondary source, it may be listed under the category of "other industrial activities."

sions into the Hudson-Raritan basin cannot be generalized to the rest of the country or to the world, three important conclusions emerge from that study:

1. Dissipative consumption contributes a significant, and in some cases, the largest fraction of total loading of metals into the environment.
2. Efforts to decrease releases of metals by way of pollution-control technology and strict regulations address only part of the problem and, in fact, increase the relative contribution from consumption-related activities.
3. Mass balance of environmental pollution by metals must include the contribution from dissipative uses, in addition to the more obvious emissions from industry and power plants.

Metals emitted into the ambient air from various sources are carried different distances by the winds, depending on their state (gaseous, vapor, or particulate) before they fall or are washed out of the air onto land or the surface of the oceans. Deposition rates to soils from atmospheric lead in selected areas of North America and Europe are shown in Table 26-2. In the case of particulate matter, particle size is the decisive factor. Most metals associated with coarse particulate matter are deposited within 10 km of the point of emission. For the gaseous phase, deposition can take place 200–2,000 km from a source (Schroeder and Lane 1988). The gaseous phase is important for the aerial transport of mercury, arsenic, cadmium, lead, antimony, selenium, and zinc (Friberg, Nordberg, and Vouk 1979). The generally short atmospheric residence times for the large fraction of

Table 26-2 *Deposition rates to soils from atmospheric lead in North America and Europe (mg/m³/yr)*

	Desposition rates
Industrial Areas	
Toronto (smelter)	>6,000
Toronto (highway)	600
Missouri (800 m from smelter)	1,265
Urban Areas	
New York City	350–547
Los Angeles	17–8,000
London	54
Madison, WI	<25
Rural Areas	6.2–34.1
Remote Areas	0.01–4.2

Source: NAS, National Research Council 1980.

airborne metals mean that changes in human activities contributing to emissions to air are reflected fairly rapidly in local ambient concentrations (Woolson 1983). Figure 26.5 shows the effects of changes in the air emissions of lead in the United States on its ambient concentrations. Clearly, the gradient in average concentration followed that of emissions within a year. This change was accompanied by a drop in average blood concentrations of lead in the population.

In addition to the local deposition in the soils and surface waters adjacent to the emission sources, the elements introduced into the atmosphere are transported over longer

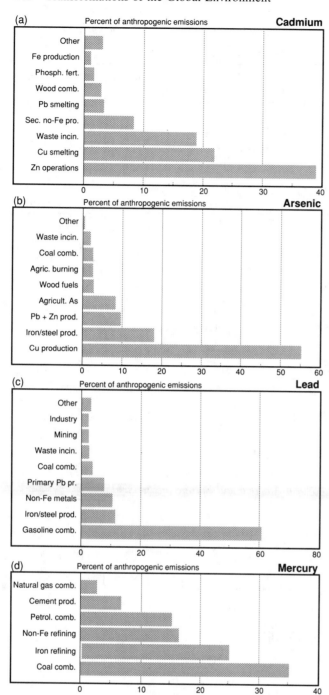

Figure 26.4 Relative contributions of various activities to total anthropogenic direct atmospheric emissions of individual metals. (a) cadmium; (b) arsenic; (c) lead; (d) mercury. Data from Nriagu 1979, 1980; Woolson 1983: 394–95.

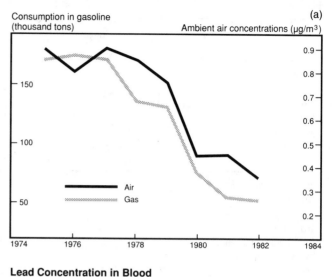

Consumption of Lead in Gasoline and Ambient Air Concentrations of Lead

Lead Concentration in Blood

Figure 26.5 Trends in lead consumption and average concentrations in the United States, 1975–1982. (a) Consumption of lead in gasoline and ambient air concentrations of lead; (b) lead concentration in blood. Data from U.S. E.P.A. 1985.

distances and are deposited on distant soils and surface waters (Schroeder and Lane 1988). Recent measurements of concentrations of selected metals in polar snow (Table 26-3) illustrate that phenomenon. There has been a dramatic increase in the concentrations of lead, cadmium, and mercury at remote sites since ancient times. The trend is most pronounced for lead, with the current concentration being about 3 orders of magnitude higher than those in the earth's crust. Recent satellite data and other remote sensing data have provided important information on the deposition of airborne particles, including metals. Two oceanic sinks for airborne particles have been identified, one located from Cape Hatteras to 1,500 km ENE of Newfoundland, and another one between southern Japan and the southwest Aleutian Islands (Chung 1986). Enrichment of lead and tin in these particular dumping grounds in the north Atlantic and the north Pacific already has been documented (Duce and Baut-Menard 1987). Lead concentrations in the waters of the

Table 26-3 *Concentrations of selected metals in Arctic snow*

Medium	Cadmium	Lead	Mercury
	(picograms per gram)		
Modern, Greenland or arctic snow	5	200	10
Ancient Greenland ice		1.4	10
Modern antarctic snow	0.26	5	10
Ancient antarctic ice		1.2	2

Source: Wolff and Peel 1985.

Atlantic Ocean have been studied, and show a decreasing gradient with depth, substantiating the effects of the deposition of airborne metals on water (Langford 1973).

Dredging, sewage disposal, industrial discharges, river drainage, and surface runoff (of industrial and consumptive origin) are, next to atmospheric deposition, significant contributors to metal pollution in surface waters. Data recently have been compiled comparing the relative contributions of metals to the waters of the North Sea from land-based sources and direct atmospheric deposition (Mance 1987). Table 26-4 presents the North Sea data for several metals in both absolute and relative terms. Land-based contributions to heavy metals in the North Sea exceed atmospheric contributions for all the metals listed except cadmium, for which land sources account for only one-half as much as atmospheric sources. It is important to note that for copper and mercury the relative contributions of the two sources are nearly equal. The data presented in Table 26-4 are consistent with the idea that consumption-related use of metals is a significant source of their total environmental emissions.

The elements introduced into the environmental compartments via atmospheric emissions and long- and short-distance transport and deposition, as well as direct discharges into soils and waters, are subject to global geochemical cycles that lead to continuous recirculation among these compartments (Fig. 26.6). The residence times of metals in environmental compartments (Table 26-5) indicate that, although sediments are the ultimate sink for these atmospheric emissions, soils and oceans also provide long-term storage.

The problem presented by the long residence times of metals in the environmental compartments suggests that the most appropriate approach to understanding the impacts of human activities on their environmental dispersion would be to examine cumulative rather than annual production and/or consumption figures. This is shown in Table 26-6 for some metals. The results are dramatic. Over the past 150 years, for example, humans have mined and processed more than 182 million t of lead, 281 million t of copper, and 112 million t of manganese.

The transport of metals through the environment is dependent on their chemical and physical form and on the processes that act to change their form during transport.

Table 26-4 *Land-based and atmospheric contributions to heavy metals in the waters of the North Sea*

Metal	Land-based (t/day)	Atmospheric (t/day)	Relative contribution (land atmospheric)
Arsenic	2.2	0.63	3.5
Cadmium	0.68	1.56	0.4
Chromium	18.3	1.83	10.0
Copper	12.9	10.8	1.2
Lead	17.9	8.0	2.2
Mercury	0.18	0.14	1.3
Nickel	11.1	4.3	2.6
Zinc	86.3	19.2	4.5

Source: Mance 1987: 324–27.

Table 26-5 *Residence times of metals in environmental compartments*

Residence times (yr)	Arsenic	Selenium	Mercury	Cadmium	Lead
Atmosph.	0.03	0.03	0.1	0.02	
Land	2,400	4,600	280	3,000	3,000
Oceans	9,400	2,300	880	2,100	
Sediments	99.8×10^6	93.5×10^6	90.8×10^6	99.8×10^6	99×10^6

Source: As, Se, Hg: MacKenzie, Lantzy and Paterson 1979; col, Cd: Nriagu 1980.

Elements associated with particles in rivers are less accessible to biota than those existing in water-soluble forms. Alkylation of mercury and its tragic consequences have been demonstrated in Minamata Bay in Japan. Thus far, only mercury and possibly cadmium are known to exhibit enhanced bioaccumulation via alkylated forms. It has been suggested that several other elements may be mobilized in the environment in organometallic form, including arsenic, tin, selenium, lead, and tellurium (Andreae et al. 1984). Changes in soil alkalinity due to acid precipitation also are known to affect the mobility of metals in soils, and thus their availability to biota (Cowling 1982).

Water-soluble forms of metals present in surface waters are readily absorbed into the flesh of aquatic organisms and in some cases can serve as a historical record for human activities. The 300-year history of utilization of lead through human action has been inscribed in the coral reefs off the Florida coast (Fig. 26.7). The ratio of lead to calcium in the dated coral bands, constant until the 1920s, has been steadily increasing, along with the global use of leaded gasoline. After reaching a peak in the mid-1970s, it appears to be declining thereafter. Interestingly, the growth and decline of lead residues in the Florida coral coincide with the use of lead in gasoline in the United States (Fig. 26.5) and not with the global mining and smelting trends (Fig. 26.3). This is consistent with an environmental transport model, in which a relatively short-range aerial transport of lead from urban areas is followed by fallout on the ocean surface and subsequent incorporation by the organisms.

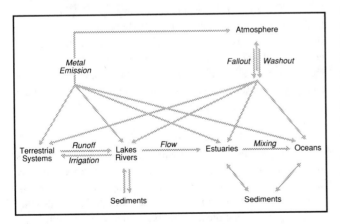

Figure 26.6 Routes of transport of trace metals in the environment.

Table 26-6 *Worldwide cumulative production of selected metals for the period 1700–1986: their toxic effects upon chronic exposure and primary routes of exposure by humans*

Metal	Cumulative production (thousands of) metric tons	Toxic effects[1]	Primary route of exposure[2]
Beryllium		respiratory cancer in humans (r), skeletal effects (o)	
Antimony	3,463	chromosomal breaks (r), emphysema (r), liver toxicity (o)	F,W,A?
Chromium	30,733	respiratory cancer in humans (r), renal toxicity (o)	W,F
Copper	281,875	aggravation of Wilson's disease (o)	F?
Magnesium	7,363		A
Manganese	112,035	neurotoxic effects (o)	F
Mercury	733	birth defects, neurologic effects (o, r)	F
Nickel	18,130	possibly cancer in humans (r), reproductive effects (o), dermititis (o)	F,W
Tin	16,516	immunosuppression (o), metabolic disorders (o)	F
Lead	182,035	neurologic effects (r, o), developmental effects (o, r), possibly kidney cancer in animals	F
Arsenic		neurotoxicity, skin lesions (o), anemia, circulatory toxicity (o, r), respiratory cancer in humans (r), reproductive effects (r, o)	W,A?
Selenium		pancreas, kidney, and liver toxicity, retarded growth (o), developmental effects (o)	F
Cadmium		renal toxicity (r, o), respiratory cancer in animals (r), reproductive effects (o)	F

[1] Not all effects occur by all routes of exposure (r, respiratory; o, oral). From Friberg, Nordberg, and Vouk, 1979.
[2] A, air; W, water; F, food. From Andreae et al. 1984.

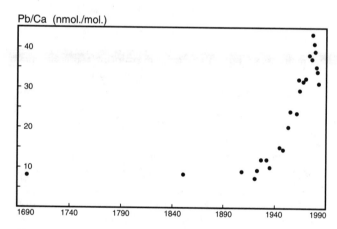

Figure 26.7 Lead concentrations in year bands of coral (*M. annularis*) from the Florida Keys. Source: Carpenter, Jickells, and Liss 1987.

Incorporation of metals residues into the flesh of aquatic organisms can also affect the food chain, where accumulation and biomagnification of the order of 10^4 to 10^5 times can occur and ultimately present a problem to humans. Recent measurements of metal concentrations on aquatic organisms in coastal and inland waters in the United States indicate that the process of food-chain contamination has been extensive. The 1976 National Marine Fisheries Service survey reported the presence of mercury, lead, cadmium, chromium, and arsenic in sea and freshwater fish at concentrations ranging from 0.12 ppm for mercury to 2.6 ppm for arsenic (Zook 1976). Some of the same metals, as well as additional ones (silver, cobalt, iron, manganese, nickel, and zinc), were found in several surveys of fish and shellfish in the New

England waters in concentrations ranging from 0.1 ppm for cobalt to 53 ppm for zinc (Capuzzo et al. 1987; Eisler et al. 1978). More recent studies of quahog clams from Narragansett Bay in Rhode Island showed contamination with cadmium, mercury, nickel, chromium, copper, zinc, and lead (Brown, Goble, and Tatelbaum 1988). Among those, cadmium, mercury, and lead have been judged to be above health-based acceptable levels for commercial use.

Adverse effects of some metals, derived mostly from observations made on occupational groups, are listed in Table 26-6. The environmental toxicology of metals is particularly complex. In addition to the limited understanding of the toxic effects of many metals at low doses and their toxicologically relevant chemical forms in the environment, risk assessors are confronted with variegated mutual interactions among metals that significantly affect the toxicity of each member in a complex mixture (Friberg, Norberg, and Vouk 1979; Liebescher and Smith 1968; Mertz 1981; Norberg 1978). Considering the undisputed global distribution of metals, especially through the food chain, further studies of their environmental fate and toxicity are among the most fascinating challenges to the risk-assessment community for the next several decades.

Organic Chemical Industry

The development of organic chemistry from its origins in the late eighteenth century has created substances entirely unknown in nature. The organic compounds present in biomass materials were the first to be exploited as feedstocks for the organic chemical industry. Fermentation, pyrolysis, and distillation of natural materials produced such new products as alcohols, tars, shellac, and turpentine, consumed in large part as naval stores (Farber 1952; Ihde 1964; Reese 1976). Later, the introduction of coal decreased the relative importance of wood and cotton as raw materials for the chemical industry (Fig. 26.8). Since the 1930s, oil and natural gas have progressively replaced both cellulose sources and coal and have opened the way for an explosive growth of the petrochemical industry.

From the late nineteenth century until the 1920s, Germany was the undisputed world leader in synthetic organic chemistry, accounting for 25% of the world's chemical industry and 85% of its synthetic dyes (Hohenbery 1967). The major industrialized nations of Europe and North America also took up the industry, with the United States emerging as the greatest volume producer in the post-World War II era. During this period, the production both of organic chemical intermediates and of plastics and resins has increased dramatically (approximately 50- and 200-fold, respectively), whereas pesticides and medicinal chemicals have increased more gradually (Fig. 26.9).

It is noteworthy that consumption of ethylene roughly parallels the production levels of the other two classes of chemicals. This is not surprising, because ethylene is a major chemical intermediate, usually consumed in the country of origin and mostly utilized by the synthetic organic chemical industry. Ethylene is, therefore, a reasonably good indicator of overall changes in synthetic organic production. Using ethylene as an indicator, trends in the worldwide production of synthetic chemicals between 1970 and 1983 are shown in Table 26-7. The table shows that although production has been concentrated in major industrial centers (such as the United States, Japan, West Germany, the Netherlands, and the Soviet Union), the recent rate of growth in some newly developing countries (such as Brazil, Mexico, Hungary, and China) has outpaced that in the established centers. As a result, the relative contribution to the world production by the major producers has dropped, and new centers of pro-

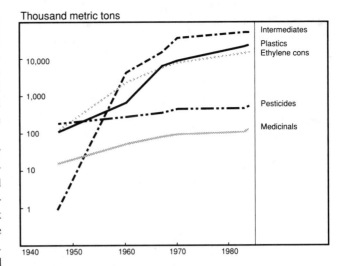

Figure 26.9 U.S. synthetic organic chemical production, 1947–1984, by production category. Sources: for 1947, 1960, Reese 1976; for 1969, 1970, U.S. Tariff Commission 1972; for 1967, 1983, 1984, U.S. International Trade Commission 1985.

duction of synthetic chemicals have emerged in eastern Europe, Asia, and possibly South America.

A similar picture of growth emerges for benzene (Table 26-8). The rate of growth in newly developing countries has outstripped that of the industrial countries, with an overall shift toward eastern Europe, Korea, India, and Brazil. Unlike ethylene, which is utilized mostly in the synthesis of other chemicals, the primary uses of benzene are in gasoline (78%) and as a solvent (13%). Benzene is, therefore, not a good indicator of chemical industry growth. Because more than 90% of benzene is ultimately released into the atmosphere, however, production levels and their geographic locations may be used to predict quite accurately atmospheric emissions of benzene.

With the exception of pesticides, most human-produced organic chemicals are not intended for release into the environment. Releases are typically the undesirable by-products of manufacturing, waste disposal, and the commercial uses of the substances. Among the organic chemicals unintentionally released into the environment, volatile organic compounds are by far the largest class. Used primarily as industrial solvents and synthetic intermediates (except benzene, which is used heavily in gasoline manufacturing), their main environmental sink is ambient air. The magnitude of emissions can be estimated from production volumes, using emission factors of the volatile intermediates. A case in point is plastics manufacturing from vinyl chloride. United States production of polyvinyl chloride in 1986 was 3,271,000 t, comprising approximately one-third of total world production. If global production is estimated at approximately 10,000,000 t and if the emission factor for vinyl chloride from polyvinyl chloride plants is assumed to be 35.5 g/kg (U.S. EPA 1978), more than 355,000 t of vinyl chloride were released into the atmosphere globally from polymer manufacturing in 1986.

Among the largest-volume volatile organic compounds in the United States (Table 26-9), emission factors are also high. Over 90% of all the benzene, trichloroethylene, and trichloro-

Percent total supply by source

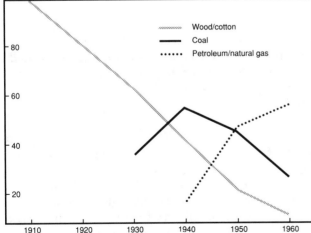

Figure 26.8 Relative contribution of fuel types as feedstocks for the chemical industry, United States and Europe. Data from Tillman 1978: 21.

Table 26-7 *Major ethylene producers in 1970 and 1983 (unless otherwise specified)*

Region	1970		1983		Growth factor relative to 1970
	$\times 10^3$ mt	% total	$\times 10^3$ mt	% total	
North America					
Canada	406	1.9	1,196	3.5	2.9
Mexico	60	0.3	645	1.9	10.8
U.S.A.	8,204	39.3	12,967	37.5	1.6
South America					
Brazil	349[b]	1.7	1,163	3.4	3.3
Western Europe					
Finland	98[a]	0.5	140	0.4	1.4
France	1,235[a]	5.9	2,046	5.9	1.7
F.R.G.	2,020	9.7	3,172	9.2	1.6
Italy	900	4.3	1,063	3.1	1.2
Netherlands	1,406[a]	6.7	1,747[c]	5.1	1.2
Spain	92	0.4	235	0.7	2.5
U.K.	998	4.8	1,155	3.3	1.2
Eastern Europe					
Bulgaria	56	0.3	213	0.6	3.8
Czechoslovakia	122	0.6	543	1.6	4.5
Greece	13	0.1	14	<0.1	1.1
Hungary	2	<0.1	261	0.8	130.5
Poland	26	0.1	198	0.6	7.6
Romania	111	0.5	316	0.9	2.8
Yugoslavia	42	0.2	168	0.5	4.0
Africa					
Algeria	37[b]	0.2	77[d]	0.2	2.1
Asia					
China	65[a]	0.3	654	1.9	10.1
India	39	0.2	102	0.3	2.6
Korea	90[a]	0.4	491	1.4	5.5
Turkey	43[a]	0.3	56	0.2	1.3
USSR	1,366[a]	6.5	2,267	6.6	1.7
Japan	3,097	14.8	3,688	10.7	1.2
TOTAL	20,877	99.8	34,577	100.3	1.7

Source: United Nations 1984.
[a] 1975; [b] 1976; [c] 1981; [d] 1982.

ethane manufactured in this country is ultimately released into the ambient air. Nonetheless, the overall trend in the total emissions of volatile organics relative to the amounts produced has been downward since the early 1970s, possibly as a result of the implementation of the Clean Air Act. A striking illustration is the approximately 30% reduction in estimated emissions of total volatile organic compounds in the United States, despite the more than 50-fold increase in chemical manufacturing during the same time, as reflected by ethylene consumption (Fig. 26.10). This growing gulf between production and releases shows that changes in technology can have dramatic effects on total emissions. It also suggests that using consumption and production figures as indicators of emissions may not be appropriate for comparisons among countries that have vastly different regulatory and technological systems. It is also likely that the recent migration of

organic chemical production from developed to developing countries, in which more permissive regulatory frameworks and control technologies exist, may involve environmental problems greater than those suggested by the changes in the distribution of world production centers shown in Tables 26-7 and 26-8.

Atmospheric chemistry largely determines the environmental fate of volatile organics released into ambient air. Agents with short atmospheric half-lives (e.g., ethylene, propylene, styrene, or butadiene) are more likely to have short-term and more localized impacts than those with longer half-lives. Limited monitoring data consistently show higher concentrations of volatile organic compounds in urban and industrial areas than in rural and remote areas (Singh, Salas, and Stiles 1982).

The direct effects of inhalation of volatile organic com-

Table 26-8 *Major benzene producers in 1970 and 1983 (unless otherwise specified)*

Region	1970 × 10³ mt	1970 % total	1983 × 10³ mt	1983 % total	Growth factor relative to 1970
North America					
Canada	406	4.0	1,196	7.7	2.9
Mexico	77	0.8	139	0.9	1.8
U.S.A.	3,753	36.7	4,094	26.5	1.1
South America					
Brazil	121[a]	1.2	1,436	2.8	3.6
Western Europe					
Belgium	64	0.6	41	0.3	0.6
France	385	3.8	627	4.1	1.6
F.R.G.	819	8.0	1,336	8.7	1.6
Italy	501	4.9	528	3.4	1.1
Netherlands	284	2.8	1,032	6.7	3.6
Spain	131	1.3	194	1.3	1.5
U.K.	463	4.5	726	4.7	1.6
Eastern Europe					
Czechoslovakia	106	1.0	268	1.7	2.5
Hungary	13	0.1	104	0.7	8.0
Romania	125	1.2	204	1.3	1.6
Asia					
India	21	0.2	92	0.6	4.4
Korea	8[b]	<0.1	159	1.0	19.9
Turkey	8	<0.1	9	<0.1	1.1
USSR	1,366[b]	13.3	2,267	14.7	1.7
Japan	1,585	15.5	1,938	12.6	1.2
TOTAL	10,236	99.9	15,433	100.0	1.5

Source: United Nations 1984.
[a] 1976; [b] 1975.

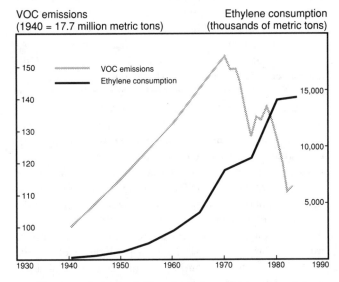

Figure 26.10 Trends in emissions of volatile organic compounds in the United States during the post–World War II years. Data from Waddams 1980 and WRI 1986.

pounds on the health of a local population are largely unknown. The documented higher incidence of lung cancer in urban and industrial centers in relation to rural areas has been attributed by some to air pollution. The contribution, if any, of volatile organic trace pollutants from chemical industry to that effect, however, is speculative at best. In fact, it is quite likely that the observed effect is due to the combined and possibly synergistic effect of a mixture of agents. If so, the volatile organic compounds, some of them known to cause cancer in animals or humans, may ultimately contribute to adverse health effects. That contribution is probably quite small, however, in comparison with other contaminants such as trace metals or inhalable particulates.

The principal indirect local effects of volatile organic emissions are ozone and smog generation, through photochemical reactions with nitrogen oxides and other oxidants. Hydrocarbons with unsaturated bonds, such as ethylene or propylene, are the most reactive of the volatile organic compounds, and, along with hydrocarbon emissions from energy generation (heat production and transportation), contribute significantly to the formation of photochemical smog in highly industrial areas.

The atmospheric fate of volatile organic compounds with

Table 26-9 *Production of volatile organic compounds in the United States and their atmospheric residence times*

Compound	Annual production (calendar year) ($\times 10^3$ mT)	Atmospheric residence time[1]
Ethylene	15,210 (87)	hours
Propylene	8,190 (87)	hours
Benzene	4,385 (84)	days
1,2 Dichloroethane	3,455 (82)	3–12 mos[2]
Vinyl Chloride	3,271 (86)	
Styrene	3,690 (87)	hours
Methanol	3,352 (87)	hours
Toluene	2,386 (84)	hours
Xylenes	2,812 (87)	hours
Butadiene	1,215 (87)	hours
Acrylonitrile	1,080 (87)	hours
Cyclohexane	1,012 (87)	hours
Tetrachloroethylene	347 (78)	
Carbon tetrachloride	332 (81)	60–100 yr
Dichloromethane	320 (84)	1–2 yr
Trichloroethane	315 (80)	
Chloroform	169 (82)	
111-Trichloroethane	612 (85)	6.5 yr
Chlorobenzenes	70 (78)	up to 4 mos
Vinylidene chloride	90 (78)	days

Source: U.S. EPA Health Assessment Documents.

[1] Residence times vary with atmospheric conditions. Different values are therefore reported among sources. The following ranges are used here: hours, from less than 1 to approximately 24 hours; days, from 1 to approximately 30 days.

[2] Calculated from a half-life reported in the literature, assuming that residence time equals five half-lives.

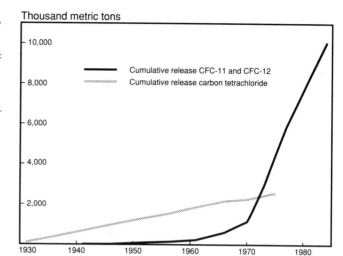

Figure 26.11 Worldwide cumulative releases of chlorofluorocarbons CFC-11 and CFC-12 and of carbon tetrachloride. Data from NAS 1978 and WRI 1986.

long atmospheric residence times is particularly interesting because of their ability to be transported over long distances and to pose, therefore, potentially adverse effects on a global scale. Among these, the halocarbons (chloromethanes, chlorofluorocarbons, bromofluorocarbons, bromochlorocarbons, bromochlorofluorocarbons, and bromocarbons) have been extensively studied in recent years because of their tendency to accumulate in the upper stratosphere and their capacity for depleting the ozone layer. Global production, atmospheric concentrations, and estimated residence times of selected halocarbons are listed in Table 26-10. Of these, CFC-11, CFC-12, and carbon tetrachloride are the most troublesome environmentally because of their combined high atmospheric concentrations, large production volumes, and very long atmospheric lifetimes (>50 years).

The cumulative amounts of carbon tetrachloride and combined CFC-11 and CFC-12 lost to the atmosphere worldwide between 1930 and 1985 are shown in Fig. 26.11. Approximately 65% of the total carbon tetrachloride was emitted before 1960, whereas 96% of the CFCs was released after 1965. Based on the data shown in Table 26-10, CFC-22 and CFC-113 are also of concern, not only because of their long lifetimes and large production volumes, but also because of their apparent rapid increase in atmospheric concentrations.

Among the halocarbons listed in Table 26-10, trichloroethane, chloroform, iodoform, and dibromoethane have shorter lifetimes than others and are removed from the atmosphere by reactions with stratospheric hydroxyl radicals. They are therefore not considered to pose a threat to the stratospheric ozone and have not been subject to the international activities aimed at reducing halocarbon production. Among these, trichloroethane (whose worldwide production has been growing steadily since the early 1950s, reaching approximately 612,000 t in 1985) is of particular interest. Because of its considerably lower toxicity than that of other chlorinated ethanes and ethylenes, its presumed very small contribution to ozone formation in the stratosphere, and its apparent lack of threat to the stratospheric ozone, this air contaminant has been consistently excluded from regulatory activities in the United States under the provisions of the Clean Air Act. As a result, its use has been steadily growing as it replaced other chlorinated ethanes and ethylenes (trichloroethylene and tetrachloroethylene, for example) whose toxicity or photochemical reactivity became of concern. As shown in Table 26-10, the worldwide production and the atmospheric concentration of trichloroethane has been increasing steadily. It is also a commonly found groundwater pollutant (Table 26-11). With no apparent adverse effects on humans or the environment at the current atmospheric levels, trichloroethane seems to be an ideal industrial and commercial solvent. While this may indeed be the case, the growing reliance on this solvent and the accompanying atmospheric releases merit attention and ongoing monitoring, especially in the stratosphere, which may be receiving some fraction of the considerable emissions into the ambient air.

In addition to the ambient air, groundwater and surface water are targets of environmental partitioning of volatile organic compounds. Contrary to the ambient emissions, which originate primarily from industrial and commercial processes, the pollution of soil and water by volatile organic solvents is largely the result of improper disposal of industrial

Table 26-10 *Global production, atmospheric concentrations, and atmospheric lifetimes of selected halocarbons*

Compound	Atmospheric concentration ppt (year)		Increase %/year (year)		Annual global production ×10³ tons (in years)		Atmospheric lifetime
CFC-11 (Cl_3F)	200	(83)	5.7	(81)	310	(82)	65
CFC-12 (Cl_2F_2)	320	(83)	6	(81)	444	(82)	120
CFC-13 (CF_3Cl)	~3.4	(80)			—		400
CFC-22 ($CHClF_2$)	~52	(80)	11.7		206	(84)	20
CFC-113	~32	(85)	10.0		140	(84)	90
CFC-114	—				13	(84)	180
CFC-115	4	(80)			—		380
CFC-116	~4	(80)			—		>500
CCl_4	~140	(79)	1.8	(81)	~830	(83)	50
CH_3Cl	630	(80)			~500	(84)	~1.5
CH_3I	~1	(81)					0.02
$CBrClF_2$	~1	2(84)				(~5?)	0.02
$CBrF_3$	~1	(84)			8	(84)	25
$C_2H_4Br_2$	~1	(84)			—		110
CH_3CCl_3	~120	(83)	9—40	(81)	0.1	(51)	~1
					7.9	(55)	6.5
					37	(60)	
					178	(70)	
					371	(75)	
					580	(80)	
					570	(81)	
					540	(82)	
					545	(83)	
					~579	(84)	
					~612	(85)	

Source: World Meteorological Organization 1985; Prinn. et al. 1987.

and commercial waste and of the underground storage of gasoline and industrial stocks. Incidents of contamination have been extensively documented in the United States. The frequency and extent of contamination suggest that surface waters are more frequently contaminated than groundwater (Table 26-11). Both groundwater and surface-water contamination have localized effects, although for different reasons. For contaminants in surface water, dilution, evaporation, and biological and chemical degradation lead to a steeply declining concentration gradient around the source. Thus the area affected by the contamination tends to be limited in extent. For groundwater contaminants, the physical boundaries of the aquifer, rather than the physicochemical and biological attrition processes, confine the problem area. These differences in confinement also explain the differences in persistence of the contamination problem. Whereas the concentration of volatile contaminants in surface water drops rapidly over time and may become negligible within days or weeks, the groundwater contaminants usually persist for decades and may become a serious water-supply problem for a local population.

Industrial countries have allocated substantial efforts over the past decade toward preventing groundwater contamination. The focus has been on all stages of the process that may lead ultimately to groundwater pollution, including:

1. severe restrictions on land disposal of domestic, commercial, and industrial liquid waste;
2. incentives for waste reduction through changes in technology;
3. strict penalties for illegal land disposal and underground storage of volatile solvents;
4. setting water-quality standards for chemicals;
5. public acquisition of lands surrounding important sources of water;
6. intense monitoring of groundwater;
7. public education.

It is interesting that a concern over potential rather than observed adverse health effects has driven these initiatives. The actual adverse health effects of drinking water polluted with small amounts of volatile organic solvents remain unknown. Attempts to document those effects through epidemiologic studies have generated mostly inconclusive results, due both to the methodological difficulties in conducting such studies and the general insensitivity of epidemiology in detecting small changes in health status of a diverse human population. Far from demonstrating the absence of adverse effects, these studies have shown that:

1. the groundwater contamination most commonly found is unlikely to produce acute illness;

Table 26-11 *(a) Occurrence of selected volatile organic compounds in finished groundwater in the United States*

Compound	Number of sites sampled	Number of positive samples	Mean* (µg/l.)	Maximum concentration (µg/l.)
Trichloroethylene	402	4.0	24.8	210
Carbon tetrachloride	432	3.0	1.7	13
Tetrachloroethylene	413	5.6	2.8	30
1,2-Dichloroethane	418	1.9	0.6	1.2
1,1,1-Trichloroethane	399	4.5	30.0	650
cIS-, trans-, and 1,1-Dichloroethylene	390	3.3	10.4	82
Methylene chloride	38	2.8	7.0	7.0
Vinyl chloride	25	4.00	76	76

* Of the positive samples.

Table 26-11 *(b) Occurrence of selected volatile organic compounds of finished surface water (EPA Surveys)*

Compound	Number of sites sampled	Number of positive samples	Mean* (µg/l.)	Maximum concentration (µg/l.)
Trichloroethylene	133	32.3	0.47	3.2
Carbon tetrachloride	144	35.7	3.46	30
Tetrachloroethylene	180	12.8	1.49	21
1,2-Dichloroethane	196	13.8	0.93	4.8
1,1,1-Trichloroethane	133	16.5	0.56	3.3
cIS-, trans-, and 1,1-Dichloroethylene	103	4.9	0.66	2.2
Methylene chloride	178	18.0	1.8	13
Vinyl chloride	133	2.3	3.43	9.8

Source: Council on Environmental Quality 1981.
* Of the positive samples.

2. the magnitude of chronic illness, such as cancer or subtle neurological disorders, often associated with many of these compounds in laboratory studies on animals, is probably not very large in any one individual.

That is not to say, however, that the aggregate effect on a large population, through increased incidence of chronic disease over a long period of time, may not occur or may not be substantial.

Our observations of the recent growth of centers of organic synthetic chemical industry in newly industrializing countries leads us to expect that the magnitude of water contamination has most likely increased in those countries and will continue to rise during the next decades. In Poland, an industrialized society, the magnitude of surface water and groundwater containing industrial waste has risen so sharply as to render them unusable even for agriculture (UNDP 1979). In the developing countries, the increase in water contamination is likely to grow faster than the rate of growth of the industry, due to the lag in investment in pollution control and chemical-waste-disposal technology and to their less stringent environmental regulations. Although cases of contamination are likely to be localized geographically, the aggregate impact of the overall trend may become significant over time.

Polychlorinated biphenyls (PCBs) are another class of unintentionally released organic synthetic chemicals that, like halocarbons, are highly persistent, but whose main environmental sinks are sediments, oceans, and biota. As shown in Fig. 26.12, the production of PCBs in the United States has declined rapidly since the peak years of the late 1960s. Concerns over the global accumulation of these persistent compounds, as well as their potential adverse health effects, have stimulated these reductions. Evidence now exists to suggest that sediments are not the final sink of PCBs, as previously thought, but are a reservoir from which PCBs may be redistributed to biota, waters, and the atmosphere (Larsson 1985). The *net* flux, however, is from the atmosphere to lakes, and thence to sediments. Environmental levels of PCBs in the air have declined, following reduced production rates (Figs. 26.12 and 26.15), and should continue to decline worldwide. The reduction will be slow, however, due to the persistence of PCBs, their ability to recycle among environmental compartments, and the large environmental reservoir (estimated in 1975 at 82,000 t). Meanwhile, PCBs still in service and in landfills, dumps, and impoundments will continue to produce local instances of high PCB levels, pending destructive disposal of these reservoirs.

Overall, the adverse health effects to humans and biota from prolonged exposures to low levels of PCBs are probably not very significant, although this class of compounds has been implicated in cancer and reproductive effects in some species. The phenomenal environmental spread of PCBs and their virtual omnipresence in all environmental compartments and in living organisms is therefore probably more important as a symbol than as an actual threat to the ecosystem. It symbolizes the irreversibility and globality of

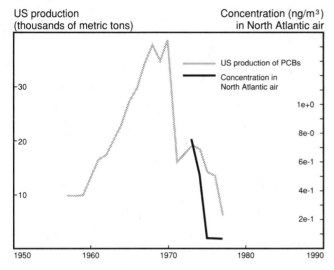

US production
(thousands of metric tons)

Concentration (ng/m³)
in North Atlantic air

Figure 26.12 U.S. production of polychlorinated biphenyls and their concentrations in ambient air over the North Atlantic Ocean. Data from Conway, Whitmore, and Hansen 1982 and NAS 1978, OECD 1979.

the effects of the release of large quantities of persistent chemicals and of short-sighted societal behavior toward the environment.

In contrast to most other organic chemicals of anthropogenic origin, pesticides are intended for release into the environment. Therefore, production and consumption figures closely parallel total releases. DDT is a prototype pesticide with a high persistence in the environment and an extensive global distribution.

Developed by Swiss chemists at Geigy laboratories in 1939, DDT won rapid acceptance due to wartime pressures for increased agricultural production, the need for a delousing agent for refugees and military personnel, and the need for protection against insect-borne diseases prevalent in the diverse climates of the war theaters. By 1945, DDT had also been released for civilian use in the United States, and it gained a quick acceptance due to its low mammalian acute toxicity, its persistence, its broad-range activity, and its relatively low cost (Perkins 1982). In 1955, the United Nations World Health Organization launched a campaign to control malaria using DDT, and by 1972 it claimed eradication of the disease in 36 countries, which would have affected 710 million people (Plimmer 1982).

While the benefits of DDT to public health programs were becoming manifest, awareness of its serious environmental hazards was growing. As early as 1950, DDT's interference with pest control by natural predators was noted (Perkins 1982). By the 1960s, DDT's persistence in the environment, due to physicochemical properties similar to those of PCBs, and its bioaccumulation and biomagnification along the food chain of various species were evident. Birds seemed especially sensitive, with eggshell thinning and bone abnormalities the most obvious effects, even with exposures in the parts-per-billion range (Garrels, MacKenzie, and Hunt 1973).

Total world consumption of DDT peaked in the late 1950s and early 1960s, and has declined continuously since (Fig. 26.13). In 1984, global consumption reached only approximately 1.5% of the previous peak value. The decline started

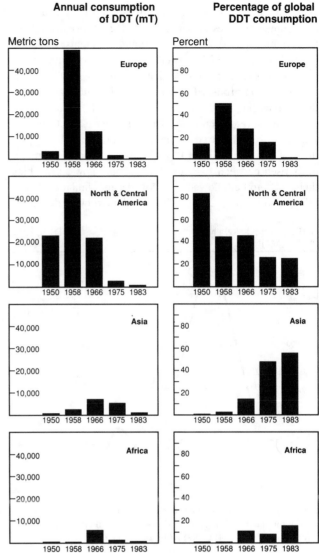

Annual consumption of DDT (mT)

Percentage of global DDT consumption

Figure 26.13 Trends in global consumption of DDT by region for selected years, expressed in metric tons and as a percentage of total annual consumption. Data from U.N. FAO Production Yearbooks.

in Europe and North America, followed by Africa and Asia about eight years later. Since the rate of decrease has been lower in Asia and Africa than in Europe and North and Central America, a dramatic geographic shift in the pattern of world consumption has occurred. Thus, Europe and North and Central America combined went from 96% of world consumption in 1958 to 26% in 1983, whereas Asia and Africa went from 3% to 74% during the same period.

The environmental effects of DDT are initially most evident in the areas of its release. For instance, in agricultural areas, DDT concentrations in the soil are as much as 10,000 times higher than in nonagricultural areas (Woodwell et al. 1975). Its physicochemical properties (moderate volatility, chemical stability, and ability to accumulate in sediments, soils, and biota), however, favor long-range environmental cycling and worldwide diffusion. Indeed, DDT residues have been detected in all environmental media and in biota. A model of the global flux of DDT residues, based on an assumed annual average consumption of 8,000 t/yr, suggests environmental fluxes of: land, 5,000 t (62%); oceans, 2,000 t (25%); atmosphere, 1,000 t (12%); and sediments, 80 t (1%) (Garrels et al. 1973; Woodwell et al. 1975). As with PCBs, one would expect a slow decline in levels of DDT and its decomposition product DDD in the environment and biota, due to recycling. There is, for example, a 20- to 25-year lag period in the reduction of DDT residues in eastern Canadian seals (Fig. 26.14). Based on the DDT data, one would expect that the concentrations of PCBs in the seals, having continuously risen between 1975 and 1982, should now be reaching their peak, to be followed by a slow decline similar to that of DDT residues (Fig. 26.15). The overall worldwide decline in

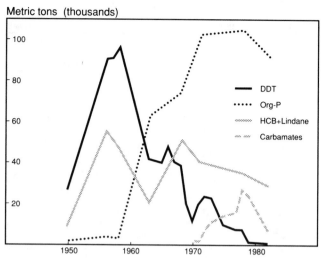

Metric tons (thousands)

Figure 26.16 Trends in global consumption of pesticides by class, 1950–1982. Data from U.N. FAO Production Yearbooks.

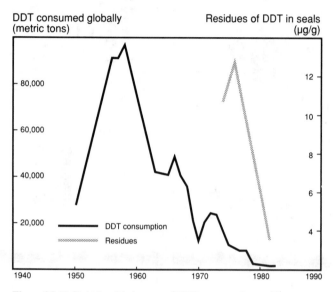

DDT consumed globally (metric tons)   Residues of DDT in seals (µg/g)

Figure 26.14 Relationship between DDT consumption and its residues in the flesh of eastern Canadian seals. Data from Addison, Brodie, and Zink 1984; U.N. FAO Production Yearbooks.

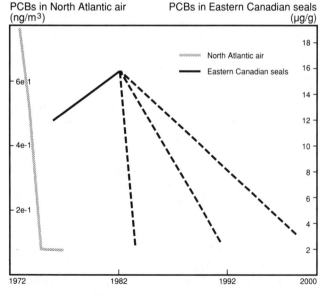

PCBs in North Atlantic air (ng/m³)   PCBs in Eastern Canadian seals (µg/g)

Figure 26.15 Concentration of polychlorinated biphenyls in North Atlantic air compared with actual and anticipated trends in biota. Dashed lines represent anticipated decline in PCB concentration in biota. Three hypothetical lines signify that the rate of decline is not known. Data from Addison et al. 1984; Conway et al. 1982.

PCB residues will likely be slower than that of DDT because of their large environmental reservoirs, greater volatility and therefore aerial transport, slower degradation rate, and greater bioaccumulation.

On a smaller scale, the rate of decline depends on the proximity of vapor reservoirs and routes of transport. Thus, whereas the levels of DDT in arctic ringed seals in the eastern arctic have declined faster than those of PCBs during the period 1972 to 1981 (Addison et al. 1986), the opposite is true for the western arctic, most likely due to a continuing supply of DDT to the western arctic via air or water from the Far East, where its use continued throughout the 1970s (see Fig. 26.16). Ultimately, the decline in PCB and DDT residues in the seals of the western arctic should approximate the pattern seen in the eastern arctic if DDT consumption in the Far East continues to decline.

The recognition of the environmental persistence of DDT and other chlorinated pesticides has led to a recent shift toward the use of chemically less stable compounds. This new generation of pesticides, exemplified by carbamates and organophosphates, are water-soluble, biodegradable, and chemically much more reactive than past agents. The time course of the rise and decline in the worldwide consumption of four major classes of pesticides is shown in Fig. 26.16. The decline in the consumption of the highly persistent hexachlorocyclobenzene, lindane, and DDT that took place during the late 1950s and early 1960s coincided with a rapid growth in the consumption of organophosphates and, later, carbamates. The consumption of carbamates, never matching the other classes in volume, declined during the 1980s, possibly due to the competition from other products and the awareness of the potential environmental build-up under special local conditions (UNEP 1986).

The physicochemical properties of carbamates and other similar pesticides allow for an environmental partitioning pattern similar to that of land-disposed volatile organic compounds. Their principal sinks are soils, surface water, and groundwater. Incidents of groundwater contamination have been well documented throughout the United States, with concentrations of various agents ranging from less than one to hundreds of parts per million (Holden 1986). As with VOCs, the environmental effects of these contaminants are mostly localized, with significantly longer residence times in groundwater than in surface waters. Recent monitoring of groundwater in 30 states in the United States has shown that about 50 to 60 pesticides have been detected.

Unlike the volatile organic compounds, carbamates, organophosphates, and other pesticides that have been introduced recently into agriculture have a fairly high acute toxicity and, when inappropriately handled or applied, can cause illness among applicators and other agricultural workers. Judging by the rapid growth of the organic chemical industry in the industrializing countries, their strong reliance on synthetic agricultural pesticides, and probably limited knowledge among users of toxicologic and chemical properties of these substances, increasing incidence of accidental poisoning should be expected. Judging by the U.S. experience, we would also expect an increasing incidence of groundwater contamination by pesticides in these countries.

Discussion

A great variety of trace pollutants has been introduced into the terrestrial environment during the past three centuries as a result of human activities. To understand their impacts, we considered quantitative and qualitative aspects of these changes; the rate of growth or decline in the releases over time, and total quantities of materials involved, as well as the types of pollutant, the spatial distribution of their key sources of release, environmental partitioning and persistence of the agents, and their effects on ecosystems, humans, and the physical environment.

Figure 26.17 shows the relative annual growth of metal mining and utilization and organic-chemical manufacturing over the past three centuries. For comparison, the relative growth in energy generation is also shown. The choice of a reference year for energy generation and metal production was driven primarily by the availability of historical data and the scope of our research questions. For chemical manufacturing, the reference year represents the actual birth of large-scale chemical manufacturing. The logarithmic scale allows us to cover a large range of changes in some activities and to get initial insights into the changes in rates of growth. The graph shows striking differences in the rates of growth of these human activities. Total energy production, measured in units of energy produced, has shown a steady growth before reaching a plateau in the past decade. The chemical industry, the most recent of the activities, has grown exponentially during the postwar years, at a rate greater than that for energy consumption, with some reduction in the rate of growth sometime around 1975. In contrast to energy generation, however, worldwide chemical production continues to increase. Metal mining and processing has exhibited the most striking increase over the past three centuries. This growth rate shows no signs of decline as of 1982.

A more detailed look at the specific pollutants generated by each of the two activities under study shows great diversity within each category. In the case of metals, the list of traditionally mined and fairly well-studied elements such as arsenic, lead, or iron has been supplemented during the past century by a large number of new ones, such as cadmium, manganese, and tungsten, whose rapid growth rate has not diminished the growth rate in the traditional elements. This increased diversity not only contributed to the rapid increase in the total volume of metals processed industrially, but also introduced a host of new questions with regard to the environmental fate and biological effects. To some of these questions no answers are readily available, as the pace of development of new materials and their uses exceeds that of research on environmental partitioning and chemistry of these new elements, as well as their interactions with organisms. Therefore, the assessment of the impacts of this activity is, to a large degree, an extrapolative process. Because of the paucity of specific knowledge about many of the metals, and the size of the task of evaluating them individually, we treat metals as a group. This treatment is justified partly on the grounds of certain common properties of metals such as indestructability; affinity for organic particles in air, soil, and sediments; solubility in acids; and general toxicity to biological systems.

The variety of pollutants, in terms of physical, biological, and environmental properties, that has been introduced by the organic chemical industry far surpasses that from metal mining and utilization. It is also the most rapidly changing group of agents, with commercial lives of some members only in the order of years. Analogously to the metals, the properties of many of these compounds are poorly understood, so that assessment of their impacts is largely judgmental in nature. Therefore, for the purpose of our analysis, we focused on the classes of organics that we considered important, either because of their large volumes introduced into the environment (volatile organic compounds, pesticides), or their unique environmental properties (persistence, for example, of DDT or PCBs), or both. Our choice was not driven by the degree of inherent toxicity or other harmful properties of the agents, although the magnitude of the releases or the persistence of the agents are clearly related to their cumulative adverse impacts.

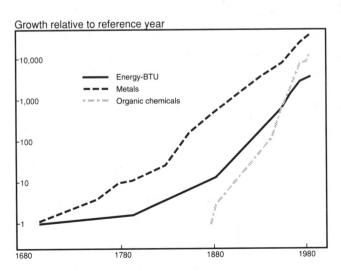

Growth relative to reference year

Energy-BTU

Metals

Organic chemicals

10,000

1,000

100

10

1

1680   1780   1880   1980

Figure 26.17 Growth trends for major human activities.

Despite the many variables and even more unknowns, the emerging picture of the past, present, and future is a surprisingly coherent one. Overall, we found that each human activity contributes to each of the four combinations of effects described in our initial two-by-two matrix. As expected, the clustering of effects into persistent/global and short-lived/local occurs, but not to an extreme extent. Thus, in addition to the global/persistent effects of DDT, metals, and some halocarbons, and the local/short-lived effects of gaseous air emissions from chemical manufacturing, we also found local/persistent effects of pesticides and solvents on groundwater and metals on soils, as well as global/short-lived effects of ubiquitous gaseous air pollutants. Finally, we found that both activities have multiple types of effects, as vividly illustrated by airborne trace metals and persistent pesticides in soils.

The story for each human activity is different and must be told separately. Our studies of the chemical industry show geographic spread in the distribution of the centers of production from the technologically advanced to the newly industrializing countries, as measured by the production of ethylene. Among the undesirable major by-products of the chemical industry are environmental releases of volatile organic compounds. Ambient air is by far the most affected by these releases, followed by surface waters, soil, and groundwater. Contamination of air with volatile compounds has local as well as global effects. For many short-lived organic compounds, the effect on the local population is that of increased exposure to toxic chemicals and the secondary effects caused by urban smog generated through photochemical reactions with airborne oxidants. Recent trends in growth of both the chemical industry and energy consumption in newly industrializing countries indicate that growing emissions of photoreactive hydrocarbons and oxides may become concentrated in the same geographic locations, thus increasing the likelihood and severity of local air-pollution problems. For the governments, environmental community, and industries in those countries, prevention of these events may be among the most important challenges in the future years.

The experience of industrial countries shows that increased chemical production and the need associated with it for proper disposal of liquid chemical waste carry a high risk of groundwater contamination. Although localized, these effects are highly persistent and become severe in the areas in which reliance on groundwater is high. The incidence of these episodes is declining in the United States, but we expect it to increase in other parts of the world.

The most persistent among the volatile organic compounds, chlorofluorocarbons, have attracted widespread attention because of their threat to the stratospheric ozone. The focus has been on CFC-11 and CFC-12, which contribute the largest fraction of the worldwide production of chlorofluorocarbons. CFC-13 and CFC-22, whose volumes are smaller, are also of concern because of the clear upward trend in their atmospheric concentrations, as is carbon tetrachloride, because of its contribution to the stratospheric ozone depletion. Our research on volatile organic compounds shows that 1,1,1-trichloroethane has a unique place among the members of that class. One of the largest-volume commercial solvents, it

has replaced several chlorinated solvents judged to be environmentally unsafe. With low toxicity, low photochemical reactivity, and a shorter atmospheric life than the fully halogenated ethanes, 1,1,1-trichloroethane appears to present little direct threat to human health or to the ozone layer and is therefore a commercially attractive and versatile agent. Not surprisingly, its increasing production and use have also been accompanied by higher ambient air concentrations and frequent presence in contaminated groundwater, as is well documented in the United States. Given the incomplete state of knowledge of its toxic properties (for example, carcinogenicity) and its environmental fate (for example, its vertical mixing into the stratosphere), 1,1,1-trichloroethane thus stands out among the high-volume volatile organic compounds as an agent whose environmental behavior should be closely monitored in the future.

Among other persistent organics, DDT and PCBs tell a story of ignorance and lack of vision. Highly persistent, both were introduced into the environment in large quantities in the 1950s and 1960s and have since become distributed throughout the globe, being present in virtually all environmental compartments and biota. DDT levels are declining, with a similar trend predicted for PCBs, but the process will take decades. Although the biological effects of DDT are most severe only to some biologic species and those of PCBs are probably generally small, the realization of their uncontrolled environmental distribution following a release has shifted the emphasis to less-persistent chemical agents, especially among pesticides. Currently used pesticides indeed have much lower persistence, but their acute toxicity and threat to groundwater are much higher than those of DDT. We therefore expect that groundwater contamination and acute accidental toxicity episodes will increase – once again mostly among rapidly developing countries, in which the growth in their use is high and the knowledge of their properties among the users is low.

The picture we have generated for metal pollution is dramatic but less clear. The extraordinary growth in the volume and variety of metals that have been mined and processed during the past 300 years, combined with direct emissions into ambient air from burning of wood, coal, and petroleum, suggest both local and global environmental impacts; on a local scale, human and nonhuman exposure through ambient air and the locally produced food chain have been fairly well documented; on a global scale, the recycling of metals between environmental compartments and their long residence times in soils and surface waters increase the likelihood of incorporation into crops and aquatic organisms. High levels of numerous metals in the flesh of fish and other seafood along the U.S. coastal and inland waters have been observed during past years. We anticipate that this trend will continue and possibly increase in the future. It is not clear what, if any, fraction of the metal residues in seafood can be attributed to the global cycling phenomenon, and what fraction to local deposition and discharges. Comparison of metal concentrations in seafood from coastal and remote locations would be helpful in addressing the question when such data become available. It will also be instructive to estimate the total amounts of metals that are released into the ambient air and waters from various production processes and from dissipative consumption. So far, reliable emission figures exist mostly for metals released through combustion of wood and fossil fuels.

Lead is the only metal for which emission reduction has become the focus of intense national and international efforts, albeit mostly in technologically advanced countries. The effects of the phasing out of leaded gasoline in the United States have been gratifying; the average concentration of lead in the blood of the U.S. population has clearly decreased. The decline is slowing down, however, and will eventually reach a plateau, simply because other sources, mostly food, dissipation of consumer products, and existing environmental reservoirs will become the major sources of long-term human exposure to lead. For other metals, ambient air will continue to be a significant pathway of exposure to populations living in the vicinity of metal-processing and energy-generating industries. On a global scale and over long time periods, however, the food chain is likely to be an important pathway of exposure.

Indeed, continuing future exposures to trace metals, globally through food chains and locally through air, merit the serious attention of the international community. Along with ozone depletion due to photoreactive halocarbons and the possible global warming from accumulation of carbon dioxide and other gases, it has the characteristics of a global problem. This is not to say that serious adverse health effects necessarily will occur. The toxicology of metals is complex, unique for each element and for each route of exposure (ingestion versus inhalation, for instance). Adverse effects at low doses are known for only a handful of the 80 elements listed in the periodic table. Among these that are better known, cadmium, lead, and mercury have been shown to produce adverse effects in humans at very low levels of exposure, possibly without a meaningful threshold level. For many others, the paucity of data does not permit defensible conclusions. Complex mutual interactions of metals in organisms, with largely unpredictable combined effects on health, virtually preclude any meaningful assessment of risks from simultaneous exposure to multiple metals. These great uncertainties in the dose-response relationships suggest that, at least on a local scale, minimizing emissions may be the most effective approach to the problem. On a global scale, where the distribution is already wide and certain to persist for a long time, accelerated studies of the toxicity of recently introduced metals and their environmental partitioning are a pressing need.

References

Adams, F. C., M. J. Van Craen, and P. J. Van Espen. 1980. Enrichment of trace elements in remote aerosols. *Env. Sci. Tech.* 14: 1002–1005.

Addison, R. F., P. F. Brodie, and M. E. Zink. 1984. DDT has declined more than PCBs in eastern Canadian seals during the 1970s. *Env. Sci. Tech.* 18: 935–37.

Addison, R. F., and M. E. Zink. 1986. PCBs have declined more than DDT-group residues in Arctic Ringed Seals (*Phoca hispida*) between 1972 and 1981. *Env. Sci. Tech.* 20: 253–56.

American Petroleum Institute. 1986. *Basic Petroleum Data Book.* Vol. VI (1). Washington, D.C.

Andreae, M. O., T. Asami, K. K. Bertine, et al. 1984. Changing biogeochemical cycles. In *Changing Metal Cycles and Human Health*, ed. J. O. Nriagu. Berlin: Springer-Verlag.

Beavington. F., and P. A. Cawse. 1978. Comparative studies of trace elements in air particulate in norther Nigeria. *Sci. Total Env.* 10: 239–44.

Beijer, K., and A. Jernelov. 1979. Sources, transport, and transportation of metals in the environment. In *Handbook of the Toxicology of Metals*, ed. L. Friberg, G. F. Nordberg, and V. B. Vouk. New York: Elsevier.

Bellinger, D., A. Leviton, H. L. Needleman, C. Waternaux, and M. Rabinowitz. 1986. Low-level lead exposure and infant development in the first year. *Neurobehav. Toxicol. Teratol.* 8: 151–61.

Bituminous Coal Institute. 1952. *Bituminous Coal Annual*. Washington, D.C.

Bowen, H. J. M. 1977. Natural cycles of the elements and their perturbation by man. In *The Chemical Environment*, ed. J. Linehan and W. W. Fletcher. Glasgow and London: Blackie and Son.

British Petroleum. 1984. *BP Statistical Review of World Energy 1984*. London.

Brown, H. S., R. L. Goble, and L. Tatelbaum. 1988. Methodology for assessing hazards of contaminants in seafoods. *Reg. Tox. Pharm.* 8: 76–101.

Capuzzo, J., M. McDowell, A. McElroy, and G. Wallace. 1987. *Fish and Shellfish Contamination in New England Waters: An Evaluation and Review of Available Data on the Distribution of Chemical Contaminants*. Washington, D.C.: Coast Alliance.

Chung, Y. 1986. Air pollution detection by satellites: the transport and deposition of air pollutants over oceans. *Atm. Env.* 20: 617–30.

Conway, R. A., F. C. Whitmore, and W. J. Hansen. 1982. Entry of chemicals into the environment. In *Environmental Risk Assessment for Chemicals*, ed. R. A. Conway. New York: Van Nostrand.

Council on Environmental Quality. 1981. *Contamination of Groundwater by Toxic Organic Chemicals*. Washington, D.C.

Cowling, E. B. 1982. Acid precipitation in historical perspective. *Env. Sci. Tech.* 16: 110A–32A.

Crawford, M. 1987. News and comments: Landmark treaty negotiated. *Science* 237: 1557.

Cronon, W. 1983. *Changes in the Land*. New York: Hill and Wang.

Dorf, R. C. 1981. *The Energy Factbook*. New York: McGraw-Hill.

Duce, R. A., and P. Baut-Menard. 1987. Metal transfer across the air-sea interface: myths and mysteries. In *Lead, Mercury, Cadmium, and Arsenic in the Environment*, ed. T. C. Hutchinson and K. M. Meema. (SCOPE 31). Chichester: John Wiley and Sons.

Eisler, R., M. M. Barry, R. L. Lapan, G. Telek, E. W. Davey, and A. E. Soper. 1978. Metal survey of the marine clam *Pitar morrhuana* collected near a Rhode Island (USA) electroplating plant. *Mar. Biol.* 45: 311–17.

Farber, E. 1952. *The Evolution of Chemistry*. New York: Ronald Press.

Friberg, L., G. F. Nordberg, and V. Vouk, eds. 1979. *Handbook of the Toxicology of Metals*. New York: Elsevier.

Garrels, R. M., F. T. MacKenzie, and C. Hunt. 1973. *Chemical Cycles and the Global Environment. Assessing Human Influences*. Los Angeles: W. Kauffmann, Inc.

Hohenbery, P. M. 1967. *Chemicals in Western Europe, 1850–1914*. Chicago: Rand McNally.

Holden, P. W. 1986. *Pesticides and Groundwater Quality*. For the Board on Agriculture, NRC. Washington, D.C.: National Academy Press.

Huisken, R. H. 1975. The consumption of raw materials for military purposes. *Ambio* 4: 211–15.

Ihde, A. 1964. *The Development of Modern Chemistry*. New York: Harper and Row.

Kreis, I. A. 1987. Department of Epidemiology, National Institute of Public Health and Environmental Hygiene, Netherlands. Personal communication.

Langford, J. C. 1973. Particulate Pb, ^{210}Pb, and ^{210}Po in the environment. In *Lead Poisoning in Man and the Environment*. MSS Information Corporation.

Larsson, P. 1985. Contaminated sediments of lakes and coeans act as sources of chlorinated hydrocarbons for release to water and atmosphere. *Nature* 317: 347–49.

League of Nations, Economic and Financial Section. 1927. *Memorandum on Coal*. Geneva.

Liebescher, K., and H. Smith. 1968. Essential and nonessential trace elements. *Arch. Env. Health* 17: 881–90.

Lindberg, S. E. 1987. Emission and deposition of atmospheric mercury vapor. In *Lead, Mercury, Cadmium, and Arsenic in the Environment*, ed. T. C. Hutchinson and K. M. Meema. (SCOPE 31). Chichester: John Wiley.

MacKenzie, F. T., R. J. Lantzy, and V. Paterson. 1979. Global trace metal cycles and predictions. *Math. Geol.* 11: 99–142.

Mance, G. 1987. *Pollution Threat of Heavy Metals in Aquatic Environments*. London and New York: Elsevier Applied Science.

Melosi, M. V. 1985. *Coping with Abundance: Energy and Environment in America*. New York: A. Knopf.

Mertz, W. 1981. The essential trace metals. *Science* 213: 1132–38.

N.A.S., National Research Council. 1978. *Chloroform, Carbon Tetrachloride, and Other Halomethanes*. Washington, D.C.

N.A.S., National Research Council. 1980. *Lead in the Human Environment*. Washington, D.C.

New York Times, February 15, 1987: 27.

Norberg, G. F. 1978. Factors influencing metabolism and toxicity of metals: a consensus report. *Env. Health Persp.* 25: 3–41.

Nriagu, J. O. 1979. Global inventory of natural and anthropogenic emissions of trace metals to the atmosphere. *Nature* 279: 409–11.

———. 1980. *Cadmium in the Environment*. New York: John Wiley.

———. 1983. *Lead and Lead Poisoning in Antiquity*. New York: John Wiley.

Nriagu, J. O., and C. I. Davidson, eds. 1986. *Toxic Metals in the Atmosphere*. Wiley Series in Advances in Environmental Science and Technology No. 17. New York: John Wiley.

OECD. 1979. *OECD State of the Environment 1979*. Paris: OECD.

Pacyna, J. M. 1986. Atmospheric trace elements from natural and anthropogenic sources. In *Toxic Metals in the Atmosphere*, ed. J. O. Nriagu and C. I. Davidson. New York: John Wiley.

Perkins, J. H. 1982. *Insects, Experts, and the Insecticide Crisis*. New York: Plenum Press.

Plimmer, J. 1982. Trends in chemical residues including reentry considerations. In *Pesticide Residues and Exposure*, ed. J. R. Plimmer. Washington, D.C.: American Chemical Society.

Prinn, R., D. Cunnold, R. Rasmussen, E. Simmonds, F. Alyea, A. Crawford, P. Frazer, and R. Rosen. 1987. Atmospheric trends and methylchloroform and the global average for the hydroxyl radical. *Science* 238: 945–50.

Reese, K. M., ed. 1976. *A Century of Chemistry*. Washington, D.C.: American Chemical Society.

Sanders, C. L. 1986. *Toxicological Aspects of Energy Production*. New York: Macmillan.

Schmitz, C. J. 1979. *World Nonferrous Metal Production and Prices 1700–1976*. London: Frank Cass.

Schroeder, W. H., and D. A. Lane. 1988. The fate of toxic airborne pollutants. *Envir. Sci. Tech.* 22: 240–46.

Schurr, S. H., and B. C. Netschert. 1960. *Energy in the American Economy, 1850–1975*. Baltimore, MD: Johns Hopkins University Press for Resources for the Future, Inc.

Singh, H. B., L. J. Salas, H. Shigeishi, and E. Scribner 1979. Atmospheric halocarbons, hydrocarbons, and sulfur hexafluoride: Global distributions, sources, sinks. *Science* 203: 899–903.

Singh, H. B., L. J. Salas, and R. E. Stiles. 1982. Distribution of selected gaseous organic mutagens in ambient air. *Envir. Sci. Tech.* 16: 872–81.

Svartengren, A., C. G. Elindor, L. Friberg, and B. Lind. 1986. Distribution and concentration of cadmium in human kidney. *Envir. Res.* 39: 1–7.

Thibodeau, L. A., R. B. Reed, Y. M. M. Bishop, and L. Kammerman. 1980. Air pollution and human health: A review and reanalysis. *Envir. Health Persp.* 34: 165–83.

Tillman, D. A. 1978. *Wood As an Energy Resource*. New York: Academic Press.

UNDP. 1979. United Nations Development Programmers; World Health Organization, Environmental Protection Project POL/RCE 001, Polish People's Republic, Ministry of Administration, Land Economy and Environmental Protection. Katowice, Poland.

UNEP, International Labor Organization, and WHO. 1986. *Carbamate Pesticides: A General Introduction*. Environmental Health Criteria 64. Geneva: WHO.

U.S. Department of Commerce, Bureau of the Census. 1985. *Statistical Abstracts of the United States 1986*. Washington, D.C.

U.S. Department of the Interior, Bureau of Mines. 1985. *Minerals Yearbook 1984*. Washington, D.C.

U.S. Environmental Protection Agency. 1978. *Source Assessment: Polyvinyl Chloride*. Washington, D.C.

———. 1985a. *Trends in the Quality of the Nation's Air*. Washington, D.C.

———. 1985b. *The Air Toxics Problem in the United States: An Analysis of Cancer Risks from Selected Pollutants*. Raleigh, NC: U.S. EPA Office of Air and Pollution.

U.S. International Trade Commission. 1985. *Synthetic Organic Chemicals. U.S. Production and Sales 1984*. Washington, D.C.

U.S. Tariff Commission. 1972. *Synthetic Organic Chemicals. U.S. Production and Sales 1970*. Washington, D.C.

United Nations. 1984. *United Nations Statistical Yearbook*. New York.

Waddams, A. L. 1980. *Chemicals from Petroleum*, 4th ed. Houston, TX: Gulf Publishing.

WHO-IPCS. 1987. *Selenium*. Environmental Health Criteria 58. Geneva: UNEP, ILO, and WHO.

Wolff, E. W., and D. A. Peel. 1985. The record of global pollution in polar ice and snow. *Nature* 313: 535–40.

Woodwell, G. M., P. P. Craig, and H. A. Johnson. 1975. DDT in the biosphere: where does it go? In *The Changing Global Environment*, ed. S. F. Singer. Dordrecht: D. Reidel.

Woolson, E. A. 1983. Man's perturbation of the sulfur cycle. In *Arsenic: Industrial, Biomedical, and Environmental Perspectives*, ed. W. H. Lederer and R. J. Fensterheim. New York: Van Nostrand Reinhold Co.

World Meteorological Organization. 1985. *Atmospheric Ozone 1985*. Vol. I. Global Ozone Research and Monitoring Project. Report No. 16.

World Chemical Outlook. 1987. *Chemical and Engineering News* 65, Dec. 14: 25–47.

Zook, E. G., J. J. Powell, B. M. Hackley, J. A. Emerson, J. R. Brooker, and G. M. Knobl. 1976. National Marine Fisheries Service preliminary survey of selected seafood for mercury, lead, cadmium, chromium, and arsenic content. *J. Agric. Food Chem.* 24: 47–53.

27

The Ionizing Radiations

MERRIL EISENBUD

All forms of life have always been exposed to a broad spectrum of naturally occurring radiations, among which are visible light, infrared, ultraviolet, and the ionizing radiations. The latter are distinguished by their ability to disrupt molecular bonds when they interact with matter, and include X-rays, gamma radiation, alpha and beta particles, neutrons, protons, and the cosmic rays, which enter the earth's atmosphere from extraterrestrial sources. Until about one century ago, the only sources of exposure to the ionizing radiations were from the undisturbed natural state. A few exceptions existed, such as uranium oxide as a coloring agent for ceramic glazes, and thorium in gas mantles, but these sources exposed relatively few people, and to only a modest degree.

When radioactivity and X-rays were discovered toward the end of the last century, the situation began to change. Radium was extracted from the earth's crust in small quantities and was used in the practice of medicine. Unfortunately, among the uses for radium were also many misuses, and the first kilogram extracted prior to World War II resulted in death from cancer of more then 100 persons. The misuses of X-rays during the same period probably resulted in a much larger toll of injuries and deaths, mainly among physicians and physicists, but also among patients and technicians. The exact figure is not likely ever to be known.

Until after World War II, relatively few members of the general public were aware of the harmful effects of the ionizing radiations. Such knowledge became more general with the bombings of Hiroshima and Nagasaki in August 1945. The association of nuclear radiation with the bombings of the two cities has left an indelible impression on the people of many nations and has resulted in widespread apprehension of the effects of radioactivity not only in war, but also in peacetime as well.

It is now almost half a century since the discovery of nuclear fission. Uranium, which is a slightly radioactive metal, is extracted from the earth in great quantities to provide fuel for the 1,000 or so nuclear reactors of various kinds that exist today in the world. These reactors produce electricity, provide propulsion for naval vessels and ice breakers, produce plutonium for nuclear and thermonuclear weapons, serve the research needs of physical and biological scientists, and produce radioactive pharmaceuticals. The infrastructure required for the operation of these reactors and the processing and use of the radioactive materials they produce results in the release of radioactive substances to the environment. The releases ordinarily occur in small quantities, but sometimes in much greater amounts as a result of accidents or abnormal occurrences, and in huge amounts when nuclear weapons are exploded (Eisenbud 1987).

Effects of Exposure to Ionizing Radiation

As a result of the many decades of international collaboration, more is known about the effects of ionizing radiation then about any of the many other noxious agents that contaminate the environment. It is necessary to begin a discussion of the effects of ionizing radiation exposure with certain dichotomies that include in part the following:

1. whether the source of exposure is external to the body (as in the case of exposure to medical X-rays) or internal (as when radioactive iodine is inhaled or ingested and then deposits in the thyroid);
2. whether the dose is from a relatively massive exposure delivered in a short period of time (less then a few days) or in small bits over a long period of time, which may extend over many years;
3. whether the effects appear soon after exposure ("acute" or "prompt" effects) or are delayed for many months or years ("delayed" or "late" effects).

The effects also should be separated according to whether they are stochastic or nonstochastic. The stochastic effects include cancer and genetic damage, for which it is believed that there are no thresholds and that the probability of occurrence increases as the dose increases, but the severity of the effect is independent of the dose.

The nonstochastic effects are seen at doses above approximately 50 rem and include suppression of bone-marrow function, damage to the gastrointestinal tract, skin burns, cataracts, and temporary sterility in males. These effects occur at doses that are so high as to be experienced in peacetime only as the result of major accidents, of which there have been relatively few throughout the world. In the United States, which has, by far, the world's largest nuclear industry, a total of seven deaths have occurred from massive radiation exposure, the last of which occurred more then 25 years ago. All of the fatalities were the results of accidents in the workplace, and no exposure of the public resulted. There also have been a number of accidents in other countries, of which the most severe was at Chernobyl in 1986, from which 31 deaths occurred among the plant workers and rescue teams. Except for Chernobyl, none of the fatal accidents, either in the United States or elsewhere, occurred from operation of civilian power plants. Although the nonstochastic effects of radiation exposure have occurred infrequently in peacetime, they would result in millions of deaths in the event of an all-out nuclear war.

The stochastic consequences (genetic and carcinogenic) may be difficult to identify in an exposed population because they occur many years after exposure. The doses received initially may be in the range of near-lethality, such as were received by some survivors of nuclear accidents or the bombings of Hiroshima or Nagasaki. Alternatively, they may be well below the dose at which the nonstochastic effects are seen. The exposures that result in stochastic effects may involve nothing more unusual then a series of chest X-rays or a life-long history of exposure to radon in a single-story home built on soil or rock in which the uranium content is elevated. Identification of the stochastic effects may be difficult because they are so few in comparison with those seen in the unexposed population. For example, the bombings of Hiroshima and Nagasaki resulted in about 200,000 deaths from the effects of blast, fires, and the acute radiation syndrome (the term used to describe the complex of effects seen soon after massive radiation exposure). The last is believed to have been responsible for about 15% of the total, or about 30,000 fatalities. These numbers must be regarded as very approximate because of great uncertainties in the casualty estimates (NAS 1980).

The survivors of the two bombings have been the subject of an epidemiological investigation supported jointly by the Japanese and U.S. governments for more the 40 years. No genetic effects have been seen among the offspring of the survivors, which does not mean that genetic effects did not occur, but rather that the effects have been so few that they could not be detected against the normal frequency with which genetic effects occur naturally in an unexposed population. It *has* been found that the incidence of certain kinds of cancer is greater than expected among the survivors and that the effect is somewhat proportional to the dose received. In round numbers, it is estimated that there will be an excess of about 700 radiation-induced cancers among the 70,000 survivors of the two bombings who have been maintained under surveillance. While not an insignificant number, it is relatively small compared to the number of initial casualties.

At the present time, the dose-response relationship for the stochastic effects is believed to take the form of a linear-quadratic equation, in which the effects are linear at low doses but become curvilinear at higher doses, as shown in

Figure 27.1. The levels of exposure to members of the public rarely have resulted in doses greater then the natural background (about 0.1 rem/yr) or less, where the effects are assumed to be governed by the linear portion of the linear-quadratic relationship.

In round numbers, the number of cancers that will develop in an exposed population may be taken to be 10^{-4} (-4) per rem.

Two facts have important implications for risk assessment and for formulation of public policy: (1) the dose-response relationship is assumed to be linear at low doses, and (2) a threshold is absent. The absence of a threshold implies that there is no such thing as an absolutely safe level of exposure. Every increment of dose above zero, however small, results in an increment of risk as well, but the risk becomes smaller as the dose diminishes. Thus, the question that must be

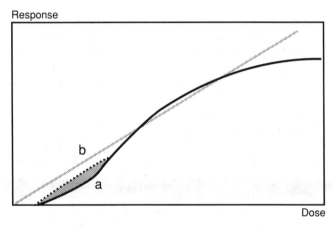

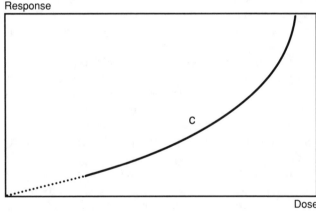

Figure 27.1 Types of dose-response curves. (a) The classical sigmoid curve, no longer considered applicable in radiobiology. At the low end, the response may be asymptotic with dose, or a true threshold may exist but be obscured by statistical uncertainties inherent in the data. The cross-hatched portion is how the dose-response would be altered if a fraction of the irradiated population should be exceptionally sensitive to radiation. (b) The linear dose-response relationship. Note that (a) and (b) may be so close together for parts of the two curves that they may be indistinguishable, particularly if the experimental or epidemiological data fall between or slightly beyond the two intercepts. (c) The linear-quadratic dose-response, in which the response is linear at low doses (dashed portion) but takes the form kD^2 at higher doses (solid portion). The slope of the linear portion may vary with dose rate. Most of the dose that the public receives is believed to lie along the linear portion of the curve.

answered is not, "What is the safe dose" but "How safe is safe enough?"

Another dilemma that arises from the assumption of linearity and the absence of a threshold is that the risk to individuals can be very small, but a finite number of cancers can result if a sufficiently large population is exposed. Most persons would regard a lifetime risk of 10^{-6} as negligible, but if the risk is extended to the world's population of 5×10^9 persons, it would be expected that 5,000 radiation-induced cancers would result – a number that would deserve the attention of public-health officials. The question of whether the permissible dose should be defined on the basis of individual or of collective risk cannot be answered by existing technical, moral, or political concepts.

Sources of Exposure: Natural Radioactivity

Ionizing radiations and radioactivity originate from natural, industrial, medical, and military sources. Our exposure to natural radioactivity is from both terrestrial and cosmic sources. The primary cosmic radiation, which originates in outer space and impinges on the top of the atmosphere, consists mainly of heavy ions that interact with the atmospheric gases in a number of ways, which have the net effect of producing a readily measurable flux of penetrating radiation at the surface of the earth. The dose received from natural sources is modified by cultural factors, such as type of housing, uses of phosphate fertilizers, air travel, and tobacco smoking.

Cosmic Rays

The dose we receive from cosmic rays is variable, depending to a slight degree on geomagnetic latitude, but mainly on altitude above sea level. This is because the shielding effect of the atmosphere is diminished progressively with altitude. The average dose at sea level is about 26 mrem/yr, but is approximately twice as high in Denver, which is 1,600 m above sea level. At an altitude of 3,200 m, such as at Leadville, Colorado, the annual cosmic-ray dose is about 125 mrem/yr.

Because of the effect of altitude, the passengers on high-flying aircraft receive additional cosmic-ray exposure. A flight across the U.S. will result in an additional dose per person of about 2.5 mrem.

The interactions of cosmic rays with atmospheric gases produce a number of radionuclides, of which Tritium (H-3) and C-14 are the most important from the point of view of human exposure. These nuclides become part of the hydrogen and carbon pools of the biosphere and find their way into water, food, and human tissue.

Carbon-14 is distributed more or less uniformly throughout the biosphere and is present in living tissue at a concentration of 7.5 ± 2.7 picocuries (pCi) per gram of carbon. The average person contains about 0.1 μCi C-14, which delivers a dose of about 0.7 mrem/yr to the skeleton. Tritium is naturally present in surface waters at a concentration of about 10 pci/l. The dose received from tritium is less than that from C-14.

The Earth's Crust

Some of the elements in the earth's crust are radioactive and result in both external and internal exposure of the body.

About 340 nuclides exist in nature, of which about 70 are radioactive and are found mainly among the heavy elements. In most parts of the world, the radioactivity of the soils and rocks varies within narrow limits, but there are places, notably Brazil and India, in which the presence of minerals that contain thorium results in levels of natural radioactivity that are ten or more times greater then normal.

The radionuclides in the earth's crust can be divided according to whether they occur singly or as members of three distinct chains that originate with U-238, U-235, and Th-232. These three long-lived radioactive parents decay through complicated chains of decay products that include more than 40 radionuclides with half-lives that range from about 10^{-6} seconds to 10^8 years. The U-238 chain is of particular importance because it includes Ra-226, a long-lived bone-seeking nuclide that is the parent of the 3.8-day isotope of the noble gas radon. U-238 is the most abundant isotope of uranium, and coexists in nature with both its radioactive descendent, U-234 (present in the amount of 0.0058%), and U-235 (present in the amount of 0.71%). The latter is the fissionable nuclide that is used in nuclear reactors.

Uranium is found in most rocks and soils in concentrations that range from 1 ppm to 4 ppm in sedimentary and granitic rocks to 120 ppm in the phosphate deposits that are exploited for commercial phosphate production in Florida and elsewhere. The fertilizers produced from these phosphate deposits contain up to 100 ppm and, when applied to agricultural soils, add slightly to the uranium that is normally present.

The main source of exposure from the U-238 series is radium-226. Because of its relatively high solubility, this nuclide readily finds its way into drinking water and food. Radium-226 decays to radon-222, which has a 3.8-day half-life and decays through a series of short-lived nuclides of five elements, including polonium, bismuth, and thalium. Radon, because of its inertness, can diffuse readily into the atmosphere, where its daughter products (which are electrically charged ions when formed) become attached to inert dust particles that may be inhaled and deposited in the lungs, mainly on the surface of the bronchial epithelium. In this way, the lungs receive a larger dose than other parts of the body. Exposure to radon is elevated within many buildings because the gas diffuses into them from soil or enters by way of well water. On average, radon and its daughter products in U.S. style houses deliver an annual dose in excess of 2,000 mrem to the bronchial epithelium, but the dose can be very much greater in places in which the uranium content of the soil or rocks is elevated.

A number of other radionuclides contribute to the dose we receive from nature. They include Pb-210 and Po-210, which are present not only in our food supplies, but also in tobacco, thereby further increasing the dose to the lungs of smokers.

The members of the uranium and thorium series also are present in coal and are released to the environment when fly ash is discharged from smokestacks or is accumulated in the ash heaps. The dose received from the coal-burning, power-plant stack discharges is often greater than that from some nuclear power plants of comparable size (Beck et al. 1980).

Another major source of exposure to natural radioactivity

is the radionuclide potassium-40 (K-40), which has a half-life of 1.3 billion years, and is present in the amount of about 800 pCi per gram of potassium. A 70-Kg person contains about 140 g of potassium, most of which is located in muscle. Our bodies receive an internal dose of about 20 mrem/yr from the potassium contained in our tissues and an average of 8 mrem/yr due to external exposure to gamma radiation from the potassium contained in rocks and soils.

From all sources, the average person receives a whole-body dose of about 80 mrem/yr from natural sources. The dose to the bronchial epithelium is very much higher because of the radon daughters.

Exceptional Exposures

Many people in the world are exposed to much higher doses because of abnormally high amounts of radioactive materials in soil or water. It has long been known that many mineral springs contain high concentrations of radium and radon, and faddists in some parts of Europe, South America, and Japan exploit such waters for their supposed beneficial effects on health. In Japan, Austria, and Czchechoslovakia, people vacation at health spas, where they can breathe air that contains high concentrations of radon and bathe in radon-containing water.

The most unusual radioactive anomalies occur in parts of Brazil and in the state of Kerala, India, where people live on sand and soil that contains such high concentrations of uranium and thorium that the dose they receive is as much as ten times the normal. The population so exposed in Brazil (6,000) has been judged to be too small to permit meaningful epidemiological studies to be undertaken. About 100,000 persons are exposed in the region of Kerala, which might be a sufficiently large population to provide meaningful information about the effects of low levels of radiation, but the required epidemiological studies have not been undertaken.

Sources of Exposure: Medical and Consumer Products

Medical and Dental Practice

In most parts of the world, the dose received from the medical uses of ionizing radiation exceeds that from any other human-made source. The dose per examination from these sources of exposure has been reduced over time because of improvements in technique, but in many countries this lower dose may have been offset by increased use of these techniques. Reports from many countries indicate that the annual frequency of radiographic examinations is in the range of 300 to 900 per 1,000 persons. In the United States, it has been estimated that the per capita dose to the adult population was 103 mrem/yr in 1970, the last year for which such an estimate is available. The U.N. Scientific Committee on the Effects of Atomic Radiation has estimated that the effective dose equivalent in the developed nations is about 100 mrem/yr. From a number of sources, the per capita dose from the medical uses of the ionizing radiations in the United States may be approximated as 75 mrem/yr.

Consumer Products

We mentioned earlier the adventitious presence of naturally occurring radionuclides in phosphate fertilizer and tobacco. In such examples, the radionuclides are present as unintended contaminants. Examples also exist of exposure that results from radioactive materials deliberately introduced into manufactured products used by the general public. Such materials have been used in consumer products since early in the twentieth century. One of the first applications was in luminous paints for the dials of timepieces, compasses, and instruments. Radium was used for this purpose until after World War II, when it was replaced by less hazardous and less costly, artificially produced nuclides such as tritium and prometheum-147. The dose received currently from these beta-emitting isotopes is small (estimated to be about 0.25 mrem/yr).

Uranium trioxide has been used in ceramic glazes, in which it produces colors that range from orange-red to lemon yellow. The dose to the hands in contact with these glazes ranges from 0.5 to 20 mrem/h for glazes produced prior to 1944, but the dose from ceramics produced since 1944 may be less – by a factor of about 5 (Menczer 1965).

Uranium also has been used at concentrations of a few hundred parts per million to enhance the appearance of porcelain teeth (Thompson 1978). The dose to a small volume of tissue within the oral cavity has been estimated to be 1.4 rem/yr. The presence of K-40 in the porcelain raises the dose to about 1.6 rem/yr.

Another general source of exposure is the presence of thorium and uranium in ophthalmic lenses (Goldman and Yaniv 1978). These elements enter the glass-making process because of their natural association with rare-earth elements used to tint the glass. The critical tissue is believed to be the germinal layer of the cornea estimated to be at a tissue depth of about 50 microns. On the assumption that an individual might wear spectacles 16 hours a day for a total of about 6,000 hours per year, the maximum annual dose to the germinal layer of the cornea has been estimated to be about 500 mrem.

Thorium has long been used for producing luminescence in gas mantles, of which an estimated 25 million are used annually in the United States, mostly by campers. Between 250 and 400 mg Th is used in each mantle (O'Donnell 1978). The dose to campers and other consumers is estimated to be less than 0.1 mrem/yr, which is sufficiently low to permit these devices to be distributed to the public without regulation.

Production of radionuclides for use in medicine, research, and industry has become an important by-product of reactor operation and particle accelerators during the past 40 years. In general, these nuclides, which have come to be known loosely as "isotopes," may be employed for a wide variety of uses, depending on their chemical and physical properties. The total quantities of the various radionuclides produced each year, the fraction of each that decays, the fraction that remains in use, and the amounts that go to waste-disposal sites, are difficult to estimate.

The importance of radionuclides as tracers and radiation sources is too well known to require elaboration. "Isotopes" are now one of the standard tools of research workers, and equipment such as scintillation counters, geiger counters, and scalers are part of the normal laboratory scenery in university, government, and industrial laboratories everywhere. The variety of radionuclides matches the number of uses to which they are put.

The sensitivity of the instrumentation used in tracer studies permits many isotopes to be used in small quantities that do not require a Nuclear Regulatory Commission (NRC) license.

Many clinical procedures also use radionuclides for either diagnostic or therapeutic reasons. It was estimated in 1980 that 10–12 million doses of radiopharmaceuticals were administered in the United States. The sales of radiopharmaceuticals in the United States increased at a rate of 25% per year during the period 1965–1975, but have since slowed to a rate of increase of 10–15% per year. Between 1966 and 1975, the annual frequency and radiopharmaceutical use in the United States increased from 3.7 to 37 per 1,000 inhabitants.

One of the most widespread uses of radionuclides is as ionization sources in smoke detectors. The first smoke detectors, introduced in 1951, contained about $20 \mu Ci$ Ra-226, but the use of that material has been discontinued in favor of Am-241 (Johnson 1978), which has made it possible to market inexpensive, efficient devices that are easily installed and can now be found in many homes and in most hotel rooms, offices, and factories. The americium is used in the form of the dioxide, which is fabricated between a backing of silver and a front cover of gold or gold/palladium alloy that is sealed by hot forging (Wrenn and Cohen 1979). Through improved design, each detector now contains from 0.5 to $1 \mu Ci$ Am-241, but the earlier designs (circa 1970) contained an average of $79 \mu Ci$. Twelve million units per year were being sold by the mid-1980s, containing a total of about 8.5 Ci Am-241 (Harris 1986).

Americium-241 has a half-life longer than 400 years, and emits both alpha and photon radiation. Because of the widespread use of smoke detectors, a great deal of attention has been given to the risk to occupants of households in which they are used. The highest dose is from external radiation and is reported to be 0.014 mrem/yr to an individual sleeping 6 ft from the detector for 8 hours per day (Wrenn and Cohen 1979). Exposure of the general population from incineration of the devices or from disposal in landfills has been shown to be less than that from external radiation.

Applications in Outer Space

The decay heat of radionuclides has been used to supply the electrical energy required for scientific instruments and communications equipment aboard space satellites. The power units are known by the acronym SNAP (Satellite Nuclear Auxiliary Power). Such devices also have been used to operate beacons and weather stations in remote places.

Between 1961 and the end of 1982, 34 radioisotope generators had been employed by the United States in 19 space systems. The first of these devices was developed for terrestrial uses in the late 1950s, with the advent of miniaturized transistorized electronic circuits with low power requirements. In 1961, the first SNAP device was launched into space to provide 2.6 W(e) of power to satellites used in the TRANSIT navigational system. The design life for the unit was 5 years, but the power plant was still operational 15 years later, when the satellite was decommissioned (Bennett, Lombardo, and Rock 1984). All of the SNAP devices used in outer space have depended on the decay heat of Pu-238, an alpha emitter with a half-life of 86.4 yr. A basic requirement in recent years is that the capsule retain its integrity under all circumstances, or at least until the Pu-238 has decayed. However, prior to adoption of this policy, a SNAP device containing 17,000 Ci of Pu-238 was volatilized by the heat of reentry about 150,000 ft above the Indian Ocean and resulted in a 50-yr dose commitment to the respiratory lymph nodes of the world's population of about 36 mrem (Shleien, Cochran, and Magno 1970). In contrast, a NASA spacecraft (Nimbus-B1), which was launched from California in 1968, was destroyed by the range safety officer at an altitude of 30 km because of a guidance error, and the radioisotope generators fell into the Santa Barbara Channel, from which the generators were recovered intact (Bennett 1981).

In 1970, the spacecraft Apollo 13 was damaged on its way to the moon, and the lunar module with its attached SNAP generator reentered the atmosphere over the South Pacific, where the generator landed in the 6-km-deep Tonga Trench. The package was never recovered, but subsequent surveys could find no evidence of radioactivity either in the atmosphere or the Pacific Ocean, leading to the conclusion that the containment remained intact.

Both the United States and the Soviet Union have developed reactors for use in outer space, but only one such device has been launched by the United States. SNAP-10A was launched in 1965, and began operation after being placed in a 4,000-yr orbit, but it shut down as a result of an electrical malfunction after only 43 days. The reactor remains in orbit. Its initial radioactive inventory contained 2×10^9 Ci of fission products, but it has decayed by now to less than 100 Ci and will diminish to less than 1 Ci after 100 years (Bennett 1981).

Nuclear Power

Generation of nuclear power requires an industrial complex that in addition to power reactors includes facilities for mining and refining uranium, fabricating reactor fuel, recycling spent fuel, and managing radioactive wastes.

Mining and Milling

Uranium mining, especially underground, involves the danger that high concentrations of radon may produce lung cancer in the miners. Such cases have occurred among miners in the southwestern United States, but this danger can be prevented by installing mine ventilation systems sufficient to meet existing standards.

The mills that produce crude U_3O_8 for shipment to refineries accumulate large heaps of "mill tailings" that contain the radium originally present in the ore. In the United States, it is estimated that the existing tailings piles contain 50,000 Ci of Ra-226. The tailings emanate radon and are a source of radium-containing dust that washes or blows into the surrounding area. In Grand Junction, Colorado, some of the tailings, which are sandlike, were used to construct buildings that were subsequently found to contain high concentrations of radon.

Nuclear Reactors

Approximately 1,000 nuclear reactors now exist in the world, of which more then 500 have been used for the generation of electricity. In addition, more than 200 reactors are used to provide power for naval vessels. Several hundred small reactors are used for research, and a much smaller number of reactors are used to produce plutonium for nuclear weapons. This discussion will be limited to reactors used for the generation of civilian power. The effects on the environment of radiation produced by these reactors can best be discussed under (1) normal operation, and (2) accidental conditions.

Nuclear power reactors under normal operating conditions produce small quantities of radioactive liquid, gaseous, and solid waste products. The doses received by persons living in the immediate vicinity of the reactors is miniscule under normal operating conditions, and can be maintained easily at a small fraction of the health and safety limits adopted by regulatory authorities. In the United States, where light-water reactors predominate, the regulations prescribe that the dose to the maximally exposed persons living near the reactors not exceed 10 mrem/yr. Under most conditions, the doses are much lower. In 1981, when 71 nuclear power plants were operating at 48 different sites, the doses received by nearby residents ranged from a low of 10^{-5} mrem/yr to 0.05 mrem/yr. The collective dose to about 98 million people living within 80 km of the reactors was 160 person rem in 1982. For the purpose of comparison, this amount should be compared to the 9,800,000 person rem received by the same population from natural sources.

Three nuclides (H^3, 12.3 yr; Kr^{85}, 10.7 yr, and C^{14}, 5,730 yr) are relatively long lived and are emitted under normal opera-

ting conditions in the gaseous or liquid wastes. They tend to accumulate in the global environment and must be considered in an evaluation of the effects of nuclear power. More will be said about them in a later section.

From the time the first reactors were built during World War II, it has been known that in the event of an accident that released the contents of a reactor core to the environment, large land areas could be contaminated and large numbers of people could be dangerously exposed. The first analytical studies of the consequences of severe reactor accidents were based on the assumption that no engineered safeguards were provided (Parker and Healy 1956; U.S. AEC 1957). These studies provided the first impetus for the need (1) to design reactors that had certain inherent safety features and (2) to provide mitigating features that would prevent the release of radioactivity in the event an accident does occur. An example of (1) is the negative coefficient of reactivity that reduces the power output of the reactor in the event of a rise in temperature. Examples of (2) include the pressure vessel within which the reactor is housed, and the hermetically sealed building that is designed to retain the steam and fission products that would be released in the event of a disruption in the reactor integrity.

It is important to note that reactor accidents rarely result in the release of large quantities of radioactive materials into the environment. During the 45-year period since the first reactor was built, 14 accidents have occurred in which the reactor core was damaged (Table 27-1). In only two of them were more than trace amounts of radioactivity released beyond the plant boundries. These accidents occurred at Windscale, England in 1957, and more recently and far more seriously, in 1986 at Chernobyl. The widely publicized accident at Three Mile Island in 1979 destroyed about 35% of the reactor core, but the engineered safeguards succeeded in preventing all but an insignificant quantity of radioactivity from escaping from the plant. The highest doses, received by a few people living near the plant, were less than 100 mrem, which is less than the dose a person receives from nature in about one year (Kemeny 1979). The Chernobyl accident was the only one in

Table 27-1 *Reactor accidents involving core damage*

Year	Location	Name of reactor	Type	Extent of contamination
1952	Canada	NRX	Experimental	None
1955	Idaho	EBR-1	Experimental	Trace
1957	United Kingdom	Windscale	Military production reactor	20,000 Ci ^{131}I
1957	Idaho	HTRE-3	Experimental	Slight
1958	Canada	NRU	Research	None
1959	California	SRE	Experimental	Slight
1960	Pennsylvania	WTR	Research	None measured
1961	Idaho	SL-1	Experimental	10 Ci ^{131}I
1963	Tennessee	ORR	Research	Trace
1966	Detroit	Fermi	Experimental power	No release outside plant
1969	France	St. Laurent	Power	Little, if any
1969	Switzerland	Lucens	Experimental	None
1979	Pennsylvania	TM-II	Power	Slight
1986	USSR	Chernobyl-4	Power	Extensive

which contamination was spread beyond national borders. Even at Chernobyl, all immediate injuries and deaths from the acute radiation syndrome occurred among the power-plant workers, firemen, and other emergency personnel.

Reprocessing Spent Reactor Fuel

When a reactor core has reached the end of its useful life, only a small percentage of the U-235 will have been consumed in fission and an additional small fraction of the U-238 will have been transmuted to Pu-239 and other trans-uranic elements. If the core is to be reprocessed for recovery of uranium and plutonium, it must be transported to a fuel-reprocessing plant, at which the spent fuel will be treated chemically (1) to convert the fission products into a waste form suitable for long-term storage, and (2) to recover the remaining U-235 and the transuranic elements.

The primary sources of possible global contamination are the gaseous wastes. I-129, a nuclide with a half-life of 17 million years is volatilized and is present in the reprocessing wastes in relatively large quantities. Because of its long half-life, it will accumulate in the environment, become part of the iodine pool, and deliver a thyroid dose to the general population that will increase in proportion to the rate of nuclear-power production (NCRPM 1983). The radioiodines can be removed chemically with caustic scrubbers or by other means, such as reactions with mercury or silver. Other radioactive gaseous releases from the nuclear fuel-reprocessing plants include Kr-85 and tritium, but the gaseous releases of the latter have been small compared to those in liquid form. The stack re-leases of Kr-85 are substantial, but have not been a source of significant exposure in the vicinity of the processing plants. The doses to the global population from the Kr-85 and tritium emissions are expected to be small but dependent on the amount of nuclear power generated and the fraction of the spent fuel that is reprocessed. A number of options are available for removing these nuclides from waste streams, should it be considered necessary to do so. Natural sources and the residual from weapons testing are expected to pre-dominate until the end of this century, at which time the dose from tritium could reach 0.02 mrem/yr. Krypton could result in a dose to the skin of about 2 mrem/yr if steps are not taken to remove and store the nuclide (half-life 10.7 years) (Eisenbud 1987).

Transportation of Radioactive Materials

About 500 billion shipments of all kinds are made annually in the United States, of which about 100 million involve hazardous materials that are flammable, explosive, toxic, or radioactive. Radioactive shipments total about 2.8 million per year, and contain about 9 million curies, not including spent fuel (U.S. NRC 1977; Wolff 1984).

The rules and regulations that govern transportation of radioactive material are complex owing to the varied types of shipments to which they are applicable (U.S. GPO 1983). In the United States, the Department of Transportation (DOT) has primary responsibility for regulating such shipments, most of which involve small quantities of radionuclides in-tended for use in research laboratories or medical facilities.

Under DOT regulations, a radioactive material is defined as one that has a specific activity in excess of 0.002 μCi/g. This definition is very conservative: the specific activity is only about 2.5 times the natural radioactivity of elemental potassium.

The exact regulatory requirements depend on the kinds and amounts of nuclides involved and on the types of vehicles being utilized. Most shipments involve relatively innocuous materials that can be shipped safely in fiberboard or wooden boxes or in steel drums designed to withstand moderately rough handling conditions (Type A packages). The require-ments vary, of course, depending on whether or not the material is in a form capable of being disseminated into the environment. Intermediate quantities of radioactive ship-ments may be required to be shipped in containers that have been tested to withstand more rigorous stresses. For more hazardous shipments (Type B), the tests include a 9-m drop to a hard surface; a fall of more than 1 m, landing on the upraised tip of a 15-cm-diameter steel bar; and 30-minute exposure to a temperature of 1475°C. A water-immersion test requires that the package be submerged for not less than 8 h under at least 1 m of water.

The many millions of shipments of radioactive materials have been involved in many accidents, most of which have occurred during handling rather than during transport. Type A packages failed 13 times during the ten-year period 1971–1981. The consequences were minor, having been limited by the small amounts of radioactive material that can be shipped in this way. No Type B packages failed during this period, al-though 45 such packages were involved in accidents (Emerson and McClure 1985; Wolff 1984). No significant accidents involved higher levels of radioactivity.

Shipments of high-level wastes, spent fuel, or large amounts of transuranic wastes occur with less frequency, but involve large quantities of radioactivity and therefore require corre-spondingly greater degrees of protection.

The casks in which such shipments are made are huge but can be accommodated either on flat-bed trailers or on rail-road cars. Special features of design are needed to remove the heat that is generated during shipment. The required shielding and the need for structural strength adds to the mass of the shipment, which may weigh as much as 100 tons. The casks are subjected to severe tests before their designs are accepted by the NRC. In one such test, a 28-ton cask was im-pacted by a rocket-propelled railroad car driven at 120 km/h. The cask was hardly damaged, despite the fact that the trailer on which the cask was mounted was bent into a U-shape around the front of the locomotive, which was badly damaged.

Radioactive Waste Management

Several kinds of radioactive wastes are classified ac-cording to their physical and chemical properties as well as according to the source from which the wastes originate. (U.S. DOE 1983).

Among the physical properties that influence the manner in which radioactive wastes should be managed are the half-life of the nuclides and the chemical form in which they exist. The categories of wastes that must be considered are:

1. Low-level wastes, which consist of residues from laboratory research, slightly contaminated paper and other laboratory debris, biological materials, scrap metal and building materials, and various weakly radioactive wastes generated at the reactor sites. In addition, two categories of low-level wastes accumulate in huge volumes at a relatively few sites. They are uranium mill tailings and wastes generated in the clean-up of uranium-, radium-, and thorium-processing plants, the so-called remedial action program of the DOE.

2. High-level wastes, which can be considered in three subcategories: unreprocessed spent fuel, liquid and solid residues from fuel, and transuranic wastes, which are mainly alpha-emitting residues from military manufacturing.

Low-level Wastes

The United States is facing a crisis in the management of low-level wastes, not because they have proved to be so hazardous, but because of widespread public concern about the potential risks of shallow land burial, which is the most favored disposal option. Although there has been no reason to believe that the public has been overexposed from past burial-site operations, there have been flaws in both design and operation of the disposal sites, all of which were correctable. The reported deficiencies were so widely publicized that widespread public opposition developed, however, which has jeopardized the nation's ability to manage its low-level radioactive wastes.

To deal with the impasse that has developed, the Congress passed a National Low-Level Policy Act, which requires individual states to provide for disposal of the wastes generated within their borders or to provide regional facilities that can serve the needs of several states that have joined in compacts for the purpose.

High-level Wastes

Several methods of isolating high-level wastes have been studied during the past 40 years, including on-site methods of solidification and disposal, use of the seabed and subseabed, injection as a grout in deep rock fissures, insertion in Greenland glaciers, and geological isolation in deep-mined cavities. Proposals have also been made that the wastes be lifted into outer space or into the sun by rockets, or be transmuted to rapidly decaying elements in giant accelerators. Such options must be considered fanciful for the foreseeable future because of economics, safety, and the current state of technology (U.S. DOE 1980). On-site solidification and disposal, use of the marine environment, and geologic isolation in mined cavities appear to be the most viable alternatives.

On-Site Solidification and Disposal.   At the Oak Ridge National Laboratory, Tennessee and in the Soviet Union, moderately radioactive wastes have been mixed with cement to form a grout, which is then injected through wells into rocks that have been fractured hydraulically (NAS-NRC 1985; Spitsyn and Balukova 1979). Recent U.S. studies have suggested that this technique might be suitable for certain defense wastes at both Savannah River, South Carolina and Hanford, Washington (NAS-NRC 1978; 1981). It has also

been shown that at these sites, wastes having intermediate levels of activity can be hardened into concrete and buried in near-surface trenches.

Subseabed Disposal.   The subseabed sediments have many attractive features as a repository for high-level wastes, and about a dozen countries are coordinating research on their possible use for that purpose. Several methods of emplacing the wastes have been proposed, of which one of the most promising is the penetrometer, which is a free-falling, ballistically shaped container that could be released from a vessel and penetrate as far as 30 m into the sediments.

The subseabed concept is in a relatively early stage of development which, to be implemented, will require that present international restrictions on "ocean dumping" be modified (U.S. DOE 1979a).

Deep Geological Repositories.   The currently favored method of disposing of high-level wastes is in deep underground mined cavities. After 25 years of political indecision as to how to deal with the high-level waste problem, the U.S. Congress enacted the Nuclear Waste Policy Act in late 1982.

Several types of rock are potentially suitable for repositories. Those that have received the most serious consideration are salt, tuff, granite, and basalt.

Methods of Risk Assessment.   There is no precedent in technology for the long periods of time for which risk assessments are required in radioactive waste management, and there is as yet no firm policy, either national or international, as to the length of time for which a given level of risk must be assured or the amounts of radioactive materials that should be permitted to enter the biosphere in future millennia. Development of criteria for the design of high-level waste repositories has been handicapped by the fact that limits of permissible dose being imposed on future generations have been slow to evolve. There is no problem insofar as limits to the maximally exposed individual is concerned, since the repositories should have no trouble in meeting the dose limits prescribed for light-water reactors, i.e., 10–25 mrem/yr. The problem is one that we have encountered before: how should we deal with the dilemma imposed by the possible imposition of exceedingly small doses to very large populations.

However, establishment of limits for collective dose is more complicated. The U.S. Environmental Protection Agency regulations stipulate that the repository should be built so that it results in no more than 1,000 deaths in 10,000 years. Using present risk coefficients for development of fatal cancers, if these risks are applied to the world's population and if one assumes that a new generation of people is born every 30 years and that the world's population will reach steady-state at 10 billion persons, it follows that there will be about 3 trillion persons born in the next 10,000 years and that the risk of dying because of radiation-induced cancer will be 3×10^{-12}. Although this level of risk is exceedingly small, it appears that the geological storage system is capable of meeting the limit (Smith et al. 1982).

The models used to predict the performance of the repository are constructed by linking together the rates at which groundwater will seep into the repository, the rates of corrosion of the canister, solubilization of the waste form, and migration of the radionuclides through the backfill and rocks. After 1,000 years or more, the nuclides reach the biosphere and then begins the task of modeling the pathways by which the nuclides reach human beings. It has been reported (Kocher et al. 1983) that the uncertainty in the dose estimates, based only on transport in the biosphere, may cover 4 or 5 orders of magnitude, and that, in the present state of knowledge, the uncertainty in the transport models used to describe the movement from the repository to the biosphere are indeterminate.

A number of investigators have used natural analogs to infer the behavior of a deep geological repository. The best known of these studies involves a natural fossil fission reactor in the Republic of Gabon, West Africa (Cowan 1976). The reactor was located in what is now known as the Oklo uranium mine about 1.8 billion years ago, when conditions in the uranium deposit were such as to sustain criticality for an estimated 100,000 years, during which time huge amounts of fission products and transuranic elements were produced. The radionuclides have long since decayed to stable nuclides, which have been measured in the environs of the fossil reactor. Most of the nuclides of interest migrated for very short distances, of the order of meters, before they decayed. The fractional mobilization rates of the individual radionuclides from the reactor zones has been estimated to be on the order of 10^{-7} to 10^{-10} years.

A second natural analog from which similar conclusions have been drawn is located in a highly weathered caldera in the state of Minas Gerais, Brazil (Eisenbud et al. 1984). A large ore body that contains thorium and rare-earth elements is located near the summit of a hill known as the Morro do Ferro, and has been studied as an analog for an ancient high-level waste repository that has been invaded by groundwater and eroded to the surface. The ore body contains about 50,000 metric tons of thorium, which is being used as a chemical analog for quadrivalent plutonium. Lanthanum, a rare-earth element, is being used as an analog for trivalent curium and americium. As at Oklo, the mobilization rates for the two analogs for the transuranic actinide elements have been shown to be on the order of 10^{-9} per year. Thus, even in this near-surface, highly weathered, wet ore body, the mobilization rates are so low as to assure in situ decay of the transuranic elements plutonium, americium, curium and, probably, neptunium (Krauskopf 1986).

One feature that Oklo and the Morro do Ferro have in common is the presence of abundant quantities of clay minerals. At the Morro do Ferro, the primary minerals in which the analog elements were originally contained have long since been destroyed by weathering, and the analog elements are presently immobilized in amorphous form associated with clays and iron oxides.

Ionizing Radiations from Military Sources

While risk assessors involved with the civilian uses of nuclear energy debate the shape of the dose response curve and whether the risk coefficients for latent cancers is 10^{-4} or 2×10^{-4} per rem, 50,000 nuclear warheads are deployed in silos, submarines, and stockpiles, ready to destroy our society in the first hour after the outbreak of a nuclear war.

It has often been said that the consequences of a nuclear war are beyond our capability to comprehend. It is of course possible to estimate the immediate casualties that will result from blast, fire, and radiation, and as early as 1959 it was predicted at a congressional hearing that 42 million people would die in the United States from the effects of a nuclear attack and that about 12 million residences would be so badly damaged as to require them to be abandoned. Since then there have been innumerable similar studies that have produced comparable numbers, some larger, and some smaller, depending on the attack scenario, and most dealing with the effects of the initial trauma of the attack. However, the long-term consequences are far more complicated to analyze, and it is those that place the ultimate consequences of nuclear war beyond comprehension.

It is significant that only during the past few years has there been consideration of the effects of the reduced solar insolation that would result from the great load of atmospheric smoke that would be produced by the fire storms of the post-attack period. It has been proposed that a "nuclear winter" would be in prospect. The effect of the smoke would be to lower the temperature on a global scale with profound effects, not only on human well being, but also on all forms of life on this planet. Although there are large uncertainties in the models used to estimate the severity of these effects, the fact that they are sufficiently plausible to even be debatable means that the nuclear-winter hypotheses must be given great weight by the superpower policymakers.

One can enumerate many imponderables at length. What would be the effect of the breakdown in the system for storage and distribution of food? How many livestock animals would survive? What would be the level of medical care? Would it be possible to repair mechanical equipment faster then it rusts into a state of uselessness? How would the surviving population behave? Would it be possible to organize the survivors into a coherent and functional society? How would epidemics be managed?

There have been several recent attempts to develop models of the "incomprehensible," but I do not believe any of them. I do not think it is possible to predict the consequences of an all-out nuclear war.

In her book, *The March of Folly*, Barbara Tuchman has chronicled how the world's leaders from the time of the Trojan Wars to Vietnam have repeatedly pursued policies that were contrary to their self-interest. Are we witnessing that kind of behavior once again? Possibly so. What a pity it would be if the society that has evolved over so many centuries should be destroyed because of ideological differences that future generations would think are trivial! How many people today can explain why the Hundred Years War was allowed to convulse and impoverish western Europe in the fifteenth and sixteenth centuries?

Concluding Comments

The exposure of the general public in the United States at the present time can be approximated as shown in Fig. 27.2. The dose estimates shown have been apportioned from various

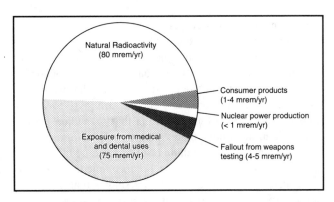

Figure 27.2 Estimates of radiation doses received by the general U.S. population from all sources.

sources, and should be considered to be only approximations. However, there is no question about the general conclusions that can be drawn. The largest portion of the dose we receive originates from natural sources which, together with our exposure to the ionizing radiations from medical practice, accounts for more then 90% of the total dose we receive. Figure 27.2 also gives the dose being received from the residual radiation from weapons tests that were conducted in the atmosphere prior to 1963. That dose, mainly from Cs-137 and Sr-90, amounts to about 4 mrem/yr, and will diminish only slowly with time because of the long lives of the two nuclides (about 30 years).

The nuclear fuel cycle has not had a measurable effect on the collective dose delivered to the United States population, but as was discussed earlier, persons living near a nuclear reactor may receive a dose of a few mrem/yr. The doses being received from the reactors are well within the range of normal variation that is found in most communities due to natural factors.

An interesting insight into the impact of the atomic energy industry on human health is provided by an EPA report (EPA 1979), the purpose of which was to estimate the numbers of cancers caused by emissions to the atmosphere from the various atomic-energy facilities other than the civilian power reactors. The study included uranium mining and refining, radio-pharmaceutical production, operation of test reactors, plutonium fabrication, and 27 Department of Energy research and production facilities. The plants and laboratories covered in the study employed 170,000 workers. It was estimated that the radioactive emissions to the environment from all of the plants and laboratories would result in less then one cancer per year. The EPA study did not include the civilian power reactors, but the Nuclear Regulatory Commission has reported that in 1981, when there were 73 power reactors in operation, the collective dose received by 98 million people living within 80 km from the reactors was 160 person-rem. This would, in round numbers result in 0.02 cancers per year (Baker and Peloquin 1985). The radioactive materials emitted by the 250 coal-fired power plants in the United States was estimated by EPA to cause 1.5 cancers per year. In short, if the current models used to estimate risk from airborne radioactivity are applied to the giagantic complex of atomic-energy facilities, the total impact is less than that of

the radioactive emissions from coal-powered power stations, and probably contributes less then one cancer per year to the hundreds of thousands of cases that result from all causes.

The public is understandably concerned also about catastrophic events, which have a low probability of occurrence, but can involve severe consequences. A study conducted by Rasmussen at MIT (USNRC 1975) used methods of probabilistic risk assessment to power reactor accidents and concluded that the risk of fatal accidents at licensed nuclear power plants is orders of magnitude lower than the risks that result from other human activities such as construction of dams, chemical explosions, and airplane accidents. The probability of reactor accidents that will result in a given number of fatalities was also found to be substantially less than from natural disasters.

The Three Mile Island accident, which was by far the most serious nuclear power plant accident in the United States, involved no overexposure of either the employees or the public, but enormous economic consequences did result because the plant was destroyed and decommissioning was expensive.

The most serious power-plant accident to data has been at Chernobyl, where, as noted earlier, 31 workers were killed. The number of delayed cases of cancer that will result from the accident will always be in doubt, but it is of interest that it has been suggested by the information that is now available, that the number of deaths will be less than the number caused by the annual emissions of coal-burning power plants in the USSR (Wilson 1987).

One cannot summarize the effects of nuclear energy in peacetime without also considering the effects of alternative methods of power generation. If one begins with the assumption that energy will be required in increasing amounts to maintain the standard of living in the developed world and improve social conditions in the less developed nations, then one must also consider the impacts on human well being of the continued burning of fossil fuels. The predicted effects of the increasing concentrations of carbon dioxide in the atmosphere become more credible with each passing year and constitute a persuasive argument for the need to preserve the nuclear option. In addition, the geopolitical risks from our continued dependence on petroleum must be considered. In 1986, nuclear energy accounted for 17% of the electricity generated in the United States and replaced the equivalent of 200 million tons of coal, or 700 million barrels of oil. In a world that is not without risks, we cannot evaluate the acceptability of any source of energy without also examining the risks associated with the available alternatives. The risks that would be imposed by *not* using nuclear energy in the years to come exceed by far the risks involved in allowing it to take its place among the modalities with which the world can meet its energy requirements. There is as yet no source other than nuclear by which energy can be produced with minimal environmental deterioration. It is the option that will avoid oil spills, reduce geopolitical tensions, eliminate the scarring of landscapes, eliminate acid deposition, and help to arrest the increase in atmospheric carbon dioxide.

The use of nuclear energy in war is another matter. Nuclear

weapons have no place in this world, and I will close with the words of Bernard Baruch, who was the U.S. delegate to the first meeting of the United Nations General Assembly in June 1946, less than one year after the end of World War II. That great statesman, who was then nearing the end of a distinguished career in which he served many presidents of both parties, said:

"We are here to make a choice between the quick and the dead. . . .

Behind the black portent of the new atomic age lies a hope which, seized upon with faith, can work our salvation. If we fail, then we have dammed every man to be the slave of Fear. Let us not deceive ourselves: We must elect World Peace or World Destruction. . . ."

That is a choice that remains to be made.

References

Albert, R. E., and B. Altshuler. 1973. Considerations relating to the formulation of limits for unavoidable population exposures to environmental carcinogens. In *Radionuclide Carcinogenesis*, ed. J. E. Ballon et al., Springfield, VA: NTIS.

Baker, D. A., and R. A. Peloquin. 1985. Population dose commitments due to radioactive releases from nuclear power plant sites in 1981. Rep. NUREG/CR-2850, PNL-4221, Vol. 3, USNRC, Wash., D.C.

Beck, H. L., C. V. Gogolak, M. Miller, and W. M. Lowder. 1980. Perturbations of the natural radiation environment due to the utilization of coal as an energy source. In *Natural Radiation Environment III*, ed. T. F. Gesell and W. M. Lowder. Washington, D.C.: U.S. Department of Energy.

Bennett, G. L. 1981. Overview of the U.S. flight safety process for space nuclear power. *Nucl. Saf.* 22: 423–34.

Bennett, G. L., J. J. Lombardo, and B. J. Rock. 1984. U. S. radioisotope thermoelectric generator space operating experience (June 1961-December 1982). *Nucl. Eng.* 25: 49–58.

Boice, J. D., Jr. 1982. Risk estimates for breast. In *Critical Issues in Setting Radiation Dose Limits*, 164–81. Proc. 17th Annual Meeting, NCRP (National Council Rad. Prot. Meas.), Bethesda, MD.

Carpenter, R., T. Jickells, and P. Liss. The Marine Environment. Paper presented at *The Earth as Transformed by Human Action Symposium*. Clark University, October 1987.

Cowan, G. A. 1976. A natural fission reactor. *Scientific American* 235: 36–47.

Cuddihy, R. G. 1982. Risks of radiation-induced lung cancer. In *Critical Issues in Setting Radiation Dose Limits*, 133–52.

Eisenbud, M. 1987. *Environmental Radioactivity*. 3rd ed. New York: Academic Press.

Eisenbud, M., K. Krauskopf, E. Penna Franca, W. Lei, R. Ballad, P. Linsalata, and K. Fujimori. 1984. Natural analogues for the transuranic actinide elements: An investigation in Minas Gerais, Brazil. *Environ. Geol. Water Sci.* 6: 1–9.

Emerson, E. L., and J. D. McClure. 1985. *Radioactive Material (RAM) Accident/Incident Data Analysis Program*. Washington, D.C.: U.S. Nuclear Regulatory Commission.

Goldman, M., and S. S. Yaniv. 1978. Naturally occurring radioactivity in ophthalmic lenses. In *Radioactivity in Consumer Products*. Edited by A. A. Moghissi, P. Paras, M.W. Carter, and R. F. Barker. Rep. NUREG/CP-0001, U.S. Nuclear Regulatory Commission, Washington, D.C.

Harris, K. 1986. Northbrook, IL: Pittway Corp.

Institute of Medicine-National Academy of Sciences. 1986. *The Medical Implications of Nuclear War*. Washington, D.C.: National Academy Press.

Ishimaru, T., M. Ichimaru, M. Mikami, Y. Yamada, and Y. Tomonaga. 1982. *Distribution of Onset of Leukemia among Atomic-Bomb Survivors in the Leukemia Registry by Dose,* *Hiroshima and Nagasaki, 1946–75*. Radiation Effects Research Foundation.

Johnson, J. E. 1978. Smoke detectors containing radioactive materials. In *Radioactivity in Consumer Products*. Edited by A. A. Moghissi, P. Paras, M. W. Carter, and R. F. Barker. Rep. NUREG/CP-0001, U.S. Nuclear Regulatory Commission, Washington, D.C.

Kemeny, J. G. 1979. *President's Commission on the Accident at Three Mile Island*. Washington, D.C.

Kocher, D.C., A. L. Sjoreen, C. S. Bard. 1983. Uncertainties in geological disposal of high level wastes: Ground water transport of radionuclides and radiological consequences. Report 5838, Oak Ridge National Laboratory, Oak Ridge, Tenn.

Krauskopf, K. B. 1986. Thorium as an analog for plutonium and rare-earth metals as analogs for heavier actinides. *Chem. Geol.*

Menczer, L. F. 1965. Radioactive ceramic glazes. *Radiol. Health Data* 6656.

NAS/NRC. 1985. *The Management of Radioactive Waste at the Oak Ridge National Laboratory: A Technical Review*. Washington: National Academy Press.

National Academy of Sciences-National Research Council (Committee on the Biological Effects of Ionizing Radiation). 1980. *The Effects on Populations of Exposure to Low Levels of Ionizing Radiation: 1980*. Washington, D.C.: National Academy Press.

National Council on Radiation Protection and Measurements. 1980. *Influence of Dose and Its Distribution in Time on Dose-Response Relationships for Low-LET Radiations*. Bethesda, MD.

———. 1983. *Iodine-129: Evaluation of Releases from Nuclear Power Generation*. Bethesda, MD.

O'Donnell, F. R. 1978. Assessment of radiation doses from radioactive materials in consumer products. In *Radioactivity in Consumer Products*. Edited by A. A. Moghissi, P. Paras, M. W. Carter, and R. F. Barker. Rep. NUREG/CP-0001, U.S. Nuclear Regulatory Commission, Washington, D.C.

Parker, H. M., and J. W. Healy. 1956. Effects of an explosion of a nuclear reactor. *Proc. U.N. Int. Conf. Peaceful Uses of Atomic Energy*. Geneva.

Shleien, B., J. A. Cochran, and P. J. Magno. 1970. Strontium-90, strontium-89, plutonium-239, and plutonium-238 concentrations in ground-level air, 1964–1969. *Envir. Sci. Tech.* 4: 598–602.

Smith, J. M., T. W. Fowler, A. S. Goldin. 1982. Environmental pathway model for estimating population risks from disposal of high-level radioactive waste in geologic repositories. Draft Report, EPA 520/5-80-002. US EPA, Washington, D.C.

Smith, P. G., and R. Doll. 1982. Mortality of patients with ankylosing spondylitis after a simple treatment course with X-rays. *Br. Med. J.*, 284: 449–60.

Spitsyn, V. I., and V. D. Balukova. 1979. The scientific basis for, and experience with, underground storage of liquid radioactive wastes in the USSR. In G. J. McCarthy, ed., *Scientific Basis for Nuclear Waste Management*. New York: Plenum.

Thompson, D.L., 1978. In *Radioactivity in Consumer Products*. Edited by A. A. Moghissi, P. Paras, M. W. Carter, and R. F. Barker. Rep. NUREG/CP-0001, U.S. Nuclear Regulatory Commission, Washington, D.C.

U.S. Atomic Energy Commission. 1957. *Atomic Energy Facts*. Washington, D.C.

———. 1974. *High-Level Radioactive Waste Management Alternatives*. Washington, D.C.

U.S. Department of Energy. 1979. *Final Environmental Impact Statement: Management of Commercially Generated Radioactive Waste*. Washington, D.C.

U.S. Department of the Interior. Bureau of Mines. 1985. *Minerals Yearbook 1984*. Washington, D.C.

———. 1980. *Management of Commercially Generated Radioactive Waste*. Springfield, VA: NTIS.

———. 1983. *Spent Fuel and Radioactive Waste Inventories, Projections, and Characteristics*. Springfield, VA: NTIS.

U.S.E.P.A. 1979. Radiological impact caused by emissions of radionuclides into air in the United States. Rep. EPA 520/7-79-006. Wash, D.C.

U.S. Government Printing Office. 1983. *Report of Fallout Prediction Panel*. Washington, D.C.

U.S. Nuclear Regulatory Commission. 1975. *Regulatory Guide 1.109 Revision 1: Calculation of Annual Doses to Man from Routine Releases of Reactor Effluents for the Purpose of Evaluating Compliances with 10 CFR Part 50 Appendix I*. Washington, D.C.: Office of Standards Development.

Upton, A. C. 1977. Radiobiological effects of low doses: implications for radiological protection. *Rad. Res.* 7151–74.

Wilson, R. 1987. A visit to Chernobyl. *Science* 236: 1636–40.

Wolff, T. A. 1984. *Transportation of Nuclear Materials*. Albuquerque, NM: Sandia National Laboratories.

World Resources Institute and International Institute for Environment and Development. 1986. *World Resources 1986*. New York: Basic Books.

Wrenn, M. E., and N. Cohen. 1979. Dosimetric and risk/benefit implications of americium-241 in smoke detectors disposed of in normal wastes. *Proc. Health Phys. Soc. 12th Midyear Topical Symp. 1979*. Washington, D.C.: USEPA.

III

Regional Studies of Transformation

Editorial Introduction

The global assessments of single variables offered in the preceding section provide one path to analysis of the transformation of the biosphere; integrative regional case studies provide another. The regional scale makes possible a manageable and meaningful integration of environmental transformations with the forces that have directly given rise to them, in the contexts in which they have occurred. It promotes recognition of two fundamental characteristics of environmental transformation. (1) The process almost invariably involves complex interactions of human and environmental variables; human uses have numerous impacts on nature, the consequences of which feed back to varying degrees onto the uses. (2) And, because of differences in both sets of variables, regions differ greatly in the kinds and scales of transformations that have taken place within them. If global changes are best regarded as something more than the mere sum of their regional parts, it is also true that the magnitudes and trajectories of the average changes in the biosphere found at the global scale are rarely duplicated within any smaller area. Indeed, we may see regions swimming strongly and for long periods against the global currents; the reforestation of the central Maya lowlands over the past 800–900 years (chap. 2) has gone directly counter to the pattern documented for the world as a whole (chap. 11).

In this section, 12 regional case studies illustrate the utility of this path to the understanding of environmental change. They offer a representative range of the broader physical and social conditions in which transformation has occurred. This range runs from equatorial to nordic and from rainforest to desert climates, from sparse to extremely dense settlement, and from poor, primarily agrarian to wealthy, advanced-industrial economies (chap. 1). A long-term view of regional change is provided by the case study of the Huang-Huai-Hai Plain in northern China. The 300-year focus is more closely adhered to in the following 11 regional studies, which have been grouped, to facilitate comparative analysis, according to selected but significant attributes of their population or environmental condition. Five groups are recognized:

1. *Tropical frontiers* (Amazonia and Borneo and the Malay Peninsula), in which recent and major deforestation has resulted from immigration and resource extraction;
2. *Highlands* (Caucasia and East African Highlands), in which industrial or agrarian economies predominate;
3. *Large plains* (the Russian Plain and the Great Plains of the United States), in which both agriculture and industry have grown rapidly over the past 300 years;
4. *Populous south* (the Basin of Mexico and Nigeria), densely settled segments of the less developed world; and
5. *Populous north* (Sweden, Hudson-Raritan Basin, and Switzerland), dominated by advanced industrial economies in which consumption, as much as production, now drives transformation.

The delimitation of "regions" as usable units for study has long been a contentious issue in geography and elsewhere. Our selection and bounding of areas and our grouping of those chosen have been guided by a range of concerns. The advantages of choosing groups of homogeneous physical environments by such purely "natural" criteria as topography and climate are evident: such a division, by holding environments constant (or at least similar), would make it possible to contrast the different transformations wrought by diverse social driving forces, and to compare the similarities in the responses of such zones to diverse uses. A classification by sociodemographic criteria offers analogous advantages, though in a study three centuries in depth, the question would arise: these criteria at what point in time? A concern for issues of management might even point to a choice of political units in spite of internal physical and social heterogeneity, for as Hägerstrand and Lohm point out in this section, most deliberate human action is still bounded within such units, even though environmental consequences flow freely across them. In light of these issues, we have chosen a more flexible arrangement that blends these criteria yet still offers some useful comparative insights and generalizations beyond those of each study taken individually.

Historical patterns and modern conditions in these regions display several fundamental characteristics of transformation that either parallel or diverge from those seen in the global view. At both scales, the kind and degree of transformation and their temporal patterns are reliably linked to patterns of population pressure and to technoeconomic development. Globally in the early stages of the 300-year period and currently in agrarian-based economies, transformation of one linked set of biospheric components dominates – loss of forest cover, depletion of species, soil erosion and degradation, stream siltation, and carbon emissions from land-use change; in contrast, in the latter stages of that period and in industrial and advanced-industrial economies, transformation of many of the less visible "flows" of the biosphere is increasingly important. The scale of these transformations historically has been related both to the fragility of the environment and to intraregional population pressures (densities), until the emergence of advanced-industrial economies with sufficient wealth, power, and technological capability to regulate or expel many harmful processes.[1] As a result of these associations, the patterns of the transformations historically have been spatially differentiated across the surface of the earth – in some cases quite dramatically so. This differentiation remains important, despite the global integration of the modern economy and the emergence of transformations that involve worldwide atmospheric flows.

A distinctive pattern of transformation has emerged within some industrial regions and all of the advanced-industrial regions, especially those of the populous north. In these cases, population growth and the emergence of industrialization initially led to major changes – in land use, forest cover, water quality, and so forth – of the kinds now evident in many less developed countries. But eventually, the amount of change in many of these variables stabilized and, in some cases, a degree of recovery has occurred. Forest cover is now greater in much of this realm than it was a century or so ago, and certain forms of pollution have been curbed. Such recovery has been promoted by the tendency of extraction and production to be transferred to less wealthy regions. A new stage of transformation in the populous north has witnessed increases in new forms of water, air, and soil pollution, the result as much of dispersed mass consumption as of production (e.g., the Hudson-Raritan Basin, Sweden, and Switzerland). But the wealth and development within these regions provides the opportunity, though one not always taken, to confront these changes directly when they come to be perceived as problems.

The nature of the relocation of damaging, or "dirty," economic activities from some regions to others is a complex matter. While its net result has apparently been to worsen many conditions in poorer nations while improving the environments of the wealthier, no simple cause-and-effect explanation can be based on this correlation. Some might argue that the transfer has stemmed in large part, save perhaps in very recent years, from economic patterns of comparative advantage in production costs rather than from conscious policies of environmental management by the developed lands. Indeed, the outflow of damaging productive activities has at least as often been resisted as promoted by residents of the wealthier nations – though often with little success – through trade barriers and industrial and agricultural subsidies. The recovery of woodland in the Hudson-Raritan Basin in this century through farmland abandonment was an environmental improvement brought about with no environmental motive behind it. As Hägerstrand and Lohm note, a goal in Sweden of preserving some degree of national "self-sufficiency" has artificially maintained much land area in agriculture, even though one result has been an increased flux of nitrogen into an already overburdened chemical environment.

Whatever its source, the spatial displacement that has occurred has contributed to the kind and scale of transformation in the industrial and agrarian regions, even those embedded within an advanced-industrial nation (e.g., the U.S. Great Plains). Perhaps this is most readily visible within the tropical forest frontiers, in which major increases in resource extraction have led to massive deforestation, sedimentation, and so on (e.g., Borneo and the Malay Peninsula), and forest clearance for new settlement may even be affecting the regional rainfall patterns and contributing to global atmospheric change (e.g., Amazonia). In other cases, high rates of population growth (e.g., the Basin of Mexico, Nigeria) increase the magnitude of transformations being wrought by global commodity production and affect local habitats once sparsely settled, contributing to forest loss and soil degradation (e.g., the East African Highlands). The pattern in these cases has been one of accelerating transformation during the latter half of this century.

If there are social patterns in regional transformation, there are also natural ones. The paper on Caucasia in this section concludes with an assessment of common features of human impacts on mountain regions. The natural fragility of the Swiss, especially the alpine, environment has made it unusual among these selected regions of the populous north in the seriousness of current transformation. The character of other environments likewise does much to shape the potential syndromes of transformation, even under relatively diverse uses. The history of agricultural transformation on the continental-interior Russian Plain and U.S. Great Plains centers on the utilization and degradation of soils, vegetation, and water resources; the islands, the high latitudes, the desert margins, and the tropical forests of the world are other generic regions that can profitably be grouped to study the response of common environments to diverse uses.

These case studies also provide insights into other, less tangible aspects of the transformation of the biosphere. Beliefs have functioned as driving agents of both unintended transformation and deliberate environmental management. The ecologically disastrous growth of Mexico City detailed by Ezcurra reflects a bias toward centralization, of many centuries' standing in national political culture, and a modern choice of development model that have overridden other considerations, although the example bears a strong resemblance to numerous cases of extreme "primate city" growth in other developing countries. Favorable attitudes toward mountain scenery that are relatively new on a historical scale have, by generating tourism, contributed in modern times to the environmental and social pressures on the Swiss Alps detailed by Pfister and Messerli. As Brookfield and colleagues observe, the rapid emergence of an ethos of exploitation for profit has contributed greatly to resource depletion in Borneo, though such attitudes in turn cannot be separated from such facilitating factors as the growth of regional demand for lumber and improvements in extractive technology.

Understanding of human impacts can also become a tool for environmental management. Most of these studies record little systematic and institutionalized intervention in this realm until the middle of the twentieth century, although the time scale varies somewhat by region. The chronology for the Russian Plain – of long-standing government concern mainly for the conservation of particular strategic resources, of elite awareness at the turn of the century of wider ecological problems, and of substantial state intervention only in recent decades – is a reasonably typical case. But this is not to deny that more diffuse and uneven awareness of much human impact has also existed throughout our study period. In some cases, indeed, early popular understanding that exaggerated the human role in perceived change served nonetheless as a basis for action. Alpine deforestation was blamed for downstream flooding in Switzerland in the mid-nineteenth century that Pfister and Messerli note was actually due to natural events, and a policy of mountain reforestation was implemented in response. Riebsame notes how the belief that afforestation and cultivation were permanently increasing rainfall on the U.S. Great Plains in the latter part of the nineteenth century promoted immigration and settlement, until a natural swing back to drier conditions discredited such optimistic forecasts.

Ironically, management responses based on incomplete understanding have themselves often produced unforeseen side-effects – today's solution becoming tomorrow's problem.

The age-old practice in China of controlling floods by confining rivers within dikes led on the Huang-Huai-Hai Plain to the building up of the rivers' beds and a catastrophic increase in the size of large floods; and the means adopted to lessen leaded gasoline emissions in the Basin of Mexico led to a sharp increase in ozone levels in the region, with new impacts on vegetation. An integrative regional approach is particularly well suited to examining such interplay among human actions and physical consequences.

The potentially distorting effects of a single global periodization against which Robert McC. Adams (foreword) warns us are, if anything, still greater at the regional scale. Massive transformations in the Basin of Mexico and the Huang-Huai-Hai Plain occurred well before 1687, while in other regions – Amazonia and the East African Highlands are cases in point – little of the significant alteration took place even in the first half of our three-century span. The variations in transformation across time as well as space require regional study as a complement to global, even now when no region is immune to substantial and often accelerating change. It is increasingly true that transformations have an international character and a global reach, but even they will be in the future, as they have been in the past, experienced differently as they interact with a global mosaic of differing physical and social contexts.

WILLIAM B. MEYER
B. L. TURNER II

Note

[1] Exceptions exist, however. For example, the sixteenth-to-seventeenth-century European "conquest" of the world had dramatic impacts on the fauna and flora and the staple cultigens of the world (chap. 41), and led to massive declines in the Amerindian populations of the New World (chap. 2).

28

The Huang-Huai-Hai Plain

ZUO DAKANG   ZHANG PEIYUAN

The physical features of the Huang-Huai-Hai Plain of north-eastern China have been altered profoundly by human activity over a much longer span of time than have those of almost any other region of the earth. Significant problems of evidence and methodology pose obstacles to the reconstruction of the historic and prehistoric transformation of the Plain, but the main outlines and some details of the consequences of the key processes of water management and land-use change provide a useful perspective on the human modification of a long-settled region.

Extent and Natural Setting

The Huang-Huai-Hai Plain, the largest plain in eastern China, covers an area of approximately 350,000 km² and accounts for 3.67% of the nation's total area. It is bordered by the foot of the Yanshan Mountains in the north and by the Huai He Mountains in the south. Its western boundary lies along the eastern part of the Taihang and Funiu mountains and extends to the Bohai and Huanghai seas in the east (Fig. 28.1). Administratively, the Plain consists of the extensive areas of the municipalities of Beijing and Tianjin and the provinces of Hebei, Henan, Shandong, Anhui, and Jiangsu.

The Plain was created as a depositional feature of three rivers, the Huang He, Huai He, and Hai He, during the Quaternary. Of the three, the Huang He is the most important, being responsible for a sediment deposit ranging from 400 to 500 m in depth. The Huang He Delta downstream of Lijin has been built up only during the past 100 years. Since the river broke its banks at Tongwaxiang and the channel shifted to its present position in 1855, a new area of more than 2,000 km² has been created by deposition on the delta. Seaward extension has proceeded at a rate of 1.4 to 1.8 km/yr.

Frequent major and minor river shifts have affected the geomorphology of the Plain; it is recorded that during the past 3,000 to 4,000 years, the Huang He has broken its banks 1,593 times. The general pattern of undulating relief characterized by hills, slopes, and depressions is liable to waterlogging due to irregular drainage. Local variations in soil-salt dynamics caused by such micromorphology are among the

principal factors held responsible for the formation of the region's saline-alkali soils. Sand ridges and sand hills have been deposited on old channels or along the main stream path of the Huang He.

The mean temperature of the coldest months on the Plain ranges from 0°C to −5°C, and the average extreme minimum temperature over a period of some years is −10°C to −20°C. Safe overwintering is possible for both winter wheat and deciduous broad-leaved fruit trees. Summers are hot; the mean temperature of the hottest months is from 26°C to 28°C. Annual precipitation ranges from 500 mm to 1,000 mm, and between 2,300 and 2,800 hours of sunshine are recorded each year. Climatically, the Plain falls into the semi-humid temperate zone, suitable for both cold-resistant and thermophilious crops.

The Plain is one of the key agricultural regions in China. Its cultivated land now makes up 18.6% of the nation's total, and the cultivation index is as high as 51.8%. Yields of grain and cotton account for 18% and 58%, respectively, of the nation's total, while the Plain also produces 25% of China's soybeans, groundnuts, and tobacco.

Early Transformation

The locations of sites of relics and cities during the Neolithic Age, the Shang and Western Zhou Dynasties (from the sixteenth century to 771 B.C.), and the Spring and Autumn and Warring States Periods (770 B.C. – 221 B.C.) are shown in Fig. 28.1. Quite an extensive area in the central part of the map is blank, in contrast to the numerous sites elsewhere. This pattern provides evidence of the inhospitable nature of that area for long-term human settlement in those periods. The Shang people lived instead in the hilly areas lying between the mountains and plains; the capital of the dynasty moved 13 times in 500 years. Agriculture apparently did not then occupy an important position in economic activities.

In considering the historical processes of human use of the Plain, primary importance must be given to the impact on the region of the Huang He and to the human activities that have themselves altered the behavior of the river. It is recorded in "Han Shu" that the construction of dikes on the Huang He

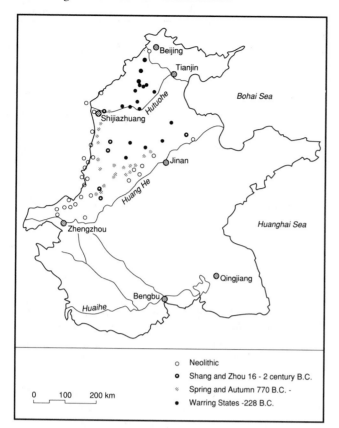

Figure 28.1 Huang-Huai-Hai Plain, showing distribution of sites of relics for the Neolithic and later.

during the Western Han Dynasty. Frequent dike breach and flooding took place as a result. Between A.D. 69 and the end of the Five Dynasties (A.D. 907–960), however, only 5 dike breaches were recorded in the first 500 years, and 16 in the next several centuries; floods in the region were most common, compared with other parts of the country, during the Tang Dynasty (A.D. 619–907). Tan Qixiang explained that land conservation was facilitated on the Plain over this long period by the substitution of grazing for farming following the migration of nomadic tribes to the middle reaches of the Huang He.

Shui Jing Zhu (Ban 1900) was a famous book on the river system over the Huang-Huai-Hai Plain during the sixth century A.D., recording all of its lakes. Figure 28.2 shows a well-developed water system over the Plain. This might indicate a wet climatic regime during that period, but human factors might also have been responsible. The importance of swamps was recognized by the ancient inhabitants. Swamps provided enough species of animals for hunting for the nobility, and also afforded numerous resources, such as fish and wood for cooking and heating. The emperors instituted many laws to protect the wetlands, and sometimes appointed officers to look after them.

Significant changes in the woodlands of the Plain as a result of human activity began somewhat later. In the fifth century A.D., the mountains north of Beijing were covered by thick forest with an abundance of animals and birds (Li 527?). Indeed, until the Yuan Dynasty (A.D. 1271–1368), the mountains of the Plain retained a thick forest cover. Because of the construction of the city of Beijing, a canal was opened

began in the period of the Warring States (475 B.C. – 221 B.C.) (Ban 1900). Detailed modern research has suggested that the project might have begun in the middle of the second century B.C. (Tan 1981). Before dikes were built, the Huang He diverged across the Plain in braided streams, making permanent settlement difficult. Even after the completion of the first system of dikes, some areas of braided channels continued to exist until at least the thirteenth century.

In the Warring States era, agricultural and water-management activities on the other rivers in the region expanded with the development of iron tools and cattle-plowing. For example, the well known Hong Gou drainage system constructed during the Wei Dynasty in 361 B.C. played an important role in the development of the Huang-Huai-Hai Plain. The project of diverting the Zhangshui River to irrigate farmland through 12 canals, which was initiated by Ximen Bao in 422 B.C., made the irrigated area the most fertile in the region (Chu 91 B.C.). However, these agricultural projects also destroyed much forest and pasture, which led to a locally serious shortage of land for cattle and sheep grazing for the Wei people.

During and shortly after the West Han Dynasty (206 B.C. to A.D. 24), channel siltation accelerated as a result of the aggravation of soil erosion in the middle reaches of Huang He River. The construction of dikes, moreover, kept the silt inside the channel, and the accumulation of considerable amounts of sediment raised the channel bed. For example, the riverbed in Henan Province rose above ground level even

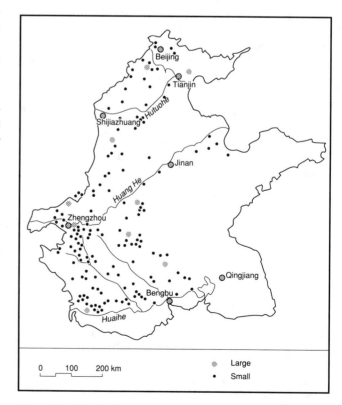

Figure 28.2 Distribution of lakes and swamps in the sixth century.

from the city to the West Mountain to transport wood and rock for building material. According to the literature, however, at this time the mountains north of Beijing still retained a dense forest cover (Zhao 1291). During the Ming Dynasty (A.D. 1368–1644), the palace derived fuel from the northern forest. By 1426–1435, the royal fuel source had been transferred to Yi Zhou, far to the east of the capital, with the aim of reserving the woods north of Beijing for defense (Shu 1520). In 1550, when peoples from the north attacked Beijing, many soldiers hid in this forest and defeated the invaders.

Forest cover elsewhere on the Plain was affected not only by demand from the cities, but also by clearance for farmland. At the beginning of the Yuan Dynasty and then during the Ming Dynasty, the rulers tried to move peasants from the Changjing Valley and Shansi Province to Beijing to reclaim wasteland. Some figures show how fast the grassland and forest could be changed to farmland. In A.D. 1375, the cultivated area in Beijing was 1,900 km^2, and by 1403, it had increased to 4,200 km^2. The remaining forest was cut during the Qing Period (1644–1911). In 1699, the Emperor Kansi gave merchants permission to transport wood from the distant northeast provinces to Beijing to supply its needs (Miao 1886), and at the end of this dynasty, all wood for construction was imported from Fujian in the northeast (Zhang 1982).

Associated with the accelerated clearance of forest and with other factors was an increase in the incidence of breaches and floods on the Plain rivers. For example, the Yongding He overflowed once every 13 years on average in the Ming Dynasty, once every 3.5 years in the Qing Dynasty, and once every 2 years between 1912 and 1939. The suggestion that high dikes be built on the banks of the lower reaches of the Huang He to "bind water and wash sand away" was made by Pan Jixun, a High Officer of River Management in the late Ming Dynasty (seventeenth century). With braided channels no longer present in the lower reaches, the breaching of dikes became more frequent on the Plain. The Huang He broke its dikes 161 times in the 267 years of the Qing Dynasty (1644–1911), and 17 breaches occurred in the quarter-century between 1913 and 1938.

The instability of the river systems on the Plain, greatly increased by the history of human management, has had serious consequences for the population. The protection afforded by dikes under normal circumstances has been offset by the artificially increased magnitude of disasters. A number of dike breaches and floods during the past 300 years have caused particularly severe and widespread damage. Figure 28.3 shows the areas affected by some of them. In 1761, the Huang He burst its banks in the section from Sanmen Gorge to Huayankou. Twelve counties in Henan Province, 12 in Shandong Province, and 4 in Anhui Province were inundated. In 1843, a peak flood discharge of 36,000 m^3/sec in Sanmen Gorge and upstream occurred, breaking a dike a kilometer in width. Eleven counties in east Henan and 6 in Anhui were affected.

In 1855, the lower Huang He changed its entire course, breaking its dikes in Tongwasheng and taking the channel of

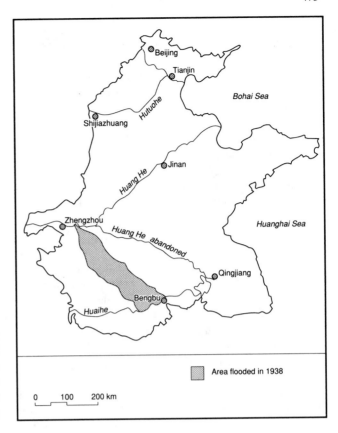

Figure 28.3 Areas affected by major floods and shifts in Huang He.

another river, the Daqing He. This was the consequence of a variety of factors, including the rise of the riverbed from siltation and failure to maintain the dikes on the river. In 1933, a great flood with a peak discharge of 22,000 m^3/sec caused a dike breach at over 50 sites along both banks. Sixty-seven counties in Hebei, Henan, and Shandong provinces were inundated, the flood-stricken area covered 11,000 km^2, and those affected numbered 3.64 million, of whom 18,000 died. In 1938, the Huayankou River was breached intentionally by the Guomintang government to obstruct the invading Japanese troops. This action placed an area of 54,000 km^2 under water, comprising 44 counties and cities in east Henan, north Anhui, and Jiangsu provinces. Some 12.5 million inhabitants were affected, and 890,000 died (Research Group 1984).

Modern Processes

Large tracts of cultivated land on the Plain were laid waste during World War II. In Henan, the area of cultivated land was 30% lower in 1946 than it had been 10 years earlier. Since the 1950s, cultivated land has been reduced also by the rapid growth in population, by economic development, and by expansion of settlement. In 1957, cultivated land in the region totaled 230,000 km^2, whereas by 1983 it dropped to 182,000, a decrease of 20%. Population between 1964 and 1982 grew from 128 million to 180 million, an increase of 41% – roughly equivalent to the growth rate for the nation as a whole.

The Huang He river-bed remains higher than the lands

outside the dikes over the region. In general, the bed of the river is 3–5 m higher than the Plain. From the Huayuankao to Dongbatou, in the highest section, it is 6–8 m above, and the maximum difference is 11 m. Since the 1950s, 400 million tons of sand have been deposited on the riverbed every year, equivalent to a rise of 1 m per decade. The discharge measured at Huayuankou is 470 hundred million m^3, or 5% of that of the Changjiang River, but the annual sand transportation is three times that of the Changjiang. In the lower reaches, the high-water-season discharge accounted for 40% of the total, and at the same time, the transportation of sand accounted for 85%. This disproportion between the transportation of water and that of sand is the main factor in causing flooding and dike breaches. As it is associated with the growth of population and economic activity, it will undoubtedly increase in the coming years.

Between 1950 and 1979, many reservoirs were constructed at the foot of the mountain ranges around the Plain and on a number of reaches of the Huang He River, and several sluices were built in the Plain. These works have changed the sediment load of the rivers. Sediment supply, which originally came from the mountain regions, now comes from the lower reaches under the impact of human activities. Because of the construction of reservoirs, some downstream sections of rivers have been scoured. Two types of impacts have been experienced in the Plain rivers. To the north of the Huang He, the Plain rivers run parallel with the Huang He. On account of receiving return water from irrigation, the average channel sediment load has been increased. To the south of the Huang He, in the Plain rivers running at an oblique angle to the Huang He, where return water is bound in the upper reaches, sedimentation has increased substantially.

Finally, because of the many locks constructed on the Plain rivers, variations in sediment load are augmented sharply. In dry years, the gates of locks are closed, and the sediment load is deposited. In wet years, the gates are left open for flood discharge, the sediment is scoured, and the sediment load of Plain rivers increases greatly (Zhao 1985).

Net Changes in the Past 300 Years

The net effect of human activity has been to reduce considerably the surface water of the region. During the seventh to twelfth centuries, 240 lakes and low-lying areas covered over 12,000 km^2 in the Huang-Huai-Hai Plain. Today only 20 of these features remain, with an area of 6,000 km^2. The south suburb of Beijing, Nanyuan, was a royal hunting field dotted with numerous springs and swamps. A survey under the Emperor Qienglung in A.D. 1771 (Yu 1774) listed

117 springs and 5 large lakes, showing little change from the surface features recorded in a survey 350 years earlier (Li 1461). Since then, the Nanyuan has become farmland and contains no spring or swamp at all. Other areas have experienced similar changes. The area of the famous Baiyangdian Lake alone has diminished by 400 km^2 during the past 23 years. The reservoirs built in 1958 and 1972 now have lost most of their usefulness because of water shortage.

In some instances, however, human activity has led to the expansion of lakes. Lake Hong Zhe was very small in the Yuan Dynasty, and was said to include some cultivated areas inside. In the Ming Dynasty, a large dam was built along its southern side. Most of the surface water of the Plain had to flow into this lake, and it has grown larger over the past 300 years.

Visibility has also decreased over time, indicating the onset of air pollution as a major problem. Evidence for comparing the past and present is provided by the scenic descriptions of early landscape writers. Four sources from the Qing Dynasty indicate a mean maximum visibility around Beijing of 55 km (Table 28-1). Modern instrumental observations indicate a maximum visibility now of 40 km. The most obvious effects of pollution on the atmosphere are on the local-scale visibility, which is sharply reduced on the "smoggy" days that occur occasionally in some cities and frequently in others.

Conclusion

Human activity has long been a key factor in environmental change in the Huang-Huai-Hai Plain, deeply affecting the rivers, lakes, and vegetation. Change in the channel of the Huang He has played the most important role in changing the surface of the Plain. The Huang He remains the most important environmental factor affecting the Plain, and control of this river is critical to environmental management.

References

Ban Gu. 1900. Chapter on Rivers and Canals Han Shu, *History of Han Dynasty*, 206 B.C. – A.D. 220, Vol. 29, rev. ed.

Chu Shaolin. 91 B.C. A Supplementary to Deeds of Ximen Ba, Appendix of "Biography of Amusing People." In *Record of the History*, Vol. 126, ed. Shi Ji.

Feng Liwen. 1982. Characteristics of drought and its variation during the growing period from 1724–1979 in Beijing. *Acta Geographica Sinica*. 31 (2):194–205.

Li Daoyuan. 527? Shue Jing Ju. *Notes on the Waterways Book*. Lu Yu Shu.

Li Xien. 1461. Da Ming Yi Tung Zhi. *Gazetteer of the Ming Kingdom*.

Miao Quanson. 1886. Shuen Tien Fu Chi. *Gazetteer of the Capital*, Vol. 8.

Table 28-1 *Best Visibility of Beijing for the Ming and Qing Dynasties and for the Present*

Visibility (km)	Location	Source
60	Great Wall (northwest of Beijing) to Bei Hai Tower	Tien Fu Guang Ji (Qing Dynasty)
60	Mt. Bai Hwa to Beijing city wall	Tien Fu Guang Ji (Qing Dynasty)
45	Mt. Shi (southwest of Beijing) to city wall	Ming Sheng Zhi (Qing Dynasty)
55	Mt. Bei Wan (northwest of Beijing) to R. Zhao Bei	ibid.
40	Haiden Observatory (north of Beijing)	Modern instrumental observation

Research Group on Harnessing Huang He. Water Conservancy Commission of Huang He. 1984. *Management and Exploitation of Huang He*, 51–52. Shanghai Education Publishing House.

Shu Fu. 1520. Ming Hue Den. *Document Collection of the Ming Dynasty*.

Song Lien. 1370. Yuan Shi. *History of the Yuan Dynasty*. Zhu Ji, Vol. 5.

Tan Qixiang. 1981. The lower reaches of the Huang He before the West Han Dynasty. *Historical Geography*, Vol. 1.

Yu Mingzhu. 1774. Ri Sha Ju Wen Kou. *Notes in the Capital*.

Zhang Peiyuan. 1982. Historical climate. In *Physical Geography of China. Historical Physical Geography*, chap. 2. Scientia Press.

Zhao Chunian. Wang Yuzhi. 1985. The sediment load and its changes in the rivers of Huang-Huai-Hai Plain. In *Management and Development of the Huang-Huai-Hai Plain*, ed. Zuo Dakang. Beijing: Science Press.

Zhao Wanli. 1291. Yuan Yi Tong Zhi. *Gazetteer of the Yuan Kingdom*, Mountains, Vol. 1–2.

Zhou Yilin. 1987. A brief narration on the changes of the lakes and marshes on the Huabei Plain during the historical periods. *Historical Geography* 5:25–39.

29

Amazonia

ENEAS SALATI   MARC J. DOUROJEANNI   FERNANDO C. NOVAES
ADÉLIA ENGRÁCIA DE OLIVEIRA   RICHARD W. PERRITT
HERBERT OTTO ROGER SCHUBART   JULIO CARRIZOSA UMANA

The "Amazon dominion" (Fig. 29.1) extends over nine countries: Brazil, Colombia, Peru, Venezuela, Ecuador, Bolivia, French Guiana, Surinam, and Guyana. It includes all the international river basin of the Amazon River and its numerous tributaries and parts of the Tocantins and Orinoco river basins. The lion's share of the region is occupied by Brazil, and represents 50% of the nation's territory, including the states of Amazonas, Pará, Goiás, Mato Grosso, Rondônia, Acre, and Maranhão, and the federal territories of Roraima and Amapá. Even so, this area holds only slightly more than 10% of Brazil's population.

With its high rainfall and subdued topography, the region is dominated by the floodplains of large rivers. The Amazon River Basin, alone occupying over 6 million km^2, is the largest hydrographic basin on earth, and discharges an average of 175,000 m^3/sec to the Atlantic Ocean. Far from being a homogeneous natural unit, Amazonia contains various ecosystems with different characteristics, including variations in geomorphology, soils, flora, and fauna. Although there are climatic variations, especially in the upper Andes, most of the region has a hot and humid climate and has soils, often of low fertility, supporting a biota extremely rich in species. The low fertility of soils, where it occurs, has posed difficulties for some systems of agricultural development. This aspect is a chief reason for the difficulties and failures of many planned or spontaneous agricultural colonization programs in the Amazon region.

Although there is still a dearth of technical and scientific information on the region, a reasonable number of studies have been completed, mainly during the past 25 years. These works are published in innumerable scientific journals; of these, *Acta Amazônica*, *Amazoniana*, and *Museo Goeldi Bulletin* are especially useful. Some books recently have tried to summarize the existing information: Dickinson 1987, Prance and Lovejoy 1985, Salati et al. 1983, and Sioli 1984. The aims of this chapter are to review the significant environmental characteristics of the Amazon dominion, particularly of soils, climate, and vegetation, and to point out some of the general problems that have resulted from human activities, especially colonization, within these environments.

The history of human development and its impact on the Amazon region can be divided into three distinct phases. The first is one of *reconnaissance and early occupation* (1500–1840), principally by the Spanish and the Portuguese. During this phase, little impact was registered on the flora and fauna, but the native communities occupying the region suffered profound changes, including drastic reductions in numbers. During the era of *forest-products exploitation* (1840–1945), the most important activity was rubber exploitation, and changes in the flora and fauna began to occur. Economic centers such as Manaus and Belém grew, and the quest for rubber resulted in the movement of 600,000 to 800,000 migrants and the occupation of many remote regions in the Amazon. The last four decades, from 1945, have been a time of intensified *modern colonization*, resulting in major environmental changes. There has also been increasing confrontation between the native communities and the colonists. Modern colonization is oriented primarily toward agriculture and cattle ranching. To provide access for colonists, highways were planned and built, crossing the region from east to west and from north to south (Fig. 29.2). As a result of these activities, an estimated 4 million ha of forest are being removed yearly. Other impact-intensive activities associated with colonization are construction of huge dams for electricity production, exploitation of great mineral deposits, petroleum exploitation, prospecting for gold and precious stones, and logging. Such forces, besides contributing to transformation within the region, may be affecting the global climate by increasing CO_2 levels and altering the earth's energy balance.

Ecological Characteristics of the Region

When examining the problems resulting from the occupation of the Amazon, it is important to consider the mechanisms leading to the present ecological equilibrium. Qualitative or quantitative changes in the processes defining such an equilibrium can produce ecological changes which, in some cases, could determine the success or failure of colonization programs (Salati and Vose 1984). Several ecological aspects will be considered first.

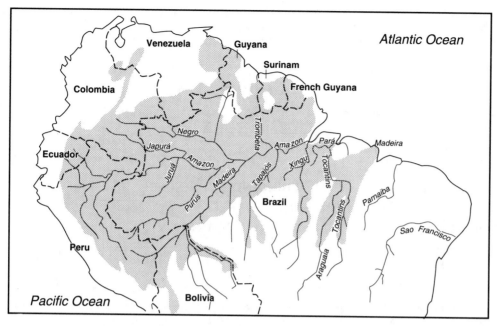

Figure 29.1 The Amazon dominion in South America.

Figure 29.2 Highways crossing Brazil and other countries in South America.

Geomorphology

The Amazon is characterized topographically by a great plain at altitudes lower than 200 m a.s.l. (Fig. 29.3). This plain is more than 3,400-km long from east to west and 2,000-km wide from north to south. It can be subdivided as follows:

1. current floodplains and swamplands consisting of Holocene sediments, slightly above water level and intermittently inundated. These lands are estimated to be about 6,000 years old.
2. Pleistocene terraces, formed during several interglacial periods, the last of which occurred 100,000 years ago, when the sea level was about 15 m above the current level.
3. the Amazon Plateau, formed of clay sediments, with altitudes between 150 m and 200 m on the east, lower in

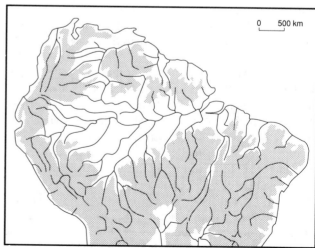

Figure 29.3 Amazon plain with altitudes lower than 200 m.

the west, distributed throughout the sedimentary basin of the Amazon, enclosed by the Guyanan and Brazilian shields. The drainage system started the division of this plateau, elaborating the various terrace levels in the interior Pleistocene.

The great plain is bounded at the north by the Guyanan Shield (Guyana Plateau), composed of ancient pre-Cambrian rocks. In this plateau, with altitudes averaging 600 m to 700 m, is the highest elevation in Brazil – Fog Peak (Pico da Nablina), 3,014 m high. To the south, the plain is bounded by the Brazilian Plateau, also composed of pre-Cambrian rocks, with average heights of 700 m (Putzer 1984); to the west, by the Andean Mountain Range, of Tertiary origin, dividing the slopes of the Atlantic side from those of the Pacific. The Andean Mountain Range forms a semicircle, opening toward the east, and has altitudes above 4,000 m. Since its emergence, the Andean Mountain Range has been the main source of sediments for the Amazon Plain. Today, about 13.5 t/sec of material is eroded from the Andes.

It is important to stress the small surface gradient along the main channel of the Amazon River; the vertical drop between Iquitos in Peru and the estuary 2,375 km downstream is only 107 m. Yet, although from a geomorphologic viewpoint the great plain exists, it is in fact divided by innumerable tributaries and streams that have cut deep furrows into the soil and created a complex microstructure of hills, gullies, and plains, with local slopes often exceeding 45°. In evaluating these lands for agriculture or cattle ranching, this fact is very important, since erosion can rapidly eliminate the fertile soil stratum after the forest cover is removed.

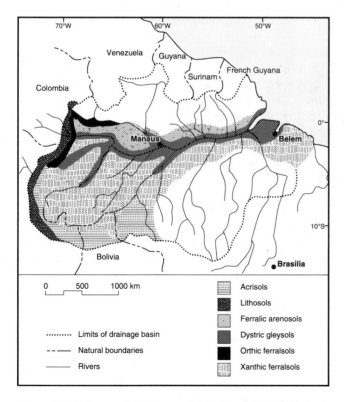

Figure 29.4 Soils map of the Amazon Basin. Source: Jordan 1985, adapted and simplified.

Soils

Developing a soil map for the Amazon has been difficult because, although much information is available, sampling densities and types of analysis have been quite variable. Brazil has carried out systematic studies with maps on a scale of 1:250,000 through the RADAM Project, and the distribution of the principal soils in the Brazilian Amazon has been mapped (Fig. 29.4; Jordan 1985). In some areas, intensive studies have provided more detailed information on soil characteristics and properties. Studies in São Carlos do Rio Negro, Venezuela, and in Peru, and research in Jurimaguas, as well in areas around Belém, Manaus, and in Rondônia, have provided a clear view of the potential and the limitations of some types of soils found in the Amazon.

As a consequence of weathering processes, Amazon soils have generally lost most of the nutrients from their mineral structure. Thus their ion-exchange capacity and fertility are generally low. A few areas with alkaline substrata have better-quality soils, such as those found in small portions of Brazil's Rondônia. The greatest impediment to agricultural development in the Amazon region is the poor quality of the soil. Difficulties in recent colonization programs, especially those along the Transamazonic and Highway 364 in Rondônia, were due to poor soil quality together with poor soil management.

Climate

Solar Energy The amount of solar energy reaching the upper atmosphere in the Amazon remains practically constant the year round. For instance, in the city of Manaus, situated in the central Amazon, the solar input varies from a maximum of 885 calories/cm^2/day in January to a minimum of 767 calories/cm^2/day in June. Solar radiation reaching the earth varies primarily as a function of cloud cover. Data are available on the extent of variations in solar energy at selected sites in the cities of Belém, Manaus, and Rio Branco (Fig. 29.5).

The yearly sun-exposure ratio in the areas mentioned is below 50% and varies during the year. The solar energy reaching the upper canopy of the forest is around 425 calories/cm^2/day (Ribeiro et al. 1982, Villa Nova, Salati, and Matsui 1976). Villa Nova calculated that 210 calories/cm^2/day are used in evapotranspiration processes and that 215 calories/cm^2/day are consumed in heating the air and are diverted into other processes. These data indicate that evapotranspiration and water balance are of great importance for the energy balance of the region.

Temperature An important characteristic of the region's climate is the small variation in the monthly average temperature, especially in the central strip below an altitude of 200 m. For instance, in the city of Belém, the highest monthly average temperature, 26.9°C, occurs in November, and the lowest, 24°C, in March. In Manaus, the highest average monthly temperature, 27.9°C, occurs in September, and the lowest, 25.8°C, between February and April, with a variation of only 2.1°C. In the city of Iquitos, the highest

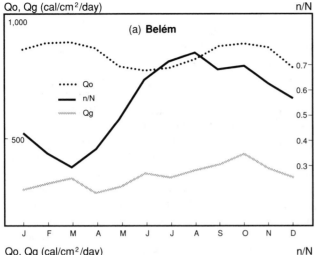

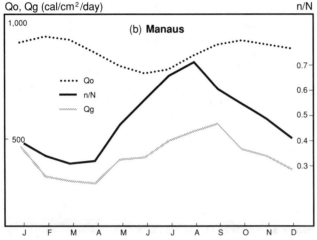

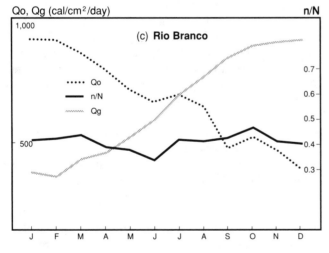

Figure 29.5 Mean monthly values of insolation ratio (n/N), solar energy at top of atmosphere (Q_o), and global radiation at the canopy top (Q_g). (a) at Belém (PA): latitude 1°28'S, longitude 67°48'W; (b) at Manaus (AM): latitude 3°08'S, longitude 60°2'W; (c) at Rio Branco (AC): latitude 9°58'S, longitude 67°48'W. Source: Salati 1985.

average monthly temperature, 32°C, occurs in November, and the lowest, 30°C, occurs in July. This isothermy results from the great quantity of water vapor in the atmosphere.

Rainfall and Water Balance   The seasonal cycle of rainfall varies across the Amazon Basin. The maximum rainfall in the north occurs in the months of June and July, whereas in the south the rainy period extends from November to March. Further west, especially in the northwest, rainfall is abundant the year round. The variation in rainfall has a major effect on river discharge, and also influences the migration and reproduction of fish. The spatial variation of rainfall in the Brazilian Amazon is indicated in the isohyet diagram (Fig. 29.6). In the Brazilian Amazon, rainfall varies from slightly over 3,000 mm/yr to 1,500 mm/yr. The highest rainfall is found on the coast, decreasing toward the west and then increasing again in the northwest regions, again attaining values of 3,000 mm/yr. Near the Andean region, rainfall increases abruptly.

The average rainfall for the region as a whole has been estimated as 2,200–2,400 mm/yr. The water balance for the Amazon Basin can be estimated, after the discharge for the Amazon River is estimated at 176,000 m³/s (Oltman 1967). From this, we estimate that the Amazon Basin receives 12 × 10¹² m³/yr of rainfall, discharges 5.5 × 10¹² m³/yr to the ocean, and returns 6.5 × 10¹² m³/yr to the atmosphere through evapotranspiration.

A more detailed study of water balance in small watersheds (Franken and Leopoldo 1984) showed that stream discharge represented approximately 25% of rainfall, whereas rain interception was about 20–25%, and transpiration around 50%. This research indicates that in dense forest, evapotranspiration can reach 75%; these values show the importance of the vegetation cover to the water balance and consequently to the energy balance of the region.

Water-Vapor Balance and Recirculation   Water vapor of the Amazon region originates primarily in the Atlantic Ocean and enters the region with the trade winds, which blow year round from the east. Marques, Salati, and Santos (1980) studied these vapor flows with the aid of existing radiosonde data. The quantity of water vapor entering the region from the Atlantic Ocean has been estimated to be of the same order of magnitude as the water vapor produced by evapotranspiration processes.

Based on this information and the results of isotopic studies, Salati et al. (1979) suggest the significance of water-vapor recirculation in the Amazon region. A simplified model (Fig. 29.7) of water recirculation is especially appropriate for the central corridor area of the Amazon Basin. Approximately 50% of the water vapor that produces rainfall comes from the Atlantic Ocean with the trade winds, whereas the other 50% is produced within the Basin by evapotranspiration from the forest vegetation, thereby establishing a crucial system of water recirculation within the region.

Hydrology

Since the beginning of colonization, the Amazon region has been famous for its great rivers. It has been referred to as the "Sweet Water Sea," because its waters intrude tens of kilometers into the Atlantic Ocean. Colonization also progressed as a function of the rivers, the cities having been built in strategic points for defense and colonization. In Fig. 29.8, the discharges of the great rivers of the planet are compared to that of the Amazon. Besides the great contribution of

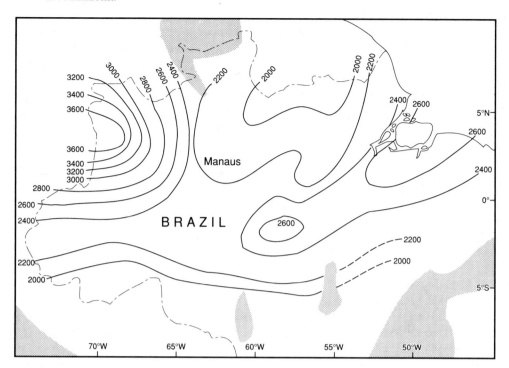

Figure 29.6 Normal precipitation in the Amazon Basin in mm/yr.
Source: Salati, Marques, and Molion 1978.

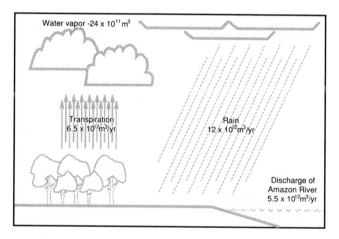

Figure 29.7 A simple model of water recirculation in the central corridor of the Amazon Basin.

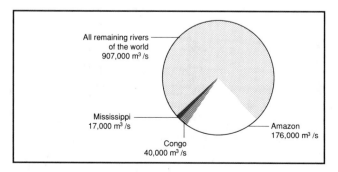

Figure 29.8 Discharges of the great rivers of the planet.

water, the Amazon delivers a great load of sediment to the ocean; it is estimated that slightly over 10^9 t of sediment are discharged to the ocean per year (Nordin and Meade 1986).

The Amazon rivers are quite variable in their physicochemical and biological characteristics. Sioli (1984) recognized three main types of waters in the Amazon region: white, black, and clear or crystalline. White-water rivers have headwaters in the Andean or pre-Andean regions. Examples are the Amazon River proper, Purus, Madeira, and Juruá. The normally yellowish color is due to carried sediment proceeding from the sources. Measurements made near Manaus show that the Amazon River contains about 0.1 g of sediment per liter and relatively high quantities of dissolved salts and has a pH around 6.5 to 7.0. These waters, which are mineralogically the richest, also have the greatest biological activity and fish production. The lands and lakes flooded by these waters are rich. The small agricultural production of the region represented by jute and manioc culture is concentrated along the white-water rivers. It is expected, due to the natural fertility, that these areas will become a focus for future colonization projects.

The black-water rivers, as exemplified by the Rio Negro, carry little sediment, and are acid, with pH values as low as 4. These rivers drain the Archean shields and Tertiary sediments. Their brown or dark-reddish hue is due to the presence of humic and fulvic acids produced by incomplete organic-matter decomposition. At high water, the forests bordering these rivers are flooded, creating a swampy habitat called *igapó*.

Clear-water rivers are normally transparent with a slightly greenish color, and carry little suspended material. Their physicochemical characteristics can vary considerably depending on their origin. The pH values can vary between 4 and 7. An example of this type of river is the Tapajos (Junk and Furch 1985).

These diverse water types together with their diverse associated flora form a complex of aquatic ecosystems containing an extremely abundant icthyofauna, with over 2,000 species of fish, of which about 1,400 have been described.

Vegetation

What first attracted the attention of researchers and explorers arriving in the Amazon was the great diversity and biomass of plants, especially in the upland forest areas. It has been estimated that more than 60,000 species of plants grow in the Amazon. A lengthy review of the forest ecosystems can be found in Murça Pires and Prance (1985).

The average areal biomass of an upland dense forest is 250 t (dry weight)/ha and a below-ground biomass of 100 t/ha, including the soil organic matter. These data are important when considering the ecological importance of Amazonia in the global carbon cycle and the consequences of large-scale deforestation on the carbon dioxide levels in the atmosphere. The biomass is distributed in different ecosystems, with varying soil and climatic conditions. In periodically flooded forests, the structure of the vegetation is closely linked to water quality. Table 29-1 presents the areas of several different vegetation units and the distribution of carbon. The total carbon is around 60×10^9 t (Fearnside 1985).

In addition to being a carbon reserve, the forest is also a reserve for chemical nutrients. In a dense forest ecosystem, a major part of the chemical nutrients is found in the forest biomass, with a much smaller portion in the mineral layer of soils. The recycling of these chemical nutrients takes place very rapidly. This fact, coupled with the physical characteristics of the soils, explains some of the difficulties and failures associated with agricultural colonization in the Amazon. The equilibrium of biogeochemical cycles is disrupted by burning and destroying the forest biomass; soil nutrients are lost to erosion and leaching. With the loss of organic material, moreover, the soil tends to become compacted.

The hot and humid climate of the Amazon usually leads to the formation of humid tropical forest. Where the climate is marginal, with lower yearly precipitation and a longer dry season, edaphic factors, such as soil drainage, become more important and can lead to the formation of enclosed fields and *cerrados* in the Hylean area. Human activity, especially forest clearing and fire, can also contribute to the formation of new savannahs and help to maintain and increase field areas of edaphic origin.

It is obvious, however, that climate is the principal factor controlling vegetation cover in the Amazon. What is less obvious, but more important to understand, is that the vegetation cover can also influence the climate. A close relationship exists between climate and vegetation, which can be characterized as a dynamic equilibrium. The role of the Amazon forest in maintaining this equilibrium is especially important. By increasing evapotranspiration, the forest acts to recycle and increase the storage time of water within the region. When water is more available, vegetation can develop even more, and so on, until a stationary state is reached. If the forest is destroyed, the system will regress from the current dynamic equilibrium to an initial state, characterized by lower annual precipitation, which would represent a climatic change.

Occupation and Ecological Alterations

Territorial Reconnaissance and Occupation (1500–1840)

During the period of discovery and occupation of the Amazon, interaction between the colonizers and the indigenes across the region was basically similar, varying somewhat according to the specific culture encountered. The Portuguese who colonized the lower portion of the Amazon Basin found densely settled areas inhabited by native populations, characterized by their primitive living conditions and by independent village structure. At the same time, the Spanish occupying the Andean portions of the Amazon encountered more complex societies that included cities linked by roadways and native populations possessing wealth in gold and silver.

Table 29-1 *Carbon Stocks in "Natural" Vegetation in the Brazilian Legal Amazon. (Masses in Gt.)*

Vegetation type	Area (1,000 km²)	Live above ground	Below ground	Litter and detritus above ground
Upland dense forest	3,063	34.69	11.90	3.239
Scrub forest (cerrado)	1,290	2.20	1.46	0.450
Montane forest	26	0.23	0.08	0.004
Other upland forest types	259	3.23	0.82	0.260
Humid savanna (upland + flooded)	165	0.53	0.24	0.050
Flooded forests (várzea + igapó)	70	0.50	0.17	0.011
Mangroves	1	0.01	0.01	0.005
TOTALS	4,874	41.39	14.68	4.02
Total Carbon = 60.09 Gt				

*1 Gt = 10^9 tons.

Source: Fearnside 1985.

Spanish discoveries of precious metals in the Incan civilization led many to believe that great treasures could be found in the Amazon, inspiring a number of expeditions to search for the legendary El Dorado. One of these expeditions, led by Captain Orellana in 1541, culminated in the first trip down the Amazon from the Andean source to the Atlantic Ocean. For the first time, the characteristics of the world's greatest river were reported, by Friar Gaspar Carvajal. From 1544 to 1546, Orellana commanded another expedition with the purpose of conquering and populating the lands south of the Amazon for the Kingdom of Castile and Leon. This expedition failed and its leader died trying to find the Amazon's main branch.

Following the Spaniards, the British, Dutch, and French also tried to establish colonies in Amazonia. Around 1615, the Portuguese, together with Brazilian colonists, instigated military campaigns and began occupying the Amazon, motivated by political and economic goals. The Portuguese plan for occupation, initiated in 1616, involved establishing sovereignty through constructing fortresses and conducting expeditions along the river; developing the region economically through sugar-cane plantations and the extraction of forest products; and undertaking religious missions with the purpose of giving religious instruction and of civilizing the Indians.

The initial plan of the Portuguese was to occupy the Amazon by establishing agricultural colonies. However, their activities were unsuccessful, the early colonists facing much the same problems of poor soils and diseases that confront settlers today.

Besides entering the river and its tributaries directly, colonists also reached the Amazon from the area of São Paulo through the Tocantins, Guaporé, and Madeira rivers. Their motivations included the search for the gold and precious stones of the city of El Dorado, and the opportunity for enslaving Indians. Gold was discovered in Mato Grosso and Goiás (southern Amazon), and many towns sprang up around these mining regions. Settlements also appeared between the Cuiabá and the Guaporé Vale after the discovery of gold there. Since the colonists were interested primarily in the extraction of gold, silver, and precious stones, few changes occurred in the natural landscape. The native population was strongly affected as a result of occupation, however, and some tribes completely disappeared.

Forest-Products Exploitation (1840–1945)

Colonization was intensified again during the "rubber boom" between 1840 and 1914. After Goodyear's discovery of rubber vulcanization in 1839, efforts to extract the product increased considerably. Rubber production increased from 367 t in 1844 to 1,935 t in 1851. Inhabitants of Brazil's northeast and foreigners of various origins migrated to the Amazon in large numbers. It is estimated that between 1872 and 1910, over 300,000 immigrants from the Brazilian northeast entered the Amazon. The population of the Brazilian Amazon increased from an estimated 137,000 in 1820, 323,000 in 1870, 695,000 by 1900, to 1,217,000 in 1910. The growth of the non-Indian population placed increasing

pressure on the native inhabitants, who migrated toward the interior of the forest and toward the headwaters of the rivers.

Several developments associated with the rubber boom began to influence the landscape, flora, and fauna of the region. They included the increase in population; the increase in river traffic, with the use of steamships carrying supplies to settlers and bringing out rubber; and the introduction of railways. Construction began on the region's first railroad, the Madeira-Mamoré line in the southwest Amazon, 364 km long, in 1872. Its operation led to the founding of the cities of Porto Velho and Guajara-Mirim, as well as to the immigration of many foreigners, including ones of British, American, Greek, Hindu, and Spanish origin. The railway was completed in 1912, when rubber production was in decline, and thus it was rarely used. Another factor influencing change in the Amazon was a related one, the development of towns and settlements. The most important of these were Manaus and Belém.

The attempted expansion of livestock production during the Amazon rubber boom was not very successful. Livestock production followed the trajectory of rubber, which peaked in 1910 and 1912 (with exports of 42,000 t), and decreased thereafter, leading to general economic and social stagnation in the region. The lack of success in producing livestock indicates that cattle production was not feasible on a sustained-yield basis.

The era of rubber exploitation was also one of social upheaval in the Peruvian and Colombian Amazon. Social disruption in these two areas was marked by the genocide of Indian groups such as the Huitotos, and human exploitation at the level of slavery. In Peru, the actions of Carlos Fermin Fitzcarrald (1862–1897) and Julio César Arana reflect this type of exploitation. The former, called the "rubber king," succeeded in accumulating a great fortune by exploiting the Ucayali. His incursions led him to discover the strait now bearing his name. Rubber extraction attracted a great migratory flux of Peruvians from the provinces of Costa, Sierrá, and Selva Alta, as well as some Brazilians and immigrants from Europe and Asia. Thus, the nonindigenous population of the region increased from 18,000 in 1876, to 36,000 in 1904, and to 120,000 in 1920 (San Román 1975). This migration gave rise to the first great farms in the lowland jungle. Initially intended for rubber extraction, the farms later turned to other products. Rubber cultivation suffered when the British and Dutch colonial plantations started production, causing a serious economic recession.

Modern Exploitation in Brazil (1945 to the Present)

From 1914 until World War II, the development of the Amazon was generally stagnant. Since 1945, the region has entered a third phase of occupation and change, spearheaded by the interests and goals associated with livestock production, principally cattle-raising. Large areas have been deforested in the conversion of forest to pasture for beef cattle, with important secondary effects on wildlife and flora through the destruction of natural habitats. Urban and industrial growth has also occurred, particularly through the creation of a duty-free zone in the city of Manaus, whose population

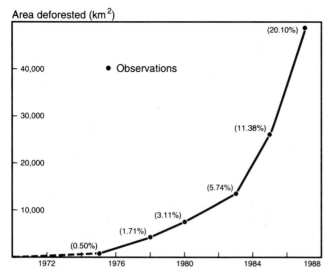

Figure 29.9 Area of deforestation for the state of Rondônia, 1970–1984. Total area of Rondônia is 244,000 km².

has increased in a few decades from 200,000 to around 700,000.

Highway Construction   The building of the new capital city, Brazilia, marked a new phase of expansion and development. Environmental impacts resulted from colonization for agriculture and cattle ranching in the upland regions that were made accessible by the building of highways. The highway development program (Fig. 29.2) began in the 1960s with the roadway from Belém to Brazilia. During the 1970s, the Transamazonic highway was built, connecting the Brazilian northwest to the western Amazon. The construction of an asphalt highway connecting Cuiabá to Porto Velho resulted in the greatest ecological impact registered in the region, due to the migration and settlement it facilitated.

Another highway project is being considered, which would link Porto Velho to Rio Branco, with the possibility of an extension to Cruzeiro do Sul. With the building of these highways and the implementation of colonization programs, especially during the past two decades, the migratory flux to the Amazon region has increased dramatically. The popula-

tion of the Brazilian Legal Amazon was estimated in 1987 to be 19,470,617.

Deforestation   The combination of agricultural and cattle-ranching projects is slowly changing the natural landscape of the region. It is estimated that during the last decade about 4 million ha/yr have been deforested. The deforestation rate is exponential, as shown in one area of Rondônia (Fig. 29.9). The area deforested in less than 12 years totals 48,930 km², corresponding to 20% of Rondônia. If the same rate of deforestation continues, the forested area of the state will be lost by 1994 (Leopoldo and Salati 1987). In spite of the dangers associated with deforestation, the number of colonization and development programs has continued to increase. The total deforestation estimate before 1988 is approximately 12% of Legal Amazon. The major modifications have occurred in the states of Pará (9%), Maranhão (20%), Goiás (11%), Acre (13%), Rondônia (24%), and Mato Grosso (24%) (Table 29-2).

Fearnside (1984) has pointed out the difficulties of effectively measuring the rate of deforestation taking place in Amazonia. The same author observes that official data are often incomplete or outdated and that no publications employ complete and updated information on the region as a whole. In some Amazonian states of Brazil, for instance Rondônia, the area deforested has been increasing at an alarming rate. From the data provided by Brazil's Institute for Forestry Development and by the National Space Research Institute (Table 29-2), it appears that the state of Rondônia lost almost 24% of its forest area between 1975 and 1988. Rondônia has been the object of some of the most accurate studies on deforestation (Fearnside and Salati 1985; Malingreau and Tucker 1987).

Besides completely deforested areas, Malingreau and Tucker (1987) identified areas that have suffered partial changes of vegetation cover. These areas have been called "disturbance areas," and reflect the beginning of the occupation process. The ratio between the disturbance area and deforestation areas is approximately 3:1 in the states of Rondônia and Mato Grosso. The value for the state of Acre is

Table 29-2 *Alteration of the Natural Vegetation Cover of the Legal Amazon of Brazil*

State or territory	Area of state or territory (km²)	Area altered (km²)				Percentage of area altered			
		To 1975	To 1978	To 1980	To 1988	To 1975	To 1978	To 1980	To 1988
Federal territory of Amapá	140,276	152.5	171.5	—	571.5	0.1	0.1	—	0.40
Pará	1,248,642	9,947.8	24,949.6	33,913.8	120,000.0	0.8	2.0	2.7	9.6
Federal territory of Rondônia	230,104	55.0	143.8	1,169.6*	3,270.0	0.0	0.1	0.5*	1.4
Maranhão	257,451	2,940.8	7,334.0	10,671.1	50,670.0	1.1	2.8	4.1	19.7
Goiás†	285,793	3,299.0	7,208.5	9,120.5	33,120.0	1.2	2.5	3.2	11.6
Acre	152,589	1,165.5	2,464.5	4,626.8	19,500.0	0.8	1.6	3.0	12.8
Rondônia	243,044	1,216.5	4,185.3	7,579.3	58,000.0	0.5	1.7	3.1	23.7
Mato Grosso	881,001	9,781.3	30,368.8	52,785.8	208,000.0	1.1	3.4	6.0	23.6
Amazonas	1,567,125	783.8	1,791.3	—	105,790.0	0.1	0.1	—	6.8
Legal Amazon	5,005,425	29,342.2	78,616.7	—	598,921.5	0.6	1.6	—	12.0

†Only part of Goiás is included in the Legal Amazon.

*1982 assessment.

on the order of 6:1. These values suggest that at least 30% of Amazonia has already suffered some sort of damage.

Mineral Exploitation in the 1980s   The search for El Dorado finally ended with the discovery in 1980 of the Serra Pelada gold mine. This mine has produced more than 40 t of gold up to 1986, and has yielded gold nuggets up to 62 kg. Many people have become rich, and today the city next to the gold mine has over 100,000 inhabitants. Gold is still being mined in the alluvium of the Amazon River, especially along the Rio Madeira, where over 500 rafts extract bed load from the river bottom. The search for precious stones goes on, and many mines have been established in the Goiás and Roraima areas.

Tin mining has also become a major industry in the Amazon region. One of the largest mining operations in the region is the Carajás Mine, which started as an iron mine and is now a multibillion-dollar mining complex with sophisticated equipment for handling several other minerals (Almeida 1986). The latest (April 1987) and perhaps the most important development was the discovery of large petroleum and natural-gas reserves on the shores of the Urucu River, one of the Jurúas affluents.

Although legislation exists, most operations are poorly controlled and often do great harm to the environment. For example, it is estimated that over 100 t of mercury have been spilled into the Madeira River during gold processing. Mining, whether carried out by firms or small companies and prospectors, produces impacts on the environment that need to be controlled by competent authorities. Stronger legislation and stricter supervision of mining activities clearly are needed. According to informal data, much of the Amazon's mineral wealth, especially gold and precious stones, is smuggled abroad, yielding little economic and social benefit to the region. It is estimated that during the last 12 years, the gold and precious stones smuggled abroad had a value of about U.S. $18 billion.

Hydroelectric-Dam Projects   The construction of hydroelectric-power projects causes impacts due to the characteristics of the reservoir formed. Because of the Amazon's low topography, reservoirs for hydroelectric plants often cover very large areas. For instance, the Tucuruí Dam on the Tocantins River flooded a forested area of about 2,000 km^2, to produce 4,000 MW. Balbina's dam near Manaus, on the Uatumã River, will flood an area of over 2,000 km^2 and produce just 250 MW when fully operational (Fig. 29.10). Other hydroelectric plants are being built, such as Samuel in Rondônia (216 MW) and Xingu. The final goal will be to exploit all of the 10 million KW of hydroelectric power estimated to exist in the Amazon affluents. Some direct consequences of dam construction are changes in the species composition of fish communities resulting from changes in current flow and from contacts between water masses, separated by the dam; changes in diseases transmitted by insect populations; and impacts on native indian communities living in the region (Junk and Nunes de Mello 1987).

Modern Developments in the Peruvian Amazon

In Peru, before the 1940s, little modern progress had been achieved in the Amazon. One noteworthy exception was the 91 km of Tambo del Sol-Pucallpa Railway, built between 1919 and 1929. Some airports also had been built, as well as some radial connections. The most important highway built in the forest connects Lima to Pucallpa. It was begun in 1937 and was completed in 1943, transforming Pucallpa into the most important trade city of Peruvian Amazon. The highway section linking Lima-Selva Central was also opened in 1943 (Oxapampa), and was extended to Villa Rica and Bocaz in 1955. In 1968, Chanchamayo was connected to Satipo, where access from Huancayo already existed. Many highways were built during this period, connecting the mountains to the high forest (Valcarel et al. 1980). Now 12 important highways exist, with various branches and links among them. More recently, the controversial Jungle Border Highway was begun. This highway was designed to connect the populated centers of the Middle Amazon, to provide greater access to the region and thereby reduce demographic pressure and social tension in other regions of the country. This project is well advanced and has generated some of the most serious environmental impacts currently occurring in the Peruvian Amazon.

The early- to mid-twentieth century marked the beginning of large-scale agricultural and cattle-ranching operations, which have continued to expand. Initially, one plan aimed to combine agricultural and cattle-ranching activities employing advanced technology appropriate to the humid tropics. The success of the experimental agricultural station at Tingo Maria, in 1942, showed that the idea had promise (Peru, Dirección de Colonizacción y Asuntos Orientales 1947). Unfortunately, economic problems led to the failure of that effort, and during the 1960s the station was transformed into a university. Two notable developments in Peru were the

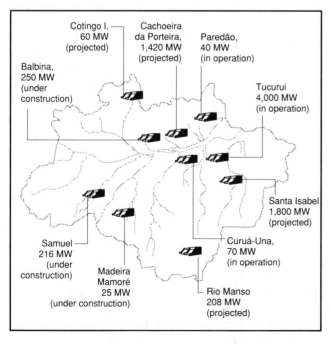

Figure 29.10 Hydroelectric plants in operation, under construction, and projected in Amazonia. Source: Junk and Nunes de Mello 1987.

establishment of the firm Le Touneau, in Tournavista (Pachitea River) and of the Summer Linguistic Institute. Le Touneau was the first cattle-ranching operation to utilize massive mechanized deforestation, which resulted in a major ecologic and economic disaster. The Summer Linguistic Institute has stimulated commercial hunting and extractive activities, and has been blamed by the local Indians for mismanaging their natural resources.

Beginning in 1970, several new developments began to have a significant impact on Peru's Amazon territory. The first was the discovery of commercially exploitable petroleum reserves in Trompeteros (Corrientes River) in 1971. Peru was already extracting petroleum from Ganso Azul, on the Pachitea River, and processing it in Pucallpa, but the quantity of oil reserves was unknown. After the discovery of the Trompeteros reserve, exploitation efforts were increased considerably, culminating in the construction of the North Peruvian pipeline. Petroleum research and exploitation has had an enormous impact on the environment, besides creating serious socioeconomic problems. The expansion of coca culture, its transformation into paste and cocaine, as well as the associated increase in traffic, has also had a major impact on the High Jungle environment.

Sucessive Peruvian governments have continued to promote Amazon occupation, promising to transform its huge area into the breadbasket of the country. Until now, the protests of scientists and long-term planners have been of no avail, even though it is evident that most of the government colonization projects have a high ecological cost. Since 1980, six large-scale colonization projects have been created with the aim of devoting millions of hectares to agriculture and cattle ranching.

More than 6 million ha of Peruvian jungle have been deforested since 1972 (Table 29-3). Clearing has greatly affected the forests and other ecosystems peculiar to the High Jungle. For example, it has resulted in the extinction of the *Podocarpus* forests, which, because of their special character and diversified fauna and flora, could well be considered separate ecosystems. It will never be known how many important species have been lost. Human impact has also been considerable in aquatic ecosystems, such as the borders of rivers in which people have settled, using *varzeas*, or floodplains.

In addition to the general impacts, some specific processes of change in Peru's Amazon region also deserve notice.

Table 29-3 *Population and Deforestation in the Peruvian Amazon, 1972–1987.*

	1972	1974	1979	1987
Total population in the forest area (thousands of people)	1,342	1,548	1,754	2,240
Rural population in the forest area (thousands of people)		929	1,018	1,148
Mean yearly deforestation (ha)		232	254	287
Accumulated deforestation (ha)		4,500	5,122	7,275

The Quina Tree (Quinine) The most widely exported plant during the missionary period was quina (quinine), or *chinchona* (*Cinchona officinalis*). The plant began to be used worldwide to fight malaria after it was given to Countess Cinchón, wife of Don Luis Jerônimo Fernandez de Cabrera, Count of Cinchón, XIV Viceroy of Peru, in 1638. As quina exploitation and export to Europe grew in importance, it started to be grown on a large scale in England's and Portugal's colonies in Asia. In 1951, Peru exported 41,168 kg of quina; this quantity was reduced to 16,134 kg in 1952 and to 6,055 kg and 8,650 kg, respectively, in 1953 and 1954 (Perú Dirección de Colonizaccion y Bosques, 1955). Although quina is of Peruvian origin, it was never successfully grown for commercial purposes in this country. Besides *C. officinalus*, there are two other species: *C. pubescens* and *C. micrantha*, both of lesser value.

Quina exploitation is a destructive process in which the entire plant must be cut in order to proceed to complete peeling. As a consequence, this species has practically been eradicated in Ecuador, Peru, and Bolivia. Ironically, it appears in Peru's national shield, together with vicuña, another species almost extinct. Although the plant is no longer exploited, natural recuperation does not occur because of its location in the most deforested area of the High Jungle. The National Agrarian University is currently studying this species with the goal of preserving the remaining genetic material.

Wood Exploitation Since remote times, wood has been exploited in the Peruvian Amazon. Cedar and mahogany were the first woods to be heavily exploited, but by now many stocks have been depleted. Exploitation has always been of a selective character, directed to semihard woods that are in greater demand. *Cedrela* and *Swietenia*, for example, constituted 60% of national wood production in 1954; cedar alone accounted for 50%. Significant quantities of *Cedrelinga catanaformis*, Podocarp (*Podocarpus* spp.), and a blend of species, called oak trees, were also extracted during this period. The ancient walnut (Juglans) exploitation had long been brought to an end. Although cedar and mahogany are still being extracted today, they constitute only a small fraction of the total harvest. The species have apparently been overexploited (Knees and Gardner 1983). Other species are now becoming marketable, and there is a slight tendency toward diversification. A dramatic case of overexploitation is that of Podocarp (*Podocarpus glomeratus, Podocarpus oleifolius, Podocarpus utilior*), which in 1954 accounted for 12.6% of sawed wood production and now is very rare.

Coca and Cudweed Coca (*erythroxilon coca*) deserves special comment. The plant has been cultivated since ancient times, using conservative methods with regard to the soil over the last millennium. It was sown on terraces and in pools and never in open declivities. In 1964, only 16,360 ha were planted in Peru. In 1970, 18,000 ha were planted. From that point, coca culture has increased enormously, and today from 150,000 ha to 200,000 ha are in cultivation. Its cultivation protected and stimulated by drug traders, coca is a multimillion-dollar illegal operation. Ecologists are particularly concerned with the highly erosive impact of the current agricultural practice of planting on declivities with bare soils. In 1972, Dourojeanni and Tovar discovered that the cavernicole bird (*Steatornis caripensis*), feeding on coca fruit as a substitute for sylvan species, was in danger of extinction, even within Tinga Maria National Park. Any protective action is hampered by the extraterritoriality of coca planting and uncontrolled erosion.

Cudweed (*Lonchocarpus utilis, L. nicoy*) is another plant that has been cultivated by the Indians since ancient times for fishing. At the beginning of this century, its toxic properties were discovered and used to control plagues. It was extensively cultivated in the Low Jungle farms, mainly in Ucauoli. In 1931, 1,392 kg were exported through Iquitos, and in 1937, this figure had increased to 393,916 kg (Wille et al. 1939). In 1964, 6,400 mt were produced, but output had already begun to decrease (Perú, CONESTCAR 1965), due to competition with new synthetic agrotoxic products being imported from abroad. Today, very little cudweed is sown, although there are possibilities of its revival.

Modern Developments in the Colombian Amazon

Even though it has a density of only 0.6 inhabitants/km^2, the Colombian Amazon Basin has also suffered major alterations over the past 25 years, characterized by accelerated colonization near the mountain ranges and along the main rivers. Completely covered with natural vegetation until the beginning of this century, 7% of the Colombian Amazon Basin has been deforested and turned into pasture. The greatest impact has occurred in the Caqueta (Carrizosa, Leyva, and Mantilla 1983) and Putumayo regions at the foot of the Andean Mountain Range and in the denuded plains and accumulation zones between the Caguan and Putumayo rivers.

The natural vegetation cover, which Humboldt called Hyllean Amazon, or rainy tropical forest, is characterized by trees with straight trunks, which sometimes exceed 45 m in height. The ecosystem was originally populated by native groups, which have since largely dispersed (Dominguez 1985). Significant transformation began in the third decade of this century, when the first highway was constructed on the eastern slope of the Andes, resulting in the deforestation of about 10,000 ha. Large-scale change, though, did not begin until the middle of the century, when politically motivated violence in rural areas, demographic expansion, rural property problems, and state financing hastened the transformation process. Instability in the Colombian Andes led to an emigration totalling about 300,000 to the Colombian Amazon between 1958 and 1986. At the same time, the national government had been promoting semiurban settlement along the frontiers of the Basin. The main settlements – Leticia on the Amazon, Puerto Leguizamon on the Putumayo, and Mituover Vaupes – are administrative and military centers whose initial purpose was to strengthen control, but which today are regional trade centers.

Native tribes still exist along the rivers and even in the wild plain hinterland; their number is unknown, but is estimated at less than 100,000. Nowadays, the territory is occupied principally by whites and mestizos involved in ranching activities. In recent years, many of the inhabitants have become involved in cocaine culture and processing. Cattle ranches are maintained with an average livestock density (including calves) of 1 per 1½ ha (PRORADAM 1979), resulting in a total population of approximately 700,000 head of cattle for the region. The humid tropical forest at the foot of the Andes has been almost completely cut down and transformed into pasture for cattle-grazing. The forest cover has been reduced to small "forest piles," kept by some owners as a wood source for consumption.

The area thus cleared is estimated to be 2 million ha, or about 7% of the area of Colombian Amazonia. Even the 26 million ha of primary forest that remain have undergone marginal changes characterized by extraction of thick trunks of valuable woods such as the cedar trees (*Cedrela* spp.); degradation of some species such as the lauraceous tree (*Beilachmiedia* sp), the black rubber (*Castilloa*), or the yellow lupine (*Leopoldina*), which have great commercial value; and degradation and disappearance of vegetation peculiar to holms and lkeas, where the first human settlements concentrated, along the Caquetá, Putumayo, and Caguan rivers.

Along the main rivers (Putumayo, Caquetá, Caguan, Yari, Vaupés, and Guainia), small human settlements of fishermen, hunters, or woodworkers who migrated from the Colombian hinterland also abound. The impact of these colonists, however, is minimal since they rarely have deforested land more than 100 m from the margin of the river.

Human Impacts on Fauna

The human impact on the biota provides a useful integrative indicator of the severity and kind of human impact on the environment of a region. It is difficult within the scope of this review to characterize the anthropogenic changes that have occurred in the fauna of the Amazon, even for a period as short as 300 years. The Amazon region has about 300 species of mammals, 2,000 species of fish, 11 species of chelonian, and 6 species of aquatic mammals. While quantitative data on animal population are lacking, some qualitative information on impacts can be gleaned from the works of various researchers (Ayres and Best 1979; Best 1984; Carvalho 1984; Dourojeanni 1985). Twenty species of fowls and reptiles already show evidence of depleted stocks. Many species of the Amazon fauna are endangered (Table 29-4; and Best 1984).

Mammals Mammals in the Amazon have suffered in varying degrees from the impacts of habitat destruction and from hunting for food, products, and international demand.

Jaguars (*Panthera onca*) have been exploited for their skins and for zoo collections. Their natural habitat has also been seriously reduced with human population increase. Originally, jaguars were distributed from Mexico to northern Argentina. They are the largest neotropical cats, the adults weighing almost 140 kg. They are highly prized for their skin, which is used in the apparel industry. In eastern Pará, with the opening of the Belém-Brazilia highway and the rapid growth

Table 29-4 *List of Species of the Fauna Possibly Endangered by Extinction*

Order	Species	Popular name	Present situation	Potential threats
Sirenia	*Trichechis inunguis*	Peixe-boi	A	2,3
Carnivora	*Panthera onca*	Onça-pintada	V	2,1
Carnivora	*Felis* spp.	Maracajás	V	2,1
Carnivora	*Atelocyrus microtes*	Cachorro-do-Mato de-orelha-curta	R	1
Carnivora	*Speothos venaticus*	Cachorro-do vinagre	R	1
Carnivora	*Pteronura brasiliensis*	Ariranha	A	2,1
Carnivora	*Lutra enudris*	Lontra	V	2,1
Edentata	*Priodontes giganteus*	Tatú-canastra	V	1,3
Edentata	*Myrmecophaga tridactyla*	Tamanduá-bandeira	V	1
Primates	*Ateles paniscus*	Coatá-Macaco-Aranha	V	1,3
Primates	*Ateles belzebul*	Coatá-Macaco-Aranha	V	1,3
Primates	*Lagothrix lagothricha*	Macaco-barrigudo	V	1,3
Primates	*Cacajao calvus calvus*	Uacarí-branco	V	3,1
Primates	*Cacajao melanocophalus*	Uacarí-cabeça-preta	V	3,1
Primates	*Chiropotes albinasus*	Cuxiú-de-nariz vermelho	V	1,3
Primates	*Chiropotes satanas satanas*	Cuxiú-preto	A	1,3
Primates	*Saguinos imperador*	Bigode, Saguí de-bigode	V	1
Primates	*Saguinos bicolor*	Saguí de colar. Sauim	A	1
Primates	*Callimico goeldi*	Callimico	R	1,2
Faleoniformes	*Harpia hurpyja*	Gavião-real ou Uiraçú	R	1
Ceconiformes	*Morpheus guianensis*	Uiraçú-menor	R	1
Galliformes	*Ciax fasciolata pinima*	Mutúm-pinima	A	1,3
Passeriformes	*Haematoderus militaris*	Anambé-vermelho	R	1
Psittaciformes	*Aratinga guarouba*	Ararajuba	V	1,2
Chelonia	*Podocnemis expansa*	Tartaruga	V	2,3
Crocodilia	*Melanosuchus niger*	Jacaré-açú	A	2
Crocodilia	*Caiman crocodilus*	Jacaretinga	V	2

(A) threatened; (V) vulnerable; (R) rare; (1) destruction of the habitat; (2) trade of the leather or meat; (3) subsistence hunting.
Source: After Ayres and Best 1979.

of farms, jaguar populations have declined markedly. Although today they are protected by law, skins are still being smuggled through the Amazon to adjoining countries. Their biology is still poorly known. While the area necessary to sustain a viable population of the species is unknown, it is presumed to be very large, because reasonable populations of prey are also necessary for its maintenance.

International demand for zoo collections has also affected the great anteater (*Myrmecophata tridactyle*), the giant armadillo (*Priodontes giganteus*), and such primates as the *Callimico goeldi*. Increased hunting for meat and hides has had a major impact on a variety of mammals in the Amazon Basin; they include the giant armadillo, the manatee (*Trichechus inungis*), and several species of deer, otter, monkeys, and peccary. Virtually all of these species have also been harmed by destruction of habitat; species not sought for other reasons and affected principally in this way include bush dogs (*Atelocynus morotis* and *Speothus venatiais*), whose meat and skins have no commercial value.

Birds So few population studies of birds in the Amazon region exist that it is difficult to appraise changes due to human activity over the past 300 years. The group most threatened, mainly by habitat destruction, are the wild fowl, such as curassows, piping guans, and jacus. They disappear

with the growth of large urban centers; the regions most affected in Brazil are Belém, eastern Pará (along the Belém-Brazilia highway) Santarém, Manaus, and most recently southern Pará, on the border with Mato Grosso. Populations of kingfishers have declined along the littoral beaches of Pará with the growth of settlement, and hunting may threaten the survival of the species.

Reptiles Reptile populations in the Amazon are endangered primarily by hunting for food. The common tortoise (*Podocnemis expansa*) has been exploited for years. It is hunted with arrows and rods, and occasionally with dragnets. The construction of hydroelectric plants in the region may also affect the structure and size of the tortoise population. The freshwater turtle (*Pondocnemis unifilis*), while less exploited than the tortoise, is also commonly encountered in the regional markets. The small chelonian (*Kinosternum scorpioides*) has long been hunted in the lower Amazon for food; today their sale is prohibited, although exploitation continues.

The alligators (*Caiman crocodilus* and *Paleosuchus trignoatus*) are hunted for food mainly in the Tapajós and Almerim rivers of the lower Amazon. *Melanosuchus niger*, formerly quite abundant in some areas, and highly regarded for its leather, has suffered a major decrease in population over the past 300 years. Large species are now quite rare.

The current hunting intensity can be gauged by the export records for Cayman in Colombia, which amount to 10 million hides between 1951 and 1976.

Fish Since the beginning of colonization, the main protein source for human consumption in the region has been fish. Recently, due to improved fishing technology, storage, and transportation facilities, fishing pressure has increased. The problem is greatest for a few species, such as tambaqui (*Colossoma macropomum*) and piracuru (*Arapaima gigos*), which have a high market value and are intensely fished. Today, in order to find large tambaquis, a fishing boat must travel 2,000–3,000 km. In the Manaus market, it is difficult to find ones above the legal minimum size of 55 cm. (Adults can reach a length of 1–1.2 m, and weigh 20–25 kg; 7 years are necessary to reach this size.) It is estimated that fish production in the Amazon Basin currently exceeds 150,000 t/yr.

Trade in aquarium fish is also quite intense in the Amazon. It occurs, for the most part, without official approval, and the statistics even for authorized trade are often falsified.

Conclusion

The pattern of resource exploitation in Amazonia and its consequences can best be understood in the context of changing socioeconomic circumstances affecting the region. Throughout Amazonia's history, such processes as the decline of animal species and the progression from local to global scales of biogeochemical changes have accelerated dramatically. The development of the entire region, when influenced by populations and economic interests originating outside of Amazonia, has been characteristically extractive in nature. Such activities as mining, logging, ranching, and farming have been managed on the basis of immediate economic returns, with little or none of the appreciation of sustainable management needed to conserve the physical environment and little understanding of the resource base needed to sustain economic development.

The first period of Portuguese and Spanish colonial exploration that initiated the extractive process had its most adverse impacts on the indigenous human populations of Amazonia. Contact and conquest were inevitable as the colonial explorers established settlements along the immense waterways and floodplains. These were the same areas occupied by and serving the hunting and gathering systems of local populations. Wherever contact occurred, native communities were removed, and eventually their numbers were greatly reduced. This type of confrontation during the early occupation by the Portuguese and Spanish had little impact on the physical environment of the region.

The first large-scale migration into Amazonia was motivated by rubber-export interests. The natural characteristics of high rainfall, a hot and humid climate, high density of forest lands, the great diversity of plant and animal species, and the abundance of rivers and streams that distinguished Amazonia from other parts of South America also facilitated the gathering of large quantities of rubber. Another feature of the region – the low fertility of native soils due to natural weathering processes – was less of a constraint in this period

of rubber exploitation than it would be in later agricultural colonization efforts.

Rubber extraction did promote wider interregional effects by increasing transportation throughout Amazonia and developing the urban centers of Manaus and Belém. The population of Brazil's Amazon region increased by almost four times between 1870 and 1910, roughly the era of the "rubber boom." In Brazilian, Peruvian, and Colombian Amazonia alike, the growth of population placed increasing pressure on the native inhabitants. The disruption caused indigenous peoples as well as some rubber tappers to increase hunting-and-gathering activities as a means of obtaining small cash incomes. Improved transportation and the needs of growing urban populations prompted agricultural and livestock expansion in nearby areas. Livestock production followed the tempo of rubber exports, increasing, and then declining rapidly between 1870 and 1912, after which the region entered a period of general economic stagnation.

The latest period of Amazonian occupation is marked by a wide range of industrial, commercial, and agricultural activities. Some of these activities are officially sponsored government projects for agricultural colonization, mining, logging, and cattle ranching. Others are spontaneous developments, in which small farmers, ranchers, and miners migrated independently from other regions to exploit Amazonia's resources. A significant volume of illicit extraction, production, and smuggling exists in all of the Amazonian countries; the multimillion-dollar coca trade is an example that has environmental as well as social effects connected with increasing deforestation and soil erosion. The modern exploitation of Amazonia (1945 to the present) has created the greatest changes in the areas of soil, water, vegetation, and the numbers and habitats of biological species. Although the type of economic activity varies considerably from one location to another, many changes occurring at a microlevel are connected at a regional level and potentially may trigger global consequences.

The large number of cattle-ranching operations combined with the homesteading activities of small-scale farm colonists have generated international concern over the loss of a major world resource – Amazonia's tropical rain forests. It is estimated that both farming and livestock operations have caused an annual 4 million ha of deforestation during the past decade. The intensity of agricultural deforestation varies greatly over the region, but the highest figures are recorded for the Brazilian states of Mato Grosso and Rondônia and are associated with the rate and direction of agricultural settlements, both those officially sponsored and those due to spontaneous streams of migration. In all parts of Amazonia, the construction of infrastructure, especially highways and hydropower dams, has encouraged similar patterns of settlement and industrial forms of exploitation; such problems as deforestation, human-vector diseases such as malaria, soil erosion, and mercury pollution follow in their path. The most immediate environmental impact is the loss of natural habitats for many of Amazonia's plant and animal species. The scale of this habitat loss is largest in Brazilian Amazonia, but developments in the Peruvian forests are significant because they take a proportionately greater toll on Peru's total natural-resource base.

The extent of recent and likely future environmental change in the region is just beginning to be understood. There is a paucity of technical and scientific information on the region, but interest and research are increasing. Part of this attention has been sparked by indications that changes in Amazonian forest cover could have global consequences, even contributing significantly to changes in world climate. The close relationship of dynamic equilibrium between vegetation and climate has been described, and the role of the Amazonian forest in maintaining the equilibrium has been emphasized in a number of recent scientific studies (Franken and Leopoldo 1984; Salati et al. 1979). One aspect relates the forest to increasing evapotranspiration by recycling and increasing the storage time of water within the region. If there is more water available due to this recycling function of the forest cover, then more vegetation is allowed to develop, until a stable stationary state is reached. The current destruction of the Amazonian forests could alter that equilibrium to the point of lowering annual precipitation. Effects on global climate through increased atmospheric carbon dioxide from deforestation are also possible.

Reversal of this destructive style of development is most likely to occur through economic factors, since many forms of agricultural production, such as livestock-raising, have proven to be unsuited to Amazonia's soil conditions. The pattern of occupation will continue, however, wherever development schemes are shown to be economically feasible, and especially where adequate infrastructure is located to support such occupation.

References

Almeida, J. M. G., Jr. 1986. *Carajás: Desafio Político, Ecologia e Desenvolvimento*. Editora Brasiliense/CNPq.

Ayres, J. M., and R. Best. 1979. Estratégias para a conservação da fauna amazônica. *Acta Amazônica* 9:81–101.

Best, R. C. 1984. The aquatic mammals and reptiles of the Amazon. In *The Amazon*, ed. H. Sioli. The Hague: W. Junk.

Carrizosa, J., P. Leyva, and G. Mantilla. 1983. La ampliación de la frontera agrícola en el Caquetá. In *Expansión de la Frontera Agropecuaria y Medio Ambiente en América Latina*. Madrid: CEPAL/CIFCA.

Carvalho, J. C. de M. 1967. A conservação da natureza e recursos naturais na Amazônia brasileira. *Atas do Simpósio Biota Amazônica*, Rio de Janeiro: CNPq, 7:1–47.

———. 1984. The conservation of nature in the Brazilian Amazonia. In *The Amazon*, ed. H. Sioli, The Hague: W. Junk.

Dickinson, R., ed. 1987. *The Geophysiology of Amazonia: Vegetation and Climate Interactions*. New York: John Wiley and Sons.

Dominguez, C. 1985. *Amazonia Colombiana*. Bogota: Banco Popular.

Dourojeanni, M. J. 1985. Overexploited and underused animals in the Amazon region. In *Amazonia*, ed. G. T. Prance and T. E. Lovejoy, 419–33. Oxford: Pergamon Press.

Fearnside, P. M. 1984. A floresta vai acabar? *Ciencia Hoje* 2(10): 43–53.

———. 1985. Summary of Progress in Quantifying the Potential Contribution of Amazonian Deforestation to the Global Carbon Problem. Workshop on Biogeochemistry of Tropical Rain Forests: Problems for Research. USP/CENA.

Fearnside, M. F., and E. Salati. 1985. Explosive deforestation in Rondônia, Brazil. *Environmental Conservation* 12.

Franken, W., and P. R. Leopoldo. 1984. Hydrology of catchment areas of central Amazonian forest streams. In *The Amazon*, ed. H. Sioli. The Hague: W. Junk.

Jordan, C. F. 1985. Soils of the Amazon rainforest. In *Amazonia*, ed. G. T. Prance and T. E. Lovejoy, 83–94. Oxford: Pergamon Press.

Junk, W. J., and K. Furk. 1985. The physical and chemical properties of Amazonian waters and their relationships with the biota. In *Amazonia*, ed. G. T. Prance and T. E. Lovejoy, 3–17. Oxford: Pergamon Press.

Junk, W. J., and J. A. S. Nunes de Mello. 1987. Impactos ecológicos das represas hidrelétricas na Bacia Amazônica Brasileira. In *Homem e Natureza na Amazônia*, ed. G. Kohlhepp and A. Schrader. Tubingen: University of Tubingen.

Knees, G. S., and M. F. Gardner. 1983. Mahoganies: candidates for the Red Data Book. *Oryx* 17(2):88–92.

Leopoldo, P. R., and E. Salati. 1987a. Estimativa do desmatamento na Amazônia Brasileira. Unpublished manuscript.

———. 1987b. Rondônia: Quando a floresta vai acabar. Unpublished manuscript.

Malingreau, J. P., and C. J. Tucker. 1987. The contribution of AVHRR data for measuring and understanding global processes: large-scale deforestation in the Amazon basin. International Geoscience and Remote Sensing. Symposium *Proceedings, IGARSS* 87. Ann Arbor, MI.

Marques, J., E. Salati, and J. M. Santos. 1979. O campo do fluxo de vapor d'água atmosferico sobre a região Amazonica. *Acta Amazônica* 9:701–703.

———. 1980. A divergencia do campo do fluxo de vapor d'água e as chuvas na região Amazonica. *Acta Amazônica* 10:133–40.

Murça Pires, J., and G. T. Prance. 1985. The vegetation types of the Brazilian Amazon. In *Amazonia*, ed. G. T. Prance and T. E. Lovejoy, 109–45. Oxford: Pergamon Press.

Nordin, C. F., and R. H. Meade. 1986. The Amazon and the Orinoco. In *McGraw-Hill Yearbook of Science and Technology*.

Oltman, R. E. 1967. Reconnaissance investigations of the discharge and water quality of the Amazon. In *Atas do Simposio sôbre a Biota Amazonica. III. Limnologia*, ed. H. Lent, 163–85. Rio de Janeiro: CNPq.

Perú, CONESTCAR. 1965. *Estadistica Agraria*. Lima.

Perú, Dirección de Colonizacción y Asuntos Orientales. 1947. *La Acción Oficial en el Desarrollo Agropecuario de la Colonización de Tingo Maria. Años 1942–1946*. Lima.

Prance, G. T., and T. E. Lovejoy, ed. 1985. *Amazonia*. Oxford: Pergamon Press.

PRORADAM. 1979. *La Amazonia Colombiana y sus Recursos*. Bogotá: Instituto Geográfico Agustín Codazzi.

Putzer, H. 1984. The geological evolution of the Amazon basin and its mineral resources. In *The Amazon*, ed. H. Sioli. The Hague: W. Junk.

Ribeiro, M. N. G., E. Salati, N. A. Villa Nova, and C. G. B. Demetrio. 1982. Radiação solar disponível em Manaus (AM) e sua relação com o brilho solar. *Acta Amazônica* 12:339–46.

Salati, E. 1985. The climatology and hydrology of Amazonia. In *Amazonia*, ed. G. T. Prance and T. E. Lovejoy, 18–48. Oxford: Pergamon Press.

Salati, E., J. Marques, and L. C. Molion. 1978. Origem e distribuição das chuvas na Amazônia. *Interciência* 3:200–206.

Salati, E., A. Dall'olio, E. Matsui, and J. Gat. 1979. Recycling of water in the Amazon basin: an isotope study. *Water Resources Research* 15:1250–58.

Salati, E., H. O. R. Schubart, W. Junk, and A. E. O. Oliveira. 1983. *Amazônia: Desenvolvimento, Integração e Ecologia*. Editora Brasiliense/CNPq.

Salati, E., and J. Marques. 1984. Climatology of the Amazon region. In *The Amazon*, ed. H. Sioli, The Hague: W. Junk.

Salati, E., and P. B. Vose. 1984. Amazon basin: A system in equilibrium. *Science* 225:129–38.

San Román, J. 1975. *Perfiles Históricos de la Amazonia Peruana*. Lima: Ed. Paulinas.

Sioli, H., ed. 1984. *The Amazon: Limnology and Landscape Ecology of a Mighty Tropical River and its Basin*. The Hague: W. Junk.

Valcarel, D. C. R. et al. 1980. *El Perú como Nación Independiente: En Historia General de los Peruanos*. Lima: Peisa.

Varese, S. 1973. *La Sal de los Cerros*. Lima: Ed. Retablo de Papel.

Villa Nova, N. A., E. Salati, and E. Matsui. 1976. Estimativa da evapotranspiração na Bacia Amazônica. *Acta Amazônica* 6:215–28.

Wille, J. E., A. Ocampo, A. Weberbauer, and D. Schofield. 1939. *El Cube (Lonchocarpus utilis) y Otros Barbascos en el Perú*. Lima: Dirección de Agricultura y Gnaderia.

30

Borneo and the Malay Peninsula

HAROLD BROOKFIELD   FRANCIS JANA LIAN
LOW KWAI-SIM   LESLEY POTTER

The equatorial countries of Southeast Asia, Indonesia and Malaysia, together with Singapore and Brunei, are, in the 1980s, the scene of more rapid transformation of their environment than are either the African or Latin American equatorial regions. Equatorial Southeast Asia is by far the most populous of the three, with an estimated population now exceeding 190 million. Growth has been rapid and accelerating. Around A.D. 1600, the whole region had fewer than 10 million people, and around 1800, about 14 million (Reid 1988). In 1930, the combined population of the four countries was only 66 million. At all times since the mid-nineteenth century, however, at least half the total population of the region has lived on the island of Java. There remain large areas with densities below 5/km^2, contrasting with the extremely high densities of the cities and some areas of intensive wet-rice agriculture.

Although a major element in recent transformation has been conversion of forest land to agriculture, on such a scale as to constitute almost a new "great age of clearance" comparable with the earlier conversions of forest to agriculture in medieval Europe and nineteenth-century North America (Brookfield 1988), most of the region is still under natural cover. Surveys made around 1982 showed that approximately 70% of the land area remained under forest, though this percentage included large areas of monsoonal scrubland and some high-montane grasslands in eastern Indonesia. About 80% of Borneo, 64% of Sumatra, and 50% even of peninsular Malaysia were still under forest in 1982. Together with western Java, these three regions represent the floristic province of western *Malesia* (Whitmore 1984), within which is found the greatest floristic variety of any forest region on earth. The forest is dominated by great stands of canopy-emergent *Dipterocarpaceae*, rising to 45–60 m over extensive areas. The flora of *Malesia* as a whole, including the eastern core-region in the island of New Guinea/Irian, was estimated by Van Steenis (1971) to include at least 25,000 species – about 10% of the world's flora. This remaining forest is not only being reduced by conversion to agriculture and by fuelwood and fodder extraction; it is also being deeply invaded by a hardwood-timber industry that has flourished

greatly since 1970. Except in reserves, not much dryland forest below 500 m a.s.l. now remains free of the marks of human interference, and large areas up to even 1,500 m are also affected.[1]

The region lies entirely within the humid tropics, but seasonally dry conditions are experienced at the latitudinal limits in the north, in Java and in eastern Indonesia, extending weakly into southeastern Borneo. The core of the region is the Sunda continental spur, around which sedimentary and volcanic rocks form the island arcs of Sumatra/Java/ southeast Indonesia and the complex systems of Sulawesi and the Philippines (Fig. 30.1). In the Malay Peninsula and Borneo, pre-Tertiary intrusives, metamorphics, and sedimentaries are maturely eroded to form low mountains and wide valleys, except in northern Borneo, where on the edge of a geosynclinal belt, the western cordillera rises to 4,100 m in Gunung Kinabalu, the highest mountain between the Himalaya and New Guinea. Extensive Tertiary sedimentaries on the lowlands and the older rocks are deeply weathered, and the dominant dryland soils are Ultisols, in which clays are concentrated in a deep B horizon, leaving the A horizon sandy, weakly structured, and very sensitive to erosion. The postglacial marine transgression first created very intricate coastlines, but they have been greatly smoothed by silt deposition and the formation of extensive lowland peat swamps.

Transformations in a Resource Frontier

Except for contextual discussion, this chapter is concerned with only a part of Southeast Asia, the whole island of Borneo (which consists of the four Kalimantan Provinces of Indonesia, the Malaysian States of Sabah and Sarawak, and independent Brunei) and peninsular Malaysia (hereafter "the Peninsula") without the State of Singapore (Fig. 30.1). These equatorial and near-equatorial regions by no means display the whole range of environmental transformation in Southeast Asia, and in particular offer a story entirely different from that of the densely peopled volcanic islands of Java and Bali; so different is the latter story, and so vast the literature, that it would require a separate study. Borneo and the Peninsula

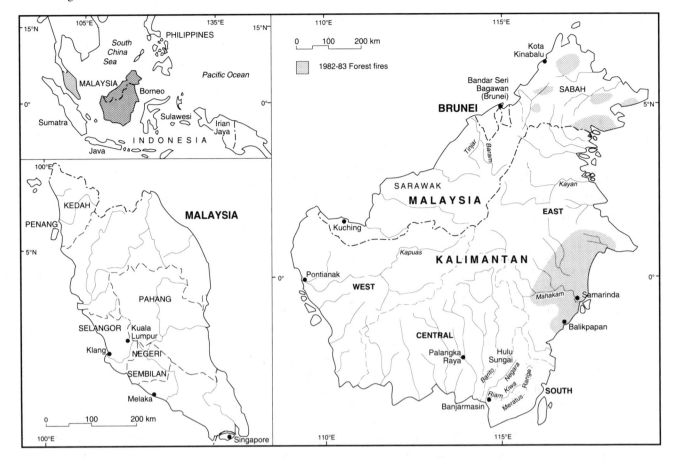

Figure 30.1 Borneo and Peninsular Malaysia showing political units, localities, and areas named in the text, and the approximate extent of the 1983 fires (from Malingreau, Stephens, and Fellows 1985).

include a substantial part of the modern "resource frontier" of Southeast Asia, and it is this resource frontier and its transformation that concern us here. Changes in the wet-rice regions due to the "green revolution" and to population growth, and the rapid expansion of large cities with all their environmental problems are excluded from treatment in this chapter.

There are some common dynamic forces of transformation, and it is a major object of this chapter to elucidate these forces and to show how they determine the manner in which resources are exploited and the earth is transformed. One major force is population growth, currently at a natural rate of about 2.5%/annum in both regions, but substantially supplemented by immigration. At the time of the 1980 censuses, the Peninsula had 11.4 million people and Borneo, 9.3 million in a much larger area. By the mid-1980s, the Peninsula had some 13 million and Borneo, almost 11 million. Substantial official and spontaneous resettlement from Java in Indonesian Borneo and temporary plus illegal migration from Indonesia to the Peninsula and to Sabah and Brunei, and from the Philippines to Sabah, boosted growth rates. Because of the large illegal element in this movement, official estimates for the mid-1980s understate the actual numbers.

The large illegal migrations reflect economic expansion, and both Borneo and the Peninsula have experienced a prolonged economic boom since the early 1960s, based both on resource use and, in the Peninsula, also on industrialization and urbanization on a large scale. This boom did not spring straight out of static traditional economies, but was preceded by an earlier boom based more exclusively on the export of primary products – tree crops and minerals – that ran from the 1880s to the onset of the Great Depression in 1930. Even before this, and far back into history, trade and the export of primary products from the rain forests and the coasts provided the main dynamic of the regional economy. From the mid-nineteenth century onward, transportation improvements, the free entry of private foreign investment, and the readiness of peasant farmers to develop new land for export products have been the means of facilitating export-led growth (Myint 1972).

The peoples of Southeast Asia have developed systems of sustaining an ecological balance – *ladang* (swiddens) under one set of conditions of ecology and population; *sawah* (wet-rice fields) and *kampung* (villages and their gardens) under another. Around both lies the resource frontier of the forests. The remarkable feature of the present phase is the manner in which this resource frontier has become the property of whole nations, developed for gain under an exploiting and modernizing ethos in an era that, in a longer historical context, looks like one of frenzy.[2]

The Historical Sequence

Antecedents

People have inhabited Southeast Asia for at least 40,000 years, and palynological and archaeological data reveal evidence of agricultural occupation of upland areas in New Guinea and Sumatra as far back as 9,000 and 7,000 years, respectively, before present (Flenley 1979). By at latest the fifth century A.D., wet-rice cultivation reached Java, and village-level irrigation systems were widely in operation several hundred years before the emergence of city-centered empires in the medieval period (Van Setten van der Meer 1979). Certainly by the fourteenth century, rice-growing Hindu states existed on the Peninsula and in Borneo.[3]

The real wealth of these latter states lay in trade, however, and continued to do so in Borneo into modern times. Gold, tin, and iron were mined and smelted by, at latest, the fifth century. The forests yielded a range of valuable products, including hunted goods (rhinoceros horn, gallstones from certain monkeys, hornbill casques, live elephants) and collected goods (camphor, damar, illipi nuts, gutta percha, rattan, and birds' nests, among others). They were supplied by indigenous tribal people who were early drawn into world trade. Some coastal places established a commanding role in this trade between the inland tribes and the seafarers from China to India.

Around 1600, the population already included a significant urban fraction (Reid 1988), and otherwise was divided among Malay and other wet-rice farmers, shifting cultivators and hunter-gatherers, and a small number of miners and metal-workers. All were linked through trade; moreover cash-cropping, principally for spices, was already established long before the Portuguese, Spanish, Dutch, and later English entered the region in search of command over trade in the highly valued commodities that Southeast Asia produced.

The Early Colonial Period

Despite the importance of trading centers on the Melaka Strait and on parts of the coast of Borneo, the direct impact of colonialism was minimal until the nineteenth century. The action of the first 300 years of the colonial period went on around Borneo and the Peninsula, not within them. The indirect impact of external change was, however, substantial. Rulers, settlers, and entrepreneurs could make large profits from cultivation of pepper from the sixteenth century onward. Pepper cultivation is recorded from both sides of the Peninsula, at Brunei in Borneo, and perhaps especially in southeastern Borneo (Idwar 1978). The two centuries of the pepper trade are said to have led to much oppression, and it seems probable that the first sustained attack on the upland forests and the creation of grasslands dates from this period.

Much of the pepper went to China, as did alluvial tin from the Peninsula and a substantially augmented quantity of forest produce. Trade with China increased during the eighteenth century, with growing European involvement. Many local rulers grew wealthy and powerful, and the stage was set for the more exploitative phase that was to follow (Andaya and Andaya 1982).

Later Colonialism and Resource Development

Although the Dutch extended control around Melaka and imposed trading monopolies on some states, and although a number of short-lived forts were set up at various coastal points, no enduring territorial colonialism existed between the original seizure of Melaka by the Portuguese in 1511 and the taking of Penang Island by the British in 1786. It was the need for control, first over mineral production and then over land for plantations, that finally brought about the spread of colonial administration over the whole of Borneo and the Peninsula.

Metallurgical developments that provided a greatly expanded market for tin were the trigger of change in the western Peninsula. The main resource is alluvial. Major discoveries took place between 1850 and 1890, and production increased rapidly after 1875, to make the Peninsula the producer of more than half the world's tin by 1895, by which time concentration of ownership into mainly European corporate hands was already well advanced (Courtenay 1972; Yip 1969). In the same early period, a shifting-cultivation type of plantation development for gambier (*Uncaria gambir*), pepper (*Piper nigrum*), and cassava (*Manihot esculenta*) laid waste large areas of forest on the interfluves between Malay wet-rice villages (Jackson 1968a). In southeastern Borneo, Dutch and other concessionaires attempted to follow the more successful Sumatran model in growing tobacco by shifting cultivation from 1886 until 1905, by which time soil exhaustion, drought, and competition brought the industry to an end.

The environmental impact of this early period of state-supported but otherwise barely controlled resource exploitation cannot be quantified, but it was certainly substantial. The Perak River in the northwestern Peninsula, which "ran clear as crystal over its sandy bed" before tin-mining began in the 1870s was already a silt-laden eyesore by the time Swettenham (1907:117) described its earlier state. The beginning of attempts to regulate burning in the interests of limiting the spread of *Imperata cylindrica*, a grass, in seasonally dry southeastern Borneo – though applied to shifting cultivators rather than to the concessionaires – dates from the same period (Klerks 1906; Lemei 1909). In the southern Peninsula, huge areas of *Imperata* marked the sites of abandoned gambier plantations in 1896 (Jackson 1968a:29). What saved the environment in both areas, but especially in the Peninsula, was the high profitability of planting *Hevea brasiliensis* rubber, first introduced at Singapore in 1877 and available for planting in quantity after 1896. The great rubber boom of the following 20 years replaced not only the grass and secondary scrub created by earlier commercial agriculture in the Peninsula, but also large areas of newly converted forest. In southern Borneo, rubber was established in 1906, replacing failed tobacco and coffee growing (Luytjes 1925), and within 15 years all available lands in the Hulu Sungai region (Fig. 30.2) were planted out, largely in small-holder rubber.

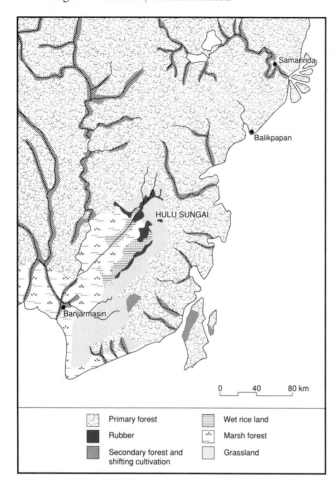

Figure 30.2 The Southeastern part of Kalimantan (Borneo) in 1924–25, compiled from contemporary maps in Van Kempen 1924; Luytjes 1925.

Legend:
Primary forest
Rubber
Secondary forest and shifting cultivation
Wet rice land
Marsh forest
Grassland

both under official transmigration schemes and by spontaneous migrants.[4]

A complete survey of all aspects of environmental transformation in Borneo is impossible here. The timber industry and its impact are emphasized, but the changes in the open agricultural areas and among the indigenous tribal people of the forests are also reviewed, using material from southeastern Kalimantan (Potter) and from the Kenyah people of northeastern Sarawak (Lian). Transmigration is only briefly discussed, for comparison with land settlement on the Peninsula. Sabah receives little mention, as do southwestern Sarawak and west Kalimantan, where important agricultural transformations are taking place (Seavoy 1980).

The principal object is to characterize what happens to the land, its forests, and its people when a resource-frontier ethos takes hold. Many politicians, entrepreneurs, officials, and skilled workers are making money out of Borneo; the interests of settled agriculturalists get lower priority, and shifting agriculture tends to be misrepresented and seen as opposed to the larger national interest. These elements of political economy have important environmental consequences, as well as consequences for the people concerned. Some of these consequences are rather clearly demonstrated by a recent "ecological disaster," as we shall see at the end of this section.

Contrasts in People and Environment

The heartland of southeast Kalimantan is the inland area of wetland and alluvial fan (Fig. 30.2) known as the "Hulu Sungai" (headwaters), the upper reaches of the Negara River and its tributaries. Here wet-rice cultivation has been practiced for centuries, without irrigation works until recent times, and in a core region that experiences seasonal flood, near Amuntai, rice is planted in the dry season. Crop failures are common, and in only one year in three or four are conditions right for producing high yields (Schuitemaker 1938). Elsewhere the *sawahs* are still largely rain-fed, so that the Banjarese people also have practiced shifting cultivation on the uplands as part of their strategy of risk minimization. This strategy includes engagement in alternative enterprises such as trade, mining, and small-scale industry, as well as out-migration to other districts when harvests fail or when prices of cash crops are low.

Most of the indigenous tribal people, by contrast, occupy the forests. Dry rice, grown in swiddens, is the main subsistence crop, but swidden-grown swamp rice is also reported from some areas (Dove 1979; Padoch 1982; 1985). Among most of the tribal groups, hunting and collection are also important activities. Some groups live mainly in this way, and practice little agriculture.

The population history of the indigenous tribal people is important in understanding their use of resources and their response to the new forces. Since at least the seventeenth century, substantial population movement has occurred in inland Borneo, the largest single force being the eastward migration of the Iban people from the northwest of the island into modern central Sarawak and Kalimantan. Warlike movements such as this have displaced other people, and

The Forests of Borneo

Borneo was, until recently, less affected either by intensive agriculture or by urban and industrial development than any other part of the region. Before this century, most of Borneo was occupied by indigenous tribal people, of whom only a minority in coastal and down-river areas were under any form of effective administration, whether by the Dutch, the British private and company regimes in Sarawak and Sabah, or the Malay sultanates. Pockets of wet-rice farming and of cash-cropping existed, the two largest being inland of Banjarmasin in the southeast and around Pontianak in the west. Between 1897 and 1910, oil was discovered and developed on both the east and the north coasts; rubber was planted in coastal and in some riverine areas, but most of the island retained a subsistence economy enriched by the ancient trade in jungle products, a trade facilitated by the new colonial peace (Black 1985). Since the 1960s, the island has become a major producer of timber and timber products. Borneo offers the contrast of a supposedly primitive indigenous tribal people practicing shifting cultivation, with a resource frontier of the most rapacious type confined to coastal areas until the 1960s, but now penetrating a large part of the island. In addition, the Indonesian part of Borneo has experienced large-scale immigration from Java and Madura, movement of whole communities still continues even though tribal warfare has ceased (Jackson 1968b; Kartawinata and Vayda 1984; Lian 1987; Padoch 1982). There is evidence of substantial depopulation in some areas, mainly as a consequence of nineteenth-century epidemics. Early visitors described much larger settlements, and more of them, than exist today (for example, St. John [1862] 1974). It is significant that numbers were larger in the past and that the shifting agriculture practiced did not cause enduring ecological damage.

The reasons for migratory behavior are various (Jessup 1981). Warfare was important, and Freeman (1955) held that land degradation forced people to move. Lian (1987) places emphasis on opportunities for trade, thus stressing that the indigenous tribal people had a traditional economy in which subsistence was only a part and not the whole. When warfare diminished late in the nineteenth century, opportunities for trade improved, and new goods became available inland, especially iron (Harrisson 1970). Some of the extensive population movements may therefore reflect the indirect impact of external change, even from ancient times. The collection of jungle produce has gone through modern periods in which particular goods have been in high demand – gutta percha until *Hevea brasiliensis* drove it from the market; jelutong (from *Dyera* spp.); and rattan at many periods, including the present. Each period of boom has established commercial links that have brought the indigenous tribal people more closely into contact with the modern trading system. Each such period has also led to serious overexploi-

tation of the resource, as in the early 1980s rattan trade from the Meratus Mountains of South Kalimantan (Lowenhaupt Tsing 1984).

It is often argued that the indigenous tribal people are subsistence farmers at the margin of existence, producing much less than a year's supply of food so that there is need for reliance on "famine foods" and a constant search for better soils by clearing new primary forest (Anderson 1978; 1980; Lau 1979; Sanchez 1976). Yields under swidden are certainly highly variable and often unpredictable, due to problems of timing the burn; insect, animal, and bird pillage; skill in weeding and maintenance; and untimely rain or drought. Yields average only around 1 t/ha, and households tend to plan their swiddens according to the amount of rice in stock, expected demand and, sometimes, the urgency of improving on a disastrous previous year. In four villages in the Tinjar Valley of Sarawak, only 19 of 181 swiddens encroached on primary forest during the two seasons 1984/85 and 1985/86 (Fig. 30.3).

Nor do swiddens produce only rice (*Oryza* spp.). Other crops, including sugar cane (*Saccharum officinarum*), bananas (*Musa* spp.), papaya, maize (*Zea mays*), leaf-mustard (*Brassica juncea*), cassava, sesame (*Sesamun indicum*), pumpkin, gourd, and cucumber (*Cucurbita* spp.) are also grown. Additionally, several items of value are obtained from the fallow. If these crops, the fallow produce, and the livestock reared are valued at current purchase prices in the upper Tinjar, the "secondary products" exceed in value the rice itself in most household farms.

Before the Timber Boom
Inland tribal people first planted rubber in the 1930s in several parts of Borneo. The 1930s also saw the beginnings of the timber industry in Borneo, though on a small scale and for a very limited range of species. The giant *Dipterocarps* still had little value on the world market. Until the 1950s, only local forestry experts and a few entrepreneurs perceived the potential value of the stands.

Before 1900 in Indonesia, timber exploitation concentrated almost entirely on the teak forests of Java. Among Borneo timbers, only ironwood (*Eusideroxylon zwageri*) was in some demand for building purposes, and a 1900 ordinance that introduced cutting licenses was a first attempt to measure volumes cut up-river. Forest surveyors were not in place until around 1921, with the tasks of mapping and inventory; methods were simple and the results unreliable (Ottow 1952; Verkuyl 1950). The general view was of a limitless supply, however – even in the coastal areas: "The [ironwood] stocks are of such large size that probably never enough population will be found to fell the yearly growth" (Van der Laan 1926:120). Yet data produced by these interwar surveys and the rough 1:200,000 maps that were prepared for all but the densely populated areas were all that were available for planning as late as the 1970s (Hamzah 1978). Sarawak did not have even this much.

It did become apparent, however, that the present province of East Kalimantan had the richest and most accessible resources. Concessions were granted at an early date over

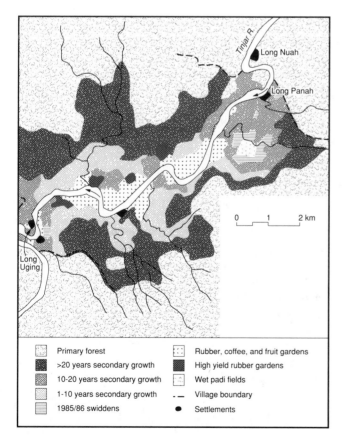

Primary forest	Rubber, coffee, and fruit gardens
>20 years secondary growth	High yield rubber gardens
10-20 years secondary growth	Wet padi fields
1-10 years secondary growth	Village boundary
1985/86 swiddens	Settlements

Figure 30.3 Land use in part of the Tinjar Valley, Sarawak, in 1985 (from field work by Lian).

forest areas north of Samarinda, but most failed. Such trade as there was lay in the hands of merchants in the towns. They financed subcontractors, who in turn provided food and tools to wood-cutting gangs far up-river. When prices fell during the Depression, many logs were left where they were, and some small tributaries of the upper Mahakam were described as choked with logs (Metz and Baretta 1937; Ottow 1952; Van der "Z" (waan) 1935).

Already in 1916 discussion arose about the need to regulate forest exploitation, and a draft ordinance in 1928 called for the delineation of protection forests, production forests, and forests that would remain the property of indigenous tribal people to be used according to their own custom. In protected areas they would have no similar rights, and their shifting form of agriculture could be prohibited (Draft Forest Ordinance 1928). The rights of the state versus those of indigenous communities were counterposed in a time when no overwhelming commercial pressure led to the issue being cast aside. The complexity of the issues and the very nature of interdepartmental politics in colonial governments, however, discouraged action. The forestry service was never able to exercise a management role or to enforce protection (Ottow 1952). Yet in this very passive environment, issues were raised that are only now again being faced after a generation of exploitation.[5]

The Great Timber Boom

International and Regional Setting   Until the 1960s, world trade in hardwood timbers was still dominated by the production of temperate regions, and tropical hardwoods constituted less than 5% of the total production of industrial wood. It was the rapid growth of Japanese demand that created commercial demand for *Dipterocarp* and other genera from the forests of western *Malesia*. At the same time, development of the one-man chainsaw, mechanized methods of timber extraction using wheeled crawler tractors and high-lead or "skyline" winching, and heavy road-construction machinery and specialized log-hauling vehicles transformed the industry. Although it remained labor-intensive, productivity was greatly enhanced. In these new circumstances, the high volume of marketable timber per hectare in the *Dipterocarp* forests – much higher than in Africa and the Americas – offered a critical comparative advantage (Kumar 1986).

By 1975, tropical hardwoods supplied about 10% of world industrial wood production. The demand in Japan and later in Korea and Taiwan has been for roundwood to supply national timber industries. Japan alone took half the world's imports of sawlogs between 1970 and 1985. A Southeast Asian view of this situation is aptly presented in Fig. 30.4. As eastern Asia came to dominate imports and Southeast Asia to dominate exports, Southeast Asian countries sought to ration supply and to acquire a much larger share of the saw-milling, veneer, and plywood industries. The Philippines began by prohibiting log exports of certain species. Peninsular Malaysia, but not the Borneo states, introduced a similar restriction in 1972 and then carried it much further. Indonesia followed suit in 1978,

Figure 30.4 A Southeast Asian view. Source: *Kompas* 1987, reprinted by permission.

and both the Peninsula and Indonesia banned log exports altogether in 1985. Sabah and Sarawak have continued to permit log exports; together with the declining production of the heavily deforested Philippines, these two states already supplied around 80% of Japan's log imports by 1983 (Hunter 1984).

These moves were also inspired by the realization, from quite an early date in the Peninsula (Editor 1967), that resources were fast disappearing. A further object of restricting and banning log exports was to conserve the resource, and for Kalimantan there was indeed a substantial drop in the rate of cutting between 1978 and 1983 (Allen, Straka, and Watson 1986; Hunter 1984). As the wood-using industries have grown, however, this decline seems to have reversed. Table 30-1, which compares low-production years in the mid-1970s and mid-1980s, and not the peak years 1972 and 1978, demonstrates the increasing role not only of Indonesia and Malaysia (with Brunei), but specifically of the whole island of Borneo in world hardwood timber production and trade, despite these changes. The share of the three countries in world production has risen from less than one-fifth to almost one-third, and exports have risen from under one-third to almost two-thirds – in 1987 exports attained 81%. The production of Borneo island has increasingly dominated the regional share, and alone constituted almost one-fifth of world production in 1985. By 1975, Borneo island was already responsible for half the world's export trade in tropical hardwood timbers, and in 1987 it accounted for almost 60% of all exports. The extent to which the world market now rests on the resources of this island is evident.

Political Economy, Policy, and Reality   Although the manner in which the timber boom was initiated was different in

Table 30-1 *Tropical Hardwood Production and Exports (percentage of world totals)*

	1965		1975		1985	
	Production*	Exports	Production	Exports	Production	Exports
Borneo: (Sabah, Sarawak, Brunei, and Kalimantan)	n.a.	24.1	16.8	48.6	15.9	50.3
Indonesia, Malaysia, and Brunei	16.6	31.6	27.6	65.7	27.5	75.8
World	100.0	100.0	100.0	100.0	100.0	100.0
World totals (million m^3)	98.9	23.2	150.3	41.2	204.0	48.4

Sources: FAO Yearbook of Forest Products 1975, 1987; Timber Trade Review 1985, 1986;
Kalimantan Timur dalam Angka, various dates
Kalimantan Tengah dalam Angka, various dates
Kalimantan Barat dalam Angka, various dates
Kalimantan Selatan dalam Angka, various dates
World Wood 1985
Government of Indonesia 1978
Biro Pusat Indonesia 1965–87
*Production = industrial roundwood. Exports = sawlogs + sawn timber + plywood (as roundwood equivalent)

each country – and within Malaysia different among the Peninsula, Sarawak, and Sabah – the differences in implementation have been of degree rather than of kind. Concessions were given to companies, most of which hired contractors – mainly Chinese – to do the work. It was much the same a little later in Sarawak, but in Sabah the concessionaires were four multinational companies that succeeded to a pre-1942 monopoly. In Kalimantan, too, where initiation was delayed until after Suharto's "new order" replaced the chaotic conditions of the Sukarno regime in 1965, large concessions went to multinational corporations, especially American and northeast Asian. By the time the boom was under way therefore, development was firmly on a private enterprise path. In both countries, the allocation of forest land was a state or provincial – rather than a national – matter, and the high proportion of timber royalties going to the state or provincial administrations became their main revenue source (Manning 1971). The allocation of timber concessions quickly became part of the political process in these circumstances.

The biggest multinational concessionaires in Kalimantan worked areas of up to almost 7,000 km^2 (Schoening 1978), and using highly capitalized methods, produced almost 1 million m^3 of timber in three years (Meijer 1974). The large concessionaires planned their enterprises, and some – particularly the American Weyerhaeuser Corporation (Fig. 30.5) – undertook substantial replanting with exotic species for a future in which the sawmills, veneer, and plywood plants and wood-chip mills which they envisaged (Schoening 1978) would require this timber. Nonetheless, both large and small concessionaires sublet much of the work to licensees and contractors whose investment in infrastructure and equipment, substantial in relation to their scale, provided both the means with which to remove the maximum volume of marketable timber and the need to do so in order to cover their fixed costs. The concessions are usually granted for 20 years only; contracts have a shorter life and subcontracts are shorter still. No one gets any pecuniary advantage from

conserving the resource, and all have a considerable interest in focusing attention on the highest-value timbers.

Both countries entered the production boom with clear forestry policies inherited from the past, further codified as events developed. The Malaysian National Forestry Policy endorsed in 1978 – with rational cutting rates, expansion of wood-processing industries, greater quality control, and higher efficiency – was termed a "new era" while it was being

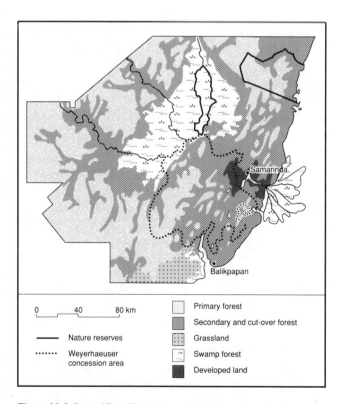

Figure 30.5 Part of East Kalimantan showing logged and unlogged areas in the mid-1970s, and planned land allocation. Sources: Voss 1983; boundary of Weyerhaeuser concession from De Pater and Visser 1979.

formulated (Sulaiman bin Haji 1977). Malaysia has its "uniform system" and Indonesia its "selective cutting system," under which the annual coupe is determined at a rate that supposedly will permit recovery of a more uniform-aged forest so as to permit successive harvests in perpetuity. But the Malaysian rate is based on a 70-year cycle and the Indonesian on a 35-year cycle, and for a long time neither was observed. In the late 1970s, the annual harvest in the Peninsula was exceeding the permitted coupe by as much as five times (Kumar 1986). The prediction that Peninsular timber resources would be unable to supply domestic demand after 1991 (Editor 1978) has become reality.

The Impact on Resources   The likelihood of a short-lived boom was foreseen by a remarkably prescient forest officer at Samarinda in East Kalimantan more than 15 years before it began. Contemplating the forests of eastern and southern Kalimantan, he asked: "Will the first felling strips be staked out by 1970? And will there be anything left by 1990?" (Verkuyl 1950). Yet "resources" have expanded as more species have become marketable and as logging methods have enabled the industry to move off the lowlands into the hills; though at a cost, timber on slopes greater than 20° can be extracted by crawler tractors, and from slopes up to 45°, by high-lead winching. With the development of wood-processing industries, the expansion of "resources" is not yet complete.

At first, development was limited to land close to the rivers with large-scale operation downstream and small-scale operation on every river down which logs could be rafted (Manning 1971), as before World War II. Later, road building made possible a great extension inland from the rivers, with some roads going as far as 60 km into the forest from raftable water. Yet estimates of resources have tended to decline through time. In East Kalimantan, 131,000 km^2 have been let out as concessions for various periods since 1967, covering most of the province, yet the largest of several estimates of the resource is 128,000 km^2 (cited in Wiersum and Boerboom 1977). Many of the 104 concessions let in East Kalimantan since 1967 have been found to contain areas bare of marketable timber. The large multinational concessionaires withdrew from East Kalimantan during the early 1980s not only because of government pressure to introduce wood processing, but also because of doubts over the future of the resource (Hoesada 1984); and these doubts are strikingly confirmed by the limited area of untouched "primary" forest (Fig. 30.5). On the other hand, early extraction was so inefficient that some concessions are now being logged a second time by new operators; this is the case in the Tinjar Valley of Sarawak.

Neither official planning nor the planning of the operators was adequately informed when the industry began, and surveys have taken place only during the event and often in haste. Designated nature reserves were found to be partly logged by the time they were surveyed (Fig. 30.5). The approximations of the 1930s, criticized well before the boom began (Ottow 1952), were relied upon only too readily. Most of the modern statistics are useless, and so also are the 70-year and 35-year cycles. Ashton (1980) points out that no

established ecological basis exists for any selective-cutting system. Though confident growth-rate figures for different whole groups of species appear in the literature (e.g., Soerianegara 1982), Whitmore (1984) insists that growth rates still are simply not known.

Selective felling is often criticized for its wastefulness. Depending on the density, the proportion felled may be as high as 30%, but commonly it is lower. Timbers that will not float – over 20% of species – are not taken from upstream concessions, where logs have to be rafted and cannot be barged. Where costs are high, the contractor is likely to take only the largest species of highest value, and the rate of extraction may fall below 5% (Mohd. Nor and Ho 1982); under optimal conditions, however, it may rise as high as 47% (Schoening 1978).

What continues to be disregarded in much of the official literature is that whatever the proportion felled, many more trees are killed or damaged. This was reported early and often (Abdulhadi, Kartawinata, and Sukardjo 1981; Burgess 1971; 1973; Grainger 1980; Hong 1987; Kartawinata 1979; 1980; Lennertz and Panzer 1983; Marsono 1980; Soekotjo 1981). Trees linked crown-to-crown by lianas are brought down with the felled tree; the falling trees smash adolescents and saplings; skidding logs crush or damage further trees, and machinery damages more, as well as compacting the ground; bare ground is readily eroded, delaying regrowth. To help them dry out, logging roads are "sunlighted," by clearing a wide belt on either side; these roads and belts interfere with drainage, killing more trees. With an extraction rate of 20%, as much as 50–55% of the standing timber is destroyed, with further loss of regrowth potential. Low utilization may be inefficient, but it does leave most of the forest behind; high utilization can, unless more than ordinary care is taken, leave no future harvest within any plannable time-horizon. The high utilization desired by professional foresters means, of necessity, a replanting program. Yet only in a few concessions is replanting even attempted. Moreover, most of the replanting is with exotics rather than the more costly "enrichment planting" with indigenous species (Whitmore 1984).

It therefore seems likely that Verkuyl (1950) may be out only a few years in his gloomy prediction. Forest will remain in the logged-over areas of Borneo, and up to half of it may still be patchy primary forest, capable either of being left to aid the regeneration of the gaps or of being harvested if the high-value timbers become sufficiently scarce and costly. The remainder will consist of low-value timbers, but it is no longer certain that even these will be allowed to remain in peace.

The fluctuation of timber prices and their generally downward trend in the 1980s, due to decline in construction demand and increasing substitution of softwoods (Leslie 1986), were in part responsible for the creation of the International Tropical Timber Organization (United Nations 1984), which, among other functions, has the role of fostering more conservationist management. East Asian demand has remained strong, however, and Japanese aid has been used for road construction in Sarawak to open new logging areas in the deep interior, with serious consequences for the hunting-and-gathering Penan people (Hong 1987; Swinbanks 1987).

Moreover, the rapid growth of timber-processing industries in the Peninsula and Kalimantan created new demand that has greatly increased the range of marketable wood.

The Effect of Introducing Timber-Processing Industries The attraction of local processing is obvious. It permits export of a higher-value product, and generates much greater employment. Using Peninsular data from the mid-1970s, Kumar (1986: 180) shows that whereas logging alone requires 32.6 ha of forest to support one employee, logging together with sawmilling, plywood manufacture, and fabrication of wood products requires only 6.7 ha per employee – less than rubber and oil palm plus their local processing. Doubt about the economic wisdom of converting forest land to tree-crop agriculture is also expressed by Burbridge, Dixon, and Soewardi (1981) in a cost-benefit exercise in the Indonesian context. Unfortunately, the data in neither exercise are sufficiently established for the results to do more than suggest that a genuine, sustainable managed forestry might sometimes be a worthwhile economic option.

Under present methods, it is not possible to contemplate the substantial expansion of wood-processing industries in the Peninsula and more recently in Kalimantan in so favorable a light. The Peninsular industry is older and much more diversified, catering to a large local market rather than to export. Both investment and output rose rapidly through the 1970s. Already by the early 1980s, however, timber was being trucked across the Peninsula from east to west to supply the mills. Expansion in Indonesia has been very rapid since 1978, with the number of plywood mills rising from 19 to 114 by 1988. The number of sawmills has also increased, but at a less dramatic rate. Most of the expansion has been for export; Indonesia now supplies over 70% of all plywood made of tropical timbers (P.T. Data Consult 1989). East Kalimantan, the principal area of concentration, had 27 plywood factories in 1988; most are concentrated around Samarinda. South Kalimantan had 14 plywood factories, and Central Kalimantan, 8. Factories without their own timber concessions derive their supply from truck operators who buy timber where they can, some of it from illegal operations by local people and transmigrants in protected forests and on concessions; much of this cutting is of immature trees. The middlemen become the effective planning managers for the small-scale logging enterprises from which they obtain supply. Rational policy is removed a further distance. Some sawmills have failed, but in 1988, most plywood factories are producing near capacity. Many employees are female immigrants from Java, and the benefits flowing to the Kalimantan people are limited. Although in the long term the establishment of timber-processing industries may require intervention to manage the transformed forest, in the short term the effect is to entrench the "gold rush" methods of the logging industry, so that the effect of log-export prohibitions has been very far from conservationist (Hunter 1984).

Changes in the Rural Economy

Indigenous Tribal Peoples The decline in Indonesian log exports after 1978 was filled partly by a major expansion in log exports from Sarawak. Employment in the industry increased from 45,500 in 1977 to 60,000 in 1984. Along the Tinjar River above the swamp-forest section, 15 timber camps have been established, and their collective male population in the mid-1980s was about as large as that of the 25 indigenous tribal longhouses in the same section of the river (Fig. 30.6).

The effect on the longhouse communities has been far-reaching. Among four sample longhouses on the Tinjar, the number engaged full-time in private sector employment – overwhelmingly the timber industry – rose from none in the 1960s to 51% of the male working population in 1985. Farming, however, has not been abandoned. The Kenyah (the indigenous tribal group discussed here) maintain combined households until the younger generation are ready to establish their own, and the household is the unit of agricultural production. Although more farming tasks have been taken over by women, male labor still is necessary for the heavy work of clearing and burning. The probability of a male working in the industry increases with the size of the household. Only a few younger married men temporarily abandon agriculture and live on their timber income.

Despite their high participation, the Kenyah and other indigenous tribal people form only a minority of the work-

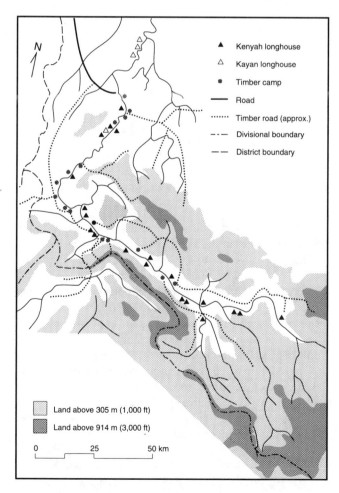

Figure 30.6 Longhouses and timber camps on the Tinjar River, Sarawak (from field work by Lian).

force, engaged mostly in the lower-paid jobs, which do not attract outsiders. Though supplemented by compensation payments and sale of produce, the share of total timber income obtained by the Kenyah is small. At one camp, 85% of gross receipts went to the four subcontractors, 9% to outside workers, and only 6% to local workers, this being a camp where the proportion of local workers is unusually high.

Yet even these incomes are far larger than those obtained from jungle produce before the 1960s, or from rubber. With so much labor now diverted to the timber industry scarcely any rubber continues to be tapped along the Tinjar. The "rubber gardens" shown on Fig. 30.3, planted in the 1960s, now resemble dense secondary forest. They are not used for swiddens, however, and the naturally sown rubber seedlings are seen as having potential value for the time when timber employment ceases in the 1990s. Adaptation is constant. Tinjar Kenyah tried wet rice in the 1970s, but the sites chosen were poor. In the mid-1980s they tried again, principally because the withdrawal of male labor demanded a system that calls for less heavy work in clearing and burning. Society itself has undergone important change as first rubber and now timber have made it possible for all to obtain income and valuables; the former economic dominance of an aristocratic class has been all but eliminated.

Beyond Timber and into a New Borneo Indigenous tribal people from remote areas have continued to move into the lower-river districts, where they have access to employment and where it is possible to acquire new tools, outboard motors, and the fuel to run them (Colfer 1983; Jessup 1981; Kartawinata and Vayda 1984; Lian 1987). In their new locations they also have access to a market for produce, which has led some – in the Mahakam system of East Kalimantan, for example – to make much larger swiddens, risking failure of the natural processes of recovery (Colfer 1983). In Kalimantan and also in Sabah, but not in Sarawak, they encounter large and growing numbers of outsiders: Banjarese and other Malay migrants from the south, Bugis from Sulawesi, Javanese both in transmigration schemes and spontaneous settlements, and Filipinos from the north.

The densely settled Banjarese core region in the Hulu Sungai was already well occupied in the 1920s (Fig. 30.2), with *sawah* on the swampland and rubber on adjacent higher ground backed by a considerable extent of *Imperata* grassland between the settled area and the forest. About this time, Banjarese began to move into the coastal swamplands around Banjarmasin to find sites on which half-tide drainage could create new *sawah*. The first Dutch colonization project in Southeast Borneo introduced Javanese settlers in 1937, successfully copying the Banjarese system of clearing by hand and cropping with rice followed by coconuts on ridges, with continuous extension into new land. More ambitious and expensive polder schemes started in the 1950s were soon abandoned for simpler techniques (Collier 1980). Most *sawahs* remain rain-fed. Since 1969, these coastal wetlands have become a major transmigrant receiving area; by 1984, almost 1,400 km^2 had been reclaimed (Van Dis 1986).

The land-use map of the early-1980s (Fig. 30.7) already

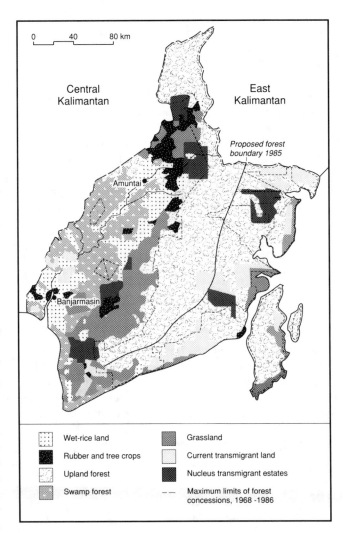

Figure 30.7 The province of South Kalimantan, showing land use in the early 1980s. From Direktorat Tata Guna Tanah, Propinsi Kalimantan Selatan, Peta "Penggunaan Tanah dan Proyek Pembangunan" (Land Use and Development Projects); Peta "HPH" (forest concessions) n.d.

reflects a major part of this change; the *sawah* area is much larger than it was in the 1920s (Fig. 30.2), both in the Hulu Sungai itself and more significantly around Banjarmasin, where formerly almost none existed. Much of this wetland, however, has serious ecological problems. Although in limited sectors of the Hulu Sungai the green revolution has been introduced successfully, large areas of the newly reclaimed wetland suffer serious problems of acidity and great depth of peat (Price and Des Bouvrie 1986). South Kalimantan has moved from a deficit to a surplus position in rice, and has taken on the role of rice supplier to its "resource frontier" neighbors, but only a minority of larger farmers are able to make good incomes from this source. The grassland belt is much wider than in 1920. The Hulu Sungai, together with many of the tidal-swamp transmigrant areas, has pockets of poverty. Its own population has ceased to grow, and is locally in decline (Potter and Hasymi 1989). Many migrant Banjarese have settled along the rivers and roads in East Kalimantan and have joined the logging business, whereas others have moved into the booming industrial cities of Samarinda and Balikpapan.

Adaptation to this shifting map of opportunities therefore involves migration, as well as the on-site changes seen in the Tinjar Valley. Kartawinata and Vayda (1984) provide a vivid picture of the dynamic situation in the hinterland of Samarinda, where shifting cultivators, timber concessionaires and unlicensed logging teams, Bugis pepper farmers and "carpet-bag" entrepreneurs from the cities are all at work, engaging in activities often very damaging to the environment. Moreover, they have done so "because these activities seemed more profitable than any perceived alternatives, and not because no other means of gaining subsistence for themselves and their families were available" (Kartawinata and Vayda 1984:119).

A rationalization of land use is certainly necessary in the resource frontier areas of Kalimantan. Such rationalization is particularly necessary where conflicts have arisen – as among the uses of forestry, indigenous cultivators, and transmigrant settlements. Only now, following the use of ground survey and aerial and satellite photography, is a clearer picture

emerging of actual land use and capability. Present plans, such as those shown for East Kalimantan in Fig. 30.8, are still very crude, however; the large extent of "conversion" forest consists of very variable land, and also includes many up-river areas occupied by indigenous tribal shifting cultivators, whom it is proposed to concentrate (Colfer 1983). The precise boundaries are under debate (TAD 1987). The Malaysian authorities also have resettlement plans for their tribal people, and the conflict of interests seems likely to continue.

An "Ecological Disaster" and Its Lessons In 1982–83, major fires occurred during a drought associated with one of the major ENSO (El Niño Southern Oscillation) events of modern times. Beginning late in 1982 and peaking in early 1983, numerous fires broke out in coastal and inland areas of East Kalimantan. In Sabah, where the drought began and ended later, an overlapping series of outbreaks occurred from early through mid-1983 (Figs. 30.1 and 30.8). Minor outbreaks occurred in other parts of Borneo and the southern Peninsula, but none to rival those in the drier east (Mackie 1984; Malingreau, Stephens, and Fellows 1985).

The causes, nature, and effects of the events are all in some measure of doubt. Drought in 1982, a weak 1982–83 wet season, and further drought in 1983 led to accumulation of large quantities of dry litter, lowered the water-table in swamp forests, and permitted fires to take hold and persist. Blame was very soon placed on tribal shifting cultivators, but in the unlogged forests, fire damage was much less than in the logged-out areas.

After initial underestimation, an aerial reconnaissance (Lennertz and Panzer 1983) led to an estimate of 35,000–37,000 km^2 as heavily damaged or destroyed in East Kalimantan alone. A significant part of this was damage by drought rather than by fire (Leighton 1984), and Wirawan (1984) showed on the basis of more careful survey that large unburned tracts remained. It is generally agreed by commentators that the multiple damage done by logging, conversion, and shifting cultivation both for subsistence and for gain created a fire hazard of an unprecedented order, so that what occurred was a largely human-made "ecological disaster".

Although the scales of interference, hence the hazard, and hence the fires, were unprecedented in 1983, it is an error to suppose that extensive fires are themselves a new event (Mackie 1984; Malingreau et al. 1985). The same dense, smoke-laden haze that in 1983 reached as far as Java and the Peninsula was reported even in the nineteenth century, and specific reports exist of extensive fires in 1914 during a drought not less severe than that of 1982–83 (Boerema 1917; Braak 1915; Van Bemmelen 1916; Van der Laan 1925). Drought is a familiar visitor in the region, affecting crop yields even in the more humid regions (Lian 1987), and major drought seems reliably associated with each large ENSO event. Fires occurred again in 1987, but on a lesser scale. Drought needs to be allowed for in all resource use planning. Up until now, only the indigenous tribal, Banjarese, and other long-settled farmers seem to have learned this and adapted their practices accordingly.[6]

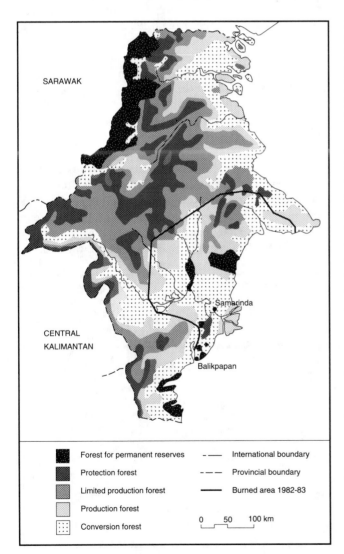

Figure 30.8 Planned land allocation in East Kalimantan. Sources: Voss 1983; 1982–83 bushfire boundary from Malingreau et al. 1985.

Conversions to Agriculture in the Peninsula

The History of Conversion

We move from consideration of a mainly extractive resource frontier to one in which extensive new agricultural land has been created in place of the forest. In terms of the wealth it has generated both for foreign capitalists and for many of its own people, the Malay Peninsula is outstanding among the equatorial lands. This fact needs to be given full weight in assessing the environmental transformation that has occurred. According to the successive surveys of land use, 64% of the whole of the Peninsula was still under forest in 1966 after already more than a decade of rapid conversion. This area was reduced to 59% by 1974 and to only 51% by 1982.

Though logging methods have been as wasteful and destructive as in Borneo, most clearance on the Peninsula has been for agriculture, and principally for oil palm and rubber. The total area under agricultural land use comprised only 21% of the Peninsula in 1966, but 39% in 1982. By the time the conversion program reaches its planned limits in the mid-1990s, only 39% of the area will remain under forest (Anon 1979) and around 45% will be under agriculture. Taking the whole period since the early 1950s, when about 73% of the area was estimated to be under forest (International Bank 1955), almost one-half of the then-existing forests will have been cleared and converted; a further one-quarter will have been logged.

An earlier phase of clearance, from the 1890s to the 1930s, was based mainly on capitalist rubber estates, and from about 1910 (Lim 1977) also on peasant small-holdings. Because it was recognized that not much further expansion of rubber could be expected from private sources, while primary production was seen as the main engine of economic growth (International Bank 1955), a Federal Land Development Authority (FELDA) was set up on the eve of independence in 1956. Its charter was to undertake planned land develop-ment for cash crops and for resettlement of villagers without land or with little land from the established rural areas. In its land-development activities, it was joined by a number of state organizations and by schemes designed to fill gaps in the rubber areas.

Within a few years, a pattern was developed through which an area was first selected after survey, then logged to extract marketable timber, then cleared, laid out, and planted – all before the settlers arrived. The annual area cleared and developed rose from about 80 km^2 in the early 1960s to over 350 km^2 in the late 1970s, by which time the land-development program had become central to the drive to eradicate Malay rural poverty under the New Economic Policy adopted in 1970 (Bahrin and Perera 1977). FELDA became a very large agribusiness enterprise, and played a leading role in the strategic shift from rubber to oil-palm production. By the mid-1970s, FELDA produced over one-third of the national palm-oil output, by then the largest in the world. By the end of the 1970s, FELDA had already developed some 4,000 km^2 of land and had settled some 250,000 people. More than two-thirds of the annual conversion is due to FELDA and other development agencies; together they had converted over 6,000 km^2 by the early 1980s (Goh 1982).

Spatial Pattern of Change in Malaysia

The spatial pattern of change is shown in Fig. 30.9a–d. The 1960s and early 1970s saw rapid expansion in the center of the Peninsula, with major assistance from the World Bank. Then in the 1970s and 1980s, great new areas were cleared, some as part of large regional development schemes, which embraced the establishment of a new urban system. The fate of the small number of tribal shifting cultivators in these regions tends not to be recorded. The remaining forest will soon take the form of two large blocks in the north, and a number of isolated and mainly upland patches elsewhere in the Peninsula. Already, one can drive across Pahang Tenggara through an entirely converted landscape all the way from the

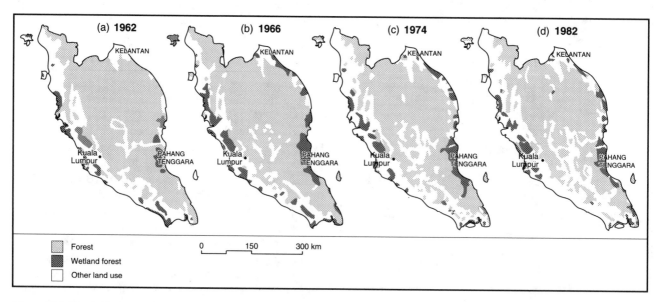

Figure 30.9 Forested areas on the Peninsula at various dates.
(a) 1962. Source: Wyatt-Smith 1964. (b) 1966. Source: Wong 1971. (c) 1974. Source: Wong 1979. (d) 1982. Source: unpublished computerized map, Jabatan Pertanian, Kuala Lumpur.

east coast to the main range in the west, and nothing now remains of the linkage between the eastern and western blocks of forest in the north.

It is not only the contiguity of planned settlements across a wide landscape that distinguishes the Malaysian program from the larger transmigration program of Indonesia. Malaysian resettlement is for cash crops; despite recent changes, Indonesian transmigrants grow mainly food crops, and on much smaller blocks of land. Between 1969 and 1983, the Indonesian program had resettled some 1.7 million people, more than three times the Malaysian achievement on the Peninsula, to which the program is almost wholly confined because there is no free migration between the Peninsula and East Malaysia. The area allocated to and worked by transmigrants in Indonesia is, however, only about the same as that converted by all agencies in the Peninsula – about 6,000 km² until 1983 (J. Hardjono, personal communication). Although a very large area is also worked by independent transmigrants in Indonesia, which has no parallel in the Peninsula, the much higher population density created by the Indonesian program is evident. The Indonesian program is population-based; it moves people out of Java. The Malaysian program is based on the twin goals of creating a rural middle class out of the poor and of increasing national wealth. Until the recent establishment of transmigrant nucleus estates, the Indonesian program has contributed little to national production of export crops; the Malaysian program contributes a great deal.

Environmental Consequences of Clearance

It is surprising that little of the international deluge of criticism by environmentalists that has descended on Indonesia (for example, Rich 1986; Secrett 1986) has crossed the South China Sea to the Peninsula. Yet the effects have been well documented by internal critics (for example, Aiken and Leigh 1985; Aiken et al. 1982; Goh 1982; Khor and Hong 1980; Mahmood 1982; Mok 1982).

The period of massive clearance after 1965 was punctuated by major floods in 1970 and 1971, after which methods were changed to incorporate contouring at an early stage. Pressure to find new land has resulted in some seriously degraded areas being selected for agricultural development (Lee 1981). As the forests have been attacked from all sides in the service of profit and of socioeconomic progress, even some watershed areas have been converted, and land proposed for national parks has been logged (Gurmit Singh 1982).

The consequences of successive waves of clearance are seen most clearly in downstream areas. The first major cause of new sedimentation was tin mining, followed over a much wider area by clearance for rubber planting, which led to the great "red floods" of 1926. On the basis of the crudest of all possible estimates – though his precise figures are not infrequently cited – Fermor (1939:149–59) opined that the contribution of rubber planting to siltation in the rivers was about twice that of mining. More specifically, resulting water shortages due to changed hydrological regimes led to the abandonment of 28 km² of rice land along the small Melaka River alone (Aiken et al. 1982:122). More recently, in the

west coast state of Negeri Sembilan, all rice lands below a recently logged watershed area now experience water shortages in periods of low rainfall (A. Samad Hadi, personal communication).

Even after revegetation of the ground under rubber, rates of runoff on rubber land were found to be 16 times higher than on slopes under undisturbed forest (Aiken et al. 1982: 173–75). Losses under oil palm, which develops a dense canopy to intercept raindrops, are of a much lower order, but oil palm is more demanding in terms of soil conditions than is rubber, so that the latter remains the dominant crop on steeper land. After 25 to 30 years, both rubber and oil palm need to be replanted, again exposing the land to severe erosion. Perhaps fortunately, the low value of rubber in recent years has caused many small-holders to allow old rubber on steep land to develop into a rubber-dominated secondary forest, as in inland Sarawak.

It seems not improbable that worse is to come before improvement. Figure 30.10 summarizes the 1980 situation at a Peninsula-wide level, and comparison with Fig. 30.9d shows the large areas still to be converted. In the process of successive redelimitations of the "permanent forest estate" and of "conversion forest", some increasingly steep land has been transferred into the conversion category. Even by 1974, there were already 1,720 km² of land with slopes greater than 20° under rubber and oil palm, compared with only 174 km² in 1966 (Chan, Wong, and Law 1978). Added to this is the growing effect of urbanization and highway construction, now biting deeply into the remaining forest. Around the capital and its conurbation, now with a population around 2.5 million, urban construction using heavy machinery to prepare large areas for development is about to extend deeply into the forests beyond the main range, where a new satellite city

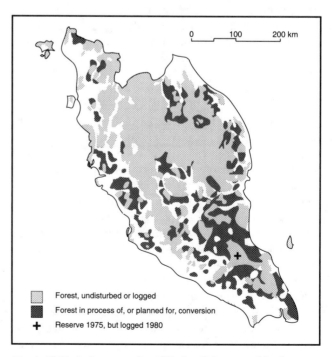

Figure 30.10 An interpretation of Peninsula forests and the future. Conversion areas modified from Shaharuddin 1983.

planned for a population of 250,000 is to be constructed. New industrial estates are being laid out elsewhere. As in Kalimantan, where the much smaller cities are growing rapidly, the urban demand on forest resources is added to the demands of forestry, of conversion for permanent agriculture, and of the shifting cultivator.

Conclusion

The equatorial lands we have surveyed were for centuries a source of profit for their rulers, then on a larger scale for the colonial capitalist system, and last, on a larger scale yet for the powerful, successful, and enterprising in the independent nations of Indonesia and Malaysia. With the possible exception of Javanese transmigrants and the poor and unemployed who have become timber cutters, those who have recently transformed the environment in damaging ways have done so for profit or in the name of development, and not from necessity. The indigenous tribal people of the forests, regarded in an earlier literature and by modern governments both as poor and as mindless in their use of the forests, are in fact neither. In some areas their activities have pressed too hard on the forests. Most of the subsistence-based farming populations, however, whether practicing swidden or wet-rice cultivation, have achieved compatibility between exploitation and conservation. Where their activities have converted the environment from one form to another, many have shown skill in adapting their technology to cope with the change.

All the cases of more rapid and destructive change we have examined have arisen from exploitation with profit as the main objective, whether by individuals, corporations, or the state. Use of swidden methods for profit has been destructive; plantations became conservationist only after their long-term crops were in place, and they exported much of their damage to downstream areas; the so-called selective commercial timber industry has been enormously wasteful and destructive; and the "bare-all" methods of preparing land for new settlement and for urban development, governed by the wish to minimize cost, have wreaked immense damage. Pollution has arisen by externalizing costs in a similar way.

Not least alarmingly, the attitudes of rural people toward their own land and its produce have changed as the profit motive has taken hold, especially on the Peninsula. With large profits obtainable from sale, less care is taken, and the investments required to use conservationist practices appear less attractive because they are less rewarding. There are antecedents in past waves of overexploitation of forest produce, and the misuse of people and land to obtain high profits from pepper farming in the early colonial period. What is new is the scale on which resources are now being viewed as a means of short-term gain, with the costs externalized to others or to later generations.

Important questions of the social ownership of resources are involved. Forest-dwelling people regard the forests as their own, but the state has claimed a superior right, and those allocated forest for exploitation by the state have kept their respect for indigenous rights to an unavoidable minimum. But in claiming rights on behalf of all the people, the state has treated the forest as a source of revenue and as a place in which it can pursue particular policies for population redistribution and economic growth. Such an approach has been aided by a dearth of real scientific knowledge about the all-important regrowth and recovery of forest resources, so that in its absence fictional notions have been allowed to serve policy in the place of real ecological understanding.

There are those who regard the forests as the property of all the people in the world, arguing that overriding interests of genetic conservation and world climate should prevail over national and private interest. Again, too much is supposed and too little proven, and evangelical fervor cannot take the place of sound argument as to why equatorial countries should forego profit from the use of their own resources. This is not to say that the worldwide conservationist movement fails to have any impact. It is to say, however, that the impact is peripheral and indirect. Ultimately the most effective force for change must lie in successful political pressure for conservation within Indonesia and Malaysia, where informed and aware groups of citizens are growing steadily in number and influence.

The role of the state has undergone great change through time. Colonial administrations seldom inhibited capitalist entrepreneurs when large profits were to be made, but sometimes did show serious concern both for conservation goals and for the rights of indigenous tribal people. Postindependence governments have given such weight to the political imperative of facilitating rapid economic development that they have tended to disregard such inherited policy constraints. Only now are some members of a new generation of decision-makers again prepared to take a longer-term view. In explaining a period of profligate resource use, it is necessary to take account of postindependence reaction against all aspects of the colonial system, good as well as bad. The strong contemporary governments of Malaysia and Indonesia, however, have embraced growth objectives and have at least until now shown a greater tendency to discourage environmental criticism of their resource-frontier policies than to incorporate conservation into the political agenda.

Acknowledgments

This chapter is abbreviated from a conference paper that also included substantial discussion of environmental change in and around the city of Kuala Lumpur, principally contributed by Low, here deleted to confine the chapter to the "tropical rain forest frontiers" theme. The authors wish to acknowledge important help from Yvonne Byron (Australian National University) in search and in editing; her contribution includes the data for Table 30–1. Dr. Abdul Samad Hadi of Universiti Kebangsaan Malaysia offered many valuable comments on an early draft. Lesley Potter acknowledges the help of Nico Dros with archival research in the Netherlands, and in Adelaide of Anneke van Woerkom with translation. The maps were prepared in Canberra by Nigel Duffy and Keith Mitchell, and the text was word-processed through its several stages by Carol McKenzie and Norma Chin. Lesley Potter acknowledges the support of the University of

Adelaide and the Australian Research Grants Scheme in field research, and Harold Brookfield and Francis Lian acknowledge the support of the Australian National University.

Notes

1. The importance of this region for world climate and possible climatic change cannot adequately be assessed by the authors. Ramage (1968) calculated that convection above the whole archipelagic region including New Guinea contributes about 29% of the total water vapor above the 500 mb level in the band between 10°N and 10°S around the world. Riehl (1979) points out the importance of this latent heat transfer to overcome net radiation cooling above the tropics and to maintain the equator-pole temperature difference. The significance of deforestation in this region for CO_2 build-up in the troposphere often forms part of agitation against deforestation. Estimates of deforestation rates in Asia as a whole run through a range in which the highest estimate is 3.6 times the lowest; a central value based on FAO/UNEP (1981) data has all Asia contributing a maximum of 26% of net carbon release from nonfallow forests in the tropics, equal to only 7% of global release from fossil-fuel combustion (Houghton et al. 1985). However, this figure does not take account of selective timber-cutting within the forest, which may substantially increase the carbon flux. Henderson-Sellers and Gornitz (1984) find that tropical deforestation, aggregated in a single block for modeling, has a significant effect on evapotranspiration, cloudiness, and daily rainfall, but that albedo change is not significant. In this fragmented region, change is probably significant at the topoclimatic scale, but we suggest that both data and modelling are as yet inadequate for firm statement about the effect of deforestation in peninsular and island Southeast Asia on world or regional climate.

2. Though our purpose is to describe, certain questions may be asked of the data. First, is it possible to manage use and transformation without damage? The process and qualities of the physical environment itself influence the direction and speed of response, and containment of damage may be impossible, though repair may be feasible and the consequences may be capable of limitation by human artifice. Second, how do we define "local," "national," "commercial," and "global" interests when evaluating the effects of transformation? What is the role of government? Is there a "world interest" in such matters as protection of the tropical rain forests, and if so who should pay its price? For a research team composed of two outsiders, one urban insider, and one rural insider, these are important questions.

3. Aggradation from both marine and terrestrial sources brought about significant coastal changes in this region even in historic times, as well as during the Holocene (Ras 1968; Van Bemmelen 1949). The changes are particularly marked in Borneo, possibly reflecting human interference, but more probably the high natural rates of river-bank erosion among unconsolidated Tertiary sediments, as Ian Douglas (personal communication) suggests.

4. "Transmigration" (transmigrasi) describes the Indonesian settlement program under which rural people from crowded areas in Java and Madura, and more recently also Bali, Lombok, and islands in southeastern Indonesia, are established in organized farming settlements on the larger outer islands. Rural resettlement schemes in Malaysia are not known by this term, which is specific to Indonesia. A comprehensive review is provided by Hardjono (1977; 1986).

5. Today it would occasion astonishment for a senior government official to react in the defense of tribal people as two Dutch residents of Southeast Kalimantan did in this period, to defend shifting cultivation as the only feasible system over much of the area (De Haan 1929), or to oppose the opening of new areas to exploitation by outsiders (Wentholt 1938). Similar changes in attitude through time are reported in Sarawak (Hong 1987; Lian 1987).

6. It is clear that many trees were killed by drought rather than by fire (Leighton 1984). Since drought is a frequent event in quite large parts of the region – particularly but not only eastern Borneo – and

seems to be highly correlated with ENSO events, it becomes important to establish the past history of their incidence. This is especially so in the light of modern ecological theory, which suggests that the persistence of ecosystem diversity is enhanced by perturbation (for example, Lewin 1986; UNESCO 1986). Unfortunately, as yet little direct evidence exists on the long record of ENSO events in Southeast Asia, though Berlage's (1931) work on tree rings in *Tectona grandis* in Java has been reinterpreted by De Boer (1951) to indicate quite frequent drought, as well as a more sustained period of negative rainfall anomalies between the sixteenth and eighteenth centuries. More recently, Allen, Brookfield and Byron (1989) have established a record back to the mid-19th century, but no record yet covers more than part of the lifetime of most of the trees in the present forests. Three major droughts have been experienced in this century – in 1914, 1941, and 1982–83 – and the drought intensity in 1914 was closely comparable with that in 1982–83. The evidence provided by Leighton and Wirawan shows that even without fire such events can cause extensive death of trees, though regeneration with secondary species is rapid (TAD 1987). These considerations should be important for the future management of the forests, as well as for the understanding of their present ecology. Moreover, it is likely that further fires, compounded by interference on the present scale, will lead to accelerated replacement of forest by grassland.

References

Abdulhadi, A., K. Kartawinata, and S. Sukardjo. 1981. Effects of mechanized logging in the lowland *dipterocarp* forest of Lempake, East Kalimantan. *Malayan Forester* 44:407–18.

Aiken, S. R., and C. H. Leigh. 1985. On the declining fauna of Peninsular Malaysia in the postcolonial period. *Ambio* 14:15–22.

Aiken, S. R., C. H. Leigh, T. R. Leinbach, and M. R. Moss. 1982. *Development and Environment in Peninsular Malaysia*. McGraw Hill: Singapore.

Allen, B., Brookfield, H., and Byron, Y. 1989. Frost and drought through time and space, II, the written, oral and proxy records and their meaning. *Mountain Research and Development* 9:279–305.

Allen, R. C., T. J. Straka, and W. F. Watson. 1986. Indonesia's developing forest industry. *Environmental Management* 10:753–59.

Andaya, B. W., and L. Y. Andaya. 1982. *A History of Malaysia*. London: Macmillan.

Anderson, A. J. U. 1978. Malnutrition among Sarawak shifting cultivators and remedies. Paper presented to Workshop on Shifting Cultivation, Kuching. Dec. 7–8.

———. 1980. Food consumption of Land Dayaks in the Tebakang Area. *Sarawak Gazette*, Feb., 27–35.

Anon. 1979. Forest resource base, policy, and legislation of Peninsular Malaysia. Paper presented at seventh Malaysian Forestry Conference. *Malaysian Forester* 42:328–47.

Ashton, P. S. 1980. The biological and ecological basis for the utilization of Dipterocarps. *Bio-Indonesia* 7:43–54.

Bahrin, T. S. and P. D. A. Perera. 1977. *FELDA, 21 Years of Land Development*. Kuala Lumpur, Federal Land Development Authority.

Berlage, H. P. 1931. Over het verband tussen de dikte der jaaringen en djatibomen en de regenval op Java. *Tectona* 24:939–53.

Biro Pusat Statistik, 1965–1987. *Statistik Perdagangan Luar Negeri Indonesia–Expor* (Indonesian Foreign Trade Statistics–exports). Jakarta: Biro Pusat Statistik.

Black, I. 1985. The "Lastposten": Eastern Kalimantan and the Dutch in the Nineteenth and Early Twentieth Centuries. *Journal of South East Asian Studies* 16:281–91.

Boerema, J. 1917. Regenval in de oostmoessonmanden en uitbreiding van het regenlooze gebied gedurende droge oostmoessons in Nederlandsche-Indie. *Natuurkindig Tijdschrift voor Nederlandsche-Indie* 76:46–63.

Braak, C. 1915. De sterke nevel in den Oostmoesson van 1914. *Natuurkundig Tijdschrift voor Nederlandsche-Indie* 74:131–40.

Brookfield, H. C. 1988. The new great age of clearance and beyond:

what sustainable development is possible? In *People of the Tropical Rainforest*, ed. J. Denslow and C. Padoch. Berkeley and Los Angeles: University of California Press.

Burbridge, P., J. A. Dixon, and B. Soewardi. 1981. Forestry and agriculture: options for resource allocation in choosing lands for transmigration. *Applied Geography* 1:237–58.

Burgess, P. F. 1971. The effects of logging on hill dipterocarp forests. *Malaysian Nature Journal* 24:231–37.

———. 1973. The impact of commercial forestry on the hill forests of the Malay Peninsula. In *Proceedings of Symposium on Biological Resources and National Development*, ed. E. Soepadmo and K. G. Singh, 131–36. May 1972. Kuala Lumpur. Malayan Nature Society.

Chan, Y. K., I. F. T. Wong, and W. M. Law. 1978. Agricultural development and land utilization in Peninsular Malaysia by year 2000. In *Proceedings of Conference on "Food and Agriculture Malaysia 2000"*, H. F. Chin, I. C. Enoch, and Wan Mohd. Othman, 471–86. July 1977. Serdang, Selangor, Faculty of Agriculture, Universiti Pertanian Malaysia.

Colfer, C. J. P. 1983. Change and indigenous agroforestry in East Kalimantan. *Borneo Research Bulletin* 15:3–21, 70–87.

Collier, W. 1980. Fifty years of spontaneous and government sponsored migration in the swampy lands of Kalimantan: past results and future prospects. *Prisma* 18:32–55.

Courtenay, P. P. 1972. *A Geography of Trade and Development in Malaya*. London: Bell.

De Boer, H. J. 1951. Tree-ring measurements and weather fluctuations in Java from A.D. 1514. *Proc. Koninklijk Nederlandsche Akademie voor Wetenschappen, Amsterdam*. Series B 54:194–209.

De Haan, J. 1929. Memorie van overgave, Zuider en Ooster Afdeeling van Borneo. Unpublished typescript, MvO No. 275, Algemeen Rijksarchief, Den Haag, Holland.

De Pater, C., and P. Visser. 1979. *Kalimantan in de Houtgreep; achtergronden en effecten van de boschexploitatie op Kalimantan*. Wageningen, Holland. Wageningen Agricultural University.

Dove, M. 1979. The Kantu at Tikul Batu: swidden ecology and economics in West Kalimantan. PhD dissertation. Stanford, Stanford University.

Editor. 1967. Forestry and conservation in the lowlands of West Malaysia. *Malayan Forester* 30:243–45.

———. 1978. The depleting resource. *Malaysian Forester* 41:209–10.

FAO. 1975 and 1987. *Yearbook of Forest Products*. Rome, FAO.

FAO/UNEP. 1981. *Tropical Forest Resources Assessment Project. Forest Resources of Tropical Asia*. Rome, FAO.

Fermor, L. L. 1939. *Report upon the Mining Industry of Malaya*. Kuala Lumpur, Government Press.

Flenley, J. R. 1979. *The Equatorial Rain Forest: a Geological History*. London: Butterworth.

Freeman, J. D. 1955. *Iban Agriculture: a Report on the Shifting Cultivation of Hill Rice by the Iban of Sarawak*. London, Her Majesty's Stationery Office, Colonial Research Studies 18.

Goh, K. C. 1982. Land use and soil erosion problems in Malaysia. In *Development and the Environmental Crisis: Proceedings of the Symposium "The Malaysian Environment in Crisis,"* Consumers' Association of Penang 109–19. Sept. 16–20, 1978. Penang, Malaysia, Consumers' Association of Penang.

Government of Indonesia. 1978. *Statistik Indonesia 77*. Jakarta: Biro Pusat Statistik.

Grainger, A. 1980. The state of the world's tropical forest. *The Ecologist* 10(1):6–54.

Gurmit Singh, K. S. 1982. More stress than energy in Malaysia's forests. In *Tropical Forests – Source of Energy through Optimization or Diversification*, ed. P. B. L. Srivastava et al., 239–44. Serdang, Universiti Pertanian Malaysia.

Hamzah, Z. 1978. Some observations on the effects of mechanical logging on regeneration, soil and hydrological conditions in East Kalimantan. In *Proceedings of Symposium on Long-Term Effects of Logging in Southeast Asia*, ed. S. Rahardjo et al.,

73–87. BIOTROP Special Publication No. 3. Bogor, India. BIOTROP.

Hardjono, J. M. 1977. *Transmigration in Indonesia*. Kuala Lumpur: Oxford University Press.

———. 1986. Transmigration: looking to the future. *Bulletin of Indonesian Economic Studies* 22(2):28–53.

Harrisson, T. 1970. *Malays of Southwest Sarawak before Malaysia*. East Lansing, MI: Michigan State University Press.

Henderson-Sellers, A., and V. Gornitz. 1984. Possible climatic impacts of land cover transformations, with particular emphasis on tropical deforestation. *Climatic Change* 6:231–57.

Hoesada, J. 1984. The contribution of American industries to the forest-based economy of Indonesia. Unpublished PhD dissertation. Nacogdoches, TX, Stephen F. Austin State University.

Hong, E. 1987. *Natives of Sarawak: Survival in Borneo's Vanishing Forest*. Pulau Pinang, Malaysia, Institut Masyarakat.

Houghton, R. A., R. D. Boone, J. M. Melillo, C. A. Palm, G. M. Woodwell, N. Myers, B. Moore, and D. L. Skole. 1985. Net flux of carbon dioxide from tropical forests in 1980. *Nature* 316: 617–20.

Hunter, L. 1984. Tropical forest plantations and natural stand management: a national lesson from East Kalimantan? *Bulletin of Indonesian Economic Studies* 20:98–116.

Idwar Saleh, M. 1978. Pepper trade and the ruling class of Banjarmasin in the seventeenth century. *Papers of the Dutch-Indonesian Historical Conference 1976*, 203–21. Leiden and Jakarta, Bureau of Indonesian Studies.

International Bank for Reconstruction and Development. 1955. *The Economic Development of Malaya*. Report of a mission organized by the International Bank for Reconstruction and Development at the request of the governments of the Federation of Malaya, the Crown Colony of Singapore, and the United Kingdom. Singapore, Government Printer.

Jackson, J. C. 1968a. *Planters and Speculators: Chinese and European Agricultural Enterprise in Malaya 1786–1921*. Kuala Lumpur: University of Malaya Press.

———. 1968b. *Sarawak: A Geographical Survey of a Developing State*. London: University of London Press.

Jessup, T. C. 1981. Why do Apo Kayan shifting cultivators move? *Borneo Research Bulletin* 13(1):16–32.

Kartawinata, K. 1979: An overview of the environmental consequences of tree removal from the forest in Indonesia. In *Biological and Sociological Basis for a Rational Use of Forest for Energy and Organics: An International Workshop*, ed. S. G. Boyce, 129–40. Southeastern Forest Experiment Station, Ashville, NC: USDA.

———. 1980. East Kalimantan: a comment. *Bulletin of Indonesian Economic Studies* 16:120–23.

Kartawinata, K., and A. P. Vayda. 1984. Forest conversion in East Kalimantan, Indonesia: the activities and impact of timber companies, shifting cultivators, migrant pepper-farmers, and others. In *Ecology in Practice, Vol. I, Ecosystem Management*, ed. F. di Castri, F. W. G. Baker, and M. Hadley, 98–121. Dublin and Paris: Tycooly and UNESCO.

Khor, K. P., and E. Hong. 1980. Resource deterioration: its economic and social consequences. In *Tropical Ecology and Development, Proceedings of Fifth International Symposium of Tropical Ecology*, ed. J. I. Furtado, 1357–62. April 1979. Kuala Lumpur, International Society of Tropical Ecology.

Klerks, E. 1906. Memorie van Overgave van de onderafdeeling Martapura. Unpublished typescript, MvO No. 472, Algemeen Rijksarchief, Den Haag.

Kompas. Dec. 21, 1987. Jakarta.

Kumar, R. 1986. *The Forest Resources of Malaysia: Their Economics and Development*. Singapore: Oxford University Press.

Lau, B. T. 1979. The effects of shifting cultivation on sustained yield management for Sarawak National Forests. *Malaysian Forester* 42:418–29.

Lee, P. C. 1981. Forest land classification in Malaysia. In *Assessing*

Tropical Forest Lands: Their Suitability for Sustainable Uses, ed. R. A. Carpenter, 186–96. Dublin: Tycooly International Publishing Ltd.

Leighton, M. 1984. The El Nino–Southern Oscillation event in Southeast Asia: effects of drought and fire in tropical forest in eastern Borneo. Unpublished project report to IUCN/World Wildlife Fund, Project US-293.

Lemei, W. 1909. Nota van Overgave, Riam Kiwa. Unpublished typescript, MvO No. 474, Algemeen Rijksarchief, Den Haag.

Lennertz, R., and K. F. Panzer. 1983. *Preliminary Assessment of the Drought and Forest Damage in Kalimantan Timur*. Report of the Fact-finding Mission by DFS German Forest Inventory Service, Ltd., Samarinda, Indonesia, German Agency for Technical Cooperation (GTZ).

Leslie, A. J. 1986. The commodity problem with tropical timber. *Timber Trade Review* (Warta Perdagangan Kayu) 15(3):13–14.

Lewin, R. 1986. In ecology, change brings stability. *Science* 234:1071–73.

Lian, F. J. 1987. Farmers' perceptions and economic change: the case of Kenyah swidden farmers in Sarawak, East Malaysia. PhD dissertation. Canberra, Australian National University.

Lim, T.-G. 1977. *Peasants and Their Agricultural Economy in Colonial Malaya 1874–1941*. Kuala Lumpur: Oxford University Press.

Lowenhaupt Tsing, A. 1984. Politics and culture in the Meratus Mountains. PhD dissertation. Stanford, Stanford University.

Luytjes, A. 1925. *De Bevolkingsrubbercultuur in Nederlandsche Indie*. Vol. II, Zuider en Ooster Afdeeling van Borneo, Weltevreden, Dept van Landbouw, Nijverheid en Handel. Published in cooperation with Native Rubber Investigation Committee Batavia.

Mackie, C. 1984. The lessons behind East Kalimantan's forest fires. *Borneo Research Bulletin* 16:63–73.

Mahmood, L. 1982. Land use conflict and its implication on sustained yield forest management in Malaysia with special reference to Kelantan. In *Tropical Forests – Source of Energy through Optimization and Diversification*, ed. P. B. L. Srivastava et al. 151–60. Serdang, Universiti Pertanian Malaysia.

Malingreau, J. P., G. Stephens, and L. Fellows. 1985. Remote sensing of forest fires: Kalimantan and North Borneo in 1982–83. *Ambio* 14:314–21.

Manning, C. 1971. The timber boom with special reference to East Kalimantan. *Bulletin of Indonesian Economic Studies* 7:30–60.

Marsono, D. 1980. The effect of Indonesian selective cutting (TPI) on the structure and regeneration of lowland tropical Dipterocarp forests in East Kalimantan, Indonesia. PhD dissertation. University of the Philippines at Los Banos.

Meijer, W. 1974. Recent developments in forestry and land use in Indonesia. *Flora Malesiana Bulletin* 27:2200–203.

Metz, T., and P. Baretta. 1937. Koetai. *Tijdschrift voor Economische Geographie* 28(4):81–91: and 28(5):113–26.

Mohd. Nor, S., and K. S. Ho. 1982. The myth of complete utilization of tropical forests. In *Tropical Forests – Source of Energy through Optimization and Diversification*, ed. P. B. L. Srivastava et al. 101–6. Serdang, Universiti Pertanian Malaysia.

Mok, S. T. 1982. Forest resource exploitation and wastage in Malaysia. In *Tropical Forests – Source of Energy through Optimization and Diversification*, ed. P. B. L. Srivastava et al., 39–50. Serdang, Universiti Pertanian Malaysia.

Myint, H. 1972. *Southeast Asia's Economy: Development Policies in the 1970s*. Harmondsworth: Penguin.

Ottow, A. 1952. De Opzet van boschexploitatie-bedrijven in de Buitengewesten, meer speciaal in Oost-Borneo. *Tectona* 42:175–281.

P. T. Data Consult, Inc. 1989. Indonesia Commercial Newsletter, 25 Sept., Jakarta.

Padoch, C. 1982. *Migration and Its Alternatives among the Iban of Sarawak*. The Hague, Martinus Nijhoff, Verhandelingen van het Koninklijk Institut voor de Taal-, Land- en Volkenkunde 98.

———. 1985. Labor efficiency and intensity of land use in rice production: An example from Kalimantan. *Human Ecology* 13:271–89.

Pemerintah Daerah Propinsi Kalimantan Barat (various dates). *Kalimantan Barat dalam Angka*, Pontianak.

Pemerintah Daerah Propinsi Kalimantan Tengah (various dates) Kalimantan Tengah dalam Angka, Palangka Raya.

Pemerintah Daerah Propinsi Kalimantan Timur (various dates) Kalimantan Timur dalam Angka, Samarinda.

Pemerintah Daerah Propinsi Kalimantan Selatan (various dates) Kalimantan Selatan dalam Angka, Banjarmasin.

Potter, L. M., and A. Hasymi. 1989. South Kalimantan: the Banjarese heartland. In *Unity and Diversity: Regional Economic Development in Indonesia since 1970*, ed. H. Hill. Singapore: Oxford University Press.

Price, O. T. W., and C. Des Bouvrie. 1986. Economic and financial aspects of lowland development in Indonesia. In Symposium on *Lowland Development in Indonesia*. Wageningen, International Institute for Land Reclamation and Improvement 3:19–44.

Ramage, C. S. 1968. The role of a tropical "maritime continent" in the atmospheric circulation. *Monthly Weather Review* 96:365–70.

Ras, J. 1968. *Hikajat Bandjar: a Study in Malay Historiography*. The Hague, Martinus Nijhoff.

Reid, A. 1988. *Southeast Asia in the Age of Commerce, 1450–1680*. New Haven: Yale University Press.

Rich, B. M. 1986. The World Bank's Indonesia Transmigration Project: potential for environmental disaster. *Indonesia Reports* 15:2–5.

Riehl, H. 1979. *Climate and Weather in the Tropics*. London: Academic Press.

Sanchez, P. A. 1976. *Properties and Management of Soils in the Tropics*. New York: Wiley.

Schoening, J. R. 1978. Forest industry development in Southeast Asia. One company's experience and observations. In *Proceedings of Conference on Improved Utilization of Tropical Forests*, ed. R. J. Auchter et al. 196–202. May 1978. Washington, D.C.: USDA Forest Service and USAID.

Schuitemaker, B. 1938. Korte Schets van den Landbouw in het Oostmoesson- Rijstgebied in de Zuider- en Oosterafdeeling van Borneo. *Landbouw* 14(12):740–78.

Seavoy, R. E. 1980. Population pressure and land use change: from tree crops to sawah in northwestern Kalimantan, Indonesia. *Singapore Journal of Tropical Geography* 1(2):61–67.

Secrett, C. 1986. The environmental impact of transmigration. *The Ecologist* 16:2/3:77–88.

Shaharuddin, Bin Mohd., I. 1983. The development and implementation of a selective management system in Peninsular Malaysia. Essay for MSc. Canberra, Australian National University, Department of Forestry.

Soekotjo 1981. Diameter growth of residual stands in logged-over areas in East Kalimantan tropical rain forest, Indonesia. PhD dissertation. East Lansing, Michigan State University.

Soerianegara, I. 1982. Socio-economic aspects of forest resources management in Indonesia. In *Socioeconomic Effects and Constraints in Tropical Forest Management*, ed. E. G. Hallsworth, 73–86. Chichester: John Wiley and Sons.

St. John, S. [1862] 1974. *Life in the Forests of the Far East*. 2 vols. Kuala Lumpur: Oxford University Press.

Sulaiman bin Haji N. 1977. Towards a new era in Malaysian forestry. in *A New Era in Malaysian Forestry*, ed. C. B. Sastry, P. B. L. Srivastava, and A. Manap, 169–88. Serdang, Malaysia, Universiti Pertanian Malaysia.

Swettenham, F. 1907. *British Malaya: an Account of the Origin and Progress of British Influence in Malaya*. London: Lane.

Swinbanks, D. 1987. Sarawak's tropical rain forests exploited by Japan. *Nature* 328:373.

TAD (Transmigration Area Development Project) 1987. *Report on the ITTO Pre-Project: The Rehabilitation of the Forest in East Kalimantan Damaged by Drought and Fire in 1982–83*.

Samarinda, Indonesia: German Agency for Technical Cooperation (GTZ).

Timber Trade Review (Warta Perdagangan Kayu) (1985 and 1986). Vols. 13, 14.

UNESCO. 1986. *Programme on Man and the Biosphere: General Scientific Advisory Panel, Final Report*. Paris: United Nations Educational, Scientific and Cultural Organization.

United Nations. 1984. *International Tropical Timber Agreement 1983*. New York: United Nations.

Van Bemmelen, R. W. 1949. *The Geology of Indonesia*. Vol. I, *The General Geology of Indonesia and Adjacent Archipelagos*. The Hague: Government Printer.

Van Bemmelen, W. 1916. Droogte-jaren op Java. *Natuurkundig Tijdschrift voor Nederlandsche-Indie* 75:157–79.

Van der Laan, E. 1925. De bossen van de Zuider- en Oosterafdeling van Borneo. *Tectona* 18:925–52.

———. 1926. Analyse der bosschen in de onderafdeeling Pleihari van de afdeeling Bandjermasin der Zuider-en Ooster Afdeeling van Borneo. *Tectona* 19:103–23.

Van der 'Z' (waan) 1935. De Bevolkingskap in Borneo. *Het Bosch* III:169–78.

Van Dis, M. 1986. The art of lowland development. In *Symposium on Lowland Development in Indonesia*. Wageningen, International Institute for Land Reclamation and Improvement 1:34–53.

Van Kempen, C. 1924. Memorie van Overgave, Zuider en Ooster Afdeeling van Borneo. Unpublished typescript, MvO No. 274, Algemeen Rijksarchief, Den Haag.

Van Setten van der Meer, V. C. 1979. *Sawah Cultivation in Ancient Java*. Canberra: A.N.U. Press Oriental Monograph Series 22.

Van Steenis, C. G. G. J. 1971. Plant conservation in Malaysia. *Bulletin du Jardin Botanique National de Belgique* 41:189–202.

Verkuyl, A. 1950. The timber resources of Kalimantan (trans.). Annual Report for 1949 of the Chief Forester, Head of the Forest Planning Brigade of Kalimantan. Unpublished typescript.

Voss, F. 1983. *East Kalimantan; Transmigration Area Development Project*, rev. ed. TAD Report No 9: Natural Resources Inventory, Hamburg.

Wentholt, J. 1938. Memorie van Overgave, onderafdeeling Marta-pura. Unpublished typescript, MvO No. 482, Algemeen Rijksarchief, Den Haag.

Whitmore, T. C. 1984. *Tropical Rain Forests of the Far East*. 2d ed. Oxford: Clarendon Press.

Wiersum, K., and J. Boerboom. 1977. The forestry situation in East Kalimantan, bijlage 5 in *Verslag van een reis naar Indonesie in het kader van de NUFFIC-projecten LHW/6 en LHW/8*. Wageningen, Dept. of Tropical Sylviculture, Wageningen Agricultural University.

Wirawan, N. 1984. *Good Forests within the Burned Forest Area in East Kalimantan*. WWF Project 1687 Field Report. Bogor, Indonesia: World Wildlife Fund.

World Wood, November 1985.

Wong, I. F. T. 1971. *The Present Land Use of West Malaysia, 1966*, Kuala Lumpur, Department of Agriculture.

———. 1979. *The Present Land Use of Peninsular Malaysia*. 2 vols. Kuala Lumpur, Department of Agriculture.

Wyatt-Smith, J. 1964. A preliminary vegetation map of Malaya with descriptions of the vegetation types. *Journal of Tropical Geography* 18:198–213.

Yip, Y.-H. 1969. *The Development of the Tin-Mining Industry of Malaya*. Kuala Lumpur: University of Malaya Press.

31

Caucasia

YU. P. BADENKOV   A. K. BORUNOV   A. F. MANDYCH   A. I. ROMASHKEVICH
AND   V. O. TARGULIAN*

The Caucasian region is a largely mountainous block of land (maximum elevation of 5,650 m a.s.l.) situated between the Black and Caspian seas in the southern USSR. Covering some 470,000 km², the region is bounded by the Azov and Black seas to the west, the Kuban and Terek river basins to the north, the Caspian Sea to the east, and the countries of Iran and Turkey to the south (Fig. 31.1). Its geographical conditions and setting have given rise to a complex mosaic of human–environment interactions. The region has a highly diverse environment, the product of the Greater Caucasus and the two large inland seas and of a location at the boundary between the moderate and subtropical thermal zones, giving rise to one of the most diverse floral and faunal subregions in the Holarctic. Its location has fostered the interaction and mixing since antiquity of various cultures from the Russian Plain, the Mediterranean, Asia Minor, and Central Asia. The historical trends in economic activities, population migration, and settlement from these diverse cultures, and their adjustments and alterations to the differing natural zones, have given rise to varied transformations.

Since antiquity and until the nineteenth century, the dominant type of human activity in Caucasia was agriculture, and particularly animal-breeding. The incorporation by Russia of Transcaucasia (during the first third of the nineteenth century) and of Northern Caucasus (in the middle of the nineteenth century) began the intensive involvement of the economy and resources of the Caucasus into the all-Russian market. Of particular importance was the long-term lease of the oil fields of the Apsheron Peninsula (the Caspian region) in 1872. Established in 1875–79, the company of Nobel, and the subsequent inflow of foreign capital, turned Baku into a major industrial center. This trend was also greatly facilitated by construction of the Transcaucasian Railway, finished in 1893, which connected the oil works of Azerbaijan with ports on the Black Sea.

*With the assistance and contributions of E. A. Belanovskaya, M. V. Davydova, E. O. Fridenberg, O. A. Kibalchich, R. A. Lotov, G. M. Nikolaeva, P. M. Polyan, E. A. Yasnyi, R. I. Zlotin, and S. V. Zonn.

In the twentieth century, the predominantly extensive economy was gradually replaced by more intensive forms: industry and recreation. At present, depending on the structure of natural and labor resources, the following types of economic activities are identifiable in Caucasia:

Mining,
Forestry,
Power production (oil, gas, hydropower),
Agro-based industry (processing of agricultural products),
Recreation (mountain-climbing, tourism, and mountain skiing),
Industry (heavy engineering).

A specific feature of mountain regions of Caucasia is the decline of the role of agriculture and the increasing role of recreation services and industrial activities. At the same time, the unique (in the USSR) agroclimatic conditions of the coastal lowlands of the Black and Caspian seas allow Caucasia to be a principal supplier of subtropical crops – tea, citrus crops, and grapes – to the domestic market of the USSR.

This chapter focuses on some of the major environmental transformations of the region that have resulted from human use and on adjustments to the habitats that have been changed. The chapter has three parts: the description and discussions of (1) the "natural" conditions of the region, (2) the major agents of change, and (3) the transformed physical conditions as they now exist.

The Physical Setting

The presence of the Greater Caucasus Ridge creates several diverse subregions within Caucasia (Fig. 31.1). Important among these are:

Ciscaucasia, including the piedmont of the southern Russian Plain and the rolling foothills and lower northern slopes of the foremost Greater Caucasus;
The Greater Caucasus, a mountain ridge extending for about 1,500 km, with a width varying from 100 km to 180 km;
The Transcaucasian Depression, including the Colchin (Rioni)

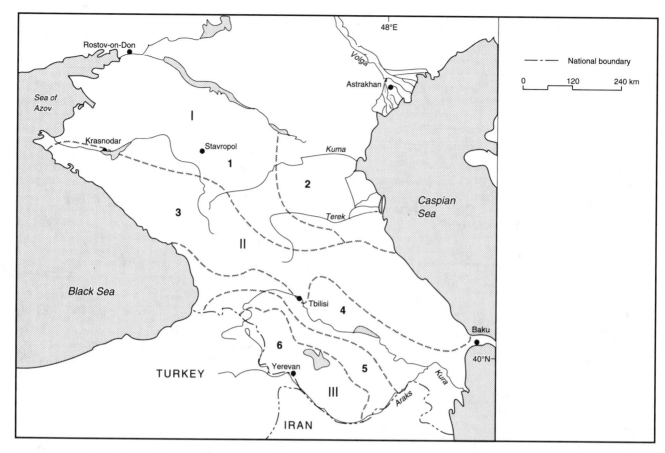

Figure 31.1 Natural regions of Caucasia. (I) Russian Plain: (1) steppic plains and highlands of Front Caucasia; (2) semidesert lowlands of the North Caspian area. (II) Caucasian mountain country: (3) forests and alpine landscapes of the Greater Caucasus Ridges; (4) Transcaucasian depression with humid forests, dry steppes, and semideserts; (5) forests and mountain meadows of the Lesser Caucasus Ridges. (III) Front Asia uplands: (6) Armenian mountain-steppe and mountain-meadow volcanic plateau. Source: *Caucasia* 1966.

lowland in the west, the Kura basin in the East, and the midmountain Suram Ridge (1,500–1,900 m) in between; and,

The Transcaucasian Highlands, including the Minor Caucasus ridges and intermontane hollows – a subregion lower (2,700–3,700 m) and less extensive than the Greater Caucasus, with no common watershed (Gvozdetskiy 1958).

The natural diversity of these subregions is accentuated by their range in latitude and elevation and by the varying geological and lithological structures, the duration and evolution of landscape formations, and the biota.

Climate

The peculiarities of Caucasian topography and location make the climatic patterns of the region very complex (*Caucasia* 1966). The Greater Caucasus Ridge divides the moderate Ciscaucasian climate belt from subtropical Transcaucasia. The major mountain ridges transform the atmospheric circulation. In addition to transforming the heat and radiation balance over the Black, Azov and Caspian seas, they are responsible for significant variations in the Caucasian subregions. Their major macroclimatic consequence is the west-to-east increase in aridity.

The region below 2,000 m is subdivided into four climatic areas: Ciscaucasia, West and East Transcaucasia, and the midmountain Armenian upland (*Caucasia* 1966). Above 2,000 m, highland climatic areas of the Greater and Minor Caucasus and the high-mountain Armenian upland are distinguished. Steppes, forest-steppes, deserts, and semideserts in Ciscaucasia change at higher altitudes into boreal forests and alpine meadows. The Mediterranean climate tends to become humid-subtropical south of Sochi. East Transcaucasia is characterized by dry subtropical deserts and dry steppes. A cool climate with relatively low humidity extends over the Armenian upland.

The orographic structure of the region affects many climatic features. Normal annual precipitation for 40°–45° N is 925–950 mm. The Kura-Araks lowland receives 15–30%, but the Colchis Depression, up to 150–250%. Precipitation is greatest (over 3,000 m) on the southwest slopes of the Greater Caucasus, decreasing eastward along the ridge line (800 mm) (The Alps – the Caucasus 1980). Radiation balance in the region also depends on the orographic structure. The isolines of total solar radiation in Ciscaucasia follow the parallels of latitude, whereas in coastal zones they are of the meridional extension.

The mean air temperature in Ciscaucasia in January is

−2°C; in the Colchis Depression, −4.6°C; and in the Minor Caucasus Ridge at 2,000 m, about −8°C (*The Alps – The Caucasus* 1980). Vertical gradients of summer temperature tend to increase eastward from 0.51°/100 m at the southern slopes of West Caucasus up to 0.64°/100 m in East Georgia and Azerbaijan. In July, the zero isotherm rises to 3,700–4,000 m. July is the warmest month in the lowlands, August in the highlands.

The mountain relief is also responsible for a significant mesoscale variability of the heat and radiation balance, as well as for other climatic processes and phenomena: intensive highland-valley circulation, orographic fohns, low temperatures, snow cover, ice crust, and fogs in winter; and droughts, heavy rainfalls, hail, floods, and mud flows in summer. On the whole, the climatic background to human activities is very diverse.

Soils

Several soil zones exist in Caucasia. The upper zone is composed of mountain-meadow and highland-meadow steppe soils, and the middle zone is composed of mainly brown forest soils; some types include mountain brown and mountain black soils. The lower zone is composed of grey wood, black, brown, and brown-grey soils, as well as of a group of humid tropics soils (red and yellow soils, pseudo-podzols). The soils in the Transcaucasian intramontane depression are of the dry-steppe and semidesert type.

Distinctions can be drawn among several types of soil terrains that are important for assessing their changes under human impacts.

1. Shallow small-earth and/or rock-debris soils over rock platform or block rocks at depths of about 20–50 cm;
2. Full-profile soils with, for example, developed profiles A-B-C or A-A2-B-C horizons overlying block rocks down to 1 m;
3. Soils of varying thickness and composition formed over ancient clay weathering material and soft sedimentary rocks;
4. Soils of different thickness and composition formed over loose rocks – heavy clay, saline sedimentary rocks, dense carbonate materials, and so on, occurring at depths of 1–2 m.

The first two groups of soils are dominant in highly dissected high- and mid-mountain areas and occasionally in low-mountain areas of Caucasia. The other groups make up the soil cover in piedmont areas, foothill valleys, vast intramontane hollows, and mountain areas of ancient humidic weathering.

Biota

The flora and fauna of Caucasia are the richest and most diversified in the whole Palaearctic; their peculiarities stem from historic, climatic, orographic, lithologic-geomorphologic, and human factors. The distribution of ecosystems in Caucasia, as in all highland systems, is governed by the law of vertical zonality. At relatively small distances from one another, ecosystems characteristic of steppes, broad-

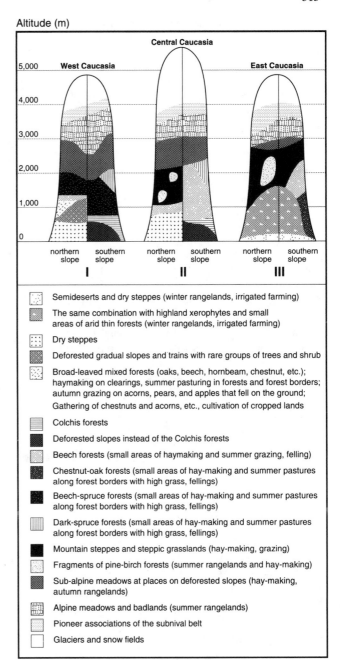

Figure 31.2 Types of modern ecosystem cover of the Greater Caucasus.

leaved and coniferous forests, subalpine and alpine meadows, and pioneer groups of the subnival zone can be found. Physical and geographic conditions, vertical zonation, and vegetation cover distinguish three zones: West, Central, and East Caucasia (Fig. 31.2).

The vertical zonality of the natural ecosystems in West Caucasia shows a classic mountain pattern comparable to that of the Alps, the Carpathians, and the Balkans. Flora and fauna had changed little here before 1700. The northern macroslope was covered by mixed forb-grass steppes (up to 400 m), oak forests with patches of meadow steppes and steppe-like meadows (800 m), beech forests (1,600 m), coniferous spruce-fir forests (2,000 m), subalpine high grass

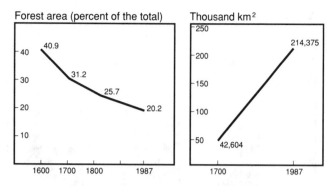

Forest area (percent of the total)

Thousand km²

Figure 31.3 Changes in forest and cultivated area. Source: curves compiled on the basis of atlases of the Soviet republics concerned.

patches and meadows, alpine meadows, and pioneer groups of subnival zone.

Central Caucasia was not as woody as West Caucasia in 1700. The river valleys and intramontane hollows of its northern slope were covered with highland meadow steppes and steppe-like meadows with birch wood patches bordering

alpine meadows. This configuration may reflect the influence of the highest Caucasus mountain peak, Elbrus (5,642 m), which is covered with a thick layer of snow and ice. On the other hand, some authors suppose that many centuries of economic activity (felling and burning of forests to clear pastures) had resulted in an almost complete denudation of the forest (Serebrianyi, Maliasova and Ilves 1981) (Fig. 31.3). Intensive use of vast areas for grazing brought about significant xerophytization of meadow communities that had succeeded woods as well as of the indigenous subalpine meadow above.

East Caucasia is the most arid subregion. The forest here is small, perhaps the result of rather early occupation. According to historicolinguistic studies, the first nomadic tribes appeared in the more convenient and accessible valleys of East Caucasia as early as the fifth and sixth centuries B.C. Since ancient times, the most widely spread vegetation communities in that region have been the arid steppes of Andropogon, upland-xerophytic vegetation of Tragacantha, derivatives of the sparsed oak, pine, juniperous, and xerophytic growth – shiblyaks and phrygana vegetation. As

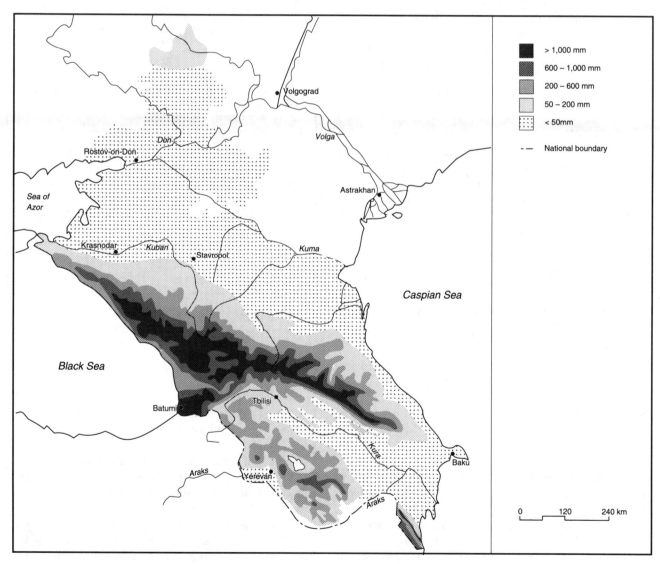

Figure 31.4 Mean annual river runoff. Source: *Caucasia* 1966.

compared to West and Central Caucasia, an additional vertical zone is present, the semidesert belt.

In the western and central portions of the southern macroslope of the Greater Caucasian Ridge, excluding the narrow coastal strip of the Black Sea, forest communities developed: submediterranean forests of *Quercus pubescens* and juniperus in the westernmost margin of the mountain system and the subtropical deciduous forests – relic ecosystems of the Colchis Depression and of the foothills with the warmest and most humid climatic regimes.

Waters

Extremely varied natural conditions in Caucasia produce a high differentiation of hydrological processes over its territory. This differentiation is reflected in intraregional patterns of mean annual runoff (Fig. 31.4) and in modification of total runoff with elevation. Most of the river runoff is formed in the belt of forest landscapes occurring from 800 m to 2,400 m (Vazhnov 1966). The majority of river watersheds over 100 km² have from 40%–50% of their area in this belt. The highest per area resources of water are in the western portion of the southern slope of the Greater Caucasus and Ajaria, the lowest in Armenia. The river runoff formed within the region is distributed equally between the watersheds of the Black and Caspian seas (Table 31-1).

The total amount of water accumulated in glaciers reaches 122 km² (Kotliakov 1966) – about equal to twice the annual runoff of all rivers in the region.

Agents of Tranformation

Climate

Work by Tushinskiy and Turmanina (1979) shows that in 1700, precipitation at timberline was at its maximum for this millennium, and since it then has continuously declined. The phase of warming that peaked in the middle of the seventeenth century was followed by a rapid decrease in mean annual air temperatures; their minimum values were

Table 31-1 *Runoff of the Major Rivers*

River	Place	Area of watershed (1,000 km²)	Runoff km³	Runoff l/s/km²
Watershed of the Black and Azov seas				
Kuban	Krasnodar	46.9	13.2	9.1
Kodori	Genakhleba	2.0	4.0	61.8
Inguri	Darcheli	3.6	5.5	48.1
Rioni	mouth	13.4	12.4	29.3
Watershed of the Caspian Sea				
Kuma	Vladimirovka	20.8	0.3	0.5
Terek	Stepnoe	35.4	9.5	8.6
Sulak	Miatly	18.1	5.5	13.3
Samur	Zukhul	3.8	2.3	19.2
Kura	mouth	188.0	18.3	3.1

Sources: Caucasia 1966.

Table 31-2 *Changes in Mass Budget of Janukat Glacier*

Years	Budget (mm)
1700–1820	−200
1820–1850	+230
1850–1910	−430
1910–1930	−320
1930–1968	−410
1968–1972	−290

Sources: Golubev et al. 1978.

registered at the very beginning of the 1800s. In the following years, a trend toward warming and decrease of precipitation was maintained in general, although with varying intensity.

An integrated indicator of climatic change in the region is the regression of the glaciers of the Greater Caucasus. According to studies by Golubev, Diurgerov, and Markin (1978), the changes in the mass budget (in millimeters) of the Janukat glacier in this period correspond to the above-mentioned climatic trends (see Table 31-2).

Superimposed upon these climatic trends were significant short-period oscillations that in some periods ran counter to the longer-term changes. This is seen most clearly in the repeated advances of the generally retreating glaciers, with

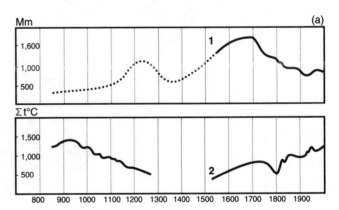

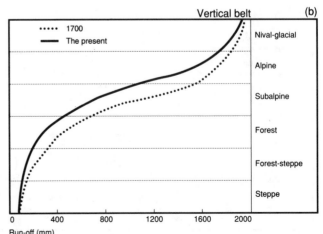

Figure 31.5 (a) Changes in annual precipitation totals (1), and sums of air temperature above 10°C at upper timberline in the Elbrus area (2). (b) Trend of runoff by vertical belts in the Elbrus area.

about 20-year periods of glacial activation (Serebrianyi, Golodkovskaya, and Ilves 1979). Secular climatic changes in the mountains and the lowlands are asynchronous (*The Alps – The Caucasus* 1980; Miagkov 1979). This asynchronicity is partially supported by the curves of temperature and precipitation changes, and illustrates the influence of the Caucasian mountain system on the synoptic processes in the region.

Long-range climatic changes have produced instability in the boundaries of the altitudinal belts – between the forest and subalpine belts, and the subalpine and alpine belts. Thus, in the period of warming in the eighteenth and nineteenth centuries, the upper timberline was 200–300 m higher than now, and cultivation was possible in Caucasia at altitudes 300–500 m higher than at present (Tushinskiy and Turmanina 1979). According to several authors, one should expect that the trend toward more continental climate over the European USSR, including Caucasia, will continue (Miagkov 1979). The

impact of temperature changes in the past 300 years on economic activities was rather mild over the whole of the region, though, and is unlikely to be significant in the next century.

Changes in hydrological regimes over the region in the period under study were due both to climatic oscillations and to economic activities. Probable changes in runoff due to climatic influence are shown in Fig. 31.5. Data on runoff changes by vertical belts are given in *The Greater Caucasus* 1984; and for 1700 the data take into account the trends of climatic change in the Elbrus region. In the latter case, it was assumed that high precipitation in the nival-glacial belt added to snow and ice accumulation, not to increased annual runoff. Taking into account significant areas under the subalpine and forest landscapes, then the runoff from these vertical belts was considerably higher (Fig. 31.5a). In 1700, glacial accumulation and river runoff from the Greater Caucasus should have been much higher than the present-day amounts.

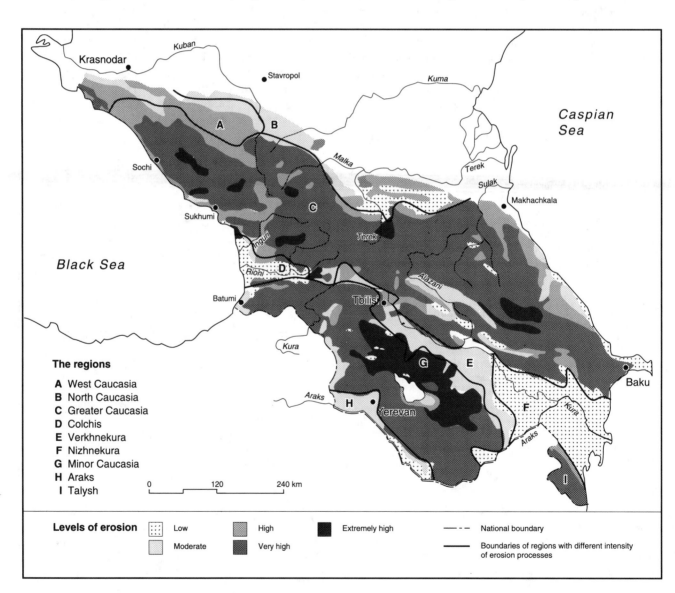

The regions

A West Caucasia
B North Caucasia
C Greater Caucasia
D Colchis
E Verkhnekura
F Nizhnekura
G Minor Caucasia
H Araks
I Talysh

0   120   240 km

Levels of erosion   Low   High   Extremely high   ----- National boundary

Moderate   Very high   ——— Boundaries of regions with different intensity of erosion processes

Figure 31.6 Patterns of erosion. The regions: I-West Caucasian; II-north Caucasian; III-greater Caucasian; IV-Colchis; V-Verkhnekura; VI-Nizhnekura; VII-minor Caucasian; VIII-Araksum; IX-Talysh.

Geodynamic Impacts

Among the most active and widespread of the natural processes important for landscape characteristics, regional environment, and human activities are those that form relief (Sergeeva 1967). The intensity of relief formation in Caucasia can be illustrated by the following data. Judging by instrumental measurements, the orogenic structure of the Greater Caucasus rises at the rate of 10–12 mm/yr and more, and the adjacent foredeeps move down at annual velocities of 5–6 mm. During the Quaternary, however, uplift was matched by denudation, and on the whole, the heights of the Greater Caucasus changed insignificantly (Voskresenskiy 1968). In an integrated form, the state of exogenic processes can be demonstrated by a map of dissection of relief, taking into account the density and depth of dissection of the territory (Fig. 31.6). Spatial diversity of the characteristics of dissection is one of the determinants of territorial differentiation of the region.

Due to the wide occurrence of carbonate rock, karst processes are very intensive over the ridges of the Greater Caucasus. Karst is found mostly in the midmountain belt. In combination with forests growing at these elevations, karst processes increase (1) the significance of the midmountain belt as an accumulator of high-quality resources of fresh water protected from economic impacts and (2) the contribution of the stable groundwater recharge in total runoff.

Avalanches pose a hazard to the population and economy of nearly one-half of Caucasia. The highest threat of avalanches is in the high-mountain alpine vertical belt and in the midmountain heavily dissected belt (Akinfieva 1970). Effects of avalanche action become weaker gradually as altitudes and dissection of terrain decrease. During winters with heavy snowfalls, however, avalanches also can form over weakly dissected low-mountain areas at altitudes of 600–1,700 m and slope gradients of 5–10°.

In Caucasia, mud flows represent one of the leading factors of denudation (*Caucasia* 1966). Their formation is facilitated by seismic activity in the region. In this century, formation of mud flows has been intensified also by human removal of natural vegetation, reducing the resistance of mountain territories to erosion. In the Greater Caucasus, this hazard increases from west to east due to greater aridity, shrinking of forest vegetation, and replacement of solid crystalline and metamorphic rocks by clayey schists and flysch strata more prone to weathering and erosion (*Caucasia* 1966). The increasing west-to-east intensity of mud flows also holds true for the Minor Caucasus and the Armenian Plateau.

Outwash from the active area of mud-flow formation by extreme floods in Central Caucasia can remove 20,000–30,000 m^3 from 1 km^2 and more (Yermakov and Yoganson 1957; Yoganson 1959). On the average, mud flows remove up to 125 t/km^2 of matter per year from the eastern areas of the Greater Caucasus within the territory of Azerbaijan, accounting for about 12% of the total solid flow of rivers (Rustamov 1954; Rustamov, Shikhailibeili, and Eiubov 1964). Over the volcanic rocks of the Minor Caucasus and the Armenian Highland, mud-flow denudation is about 75 t/km^2 per year on average.

Besides their significance for sediment transfer, mud flows create serious threats to the population and economy of Caucasia. The capital cities of Yerevan and Tbilisi are located within the zone of mud-flow threat, as are the Military-Georgian road, the Transcaucasian railway in the region of the Suram Pass, the railroads from Yerevan to Tbilisi and from Yerevan to Baku, and other important features (*Caucasia* 1966).

Population and Economy

The Caucasian region was densely populated long ago at a high level of economic and cultural advancement. Long wars and feudal conflicts, however, resulted in a significant decline in population and even in complete depopulation of some regions. At the beginning of the nineteenth century, the population of Transcaucasia amounted to 1.4 million persons, including about 700,000 in Georgia, 500,000 in Azerbaijan, and 200,000 in Armenia (*Geography of Economy . . .* 1966). At present, this region is inhabited by over 50 nationalities. Total population exceeds 26 million, and the most numerous nationalities are: Russian (8,642,000), Azerbaijan (5,458,00), Armenian (4,060,000), and Georgian (3,969,000) (Fig. 31.7).

Early settlement patterns in Caucasia evolved not only in correspondence to the suitability of environment for human life and the availability of cultivable areas, but also to a significant extent according to the concern of defense against invasions. Therefore, practically all convenient lands in the midmountains and in the lower portions of the high-mountain belt were developed before 1700. The patterns of rural settlement that evolved then have changed little until now.

The main features of this settlement system date back to the period 1780–1860, when North Caucasia, Georgia, Armenia, and Azerbaijan joined the Russian state. At that time, settlement patterns were to a certain extent determined by such military considerations as the location of fortresses, fortification works, and defense lines. The three decades from 1860 to 1890 saw a massive migration of the former serfs (who were freed in 1861) from the central and western provinces to North Caucasia. This migration resulted in the intensive agricultural colonization of practically the whole of Ciscaucasia.

The subsequent construction of railroads from Rostov-on-Don to Stavropol, Vladikavkaz (Orjonikidze), Baku, and Novorossiysk promoted industrial-commercial specialization in the region. Grain production acquired a clear commercial (even export-oriented) character, and processing industries sprang up in the cities. Oil refineries and auxiliary industries concentrated in the urban centers of Baku and Groznyi. By 1897, North Caucasia was populated by 3.8 million persons at a mean density of 20/km^2. In some areas, such as Krasnodar, Kavkaz (Tikhoretskiy), Armavir, and Piatigorsk Districts, population density was twice as high.

The political stability and sustainable socioeconomic development established after the Great October Socialist Revolution (1917) has resulted during the twentieth century in intensive economic and population growth in all of the republics of the Caucasian region. Advancement of the technologies of irrigated farming on lowlands, increases in the productivity of highly mechanized agriculture there, and

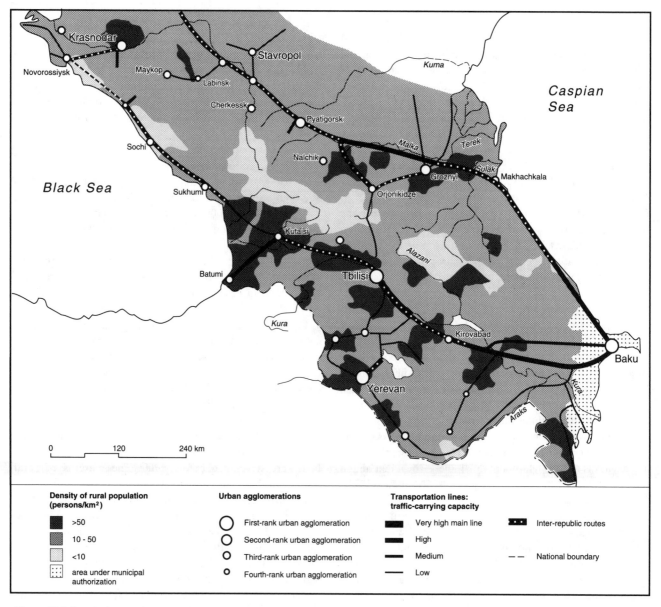

Figure 31.7 Population, settlement, and transportation, 1979.
Modified from *Atlas of the World Nations* 1964.

development of industry and transportation resulted in an outflow of population from the higher altitudinal belts to the foothills and lowlands. The consequences included the growth of cities and the formation of new settlements in the lower altitudinal belts. With local variations, the increase of population in the lower belts took place throughout the region.

The distribution of population by vertical belts, other things being equal, is a good index to the favorability of environmental conditions for human life and economy. As a rule, the upper line of permanent settlement coincides with the upper line of crop cultivation (2,000–2,400 m), but in some instances it can move even higher. For example, the *aul* (rural settlement) Kurush in Daghestan is 2,700 m above sea level (Sergeeva 1967). Below this line, patterns also vary to some extent, owing to specific features of the environments and of historical evolution.

In Georgia, an increase of population was registered in this century in all vertical belts, but it was most intensive in the lowland-foothill belt (up to 500 m). As a result, from 1926 to 1959, the proportion of mountain population (from 500 to 1,000 m) decreased from 15.7% to 11.1%. In the same period, the proportion of urban population increased from 22.2% to 42.4% (Jaoshvili 1964). High rates of industrial development, new cultivation of tens of thousands of hectares of lands in the Colchis Lowland and in dry steppes of eastern Georgia, rapid urban growth, and the emergence of new urban and rural settlements both reflected and promoted migration of the mountain population to the lowland-foothill belt. Thanks to the favorable environment, however, population is now stable or even slowly growing in mountains up to 1,500–1,800 m.

The lands suitable for cultivation and settlement in Georgia do not exceed 20% of the total area of the Republic.

According to data of 1959, about 90% of the population was concentrated in about 46% of the total area. Mean population density up to 1,000 m was 113 persons/km², and above 1,000 m it was not more than 12 persons/km² (Jaoshvili 1964).

In Armenia, half of the total population and about 67% of the urban population is concentrated on 10% of the territory, within the range of altitudes from 400 to 1,000 m. In the period from 1939 to 1959, the population of the mountain belt (1,500–2,000 m) in the Armenian SSR decreased from 46.6% to 34.4%, while rural population also decreased in absolute figures (Grgearian 1964). Growth of population in the mountain belt is hampered by its limited potential for development of agriculture and industry. The Ararat Plain is the region of the most ancient settlement. The next clusters of population in the Republic correspond to the altitudinal steps 1,500–1,600 m (Shirak Plateau) and 1,900–2,000 m (Sevan Depression). In the two latter cases, local relief conditions are especially favorable for settlement and for cultivation. Less populous is the zone 400–700 m, where arid climates and lack of convenient water sources hinder development of farming.

The influence of history on present settlement patterns is evident in Daghestan. In the period from 1890 to 1959, the major portion of the population inhabited the midmountains and the lower portion of the high-mountain belt. These altitudinal belts have the lowest amount of cultivable lands (Sergeeva 1967), but the necessity of protecting themselves from invasions from outside had driven the people to colonize these lands and to develop terrace agriculture that became widespread in the mountains of Daghestan.

From 1926 until 1959, the number of settlements in the lowland belt increased from 2.7 to 4.4/100 km². During this period, 453 new settlements appeared, while in the midmountain and high-mountain belts, their number remained practically the same. By 1959, about 26% of the rural population was concentrated in the lowland belt, up to 500 m. Together with the urban population, this belt had about 55% of the total population of the Republic (*Geography of Economy . . .* 1966). Despite the fact that rural population within the altitudinal belt 1,500–2,000 m is the most numerous, the highest density is within the range of altitudes 1,000–1,500 m, which in 1959 reached 32.1 persons/km². The trend toward above-average rates of population growth in the lowland-foothill belt will persist in Daghestan in the near future.

Population of the Kabardino-Balkarskaya ASSR increased from 112,900 to 495,600, or by 4.4 times, in the period 1890–1964 (Doguzhaev 1965). Changes of population distribution by the vertical belts in this period included a sharp depopulation of the high-mountain belt and a relative reduction of population in the lowland-foothill belt within the range of altitudes up to 500 m.

Favorable climatic conditions led to the concentration of over 55% of the population of Kabardino-Balkaria in the foothills within altitudes 300–700 m, which accounts for only 18.1% of the total area of the Republic. This area has diversified agriculture and concentrates the greater portion of the industrial facilities of the Republic (Doguzhaev 1965).

Only 31% of the population is found in the lowland belt, even though its area is greater than that of the foothills; this is due to the arid climate and limited water resources.

These data on population distribution in Caucasia can be taken as one index of human pressure on the natural environment. No less important is a very specific feature of the regional economy, the breeding of sheep and their seasonal grazing in the subalpine and alpine vertical belts. Practiced for many centuries, this form of animal-breeding is common throughout the region. It has produced, and continues to produce, a strong influence on the mountain meadows, and to a lesser degree, on the forest belt.

The Transformation of the Environment

Soil Cover

Long before 1700, the environmental background to soil genesis in Caucasia was strongly modified by anthropogenic pressures. By 1700, the regions most densely populated and modified were Transcaucasia and Daghestan within the zones of the seasonally humid and dry subtropics, the mountain steppes, and to a lesser degree the mountain forests and meadows of Georgia, Armenia, Azerbaijan, and Daghestan. Before 1700, the main agricultural lands used for dry and irrigated farming and pasturing were concentrated in these territories (Fig. 31.8). The sparse low-mountain, semidry, and dry forests were heavily felled, and the soils that developed under these forests were devoted, after clearing, to cultivation and grazing.

In Caucasia the anthropogenic pressures varied significantly by region (Fig. 31.8). Mountain meadows were used as rangelands, causing degradation of the soil humus horizons, destructuring, and partial erosion. The midmountain belt of the brown forest and podzolic soils was influenced by selective clearings with the subsequent regeneration of secondary forests, and sometimes formation of forest-grassland rangelands causing insignificant soil changes. The low-mountain and foothill forests and steppes of North Caucasia with brown forest soils (mostly pseudopodzolic), grey forest soils, chernozems, and chestnut soils were little cultivated, and were used only in fragments as rangelands, due to the comparatively low population in these regions of Caucasia.

By 1700, some 30–50% of the humid-subtropical forests of western Transcaucasia in the foothills and low mountains were cleared for plowing cultivation. In conditions of high humidity, the soils of this region (krasnozems, zheltozems, pseudopodzols) experienced partial erosion of the humus and subhumus horizons. Impacts on all elements of the landscape, including subsoil ground layers, were produced by the century-long practice of terraced agriculture on the mountain slopes of Daghestan and Transcaucasia. The semidesert and dry-steppe areas of Transcaucasia and East Caucasia were used as rangelands, with islands of irrigated farming that experienced degradation of rangeland soils and fragmented salinizations.

Up to 1700, the anthropogenic impacts over the major portion of Caucasia had a pulsatory character. Periods of

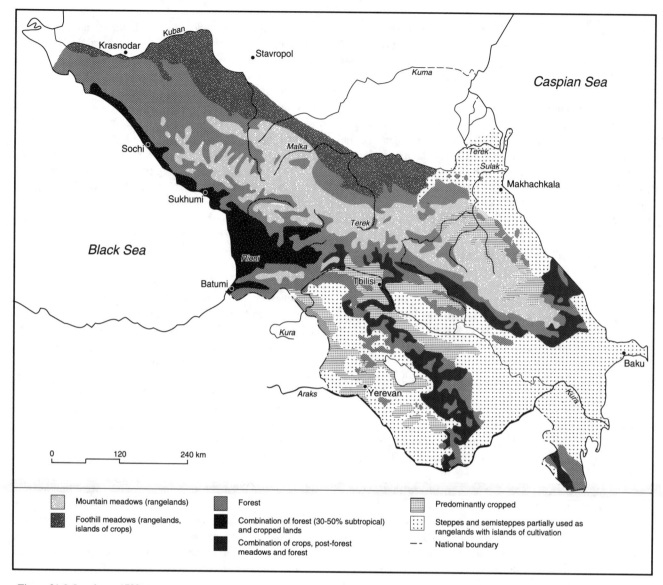

Figure 31.8 Land use, 1700.

expansion of rangeland and cultivated areas coincided with periods of peace and the consolidation of states; interruptions in cultivation and shrinking of rangelands and plowed areas coincided with invasions, local wars, and epidemics. During the latter times, many degraded soils were left fallow, revegetated and preserved from active erosion, allowing the restoration of humus and structure.

The soils in 1700 fell into the following groups:

1. natural soils and landscapes;
2. soils with degraded or modified natural vegetation, but with preserved profile (1 and 2 apparently dominant in Caucasia);
3. soils under rangelands and plowed cultivation with average or low levels of erosion and/or overcultivated (dehumified and destructured),
4. soils of ancient irrigation: reclaimed (agroirrigated) and depleted, eroded, and salinized;
5. terraced soils sand landscapes;
6. areas of "grazing" and "farming" badlands: soils eroded

to bedrock or to loose "ecologically discomfortable" mountain rocks.

Both natural and anthropogenic processes affected soils and soil covers in Caucasia. Natural impacts were of local character and their total contribution to changes of the soil cover was relatively small during the whole of the 300-year period. The principal factors of landscape and soil transformations in Caucasia for the past 300 years have definitely been of an anthropogenic character, acting over the complicated background inherited from the previous phases of development.

The main sources of anthropogenic impact on the Caucasian soil cover during the total 300-year period were and still are animal-grazing, forestry, and farming (Fig. 31.9). These impacts have drastically accelerated since the middle of the nineteenth century. The forested area has decreased by a factor of two (Fig. 31.10), plowed area has increased nearly five times, and the population of domesticated animals has increased significantly.

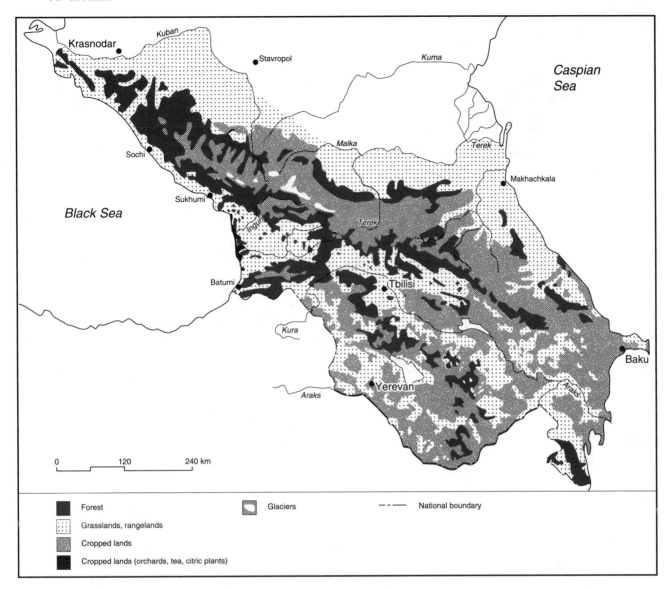

Figure 31.9 Land use, 1986.

The impacts of animal grazing can be subdivided into weak (modification of vegetable associations only), and strong (transformation of the sod and of surface soil horizons). The impact of grazing has long been felt in Caucasia; until 1700, it influenced mostly mountain meadows, and also mountain and low-mountain forests, steppes, and semideserts. For 300 years, the area of rangelands has shrunk considerably throughout Caucasia (except for mountain meadows) through their replacement by plowed lands, most extensive in the steppe and low-mountain forest zones. In consequence, the grazing pressures have significantly increased in the mountain-grassland zone and in the dry steppes and semideserts of East Caucasia and Transcaucasia. They became the regions of summer grazing for the continuously expanding animal population from the intramontane depressions and piedmont.

Forest clearing, depending on technology, area, and purpose of fellings, produces varied influences on soils. One should distinguish among:

1. Selective felling for local use, which employed "sparing" technologies of hand-felling and horse transportation in the eighteenth and nineteenth centuries;
2. Felling by machinery in the twentieth century, but on a limited area and with replacement of the cleared forests by regenerated secondary forests;
3. Clearing of forests for rangelands, cropped areas, and plantations, with continuous felling and extraction of stumps and the complete replacement of forested by cleared landscapes.

The agricultural impacts on soil vary in intensity and depth. They include:

1. Surface (shallow) disruption without irrigation, involving large areas of foothills and foothill lowlands in North Caucasia;
2. Deep disturbance of the cultivation type, widely spread in semidry and humid subtropics;
3. Terracing, the most radical reconstruction of landscapes

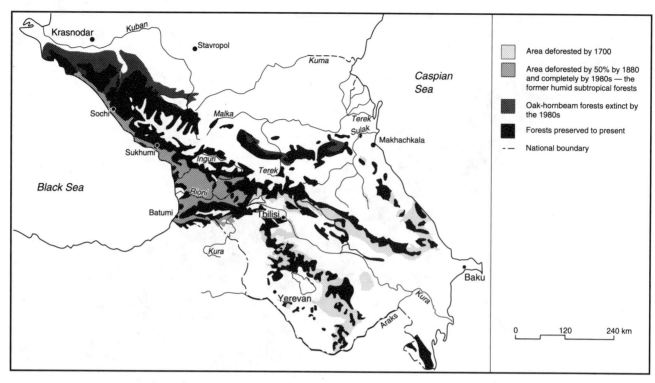

Figure 31.10 Changes in forested areas. Map compiled by A. I. Romashkevich.

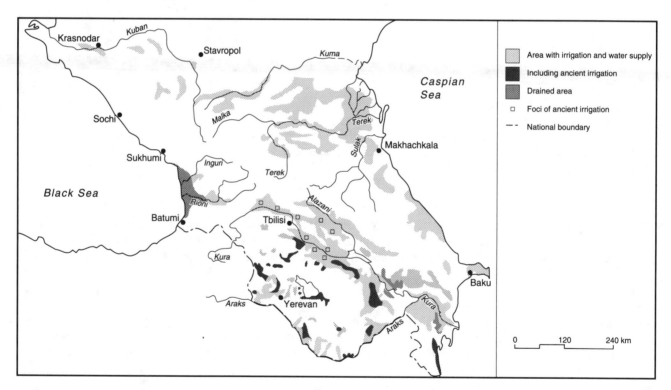

Figure 31.11 Land reclamation. Map compiled by A. I. Romashkevich.

and soils, which practically "conquered" an important portion of the humid subtropics of Georgia and was widespread in Daghestan long ago;

4. Irrigation, widely practiced in intramontane depressions, eastern coastal areas, and foothills in the northeastern regions of Caucasia (Fig. 31.11);

5. Drainage reclamations, which spread only over the Colchis in the Caucasian humid subtropics.

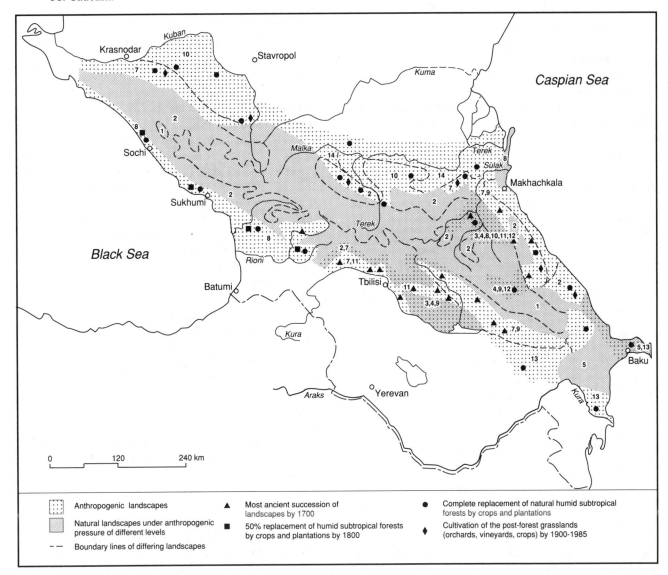

Figure 31.12 Landscape transformations. (I) Natural landscapes under different levels of digression due to anthropogenic impacts: (1) mountain meadows (humid alpine-type highlands, humid monoclines, and uplifted depressions, dry meadows of Daghestan and Azerbaijan); (2) mountain forests (beech and coniferous forests, oak and oak-hornbeam forests); (3) subtropical Andropogon steppes; (4) steppic meadows and dry steppes in combination with shibliak and phrygana; (5) semideserts; (6) coastal sands; (II) Anthropogenic landscapes: (7) cultivated areas, plantations, rangelands in the areas of the former beech, beech-hornbeam, oak-hornbeam forests, and post-forest vegetation; (8) cultivated areas, crops, plantations in the areas of the former humid subtropical forests; (9) cultivated areas, crops, and plantations (with irrigation) in the areas of the cleared light forests and post-forest vegetation; (10) plowed areas replacing foothill herb-grass steppes and steppic meadows; (11) crops and plantations replacing the subtropical Andropogon steppes; (12) crops and plantations with irrigation replacing dry steppes and steppic meadows in combination with shibliak and phrygana; (13) crops with irrigation replacing semideserts; (14) cultivated areas, including rangelands on flooded meadows, partially bogged and·salinized.

The past 300 years have witnessed a powerful shift of anthropogenic pressures on soil cover in Caucasia, mostly due to the expansion of farmland (Fig. 31.12), including plantation economy, practicing cultivation and terracing technologies. This shift in farming economy has included a major growth of irrigated farming.

The transformation patterns of soils and soil cover in the recent 300 years follow several major trends. "Natural" soils in rangeland areas have been degraded and new foci of erosion developed. There has been a sharp increase in the percentage of soils with disturbed profiles and superposition of young pedogenesis occurring in deforested areas over the total area of natural soils of forests. Soil erosion of all types (water, wind, and irrigation-induced) has intensified in the areas of new agricultural development. There has been reclamation for cultivation of the loose sedimentary rock and crusts of weathering that have been exposed by ancient and modern erosion and development of young soils. Irrigated farming has expanded significantly with different trends of soil transformations, both in irrigated soils and in soils of the adjacent areas without irrigation. Least modified under anthropogenic impacts are the soils of the mountain-forest and mountain-grassland belts that were not subject to continuous clearing and overgrazing (brown and grey forest soils, mountain-grassland soils).

Despite the diversity of anthropogenic impacts on the soils of Caucasia during the past 300 years, their most important specific feature and the major threat to future environments and human activities is expansion and intensification of soil erosion in all belts and regions of this mountain system. Comparison of the maps of transformation of natural landscapes of the Greater Caucasus (from their original state to the present) shows that during a comparatively short period, the new areas of agricultural development in Caucasia have been eroded to a degree that is comparable to that of the regions of ancient cultivation.

The expansion and intensification without antierosion measures of practically all economic activities (agriculture, animal-breeding, felling, construction, and so forth) threaten the irreversible loss of the ecologically "comfortable" loose cover necessary for the life of natural and agrotechnological systems. Formation of natural soils, crusts of weathering, and loose sediments takes thousands and even millions of years. The rate of their destruction by human-induced erosion is several orders higher. Thus, it is impossible to restore the generally shallow, loose, soil-ground cover in Caucasia, similar to other mountain countries, through natural processes within the scale of human time.

Biota

The biota of Caucasia have long been affected by land cultivation, grazing, hay-making, deforestation, and hunting. By the beginning of the twentieth century, such economic activities had become so intensive that at present the leading role in the formation of ecosystems in Caucasia belongs to such anthropogenic factors, with natural factors now of secondary importance. Recent decades have seen the addition of new types of anthropogenic impacts, such as recreation, construction, and industrial activity. Long and intensive economic development depletes the species composition, degrades the structure, decreases the productivity, and even destroys the integrity of original ecosystems, replacing them with secondary ones that are usually less valuable and less productive.

Transformation of the forest cover began with the earliest stages of human development of the region. The forests had previously occupied practically the whole of the mid-mountain belt of the Greater Caucasus, except for the dry subtropical and semidesert regions adjoining to the southeast. In the past three centuries, North Caucasia lost 1.4 million ha of forests, and Transcaucasia, 1.7 million ha (Kazankin 1984). The forest area in the Greater Caucasus had changed in the following way: from 98% to 41% in the watershed of Rioni (humid subtropical environments of Transcaucasia), from 80% to 48% in the watershed of Bolshoi Zelenchuk (north Caucasia), from 68% to 42% in the watershed of Alazan (semidry and dry subtropics of Transcaucasia), and from 50% to 60% to 8% to 11% over the total area of present-day Daghestan.

In mountain Azerbaijan and in the rest of North Caucasia (except for Daghestan), the main role in clearing of forests was played by shifting cultivation. Light forests and, to a considerable extent, the oak-hornbeam forests in the foothills and midmountains of the subtropical belt were practically cleared out. After clearing, the former forest areas were used either for cultivation or for grazing; many of the former forested areas have entered the stage of steppic or grassland associations (Shiffers 1953).

In West Caucasia at the end of the eighteenth century, the plant cover and animal population remained in an almost primeval state. Forb-grass steppes (up to 400 m), oak forests with fragments of meadow steppes and steppic meadows (800 m), beech forests (up to 1,600 m), dark-coniferous fir-spruce forests (up to 2,000 m), and subalpine high grasslands and meadows, alpine meadows, and pioneer associations of the subnival belt (above 2,000 m) represented the vertical patterns of vegetation.

In Transcaucasia, by contrast, the lowland-foothill dry and semidry subtropical forests were completely cleared as early as the Middle Ages. Semidesert and dry steppic areas of Transcaucasia and East Caucasia were used as rangelands, and in isolated spots for irrigated farming. Even under light pressures of grazing, the vegetation and soils of the semideserts changed significantly. The lowland-foothill humid subtropical forests were also destroyed long ago, although about half of them were preserved until the middle of the nineteenth century. Comparison of the profiles of the reconstructed and contemporary structures of the vertical zonation and also of the maps of reconstructed and contemporary ecosystems cover reveals the main regional and zonal types of transformations of plant and animal population (*The Alps – The Caucasus* 1980).

In the Greater Caucasus, the lowland ecosystems were completely destroyed. The northern macroslope steppe areas are nearly fully plowed for cereals, melons, and forage. Irrigated farming produces soil salinization and development of secondary halophyte associations. Over dry hill slopes, islands of degraded steppes are used for grazing. These associations are characterized by low cover, insignificant grass height, and an abundance of rangeland weeds. At present, the animal population of the steppe is composed basically of some specialized pests of crops and a small group of species adapted to the high level of economic development. Because of plowing, many typical steppe species have almost completely disappeared, such as the bustard and the steppe eagle. In the foothill forest-steppe, the islands of oak forests are nearly completely cleared out. Suitable areas are used for cultivation. Those unsuitable for cultivation are used for orchards. Large areas are occupied by hay-making and grazing lands.

In the lower part of the forest belt, small areas of secondary oak-hornbeam and hornbeam forests have formed after selective felling, replacing the oak forests. Large areas over fully deforested gradual slopes are occupied by postforest steppic grasslands and grass steppes with curtains of shrub used for hay-making and grazing. This technology of exploitation of associations results in depletion of species composition, spread of weeds, and degraded ecosystem structures.

On the southern macroslope of the Great Caucasus, the

greatest damage due to economic activities occurs in the low-mountain oak forests, the subtropical broad-leaved forests of the western and central parts, and the steppic and semidesert ecosystems of the eastern part. The mediterranean forests of pubescent oak have been cleared from vast areas. What was left was transformed into growth of shrubs of oaks and oriental hornbeam, into shibliak (growth of thornbush), or into secondary steppe vegetation. Mixed, broad-leaved subtropical forests are now replaced by agricultural lands. The crops include tea, citric plants, mulberry, tobacco, and also maize. In places, islands of forests are still found, but they too are being transformed into degraded hornbeam forests and thick thornbush. Oak forests on the southern macroslope are replaced by hornbeam forests after selective felling, and, after complete felling aggravated by grazing, by the growth of oriental hornbeam, shibliak, and phrygana-type vegetation. Thus, in the low-mountain belts of Transcaucasia, irrespective of the indigenous types of forest or the humidity of the climate, the vegetation cover becomes more uniform under anthropogenic pressures.

Beech and dark coniferous forests of the Greater Caucasus growing in midmountains in conditions of sufficient humidity have been damaged less in the past 300 years than the low-mountain oak forests. After selective felling in beech forests, pure hornbeam or maple-tree growth has developed, and in fir-spruce forests, maple trees. Both types of forests after complete clearing, however, are replaced by shrubs and high grasses.

In high-mountain belts, the subalpine and alpine meadows are subject to two major agents of change, hay-making and grazing. Due to hay-making, on the north-facing slopes and on southern slopes of west Caucasia in conditions of excessive humidity, high-grass subalpine meadows with curtains of shrub are formed. On cut-over meadows of the dry southern slopes in central and east Caucasia, the elements of high grasses disappear, the number of moisture-loving species decreases, and the subalpine middle-grass meadows spread.

On the grazed areas of meadows, the grass cover decreases in height and density, and productivity goes down sharply. Intensive grazing produces degradation of the species composition of meadow associations; on humid and dry slopes in the high mountains of the Greater Caucasus, low-grass high-mountain meadows are formed. In this case, the species patterns change: some middle partly-rosette and soddy grasses disappear, and are replaced by grazing-resistant and stamping-resistant, low-grass rosette species and by rapidly growing, soddy, densely tufted grasses and sedges. Because of weak competition, inedible and poisonous species are spreading. Such light-demanding species as xeromesophytes, petrophytes, and talus become more diversified.

Anthropogenic pressures in the Greater Caucasus have deformed and degraded ecosystem structures. Disturbance of continuity promotes sharp transitions from steppe to forest communities, and from forest to meadow communities in the disappearance of the forest-steppe and forest-meadow strips – lowering the resistance of the biota to ecological and anthropogenic pressures.

Economic activities have produced a simplification of the

ecosystems of the Greater Caucasus. The character of transformations and the resistance or degradation of ecosystems depend on the form of economic impact, on the intensity of land use, and on the environmental situation, especially on the moisture supply on the slopes. Thus, the level of transformation of ecosystems under similar pressures is higher in East and Central Caucasia than in humid West Caucasia, and over dry southern slopes as compared to moister northern slopes. The transformation of ecosystems also increases from the midmountains to the lowlands and highlands.

Hydrology

Human impacts on water resources and natural runoff in Caucasia involve mostly water withdrawal for consumption by population and industry, for irrigation of cultivated areas, and for production of electric power. Human transformation of vegetation, soils, and the geological substratum has also changed the water regime, but these changes have differed throughout the region. On the whole, human-induced transformations in the region from 1700 to the 1920s remained within the limits of the natural fluctuations of the water systems. The essential hydrological problem of that period was the adaptation of population and economy to the natural runoff regime and to the technology of water supply. The case of one of the most water-intensive industries, irrigated farming, provides an illustration.

Irrigated farming in the heat-abundant, arid lowlands and foothills of the region is an age-old practice. In Armenia, Azerbaijan, and Daghestan, fields were irrigated as early as the first millennium A.D. In North Caucasia, irrigation became important after the middle of the nineteenth century. As population fluctuated in these regions, irrigated areas remained small and dispersed. Water withdrawals for irrigation were limited and did not significantly influence the regimes of rivers and the other sources. A shortage of water

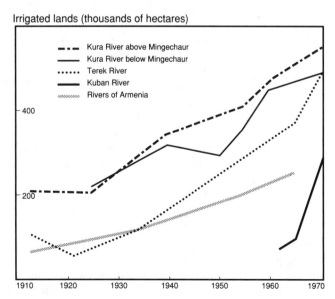

Figure 31.13 Changes in irrigated lands.

for irrigation was noticed only in years of unusually low flow.

A significant and uninterrupted increase in irrigated area started in the second and third decades of the twentieth century (Fig. 31.13). From the 1920s to 1970, the irrigated area in the Kura-Araks basin increased by 2.7 times. A remarkable expansion of reclamation has also been registered in the past 30 to 35 years, and has included drainage of low bog lands, elimination of reed growth, construction of several water reservoirs, and increased water consumption by industry and municipal users. Within eastern Georgia, 20,000 ha had been drained by 1970.

Increased economic activities in the Kura watershed and reclamation projects reduced the mean annual runoff by 5%, and in years of low runoff, by 15–20% (Shiklomanov and Smirnov 1973). In 1970, total irreversible losses of water for economic consumption in the watershed of Kura down to Mingechaur were assessed at 5 km³/yr.

More important changes of runoff took place at the tributaries of the Kura River, and especially in the upper elements of its left-bank hydrographic net. Thus, in the watershed of the Alazen River from 1917 to 1960, the irrigated area increased by nearly seven times and annual runoff decreased by 13% (Kochiashvili and Marianashvili 1980). A high population density and high level of economic development in the area resulted in the serious depletion of water resources. The situation in this region is aggravated by the fact that the time of maximum water consumption does not coincide with the seasonal peak of river runoff (Kolesnikov 1980).

The rather low net changes in the mean annual runoff of the Kura River, despite the growing intensity of direct and indirect impacts on water resources, can be attributed to compensating effects on the water budget of the area (Glinskaya 1982). Flooding of moisture-demanding vegetation by reservoirs (evapotranspiration from this vegetation was assessed at 1,600–1,800 mm/yr [*Resources of Surface Waters*, 1971]), and draining of bog lands have considerably lowered the total evapotranspiration from the watershed. Thus, evaporation even from the surface of water reservoirs in this region does not exceed 1,000 mm/yr (Shiklomanov and Smirnov 1973). An additional compensating factor is the better drainage of soil-ground waters by the diversified network of channels of irrigation systems.

The natural potential of the rivers of the Kura watershed to absorb anthropogenic pressures is now exhausted. Further increases in water consumption will produce a rapid and significant decrease in runoff. The sustainable development of water-using industries and the maintenance of the natural potential of the territory in the optimal state require more economical use of water.

In the watershed of the Terek River, intensive development of irrigation began in the 1920s. From 1914 to 1970, the irrigated area increased almost eightfold, from 650 km² to 5,000 km². The major withdrawal for irrigation is in the middle part of the river; here, the mechanism of natural compensation for this withdrawal described for the Kura River does not operate. As a result, in a decade 1960–1970, the annual runoff of the Terek River was reduced by about 20%, and in the warm season by 25% (Shiklomanov and Smirnov 1973). Runoff of this river in the 1980s was about 50% below the level of 1970.

Between 1960 and 1970, the irrigated area in the watershed of the Kuban River increased by 3.7 times. Due to the destruction of vegetation on floodplains in the lower part of the river and the better draining of the basin by the irrigation network, however, this increase did not produce any significant decrease in the annual runoff of the river. Only in the low-water years, such as 1969 and 1970, did human impact result in a lowering of the annual runoff by as much as 15% (Shiklomanov and Smirnov 1973).

Another type of transformation of water resources of an area is illustrated by the watershed of the Rioni River, which drains most of very humid western Georgia. The draining of the Colchis lowland bogs (about 500 km²), the irrigation of about 380 km², and the construction of several hydropower plants with reservoirs on the main river and its tributaries are the main human impacts on natural waters in the watershed under study in the twentieth century. An outcome was a noticeable increase in the annual runoff of the Rioni River. According to an assessment made by Khamaladze (1982), between 1937 and 1975 the annual runoff of the Rioni River increased by 20%; the author attributes this phenomenon both to human impact and to higher precipitation in western Georgia in this period. Although the role of anthropogenic factors in this case is uncertain, one can surely affirm that reclamation of the lowland areas of the river watershed has improved the drainage system, and thus has reduced water loss by evaporation.

In the Armenian SSR, the total area with soils transformed by irrigation throughout the historical time is about 1,200 km². In different periods, the irrigated area was different, but never above this level. By the beginning of the 1920s, irrigated land in Armenia covered no more than 600 km², but by 1971 that number had increased up to 2,620 km², or 4.4 times (Ananian 1974).

In Armenia, the sources of water are rivers, the Sevan Lake, and groundwater. The average river runoff formed in the territory of Armenia is 6.3 km³, and withdrawal of groundwater, about 1 km³ (Ananian 1974). Total demand of water by population and economy is now assessed at approximately 2.3–2.7 km³ per year, including 1.8–2.1 km³ per year accounted for by irrigated farming. This demand has required the use of all sources of water and has created significant pressures on several water bodies.

To use the favorable natural conditions for the generation of hydropower, several reservoirs were constructed on rivers in Caucasia during the twentieth century. In most cases, the goal was only producing power, but these reservoirs also improved water supply to irrigated farming, industry, and cities, and regulated the unfavorable effects on the economy of floods and periods of low water. By 1985, the number of water reservoirs in Transcaucasia had reached 53 (Georgia, 14; Armenia, 24; Azerbaijan, 15) and five more reservoirs were completed on the Inguri, Aragvi, Kura, Algeti, and Vorotan rivers (Metreveli 1985).

Most of the impoundments were constructed in Transcaucasia in the past four decades. Several of them have formed cascades of reservoirs. Because about 80% of the reservoirs are in mountains, they have submerged relatively small areas. Several natural lakes also had been transformed into reservoirs, such as Arpa Lake and Kumisi Lake. The storage capacity of several reservoirs permits the multiyear control of river runoff. The full volumes of the largest Transcaucasian water reservoirs are: Mingechaur, 16 km³; Javar, 1.09 km³; and Araks, 1.35 km³ (Shiklomanov and Smirnov 1973; Metreveli 1985).

Due to the massive amount of construction of large and small reservoirs, the anthropogenic impact upon the hydrological cycle has sharply increased in the region. The artificial supply of large quantities of water to watersheds for irrigation and the infiltration of water from reservoirs to indigenous rocks in some areas significantly transform the water budget within the foothills and lowlands.

Coastal Areas

The indirect consequences of water impoundment, combined with other anthropogenic and natural factors, can be seen in the disturbance of the stability of the coastal zones of the Caspian and Black seas. The persistent trend toward lower discharge of rivers in the region and the diverse economic activities within the river watersheds have greatly affected the coasts of the two inland seas.

Until the 1880s, there was a net aggradation of the coast at the Colchis depression. Subsequently, accumulation was replaced by ever-increasing erosion, which now occurs at the rate of 2–5 m/yr (Zenkovich 1987). At some points on the Black Sea coast, this process has had catastrophic effects, when the zone of coastal disturbance has encroached upon the transportation and settlement networks. Acute destabilization of the coastline stemmed from the decrease of sediment load because of construction of dams and mining of loose material in river channels and hydrotechnical construction in the coastal zone. The following examples illustrate the magnitude of such impacts. Since the construction of the Inguri Hydro Power Plant in 1978, transportation of beach-forming sediments by the Inguri River has decreased from 369,300 m³ to 29,400 m³; 24% of 2.5 million m³ of beach-forming rock transported by the Chorokh River are mined from the river channel for construction purposes, 73% migrate to the abyssal zone of the Black Sea, and only 3% move to the sea coast (Jaoshvili 1987).

Erosion of the beaches of the coast of the Caspian Sea began around 1970. The erosion, which gradually has become more intense, has now reached the rate of 1–4 m/yr, and in some areas, 15 m/yr and more (Gvozdetskiy 1974). Again, the main reason for the development of this process was reduction of sediment load by economic activities in the watersheds. According to preliminary assessments, annual transportation of sediments by rivers to the western coast of the Caspian Sea has decreased from 50 million m³ to 27–29 million m³. Construction of the Mingechaur water reservoir on the Kura River in 1953 reduced its solid runoff from 18.3 million m³/yr to 7–9 million m³/yr.

The rapid transformation of the coastal zone of the Caspian Sea can be accounted for by a combination of factors: the reduction of solid runoff from rivers because of construction of hydropower plants, withdrawal of large volumes of river water for irrigation, and continuing increase in sea level. All this results in losses of agricultural lands, threatens coastal enterprises, and hinders recreational development.

The disturbance of coastal stability in the Caucasian region illustrates the anthropogenic aggravation of natural trends in regions that evolve under the influence of both local processes of land-sea interaction and processes going on in vast river watersheds. Human actions have sharply accelerated the transformation of sea coasts and have hampered adaptation of population and economy to the changing environments.

Summary and Comments

By 1700, the beginning of the period under study, Caucasia had already undergone a long history of uninterrupted economic development. The areas most actively developed were the semidry and dry subtropics. Grassland and forest ecosystems of Caucasia had been only weakly transformed. The period from 1780 to 1890 – after the incorporation of North Caucasia, Georgia, Armenia, and Azerbaijan into the Russian Empire – was the time of large-scale development of natural resources and of cultivation of new lands, mostly in the lowlands and foothills of North Caucasia. The principal outlines of present settlement were formed at that period, both by an influx of immigrants from Russia and by intraregional migration.

The 1920s saw the beginning of rapid growth in population and in the number of settlements in the foothills, lowlands, and plains. These regions saw the active development of irrigation, industry, and transportation. Pressure on forest resources and rangelands also increased. In this period, the clearing of the main forests in the foothills and lowlands was completed, and the lands were converted to cultivation. The shrinking area of pasture-lands in the lowlands and foothills increased the pressure of grazing on all forest ecosystems, and especially on the alpine meadows. The deep transformation of the vegetation cover also produced radical changes in soils, including disturbance of soil profiles, reduction of fertility and acceleration of erosion. Rapid growth of water consumption and control of river runoff in recent decades has disturbed the hydrological regimes. Urgent ecological problems have accompanied the overall positive effect of land reclamation: disturbance of equilibrium in the coastal zone (because of shortage of sediment) and erosion of the beaches of the Black Sea coast.

The present state and the trends of transformation of the Caucasian landscape in the system of economy that had evolved by the mid-1980s can be distinguished by altitudinal zone.

The nival-glacial alpine belt shows a continuation of the natural trends of change. The main human impacts are from tourism and recreation. In the mountain-meadow belt, the factors of transformation are grazing (with seasonal migrations of animals) within the whole belt and limited island-type mining, resulting in the destruction of vegetation cover and the transformation of soils through consolidation, loss of humus, and erosion down to bedrock, creating stony deserts. The pressure of grazing continues to increase. Mining requires localized withdrawal of lands suitable for cultivation. These impacts are constantly expanding in magnitude and intensity.

The mountain-forest belt at present experiences less anthropogenic pressure than does any other zone save the nival-glacial. It has contracted in extent due to felling at the lower and upper timberline; at the upper timberline, the risk of avalanches has increased. The lower timberline has risen because of expansion of the plowed areas (especially in the subtropics and in the Black Sea coastal region). Indigenous forests are replaced by secondary ones, and pine-forest planting increases the area of monoculture. Expansion of preserves helps to stabilize natural processes.

In the mountain-steppe belt, cropland is expanding at the expense of rangelands. Techniques of dry farming intensify wind and water erosion. Development of irrigation carries along with its significant positive effect (reclamation of soils), certain negative effects as well (salinization and bogging).

The semideserts, including the intramontane depressions of North Caucasia, are in active use for winter grazing and irrigated farming. Vast areas are intensively reclaimed. The humid subtropics have been developed for tea and citrus fruits, with transformation of relief and soils. Erosion is sharply accelerated by the construction of terraces, especially on crusts of weathering. In the coastal zone of the Black and Caspian seas, land has also been withdrawn for recreational and transport use.

These conclusions are of a rather specific character, but they can be generalized to apply to most of the mountain regions of the world. Such problems of development as activation of erosion, degradation of rangelands, and disturbance of the hydrological regime of mountain rivers are present in most mountain countries, although differing in magnitudes, intensity, and significance. Analysis of the historical processes of nature transformation in Caucasia makes it possible to formulate several general principles explaining the successive changes in the colonization and development of a mountain territory.

The first is *the principle of inherited development.* The regions of the longest history of occupation and development are the ones most highly subject to the processes of transformation. Contemporary areas display this general trend of the attraction of population and economy to the place with the most "comfortable" conditions for development.

The principle of inherited development is linked with another interesting phenomenon, *the principle of adaptation to risk.* The essence of this principle is that the stability of settlement and economic development in "comfortable" conditions ignores the known risk of natural catastrophe. A vivid illustration is the rebuilding of cities that are periodically destroyed by earthquakes, such as Shemakha. The adaptation of population to the conditions of habitat "annihilates the memory" of the catastrophes.

The third principle is that of *polarized development.* In the process of historical development, economic activities and environmental transformations become more and more spatially concentrated. Lowlands and river valleys undergo the most active development against a background of decelerated highland development. The formation of secondary growth foci (recreation, hydropower industry, and mining) in the mountains displays this trend at a different scale.

In mountain areas, the *territorial discontinuity of the "factors" and "consequences"* is evident. Deforestation in highlands (the factor) produces landslides, mudflows, and deterioration of conditions for economic activities in river valleys and lowlands (consequences). In the same way, control of runoff of mountain rivers leads to beach erosion in the coastal zone.

Finally, *the principle of natural instability in mountains* is predetermined by the high dissection of the topography and the high potential of mass and energy circulation, responsible for the fragility of the mountain ecosystems and the higher risks of resource development and economic activities.

Disregard or deliberate violation of these general principles produces acute ecological problems. The euphoria of technological omnipotence should give way to realistic scientific analysis, taking into account the age-old experience and traditions of human life in mountains.

References (titles translated from the Russian)

Agricultural Atlas of the USSR. 1960. Moscow: GUGK.

Akinfieva, K. V. 1970. The Caucasus. In *Avalanche-Prone Regions of the Soviet Union.* Moscow: Moscow University Press.

Ananian, A. K. 1974. The Sevan Lake and the problems of land reclamation in the Ararat Valley. In *Reclamation with Water in the USSR*, 65–70. Moscow: Nauka.

Atlas of the Armenian SSR. 1961. Yerevan-Moscow.

Atlas of the Azerbaijan SSR. 1963. Naku-Moscow: GUGK.

Atlas of the Chechen-Ingush ASSR. 1978. Moscow: GUGK.

Atlas of the Daghestan ASSR. 1980. Moscow: GUGK.

Atlas of the Georgian SSR. 1964. Tbilisi-Moscow: GUGK.

Atlas of the North-Osetin ASSR. 1967. Moscow: GUGK.

Atlas of the Stavropol Krai. 1968. Moscow: GUGK.

Atlas of the World Nations. 1964. Moscow: GUGK/Institute of Ethnography named after N. N. Miklukho-Maklai.

Bazilevich, N. I. 1986. New maps of ecosystems' productivity in the USSR and the quantitative ratios of their primary and secondary production. In *All-Union Workshop on General Problems of Biogeocenology, Abstracts*, 33–35. Moscow: USSR Academy of Sciences.

Belanovskaya, E. A., R. P. Zimina, and E. V. Yasnyi. 1984. The Greater Caucasus: vegetation and animal population. In *The Greater Caucasus – Stara Planina.* Moscow: Nauka.

Caucasia. 1966. Moscow: Nauka.

Davydova, M. V. 1986. Productivity of the mountain-steppic rangelands of the Caucasus. In *Productivity of Haying Grounds and Rangelands*, 70–73. Novosibirsk: Nauka.

Doguzhaev, V. B. 1965. Vertical belticity in distribution of economy and population of Kabarda-Balkaria, 25–33. *Proceedings of MGU.* Series V. Geography, No. 6.

Gabeev, M. D. 1971. The state and prospects of reclamation of the mountain rangelands and haying grounds of the North Caucasus. In *Geographical Problems of Research and Development of Resources of the Lower Don and Northern Caucasus*, 155–56. Rostov-on-Don.

Gasanov, Sh. G. 1985. Land resources in mountain regions of the Azerbaijan SSR. In *Problems of Socioeconomic Development of the Mountain Regions.* Yerevan.

Geography of Economy of the Transcaucasian Republics. 1966. Moscow: Nauka.

Glinskaya, L. V. 1982. Structure of water budget of the irrigated territories of Eastern Georgia. *Proceedings of ZakRNII* 77(83): 125–31.

Golubev, G. N., M. B. Diurgerov, and V. A. Markin. 1978. The Janukat Glacier. In *Ice, Water, and Heat Budget in the Mountain-Glacial Basins of the USSR*. Leningrad: Hydrometeorology Press.

Grgearian, A. K. 1964. Distribution of population of the Armenian SSR by vertical belts. In *Geography of Population in the USSR: Major Problems*, 230–38. Moscow-Leningrad: Nauka.

Gvozdetskiy, N. A. 1954. *Physical Geography of the Caucasus.* Moscow: Moscow University Press.

———. 1958. *Physical Geography of the Caucasus*. Lectures, Part II. Moscow: Moscow University Press.

———. 1974. *Mountain Countries of the European USSR and Caucasus*. Moscow: Nauka.

Isakov, Yu. A., R. P. Zimina, and D. V. Panfilov. 1966. Animal life of the Caucasus. In *Caucasus*, 256–306. Moscow: Nauka.

Jaoshvili, V. Sh. 1964. Principal shifts in vertical distribution of population in Georgia. In *Modern Problems of Geography. Scientific Reports of the Soviet Geographers to XXth International Geographical Congress*, 66–71. London. Moscow: Nauka.

———. 1987. Budget of solid sediments in the river-mouth – coastal areas of Georgia. In *Natural Foundations of Coast Protection*, 57–62. Moscow: Nauka.

Kaloev, B. A. 1981. *Agriculture of the Nationalities of Northern Caucasia*. Moscow: Nauka.

Karachaevo-Cherkessia at the 50th Anniversary of the USSR. 1972. Cherkessk: Stavropol Publishing House.

Kazankin, A. P. 1984. Assessment of the level of anthropogenic degradation of mountain ecosystems on the basis of changes in forested area in river watersheds: The case of the Caucasus and Tien Shan. *Ecology* 6:12–17.

Khamaladze, G. N. 1982. Influence of anthropogenic activities on river runoff of Rioni and Kura. *Proceedings of ZakRNII* 77 (83):10–23. Leningrad: Hydrometeorology Press.

Kochiashvili, B. M., and M. A. Marianashvili. 1980. On assessment of the influence of irrigation on annual runoff of the Alazan River, *Proceedings of ZakRNII* 72(78):43–48.

Koford, A. A. 1903. The Black Sea province agriculture. *Proceedings of the Emperor's Royal Geographical Society* 39:571–616.

Kolesnikov, V. I. 1980. On the problem of use of the Kura River waters, and of resources of its tributaries. *Proceedings of ZakRNII* 72(78):25–29.

Kotliakov, V. M. 1966. An attempt to calculate water reserves accumulated in mountain glaciers of the Soviet Union. *Proceedings of the USSR Academy of Sciences*. Geographical Series 3:43–48.

Kovalevskiy, P. I. 1915. *Caucasus. Vol. II: The History of the Conquest of the Caucasus*. St. Petersburg.

Kuteeva, E. N. 1963. *Nations of the Northern Caucasus and Their Relations with Russia from the Second Half of the 16th Century to the 1730s*. Moscow: Nauka.

Metreveli, G. S. 1985. *Water Reservoirs of Transcaucasia: The Armenian and Georgian SSRs*. Leningrad: Hydrometeorology Press.

Miagkov, S. M. 1979. History of climate in our era in Europe and its relationship with the problem of rhythmicity and prognosis of trends of the glacial processes. In *Rhythms of Glacial Processes*, 7–23. Moscow: Moscow University Press.

Resources of Surface Waters in the USSR. 1971. Vol. 9, issue 4. Leningrad: Hydrometeorology Press.

Rustamov, S. G., E. M. Shikhailibeili, and E. D. Eiubov. 1964. Azerbaijan. In *Mudflows in the USSR and Counteraction*. Moscow: Nauka.

Serebrianyi, L. R., N. A. Golodkovskaya, and E. O. Ilves. 1979. Oscillations of glaciers in the Caucasian highlands in the historical period, by lichenometric and radiocarbon data. *Proceedings of the VGO* 1:11–18.

———. 1981. On the history of anthropogenic impact on highland vegetation in the central Caucasus. In *Anthropogenic Factors in Evolution of the Modern Ecosystems*, 113–25. Moscow: Nauka.

Sergeeva, K. P. 1967. Distribution of rural population in the Daghestan ASSR by vertical belts. *Reports of the Sections and Commissions of the USSR Geographical Society. Vol. I, Economic Geography*, 101–14, Leningrad.

Shiffers, E. V. 1953. *Vegetation of the North Caucasus and Its Natural and Forage Lands*. Moscow-Leningrad: Press of the USSR Academy of Sciences.

Shiklomanov, I. A., and L. E. Smirnov. 1973. Impact assessment of economic activities on the runoff of the major rivers of the Caucasus (Kura, Terek, Kuban). *Proceedings of the State Hydrological Institute*, issue 206, 92–121. Leningrad.

Tembotov, A. K. 1972. *Geography of Mammals in the Northern Caucasus*. Nalchik: Elbrus.

The Alps – The Caucasus: Modern Problems of Constructive Geography of Mountain Counties. 1980. Moscow: Nauka.

The Greater Caucasus – Stara Planina (the Balkans). 1984. Moscow: Nauka.

Tuskinskiy, G. K., and V. I. Turmanina. 1979. The rhythms of glacial processes in the recent millennium. In *Rhythms of the Glacial Processes*, 154–60. Moscow: Moscow University Press.

Vakhushti Bagrationi. 1904. *Geography of Georgia*. Translated by M. G. Jaoshvili. ZKORGO, Tiflis 24, issue 5.

Vazhnov, A. N. 1966. *Analysis and Prediction of Runoff of the Caucasian Rivers*. Moscow: Moscow Section of the Hydrometeorology Press.

Vendrov, S. L., and K. N. Diakonov. 1976. *Water Reservoirs and the Environment*. Moscow: Nauka.

Vereshchagina, A. K. 1959. *Mammals of the Caucasus*. Moscow-Leningrad: Press of the USSR Academy of Sciences.

Voskresenskiy, S. S. 1968. *Geomorphology of the USSR*. Moscow: Higher School Publishing House.

Yasnyi, Ye. V. 1968. Anthropogenic transformation of biogeocenoses in the piedmont forest-steppe of the Northern Caucasus. *All-Union Workshop on the General Problems of Biogeocenoses. Abstracts of Reports*, 33–35. Moscow: Press of the USSR Academy of Science.

Yermakov, A. V., and V. E. Yoganson. 1957. Conditions for mudflow formation at the Terek tributaries in the region of the Military-Georgian Highway. In *Mudflows and Counteraction*. Moscow: Press of the USSR Academy of Sciences.

Yoganson, V. E. 1959. Mudflows in the region of the Military-Georgian Highway and hydrometeorological conditions of their formation. *Proceedings of the Third All-Union Hydrological Congress*, Vol. 7, 231–40. Section of Hydrology, Leningrad: Hydrometeorological Press.

Zenkovich, V. P. 1987. Studies of the Black Sea coastline within Georgia. In *Natural Foundations of Shore Protection*, 45–51. Moscow: Nauka.

32

East African Highlands

LEONARD BERRY   LAURENCE A. LEWIS   CARA WILLIAMS

The East African highland region has no standard demarcations, despite the common vernacular use of the term. Here the region is defined as the higher elevated areas of Burundi, Kenya, Rwanda, Tanzania, and Uganda. Some uses of the term include the highlands of Ethiopia, but these have been excluded from this assessment because of their geologic and climatic differences with the highlands under discussion.

The East African highlands, including both uplands and montane areas, are vital from several perspectives. They serve as the major area of water supply for most East African river basins, as well as a major component of supply for the Nile River system, as a source of diverse plant types, as lands of high agricultural potential and production, and as areas themselves supporting dense populations. Only about 3% of Kenya and Tanzania regularly receive annual rainfall in excess of potential evapotranspiration (Morgan 1973:109). Furthermore, only 15% of Kenya receives over 750 mm of rain in 4 out of 5 years, and most of these areas are in the highlands. This precipitation is the limit of profitable maize growing. Over 80% of Rwanda and Burundi have rainfall in excess of 750 mm (Lewis and Berry 1988:249). Because of their relatively good moisture conditions, the highlands are crucial for meeting the present and future food and water demands of their immediate countries and of those situated downstream (Sudan and Egypt).

The past 300 years have been a period of profound environmental change in the highlands: from forest to cultivation, from sparse to dense population, from paleotechnic to neotechnic commercial farming systems, and from rural to metropolitan occupance. The region has witnessed environmental adjustments to population fluctuations and changes in the political organization of production. During the past 50 years in particular, population densities have increased significantly, and commercial agriculture has gradually become more important. These demographic and socioeconomic changes have major implications for land use and the consequent state of the environment.

The current mosaic of highland environments was created by the historical action of spatially differentiated factors of change. This chapter examines the nature of change in the highlands, focusing on several areas in particular, owing to the scarcity of historical data for the region in general. Specific sites were chosen to illustrate the particular manifestations of change in individual places, as well as to indicate trends in the general environmental condition of the region.

Highland Environments and Society in East Africa

Environment

In terms of climate, soils, and vegetation, the highlands are distinctive and potentially productive environments for various uses; the combination of advantages has attracted agriculturalists from the surrounding lower areas. Highland environments differ significantly from lowlands in regard to climate, soils, and vegetation. Even so, delineation of the boundary between the two in terms of the biota and the types of ecosystems remains a matter for debate.

The natural upland vegetation of East Africa corresponds to broad altitudinal belts. While it is commonly assumed that the gradual decrease in temperature with altitude is the primary cause of this zonation, available water, net solar radiation, competition, and human activity must also be considered. The natural vegetation existing at any elevation does reflect overall moisture conditions to some degree; one approach to explaining the altitudinal zonation is based on "effective rainfall" as it describes potential conditions for plant growth.

Anderson (1982) found that, in the vicinity of Mt. Kilimanjaro, the average rainfall for the upper (1,460–1,820 m a.s.l.), middle (1,160–1,460 m), and lower (850–1,160 m) altitudinal zones was 1,839 mm, 1,352 mm, and 976 mm, respectively. The effectiveness of this rainfall increases with elevation because of the decrease in potential evapotranspiration with altitude resulting from lower temperatures and the decreasing solar irradiation due to cloud cover. Potential evapotranspiration is over 2,500 mm/yr in the semiarid and arid areas of Kenya and Tanzania, based on Penman's (1948) method of estimation. In the cloudier and cooler highlands (above 2,750 m), it is 1,000 mm or less. Although these estimates of moisture demand are higher than actual evapotranspiration, the relations of altitude to moisture conditions are evident.

Rainfall is not uniform within altitudinal zones. Slope aspect, wind systems, air currents, and proximity to the ocean play a part in determining the precipitation characteristics at any highland locale. Seasonality of rainfall is associated with the latitudinal shifting of the sun. The Kenyan highlands and Kilimanjaro have "long rains" in April and May and "short rains" in November and December. Rwanda's highlands likewise have two major rainy seasons, which occur in September to December and February to May (Division de Climatologie 1985).

Two main schools of thought exist regarding the nature of altitudinal variation in biota. By one group, the forest vegetation is divided into two well-defined and altitudinally distinct ecosystems – lowland and montane – with few species transgressing the boundary between them. Moreau (1966) argued that this boundary normally lay at an altitude of about 500 m during the Pleistocene. He recognized that a number of species occurred in patches of montane forest geographically isolated from one another, and believed that the biotic homogeneity of montane forests was due to the spread of species during glacial periods. During glaciations, the combination of lower temperatures and enhanced rainfall was responsible for lowering the lowland/montane forest boundary by 500 m, allowing a great increase in the extent of montane forest in tropical Africa. The boundary retreated to today's higher levels with the end of the Pleistocene.

The second school of thought holds that on a broad geographic scale, there is continuous biotic change in forest composition with increasing altitude and that boundary demarcation is, therefore, arbitrary. Hamilton (1982), a proponent of this view, argues that researchers in East Africa generally have been inclined to accept a sharp division between lowland and montane forests because in drier areas forests appear at about 2,000 m. In humid areas, the altitudinal band between 1,500 and 2,000 m has proved attractive to cultivators, resulting in widespread forest destruction. The lower boundary for a "montane" forest was consequently often set at a level that is too high (2,000 m) in humid cultivated zones.

For the purpose of this chapter, a lower boundary of 1,000–1,500 m defines the highland environments of East Africa (Fig. 32.1). The area thus defined is distributed as follows: 19 million ha in Tanzania, 11 million ha in Kenya, 3 million ha in Uganda, and 1.5 million ha each in Burundi and Rwanda (Lewis and Berry 1988:246–48). The choice of this boundary reflects a loose interpretation of "natural vegetation" zones and the understanding that human activity over the past 400 to 500 years has gradually transformed the natural environment. The East African highlands are a discontinuous region covering some 360,000 km^2.

Parent materials, climate, topography, age, vegetation, and land use interact to produce a considerable variety of soil types in this region. In the highlands, climate and topography play especially important roles. Regions with an average rainfall of 1,500–2,000 mm or more nearly always have red soils, or oxisols. Given sufficient rainfall and free soil drainage, these red soils develop over a wide range of parent materials. Topography determines soil drainage at specific points on the slope. The combined effects of increased rainfall with altitude and variable leaching rates for each slope segment create distinctive soil series in the highlands. Milne (1935) developed the idea of "soil catena" to describe parts of East Africa with these characteristic bands of soil associated with the undulating topography.

Political Economy and Land Tenure

The Precolonial Period   It is, perhaps, an erroneous oversimplification to view the socioeconomic and land-tenure systems of the precolonial period as uniform, particularly in a region marked by various combinations of agriculturalists, pastoralists, and agropastoralists, and by an ethnic diversity including Nilo-Hamitic and Bantu groups (Oliver and Mathew 1963). Rather than attempt an exhaustive overview, here we briefly sketch several representative examples of precolonial economies and land systems that existed in the highlands. For the most part, this region was the domain of agricultural and agropastoral groups.

Among the Chagga of northeastern Tanzania, land traditionally belonged to the chiefs, each of whom owned tracts of land cascading down the slopes of Kilimanjaro. Use of the land required the chief's permission, which was given on payment of a gift (Maro 1974: 44). Agriculture apparently intensified gradually from shifting cultivation to more permanent types as population density increased. In certain areas, the shortage of land prompted the building of irrigation channels and ditches to carry water across the slope to fields. Each ridge of Kilimanjaro was served by these "water" furrows by the time of European intervention. The Chagga land was fertile, and the crops grown included yams (*Dioscorea*), beans (*Phaseolus*), peas (*Pisom sativum*), and millet (*Setaria*). Stands of bananas (*Musa*) were grown as a staple crop, as fodder for stall-fed cattle, and as a building material. Cattle manure was used as a fertilizer and land was kept under short fallow (two years) after three years of cropping. The irrigation system virtually assured a third cropping season per year beyond the two normally connected with the long and short rainy seasons.

Chagga society was not entirely introverted. Trading with the pastoral Masai and Pare to the southeast was common from at least the mid-eighteenth century onward (Kimambo 1969: 205). By the 1850s, strong trading links had been developed with the coast and with neighboring tribes. The productivity of the area was sufficient to support the subsistence of the population, expropriation of surplus by the chiefs, trade with "outsiders," and intertribal warfare.

Like the Chagga, the Kikuyu of the Kenyan highlands are Bantu-speaking, but there has been much cultural interchange among the Kikuyu, the Masai (Nilo-Hamites), and the Athi and Ndorobo hunter-gatherers. The proto-Kikuyu migrated south into Kiambu and Murang'a in the sixteenth century, and claimed territory in those areas. Land rights in Kikuyu society were controlled and inherited by lineage (Sorrenson 1967: 3–7). Apparently, shifting cultivation of

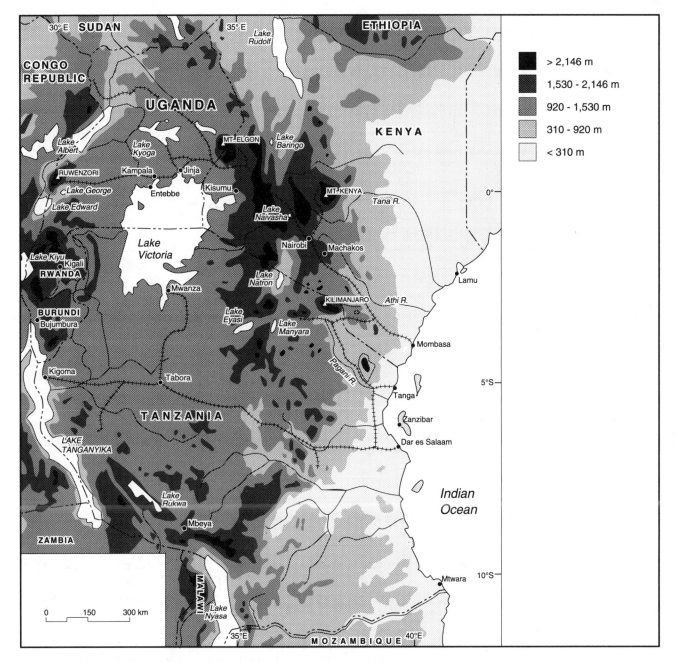

Figure 32.1 The East African Highlands. Adapted from Stamp and Morgan 1972.

varying fallows predominated, although annual cultivation probably marked the more populous areas; cultigens included beans, yams, cow peas (*Vigma umguiculata*), millet, sorghum (*Sorghum*), bananas, and arrowroot (*Maramta arundimacea*), grown at various elevations on the ridge to take advantage of different soil types. Cattle were raised on adjacent grazing land.

Kikuyu country was fertile, and enough surplus was produced to support trade in foodstuffs with the Masai and the Kamba. While much has been written about continual raiding that occurred between the Kikuyu and the Masai pastoralists, it has been suggested by others that economic cooperation between the two groups was the norm, even during times of increased raiding brought on by hardship among the Masai. In the early nineteenth century, Kikuyu

trading with the Kamba increased with the advent of Arab and Swahili caravans connecting the interior with the coast (Ogot 1976:111). By the 1850s, the Kikuyu supplemented their predominantly agricultural activity with regular trading with the Swahili caravans.

The earliest occupants of Rwanda and Burundi were primarily hunters and gatherers. They were concentrated in the forests in the southwest of the country (*Forêt de Nyungwe*). The Hutu, who arrived in Rwanda in the tenth century, lived by cultivation and small-scale livestock rearing. The largely pastoral Tutsi migrated into central Africa in the fourteenth and fifteenth centuries. By the nineteenth century, the Tutsi chiefs had imposed their authority over most of present-day Rwanda and Burundi.

Tutsi rulers exacted various forms of tribute, including both agricultural commodities and livestock. To meet these demands required an increase in production, which was probably achieved through cropland expansion. Although written accounts and archaeological data are scarce, it may be assumed that growth in population and demand from the Tutsi chiefs caused large amounts of forest to be cleared for cultivation. The result was a very small amount of forested land remaining in Rwanda at the end of the nineteenth century; it is estimated that 75% of the country's forests had been cleared by that time (Prioul and Sirven 1981). The dominance of banana-planting in the traditional farming system, however, minimized soil erosion and other destructive effects. By contrast with the western hilly highlands, the eastern uplands in Rwanda remained relatively unaltered throughout the precolonial era, mainly because of the prevalence there of tsetse fly and malaria.

The Colonial Period The advent of European colonial rule began a period of dramatic change in the political economy across Africa, but the nature and effects of colonialism varied considerably within East Africa. The first significant European environmental impact was indirect – the rinderpest epidemic that spread among cattle from the Italian presence in Ethiopia in the late nineteenth century – but the establishment of colonial rule brought wider and deeper impacts, especially on agriculture and land use.

Kenya, a settler colony from the early 1900s onward, experienced the most intrusive form of colonialism over the longest period. The government annexed large tracts (43,300 km²) of high-quality agricultural land (Brett 1973:172) as part of a policy of enclave development planned to allow Europeans to produce cash crops with African labor for export. The reluctance of Africans to work for extremely low wages on the new plantations led to the institution of hut and poll taxes, forced labor, and eviction from crown lands. This promoted movement of the displaced population to environmentally sensitive areas, dramatically increasing the pressure on those lands and creating a situation that continues to this day. Colonial policies not only affected land tenure, but also led to changes in the types of crops grown by the peasants. The taxes levied on Africans forced them to earn cash income, which they could acquire only by wage labor or by trading agricultural products in the market.

Colonialism in Tanzania (Tanganyika) began with a period of German rule (1885–1918), during which time many uprisings and a world war limited the ability of the colonial power to change African society in the interior. A number of sisal (*Agave sisalama*) plantations were established in the Pare District in the northeast, and coffee was introduced in the 1890s to the Chagga of Kilimanjaro. After World War I, the British gained control of the Tanzanian territory. In contrast with the policies pursued in Kenya, the administration sought to control the indigenous economy in an indirect fashion. Rather than alienate vast tracts of land for English settlers, the authorities encouraged African small-holders to grow coffee as a cash crop (Brett 1973:217–34). The increasing commercialization of agriculture was accompanied by fragmentation and commercialization of land holdings and by landlessness as an endemic problem.

Rwanda and Burundi also experienced two periods of colonialism. During all of German rule (1895–1918) and most of Belgian (1918–1962) rule, the two nations were administered jointly as Ruanda-Urundi, with the administrative center in Usumbura (Bujambura, Burundi). Both colonial powers took much less interest in Rwanda than in their other possessions, seeing it as valuable primarily for strategic reasons. European administrators left the local structure of Tutsi supremacy unchallenged. Although German rule left little imprint on the land, the Belgian period did effect some changes in agricultural patterns. Some attempts were made to commercialize agriculture, coffee was introduced as a cash crop, and *paysannat* schemes (government-initiated clearing and rural resettlement involving coffee production) were initiated to ease population pressure in the higher zones. With continued clearing for agriculture, the two remaining major forested areas in the northwest (Gishwati) and in the southwest (Nyungwe) of Rwanda were reduced by over 50% between 1916 and 1948.

Independence The end of colonialism in the early 1960s marked a further change of administration for Rwanda, Burundi, Kenya, and Tanzania; a coup in Rwanda in 1961 also ended the era of Tutsi domination. In preindependent and independent Kenya, land was reallocated to peasants through government schemes such as the 1956 ALDEV Plan (Heyer, Ireri, and Morris. 1976; Owako 1971). By 1970, almost 27% of the formerly European area was reallocated to small-holders through settlement schemes, but much of the superior agricultural land remained in the hands of large, though African, landowners. The 1967 *ujamaa* principle marked the beginning of socialist-style development in rural Tanzania, with villages organized into cooperatives, but the policy did not much affect the Kilimanjaro area, as the lands were already densely settled and organized into agricultural cooperatives (Smith 1980). Almost no large landholdings existed in Ruanda-Urundi prior to independence, and small farms have continued to characterize the landscape. The emphasis of the Hutu-dominated government in Rwanda on the production of foodstuffs to feed the growing population has diminished the land held for grazing and increased the area under cultivation.

The Dynamics of Environmental Change

The catalysts of change in the highlands during the twentieth century include high rates of population growth, increasing rural population densities, rapid urbanization, increasing landlessness, and land-use change, which have contributed to myriad environmental transformations, of which deforestation, soil erosion, and water pollution are the most important. The impacts of these processes are not uniform. The degree to which these processes initiate and sustain environmental change reflect details of local physical and social settings.

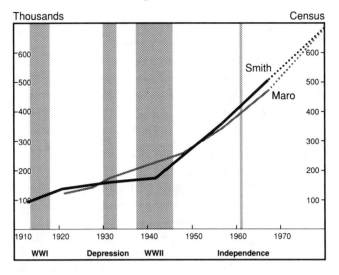

Figure 32.2 Population of Tanzania, 1915–1980. Sources: Maro 1974; Smith 1980.

Table 32-1 *Kilimanjaro Growth Rate*

(a) Regional

Year	Population	Growth Rate (per annum)
1948	353,500	+3.31
1957	473,900	+3.25
1967	652,700	+2.99
1978	902,400	

(b) Kilimanjaro District

Year	Population	Growth Rate (per annum)
1913	99,000 (E)	+3.3
1921	128,443 (M)	+1.6
1928	143,013 (M)	+2.8
1931	155,337 (M)	+0.9
1942	172,000 (S)	+7.7
1948	267,700 (C)	+3.5
1957	365,000 (C)	+3.2
1967	500,800 (C)	+3.0
1978	694,246 (C)	

Sources: E = estimate; M = Maro 1974: 11; S = Smith 1980:30; C = Census of Tanzania 1948, 1957, 1967, 1978.

Population Growth, Migration, and Urbanization

The highlands have experienced rapid growth in population in this century, clearly precipitated by declining mortality rates and increased life expectancy. Tanzanian data, for example, suggest that a rapid increase began after World War II (Fig. 32.2). Catastrophes such as the rinderpest epidemic, smallpox, famine, and the toll of World War I may have subdued natural increase between the 1890s and the 1920s. Growth since 1942 has maintained an annual rate above 3%, as it has in the Kilimanjaro region and the Kilimanjaro district (Table 32-1). Kenya has shown a similar national pattern (Fig. 32.3). In the highland districts of Kiambu, Murang'a, Machakos, and Nyeri, annual growth

Table 32-2 *Population Growth Rates in Selected Regions of Kenya*

District	Growth Rates per Annum	
	1962/69	1969/79
Kiambu	+2.2	+3.8
Murang'a	+3.7	+3.8
Nyeri	+5.2	+3.0
Machakos	*	+3.7

* Data not available.

rates have mostly exceeded 3% (Table 32-2). In 1962, the population of Rwanda reached 2.5 million; by 1978, it stood at 4,831,527. Between 1978 and 1984, the population grew by another 15% to 5.5 million, and today it exceeds 6 million, whereas the population of Burundi is in excess of 5 million (ECA 1982). The total population estimated for 1988 for the highlands region as defined here approaches 55 million (ECA 1982).

One simple indicator of population pressure in an area is density. Table 32-3 shows density figures for Kenya, Tanzania, and Rwanda for much of this century. Such average national figures are misleading because actual densities in the highland areas are generally much higher than in the lowlands. This is reflected in the higher population densities of Rwanda, almost a completely highland nation. The population density of the East African highlands as defined here exceeds 150 persons/km^2.

Regional population densities for three representative highland areas are presented in Table 32-3. In 1967, average densities in the Kilimanjaro region ranged from 94 to 270 persons/km^2 (Maro 1974:7). The average density, calculated by agricultural land available, was 203.2 in 1967. Projections suggest that densities as high as 430/km^2 may be reached by 1990. The situation in the Kenyan highlands is similar; the

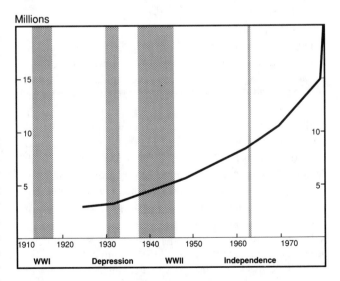

Figure 32.3 Population of Kenya, 1925–1979. Sources: Census Bureau 1948, 1962, 1979; Hailey 1945; World Bank 1986.

Table 32-3 *Population Densities in East Africa, 1940s to Present*

(a) Population Density by Total Land

	Density (persons/km²)		
Year	Rwanda	Kenya	Tanzania
1948	77.0	9.0	8.4
1960	108.5	14.1	10.8
1965	123.4	16.3	12.3
1970	140.3	19.3	14.1
1975	165.5	23.5	16.7
1980	196.2	28.6	19.6

Source: World Bank 1983.

(b) Population Density in Selected Upland Regions

	Population Density	
Region/Country	Regional	National
Kiambu (Kenya)	280.4 (1974)	26.6 (1979)
Kilimanjaro (Tanzania)	131.3 (1978)	19.1 (1987)
Ruhengeri (Rwanda)	421.4 (1966)	203.2 (1967)

Data sources: Census data for each country and region.

Table 32-4 *Percentage of Population That Is Urbanized in East Africa*

Country	Percentage Urbanized	Year
Kenya	15.1	1978
Tanzania	12.9	1978
Rwanda	4.0	1980

average densities of Kiambu, Murang'a, and Nyeri districts were 280, 262, and 148 persons/km², respectively in 1978. These figures are diluted by the inclusion of the nonhighland portions of each district. Some highland zones reached 515/km² in 1978. The average *préfecture* densities in Rwanda exceeded 350/km² in 1982.

These figures raise the issue of whether the environment has the capacity to support the ever-growing population under current agricultural systems. The population has grown by 700% in 80 years. To compensate, land under fallow has decreased, and cultivation has expanded into more fragile lands. There seems to be very little additional room for agricultural expansion under existing systems, and it is not clear that intensification of production has kept pace with demand. Yet although population density gives an indication of human pressures, it is not the only factor in operation, and in some cases may not be the principal determinant of environmental degradation.

The percentage of urban population differs among the three countries (Table 32-4). Mass migration to the cities began in Kenya and Tanzania when colonial restrictions on the movement of Africans were lifted. Urban growth rates in Kenya and Tanzania now run twice the national growth rates. For example, Moshi, situated in the Tanzanian highlands, has grown at an annual rate of over 6% for the past 30 years. Nairobi, Kenya, grew at a rate of 6%/yr between 1948 and 1962, 9.6% between 1962 and 1967, and 5% between 1969 and 1978. This rapid increase is mostly due to immigration from the rural areas. Rural-urban migration is a response to land scarcity, rural poverty, and rural-urban income differentials. In contrast, only a small percentage of the Rwandan population lives in urban areas. Burundi, while slightly more urbanized than Rwanda, has only about 6% of its population in urban areas. Over 80% of its urban population is in its capital (Lasserre and Menault 1979). Rural-to-rural migration has become common in Rwanda and Burundi as land shortage has grown more severe.

Rural Land Use and Landlessness

All of the highland areas have witnessed increased agricultural commercialization, a trend more apparent in Kenya and Tanzania than in other areas of the highlands, although subsistence crops have remained an important part of the production strategy of the small farmer. The types of crops grown affect environmental conditions. Perennial crops, such as bananas, compared to annual crops (e.g., tobacco), usually result in lower soil losses. Likewise, crops that provide relatively good ground cover (e.g., beans) compared to those providing poor ground cover early in the rainy season (e.g., maize), help reduce environmental problems (Lewis 1988). Most patterns of highland vegetation today reflect the local agricultural economy, as most land, save that at the highest elevations or which is already severely degraded, is under some form of cultivation (Lewis and Nyamulinda 1989).

Agriculture in Kilimanjaro is increasingly commercial. Coffee is the major cash crop in this region. Its adoption was especially rapid after the 1950s (Fig. 32.4), and it contributed 58% of Tanzania's market production by the mid-1970s. Banana production in Kilimanjaro accounts for 34% of the national marketed production (Smith 1980:12). Besides commercial crops, the region produces a wide range of food staples: maize (50,000 mt in 1980), potatoes (10,000 mt in 1972), and millet (5,500 mt in 1980). The mountain slopes are a patchwork of *kihamba* plots, with mixed stands of bananas, coffee, tubers, cereals, and beans (Maro 1974; Smith 1980).

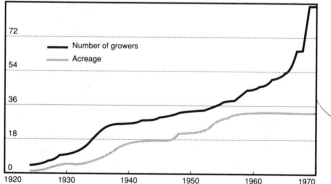

Figure 32.4 Coffee growers in Kilimanjaro, 1920–1970. Source: Maro 1974.

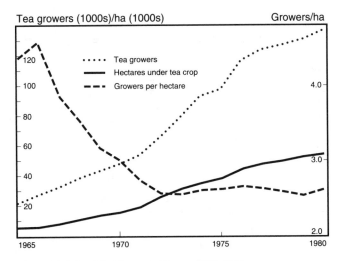

Figure 32.5 Small-holder tea in Kenya, 1965–1980.

The economy is land-intensive; the average holding is less than 1 ha.

The highland areas of the Central Province (Kenya) combine subsistence and cash-crop agriculture. Most farmers in the Kiambu and Murang'a districts are heavily involved in agricultural marketing, and many households have a diversified strategy for survival that includes off-farm employment. Only one in five small-holders (owning less than 12 ha) remains a true subsistence farmer (90% of production for direct consumption). Coffee and tea production are a major component of commercial cropping (Fig. 32.5). Tea is grown in the higher elevations, whereas coffee is found in the lower portions of the highlands. In 1978–79, 70% of all Kenyan small-holders growing coffee lived in the central highlands.

Land-use patterns in Rwanda have changed with population growth. The increasing numbers of people and the sparse industrial sector have promoted fragmentation of the land. Today, each household (approximately six people) has an average of only 1.2 ha, divided into four to five fields. Agriculture is predominantly subsistence, as local markets are few and and the international transportation of cash crops is prohibitively expensive. Coffee is the major exception to this rule. As land pressures increase, a shift in crop mix is occurring. While bananas, beans, and sorghum remain staples, crops that yield more calories per hectare, such as tubers, are becoming increasingly important (Clay and Mazmani 1986).

Deforestation

Deforestation is a critical issue in the highland region. Forest cover has declined steadily throughout the region during this century, although increasingly there are concerted efforts to maintain wood reserves for fuel and timber, to conserve "natural" forests, and to replant. Despite such efforts, many densely populated areas in the highlands are actively cut – a situation that has serious implications for local energy needs and soils. Today, forest covers only a small proportion of the region.

Kenya and Tanzania lost much of their highland forest during the nineteenth and early twentieth centuries, despite government attempts at conservation. The woodlands of Kilimanjaro have been gradually cut for the expansion of cultivated land, although this advance has been halted to a degree by the creation of a forest reserve. Outside this, woodland today is found only along rivers. Deforestation is slightly offset by the hedges and shade trees that bound each farm plot (Maro 1974:93). In Kenya, cropland expansion at the expense of forest is still evident. In the Moi area, for example, 10% of the forested land was lost in a 5-year period between 1973 and 1978 (Berry 1980:4); in Kiambu District, active deforestation due to agricultural expansion is occurring on lands previously planted in wattle (Lewis and Berry 1988).

While widespread planting of trees, especially pines and eucalyptus, has increased since independence in Rwanda, the long-term trend of vegetation change from tree cover to either crops or pasture shows no sign of abating. Before the 1950s, Rwanda's population was concentrated almost entirely in the high-potential agricultural areas of the western and south-central portions of the country. Today, continuing population growth has left little unaltered vegetation anywhere. The land-cover transformation in Rwanda began with conversion of forest to small-scale farming systems on the hillslopes. The second phase involved farming the more poorly drained valley bottoms in the western and central areas; cultivation has finally expanded into the lower-potential areas of the north-central section and the savanna lands in the east. The early replacement of woodland by cultivation and pasture has thus been followed by substantial forest removal in the past 80 years. Of the deforested area, however, 33% is covered with banana, which minimizes the effects of deforestation.

Impacts on Soil and Hydrology

In the East African highlands, conditions are favorable for rock weathering and deep soil formation. The climate is warm and seasonally humid. Volcanic and granitic rocks, which decompose easily under such climatic conditions, are widespread. Periods of surplus moisture, intense rains, deep weathering, and the steep slopes found in these areas create a potential for surface waters to erode large quantities of soil. Under natural conditions, however, the vegetation cover largely negates this potential. The natural vegetation in the highlands is dense forest and woodland, except at the highest altitudes. The forest is typically multistoried. The tall trees, smaller trees, shrubs, and underlayer of ferns and mosses form a series of protective layers between the falling rains and the soil.

Although distinct rainy and dry seasons occur in the highlands, streams in forested areas have relatively constant annual flow regimes. Their discharges are usually clear, carrying little sediment. The streams are largely fed by groundwater, since a large percentage of precipitation is intercepted by the forest canopy and groundcover. This interception reduces the rainfall intensity at ground level, and a large percentage of the rainfall infiltrates into the soil. The infrequent landslide after exceptionally heavy rain is the most dramatic form of soil movement under these conditions. The forest cover also helps to maintain a humid microclimate at ground level.

The physical impacts of forest removal in the highlands are far from uniform; they depend upon the interaction among a number of factors. These factors include existing conditions, such as slope, soil characteristics, and rainfall. They also include the conditions of transformation, such as the nature of land use, the density of occupance, and the type of conservation measures. Other human activities, such as quarrying and road building, also play a role. Some of the physical impacts are direct and local, such as soil loss from farm plots; others are indirect and regional, such as increased silt and clay load in streams.

In general, the effects of land clearing are what would be expected. Soil loss and sediment load in streams have continued to increase. Stream and river regimes have become erratic, fluctuating with the seasons (Pereira 1962; Rapp et al. 1972). Smaller river basins that had permanent streams with little seasonal variation in their flow under natural conditions now are often occupied by torrents after heavy rains and low-flow streams by the end of the dry season. This situation reflects the alteration in critical portions of the hydrologic cycle through the change in the vegetation cover. It is important, however, to look at the regional differences.

A general transformation widespread in these highlands is the planting of tea in the higher zones, merging with coffee at the middle altitudes. Although food crops are found throughout the area, maize, beans, and cattle dominate the lower altitudes. Each crop substitution alters the environmental situation. Pereira (1962) shows that the sequence from forest to tea corresponds to several stages of soil and water conditions. Although soil and water are greatly disturbed as the tea matures, the crop increasingly protects the soil and restores some balance to the system. Lewis (1985) shows that maize cultivation often results in dramatic negative changes. Runoff is greatly increased, soil loss can be many times that under natural conditions, and in some areas the productivity of soils diminishes. In some steep portions of the Pare and Usambura mountains in Tanzania, clearing, cultivation, and abandonment have all occurred in the span of 5 years. Fortunately, the major mountainous areas have so far escaped the worst impacts.

In spite of massive deforestation, total soil loss in Rwanda appears to have been slight to moderate (Lewis, Clay, and Dejaegher 1988), which probably reflects the continuing dominant role of bananas in the farming system. This species minimizes soil disturbance, and through its broad leaves and mulching properties, protects the soil from erosion. As a result of increasing land scarcity, however, both a rapid decrease in lands under fallow and a shift toward tubers is occurring throughout the country. Already, 13% of all cultivated fields and, in the most densely populated areas, 46% of total crop production is in tubers (Ministère de l'Agriculture 1985). If these trends continue without conservation and management innovations, it is likely that soil erosion rates in Rwanda will increase, becoming similar to those in highland Kenya, and agricultural yields will drop. This drop will exacerbate the pressure on the remaining

Table 32-5 *Siltation Rates in Selected Reservoirs*

Country	Reservoir	Annual Siltation Rate (mt)	Years until Full of Silt
Tanzania	Matambulu	19,800	30
Tanzania	Kisongo	3,400	15

agricultural lands, affecting the overall environmental situation in the country.

Soil loss has raised concern for the long-term viability of the highlands (Anderson 1982), and its impacts extend outside the region. Through a combination of cultivation practices, quarrying, poorly engineered road cuts, and runoff from roads, soil and sediment losses from the highlands of Kenya and Tanzania have increased to crisis proportions. In Kenya, the waters of the uplands run red with sediment after a storm. Sediment in the country's major river, the Tana, has reached record levels, and the river has lost much of its potential for hydropower and irrigation. In Kilimanjaro, the situation is similar, although the Pagani is not as crucial to Tanzania as the Tana is to Kenya. Reservoirs have accumulated silt at rates far in excess of those forecasted as a result of accelerated highland erosion (Table 32-5). Heavy sediment loads in the Athi and Galana rivers have had a serious impact on the coastal environment, destroying coral reefs and damaging mangrove swamps (DuBois 1984).

Summary and Comments

In Kenya, vast population movements into agriculturally marginal areas led to environmental deterioration during the colonial period, and the problems have returned with recent population growth and agricultural commercialization. The long tradition of commercial agriculture in Tanzania remained undisturbed even during the colonial period; with population growth, land has become fragmented, and landlessness and environmental stress have become increasingly common. Rwanda and Burundi, with their land-locked position and history of less intrusive colonial rule, have not been as much involved in commercial agriculture as have Kenya and Tanzania. The shortage of land for subsistence, however, is increasing, as are deforestation, soil losses, and soil impoverishment.

Differences in population growth, land use, and political and economic history for the countries of the region seem to provide a partial explanation of the differences in environmental change (Tables 32-6 and 32-7). Three hundred years

Table 32-6 *Resource Changes in East Africa*

Resource Change	Rwanda	Kenya and Tanzania
Vegetation decrease	High	Moderate-high
Soil loss	Moderate	Moderate-high
Productivity loss	Slight	Low-moderate
Water regime change	Moderate	Moderate-high

Table 32-7 *Factors of Change in East Africa*

Factor of Change	Rwanda	Kenya	Tanzania
Population growth	High	High	High
Population density	Very high	Moderate-high	Moderate-high
History of trading	Short	Long	Long
Commercialization of agriculture	Limited	Moderate	Moderate
Involvement in war/civil war	Short-term	Short-term	Short-term

ago, agriculture had begun to make some inroads into the original forest cover, but the general pattern of forest had not been broken up. The major period of deforestation in Rwanda began long before European influence. In Kenya and Tanzania, it occurred in the past 100 years and still continues, although with fewer areas left to be deforested. The remaining forest reserves on the highlands of the three countries are extremely important as the remaining protection for agricultural and hydrologic systems.

In Kenya and Tanzania, the conversion of land to farming has greatly increased the flow of materials from fields, and the movement of this sediment through the hydrologic network is a great problem. The current impact of these changes on overall agricultural productivity is not yet high. In some areas of steep slopes, landsliding is a problem; in other areas, cleared slopes have degraded rapidly to unproductive land; but generally productivity remains high. Prediction for the future is difficult, but given current rates of soil loss, improved conservation measures and cropping practices will be needed to maintain production.

In Rwanda and Burundi, the transformation of forest to agriculture is almost complete, and rural population densities are very high. Various circumstances, including the mixture of crops grown and the nature of the soil, have meant a much lower rate of soil loss and sediment flow in the streams. Population densities are increasing at very high rates, however, and the system appears to be on the verge of requiring large adjustments. The impacts of continued growth in the next few years are likely to be large.

The landscape of the highlands is now highly altered. What was forest is now intensively used for agriculture, or in some cases, is already degraded and abandoned or covered by settlement and towns. This chapter has not dealt with the more global issues of species diversity and the climatic impacts of vegetational and other changes. The first is clearly important and the second is of potential regional and wider concern. Even without consideration of these issues, it is clear that change in the East African highlands has brought the region to the edge of important thresholds. The actions taken in the next few years may well determine the prospects of these key regions for many years to come.

References

Anderson, G. D. 1982. *The Soils and Land Use Potential of the Southern and Eastern Slopes of Kilimanjaro. Tanzania.* Dar es Salaam: Institute of Resource Assessment and International Development Program. Clark University.

Berry, L. 1980. *Kenya: East African Country Profile.* Worcester, MA: Program for International Development.

Brett, E. A. 1973. *Colonialism and Underdevelopment in East Africa: The Politics of Economic Change 1919–1939.* London: Heinemann.

Census Bureau. 1948, 1962, 1979. *Population Census.* Kenya.

Census of Tanzania. 1948, 1957, 1967, 1978. Dar es Salaam.

Central Bureau of Statistics. 1973, 1976, 1979, 1982. *Economic Survey.* Republic of Kenya.

Clay, D. C., and R. J. Mazmani. 1986. The human ecology of farming systems: toward understanding agricultural development in Rwanda. Washington, D.C.: International Statistical Programs Center, U.S. Bureau of the Census.

Division de Climatologie. 1985. *Bulletin Climatologique Année 1984.* Kigale: Ministere des Transports et des Communications.

DuBois, R. 1984. Catchment Land Use and Its Implications for Coastal Resources Conservation. Center for Technology, Environment, and Development. Worcester, MA.

Economic Commission for Africa. 1982. *Handbook for Africa 1982.* Economic Commission for Africa. Addis Ababa.

Hailey, Lord. 1957. *An African Survey.* London; Oxford University Press.

Hamilton, A. C. 1982. *Environmental History of East Africa: a Study of the Quaternary.* London: Academic Press.

Heyer, J., D. Ireri, and J. Morris. 1976. *Rural Development in Kenya.* Nairobi: East African Publishing House.

Kimambo, I. N. 1969. *A Political History of the Pare of Tanzania: ca 1500–1800.* Vol. 3, *Peoples of East Africa.* Nairobi: East African Publishing House.

Lasserre, G., and J. Menault, eds. 1979. *Atlas du Burundi.* Paris: Ministere de la Coopération de la République française.

Lewis, L. A. 1985. Assessing soil loss in Kiambu and Murang'a Districts, Kenya. *Geografiska Annaler* 67A: 273–84.

———. 1988. Measurement and assessment of soil loss in Rwanda. *Catena Supplement* 12:151–65.

Lewis, L. A., and L. Berry. 1988. *African Environments and Resources.* London: Unwin Hyman Ltd.

Lewis, L. A., D. C. Clay, and Y. M. J. Dejaegher. 1988. Soil loss, agriculture and conservation in Rwanda: toward sound strategies for soil management. *Journal of Soil and Water Conservation* 43:418–21.

Lewis, L. A., and V. Nyamulinda. 1989. Les relations entre les cultures et les unites topographiques dans les regions agricoles de la bordure du lac Kivu et de l'Impara au Rwanda: Quelques strategies pour une agriculture soutenue. *Bulletin Agricole du Rwanda* 22:143–49.

Maro, P. S. 1974. Population and land resources in northern Tanzania: The dynamics of change 1920–1970. Ph.D. dissertation. University of Minnesota.

Milne, G. 1935. Some suggested units of classification and mapping, particularly for East African soils. *Soil Resources* 4:183–98.

Ministère de l'Agriculture, de l'Elevage et des Forêts. 1985. *Resultats de l'enquête nationale agricole 1984.* Kigali, Rwanda.

Moreau, R. E. 1966. *The Bird Faunas of Africa and Its Islands.* New York: Academic Press.

Morgan, W. T. W. 1973. *East Africa.* London: Longman.

Ogot, B. A. 1976. *Kenya Before 1900: Eight Regional Studies.* Nairobi: East African Publishing House.

Oliver, R., and G. Mathew, eds. 1963. *History of East Africa.* Oxford: The Clarendon Press.

Owako, F. N. 1971. Machakos land and population problems. In *Studies in East African Geography and Development,* ed. S. H. Ominde, 177–92. London: Heinemann.

Penman, H. L. 1948. Natural evaporation from open water, bare soil, and grass. *Proceedings of the Royal Society A* 193:120–45.

Pereira, H. C. 1962. Hydrological effects of changes in land use in some East African catchment areas. *East African Agricultural and Forestry Journal*, Special Issue 27.

Prioul, C., and P. Sirven, eds. 1981. *Atlas du Rwanda*. Paris: Ministère de la Coopération de la République Française.

Rapp, A., V. Axelsson, L. Berry, and D. H. Murray-Rust. 1972. Soil erosion and sedimentation in Tanzania. *Geografiska Annaler* 54A, 3–4.

Smith, C. H. R. 1980. *The Changing Economy of Mt. Kilimanjaro, Tanzania: Four Essays on the Modernization of Smallholder*

Agriculture. Utrecht: Utrechtse Geographische Studies 19.

Sorrenson, M. P. K. 1967. *Land Reform in Kikuyu Country: A Study in Government Policy*. Nairobi: Oxford University Press.

Stamp, L. D., and W. T. W. Morgan. *Africa: A Study in Tropical Development*. 3rd ed. New York: John Wiley and Sons.

World Bank. 1983. *Social Data*. Vol. 2. Rome: World Bank. World Bank. 1986. *World Development Report*. Rome: World Bank.

33

The Russian Plain

E. B. ALAYEV   YU. P. BADENKOV,   N. A. KARAVAEVA*

The Russian Plain is the world's most extensive extratropical plain; its 462.8 million ha (4,628,000 km^2) occupy one-half of Europe (Fig. 33.1). The larger portion of the Plain (356.5 million ha) lies in the temperate zone, the remainder (106.3 million ha), in the boreal and cold-belt zones.

The territory of the Russian Plain – Novgorod, the interfluvial area between the Oka and upper Volga rivers with Vladimir, Suzdal, Rostov and, starting from the thirteenth century, Moscow – was the historical center of the Russian state. Throughout Russian history, the Plain has been the economic and social core of the state, possessing the most highly developed industry, agriculture, and transportation, as well as the highest density of population and degree of urbanization. At present, about 70% of the population of the USSR lives on the Plain, at a density of 32 persons/km^2 (the average density in the USSR is 11 persons/km^2); the Plain supplies 75% of the country's industrial products and 60% of its agricultural products.

The vastness of the Plain accounts for the variation of climates and natural zones within its territory, and provides a chance to study human activities and the resulting transformations in different landscape situations. A diverse array of human transformations, varying in specific features and intensities, taking place against contrasting landscape backgrounds, makes the Russian Plain a representative area in which to study human impact on a temperate plains environment.

Approaches to Research

This chapter is organized as an examination of the factors and consequences of anthropogenic impact on nature, and the responses of society to such environmental transformations.

The factors affecting nature are grouped into the following categories:

Population (increase, density, and distribution, both of urban and of rural population)

Urbanization (the emergence, growth, and distribution of towns and cities)

Agriculture (location, productivity, land use, degree of agricultural development and land improvement)

Industry (mining, processing, and energy production)

Transportation (expansion of road networks, railroads, and waterways).

Indices reflecting the nature of human impacts were selected for research:

Degree of forest cover;

Difference in biological cycle of natural and agricultural ecosystems;

Trends in the alteration of soil structure and chemistry;

Major trends in the alteration of volume, regime, and chemistry of surface water and river flow;

Types and intensity of anthropogenic erosion;

Disturbance of natural relief;

Characteristics of air, water, and landscape pollution.

The social factors significant to transformation include both the economic development of the region and measures taken specifically for the amelioration of harmful impact on nature. The period under study begins at the close of the seventeenth century, coinciding with the changes introduced by Peter the Great. During the following 300 years on the Russian Plain, feudal relations were replaced by capitalist, and capitalist relations by socialist. These successions are associated with specific dates – the transition to capitalism with the abolition of serfdom in 1861, and to socialism with the October Revolution in 1917.

The third stage is very clearly subdivided into two parts – the years prior to World War II (1917–1941), and the postwar period, whose beginning almost coincided with the beginning of the scientific and technological revolution. These two periods are separated by the spell of the worst anthropogenic impact, World War II, which brought about loss of human life, material loss, and landscape destruction in the zones of military action. While social responses to

* With the assistance of L. N. Bylinskaya, G. A. Golts, S. N. Zharikov, N. I. Koronkevich, A. A. Tishkov, and L. K. Tselishcheva.

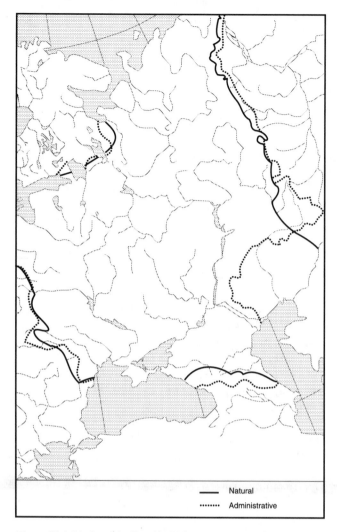

Natural
Administrative

Figure 33.1 Limits of the Russian Plain.

transformation have long been taken, their integrated development is a feature of the past few decades.

Environmental Background

Relief and Lithology

The Plain's diverse relief is represented by several uplands, separated by a system of lowlands. The northern part of the Plain consists largely of glacial landforms and rocks of glacial genesis, moraines with different physical textures, fluvioglacial sands, lake-glacial clays, and, outside the area of the last Valdai glaciation, blanket loess loams. On the whole, the northern part of the Plain is much less characterized by erosion or denudation features than the southern. The extraglacial southern part of the Russian Plain is composed of mature erosional uplands and relatively young accumulative lowlands. Relief is more rugged and the river systems more dense than in the north. Friable surface deposits here are represented mainly by blanket loess rocks. These differences in relief have determined different degrees of tolerance of human impact. Tolerance of erosion, for example, is higher in the north than in the south.

Climate

The climate of the Russian Plain is moderately continental on the whole, and continental in the southeast. Thermal indices, precipitation, and humidity vary with latitude and longitude. Winter is generally cold in the northeast (the average January temperature is −17°C), and mild in the south (−3°C). Two types of winter predominate: a moderately cold, stable winter (−10°C to −17°C) in the central and eastern parts of the Plain, and a moderately soft, unstable winter in the western part (−10°C). Two types of summer also prevail: moderately warm (average July temperature is +14°C to +18°C), and warm (+18°C to +22°C). In the south, especially in the southeast, the summer is very warm (+22°C to +26°C), whereas at the northern coast, the summer is moderately cool (+10°C to +14°C) to cool (0°C to 10°C).

Annual precipitation decreases to the east and southeast, from 675–852 mm in the taiga-forest zone to 456–558 mm in the steppe and 249–389 mm in the desert. Overall precipitation exceeds potential evapotranspiration in the northern half of the Russian Plain, especially in the northwest, where the excess of moisture is 50–100 mm/yr. Most southern areas of the Plain have a substantial moisture deficit of some 700–800 mm/yr. Summer heat in these areas is often accompanied by droughts, strong dry winds, and "black storms" of active wind erosion.

Landscape Zones and Subzones

The Russian Plain displays an almost ideal succession of landscape zones and subzones from north to south. The moderately continental climate accounts for the smooth transition and wide variety of landscapes. From north to south, the following soil and vegetation zones and subzones can be found (Fig. 33.2):

1. Tundra (typical, southern, and forest tundra subzones);
2. Taiga (northern, middle and southern subzones);
3. Mixed-forest (coniferous–broad–leaved and broad–leaved subzones);
4. Steppe (forest-steppe, moderately arid steppe, and arid steppe subzones);
5. Desert.

During the past 300 years, few substantial natural changes could have occurred on the Russian Plain, although there must have been regular periodic climatic fluctuations followed by biotic adjustments. It can be assumed that the considerable changes in the Russian Plain over this time have been largely due to human activities.

Human Impact on the Environment over 300 Years

The period under examination witnessed qualitative social transformations (feudalism, capitalism, socialism), drastic changes in the structure of social production, and several technical and technological revolutions. Accordingly, analysis was undertaken over the three historical stages (1700–1861, 1861–1917, post–1917), focusing on four selected major agents of anthropogenic impact – population, agriculture, industry, and transportation – and the dynamics of their development.

Feudal Development: 1700–1861

By the beginning of the eighteenth century, the Russian Plain was inhabited by 17 million people, of whom 15 million lived in the territory of the Russian state. Although at that time Russia's population was the largest in Europe, its density of 3–4/km^2 was not high. The areas most densely settled were the center around Moscow and the zone of mixed and broad-leaved forests (12/km^2), where population was not attached to a few centers but was distributed across the area. In the taiga, the population was concentrated around a few settlements. As the inroads of nomadic tribes and other enemies diminished, the steppe was colonized, and the rate of population growth was especially high there.

In 1700, 253 settlements with the status of a town existed on the Russian Plain, but all of them, except Moscow, were small, and their 600,000 inhabitants represented no more than 4% of the total population. By the end of the feudal period, 441 towns held 6% of the population (3.4 million). The founding of Petersburg (now Leningrad) in 1703 as the seat of government played an important role by forming another center of attraction and development in addition to Moscow.

Agriculture dominated the economy of the Russian Plain through the end of the nineteenth century. Indeed, in some areas its leading role was preserved until the 1930s, when the policy of industrialization was adopted. During the period of feudal relations, agricultural development was slow (Table 33-1). By the end of the period, yields even went down, and the demands of the growing population were satisfied only through an extension of arable lands. Forests were cut and new territories were developed.

The human pressure on nature was felt mainly in the depletion of soils (which was one of the causes of lowered yields). Even so, it cannot be asserted that agriculture failed to develop. Many new cultivars were introduced during the eighteenth and nineteenth centuries. At the end of the seventeenth century, 55 cultivars existed; by the end of the nineteenth century, they numbered 115. However, newly introduced crops, as a rule, occupied small areas, save for potatoes (*Solarium* spp.) and sunflower (*Helianthus annuus*) in the south.

Two branches of agriculture – land cultivation and cattle-breeding – developed more or less in harmony. Organic fertilizers were widely used in field-crop cultivation, especially on podzolic soils. The yields obtained in the north were not

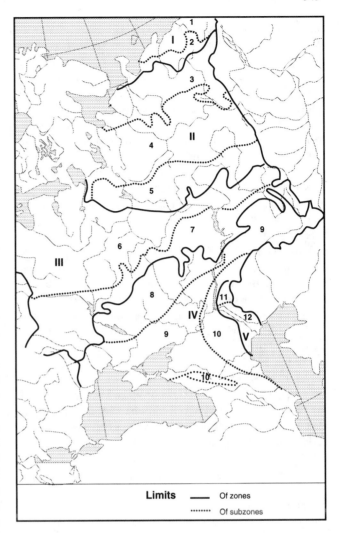

Limits —— Of zones
·········· Of subzones

Figure 33.2 Soil-vegetation zones. Zones: (I) tundra; (II) taiga; (III) mixed and broad-leaved forests; (IV) steppe; (V) desert. Subzones: (1) tundra; (2) forest-tundra; (3) northern taiga; (4) middle taiga; (5) southern taiga; (6) mixed forests; mixed and dark coniferous forests; (7) broad-leaved forests; (8) forest-steppe; (9) moderately arid steppe; (10) dry steppe; (11) semidesert; (12) desert.

lower and were sometimes even higher than the average, owing to the use of organic fertilizers that delayed the process of soil depletion.

The region, at least in the early stages of development, was not rich in usable mineral resources, with the exception of construction materials. At every historical stage, however, certain types of resources provided raw materials for industry. At the end of the seventeenth century, at least 30 types of manufacturing in metallurgy and chemistry existed, including iron, steel, copper, bronze, ceramics, glass, niter and gunpowder, and soap. The first half of the nineteenth century saw the production of nitric, sulphuric, hydrochloric, and acetic acids, methyl alcohol, sodium carbonate, concrete, silver, lead, and tin. The number of industries increased to 50. Forests were severely damaged as a consequence, since wood was at once the principal fuel, the major construction material, and a raw material for many industries. The feudal system inhibited the further development of industry. Although it possessed considerable resources, Russia in 1861

Table 33-1 *The Russian Plain. Yield of Grain Crops from 1600 to 1850 (in centners per hectare)*

Zone	1600–1650	1750–1800	1800–1850
Northern (taiga)	4	4.9	4.3
Mixed-forest zone	4.4	4.4	4.1
Steppe and forest-steppe	5.1	5.6	4.5

imported 87.3% of its consumption of cast iron, 69.8% of its chemical products, 50% of its steel, and 46% of its linen cloth. Imports of copper and iron also exceeded exports.

A clear pattern existed in the location of industrial enterprises. Extractive industries were located near mining fields, whereas processing industries concentrated in such established centers as Moscow, Nizhni Novgorod, and Tula. As natural resources became scarce in the central region, the extraction of raw materials shifted toward the periphery, to the Urals, the Volga region, and the Ukraine. The nature-conservation policy pursued by the government, including a prohibition on tree-cutting for industrial purposes in a 200-km radius from Petersburg to Moscow, also promoted such decentralization.

Before large-scale railroad construction at the end of the nineteenth century, horse-drawn vehicles were the principal means of transportation, and in rural areas they maintained their leading role until the beginning of the automobile era in the 1920s and 1930s. All major cities were connected with roads, with special coach service that provided relatively rapid travel (the 670 km from Moscow to Petersburg could be covered in 3 to 5 days).

Water transportation played its principal role in the movement of large-tonnage cargoes. When a waterway linked the Baltic Sea with the Volga Basin (the Mariinsk system), it meant the connection of two major regions of the country. As early as 1833, 40 steamers were used on rivers, and by 1860 their number had increased tenfold. Since Russia was becoming a major exporter of grain (grain exports, which amounted to 12,000 tons in 1760, reached 200,000 tons at the beginning of the nineteenth century, and exceeded 1 million tons in 1856–1860), it began to develop sea-transport and harbor facilities.

In 1837, the first railroad was constructed between Petersburg and Tsarskoye Selo. In 1851, Petersburg and Moscow were connected, and in 1880 the total length of railroads exceeded 20,000 km.

Capitalist Development: 1861–1917

The stage of capitalist development was associated more with structural changes in population (the formation and development of the working class, and the acceleration of urbanization), than with spatial changes, since the colonization of annexed lands was largely completed. The number of industrial workers grew from 706,000 in 1865 to 2.2 million in 1900–1903, and before World War I the total number of wage laborers reached 15 million, 4 million of whom were in the industrial and transportation sectors.

Although the capitalist period saw only a very small increase in the number of towns, towns grew rapidly with the influx of rural population. The percentage of town population tripled from 6% in 1861 to 18% in 1913, and the number of town-dwellers reached 22.7 million out of the total 126.2 million living on the Russian Plain. Agglomerations of large settlements sprang up around Moscow, in the interfluvial area between the Volga and Oka rivers, around Petersburg, and in Donbass.

Table 33-2 *Growth of Industrial Production on the Russian Plain: 1860–1913*

Types of products	(million tons)		
	1860	1900	1913
Coal	—	16.9	33.3
Cast iron	0.3	2.9	4.6
Steel	0.2	2.2	4.2

Industry became the leading force in economic development and anthropogenic impact on the environment. By the end of the feudal period, several hundred small industrial enterprises existed. Before World War I, there were as many as 250 iron and steel plants, 560 enterprises in the coal industry, and 1,800 plants of various sizes in engineering. Large enterprises of more than 500 workers employed 56.7% of the labor force.

At the beginning of the nineteenth century, industrial production in Russia was seven times less than in France and nine times less than in Germany. By the start of World War I, Russia had become a country with an average level of capitalist development, whose gross industrial production was fifth in the world and fourth in Europe (Table 33-2).

Still greater changes took place in transportation, especially in the growth of the railroad system. By 1851, its length reached 1,000 km. During the 1860s, 1,500 km of new lines were built annually, and in the 1890s, 2,500 km. At the beginning of the twentieth century, there were 55,000 km, and by 1913 not less than 65,000 km of railroads on the Russian Plain (out of 72,000 km in the whole of Russia).

The development of railroad transportation went hand in hand with the clearing of forests. Wood, as well as being an important item of export, was used as fuel and to make sleepers; until the end of the nineteenth century, wood was the principal fuel for steam locomotives. All in all, 28 million ha of forest were cut down. River transportation also expanded, the number of steamers exceeding 6,500. By 1914, motor vessels numbered 70 (87% of their total number in the world).

Despite some resurgence after the abolition of serfdom, agriculture remained backward. Growth in production was achieved mainly through extensive methods. The yield of grain crops increased slightly, reaching, on the average, 400 kg/ha, which was three times less than in Germany or Belgium. The maximum harvest, taken in 1913, amounted to 80 million tons. Russia's dependence on imported machinery, equipment, and chemical products stimulated the export of grain (in 1910 it amounted to 13.5 million tons), even though there was a deficiency of grain in the country.

To sum up the development of anthropogenic impact during this period, forests and soils were the most severely damaged aspects of nature. Forests were practically destroyed over large territories. Soils were depleted on peasant farms, which occupied about 70% of all arable lands. Intensive technologies were used only on landlords' farms, and on only some of these.

Socialist Development: 1917–1987

The force of human impact during the third stage and the rate of its development are unparalleled. Continuity with previous rates of growth was preserved only with regard to population, although the structure of growth changed. The birth-rate was halved, but since the death-rate went down even more, natural increase remained high until the 1960s, when it fell as a result of a demographic transition characterized by families with few children. In 1979, 153.7 million people lived on the territory of the Russian Plain, and the estimate for 1987 is 161 million. During the past 300 years, the population of the region has increased tenfold.

Considerable changes have occurred in the distribution of population between city and countryside. Industrialization resulted in the growth of the number of towns and cities. After 1917, 445 new towns emerged on the Russian Plain – almost as many as during the whole preceding period – and their number now exceeds 900. Urban population also started to grow rapidly; during 70 years, it has increased almost by a factor of five, and now has reached 110 million (68% of the total). The proportion of rural population is constantly decreasing. This distribution was mainly a result of rural migration to towns (56%); natural increase in towns provided 26%, and the remaining 18% came from administrative transformations, from which rural settlements were redesignated as urban settlements (Fig. 33.3). Starting in 1950, the decrease of rural population on the Plain became not only relative, but absolute. On the whole, it is a progressive process, reflecting the higher productivity of agricultural production. The number of rural settlements has also decreased with the abandonment of small villages.

The volume of industrial production has increased more than 70 times since 1913. New industries have been created; mining in particular has become much more developed. New deposits of oil were found in the Komi ASSR, and the Ukraine and the middle Volga regions were called "another

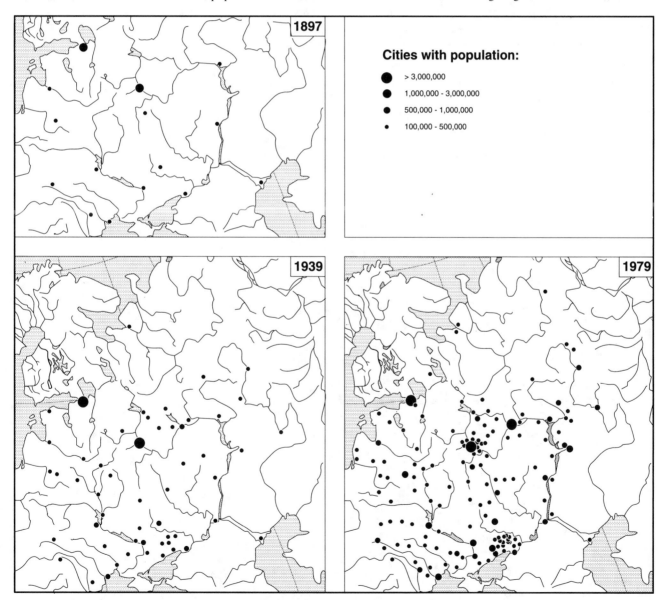

Figure 33.3 Locations of large cities: 1897, 1939, and 1979.

Baku''; in 1950–1960, this region produced 70% of the oil in the USSR; coal (Vorkuta); brown coal (45 million tons between 1940 to 1950 in the Moscow area); iron ore (the Kursk magnetic anomaly); phosphorites (the Moscow, Estonia, and Kirov regions); and other minerals. Although many fuel industries moved east, about half the country's fuel and at least 60% of its electric energy are still produced on the Russian Plain. Shortage of energy in the region has required the development of nuclear power plants. Out of 23 Soviet nuclear plants in operation or under construction, 20 are on the Russian Plain.

It is estimated that settlements, roads, industrial works, and quarries occupy 120,000 km², or 2% of the territory of the Russian Plain (Fig. 33.4). The development of industry intensified anthropogenic impact in numerous ways. Lands were taken up by new industrial (and municipal) construction, by opencut mines, and by terriconics and burial grounds of wastes. Atmospheric emissions of carbon dioxide and harmful chemical compounds, oxides of sulfur, nitrogen, and phosphorus, as well as dust and aerosols, increased, as did water consumption, not only for industrial purposes, but also to dilute industrial wastes.

Transportation has undergone some qualitative changes. Traditional types of transportation by rail (the length of railroads has reached 100,000 km) and water were supplemented by automobiles, aviation, and pipelines. On railroads, motor and electric locomotives replaced steam, and motorboats are now the most common type of vessel on seas and rivers. Individual automobile transportation developed rapidly after World War II. The length of hard-cover roads increased from 30,000 km in 1913 to 600,000 km in 1975, of which about 300,000 km are high-quality cover.

Agriculture has also changed greatly. It is now represented mainly by large-scale collective and state farms (kolkhozes and sovkhozes). Production has experienced a major turn toward intensification through the greater use of machinery, electricity, and chemicals. The yield of grain crops increased from 450 kg/ha in 1913 to 900 kg/ha in 1986. The productivity

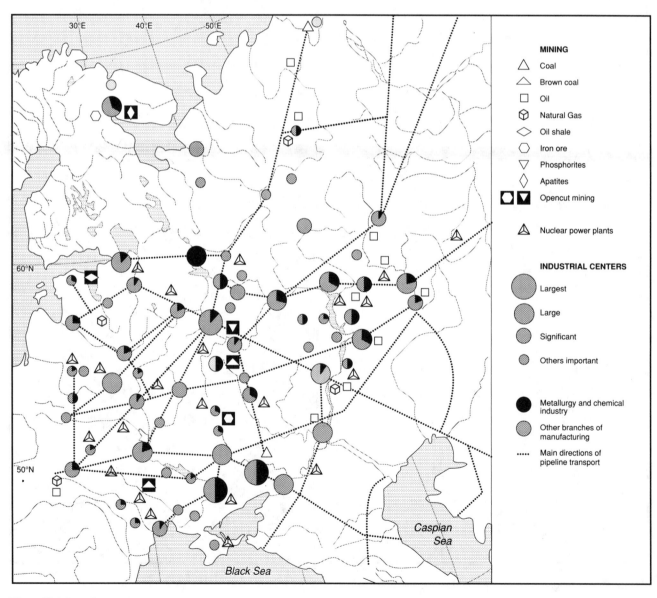

Figure 33.4 Location of industry in the 1980s.

of stockraising has gone up considerably, and the yield of milk per cow has doubled, reaching 2,500 kg/yr. Such intensification, however – especially the use of mineral fertilizers and chemical pesticides and weed controls – has made the industry one of the major anthropogenic agents affecting the environment.

A peculiar feature of the third stage of development was World War II (known as the Great Patriotic War in the Soviet Union), which lasted from June 1941 until May 1945. The war brought severe damage not only to population (the prewar level was reached again only in 1955), agriculture (the prewar area under cultivation was restored by 1950), and industry (the prewar level of production was restored in 1953–1955), but also to the environment. Military operations were conducted across a territory of 3.5 million km^2. Forest cover shrank considerably, and soils went untended. The overall damage caused by the war to the Soviet Union is estimated at 2.5 trillion roubles (expressed in prewar prices). The rehabilitation of the economy required great material and human resources, and considerably retarded postwar development.

Land Use in Historical Perspective

Two major historical trends have occurred in land use on the Russian Plain: the expansion of lands used for agriculture and the increased alienation of lands for industrial, social, transportation, and other nonagricultural purposes. The expansion of territory occupied by arable lands (fields) was most rapid at the end of the nineteenth and the beginning

of the twentieth century. It increased in the steppe and forest-steppe zones mainly through deforestation and through the conversion of other types of agricultural lands into plowed fields; in the forest zone, by deforestation. On the whole, during the capitalist period of development, the area of plowed lands decreased somewhat only in the center of the Russian Plain, while on the periphery, especially in the south, southeast, and east, it increased by 1.2–1.5 times as compared with the feudal period (Fig. 33.5; Table 33-3).

In the mid-1960s, the expansion of territories occupied by agricultural lands, and by arable lands in particular, continued. The territory of arable lands has almost doubled as compared with the end of the nineteenth century. Today, territories with an immediate productive value (agricultural lands, exploited forests, and lands occupied by industry, settlements and transportation) make up 90–91% in the southern Plain. Thus, almost all lands are productively used.

Alienation of lands for nonagricultural purposes is a result of growth in industry and transportation and of the increase in settlements. At the beginning of the 1970s, nonagricultural uses took up less than 5% of the northern Russian Plain and about 5.5% of the southern Plain but in industrially developed areas, such as the Donetsk-Dnieper region, they occupied 7%. In the past decade, about 400,000 ha annually have been taken up by construction sites and roads; 45% of this land is subtracted from agricultural use, and even more in the southern Plain. It will be an important task to reduce areas occupied by settlement and industry, to limit the development

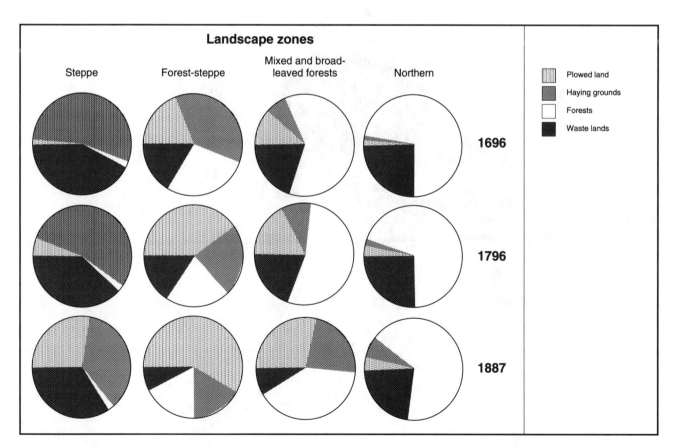

Figure 33.5 The structure of land use for the period since the end of the seventeenth century and until the end of the nineteenth century.

Table 33-3 *Changes in Land Use on the Russian Plain between the Late Nineteenth Century and the 1960s (Using Categories from the Earlier Period)*

Structural components of lands	Percentage of total area of the Plain	
	1877	1966
Arable lands (fields)	20.0	41.4
Hayfields and other used lands	14.6	22.0
Forests	42.3	30.2
Badlands (swamps, sands, ravines, etc.)	23.1	6.4

of "land-consuming" industries in valuable agricultural regions, and to devote lands unfit for agriculture to urban and industrial construction.

Major Environmental Transformations

Each of the socioeconomic periods described made its own contribution to the anthropogenic evolution of nature on the Russian Plain. Each prompted the emergence or aggravation of certain critical situations, followed by certain social responses to negative transformations.

Vegetation

The forest cover on the Russian Plain in the seventeenth century had already been affected by traditional types of economic activities; the problem of forest protection and regrowth had already emerged during the reign of Peter the First. In the taiga zone, changes were focused around settlements or in belts along rivers. At the end of the seventeenth century, forest cover in the taiga remained very high (83.9% of the total taiga area), whereas farmlands made up only 4.5%. The subzone of broad-leaved forests, however, was already so much changed that it did not exist as an uninterrupted band. Forest coverage on the Russian Plain has declined continuously during the past 300 years (Fig. 33.6) from 52.0% to 32.5% of the total area. Deforestation was greater in the southern taiga-forest area and the steppe; in the zone of mixed and broad-leaved forests, forest cover has now diminished by one-third; and in the steppe zone, by one-half (Figs. 33.7, 33.8). The process was most intensive from the end of the seventeenth until the end of the nineteenth century. This period witnessed the active development of the fleet, the building up of metallurgy, salt-making, and potash production, charcoal burning, and the expansion of plowlands. But deforestation was still focal in its pattern (except

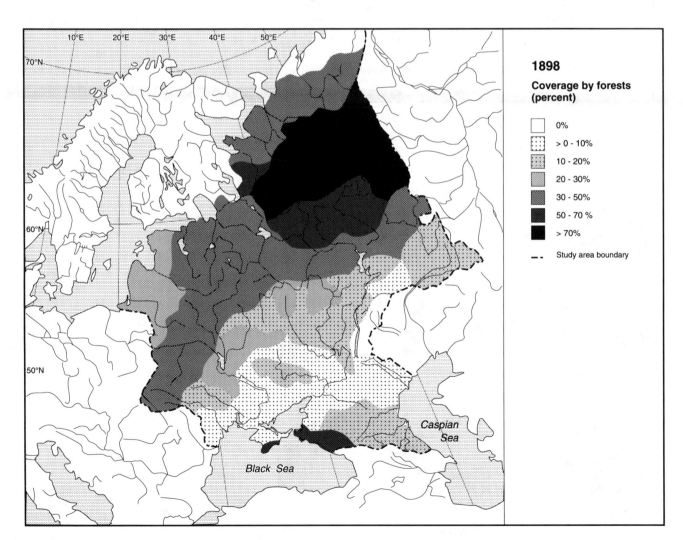

Figure 33.7 Forest resources, 1898. Coverage by forests in percent.

Coverage by forests (percent)

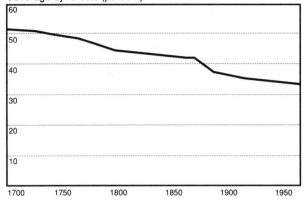

Figure 33.6 Forest area on the Russian Plain, seventeenth to twentieth centuries.

nineteenth century, but its impact was substantial from the very beginning. Steppe biomes, like the biomes of the broad-leaved forests, have been entirely transformed during the past 100–150 years. Today, virgin lands exist only in reserves. Intensive transformation of vegetation on the floodplains of medium-sized and large rivers began as late as the second half of the nineteenth century and reached a maximum in the 1950s and 1960s, due to the construction of a cascade of dams on the Dnieper, Volga, Don, Kama, and other rivers. Before this, floodplains had been used for hay-making, lumbering, and limited plowing.

Assessments of the degree of transformation of zonal biomes on the Russian Plain over the past 300 years provide the following rather rough figures: for the tundra, 15–30%; for the taiga, 30–50%; for the mixed and broad-leaved forests, 40–60%; for the steppe, 60–90%; and for the semiarid lands, 50–70% of the total area of the corresponding natural zone is characterized by transformation of its biomes.

for areas around large towns and northern territories) and was associated with rivers down which timber was floated.

Agricultural development in the steppe began only in the

Soils

As in the case of vegetation, the transformation of soils as a result of human activities stems mostly from agriculture.

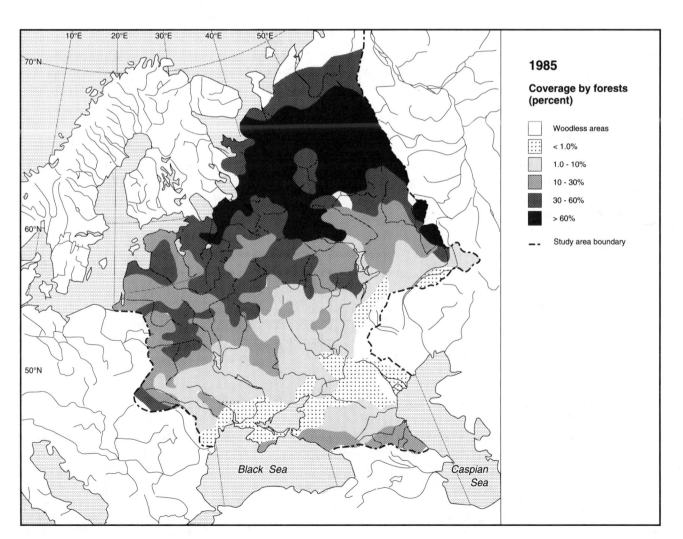

Figure 33.8 Forest resources, 1985. Coverage by forests in percent.

Distribution

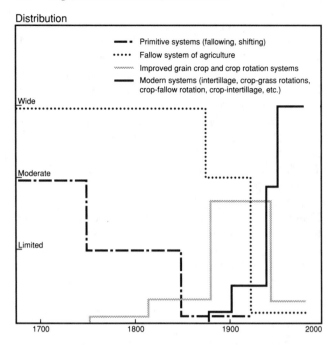

Figure 33.9 The spread of agricultural systems on the Russian Plain, 1700–1985.

As natural cover is replaced by farmland of any type, the principal changes in the process of soil formation are caused by changes in the chemistry and the amount of biological cycling; fertilizers added to the soil; mechanical disturbance of either the upper profile by shallow plowing, pastures, or hay-fields, or of the entire profile by deep plowing or certain types of drainage; and changes in the hydrological and thermal regimes.

Three major groups of farming systems succeeded each other historically on the Russian Plain (Fig. 33.9). Primitive systems included slash-and-burn, woodland, long-fallow and, swidden systems; the two former prevailed in the forest zone, and the two latter in the steppe. In all of these systems, the natural vegetation was destroyed and the plot was turned into a plowland for up to 10 years. Plowing was shallow and fertilizers were not applied. When yields went down, the plot was abandoned to revegetate naturally.

The fallow and three-course systems involved the succession of grain crops and fallow (in the forest zone: barley, oats, fallow; rye, oats, fallow). The systems permitted a three- to fourfold increase in the area planted with grain, but ecologically they put much greater demands on the soil; and given the lack of fertilizers, they brought about soil degradation.

The present-day lea system relies on crop rotations of varying duration (usually 5–9 years): intertilled, grain-tilled, grain-grass, and others. The soil is in use constantly. This system is the most hazardous ecologically, because it requires deep plowing (to 35 cm) and large amounts of fertilizer; where agricultural technology is poor and fertilizers are deficient, the soils are exhausted. Crop rotations including grass have the mildest effect, whereas those including intertilled crops have the strongest.

By 1700, the fallow system was already widespread, but it was combined with primitive systems that lasted until 1930. At that time, the modern lea system was actively used; it had been introduced at the end of the nineteenth century. The late nineteenth and early twentieth centuries were characterized by a diversity of land-use systems; during this period, all systems were applied, including ones intermediate between fallow and lea-improved grain and fruit rotation, used mostly in the western regions.

Two related indices, fertilizers and yields, indirectly describe the state of the soil as a natural resource in different periods. Most farmlands were not fertilized with manure before the 1930s, whereas mineral fertilizers were widely used only in the 1950s and 1960s. The active use of chemicals in agriculture undertaken during the past decade has not so far established a deficit-free type of farming over the entire territory of the Russian Plain. Unlike some regions, located mostly in the western Plain, center and eastern areas still suffer from shortage of organic and mineral fertilizers.

Throughout the 300-year period, the productivity of grain crops has increased constantly with the advance of farming systems and agricultural technology. If at the beginning of the eighteenth century it was 200–250 kg/ha, by the end of the nineteenth century it reached 250–500 kg/ha over most of the territory, and at the beginning of the twentieth century, it amounted to 375–625 kg/ha. In the 1980s, the mean productivity of grain crops over the entire Russian Plain remained low (900 kg/ha), although in western areas and on advanced farms it ranged from 1,500 to 3,000 kg/ha.

The overall low productivity and the shortage of fertilizers suggest that some soils on the Russian Plain have been degraded and that their natural productivity has been exhausted as a result of their extensive exploitation over the period in question. The chernozems were most severely damaged, because it had been long believed that they needed no fertilizers at all. At present, agriculture on the Russian Plain, as in the whole of the USSR, aims at establishing intensive and deficit-free farming over the entire territory.

Drainage was conducted locally in Russia, even before 1700, for construction purposes in towns and monasteries, and for the regulation of river flow in densely settled areas. The first major drainage project was undertaken during the construction of Petersburg (1703) and the improvement of its vicinity. The most important early drainage operations for transportation purposes were the Vyshny Volochok system, which joined the Volga and Neva rivers, and the Ladoga channel. Little agricultural drainage was undertaken because of the abundance of free land. Reclaimed wetlands were usually planted with rye, and later used as pastures and haylands (Table 33-4).

In the nineteenth century, drainage was more widely undertaken, with particular attention given to turning swamps into pastures, haylands, and grain fields. Another purpose was peat-mining near Petersburg, in the northwest, and in some central districts. At the beginning of the nineteenth century, tile drainage came into use. The drainage of swamps and bogged lands became still more extensive under capitalist development in the late nineteenth and early twentieth centuries; the purpose was to improve natural forests and

Table 33-4 *Development of Soil Drainage on the Russian Plain after 1917 (1,000 ha)*

Areas	Years					
	1913	1921–23	1928	1932	1967	1980
Russian Federation	800	420	1,430	2,000	1,640	3,860
Byelorussia	290	110	290	380	290,000	6,400,000
The Ukraine	44.0	20.0	73	160	537	681
Lithuania	64.0	—	—	—	970	2,180

haylands, as well as to provide waterways for wood floatage.

During the socialist period, major drainage projects were undertaken for the regulation of river flow in the center of the Plain and for large-scale hydrotechnical construction. The latter application required a very deep drainage (down to 4 m). Drainage also was performed widely for agriculture, especially after the 1960s. Mineralized lands are now reclaimed using closed drainage and moling, requiring deep soil loosening and liming; in swamps, dense open drainage is still in use. From 1913 to 1980, drained lands increased from about 2 million ha to over 12 million ha, and irrigated lands from less than 1 million to over 5 million ha.

Until the nineteenth century, irrigation was confined to small plots in the south of the Plain due to the complexity of the work and the low density of population. Irrigation projects at that period included the Volga bottomland (Verkhnyaya Akhtuba), 2–4 ha plots occupied by gardens, vegetable gardens, grain crops, and meadows. During the nineteenth century, the extent of irrigated lands steadily increased, mostly in southeastern Russia, where a slightly hilly terrain prevailed. Estuarine irrigation based on the accumulation of spring water predominated. Water reservoirs, ponds, and entire systems were constructed in the Ukraine and the lower reaches of the Volga on steppe chernozyoms and chestnut soils.

At the end of the nineteenth and the beginning of the twentieth centuries, vast territories were provided with regular irrigation in units of up to 1,000 ha and more. Methods included gravity irrigation from ponds; inundation of small plots and check-plots came into use. Irrigation began to spread westward and into the Black Sea region. Beginning in 1894, land improvement became a state matter, with the establishment of the Department of Land Improvement in the Ministry of Agriculture. After the drought of 1901–1907, estuarine irrigation was introduced widely into the Volga regions that had been most severely damaged.

After 1917 and up to World War II, irrigation channels and water reservoirs were constructed in the Rostov region and on the Kuban River. From the 1960s through 1980, irrigation was used throughout the southern Russian Plain. Although estuarine irrigation was still in use, new methods appeared, including sprinkling and inundation of check-plots and markets. By 1980, irrigated lands made up as much as 5–6% of the total tilled area in the southeastern Plain.

Tillable lands on the Russian Plain over the 300-year period were largely sod-podzolic soils in the forest-taiga zone, grey forest soils in the zone of broad-leaved forests, and cherno-zems in the steppe. Transformations of those three types of soils will be the focus of this discussion.

The transformation of general soil properties (chemical, physiochemical, and physical) in agriculture is determined by the level of land management and the degree of fertilization. Those conditions also determine the evolution of anthropogenic sod-podzolic soils. At a low level of land management and with a scarcity of fertilizers, the soil remains acid. The content and reserves of humus considerably diminish; its composition remains fulvic and its mobility is even slightly increased. Absorption capacity and amount of absorbed bases (Ca, Mg) decreases. Physical properties are considerably impaired: the density of soil goes up while its porosity goes down; the fine fraction is partially lost and its mechanical composition becomes somewhat light. Aggregate composition is characterized both by a decreased amount of particles of the most valuable size, which are crushed, and an overall reduction of the structure's water-resistance. All of those changes abruptly increase the erodibility of such soils. Their result under poor management and scarcity of fertilizers is a podzolization (acid eluviation), just as in natural soils. But in contrast to natural conditions, podzolization takes place under a much narrower biological turnover, and therefore proves more destructive to the soil mass. Removal processes occur in the entire topsoil. Such evolution produces degraded, overtilled, low-yield, sod-podzolic soil.

If the level of management is high and fertilizers are abundant, the properties of arable sod-podzolic soils change considerably as compared with their natural analogs. Acidity disappears; the content and reserves of humus, NPK amount, absorption capacity, and absorbed bases increase; and composition becomes humate or fulve-humate. Physical properties experience the same negative tendencies as under poor land management, but they are not so clearly manifested. Cultivated sod-podzolic soils are less subject to erosion than degraded soils, but more so than natural soils. Their evolution progresses toward a humus-accumulative (mollic) neutral state whose properties are favorable for farming. The analysis of processes in such soils, however, shows that this trend is not inevitable and that it needs to be artificially maintained. At lower levels of land management, cultural sod-podzolic soils are also degraded, though rather slowly.

While tillage changes the basic properties of grey forest soils to the same extent and in the same direction as in the case of sod-podzolic soils, there are also differences. These differences stem from the fact that these soils lie in the territory with a moisture coefficient of about 1.0 (which accounts for a potential steppe invasion after deforestation), and from their long-time extensive use at a threshold intensity of tillage (when forest landscape is replaced by forestless over huge territories). The result is soil "xerophytization and steppization," which above all, affects the nature of biological turnover and the state of humus. In this zone, when natural vegetation is replaced by grain fields, the addition of organic substances to the soil diminishes four- to six-fold. Tillage intensifies the biological decomposition and mineralization of organic substances, which brings about an intensive removal of humus, nitrogen, ash, and absorbed calcium from the topsoil. Data showing these trends are available for grey forest soils in Tataria over the past 40 years. The same regularity is found in the central regions of the Plain, where the content of humus and its reserves in grey and dark-grey forest soils decreased considerably as compared with their forest analogs. The loss of humus intensifies from the north to the south of the grey forest soil zone since the rate of mineralization and the history of exploitation increase in the same direction. The loss of humus results in a considerable deterioration of physical properties and severe disaggregation of the topsoil, abruptly intensifying erosion, which is also facilitated by the broken relief and adequate rainfall.

Large-scale plowing of chernozems started in the nineteenth century. Nowadays chernozems occupy 82–94% of the tilled lands. The long-term use of these soils has brought consider-

able changes in the content and reserves of humus. The work of V. V. Dokuchaev, from the 1880s, provides data with which to assess the development of this process. At that time, virgin steppes were still in existence, and the researcher could compare the state of humus in natural and cultivated soils. Another study was conducted on the same territory in the 1980s, and its results were compared with those of Dokuchaev (Figs. 33.10, 33.11).

The most significant losses of humus in the last century occurred in chernozems on the eastern Russian Plain (Table 33-5). At present, a humus equilibrium is not achieved on the whole of the chernozem zone. The doses of organic and mineral fertilizers applied in recent years on the Ukrainian forest-steppe and steppe chernozems still leave a mean annual humus deficit of 0.45–0.55 t/ha. A deficit-free humus equilibrium will be achieved when manure is applied in the following doses: in forest-steppe, about 8–15 t/ha; in steppe, 9–10 t/ha.

Humus is lost from soil not only by its mineralization and removal with crops, but also through erosion. In slightly eroded soils, humus content diminishes by 5–10%, and in strongly eroded, by 30–40%, as compared with noneroded arable chernozems.

Dry-land farming also changes other properties of chernozems. Chernozems clearly are acidified as they continue to be used without fertilization (by 0.3–0.5 pH unit as compared

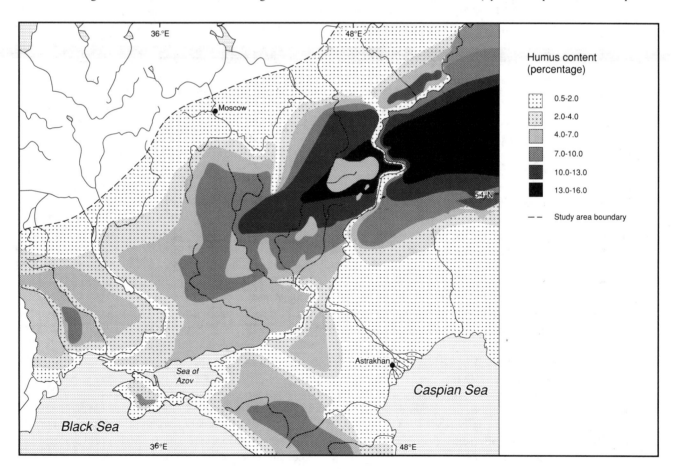

Figure 33.10 A schematic map of humus content in the upper horizon of soils in the chernozem zone, 1883. Compiled by V. V. Dokuchaev.

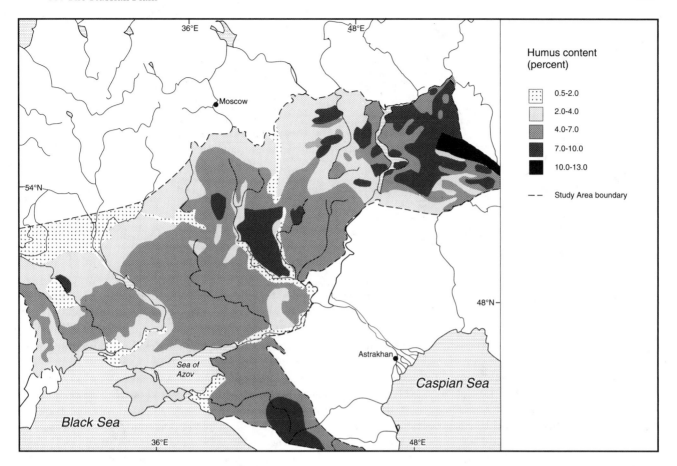

Figure 33.11 A schematic map of humus content in the upper horizon of soils in the chernozem zone for the 1960s through the 1980s.

with "virgin" lands). Absorption capacity and the content of exchange bases goes down. In the forest-steppe, chernozem absorption capacity fell from 47 to 39 m.eq./100 g; the loss of calcium amounts to 215 kg/ha out of the 0–35-cm layer during the 20-year period.

If fertilizers are not provided, physical properties also degrade. The structure is destroyed, density increases, and porosity decreases, as does the soils' erosion resistance. Manure is a universal fertilizer for chernozems, improving all of its properties, while the effects of mineral fertilizers remain ambiguous.

Irrigation produces a very strong effect on chernozems; it has been widely used since the 1960s, and in the past 15 years the area of irrigated chernozems grew 2.5–3.5 times. Irrigation results in a rise of groundwater within the range of the irrigation system and in the waterlogging of soils. Irrigation water comes in contact with rising groundwater, causing deterioration in the chernozems' water regime and in the landscape hydrology in general. A nonpercolative automorphic regime of chernozems (depth of groundwater 5–30 m) is replaced by a semiautomorphic percolative regime (groundwater depth 2.5–5.0 m) or even by a hydromorphic evaporative regime (1.2–2.5 m). The loess soil and ground column contains, as a rule, buried salt layers; following such changes in the water regime, salts gradually rise to the surface

and increase the soil's salinity. Sagging events take place and deform the surface. Lamination of the soil and ground column produces temporary or permanent lenses of surface water. Large regional hydrogeological basins are created on the periphery and within the range of irrigation systems. On the whole, secondary salinization of chernozems through irrigation is local, but by no means is it unusual. The hazard of secondary salinization is avoided if the groundwater level is not higher than 5–6 m.

Irrigated chernozems rapidly collapse and become lumpy, with a tendency to develop a crust after watering and rains. The state of humus also changes: at the beginning of irrigation its supply goes down and then rebounds, but the content of humus in the topsoil always diminishes. Experience shows that on chernozems irrigation should be minimal, used only to supplement natural precipitation. The irrigation system should be contained in closed pipelines to prevent seepage from channels.

Chernozems are particularly subject to damage when used for rice production. Because of irrigation, the redox regime and chemical properties change: elements with variable valence are redistributed and removed; and drainage water develops considerable amounts of silicon, iron, and aluminium. Soils become poor in humus – after 4 years of rice planting, 8–10% of the humus is lost. Soil-formation pro-

Table 33-5 *Changes of Content and Reserves of Humus in the Arable Layer (0–30 cm) of the Chernozems of the Russian Plain from 1881 to 1981*

Subtypes of chernozems	Regions	Content and reserves of humus				Losses of humus for 100 years (t/ha)	Annual average losses of humus (t/ha)	Losses of humus from the initial reserves (%)
		1881		1981				
		Content (%)	Reserves (t/ha)	Content (%)	Reserves (t/ha)			
Forest-steppe chernozems								
Typical	Central Plain	10–13	300–330	7–10	210–300	90	0.9	23–30
"	Southeastern Plain	13–16	390–480	8–10	240–300	150–180	1.5–1.8	38–39
Leached	Ciscaucasia	7–10	221–315	4–7	150–263	67–81	0.7–0.8	20–34
"	Volga region	13–16	390–480	4–7	120–210	270	2.7	56–69
Steppe chernozems								
True	Central Plain	7–10	221–315	4–7	150–263	52–71	0.5–0.7	17–32
"	Moldavia	4–7	126–221	2–4	75–150	51–71	0.5–0.7	32–40
"	Southeastern Plain	9–11	270–330	6–8	180–240	90	0.9	27–33

cesses change radically, and the chernozem is transformed into a different type of soil.

The transformation of chernozems in the course of agricultural use is diverse. In dry-land farming two states are possible: one close to the natural, with optimal fertilization and high level of land management; the other, degraded chernozems with humus reduction, acidification, decrease of exchange capacity and exchange bases, and deterioration of physical properties. Such negative transformations are in most cases reversible. In irrigation, the changes (mostly negative) cover a wide range, but they also can be reduced to two principal trends; chemical and physical degradation including progressive salinization; and the transformation of chernozems into gray-eluvial degraded solonetz soil after being used for rice production.

Relief

Human impact on geomorphological patterns and processes during the past 300 years has varied across the Plain. The consequences can be divided into two groups. Some human activities intensify, attenuate, or modify natural processes. They include different types of erosion and accumulation of soils and surface deposits, including artificial levelling of relief and the sagging of rocks caused by underground mining. They reflect a combination of natural and anthropogenic processes. Other forms of human impact are entirely different from natural processes. Examples include the creation of vast areas of open-pit quarries for the extraction of minerals and construction materials, producing unwelcome reliefs; the construction of terriconics and other tailings extracted during closed-pit mining; and hydrotechnical, transportation, and construction work that produces relief rising over the natural background. Both groups are considered here.

By 1700, soil erosion was already manifest on the Plain in the broad-leaved forests and the northern forest-steppe, areas of grey forest soils and forest-steppe chernozems. Data show

falls in yields and silting of minor rivers and water bodies as early as 300 years ago.

In the forest-taiga zone of sod-podzolic soils, the most dominant type of erosion has been caused by snowmelt. It has been estimated that during the past 100 years, sod-podzolic soils lost 1,217.9 t/ha of the fine soil fraction because of erosion triggered by agriculture; also 10,950 kg/ha of humus, 7,100 kg/ha of potassium, 610 kg/ha of phosphorus, 915 kg/ha of nitrogen were lost. From 2.5% to 14% of the total arable territory of this zone is eroded; the average for the zone is 6.6%. In the broad-leafed forests and northern forest-steppe, long-continued erosion brought considerable changes in mesorelief. Many gullies appeared, which observations over the past 50-year period show have continued to grow despite special steps to prevent erosion. The degree of gullying of this zone is very high. Autumn plowing has slowed down this process by reducing the amount of spring runoff, but has failed to eliminate it altogether. The transformation of relief in this territory can be attributed only to human activities, mostly agriculture.

In the steppe, tillage caused even more extensive gullying than in the forest-steppe. A new denudation process developed, moreover, that had been absent from the natural steppe – wind erosion in the form of dust or "black storms." The scope of such deflation can be great. A storm in 1960, with wind speeds up to 28 m/sec, completely blew away a 40-cm arable layer from a chernozem field not far from Donbass. Depressions are sometimes formed 10 m in diameter and up to 1.5 m in depth. In the south of the Ukraine, a sandstorm moved 1.2–1.6 km^3 of solid material, which amounts to 960–1,280 million tons of fine soil. Soil erosion by this and other processes is widespread in the steppe zone. 24.9% of the chernozem soils in the Ukraine are eroded, 17.8% slightly eroded, 5.2% moderately eroded, and 1.9% heavily eroded. Their location and the distribution of gullies identify erosion-hazardous areas (Fig. 33.12).

The environment, including relief, is heavily affected by coal and by iron-ore and oil-and-gas-extracting industries.

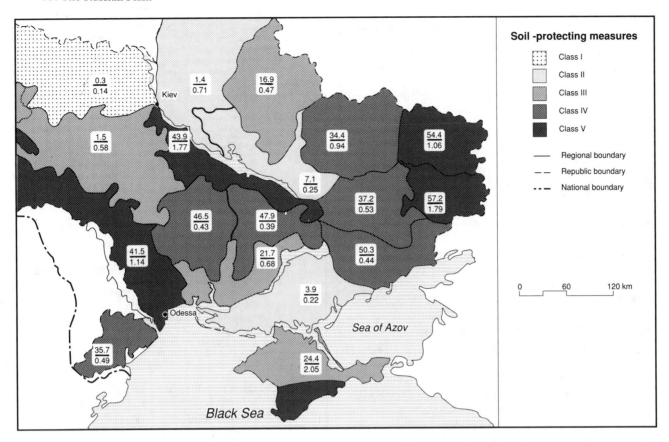

Figure 33.12 Regionalization of eroded lands (fractions) and soil-protecting measures (points I to V) within the Ukrainian SSR. In the numerator: area of eroded lands in percentage of the region's area; in the denominator: the area of gullies in percentage of the region's area.

The extraction of surrounding rock is several times greater than the amount of the basic mineral. During the 80 years' exploitation of the Krivoy Rog iron-ore basin, 560 million tons of raw ore were extracted. Quarries in the Kursk magnetic anomaly occupy an area 2–12 ha and more. Areas of extraction form large depressions (or saggings), while strip-mine tailings on the surface form raised mesorelief. Both processes destroy the natural landscape.

Maps of an iron-ore basin in the center of the Russian Plain contrast natural relief 200 years ago with modern, technologically transformed relief. In addition to overall changes in the pattern of the relief and its much increased spatial diversity, there has been a substantial change in the absolute and relative heights of its elements. The height of the newly created relief differs from that of natural relief by 200 m.

Hydrology

The trend toward the reduction of mean annual runoff of major rivers on the Russian Plain under the impact of human activities is evident. At present, it is most marked in rivers flowing to the south (Fig. 33.13), especially in their lower reaches. This is due to the high population density and water consumption in the southern Plain, with its developed industry and agriculture. The total irreversible water consumption on the Russian Plain in 1900 was 5 km³; in 1980, 45–60 km³. This growth took place in all spheres of water

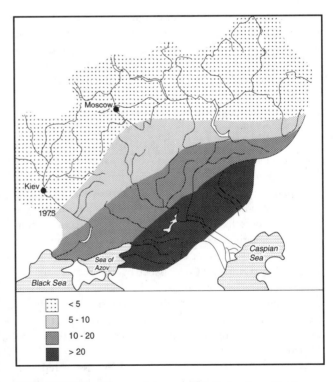

Figure 33.13 The decrease of river runoff in the southern Russian Plain under the influence of irrigated agriculture (in percentage of the period up to 1950).

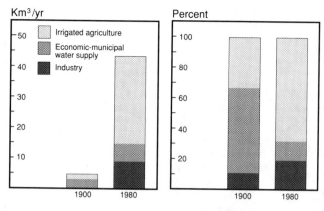

Figure 33.14 The structure of consumptive water use within the Russian Plain.

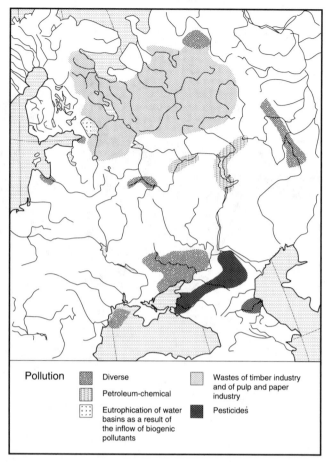

Figure 33.15 Regions with the greatest pollution of surface water, modern period.

consumption, particularly in industry and irrigated agriculture (Fig. 33.14). Before 1900, the Plain had only 6 large reservoirs, with a total storage capacity of 3 km^3; before 1950, another 31 reservoirs were built, with the total storage capacity of 68.6 km^3; and before 1960, 95 more, with the total storage capacity of 336 km^3. The reduction of annual runoff of regulated rivers is, in part, also a result of additional evaporation from the surface of the reservoirs. Losses caused in this way by the construction of a cascade of electric power stations on the Volga amount to 13 km^3/yr. High water losses are also typical of connecting and irrigation channels. Here, in addition to evaporation, water is lost by seepage through channel walls. A number of areas are already faced with the problem of adequate water supply of population and economy.

Along with decreasing water resources, there is an increase in salinity and water pollution (Fig. 33.15). This is most evident near large cities, near centers of mining and processing, in agricultural territories with a high level of mineral fertilizer use, and locally near cattle-breeding complexes.

Social Responses to Negative Consequences

By the beginning of the period examined, the Russian people had already developed certain traditions of careful management of those natural components that directly influenced production. Slash-and-burn farming, for example, was almost everywhere replaced by three-course farming, with the introduction of fallowing. Hunting and fishing were limited in reproductive periods. Measures for conservation had been incorporated into state legislation as early as the "Russkaya Pravda" in the eleventh century. The "Sobornoye ulozheniye" (Cathedral Code) issued by Tsar Alexei Mikhailovich contained as many as 20 articles dealing with conservation, especially of forests. Reserved territories included Belovezhskaya Pushcha since the fourteenth century, the bird reserve "Semiostrov" on the White Sea, and forests near Moscow.

Many nature-conservation documents are associated with Peter the First; they dealt with the contamination of rivers, bank fixation, the reservation of forests along rivers (20–50 km wide) and fishing regulations. The practice of introduc-ing game animals and birds into forests near Moscow and Petersburg dates back to 1737. Stricter hunting regulations were introduced in 1773. Conservation of the environment, moreover, was indirectly promoted by certain measures having a different purpose, including the planting of timber woods for the nation's fleet and the preservation of woods along the southern boundaries of the state in the interests of defense.

During the rule of Catherine II (1763–1796), the aristocrats procured the right to use forests at their will. Woods were cut down, the main consumer being developing industry in general. Forest cutting intensified after the mid-nineteenth century with the development of railroads, as noted. Between 1888 and 1914, 26 million ha of forests were obliterated, whereas afforestation efforts covered only a little more than 1 million ha.

The dawn of the twentieth century saw the beginning of public action for the protection of the environment in general, rather than of its separate components. It was at that time that the term "environmental protection" came into use. Between 1905 and 1912, nature-conservation societies appeared in Moscow, Petersburg, Kazan, Kharkov, and Ekaterinoslav, and a permanent committee for nature con-servation was established in the Geographical Society. Never-theless, the last decades of the capitalist stage were charac-terized by an acceleration in the exploitation of natural resources, aggravated by the negative consequences of World War I.

The first Soviet decrees were attempts to change radically the situation in the sphere of nature use. All natural resources were removed from private ownership and declared the property of the state. In 1918, a decree on the protection of forests was adopted; in 1919, on hunting regulations, and the protection of health resorts; in 1920, on the protection of all natural and "man-made" forests and shrubs; and in 1921, on the protection and restoration of fish stocks and the protection of cultural monuments. The existing reserves were transferred to the state (Askaniya-Nova) and new reserves were set up in the European part of the USSR. In 1924, the All-Russian Society for the Protection of Nature was formed.

In the first years of Soviet rule, the greatest attention was paid to restoring forests and soils, those natural components that had been most severely damaged in earlier years. Afforestation was conducted on a planned basis. Before 1948, 468,000 ha of shelterbelt forests, 266,000 ha of sand-fixing forests, and 181,000 ha of gully-control forests were planted.

The natural environment was gravely damaged by military actions and extreme economic conditions during World War II (1941–1945). The western, southern, and central parts of the Russian Plain were turned into battlefields. Entire landscapes in vast territories were transformed into defense earthworks (trenches, ditches, dug-outs) several meters deep, damaged by bomb- and shell-holes and passing heavy war machines, and their vegetation destroyed by fire. As a rule, there are no large forests more than 40 years old in the area occupied by Germany, since those forests had to be restored after the war. The requirements of the economy at that period, including military-oriented industries, meant and intensified exploitation of all natural resources. Even later, until the end of the 1950s, as the country rehabilitated the economy disrupted by the war, nature-conservation problems were not of primary importance.

At the end of the 1950s, however, the Soviet government adopted the first postwar decrees aimed at harmonizing the use of certain types of natural resources, namely, of lands (1954) and game animals (1959). Attention was paid to reducing the lands allocated for nonagricultural purposes, as well as to a strict observation of hunting regulations, and the overall protection of many species of animals.

Starting in the 1960s, "State Measures on Rational Utilization and Protection of the Environment" became part and parcel of domestic policy. The adoption of a legislative program and state laws dealing with specific natural components was the most important step taken in the past 25 years. These laws have included the framework of land-oriented legislation in 1968 (protection of lands, enhancement of soil fertility, creation of green belts, and strict protection of reserves), of water-oriented legislation in 1970 (organization of state control of the utilization and protection of water resources and of construction affecting water quality), and of forestry-oriented legislation in 1977 (protection and restoration of forests, survey of their composition, age, and acreage, and control of lumbering operations); legislation on the protection and utilization of the fauna in

1980 (reproduction and control of population strength and species composition of the fauna) and the Law on the USSR Red Data Book, 1983; and the Law on Atmospheric Protection in 1980 (standards for maximum permissible levels of emissions of contaminants into the atmosphere, creation of a unified system to take account of harmful effects and state control of air quality).

Between the end of the 1950s and the 1970s, all of the union republics adopted laws on the protection of nature. In the 1980s, such laws were adopted country-wide, and regional projects for the protection of nature were developed. Starting in the 1970s, the programs for the development of the USSR national economy for five-year periods have contained a section dealing with environmental protection and rational use and restoration of natural resources.

During the postwar period, the Soviet government issued many decrees dealing with specific natural components and with unwelcome processes caused or exacerbated by human activities. They addressed the reclamation, erosion, and recultivation of lands; control of forest and peat fires; the prevention of water pollution (including the Volga and the Ural rivers, the Baltic Sea basin, Lake Ladoga, and others); the protection of minor rivers from contamination and depletion; the protection of fish stocks and of wetlands that have an international significance as habitats of waterfowl; the preservation and reproduction of the population of polar bears; and many other nature-protection issues.

In the 1960s–1970s, the number of reserves and partial reserves (60 exist today) was considerably increased, their locations selected with a view to preserving natural examples of major landscapes on the Russian Plain.

Summary and Comments

The Russian Plain displays a diversity of natural landscapes. This natural mosaic has been overlain by the mosaic of human impacts. In the past 300 years, environments in the Plain did not undergo significant cumulative changes of a natural character, only the usual long-period fluctuations. Most transformations of the natural environment can be considered the results of exclusively anthropogenic influences. The central feature of nature–society interactions has been the extreme acceleration of anthropogenic pressures in the past 100 years, their concentration in this short time interval accounted for by the history of Russia during the twentieth century.

During most of the 300-year period, agriculture and forestry, among the branches of the economy, had the most extensive influence on nature; since the middle of the twentieth century, the influence on nature of some forms of mining and processing became more and more intensive. Nature-society interaction generally begins with the exploitation of a limited number of resources, followed by an increase of scope, up to the present day, when practically all components of nature are brought within the sphere of human activity. The consequence is a substantial increase in the threat to the biosphere of the earth as a whole and of its individual regions.

At present, all landscapes of the Russian Plain are to some degree transformed, except for some areas in the extreme north and in nature reserves. The most significant changes can be observed in the biota and soil cover. Forests cover a smaller area and are degraded in species composition. Areas under natural forest-steppe landscapes have greatly diminished, with the practical extinction of the natural steppe outside of nature reserves and a profound transformation of the floodplain vegetation. Depletion and transformation of the species composition and ratios of the major groups of animals and fish has included the extinction of several species. Soils have undergone degradation and erosion. Decrease of the mean annual runoff of the major rivers, and especially of small rivers, has been combined with higher mineralization and pollution of waters.

The principal problems on the Russian Plain are the protection and reconstruction of the valuable forest cenoses; restoration of the fertility of agricultural lands; deceleration and elimination of erosion; recultivation of disturbed industrial lands; and purification and protection of water resources. An important general task is to maintain and expand the areas of natural landscapes as the natural systems most "perfectly" organized for many purposes, including conserving the gene pool and studying and artificially reproducing natural relationships. Many of these problems are found in the majority of countries; the list has a global character.

Possible solutions to these problems include optimal use of resources, nonconsumptive agriculture ecologically safe animal-breeding, new technologies in industry that ensure more efficient water consumption, full purification of industrial sewage, and control of emissions to the atmosphere. The actual measures adopted should undoubtedly be region-specific.

Past social responses to negative transformations of the natural environments took the form of nature-protective legislation, which reduced the negative effects of economic activities in the Russian Plain. It is clear, however, that these social responses were never of the optimal character. They were not based on an "ecological" investigation of the problems, but were oriented toward the restoration of individual degraded components, ignoring the state of the natural environment as a whole. The solutions and tools that were adequate for a certain historical period proved inadequate in later years, when the discrepancies between human demands and natural potential produced new problems. The experience suggests that we reexamine the current strategies of environmental policy in regard to their safety and the protection of the interests of future generations.

The major criteria for assessing the needs and priorities of social response to negative transformations should be the rates of increase of the transformations; the likelihood of spatial expansion; the possible development of feedbacks that are often difficult to predict; and the need for long-term action to eliminate or reduce the damage inflicted. Pollution of the environment is one such key transformation. Its influence is already quite noticeable over considerable areas. The accident at the Chernobyl nuclear power plant produced the largest and ecologically most damaged area, but it is known that changes due to other types of pollution that evolve in a slow noncatastrophic way can also transform problem situations into crises. The place of priority in social response should be given to the problem of environmental pollution – which is probably true not only for the Russian Plain – and the spectrum of responses should cover the greatest possible range of negative transformations.

Note

1. The region incorporates most of the European territory of the USSR. Physicogeographical and economic-statistical boundaries of the Russian Plain do not coincide everywhere (Fig. 33.1); the economic and statistical boundaries of the Russian Plain used in this chapter in the description of economic and social indices have always included the whole of the lowland territory of European Russia, with Karelia and the Kolsk Peninsula.

Principal Works Consulted (titles translated from the Russian)

Agricultural Atlas of the USSR. 1960. Moscow: Main Department of Geodesy and Cartography.

Agriculture and Forestry of Russia. 1898. St. Petersburg.

Dulov, A. V. 1983. *Geographical Environment and the History of Russia. Late Fifteenth–Middle of Nineteenth Centuries.* Moscow: Nauka.

Economic-Statistical Atlas of European Russia. 1869. St. Petersburg.

Geography of Agriculture; Problems and Methods of Study. 1970. Moscow: Mysl.

Geography of Russia in the Fifteenth through Eighteenth Centuries: By the Evidence of Foreigners. 1984. Leningrad: Press of the All-Union Geographical Society.

Natural Resources of the Russian Plain in the Past, Present, and Future. 1976. Moscow: Nauka.

On Conservation of the Environment. A Collection of Documents of the Party and Government 1917–1985. 1986. Moscow: Political Press.

Problems of Rational Use of the Soils in the Nonchernozem Zone of the Russian Federation. 1978. Moscow University Press.

Russian Chernozem. 100 Years after Dokuchaev. 1983. Moscow: Nauka.

Semionov-Tien-Shanskiy, V. P. 1910. *City and Countryside in European Russia.* St. Petersburg.

Tsvetkov, M. A. 1957. *Change of Forest Area in European Russia since the End of the Seventeenth Century to 1914.* Moscow: Press of the USSR Academy of Sciences.

34

The United States Great Plains

WILLIAM E. RIEBSAME

From any vantage point in the vast, "treeless" region called the Great Plains of the United States, the earth-transforming effects of human activity are apparent. Agricultural settlement of this semiarid plain over the past century pervasively altered its floral, faunal, pedologic, hydrologic, and biogeochemical faces and flows. Prehistoric human inhabitants also changed the Plains environment, but the massive transformations examined in this chapter result from a century of settlement and use of the region by immigrants who established a dryland farming system that has become pivotal to world grain supplies.

The frontiers of cultivation offer an especially useful laboratory for studying the process of transformation. Clark (1962: v) commented that:

From the time of our earliest archeological records of western civilization, one of the most important and interesting kinds of geographical line has been that between "the desert and the sown." This boundary, between land used by man for the grazing or hunting of animals that live on steppe grass or desert shrub and land plowed and used for growing crops, rarely has been fixed in any area for long periods of time.

The progress of Plains settlement was often viewed as fulfillment of a national destiny, or as the "wooing of the earth," to use Dubos' (1980) phrase for the human creation of socially nurturing landscapes. Others, however, felt that the grassland was too fragile for extensive farming, and urged caution as the settlement wave moved westward (e.g., Sears 1980). After a century of settlement and transformation, the Great Plains still spark controversy over the proper human use of semiarid grasslands.

This chapter first describes the nature and extent of physical transformation of the Great Plains, fitting landscape changes into a descriptive typology. The region's transformation is then examined in the context of historical social forces, institutions, and specific technologies that were instrumental in the creation of the world's most productive dryland wheat region.

The Great Plains

In the middle of the North American continent lies a broad topographic plain of semiarid climate, grassland ecology, and agricultural economy (Fig. 34.1). Its western border is marked dramatically by the front ranges of the Rocky Mountains. The other borders of this roughly rectangular region are less distinct, marked by subtle gradients of climate and vegetation (cf. maps by Kuchler 1949; Shantz 1923). To the north, along the 53rd parallel in Canada, the grasses interdigitate with the aspen forests that border the circumpolar taiga. At its southern boundary, in Texas and New Mexico, the grassland gives way to desert scrub (oak and mesquite). The eastern margin has been variously delineated by the 98th meridian, the 700–760 mm annual isohyets, and the edge of the bluestem grasses that skirt most of the eastern Plains (e.g., Great Plains Committee 1937). The United States Great Plains, the focus of this chapter, includes an area of roughly 1,314,500 km^2, with 6.2 million inhabitants and a population density of 4.74 persons/km^2.

Two great climatic gradients characterize the Plains: a south-to-north decrease in mean temperatures, and an east-

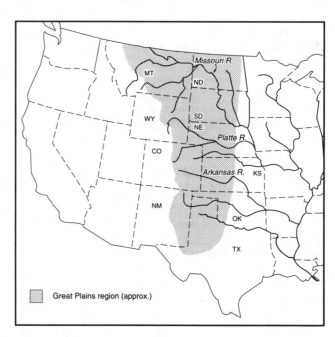

Figure 34.1 The Great Plains region of the United States.

to-west decrease in precipitation. Finer details of both contemporary and past Great Plains climate have been carefully documented (Barry 1983; Borchert 1950), but these two gradients overshadow many other factors in determining the region's environmental characteristics. Moreover, they have interacted in a fundamental way with human settlement and use of the region. Whereas primeval human immigration probably progressed from north to south, toward more accommodating climates, agricultural settlement proceeded east to west – down the precipitation gradient toward greater aridity and more frequent drought. This pattern had important implications for the region's transformation, as agriculture was extended into increasingly risky environments, and farmers worked closer to the margin of survival and resource sustainability (e.g., Hewes 1979).

Risk and marginality also define the social environment of the Plains. A fuller understanding of the region transformed is achieved by analyzing not only its physical attributes, but also its symbolic and historic role in the development of American society. The Great Plains has long evoked strong, often contradictory, images in people's minds (Blouet and Lawson 1975). Seen variously as the "Great American Desert" (Bowden 1975), as part of the alluring frontier that shaped the American experience (Smith 1950), as the stage on which the tragedy of the Dust Bowl was played out (Gray 1967; McDean 1986), or as "breadbasket to the world," the Great Plains stands out in history and in the American consciousness. The history of agricultural settlement is one not only of physical transformations, but also of the transformation of ideas and institutions.

The Great Plains Transformed[1]

The vegetation, soil, topography, and hydrography of the Plains have been altered by a society gripped by an agrarian vision articulated by its leaders, supported by its values, and pursued with the tools of both pseudo-science and technology. It is a seminal historical fact that the Great Plains region of the United States was originally settled in the late 1800s under a federal policy of disposing public land into private hands as quickly as possible. This disposal policy ended in the early 1900s in response to private abuse of resources, especially of forests in the East and Midwest, and in keeping with a growing movement for efficient resource utilization under government management (Hays 1975). By then, however, the basic pattern of Great Plains settlement had been set. The region was divided into farms of from 0.6 to 2.6 km^2, fulfilling a symbolic vision of independent farmers owning and working manageable units of land.

Great Plains settlement proceeded rapidly after a series of laws, beginning with the Homestead Act of 1862, established and strengthened the mechanisms for quick, cheap land acquisition. Despite drought-induced setbacks in the mid-1890s and 1910s, population grew quickly through 1930 (Fig. 34.2). Only two Great Plains counties lost population between 1920 and 1930 (Thornthwaite 1936), and even the drier, western areas had achieved rural population densities of up to 6 persons/km^2 by 1930 (Fig. 34.3), marking the zenith of rural settlement on the Plains.

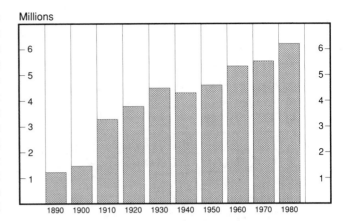

Figure 34.2 Great Plains population. All regional statistics apply to the area mapped in Fig. 34.3. Source: U.S. Census Bureau.

Like many other aspects of Great Plains development, population patterns and trends changed markedly in the 1930s due to drought and depression. Though overall regional population continued to increase (Fig. 34.2), rural population began to decline, balanced by urban growth (Fig. 34.4). Recognition that the original homesteads were too small to survive led to farm consolidation and declining farm numbers (Fig. 34.5). Farm size averaged 1.8 km^2 though 1935, but had doubled by 1960 and tripled by 1980 (Baltensperger 1987). These enlarging, capital-intensive farms are the basic social institution through which human transformation of the region has occurred.

The Chief Transformations

The major human transformations of the Great Plains are listed in Table 34-1. Most obvious to the casual observer are tillage (termed sodbusting when the original grass cover is plowed), crop cultivation, tree planting, and water impoundment. Less obvious are human impacts on runoff, groundwater, and soil structure.

A simple classification of transformations is also offered in Table 34-1, under the headings of areal extent (region-wide, subregional, local), dispersion of the impact through the environment (a continuum from diffuse to concentrated),[2] and "naturalness" (a continuum from natural to nonnatural). The last attribute indicates the similarity between the

Table 34-1 *Major Human Transformations of the Great Plains*

Transformation	Areal extent	Dispersion	Naturalness
Tillage, cropping	Regional	Diffuse	Natural
Tree planting	Subregional	Concentrated	Seminatural
Runoff change	Subregional	Diffuse	Seminatural
Water impoundment	Local	Concentrated	Nonnatural
Groundwater depletion	Subregional	Diffuse	Nonnatural
Soil structure change	Regional	Diffuse	Nonnatural
Soil chemistry change	Regional	Diffuse	Nonnatural
Soil and water pollution	Regional	Diffuse	Nonnatural

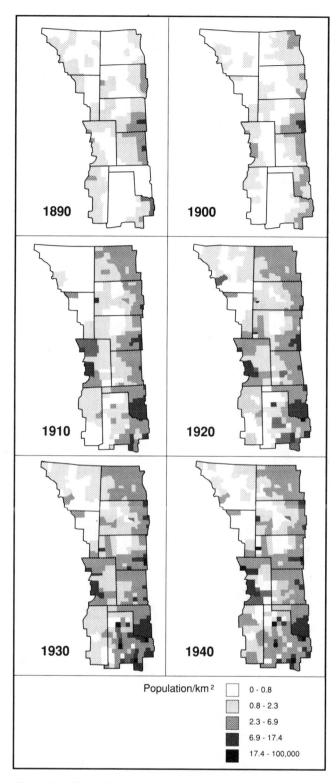

Figure 34.3 Great Plains population density. Maps for 1890, 1900, and 1910 were derived from Thornthwaite 1936, and 1920, 1930, and 1940 data are from the U.S. Census Bureau. Other data presented in this chapter apply roughly to the area mapped here.

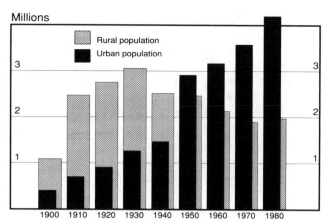

Figure 34.4 Great Plains urban and rural population. Source: U.S. Census Bureau.

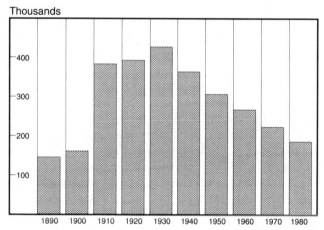

Figure 34.5 Total number of commercial farms on the Great Plains. Sources: U.S. Census Bureau and state statistics.

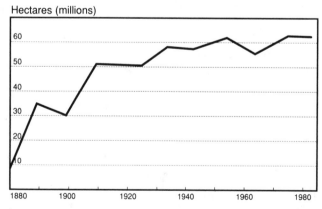

Figure 34.6 Total Great Plains cropland. Sources: U.S. Census Bureau and state statistics.

transformed environment or environmental element, and the presettlement state or component it replaced. For example, wheat in many ways is a facsimile of the short- and tall-grass vegetation complex it replaced (such as drought resistance, surface roughness, albedo, and seasonal cycle) it thus resides near the natural end of the natural/nonnatural continuum. Tree planting and water impoundment fall closer to the nonnatural end.

Tillage and Crop Cultivation

The central human transformation of the Great Plains has been the conversion of grassland to cropland. Over 90% of the land of the Plains is in farms and ranches. Roughly 75% of this land is cultivated, with wheat the dominant crop; the remainder is grazed. The non-farm land is divided between urbanized areas, infrastructures such as highways and railroad rights-of-way, and public preserves including parks, national grasslands, and wildlife refuges.

Small grains cropping is a widespread but relatively natural transformation that creates an environment not too dissimilar to the presettlement grassland, though one with reduced species diversity. Large, continuous tracts of dryland wheat and other small grains are cultivated throughout the region, even in the western, drier reaches. The area under cultivation began to increase quickly around 1890, expanding rapidly through the 1920s (Fig. 34.6). Slower growth ensued as the agricultural frontier approached the Rocky Mountains, and as droughts and economic downturns interceded. Yet, despite occasional set-backs, expansion is the dominant characteristic of the record to modern times; a new maximum of cultivated area was set in 1983.

The decadal census of cultivated land, however, obscures large, short-term swings, which emerge in the annual record of the region's dominant crop, wheat. Much as an ecologist identifies a key species as indicative of a particular habitat or certain environmental factors, wheat is an "indicator species" of human use of the Great Plains.[3] The crop's rise and fall (Fig. 34.7) reflects the impacts of physical and social forces, both internal and external to the region. The initial trend of steady expansion endured, with a set-back due to drought in the mid-1890s, until economic depression and drought made wheat production unprofitable and, in places, impossible during the 1930s. This was the Dust Bowl epoch of farm failure and outmigration.

Despite efforts to reduce crop area through land retirement programs, wheat cultivation rebounded quickly after the 1930s as war demand took effect. More lasting land retirement was effected only after the second major Plains drought developed in the 1950s. Even then, relatively low grain prices and technology-based yield increases were probably as

important in achieving land retirement as any commitment to conservation or the decreasing availability of grassland for expansion. When the economic signals again suggested expansion, it followed quickly.

Indeed, dramatic cultivation increases in the 1970s – associated with large export demand – provoked the current concern over "sodbusting," the plow-up of remaining, mostly marginal and highly erodible, grassland. Data on sodbusting are poor, but rough surveys show that much of the Plains includes large cultivated areas in highly erodible and marginal land classes (Table 34-2). Additional large tracts of land are susceptible to future plowing if market conditions (e.g., low cattle prices and high wheat prices) encourage it. These conditions prevailed in 1972, when world grain prices rose dramatically due to droughts and export demand (see Garcia 1981). Depressed livestock prices and aggressive international marketing helped increase wheat area by 50% between 1970 and 1975; for the first time, more than half of all U.S. wheat was exported (U.S. Department of Agriculture 1985:38).

The largest single-year cropland increase occurred in 1973–74, when $16,000 \text{ km}^2$ were added to the U.S. total, including some $8,000–12,000 \text{ km}^2$ of new cropland in the Great Plains (Grant 1975). Up to $21,000 \text{ km}^2$ of grassland were converted to cropping in the central and northern Plains in another surge of cultivation during 1979–81. Though recent price declines and reinvigorated government conservation programs have tempered this latest plow-up (U.S. Soil Conservation Service 1987; see also Heimlich 1985), expansion of cultivation on the Plains continues, especially on the western fringes (Huszar 1985).

Tree Planting

The urge to plant trees on the Great Plains is rooted in people's values about the environment and their beliefs about its potential modification. From early settlement to the present, Plains folk have believed that trees ameliorate the harsh physical environment, both locally and regionally. Trees have been ascribed an almost magical power to modify the climate and otherwise improve the land for human habitation, and tree planting was part of the "rain follows the plow" syndrome, which is discussed later (Kollmorgen and Kollmorgen 1973).

Table 34-2 *Highly Erodible Cropland* in the Northern and Central Great Plains*

State	Cultivated Area (km²)	Potential New Cultivation (km²)
Colorado	109,075	427,868
Kansas	70,077	223,972
Montana	94,588	475,422
Nebraska	95,982	394,630
North Dakota	59,700	98,525
South Dakota	40,328	234,838
Wyoming	20,700	345,258

* Includes Soil Conservation Service soil classes 4e, 6e, 7, and 8.

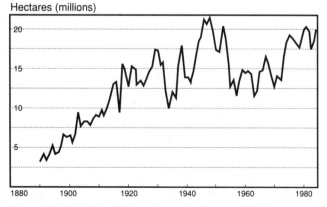

Hectares (millions)

Figure 34.7 Total Great Plains wheat area. Sources: U.S. Census Bureau, U.S. Department of Agriculture, and state statistics.

Tree cultivation on the Plains, referred to here by the title given early efforts – the "shelterbelt" program – is one of the few documented, historical cases of conscious and concerted effort to transform the environment of an entire region. How well it succeeded, and whether the program should be continued or perhaps revitalized, is still debated today.

In *Man's Role*, Clark doubted the success of the shelterbelt program, but it also has been called the Plains' salvation. Though trees were planted by early settlers, the shelterbelt program began formally in the 1930s, when President Franklin Roosevelt, impressed by soil erosion during the Dust Bowl, issued an executive order establishing the Prairie Forestry Program (something of a contradiction in terms). Huntington (1934) predicted at the outset that the effort to forest the Plains would founder on ecologic and economic realities. Yet the shelterbelt movement gathered momentum even in the absence of any credible evaluation of its effectiveness. Today it is difficult to assess just how widespread and successful tree planting was; official numbers differ widely and no definitive survey has been conducted. There is little doubt, though, that millions of trees have been planted in rows along field margins since the 1930s; the shelterbelts are a conspicuous feature of the landscape, even in the drier, western Plains. Tree planting is thus a widespread, unnatural transformation with mostly local or even microscale impacts. Widespread and conspicuous, however, does not necessarily mean efficacious.

Roosevelt's original vision of a 260-km swath of trees covering roughly 300,000 km^2 along the 100th meridian touched off a scientific controversy over its feasibility, and an economic debate over its practicality, but surprisingly little debate over its expected physical benefits, including both local and regional climate amelioration (Zon 1935). Despite conflicting opinions within the government, the program went forward, and its accomplishments have been variously estimated by numbers of trees planted, area "protected," or the total length of rows of tree. Between 1934 and the mid-1940s, when planting slowed due to decreased funding and increased rainfall, over 46,000 km of shelterbelts, encompassing perhaps over 200 million trees, were planted (Gilbert 1977). The total length of windbreaks was probably never over 65,000 km, despite arguments in early plans and by contemporary shelterbelt supporters that 400,000 km of trees are needed to "adequately protect" the region (Griffith 1976). Half-hearted planting programs aimed mostly at maintaining and replacing original shelterbelts continue to the present. Most new planting has been in farmstead windbreaks that improve the microclimate for livestock and people.

The shelterbelts today are deteriorating and are being removed (Griffith 1976; U.S. General Accounting Office 1975; U.S. Soil Conservation Service 1977) – a detransformation process of sorts. Occasional shelterbelt surveys were conducted after the 1940s, but as Sorenson and Marotz (1977) pointed out, inconsistent sampling methods make any trend difficult to detect. A government survey in the late 1970s concluded that shelterbelt removal (chiefly to accommodate larger fields) was being balanced by new plantings, such that there was a 2.5% increase between 1970 and 1975 (U.S. Soil

Conservation Service 1977). Sorenson and Marotz's (1977) more detailed survey in Kansas, however, indicated a 20% reduction between 1956 and 1970. They question more positive government surveys and argue that the shelterbelt is degrading for several reasons, including the old age of the trees, pest infestations, and field configurations required by larger machinery.

Even Sorenson and Marotz are convinced that the original rationale for planting trees on the Plains remains valid, arguing that windbreaks conserve soil, save moisture, and improve crop yields. This view was originally derived of reports from the Soviet New Lands region that windbreaks were crucial to successful agriculture on the Asian steppes (e.g., Bolyshev and Solov'yev 1958). But, not all empirical studies support it. Greb and Black (1962), working at the Central Great Plains Experiment Station near Akron, Colorado, found that the extension of tree roots into fields extracted moisture and nutrients and thus actually reduced adjacent crop yields. Studies of soil erosion have showed mixed results from windbreaks, and the debate continues.

Transformations of the Hydrologic Cycle

Human intervention in the hydrologic cycle on the Plains affects four principal variables: runoff, soil moisture storage, surface storage, and groundwater.

Changes in Runoff due to Cultivation Most researchers agree that cultivation of grasslands increases runoff, at times quite dramatically (see Glymph and Holtan 1969 for a review). Longitudinal field studies of this effect are rare, however, and some conflicting evidence exists. More detailed studies in the region just east of the Plains led Sartz (1975:92) to conclude that "tilled cropland is by far the greatest source of flood runoff and stream sediment. . . . Rainfall runoff from tilled land may be as much as 10 times greater than from hayland or pasture." Long-term studies in several humid watersheds in the eastern United States support this view (Glymph and Holtan 1969), but the evidence from semiarid grasslands is not as compelling. Indeed, Shiklomanov (1983) showed that intensive fall plowing on the Soviet steppes actually decreased runoff.

Experimental watersheds monitored for a few years in the 1930s showed that both total runoff and peak runoff rates were slightly higher in cultivated than in grassland catchments on the southern and central Great Plains (Fig. 34.8; also Allis 1948), but no long-term data are available, and the same may not hold under different tillage practices. Comparative studies conducted during a brief period in the 1940s and 1950s in three small (2-to-3-km^2) watersheds near Hastings, Nebraska, lend support to the notion that grassland cultivation enhances runoff (Allis 1952; Allis and Kelly 1958), but also showed that certain tillage practices could reverse the effect. After observing runoff from two watersheds farmed in the traditional straight-row plowing method for seven years, researchers intervened in one by instituting conservation tillage. These practices essentially emulate the precultivation condition; for instance, natural drainage-ways are seeded to grass (the grassed area in the experimental watershed

Runoff (m³/second)

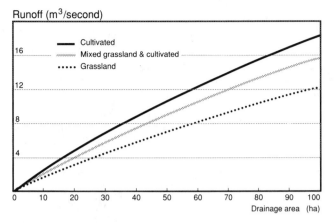

Figure 34.8 Peak runoff rates for different land covers in the central Great Plains. Source: Allis 1948.

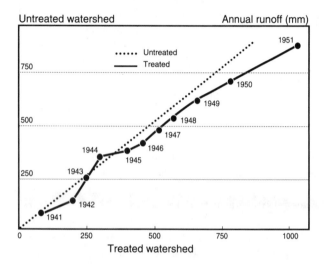

Figure 34.9 Accumulated runoff from two watersheds, showing a small decline in runoff from the "treated watershed" after conservation techniques were implemented in 1944. Source: Allis and Kelly 1958.

increased from 10% to 17% over five years), and crop stubble is not plowed under. A modest reversion to precultivation hydrologic conditions occurred in the experimental watershed (Fig. 34.9).

Because modern conservation tillage practices, including less plowing and disturbance of surface crop residue, result in demonstrated increases in soil moisture, it can be inferred that greater tillage exacerbates runoff. Brunn and colleagues (1981) found that much of eastern North Dakota, where 80% of the land is cultivated, exhibited a statistically significant increase in streamflow since about 1940, without an increase in areally averaged precipitation. No streamflow change was found in western North Dakota, where less than half the land is cultivated and where cultivation grew more slowly during the period (Vining et al. 1983). A study of flood flow characteristics in the same area, however, showed no change over time (Miller and Frink 1984), suggesting that not all of the enhanced streamflow found by Brunn and his team

derives from runoff. An alternative explanation is that soil moisture accumulated under conservation tillage may be contributing to increased base flow – at least for rivers in the eastern Plains.

It has been demonstrated throughout the Great Plains that certain cultivation practices – alternate-year fallowing, minimum tillage, and stubble mulching – reduce soil moisture loss, thus increasing crop yields (see, for example, Greb 1979; U.S. Department of Agriculture 1974). Summer fallow and minimum tillage can reduce soil evaporation by 30% or more, and now dominate cultivation throughout the Plains (U.S. Department of Agriculture 1974). Spath (1987) notes that minimun-tillage strategies on fallow in northeastern Colorado achieve moisture efficiencies (the proportion of fallow-season precipitation retained in the soil profile) of 30–45%.

Indeed, summer fallow is so moisture-efficient that, especially in the northern Plains, it has led to the development of saline seeps by creating perched water tables. Over 325 km² of farmland in eastern Montana and up to 400 km² in North Dakota have been damaged by salinization from seeps (Halvorson and Black 1974). Some estimates put growth of salinized areas at 10% annually. Saline seeps associated with dryland farming have been recognized in other parts of the Plains (Brown et al. 1982) and in other dryland farming regions of the world, but the problem has been studied less than seeps and salinization associated with irrigation.

Surface Water Impoundment   Small-scale runoff impoundment is common throughout the Plains. Farmers have created thousands of small ponds to hold water for livestock, to allow water spreading in hay fields, to reduce erosion, and to attract wildlife. In North Dakota alone, for example, roughly 50,000 small ponds have been created with government assistance since the 1930s, and over a million human-made ponds now exist on the Great Plains, most covering only a few acres (U.S. Geological Survey 1970:167). Impoundment is thus a widespread, but only locally significant, intervention in normal water runoff, storage, and evaporation.

The Plains region is not known for large lakes or reservoirs, though a few have been constructed: Fort Peck Reservoir in Montana, Lake Sakakawea in North Dakota, Oahe in South Dakota, McConaughy in Nebraska, Wilson in Kansas, and Meredith in Texas, each inundating several hundred thousand square kilometers (cf. Fig. 34.1). The combined storage volume of large (over 0.5 km³) reservoirs on the Plains equals roughly 41.5 km³ – only a small proportion of the runoff either generated on the Plains or traversing the region from montane watersheds to the west. Even so, a significant proportion of total runoff can be stored in some basins. The Missouri basin in the northern Plains produces roughly 30 km³ of average annual runoff, and encompasses a developed storage capacity of 35 km³ (some of this in the mountains to the west of the Plains). Yet, even this large storage irrigates little crop land; the Oahe Reservoir stores 14 km³ of water, but provides irrigation to only 770 km². In 1982, only 75,000 km², or 12% of all Great Plains cropland, were irrigated, over half with groundwater.

Although humans have not intervened significantly in surface storage and distribution of water on the Great Plains proper, growing water use to the west, in the Rocky Mountain foot hills, is increasingly affecting the hydroecology of Plains rivers. For example, the Arkansas River is usually completely dewatered before it reaches the Colorado–Kansas border, and interstate and environmentalist conflicts have developed over the decreased flow of the Platte and Missouri rivers. Planned water storage facilities for metropoli in Colorado's front-range urban corridor could lead to significantly reduced flow of the Platte and other rivers that, among other uses, provide critical habitats for species such as the whooping crane (see U.S. Army Corps of Engineers 1987).

Groundwater Changes The hydrological intervention needed to support 40,000 km^2 under irrigation on the Plains is focused on groundwater, not runoff. Changes in aquifers, such as the Ogallala that underlies much of the southern and central Great Plains, are described in detail elsewhere in this volume and will be mentioned only briefly here.

Irrigation by center-pivot sprinkler systems in the Ogallala area expanded rapidly after World War II as crop prices remained high, deep-well and sprinkler technology improved, and energy became cheaper (High Plains Associates 1982). Demand on the aquifer increased dramatically (see chap. 15). Because the Ogallala experiences no natural recharge under current geoclimatological conditions, the inevitable occurred: water levels dropped drastically in some areas, the cost of pumping went up, and the complex physical and economic infrastructure built around center-pivot irrigation was threatened. In response, the U.S. Congress mandated a detailed study of water supply alternatives for the region (see High Plains Associates 1982:35). The study concluded that the Plains would require water imports by the turn of the century or face serious social disruption, a conclusion that partly derived from the other major conclusion: that irrigated farmers could not easily revert to dryland agriculture because of altered soil conditions and economics.

An emerging groundwater problem in the region is fertilizer and pesticide pollution. Groundwater contamination by fertilizer nitrates has been reported in all parts of the Plains (see Canter 1987; and Fairchild 1987, for surveys of the problem). Studies in the central Plains (reviewed in Canter 1987) show that average groundwater nitrate amounts increased 25% from the mid-1960s through the mid-1970s. Nitrate-nitrogen concentration exceeded the standard public health threshold of 10 mg/1. in 70% of the samples taken from 256 wells in Nebraska during 1976–77. Nitrate concentrations from 45 to 170 mg/1. have been found in many parts of the Ogallala aquifer, and reported in most other Great Plains states (Fairchild 1987). Pesticide contamination is probably only slightly less widespread, and is increasing with the adoption of minimum-tillage cultivation, which requires greater pest control (Baeumer and Bakermans 1973). The common no-till pesticides Atrazine and Alachlor are already present in groundwater in central Nebraska (Fairchild 1987), although Atrazine carry-over on the surface is relatively small (Smika and Sharman 1984).

Soil Transformations

Like groundwater changes, soil transformations are not obvious to the casual observer, but may be critical to long-term resource sustainability. Chief among these transformations are soil profile disturbance due to tillage, compaction by heavy machinery, subtraction and addition of nitrogen and phosphorus, soil erosion, and the accumulation of toxic materials.

Soil Structure No region-wide assessment of soil structure transformation has been conducted, but a few site studies show that common tillage practices disrupt at least the upper soil horizons, breaking down natural clods and mixing topsoil with subsoil (Langdale et al. 1984). Subsoil effects are less obvious, but potentially serious. Smika and his colleagues at the Central Great Plains Experiment Station claim that a "tillage pan," an impervious, compacted subsoil layer caused by frequent working with heavy machinery, has developed in many areas of the central Great Plains. It disrupts water percolation, root growth, and the effectiveness of fertilizers. Perhaps half of the cultivated land in the Plains is affected by this condition.

Soil Chemistry Human intervention in soil chemical cycles, especially the nitrogen cycle, is a fundamental element of agriculture. From settlement until the mid-1900s, Great Plains farmers relied mostly on natural nitrogen cycling (enhanced by certain crop rotations and occasionally supplemented by manure) for soil fertility. Crop harvesting and export, especially under early practices that left little stubble, depleted the nitrogen store developed under the orginal grassland. Over the past century, roughly half of the nitrogen, 30–40% of the sulfur, and 10–30% of the potassium have been removed from cultivated Great Plains soils (Bolin et al. 1983:23). Consequently, crop yields declined until about the mid-1950s, when artificial fertilizer application became widespread. By this time, the depletion of key chemical com-

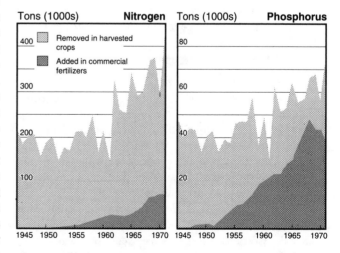

Figure 34.10 Nitrogen and phosphorus (a) removed via harvesting and (b) added chemically in North Dakota. Source: North Dakota Agricultural Statistics.

pounds had progressed to the point that small additions produced large increases in yields, and fertilizer application caught on quickly (Fig. 34.10). Even in the last decade, however, removal has outstripped addition, and the "mining" of soil chemical compounds critical to fertility continues.

Soil Erosion　Both water and wind erosion of soil has been exacerbated by human use of the Plains. Erosion by water is perhaps the most controversial human impact on agricultural lands. Some analysts (e.g., Pimentel et al. 1976) feel that it threatens the future productivity of the U.S. granary. Other studies are less certain, and the evidence remains mixed. The U.S. Department of Agriculture (1980) estimated that 16% of the Great Plains cropland exhibited serious water erosion (compared to 23% nationwide), but perhaps 25% suffered serious wind erosion – the largest of any U.S. farming area. Crosson (1986), however, analyzing these and other data, concluded that even if current erosion rates were sustained for the next 50 to 100 years, related yield declines in the Midwest and Great Plains would be less than 10%, and perhaps only 2%.

Wind erosion is the chief concern in the Plains. Indeed, it is the raison d'etre of many conservation programs, including the shelterbelt. The U.S. Soil Conservation Service (SCS) had its origin in the "black blizzard" dust storms of the 1930s. Yet data on wind erosion are of questionable quality, and the effectiveness of many prescribed conservation methods is judged more by assumption than by analysis, the case of shelterbelts being a good example.

Uncertainty over the importance of soil erosion is partly due to poor historical data and lack of standardized measures of erosion rates and impacts. Although little doubt exists that cultivation increases soil erosion, debate rages over the rate of erosion that is "damaging" and how to measure it (National Research Council 1986). Erosion in some parts of the Great Plains removes up to 10 or more megagrams per hectare per year, and recent surveys suggest that over half of the region's farmland is on soils and slopes susceptible to significant erosion (U.S. Department of Agriculture 1980). These studies, however, remain ambiguous as to the ultimate threat that soil erosion poses to long-term sustainability in the Great Plains.

Summary of Transformations

This survey of human transformations of the Great Plains environment outlines the major changes associated with agricultural development of the region over the past century. Several other human impacts have been neglected, the most notable being those associated with the limited urban development in the region: heavy-metals accumulation in soils, industrial-site wastes, air pollution, the effects of coal mining and oil drilling, and the multifarious aspects of urban sprawl associated with the few cities within the region (e.g., Bismarck, North Dakota) and the fringe metropoli (e.g., Kansas City, and the Colorado front range urban corridor). These impacts are overshadowed, however, by agricultural impacts in this predominantly rural region.

Historical Contexts of Agricultural Development

Explanations of regional development typically focus on "fundamental" causes, such as population pressures, economic imperatives, and environmental attributes, or on such proximate factors as infrastructural improvements that accompany and assist development. These explanations figure prominently in the Great Plains literature, ranging from Thornthwaite's (1936) benchmark analysis of population growth and decline, to Borchert's (1987) recent analysis of northern Great Plains settlement patterns and transportation systems.

However, transformation of the environment is accomplished by people either consciously or unconsciously seeking certain goals within more broadly defined social and institutional guidelines. Thus, the explanatory approach used here is to describe the historical social contexts of transforming human activities. A descriptive historical model of regional development is created by dividing the last century into periods characterized by dominant development ideas and the associated institutional and individual behaviors that coalesced to create the modern human and physical landscape.

Development of the Great Plains Agricultural System

The dominant historical pattern of Great Plains agricultural development is its consistent trend toward both expansion and intensification of dryland small-grains production and marketing by owner-operated ("family") farms.[4] Except for minor set-backs, this pattern has been insensitive to negative feedback from the environment, in the form of droughts and resource constraints, and from the economy – the "invisible hand" of grain prices and input costs. Yet, despite enduring expansion and intensification of dryland farming, predictions about Great Plains social development and prescriptions for its appropriate direction are based on normative, homeostatic principles emphasizing the creation of a diverse and presumably more stable social system (e.g., Great Plains Committee 1937; Ottoson et al. 1966). In the prescribed system, risks from environmental and market fluctuations would evoke scientific land-use and farm-management strategies centered on diversification. Since first settlement, however, Great Plains agriculture has tended toward a rather uniform pattern of small-grain farms growing in size and in the level of technological input, rather than in ecological planning or enterprise diversification.

Indeed, Plains scholars are often surprised and dismayed by persistence of the monocultural wheat farm typical of the region. Despite John W. Powell's presettlement prescription for diversified land use centered on cattle grazing, the Great Plains Committee's recommendations in the 1930s that land use be matched to diverse land capabilities, and contemporary observers' often strident calls for diversification and/or abandonment (see, for example, Lockeretz 1978; Popper and Popper 1987 and Worster 1979), Great Plains farmers remain committed to dryland grain production on a massive scale. This persistent pattern of development is better explained as the result of historical social values, institutions, and symbols, rather than the guiding force of Darwinian adaptational mechanisms.

Social Factors in Great Plains Development

Though exhibiting some changes in technique and strategy over the past century, Great Plains farming has not undergone the more fundamental structural transitions experienced in other agricultural regions (de Janvry and LeVeen 1986), including the adjacent "corn belt" (Hart 1986). Throughout its history, Plains farming fits Turner and Brush's (1987) category of a neotechnic commodity system marked by monocultural management and large technical inputs.

In the face of shifting selective forces (emanating from the market, government, environment, and community, see Bennett 1982), the ideas and institutions supporting, justifying, and encouraging development were changed, but the basic institutional and individual goals for use of the Great Plains as an extensive small-grains region remained. Except during the 1930s, when the signals for a fundamental change in course were briefly overwhelming, expansion of dryland farming in the region has been continuously justified by new or revived development theories articulated by farmers, technologists, outside investors, and government officials. At least five development themes can be identified in Great Plains history:

1. Boosterism, mythical bounty, and anticipated climate amelioration during the frontier years;
2. Pseudo-scientific adjustment of farming methods to match the environment during the so-called dry-farming movement;
3. Social and ecological adjustment in the 1930s – which temporarily weakened expansionary pressures;
4. Technological manipulation of the environment especially after the 1940s;
5. Marketing and business efficiency during the 1970s and 1980s.

Though other observers might identify different sets of themes, these five appear to encompass rather neatly the changing social contexts of Great Plains development.

Boosterism and Early Settlement

The original grassland plow-up, the most obvious human transformation of the Plains, occurred especially rapidly in the first few decades of settlement. The critical condition for creation of commodity agriculture on the Plains was the region's transformation from a grassland, seen through eastern eyes as relatively unproductive and underutilized (Kollmorgen and Kollmorgen 1963), to intensive cultivation. Several cultural forces promoted rapid settlement. The nation's leaders felt a strong need to expand settlement to the western lands, and the mythical and real American frontier offered powerful symbolic opportunities (Cummins and White 1972).

Bennett (1982) notes that "the political pressures to open the western lands to the burgeoning populations of the East, especially during periods of industrial unemployment, were simply too strong to resist . . . " (p. 39). The historical record indeed shows little resistance. Rapid growth was propelled by government land grants and empowerment of railroad corporations to build lines and create towns. Settlers were attracted by land grants under the well-known 1862 Homestead Act and subsequent legislation and by the flood of propaganda or "boosterism" that was part hucksterism and part expression of the American spirit of optimism (Baltensperger 1974; Emmons 1971). The newly formed Great Plains states proclaimed their virtues, as illustrated by statements issued by the Dakota Commissioner of Immigration:

> The great extent of magnificent soil, of cheap lands easily tilled, and yielding a bountiful return for the husbandman's efforts, is rapidly crowding the Territory toward her eventual position as the garden spot of the Nation; the depot for the food supplies of the Union. The East can never compete with Dakota in the cheapness of the production of a bushel of wheat, no more than can she raise wheat of an equal quality. (1891:81).

A staple of the booster literature was the quasi-scientific myth – promulgated by hucksters and some government scientists – that the region's semiarid climate would be permanently ameliorated by cultivation – a myth encapsulated in the phrase "rain follows the plow" (Kutzleb 1968). The theory was baseless, but widely believed, because, according to Kollmorgen and Kollmorgen (1973), the treeless Great Plains landscape evoked a syndrome of "landscape meteorology" in which people's intuitive links among humid climate, trees, and lush crops was stood on its head in the notion that the climate could be changed for the better by the addition of trees and crops.

Few questioned the wisdom of rapid Plains settlement, despite Powell's admonition that only limited agricultural settlement be allowed in carefully selected sites (Stegner 1953). As Hewes (1975:203) put it, "those who broke and farmed the dry grassland did not know of Powell's warning or perceived the plains differently." The goals and mechanisms of rapid development, based predominantly on national priorities and agricultural strategies conceived in eastern, more humid contexts, remained unexamined until the first postsettlement drought hit the region in the 1890s.

The Pseudo-Scientific Solution

Many parts of the Great Plains achieved their greatest population densities between 1890 and 1910, though some environmental and economic problems began cracking the facade of boosterism during the same period. The frontier attitude that ignored the risks of cultivating even the most marginal land, belittling the record of increasing farm failure due to drought, pests, finances, or simple ineptitude, paled slightly in the face of drought-induced reverse migrations after 1890. Warrick and Bowden called the mid-1890s drought:

> a disaster. . . . After a number of years in which optimistic agriculturalists flooded into the largely uncultivated margins of the frontier, the region experienced a net displacement of nearly three hundred thousand people. Many areas lost between half and three-quarters of their population (1981:126)

Barrows called it the "first great crushing defeat" of American farmers (1962:231).

With the system apparently in need of propping up, external forces poised the region for another round of expansion after about 1910, which would come to be known as the "second great plow-up." U.S. Department of Agriculture officials promoted the notion that greater Plains cultivation was necessary to avoid famine and to compete on international markets (Secretary of Agriculture 1909). The droughts faded (physically and symbolically), and two factors made expansion both possible and profitable: tractor power dramatically increased farmers' ability to work larger areas, and prices began climbing toward a maximum induced by World War I.

Still, a new development rationale was needed to assuage the concerns raised by the first busts. The discredited booster notion that the region's dry climate would be modified by human action could, theoretically, have been replaced by changed goals for regional development or by a new development theory that supported further expansion. Farmers and government officials in a position to lead opinions and set policy believed that the system could be maintained. A large investment – by the railroads, the government, eastern entrepreneurs, and farmers – was threatened by the prospect of postboom retrenchment. It would have been difficult for them to admit that homesteading, sodbusting, and monoculture farming were mistakes.

An alternative to the myth of frontier bounty enhanced by human settlement was found in its antithesis: that human use of the region could be modified to fit the environment. This theory required little change in the fundamental goals of agricultural expansion and intensification, and entailed no alteration of basic values and attitudes. Rather, it required faith that human technology could be modified to suit the environment, a shift that also suited the progressive thinking of the period. Thus it drew on a basic American belief: that technology can overcome all obstacles (see Zelinsky 1973).

What was needed was an appealing, reasonable-sounding idea concisely stated, some feasible way to apply it, and no immediate, overwhelming evidence against its validity. The so-called dry-farming movement of the early 1900s had all these characteristics. Dry-farming, extensively documented by Hargreaves (1957), was based on a new set of farming implements and strategies linked to intuitive, but unscientific, notions of how water is stored and transported in the soil. The dry-farming concept sprang originally from one South Dakota farmer, Hardy Webster Campbell, as he sodbusted thousands of acres of northern Plains grassland. The key ingredients of dry-farming were deep plowing, subsurface soil compaction, and maintenance of a "dust mulch" – a thoroughly loosened surface layer that supposedly blocked evaporation. As his system caught on, Campbell – backed by official sanction and eastern investment – designed dry-farming implements, promoted dry-farming through pamphlets, magazine articles, and books, and even created a dry-farming congress that traveled around the Plains.

The strategy was patently unsafe in the windy Plains, yet it caught on quickly in the relatively benign climate before the 1930s droughts. The railroads and the government supported dry-farming by establishing demonstration farms, though later analysis showed that many dry-farming techniques were worse than useless (it had even been suggested that trouble-some soils be loosened with dynamite!), and most were eventually debunked by government studies (see Chilcott et al. 1915; Chilcott and Cole 1918). Nevertheless, the dry-farming movement magnified human transformation of the region by offering an apparently safe way to expand cultivation on the dry uplands and into the drier western Plains just when enthusiasm for such endeavors had waned. It was a pseudo-science that rekindled the belief that most of the Plains could be successfully farmed, even among those suspicious of its methods (Hargreaves 1957). The result was the second great plow-up that propelled Plains crop acreage to a new maximum just before the Dust Bowl droughts of the 1930s.

The Social Adjustment Solution

Indications that Plains agriculture was misfit to the environment, and might even be degrading it beyond recovery, were multiplied when the agricultural system broke down due to drought and depression in the mid-1930s – the so-called Dust Bowl. Worster (1979) cites the Dust Bowl, with its soil loss, abandoned farms and out-migration, as an ecological catastrophe comparable to the desertification of the African Sahel. It takes a central place in any discussion of human transformation of the Plains; the questions it raises reflect an interpretive tension common in nature–society scholarship. This tension centers on the relative roles of natural drought on the one hand, and maladapted farming practices and social institutions, on the other, in creating the infamous soil erosion and farm abandonment that made the term "Dust Bowl" a vivid symbol of human abuse of the land (Riebsame 1986). Some scholars (e.g., Bonnifield 1979) see the climatic severity of the drought – something to be expected less than once in several hundred years – as the chief culprit, and marvel at the tenacity of farmers who survived and recovered. Others, such as Worster (1979) and Sears (1980), interpret the episode as the product of heinous human abuse in which resource conservation was sacrificed to driving economic greed. Some observers of the contemporary Great Plains warn that the "lessons of the Dust Bowl" – whatever they are – have been forgotten and that it might return (Lockeretz 1978).

While the disaster strengthened efforts to develop drought-resistant crops and new cultivation technologies, it is most important for the social adjustments it provoked: land retirement, adjusted land-tenure systems, resettlement, commodity credit programs, subsidized crop insurance, economic diversification, and other prescriptions for curing what had finally come to be viewed as persistent social maladaptation on the Great Plains (see, especially, the report of the Great Plains Committee 1937). For once, the basic tenets of agricultural development were questioned, and the opportunity to deflect further rapid development emerged.

Much was accomplished: a large area was protected as federal grassland (Hurt 1986); many dry-farming techniques were abandoned; conservation tillage practices, long known, were more widely adopted; trees were planted; and farm size was increased. Yet pressures for continued agricultural development soon regained their former dominance, as shown in the fate of land-use planning, the most promising adjustment of the period. Planning encompassed most other resource-use prescriptions, with the provision that they be applied through collective planning (Hargreaves 1976). State and county land-use committees were established under the aegis of such federal agencies as the Agricultural Adjustment Administration and the Soil Conservation Service in the first attempt to apply strategic, top-down planning to the region. Guidance came from the national level, where the National Resources Board and other new institutions reflected a philosophy of rational resource use (Hays 1975).

Although the land-use program had established 1,891 county committees on the Plains by 1942, it was scuttled in the middecade by wartime demand, increased rainfall, and opposition from groups, like the Farm Bureau, that called it a violation of private rights (Ottoson et al. 1966). Reflecting on the work of the Great Plains Committee, which championed the approach, White (1986) commented that:

the ability and willingness of a democratic society to change its management processes in a few decades was completely misjudged. . . . The committee envisaged a degree of acceptance of social change to achieve "best land use" that proved only superficial. (92)

. . . the major directions in which it went astray were in overly modest assumptions about technological change and overly optimistic assumptions about the receptivity of society to radical alterations in traditional processes. (93)

It was not long before those processes, notably market competition and technological innovation, were again guiding Great Plains development.

The Technological Fix

The rapid innovation and adoption of new technology for overcoming environmental constraints alluded to by White marked the emergence of a new era in Great Plains development after World War II. Yields increased dramatically as farmers increased inputs of fertilizer, pesticides, and new hybrids – which, in combination with strong demand, pushed crop production to an all-time high in the late 1950s. Drought in the mid-1950s provoked some renewed interest in social adjustment, and the Soil Bank Program established in 1956 was slightly more effective at retiring marginal land than were the land-use plans of the 1930s (Hewes 1967; Warrick et al. 1975). But the move toward larger technical input put farmers in a tighter cost-price squeeze that could be lessened only by placing more land into production. This pattern was supported by a national economy marked by growth, rising consumer demand, and growing capital investment in agriculture (Drache 1976).

These innovations marked a new pattern of human transformations. More subtle, cumulative changes in soil chemistry, water quality, and groundwater levels, described earlier, were added to the more obvious changes in the landscape like sodbusting and tree planting.

Marketing and Business Management

Technological inputs are still an important force in the transformation of the Great Plains, though perhaps some lessening of their impacts has stemmed from the environmental protection movement of the 1970s. However, a new development principle is now guiding human use of the region, exemplified by the federal government's decision in the early 1970s to loosen crop area restrictions and to encourage expansion in order to capture more of the burgeoning international grain market. Marketing, and the business-management skills needed to compete, now drive further transformation of the region.

The most dramatic manifestation of this new development paradigm was the Secretary of Agriculture's call, in 1972, for "fence-row to fence-row" planting to "feed the world." Food exports were seen as a way to ease the country's negative trade balance, and crop land became a speculative investment.

The impact of this new management philosophy was immediate and dramatic: crop area increased sharply, as did fertilizer and pesticide application. Grassland plowing and soil erosion quickened. Caught off-guard by the rapid expansion, the U.S. Soil Conservation Service (SCS) was forced to create a new conservation program (Grant 1975). Reflecting the need to resolve the basic antithesis of increased production and resource protection, the SCS program was heralded by the contradictory slogan, "produce more, protect more." The agency director managed to persuade the Secretary of Agriculture to temper his unabashed enthusiasm for expansion with statements warning farmers not to cultivate "soil that cannot adequately be protected" in order to avoid "starting another Dust Bowl" (Grant 1975:30). Yet, sodbusting increased (Heimlich 1985), and various efforts to reduce acreage in the early 1980s, such as the 1983 Payment-in-Kind Program, have been largely ineffective (U.S. General Accounting Office 1985). Only poor crop prices have slowed this latest episode of expansion and intensification.

Another impact of the expanded grain markets has been to make Great Plains farms into a unique hybrid of family operation and modern business firm. Increased farmer control over production and marketing provided by developments such as on-farm grain storage, higher land values, and a grain trade that rewards speculation and shrewd business management, have transformed farmers from agronomists to businessmen (Shertz 1979). While a large proportion of Great Plains farms (about 85%) are still operated by their owners, farmers now behave much more like the firms at which most normative economic analysis is aimed. Flexible and speedy harvesting, on-farm storage, improved highway transportation, and computer marketing give the farmer control over many aspects of the enterprise that were once controlled by institutions like grain-elevator companies and railroads (see, for example, Drache 1985).

What the marketing trend portends for the further transformation of the Great Plains is difficult to say. Conventional wisdom holds that a business approach distances the farmer from the land, heightening the attitude – bemoaned by Kraenzel, Worster, and other Great Plains scholars – that the environment is simply another factor of production, not a special underpinning for sustainability and continued social well-being. Sodbusting associated with recent acreage swings offers evidence for the power of market economics to affect the environment (Grant 1975; Huszar 1985). Yet some aspects of business farming, such as higher land values, might also encourage conservation practices aimed at slowing or even reversing land degradation.

More careful analysis is needed to disentangle the emerging relationships among market-oriented Great Plains farms, global markets, and impacts on the land. For example, Huszar (1985) shows that institutional factors commonly blamed for encouraging sodbusting – easy credit and tax breaks – may be minor compared to the simple economics of business expansion and efficiency in a competitive market. A major government study of recent economic changes in agriculture, however, fails even to raise the question of their environmental implications (Shertz 1979). A more business-like approach to Great Plains farming will at the least probably exacerbate the transformations associated with intensified land use, and may lead to new types of transformations.

Development Themes and the Pattern of Transformation

The social and technical forces arrayed for intensive agricultural development of the Great Plains, from myth-based boosterism to the recent marriage of technology and business management, have produced a trajectory of transformation that is remarkably consistent through time. Basic human goals, and attitudes about the propriety of human transformation of the region, have changed little. What have changed over the last century are the the social institutions and ideas driving the system toward extensive and intensive agricultural development.

The Bias for Growth

This view of Great Plains development differs from the paradigmatic human-ecological model of relationships between nature and society. Particularly in variable or marginal environments like the Plains, human-ecological ideas stress the role of dampening feedbacks from the physical or social environment (e.g., occasional droughts, worsened soil erosion, or financial hardship), which supposedly mold the social system into a more adapted form. Although these adaptive forces have led occasionally to retrenchments and altered farm strategy, they have been attenuated by both an internal and an external bias toward growth – evident in the guiding rationales just described. The human imprint on the Plains is thus enlarged and enlarging. Now, even when global grain markets – the latest driving force behind human use of the Plains – soften, government programs and speculative investments continue to encourage extensive cultivation, or at least hinder retirement of significant amounts of marginal land (Riebsame 1983; Opie 1987).

In understanding human transformation of the Great Plains, two factors appear to deserve more attention: social institutions and symbols. Although environmental and economic factors are reasonably well understood, and are typically cited as forces for adaptation, it can be argued that the social institutions in which dryland farming is embedded, and the symbolic attributes that have accrued to Plains farming, often counter these forces, encouraging unidirectional develop-

ment despite shifting economic and environmental variables. One of the institutions driving expansion is a formal government policy of cheap food, requiring public subsidy of extensive grain farming. According to Opie (1987):

American agriculture has been deeply and probably irrevocably committed to a scientific, industrial and government infrastructure in which low prices and high production have the highest priority. (187)

Supporting this institutional structure is a strong symbolic mythology centered on the family farm. Mostly symbolic forces created the original urgency for settling the virgin lands (so-called manifest destiny and the yeoman farmer creating the Jeffersonian agrarian ideal). These symbols affect contemporary farm policy. Opie argues that:

American farmland policy is still closely connected to the patriotic pieties of frontier individualism and Manifest Destiny. Congressional rhetoric still reflects the lasting public faith in the independent farmer, who remains a persistent national hero. (191)

The family farm is a symbol that Americans support through programs meant to protect it from both environmental and economic shocks. This puts a boundary on how much the agricultural system can adapt to its physical and social environment, and affects the choices that farmers make in land use and in other strategies.

The symbolic message of transformation is thus congruent with the values of the collective consciousness of both the region and the nation. It may not be congruent, however, with sustainability. Future Great Plains analysts should ask whether this transformation is akin to Dubos' (1980) "wooing of earth" – the creation of a human landscape that supports positive social development – or whether it is more destructive than constructive. Dubos' optimism for the future of nature-society relationships stems partly from his focus on "successful landscapes," especially the European pastoral, though he recognizes failures such as the deforestation of northern Europe and the denudation of the Mediterranean lands. Perhaps the wheat field, the farmstead, and the shelterbelt are elements of the successful transformation of the Great Plains into a nurturing human landscape. Yet the wheat field's potential for failure during the next drought, and the cumulative modification of both the physical and social environment required to maintain a dryland agricultural commodity system in a variable environment, deserve more critical examination.

Future Trends, Future Surprises?

The most likely future path of Great Plains transformation is simply an extrapolation of the past trend: more extensive and intensive dryland farming to produce small grains for global markets. Is there, however, potential for major change or for a surprising shift in this pattern? Some scholars see, in the economic slump in agriculture during the 1980s, both the cause and the rationale for abandoning much of the region's dryland fields – and, indeed, they forecast an eventual ecological and social collapse unless dryland farming is reduced (Popper and Popper 1987). Others expect persistence, supported by the region's symbolic appeal, improved technology, and the social contract that places farmers at risk to produce huge amounts of grain when needed to prop up exports and to keep food prices low (Borchert 1971; Opie 1987).

The potential sources of surprise are many. They may come from the markets, perhaps in the form of increased Third World food independence or stronger competition from grain-producing countries like Canada and the Soviet Union. Surprise might also emanate from the environment, as in the threat of global warming due to the greenhouse effect – which could increase drought frequency in this already climatically marginal area. Global warming could also change the economic viability of Plains agriculture by improving or worsening the lot of other small-grain farming regions. Despite the growing scientific credibility of global warming predictions (World Meteorological Organization 1985), agricultural resource planning in the Great Plains is based on the assumption that the future will emulate the past. This attitude ensures that the effect on the region, if any, will come as a surprise. Given such uncertainties, there is no unimpeachable way to determine whether the evolving Great Plains human landscape can, in a humane and sustainable way, continue to provide food and livelihood to the local, national, and global communities that depend on it.

Notes

1. Two industrialized nations, the United States and Canada, occupy the North American Great Plains. This chapter, however, is limited to the United States Great Plains due to the author's better access to that country's data archives.
2. These two characteristics were applied to the description of natural hazards by Burton, Kates, and White (1978).
3. Roughly half of the Plains cropland is planted to wheat or lies fallow between wheat crops in any year. The rest is divided chiefly among sorghum, oats, maize, and barley. The sorghum and maize are grown chiefly on the $40,000 \, \text{km}^2$ under irrigation. Land seeded to perennial grasses and regularly cropped for hay accounts for up to a fifth of the reported cultivated area.
4. Expansion (more land in production) and intensification (greater yields per land area) are complementary trends, both resulting in increased total production. There is some trade-off between the two, as larger yields reduce the pressure for cultivating more land. Similarly, government programs to reduce total acreage, aimed at protecting especially erodible land and stabilizing grain prices, may have the effect of intensifying production on remaining crop land.

References

Allis, J. A. 1948. *Rates of Runoff for the Design of Conservation Structures in the Central Great Plains of Nebraska and Kansas.* Technical Publication No. 69. Washington, D.C.: U.S. Soil Conservation Service.

———. 1952. The story of two watersheds. *Journal of Soil and Water Conservation* 7:243–45.

Allis, J. A., and L. L. Kelly. 1958. Runoff from small watersheds. *Soil Conservation* (March): 164–66.

Baeumer, K., and W. A. P. Bakermans. 1973. Zero tillage. In *Advances in Agronomy*, ed. N. C. Brads, 77–123. New York: Academic Press.

Baltensperger, B. 1974. Plains Promoters and Plain Folk: Premigration and Postsettlement Images of the Central Great Plains. Unpublished Ph.D. dissertation. Clark University.

———. 1987. Farm consolidation in the northern and central states of the Great Plains. *Great Plains Quarterly* 7:256–65.

Barrows, H. H. 1962. *Lectures on the Historical Geography of the United States as Given in 1933*, ed. (W. A. Koelsch.) Department of Geography Research Paper No. 77. University of Chicago.

Barry, R. G. 1983. Climatic environments of the Great Plains, past and present. In *Man and the Changing Environments in the Great Plains: Transactions of the Nebraska Academy of Sciences* 11:45–55.

Bennett, J. W. 1982. *Of Time and the Enterprise.* Minneapolis: University of Minnesota Press.

Blouet, B. W., and M. P. Lawson, eds. 1975. *Images of the Plains: The Role of Human Nature in Settlement.* Lincoln: University of Nebraska Press.

Bolin, B., P. J. Crutzen, P. M. Vitousek, R. G. Woodmansee, E. D. Goldberg, and R. B. Cook. 1983. Interactions of the biogeochemical cycles. In *The Major Biogeochemical Cycles and Their Interactions*, ed. B. Bolin and R. B. Cook, 1–39. New York: John Wiley and Sons.

Bolyshev, N. N., and Solv'yev. 1958. Soil investigation methods on state farms organized on virgin soil. *Soviet Soil Science* 4:388–96.

Bonnifield, P. 1979. *The Dust Bowl.* Albuquerque: University of New Mexico Press.

Borchert, J. R. 1950. Climate of the central North American grassland. *Annals of the Association of American Geographers* 40:1–39.

———. 1971. The Dust Bowl in the 1970s. *Annals of the Association of American Geographers* 61:1–22.

———. 1987. *America's Northern Heartland.* Minneapolis: University of Minnesota Press.

Bowden, M. J. 1975. The Great American Desert in the American mind: the historiography of a geographical notion. In *Geographies of the Mind*, ed. D. Lowenthal and M. J. Bowden, 119–47. New York: Oxford University Press.

Brown, P. L., A. D. Halvorson, F. H. Siddoway, H. F. Mayland, and M. R. Miller. 1982. *Saline-seep Diagnosis, Control, and Reclamation.* Conservation Report No. 30. Washington, D.C.: U.S. Department of Agriculture.

Brunn, L. J., J. L. Richardson, J. W. Enz, and J. K. Larsen. 1981. Streamflow changes in the southern Red River Valley of North Dakota. *North Dakota Farm Research* 4:11–14.

Burton, I., R. W. Kates, and G. F. White. 1978. *The Environment as Hazard.* New York: Oxford University Press.

Canter, L. W. 1987. Nitrates and pesticides in ground water: An analysis of a computer-based literature search. In *Ground Water Quality and Agricultural Practice*, ed. D. M. Fairchild, 155–74. Chelsea, MI.: Lewis Publishers.

Chilcott, E. C., J. S. Cole, and W. W. Burr. 1915. *Crop Production in the Great Plains Area: Relation of Cultural Methods to Yields.* Agricultural Bulletin No. 268. Washington, D.C.: U.S. Department of Agriculture.

Chilcott, E. C., and J. S. Cole. 1918. Subsoiling, deep tilling, and soil dynamiting in the Great Plains. *Journal of Agricultural Research* 14:481–521.

Clark, A. H. 1956. The impact of exotic invasion on the remaining New World midlatitude grasslands. In *Man's Role in Changing the Face of the Earth*, W. L. Thomas, Jr., 737–62. Chicago: University of Chicago Press.

———. 1962. Editor's note. In *On the Margins of the Good Earth: The South Australian Wheat Frontier, 1869–1884*, ed. D. W. Meinig, v–vi. Monograph No. 2 of the Association of American Geographers. Washington, D.C.

Crosson, P. R. 1986. Soil erosion and policy issues. In *Agriculture and the Environment*, ed. T. T. Phipps, P. R. Crosson, and K. A. Price, 35–73. Washington, D.C.: Resources for the Future.

Cummins, D. D., and W. G. White. 1972. *Inquiries into American History: The American Frontier.* Beverly Hills, CA: Benziger.

Dakota Commissioner of Immigration. 1891. *The Resources of Dakota.* Sioux Falls, Dakota Territory.

de Janvry, A., and E. P. LeVeen. 1986. Historical forces that have shaped world agriculture: a structural perspective. In *New*

Directions in Agriculture and Agricultural Research, ed. K. A. Dahlberg, 83–104. Totowa, NJ: Rowman and Allanheld.

Drache, H. M. 1976. *Beyond the Furrow: Keys to Successful Farming in the Twentieth Century*. Danville, IL: Interstate.

———. 1985. *Plowshares to Printouts*. Danville, IL: Interstate.

Dubos, R. 1980. *The Wooing of Earth*. New York: Charles Scribner's Sons.

Emmons, D. M. 1971. *Garden in the Grassland: Boomer Literature of the Central Great Plains*. Lincoln, NB: University of Nebraska Press.

Fairchild, D. M., ed. 1987. *Ground Water Quality and Agricultural Practice*. Chelsea, MI: Lewis Publishers.

Garcia, R. V. 1981. *Drought and Man: The 1972 Case History*. Oxford: Pergamon Press.

Gilbert, R. H. 1977. Measuring windbreaks from the air. *Soil Conservation* (August):7–8.

Glymph, L. M., and H. N. Holtan. 1969. Land treatment in agricultural watershed in hydrology research. In ed. *Effects of Watershed Changes on Streamflow*, W. L. Moore and C. W. Morgan, 44–68. Austin, TX: University of Texas Press.

Grant, K. E. 1975. Erosion in 1973–74: The record and the challenge. *Journal of Soil and Water Conservation* 30:29–32.

Gray, J. H. 1967. *Men Against the Desert*. Saskatoon, Saskatchewan: Western Producer Prairie Books.

Great Plains Committee. 1937. *The Future of the Great Plains*. House of Representatives Document No. 144, 75th Congress. Washington, D.C.: U.S. Government Printing Office.

Greb, B. W. 1979. Technology and wheat yields in the central Great Plains: commercial advances. *Journal of Soil and Water Conservation* 34:264–68.

Greb, B. W., and A. L. Black. 1962. Effects of windbreak plantings on adjacent crops. *Journal of Soil and Water Conservation* 20:223–27.

Griffith, P. W. 1976. Introduction of the problems. In *Proceedings of the Symposium on Shelterbelts on the Great Plains*. Publication No. 78. Lincoln, NE: Great Plains Agricultural Council.

Grossman, L. 1977. Man-environment relationships in anthropology and geography. *Annals of the Association of American Geographers* 67:126–44.

Halvorson, A. D., and A. L. Black. 1974. Saline-seep development in dryland soils of northeastern Montana. *Journal of Soil and Water Conservation* 29:77–79.

Hardesty, D. L. 1986. Rethinking cultural adaptation. *Professional Geographer* 38:11–18.

Hargreaves, M. W. M. 1957. *Dry Farming in the Northern Great Plains: 1900–1925*. Cambridge, MA: Harvard University Press.

———. 1976. Land-use planning in response to drought: The experience of the thirties. *Agricultural History* 50:561–82.

Hart, J. F. 1976. Change in the corn belt. *The Geographical Review* 76:51–72.

Hays, S. P. 1975. *Conservation and the Gospel of Efficiency*. New York: Atheneum.

Heimlich, R. E. 1985. Soil erosion on new cropland: A sodbusting perspective. *Journal of Soil and Water Conservation* 40:322–26.

Hewes, L. 1965. Causes of wheat failure in the dry farming region, Central Great Plains, 1939–1957. *Economic Geography* 41:313–30.

———. 1975. The Great Plains one hundred years after Major John Wesley Powell. In, *Images of the Plains: The Role of Human Nature in Settlement*, ed. B. W. Blouet and M. P. Lawson, 203–14. Lincoln: University of Nebraska Press.

———. 1979. Agricultural risk in the Great Plains. In *The Great Plains: Environment and Culture*, ed. B. Blouet and F. Luebke, 157–85. Lincoln, NE: University of Nebraska Press.

High Plains Associates. 1982. *Six-State High Plains Ogallala Regional Resources Study*. High Plains Associates. Austin, TX.

Huntington, E. 1934. Marginal land and the shelter belt. *Journal of Forestry* 32:974–77.

Hurt, R. D. 1986. Federal land reclamation in the Dust Bowl. *Great Plains Quarterly* 6:94–106.

Huszar, P. C. 1985. Dusting off the sodbuster issue. *Journal of Soil and Water Conservation* 40:482–84.

Kollmorgen, W., and J. Kollmorgen. 1973. Landscape meteorology in the Plains area. *Annals of the Association of American Geographers* 63:424–41.

Kuchler, A. W. 1949. A physiognomic classification of vegetation. *Annals of the Association of American Geographers* 39:201–10.

Kutzleb, C. R. 1968. Rain follows the plow: The history of an idea. Unpublished Ph.D. dissertation. University of Colorado.

Langdale, G. W., W. Frye, D. K. McCool, R. I. Papendick, D. E. Smika, and D. W. Fryrear. 1984. Conservation tillage for erosion control. *Journal of the Soil Conservation Society of America* 38:144–51.

Lockeretz, W. 1978. The lessons of the Dust Bowl. *American Scientist* 66:560–69.

Malin, J. C. 1956. The grassland of North America: its occupance and the challenge of continuous reappraisals. In *Man's Role in Changing the Face of the Earth*, ed. W. L. Thomas, Jr., 350–66. Chicago: University of Chicago Press.

McDean, H. C. 1986. Dust Bowl historiography. *Great Plains Quarterly* 6:117–26.

Miller, J. E., and D. L. Frink. 1984. *Changes in Flood Response of the Red River of the North Basin, North Dakota–Minnesota*. Water-Supply Paper 2243. Washington, D.C.: U.S. Geological Survey.

National Research Council. 1986. *Soil Conservation: Assessing the National Resources Inventory*. Committee on Conservation Needs and Opportunities, Board on Agriculture. Washington, D.C.: National Academy Press.

Opie, J. 1987. *The Law of the Land*. Lincoln, NB: University of Nebraska Press.

Ottoson, H. W., E. M. Birch, P. A. Henderson, and A. H. Anderson. 1966. *Land and People of the Northern Great Plains Transition Area*. Lincoln, NB: University of Nebraska Press.

Pimentel, D., et al. 1976. Land degradation: Effects on food and energy resources. *Science* 194:149–55.

Popper, D. E., and F. J. Popper. 1987. The Great Plains: from dust to dust. *Planning* (December): 13–18.

Riebsame, W. E. 1983. Managing agricultural drought: the 'Great Plains experience. In *Beyond the Urban Fringe: Land Use Issues in Non-Metropolitan America*, ed. R. Platt and G. Macinko, 257–70. Minneapolis: University of Minnesota Press.

———. 1986. The Dust Bowl: historical image, psychological anchor, and ecological taboo. *Great Plains Quarterly* 6:127–36.

Sartz, R. S. 1975. Controlling runoff in the driftless area. *Journal of Soil and Water Conservation* 30:92–95.

Sears, P. B. 1980. *Deserts on the March*. 4th ed. Norman, OK: University of Oklahoma Press.

Secretary of Agriculture. 1909. *Annual Report*. Washington, D.C.: U.S. Department of Agriculture.

Shantz, H. L. 1923. The natural vegetation of the Great Plains region. *Annals of the Association of American Geographers* 13:81–107.

Shertz, L. P., ed. 1979. *Another Revolution in U.S. Farming?* Washington, D.C.: U.S. Department of Agriculture.

Shiklomanov, I. A. 1983. The effects of agricultural land use on river runoff. In *Environmental Management of Agricultural Watersheds*, ed. G. Golubev, 35–54. Laxenburg, Austria: IIASA.

Smika, D. E., and E. D. Sharman. 1984. Atrazine carryover in conservation tillage. *Journal of the Soil Conservation Society of America* 38:239.

Smith, H. N. 1950. *Virgin Land: The American West as Symbol and Myth*. Cambridge, MA: Harvard University Press.

Sorenson, C. J., and G. A. Marotz. 1977. Changes in shelterbelt mileage statistics over four decades in Kansas. *Journal of Soil and Water Conservation* 32:276–81.

Spath, H. J. W. 1987. Dryland wheat farming on the central Great Plains: Sedgwick County, northeast Colorado. In *Comparative Farming Systems*, ed. B. L. Turner II and S. B. Brush, 313–44. New York: The Guilford Press.

Stegner, W. 1953. *Beyond the Hundredth Meridian: John Wesley Powell and the Second Opening of the West*. Boston: Houghton Mifflin.

Thornthwaite, C. W. 1936. The Great Plains. In *Migration and Economic Opportunity: The Report of the Study of Population Distribution*, ed. C. Goodrich, 202–50. Philadelphia: University of Pennsylvania Press.

Turner, B. L., II, and S. B. Brush, eds. 1987. *Comparative Farming Systems*. New York: The Guilford Press.

United States Army Corps of Engineers. 1987. *Metropolitan Denver Water Plan*. Omaha, NE.

U.S. Department of Agriculture. 1974. *Summer Fallow in the Western United States*. Conservation Research Report No. 17. Washington, D.C.

———. 1980. *Appraisal: Soil, Water, and Related Resources in the United States*. Vol. I. Washington, D.C.

———. 1985. *Factbook of Agriculture*. Miscellaneous Publication No. 1063. Washington, D.C.

U.S. Soil Conservation Service. 1977. *Field Windbreak Removals in Five Great Plains States, 1970 to 1975*. Washington, D.C.

———. 1987. Progress in soil conservation. *Soil Conservation* (December): 8–9.

U.S. General Accounting Office. 1975. *Action Needed to Discourage Removal of Trees that Shelter Cropland in the Great Plains*. Washington, D.C. Government Printing Office.

U.S. General Accounting Office. 1985. *1983 Payment-in-Kind Program Overview: Its Design, Impact, and Cost*. Washington, D.C.: Government Printing Office.

U.S. Geological Survey. 1970. *The National Atlas of the United States*. Washington, D.C.

Vining, R. C., L. J. Brunn, J. W. Enz, and J. L, Rishardson. 1983. An analysis of streamflow variability in three rivers in North Dakota. In *Preprints of the Fifth Conference on Hydrometeorology, Tulsa, Oklahoma*. Boston, MA: American Meteorological Society.

Warrick, R. A., P. B. Trainer, E. J. Baker, and W. A. R. Brinkmann. 1975. *Drought Hazard in the United States: A Research Assessment*. Monograph No. 4, Natural Hazards Research and Applications Information Center. Boulder, CO: University of Colorado.

Warrick, R. A., and M. J. Bowden. 1981. The changing impacts of drought in the Great Plains. In *The Great Plains: Perspectives and Prospects*, ed. M. P. Lawson and M. E. Baker, 111–37. Lincoln, NB: University of Nebraska Press.

White, G. F. 1986. *The Future of the Great Plains*, revisited. *Great Plains Quarterly* 6:84–93.

Worcester, B. K., L. J. Brun, and E. J. Doering. 1977. Growth and development of saline seeps. *North Dakota Farm Research* 35:16–17.

World Meteorological Organization. 1985. *Report of the International Conference on the Assessment of the Role of Carbon Dioxide and of Other Greenhouse Gases in Climate Variation and Associated Impacts*. WMO No. 661. Geneva.

Worster, D. 1979. *Dust Bowl: The Southern Great Plains in the 1930s*. New York: Oxford University Press.

Zelinsky, W. 1973. *The Cultural Geography of the United States*. Englewood Cliffs, NJ: Prentice-Hall.

Zon, R. 1935. Shelterbelts: futile dream or workable plan. *Science* 81:392.

35

The Basin of Mexico
EXEQUIEL EZCURRA

Enclosed by the mountains of the Central Volcanic Axis, the Basin of Mexico has long been, and remains, the economic, social, political, and cultural center of the Mexican nation. It is also the site of perhaps the largest urban complex in the world, Mexico City, one of the most striking examples of the consequences of unplanned growth and of the Third World "rush to the cities." The old Tenochtitlan, the glorious capital of the Anahuac, the colonial City of the Palaces that enthralled von Humboldt (1811), is now the twentieth-century epitome of urban disaster.

Before the Spanish conquest, the Basin was occupied by a set of cities dominated by Tenochtitlan-Tlatelolco, sharing a highly developed lacustrine civilization. The *chinampa*, an intensive and highly productive agricultural system formed by a succession of elevated fields within a reticular canal network, cycled nutrients very efficiently and produced abundant crops for the population, which modern estimates put in the millions. Already, however, the civilizations of the Basin depended to some extent on foreign goods, in the form of tribute, which subsidized the local economy. With the conquest, the cities were redesigned following the Spanish patterns, and the lacustrine surface of the Basin came to be considered incompatible with the new urban and rural land-use plan. From the seventeenth century onward, drainage works of increasing size and complexity were set up to rid the city of floods and to dry up the muddy subsoil of the lake. These developments gradually produced important changes in the environment of the Basin, with traditional agriculture as one of the main casualties.

The situation has deteriorated very quickly during the past 40 years. As in many other parts of Latin America, the industrialization of Mexico accelerated the migration of rural inhabitants to the large cities. The rapid growth of Mexico City engulfed the satellite towns of the old capital and created a large megalopolis within the Basin. This urban conglomerate occupies most of the Federal District and also part of the neighboring State of Mexico. The mountains south and west of the city, which had been until recently little affected by the urban expansion, have now succumbed to rapid development. The Basin, which occupies only 0.03% of the country's territory, is the home of 23% of the population and poses massive social, economic, and environmental problems.

The Environmental Setting

The Basin of Mexico lies within the Central Volcanic Axis, an upland formation of Late Tertiary origin. It is a naturally closed (but now artificially drained) hydrological unit of approximately 7,000 km² (Fig. 35.1). The lowest part, a lacustrine plain, has an elevation of 2,240 m above sea level. The Basin is surrounded on three sides by a magnificent succession of elevated volcanic sierras (the Ajusco to the south, the Sierra Nevada to the east, and the Sierra de las Cruces to the west). To the north, it is bounded by a series of low ranges (Los Pitos, Tepotzotlan, Patlachique, Santa Catarina, and others). The highest peaks (Popocatepetl and Ixtaccihuatl, with altitudes of 5,465 m and 5,230 m, respectively) lie southeast of the Basin. Many other peaks reach elevations of around 4,000 m. These peripheral ranges present a strong physical limit to the modern urban development of the Basin.

The Basin is located in the central part of the Mexican Transversal Volcanic Belt, a geologic formation 20–70 km wide running from the Pacific to the Atlantic (Mosser 1987). Both by the existence of numerous faults along the Belt and by its proximity to the Pacific Trench, tectonic instability, volcanic processes, and earthquakes have been outstanding natural features in the history of the area.

Before the rise of the Aztec state, around A.D. 1000, the lacustrine system at the bottom of the Basin of Mexico covered approximately 1,500 km² and was formed by five shallow lakes running in a north-south chain: Tzompanco, Xaltocan, Texcoco, Xochimilco, and Chalco (Fig. 35.1). The two southernmost lakes, Chalco and Xochimilco, and the two northernmost lakes, Tzompanco and Xaltocan, were higher, and their fresh waters flowed toward the central and lowest lake, Texcoco, where runoff from the whole Basin accumulated and evaporated. The waters of Texcoco, in consequence, were briny.

Sanders, Parsons, and Santley (1979: also Sanders 1976b)

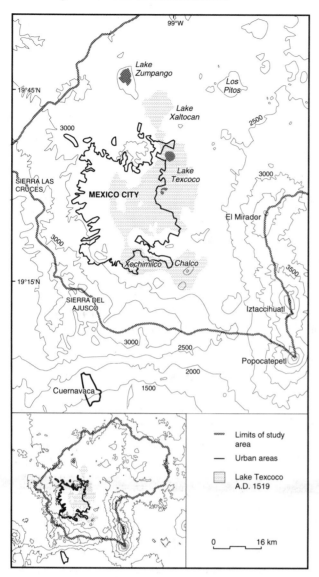

Figure 35.1 The Basin of Mexico.

recognized nine major environmental zones within the Basin before extensive human transformations began:

1. The lake system, which was an important resting point for migratory waterfowl;
2. The saline lakeshore, with halophyllous plants;
3. The deep soil alluvium, covered by sedges and swamp cypresses (*Taxodium mucronatum*);
4. The thin soil alluvium, dominated by grasses and agaves;
5. The upland alluvium, vegetated by oaks and acacias;
6. The lower piedmont, gently sloping and with low oak forests;
7. The middle piedmont with broadleaf oaks;
8. The upper piedmont, occupying elevations above 2,500 m and vegetated by oaks, tepozanes (*Buddleja* spp.), alder (*Alnus* sp.), and madrones (*Arbutus xalapensis*);
9. The sierras, occupying sites above 2,700 m and harboring temperate plant communities with pine, fir, and juniper.

Rainfall is concentrated in summer, mostly from June to September. A marked precipitation gradient exists in the Basin, from high-rainfall areas toward the southwest to

semiarid conditions toward the northeast. Mean annual temperatures in the bottom of the Basin are approximately 15°C, with an amplitude of 8°C between mean monthly summer and winter temperatures. Night frosts occur in winter throughout most of the Basin, and their frequency increases considerably with elevation and aridity (Jáuregui 1987).

History

Pre-Hispanic Period

The first human settlers of the region, forming small nomadic groups of hunters and gatherers, arrived around 20,000 B.C. When agriculture started to develop in the Basin of Mexico, toward 3000 B.C., human groups became sedentary and formed small villages on some parts of the low Basin that combined good agricultural potential with adequate protection against floods. Toward the beginning of the Christian era, the population of Texcoco, east of the Basin, was around 3,500 inhabitants. At that time, development of the urban and religious center of Teotihuacan was starting northeast of the lake system and away from the flood-prone areas. In A.D. 100, Teotihuacan had 30,000 inhabitants, and by A.D. 650, before its collapse, the population of Teotihuacan was in excess of 100,000, falling to one-tenth of that only a century later (Parsons 1976). One explanation of this collapse cites overexploitation of the surrounding semiarid natural resources, together with the lack of a technology to use the lake waters and the more productive but flood-prone lands of the bottom of the Basin (Sanders 1976a; Sanders et al. 1979).

Various cultures existed on the lake margins before and during the arrival and settlement of the Aztec tribes. The lacustrine system at the bottom of the Basin became surrounded by a cluster of towns, and the development of new agricultural techniques, based on irrigation, canals, and flood-control systems, allowed a tremendous increase, in population densities. Around A.D. 1325, the Aztecs – or Mexicas – founded their city on a low, floodable island, which became in a few centuries the capital of the powerful Aztec empire and the political, economic, and religious center of the whole of Mesoamerica.

Between A.D. 1200 and 1400, a tremendous succession of cultural and technological changes occurred in the Basin, both before and after the foundation of Tenochtitlan. It is estimated that during the late fifteenth century, the population of the Basin reached 1.5 million inhabitants, distributed in more than 100 towns. At that time, the Basin of Mexico was probably the largest and most densely settled urban area in the world. When the Spaniards arrived in 1519, the Basin of Mexico was occupied by a well-developed civilization, founded on the cultivation of the surrounding *chinampa* fields. Its magnificent green areas so impressed Hernán Cortés that he wrote a long description of the gardens of Tenochtitlan to the Spanish Emperor, Charles V, on his *Cartas de Relación*. The two large islands of the lake, Tenochtitlan and Tlatelolco, had been joined by roads with a group of smaller islands, forming a large urban conglomerate surrounded by water and linked to the lake margins by three elevated roads made of wood, stone, and compressed mud. Two aqueducts, made of stuccated mud pipes, brought drinking water into the center of Tenochtitlan: one came from Chapultepec by the road to Tlacopan, and the other came from Churubusco by the road to Iztapalapa. To control floods, a dam had been built in the eastern border of the city, separating it from Lake Texcoco.

The admiration of the Spaniards for the Aztec culture, however, was rather short-lived. After a siege of 90 days, the soldiers of Cortés, backed by a large army of local allies that wanted to get rid of the Aztec dominion, took over Tenochtitlan, and in a very short time dismantled the Aztec social structure. The city itself, symbol of the Aztec cosmology and way of life, particularly suffered a deep transformation (DDF 1983). Based on the cheap labor provided by the conquered population, the Spaniards completely redesigned the city, erecting colonial, Spanish-style buildings in place of the old Aztec palaces and temples.

With the Spanish conquest, horses and cattle were introduced to Mexico, and both the transportation and the agricultural structure changed accordingly. Many of the Aztec canals were filled to make roads for horses and carts. Thus, the *chinampas* were displaced away from the center of the city, and an aqueduct was built to carry drinking water from Chapultepec to the new urban center. Cattle, sheep, goats, pigs, and chickens provided new sources of protein. The land use and physiognomy of the surrounding mountains started to change, mostly through cattle grazing and timber logging. The Spanish conquest also brought a tremendous population decline in the Basin (León-Portilla, Garibay, and Beltrán 1972). A century after the Spanish conquest, the total population of the Basin had fallen below 100,000.

The Colony

The Spaniards, however, also were changed by the indigenous culture, in a perhaps more subtle but equally irreversible manner. The Mexican colony became a synthesis of both the Aztec and the Spanish cultures, of which the latter had itself been strongly influenced by centuries of Arab occupation of the Iberian peninsula. The highly developed agriculture of the Basin and the traditional use of the rich Mexican flora matched perfectly the Arabian-Spanish tradition of interior gardens and patios. Another element common to the Aztec and Spanish cultures was the existence of an open area in the center of the city, surrounded by the main ceremonial and government buildings, and usually near the city market. Thus, the *plazas*, or town squares, became the centers of colonial life, the places in which Aztec and Spanish elements blended into a new culture.

Some persistent cultural differences led to landscape transformations. From early colonial times, it became clear that the new city plan was incompatible with the lacustrine landscape of the Basin (Sala Catalá 1986). The filling of the Aztec canals to build elevated roads obstructed the surface drainage of the city and created large surfaces of stagnant water (Anonymous 1788), while the grazing and logging of the slopes surrounding the Basin generated more surface runoff with the intense, monsoon-type summer rains. The first severe flood occurred in 1553; new floods recurred in 1580, 1604, 1629, and thereafter at shorter intervals. The low

altitude of the northern ranges and the existence of near-level passes between them drove the colonial government to plan the drainage of the Basin toward the north, from Lake Zumpango. The first drainage canal, "El Tajo de Nochistongo," was 15 km long and opened the Basin toward the Tula Basin in 1608 (Lara 1988). The larger works of the Canal de Huehuetoca began in the late sixteenth century and continued until the early twentieth century. At first, the canal served only as a spillover system, but with the construction for drainage of the auxiliary Canal de Guadalupe in 1796, the lacustrine area in the Basin of Mexico began to shrink rapidly. In 1769, there was for the first time a debate within the colonial government over the desirability of eradicating the lakes. Only José Antonio Alzate, a pioneer Mexican naturalist, opposed draining the whole lake system, suggesting instead the construction of a canal to control the level of Lake Texcoco while maintaining the lake surfaces of the Basin (Trabulse 1983). In spite of the drainage works, navigation by canals was still very popular toward the end of the colonial period. Boats departed regularly to Xochimilco and Chalco from a pier near the old market of La Merced, east of the Central Plaza, known as El Zocalo (Sierra 1984). The "Canal de La Viga," among many others, remained active throughout all of the colonial period, and represented both an important trading route for agricultural products between the *chinampas* of Xochimilco and the City and a favorite promenade for many colonial Mexicans.

Independence

The War of Independence (1810–1821) brought little change to the general physiognomy of the city (González Angulo and Terán Trillo 1976). The city squares continued to be the centers of city life. During the nineteenth century, many improvements were made in these open areas, particularly during the French intervention, when the Emperor Maximilian replanted many of the squares following the design of the French "romantic gardens." Drainage works in the Canal de Huehuetoca were greatly extended during that century, and for the first time, some people began to worry about the environmental consequences of draining the lakes. One consequence was becoming evident to garden-lovers: a saline crust was forming on the topsoil of many areas in the lower Basin.

During the prolonged dictatorship of Porfirio Díaz, in the late nineteenth and early twentieth centuries, the Industrial Revolution was imported to Mexico. Factories and railroads were built, and the City was modernized for the benefit of a small, centralist, and very powerful bourgeoisie, whose aim was to transform the wealthier quarters of Mexico, copying the plan of contemporary European cities. Iron parts, cast in European foundries, were incorporated into the architecture of public buildings. Pavillions for musical bands, in the style of the Brighton Royal Pavillion, were built in most parks, generating a tradition of band music in Mexican squares that is still very much alive at present. For the first time, the Basin ceased to be regarded as a series of separated cities linked more by commerce than by a central administration, and started to be considered by many as a single unit. The newly

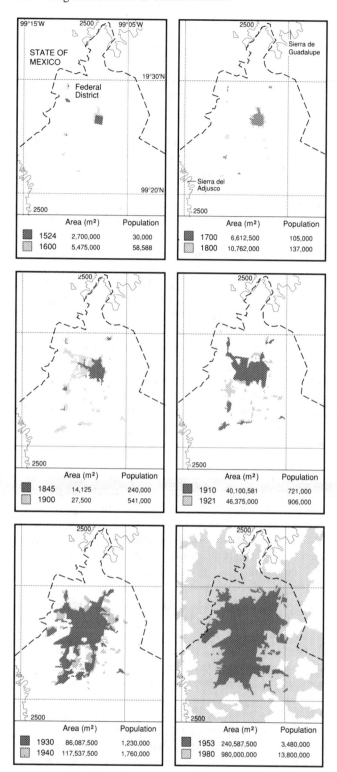

Figure 35.2 Urbanized area in the Basin of Mexico at selected times between 1524 and 1980.

Table 35-1 *Evolution of Urban Area and Population Densities in Mexico City from 1600 to 1980*

Year	Area (km²)	Population (thousands)	Urban Density (persons/km²)
1600	5.5	58	10,584
1700	6.6	105	15,885
1800	10.8	137	12,732
1845	14.1	240	16,985
1900	27.5	541	19,673
1910	40.1	721	17,980
1921	46.4	906	19,534
1930	86.1	1,230	14,287
1940	117.5	1,760	14,974
1953	240.6	3,480	14,464
1980	980.0	13,800	14,082

Source: DDF 1986.

Porfirian bourgeoisie, which defended its privileges, and other social sectors demanding more participation in the distribution of the national wealth. Mexico City had at that time approximately 700,000 inhabitants and, unexpectedly, suffered little damage. The Revolution was mostly a rural movement, and the City became a haven for middle-class provincial families, who flocked into the Basin of Mexico searching for cover under the new bureaucracy and the rising industries (Table 35-1).

The Revolution became institutionalized with the presidency of Plutarco Elías Calles in 1924, and peace finally returned to Mexico. Industrialization returned to the City, bringing marked improvements in transportation, which allowed the expansion of the urban area and, consequently, a sharp decline in urban population densities (Table 35-1). The progressive President Lázaro Cárdenas (1934–1940) attached great importance to the creation of national parks and reserves in the mountains surrounding the Basin and to the creation of parks within the City. The national parks Desierto de los Leones and Cumbres del Ajusco were created to the west and south, as a way of restricting the deforestation of the Basin slopes. Unfortunately, during the presidency of Miguel Alemán (1946–1952) a good part of the Ajusco park was given to the paper mill Loreto y Peña Pobre, which started an ambitious timberlogging program (DDF 1986). Although this company also planted some pine forests, the elimination of the park and the deforestation of areas near the City opened the way for the urban occupation of the land (Fig. 35.2).

laid railroads brought peasants looking for employment in the new industries, and some of the smaller towns near the center of the city, like Tacuba, Tacubaya, and Azcapotzalco, were engulfed into the urban perimeter (Fig. 35.2).

The Revolution

Between 1910 and 1920, the Mexican Revolution brought a decade of ruthless confrontation between the old

Modern Mexico

During the post-revolutionary period, and particularly after World War II, the industrial growth that had been heralded by the Porfirian government became a reality. Mexico City became an industrial city, and a massive migration started from the country into the City. In less than 80 years, the population of the urban conglomerate jumped from 700,000 to a total of nearly 18 million in 1987. Peripheral cities, like Coyoacán, Tlalpan, and Xochimilco, were incorporated into the urban perimeter (Figs. 35.1 and 35.2). A deep drainage system was built to remove the torrential urban runoff from the Basin, and most of the old lake beds became dry. The draining of the underground aquifer and the contraction of the expansive clays of the lake bed depressed the center of the City by approximately 9 m from 1910 to 1987. The extremely low wind speeds in the high-altitude plateau, together with intense industrial activity and the emissions of 3 million vehicles, have degraded the quality of the atmosphere in the Basin to levels that are dangerous to human health. In the next sections, these changes are analyzed and their consequences for the future explored.

Rates and States in a Changing City

Population and Land Surfaces

The population of the metropolitan area of Mexico City (which at present includes the Federal District plus the urbanized area within the neighboring State of Mexico, all referred to in the remainder of this chapter as Mexico City) has increased steadily since the end of the Mexican Revolution. From 1950 to 1986, the average annual growth rate was 4.8% (Table 35-2)[1]. The population has grown more quickly in the industrial area of the neighboring State of Mexico, north of the Federal District, where the average rate of increase has been 13.6%, compared to 3.3% in the Federal District. Much of the high growth rate of the City is due to the continuous arrival of migrants from the economically depressed rural areas (Goldani 1977; Stern 1977; Unikel 1974). Between 1970 and 1980, for example, 3,248,000 immigrants arrived in Mexico City (Calderón and Hernández 1987). If this effect is taken into account, the intrinsic annual growth rate of the City can be calculated as approximately 1.8%, considerably lower than the national average, which was around 3.0% for the same period. In short, it is immigration more than reproductive growth that maintains the high rate of increase of the population of Mexico City. Applying the 1980 rates to the 1987 population of 18 million, it can be calculated that every day, approximately 900 babies are born, whereas 1,500 new immigrants arrive to stay in the Basin of Mexico. Many of the babies, of course, are born to recently arrived immigrants, which further increases the growth rate of the population by elevating the natural birth rates (Goldani 1977).

The growth rate of the city in spatial extent, estimated from the urban areas measured on aerial photographs, is close to that of the population (5.2%). In 1953, the urban area covered 240 km² (8% of the Basin), whereas by 1980, it has increased to 980 km² (33% of the Basin). The expansion, however, has not kept the old style of urbanization. The new developments are more dense and less planned, and generally include less open space. Many developments are now built on hillslopes, generating a considerable amount of soil erosion and a significant increase in flash floods after rainstorms (Galindo and Morales 1987). In 1950, the urban area included a large proportion of agropastoral fields, together with numerous empty lots, parks, and public spaces. The relative

Table 35-2 *Population in Mexico City from 1519 to 1986 (in millions)*

Year	Federal District	State of Mexico	Total
1519 (Conquest)*	0.3	—	0.3
1620 (Colony)	0.03	—	0.03
1810 (Independence)	0.1	—	0.1
1910 (Revolution)	0.7	—	0.5
1940 (Cardenist period)	1.8	—	1.8
1950	3.0	—	3.0
1960	4.8	0.4	5.2
1970	6.8	1.9	8.7
1980	8.8	5.0	13.8
1986	10.0	6.7	16.7
Estimated yearly growth rate (1950–86)	3.3%	13.6%	4.8%
Standard error	0.3%	1.7%	0.2%

* Pre-1950 dates have been chosen as approximate indicators, and correspond with important historical dates, which are indicated in parentheses.
Source: DDF 1987.

Table 35-3 *Rate of Change of Green Areas within the Metropolitan Area of Mexico City from 1950 to 1980.*

Land use	Relative area (%)* 1950	1980	Yearly change (%)
Parks and public spaces	13.1	8.3	−1.5
Empty lots	8.1	3.2	−3.1
Agropastoral fields	21.2	2.3	−7.4
Total	42.4	13.8	−3.7

* Measured as a percentage of the total City area and estimated from aerial photograph samples.
Source: Lavín 1983.

frequency of these open spaces within the City has decreased considerably with the new industrial style of urbanization. All kinds of open space within Mexico City are decreasing (Table 35-3), but at different rates. Agropastoral fields, previously very important within the city as dairy farms, and domestic maize fields (or *milpas*) have been disappearing at an annual rate of 7.4%, and are now practically nonexistent within the City. Most of these areas are occupied by industrial buildings and housing developments. Parks, private gardens, and public spaces have been somewhat better conserved, disappearing from the city at an average rate of 1.5%. New roads have accounted for most of the loss. Overall, vegetated areas have been decreasing at an annual rate of 3.7%.

Lavín (1983) made an analysis of the rate of change of vegetated ("green") areas within different sectors of Mexico City from 1950 to 1980. She found that the total rate of change of green areas varied considerably from one sector of

Table 35-4 *Rate of Change of Green Areas within Different Sectors of the Metropolitan Area of Mexico City from 1950 to 1980.*

Sector	Relative area (%)*		Yearly change (%)
	1950	1980	
North	52.6	21.8	−2.9
South	41.6	14.7	−3.5
East	23.5	4.0	−5.9
West	62.5	28.1	−2.7
Center	5.0	3.7	−1.0

* Measured as a percentage of the area of the sector and estimated from aerial photograph samples.
Source: Lavín 1983.

the city to another. The east of Mexico City, where the larger proletarian settlements lie (in particular, Ciudad Netzahualcoyotl with some 5 million inhabitants), is the area changing most quickly; nearly 6% of its open space disappeared each year (Table 35-4). Open spaces are disappearing most slowly in the old center of the city (−1.0%). The rate of change within urbanized areas depends on the social position of their inhabitants and on the time of their establishment. In the poorer and more recently established areas, vacant land is transformed quickly into new houses, leaving less green areas per person. The distribution of green areas, like the distribution of wealth, is very uneven at present, and varies considerably from one part of the city to another. Although some quarters have more than $10 \, m^2$ of green land per person, others have much less. Azcapotzalco, an industrial quarter with a population of some 700,000, has at present $0.9 \, m^2$ of green areas per inhabitant (Barradas and J-Seres 1987; Calvillo-Ortega 1988; Guevara and Moreno 1987).

The drainage and drying-up of the lake beds has also produced a seasonal phenomenon of dust storms between February and May. The midday air temperatures during the dry season generate strong advective currents that elevate salt and clay particles from the former lake bottom. These particles are later blown into the city by the prevailing easterly winds. The problem of dust storms, however, reached a peak in the 1970s and has declined slightly since (Jáuregui 1983). The decline (or at least the lack of increase) of soil particles in the atmosphere during the dry season seems to be associated with successful government efforts to vegetate the dry mud-bed of the former Lake Texcoco (Jáuregui 1971, 1983), which has now become a pasture of halophytic grasses and forbs. In spite of this moderate success, fecal contamination from sewage water is still common in the lake-beds, and the dust storms remain a potential source of infection. The concentration of fecal bacteria in the rainwater of Mexico City is 100–150 microorganisms/l. (Soms Garcia 1986). Gamboa (1983; cited in Bravo 1987) sampled the microorganisms suspended in the air of Mexico City, and found a significantly high frequency of potential pathogens.

Water Supply

During this century, the Basin has gone from a high level of self-sufficiency in natural resources to a complete dependence on imports from other parts of Mexico. The best soils of the Basin are now occupied by houses, the underground aquifer has gone down in some parts more than 9 meters, and much of the water in the Basin is heavily polluted. These changes are obvious in the satellite town of Xochimilco, south of the city, where *chinampa* agriculture is still carried on, but is quickly disappearing because of the descending water table and the high pollution levels of the canal waters. Thus, most of the food and water consumed within the Basin comes from outside its boundaries.

The problem is particularly critical in the case of water, which is brought at high expense from other basins, where it is also badly needed. In 1976, the City used 1,293 million m^3 of water at an average rate of $41 \, m^3/s$. Of this amount, 30% ($12 \, m^3/s$) came from the Lerma Basin (DDF 1977). At present, the City uses $60 \, m^3/s$ of water (Enciclopedia de Mexico 1985), of which $18 \, m^3/s$ (about 570 million m^3/yr) are pumped from the Lerma and Cutzamala basins. The average daily supply of water in Mexico City is around $300 \, l$/person – more than in many European cities (Alvarez 1985). Even so, many parts of the city suffer from chronic water shortages. Industrial use is very inefficient, water recycling uses only 7% of the sewage, and nearly 20% of the water supply is lost through deficient pipe systems. Pipe breakage in the muddy subsoil of the old lake bed also represents a continuous health hazard, as microorganisms from the sewage system can contaminate the fractured pipes. Thus, gastrointestinal diseases are among the most frequent health problems in the Basin of Mexico and are a primary cause of infant mortality.

Waste

Approximately $4–5 \, m^3/s$ of sewage water are treated and used mainly for irrigation in parks and public spaces (DDF 1974). The remainder is eliminated from the Basin by means of the deep drainage system that was built in the early 1970s and by the old surface drainage canals, and is used mostly in the State of Hidalgo for irrigation. The untreated sewage used for irrigation is an important source of agricultural pollution. According to Ibarra et al. (1986), some of the fields of Hidalgo can receive in one year as much as 470 kg/ha of heavy metals, 710 kg/ha of boron, and 2,300 kg/ha of detergents.

The City produces approximately 9,000 t of domestic garbage every day. Around 50% of it is organic litter, and the remainder is formed by paper (17%), glass (10%), textiles (6%), plastics (6%), metals (3%), and other refuse (9%). In contrast to developed countries, which generate litter with a low proportion of organic residues, the garbage of Mexico City is rich in vegetable and fruit waste (Restrepo and Phillips 1985). Until 1987, most of these residues were disposed of in open yards, which represented high health risks. The most important of these yards were Santa Cruz Meyehualco and Santa Fe, although many smaller, and very often clandestine, disposal yards existed, and still exist, throughout Mexico City (SAHOP 1977; SMA 1978a). Recently, a more modern system of sanitary filling into dredged pits has been inaugurated east of the City to solve, in part, the tremendous environmental problem posed by the disposal of garbage. Many experts, however, believe that waste disposal will remain a problem until a better disposal service is implemented, more strict regulations are applied (Aguilar Sahagún 1984), and above all, waste-processing plants are built to cope with the large output of garbage produced by the city (Monroy Hermosillo 1987; Trejo Vázquez 1987). Because of its high content of organic residues, the litter generated by Mexico City could be used for making compost at a relatively low cost.

Air Quality

Perhaps the worst problem associated with the uncontrolled growth of the City is the high level of atmospheric pollution within the Basin (SAHOP 1978; SMA 1978b, 1978c). This problem is particularly critical during the cold season (December to February), when the low temperatures stabilize the atmosphere above the Basin and the air pollutants accumulate in the stationary mass of air that covers the city (SEDUE 1986; Velasco Levy 1983). Studies of the lead and bromine content in the air particulate pollutants in Mexico City have shown that most of the air pollution originates from automobile exhaust (Barfoot et al. 1984; Sigler Andrade, Fuentes Gea, and Vargas Aburto 1982). SEDUE (1986) estimated that motor vehicles are responsible for 85% of all atmospheric pollutants in Mexico City. In some parts of the city, particularly toward the eastern-central, the concentration of total suspended particles exceeds the Mexican and the international air-quality standards more than 50% of the time (Fuentes Gea and Hernández 1984). Although air quality during the rainy season has remained more or less constant for the past 10 years, the total of suspended particles during the dry season is increasing at approximately 6% per year (calculated from Fuentes Gea and Hernández 1984). In accordance with the idea that most of the atmospheric pollution derives from automobile exhaust, the number of cars in the City is also increasing at an annual rate of 6% (there were some 2 million cars in 1979 and more than 3 million in 1987). According to these data, the deterioration of the air quality in the Basin of Mexico during the dry season is much quicker than the population growth and the urban expansion. It is predictable that, if the trend continues, in a few years the atmospheric pollution will exceed the acceptable air quality standards most of the time, with very serious consequences for the health of the entire population.

According to Bravo's (1987) detailed report, vehicles produce most of the carbon monoxide and hydrocarbon residues in the Basin, but fixed sources are responsible for most of the particles, sulfur dioxide, and nitrogen oxides (Table 35-5). Particulate pollution is highest toward the eastern-central portion of the City, but sulfur dioxide is highest in the north, where most of the industries are located. Until 1986, lead was probably the worst pollutant in the atmosphere of the Basin (Salazar, Bravo, and Falcón 1981). Only leaded gasoline was sold in Mexico City, and the con-

Table 35-5 *Atmospheric Emissions Estimated for the Metropolitan Area of Mexico City in 1983.*

Pollutant	Fixed sources		Vehicles		Total	
	ton/yr	%	ton/yr	%	ton/yr	%
Particles	141,000	2.9	12,800	.3	153,800	3.1
Carbon monoxide	120,000	2.4	3,600,000	72.8	3,720,000	75.3
Hydrocarbons	140,000	2.8	385,000	7.8	525,000	10.6
Sulfur dioxide	400,000	8.1	11,000	.2	411,000	8.3
Nitrogen oxides	93,000	1.9	39,000	.8	132,000	2.7
Total	894,000	18.1	4,047,800	81.9	4,941,800	100

Source: Bravo 1987.

centration of lead in the air increased steadily with the number of cars, reaching an average value of $5\,\mu g/m^3$ in 1968 (Halffter and Ezcurra 1983) and approximately $8\,\mu g/m^3$ in 1986 (5 times the Mexican standard of $1.5\,\mu g/m^3$). The problem became so critical that in September 1986, the national oil company (PEMEX) replaced leaded gasoline in the Basin with low-lead-content fuel, in which synthetic oxidizing additives (olefines) replaced the action of leaded compounds. The change produced unexpected side-effects (Fig. 35.3). While the atmospheric concentration of lead did indeed fall, ozone concentrations above the City rose quickly as a result of a

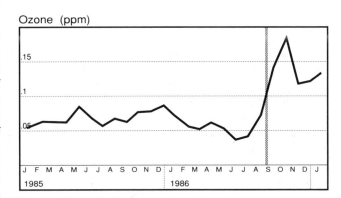

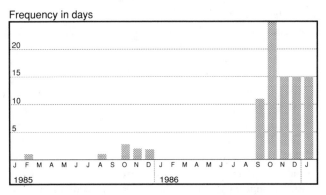

Figure 35.3 Mean monthly ozone concentrations in the atmosphere above Mexico City, and number of days in which the ozone standard (0.11 ppm) was violated. The broken line (September 1986) indicates the period in which leaded gasoline was replaced by unleaded gasoline, with a higher concentration of photochemical oxidants. Source: Bravo 1987.

reaction between ultraviolet solar radiation, atmospheric oxygen, and the oxidizing effect of the new gasoline additives. The present mean ozone concentration is on average approximately 0.15 ppm (300 µg/m³) – 10 times the normal atmospheric concentration, more than double the maximum limit in the United States and Japan (Avediz Aznavourian 1984), and high enough to damage most of the urban vegetation (Skärby and Sellden 1984). Because of the time lag involved in ozone formation, the highest ozone levels are registered toward the southwest of the City in the direction of the prevailing winds. During the winter of 1987–88, the ozone levels in this area exceeded the maximum allowable standard (0.11 ppm) more than 50% of the time, and generated continuous health complaints from the population. Ironically, while low ozone concentrations in the stratosphere are a major environmental concern at a global scale, excessively high ozone concentrations are now one of the main problems in the Basin of Mexico.

Much could be done, however, to control atmospheric pollution in the Basin of Mexico. Catalytic converters still are not used in cars, and the Mexican standard for maximum allowable exhaust emissions in new vehicles is 2 to 3 times more permissive than that of, for example, the United States. More widespread use of public transportation, coupled with restrictions on the use of private vehicles, would certainly ease the air-pollution problem. Buses, metro trains, trolley buses, and taxis are responsible for only 23–30% of all vehicular emissions, but they transport 81% of all passengers (Bravo 1986). The average emission of pollutants per passenger using private vehicles is 10 times higher than that of passengers using public transportation. If these simple measures (emission control plus encouragement of public transportation) were put to work, a marked improvement in the quality of the air could be expected in a relatively short time.

Atmospheric pollution also has a considerable influence on the quality of rainwater. Páramo, Guerrero, Morales, Morales and Baz Contreras (1987, see also Bravo 1987) reported, for the 1983–1986 period, a significant decrease in the pH of incoming rainwater in Mexico City due to the increasing concentration of sulfur and nitrogen oxides in the air. In the urban parts of the Basin, the average pH of rainwater is approximately 5.5, and a few rain events have been registered with pH values as low as 3.0. Although little information exists on the matter, it is known that the effects of air pollution are not restricted to the urban areas; they can also have considerable impact on the natural ecosystems surrounding the Basin. Hernández Tejeda, Bauer, and Krupa (1985; see also Bauer, Hernández Tejeda, and Manning 1985; Hernández Tejeda, Bauer, and Ortega Delgado 1985; and Hernández Tejeda and Bauer 1986), for example, have found that the ozone produced above the City and carried by the dominant winds to the Sierra del Ajusco, southwest of the Basin, significantly reduces the chlorophyll content and the growth of *Pinus hartwegii*, the dominant pine species in the high mountains around the Basin (ca. 3,500 m). One of the main functions of these forests is the collection of water for the City. Thus, atmospheric pollution may have a considerable impact on the water balance on the hillslopes of the Basin,

and consequently on the availability and quality of water for human consumption.

Ecological Subsidies

The rapid rise and the enormous power of the Aztec state were based on the political control of much of Mesoamerica and on the subordination of hundreds of different groups that paid tribute to the emperor. Aztec wealth depended to some extent on the concentration of high-quality goods (e.g., metals, obsidian, tropical fruits, and high-protein food) and labor collected as tribute from conquered groups. The Basin of Mexico, which initially allowed the surge of the Aztec culture through the appropriation and use of the highly productive *chinampa* technology, became a partly subsidized ecosystem receiving inputs of matter and energy from other areas.

This tradition, maintained under Spanish rule, has now reached immense proportions. Few ecosystems in the world are so far from self-sufficiency as is the Basin of Mexico at present. With much of the forests cut, most of the *chinampa* lands turned into urban developments, and practically all of the lakes dried up, the supply of raw materials and energy generated within the Basin does not suffice for even a small fraction of the 18 million residents. Thus, the Basin of Mexico imports vast amounts of food, energy, wood, water, building materials, and many other products from other ecosystems that, in effect, subsidize the water and energy flows of the Basin. With 22% of the population of the country, the Basin consumes around 27% of the country's oil and nearly one-third of its electricity (Table 35-6).

In spite of the severe environmental problems, the Mexican model of development has given priority to improving the quality of life in the large cities, where the social demand is more concentrated, at the expense of the rural areas, which have become comparatively poorer. From 1950 to 1980, the Basin experienced marked improvement in demographic and domestic indicators of quality of life (Table 35-7), but the

Table 35-6 *Energy Consumption in the Mexican Republic and in the Basin of Mexico between 1970 and 1975.* *

Year	1970		1975	
Whole country				
Oil	34,060,003		48,081,005	
Electricity	2,320,482		3,708,698	
Coal	1,470,000		2,616,000	
Total	37,850,485		54,405,703	
Basin of Mexico				
Oil	9,215,600	(27.1%)	13,202,132	(27.5%)
Electricity	753,874	(32.5%)	1,065,554	(28.7%)
Coal	0		0	
Total	9,969,474	(26.3%)	14,267,686	(26.2%)

* In m³ of oil or their equivalent. The numbers in parentheses indicate the proportion used by the Basin of Mexico with respect to the whole country.
Source: Ibarra et al. 1986.

Table 35-7 *Evolution of the Quality-of-Life Indicators for the Basin of Mexico from 1950 to 1980.*

Year	1950	1960	1970	1980	1980–MR*
Life expectancy at 1 year of age (yrs)	55.0	60.8	63.2	65.2	64.4
Infant mortality (%)	12.0	7.9	7.4	4.3	7.1
Adult literacy (%)	83.8	88.4	92.6	95.6	83.0
Proportion of houses with running water (%)	n.a.	35.0	53.0	67.0	n.a.
Proportion of houses with drainage (%)	n.a.	33.0	63.0	81.3	n.a.
Proportion of houses owned by their residents (%)	n.a.	34.0	50.0	52.7	n.a.

*Values for the Mexican Republic (MR) are given for comparison.
Source: Ibarra et al. 1986.

changes at the national level have been lower. This difference in trends is, of course, much more marked if the Basin of Mexico is compared with the depressed rural areas from which most of the immigrants come. Although the data were not available at the time of writing, it is evident that such public services as education, running water, and drainage are scanty in the poorer areas of central and southern Mexico that provide at a cheap price many of the products that are consumed in the Basin and that also generate most of the new immigrants that move into the area.

Through this system of ecological subsidies, many of the problems generated by the growth, or by the sheer size, of Mexico City are in effect exported to neighboring areas. The chronic shortage of water in the Basin, for example, is in great part transferred to the Lerma and Cutzamala basins, from which water is imported at a rate of 18 m³/s (Bazdresch 1986). Sewage water, on the other hand, is drained into the Tula Basin, in the State of Hidalgo. In this way, water pollution is exported into the Tula system.

Apart from the ecological interpretation of these subsidies, the urban concentration of Mexico City has also involved the concentration of wealth and an economic subsidy implicitly granted by the rest of the nation to the residents of the capital city. Public transportation in Mexico City (buses, trolleybuses and the metro train) now costs approximately U.S. $0.04 per trip, a fixed tariff that is independent of the distance traveled. The metro, which transports 3 million passengers per day (Bravo 1986), thus generates a revenue of U.S. $120,000 per day, but the real cost of operating the system is in the order of U.S. $1.5 million per day (Bazdresch 1986). The difference is ultimately met by all taxpayers, many of whom do not benefit from the service in any way. Water costs approximately U.S. $0.10/m³ to distribute in Mexico City. This price is largely due to the high costs of pumping water into the Basin of Mexico from the Basin of Lerma (Bazdresch 1986). The government spends approximately U.S. $150 million per year to supply water to the Basin of Mexico. The revenue obtained from the service, however, is on the order of U.S. $42 million, less than 30% of the total cost. Other services, such as electricity, gas, garbage collection, and road maintenance, are subsidized for the whole country and not only for the Basin of Mexico. Because the city receives these services in a higher proportion than the rest of the nation, however, it receives a higher share of the subsidy, as in the

Table 35-8 *Population, Total Urban Area, and Vegetated Areas per Person for the Metropolitan Area of Mexico City in 1950 and 1980, and Projected Values for the Year 2000*

	1950	1980	2000
Population (millions)	3.0	13.8	32.7
Total urban area (km²)	215	980	2700
Total urban green areas (m²/person)	29.0	9.9	5.6
Parks and recreational areas (m²/person)	9.0	5.9	5.0

case of energy, previously discussed. This is, again, particularly true for rural areas that export their produce to the city but that do not benefit from the cheap urban services.

Conclusion: A Development Model in Crisis

The projection of present trends (Fig. 35.4 and Table 35-8; see footnote 1 for methodology) shows that, by the year 2000, Mexico City will spread over 2,700 km², possibly spilling over the boundaries of the Basin into the adjacent cities of Toluca, Querétaro, Cuernavaca, or Puebla. Most (92%) of that immense urban area will be houses and roads, whereas only 6% of it will be occupied by parks, private gardens, and public spaces. Approximately 30 million people will live on the Basin, enjoying only 5 m² of green area per person (Table 35-8). In some parts of the city, the situation will be substantially worse; many inhabitants of the future city will have less than 1 m² of open public spaces for their recreational use, as is already the case in Azcapotzalco. Mexico City will have changed from the patchy mixture of urban and rural environments that was typical of the first half of this century to an overcrowded urban environment with little vegetation and open space for its inhabitants (Fig. 35.4). By that time, approximately 100 m³/s of water will have to be pumped from outside the Basin, unless new and more efficient methods of recycling sewage are adopted soon. The source for this future hydrological subsidy from other watersheds into the Basin of Mexico is not yet clear. What is clear is that the extension of the city to its future area of 2,700 km² necessarily will mean the deforestation of many of the surrounding areas that now act as hydrological regulators for the already severely disrupted water cycle of the Basin. One cannot be optimistic about the future prospects; it would

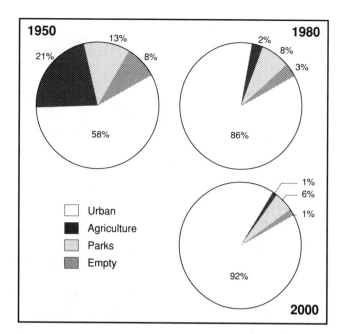

Figure 35.4 Evolution of the distribution of land surfaces in Mexico City from 1950 to 1980, and projected values for the year 2000.

appear by any interpretation that Mexico City is rapidly reaching its ecological limits, given its technology. The greatest challenge at present is to promote action before matters get completely out of control.

Although most of the environmental problems in the Basin of Mexico have reached critical proportions in the late twentieth century, industrial development is not solely to blame. Urban primacy and political centralism have been a tradition in Mexican society since the Aztec empire. The Basin of Mexico, for nearly two millennia one of the most densely populated areas of the world, has used its preeminent administrative and political position to obtain advantages over other areas of the nation. But modern industrialization has exaggerated this historical trend to dramatic proportions, and is indeed responsible for the disproportionate urbanization and the biased distribution of population and wealth in the Basin of Mexico.

Since the Revolution, a brand of economic development, which Sandbrook (1986) has called "conservative modernization," developed in Mexico through the alliance of three dominant sectors: the paternalistic postrevolutionary government, local private enterprises, and foreign capital. The goal of this alliance has been massive industrial development, often at the expense of social equality. Public resources have been largely allocated to the industrial sector, and this, in turn, accelerated urban growth. The Basin of Mexico concentrates government, public bureaucracy, a large middle class with a high capacity to consume, infrastructure such as electricity and roads, health services, and industries eager to profit from this growing market. These sectors have formed the "modern" part of the City, with skyscrapers, large shopping centers, highways, and residential suburbs. Most of the City, however, is formed by poor quarters inhabited by workers and subemployed persons who only a generation ago

were peasants in rural Mexico and migrated into the Basin looking for a share in some of the services and goods that industrialization seems to promise. This migratory trend continues, and the City is still sprawling over forests and fields. Quite obviously, only a strong decentralization policy promoting migration to smaller cities, favoring life in rural areas, and heavily taxing residence in the Basin of Mexico can stop the process. But such a policy would cost hard currency in a country with a foreign debt of over U.S. $100 billion, would go against the interests of both national and multinational industries, and might also go against the short-term interests of the workers of Mexico City. People must be made aware of the seriousness of the environmental problem before action for decentralization can be taken.

The future of the Basin of Mexico is inextricably linked with the economic future of Latin America and with the political and social model that the country adopts in the next decade. But the story of the Basin is one of growth, collapse, and cultural rebirth, of catastrophic disintegration and cultural reorganization. Although more acute than ever before, many of the problems of the Basin are not new. It is in the hands of modern Mexicans to find innovative answers to both the old and the new questions posed by the industrial development of the former capital of the Anahuac.

Note

1. Modeling and projection methods are explained here. To evaluate the magnitude of the changes that have occurred in the past decades in the Basin of Mexico, a technique commonly employed in demography has been used. Let us assume that within a certain time interval the relative rate of change of some variables is constant, or nearly so (obviously, the validity of this assumption decreases with the length of the time interval considered). This means that for a given period, the per capita growth rate of certain variables, like the population density, the urban area, or the number of cars, can be considered to be more or less constant. That is, that the number of live children per adult, the number of new cars per car on the road, or the number of new urbanized hectares per urbanized hectare does not change as quickly as the variables themselves (population density, number of cars, or urban area). In mathematical terms this can be written as

$$\frac{1}{X} \cdot \frac{dX}{dt} = k \qquad (1)$$

where X is the variable in question, and k is the relative growth rate and can show negative values for variables that tend to decrease with time. Integrating equation (1), we get

$$X(t) = X(0) \cdot e^{kt} \qquad (2)$$

which is the typical exponential growth curve used in demography to estimate future population numbers when the relative growth rate (k) is known.

If only two points are known, the relative growth rate can be estimated from equation (1), by rewriting it as

$$\frac{d(\ln(X))}{dt} = k \qquad (3)$$

and approximating its value from the difference equation

$$k \cong \frac{\Delta(\ln(X))}{\Delta t} \qquad (4)$$

Alternatively, if more than two points are known, an estimator can be derived by rewriting equation (2) as

$$\ln(X(t)) = \ln(X(0)) + kt \qquad (5)$$

where, obviously, k can be estimated as the slope of the regression line between the log values of the variable under study (X) and time (t).

After the values of the relative rate of change of the main variables have been estimated, they can be used to project the behavior of the system to the future. Obviously, these projections will be valid only if the k values remain fairly constant in time. Although absolute certainty does not exist that this will be the case, the projected values are at least good indicators of the future consequences of maintaining a present trend.

References

Aguilar Sahagún, G. 1984. Reglamentación en problemas de desechos sólidos. *Proceedings. I Reunión Regional sobre Legislación Ambiental. Monterrey. Nvo. León*, 35–45. México, D.F.: Secretaria de Desarrollo Urbano y Ecologis.

Alvarez, J. R., Coord. 1985. *Imagen de la Gran Capital*. Mexico, D.F.: Enciclopedia de México.

Anonymous. [1788] 1984. *Reflexiones y Apuntes sobre la Ciudad de México*. Compiled and edited by Ignacio González Polo. Departamento del Distrito Federal. México, D. F.: Colección Distrito Federal, No. 4.

Avediz Aznavourian, A. 1984. Normas de calidad del aire en México. *Proceedings. I Reunión Regional sobre Legislación Ambiental, Monterrey, Nvo. León*, 101–120. México, D. F.: Secretaria de Desarrollo Urbano y Ecologia.

Barfoot, K. M., C. Vargas-Aburto, J.D. MacArthur, A. Jaidar, F. Garcia-Santibáñez, and V. Fuentes-Gea. 1984. Multielemental measurements of air particulate pollution at a site in Mexico City. *Atmos. Env.* 18:467–51.

Barradas, V., and J-Seres, R. 1987. Los pulmones urbanos. *Ciencia v Desarrollo* 79:61–72.

Bauer, L. I., Tejeda, Hernández and W. J. Manning. 1985. Ozone causes needle injury and tree decline in *Pinus hartwegii* at high altitudes in the mountains around Mexico City. *J. Air Pollut. Control Assoc.* 35(8):838.

Bazdresch, C. 1986. Los subsidios y la concentración en la Ciudad de México. In *Descentralización y democracia en México*, comp. B. Torres, 205–218. Mexico, D.F.: El Colegio de México.

Bravo, H. 1986. La atmósfera de la Zona Metropolitana de la Ciudad de México. *Desarrollo y Medio Ambiente: Fund. Mex. Rest. Ambiental* 2:2–3.

———. 1987. *La contaminación del aire en México*. Mexico, D.F.: Fundación Universo Veintiuno.

Calderón, E., and B. Hernández. 1987. Crecimiento actual de la población de México. *Ciencia y Desarrollo* 76:49–66.

Calvillo-Ortega, M. T. 1978. Areas verdes de la Ciudad de México. *Anuario de Geografia* 16:377–82.

DDF (Departamento del Distrito Federal). 1974. *Plantas de tratamiento de aguas negras en la Ciudad de México*. Mexico, D.F.: Departamento del Distrito Federal, Dirección General de Obras Hidráulicas.

———. 1977. *Volumen de agua potable para la Ciudad de México, datos estimativos 1976*. Mexico, D. F.: Departamento del Distrito Federal, Dirección General de Obras Hidráulicas.

———, Comp. 1983. *La Ciudad de México antes y después de la Conquista* (a compilation of texts from early colonial times). Mexico, D.F.: Colección Distrito Federal No. 2.

———. 1986. *Manual de planeación, diseño v manejo de las áreas verdes urbanas del Distrito Federal*. Mexico, D.F.: Departamento del Distrito Federal.

———. 1987. Programas de desarrollo urbano del Distrito Federal, 1987–1988. Mexico, D. F. Published in all Mexico City newspapers on January 8, 1987.

Fuentes Gea, V., and A. A. C. Hernández. 1984. Evaluación preliminar de la contaminación del aire por particulas en el Area Metropolitana del Valle de México. *Memorias del IV Congreso Nacional de Ingenieria Sanitaria y Ambiental* 523–26. Mexico, D.F.: Sociedad Mexicana de Ingenieria Sanitaria y Ambiental.

Galindo, G., and J. Morales. 1987. El relieve y los asentamientos humanos en la Ciudad de México. *Ciencia y Desarrollo* 76:67–80.

Gamboa, M. T. 1983. *Identificación y cuantificación de microorganismos (bacterias y hongos) y su relación con la distribución del tamaño de particulas en cuatro sitios de la atmósfera de la Ciudad de México*. Mexico, Facultad de Ciencias, Univ. Nac. Aut. de México. Unpublished thesis.

Goldani, A. M. 1977. Impacto de los inmigrantes sobre la estructura y el crecimiento del área metropolitana. In *Migración y desigualdad social en la ciudad de México*, comp. H. Muñoz, O. de Oliveira, and C. Stern 129–37. Mexico, D.F.: Instituto de Investigaciones Sociales, Univ. Nac. Aut. de México and El Colegio de México.

González Angulo, J., and Y. Terán Trillo. 1976. *Planos de la Ciudad de México 1785, 1853 y 1896*. Mexico, D. F.: Instituto Nacional de Antropologia e Historia, Colección Científica, No. 50.

Guevara, S., and P. Moreno. 1987. Areas verdes en la zona metropolitana de la Ciudad de México. In Garza, G. (comp.) *Atlas de Ciudad de México*, comp. G. Garza 231–36. Departamento del Distrito Federal and El Colegio de Mexico. Mexico, D. F.

Halffter, G., and E. Ezcurra. 1983. Diseño de una politica ecológica para el Valle de México. *Ciencia y Desarrollo* 53:89–96.

Hernández Tejeda, T., and L. I. de Bauer. 1986. Photochemical oxidant damage on *Pinus hartwegii* at the "Desierto de los Leones." Mexico, D. F. *Phytopathology* 76(3):377.

Hernández Tejeda, T., L. I. de Bauer., and S. V. Krupa. 1985. Daños por gases oxidantes en pinos del Ajusco. *Memoria de los Simposia Nacionales de Parasitologia Forestal II y III*. Mexico, D.F., Secretaria de Agricultura y Recursos Hidráulicos. Publicación Especial No. 46, 26–36.

Hernández Tejeda, T., L. I. de Bauer, and M. L. Ortega Delgado. 1985. Determinación de la clorofila total de hojas de *Pinus hartwegii* afectadas por gases oxidantes. *Memoria de los Simposia Nacionales de Parasitologia Forestal II y III*. Mexico, D.F., Secretaria de Agricultura y Recursos Hidraúlicos. Publicaión Especial No. 46, 334–41.

von Humboldt, A. [1811] Published in Spanish in 1966. *Ensayo politico sobre el Reino de la Nueva España*. Porrùa Editores, Mèxico, D. F.

Ibarra, V., F. Saavedra, S. Puente, and M. Schteingart. 1986. La ciudad y el medio ambiente: El caso de la zona metropolitana de la ciudad de Mèxico. In *La ciudad y el medio ambiente en América Latina: seis estudios de caso*, comp. V. Ibarra, S. Puente, and F. Saavedra, 97–150. El Colegio de México. Mexico, D.F.

Jáuregui, E. 1971. La erosión eólica en los suelos vecinos al Lago de Texcoco. *Rev. de Ingenieria Hidráulica* XXV:103–118.

———. 1983. Variaciones de largo periodo de la visibilidad en la Ciudad de México. *Geofisica Internacional* 22–23:251–75.

———. 1987. Climas. *In Atlas de Ciudad de México*, Comp. G. Garza, 37–40. Departamento del Distrito Federal and El Colegio de Mexico. Mexico, D. F.

Lara, O. 1988. El agua en la Ciudad de México. *Gaceta UNAM* 45(15):20–22.

Lavín, M. 1983. *Cambios en las áreas verdes de la zona metroplitana de la Ciudad de México de 1940 a 1980*. Mexico, D.F.: Internal report, Instituto de Ecologia.

León-Portilla, M., A. M. Garibay, and A. Beltrán. 1972. *Visión de los vencidos: Relaciones indigenas de la conquista*. Mexico, D. F.: Universidad Nacional Autónoma de México.

Monroy Hermosillo, O. 1987. Manejo y disposición de residuos sólidos. *Desarrollo y Medio Ambiente* 2:2–7.

Mosser, F. 1987. Geologia. In *Atlas de Ciudad de México*, comp. G. Garza, 23–29. Departamento del Distrito Federal and El Colegio de Mexico. Mexico, D. F.

Niederberger, C. 1987. De la prehistoria a los primeros asentamientos humanos en la Cuenca de México. *In Atlas de Ciudad de México*, comp. G. Garza, 40–43. Departamento del Distrito Federal and El Colegio de Mexico. Mexico, D.F.

Páramo, V. H., M. A. Guerrero. M. A. Morales, R. E. Morales, and D. Baz Contreras. 1987. Acidez de las precipitaciones en el Distrito Federal. *Ciencia y Desarrollo* 72:59–66.

Parsons, J. R. 1976. Settlement and population history of the Basin of Mexico. In *The Valley of Mexico: Studies in Prehispanic Ecology and Society*, ed. E. R. Wolf, 69–100. Albuquerque, NM: University of New Mexico Press.

Restrepo, I., and D. Phillips. 1985. *La basura: Consumo y desperdicio en el Distrito Federal*. Mexico, D.F.: Centro de Ecodesarrollo.

SAHOP (Secretaria de Asentamientos Humanos y Obras Públicas). 1977. *Memoria descriptiva del flujo de agua, energéticos y alimentos en el área metropolitana de la ciudad de México*. Mexico, D.F.: Secr. de Asentamientos Humanos y Obras Públicas, Subsecretaria de Asentamientos Humanos, Dirección General de Ecologia Urbana.

———. 1978. *Diagnóstico de la calidad atmosférica del Valle de México*. Mexico, D.F.: Secr. de Asentamientos Humanos y Obras Públicas, Subsecretaria de Asentamientos Humanos, Dirección General de Ecologia Urbana.

Sala Catalá, J. 1986. La localización de la capital de Nueva España, como problema científico y tecnológico. *Quipu* 3:279–98.

Salazar, S., J. L. Bravo, and Y. Falcón. 1981. Sobre la presencia de algunos metales pesados en la atmósfera de la Ciudad de México. *Geofísica Internacional* 20:41–54.

Sandbrook, R. 1986. Crisis urbana en el Tercer Mundo. In *La ciudad y el medio ambiente en América Latina: seis estudios de caso*, comp. V. Ibarra, S. Puente, and F. Saavedra, 19–27. Mexico, D. F.: El Colegio de México.

Sanders, W. T. 1976a. The agricultural history of the Basin of Mexico. In *The Valley of Mexico: Studies in Prehispanic Ecology and Society*, ed. E. R. Wolf, 101–159. Albuquerque, NM: University of New Mexico Press.

———. 1976b. The natural environment of the Basin of Mexico. In *The Valley of Mexico: Studies in Prehispanic Ecology and Society*, ed. E. R. Wolf, 59–67. Albuquerque, NM: University of New Mexico Press.

Sanders, W. T., J. R. Parsons, and R. S. Santley. 1979. *The Basin of Mexico: Ecological Processes in the Evolution of a Civilization*. New York: Academic Press.

SEDUE. 1986. *Informe sobre estado del medio ambiente en México*. Mexico, D. F.: Secretaria de Desarrollo Urbano y Ecologia.

Sierra, C. J. 1984. *Historia de la navegación en la Ciudad de México*. Mexico, D. F.: Departamento del Distrito Federal, Colección Distrito Federal, No. 7.

Sigler Andrade, E., V. Fuentes Gea, and C. Vargas Aburto. 1982. Análisis de la contaminación del aire por particulas en Ciudad Universitaria. Vol. II, *Memorias del III Congreso Nacional de Ingenieria Sanitaria y Ambiental*. 1–13. Mexico, D.F.: Sociedad Mexicana de Ingenieria Sanitaria y Ambiental.

Skärby, L., and G. Sellden. 1984. The effects of ozone on crops and forests. *Ambio* 13:68–72.

SMA (Subsecretaria de Mejoramiento del Ambiente). 1978a. *Desechos sólidos*. Mexico, D. F.: Secretaria de Salubridad y Asistencia. Subsecretaria de Mejoramiento del Ambiente.

———. 1978b. *Fuentes emisoras en México. Industrias altamente contaminantes*. Mexico, D. F.: Secretaria de Salubridad y Asistencia. Subsecretaria de Mejoramiento del Ambiente.

———. 1978c. *Situación actual de la contaminación atmosférica en el área metropolitana de la Ciudad de México*. Mexico, D.F.: Secretaria de Salubridad y Asistencia, Subsecretaria de Mejoramiento del Ambiente.

Soms Garcia, E. 1986. *La hiperurbanización en el Valle de México*. Vols. I and II. Mexico, D. F.: Univ. Aut. Metropolitana.

Stern, C. 1977. Cambios en los volúmenes de migrantes provenientes de distintas zonas geoeconómicas. In *Migración y desigualded social en la ciudad de México*, comp. H. Huñoz, O. de Oliveira, and C. Stern, 115–28. Mexico, D.F.: Univ. Nac. Aut. de México and El Colegio de México.

Trabulse, E. 1983. *Cartografía mexicana: Tesoros de la Nación, siglos XVI a XIX*. Mexico, D. F.: Archivo General de la Nación.

Trejo Vázquez, R. 1987. La disposición de desechos sólidos urbanos. *Ciencia y Desarrollo* 74:79–90.

Unikel, L. 1974. *La dinámica del crecimiento de la Ciudad de México*. Mexico, D. F.: SEP-Setentas.

Velasco Levy, A. 1983. La contaminación atmosférica en la ciudad de México. *Ciencia y Desarrollo* 52:59–68.

36

Nigeria

REUBEN K. UDO   O. O. AREOLA   J. O. AYOADE   A. A. AFOLAYAN

Nigeria is neither a physically nor a culturally homogeneous region. It is, rather, a political region of West Africa that straddles a number of environmental zones, from the wet tropical coasts to the dry Sudan-Sahelian interior, and is occupied by a variety of ethnically and once economically diverse groups. These factors, coupled with its colonial history, make Nigeria in many ways a microcosm of the larger nature–society problems that confront much of sub-Saharan Africa. These problems and the human causes and adjustments to them are too many and varied to document in detail for the past 300 years, even if the data were sufficient to do so. Therefore, the strategy followed here is first to address briefly the three major socioeconomic periods that make up those 300 years, emphasizing impacts on vegetation and soil by period, and second to summarize some of the net transformations and major agents of change, focusing on wildlife, atmosphere, and water resources.

The Setting

The Physical Environment

Nigeria displays a great variety of landscapes and climates. Although it has no high mountains, the rugged hills of Obudu and the Shebshi-Mandara ranges of the eastern borderlands with the Republic of Cameroon are highland areas with a semi-temperate climate. Other prominent landforms include the heavily dissected Enugu-Okigwi escarpment, the 4,200-foot Jos Plateau, and the lagoons and swamps of the Atlantic coastlands and the Niger Delta (Fig. 36.1). The extensive crystalline plateau surfaces of Hausaland and northern Yorubaland are, like the plateau surfaces of Tanzania and Zambia in High Africa, characterized by vast plains, whose monotony is broken here and there by inselbergs, which appear singly or in groups.

By virtue of its location just north of the equator (lat. 4°N to 14°N), Nigeria is hot throughout the year, with shade temperatures of almost 100°F in the dry season. The fact that it is bordered in the south by the Gulf of Guinea and in the north by the Sahara Desert is important not only in determining features of the climate of the various macroregions, but also in explaining the course of human history

before and during the past 300 years. The rain-bearing winds from the southwest keep the southern third of the country hot and wet for most of the year. Rainfall decreases northward toward the desert. The northern third of the country has a long dry season of about 6 months, during which the cold, dry, and dusty *harmattan* wind from the Sahara blows for about two months. The open character of the northern grasslands derives from the interior location of the area, just as the forest cover of the south is made possible by the heavy rainfall near the coast (Figs 36.2 and 36.3). A zone of transition separates the north from the south, and is usually called the middle belt.

A great variety of landscapes is associated with these physiographic and climatic attributes of various parts of the country. It is the combination of these landscapes and the varied ethnic composition of the population that has produced in Nigeria examples of environmental changes representative of those caused by human action throughout tropical Africa. They have also combined to give distinctive physical and cultural characteristics to the three macroregions (the south, the middle belt, and the Nigerian Sudan), into which the country is divided for the purpose of this study. Physical, but largely cultural differences, however, also occur within these macroregions, as in the case of Yorubaland and Iboland in the south.

The Population Pattern

Within its territory of 922,280 km², which is only 3.05% of the area of Africa, Nigeria now supports a very large population of about 120 million, which is about 23% of the total population of the continent. The very uneven distribution of population has contributed greatly in the past and present to the variation in the changes caused by settlement in areas of similar physical environmental characteristics (Fig. 36.4). The very densely populated rural districts of Okigwe, Orlu, and Mbaise in Iboland, like the rural districts of Ikot-Ekpene, Abak, and Uyo in the Annang and Ibibio homelands, now support about 400 persons/km². Similar concentrations of rural population occur in parts of Yorubaland, notably in Ijebu-Remo, Ekiti, and the Ibadan-Ife area. In the far north, the major areas of concentration are the Sokoto home districts, the Kano closed-settled zone, and the Katsina

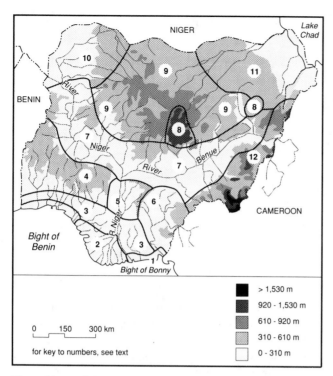

Figure 36.1 Relief and physical regions of Nigeria. (1) coastal creeks and lagoons; (2) Niger Delta; (3) coastal plain; (4) western or Oyo plains; (5) scarplands of south-central Nigeria; (6) Cross River Basin; (7) Niger-Benue Valley; (8) Jos and Biu plateaus; (9) high plains of Hausaland; (10) Sokoto-Rima plains; (11) Chad Basin; (12) eastern mountains. Source: Udo 1978.

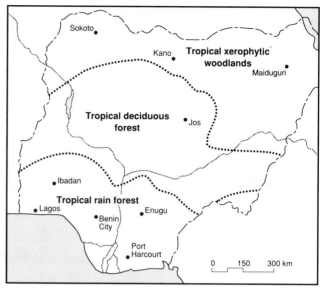

Figure 36.2 Original vegetation belts of Nigeria.

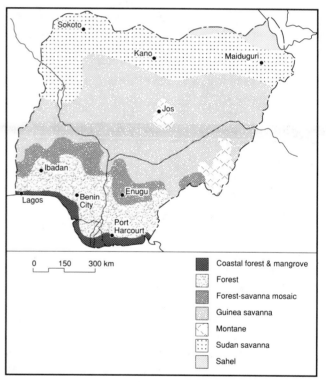

Figure 36.3 Present vegetation belts of Nigeria.

home districts, each of which supports a population of about 200/km². Although these northern districts are less congested, the lower rainfall and the comparatively drier conditions impose even greater stress on the local resources than in the more congested but wetter districts of the southern states.

By contrast, parts of the country contain vast areas that are very sparsely settled or virtually uninhabited. Such areas include the forests of the Oban and Obubra Districts in the Cross River State, the Middle Benue Basin, and the Niger Delta. The Chad Basin, the Kontagora District, and the northern Yoruba grassland areas of the Kishi and Shaki Districts are also lightly populated. Often the densely settled areas share internal political boundaries with the sparsely settled areas, a situation partly caused by the fact that each ethnic group occupies a territory to which it lays claim by right of first occupance (Fig. 36.5).

The rate of ecological change in Nigeria, like the rate of growth of the human population, has increased greatly during the twentieth century, and especially since about 1945. Three hundred years ago, the major process that affected the human occupation of the country was the slave trade, which resulted in the destruction of human lives and settlements in various parts of the country and the relocation of a large number of people. Other major events include the introduction of new food crops, the spread of Islam, the Fulani conquest of Hausaland and northern Yorubaland, and the Yoruba civil wars. Finally, toward the end of the nineteenth century came the imposition of British colonial rule, which lasted until

1960. The importance of these events in shaping the contemporary landscape of Nigeria is discussed in this study over three time periods, namely the precolonial period (1650–1902), the period of effective British control (1902–1960), and the postcolonial period (starting in 1960).

The Precolonial Period: 1650–1902

Documentary evidence of events before 1800 is fragmentary and in some cases speculative.[1] Abundant evidence

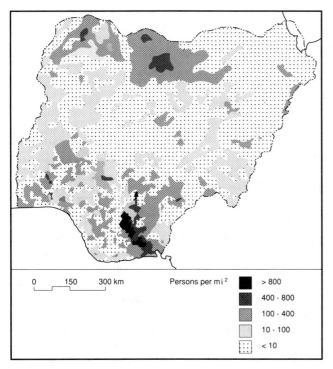

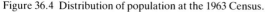

Figure 36.4 Distribution of population at the 1963 Census.

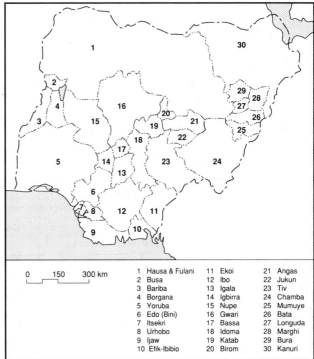

Figure 36.5 The major ethnic/cultural areas.

shows, however, that almost all parts of the country supported a sedentary population of farmers as of 1650, with the possible exception of the dense forests of the eastern borderlands between the Cross River State and western Cameroon. The population of Africa in 1650 is estimated to have been 100 million (Willcox 1940). Given the large number of slaves taken from West Africa, including Nigeria, it appears reasonable to assume that Nigeria's share of this total population was not much less than it is today. The country probably had a total population of about 20 million in 1650, with major concentrations around Kano, Zaria, Katsina, Bida, southern Tivland, and the Ibo and Ibibio homelands in the east.

The major events that shaped the cultural landscapes of Nigeria during this period, much of which coincides with the peak period of the European slave trade, revolved around the politics of the various city-states and empires. The populations and land areas of the states and empires differed considerably, as did the systems of government and the organization of the economy. These differences were particularly marked as between the far north, or Nigerian Sudan, and the forest belt in the south. The open nature of the grass-covered plateau landscapes of the north facilitated the movement of large armies and the use of animal transportation. It thus contributed greatly to the ability of the Hausas, and later the Fulanis and Kanuris, to establish and police states and empires covering much more extensive areas than those of the forest belt or the Niger Delta. The Nigerian Sudan conducted external trade northward across the Sahara, whereas the south traded with Europe by way of the Atlantic Ocean.

Political Instability, Population Movements, and Urbanization

By 1650, the northern city-states, most of which later became part of the Fulani empire, were already fully established. All of them carried on considerable trade with the forest kingdoms in the south and with Europe and Asia, and several served as major entrepots in the trans-Saharan trade. Political conflicts and trade rivalry resulted in periodic and sometimes prolonged warfare among the city-states. The resultant insecurity strongly influenced the sites chosen for settlements, the settlement patterns, and the grouping and relocation of population. Accounts of the destruction occasioned by these conflicts and warfare abound in the journals of European travelers. In the boundary districts between Borno and Hausaland, for example, Barth (1857a, 1857b) described how a flourishing and populous area that he visited in 1851 was reduced to a state of ruins and misery three years later as a result of civil wars. Intergroup warfare and slave raids were also responsible for the destruction of villages and farms in much of the middle belt, notably the Kontagora and Yelwa districts.

Political instability in these northern districts led to considerable migration. Large concentrations of population emerged around the seats of powerful rulers such as those of Kano, Katsina, and Sokoto, who were able to offer protection to their subjects. Large areas of the outlying districts were depopulated as people left to settle in more peaceful locations. Throughout the precolonial period, and especially during the slave trade, a close positive relationship existed between population density and the state of social security in a given rural district. The establishment of hill settlements and of walled villages was a common defensive strategy at this time. All of the major cities were also surrounded by walls of mud and by moats, relics of which may be seen today.

In the densely forested south, save in parts of Yorubaland, the territories of the city-states were generally smaller. Recent archaeological finds suggest the existence of a large Ibo city-state based at Awka, but at the time of British conquest no large city-states existed in the eastern forest belt. Indeed, outside Yorubaland the only large and prominent city-state in the forest belt was the kingdom of Benin. The large concentration of urban centers in Yorubaland is one of the unique features of precolonial urbanization in Africa. The largest native towns in Nigeria, and indeed in sub-Saharan Africa, are concentrated in Oyo State in Yorubaland (see Andah 1960; Ojo 1966). According to Mabogunje (1962), before the nineteenth century, the largest of the Yoruba metropolitan towns, each with a crowned *oba* (king), had populations of not more than 30,000 each. The outlying towns of each of the Yoruba feudal states were much smaller, each with populations of about 5,000.

Agricultural Land Use, Grazing, and Forest Clearance

Throughout the precolonial period, agriculture involved primarily food production for the family and for local exchange. Kola nut (*Cola nitida*), which is produced in the forest belt, was exported to the north in exchange for such valuable commodities as natron (carbonate of soda), horses, and cattle. There were, however, no such large plantations of kola nut or of any other tree crops as occur today. Because only annuals were cultivated in both the forest and the savanna regions, the pattern of land use was broadly similar all over the country, except that farms were larger in the grassland areas. The ruling class and the rich depended mostly on slave labor, hence the large number of domestic slaves in the city-states. Often, as at Nike near Enugu, at Calabar, and among the Hausa city-states, most of the slave farmhands lived in villages away from the settlements of the free-born. Some of these slave villages provide good examples of the influence of a centralized political authority in the spatial redistribution of population in precolonial Nigeria (Gana 1978).

Most of the central Iboland and the Annang and Ibibio territories to the south were already densely settled and under intensive cultivation. The forest belt west of the lower Niger Valley was, however, very sparsely populated. Indeed, as Morgan (1959) has pointed out, large-scale clearance of the rain forest in the southwest did not begin until the early nineteenth century, when the Fulani armies invaded northern Yorubaland, destroying a large number of settlements. The refugees who flocked into the forest belt cleared large areas around their new settlements and in the neighborhood of the older but crowded cities for farmland. Extensive areas of forest, however, survived into the colonial period; some were later set aside as forest reserves by the colonial government.

In the savanna region, the long period of political

instability and warfare disrupted normal economic activities. A large number of defensive hill settlements, some of which have survived until today, were established at this time. Many of the areas laid waste in the course of this warfare were never resettled and have since reverted to savanna woodland. The site of Old Oyo and a large part of northwestern Yorubaland, for example, had become a desolate wilderness by the middle of the nineteenth century, making possible the creation of the 2,000-square-mile Oyo Division Forest Reserve (Adejuwan 1974).

The period through 1885, when cocoa (*Theobroma* spp.) was brought to Nigeria from Fernando Po, saw many new cultivars introduced into the country. Most of them, notably cassava (*Manihot esculenta*), sweet potatoes (*Ipomoea batatas*), maize (*Zea mays*), lima beans (*Phaseolus lunatis*), and groundnut (*Arachis hypogaea*), are said to have been introduced by Portuguese slave traders to ensure a reliable supply of food for the slave ships. It was at about the same time that Muslim pilgrims introduced such important cultivars as the water yam and coco yam (*Dioscorea* spp.), swamp rice (*Oryza sativa*), plantain (*Musa paradisiaca*), and mango (*Mangifera indica*) from Asia. At the beginning of the colonial period, these crops had already diffused to many parts of the country.

During the first decade of the nineteenth century, Yorubaland, or most of southwestern Nigeria, became involved in a series of political upheavals and in warfare that continued almost without a break until 1893, when the British finally occupied all of the area. The events started with Fulani raids on northern Yorubaland, which were followed closely by a series of fratricidal wars among rival Yoruba states, notably Ibadan, Egbas, Ekitis, and Dahomeans. The extensive destruction of lives and property in these wars brought about far-reaching changes in the cultural landscape of southwestern Nigeria, large-scale shifts of population from the Yoruba grasslands into the forest belt, the total destruction of such historic cities as old Oyo, Owu, and Ketu, and the emergence of new large cities including Ibadan, Ijaiye, Abeokuta, and New Oyo.

After the establishment of political control over the Hausa city-states between 1802 and 1807, the Fulanis, under the pretext of spreading Islam, began the steady and continuous devastation of farms and settlements in northern Yorubaland. Refugees fleeing south from these raids swelled the population of the major Yoruba towns. At about the same time, the ruler of neighboring Dahomey, now free from the domination of the Alafin of Oyo, set about raiding and destroying Egbado Yoruba settlements to obtain slaves for export to the Americas. Between 1830 and 1848, about 143 settlements in the borderlands between Nigeria and the Benin Republic were completely destroyed (Asiwaju 1976). In 1886, the Dahomeans sacked and burned the large walled city of Ketu, carrying away thousands of its citizens as slaves. Eye-witness accounts of the destruction caused by both the Fulanis and the Dahomeans in this part of the country have been left behind in the journals of early European explorers, notably Clapperton (1829) and the Lander brothers (Lander and

Lander 1832), who passed through several settlements that had been destroyed.

The pre-colonial coastal and Niger Delta city-states belong to a special category, in that they achieved prominence and wealth through trans-Atlantic trade with Europe in slaves and later in palm oil. With the onset of the Portuguese slave trade, these erstwhile fishing settlements assumed the role as collecting points for slaves from the interior and later for palm oil, also from the rain-forest belt. Their prosperity and political influence rested on their middleman role in the trade with Europe, since none of the trade goods was produced along the coast. Their wealth and importance vanished almost as rapidly as they were achieved following the establishment of colonial rule over Nigeria and the consequent collapse of the monopoly that the coastal city-state rulers had over trade with Europe (Udo and Ogundana 1966). The cultural imprint left by these coastal states on the landscape has been ephemeral and minimal.

Livestock has always been an important aspect of the native economy of the savanna areas. Indeed, the Fulanis, who later became the rulers of Hausaland, originally went there as nomadic herdsmen, although those who had adopted Islam settled in the cities. In addition to cattle, the Nigerian Sudan supported a large population of goats and sheep. Evidence of overgrazing, soil erosion, and the silting and deterioration of river beds includes rising flood heights, resulting in the destruction of farms and settlements on the floodplains, and the blocking of the mouth of the Rima River. By the end of the last century, the Rima River, which flows past Sokoto city, had no major channel connection with the River Niger. The whole mass of its water flowed into a marsh in the lower reaches, where it was lost through evaporation, leaving only a trickle to flow into the Niger. It was not until 1903 that the British colonial administration cut the present channel linking the Rima with the Niger (Burdon 1904). The silting of the Rima Valley was also responsible for the deterioration of the harbor of Birnin Kebbi, an important riverside town and market during the eighteenth and nineteenth centuries.

The land-use and management practices adopted in the marginal areas of the far north by the Tuaregs and Fulani pastoralists and by the Hausa and Kanuri settled cultivators suffered considerable stress as a result of increases in the human and livestock population. Usually in periods of successive wet years, farming and grazing were extended further into the desert, only to be forced to retreat in successive dry years, in which famines occurred and the environment became more desolate. Drought was largely responsible for the famines of 1835–37, 1847, 1855, 1873, 1888, and 1889–90 in the northern states.

Immediately preceding British colonial rule, the forests of Ondo, Benin, and Ijebu provinces became a major source of wild rubber export, which began in 1893. The latex came from indigenous wild rubber-bearing plants, notably the *Funtimia elastica* tree and the West African rubber vine (*Landolphia*), which grew in the dense forests in the south and in the derived savanna woodlands of Igalla District. In the rush that ensued, wild rubber exports rose from only 56 lb in 1893 to over 5 million lb in 1895, valued at about £2.4 million sterling. By 1900, the rubber boom was over as a result of reckless tapping which destroyed the plants; the export for that year was only 600,000 lb. This rapid destruction of the local rubber resources provides a clear example of the human role in changing local ecosystems. In this case, the government decided to introduce the para rubber (*Hevea brasiliensis*), which was to dominate the cultural landscape of large areas in the Sapele-Benin-Ondo region from the early years of the colonial period to the present.

Mining and the Charcoal-Iron Industry

Between 1650 and 1900, mining in Nigeria was restricted to localized exploitation of lateritic iron ore for making farming and hunting tools and weapons. Lead and zinc also were mined in the Abakaliki area for casting bronze and copper artifacts. Tin was mined in the Jos Plateau, and it was information obtained from Hausa traders, selling locally made tin wares, that led British geologists to the source of tin in the Jos area.[2]

Iron mining and smelting had little direct impact on the landscape because of the small scale of operations and the rather primitive methods of extraction in widely dispersed locations. The salt-mining pits of the Awe-Azara-Keena areas of the Benue Valley left much larger and more lasting scars on the landscape. It was indirectly, through its demands for firewood and charcoal, that the local iron industry had a major impact on the environment. The concentration of iron-smelting sites in the savanna region contributed greatly to woodland destruction and environmental deterioration, especially in the far northern districts of Sokoto, Katsina, and Borno.

Precolonial Urban Landscapes

Nigeria's precolonial cities were restricted to the Niger Delta and to coastal areas, the Yoruba cultural area of the southwest, and the Hausa-Kanuri cultural areas of the far north. Virtually all of the rudimentary manufacturing of this period was found in these cities. Availability of an adequate water supply was a major consideration in the location of cities, and in the Nigerian Sudan, all the cities were located close to rivers. Almost all of the rivers, however, dried up in years of severe drought, and were reduced to disconnected pools of water in years of less severe drought. The emergence of large urban centers and a restricted water supply created serious problems of sanitation.

The description by Denham, Clapperton, and Oudney (1826) of the townscape and the state of environmental sanitation in Kano City in 1825 gives a good idea of the situation in the walled cities of the Nigerian Sudan. Kano City, they wrote, "is rendered very unhealthy by a large morass, which almost divides it into two parts, besides many pools of stagnant water, made by digging clay for houses. . . ." The city had an estimated population of 30,000 in 1851 (Barth 1857a; 1857b), and was surrounded by a wall about 15 miles in circumference, with 15 gates. Only a quarter of the space thus enclosed was built up, the rest being used as farmland. Sanitation was extremely poor, especially during the rainy season, when the large morass in the heart of the city overflowed to engulf parts of the built-up areas. Because water obtained from the city wells was not fit for drinking, due to pollution, many women carried on a flourishing trade by hawking water obtained from a favorite stream.

In the Yoruba cultural area, the sudden increase in the population of the pre-Islamic cities created serious problems of congestion and poor sanitation. Water was also a problem here, largely because the bulk of the household refuse generated by the population of these cities was dumped into the streams to be carried away to running water. Aside from polluting the drinking water for people further downstream, this practice proved to be a serious menace during the rainy season, when the smaller stream channels became blocked, often giving rise to localized but destructive floods.

A high water table and too much rainfall, resulting in very poor drainage, coupled with the shortage of adequate dry land for constructing houses, likewise made the coastal cities of Lagos, Warri, Bonny, Akassa, and Opobo Town rather unhealthy and filthy, especially during the rainy season. Good drinking water was in short supply in most cases, and the uncoordinated disposal of human and household wastes into the creeks resulted in a highly polluted environment that was prone to epidemics.

The Colonial Period: 1902–1960

The colonial period started in the southwest of Nigeria with the British occupation of Lagos in 1850, involved expansion across the land until the turn of the century, and ended with the granting of political independence in October 1960. This comparatively short period, spanning not much more than 50 years for the greater part of the country, left great and lasting evidence of human exploitation of the natural environment for food, clothing, shelter, and industrial raw materials. The evidence is substantial, largely because it was created in the recent past by advanced technology, sometimes involving sophisticated equipment and machinery. It was during this period that extensive areas of natural forests were destroyed and replaced with small-scale cocoa and rubber farms, as well as with extensive forest plantations and large-scale commercial plantations of oil palms (*Elaeis guineensis*), cocoa, and rubber. Extensive surface mining of tin, gold, lead, and gravel started under colonial rule and left permanent scars on the landscape of the affected districts. Above all, the unprecedented increase in the population of certain parts of the country resulted in overcultivation and overgrazing of such areas, portions of which have since been destroyed by gully erosion.

The Transformation of the Settlement Pattern

The foremost concern of the early British colonial officers was to ensure the peaceful coexistence of the ethnic groups in their assigned territories. The establishment of intergroup boundaries, like that of forest reserves, meant the restriction of still-expanding groups such as the Ibos, Ibibios, and Tivs to territories that were to prove too small for them

before the beginning of World War II; hence the pressure of population was great on farmland in some of these districts. Often, as in Ozubulu in Anambra State, the increase in the demand for land, coupled with the land inheritance system, resulted in a complete disintegration of the original nucleated settlement (Udo 1965), as individuals moved out of the village to build on one of the plots that they had inherited or bought.

Road building was another important factor in the location and relocation of settlements. New settlements grew at key road junctions, whereas small settlements not served by roads declined. Many hill settlements founded during the turbulent days of the slave trade moved downhill to more accessible locations (Gleave 1964). The new state of social security also made it possible for people to build houses outside the city or village walls, while many people from land-hungry districts became migrant tenant farmers in other parts of the country.

The new administrative structure introduced by the colonial government also contributed to the considerable change in the distribution of urban centers. The functions of the larger traditional cities selected to serve as administrative headquarters were greatly diversified. The older walled native cities expanded as new residential areas were created outside the city walls to accommodate Europeans and other ethnic groups. In the eastern states and the middle belt provinces, where the traditional cultural landscapes are characterized by scattered homesteads and small villages, many new towns were established to serve as administrative headquarters for the districts, divisions, and provinces created by the new government. As a rule, the headquarters selected was an existing village that was both readily accessible and centrally located within the administrative unit concerned. The population of regular wage earners in these new administrative centers made possible the replacement of weekly periodic markets by daily markets. A few new towns, notably Port Harcourt, Enugu, and Jos, grew up to serve the coal- and tin-mining industries.

Large-scale movements of people from one cultural area to another started with the opening of the Lagos-Kano and the Port Harcourt-Kaduna railway lines. Public servants, including those employed in the government-owned railways, police, postal services, hospitals, and schools, figured prominently in this wave of migrations, which was directed mainly to the larger towns. Another large component of this migration stream consisted of the ever-increasing number of traders dealing in foodstuffs, manufactured goods, and agricultural exports.

Agricultural Land Use and Forestry

In the rural areas, the major factor of landscape change during the colonial period was the clearing of forest for agriculture. At that time, the proportion of people engaged in farming was much larger than it is today. Even so, except in the grassland areas of the north and in the very densely settled areas mentioned earlier, where the great pressure of population on land had resulted in permanent cultivation, bush clearing for food cultivation did not leave behind lasting modification or destruction of the environment. Only small patches of forest land were cleared for cultivation every year, and in most districts these small farmlands were allowed to revert to fallow bush after a few years. In the very sparsely settled areas, where the fallow periods exceeded 10 years, the original forest regime was almost restored.

The decision to create forest reserves was made rather early, and the first forest reserve was created at Ibadan in 1899 (Morgan 1959), even though the Forestry Ordinance was not enacted until 1916. The rapid destruction of Nigeria's wild-rubber resources through reckless exploitation contributed to this early and commendable action. However, the withdrawal of 92,740 km² for forest reserves during the colonial period contributed to high rural population densities, leading in some cases to overcultivation, soil impoverishment, and environmental degradation. The largest forest reserves, however, were established in the very sparsely settled rainforests of Benin, Ijebu, Ondo, and the Cross River districts (Table 36-1).

Paradoxically, while the colonial government created forest reserves, it also initiated certain policies and measures that were to accelerate the destruction of unreserved forests. These measures included the introduction and promotion of tree-crop cultivation of cocoa, rubber, and oil palm for export, the granting of timber-felling concessions to foreign firms, and the establishment of forest plantations of exotic tree species. The result was a steady reduction in the area of closed forests outside the forest reserves. Thus, in sparsely settled areas of the Cross River, Ondo, Ogun, and Bendel states, extensive areas of dense rain forest were cut down and planted with more homogeneous human-made forests of rubber, cocoa, and oil palm. The situation in the Yoruba cocoa belt is one of very high intensity of tree-crop cultivation in more than one-third of the region, with cocoa accounting for 30% of the agricultural land use in some districts. By the

end of the colonial period in 1960, rubber farms covered approximately 2,184 km² (6% of the total area of Bendel State); and in the rubber-growing districts, the proportion of land under rubber varied from 7.2% to 27.4% (Agboola 1979).

The forest plantations established in the savanna region have served largely as firewood reserves. The bulk of the wood used in the homes, for cottage industries, and even in government institutions such as boarding schools and prisons, came from land under fallow or from farmlands. The complete depletion of the woodlands near the large grassland cities such as Kano, Zaria, Kaduna, and Jos has been caused partly by the continuing and rising demand for firewood and charcoal in these cities. Unfortunately, the very low annual rainfall in these regions does not permit a rapid growth of woody vegetation as in the south; hence the near-total destruction of vegetation for firewood, which along with overgrazing, has contributed to the now chronic drought situation in the Sahel section of the Nigerian Sudan.

Mining and Mining Landscapes

Mining on a large scale started during the early years of the colonial period, following the discovery and exploitation of tin in 1905, and later of columbite in the Jos Plateau and of coal in the Udi District of Anambra State. Considerable alteration of the land surface of the tin-mining districts occurred, because tin is obtained by open-cast mining. The Jos-Bukuru area, for example, became an anthropogenic "lakes district," featuring many small dammed lakes for producing hydroelectricity, as well as a large number of water ponds or paddocks (Fig. 36.6). Many paddocks were created during the early years by independent freelance mining laborers, who worked for mining companies and were paid by results. These abandoned ponds now are used for watering

Table 36-1 *Forest Reserves in Nigeria, 1968*

Territorial unit	Area of Forest Reserves			Total forest reserves (km²)	High forest as percentage of state forest reserve	High forest as percentage of total area of forest reserve	Total state forest as percentage of national forest reserve
	Mangrove (km²)	High forest (km²)	Savanna (km²)				
Benue/Plateau	—	139.9	4,006.7	4,146.6	3.4	0.7	4.4
Imo/Anambra	—	367.8	36.3	404.0	9.1	1.9	0.4
Kano	—	—	2,178.2	2,178.2	—	—	2.3
Kwara	—	945.4	10,041.4	10,986.8	8.6	5.0	11.8
Lagos	5.2	15.5	—	20.7	7.5	0.08	0.02
Bendel	20.7	5,029.8	676.0	5,726.5	87.8	26.7	6.2
Kaduna	—	114.0	9,484.6	9,598.5	1.2	0.6	10.2
Borno/Bauchi/Gongola	—	80.3	16,063.2	16,143.5	0.5	0.4	17.4
Sokoto/Niger	—	64.7	24,053.3	24,118.0	0.3	0.3	26.0
Rivers State	—	—	—	—	—	—	—
Cross River	116.5	6,156.4	139.9	6,412.8	96.0	32.7	6.9
Ogun/Ondo/Oyo	—	5,946.6	7,057.7	13,004.4	45.7	31.6	14.0
TOTAL	142.4	18,864.0	73,737.3	92,740.0	—	100.0	100.0

Note: After Adeyoju, S. K. (1975)
Source: Compiled from the Annual Reports on the Forest Administration of Eastern, Midwestern, Northern, and Western Regions (Lagos Government Printers)

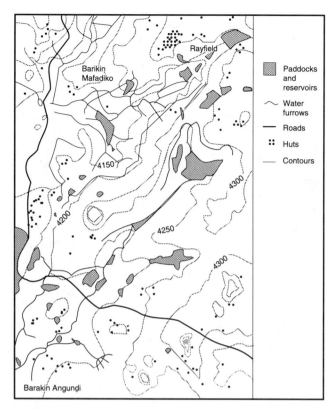

Figure 36.6 Tin-mining landscape of the Jos Plateau. Source: Udo 1970.

stock by Fulani pastoralists and for pump irrigation by some local farmers.

Loss of farmland to mining has been minimal because mining is often carried out on land that is not suitable for farming. Tin mining, however, brought a large influx of migrants into the mining towns of Jos and Bukuru, and of migrant farmers and cattle rearers into the nearby rural areas. The large increase in the demand for firewood and charcoal that followed this upsurge in population has contributed significantly to the total deforestation of the Jos Plateau. In many localities, overcultivation and overgrazing of these treeless grass plains resulted in soil impoverishment and severe soil erosion. Before the end of the colonial period, the Jos Plateau, which receives more rainfall than the Ibadan area, had been converted into a treeless savanna, whereas a dense vegetation of deciduous forest survived in the Ibadan area.

In the coal district of the southeast, mining has left little or no trace on the surface, because the coal is obtained from adits (shafts) driven into the hillsides. Of the other materials exploited during the colonial period, only the quarrying of limestone for cement and of gravel and sand for roads and building has left considerable scars on the landscape.

The Postcolonial Period: 1960–1987

The postcolonial period of just under 30 years, which started in 1960, has witnessed many serious political crises, the most traumatic of which was the 3-year civil war (1967–1970), closely followed by the oil boom of the 1970s.

Rapid social changes have led to the appearance of novel forms of environmental transformation, as well as to the intensification of familiar ones.

The war and the oil boom were largely responsible for the rapid and uncontrolled influx of Nigerians into the larger urban centers and the construction, by the new rich, of large but mostly substandard houses at urban locations, many of which have no access roads. The most obvious results of this urban influx are the areal expansion of such cities as Ibadan, Lagos, Kano, Port Harcourt, and Enugu; urban congestion, featuring unmanageable filth and pollution from untreated sewage and solid wastes; and urban floods, caused partly by blocked river channels and gutters. The population of Lagos, the nation's capital city, increased from about 1.09 million in 1963 to about 4.5 million in 1980. To accommodate the ever-increasing population, dredging and reclamation of marshlands and mangrove swamps along the coast and the lagoons had to be undertaken. The erosion of the eastern part of Victoria Island has been caused largely by human interference in the form of ditch construction, removal of bush vegetation, and reclamation.

In the rapidly growing coastal cities of Lagos, Port Harcourt, Warri, and Calabar, waste water and sewage is discharged mostly into the swamps and creeks. With the possible exception of Calabar, these coastal cities are given to extensive flooding during the rainy season, which lasts for about 8 months in Lagos and about 10 months in the other cities. Because household waste is left along the streets and waste water from kitchens and bathrooms drains into the open wayside gutters, flooding during the rainy season produces a rather noxious and unhealthy environment. The situation is particularly deplorable in the very high-density, low-income residential areas, where tarred roads rarely exist and where refuse is dumped by the wayside or into the drains.

Rural areas, including the sparsely settled ones, have not been spared the dramatic and sometimes destructive landscape changes effected by the sophisticated technology of the post-independence period. The construction, mostly in the northern states, of multipurpose dams for electricity and irrigation has covered large areas of land with reservoirs such as those at Kainji (1,230 km²), north of Jebba, at Baguada, near Kano city, and at Bakolori in Sokoto State. The construction in 1968 of the Kainji Dam, for example, drowned about 127,300 ha of land. About 43,000 inhabitants living in 221 villages were displaced from the lake basin and were resettled in 121 new villages and in two new towns (Mabogunje 1973). Downstream of each dam, the disruption of the river regime has had adverse effects on ecosystems and on the occupations of the people. A marked decline in annual fish yield from 28,000 t to 8,000–10,000 t occurred in the Kainji lake area within a few years of the formation of the lake.

Although a recent phenomenon on the Nigerian economic scene as compared with agriculture or with tin- and coal-mining, crude-oil extraction has had profound and widespread influence, direct and indirect, in modifying the landscape of various parts of the country (Fig. 36.7). The importance of oil in the post-civil war economy of Nigeria is clear from the fact that the revenue from oil leaped from U.S. $771 million in

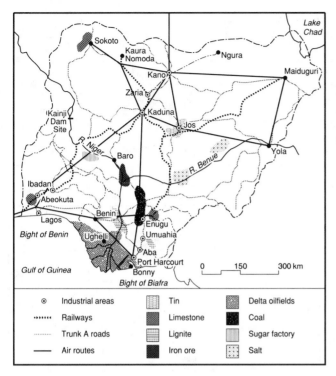

Figure 36.7 Industrial and transportation patterns.

1970 to U.S. $20.15 billion in 1983. By 1975, the economic and social life of Nigerians showed signs of abrupt changes made possible by the huge and increasing revenue from oil. Capital-intensive projects, such as the Ajaokuta steel plant, the Aladja steel complex near Warri, the steel-rolling mills at Oshogbo, Jos, and Katsina, car-assembly plants, and petro-chemical plants, were established in various states. At Aladja and Ajaokuta, new towns grew up to serve the two more elaborate steel projects.

The oil boom also made possible the rapid expansion of the Lagos metropolitan district, with the addition of such new towns as Festac, Satellite, and the Orogun industrial town. Medium-scale industries grew up in most state capitals and in other large towns. The new national capital city of Abuja was probably the most gigantic project embarked upon during the short-lived oil boom, and it turned out to be a major factor in the crash of the Nigerian economy. As many as 7 new universities and a much larger number of colleges of education and of technology were established between 1970 and 1980. Education was made free at all levels in most states, necessitating the construction of hundreds of new primary and secondary schools.

The greatest effects of these projects were the great boom in the construction industry and the proliferation of consult-ancy and architectural firms. The influx into the larger cities greatly strained the available infrastructure and facilities, resulting in extreme congestion and filthy neighborhoods. The prestigious flyovers (elevated roads) of the Lagos metropolitan area merely eased, but failed to eliminate, the traffic holdups. Even as the demand for and the prices of foodstuffs in the cities soared, local production declined because many farmers had left the land for city construction

sites. The food import bills rose by leaps and bounds, increasing from U.S. $189.45 million in 1973 to U.S. $2.82 billion in 1980.

In the oil-producing areas, the crude oil industry had brought varied and sometimes quite destructive changes to the landscape. The more obvious and positive changes include the impressive growth of manufacturing, retail business, and modern middle-class residential districts in the oil cities of Port Harcourt and Warri and, to a lesser extent Eket, Ughelli, and Ahoada. In the low-income residential suburbs of these towns, as well as in the villages of the oil belt, most traditional mud houses have been replaced by modern two: or three-room houses with concrete walls and corrugated sheet-iron roofs. The oil fields are dotted with wells, exploratory and production camps built on land reclaimed from mangrove swamps, and steel and concrete jetties. A network of pipelines traverses the swamps and forests that constitute the delta oil fields, which are served by good roads and bridges strong enough to carry heavy drilling equipment to the oil wells. The negative and destructive changes that the oil industry has brought upon the environment include the fires from gas-flaring sites, which constitute a serious nuisance to both plant and animal life, including the local human population.

Some Net Transformations

It is most difficult to produce quantitative estimates of environmental transformations for the entire 300 years in question. Broad surrogate indices might be used to recon-struct some aspects of change, but pending intensive study, the results would have a large degree of error. Therefore, the net transformations addressed here are done so primarily by qualitative assessment.

Wildlife

Outside the few game reserves, notably the Yankari Games Reserve in Bauchi, the Borgu Game Reserve, and the Lake Kainji National Park, very little information exists on the wildlife resources of Nigeria. This situation may be explained by the fact that wildlife as a resource has long been considered as subsidiary to forestry, and hence has been given only peripheral attention. There is, however, general agree-ment on the devastating impact of human activities on the game population. Nigeria's rural population always has depended on the harvesting of these animals for its animal-protein consumption. In recent years, urban dwellers have also developed a taste for wild game, popularly referred to as "bush meat," and are willing to pay high prices for it. Charter (1970) estimated that locally produced animal protein in southern Nigeria includes about 19% from wild game, valued at about $30 million (N20 million). The most valued game animals include wild boar, bush cow, antelopes, guinea fowl, grasscutters, porcupine, snails, and forest snakes (FAO 1974).

The pressure on the wild-game population has resulted in marked scarcity of game in areas that were once well stocked, including forest reserves (Table 36-2). Traditional methods of hunting remain crude and detrimental to sustaining the

Table 36-2 *Estimates of Livestock Population and Mortality in Northwestern Nigeria in 1972/73*

Division	Cattle		Sheep and Goats		Horses and Donkeys	
	Population	Mortality	Population	Mortality	Population	Mortality
Sokoto	1,007,100	201,420	3,384,693	676,337	658,041	121,608
Argungu	147,270	29,454	263,769	52,744	46,534	9,111
Gwandu	356,545	71,289	729,588	145,918	163,269	32,581
Total	1,510,815	302,163	4,378,050	874,999	867,864	163,300

animal population, since many more animals are wounded than are caught. Further, there is indiscriminate killing of pregnant females and young animals (Afolayan 1975). Forest clearance and bush burning continue to destroy the habitats of much wild game, making the game reserves their last remaining refuge, especially in the savanna areas. Yet many game reserves have been the scene of illegal grazing of livestock and unauthorized settlement by local people engaged in illegal harvesting as well as poaching and bush burning.

The Soil

Agricultural practices (Fig. 36.8) contribute significantly to environmental transformation. The impact of human activities that remove or alter vegetation is clearly displayed in the damage caused to soil in various parts of the country. In parts of the middle belt that are heavily grazed and burnt regularly, for example, the topsoil has been removed completely, thereby exposing the clay-enriched, highly sesquioxidic B horizons, which harden upon exposure to intense insolation (Fagbami, Babalola, and Areola 1984). The three soil-related problems linked directly to human activities and interference with the vegetation are soil deterioration, soil desiccation, and accelerated soil erosion.

The inherent fertility of Nigerian soils is not very high, and most soils suffer from the exhaustion of major nutrients after 2 or 3 years of cultivation. The traditional method of restoring the soil fertility is to leave the land fallow for many years, usually up to 20 years in the past, when the demand for farmland was low. Rapid increase in the population during the present century and the consequent high demand for land have led to the drastic reduction of fallow periods to under 10 years in almost every part of the country. In parts of the very densely settled districts, there is now no fallow period.

The consequences of soil deterioration are seen in reduced crop yields, the proliferation of weeds, increased susceptibility of crops to pests and disease infestation, and the eventual structural breakdown of the soil itself. In many parts of the Ibo heartland, for example, large areas of sandy soils have broken down completely, resulting in serious soil erosion. Soil desiccation, by comparison, is the progressive drying out and hardening of the soil, an irreversible process that, in many areas, has led to the formation of clay pans and lateritic crusts. In some areas, the patched, hardened soil surfaces are completely bare of vegetation, and in those areas with sandy soils, such as the Chad Basin and the coastal districts, such desiccated soils have become extremely loose and unproduc-

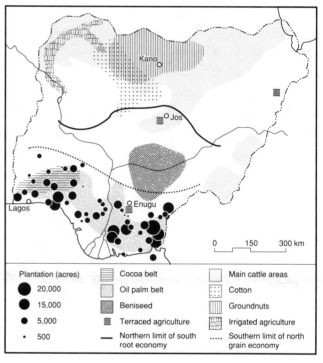

Figure 36.8 Generalized agricultural land use.

tive. Currently, the areas most affected by soil desiccation are the Sahel and Sudan savanna districts of the far north.

Accelerated soil erosion now constitutes a threat to life and property in many parts of Nigeria, especially in those parts of Imo and Anambra states where the extensive damage caused by gully erosion is well documented (Floyd 1965; Ofomata 1965). Ofomata in particular has stressed the human role in inducing soil erosion through farming, road construction, and various excavation works. Because of its spectacular nature, gully erosion has attracted more attention than sheet erosion, which is more widespread and is probably more destructive of soil. Sheet erosion, which is caused by wind and running water, washes away the clay, humus, and nutrient content of the topsoil. The areas that have suffered most from sheet erosion are the low-lying districts of the far north and parts of the Jos and Udi-Nsukka plateaus.

The Forest-Savanna Boundary

The forest-savanna boundary in Nigeria is clearly defined, especially on aerial photographs, and changes in it are easy to delimit and verify. Morgan and Moss (1965) concluded that "the forest-savanna boundary in [western Nigeria] seems to be relatively stable . . . despite the increase in population that has taken place in the last ten years." They went on to observe that there was rather more evidence of minor forest advances, particularly in the vicinity of forest reserves, than of forest retreat, and that the importance of edaphic factors as critical controls was strongly indicated.

Stebbing (1935) mapped and estimated the rate of advance of the Sahara Desert southward. His controversial views were rejected by Jones (1938), who argued that the empirical evidence, such as declining rainfall and falling water tables over a long period of time or the southward extension of the frontiers of settlement, did not exist. His argument was upheld a few months later by the report of a Royal Commission on the subject. Later events, such as the marked increase in the rainfall in the 1950s and 1960s, have since vindicated the views of Jones and the stand of the Royal Commission. What is now clear is that in the ecologically precarious northern districts of Nigeria, a run of drought years can increase the risk of desertification, especially if activities such as grazing and woodcutting are not controlled. Such a process of desertification should not be regarded as an advance of the desert frontier; rather, it should be viewed as a predictable interaction between a precarious dryland environment and an intensified occupation and use of it (UNO 1977).

The human impact on the hydrological and atmospheric environment of the Niger Delta was minimal until the discovery and mining of crude oil in the late 1950s. The impact has been largely destructive and is associated with the various types of environmental pollution caused through operational discharges and accidental oil spills (Table 36-3). Most of these oil spills were traced to accidental blowouts of wells, sudden release from damaged crude-oil storage tanks, and sabotage. In January 1980, for example, a devastating blowout occurred at the Funiwa No. 5 oil well, resulting in the release of over 400,000 barrels of crude oil into the marine environment (Ekekwe 1981). Within 6 months of this particular oil spill, the mangrove vegetation in the affected area started to dry out, while dead crabs, mollusks, and periwinkles were found in the contaminated water. Offshore production facilities and discharges from ballasts and tank washings are other important sources of oil spills.

Table 36-3 *Yearly Distribution of Oil Spills (1976–1983)*

Year	Number of spills	Net volume (barrels)	Total production (barrels)
1976	128	20,023	758,055,728
1977	104	31,144	764,646,983
1978	154	97,250	696,310,212
1979	157	630,405	842,222,523
1980	241	558,053	747,915,679
1981	233	22,840	525,291,091
1982	213	33,612	470,638,382
1983	130	32,337	450,961,226

Source: NNPC Petroleum Inspectorate Division, Annual Report.

Air pollution is also a major hazard of the Delta oil fields. It has been attributed in part to the high rate of evaporation of the light to medium crudes produced in the Delta. The main source of atmospheric pollution in the area is, however, gas-flaring. In 1981, for example, 84% of the gas produced every day, or $14.50 \times 10^6\,m^3$, was flared. The burning of such large quantities constitutes a major hazard to the environment and is a source of embarrassment to the villagers who suffer from the perpetual bright nights.

The section of the forest-savanna boundary examined by Morgan and Moss happens to lie in the area that suffered much devastation from intergroup wars during the precolonial period. The depopulation resulting from these wars made possible the creation of many forest reserves in the savanna regions of Kabba, Ilorin, and Oyo provinces during the early colonial period.

The situation in the eastern part of the boundary zone is very different. Here, high rural population densities have resulted during the past several decades in a much greater southward extension of the savanna into the forest belt. The importance of population pressure to the boundary is strongly supported by the fact that in the sparsely settled Cross River districts of Akampa, Obubra, Ogoja, and Ikom, the forest-savanna boundary remains much further inland – by as much as about 60 km – compared with its position in the very densely populated districts west of the Cross River Valley. It is fair to add, however, that the rainfall in the districts east of the Cross River Valley is higher than that in most parts of the area west of the river.

Climate and Hydrology

Lying on the great Sudan-Sahelian transition zone between the wet tropics and the Sahara Desert, much of Nigeria has been characterized by fluctuating climatic patterns. Analysis of cores taken from Lake Chad provides a backdrop for the modern period.[3] After almost 1,000 years of intense desiccation that ended about A.D. 1500, rainfall increased considerably in the Lake Chad Basin between 1500 and 1700, bringing the lake level to above 280 m above sea level. A period of fluctuating but generally declining rainfall followed, until the end of the nineteenth century. The reconstruction of the surface levels of Lake Chad from 1870 to 1970 indicates that until 1900, high rainfall was experienced. Then followed a general decline in the rainfall, except between 1950 and the late 1960s, when a small increase was recorded. The droughts of 1913 and the early 1940s are reflected in the falls of the level of the lake.

Historical records indicate that droughts have occurred frequently in the past throughout Nigeria, but more often in the northern states. Extremely low rainfalls in Yorubaland resulted in severe famines in 1903–4 and in 1945–46, while Nupeland and Hausaland experienced severe famines in 1934–35 and 1943–46 respectively. All over the country, rainfall was generally good through the 1950s and 1960s. A decline that started in 1968 peaked in several places in 1972–73, heralding the great Sahelian drought that drew world attention to the suffering of people and animals in this part of West Africa (Franke and Chasin 1980; Watts 1983).

The extreme northern parts of Nigeria suffered greatly, with the deaths of over 1.3 million domestic animals and a great decline in crop yields (Table 36-2). The drought also induced large migrations of rural people into urban centers all over the country.

The 1972–73 drought produced many adverse environmental consequences, and fears of the southward extension of the Sahara Desert, first expressed in 1921 (Bovill 1921; Migeod 1921) were reechoed. The impacts of this drought are well noted (Franke and Chasin 1980; Watts 1983). The role of humankind has been stressed in some of the explanations offered for the Sahelian drought of 1972–73. Bryson (1973) contends that the increase in carbon dioxide and particulate matter in the atmosphere caused by world-wide industrial, commercial, and agricultural activities contributed to suppressing the monsoons – the rain-bearing winds – that water the region. The view of Charnley (1975) is that the decline in the rainfall received in the West African Sahel in 1968–73 was due to loss in vegetation cover, caused by overcropping, overgrazing, and woodcutting. An increase in surface albedo, which usually leads to an increase in net radiative loss, followed. The result of all these changes was increased subsidence, sustained thermal equilibrium, and much lower rainfall. This ascription of the meteorological drought to human activity is by no means universally accepted, but many of the consequences of drought are affected by social processes.

Curiously, both the local authorities and the people of the various states always appear to be taken unawares by the incidents of severe droughts, despite their repeated occurrence during the past 30 years. For many of the people, however, this appearance may be more the product of practical constraints on action than of any unawareness of the drought hazard. Local authorities and the federal government engage in relief efforts, but their long-term solutions seem to be fixed on technological measures. The federal government has built large and expensive dams. Numerous boreholes have been drilled by both the central and the state governments to increase the water supply in drought-prone areas. Most of the large dams built for irrigation are located in the drier savanna areas of the Nigerian Sudan, where the problems of drought and water shortages are most acute.

Many justifiable criticisms have been made of these technological solutions to the drought problem. One is that the dams and ancillary works are capital-intensive and are very expensive to build and maintain. Secondly, although thousands of people are usually displaced and resettled elsewhere at great cost to the state, it is only a comparatively few people who usually benefit from the various irrigation schemes. Further, the damming of rivers has adverse effects on *fadama* (seasonally flooded) agriculture in the areas located downstream from the dams, while several ecological problems have been created within and around the new reservoirs.

Measures that help to control or manage droughts are, in effect, also measures to control desertification, since drought is usually the precursor of desertification. Any scheme that seeks to combat desertification must, however, be based on sound land-use planning and management. Effective land-use management is feasible only if the human and livestock populations are kept under control, especially in the marginal dryland ecosystems of the northern Sudan and Sahel regions. Here, incongruencies exist between the needs of individuals to procure a livelihood and the need to take conservation measures. Currently, the most popular measure to control desertification is reforestation. A tree-planting program, started in the northern states following the 1972–73 drought, has since been extended to the south. A savanna shelterbelt program was also started about 1973 to check wind erosion and desert encroachment. The tree species presently used for the shelterbelts include *Eucalyptus camaldulensis*, neem (*Azadirachta indica*), and acacia.

It is in the major centers of population that human impact on the hydrologic environment is most obvious and has consequently attracted the most attention. In these large urban areas, the pervious surfaces of fields, farms, forests, and swamps have been replaced with impervious human-made surfaces of concrete, stone, bricks, and asphalt. The floodplains of the rivers flowing through the city of Ibadan have been heavily built up with concrete structures. Many of the hills and ridges within the city have been deforested and built up. All of these activities have resulted in a great increase in surface runoff and in the rapid silting of river beds. The common practice of discharging and dumping industrial and solid wastes into urban watercourses has, in addition to polluting the water supply from these rivers (Table 36-4), often rendered them incapable of efficiently carrying and discharging flood waters; hence, many major flood disasters have occurred in Nigerian cities during the past 30 years.

The study by Ledger (1961) of the recent hydrological changes in the Rima Basin of Sokoto State attributed rising flood heights and the consequent retreat of the settlement frontier from the valley to the interfluves to the deterioration of the river beds through silting. These changes, like the important hydrological changes in the central Potiskum District of the Lake Chad Basin, featuring the appearance of many new springs, streams, and lakes (Carter and Barber 1956), have in turn been attributed to extensive clearance of woodland for cultivation and to overgrazing. Geomorphological and hydrological processes also have been affected by mining and quarrying activities, especially in the Jos Plateau and the Niger Delta.

The construction of large dams has influenced the water balance and flow regimes of many rivers. Since the construction of the Kainji Dam, for instance, the peak discharges of the Niger River downstream at Jebba have decreased from about $6,000 \, m^3/s$ to below $3,500 \, m^3/s$. By contrast, low flows have tripled to about $600 \, m^3/s$. This regulation of the flow regime of the Niger has caused the contraction of the floodplain by about 70–95%. At the same time, the many pools and sand banks that formerly characterized the river channel during the dry season are now submerged, owing to increase in low flows (Oyebande et al. 1980).

Human Responses to Transformation

Generally, the ways in which Nigerians have reacted to, and have tried to modify, the effects of undesirable changes in the environment have depended largely on their perception

Table 36-4 *Land Use and Surface Water Pollution in the City of Ibadan, Nigeria*

Variables	Low-density area	High-density area	Traditional core	Commercial zone	Agricultural zone	Industrial zone	WHO Limits (1963)
Acidity (ppm)	0.0	40	15.8	83.8	147.8	60	—
Alkalinity (ppm)	118.8	19.3	114	27.50	0	75.5	—
Chloride (mg/l.)	2.0	3.65	4.5	4.0	5.3	5.8	600
Color (hazen units)	102	209	630	546	135	130	50
Copper (mg/l.)	0.03	0.19	0.21	0.05	0.01	0.01	1.5
Fluoride (mg/l.)	5.6	19.20	28.3	21.8	2.70	1.9	1.5
Hardness (mg/l.)	135	195	405	350	142.5	175	100
Iron (mg/l.)	0.03	0.02	0.4	0.03	0.94	0.38	1.0
Manganese (mg/l.)	0.39	1.4	1.4	2.1	7.7	3.8	0.5
Nitrate (mg/l.)	2.5	0.95	0.5	0.9	33.7	13.7	50
Dissolved O_2 (ppm)	6.5	0.98	0.2	0.25	7.4	2.3	—
pH	7.5	6.3	7.3	6.3	6.1	6.5	Less than 6.5 or greater than 9.2
Phosphate (mg/l.)	16.7	14.8	20	17.5	34.5	28.1	—
Suspended Solid (mg/l.)	7.0	222	260	182	15.5	41.3	—
Turbidity (turbidity units)	23.5	275	325	228	24	57.5	25
Temperature (°C)	24.1	26	27.5	25	24.8	28.3	—

Source: Akintola and Nnyamah in Oguntoyinbo el al., eds. 1978.

of the causes of the problems, and partly on the level of technology available, but more so on their ability to meet the costs of projects to control or to modify the effects of the changes in the environment. The oldest major environmental problem in Nigeria, drought, has resulted in the decline and complete abandonment of some settlements in the far north. The inhabitants of the Sudan and Sahel regions have, therefore, developed social, economic, and land-use systems that have helped to ensure their survival in these environments – the practice of pastoral nomadism. Although an increasing number of Nigerians now understand that wrong use of the land can encourage or exacerbate the effects of droughts, the immediate reaction of many to the incidence of drought is to offer prayers or sacrifices to ward off the impending disaster. Farmers who are more knowledgeable about soil and ecological conditions try to adapt by watering crops by hand, mulching, shifting farms downslope onto hydromorphic soils, or switching to cultivars that demand less water. Thus, during periods of droughts, cassava is given preference over yams in the southern states, while millet is preferred to guinea corn in the north.

Soil exhaustion and deterioration in many parts of the country is another undesirable situation that has been created by overcropping and overgrazing. A variety of methods have been adopted to limit the incidence of crop failures and famines in such areas. In the densely settled rural districts, there is a noticeable expansion, wherever possible, of the compound land, which is the homelot area kept under permanent cultivation by the lavish application of household manure. Chemical fertilizers are used by those who can afford and know how to use them. Many others, however, prefer to adopt cultivars like cassava, sweet potato, or millet, which are more tolerant of impoverished soils.

During the past 50 years, soil erosion, especially gully erosion, has destroyed extensive areas of farmland in various parts of the country. As with drought, many rural dwellers attribute the destruction to the anger of the gods, and apart from abandoning the houses threatened by advancing gullies, very little is done to combat such erosion. The central government and some of the state governments have, since about 1975, spent large sums of money toward rehabilitating badly eroded landscapes in various parts of the country. In 1981, for example, the central government paid out $21 million (N $15 million) toward controlling soil erosion and rehabilitating land devastated by gullying in parts of Anambra State.

Outside of the crude-oil-mining areas of the country, there has been very little reaction by the citizens to the problem of air and water pollution in Nigeria. This situation largely can be attributed to the general tendency at the early stages of industrial development to emphasize the tangible aspects of basic human needs, such as food, potable water, and energy, rather than the qualitative aspects of a clean, wholesome, and healthy environment. Antipollution laws were, until recently, never invoked, even in the heavily industrialized cities of Lagos, Kano, and Port Harcourt.

Several provisions related to water pollution exist in the recent River Basins Development Authorities Act of 1976 and the Sea Fisheries Act of 1971. Anti-water-pollution provisions also abound in various laws governing petroleum exploration and exploitation in the country. Under the Oil Pipeline Act of 1963, for example, it is mandatory for oil pipeline licensees to obey any regulations that may be provided from time to time to prevent oil pollution of both land and water. The Oil in Navigable Waters Act of 1968 prohibits the discharging of crude oil, fuel oil, lubrication oil, and heavy diesel oil in the country's territorial waters, including inland waters. Anti-air-pollution provisions also exist in several laws. Existing legislation, however, has rarely been enforced. An up-to-date harmonization of existing antipollution laws under a general and comprehensive environmental act is long overdue. The Environmental Protection Law, which has been mooted since 1986, may well provide such a comprehensive framework for the control of all aspects of pollution in Nigeria.

The one common response noticeable in any area of environmental stress, whether caused by drought, soil impoverishment, gully erosion, desertification, or environmental pollution, has been migration. Thus the severe Sahelian drought of 1972–73 brought large numbers of rural people from the Niger Republic, Chad, and the far north of Nigeria into urban areas in Nigeria, including those as far south as Lagos, Abeokuta, Benin, Warri, Port Harcourt, and Calabar. It is also known that a large number of rural-rural migrants in the country originate in the very densely populated areas, in which soils are impoverished and large areas have been destroyed by erosion. Extensive damage to the fishing grounds and to farmland in the Niger Delta by oil pollution has also contributed to the large-scale migration of people from the affected rural areas into the oil cities of Port Harcourt and Warri.

Summary and Comments

Humankind has obviously been instrumental in the transformation of Nigeria's environment. These changes have been largely the product of increasing demand on resources stimulated by increasing population, but in varying forms through three major socioeconomic periods and within the regional environments. Purely natural causes of transformation have been localized, such as the lava flow near Idah in Benue State in November 1987; more commonly, human activity has been the major agent of change. Long-term and persistent uses of resources have resulted in slow but cumulative transformations, such as the extensive soil erosion that has ultimately developed throughout souteastern Nigeria in the very densely populated zones. Accelerated and intensified use of marginal environments for agriculture, such as the historic ebb-and-flow of cultivation in the Sudan-Sahel zone of northern Nigeria has had more recent and dramatic impacts, as has urbanization.

No major decreases seem likely in the demands that will be placed upon the environment of Nigeria in the immediate future, and alternative resource strategies will be instigated probably only slowly, given the economic conditions. The types and scale of transformations that are currently underway will most likely continue for some time.

Notes

1. Much of the literature on this period deals with the empires and the city-states of the western Sudan which, like the Yoruba city-states, extended beyond the boundaries of present-day Nigeria. Considerable documentation also exists on the Benin Empire, which dates back to the twelfth century A.D. as well as on the city-states of the eastern coastal districts of the Niger Delta and the Cross River estuary.

2. The working of iron ore was widespread, as is evidenced by physical remains. Writing about Ketu in western Yorubaland, for example, Bowen (1857), recorded that the people excelled "all the tribes . . . in working lead, brass and iron . . . ," and the remains of iron smelting still can be identified at Ilobi, Imeko, and many other western Yoruba settlements (Asiwaju 1976). Other areas in which iron ore was mined and processed include Awka, the Ishan Plateau, which supplied Benin city with much of its iron requirements, and the hilly districts of the Jos Plateau. In Idoma District of the Benue Valley, iron smelting in the area north of Bopo continued far into the colonial period, until it was forced to close down by the importation of cheap and better-quality iron and steel from Europe. The Hausas and the Kanuris also smelted iron. Kano city, which later grew to become a major trading center in the western Sudan, started originally as a small iron-smelting village at the foot of the Dalla Hill.

3. In Nigeria, meteorological observations began in Lagos in 1892, and several other stations were established during the first decade of the twentieth century. Information on the climate before this period is, therefore, based on indirect evidence that is biological, anthropological, and geomorphological in nature. The two problems that arise in trying to trace the history of climatic fluctuations in this way are (1) how to translate the indirect evidence into climatic terms, and (2) how to date accurately the events involved (Grove 1973). The same evidence has sometimes been interpreted differently by different workers, especially geomorphological evidence such as pedimentation, multiconcave valley profiles, and the occurrence of laterites (Jeje 1980). On the whole, biological evidence has been more reliable than geomorphological.

References

Adejuwan, J. O. 1974. Geographical patterns with precolonial antecedents in western Nigeria. *ODU: A Journal of West African Studies*, No. 9:64–79.

Afolayan, T. A. 1975. Wildlife management in Nigeria. *Obeche* 11:12–20.

Agboola, S. A. 1979. *An Agricultural Atlas of Nigeria*. London: Oxford University Press.

Andah, B. A. 1960. An archaeological view of the urbanization process in the earliest West African states. *Journal of Historical Society of Nigeria* 8, No. 3.

Asiwaju, A. I. 1976. *Western Yorubaland Under European Rule, 1889–1945*. London: Longman.

Barth, H. 1857a; 1857b. *Travels and Discoveries in North and Central Africa, 1849–55*. Vols. 1 and 3.

Bovill, E. 1921. Encroachment of the Sahara on the Sudan. *Journal of African Society* 20:174–85; 259–69.

Bowen, T. J. 1857. *Adventures and Missionary Labours in Several Countries in the Interior of Africa from 1849–56*. Charleston, S. C.: Southern Baptist Publication Society.

Burdon, J. A. 1904. Discussion after paper by G. S. Elliot on "The Anglo-French Niger-Chad boundary." *Geographical Journal* 24:520.

Bryson, R. A. 1973. Climatic Modification by Air Pollution II: The Sahelian Effect. Report No. 9 of the Institute of Environmental Studies. University of Wisconsin.

Carter, J. D., and W. Barber. 1956. The rise in the water table in parts of Potiskum Division, Bornu Province. *Records of the Geological Survey of Nigeria* 5–13.

Charnley, J. G. 1975. Dynamics of deserts and drought in the Sahel. *Quarterly Journal of the Royal Meteorological Society* 101:193–202.

Charter, J. R. 1970. The economic value of wildife in Nigeria. Paper presented at the First Conference of the Forestry Association of Nigeria. Ibadan, Nigeria.

Clapperton, H. 1829. *Journal of a Second Expedition into the Interior of Africa from Benin to Soccato*. London: J. Murray.

Denham, D., H. Clapperton, and W. Oudney. 1826. *Narrative of Travels and Discoveries in Africa*. London: J. Murray.

Ekekwe. 1981. The Funiwa-5 oil well blowout. *Proceedings of the International Seminar on the Petroleum Industry and the Nigerian Environment*, 64–68.

Fagbami, A. A., O. Babalola, and O. Areola. 1984. A preliminary study of the soil features and land use of the basalt plain below the Jos Plateau escarpment of Nigeria. *Agrochemical* 28:26–39.

FAO. 1974. *Wildlife Management in Nigeria*. Department of Forestry, University of Ibadan.

Floyd, B. N. 1965. Soil erosion and deterioration in eastern Nigeria. *Nigerian Geographical Journal* 8:33–43.

Franke, R., and B. Chasin. 1980. *Seeds of Famine: Ecological Destruction and the Development Dilemma in the West African Sahel*. Montclair, NJ: Allenheld & Osmun.

Gana, J. A. 1978. Rural settlements. In *A Geography of Nigerian Development*, 138–55. J. S. Oguntoyinbo, O. Areola, and M. Filani, eds. Ibadan: Heinemann.

Gleave, M. B. 1964. Hill settlements and their abandonment in western Yorubaland. *Africa* 33:343–53.

Grove, A. T. 1973. Desertification in the African environment. In *Drought in Africa*, ed. D. Dalby and R. J. H. Church. London: School of Oriental and African Studies.

Jeje, L. K. 1980. A review of geomorphic evidence for climatic change since the late Pleistocene in the rain forest areas of southern Nigeria. *Palaeogeography, Palaeoclimatology, and Palaeoecology* 31:63–86.

Jones, B. 1938. Desiccation and the West African colonies. *Geographical Journal* 91:401–22.

Lander, R., and J. Lander. 1832. *Journal of an Expedition to Explore the Course and Termination of the Niger*. London: J. Murray.

Ledger, D. O. 1961. Recent hydrological changes in the Rima Basin, northern Nigeria. *Geographical Journal* 127:477–86.

Mabogunje, A. L. 1962. *Yoruba Towns*. Ibadan: Ibadan University Press.

———. 1973. *Kainji, A Man-made Lake*. Vol. II, *Social and Economic Conditions*. Ibadan: NISER.

Migeod, P. M. H. 1921. Some notes on the Lake Chad region in British territory. *Geographical Journal* 60:347–59.

Morgan, W. B. 1959. The influence of European contacts on the landscape of southern Nigeria. *Geographical Journal* 125:48–64.

Morgan, W. B., and R. P. Moss. 1965. Savanna and forest in western Nigeria. *Africa* 35:286–93.

Ofomato, G. E. K. 1965. Factors of soil erosion in the Enugu area of Nigeria. *Nigerian Geographical Journal* 8.

Ojo, G. J. A. 1966. *Yoruba Cultures: A Geographical Analysis*. London: University of London Press.

Oyebande, L., et al. 1980. The effect of Kainji Dam on the hydrological regime, water balance and water quality of the River Niger. In *International Association for Hydrological Sciences Publication* 130:221–28.

Stebbing, E. T. 1935. The encroaching Sahara, the threat to the West African colonies. *Geographical Journal* 85:506–24.

Udo, R. K. 1965. Disintegration of nucleated settlements in Eastern Nigeria. *Geographical Review* 55:53–67.

Udo, R. K., and B. Ogundana. 1966. Factors influencing the fortunes of ports in the Niger Delta. *Scottish Geographical Magazine* 82:169–83.

UNO. 1977. *Desertification: Its Causes and Consequences*. Oxford: Pergamon Press.

Watts, M. 1983. *Silent Violence*. Berkeley: University of California Press.

Willcox, W. F. 1940. *Studies in American Demography*. Ithaca, NY: Cornell University Press.

37

Sweden
TORSTEN HÄGERSTRAND   ULRIK LOHM

Human action in the landscape is, as a rule, contained inside spaces with socially defined boundaries. The land surface is divided into "pockets of local order" of different rank. Among these, the most power is assigned to the property unit and the national territory. In both cases, the purpose is to protect belongings and activities against unwanted intrusion from the outside.

But human action also requires mobility of people, goods, and messages. The degree of mobility defines how far actors are able to combine inputs from dispersed sources for projects they want to undertake in their domains. The transformation of nature through human action is thus framed by the territorial competence of actors and the means of movement at their disposal. Then, unintended, secondary effects are more often the rule than the exception.

In accordance with this conceptualization, the following review of the impact on nature caused by the Swedish population since the end of the seventeenth century focuses on direct and indirect consequences of changes in patterns of territorial competence and in circulation. While territorial competence has always undergone continuous marginal changes, Sweden has also witnessed some revolutionary changes in this realm. Circulation has expanded from a predominantly local to a global range. At the beginning of the period, there existed a certain correspondence between the structure of domains and the spatial range of circulation. This is no longer the case, and the contradiction contains a central problem for future management of the human relation to nature.

The Stage and the Actors

A comprehensive idea of the physiography of Sweden can be derived most easily from the distribution of farmland and forest (Fig. 37.1). The main outlines of this distribution have been quite stable over the centuries, but various qualitative changes have been considerable. The solid agricultural belt in the middle and the narrow serrated zones along the coasts correspond to areas of marine transgression before the land rebounded from glacial depression. The major exception is the southwest corner, where farming thrives on a lime-rich moraine brought up from the bottom of the Baltic Sea. Forests and glacial deposits go together, but forests are sprinkled with thousands of small clearances, where fine-grained moraines on hilltops or smaller fractions of glacio-fluvial material in the valleys offered opportunities for cultivation.

Sweden is warmer than are other areas in the same high latitudes because of the cyclonal inflow of air from the south and southwest during winter. The long summer days to a large extent compensate for the dark and cold winters. The growing season is around 240 days in the south and 150 days in the north. Annual precipitation varies from around 1,000 mm in the southwest to 500 mm on the islands in the Baltic Sea. Rain is most abundant in August, which is quite the reverse of the ideal for farming.

From 1650 to 1985, the Swedish population increased from slightly below 1 million to 8.4 million. The demographic transition began around 1820, when mortality began to decline (Fig. 37.2). Administratively, Sweden has been and is a very centralized state. While a rather personal royal government dominated shorter periods, most of the time government and people have joined in holding their own against aristocratic expansion. Feudalism never gained a foothold, and after the reduction of noble land before 1700, the aristocracy developed into a class of civil servants.

The Old Order

In the middle of the seventeenth century, when a modern state organization had taken shape and Sweden's Baltic empire had reached its maximum extent, the majority of the Swedish population were peasants, almost entirely reliant upon locally available resources for their needs. Everything within reach had to be used not only for preparation of food, but also for meeting nearly all other needs. Subsistence practices were clearly not uniform across the vast country. Plains and woodlands, coasts and mining

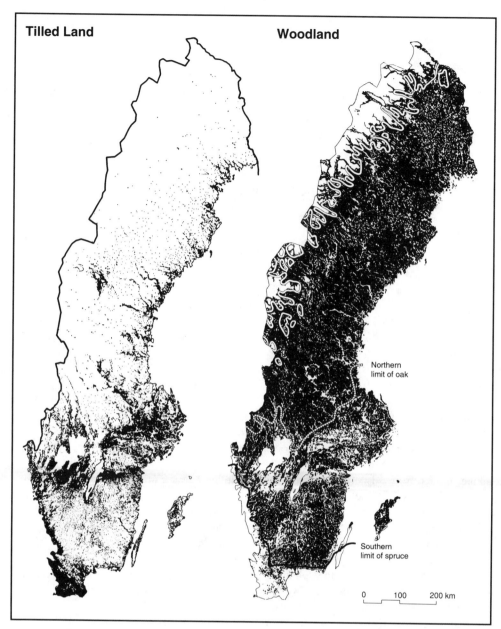

Figure 37.1 Distribution of tilled land and woodland in Sweden around 1950. Note on the woodland map the southern limit of spruce and the northern limit of oak. The limit of mountain vegetation is also marked along the Norwegian boundary. Source: Jonasson et al. 1937.

districts afforded different spectra of resources. But so many traits were common, and change so slow, that it is possible to identify one basic model behind the variations.

Tillage and Meadow

The nucleated village was the center of economic and social life. The number of farms in each varied from perhaps 50 on the plains and in the northern river valleys, to two to four in the forest districts. Isolated farms also existed, normally representing a later stage of cultivation. The settlements were encircled by an infield of tilled land and meadows, followed by the outfields – woodland in most of the country, but more open grazing land on the densely cultivated plains. The outfield was common land, whereas the infield

was divided in narrow strips. The guiding principle was that every holding should have its share of all qualities of soil.

The overriding problem of the peasant was to maintain yields. One method was to let one-half or one-third of the tilled land lie fallow. In most of the southwestern woodland, the acreage was too small for fallow and was planted year after year. A further practice was to use cattle and sheep as collectors of nutrients found beyond the tillage. Hay and leaves were cut in the meadows in the middle of summer and dried for winter use. All hay within reach, including that from glades in the forest, was collected and brought home. The practice just described resulted in a widespread type of landscape around the settlements called *löväng* (approximately, park meadow). It was not the same as the Continental

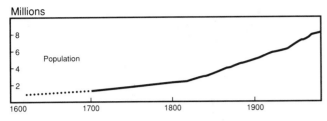

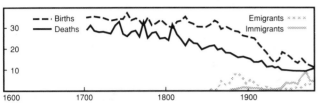

Figure 37.2 Population development in Sweden. Total population
is given in million births and deaths, as well as emigrants and
immigrants per 1,000 inhabitants. Source: Swedish official statistics.

"sprout forest"; it was a plant community of sparsely grown
deciduous trees with clusters of shrubs.

Multiple Use of Forests

Coniferous forests dominated in most of the country.
Spruce, which had spread from the northeast, just reached
its southern limits on the slopes of the southern Swedish
uplands. Deciduous woods were maintained as islands around
villages and farms. Much evidence indicates that southwestern
Sweden at this time possessed more continuous tracts of oak,
beech, and hazel than the remainder of the country. Here
acorns and a rich grass vegetation provided exceptionally
good conditions for cattle-breeding.

Forests were strongly affected by human use in the settled
parts of the country – in southern and central Sweden and
along the coastal belt and in the lower river valleys of the
north. The practice was to let the animals graze in the forest
during summer. In the woodlands of middle Sweden and in
those still limited parts of the north that were settled by
peasants, animal husbandry was even more dominant than
further south. Here, in order to increase access to pasture,
the cattle herds were driven up from the villages to distant
summer chalets (*fäbodar*), where women stayed with them,
making butter and cheese.

Large tracts of the Swedish forests have been affected by
burn-beating. The practice has a long history. It is mentioned
in medieval provincial legislation, but seems to have been
intensified by Finnish immigrants in the sixteenth and
seventeenth centuries. It became widespread during the
eighteenth and the first half of the nineteenth century. A
forest area of less than half a hectare was selected in early
summer. Trees were felled to cover the surface, and the plot
was left over the winter and burned the following June. Rye
was then sown before the ash blew away. After some 10 years
of rye, hay, and grazing, birch and alder made their way into
the beat-burned land. Reports from the time tell of surprisingly high grain yields, ten- to twentyfold or more, in contrast
to the four- to sixfold yields of the tillage.

Forests also contributed to diet in other ways. Blueberries,

lingonberries, raspberries, and cloudberries were available in
large quantities. Their food value was not high, but they
provided protection against scurvy. Porridge made of dock,
sorrel, nettle, and other plants is mentioned as poor people's
food (Hyltén-Cavallius 1868).

Wood was the sole fuel for heating in countryside and town
alike, as well as for modest light in farmhouses. Buildings,
fences, furniture, carts, and tools were made of wood, while
fencing took a large toll of young trees. Tar boiling and
production of potash were also important, particularly in the
coastal areas of Norrland. Tar, which made up 8–10% of
Sweden's export, was distilled from stumps of pine and
potash made from birchwood.

The sparse human population left plenty of space for birds
and other useful game. The hunting of edible game by
villagers as owners or tenants of land was severely limited,
however, because of privileges reserved for the nobility. Laws
also required peasants to participate in regular hunts for such
predators of cattle and sheep as the bear, wolf, lynx,
marten, and fox. Fisheries along the coast and in the large
rivers of the north were of great importance for the local
population. Dried or salted fish became an important
commodity for sale at an early date.

Water was an important source of energy everywhere.
Watermills for grinding were in use already in the thirteenth
century. Sawmills were introduced in the fifteenth century. The
wealth of rivers and streams provided approximately equal
opportunities for small waterwheels across the whole country.

Iron production in Sweden dates from prehistoric times. It
was originally based on lake and bog ore, widely available in
areas above the highest postglacial coastline. At about A.D.
1200, rock ore began to be mined in central Sweden, and the
industrial region called Bergslagen gradually took shape. The
famous Falu copper mine is situated in this region.

Pig iron made up 70% of Sweden's exports. Although
establishments were in private hands, the state exercised
strict control through its *Bergskollegium* (Council of Mines),
set up in 1683. The people of Bergslagen lived on small farms,
but many of their activities were related to the mines and
ironworks. Forest, water, and ore were vastly more important
than tillage.

Famines and Reserve Food

Climate in Sweden, even in "normal" years, is not
particularly favorable for crop production. Precipitation is on
the average low in the beginning of the period of vegetation,
and reaches its maximum in late summer. This pattern is the
reverse of what the farmer would wish. A cold winter with a
late spring shortens the period of vegetation. In addition,
sudden waves of cold air, causing night frost, set in even
during the warm season.

Estimates of the food potential vary and are quite
uncertain. Feeding allowances in kind for workers under the
Crown and on some private estates state a consumption per
day that seems to have guaranteed a satisfactory level
(approximately 3,000 kcal/person per day). Some further
calculations (Table 37–1) have been attempted, based on
what is known about cultivated area, yields, number of cattle,

Table 37-1 *Production of Food on Average Peasant Farms in the Seventeenth Century*

| Type of household | Outcome of harvest | kcal/person/day | Source of Kcal | | |
			Grain (%)	Cattle (%)	Other (%)
Farm on the plains	Good	3.800	68%	21%	11%
	Bad	2.400	58%	25%	17%
Farm in woodlands	Good	2.000	40%	40%	20%
	Bad	1.300	23%	46%	31%

Source: Hannerberg 1971.

and size of taxes (Hannerberg 1971). These estimates indicate that farms on the plains produced more than enough in good years and were able to manage in bad ones. Smaller farms in the hilly woodlands, on the other hand, do not appear to have reached a sufficient level even in good years, although it must be noted that crops derived from burn-beating are not included. On the whole, milk products and meat, as well as food from forests and streams, were more important for these households than was their own production of grain. A regional trade in grain also took place, the woodland inhabitants delivering timber and firewood in exchange. A tradition of handicrafts for sale took shape in areas in which farms had exceedingly small plowlands.

A variety of attempts were made to broaden the diet. The peasantry and the landless relied on their own traditional emergency reserves. The prevalent procedure was to make bread from a mixture of flour and bark from pine, spruce, and birch. Pounded straw was commonly used for the same purpose. Efforts to introduce lichens as a reserve food were not successful (Nelson and Svanberg 1987). Much effort was devoted to the dissemination of the potato from the beginning of the eighteenth century. This effort was not very successful until the end of that century, when it became clear to people that cereals could be saved by the distillation of alcohol from potatoes. In the nineteenth century, potatoes very rapidly became an essential food as well.

Because many peasants lived very close to a minimal subsistence level even during normal years, crop failures inevitably led to famines. The most severe and most widespread famines are clearly visible in the mortality figures (Fig. 37.2), including those from 1771–73 and also the years around 1810. The high death rate does not necessarily mean that many people actually starved to death, but rather that susceptibility to diseases increased. Even the ordinary high mortality of the period reflected a background of widespread ill health. Shortage of food was reflected also in other ways that cannot be shown by statistics. The better-situated families took care of endangered relatives and friends as lodgers. But as a consequence of the distress of the landowners, unemployment increased and the purchasing power of many people was diminished. The poorest had to go begging, frequently far away from home, although authorities sought to prevent this by forcing parishes to care for their own beggars.

Limitations of Territorial Competence

Until 1718 Sweden pursued a Great Power policy that, among other goals, aimed to make the Baltic Sea into a Swedish inland water. Foreign wars imposed a heavy burden on the small population, as the Crown seems to have viewed the peasantry predominantly as an object of taxation and a producer of soldiers for army and navy. Strict regulations were also imposed on the use of some natural resources. The forest legislation of 1647 declared that oaks and pines that were suitable as ships' masts were royal property. This rule irritated peasants in middle and southern Sweden, because oaks grew to a large extent in the infields and even in tilled land.

The political situation of the country made the domestic production of gunpowder indispensable. Sulfur was readily available, since it was produced as a byproduct in copper mines. Access to crude saltpeter, however, required a peculiar kind of mining. The soil under stables was made royal property because of its high content of nitrogen. Peasants had to accept that their stable floors would be broken up and the underlying soil transported to the gunpowder works (Lindberg 1964).

In 1641, the practice of burn-beating was forbidden. This measure was intended to guarantee adequate supplies of firewood and charcoal for the iron industry. It hurt in particular the Finnish settlers in central Sweden, who only a few decades earlier had been invited to exploit what King Gustaf Wasa called the "useless forest." The legislation was not very effective; indeed, the mine owners themselves recommended burning as a method to improve the regrowth of forests (Nelson 1913).

The Break-up of the Old Order

Swedish supremacy over the Baltic came to an end in 1720. This was a major shock, but it also had liberating effects. Leaders turned their attention toward "peace instead of war, prosperity instead of power" (Heckscher 1941). Modernization of Sweden began, at least in theory. The eighteenth century is interesting for its youthful ideas, experiments, and debates, but its practical achievements were limited. The country was poor, and the belief was still dominant that mercantilistic rules and regulations would lead to desired outcomes. There was no real take-off until after the next major shock, the loss of Finland in 1809. The old order came under attack, and a capitalistic market economy gradually took shape.

The breaking up of the old order was conditioned by two processes. One was a reorganization of territorial competence in villages and forests. The other was the upward leap in mobility made possible by the steam engine. Profound changes in the use of natural resources followed. Here only three chapters of this story will be treated: (1) the transformation of farmland and water-flow; (2) the depletion and repair of forests; and (3) the expansion and diversification of flows of substances. Consideration of the colonization of the northern interior regions and relations between Lapps and Swedes are omitted.

Redistribution of Land

The remolding of Swedish agriculture began in the eighteenth century, but its most intensive phase coincided with the decreasing mortality and the accelerated growth of population. This transformation should not be viewed primarily as a direct response to increasing demands for food; other interests also were involved. Different social groups addressed the challenge from different conditions and motivations. One could argue that in many cases it was simply the supply of young workers after 1820 that made possible major investments in land reclamation, ditching, and building.

In eighteenth-century debate, one can discern a humanitarian streak of thought, predominantly among intellectual aristocrats who wanted to improve the living conditions of the broad strata of the population. Otherwise, thinking was dominated by the economic interests of the state. Taxes paid by farms made up the bulk of the financial base of the state, after efforts to introduce manufacturing had failed. Grain had to be imported. It was also strongly believed that large unused supplies of land lay available for cultivation. At this time, it was taken as self-evident that increased production required, first of all, more land area. Because that required more people, the state pursued a positive population policy that included the organization of population censuses from 1750 onward.

A radical land reform was conceived under the influence of the same ideas. As long as each holding comprised a great number of scattered and narrow strips of land in the infield, peasants had to coordinate their work in ways that largely prevented individual initiatives. Agricultural innovations already visible abroad could not be introduced until the constraints imposed by the division of land had been removed.

A redivision of land came to be carried out in three steps: *storskifte*, in 1757; *enskifte*, in 1803; and *laga skifte*, in 1827. The purpose of the first was simply to consolidate the many strips of each individual holding into a few larger blocks, without touching the nucleated villages as such. Later, in 1803, the goal was to provide each holding with just one block of land and to move the farmstead out from the village to its center. For purely topographical reasons, this radical program could be realized only on the open plains. In these areas, the agricultural landscape was entirely reshaped over a few decades. Finally, the legislation of 1827 was a compromise,

more attuned to conditions in most of the country. It also required many farmsteads to move out from the village, but it permitted more than one parcel per holding (Figs. 37.3 and 37.4).

Peasants now had to leave an archaic collective existence and become their own masters. The outfields – grazing enclosures and forests – were converted from commons to privately owned land. This huge reorganization reached its climax at the middle of the nineteenth century, but continued into the present century in distant parts of the country. One of the reasons for the relative speed and uniformity of the process was the rule, established in 1757, that required enclosure even if only one landowner in a village requested it.

Individual territorial competence also changed in other respects. Along with the land reform, the state sold off much of the Crown land to the tenants at a low price. Noble land could also be gradually acquired by others than members of the nobility. Independent family farmers became the dominant actors in the landscape. In Norrland, the settlers who had moved inland from the coast had traditionally been permitted to use widely scattered meadows and lakesides on Crown land for their haymaking. During the general reorganization of land ownership, strict boundary lines were finally laid out, both between individual settlements and between private and Crown land. Because reigning doctrine favored undivided property units, settlers received much larger compact areas than the scattered patches that they had used earlier to feed their cattle and do their fishing. This arrangement came to be of crucial importance for the paths taken by the exploitation of the forests when timber began to rise in value.

At this point a statistical overview of the development of agricultural land use up to the present is in order. Official data are not very reliable until the 1930s. Drawing upon local studies and various primary sources, however, Hannerberg (1971) has made estimates for earlier periods. The figures (Table 37-2) are the best now available for Sweden as a whole. Corresponding national figures have not been calculated for periods before 1800. But estimates exist (Table 37-2) for the province of Närke (in the middle of Svealand) and should give at least an indication of the general situation.

The data, national as well as regional, support the conclusion that reclamation already kept pace with the number of inhabitants in the eighteenth century. It increased considerably faster than that during the period after 1820, when the growth of population reached its highest rate. In the present century, on the other hand, the continued growth of agricultural output reflects increased yields per unit areas, not increases in total area under cultivation.

The changing pattern of land use became manifest in other ways than the expansion of farmland belonging to the old holdings. The number of holdings grew little, but the population continued to increase. A proletariat that emerged outside the limited circle of landowners was allowed to clear small plots in the outfields, frequently smaller than half a hectare. The potato was their lifesaver. Landowners helped by providing grazing for a cow and a few sheep in the vicinity. In return, they could count on extra labor within easy reach

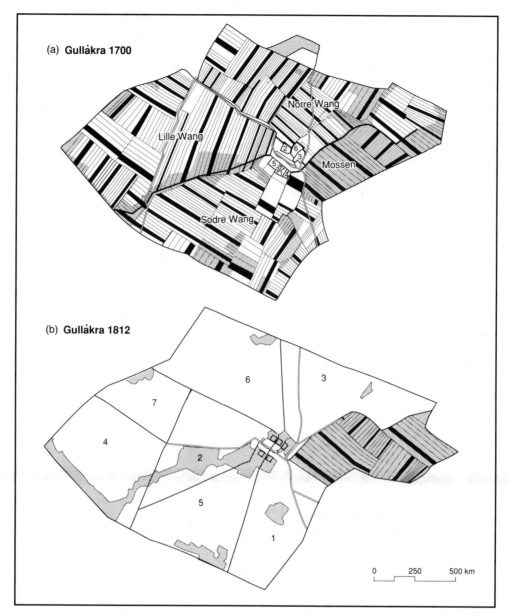

Figure 37.3 The village of Gullåkra in the province of Skane (a) in the year 1700 and (b) after *enskifte* in 1812. Black strips mark land allocated to farm number 1. In 1812 this farm has its land concentrated in the southern corner of the village area. But note that the bogland east of the settlement was not included in the redistribution. Source: Wester 1960.

when needed. The rent consisted of work by the day and delivery of berries and handicraft products such as fabrics. Around 1880, when the rural population reached its maximum, the outfields were full of this class of people, and additional useful plots were scarce in Götaland and Svealand. In the span of 50 years, the number of rural habitations had increased fivefold (Fig. 37.5).

Reclamation

It was during the nineteenth century that land reclamation was most intensive in Sweden. In southern and central regions, meadows were converted to plowland, lakes and wetlands were drained and tilled, and outfields were sprinkled by the small clearings of crofters. In the north, colonization of inland areas gained momentum. New farming practices were introduced gradually.

In the redistribution of land authorized by the *skiftes* laws, soils were carefully graded according to quality measures of the time, and lower quality was compensated for by increased area. Holders who had to move out to the periphery could obtain much untilled but cultivable land. The land reform not only made reclamation easier than before, but also rendered it a necessity for many. Between 1800 and 1850, the area of tilled land increased by more than 70%. The number of hectares per 100 inhabitants increased from 64 to 75, and yields per hectare nearly doubled. Reclamation then continued at a slower pace until the 1920s (Table 37-2).

The old tillage had, as a rule, been located on light and dry soils, on the tops and slopes of hills in many regions. Reclamation to begin with consumed adjacent meadows, which meant the cutting of trees and the removal of stones. The land surface above the upper marine limit is frequently

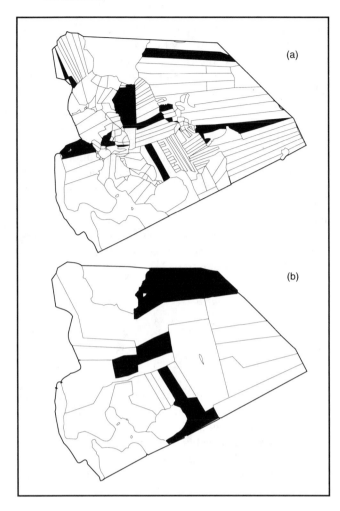

Figure 37.4 The village of Vrångfall in the southern upland area (a) before and (b) after *laga skifte* in 1862. Black areas mark the land allocated to the same farm. *Laga skifte* permitted several parcels per farm. Source: Gerger 1984.

Table 37-2 *Development of Agricultural Land Use in Sweden*

Year	Tilled land (ha)	Hectares per 100 inhabitants	Yield (kg/ha)
For one province			
1630	17,000	70	
1690	22,000	60	6–700
1780	30,000	60	
For the nation			
1800	1,500,000	64	8–900
1850	2,600,000	75	
1880	3,400,000	74	14–1,500
1920	3,800,000	64	17–2,000
1950	3,600,000	51	21–2,500
1980	3,000,000	36	33–4,300

ilitated the removal of stones, which were frequently used in making broad walls to mark the new property boundaries. The stone walls are striking features of today's landscape, forming a unique kind of human-made biotope.

Extension of tillage at the expense of former meadows was only the initial step in the reclamation movement. From the beginning of the nineteenth century and until almost the 1950s, agricultural thinking was permeated by the hope of gaining additional fertile land by lowering the level of lakes and by draining wetlands. It was also believed that drainage would produce a more favorable climate.

A century and a half of effort has radically reshaped the hydrography of Sweden. Apart from stretches of remote bogland, hardly any lake, river, stream, or marsh has not been subjected to some sort of regulation. The nineteenth century was dominated by the demands of farming and transportation. In the present century, efforts have been directed more toward the development of water power and the provision of water and sewage systems for industry and cities. The focus will here rest only on changes related to farming.

The Royal Academy of Agriculture, established in 1811 by the new French-born Crown Prince Jean Bernadotte, devoted much of its activity to the problems of drainage and land reclamation. So, too, did the country agricultural societies,

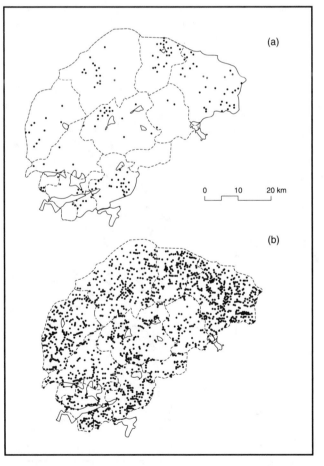

Figure 37.5 The multiplication of crofters in a woodland district of southern Sweden between (a) 1745 and (b) 1860. Source: Nordström 1952.

full of boulders, which posed few problems as long as only light, wooden tools or the ard was in use, but they became impediments on old as well as new tillage for the mould-board plough that came into common use. *Lage skifte* also fac-

which were organized somewhat later. To help to keep up with developments abroad, a ditching consultant, George Stephens, was called in from Scotland. Scholarships were awarded for study trips to the continent, and gradually a developing corps of agricultural engineers applied their skills in every province. Public support was considerable and consistent. The Parliament surprised even the government itself by making subsidies and loans available annually from 1841 onward.

No quantitatively documented record exists of how the transformation of land use and waterflow actually proceeded. Only scattered local investigations and partial statistics are available. It has been estimated that lakes and mires contributed 600,000 ha, or 1/6 of the tilled area in Sweden, around 1950 – an estimate that probably omits areas that had been tried and abandoned.

The largest single undertaking, centered on Lake Hjälmaren in middle Sweden, illustrates both success and failure in reclamation. The lake is the fourth largest in the country and is located on a fertile plain. As long as hay for winter fodder was the critical resource, estate owners and villagers around the lake were satisfied with their rich harvests of grass on the wide wetlands. In 1783, for example, a single farm at Lake Hjälmaren cut 880 loads of hay. Because only 300 loads were needed for the farm itself, nearly two-thirds of the harvest could be exchanged for timber and firewood from the woodlands beyond the plain (Rönnby 1942). In certain years, however, severe flooding of the wetland had disastrous consequences for the economy. Efforts were made on several

of these occasions to get rid of the surplus water by removing dams and other obstacles downstream. The state intervened in 1757 and cleared the channel outlet. Various plans for improvement were aired until the 1820s. Their purpose was still not to obtain new arable land but to protect the production of hay.

The radical repartitioning of land by enclosure created a new situation. With entrepreneurship no longer hampered by village organization, farmers began to give priority to the expansion of cropland. Beginning in 1849, plans were made on behalf of a consortium of larger farms for the regulation of Lake Hjälmaren. The smaller holders still opposed the plans, fearing the capital costs. Finally, the Parliament granted a loan, and work began in 1877. This, the most wide-ranging drainage enterprise ever undertaken in Sweden, and at that time also the largest in Europe, was completed in 1888. The enterprise turned out to be four times more expensive than first calculated, but it increased the arable acreage in the area by 41% (Laurell 1886).

The case of Lake Hjälmaren became the flagship for the drainage movement, and it was preceded and followed by thousands of less demanding undertakings. Stephens had already begun to attack the big mires on the isle of Gotland in the 1820s, despite the distrust of most farmers who were not ready to give up haymaking and fishing. He was followed by other entrepreneurs until, by 1950, only 10% of the original wetland surface remained on the island (Fig. 37.6).

The drainage of mires on Gotland was, in part, a disaster from the very beginning. The mires had previously yielded

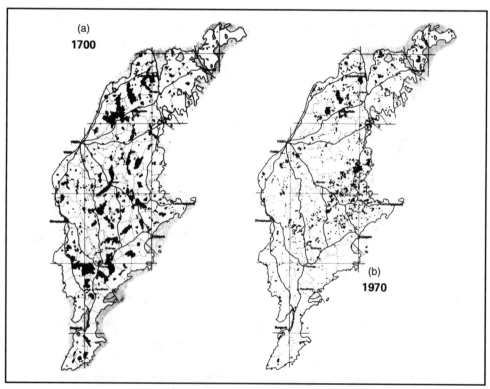

Figure 37.6 Disappearance of open-water surfaces on the island of Gotland in the Baltic between (a) the eighteenth century and (b) the present. Source: *Blågul miljö* 1982.

good harvests of both hay and fish, and they provided sedge, generally used as a cheap roofing material on the island. Stephens was guided by the humus theory. But, unlike situations encountered before, in the Gotland mires the humus layer rested on a subsoil of pure lime. When the running water was diverted from this complex, minerals from the higher ground ceased to percolate downward, and the conditions for continued plant growth deteriorated rapidly (Romell 1947).

An unknown number of smaller undertakings elsewhere in Sweden led to disappointment because the soils did not have the expected qualities, although for other reasons than on Gotland. Originally successful cultivation of organogenic soils too has turned out to be problematic in the long run. The case of Lake Hjälmaren again offers a good illustration.

Grain productivity in the Lake Hjälmaren region was very high until about 1920, a fact of great significance for providing bread during the World War I. But later difficulties arose. When the water level is lowered and the organicogenic soil plowed, oxidation sets in. The surface shrinks and comes once again within reach of high water. Between 1888 and 1955, the fields at Lake Hjälmaren sank 0.7 m. Embankments had to be built and pumping plants installed in order to make further farming feasible. In another case further north (Persson and Lohm 1977), the soil surface sank up to 1 meter between 1927 and 1967. Water control had been implemented in 1905–1910, and farming was given up in the 1960s. Thousands of smaller similar areas around the country have been abandoned, particularly where the subsoil consists of stony moraine instead of clay and sand. Afforestation is a common further step in their use.

Around 1920, experience had led to a general use of embankments and pumping from the very beginning of larger undertakings. But still several decades later a leading agronomist felt compelled to suggest that Swedish water management needed a more hydrogeological and less stereotyped technical approach. To "regulate and distribute water should be more important than just finding the simplest way of getting rid of it" (Malmström 1951). Apart from changes in land use, brought about by the drainage movement of the past one and a half centuries, there is hardly any doubt that farmland was made more susceptible to drought. The transformation of the partly groundwater-fed soils in the formerly undrained-groundwater-discharge zone made the new well-drained soils wholly dependent on precipitation. Today one even finds formerly drained areas periodically under irrigation.

Heydays, Crisis, and Recovery

The transformation of meadows to tillage turned out to be an economic success for a few decades. Yields were good, particularly where low-lying meadows, rich in topsoil, had been reclaimed. Investments in new buildings, roads, wells, fences, and ditches gave work and income to many of the landless. Grain cash-crops also became attractive, at least for larger farm-owners. Demand for farm products grew within Sweden as transportation improved and economic life in general began to diversify. The relaxation of British protec-

tionistic barriers in the 1840s offered a new market to the grain trade. For more than three decades, Sweden was a major supplier of oats for the horses of London. Oats began to be grown year after year, and rapidly became a dominant crop in most of the country, reaching more than 75% of the total harvest in the western districts (Fridlizius 1957).

The prosperity of the decades after 1850 rested on unstable ground. In this new era of mobility, the world market replaced the local weather as the leading source of hazard. In the 1880s, competition from American and Russian grain brought commercial farming into a crisis that introduced a second stage in the modernization of agriculture.

The practice of crop rotation had already been tried in scattered places. More widespread by 1880, it became the rule in a few decades. The sale of dairy products and meat gained in importance. For the first time, arable fields provided both grazing and winter fodder, although hay-making on remaining meadows as well as woodland grazing still continued to some extent. Root crops facilitated combatting weeds. Modest amounts of artificial fertilizers, mainly phosphates, were imported, and a certain amount of mechanization of labor was achieved.

The period until 1945 has been judged as well-balanced from a biological point of view (Mattsson 1985). Crop production and the raising of cattle and horses were well integrated. Plant nutrients still circulated to a large extent inside the farm unit. Yields continued to increase as a result of improved tools, development of new strains, and cleaner seed. The cessation of imports during World War I did, of course, cause some hunger, but the nation survived World War II without serious food shortage. A provisional supply of phosphates was derived from the apatite ore in the mines of the far north, compensating for interrupted imports.

The sources of inputs in farming changed radically after the 1940s. A new agricultural policy sought to retain the family farm as the basic unit of production, but under conditions that kept the level of income comparable to that of industrial workers. This required a new redistribution of land, leading to bigger holdings and to accelerated growth in the productivity of both land and labor. The number of holdings was reduced from 300,000 in 1945 to the present 100,000. The area under cultivation was not affected to the same extent; it declined only from 3.6 million ha to 2.9 million ha.

Beside rural depopulation – which in reality had started much earlier – the result has been a high degree of mechanization and specialization. One-third of the farms have no cattle and rely entirely on artificial fertilizers for their production of grain (Fig. 37.7), and farms that specialize in dairy products buy much of their fodder. High productivity is supported by plant and animal breeding, control of seed, and use of pesticides (Fig. 37.8). The circulation of substances in modern agriculture has moved far from the principles of the old order and even from those employed as late as the 1930s. An example taken from a farm in southern Sweden (Table 37-3) shows how production is integrated now in a global network of links.

Sweden's postwar agricultural policy was oriented toward national self-sufficiency in preparation for a possible future

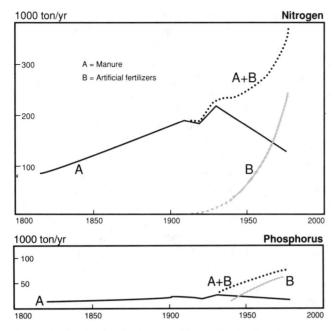

Figure 37.7 Amounts of nitrogen and phosphorus used in Swedish farming from 1800 until 1980. A, manure; B, artificial fertilizers. Source: Anderson 1982.

Table 37-3 *Origin in 1978 of Selected Inputs to the Farm Östergårda* in Southern Sweden*

Country	Machines	Pesticides	Fertilizers	Fodder
Norway			x	
Denmark	x	x		
Iceland				x
West Germany	x	x	x	
Netherlands	x	x		
United Kingdom	x	x		
France		x	x	
East Germany			x	
Poland			x	
Soviet Union			x	
United States			x	x
Mexico				x
Brazil				x
Argentina				x
Morocco		x		
Philippines				x
Indonesia				x

* Östergårda comprises 48 ha of arable land, of which 11 ha are rented, 12 ha are pasture land, and 11 ha are woodland. Income is derived from some grain for sale, 25–30 milk cows, 40 other cattle, and 1,200 pigs per year. The farm supports two families.
Source: Göransson 1978.

period of isolation. The present outcome is a large overproduction, but the self-sufficiency is clearly an illusion, because of the overwhelming dependence on imported inputs.

Depletion and Repair of Forests

The meager sources indicate that at the dawn of the eighteenth century, the forests already had been strongly affected by the inhabitants in the settled parts of the country. On the other hand, the vast stretches of primeval forest in the interior of Norrland had developed more or less undisturbed since deglaciation. Before the beginning of the eigh-

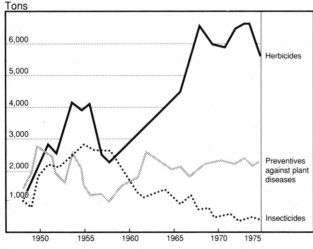

Figure 37.8 Amounts of herbicides, preventives against plant diseases, and insecticides used in Swedish farming from the 1940s until 1975. Source: *Blågul miljö* 1982.

teenth century, some of the forest fires that broke out a few times per century and renewed the growth, however, might have been caused by Lapps or hunters from the coastland (Fig. 37.9).

During this early period, the forest was, on the whole, seen by both peasants and government as self-replenishing. Learned men of the eighteenth century discussed the principles of sustainable forestry, but very few of their ideas were put into widespread practice. On the other hand, the state made numerous efforts to regulate the use of forest resources, particularly in the interest of exports and of military requirements.

Consumption of charcoal remained fairly constant during the eighteenth century. It has been calculated that the output of 50,000 t of bar-iron per year required 1 million m^3 of wood in the mines and 3 million m^3 for charcoal burning (Lindqvist 1984). By the nineteenth century, technical improvements, such as the use of powder in the mines, permitted some increase in iron production without an increase in wood consumption. Other forms of production also consumed firewood, such as glassworks, limeworks and saltpeter burning.

The large tracts of oak and beech in southwestern Sweden became radically transformed in the same century. Heatherclad moors evolved in their places (Fig. 37.10), a landscape of the same type as that on Jylland in Denmark, though less continuous. The relative roles played by various actors in the change are not well known. Peasants probably did not respect the prohibition on the felling of oak. Overgrazing is another factor to take into account. The state itself may have

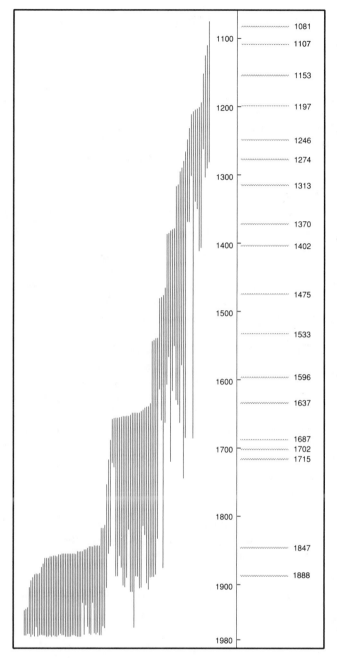

Figure 37.9 Establishment of stands of pine in relation to forest fires over a period of 800 years on Haradsheden, upper Norrland, not far from the polar circle. Dating was carried out by dendro-ecological methods applied to living as well as dead trees. Average time between fires has been 47 years. A particularly striking rejuvenation of the pine forest took place after the fires of 1637 and 1847. Source: Zackrisson 1977.

grow at smaller waterfalls and was slowly expanding. After Britain lowered its import duties in the 1840s, timber exports increased explosively. A Swedish joint-stock company law of 1848 allowed larger units than before to operate. The steam engine, introduced to the sawmills in 1849, permitted processing to be relocated from the inland waterfalls to the river mouths, where sorting of floated timber, production, and sea transportation could be combined at one place.

The new export situation had its most sweeping effects in Norrland, where forests had been exploited only in scattered patches before 1850. New areas for cutting were opened up by removing impediments for floating down the rivers. The new sawmill companies extended their influence over wide areas by acquiring forests belonging to farmers and colonists, many of whom found that the earlier principles of land

Figure 37.10 Heather-clad moorland in southwestern Sweden around 1897. Only insignificant remnants still exist after successful reforestation in the present century. Source: Schager 1909.

exploited the oak stands for its own purposes. Finally, it must be kept in mind that as soon as the heather had established itself, people living in the area burned it regularly to get fresh growth for cattle and sheep to feed on.

Free Exploitation

Already during the latter part of the eighteenth century, a market-oriented sawmill industry had started to

division had unexpectedly given them a valuable resource. Initially, companies bought only cutting rights, but a growing criticism of this arrangement led to restrictive legislation in 1889, which limited such rights and accelerated the outright purchase of land by the companies.

As exploitation of the primeval forest in the north continued, a debate began in the middle of the century about the size of the total forest resource and the need to take measures for reforestation. Concern existed about foreign businessmen who lumbered and then disappeared (Ljungberg 1874). Nevertheless, the general opinion prevailed – at least as interpreted by the government – that free handling of resources by private owners was the best guarantee of wise use. The debate, however, prodded the state now to tend its own forests with the goal of instructing by example. A central board for the state forests was set up in 1859.

Burn-beating practices continued, even becoming easier to arrange now that the outfields no longer were common land. In some parts of the country, burn-beating became more intense than ever before, particularly in the woodlands of southern Sweden. Only after the railways arrived did trees become too valuable to be burned (Larsson 1980).

In 1906, companies in Norrland and later in the whole country were prohibited by law from purchasing more land than they already had. The motivation for this drastic step was primarily social. The farming interests who dominated Parliament wanted to protect the traditional ties between farm and forest. Particularly in the north, farming was not viable without access to woodland grazing. The legislation froze forest ownership in proportions that are still in force, namely, state 25%, companies 25%, and farmers 50%.

Compulsory Restoration

The poor condition of the Swedish forests at the end of the nineteenth century made it clear that natural renewal was not sufficient for maintaining the forest capital. New legislation ensued. In 1903, the rebuilding of forest capital on private land was entrusted to regional forestry boards. They were composed of a few laymen and staffed by trained foresters. These boards proved to be quite successful because they did not in general act by coercion, even if they had the legal power to do so. Instead, their officers worked as friendly advisers, using the long-term benefit of the landowners themselves as their main argument. The key words recommended by the state were "information" and "cooperation." Clearly, time was needed to convert farmers from their traditional view of the forest as a multiple-use resource particularly valuable for grazing to an acceptance of the forest as a single-purpose producer of wood. The 1906 act forbidding companies to buy land exerted a psychological pressure by giving farmers a privileged position as owners of forest and making them feel obliged to meet expectations.

The work of the regional forestry boards over half a century resulted in a "negotiated order" (Stjernquist 1973). A measure of their growing influence is given by the numbers of field officers. From about 80 in the beginning of the century, they increased to more than 500 by 1960. For the

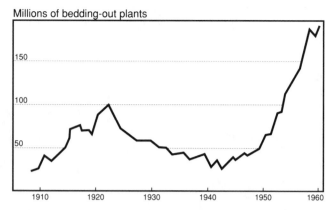

Figure 37.11 Number of forest plants distributed by the regional forestry boards from the beginning of the century up to 1960. Source: Stjernquist 1973.

country taken as a whole, planting became the leading effort and increased until about 1920 (Fig. 37.11). During this period, the forestry boards managed to create something of a popular movement around afforestation.

The proportions of different species of trees have shifted. The stands of spruce increased by 80% just between 1925 and 1950. The spruce has surpassed the pine as the dominant species through both natural spread and planting. The area of deciduous woods and mixed forests has diminished. From 40% in 1920, and still 35% in 1960, it shrank to 14% by 1977. Breeding of indigenous trees began in the 1960s. By then, also, the high-yielding North American *Pinus contorta* was imported and planted predominantly in the state and company forests in the north.

The Debate about Wood Shortage

A recurrent theme in economic debates ever since 1650 is that, despite the vast area of forests in Sweden, harvests

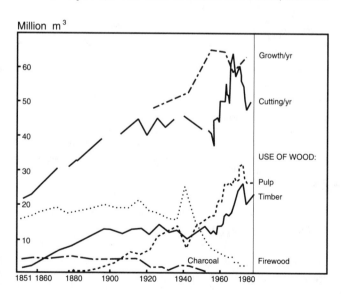

Figure 37.12 The Swedish forest budget from 1850 up to 1980. Note that the amount of annual growth is well known only after the 1920s, when systematic field estimates were introduced. Source: Stridsberg and Mattson 1980.

tend to outstrip new growth. Such opinions have had a pervasive influence on policies. What were the realities behind former fears of wood shortage?

Clearly, there was a genuine risk of local shortages at the time when firewood and charcoal had to be collected within a short radius for use in mines and furnaces. After a careful calculation, Wieslander (1936) concluded that about 1750 a regional deficit probably existed in central Sweden. Other calculations show an approximate equilibrium (Arpi, Nordquist, and Nordstrom 1959) on the regional scale.

A regular nationwide and statistically reliable assessment of forest resources was introduced in 1923. It was soon found that yearly volume of wood extracted was less than the volume added by growth, despite the fact that harvests had presumably doubled since the middle of the nineteenth century (Fig. 37.12). Until 1960, the amount of cutting remained between 40 and 45 million m^3. This stability was due to the circumstance that the increase in demand for pulpwood approximately equalled the decrease in the use of charcoal and firewood. World War II had brought about a temporary increase in the consumption of firewood. The sales of timber had already stagnated at the turn of the century.

After 1950, the expanding market in Europe and the growing gap between forest growth and cutting stimulated investment in the forest industry and a corresponding increase in cutting, until trees cut finally exceeded growth in the mid-1970s. The pulp industry then began to import its raw materials, at the same time that pressure grew to try to increase forest yields.

The total amount of wood decreased in the north and in the northern part of central Sweden until 1950, when it slowly began to increase again. During the same period, the amount of forest grew considerably faster in the remainder of Sweden because of a larger annual growth rate. The time required for regeneration in the north is about 150 years, whereas in the south it is half as long.

In the 1980s, the question of shortage has entered a new phase. The forest industries exert a strong pressure to employ all possible means to increase productivity. Economic legislation supports this tendency because the export of forest products represents a large share of national income. However, forestry today is stamped by a number of controversies. Since few owners (10%) are economically dependent on their forests, economic incentives have little force. A new era of legal regulation of forest management is therefore taking shape.

Expansion and Diversification of Flows of Substances

One of the pervasive characteristics of the nineteenth and twentieth centuries is the globalization and diversification of flows of substances from natural sources through the economic system and back again at dispersed places, either as emissions along the route or as waste after the useful life of products. In particular, since World War II, horizontal interconnections have grown explosively. A "technosphere," superimposed upon the geo- and biospheres, temporarily draws an immense number of elements into its orbit, until

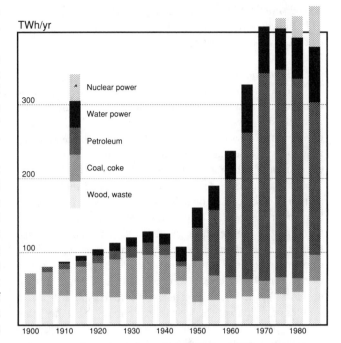

Figure 37.13 Carriers of energy in Sweden from 1900 until the present. According to plans adopted by the *riksdag* (parliament), nuclear energy is going to be liquidated before 2010. Source: Swedish official statistics.

they are sent back again, as a rule at many more localities from which they originally came. According to one estimate, around 70,000 substances are now in commercial circulation.

Energy

The most easily available general indicators of the evolution of circulation in industrial society are the carriers and quantities of energy used (Fig. 37.13). Firewood and charcoal were the dominant sources of energy in Sweden until 1900. Before the 1830s, the import of mineral coal and coke amounted on the average to not more than 5,000 t/yr. Then an increase occurred, probably because of the introduction of steamboats. The next leap upward took place in the 1860s (340,000 t/yr). Railways were responsible for 11% of this use, a share that went up to 25% before World War I. Petroleum had an insignificant share prior to 1945, at which time an unparalleled expansion began. Motorism and central heating, as well as industrial use, created a new world of mobility, productivity, and convenience. Finally, recent figures reflect political efforts to cut back dependence on imported fuel for reasons of national security, as well as to lower levels of energy consumption, in general because of environmental concerns.

The reliance on imported energy and motorism caused considerable changes in the use of land and water. The road-net was rebuilt step by step to accommodate fast and heavy traffic. Trains ceased to run on a great number of branch lines. Because of the advantages of moving timber by truck, logs were no longer floated on the large rivers, a change that removed an obstacle to full-scale development of water power. The horse disappeared from farm and forest. The

600,000 horses of the 1940s were replaced by 200,000 tractors. This allowed hay-producing tillage to be used for other crops or taken out of production.

Emissions in Time Perspective

In a historical perspective, one faces a central question of the extent to which those environmental problems that are recognized today (eutrophication, acidification, and pollution of heavy metals) are the outcome of accumulation over a long time or are essentially due to the exceptional pattern of circulation of substances set in motion after 1945.

Historical records reveal little awareness of the environmental damage caused by pollution. The major exceptions in Sweden are reports by visitors to the Falu copper mine, once the largest copper producer in the world. The famed botanist Linnaeus noted damage to the vegetation within reach of the smoke. Today it is known that the old heaps of waste in Bergslagen, where ores of various kinds have been brought up from the bedrock for at least 800 years, are still active sources of pollution. The heaps contain many substances that were beyond the technical capability of people of earlier periods to separate. Much has been recovered by modern methods, but when the sulfides in the remaining heaps come in contact with water and oxygen, sulfuric acid and free metals are released. As buffering basic substances are gradually used up, metals begin to leak out (Södermark 1981). Several lakes in central Sweden are now seriously damaged.

The use of natural objects from field sites or museums, such as herbarium plants, sediment cores, and mussel shells, for measuring the accumulation in nature of anthropogenic substances has shown that there have been many sources of pollution other than the old mines (Fig. 37.14; also Renberg and Wik 1985). It is evident that the time series of soot-sphere accumulation in varved lake sediments corresponds very closely to the general development of coal and oil combustion in Sweden. This result is remarkable because the sample was taken at a location in the coastal zone of Norrland, 600 km away from the industrial and urban heartland of the country.

The accumulation of lead is another example (Fig. 37.15). The general outcome is similar to that for soot pollution, but

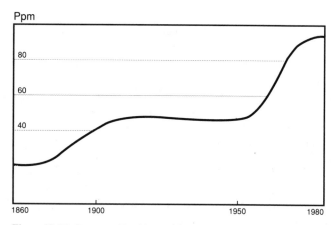

Figure 37.15 Content of lead in mosses preserved at the Botanical Museum of the University of Lund. Content is defined as microgram of metal per gram dry substance of moss. Source: Blågul miljö 1982 after Tyler.

lead has a much longer history of use than coal and oil. By 1700, 120 t/yr were imported to Sweden – about one percent of the present annual import. Because of the multiple uses of lead, one must assume that the substance has come to be deposited in a pattern closely associated with the general distribution of population.

Observations made in "natural archives" cannot, however, reveal the total quantities in circulation of those substances that have left traces. A case can be made for a complementary approach that seeks to estimate the total magnitude of the historical loadings. A few figures are available from an ongoing study (Anderberg, Bergbäck, and Lohm 1989). The substances selected were sulfur, metals in general, and chrome in particular. Such estimates are clearly full of pitfalls, as it is difficult to find out about earlier technologies and about the quality of input material.

During the past century, the wood industry has probably been responsible for 75% of all emissions to water of organic material. The wood-pulp industry has also generated considerable atmospheric emissions, in particular sulfuric compounds. A maximum was reached in the 1960s. Since then, emissions have been much reduced, particularly in the amount of dust.

In 1830, Sweden had 600 furnaces and foundries employing around 8,000 workers, and 85% of the production took place in Bergslagen. Dramatic changes occurred in the following decades. Bar iron was replaced by cast steel, and furnaces and ironworks became fewer and larger. Restructuring has continued over the years, and in 1980, 37 works remained with 46,000 employees.

The environmental impact of the iron industry consists above all of emission of metals to both air and water. Besides iron, there are also titanium, chrome, nickel, vanadium, manganese, zinc, and lead. Table 37.4 compares the accumulated quantities of emissions with the present annual emissions. 1920 is chosen as the base year for metal, because the charcoal-based production of bar-iron accounted for 90% of total production and little can be known about emissions. The modern steel industry with its bar-iron based on coke and

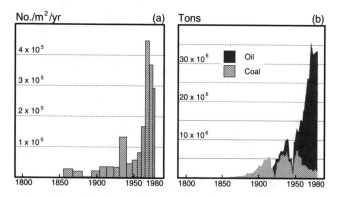

Figure 37.14 (a) Accumulation of soot spheres over time in the sediments of Lake Gråvästjärn, located in the coastal zone of Norrland, compared with (b) combustion of coal and oil in Sweden in corresponding years. Source: Renberg and Wik 1985.

Table 37-4 *Emissions from Wood-Pulp and Iron Industries in Sweden*

Emission	Period	Accumulated quantity (tons)	Present annual emission (tons)	Present emission in percent of accumulated quantity
Lignin	1870–1980	43,000,000	290,000	0.7
Sulfur	1870–1980	4,500,000	43,000	1.0
Metals to air	1920–1980	3,200,000	42,000	1.3
Metals to water	1920–1980	343,000	2,600	0.8

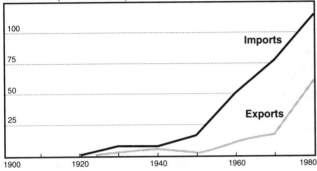

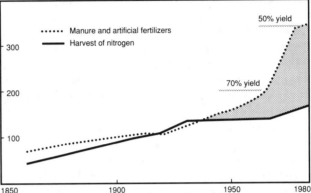

Figure 37.16 Import and export of chrome. The difference is present in Sweden in industrial products or has been dispersed as pollution. Source: Anderberg et al., 1989.

Figure 37.18 Input and harvest of nitrogen in Swedish farming. At present, only 50% of the added nitrogen (manure + artificial fertilizers) are utilized by the crops. Concerning proportions between manure and artificial fertilizers, see Fig. 37.7. Source: Andersson 1986.

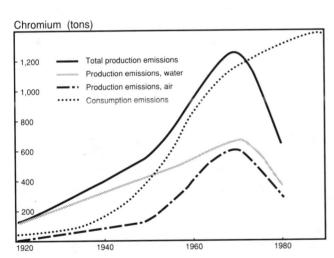

Figure 37.17 Consumption emissions of chrome compared to the development of production emissions. Source: Anderberg et al., 1989.

achieved during the 1970s, but this is only part of the total picture. Products move out, primarily as steel in tools, ball bearings, and stainless equipment, but also in leather, paint, solutions for wood impregnation, and chrome-plated objects. Such uses imply a diffuse emission. According to the best estimates that can be made at present, diffuse emission now represents the largest and the still growing part of the total.

Recent Changes

Today, the use of fertilizers – above all nitrogen – in farming has become a difficult problem. The input of nitrogen over a century relates to the amount of nitrogen in the harvest (Fig. 37.18). A rather balanced situation existed until about 1930. But the subsequent, very quickly increasing input has been accompanied by a relatively small increase in harvest. Half of the input flows away to the atmosphere and to ground- and surface-water. The outcome is nitrate pollution of groundwater and, in the end, fertilization of the coastal waters.

The situation is particularly serious in the waters that connect the Baltic Sea with the North Sea. The outflow of nutrients gives rise to hypertrophication, which in turn, causes oxygen deficits. In this process organisms at the bottom are eradicated, and finally the fisheries in the area are destroyed. Other countries, of course, add to the total loads. The short growing season characteristic of grain causes more losses of nutrients than occur from arable land, which is vegetated during autumn and winter. On farms with an

its ferro-alloys developed later. The proportions between accumulated and present annual quantities all turn out to be around 1%. Thus, reduction of emissions today has little immediate impact on the total load already emitted to the geobiosphere.

Chrome, as a key component in stainless steel and other new kinds of steel, has been singled out as a special case. Its use has increased very rapidly in the twentieth century. Because Sweden has no deposits worth mining, import and export volumes (Fig. 37.16) give a good picture of the total volume in circulation. As Fig. 37.17. shows, a quite successful reduction of emissions of chrome from production plants was

"industrial" production of pigs and poultry, the sown area is frequently too small for the large quantities of manure produced (Andersson 1986).

Phosphorus also leaks out from farmland to some extent, mainly through surface runoff. It is feasible to make retrospective budget calculations based on historical statistics, because phosphorus has a less complex pattern of circulation than nitrogen. Such a calculation, referring to a watershed in middle Sweden, indicates that around 1880 – when artificial fertilizers were not yet in general use – the land use caused a net loss of phosphorus amounting to about 1 kg/ha per year (Karlsson and Löwgren, 1990). The figure corresponds well to an estimate for the 1680s based on observations of lake sediments (Dearing et al. 1987). This obviously protracted net loss – which ends up on the bottom of lakes and seas – has continued during this century, but now so much fertilizer is imported from abroad that an annual net accumulation takes place in arable lands with an amount slightly larger than the earlier net loss.

Public awareness of eutrophication was first awakened not by farming but by the visible waste from towns and manufacturing industries. A debate about water pollution began around the turn of the century, but had little effect on political action. By 1930, for example, only five cities had sewage-treatment plants, and around 1940, only 10 more had acquired them. It became obvious, however, that the increased inflow of organic material was filling lakes with vegetation – causing fish to die out, swimming places to disappear, and bad odors to occur. Legislation was hesitantly initiated in 1942, and then was gradually strengthened. The 1960s, when suburbanization and house building reached a climax, was a favorable period also for the construction of sewage plants (Fig. 37.19). By 1985, 83% of the Swedish population was served by such plants.

Acidification of water and soils was the next major problem to attract attention. Acidification has been occurring since the Ice Age. The layer of soil is shallow and rests upon a polished bedrock that resists weathering and is deficient in lime. The natural process was very slow compared to present change. The oxides of sulfur and nitrogen, which are seen as major causes, emanate from both domestic and foreign sources. The "imported" pollution is now estimated to contribute more than half of the deposition. That the proportion is this high despite the considerable emissions from Swedish sources is due to the fact that perhaps two-thirds of the latter moves eastward.

Of Sweden's 85,000 large and middle-sized lakes, 18,000 are now classed as acidified. In half of them, the stock of fish has been negatively affected; 4,000 lakes show grave biological damage. Acidification is most advanced in the southwestern part of the country, where the highest annual precipitation falls.

The emerging chemical environment also has some paradoxical effects on plant life. This is most clearly seen in the case of forest growth. There is much anxiety about "forest death." Although Sweden has no large dying forest stands of the middle European type, individual trees are affected, and some zones show a higher frequency of damage than others, particularly locations downwind from polluting factories.

Yet never in history has there been such a large annual growth of forest as at present. This is due in part to the higher density of spruce (Tamm 1987), but the increased flow of nitrogen – quite apart from its role in the acidification process – probably also acts as a fertilizer. Some trees may indeed be forced to grow to death because other necessary nutrients are no longer able to match the intake of nitrogen. Because of acidification, leakage may be magnifying this imbalance by washing out minerals emanating from the weathering bedrock. The net result may, however, be an enrichment over the whole surface of our originally relatively poor soils.

Discussion

It is striking to note how consistently one type of process has occurred time and again over the period. Economic pressure, economic expectations, or perhaps pure imitation have led actors to continue a practice to the verge of its breakdown.

The mercantilistic period saw the overexploitation of charcoal and firewood forests in scattered localities around mines and ironworks. Overcutting and probably overgrazing during the eighteenth and nineteenth centuries transformed the deciduous forests of southwestern Sweden into heather-clad moors notorious for their poverty, until the beginning of the present century. During the nineteenth century, the unchecked cutting of forests led to a nationwide depletion of this resource before the movement for repair gained momentum around 1900. During the same time, the opening of a British market for oats resulted in three decades of specialization that ended suddenly in the economic crisis of the 1880s, leaving soils depleted. The century of drainage saw many local failures, but the enthusiasm for getting rid of water kept

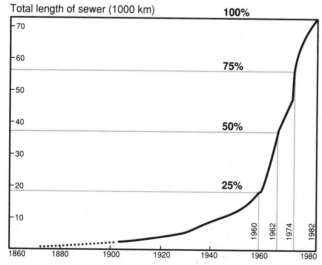

Figure 37.19 Total length of municipal sewers in Sweden for different years. The rapid growth in recent decades is partly due to the introduction of separate storm sewers. Also trenching costs were greatly reduced when excavators came into use around 1950. Source: Bäckman 1984.

its grasp on most minds until World War II. Finally, in the past four decades, the strong belief in endless growth has been shaken by the surfacing of unexpected problems.

Nevertheless, there are grounds to conclude that before 1950 the biological resources were never misused beyond repair. The situation now may be more difficult to escape than any earlier one because no longer is any outside realm uninvolved.

Certain changes have occurred that are definitely irreversible, foremost among them the radical remodeling of water flows and the depletion of mineral resources. Other changes are of a more oscillatory nature. Every corner of the rural seventeenth century landscape was stamped by multiple use; the transition from tillage to deep forest was gradual. Beginning a century ago, and in particular after 1950, the key concept became functional specialization. Today, sharp boundaries separate one-sided farming from one-sided forestry. The former displays large, smooth fields and the latter, stands of equal age. Conditions for wild plants and animals have been transformed. The floral splendor of park meadows and weedy fields has vanished. The great beasts of prey have been reduced to a few survivors in the mountains, but elk and roe are more common now than ever before. When cattle and sheep finally were driven out of the woods, foresters found to their surprise that other grass- and leaf-eaters replaced them.

The observed changes are closely related to the expansion of mobility. The low mobility of goods, people, and messages until 1800 affected every aspect of the old order. Through-going roads were few and carts were unsuited to heavy loads. Weighty goods had to be carried out on snow and ice during the winter. The transportation revolution of the nineteenth century was an extension toward the European periphery of earlier developments in the center. Steamboats were introduced and a few canals constructed, but most projects were not realized before the beginning of the railway era in the 1850s. Railways and draft animals on gradually improved gravel roads came to dominate land transportation up to World War II. After that, motorism took over with an almost explosive speed.

The specialization we have witnessed is conditioned upon inputs from distant sources and outputs to distant markets. The new range of circulation of all kinds has resulted in new types of conflicts; there are probably many more sources of conflicts than before, because interests overlap much more in space. We see in part the consequences of a real shortage of elbow-room, in part divergences in values between groups.

The old order generated conflicts mainly between neighbors. Conflicts arose along boundaries at the level of both farms and states. These conflicts have by no means disappeared, but in addition one now sees wide-ranging international conflicts over atmospheric pollution and safety standards. The use of chemical substances in farming, forestry, and industry threatens fisheries along the coasts and the quality of waters reserved for human consumption.

As long as circulation was locally contained, actors in the landscape could easily see how events held together, even if deeper scientific understanding was limited. Today, corresponding relationships are much less evident; we no longer know who produced our food or where. The traditional division of space into bounded domains, from the property unit to the state, was an obviously rational form of organization in a society with low mobility. Apart from minor adjustments of scale, the old principles of territorial competence have persisted. This situation makes it easy for environmental management to set off bounded nature reserves and to try to delimit the territorial competence of classes of actors in the landscape. The system is very weak, however, in its ability to monitor and control flows from beginning to end. This is made clear by the difficulties that exist in arranging cascading systems, the recycling of material in industry, or workable systems of water management for river basins. The whole area seems to be ripe for innovative thinking.

Acknowledgments

The many helpful comments and suggestions from colleagues are gratefully acknowledged. Financial support was provided by the Bank of Sweden Tercentenary Foundation.

References

Anderberg, S., B. Bergbäck, and U. Lohm. 1989. Flow and distribution of chromium in the Swedish environment: A new approach to studying environmental pollution. *Ambio* 18:216–20.

Andersson, R. 1982. Växtnäringsförluster från åker och skog. *Vatten* 38: 205–25.

———. 1986. *Förluster av kväve och fosfor från åkermark i Sverige.* Sveriges Lantbruksuniversitet, Uppsala.

Arpi, G., M. Nordquist, and L. Nordström. 1959. *Sveriges skogar under 100 år.* Parts I and II. Stockholm.

Bäckman, H. 1984. Avloppsledningar i svenska tätorter. En översiktlig historik. *Vatten* 40:177–87.

Blågul miljö. 1982. Miljödatanämnden, Stockholm.

Dearing, J. A., H. Håkansson, B. Liedberg-Jönsson, A. Persson, S. Skansjö, D. Widholm, and F. El-Daoushy. 1987. Lake sediments used to quantify the erosional response to land use change in southern Sweden. *Oikos* 50:60–78.

Fridlizius, G. 1957. Swedish corn export in the free trade area: Patterns in the oats trade, 1850–1880. *Samhällsvetenskapliga studier* 14, Lund.

Gerger, T. 1984. *Patterns of Jobs and Geographic Mobility.* Stockholm: Almquist and Wiksell International.

Göransson, G. 1978. Östergärda – är det sårbart? *Det sårbara samhället,* 2. Sekretariatet för framtidsstudier, Stockholm.

Hannerberg, D. 1971. *Svenskt agrarsamhälle under 1200 år. Gård och åker. Skörd och boskap.* Stockholm.

Heckscher, E. 1941. *Svenskt arbete och liv. Från medeltiden till nutiden.* Stockholm: Bonnier.

Hyltén-Cavallius, G. O. 1868. *Wärend och Wirdarne.* Ett försök i Svensk Ethnologi, Stockholm.

Jonasson, O., E. Höijer, and T. Björkman. 1937. *Jordbruksatlas över Sverige.* Stockholm.

Karlsson, G., and M. Löwgren. 1990. Phosphorus transport as controlled by large-scale land use changes. *Acta Agr. Scand.* 40: 149–62.

Larsson, L. J. 1980. Svedjebruket i Småland. *Kronobergsboken* 1979, 80:65–77. Växjö.

Laurell, P. 1886. Sjöarna Hjelmarens och Qvismarens sänkning. *Ymer* 6:165–86.

Lindberg, A. 1964. Salpeterframställningen in Sverige fram till 1642. *Ymer* 84:267–82.

Lindqvist, S. 1984. Naturresurser och teknik. Energiteknisk debatt i Sverige under 1700-talet. In *Paradiset och vildmarken*, ed. T. Frängsmyr, 82–108. Stockholm.

Ljungberg, K. 1874. Om skogssköfvlingen i Sverige. Stockholm.

Malmström, C. 1951. Om den svenska markens utnyttjande för bete, åker, äng och skog genom tiderna och orsakerna till rörligheten i utnyttjandet. *Kungl. Lantbruksakademiens Tidskr.* 90:292–314.

Mattsson, R. 1985. Jordbrukets utveckling i Sverige. *Aktuellt från lantbruksuniversitetet* 344. Uppsala.

Nelson, C. M., and I. Svanberg. 1987. Lichens as food: Historical perspectives on food propaganda. *Svenska Linnésällskapets Årsskrift*, 1986–87, 37–51. Uppsala.

Nelson, H. 1913. En bergslagbygd. En historiskt-geografisk öfverblick. *Ymer* 33:278–344.

Nordström, O. 1952. *Relationer mellan bruk och omland i östra Småland 1750–1900*. Lund.

Persson, T., and U. Lohm. 1977. Energetical significance of the annelids and arthropods in a Swedish grassland soil. *Ecological Bulletins* 23.

Pleijel, H., B. Wastenson, and L. Wastenson. 1987. *Luftföroreningar och naturmiljö i Göteborgs och Bohus län, Älvsborgs län*. Göteborg.

Renberg, I., and M. Wik. 1985. Carbonaceous particles in lake sediments: Pollutants from fossil fuel combustion. *Ambio* 14:161–63.

Romell, L. G. 1947. Det gamla Gotland. *Ymer* 67:108–26.

Rönnby, E. 1942. Orsakerna till sänkningen av sjöarna Hjälmaren och Kvismaren – jordbrukets inriktning och omdaning. *Svensk Geografisk Årsbok* 18:190–96.

Schager, N. 1909. De sydsvenska ljunghedarna. *Ymer* 29:309–35.

Stridsberg, E. and L. Mattsson. 1980. *Skogen genom tiderna*. Helsingborg.

Södermark, B. 1981. Gruvindustrins avfallsproblem. *Statens Naturvårdsverk PM*. Stockholm.

Statens offentliga utredningar 1976:28. *Vattenkraft och miljö 3*. Stockholm.

Stjernquist, P. 1973. *Laws in the Forests. A Study of Public Direction of Swedish Private Forestry*. Lund.

———. 1983. Från enskild mot offentlig förvaltning i skogspolitiken. *Statsvetenskaplig tidskrift* 86:297–307.

Tamm, C. O. 1987. Tveksamt att använda ordet skogsdöd. *Svenska Dagbladet 16/7 1987*.

Wester, E. 1960. Några skånska byar enligt lantmäterikartorna. *Svensk Geografisk Årsbok* 36:162–80.

Wieslander, G. 1936. Skogsbristen i Sverige under 1600 – och 1700-talen. *Svenska skogsvårdsföreningens tidskrift* 34:593–663.

Zackrisson, O. 1977. Influence of forest fires on the north Swedish boreal forest. *Oikos* 29:22–32.

38

The Hudson-Raritan Basin

JOEL A. TARR   ROBERT U. AYRES

During the past three centuries, the Hudson River Basin and the Hudson-Raritan estuary have experienced many alterations as human settlement and development have vastly increased. Changes have included the reshaping of the face of the landscape through such activities as the removal of forests, the damming and dredging of rivers, the filling of wetlands, and the construction of railroad lines, highways, bridges, and other structures. Less visible, but at least as significant, have been the pollution flows generated by urbanization and industrialization. This chapter describes some of these changes for the period from 1700 to 1980, focusing on emissions into the estuarine environment resulting from the major pollution-generating human activities.

The Region

The study area (Fig. 38.1) covers 32,341 km^2, including 21 counties in New York and 10 in New Jersey. The Hudson, Raritan, and Passaic rivers flow into the Hudson-Raritan estuary, one of the most important in the eastern coast of North America. Estuaries are open bays, back bays, and parts of river systems in which saline waters from the ocean mix with fresh waters from the land and where water levels are affected by oceanic tides.

The section of the Hudson under study stretches 248 km from Manhattan to Troy, New York, and is known as the Lower Hudson. The Federal Dam at Troy, located less than 3 km downstream of the confluence of the Mohawk and Hudson rivers, is the head of tidewater where tidal influence ends. From Manhattan to Troy, the river's surface elevation does not drop, and a powerful flood tide keeps a substantial stretch of the river saline or brackish. Because the river has no gravity flow below its confluence with the Mohawk River at Troy, it has not built up a floodplain. The river discharges into the Upper New York Bay and subsequently through the Verrazano Narrows into Lower New York Bay, which is an arm of the Atlantic Ocean. The drainage area encompassed by this stretch of the river is approximately 12,800 km^2.

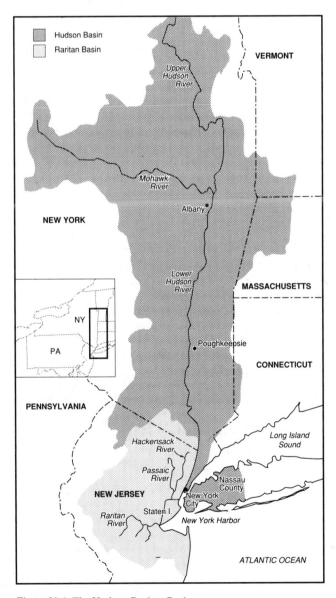

Figure 38.1 The Hudson-Raritan Basin.

The Raritan River, the second largest in New Jersey, is formed by the junction of the North and South branches and flows southeasterly to Raritan Bay. It is a tidal river to a point about 6.5 km above the city of New Brunswick. The drainage area of the entire river system is 2,862 km². The upper part of the drainage system is located in a hilly area, but the terrain flattens out toward the Raritan Bay, with the river cutting through low and marshy land (Rudolfs and Heukelekian 1942).

The Passaic River flows approximately 145 km from Mendham, New Jersey, northeast and finally south into Newark Bay. The drainage basin covers 2,453 km², including large portions of 11 New Jersey counties and a portion of southern New York. A dam constructed at Passaic in order to generate waterpower marks the upper limit of tidewater. From approximately 5 km below the dam, the river begins to flow through an open plain. Much of this area consists of wetlands, including the Newark meadows near the mouth of the river at Newark Bay and the Hackensack meadowlands between the Passaic and the Hackensack rivers (Brydon 1974).

The locations of the two major metropolitan complexes in the region today, both intimately related to the river systems, have been the sites of the region's major cities since the late eighteenth century. The larger is known as the New York Metropolitan Zone. Historically, the most extensive development in the Zone has been in sections of New York and New Jersey adjacent to the Port of New York (Fig. 38.2). The port area includes five main divisions: the Lower Bay, the Narrows, the Upper Bay, the Hudson River, and the East River. The bay complex forms part of one of the world's busiest seaports, and the great New York metropolitan area has developed in the flat areas of the central plain around it, as urban uses have steadily encroached upon surrounding wetlands and upon lands formerly devoted to agricultural uses (Carey 1976). The second urban complex in the region is the Upper Hudson Metropolitan Zone, focused on the urban centers of Albany, Schenectady, and Troy, around the confluence of the Hudson and Mohawk rivers. The growth of this urban cluster also has historically been strongly related to transportation and trade. Here, the Hudson itself, the Erie Canal, the New York State Barge Canal, the various railroads constructed over time, and the New York State Thruway have successively played critical roles (Richardson and Tauber 1979).

From a geomorphic and historical perspective, the Hudson River Basin has been of particular importance because it provides a convenient lowland route between the densely settled New York City area and the country's interior. It is composed primarily of soft sedimentary rocks and overlying glacial deposits that have been eroded to produce several different types of terrain. Forest originally covered nearly the entire basin's land area. Much of it was cleared for farmland and lumber in the nineteenth century, but more recent decades have seen forested land increase. The forests of the

Figure 38.2 New York Metropolitan Zone counties.

region are primarily oak, which occupies the warmer areas and thinner soils, and northern hardwoods, which flourish in deeper soils but also in somewhat cooler highlands (Cronon 1983).

Although the greatest amount of transformation occurred after European settlement, the previous human inhabitants, the Amerindians, also shaped the environment. Before Europeans arrived in the Hudson-Raritan Basin in the seventeenth century, an Algonquin and Iroquoian population of approximately 40,000–60,000 had long resided there. Primarily agriculturists by the time of European arrival, they used a slash-and-burn method to clear the forest, primarily to grow maize (corn). Small village and planting sites were subjected to intense human use for agriculture, waste disposal, and firewood gathering. By moving their habitat according to the seasons, tribes were able to hold their impact on the ecosystem to a minimum. Selective burning created a mosaic forest environment in many different stages of succession (Cronon 1983).

Social Processes and Changes

The historical trends in pollution flows, as well as in other environmental transformations, in the Hudson-Raritan Basin reflect changing patterns of human activity. Of particular importance have been the related processes of population concentration and deconcentration and the location of economic activities.

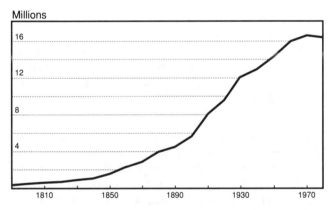

Figure 38.3 Population of the Hudson-Raritan region, 1790–1980.

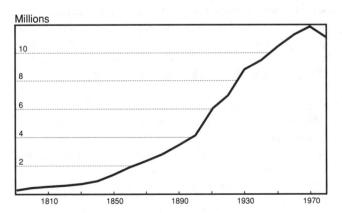

Figure 38.4 Population of the New York Metropolitan Zone, 1790–1980.

Population History

Although the Hudson-Raritan region had extensive agricultural development in the nineteenth century, its population history is primarily the story of urban growth. Urban sites were present from the beginning of European settlement, but it was the growth of port activity and the creation of transportation links with the western hinterland that accelerated urbanization in the first half of the nineteenth century (Lampard 1986). The largest of the urban complexes today, the New York Metropolitan Zone, encompasses a 21-county area in New York and New Jersey. The second complex, the Upper Hudson Metropolitan Zone, encompasses a three-county area.[1] The growth of both of these urban clusters has been related historically to transportation and trade, but site advantages and railroad links caused New York to outstrip the Upper Hudson Zone in growth rapidly in the early nineteenth century (Carey 1976; Pred 1966; Richardson and Tauber 1979).

Originally, urban population was densely concentrated, with cities occupying only a small amount of the land area of most counties. Transportation limitations restricted cities to walking distances until about the middle of the nineteenth century, when a series of innovations – omnibuses, horsecars, and commuter railroads – permitted them to grow far beyond their original cores (Jackson 1985). Since the late nineteenth century, further transportation innovations – electric streetcars, rapid transit, and the automobile – have facilitated urban spread. In the twentieth century, metropolitan growth has been accompanied by movement from the urban core, by declines in population densities, and by a flattening of the density curve between central and outlying areas as population moved toward an ever-receding urban periphery (Berry 1976). The abrupt transitions between "city" and "country" that characterized eighteenth- and nineteenth-century landscapes were replaced by more gradual population and development slopes, as a symbiosis of urban and rural land uses occurred. Thus, the proportion of the land devoted to urban uses (defined as residential, commerical, industrial, institutional, and transportation) has steadily increased even though urban densities have declined. Peripheral urbanization, however, often advanced in hop-scotch fashion ("scatteration of uses") rather than like a wave (Richardson and Tauber 1979). This intermingling of urban and rural occurred in a context of declining agricultural land use, and farming decreased in importance in the region (Gottmann 1961).

These population trends can be explored in more detail by dividing available census data into three periods: 1790–1880, 1880–1940, and 1940–1980 (Figs. 38.3 and 38.4). Within these periods, overall trends of growth or decline have differed sharply within the spatial zones of the region. To comprehend better these changes in the most urbanized area, the 21 counties in the New York Metropolitan Zone have been divided into a core and inner and outer rings.[2] Between 1790 and 1880, a period of agricultural expansion as well as the growth of industrial cities, the total population of the Hudson-Raritan region grew from 419,538 to 4,031,765, with percentage increases highest in the 1840s, the 1850s, and the 1870s. By 1880, almost 85% of the region's population lived in the New York Metropolitan Zone, with another 7% in the Upper Hudson Metropolitan Zone. In the New York Metropolitan Zone, the core counties – New York (Manhattan), Hudson, Kings, Queens, and Westchester – increased their population from 110,544 to 2,193,300, as key cities developed very high densities.[3] In 1800, the core contained 55.2% of the zone's population; in 1860, it contained 72.4%; and in 1880, 66.2%. The inner-ring counties of Bergen, Essex, Passaic, and Union in New Jersey, and Richmond and Nassau in New York, grew especially rapidly after 1850, and by 1880 the inner ring's percentage of the zone had reached 21.8%. Many of these counties were in New Jersey and included growing industrial cities such as Newark, Paterson, Passaic, and Elizabeth. The much more modest growth of the outer-ring counties of Rockland, Orange, Putnam, Dutchess, and Suffolk in New York and Middlesex, Morris, Monmouth, and Somerset in New Jersey reflected their continued rural and agricultural nature.[4] The outer ring's share of the population of the New York Metropolitan Zone dropped steadily from 23.8% in 1800 to 11.8% in 1880, as the core and the inner ring became more urbanized.

Between 1880 and 1940, the total population of the Hudson-Raritan region grew from 4,031,765 to 12,965,642, with the share of the New York Metropolitan Zone increasing to almost 92%, while that of the Upper Hudson Metropolitan Zone decreased to 3.6%. Although there was increased suburbanization in the New York Metropolitan Zone, most of the area's population remained concentrated in New York City and surrounding urban centers such as Yonkers, or Jersey City and Newark in New Jersey. Central cities actually absorbed more than half the basin's increase in urban population between 1920 and 1940. The core and the outer-ring counties lost some of their share of the zone's population by the end of the period, while the inner-ring counties increased their share.[5] New York City itself grew from 1,911,698 to 7,454,995, largely by consolidating with adjacent areas such as Brooklyn and Queens. After 1920, central city densities began to decline, whereas those in more outlying boroughs, such as Queens, increased sharply, as rapid transit lines and the automobile provided improved access. Densities also increased in outer-ring counties such as Nassau on Long Island and Bergen in New Jersey, but from a much smaller base, and they did not experience explosive growth until after World War II.

By 1980, the total population of the Hudson-Raritan region had reached 17,506,382. The New York Metropolitan Zone grew to 14,973,972 but shrank to 85.5% of the region's population, while the Upper Hudson Zone increased to 587,038, or 3.8%. The New York Metropolitan Zone experienced dramatic shifts in population between cities and suburbs and rural areas. Suburban areas grew rapidly, while cities in both the core and the inner ring of counties stagnated, and after 1960, actually lost population. The core counties and especially their central cities suffered the heaviest losses. By 1960, the core's share of the Zone's population had dropped to 55.1%, and by 1980 to 48.4%. New York City and other older cities such as Jersey City and Hoboken suffered a net population loss. The inner-ring

counties grew in the immediate postwar decades, increasing their share of the Zone's population to 33.4%, as counties such as Essex and Union in New Jersey and Nassau on Long Island rapidly suburbanized. Older New Jersey industrial cities like Newark and Passaic showed either losses or no change. From 1960 to 1980, population growth in the inner-ring counties nearly stopped, and population share remained steady, as land became fully developed. The major growth in the Zone occurred in the outer ring of counties, where population advanced to 2,549,630; by 1960 the outer ring's share had increased to 11.5%, and by 1980 it was over 17%. Driving the peripheral movement was a preference for low-density living, increased automobile ownership, new expressways and interstate highway systems, and the availability of mortgages at affordable rates with help from the Federal Housing Administration and the Veterans Administration (Jackson 1985).

In the decade 1970–1980, the Hudson-Raritan region underwent the first population loss in its history, declining from 17,560,739 to 17,506,582. Urbanized land, however, increased from 6,595 to 7,685 km^2 as peripheral growth continued into the non-Metropolitan Zone rural counties and a nonfarm population of long-distance commuters developed. The decentralization of population out of central cities and the older areas of the metropolitan zones ("counterurbanization") had become the dominant force shaping the region's settlement pattern (Berry 1976).

Economic Development

The region has long been a preeminent economic center in the United States and indeed in the world, but the specific activities carried on within it have varied significantly over time with changing circumstances and factors of economic location.

Early Development Seventeenth- and eighteenth-century settlement tended to be slow, and usually close to the riverbanks. Except for the eastern bank of the Hudson, the hill country of the region remained almost unbroken forest at the time of the American Revolution (1776–1783). Well into the nineteenth century, much of the land in the Hudson River Valley lay in large estates established during the colonial period. These estates were either held for speculation or rented to tenants. After independence, however, some of the large estates were broken up, and small farmers became more numerous, while tenant farmers worked the land on the remaining large estates. The forests were rapidly cleared, and the land was cropped until exhausted, with the principles of rotation and fertilizer use ignored (Ellis et al. 1967).

In the years after the Revolution, settlement and agriculture spread rapidly through the bottomlands of the Hudson and Mohawk river valleys, as transportation improvements and urban growth, especially after 1820, created commercial opportunities. Canals and railroads, however, also exposed New York farmers to competition from western produce. New York shifted away from wheat and developed as an important center for specialized products such as vegetables, wool, and dairy products (Ellis et al. 1967). Although commercial opportunities often produced exploitative cropping practices, the rise of an urban market for garden and dairy products spurred farmers to improve their methods by adopting fertilizers, rotating crops, and following selective breeding practices.

From before the Revolution through the 1820s, manufacturing in the Hudson-Raritan counties was largely decentralized. The main elements were the gristmill, the sawmill, and the country forge, which used the waterpower supplied by the area's abundant streams and served the surrounding region. By 1820, consolidation had replaced the proliferation of tiny gristmills and small tanneries with a few large mills near major waterfalls (Ellis et al. 1967). Within the cities themselves, craftsmen and artisans worked in relatively small shops and produced the preponderance of goods, although larger operations were emerging in such industries as tanning, shipbuilding, sugar refining, printing, and construction (Wilentz 1984).

Between 1825 and 1850, New York became the nation's leading manufacturing state, and New York City, the most productive manufacturing city, having overtaken Philadelphia. Transportation improvements, including the opening of the Erie Canal (1825), the construction of other canals, and the building of railroads, connected the city to a growing urban network. They strengthened the Hudson-Mohawk axis of traffic and development, and made New York the main port for export of grain and other agricultural products from the Midwest to Europe. Railroad construction began after 1836, and by 1855 provided a direct link between Lake Erie and New York City as well as joining other cities (Lampard 1986). Manufacturing increasingly clustered at urban locations at important canal and railroad nodes, and the number of small mills scattered at rural locations diminished yearly (Meinig 1966a; Meinig 1966b).

Until after the Civil War, however, large factories and manufacturing establishments, with or without mechanical power, were highly unusual. The light handicraft industries, especially in building and in consumer finishing trade, remained the most important sectors of the economy. Heavier industry was concentrated in the areas of iron casting and forging, machine and toolmaking, brewing, distilling, sugar refining, and manufactured gas production (Chandler 1977; Spann 1981; Wilentz 1984). The advent of steam liberated mechanical production from major sites of waterpower, although streams remained essential for the disposal of wastes in many industries.

Economy from 1860 to 1940 In the decades after the Civil War, the regional economy completed its transition from an agricultural and commercial-mercantile base to an industrial-urban one. Between 1850 and 1900, the amount of farmland in the region stayed steady at about 2.43 million ha. Lumbering was another significant activity in the rural parts of the region. During the latter part of the nineteenth century, New York stood among the nation's first 10 lumber producers. Pine, spruce, and hemlock from "virgin" stands were most frequently harvested. The state was also an important producer of wood pulp, providing about 30% of the national total at this time (Thompson 1966; Williams 1982).

In the years after 1900, land in farms steadily diminished. The unprofitability of farming in areas of poor soil, compared with more fertile regions whose products were readily exported was the prime reason, but the spread of urbanization due to new modes of transportation, especially the automobile, also played a role (Meinig 1977). From 1900 to 1920, over 400,000 ha of farmland disappeared. Another 400,000 ha were lost in the 1920s, and 200,000 from 1930 to 1949, leaving a little over 1.2 million ha in farmland in 1950.

Manufacturing output grew more rapidly than did urban population, as innovation interacted with growing demand. Significant shifts occurred in the character of the region's production. The industries that declined after 1880 were those in which the costs of moving raw materials to plant and/or finished product to market were of prime importance. These years saw the decline of transportation-sensitive industries such as iron and steel, lumber, glass, pottery, and locomotive manufacture, which reduced their total transportation costs by locating closer to sources of materials (Lichtenberg 1960). For instance, the steel industry moved west to Pittsburgh (near supplies of bituminous coal) and beyond, and the older charcoal and anthracite-based iron-smelting operations declined in importance. Simultaneously, the New York Metropolitan Zone was becoming the nation's center for many industries for which such transportation costs were relatively less important.

Metal production was extremely important in the Zone from 1880 through 1922, but the role of nonferrous metals – especially copper and brass – increased dramatically as compared to the iron-steel segment. In 1880, New York City, Brooklyn, Jersey City, and Newark had 483 firms producing foundry and machine-shop products, with almost 16,000 workers, making it by far the nation's largest concentration of metal-working activity (Bureau of the Census 1880). Between 1900 and 1922, the number of metal-products plants in the region increased from 3,216 to 9,426, or by 192.8%, and the number of employees increased from 150,461 to 269,079, or a rise of 78.8%. In 1922, there were 1,283 machinery firms in the Zone, with 83,508 employees (Lanfear 1928). During this period, the region shifted from the manufacture of predominantly heavy metal products such as castings, rails, and girders to light metal products. Many of the plants producing heavy products moved out of Lower Manhattan, some of them out of the Basin.

In the late nineteenth century, the New York Metropolitan Zone became an important center for copper refining by the "fire" and electrolytic process, with some associated smelting of imported ores from Mexico and South America. Copper refining centered in New York because of the availability of electric power and the proximity of the copper-consuming electrical manufacturing industry (Navin 1978; Trescott 1981). By 1918, 63% of U.S. copper refinery output came from the New York region. Although the percentage dropped after this date, as late as 1970, the Zone still accounted for 25% of U.S. copper refining (Lanfear 1928; Navin 1978; U.S.

Bureau of Mines 1975). Copper smelting, as compared to refining, was relatively limited in the region.

A second major industry that centered in the New York Metropolitan Zone beginning in the 1890s was inorganic chemicals. By the turn of the century, the region had become the nation's largest chemical producer. Again, New York was favored partly because of the availability of electric power and partly because of access to markets, including exports. In 1900, there were 660 "chemical plants" in the New York metropolitan area; by 1922, the number had increased to 1,351, and between 15% and 20% of the nation's chemical production and of the chemical industry work force was located in the New York Metropolitan Zone (Newcomer 1928). An important related activity involved the production of paints, dyes, inks, and varnishes. The availability of petroleum-based solvents such as benzene and naphtha from the large New Jersey refineries was a factor. Pigments for paints also provided early markets for companies manufacturing inorganic chemicals from copper, chromium, lead, and zinc. Total employment in this manufacturing sector nearly doubled between 1900 and 1922, increasing from approximately 6,000 to 12,000 workers (Newcomer 1928).

Beginning in the 1870s, petroleum refining became one of the Zone's fastest-growing industries. The first pipeline from the Pennsylvania fields was completed in 1879. Standard Oil of New Jersey centralized its refinery activities in Bayonne, to serve both the New York market and the even larger export market for illuminating oils. By 1920, 12 major refineries were located there, making the New York Metropolitan Zone the world's largest refining center. Most of the oil processed came from wells in western Pennsylvania; as the center of petroleum production moved to Texas after 1900, the refineries depended more on tankers. After 1930, the New York area refineries expanded, but no new ones were built, and the zone accounted for a steadily declining fraction of the nation's capacity (Larson, Knowlton, and Popple 1971).

Recent Decades (1940–1980)   In the postwar decades, rapid suburbanization, as well as the unprofitability of farming, drove total farm area to even lower levels. In the five-year period from 1949 to 1954, land was removed from farming at twice the rate of the previous 20-year period (Gottmann 1961). By 1969, only 726,000 ha were in farmland, with little change in the next decade, as the proportion of forestland greatly increased (Richardson and Tauber 1979). By the 1970s, high-value commercial crops such as dairy, fruit, and vegetables dominated Hudson Valley production, especially in lowland areas. Agricultural area was in decline, though production per unit area and per farm was increasing. Today, in spite of relatively dense settlement, forests again cover large areas of the Hudson-Raritan region, and more trees exist in the area than did 50 years ago. Forest resources, however, are declining in quality. Much of the woodland exists largely for amenity purposes in spread suburbs and parks rather than for productive purposes (Gottmann 1961; Richardson and Tauber 1979).

Between 1947 and 1977, the total number of manufacturing jobs in the Hudson-Raritan counties dropped from 1,750,000

to 1,452,700. The largest growth sectors in the region were in services rather than in manufacturing. By 1982, approximately one-fifth of the jobs in the New York region were goods-producing, with 79% in the service and information-producing sectors (Regional Plan Association 1986). The continuing decline in manufacturing was graphically illustrated in chemicals and fabricated metals, traditionally two of the region's strongest industries. Employment in chemicals within New Jersey and New York, almost all of it located within the Zone, dropped from approximately 95,000 in 1977 to about 84,000 in 1985; in fabricated metals, from 58,000 to 50,000 in the same period (U.S. Bureau of the Census 1985). Within the manufacturing sector, there was a large degree of change during these years. The New York Metropolitan Zone saw a continuation of trends begun earlier in the century, as heavy industry moved west of the Alleghenies and out of the region, while newer industries continued to shift toward the region's periphery. New plant construction took place overwhelmingly in the outer ring of counties (Hoover and Vernon 1959; Lampard 1986). Here, cheap land and access to freeways rather than to railways and harbors, as earlier, were the dominant factors in location.

Pollution Flows and Organic Wastes

Until the late nineteenth century, most studies of environmental conditions in the cities of the region focused on the land and the waterfront rather than on the water itself, except in the case of obvious nuisances. Sanitary conditions and their supposed relationship to the public health rather than water quality per se were the concern of investigators (Citizens' Association of New York 1866; Duffy 1974). Serious pollution problems were created by such nuisance trades as slaughterhouses, rendering factories, and gasworks, and municipal ordinances often relegated these industries to fringe locations, including riverbank sites. Many accounts, however, record a great abundance of fin- and shellfish in the waters of the estuary throughout the century, suggesting that pollution, at least in the middle decades, had only a limited effect on water quality in the rivers and bays (Esser 1982; Franz 1982).

In the late nineteenth century, municipalities invested heavily in sewage works for the rapid and systematic removal of sanitary and storm-water wastes. These systems commonly discharged raw sewage into the rivers and the bays, greatly increasing their pollution and raising concern over threats to the public health, although disposal practices were justified at the time by the belief that wastes were purified by running water. Growing industrial effluent added to the problems. The legal response to water pollution, however, was minimal. Two laws – one federal and one state – were passed in the late nineteenth century, which addressed navigation impediments and the injurious effects of industrial wastes on shellfish (Klawonn 1977; Mersereau 1887).

By the beginning of the twentieth century, population growth accompanied by the expansion of municipal sewerage systems that discharged raw sewage into waterways had increased the waste load carried by the Basin's rivers and the estuary. The growth of industry, especially of metallurgical and chemical manufacturing that produced oxygen-consuming and toxic wastes, increased the pollution. Dilution in the rivers and bays and tidal action were relied upon to disperse the sewage. As loads increased, however, water quality deteriorated, as reflected in terms of visible offense and bacterial and chemical measures. Trends in pollution during this century are best followed through the major water-quality surveys undertaken by various government agencies; they are the principal sources drawn upon in the following discussion, and are supplemented by the results of materials-balance calculations.

In 1902, the U.S. Geological Survey conducted the first major examination of sewage pollution in the major rivers of the Hudson-Raritan Basin. The study did not examine conditions in the New York, Raritan, or Newark bays per se, but it is important for the picture that it supplies of river pollution at the turn of the century. Although specific local nuisances existed in the Hudson below the larger cities such as Albany and Poughkeepsie, the report found that the river's capacity for dilution sufficed to prevent "material damage" that would require sewage treatment. Conditions in the Raritan River were found to be similar, with pollution noted in only a limited area about the mouth of the stream. Water in many of the Raritan's tributaries was potable without treatment and "fisheries have been preserved intact." Conditions had deteriorated most in the Passaic, the smallest of the three rivers, which was badly polluted by both sewage and industrial wastes. Fishing had been destroyed in the lower river, the water was not potable, the natural-ice industry had been damaged, and the water was unsuitable for industrial purposes (Leighton 1902).

Concern over the increasing pollution of New York harbor led to a series of detailed pollution studies in the decades before World War I. The Metropolitan Sewage Commission (MSC) (1907–1914) produced the most intensive and thorough examination of the estuary conducted during the first half of the twentieth century. The MSC found that while the Lower Bay was not "badly polluted by sewage," the Upper Bay was, with evidence of floating sewage solids, large areas of greasy sleek, and turbid water conditions. The lower Hudson above New York City absorbed sewage mostly from Manhattan and was not visibly polluted. In contrast, the East and Harlem rivers were turbid, filled with floating sewage solids, and foul-smelling. The waters of Newark Bay were especially turbid and brown, with oil slicks and sewage pollution near the mouths of the Passaic and Hackensack rivers. Studies of bacteria revealed that the Upper Bay, the Harlem River, and the Passaic River were the most polluted. According to one recent investigator, the areas examined by the MSC that would not have met "present-day" (1981) standards for dissolved oxygen for substantial periods were the Upper New York Bay, the Passaic River, and the East River below Hell's Gate (Mytelka et al. 1981).

Under its mandate from the Oil Pollution Act of 1924, the U.S. Army Corps of Engineers conducted an intensive but unpublished investigation of pollution conditions in the Hudson River Basin and estuary. The report noted that since the investigations of the MSC, almost no "corrective meas-

ures" had been carried out, and that conditions had accordingly deteriorated. Pollution was now driving the fishing industry from the waters near New York City, and oyster culture was rapidly declining. The dissolved oxygen (DO) average in the harbor had declined from 62% in 1911 to 43% in 1925, and the 130-km^2 area between the Narrows, Spuyten Duyvil, and Throgs Neck did not contain "enough oxygen during one-third of the year to permit active fish to live, and the remainder of the time it is impossible for even sluggish varieties to thrive." The amount of raw sewage discharged in the New York metropolitan area had increased from 2,353 mld (million liters per day) in 1910 to 2,797 mld in 1920, emptied through 375 outlets. The East River received half of the sewage, the Hudson River 20%, and the Harlem River and Upper Bay about 10% each, while the remaining 10% was discharged into smaller waterways.

Industries also discharged some 183.5 mld of trade wastes into the district waters in 1920; most came from factories located in a narrow strip along the waterfront. Laundering, cleaning, and dyeing establishments produced the largest group of wastes, consisting of soap, soda, bleach, inorganic acids and bases, and organic dyes, as well as the filth removed from textiles and clothes. The Corps noted that oil pollution was widespread, stemming from shipping, from industrial processes, and from the sewers. Intermittent patches of oil were always visible in the river and the harbor, though the report concluded that oil pollution had been considerably reduced between 1922 and 1925, suggesting the severity of the problem before then. Problems of gas-manufacturing wastes were highlighted in the Corps report, and had been an object of particular concern in both New York and New Jersey. In 1908, for instance, the New Jersey State Sewerage Commission sponsored an investigation into gas-house pollution that noted the existence of over 50 gasworks in New Jersey alone, which produced highly toxic wastes and created many nuisances (Whipple 1908).

The 10 years from the mid-1920s through the mid-1930s saw no major pollution investigations in the New York estuary comparable to those of the MSC or the Corps of Engineers, although there were some smaller-scale inquiries. Various New York City departments monitored chemical, bacterial, and oxygen water-quality indicators, the New York Department of Conservation investigated pollution conditions in the Upper Hudson, and several New Jersey groups explored the deterioration of the Raritan River and the Raritan Bay (Mytelka et al. 1981; New York State Department of Health 1925; 1926; 1929; Remington, Vosbury, and Goff 1930). All reported general environmental deterioration since earlier in the century. Two major technological improvements made during this decade, the Bronx Valley Sewer and the Passaic Valley Trunk Sewer (which provided primary treatment to its discharges), threatened to pollute the harbor further. New York City unsuccessfully attempted to block their construction in the courts on these grounds (New Jersey Passaic Valley Sewerage Commissioners 1926; New York City Sanitation Department 1931).

During the 1930s, due in large part to funding supplied by public works programs of the federal government, a number of sewage-treatment plants were constructed in cities of the river basins and estuary (National Resources Committee 1936). The most important of these were in New York City. In 1939, in the Hudson River Valley (Hudson and Mohawk rivers), the sewage of 561,575 people was treated, while a population of 287,277 discharged raw sewage into the rivers. Of the 32 treatment plants in operation, 25 were constructed during the years from 1930 to 1939 (New York State Legislature 1939). In addition, a number of treatment plants were built along the Raritan River in New Jersey, and the capacity of the primary treatment plant of the Passaic Valley Sewerage Commission was enlarged (Rudolfs and Heukelekian 1942).

In 1936, New York and New Jersey formed the Interstate Sanitation Commission for the purpose of abating existing and controlling future pollution in the tidal waters of the metropolitan area. Connecticut joined the compact in 1941. One of the Commission's first tasks was, with the help of the Federal Works Agency, to monitor the district water quality conditions using standard parameters such as DO and coliform counts. In its first survey in 1938, the Commission reported that the district's maximum pollution occurred in the East and Harlem rivers, while the Upper Bay, the Narrows, the Kills, and Newark Bay were also badly polluted. Conditions in the Lower Bay, Raritan Bay, and Sandy Hook Bay were found to be satisfactory (Federal Works Agency 1939).

The 1940 studies of water-quality measures, however, showed improvements in DO conditions in the East and Harlem rivers (probably due to the various new sewage-treatment plants in New York), and long-term decreases in Jamaica Bay, the Kill Van Kull, and the Arthur Kill (Mytelka et al. 1981). Further improvements were reported in a study of the Raritan River and Bay, published in 1942, which compared water-quality measures from 1927–28, 1937–38, and 1940–41. "It is difficult to visualize," observed the authors, "what the condition of the river would be if municipal sewage plants and several of the larger industrial treatment works had not been built and operated" (Rudolfs and Heukelekian 1942).

Environmental conditions deteriorated during and after World War II, particularly in regard to industrial pollution. Extremely important was a shift in the source of fish kills occurring because of industrial wastes. For most of the first half of the century, canneries and milk-product plants had been the leading producers of oxygen-reducing wastes (New York Department of Conservation 1946). In 1948, however, the New York Department of Conservation reported that firms using chemical methods in manufacturing, especially cyanide processes, had become the worst offenders (New York Department of Conservation 1948). Industrial wastes also became more important in the Raritan River. While the municipal load had a population equivalent (PE) of about 220,000 persons, a 1951 study showed that separate industrial-plant discharges were equal to a PE of 450,000 persons. A substantial amount of the municipal load was also due to industrial wastes (Metcalf and Eddy 1951).

Reflecting this new situation, in 1951 the Interstate Sanitation Commission published its first Industrial Waste Inventory, which surveyed approximately 1,500 of the district's 29,000 industrial plants along 2,400 km of coastline. Of these, 300 discharged directly into District waters, and the remainder into the sewers. The heaviest concentrations of plants were in Brooklyn, Queens, the Arthur Kill, Kill Van Kull, and Bridgeport, Connecticut. Of the total wastes discharged, 65% came from the petroleum industry, 14.4% from utilities, and 10.1% from the chemical industry. The Commission estimated that the biological oxygen demand (BOD) of the industrial wastes equalled that of the raw sewage that would be discharged by 2,100,000 people. Study was also made of such parameters as toxicity, grease and oil, acidity, suspended solids, and color, which had not appeared in earlier pollution reports (Interstate Sanitation Commission 1951).

Public concern over water pollution increased sharply in the 1950s, resulting in passage of federal and state statutes. From 1952 to 1963, nine major plants providing primary treatment (six in New Jersey and three in New York) were constructed with the help of federal matching funds; by 1962, about 70% of New York City's sewage was being treated. Legislation also required the classification of the state's water resources, and the New York State Health Department conducted studies of the major drainage basins, exploring the hydrology, uses, and pollution conditions of the state's waters and classifying them for best usage. Studies of the New York estuary showed that industry was the most serious polluter of the Arthur Kill and the Kill Van Kull. Municipal sewage discharge had the most impact on the water of the Hudson opposite New York City and in the Upper Bay.

In 1964, as a result of these water-quality surveys, the New York State Water Resources Commission adopted a pair of official classifications: class I: fishing; class II: water not primarily for recreational purposes, shellfish culture, or development of fish life. Standards used in the scheme were based on such traditional parameters as floating solids and DO as well as measures of toxic wastes that might affect "edible fish and shellfish." The waters of the Hudson River from the New York–New Jersey state line to the Battery, Upper New York Bay, and the Harlem River from George Washington Bridge to its junction with the Hudson were placed in class I, while the Kill Van Kull, the Lower East River, and the Harlem River from its juction with the Lower East River to the George Washington Bridge were placed in class II.

In 1965, the U.S. Public Health Service reported that a total of 74 municipal sources on the Hudson discharged wastes, with a total PE of 10 million. Six municipalities provided secondary treatment, 44 primary treatment, and 24 no treatment. Raw-sewage flows were heaviest in the upper Hudson from Troy south to the Ulster County line and in the New York City area. Pollution of the bays came two-thirds from New York and one-third from New Jersey, with the Passaic Valley Sewerage Commission being the leading offender. DO measures reflected the extremely polluted condition of the river. Depressed oxygen conditions existed for 100 km downstream from the Troy dam, while the river was essentially devoid of dissolved oxygen for 30 km from Albany downstream. The river did not return to a state of relatively complete oxygen saturation until it reached the ocean in the New York Bight. The maximum DO levels were near the Tappan Zee Bridge, while the low point in the Hudson south of the Bridge was found between the Battery and 42nd Street. Vast quantities of sludge deposits were also noted on the bottoms of the East River, the Newark River, and parts of the Hudson River (U.S. DHEW 1965).

The 1965 pollution measures, however, represented a peak, and declined sharply in the following decade. By 1972, New York City treated almost 90% of the wastes that it was discharging daily (Gunnerson 1981). A 1974 study by the Hudson River Environmental Society showed that while wastewater flows into the river had increased with population growth, inputs of organic material (measured in BOD) had

been reduced by about 35% over the previous 10 years (Hetling 1974). The construction of new secondary sewage-treatment plants and the upgrading of existing facilities were responsible for these improvements. In the 1970s, in response to the 1972 Clean Water Act (PL 92), further upgrading of municipal facilities took place. Studies in the early 1980s by the Interstate Sanitary Commission showed further improvements in most areas for the lower river and the estuary, including higher DO and lower coliform bacteria counts.

It is possible to supplement the descriptions in these reports with estimates of the organic waste, nitrogen, and phosphorus emissions into the Basin over the past century and the impact of sewage treatment on those inputs (Table 38-1). In recent decades, detergents have added significantly to phosphorus emissions (though this contribution is again declining), and synthetic nitrate fertilizers and other chemicals have contri-

Table 38-1 *Carbon, Nitrogen, and Phosphorus Emissions*
(a) Organic Carbon Loadings

Year	Urban Population	Urban Horse Population	Organic Carbon from Human Waste (t)[a]	Organic Carbon from Horse Waste (t)	Fraction of Human Waste Drained to Sewers[b]	Fraction of Horse Waste Drained to Sewers	Fraction of TOC Removed by Sewage Treatment[c]	Total Organic Material (t)
1980	15,188,490	0	803,851	0	1.03	1.00	0.6824	262,966
1970	16,148,898	0	854,680	0	1.00	1.00	0.3544	551,803
1960	14,893,389	0	788,233	0	0.99	0.99	0.1439	668,050
1950	13,189,415	0	698,050	0	0.97	0.97	0.1025	607,705
1940	11,602,963	0	614,087	0	0.95	0.95	0.0663	544,722
1930	10,938,588	0	578,925	0	0.92	0.92	0.0581	501,677
1920	8,597,704	115,884	455,033	113,964	0.90	0.90	0.0188	502,495
1900	5,121,033	178,786	271,031	175,823	0.75	0.75	0.0005	334,980
1880	2,950,314	250,014	156,145	245,871	0.33	0.50	0	174,463

[a] Based on urban population.

[b] Note that some non-urban human waste reaches sewers from outer suburbs. This accounts for the fraction being slightly greater than unity in recent years.

[c] Estimated by Tarr and McCurley.

(b) Point-Source Loadings of Nitrogen and Phosphorus in the Hudson-Raritan Basin

	Urban Population		From (Urban) Human Waste (t)		From Horse Waste (Urban) (t)		Phosphorus from Detergents (t)	Urban Population with Sewers (%)	Urban Horse Wastes Drained (%)	Nitrogen and Phosphorus Removed by Sewage Treatment (%)	Discharge	
Year	Human (millions)	Horse (thousands)	Organic Nitrogen	Organic Phosphorus	Organic Nitrogen	Organic Phosphorus					Nitrogen (t)	Phosphorus (t)
1980	15.2	0	55,438	13,859	0	0	18,000	1.03	NA	0.194	46,024	26,449
1970	16.1	0	58,943	14,736	0	0	25,100	1.00		0.150	50,102	33,861
1960	14.9	0	54,361	13,590	0	0	13,600	0.99		0.108	48,005	24,011
1950	13.2	0	48,141	12,035	0	0	5,000	0.97		0.100	42,027	14,872
1940	11.6	0	42,351	10,588	0	0	0	0.95		0.094	36,452	9,113
1930	10.9	0	39,926	9,981	0	0	0	0.92		0.088	33,500	8,374
1920	8.6	115.9	31,382	7,845	1,692	423	0	0.90	0.90	0.050	28,278	7,069
1900	5.1	178.8	18,692	4,673	2,610	653	0	0.75	0.75	0.008	15,849	3,963
1880	3	250	10,769	2,692	3,650	913	0	0.33	0.5	0	5,379	1,345

Table 38-1 (*cont.*)

(c) Historical Nitrogen and Phosphorus Loadings in the Hudson-Raritan Estuary (units = 1,000 t)

	Nitrogen			Phosphorus		
Year	Runoff	Point Sources	Total	Runoff	Point Sources	Total
1980	66.7	46.0	112.7	5.36	26.45	31.81
1970	67.8	50.1	117.9	5.56	33.86	39.42
1960	68.7	48.0	116.7	5.65	24.01	29.66
1950	69.0	42.0	111.0	5.68	14.87	20.55
1940	70.0	36.5	106.5	5.73	9.11	14.84
1930	67.2	33.5	100.7	5.48	8.37	13.85
1920	66.0	28.3	94.3	5.23	7.07	12.30
1900	68.0	15.8	83.8	5.28	3.96	9.24
1880	75.0	5.4	80.4	5.78	1.34	7.12

buted significantly to the nitrogen emissions. Both point sources and surface runoff are considered; runoff models have been built to estimate the contributions of various pollutants as a function of land use and rainfall. (In the case of total organic carbon, the two categories are combined.) The figures indicate the improvements that have occurred in very recent years, which are mainly attributable to environmental management.

Pollution Flows: Metals and Chemicals

Although traditional waste loads have been reduced, new pollutants have been identified and water quality standards have been raised in the Hudson-Raritan Estuary. Both expectations and concerns have risen. The pollutants of relatively recent concern having significant environmental as well as health effects include heavy metals and chlorinated hydrocarbons such as pesticides; polychlorinated biphenyls (PCBs) are a matter of special concern in the region. The historical reconstructions summarized in this section have been constructed using a mass-balance approach (Ayres, McMichael, and Rod 1987). The pollutants described are heavy metals, pesticides, PCBs, and oil and grease. Of these, heavy metals are released into the environment in three ways: (1) by production processes; (2) by fossil-fuel combustion; and (3) by dissipation of intermediate or final products. We discuss the histories of these sources and pollutants briefly in order.

Metallurgical Refining Processes

Although the Hudson-Raritan Basin was an important producer of iron in the middle of the nineteenth century, in the years after 1880 its share of the U.S. iron/steel industry was small. In contrast, as noted previously, the copper and lead-refining industries were important in the region from the 1890s to the 1920s, and to some extent ever since then.

The metallurgy of copper is complex, with each smelter and refinery having a different pattern, depending on the available ores or concentrates. Gaseous waste streams are generated primarily from copper smelters and converters, while slag is the major solid waste. Typically, 3 tons of slag are produced

per ton of blister copper from concentrate, but the ratio was as high as 10 to 1 for the concentrates used in the New Jersey–New York smelters. Slag is mostly inert silicates and oxides, but it does contain some copper and other trace metals that leach slowly. Arsenic is a byproduct of the processing of copper ores and is emitted both in gaseous form and as a component of slag. The slag was normally disposed of in landfills, often on the refinery sites, which were located in low-lying marshy areas. A major source of copper pollution in the region may well be leaching from old slag piles. "Acid rain" probably accelerates the process.

Other toxic materials, such as arsenic, cadmium, silver, and lead, are associated with copper and zinc ores. Some is lost in mining and ore-processing operations, Until recently, one zinc mine was operating in New Jersey on a tributary of the Hudson that produced 29,000 t of recoverable zinc in 1980. In addition, there was one plant manufacturing zinc oxide and a secondary zinc recovery plant in New Jersey.

Lead refining and desilverizing from imported ore or bullion was very important in the region from the 1890s through the 1960s. Three major lead refineries existed in the first half of the twentieth century. In 1899, two of them accounted for 32.5% of the total of 222,000 t of refined lead in the United States. Lead refinery output in New Jersey peaked probably sometime before World War I, although one refinery operated until 1945 and a second until 1961. Refinery emissions would have been in the form of particulates escaping with gaseous wastes.

Control of emissions from copper and lead smelters began early in the twentieth century, driven by the damage observed to plants and animals near copper smelters in Tennessee, Arizona, Montana, and Ontario. The first approach to emissions control was mechanical, using techniques such as baffles, expansion chambers, and "bag houses." In 1907, F. G. Cottrell of the University of California developed the first successful electrostatic precipitator, which was quickly applied in the primary copper-smelting industry for economic reasons. By the end of the 1920s, most copper smelters had "Cottrell treaters," usually operating at 90% efficiency or better. Taking into account average uncontrolled emissions from metallurgical processes (from EPA data), and our estimates of historical increases in airborne emissions control efficiency, it is possible to obtain an estimate of metallurgical emissions for the region (Table 38-2).

Heavy Metals Released from Fossil-Fuel Combustion

Until the 1820s and 1830s, wood was the primary fuel used by both urban and rural inhabitants of the Hudson-Raritan region. At this time, however, anthracite coal from eastern Pennsylvania began to move into the urban markets, and by the middle of the century, it was the dominant domestic and industrial fuel (Binder 1974). Bituminous coal from western Pennsylvania began to capture industrial markets in the late 19th century and, by 1900, although anthracite was still the primary fuel used in New York State and New York City, bituminous was increasingly used in industry (Chandler 1977). Anthracite reached a peak in 1920, but by 1925 had declined to its 1900 level of use. Bituminous

Table 38-2 *Average Annual Emissions from Metallurgical Operations in the Hudson-Raritan Valley (units-metric tons)*

Year	Arsenic		Cadmium		Chromium		Copper		Mercury		Lead		Zinc	
	Low	High	Low	High	Low	High	Low	High	Low	High	Low	High	Low	High
1980	4.9	5.5	.0	.0	0.02	0.02	0.9	1.8	0.00	0.00	43	51	1.6	3.5
1970	33.8	74.1	0.1	0.4	0.00	0.00	3.3	12.5	0.01	0.02	112	261	13.8	35.1
1960	125.3	275.3	0.4	1.1	0.07	0.15	7.7	28.0	0.03	0.04	295	688	30.8	82.3
1950	131.2	462.0	0.6	1.6	0.07	0.26	10.3	52.7	0.04	0.06	564	2,173	43.0	163.8
1940	150.3	462.1	0.7	1.8	0.33	1.02	9.8	43.8	0.04	0.05	957	3,163	47.3	194.1
1930	163.6	445.6	14.2	24.9	0.20	0.55	9.7	40.3	0.11	0.16	864	2,306	43.5	149.2
1920	168.0	373.9	20.2	49.3	0.51	1.11	9.9	37.8	0.16	0.31	1,254	2,902	43.7	167.9
1900	89.5	108.6	1.6	3.7	0.46	0.50	6.6	18.4	0.05	0.08	2,328	3,436	39.6	82.3
1880	12.1	13.1	0.4	0.6	0.47	0.51	2.3	3.7	0.01	0.01	16	23	5.7	31.3

was the preferred fuel for industry, and especially in the growing electrical utility industry. In addition, by the 1920s, both residual and distillate oil had become important fuels. In 1940, bituminous and anthracite were used about equally in the state, with bituminous preferred for industrial and electrical utility use and anthracite for domestic purposes. The use of fuel oil also accelerated, about equally divided among electric utilities, industry, and domestic use. In 1940, about 60% of households in the New York metropolitan area burned coal for fuel, about 25% used oil, and the remainder used gas or wood (Bureau of the Census 1940).

By 1950, bituminous coal was being used in the state at a ratio of about two to one over anthracite; electrical utilities and industry continued to be the heaviest users. Fuel oil had made sharp inroads into the domestic markets in the New York Metropolitan Region, and was now about even with coal in shares of household users (Bureau of the Census 1950). By 1960, anthracite use in the state was down sharply, to a total of 1.6 million t, while bituminous had soared to over 23 million t. Fuel-oil consumption was also up sharply in all areas of use. In 1960, coal was used by only 434,817 households in the New York Metropolitan area, whereas oil was the fuel for over 2.5 million users. Another 700,000 households used gas for fuel. The 1970s witnessed the energy crisis and rising oil prices. Oil use by utilities and households in the state diminished sharply, but remained high in industry. Bituminous-coal use was also down considerably, while anthracite use dropped nearly to zero. Natural gas made up the difference, especially for households.

Minor trace metals are found in coal ash and can be mobilized by coal combustion to an extent comparable with natural processes or mining. The quantities of trace metals actually released to the environment depend on the fraction that escapes as vapor and the fraction that condenses on very small particulates, most of which are now captured by electrostatic precipitators (ESPs).

Three distinct phases exist in the history of coal-ash control. In the first phase (before 1920), a large fraction (about 50% of stoker-fired coal combustion) of the ash was collected and removed in solid form and usually deposited in landfills, although means of recovering fly-ash did not exist (Hering and Greeley 1921). In the second period, after 1915, the use of mechanical baffles, filters, and cyclones to reduce soot was balanced by the increasing use of pulverized fuel. In 1929, however, electrostatic precipitators with about 90% recovery efficiency were adopted by New York Edison Company and other utilities (Carleton-Jones 1974). Substantial nonutility coal use without fly-ash controls by households and industries continued, however, until 1950. Averaging over all users, we estimate 50% control for 1930, 60% for 1940, 70% for 1950, 90% for 1960, and 97% by 1970. Estimates of heavy-metal emissions can be derived by synthesizing these estimates (Table 38-3).

Heavy Metals Released by Dissipation of Products

Emissions of copper prior to 1920, of chromium prior to 1930, of cadmium prior to 1940, and of lead prior to 1950 were primarily the result of production processes. During the

Table 38-3 *Metallic Emissions due to Combustion of Fossil Fuels in the Hudson-Raritan Basin (units = metric tons)*

Year	Arsenic	Cadmium	Chromium	Copper	Mercury	Lead	Zinc low	Zinc high
1980	4.1	31.5	41.7	10.1	.0	5,312.4	0.5	0.6
1970	6.1	46.6	63.4	16.4	0.1	9,684.3	1.2	1.7
1960	3.0	22.8	40.4	16.4	0.2	7,203.1	3.2	5.5
1950	2.2	17.2	48.5	30.7	0.3	4,884.2	8.1	14.3
1940	1.5	11.9	79.9	66.0	0.7	2,504.3	19.6	34.7
1930	1.3	10.5	110.1	96.3	1.0	266.4	29.2	51.7
1920	2.9	24.6	362.4	326.8	3.5	73.9	100.0	177.1
1900	2.6	23.2	444.8	408.0	4.2	91.9	125.5	222.3
1880	0.8	7.1	136.4	125.1	1.3	29.4	38.5	68.2

past 30 to 40 years, the principal source of heavy-metal emissions in the Hudson-Raritan estuary has shifted from production-related to consumption-related processes. There are now various consumption uses that release heavy metals into the environment in ways that contribute to water pollution through surface runoff. These more recent sources of heavy metals vary in their degrees of dissipation in use and their modes of release to the environment.

Since 1950, tetraethyl lead (TEL), used as an "anti-knock" additive for gasoline, has been the principal source of lead emissions to the environment and the most significant consumption-related source of any one heavy metal. (Before the 1950s, pigments for paints – "white lead" and "red lead" – were the major dissipative use of lead.) Consumption of alkyl lead in any region can be assumed to be roughly in proportion to the gasoline consumption of the region. For purposes of estimating gross magnitudes, the gasoline consumption of the Hudson-Raritan watershed area in 1970 was 6.65% of the U.S. total. On this basis, it can be assumed that close to 6.65% of the 246,000 t of lead consumed in gasoline in 1970, or 16,400 t, was consumed in the Hudson-Raritan Basin. Corresponding ratios for other years can be estimated.

Of the total consumption of lead as TEL in 1970, about 70%, or 11,500 t, must have been emitted directly to the air of the Basin, the rest being retained in auto exhaust systems, oil filters, and waste motor oil. Approximately 32% of all motor oil is burned or lost by leakage onto city streets, from whence it is washed into the sewers. Some waste motor oil is dumped "privately," and, of this, some is commingled with refuse. In urbanized areas, much of it is ultimately incinerated. Some oil is collected and used later as fuel. This may account for the high lead content in some incinerator emissions. In any case, most of the lead emitted by motor vehicles is deposited locally, and most of it finds its way into watercourses via runoff.

For heavy metals as a group, we have identified 10 categories of consumption that are readily distinguishable in terms of their different degrees of dissipation in use and different modes of release into the environment. They are as follows:

1. Metallic uses, such as in alloys. Environmental losses occur mainly in the production stage (discussed pre-

viously) and as a result of corrosion or discharge to landfills.
2. Plating and anodyzing (excluding paints and pigments) generate some losses in the plating or treatment process and some corrosion loss.
3. Paints and pigments generate losses at the point of application and from weathering and wear. Some are ultimately disposed of to landfills along with discarded objects or building materials.
4. Batteries and electronic devices have relatively short useful lives of 1 to 10 years. Production losses can be significant. Most are discarded to landfills.
5. Other electrical equipment, as above, but may be longer-lived.
6. Industrial chemicals and reagents (such as catalysts and solvents) that are not embodied in products have short useful lives. Catalysts and solvents are partially recycled; others are lost directly to air or water.
7. Chemical additives to consumer products, including fuel additives, rubber vulcanizing agents and pigments, detergents, plasticizers, and photographic film. They are disposed of mainly to landfills or incinerators. There is no recycling.
8. Agricultural pesticides, fungicides, and herbicides are used dissipatively on farms and nurseries. Most are immobilized by soil or are biologically degraded and volatilized. There is some uptake into the food chain and a small amount of loss via runoff.
9. Nonagricultural biocides, including the above, as used in homes and gardens. These uses are dissipative, but most biocides, again, are immobilized by soil.
10. Pharmaceuticals and germicides are used in the home or in health-service facilities, and are largely discharged via sewage or to incinerators.

The term "emission coefficient" will be used to mean the fraction of the material in question that is released in mobile form within a decade (more or less). We exclude wastes that are recycled or disposed of in landfills or in sludge dumped offshore. In a few cases, we also include production-related losses that were not included in the earlier discussion, such as process wastes in the plating, tanning, and chemical industries.

It is curious and unfortunate that almost no data have been

Table 38-4 *Consumption-Related Emissions Factors*

Symbol	Metal	Metallic Use	Plating & Coating	Paint & Pigments	Electron Tubes & Batteries	Other Electrical Equipment	Chemical Uses, Not Embodied	Chemical Uses, Embodied	Agricultural Uses	Non-Agricultural Uses	Medical, Dental	Misc. (NEC)
Ag	Silver	0.001	0.02	0.5	0.01	0.01	1	0.4	na	na	0.5	0.15
As	Arsenic	0.001	0	0.5	0.01	na	na	0.05	0.5	0.8	0.8	0.15
Cd	Cadmium	0.001	0.15	0.5	0.02	n	1	0.15	na	na	na	0.15
Cr	Chromium	0.001	0.02	0.5	na	na	1	0.05	na	1	0.8	0.15
Cu	Copper	0.005	0	1.0	na	0.1	1	0.05	0.05	1	na	0.15
Hg	Mercury	0.05	0.05	0.8	0.2	na	1	na	0.8	0.9	0.2	0.5
Pb	Lead	0.005	0	0.5	0.01	na	1	0.75	0.05	0.1	na	0.15
Zn	Zinc	0.001	0.02	0.5	0.01	na	1	0.15	0.05	0.1	0.8	0.15

published on emissions coefficients for consumption activities. Obviously, most analysts have not considered such activities to be "sources" of pollutants. In the absence of systematic research, we are led to a rather ad hoc choice of emissions coefficients (Table 38-4). It must be pointed out that, while the numerical estimates in many cases are very uncertain, sometimes even by a factor of two or three, there are only a few important routes that dominate the rest for each metal.

In the total metal emissions for the Hudson-Raritan Basin (Table 38-5), comparing the various sources that have been discussed, a major finding stands out. In recent decades, consumption-related emissions have dominated production-related emissions by a large factor. The apparent exception, lead in gasoline, is really a classification problem, as TEL is listed under "fossil fuel."

Pesticides

Before World War II, arsenic was the most widely utilized insecticide in the United States. Arsenic sprays were in especially wide use in fruit orchards (Whorton 1974). Mercury-based fungicides for agricultural purposes were also quite important from the 1930s through the 1950s, with rapid decline after 1968. Most of these pesticides, fungicides, and herbicides are immobilized by the soil or are biologically degraded and volatilized. A small amount, however, is lost via runoff.

All of the chlorinated hydrocarbon pesticides and herbicides are considered as a group, due to their similarities. Chlorinated pesticides were in use from 1946 through the early 1970s, but restrictions began in the early 1960s, beginning with DDT. The major farm uses, from the outset, were to control pests of cotton and corn, whereas lesser amounts were used on soy beans, tobacco, potatoes, apples, citrus fruits, and other crops. Figures on pesticide use by farms, by crop, are available from USDA stratified-sample surveys. Major shifts that occurred from 1964 to 1976 are clearly attributable to the fact that many of the chlorinated pesticides that were important in 1964 had been banned by 1976.

It is significant that the Hudson-Raritan Basin as a whole, with roughly 8% of the nation's population, produces less than 0.1% of the nation's wheat, less than 0.01% of the nation's corn and oats, and around 0.02% of its potatoes. Deciduous fruit (e.g., apples) is by far the most important crop in the region, accounting for 4.5% of the national total in 1950, but less than 2% now, with hay being next in regional importance.

The available data do not permit a complete allocation of

Table 38-5 *Emissions of Selected Metals in the Hudson-Raritan Basin (units = t)*
(a) Average Annual Silver and Arsenic Emissions

Year	Silver (Consumptive Only)	Arsenic Metallurgical Operations		Arsenic Fossil Fuel Combustion	Arsenic Consumptive Uses	Arsenic Total Emissions	
		low	high			low	high
1980	59.6	4.9	5.5	4.1	672.4	681.4	682.0
1970	49.4	33.8	74.1	6.1	1,020.7	1,060.6	1,100.9
1960	39.6	125.3	275.3	3.0	755.9	884.1	1,034.2
1950	37.7	131.2	462.0	2.2	821.1	954.5	1,285.3
1940	18.6	150.3	462.1	1.5	1,363.4	1,515.2	1,826.9
1930	12.5	163.6	445.6	1.3	974.6	1,139.5	1,421.5
1920	10.3	168.0	373.9	2.9	551.4	722.3	928.2
1900	5.2	89.5	108.6	2.6	151.8	243.9	263.0
1880	1.3	12.1	13.1	0.8	43.9	56.8	57.8

(b) Average Annual Cadmium Emissions

Year	Metallurgical Operations		Fossil-Fuel Combustion	Consumptive Uses	Total Emissions	
	low	high			low	high
1980	.0	.0	31.5	20.8	52.3	52.3
1970	0.1	0.4	46.6	71.5	118.3	118.6
1960	0.4	1.1	22.8	80.9	104.1	104.8
1950	0.6	1.6	17.2	71.7	89.4	90.4
1940	0.7	1.8	11.9	69.0	81.5	82.6
1930	14.2	24.9	10.5	20.7	45.4	56.1
1920	20.2	49.3	24.6	3.0	47.8	76.9
1900	1.6	3.7	23.2	0.0	24.8	26.9
1880	0.4	0.6	7.1	0.0	7.5	7.6

Table 38-5 (cont.)

(c) Average Annual Chromium Emissions

Year	Metallurgical Operations		Fossil Fuel Combustion	Consumptive Uses	Total Emissions	
	low	high			low	high
1980	0.02	0.02	41.7	837	878.7	878.7
1970	0.00	0.00	63.4	1,463	1,526.4	1,526.4
1960	0.07	0.15	40.4	1,612	1,652.4	1,652.5
1950	0.07	0.26	48.5	1,449	1,497.6	1,497.8
1940	0.33	1.02	79.9	1,513	1,593.2	1,593.9
1930	0.20	0.55	110.1	428	538.3	538.6
1920	0.51	1.11	362.4	300	662.9	663.5
1900	0.46	0.50	444.8	254	699.3	699.3
1880	0.47	0.51	136.4	24	160.8	160.9

(d) Average Annual Copper Emissions

Year	Metallurgical Operations		Fossil Fuel Combustion	Consumptive Uses	Total Emissions	
	low	high			low	high
1980	0.9	1.8	10.1	1,109	1,120.0	1,120.8
1970	3.3	12.5	16.4	1,222	1,241.7	1,250.9
1960	7.7	28.0	16.4	973	997.1	1,017.4
1950	10.3	52.7	30.7	1,145	1,186.0	1,228.4
1940	9.8	43.8	66.0	1,309	1,384.9	1,418.9
1930	9.7	40.3	96.3	550	656.0	686.7
1920	9.9	37.8	326.8	541	877.8	905.7
1900	6.6	18.4	408.0	309	723.6	735.4
1880	2.3	3.7	125.1	109	236.4	237.8

(e) Average Annual Mercury Emissions

Year	Metallurgical Operations		Fossil Fuel Combustion	Consumptive Uses	Total Emissions	
	low	high			low	high
1980	0.00	0.00	0.03	64.1	64.2	64.2
1970	0.01	0.02	0.10	106.3	106.4	106.4
1960	0.03	0.04	0.16	56.6	56.8	56.8
1950	0.04	0.06	0.32	66.4	66.7	66.8
1940	0.04	0.05	0.71	66.0	66.7	66.8
1930	0.11	0.16	1.04	57.8	58.9	58.9
1920	0.16	0.31	3.54	48.9	52.6	52.7
1900	0.05	0.08	4.21	27.7	31.9	31.9
1880	0.01	0.01	1.28	27.9	29.2	29.2

pesticide use for all years. It is sufficiently clear from available information, however, that agricultural uses in the Hudson-Raritan Basin accounted for an insignificant proportion of national use for all of these chemicals over the entire relevant time span. In effect, we are able to conclude that only nonagricultural pesticide uses were significant (Table 38-6).

PCBs

The emissions of PCBs into the Hudson River are largely due to a single point source. Two General Electric capacitor plants at Fort Edward and Hudson Falls in the upper basin purchased about 35,000 t of PCBs during the nine years 1966–1974 inclusive. This constituted about 15% of the total U.S. consumption during that period, and 25% of U.S. consumption for electrical equipment. Assuming similar patterns of U.S. consumption during the earlier period 1948–1965, for which GE data are lacking, the total amount used at these locations must have been around 75,000 t. Given the amounts known to have been removed by dredging and the amounts known to remain in sediments, there must

Table 38-5 (*cont.*)

(f) Average Annual Lead Emissions

Year	Metallurgical Operations		Fossil Fuel Combustion	Consumptive Uses	Total Emissions	
	low	high			low	high
1980	43	51	5,312	95	5,451	5,458
1970	112	261	9,684	199	9,994	10,143
1960	295	688	7,203	126	7,625	8,017
1950	564	2,173	4,884	81	5,529	7,138
1940	957	3,163	2,504	18	3,480	5,685
1930	864	2,306	266	13	1,144	2,586
1920	1,254	2,902	74	14	1,342	2,991
1900	1,470	1,708	92	0	1,562	1,800
1880	16	23	29	0	45	53

(g) Average Annual Zinc Emissions

Year	Metallurgical Operations		Fossil Fuel Combustion		Consumptive Uses	Total Emissions	
	low	high	Low	high		low	high
1980	1.6	3.5	0.5	0.6	7,870	7,872	7,874
1970	13.8	35.1	1.2	1.7	10,225	10,240	10,262
1960	30.8	82.3	3.2	5.5	8,720	8,754	8,808
1950	43.0	163.8	8.1	14.3	9,170	9,221	9,348
1940	47.3	194.1	19.6	34.7	8,500	8,567	8,729
1930	43.5	149.2	29.2	51.7	7,280	7,353	7,481
1920	43.7	167.9	100.0	177.1	5,560	5,704	5,905
1900	39.6	82.3	125.5	222.3	1,550	1,715	1,855
1880	5.7	31.3	38.5	68.2	470	514	569

Table 38-6 *Use of Chlorinated Pesticides in the Hudson-Raritan Basin (1945–1980) (units = t)*

Year	DDT	BHC/Lindane	Aldrin	Chlordane	Dieldrin	Endrin	Heptachlor	Toxaphene
1980	0	0	0	0	0	0	12.6	2.0
1976	0	8.6	0.4	78.8	1.2	0.4	11.6	4.1
1971	48.0	8.6	0.7	295.9	1.7	0.5	13.0	5.0
1966	124.9	18.6	1.2	206.5	4.7	0.7	12.6	5.2
1964	135.3	25.6	0.8	162.5	4.8	0.8	11.6	5.4
1960	187.7	66.8	0.5	159.3	13.8	0.9	10.8	5.3
1955	165.4	333.6	0.6	159.3	13.4	0.9	9.5	5.3
1950	154.2	147.6	0.1	159.3	2.6	0.4	7.0	3.7
1945	84.6	86.9		15.8				

have been a total accumulation of at least 500 t in the upper basin, corresponding to a loss rate from the capacitor plants of 0.67%. Roughly 50–60% of this is now immobilized on dump sites from dredging in 1978–80. Around 64 t remained in the riverbed of the upper basin as of 1978.

Oil and Grease

Oil and grease are major water pollutants, and are a problem in the Hudson-Raritan estuary, though not in the basin generally. There are two significant sources: (1) bilge washings and spills from tankers bringing crude oil or petroleum products into New York harbor, and (2) waste motor oil that finds its way into the rivers, primarily via runoff. Motor oil carries with it a residue of lead, originating from tetraethyl lead in gasoline, and was discussed earlier briefly under that heading. Historical trends have been estimated for oil and grease losses (Table 38-7).

Conclusion

Major changes have occurred in patterns of population and economy in the Hudson-Raritan Basin over the past three centuries. These changes have, in turn, had important

Table 38-7 *Historical Oil and Grease Loading in the Hudson-Raritan Estuary*

Year	Oil and Grease (1,000 t)		
	Point Source	Runoff	Total
1980	45	59	104
1970	507	57	564
1960	325	61	386
1950	234	53	287
1940	156	45	201
1930	128	45	173
1920	55	28.5	83
1900	18.5	4.5	23
1880	6.0	2.0	8

consequences for the types and magnitude of pollution flows into the environment. This chapter has examined the most important of these pollution flows, both through a study of the documentary record in regard to pollution and by utilizing a materials-balance accounting principle to estimate residual flows from the processes of production and consumption. The latter makes possible a quantitative estimate of past emissions into the environment of pollutants that were not being measured at the time.

The record suggest that the environment in the Hudson-Raritan Basin was most heavily abused in the decades from about 1880 through 1970. These were decades of intensive agricultural land use, of rapid industrialization, and of extremely rapid city growth. More recently, there has been a good deal of environmental restoration and regulation of pollution, aided by the withdrawal from the region of a substantial share of manufacturing activity, but severe burdens are still placed on the environment. Industrial pollution remains a problem. One recent study of point-source pollution in the Hudson found 147 industries and utilities that had discharged at least one toxic chemical into the river from 1978 through 1983; many firms discharged more than one toxic stream (Rohmann 1985). In addition, many of the plants that once operated in the inner- and outer-ring counties, especially in New Jersey, because of the ease of waste disposal, have left a heritage that persists today in the form of existing and abandoned waste dumps.

Current pollution burdens are the product of several factors, including continued leaching from wastes discarded in the past, the unprecedentedly large sprawl of population and settlement into areas not formerly urbanized, and the unanticipated effects of new products. Success in controlling pollution from processes of production has not been matched by control of pollution from now widely dispersed processes of consumption, which have become the principal source of heavy-metals emissions, although the regulation of leaded gasoline, for instance, has led to noticeable improvements. In addition, we now have not only higher standards of environmental quality, but also the ability to measure injurious substances in much smaller quantities than was possible in the past. The future will almost undoubtedly bring with it both more stringent regulation of traditional pollutants and the discovery of injurious effects from unsuspected sources.

Acknowledgments

The research for this chapter was originally conducted under grants from the National Oceanic and Atmospheric Administration (Nos. NA82RAD00010 and NA83AA-D-00059) and the National Science Foundation (No. SES-8420478). For the full reports on this material, see Joel A. Tarr and James McCurley III, *Historical Assessment of Pollution Impacts in Estuaries: The Potomac, Delaware, Hudson, Connecticut and Narragansett*, A Report to the National Oceanic and Atmospheric Administration (Pittsburgh, 1985); and Robert U. Ayres (principal investigator), Leslie W. Ayres, Joel A. Tarr, and Rolande C. Widgery, *An Historical Reconstruction of Major Pollution Levels in the Hudson-Raritan Basin: 1880–1980*, NOAA Technical Memorandum NOS OMA 43 (Rockville, MD, October 1988). The authors would like to thank James McCurley III, Mitchell Small, Samuel R. Rod, and Martin Marietta Environmental Systems for aid in collecting and analyzing the data.

Notes

1. The counties are Albany, Rensselaer, and Schenectady.

2. This follows the schema used by the Regional Plan Association in its 1950s study of the New York Metropolitan Region, except for deletion of Suffolk County (Hoover and Vernon 1959). The rationale for deletion is that the county's runoff patterns are not toward the estuary. In 1968 the Regional Plan Association increased the number of counties it designated as part of the region to 31.

3. Until 1879, the Bronx was part of Westchester County, which has been included in the core for this period in order to capture its rapid population increase.

4. The transportation improvements of the 1840s and 1850s, however, allowed these counties to become the source of garden crops and dairy products for the core cities. See Ellis et al. 1967.

5. Bronx County was formed early in the century and becomes part of the core totals in 1920. Westchester County is added to the inner ring for that time.

References

Ayres, R. U., F. C. McMichael, and S. R. Rod. 1987. Measuring toxic chemicals in the environment: A materials balance approach. In *Toxic Chemicals, Health and the Environment*, ed. L. Lave and A. Upton. Baltimore, MD: Johns Hopkins University Press.

Berry, B. J. L., ed. 1976. *Urbanization and Counter-Urbanization*. Urban Affairs Annual Reviews, Vol 10. Beverly Hills, CA: Sage Publications.

Binder, F. M. 1974. *Coal Age Empire: Pennsylvania Coal and Its Utilization to 1860*. Harrisburg, PA: Pennsylvania Historical and Museum Commission.

Brydon, N. F. 1974. *The Passaic River: Past, Present, Future*. New Brunswick, NJ: Rutgers University Press.

Carlton-Jones, 1974. Electrostatic precipitation of fly-ash reaches fiftieth anniversary. *Journal of the American Pollution Control Association* 24:11.

Carey, G. W. 1976. *New York New Jersey: A Vignette of the Metropolitan Region*. Cambridge, MA: Ballinger Publishing Co.

Chandler, A.D., Jr. 1977. *The Visible Hand: The Managerial Revolution in American Business*. Cambridge, MA: Harvard University Press.

Citizens' Association of New York. 1866. *Report Upon the Sanitary*

Condition of the City. New York: D. Appleton and Co.

Cronon, W. 1983. *Changes in the Land: Indians, Colonists, and the Ecology of New England.* New York: Hill and Wang.

Duffy, J. 1974. *A History of Public Health in New York City, 1625–1966.* 2 vols. New York: Russell Sage Foundation.

Ellis, D. M., J. A. Frost, H. C. Syrett, and H. J. Carman. 1967. *A History of New York State.* Ithaca, NY: Cornell University Press.

Esser, S. C. 1982. Long-term changes in some finfishes of the Hudson-Raritan estuary. In *Ecological Stress and the New York Bight: Science and Management,* ed. G. F. Mayer. Columbia, SC: Estuarine Research Federation.

Federal Works Agency. 1939. *Chemical and Bacteriological Analyses of the Water in the Natural Waterways of the Interstate Sanitation District 1937–1938.* New York: The Interstate Sanitation Commission.

Franz, D. R. 1982. An historical perspective on molluscs in lower New York Harbor, with emphasis on oysters. In *Ecological Stress and the New York Bight: Science and Management,* ed. G. F. Mayer. Columbia, SC: Estuarine Research Federation.

Gottmann, J. 1961. *Megalopolis.* Cambridge, MA: MIT Press.

Gunnerson, C. G. 1981. New York City: Costs, financing, and benefits of conventional sewerage. In *Project Monitoring and Reappraisal in the International Drinking Water. Supply, and Sanitation Decade,* ed. C. G. Gunnerson and J. M. Kalbermatten. New York: American Society of Civil Engineers.

Hering, R., and S. A. Greeley. 1921. *Collection and Disposal of Municipal Refuse.* New York: McGraw-Hill.

Hetling, L. 1974. *An Analysis of Past, Present, and Future Hudson River Wastewater Loadings.* Albany NY: New York State Department of Environmental Conservation Technical Paper 37.

Hoover, E. M., and R. Vernon. 1959. *Anatomy of a Metropolis: The Changing Distribution of People and Jobs Within the New York Metropolitan Region.* New York Metropolitan Region Study. Cambridge, MA: Harvard University Press.

Interstate Sanitation Commission. 1951. *Industrial Waste Inventory.* New York.

Jackson, K. T. 1985. *Crabgrass Frontier: The Suburbanization of the United States.* New York: Oxford University Press.

Klawonn, M. J. 1977. *A History of the New York District U.S. Army Corps of Engineers, 1775–1975.* New York: U.S. Army Engineer Corps – New York District.

Lampard, E. E. 1986. The New York metropolis in transformation: History and prospect. A study in historical particularity. In *The Future of the Metropolis: Berlin, London, Paris, New York,* ed. H.-J. Ewers, J. B. Goddard, and H. Matzerath. New York: Walter de Gruyter.

Lanfear, V. 1928. *The Metal Industry.* Monograph No. 2. Regional Plan of New York and Its Environs. New York: Regional Plan Association.

Larson, H. M., E. H. Knowlton, and C. S. Popple, 1971. *History of Standard Oil Company (New Jersey).* Vol. 3: *New Horizons 1927–1950.* New York: Harper and Row.

Leighton, M. O. 1902. *Sewage Pollution in the Metropolitan Area Near New York City and Its Effect on Inland Water Resources.* USGS Water-Supply and Irrigation Paper No. 72. Washington, D.C.: GPO.

Lichtenberg, R. M. 1960. *One-Tenth of a Nation: National Forces in the Economic Growth of the New York Region.* New York Metropolitan Region Study. Cambridge, MA: Harvard University Press.

Meinig, D.W. 1966a. Geography of expansion. In *Geography of New York State,* ed. J. H. Thompson, 140–171. Syracuse, NY: Syracuse University Press.

———. 1966b. Elaboration and change. In *Geography of New York State,* ed. J. H. Thompson, 172–96. Syracuse, NY: Syracuse University Press.

Mersereau, J. W. 1887. Report of J. W. Mersereau, State Oyster Inspector. In *Report of Oyster Investigation and Shellfish Commissioner.* New York State Assembly Document No. 37, 1888.

Mytelka, J. A., M. Wendell, P. L. Sattler, and H. Golub. 1981. *Water Quality of the Hudson-Raritan Estuary* (draft) New York: Interstate Sanitation Commission.

Navin, T. R. 1978. *Copper Mining and Management.* Tucson, AZ: University of Arizona Press.

Newcomer, M. 1928. The chemical industry. In *Regional Plan of New York and Its Environs.* New York: Regional Plan Association.

New Jersey Passaic Valley Sewerage Commissioners. 1926. *Report.* Newark, NJ.

New York City Sanitation Department. 1931. *Preliminary Reports on the General Plans for Sewage Disposal for the City of New York.* New York.

New York Metropolitan Sewerage Commission. 1912.

New York State Department of Conservation. 1946, 1948. *Annual Reports.* Albany, NY.

New York State Department of Health. 1925–1940. *Annual Reports.* Albany, NY.

———. 1965. *Lower Hudson River.* Lower Hudson River Drainage Survey Report No. 9. Albany, NY.

New York State Legislature. 1939. *Report of the Hudson Valley Survey Commission to the New York Legislature.* Legislative Document No. 71. Albany, NY.

Pred, A. R. 1966. *The Spatial Dynamics of U.S. Urban Industrial Growth: 1800–1914.* Boston, MA: MIT Press.

Regional Plan Association. 1986. *Outlook for the Tri-State Region Thru 2000.* New York: Regional Plan Association.

Remington, Vosbury, and Goff. 1930. *Methods for Abatement of the Pollution of the Raritan River.* Report to the Port Raritan District Commission. New Brunswick, NJ.

Richardson, R. W., and G. Tauber, eds. 1979. *The Hudson River Basin: Environmental Problems and Institutional Response.* 2 vols. New York: Academic Press.

Rohmann, S. O. 1985. *Tracing a River's Toxic Pollution: A Case Study of the Hudson.* New York: Inform, Inc.

Rudolfs, W., and H. Heukelekian. 1942. Raritan River pollution studies: Comparison of results obtained in 1927–28, 1937–38, 1940–41. *Sewage Works Journal* 14:839–65.

Spann, E. K. 1981. *The New Metropolis: New York City, 1840–1857.* New York: Columbia University Press.

Thompson, J. H., ed. 1966. *Geography of New York State.* Syracuse, NY: Syracuse University Press.

Trescott, M. M. 1981. *The Rise of the American Electrochemical Industry 1880–1910.* Westport, CT: Greenwood Press.

U.S. Bureau of the Census. 1940. *Census of the United States.* Washington, D.C.: U.S. Government Printing Office.

———. 1880. *Census of the United States.* Washington, D.C.: U.S. Government Printing Office.

U.S. Bureau of the Census. 1985. *Census of Manufactures.* Washington, D.C.: Government Printing Office.

U.S. Bureau of Mines. 1975. *Mineral Facts and Problems.* Washington, D.C.: GPO.

U.S. Department of Commerce, Bureau of the Census. 1790–1980. *Population Report.* Washington, D.C.: GPO.

———. 1809–1985. *Census of Manufactures.* Washington, D.C.: GPO.

U.S. Department of Health, Education, and Welfare. 1965. *Report on Pollution of the Hudson River and Its Tributaries.* Washington, D.C.: Public Health Service.

Whipple, G. C. 1908. Gas wastes. In *Report of the New Jersey State Sewerage Commission.* Somerville, NJ.

Whorton, J. 1974. *Before Silent Spring: Pesticides and Public Health in Pre-DDT America.* Princeton, NJ: Princeton University Press.

Wilentz, S. 1984. *Chants Democratic.* New York: Oxford University Press.

Williams, M. 1982. Clearing the United States forests: Pivotal years 1810–1860. *Journal of Historical Geography* 8:12–28.

39

Switzerland

CHRISTIAN PFISTER   PAUL MESSERLI

Switzerland is a small country of 40,000 km^2 in the heart of Europe. It is dominated by three main physiographic zones: high mountains and valleys of the Alps, lower mountain ranges and plateaus in the Jura, and a central plateau in between (Fig. 39.1). Beyond hydropower and the appeal of its mountains to tourists, Switzerland has few "natural" resources, as reflected in land-use patterns (Fig. 39.2). The bulk of the 6.6 million inhabitants live in the central plateau.

Analysis of the transformations of Switzerland over the past 300 years is facilitated by the use of temporal subdivisions corresponding to the kinds and amount of energy inputs. Until A.D. 1875, the economy was essentially a solar-energy system, characterized by low-scale inputs. The railroad made possible the importation of coal; a fossil-fuel system allowed energy consumption to increase gradually, corresponding to the slow pace of economic growth up to 1950. Since then, the modern system based on oil has been associated with exponential growth in energy consumption, as elsewhere in central and western Europe.

Analysis of transformation is also facilitated by an integrative approach in which society is seen as embedded within and dependent upon physical habitats. Human action traditionally has been examined in terms of three fundamental frameworks: economics, social values and institutions, and biological sciences. The three are divergent because they focus on different facets of human existence: the role of a self-oriented, optimizing agent in the marketplace and creator of technological change; the role of a social being, driven by the need for status within society and regulated by the values, rules, and organizations of that society; and the role of a biological organism requiring inputs and producing outputs (Svedin 1985).

Institutional economics may offer a means to synthesize coherently these divergent frameworks. It views the human or social system as composed of a set of interconnected elements, including natural resources, population, technology, institutions, economic inputs, and cognitive and behavioral patterns (Steppacher 1985). The basic goal of society – the overall effort to keep scarcity away – is expressed in the effort of a combined system, which, over many years, adjusts

to changes in the natural and social environment. Our analysis of Switzerland from 1687 to 1987 draws upon this kind of synthesis.

This case study is organized as follows. Three main variables of change – climate, population, and technology – are identified and discussed as they have operated in both lowland and mountain settings. Attention in detail is then given to the modern period of exponential growth for Grindelwald, a tourist resort that has been the subject of study by the Swiss *Man and the Biosphere* Program. Finally, the institutions and cognitive patterns emerging from the analysis are discussed briefly.

Broad Changes in the Main Variables

Climate

The preindustrial economy operated as a solar-energy system (Sieferle 1982). The carrying capacity or food production of the system was comparatively low. Fuelwood consumption could not exceed the pace of tree growth without long-term degradation of the environment. While output was low, however, the energy supply was, on average, constant. This constancy was not, however, evident on a day-to-day basis at any given locale. Solar energy varies according to atmospheric conditions, and therefore, the economy was affected by fluctuations in weather.

In order to include climatic variability in a study of environmental transformation, data are needed for specific months from which temperature and precipitation patterns may be distinguished. At the University of Bern, a new method has been developed that permits monthly estimates to be derived from historical sources. At present this record dates back into the early sixteenth century (C. Pfister 1984).

From these data it has been demonstrated that a prevalence of warmth and sunshine during the growing season was connected to a higher agricultural output and, in the long term, to more rapid population growth. Given the low yields and the small size of herds, ecosystems were less sensitive to drought than today. Major setbacks in overall agricultural output were connected to meteorological constellations that

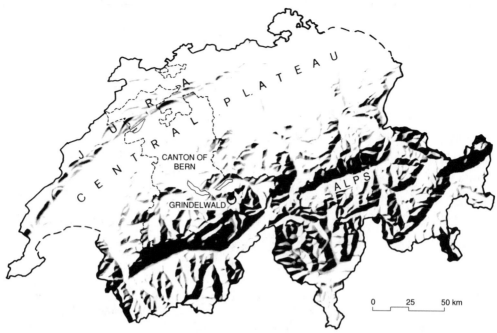

Figure 39.1 The major landscapes of Switzerland.

included a cold spring and a wet midsummer. In a chilly spring, grains perished under the snow, and fodder for the livestock ran short; long wet spells during the grain harvest promoted the sprouting of the ears and caused huge losses from mold and insects during storage. A long sequence of rainy days during the harvest washed nutrients out of the hay; as a consequence, milk output dropped in the following winter and spring. The demographic impact of crises depended on the efficiency of the various social and regulative strategies that could buffer the consequences of bottlenecks and shortages of food, such as the crop mix, the size of public stocks, and the organization of relief for the poor.

Meteorological hazards are often attributed to anthropogenic causes, whereas the inherent variability of climate as an alternative explanation is disregarded. For instance, deforestation in the Alps and poor management of water were denounced as the primary cause of the floods in the early 1850s. However, a careful legal opinion given by a scientist

revealed even then that the frequency of severe floods was due to the recurrence of specific meteorological patterns (C. Pfister 1984).

Population

The "demography of scarce resources" (Mattmüller 1987) is a major theme associated with solar-energy societies. The limited availability of cultivable land, the levels of agricultural productivity, and, in the long run, the supply of energy, set upper limits to the growth of population. It was left to early modern societies to establish reproductive behavior so nicely tuned as, on the one hand, to ensure the survival of society and, on the other, not to swamp it with human beings, who, in the circumstances of the day, could provoke even more severe culling by famine crises (Flinn 1981). Indeed, despite the great potential for exponential growth of human populations, early modern societies in Europe witnessed very modest growth of less than 1% per annum. This gradual increase is connected to the slow rise in food production, which in turn depended on the uptake of new land for cultivation and the creation and diffusion of innovations. For England, Wrigley and Schofield (1981) have convincingly demonstrated that the growth rates of population and food prices were negatively correlated. This balancing of population growth and food capacity was achieved by a set of interrelated economic, biological, and social factors.

While the debate is still going over the extent to which changes in mortality were connected to exogenous, mostly epidemiological and climatic variables (Perrenoud 1985), there is agreement that the regulation of growth was achieved by controlling fertility in response to changing levels of mortality and economic capacity. Hajnal (1965) has shown

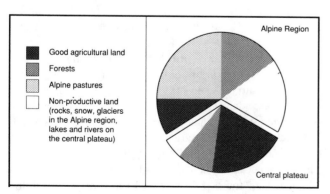

Figure 39.2 Land use in Switzerland.

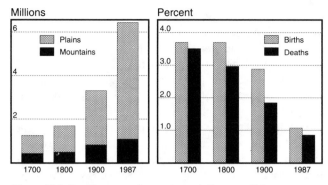

Figure 39.3 Fertility, mortality, and population growth in Switzerland, 1687–1987.

Switzerland (Fig. 39.3) are consistent with those observed elsewhere in western Europe.

It is not yet clear why population growth in western Europe after 1750 was no longer interrupted by major setbacks. Improvements in nutrition standards [perhaps connected to declining (child-) mortality and rising fertility], improvements in medical knowledge and standards of hygiene, and exogenous changes in the relationship between pathogenic agents and people are mentioned as the main causes (Frisch 1978; McKeown 1983; Perrenoud 1985). Rapid growth was avoided, however, because social checks were still operative: In Switzerland 20% of the women born between 1806 and 1830 remained single, and the mean age at marriage for women stood at 28 years. Infant mortality, moreover, was still at the high level of 25% in the 1870s (Höpflinger 1986).

The subsequent changes are known as the demographic transition. From the 1880s, mortality declined in the long term, when new standards in personal hygiene were set and the quality of medical services improved. The change was slow and gradual; it took 60 years for death rates to fall from 20% to 10% (Diserens 1985). Birth control spread shortly after the onset of mortality decline. In order to determine the social and economic conditions that prevailed when the modern reduction in the rate of childbearing began in Europe, a detailed, quantitative study of fertility in each of the several hundred provinces was undertaken (Coale and Watkins 1986). The results require that the classic descriptions and explanations of the demographic transition in Europe be modified. It turns out that fertility declined under a wide variety of social, economic, and demographic conditions. Cultural setting influenced the onset and the spread of fertility declines independently of socioeconomic conditions. In Switzerland, compulsory schooling (beginning in the 1870s), the prohibition of factory work for minors (1877), and urbanization all favored the onset of fertility decline. The

that the marriage pattern of most of Europe during the two centuries before 1900 was unique in the world, distinguished by a high age at marriage of women and a high proportion of people who never married at all. This pattern was intimately tied in with the performance of the economy. In early modern Europe, the household was the principal unit of economic production as well as of consumption. Religion, norms, and social control prevented the formation of a new household until the young couple could establish an independent livelihood; in societies outside Europe, a new family was incorporated into a larger economic unit, such as a joint family. The efficiency of late marriage as a "social birth control" is evident: a rise in the age at marriage from 20 to 25 years is equivalent to a drop in fertility of 25% (Knodel 1977). People who remained single were taken out of the reproductive process altogether; in France their percentage doubled from the time of Louis XIV to the Revolution (Henry and Houdaille 1978). Various forms of birth control were also practiced from the seventeenth century (Perrenoud 1974; U. Pfister 1985). The patterns of fertility and mortality in

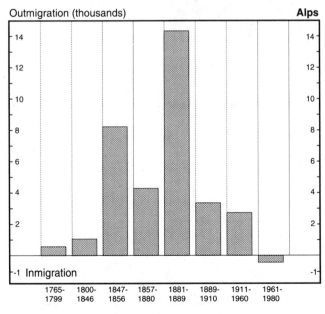

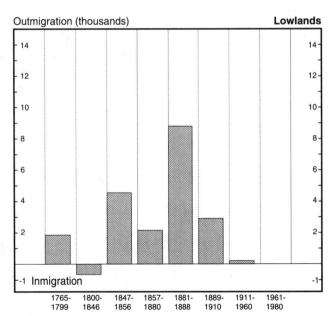

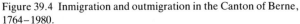

Figure 39.4 Inmigration and outmigration in the Canton of Berne, 1764–1980.

falling trend was interrupted from 1940 to 1964. Today, natural increase is close to zero, and negative growth is expected from the 1990s (Diserens 1985).

Population growth has been very uneven in the lowlands and in the Alps over the past 300 years (Fig. 39.4). The size and the direction of migratory flows are known to have varied according to the relationship of push factors (poverty, economic outlook, a series of bad crops) and pull factors (economic opportunities outside the region). From the early nineteenth century, the flow from the alpine region was directed mainly to the lowlands, where agricultural growth, urbanization, and industrialization required more manpower.

When the knowledge of new opportunities overseas spread and the cost of transportation declined, emigration became a temporary safety valve during the crises of the 1850s and the 1880s. The periods of maximum out-migration 1846–56 and 1881–88 are connected to sequences of poor crops. Some of the migrants went overseas. However, the loss of 500,000 people through emigration was almost balanced by immigration in the economic boom period after 1890 (Gruner 1980).

It may be concluded that social regulation of population has been a key factor in slowing the rate of transformation in preindustrial societies. This is illustrated in the following hypothetical model: had population grown continuously at a rate of 2% during the nineteenth century, Switzerland would have been burdened with almost 10 million people on the eve of World War I; the actual population was 3.8 million. Migration was also crucial in diverting the brunt of human impacts from the mountains to the lowlands.

Technological Change in Solar-Energy Society

Until the coming of the railroad, technological innovations focused mainly upon a greater efficiency in the various forms in which solar energy could be captured (water-power, agriculture, forestry) and also upon a more efficient application of manpower (soft mechanization of agriculture and cottage industries).

The Lowlands   Within the three-field system, carrying capacity was moderate because yields were poor and because only part of the land was cultivated (Thut and Pfister 1986) (Fig. 39.5). Fields, meadows, and forests provided most of the basic needs of the population. Subsistence crises were triggered by poor harvests. Cultivation expanded slowly, at the expense of marginal and forested areas.

Grain yields did not increase in the long run because manure was in short supply. This in turn resulted from the low number of cattle in proportion to the surface of the arable fields. The shortage of hay, which was connected to the shortage of meadows, blocked the possibility of increasing the size and productivity of animal herds. And, to complete the circle, the risk of expanding the meadows was not taken, given the poor grain yields. One-third of the fields lay fallow every year from lack of manure (C. Pfister 1984). Frequent plowing undertaken to discourage weeds promoted gully-erosion (Blaikie and Brookfield 1987:126ff).

A nexus of four interrelated innovations constituted an "agricultural revolution." The seeding of clover in the fallow, the large-scale planting of potatoes, the feeding of cattle indoors during summer, and the construction of underground reservoirs for collecting dung-water made it possible to break out of the vicious circle of meager meadows and poor grain yields. The cultivation of clover tapped new biological resources of nitrogen; the potato was twice as effective in assimilating the sun's energy as grain, hence its superior productivity (Kleiber 1967); the amount of manure that could be brought into the fields doubled, as soon as the livestock were kept indoors in summer; and the dung-water, which previously had not been collected, was used as a fertilizer for

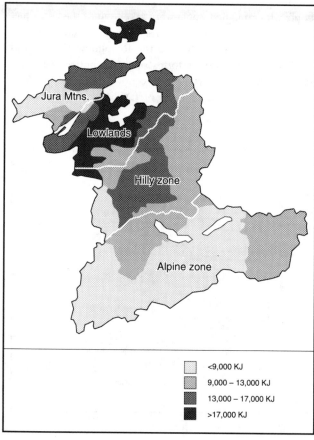

Figure 39.6 Food production per capita in the Swiss Canton of Berne.

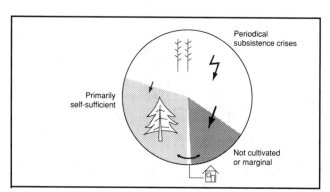

Figure 39.5 Land use in the Swiss lowlands prior to the agricultural revolution.

the meadows (Hauser 1974). These innovations were promoted by agricultural societies from the late eighteenth century.

The additional supply of nitrogen allowed more land to be cultivated: the fallow was abolished and the commons were converted into potato fields for the poor. Agricultural intensification required additional inputs of labor. For some decades, food production and population growth were positively related in a self-reinforcing process (Pfister 1984), as it has been described by Boserup (1965). This explains why large parts of the country remained self-sufficient after a century of population growth (Fig. 39.6).

On the other hand, land reclamation and intensification consumed natural habitats. Marshes were drained, shrubs and hedges were cut down, and the application of dung-water to meadows reduced floral and faunal diversity. The forests no longer met the energy requirements of the population (Fig. 39.7), nor did housing keep pace with numbers. Land became a scarce resource. The rising price of building ground (and of energy) caused households to draw together (Thut and Pfister 1986).

We may conclude that a substantial increase in food capacity was obtained by increasing the efficiency of the existing solar-energy system and by expanding the cultivated area at the expense of marginal land. This process absorbed part of the growing population.

The Alps Many parts of the Alps were self-sufficient at the turn of the eighteenth century. Cereals were grown on small plots in the valleys; most of the cultivated surface was devoted to dairy production. Meadows provided hay for feeding cattle in the winter. During the growing season, the animals grazed on the pastures at higher altitudes. The fodder potential in the valleys was rarely in balance with the size of the pastures on the Alps. In order to use fully the given fodder potential, many regions had to sell their excess cattle in the fall to markets in the lowlands and to buy (or rent) young animals in the following spring. They were thus bound into an interregional trading system.

The forests in the Alps and those in the adjacent hilly zone were a major source of firewood and lumber for the resident population and for the lowlands. Cheese manufacturing and a few local iron mills and saltworks drew on the resources. The bulk of forest produce was consumed for cooking and for heating the houses of the local population; the importance of the urban centers and the mills should not be overestimated. To take two examples: the demand of the saltworks near Aigle (western Switzerland) did not exceed the requirements of a small parish (Hahling 1985); and 30,000 fireplaces in the Austrian province of Carinthia burned 50% more fuel than did the large ironworks of this same region (Sieferle 1982).

Surges of population in the Alps (and long-term drops in winter temperatures) had the greatest overall impact upon ecological resources. The demand for firewood went along with a demand for new pastures; when the growing season was shortened for several subsequent years by climatic fluctuations, people increasingly turned to goats, which could feed on steep patches of grassland and on the produce of forests.

Between 1700 and 1900, the resident population of the Alps almost doubled. In some districts of the Canton of Appenzell, population density was more than 200 persons/km^2, exceeding the carrying capacity of the local ecosystem (Tanner 1982). Such growth, very moderate in comparison to that of the lowlands, was based upon cottage industry and the potato. In the mountains of eastern Switzerland, most families had acquired a loom, which was almost as common and indispensable as a table and benches (Braun 1984). The potato is first mentioned in the early eighteenth century. Until the 1850s, it had spread through most of the alpine area without, however, brushing grain cultivation completely aside (C. Pfister 1986).

The planting of potatoes on land formerly sown with wheat or barley may have nourished 26–28% of the total population increase registered in the Bernese Alps between 1764 and 1850. Contemporaries already assumed that the new staple spurred population growth (Schneider 1848). Frisch (1978) has shown evidence for a direct effect of nutrition on reproductive ability. Anthropologists have inferred the operation of similar processes in Tibetan and Nepalese localities that they have studied (Fürer-Haimendorf 1964; Goldstein 1978). Netting (1981) has shown this relationship for a village in the Swiss Alps. During the early nineteenth century, population growth in the highlands was accompanied by pauperization and environmental degradation. From 1790 to 1847, the number of cows per capita fell by one-third, and the number of goats by one-quarter in the Bernese Alps (C. Pfister 1984).

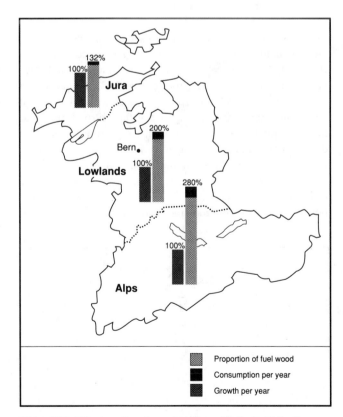

Figure 39.7 Tree growth and wood consumption in the Swiss Canton of Berne, 1885.

In 1885, the yearly growth of trees (crippled by the teeth of countless goats) replaced only 38% of the consumption of fuelwood (Fig. 39.7).

We may conclude that population growth in the alpine area, though moderate, exceeded the long-term carrying capacity of the forests in the nineteenth century. Emigration, the railways, and the coming of hydroelectric power may have prevented the Alps from going the way of the mountain areas around the Mediterranean, which became denuded and sterile as a consequence of deforestation.

Technological Changes in Fossil-Energy Society

The Lowlands   The transformation of the lowland landscape centered upon the process of urbanization. New transportation networks – the railways in the late nineteenth century, and the expressways in the late twentieth century – spearheaded change by marking out the range in which market forces were most effective. For the Canton of Bern, the modifications from the beginnings of the railway age in 1865 have been quantified (Fig. 39.8). While these estimates require some assumptions, their validity is sufficient to support the conclusions.

In 1865, many families still lived in tiny, filthy tenements without bathrooms or other facilities; the per capita values at that time include working areas, public buildings and facilities, parks, playing-fields, and the like. The increase in residential space per person up to 1950 improved this situation. Because urbanization was connected to public transportation, it was relatively sparing of land. New suburbs expanded in walking or biking distance around railway stations and streetcar stops. Outside the range of public transportation, the landscape remained unaffected (Thut and Pfister 1986). Between 1885 and 1945, federally subsidized

drainage and land-reclamation projects enlarged the cultivated area by 1,153 km^2 at the expense of marginal lands (Egli 1986).

After 1960, a network of expressways was created. It opened up large zones as residential areas for commuters or as building sites for shopping centers and service facilities (C. Pfister 1973). Connected to mass motorization, settlement spread widely in those areas from which the urban centers could be reached by the expressways in a short time. Rising incomes and mass consumption stimulated demand for residential space. In the city of Basel, for example, the residential surface per capita almost doubled between 1950 and 1980. The expansion of workspace within the centers sent prices for real estate upward; noise and pollution led to a decline in the quality of life. As a consequence, the residential population was pushed to the periphery. In the Canton of Thurgau, 14,000 new apartments were built in the 1970s, whereas population remained stable. In contrast, many empty buildings and unused roads in the zones of heavy outmigration were not reconverted to productive use. As a consequence, the building-over of the landscape is changing the face of the country at a rate much faster than the rate of population growth (Fig. 39.9). Losses occur mainly at the expense of the most fertile soils, which are at the same time those best suited for mechanical cultivation. More than 1,000 km^2 of fields and meadows were irreversibly transformed to residential areas, service facilities, and expressways from 1942 to 1967. The urbanized area doubled as a consequence. The productive land is dwindling at a rate of 1 m^2/sec today (Bundesamt für Raumplanung 1986). Natural biota have almost disappeared.

The Alps   With alpine agriculture shifted to the periphery by the availability of food from elsewhere, a new economic base was created by classical tourism. In the eighteenth and early nineteenth centuries, descriptions of the mountains and glaciers published by foreign travelers created an image of the country that, after the coming of the railroad, provided the basis for tourism in large numbers. Where recreational development created new opportunities, such as part-time jobs for mountain farmers, the exodus of the population could be slowed down or reversed. Technological innovations in the domains of energy (long-distance transfer of electric power) and transportation (rack-railway and cable car) pro-

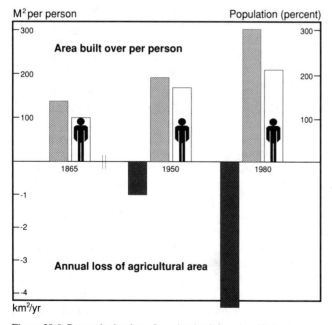

Figure 39.8 Per capita land use for urbanization and traffic in the Swiss Canton of Berne compared to losses of productive soil, 1865–1980.

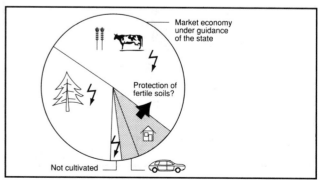

Figure 39.9 Land use in the Swiss Lowlands today.

moted the transformation of the higher parts of the upland zone. The outbreak of World War I put an abrupt end to this period of classical tourism. The *Grand Hotellerie* fell into an economic crisis, because an indigenous guest potential did not yet exist for substitution. In addition, the construction sector suffered from this breakdown.

Renewed demand for touristic activities was interrupted again by the worldwide crisis in the 1930s, which brought the end of tourism in smaller stations. Given the insufficient operational *hotellerie* in those places, middle- and working-class people made up the majority of visitors at the eve of World War II. This new demand for modest accommodation led to the creation of guest houses and rooms for rent by residents. This alternative to the hotel sector spread throughout the mountain areas and led to a mushroomlike growth of *parahotellerie* (for rent) and second homes (privately owned and used).

The "new age" in tourism began with a tremendous growth in both traditional and new supply elements in the early 1950s. The take-off took place first at the traditional resorts, but then spread out all over the alpine region, creating new vacation areas. Increase in income and leisure time, and the mobility created by automobiles (which increased in Switzerland from 147,000 units in 1950 to 2.6 million in 1986) acted as push factors to this development. The attraction of the mountains – at first for summer vacations, later for winter sports – is the overall pull factor for a population living more and more in urban areas (Fig. 39.10).

Today more than 250,000 jobs depend directly or indirectly on such mass tourism. A new alpine development pattern has emerged. Industrialized zones and centers of tourism have increased their income level, while side valleys inaccessible to

tourism and dependent upon agriculture are still losing population. Disparities and migrations thus occur within the mountain area.

The decline of mountain agriculture was halted during World War II. In 1955, approximately 70,000 farm holdings still existed; only 47,000 remained in 1985 (only 37% of them full-job farms). During the past decade, mountain agriculture has recovered somewhat as a consequence of modernization and hobby farming on tiny plots. The abandonment of farmland – 800 km² in 1972 – (Surber, Amiet, and Kobert 1973) was another consequences of the decline. There has been, however, a recent wave of fallow reclamation as a reaction to the increase in natural hazards (avalanches, fire) and the loss of productive potential (Walther and Julen 1986).

Until World War II the supply of water power was less than 2 million kW, and the surface of artificial reservoirs was only approximately 40 km². A tremendous expansion of water-power utilization took place between 1955 and 1970, when the 10-million-kW limit was reached. Today, the economically usable water-power potential is almost completely exploited. The total surface of artificial lakes has reached 120 km² (Bundesamt für Wasserwirtschaft 1980; Leibundgut 1984).

Forest management is plagued with the problem of insufficient utilization, a reversal of the serious overexploitation in the nineteenth century. In order to ensure sustained forest tending, fellings should be increased by 50%. This is probably not feasible in the foreseeable future. The consequences of inadequate management are aggravated by those of air pollution. Surveys taken after 1983–85 suggested that *Waldsterben* was spreading continuously (Fig. 39.11). However, conditions have not worsened any more in the second half of the decade (Sanasilva 1989).

The trees at the upper timberline are particularly affected because the toxic substances concentrate just below the inversions that are often located at this altitude (Eidg. Department des Innern 1984). Since 1950, the mileage covered by motorcars has increased fifteenfold. Over this period, CO emissions have grown fivefold, HC emissions sevenfold, and NO_x emissions nineteenfold (Fig. 39.12). Technology offers a solution in the form of the catalytic converter, which has been made compulsory for new cars. Reductions in HC and NO emissions are expected as a result. It is not yet clear, however, whether this reduction will suffice to prevent an ecological breakdown of the forests.

We may conclude that the tapping of fossil energy and the adoption of new technologies have brought the Swiss population an increase in wealth and individual well-being that is outstanding by historical and global standards. On the other hand, the human impact upon the environment has been multiplied by an ever-rising consumption of land and energy, on the one hand, and by the production of pollution, on the other. Today, the level of pollution has become the limiting factor for further improvement.

Exponential Growth: Tourism, Agriculture, and Natural Resources in Grindelwald

Grindelwald – the second tourist resort (after Interlaken) in the Bernese Oberland – has, since the middle of the

Overnight stays (millions)

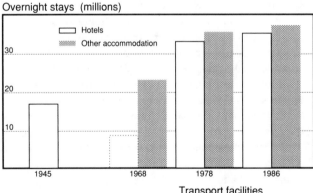

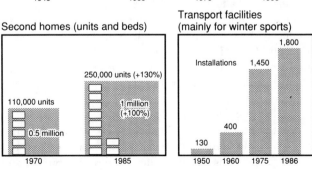

Figure 39.10 Growth of demand-and-supply structure in Swiss tourism.

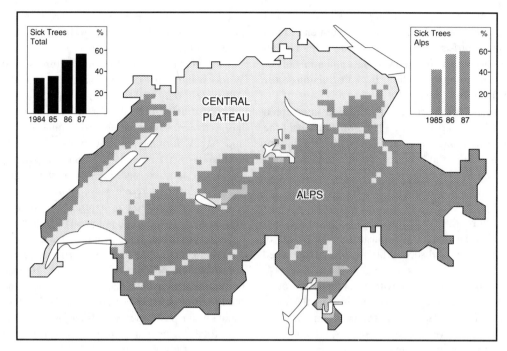

Figure 39.11 Percentage of trees suffering from *Waldsterben*, 1985–1987. Source: Sanasilva 1987

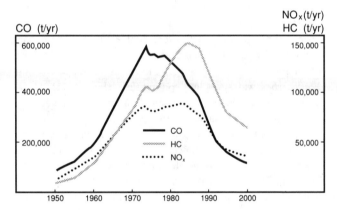

Figure 39.12 Output of CO, HC, and NO$_x$ from private motors in Switzerland, 1950–2000. (Extrapolation to the year 2000.)

last century, undergone all of the phases of recreational development, from the pioneering days of alpinism up to the expansion of the 1960s and 1970s. Today, with 3,500 inhabitants and 9,000 beds, there are still 260 farms, though over 80% are operated only part-time. There is almost no fallow land. Over a long period of assimilation, economic and social links between agriculture and tourism have been established, to the benefit of local development. The regulation of agricultural land use, dating back to A.D. 1404, provides control over resources. Exponential growth, however, is weakening the surviving links between agriculture and tourism, leading to environmental degradation.

The Dynamics of Modern Tourism

Growth processes can often be understood as self-intensifying spirals that persist until the resources required for development are exhausted or substitutes are found. The

growth in tourism of the 1960s and 1970s was based on the explosive expansion of winter sports, and is the result of a constant process of adjustment between local accommodation, transportation, and ski-run capacities. Under conditions of growth, overcapacities can always be justified with forward planning, but they inevitably generate a pressure on the lagging sectors to adjust (Krippendorf 1984). Where there are no real economic alternatives, the development of tourism follows this model, leading increasingly down a one-way street in which the entire economic structure becomes more and more dependent on tourism. This "touristification" of a local or regional economy leads to an increasing uncoupling of the traditional occupations, particularly those of agriculture and associated small trades, and to a centralization of the tourist infrasturcture and the local supply structure. Equally, the tourist sector generally does not develop as an integrated economic whole, but separates into a service and a construction sector. In the latter, a strong building trade presses forward with the building of chalets and second homes. The political control of this process is very difficult, since it endangers jobs in the building sector, clearly preferred to those in tourism by the resident population. The basic model of this dynamic, with the main effects, is shown in Fig. 39.13 (Messerli 1987). This model guides the following discussion of the economic, societal, and environmental effects of the exponential growth of tourism.

Economic and Social Effects

The positive correlation between tourist development and population growth must not obscure the fact that this development does not meet the vocational aspirations of resident people. The emigration of qualified young people who represent a potential for innovation in other economic

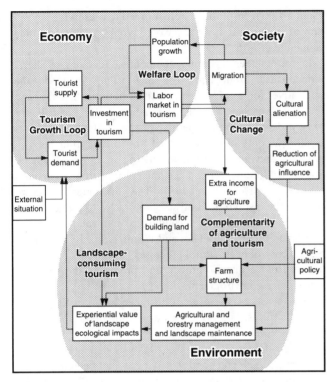

Figure 39.13 A basic model of tourism, agriculture, and the natural environment.

sectors cannot be prevented. For others, construction and services for tourism create two labor markets that clearly differ with respect to qualifications and attractiveness. Young people and the resident population prefer construction, which intensifies the pressure on the construction sector to provide jobs. Anyone who suggests "zero growth" provokes political opposition from wide sections of the population. Thus, any community with a substantial construction sector is unable to act as long as exogenous demand for construction continues, and the potential labor force cannot be displaced to other regions (Wiesmann 1986).

The strong pressure on mountain agriculture to rationalize is dampened in tourist areas by the possibilities of part-time employment. The maintenance of land-use and resource protection requires a sufficient number of farms and a variety of farm types. There are three central links between agriculture and tourism: the labor market, the land market, and the development of the spatial infrastructure. The relationships with regard to the labor market are generally positive, and the cultivation of lots and alpine meadows is facilitated by the construction of access roads. The greatest conflicts occur in the land market (Nägeli 1986). The loss of ownership and control of land by agriculture is regarded as "expropriation."

The social and cultural changes produced by the emergence of mass tourism are manifested in a coexistence of traditional and modern values and behaviors in the local society. Postwar tourism has initiated an economic and social revolution with lasting effects on the rural community. The economic opening of a village or region, necessary for its continued viability, is always a social and cultural threat. It is often overlooked that these rural communities feel far less threatened and troubled by tourists than by the immigration of new residents. The infiltration by these immigrants represents a threat to traditional village societies; their permanence is given greater emphasis than the temporary presence of tourists, who can be more easily kept at a distance. However, the sociocultural and political boundaries between natives and immigrants are exactly where social and cultural change in the village societies takes place (Meyrat-Schlee 1983).

The social and cultural ability of local and regional societies to adapt to new economic realities and new patterns of behavior are defined by the growth dynamics of tourism. Rapid growth allows no time for the assessment of the situation and the evolution of new, genuine objectives. Only an adequate supply of time allows an opening to new ideas and a critical evaluation of new facts against a familiar background. In this way, social and cultural change takes place without abrupt breaks in continuity.

Effects on Natural Systems and Landscapes

The continued high natural diversity of species and landscape types in Grindelwald shows that mountain agriculture regulates and preserves resources. Over generations, agriculture has maintained an equilibrium of uses that guaranteed its outputs and a secure living space. Where it changed natural vegetation, the new habitats contributed to the diversity of the landscape. Through site-adapted use that remained unchanged over long periods, mountain agriculture was a dependable partner of the indigenous fauna and flora (Price 1987).

Two phenomena characterize the current utilization of the alpine cultural landscape. Where the potential revenues from land are especially low, the area used for agriculture tends to decrease or to be used less intensively. This also applies to forests, in which large areas remain unused because wood prices are low or because access is inadequate. Conversely, use is intensified where mechanical cultivation is possible or where land rents become particularly high as a result of tourist demand. Linked to this are considerable ecological risks, such as those associated with fallow land, unstable and critical forests, and the development of new areas and uncontrolled tourist sprawl (Price 1987).

The diversity of animal and plant species decreases as altitude increases. Consequently, it is wrong to think that higher areas still undisturbed by tourism are suitable retreats for threatened species. The greatest conflicts with the preservation of a diverse fauna and flora occur around settlements in which tourism consumes the most land, since agricultural intensification has also made the greatest advances close to settlements (Schiess 1984).

For the winter sports, the alpine landscape is almost completely substitutable, whereas for aesthetic experience and recreation it is not. The beauty and individuality of the landscape play a central role in tourism. For the local resident, this landscape provides identity through its symbolic value; the discussion about the preservation of the landscape must focus on all of these affected populations.

The Lessons

There is a reasonable suspicion that the dynamics of the growth spiral, shown in Fig. 39.13, typically prevail over political control and leadership, with consequent sociocultural and ecological "erosion." An escape from tourism's beaten track of development calls primarily for a strategy carefully directed at gaining time and markedly slowing growth. Unless time can be gained, there is no hope that aims and means of future development can be established in an opinion-leading process with wide political support. Consequently, the definition of clear limits to growth is indispensable. In addition, the most recent discussions of "qualitative developments" in tourism show how easily qualitative objectives can be linked with quantitative growth. All political declarations are useless if the instrumentation to enforce their objectives is not developed simultaneously.

Institutions and Cognitive Patterns

The technological change that ultimately leads to environmental transformation should be interpreted in the context of institutions and values, for the application and expansion of new technologies is undertaken within the institutional framework of a society. Institutions may block, regulate, or unleash the introduction of technological innovations, whereas action or inaction is justified with reference to the set of values and norms that underlie the coherence of a society.

Human–environment interactions of old societies were, in most cases, regulated by local elites at the level of the village community. It is true that the cantons (which were still independent states at that time) sought to regulate flows of matter and energy through the allocation of manure and the conservation of wood (Schuler 1980). In many cases, though, the cantonal administrations were too weak to enforce their edicts. For the most part, the economies of sovereign territories were composed of domestic rural economies, each primarily geared to establish a labor-consumer balance. Land use was attuned to a maximum of self-sufficiency. Only excess production was traded. The static image of society reflected the reality of a zero-growth economy.

Regulation was directed toward the management of scarce resources. This included fixing the load and the kind of animals on communal forests and pastures and their temporal and spatial allocation, caring for the maintenance of pastures, scheduling seeding and harvesting in order to allow prior and subsequent pasturing on the fields and meadows, and building and maintaining flood-control works (Thut and Pfister 1986). Entitlement to communal resources was restricted to a small number of households, the burghers. Competition was restricted by checking immigration and marriages. Because leaving the village community involved considerable losses, mobility was low. Fields could not be converted into meadows without the consent of the central authorities, the owners of the tithe and the village community (C. Pfister 1984). This was one of the reasons for the stagnation of yields in the long run. This static order was given religious justification. Natural disasters were interpreted as divine punishment and were made a pretext for repressing undesirable activities

(Simon 1981). Institutions were attuned to preserving a given flow of resources in favor of a closed group, not to promoting economic growth.

In the nineteenth century, the political ideology of liberal individualism triumphed. The new values overrode the normative force of religion and tradition. Science and technology became a fetish. The "new society" was believed to be ordered by the competitive market in the best interests of all. The duty of the individual was to look after his own interests and abstain from interfering in those of others. Social institutions derived legitimacy only from their conformity to reason (Langer 1987). The government sought to remove the institutional and social obstacles to free competition. The application of technological innovations was left entirely to the market (Thut and Pfister 1986). By increasing human control over natural processes, new modes of production spurred economic growth and promoted the transformation of the environment.

New measures, however, were taken in order to contain natural hazards. Following the devastating floods that struck the Swiss lowlands in the 1850s, the "ecological anarchy" that permitted deforestation in the Alps was denounced as the primary cause. Flood control previously had been limited to damming and diverting rivers in the lowlands (Vischer 1986). This time, measures for safeguarding and restoring the alpine forests were demanded. The Federal Constitution of 1874 gave the Confederation (founded in 1848) the right to control river embankments and forests and to lay down the regulations required to preserve existing forests. A first law was promulgated in 1876 to protect and restore the forests in the upland zone. Today, cutting within the forests always must be compensated for by at least an equal area of new planting (Luck 1985). Also the Confederation has enacted a great number of measures promoting mountain agriculture in order to prevent those lands from being abandoned (Bussmann 1984).

Decisions regulating the use of environmental resources are taken today at three levels: (1) the communities, at the lowest, still have a considerable degree of self-administration; (2) most of the decision-making, legislation, and execution takes place at the intermediate level of the cantons; (3) at the level of the Confederation, guidelines for cantonal legislation are provided. The weight of public opinion in political decision-making is unique in Switzerland. The instrument of the referendum allows groups of citizens to interfere directly in the process of legislation. Citizens may also propose amendments to the constitution. Daily political decision-making is tightly bound to current trends in public opinion.

Discussion in the media and popular votes suggest that a profound change in values is underway. The ethic to do no harm to the biosphere is widely shared. Concern for nature has reached the top of the political agenda; hence the readiness to invest in new technologies (such as the catalytic converter) to improve the quality of the environment. On the other hand, the new values are not strong enough yet to bring about changes in the way of life – unlimited mobility by automobile has become a fundamental right – or to check the

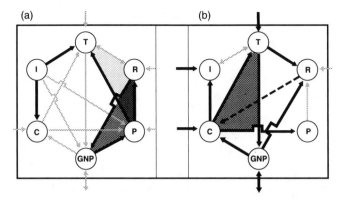

Figure 39.14 Structure and interaction of the main variables within (a) a "society of scarcity" and (b) a "society of abundance." C = cognitive patterns, I = institutions, GNP = gross national product, P = population, R = resources, T = technology.

market system in those domains in which it obviously promotes environmental degradation.

Struggling with Scarcity and Abundance — A Summary

In western Europe, society has been successful in its long-term struggle to avoid scarcity. The unbridled abundance and mass consumption that represent the achievement of this goal, however, are undermining the ecological foundations of human existence. As a consequence, societal action focuses more and more upon improving environmental quality. These changes are reflected in the strength and direction of the links between the variables within the social system, which have in their turn directed environmental transformation (Fig. 39.14).

The solar-energy economy was based upon natural resources and was embedded within a societal framework controlled by institutions. Most activity was directed toward achieving food security. In order to balance food capacity and population growth, the authorities attempted to buffer fluctuations in output in the context of climatic fluctuations in the short term and to adapt population size to the given technology in the long term. Environmental transformation was usually reversible, and varied according to the rate of population growth. In many places, in particular in the Alps, it exceeded the long-term carrying capacity of the forests.

In the market economy, the controlling capacity of institutions was abolished. Technological innovations and market forces stimulated economic growth with an increasing input of fossil energy. The democratic institutions created were controlled by public opinion and economic pressure groups. In order to handle the social tensions associated with economic growth and disparities, social security in the context of a social market economy became the prime aim of society, a goal to be achieved through economic growth. Compared to the situation in the Old Regime, the direction of control was reversed. Society was subjected largely to economic forces, whereas those forces previously had been contained by social institutions. According to the moderate dynamic of economic growth, environmental transformation before 1950 was gradual. Only within the last decades has it become exponential. The ability of democratic institutions to intervene in this

process will depend on the degree to which the emerging ideal of an 'ecosocial market economy' is adopted by a majority of citizens.

Acknowledgments

This research has been supported by the Swiss National Science Foundation. Acknowledgment is due to A. Brodbeck for drawing the original versions of the figures.

References

Blaikie P., and H. Brookfield. 1987. *Land Degradation and Society.* London: Methuen.

Boserup, E. 1965. *The Conditions of Agricultural Growth. The Economics of Agrarian Change under Population Pressure.* London: Aldine.

Braun, R. 1984. *Das Ausgehende Ancien Régime in der Schweiz.* Göttingen: Vandenhoeck and Ruprecht.

Bundesamt für Raumplanung, ed. 1986. Der Wettstreit um den Boden. Bern: EDMZ.

Bundesamt für Wasserwirtschaft. 1980. Oral information.

Bussmann, W. 1984. Distribution of tasks among the different levels of government and problems of federalism. In *Transformation of Swiss Mountain Regions*, ed. E. Brugger, G. Furrer, B. Messerli, and P. Messerli, 567–79. Bern: Haupt.

Coale A. J., and S. C. Watkins 1986. *The Decline of Fertility in Europe.* The Revised Proceedings of a Conference on the Princeton European Fertility Project. Princeton, NJ: Princeton University Press.

Diserens, M. 1985. Sterblichkeit. Bevölkerungsprojektionen. In *Sterben die Schweizer aus?* Kommission "Bovölkerungspolitik", ed. Bern: Haupt.

Egli, H. R. 1986. Ländliche Neusiedlung in der Schweiz vom Ende des 19. Jahrhunderts bis zur Gegenwart. *Erdkunde* 40:197–208.

Eidg. Department des Innern (Hg.) 1984. Waldsterben und Luftverschmutzung. Bern: EDMZ.

Flinn, M. W. 1981. *The European Demographic System, 1500–1820.* Baltimore, MD: John Hopkins.

Frisch, R. 1978. Population, food intake and fertility. *Science* 199:22–30.

Fürer-Haimendorf, C. V. 1964. *The Sherpas of Nepal.* Berkeley, CA: University of California Press.

Goldstein, M. C. 1978. Pahari and Tibetan polyandry revisited. *Ethnology* 17:325–338.

Gruner, E. 1980. Immigration et marché du travail en Suisse au XIXème siècle. In *Les migrations internationales de la fin du XVIIe siècle à nos jours*, ed. G. Dupeux, 175–94. Paris: Centre de la Recherche Scientifique.

Hahling, A. 1985. Dans les Alpes Vaudoises, durant 3 siècles: Point de bois-point de sel. Difficultés et solutions. In History of Forest Utilization and Forestry in Mountain Regions, ed. A. Schuler. *Beiheft zur Schweiz Zeitschrift für Forstwesen* 74: 137–52.

Hajnal, J. 1965. European marriage patterns in perspective. In *Population in History*, ed. D. V. Glass and D. E. C. Eversley. London: Edward Arnold.

Hauser, A. 1974. Güllewirtschaft und Stallmist – zwei grosse Erfindungen der Landwirtschaft. *Schweiz. Landw. Forschung* 13:15–26.

Henry, L., and J. Houdaille. 1978. Célibat et âge au mariage aux XVIIe – XIXe siècles en France. I: Célibat définitif. *Population* 33:43–84.

Höpflinger, F. 1986. *Bevölkerungswandel in der Schweiz.* Grüsch: Rüegger.

Kleiber, M. 1967. *Der Energiehaushalt von Mensch und Haustier. Ein Lehrbuch der Tierenergetik.* Hamburg: Parey.

Knodel, J. 1977. Family limitation and the fertility transition: evidence from the age patterns of fertility in Europe and Asia. *Population Studies* 31:219–49.

Krippendorf, J. 1984. The capital of tourism in danger. In *The Transformation of Swiss Mountain Regions*, E. Brugger, G. Furrer, B. Messerli, and P. Messerli, ed. Bern: Haupt.

Langer G. F. 1987. *The Coming of Age of Political Economy 1815–1825*. New York: Greenwood Press.

Leibundgut, 1984. Hydrological potential-changes and stresses. In *The Transformation of Swiss Mountain Regions*, E. Brugger, G. Furrer, B. Messerli, and P. Messerli, ed. 167–96. Bern: Haupt.

Luck, M. 1985. *A History of Switzerland. The First 100,000 Years: Before the Beginnings to the Days of the Present*. Palo Alto, CA: SPOSS.

Mattmüller, M. 1987. *Bevölkerungsgeschichte der Schweiz 1500–1700*. Basel: Helbling and Lichtenhahn.

McKeown, T. 1983. Food, infection and population. *Journal of Interdisciplinary History* 14:227–47.

Messerli, P. 1987. The development of tourism in the Swiss Alps: Economic, social and environmental effects. Experience and recommendations from the Swiss MAB Programme. *Mountain Research and Development*, 7 (1):13–24.

Meyrat-Schlee, E. 1983. Werte und Verhalten. *Bedeutung und Wirkungsweise von Wertsystemen im Entwicklungsprozess einer Berggemeinde, aufgezeigt am Beispiel von Grindelwald*. Schlussbericht schweiz. MAB-Programm Nr. 2. Bern: Bundesamt für Umweltschutz.

Nägeli, R. 1986. Die Berglandwirtschaft und Alpwirtschaft in Grindelwald. Schlussbericht schweiz. MAB-Programm Nr. 21. Bern: Bundesamt für Umweltschutz.

Netting, R. 1981. *Balancing on an Alp. Ecological Change and Continuity in a Swiss mountain Community*. Cambridge: Cambridge University Press.

Perrenoud, A. 1974. Malthusianisme et protestantisme: "un modèle démographique Weberien". *Annales E.S.C.* 29:975–88.

———. 1985. Le biologique et l'humain dans le déclin séculaire de la mortalité. *Annales E.S.C.*, 113–35.

Pfister C. 1973. Landschaftswandel im Bereich von Autobahnanschlüssen. Die Bedeutung des neuen Verkehrsträgers für die betriebliche Standortwahl und die Raumordnung am Beispiel der N1 zwischen Bern und Rothrist. *Geographica Helvetica* 4:200–217.

Pfister, C. 1984. Bevölkerung, Klima und Agrarmodernisierung 1525–1860. Das Klima der Schweiz von 1525–1860 und seine Bedeutung in der Geschichte von Bevölkerung und Landwirtschaft. Bern: Haupt.

Pfister, C. 1986. Bevölkerung, Wirtschaft und Ernährung in den Berg- und Talgebieten des Kantons Bern 1760–1860. In Wirtschaft und Gesellschaft in Berggebieten, ed. M. Mattmüller. *Itinera* 5/6:361–91.

Pfister, U. 1985. Die Anfänge von Geburtenbeschränkung. Eine Fallstudie (ausgewählte Zürcher Familien im 17. und 18. Jahrhundert). Bern: Peter Lang.

Price, M. 1987. Tourism and forestry in the Swiss Alps. Parasitism or symbiosis. *Mountain Research and Development* 7 (1):1–12.

Sanasilva Waldschadenbericht 1989. Eidgenöss. Anstalt für das Forstlitche Versuchswesen CH8903 Birmenstorf.

Sanasilva Waldschadenbericht 1989. Eidgenöss. Anstalt für das forstiche Versuchswesen CH8903 Birmenstorf.

Schiess, H. 1984. Erhaltung und Gefährdung der Tierwelt durch landwirtschaftliche und touristische Nutzung und Nutzungsänderungen. In: *Die Berglandwirtschaft im Spannungsfeld zwischen Oekonomie und Oekologie*, 47–56. Bern: Bundesamt f. Landwirtschaft.

Schneider, J. R. 1848. *Vortrag der Direktion des Inneren an den Regierungsrat zu Handen des Grossen Rates über die Angelegenheit der Auswanderung*. Bern: Wyss.

Schuler, A. 1980. Wald- und Holzwirtschaftspolitik der alten Eidgenossenschaft. *Beiheft zu den Zeitschriften des Schweiz. Forstvereins* 68.

Sieferle, R. 1982. *Der unterirdische Wald. Energiekrise und industrielle Revolution*. München: Beck.

Simon C. 1981. *Untertanenverhalten und obrigkeitliche Moralpolitik. Studien zum Verhältnis zwischen Stadt und Land im ausgehenden 18. Jahrhundet am Beispiel Basels*. Basel: Helbling & Lichtenhahn.

Steppacher, R. 1985. Institutionalismus. In: *Die Zukunft der Oekonomie. Wirtschaftswissenschaftliche Forschungsansätze im Vergleich*, ed. J. Jarre, 30–95. Rehberg-Loccum: Evangelische Akademie.

Surber E., R. Amiet, and H. Kobert. 1973. Das Brachlandproblem in der Schweiz. Bericht Nr. 112 der Eidg. Anstalt für das Forstliche Versuchswesen. Birmenstorf.

Svedin, U. 1985. Economic and ecological theory: differences and similarities. In *Economics of Ecosystem Management*, ed. D. O. Hall and N. Myers 31–40. Dordrecht: Junk.

Tanner, A. 1982. *Spulen-Weber-Sticken. Die Industrialisierung in Appenzell Ausserrhoden*. Zürich: Eigenverlag.

Thut, W., and C. Pfister. 1986. *Haushälterischer Umgang mit Boden. Erfahrungen aus der Geschichte*. Pilotprojekt zum Nationalen Forschungsprogramm 22 "Nutzung des Bodens in der Schweiz". Bern: Programmleitung Boden, Schwarzenburgstr. 179, CH3097 Liebefeld-Bern.

Wiesmann, U. 1986. *Wirtschaftliche, gesellschaftliche und räumliche Bedeutung des Fremdenverkehrs in Grindelwald*. Schlussbericht schweizerisches MAB-Programm Nr. 24. Bern: Bundesamt für Umweltschutz.

Wrigley, E. A., and R. S. Schofield. 1981. *The Population History of England*. London: Arnold.

IV

Understanding Transformations

Editorial Introduction

No aspect of the transformation of the earth is more controversial and problematic than the question, "Why do we transform the environment in the way that we do?" This question has been met with at least two broad types of answers. The first type focuses on the human action per se, such as industrialization causing pollution or agricultural settlement producing deforestation in a frontier region. In these interpretations, the second part of the question ("in the way that we do") is emphasized, making the kind and magnitude of the transformation the dependent variable. The cause then becomes the immediate action or policy that seems to have triggered the environmental consequence(s), not unlike the driving forces examined in Section I. The second type focuses on the reasons for the action or policy, and emphasizes the first part of the question, seeking the underlying forces of human behavior – commonly nonmaterial – that ultimately generate transformation. Here the transformation question is viewed as a subset of a greater question: "Why do we behave in the way that we do?"

To examine the transformation of the biosphere in this second way is to engage fully the social and human sciences, and in so doing, to encounter their distinctive problems of understanding and explanation. They include:

The structure of explanations claiming to be "general," a subject of extensive and diverse philosophical discourse such that the very definition of explanation is controversial;
The difficulty of general causal explanations for humans as "reflexive agents," able to perceive and alter their actions;
The contested identity of the fundamental "driving forces" of human behavior, with many positions claiming but failing to achieve acceptance as the standard;
The minimal attention given in modern social science to the development of a theory of human–nature (or nature–society) relationships, despite the antiquity of the search.

In part because of these circumstances, and also because of the primary focus on a basic stocktaking of transformation in this volume, we can only briefly explore some of the broad avenues through which human behavior is linked to environmental transformation. This exploration is based on a tripar-tite division of the realms of explanation, following Sack (chap. 40), from which theories that purport to provide the keys for this behavior can be said to emanate. The three realms are meaning, social relations, and nature. The chapters in this section are not intended to be exhaustive reviews of the theories in each realm that can be linked to environmental transformation. Rather, by offering examples of the themes characteristic of each realm, they serve to illustrate the strengths, weaknesses, and utility of each.

The first chapter, by Sack, has three objectives. First, it introduces the entire section by discussing the role of reflexivity in explanations of the causes of human behavior. Second, it outlines, with illustrations, the typology of the three explanatory realms. Third, it explores the realm of meaning, with an emphasis on meaning in everyday life. Reflexivity raises philosophical and methodological problems about explanation that are not encountered in most of the physical sciences, suggesting an incongruence between the underlying explanatory constructs of the two basic components of the relationship in question: *human* and *nature*. Real or not, the apparent incongruence can act as a wedge between the physical and human sciences in a pragmatic sense; physical scientists are steeped in the tradition of empirical relationships as central to verification, whereas many social scientists question the usefulness of this particular form of verification for their subjects of inquiry. Sack argues that each of the three realms of knowledge has given rise to theories that claim explanatory priority over those situated in the other two. While these theories of human behavior, and ultimately human–nature relationships, are competing for dominance, however, none has so far achieved this status, because each realm has its own basis of judgment and because most theories undervalue the role of reflexivity.

With the stage thus set, an alternative approach is offered based on the everyday experience of "mass-consumption culture," an experience that Sack believes combines the three realms and reflexivity in a practical way. The basic argument is that western cultures have been largely divorced from serious, day-to-day contact with nature except through consumption, which has transcended sustenance to embrace the very meaning or expression of ourselves. We consume, in part, to display identity, and in so doing, we utilize and transform part of nature. This impact, however, is disguised in various ways. Production is not seen, but the illusion of advertisements, many of which invoke environment, is. Mass culture, so distant from the production process of any consumed good, is hidden from the environmental impact, until that impact affects the ability to consume. The message for those interested in the transformation of the biosphere is clear: mass-consuming culture transforms nature in the way that it does because meaning in everyday life is found through consumption, which is divorced in everyday life from the nature-production matrix.

Inasmuch as this approach emphasizes image and agency as keys to behavior, it may be seen as emanating largely from the *realm of meaning*, although its ties to economics and social relations are readily apparent. Elaboration will be needed, particularly in regard to the issue of the ultimate primacy of the various components. Does mass culture constitute a driving force independent of the larger socioeconomic context; or, as some would contend, does the political economy give rise to mass culture? Does a synergistic relationship rather than one of dominance exist among the components? As do others from the social and human sciences, Sack's argument implies a challenge to the notion that a strong "science-based" environmental awareness is present in mass culture.

The next chapter, by Merchant, takes us into the *realm of social relations*, which emphasizes the influence of the sociopolitical and economic structure of society on human behavior and, ultimately, on the transformation of nature. Certain philosophies/perspectives situated in this realm lay claim not only to a well-developed theory of human behavior, but also to one of human-nature relationships. Briefly, this conceptualization (in a synthesis of its multiple forms) insists on the unity of nature and society, in which nature has meaning only through its human use – the labor process – that leads to the transformation not only of nature, but also of the nature–human relationship itself. Although society cannot transcend the laws of nature, the interpretations of those laws and the use made of nature depend on social structure because relations with nature are "socially constructed," and the use of nature's resources requires social relations. The source of social relations is found in the mode of production as it has emerged in specific contexts. It follows, therefore, that the kind, if not the scale, of transformation at any locale is the product of the socioeconomic structure.

This theoretical foundation has been developed, in part as a critique of the theories of transformation more readily housed within the other two realms, and has not itself received extensive critical examination. While this introduction is not the place for such an examination, several observations specific to understanding human-induced, global transformation may be useful. First, such work to date has proven more intriguing as a philosophy or "optic" of interpretation than as the foundation for a rigorous explanatory framework. This is, in part, because its coherence exists at a high level of abstraction that is not only difficult to employ, but also has not consistently yielded results that cannot

apparently be generated by other means. Second, its call for historical and spatial context as critical to the details of the transformations in question can be used inconsistently with the uniform or common behavior postulated for any mode of production; it is critical of generalizations associated with other theories, but then implies its own through common classes of political economy. Third, and perhaps most importantly, this perspective must logically find significant differences in the kind and, presumably, the scale of transformations associated with different modes of production. Here the reader is referred to chap. 1, where it is argued that empirical documentation of this kind has not been forthcoming beyond the broad sociotechnological sweeps of history, which are uniformly associated with major increases in population. These comments notwithstanding, theories of social relations have much to offer to the understanding of transformation and have been particularly important in emphasizing the role of structure and context as important forces that give rise to the way in which humans make this transformation.

Merchant's chapter on the role of social relations as a basis for understanding the transformation of the biosphere assumes that the basics of such approaches (noted above) are understood, and proceeds ambitiously to critique and expand upon the theme. Critical to understanding transformation, Merchant asserts, is the replacement of the dominating "scientific" paradigm, which segments a process that can be understood only as a whole, and encourages approaches that are synchronic and noncontextual. Dialectical theories from the realm of social relations can avoid these errors for the reasons previously discussed, but can do so adequately only by expanding theory to include reproduction and gender.

The sweep of transformation history, according to Merchant, can be viewed as great changes by way of "ecological revolutions," in which existing human-nature relationships break down and new ones arise. These revolutions are intimately linked to shifts in the mode of production. She draws as an example the changing modes of production in New England, from the subsistence-based Amerindians, to the rise of colonial agriculturalists, mercantile capitalists, nineteenth-century industrialists, and a twentieth-century global service economy within the region – each mode associated with different demands upon and perceptions of the resources of the region. Although production is most directly linked to this transformation, Merchant delves further into the rationale of production by focusing on a second-tier linkage – the changing status of women within different modes, and the internal dynamics of gender-reproduction relationships. In this scheme, gender-reproduction relationships themselves have a synergistic relationship with production, and together they explain the human conditions that give rise to transformation in a specific environmental context. Again, illustrations are drawn from the history of New England.

The typology of "ecological revolutions," the emphasis on context, and the broader dimensions of the association between changing modes of production and changing "modes of transformation" are important for understanding environmental history. Yet demonstration that the environmental impact differs among contemporaneous but varying modes of production – especially those with similar population densities and technologies – will require research expanded beyond individual case studies. Pending such demonstration, the adequacy of the argument remains an open question. Furthermore, the second-tier status given to reproduction-gender implies an indirect relationship with transformation: in this case, as if changing the question from what affects environmental change (production) to what affects production (reproduction-gender).

At least two broad categories of theories emanate from the *realm of nature*. The first is directly associated with the earth and the biological sciences, in that primary explanatory status is given to physical variables that lie in their domain of study. Environmental determinism, or environmentalism, is one such theory, which explains cultural development and, indirectly, environmental transformation in terms of the physical geography of a place or region. Although it largely was abandoned after the first half of this century, elements of it – that is, the primacy of these variables – can be found in a wide assortment of nature–society theories, including some associated with the realms of meaning and social relations. Sociobiological theories offer another example, although they are only ephemerally linked to transformation. The second category of theories draws not upon these variables per se, but upon theoretical analogies and principles largely developed in the physical sciences, especially within ecology. These theories, often labeled cultural/human-ecological, are marked by various systems frameworks. A distinction can be drawn between those that are deductive and synchronic (or at least strive to be) and those that are inductive and diachronic.

It is the latter approach that Butzer offers in this section. After a brief survey of cultural/human–ecological approaches to nature–society relationships, he embarks upon an inductive microstudy that captures many of the attributes of historical cultural–ecological approaches. The subject is the environmental transformation of the village of Aín, in eastern Spain, over the past 375 years, as interpreted through the sociocultural changes in the village, region, and state. From this study, generalizations are derived for agricultural communities and are assessed in terms of ascending spatial scale.

Utilizing systems as a heuristic device, Butzer homes in on a dozen lessons about decision-making, adaptation, and adjustment in Aín, centered on land use and food production, but always in the context of the sociocultural matrix in which the villagers were situated. In this case, environmental transformation resulted from continual trial-and-error adjustments to sustain the family and village, adjustments predicated on a mini-max strategy that balanced short- and long-term needs. Some of these lessons are then examined at the next scale of analysis by way of the population trends of Spain over the past 2,000 years, from which Butzer concludes that population rarely approached the bounds established by the sociotechnological components of the system, and did so only under "unusual" politicoeconomic conditions. While the characteristics of these conditions are not elaborated, Butzer notes that metastable conditions were ultimately met, in which population declines were associated with political devolution. The lesson here is that at varying regional scales,

political economic disruption and population decline have been by no means rare in history, and that while these conditions are obviously related to environmental transformation, the directions of the linkages among these parts of the system have not been documented (see chap. 2). The systems approach does emphasize that almost all human systems are latently unstable and that their overall trajectory has been toward a condition best described as metastable. Interestingly, it is precisely the changes from one state of the system to another that are typically captured in the paleoecological record as periods of major environmental disruption, promoting explanations of simple ecological collapse. Butzer offers a convincing case that the human-nature relationship is much more complex than such themes imply. He concludes by noting that the contemporary global economy shows every sign of an unstable system.

Some criticisms of the systems approaches have focused primarily on the problems inherent in the sheer complexity that hinders closure of the system for analysis. Others cite the often tautological nature of "functionalist" or "adaptationist" explanations of human behavior, and the avoidance of the behavioral and structural foundations of the actions that give rise to the adaptation and/or transformation. Butzer avoids many of these problems by using notions of ecological systems and adaptation as heuristic devices and not as explanatory themes per se. Generalizations about individual behavior and structure are embedded in the analysis, although they are not explicitly connected to standard "isms." In avoiding these pitfalls, the coherence of what is commonly taken for a "general" explanation is lost; Butzer argues, however, that the generalizations gained from the study of Aín are applicable only for cases in similar context and that explanatory variables change as the context and the spatial scale of analysis change.

What then do these chapters tell us about understanding transformation beyond their individual foci and associated explanatory realms? Taken as a whole, they indicate that our transformation of nature stems from complex mixes of behavioral and structural factors that are associated with the prevailing character of the scale and kind of demand, technological capacity, social relations affecting demand and capacity, and the nature of the environment in question. Context matters. They demonstrate that this mix of factors has changed dramatically but unevenly, in a geographical sense, over the 300-year period examined in this volume and that the manner in which aspects of the nature–human relationship are addressed most probably should change as the spatial scale changes. Understanding transformation, then, at least from the view of human behavior, requires multiple forms of analysis, and although practitioners of the subject may be on the verge of identifying the more useful analytical forms by scale (both of space and of complexity), it is doubtful that a relatively simple general explanation of "why we transform the environment in the way that we do" is forthcoming.

B. L. Turner II

40

The Realm of Meaning: The Inadequacy of Human-Nature Theory and the View of Mass Consumption

ROBERT D. SACK

An understanding of human transformation of nature involves understanding not only what we are doing to affect nature, but also why we do it. Describing "what" – in the sense of the volumes of carbon dioxide released into the atmosphere, the amount of soil depleted, or the ozone removed – can be accomplished up to a point without considering social and individual motivations. These motivations, however, must be included in the "why" of human behavior, and knowing the "why" is essential if we expect to change "what" we do. Describing what happens assumes some theoretical view, and verifying theories requires describing the facts.[1] Yet distinguishing between what and why will be useful in this discussion if we do not lose sight of the fact that they are ultimately interrelated. Why we behave the way we do means understanding ourselves as agents and the kind of life we wish to lead, and this understanding may well raise questions about ourselves that are difficult for conventional scientific methods to handle. Much of the "why" in human–nature relations can be understood only through the social side of the equation – that is, through understanding the nature of individuals and societies that create the "what".

Insights into human behavior can come from any method, but in our age, a socially sanctioned and "scientific" understanding of ourselves is preferred and often expected to emerge from theories that are based in concepts from the social sciences. These are often referred to as social theories; here, however, they are called social-science theories. The term social theories is used as a more inclusive category that incorporates "scientific" attempts at understanding human behavior, whether or not they be from the perspective of social science. The term is not used in the more restrictive sense that it has acquired from neo-Marxist approaches. Thus sociobiology, environmental determinism, psychoanalysis, neoclassical economics, and Marxism are all social theories.

The general import of my remarks is skeptical. Although existing social theories contain many useful and provocative insights into our behavior, they do not, and may never, provide us with a general understanding of ourselves as agents transforming ourselves and nature. The reasons for skepticism are far too complex to review comprehensively in this chapter. What I do here is provide a particular framework that maps several of the more important issues.

The framework, or intellectual map, is intended to portray the theoretical interconnections among three well-known problems. The first is the fragmented and partial nature of social theories, and especially social-science theories. The second is the difficulty in developing a science of human nature that has as its subject conscious, reflective, and intelligent human agents. The third is the incongruity between what social theory tells us about the relationships between people and nature, and what our everyday experiences suggest, especially as they are molded by mass consumption. This last issue needs to be raised if we, as reflexive agents, expect our theories to match our experiences. The three are interrelated.

The first section of the chapter considers the problems of reflexivity in the context of causality and free will. The second section is a wide-ranging survey of social theories, focusing on what they have to say about why we transform nature. Their truth or validity is not evaluated. Rather, these theories are used as critiques of one another to show that there is very little common ground to which an objective truth can be anchored, because the theories tend to consider three very different realms as the sources of power over humans – the realms of nature, meaning, and social relations – and because all underestimate the importance of reflexivity or free agency. The third section concentrates on one important component of modern, western, everyday life – that of being a consumer of mass-produced goods and services. Virtually everyone in the West is a consumer in a consumer society. Indeed, our economies are geared to increase people's desires for goods. Mass consumption powers the economy, but it does more. Since mass consumption transforms nature and since the economy of mass consumption dominates the world, these transformations have a global reach. Therefore, each of us, as a consumer in everyday life, becomes intimately involved in this transformation process. In addition, mass consumption provides us with an everyday experience of combining nature, meaning, social relations, and reflexivity (or agency) – a synthesis that is presently beyond the powers of social theory.

The section then examines this everyday experience, focusing in particular on how it molds our attitudes and values toward nature.

Reflexivity

Social theories consist of a multitude of suggestions based on different conceptions of what people are and how they can and should be studied. One of the major cleavages arises from the tensions between scientific method and the nature of the human subject. Much social theory attempts, with the aid of the philosophy of science, to emulate what it conceives to be the structure of natural science. Its overall ideal is to phrase its observations in the form of interrelated (and often deductively linked) generalizations that are subjected to verification and testing. This often implies that empirical associations reveal some sort of deeper causal structure and even a necessity. This chain of inference is not ironclad. Empirical regularities and generalizations do not have to imply causality, and causality does not have to lead to necessity (Bunge 1963; Keat and Urry 1975; Nagel 1986). But they can be linked, and the desire of many social scientists to unearth laws and theories that will explain and predict human behavior seems to suggest that they have the forging of such a chain in mind. Even the embedding of correlation and regression within a hierarchy of structural equations and LISREL models suggests that most social scientists view statistical associations as part of the search for causal connections.[2]

This search further suggests a particular conception of human behavior – one of unfree and unreflexive agents compelled to act by forces beyond their control. Certainly causality can exist side by side with degrees of indeterminism and theoretical incompleteness, but these characteristics are not equivalent to a sense of humans as free and reflexive agents (even when the realm of their agency is restricted). Learning, motivation, and purpose can be included in social-science models, and these models, moreover, can apply uniquely to humans, and thus truly separate us from the rest of creation. Nevertheless, these models are based on rules that generate regular and predictable behavior and, in the long run, either replace free agency with cause or reduce free agency to an appearance or sensation that can be explained away by a more comprehensive analysis of forces controlling us (Nagel 1986: 110–26).

Thus the use of scientific method itself may incline researchers to assume a model of human behavior that relies very little on individual free will and much on structural constraints. It is important to note that constraints need not take the form of causal laws. In fact, constraints most often appear to us in the form of rules and regulations over which we seem to have little or no control.

Still, most of us believe that our sense of agency is not an illusion. Even though our actions are constrained by rules or laws, we are still able to create projects. We set our own goals and attempt to attain them. In so doing, we are reflexive. We provide our own explanations for human actions and learn, evaluate, and react to the theories or explanations of others. Thus, unlike the situation in the natural sciences of subjects studying objects, the social sciences have the problem of subjects studying subjects. This freedom and reflexivity mean that theory can transform its own object (Giddens 1984: 348). From its very beginnings, social science has held this view, as well as a causal or structural one, and has developed attendant methodologies, including *Verstehen* and empathetic understanding, that are quite different from those of the natural sciences (Weber 1947).

Reflexivity complicates the already thorny issue of verification. Evidence is extremely important in a society committed to science, and people, who in their everyday lives theorize about their own behavior as well as the behavior of others, must have their explanations somehow conform to their own experiences. But many of the concepts and posited structures of social theory seem remote from our day-to-day experiences of people and nature. When individuals can provide their own reasons for their own behavior, they may be skeptical of social theories that postulate hidden forces and undisclosed meanings. Because of social science's subject/subject relationship, it matters that social theories are remote from everyday experiences, and this must be taken into account when evaluating social theory. This remoteness is explored here when considering the ways that mass consumption provides a day-to-day structure connecting society to nature.

Reflexivity is a fundamental problem of social science, and social theorists from Marx to Weber to Giddens have struggled to find how it can be contained. Reflexivity is also central to the entire question of why we transform nature in the way we do. An emphasis on the importance of causes or structures tends to make the human realm less autonomous, whereas the opposite is true when we emphasize free agency. When we believe that the most significant part of our behavior is reducible to natural or physical forces, structure is obviously emphasized. This emphasis can still admit that humans, like volcanoes and earthquakes, have an enormous capacity to transform nature, but it insists that the explanation of why we do what we do falls within the province of the natural sciences and that we ultimately have little control over our behavior. Even if we believe that humans are essentially different from other agencies and that the sources of our actions come from particularly human conditions, our actions still could be "structured" and caused if they can be disclosed by natural-science like methods of hypothesis formation and testing. If, however, the reflexive and creative capacities of human nature are emphasized, then little about our behavior toward nature is beyond our capacity to change (if we have the will to do so), but also little about our behavior would then be predictable.

If the duality of causality and free agency (or structure and agency, as it is often termed) is not bridgeable in theory, modern mass consumption – a process changing the biosphere on a global scale – at least provides the illusion of a link between the two. Consumption in this culture both constrains and enables the consumer, and does so by drawing together elements from the realms of society, nature, and meaning (Fig. 40.1). These three realms, in fact, constitute the major territories on our intellectual map of social theory. These three realms are difficult to connect theoretically and, impor-

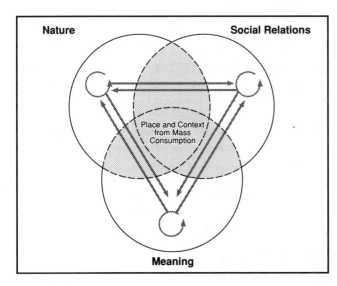

Figure 40.1 The intellectual surface.

tantly, each provides claims for sovereignty over the others. This map will serve as a guide in our discussion of social theory.

Social Theory

I would have us consider nature, social relations, and meaning as interpenetrating conceptual realms identifying important components of modern thought. The three circumscribe separate loci of power in an intellectual terrain roughly embracing the academic domains of the natural sciences, the social sciences, and the humanities. Each realm contains the raw materials to develop theories that claim to explain human nature and also to reduce or subsume the others, but their primary efforts have been confined to issues within their respective domains. The realm of meaning and especially the realm of social relations have generated what I have termed social-science theory. It is in these realms that many of the chapters in this volume place the locus of environmental change, either implicitly or explicitly. And it is within these two realms that the structure/agency debate occurs (indicated by the stippling in Figure 40.1).

The map (Fig. 40.1) illustrates the relationships among these realms, even though by using it, the risk is run of having the divisions appear more rigid and exclusive than they actually are. The arrows portray lines of analysis emanating from theories of a particular realm. Most of the theories examine issues within their own domains and are represented by small, semicircular arrows. Indeed, many chapters in this volume are concerned primarily with the interconnections among natural-science forces and thus focus exclusively upon the realm of nature. The theories explored here are those that have something to say about the other realms. These theories, of course, can be quite complex, passing through two realms, with numerous feedback loops. To simplify, they are represented by straight arrows.

Each realm emphasizes a particular kind of power that controls human beings. The *realm of meaning* draws upon the mind and its power to construct reality. It includes theories

that emphasize the power of ideas, values, and psychological relationships in shaping nature and social organizations. The mind, as the locus of power, molds reality and creates change. This position embraces theories that draw attention to the fact that humans are symbol makers and users. Although reality may exist independently of the mind, it is only through symbolic systems (including ordinary language, art, and science) that the world takes shape. At first glance, it may appear that the realm of meaning implies a commitment to agency over structure: to unbridled creative mental power. However, this is not the case. Some theories of mind do see mental energy in this way, but many propose complex patterns of thought that constrain the form that thought takes.

The *realm of nature* emphasizes the power of those forces that the natural sciences recognize. Here we find theories of environmental determinism that emphasize the power over humans of climate and other aspects of nature, or the theory of sociobiology, which emphasizes genetics as a force in human actions. These forces from the realm of nature are supposed to explain the broad range of human actions, including the realms of society and meaning.

The *realm of social relations* situates the forces controlling human actions in social, economic, and political structures. Here we find theories about the power of bureaucracy, as in Weber; or market economy, as in classical economics; or economic class, as in Marx. Social relations such as these are argued to affect other social actions, and also to mold the realm of meaning and to propel our transformations of nature.

The conceptual development, separation, and difficulty of recombining these three realms is a particularly modern and intellectual phenomenon. The basic cleavages, however, may have their roots in consciousness itself. For instance, the separation between realms of meaning and nature elaborates the basic distinction between being aware both of the world and of oneself as an observer of that world (Nagel 1986). Different societies handle this tension differently. In the modern West, it has become elaborated (since the seventeenth century) into the objective realm of nature and its universal properties, and the subjective realm of meaning, value, and the mind. The social realm, in turn, became separated from both the mind and nature (in the eighteenth and nineteenth centuries, with the rise of social science) in that it is corporeal because it includes the physical properties of people, their symbols, and their artifacts, and yet it is produced by humans and thus distinct from the rest of nature.[3]

Several theories attempt to incorporate all three realms, but even these draw their primary rationale and model of human behavior from one realm, tending to make the others derivative. Theories from different realms make fragmented and competing claims. This is why the arrows do not emanate from the center of the diagram or even traverse it, for the center represents a balanced synthesis drawn from elements (though not necessarily theories) of all three realms equally. At the level of theory, fragmentation, not synthesis, prevails.

The center, however, is approached in everyday practice.

Here our lives are lived within the realms of nature, meaning, and social relations. Moreover, the interconnections of the three in everyday life are important to our discussion of theory because of the subject/subject character of social science. It is important for both theory and practice to know whether our theories synthesize the three to coincide with the way they appear in everyday practices.

Several mechanisms operate to draw parts of the three together at the level of everyday life. One is the ordinary, personal experience of being in place. This sense of place captures elements of all three realms, but it is a personal synthesis that is achieved simply by being in place. Its elements differ for each of us, which makes this sense of place difficult to communicate in our highly complex, hierarchical, and specialized world. Another and more public mechanism is our material constructions and symbols of place as played out in mass consumption. It builds on the first by allowing the consumer to use mass-produced goods to create places as contexts. Because mass consumption draws on elements of all three realms, it affects our everyday experiences of the three; and these experiences, in turn, are used by consumers, as reflexive agents, in their evaluation of the theoretical perspectives.

A later section of the chapter considers the role of consumption in drawing the three realms together in creating context, including environmental context, but it will empha-size the link between consumption and meaning. Before con-sidering the role of consumption, however, we first must explore the theoretical attempts to draw the three realms together. We begin with theories from the realm of meaning.

Meaning

Innumerable examples exist of the assumption that the mind provides the primary power for affecting human nature and our transformation of the world. Some of these are simple, others complex. Some give more emphasis to struc-ture, others to agency. Here only three are explored. The first is the well-known position expressed by Lynn White (1967) in his article "The Historical Roots of Our Ecologic Crisis." It is the simplest of the three and represents the way many intellectual historians would portray the mind as a dynamic independent element transforming the world. The second and third examples are progressively more complex. The second, from Lévi-Strauss, explores how the mind constructs a view of nature and social relations, albeit a static one. The third example is from Sigmund Freud, and examines how the mind uses forces from the biological portion of the natural realm continuously to develop complex systems of social relations. Freud's theories are enormously complex. Although his work is primarily about the mind, it serves also as a transition to our discussion of nature.

Lynn White's position is that the responsibility for our ecological crises can be laid at the doorstep of Christianity. Christianity has taught that humanity has dominion over nature. This belief has come to be so much a part of our values that we act without concern for nature, which we treat simply as a resource to be dominated and transformed. "Christianity . . . not only established a dualism of man and

nature but also insisted that it is God's will that man exploit nature for his proper ends" (White 1967: 107). White claims that the "victory of Christianity over paganism was the greatest psychic revolution in the history of our culture" (White 1967: 106). This victory instilled in us not only the sense of domination over nature, but also the sense of progress that sees the cumulative weight of our actions as improvements. It is true that the idea by itself did not transform nature. Rather, it set in motion a complex web of practices, including the development of science and tech-nology, through which this mental commitment operates. Still, the motor for this transformation is squarely within the realm of ideas. White's commitment to the mind as the primary source of change also is revealed by the fact that he believes the primary means by which we can mend our ways is to change our values. "We shall continue to have a worsening ecologic crisis until we reject the Christian axiom that nature has no reason for existence save to serve man" (White 1967). He proposes as an alternative the view of St. Francis of Assisi, who "tried to substitute the idea of the equality of all creatures, including men, for the idea of man's limitless rule of creation" (White 1967: 114).

Even though we must act through social organizations and institutions, as in the case of religion, "men do what they think" (Schaeffer 1975: 13). We are free to choose, although the range of choice varies. Instead of attacking the unre-strained role of agency implied by White, some critics have questioned his interpretation of Christianity. Schaeffer (1975), for example, proposes an alternative Christian ethic that he believes would allow humanity to exist in harmony with nature. Others, though, have challenged White's assumption about the power of ideas, simply by asking if any evidence really exists that our attitudes affect the way we behave toward nature. An excellent example of such a challenge is Tuan's (1968) comparison of Chinese Taoist attitudes toward nature and China's effects on the land, on the one hand, and western Christian attitudes and uses of the land, on the other. Tuan argues, along with White, that the predominant western view is that humanity should dominate nature, whereas the predominant view in China – the Taoist view – is one of harmony with nature. Yet, in comparing the environ-mental changes wrought by both civilizations until the rise of the Industrial Revolution, Tuan is hard-pressed to find a difference: the transformations wrought in the two traditions were comparable. The lesson, then, is that attitudes may have little effect on environment at this scale of analysis.

Even if we accept the argument that Christian values have influenced our transformation of nature, other complicating factors abound in interpreting the specific form of these particular values. For example, Protestantism, and especially the Puritan ethic, has tended to encourage individualism and acquisitiveness, which, as many have pointed out, are necessary values in the modern consumer world. Consumers must believe not only that they should transform nature to meet their needs, but also that their needs are potentially unlimited and are worth satisfying at all costs. But is unbridled acquisitiveness primarily a product of particular forms of Christianity, or is it a product of other forces? Such a question points out that another means of attacking positions like White's is to argue that Christian values in particular, or our realm of meaning in general, are not autonomous seats of power, but rather dependent on one of the other realms. Thus, particular forms of Christian values, individualism, and unbridled acquisitiveness could reinforce one another and yet be outgrowths of particular social relations such as capitalism; and it is really these social relations that are the primary factors transforming nature.

Lévi-Strauss's theory of "structuralism" is a more complex set of ideas about how the mind creates a world of nature and of social relations (Leach 1976; Lévi-Strauss 1963). Lévi-Strauss argues that the mind works by forming categories of extreme oppositions and mediation. These categories are most clearly revealed in the mythical structures of preliterate societies. A myth's content in a sense is secondary to its structure, which reveals the inner workings of the mind. For the most part, these mental processes are unconscious. According to Kirk (1970: 44), Levi-Strauss does not claim to show how men think in their myths, but "how myths think themselves in men, and without their awareness." The structural oppositions reflect irreconcilable mental categories such as life/death, man/god, good/evil, male/female, up/down, front/back, and so on. These and others provide a scaffolding for our ideas about nature and society. Lévi-Strauss's examples are often extremely complex and assume a considerable background in the ethnography and environment of a people. Therefore, I will take a short cut and consider the application of his method to a western view about people and nature, with the understanding that the method seems to be exemplified best in simpler, preliterate societies. A prime example comes once again from Christian thought. To a Lévi-Straussian, the characteristics of Christ – his being the son of God, his having been immaculately conceived, and his death and resurrection – are a product of our attempts to reconcile contradictory categories. God is immortal. God is unchanging. God is perfect. Man is mortal. Man changes. And Man is imperfect. How can these extremes be reduced? By developing a set of mediations that can also reduce the tensions between other and related categories. A primary mediating concept is Christ the man/god. He is both man and a god, and he can die and yet be immortal. The structure can develop further through other intermediaries such as priests, bishops, archbishops, and the Pope. Another set of intermediate positions could be developed to close the geographical gap between heaven and earth. Various earthly places can bring us closer to heaven and, after death, heaven itself is reached through various steps or levels.

Another example, closer to home, is an interpretation of one of our contemporary conceptions of wilderness (Tuan 1971; Graber 1976). Wilderness can be thought of as part of a modern western opposition. Wilderness recently is often valued positively. It is natural, pure, and unchanging. Earlier, it had been thought of as hostile and something to conquer. It is also a place with little or no human activity. The relative absence of man is what makes wilderness pure. Its opposites are the areas of greatest human habitation and control, places such as cities. They are almost completely human-made

environments, and yet they are, relatively speaking, often seen as unnatural, impure, and impermanent. Still, these oppositions contain elements of the other. Wilderness requires human intervention. It must be protected, and it is there for humans to visit. Cities are not completely immune from nature. Natural elements can still wreak havoc. In order to reduce the oppositions, we create intermediate categories and places, such as suburbia, city parks, and zoos.

Our analysis can continue almost indefinitely, but this may be sufficient to illustrate the position that the power of the mind creates oppositions and mediations that order the natural and social worlds. Both White and Lévi-Strauss conceive of the realm of meaning as the locus of power. But unlike White, who emphasizes the role of the agent, Lévi-Strauss presents a mental structure that (he argues) cannot be escaped. Yet another difference is that for all of its complexity, Lévi-Strauss's model is primarily static, whereas White's is dynamic. (Others have attempted to make structuralism dynamic [e.g., Sahlins 1981; 1985]). Finally, we should note that Lévi-Strauss's oppositions themselves may not be so much a product of the mind, as mental reflections of deeper antitheses in social relations.

Freud, the founder of modern psychoanalysis and other branches of psychology, focused his attention on the nature of psychological forces. He sees the principal sources of psychic energy as stemming from our biological drives and instincts. Freud's efforts lie in understanding the way in which the mind draws upon and transforms these forces and how they lead to social relations. In his most succinct discussion of these relationships, Freud (1952) argues that civilization creates frustrations by placing obstacles in the path of the immediate gratification of our desires and drives. This might appear to mean that social relations dominate psychological and even biological ones, yet civilization itself is a product of displaced psychological forces, so that the effects of civilization are something like feedback loops within a psychological system.

In its simplest form, the model is built on the dynamic interrelationships among the id, the ego, and the super-ego. The id includes our internal drives and our need to satisfy them. Among the most general drives are the pleasure principle and aggressive instincts. The ego includes our learned instrumentalities for satisfying these urges; it furthers the aims of the id (Hall and Lindzey 1978). The super-ego refers to our socially derived norms or social facets of our personality: our conscience. The super-ego is instilled by social organization such as the family and school, and represses, displaces, and postpones many of our drives. This causes frustration. But these social institutions in turn are based on displaced and sublimated psychic energy, particularly the energy from the guilt over conflicts between fathers and sons. In other words, civilization is a result of psychic forces, and may itself exhibit a psyche and a cultural super-ego. On the one hand, its institutions are essential in providing individuals with a nurturing environment. On the other, they draw their force by inhibiting our drives – hence our ambivalent attitudes and even hostility toward civilization.

It is clear from Freud's dynamic theory that biological nature ultimately is at the base of our psychological drives but that psychological forces transform this part of nature and lead to the development of civilization. Moreover, civilization dominates the rest of nature – the biosphere – to provide us with a nurturing environment. Indeed, the highest forms of civilization are measured by their power to control nature (Lowenthal's reference to Freud, chap. 8). These are the primary structures, and they drive the system despite the wishes of individual agents.

Nature

Freud's theory draws on biological forces but emphasizes the role of the mind. Other, more direct claims have been made about the power of the natural world in determining human behavior, and they will be discussed here under the realm of nature. They include theories that reduce meaning and social relations to the forces recognized by the natural sciences. This reduction not only places the natural forces in a position to determine the conditions of the other realms, but it also presents a view of the influence of the human on the nonhuman realm as simply a subsystem affecting a larger system. First, those theories that have nature driving human action are considered, followed by those dealing with the effect of human activities, conceived in natural terms, on nature. Finally, human ecology is examined as a bridge between natural and social-science theories.

Entire fields such as neurophysiology and sociobiology are dedicated to the reduction of human behavior to biological, chemical, and physical processes. Reduction is a complex concept in philosophy, but to scientific practitioners it usually means the capacity to use the concepts and theories of a more basic discipline to understand processes in another field (Bergmann 1954: 170–71; Brodbeck 1968). In this case, it means the use of the natural sciences to understand human actions. Claims that our mental and social processes are affected by chemical states, biological instincts, or drives are examples of reduction.

Precise, but narrow, links have been established between certain chemical and electrical states of the brain, and certain mental dispositions and activities. On a broader, but less precise, level assertions have been made that social organizations, social hierarchies, territorial behavior, and the like can be structured by our biological instincts and drives that evolved within the "pristine environments" of our ancestors. So too are such attitudes and values as love of family and self-sacrifice. Some have gone so far as to claim to predict which type of relative one would most likely sacrifice onself for, by considering which ones would perpetuate more of one's own genetic pool (Wilson 1975: 118–26). Extending this logic, I would be more likely to sacrifice my life for my brother than for a first cousin, but more likely to sacrifice my life for nine first cousins or three uncles than for a brother.

Biology, of course, is one part of the natural sciences. Other parts focus on the power of climate and the entire biosphere as driving mechanisms affecting human behavior. Perhaps the most comprehensive environmental theory – and one that still has residual effects – was the classical doctrine of elements and humours. Through the correspondences of the elements of air, water, earth, and fire with the humours of phlegm, bile, black bile, and blood, the theory was able to link natural forces that originated in the stars and planets at one end with mental and social behavior at the other (Glacken 1967: 10–12, 80–82). The position of the planets and stars affected the distribution of elements, which in turn affected the internal balance of the body through the distribution of humours, and they determined mental and social states, as well as a person's physical well being. The more recent theories of environmental determinism are far less sweeping. Ellsworth Huntington viewed the local environment as a determining factor, and supported his claims with specific relations such as associations between temperature and barometric pressure and the expansion of the Mongols, and between temperature extremes and higher forms of civilization (Grossman 1977: 127).

All together, these theories emphasize nature's constraints on human behavior. They can make room for randomness and incompleteness, but there is no room for the individual as a reflexive agent. The concept of reflexivity is beyond the natural sciences; it belongs solely to the realms of meaning and social relations. Thus the natural realm views our transformations as inevitable because we act according to our nature. If this means fouling our nests or depleting our resources, then that is the way it is. And even then, we may survive. After all, we have so far. We are increasing in number. We continue to settle in practically every nook and cranny of the globe, and we are even thinking of colonizing outer space. It is the implications of inevitability, more than anything else, that make many social scientists recoil from social hypotheses that are drawn from the realm of nature.

This part of our discussion has drawn attention to theories in which the forces of nature, through some kind of causal chain, affect the realms of meaning and social relations. But the same chain can be used in the opposite direction to analyze the human impact on nature by considering humans as subsystems within the larger natural realm. This means examining the physical, chemical, and biological outputs of human behavior without entering the social or mental realms to look for the sources of such output, much as one would examine the outputs of volcanoes. Such an approach is essential in order to find out what humans in fact are doing to the natural world (and several of the papers in this volume are examples of such analysis). But without explaining this output by embedding it within a broader social theory (from any of the realms), learning is restricted to "what" we are doing to nature, and not "why."

One exception might be the use of biological explanations, as in a loose interpretation of competition among the species. This analysis could argue that it is natural that humans, like any other species, try to survive. If in so doing, humans have altered and even simplified the natural environment, that is just the way it has to be. Even so, we may continue to succeed. Success could be assured not only because it is in our nature, but becuase the rest of nature is designed to accommodate us. This idea of a forgiving nature does not have to lead us to a biblical interpretation of design (Glacken 1967: 42–44, 403–404). Rather, it can lead us off the beaten track of conventional science to the byways of functional and teleological systems. Lovelock (1979), for one, in his Gaia hypothesis, has argued that much of ecology fits into place scientifically if the biosphere is thought of as designed to support life.

In its broadest sense, human ecology provides the conceptual foundation for the most comprehensive description of the complex links between people and nature. Ecology and ecosystems stress connectivity and mutual causality among the natural and human components. In Ellen's (1982: 76) words,

in the ecosystem view, all social activities impinge directly or indirectly on ecological processes and are themselves affected by these same processes. . . . The approach thus emphasizes the two-way character of causality and avoids the deterministic-possibilistic fallacy, although the relative influence in reciprocally causal relationships is never equal and may be very unequal.

We shall turn to the issue of relative influence shortly, but first note that the primary, though by no means only, device that ecologists employ to connect human and natural systems is, to put it positively, to focus on characteristics that both systems possess, or to put it slightly negatively, to reduce human actions to physical ones. One of the most important and elemental means is the flow of energy. A web of energy and material relations allows the ecosystems approach to draw together the natural and human processes (Coomes 1987). This focus on common components in an interconnected system provides an important means of specifying how nature and society are in fact interrelated: how, for example, the slightest changes in irrigation processes (along with the human energy required to initiate and sustain them) change the caloric yield of crops, and how changes in precipitation can also affect yields. The analysis can be extended to the inorganic. It can help us trace the effects of agricultural practices on erosion, and this erosion on stream morphology and flooding. We can use it to trace the effects of effluents throughout the material and biotic systems, if we know the energy and material flows. Indeed, many chapters in this volume do precisely these things.

But once again, what causes these flows? It is at this point that subsumption of people and nature within a single web becomes unravelled by the various theoretical tugs from the three realms, but primarily from the realm of nature. An ecological concept that is particularly sensitive to these pulls is adaptation.[4] A narrowly biological sense of adaptation will once again place the primary emphasis squarely within the realm of nature. Two other interpretations that are more distant from the biological are functional adaptation, which is usually a part of "ecosystemicism" (Bennett 1976: 166), and strategic adaptation, which is part of adaptive dynamics. The former, of course, involves an understanding of the purpose of the system and thus invokes teleology and its attendant criticisms, and places human actions in the context of homeostatic adaptations. The latter views adaptation as the

process of individual choice and alteration to attain individual goals. The individual is both purposeful and innovative. As a biological person, he has definable needs . . . [he] is tethered by available

material conditions of the environment (nature and culture) and by available cultural institutions, rules, values, etc. He is not reducible to either, however, but plays the key selective role that underlies the dynamics of . . . a revised adaptationism (Earle 1984: 407).

Conceiving of adaptation as a series of strategic choices is helpful because it focuses the analysis on the decisions and actions of individuals, not populations or cultures; avoids teleological explanation; and opens the analysis to interesting methods such as game theory. Yet in the shift from adaptation to strategy, we lose purpose and direction and run the risk of seeing any action as "strategic" and thus "adaptive" (Ellen 1982). To go beyond is to seek causes.

Non-natural-science causes or reasons for human actions are found in the realms of both meaning and social relations. We have discussed theories from the former, and it is now time to examine theories from the latter.

Social Relations

The realm of social relations provides a host of social-science theories offering explanations of why humans act the way they do. Only a few focus directly on the human transformation of nature, although it is possible to draw from most of the others implications that pertain to the question of the human impact on nature. Those social-science theories that explore such quantitative aspects of human actions as movement in space and time, and energy expended, can be linked directly to the human-ecological models and can even drive them – but not necessarily in the direction of equilibrium or adaptation. One such link can be forged along the lines of ecology. Ellen (1982: 122), for example, considers human society, along with other biological systems, in terms of energy production, utilization, and exchange, and these processes provide "the material basis of human existence." Energy is the starting point for "a materialist explanation of human social relations and the history of these relations." Where a materialist link leads us will be discussed later. First I consider another chain that can also transmit flows of energy. This one, however, is forged by a more conventional social-science perspective on human behavior, of humans as seekers of pleasure, and forms the basis of what we shall term conventional social theory.

Schnaiberg (1980: 17–19), who discusses human and other biological systems in terms of energy, notices that one important area wherein human systems diverge from other biological systems is in the

creation and disposition of surplus energy. . . . [If] the ecosystem changes over time from [a] simpler, faster-growing one to a more complex, slower-growing entity, almost the reverse is true of human economies whereas the ecosystem reaches a steady-state by permitting the growth of just enough species and populations to offset the surplus, societies tend to use the surplus to accumulate still more economic surplus in future periods. . . . Thus societies operate to multiply their surpluses, particularly industrial capitalist societies. In contrast, ecosystems tend to mature by stabilizing numbers of consumers and levels of consumption.

The social question then is, "What drives society?" And the conventional social-science theory answer is the deceptively simple one: our individual pursuit of pleasure.

Conventional social-science theory is built upon a political-economic tradition that emphasized the importance and sovereignty of individuals – from the exaltation of the individual in Renaissance thought, to the development of individual liberties in Enlightenment political theories and constitutions, to the development of neoclassical economics. Contemporary social science has crystallized these forces into a series of propositions built upon the assumption that people are motivated to seek pleasure and avoid pain, and society is, or ought to be, structured to facilitate such a pursuit. Pleasure and pain can, of course, take innumerable forms. Freud uses the concept of pleasure in his psychological theories, and other branches of psychology (as in stimulus-response theory) discuss it in a slightly different way. Utilitarians use a conception of it in their theories about the greatest good for the greatest number, and economics, as well as economically oriented approaches in political science, sociology, and geography, discuss it in terms of utility functions. The latter concept can be made quantitative and public when money becomes the measure of utility or pleasure.

The pursuit of pleasure alone may not be a particularly human trait, but it becomes more so when combined with human learning and rationality (which in conventional social science usually means the capacity constantly to compare often novel alternatives and evaluate their outcomes in terms of their respective utilities), and when these utilities are quantified in terms of a scale like money. Then we have the basic components of a social motor that can drive society to "multiply its surpluses," consume more energy, and transform nature. The object of human behavior is then to maximize income or wealth, or to minimize costs, and so on.

The pursuit of pleasure does not necessarily lead to a need for more and more. Some certainly are satisfied with what they have, and others want even less. But the motor tends to (and some interpretations say ought to) push us in the direction of more because of the way in which the parts are interconnected (Leiss 1976). It is at this level of design that we find different and numerous subtheories within the major thesis of pleasure – each providing different means of discussing the role of the agent within the powerful structure.

Neoclassical economic theory, for example, presents the agents as free to pursue pleasure and avoid pain, and this can even mean free to be irrational, by not maximizing pleasure. However, such freedom is constrained by several structures that make "more" even more compelling than "less." For example, economies of scale, which in neoclassical economics result from specialization and division of labor, mean that more can be produced more cheaply. This sets in motion the need for firms competing in the market to take advantage of economies of scale in order to survive. Once they do, the consumer is presented with even more to consume. The economy itself encourages an ideology of "more is better." More means success, more means a higher standard of living, and more is progress. This ideology is, of course, encouraged by advertising, which may do more to promote the expectation that more is better, and thus grease the wheels of consumption, than to increase the sales of one item over another. In addition, people may simply want more, even without these extra pushes.

Once set in motion, these factors reinforce one another and become embedded within institutions, each trying to maximize its own sphere of interests. Which ones are significant, how, and why are, of course, the critical issues that distinguish the particular theories within the classical social-science paradigm. Thus, in some cases, the various realms of government – state and local – and their several branches must be distinguished from types of business interests; and these, from labor unions; and these, from classes of civil servants; and these, from nonunionized; and these, from home owners and apartment dwellers, males and females, age cohorts, regional areas, and so on.

Some theories see organizations of all kinds behaving in generally the same way (as in bureaucracies being driven by their interest in perpetuating themselves [Michels 1958]), and others require distinctions among the different goals of organizations and the individuals within them. These institutional contexts can appear so important that the entire idea of free agents pursuing their own self-interest loses ground to the notion of agents following a script for a role in an institution. What is more, the competing interests and institutions can have the net effect of thwarting the tendencies to produce and consume more. This would have environmental consequences, for it would mean that social production may not "necessarily require increased environmental withdrawals and additions" (Schnaiberg 1980: 423). Overall, then, even within the conventionl paradigm, there is little consensus about the identity of society's significant components, their relative weights, and their causal efficacy. These contradictions and vagaries are magnified when simplified models of the human system are linked to simplified models of the natural system to create instruments of analysis, such as global-simulation models.

Conventional theories forge chains not only to nature, but also to the realm of meaning. Conventional social science can be used to explain or reduce this realm to social relations. This is, of course, one of the projects of stimulus-response theories in several branches of psychology. Other links between social relations and meaning have been explored by social scientists examining the connection between social and economic status, and between political and religious values and beliefs. More inclusive attempts at reducing meaning to social relations come from theories that are only partially based in the conventional paradigm, for instance in ethno-science, the sociology of knowledge (Mannheim 1936), and the social construction of reality (Berger and Luckmann 1966). These approaches share the assumption that ideas and meaning, including our attitudes and beliefs about nature, are molded by various forms of social relations. Hence the mind once again constructs nature and reality, but this time the mind itself is molded by society.

Marxism too draws on the concept of self-interest and the pursuit of pleasure, but with a different emphasis and purpose. Marx tended not to isolate and abstract individuals conceptually and theorize about their interests apart from their particular social contexts and constraints. Perhaps the most basic context, and the one that makes Marxism a materialist philosophy (and thus a potential bridge constructed through flows of energy between nature and society) is that humans and nature are dialectically connected through labor. As with all other living organisms, humans too must consume and thus transform nature. This is accomplished through our labor, which is natural, and yet which has particularly social qualities. One quality is labor's superiority over nature. To paraphrase Schmidt (1971: 30), at bottom there existed only human beings and their labor on the one side, nature and its material on the other. Human beings construct the world on the model of their contemporary struggle with nature. Historically, the struggle favors humans.

Labor then, according to Marx, forges the links between humans and nature. The power of labor is elaborated through the mode of production, which includes the forces and relations of production. The forces refer to resources and technology, and the relations refer to the social organization of work and the ownership of the means of production and of surplus. Historically, we find different modes of production, including primitive, feudal, and capitalist. (The number and characteristics are unsettled issues within Marxist theory [Hindess and Hirst 1975]). Each not only affects material production and our use of nature as well as the distribution of wealth, but also provides the basic organizing principle (or "base" in the vulgar materialist term) for other social organizations (such as education, childrearing, and leisure) and also for the realm of meaning (or superstructure). Vulgar materialists would say that the realm of meaning, or the superstructure, is an epiphenomenon reducible to the mode of production.

One can argue that because Marxism is a form of materialism, its proper location on our map is within the realm of nature. I believe, however, that the material link is not the primary one, because human behavior is seen by most Marxists as a struggle to overcome and transform nature (although we can quibble about whether this itself is natural), and is driven by forces squarely within the realm of the social – forces that in capitalism are especially those of class relations. Capitalism is thus far unique in the scope and scale by which it has transformed nature. Within the biosphere there is now virtually no "nature" that is not in some way affected by the activity of labor (Smith 1984). But Marx does not tell us much about what to expect after the demise of capitalism. According to Marx, we never escape from the necessity of labor, and thus the transformation of nature (Marx 1967: 820, as quoted in Smith 1984: 64).

As noted, Marxist theories exist that interpret materialism far more literally, so that nature does indeed become the determining force (e.g., Wittfogel 1957). Such theories are very difficult to distinguish from those of environmental determinism. By the same token, some Marxists emphasize the "relative" autonomy of the realm of meaning and see that realm as in turn affecting the realm of social relations (Thompson 1978; Williams 1978). Meaning or culture then is not a superstructure, but rather an integral component in the "production" of society.

Marxism, like the conventional paradigm, is not monolithic. A narrow Marxism based on the mode of production and class conflict as the necessary and sufficient social forces may appear logically coherent but also highly unrealistic. A broader interpretation that attributes power to other forms of social relations and to other realms faces the problem of logical incoherence. In addition, Marxist theory contains the problem of the autonomy of the agent vis-a-vis any structure. Marx (1963: 15) wrote that "men make their own history." Yet the power of specific structures – especially class relations – is emphasized by Marxism to such a degree that it casts the power of the agent into doubt. It is important to note that technology, bureaucracy, and population pressure are parts of social relations, and have been mentioned frequently in chapters of this volume as tripping functions causing environmental transformations. Moreover, ever since Malthus, important social theories have viewed population and technology as major transforming forces. Both conventional social science and Marxism recognize that demography is important, that institutions tend to have a life of their own, and that technology can lead to numerous and alienating consequences. But these theories do not see population and technology as root causes of the transformation of nature. Rather, they see them as particulars of social relations that are driven by deeper social structures.

Social Theory: Summary

At this point we come full circle. We have examined arguments that claim meaning can shape nature and social relations; that nature can shape meaning and social relations; and that social relations can do the same for meaning and nature. Within this circularity lie the undercutting issues of reflexivity. Where then do we turn? Each position purports to tell us something about the causes for human alteration of the environment. But each can be undermined by another. Even if we assume that we are facing severe ecological crisis, as in Schnaiberg's (1980: 423–24) dialectic, we still are left directionless about its causes. Are they psychological? Are they matters of individual values? Are they based on social relations? Are they simple natural? In terms of our map, this circularity means that none of the theories provides a balanced picture of the center.

The partial and competing theories also raise fundamental doubts about the possibility of objective knowledge. A profound relativity pervades the realms of meaning and social relations, and even extends to the natural sciences through the thesis that reality is mentally and socially constructed. Contemporary philosophy and history of science have been unable to demonstrate how it is possible for science to be "objective," given the fact that models and theories are human creations; but these problems have not (perhaps fortunately) affected the everyday conduct of the natural sciences. Even though philosophers cannot show us how particular theories are truer than others, science still seems to work. Its own structure confidently supports or rejects statements about reality that are far removed from everyday experience.

The issue is quite different, though, for the realms of meaning and social relations. Here no single theory has the scope and consistency of the paradigms of the physical sciences. This alone can make the problem of relativity more acute. But the problem penetrates to the core of the entire social-science enterprise when it is allowed that the subjects of the theories themselves, as agents, are also their own theorists in everyday life, and thus social science has subjects

not make objectivity evaporate altogether, but it does make it more difficult to grasp. One possibility of reconstructing it is to build on our shared experiences in everyday life, for these are the ones that most people draw on to construct their own theories about people and nature.

One such experience is the sense of place. Being in place is central to everyday life, and also at the center of our diagram, for it draws equally on elements of meaning, nature, and social relations. When the experience is conveyed to others in dynamic societies such as ours, however, it too fragments along the lines of the theories discussed (Sack 1980). One way in which we can construct our personal worlds, or contexts, and do so through a public language, is through the everyday activity of mass consumption. Mass consumption draws on all three realms, but the synthesis it achieves is only partial, and what is more, it does not speak to the theories addressed. Nevertheless, even this incomplete synthesis is important. It stays, albeit temporarily, the contradictions that the theoretical realm cannot resolve, and it makes us party to transforming nature while presenting us its own view of this transformation.

I have said that consumption allows us to draw upon and affect all the realms equally. The full mechanism of consumption cannot be described here (see Sack 1988). Rather, this synthesis is sketched primarily from the meaning consumption creates. The meaning of mass-produced commodities is readily accessible to everyone because advertisements are the primary means by which such information is conveyed.

Consumption and Meaning

The creation of ever more products and goods to consume is the fuel for our economy; and in consuming them, each of us in daily life becomes an active agent transforming nature. What we have to say about consumption pertains for the moment especially to the more developed western economies. Still, the nature of consumption has broader implications because the desire for mass-produced goods is spreading. With the assistance of advertising, these goods have penetrated virtually all economies, and many of the developing countries aspire to a standard of living like that of the West. This standard is difficult to separate from a consumer society. Focusing on mass consumption can help disclose how most of us in everyday life affect nature and one important and widespread way we conceive of this effect.

Many claim that people in advanced capitalist societies live in a consumer's world – a world in which the things we are and do count less as common bonds than the things we consume. We live by consuming mass-produced products, whether we wish to or not. Consumption forms a mass culture, and each act of consumption or purchase draws together the realms of meaning, nature, and social relations, and in turn transforms them (Sack 1988). Consumption draws the three together because each mass-produced product contains elements of all three.

A product – whether it be a Coke or an automobile – embodies social and economic relations. It is produced and consumed within specific historical contexts. The social history of an automobile, for example, can include the efforts of thousands who extract the raw materials from various parts of the world, assemble them (often in different countries under different working conditions), and then ship them to dealers and finally to the public. A product is also part of nature. Its history and present location take place in physical space, which is a property of nature. The product is drawn from material objects and becomes an important part of the modern "consumer" landscape. Also, a product embodies meaning, especially through the aid of advertising. Advertising tells us that an automobile is more than a means of transportation; it is a life style.

Purchasing or consuming products activates these relationships and allows us to draw together the realms to create contexts, with ourselves as the center. The blueprint for such contexts is provided by advertising. A Coca-Cola advertisement shows how possession of this drink can make the consumer the center of a happy, attractive group of young adults; and an automobile ad tells us how possession of this particular car can make the consumer the center of attention, and how he can feel at ease anywhere and anytime.

Consumption then purports to give the consumer the power to create his own context, place, or world. Because the meanings of products are addressed through the ubiquitous medium of advertisements, the meaning of their contexts and their content is part of the realm of public discourse. In other words, consumption is also a public language, which people can and do use to communicate (Leiss 1976). They make statements about who they are or wish to be through the products they consume. One may not wish to participate in this discourse, yet our very act of not purchasing products is still communicating – but through silence. As with any language, that of consumption both constrains the consumer, in that it provides the basic codes and syntax, and enables the consumer to create his own mixtures and meanings, and perhaps even change the structure of the language.

We must recognize that people react skeptically to advertising. They might not take any ad literally, and they know that exaggeration and indirection are advertisement's stock in trade. Even through such skepticism is rampant, the virtual ubiquity of advertisement assures that people come to think of products as having the potential to do more than serve utilitarian goals. Advertisements present a picture of this potential. They impart meanings to products.

These meanings affect our attitudes to and uses of nature. A most obvious but enormously important point is that advertising rationalizes the consumption of ever more products. Since most of what western economies do to the natural world is for the purpose of providing consumers with commodities, advertising can be seen as a justification of such transformations. But, as we shall see, advertisements really do not address the details of this transformation. In fact, they disguise them by focusing on new contexts that commodities are supposed to provide. These commodities become fixtures in homes, in offices, and on the road; and often the homes and offices themselves are literally mass-produced. Thus, mass-produced products populate the built environment, which is the one in which we spend most of our time. Something of their meanings then adheres to the real places that products create.

The meaning of commodities affects our contexts in other ways. The products are often sold in places that are themselves like advertisements, and these places too are often mass-produced. I refer here to the fast-food chains, the department stores, and the shopping malls – all of which are places devoted solely to the world of mass consumption. Even a physical place itself can be turned into a mass-consumed commodity or a place consumed en masse. These include amusement and theme parks and resorts. Hawaii, Miami, and the beaches of Jamaica and Majorca become mass-consumed commodities of sun, surf, and sand, The modern consumer spends much of his leisure time within these "landscapes" (and a good portion of the service sector spends much of its workday there too), and an even greater amount of time viewing the advertisements that promote commodities. The overwhelming message of these places is that the road to the good life is consumption.

The road, of course, can be quite literal, in the sense of a string of physical places that are intimately related to consumption. There is the house, which contains the mass-produced products. Within it individuals are linked to the outside world of consumption through the advertisements in television, radio, magazines, and newspapers. The trips to shopping centers, department stores, and malls are along roads containing signs and billboards and buildings with facades presenting a context for their products. Longer trips and vacations are often undertaken in vans or caravans that contain TVs and have as their destination the amusement parks and the resorts.

As mass consumption draws together meaning, nature, and social relations, it transforms nature, and yet disguises this transformation. Mass-produced products require the extraction, assembly, and distribution of vast amounts of raw materials, the establishment of enormous technical and physical infrastructures, the development of an elaborate "built" environment, and the dumping of large amounts of waste. Yet advertising and the consumer landscape present these same products to us as though they require no such effort, have no such impact, and possess no such history – the biosphere has been unchanged. It is as though through some form of magic the products appear out of nowhere and from no time, to be available instantaneously anywhere and anytime. The global economy can exacerbate this view by locating the source of raw materials continents away from the location of consumption. Only money is needed to purchase the product and it is yours.

On occasion, advertising may describe something of the product's social history or its natural ingredients, as when an American beer is described as being made the American way or an automobile is built with German technology. But these are extremely general and often misleading descriptions of the origins of products. Yet these same products that appear to have no real context are presented as though they can create contexts anywhere. They can draw strangers together. They can make nature into culture and make culture seem natural. They can make you happy, well, and popular. They never make you sorry, poor, or ill, nor do they every harm a particular group or a natural environment. Since each product creates its own instantaneous context, each place then is a discontinuous and isolated world. A consumer who has the money can pass through the environment of Coca-Cola to that of a Le Mans automobile, to that of a Danish modern interior or an American ranch-style house. There is no external logic to connect one context to another except the individual acts of consumption. It is as though products empower individuals with something like magical properties to create things out of nowhere and to transform them into one context after another.

We find this same magical and fantastic sense of context in the places dedicated to selling mass-produced products. Restaurant chains, department stores, malls, amusement parks, and resorts offer versions of contexts that are entire, isolated from one another, and often in no place at all. This sense of place that is no place has been a major part of the geographic critiques of modern landscapes, which have been called pastiches, veneers, generic, inauthentic, and placeless (Relph 1976). Although we cannot address this here, we should note that the sense of contexts out of context, of places that are no place, that result from mass consumption, are reinforced by the workings of mass communications (Meyrowitz 1985).

Consumption, then, allows the individual to create contexts that draw together elements from nature, meaning, and social relations. These contexts form part of our everyday experience and become components in how we, as agents, conceive of the integrations of society, nature, and meaning. These integrations are not only mental. They involve real actions that transform nature. But consumption disguises these transformations and offers a magical world instead. In this respect, consumption stands in opposition to virtually all of the theoretical positions we have discussed. Even though they vary enormously, the theories at least share the assumption that actions have consequences (though not always necessary ones) that extend beyond a single point in time and space, and that these consequences are connected to others, forming some type of chain. It is this broader sense of continuity and context, which in the natural sciences became embodied in the principle of action by contact (Bunge 1963; Sack 1980: 9–19), that is violated in the consumer's world. Here mass consumption can produce a sense of context in which action has no origin or consequence. In short, it creates an egocentric, magical, and irresponsible world – a world virtually divorced from the biosphere in which it is situated. It is precisely this "meaning" that helps explain some of the western world's attitudes about nature and transformation.

I have raised the issue of consumption not to condemn it, but rather to have us recognize its importance in forming our own, everyday sense of our power over nature. According to many social-science theories, human beings are their own theorists. They draw upon their own experiences to explain human behavior. This then makes the consumer's world an important part of reality. People use it to evaluate theoretical positions and to justify their own actions.

Summary

An intellectual terrain has been constructed to illustrate the range of issues involved in judging theories of humans and nature. This intellectual terrain is brought into focus when we consider the range of social theories explaining why we behave the way we do. The terrain is a composite view of such theories: a view from nowhere (Nagel 1986). The terrain recedes into the background as our view centers on a single perspective and how it portrays what our behavior toward nature is like. (Once again I am aware of the basic and ultimate interconnectivity between "what" and "why," and consider them distinct only in terms of the issues they emphasize.) This does not mean that analyzing "what" is at all a simple matter. Rather, it means that for such a purpose we can in effect work within one framework. We can, for example, reduce human actions to physical ones, and trace the results within the environment. We could even draw attention to the severity of such impacts and describe how they can be life-threatening. And all the time, the analysis would take place within just one of the modes of inquiry, and in this case the least philosophically controversial one: the natural mode.

Commitment to only one of the perspectives obviates the others so that the terrain itself evaporates under the gaze of the committed. I do not wish to challenge commitment, but only to bring to light a range of issues that need to be addressed if others are to be persuaded. By suggesting the strengths and weaknesses of various perspectives, the terrain maps out a domain of discourse that a comprehensive social theory might have to address.

The intellectual terrain also stresses the significance of the center: a position that a comprehensive theory would have to occupy. Yet the center is occupied in everyday life, and consumption helps draw elements of the three realms together and shape their meaning. It literally offers a magical sense of context and causality that opposes all of the other theoretical positions. It is a sense that must be reckoned with even in an age of science. To find out how this sense of context comes about and how people can be persuaded to disregard it leads us back again to the divergent and competing social theories.

Notes

1. The interconnections among description and explanation are revealed primarily through research in the history of science (e.g., Kuhn 1962) and in the philosophy of social science (e.g., Keat and Urry 1975). These issues are similar to those involved in perception and conception and in seeing and knowing (Dretske 1969).

2. LISREL, an acronym, is a well-known social-science synthesis of statistical techniques (Cadwallader 1986). Goldberger (1973), a major contributor to these models, has stated that the role of statistical methods in social science is to disclose real causal relations.

3. The contours of the realms do not neatly conform to the underlying bedrock of philosophical ontologies. This disconformity is not bad, considering that the limitations and contradictions of ontological systems made the bedrock itself a weak and unstable foundation. Nevertheless, in some instances the contours to some extent coincide with ontological positions. For example, the primacy of the mind and its concepts conforms to many facets of idealism. The realm of nature assumes that the constitution of reality is what natural science says it is. This view can be ontologically undergirded by various combinations of naturalism and realism. Of the three, the social realm rests least comfortably on a single well-developed ontological substructure. Rather, it draws upon elements of idealism, naturalism, and materialism.

4. I am much indebted to Oliver Coomes' (1987) paper for definition and references on cultural adaptation.

References

Bennett, J. 1976. *The Ecological Transition: Cultural Anthropology and Human Adaptation*. New York: Pergamon.

Berger, P., and T. Luckmann. 1966. *The Social Construction of Reality*. New York: Doubleday.

Bergmann, G. 1954. *The Metaphysics of Logical Positivism*. Madison, WI: University of Wisconsin Press.

Brodbeck, M., ed. 1968. *Readings in the Philosophy of the Social Sciences*. New York: Macmillan.

Bunge, M. 1963. *Causality: The Place of the Causal Principle in Modern Science*. New York: Meridan Books.

Cadwallader, M. 1986. Structural equation models in human geography. *Progress in Human Geography* 10:24–47.

Coomes, O. 1987. The concept of cultural adaptation in cultural ecology: A critical appraisal of functional and strategic interpretation. Department of Geography, University of Wisconsin. Madison, WI.

Dretske, F. 1969. *Seeing and Knowing*. London: Routledge and Kegan Paul.

Earle, T. 1984. Comment. *Current Anthropology* 25:406–407.

Ellen, R. 1982. *Environment, Subsistence and System*. New York: Cambridge University Press.

Freud, S. 1952. *Civilization and Its Discontents*. Vol. 54. Chicago: Great Books.

Giddens, A. 1984. *The Constitution of Society: Outline of the Theory of Structuration*. Berkeley, CA: University of California Press.

Glacken, C. J. 1967. *Traces on the Rhodian Shore: Nature and Culture in Western Thought from Ancient Times to the End of the Eighteenth Century*. Berkeley: University of California Press.

Goldberger, A. 1973. Structural equation models: an overview. In *Structural Equation Models in the Social Sciences*, ed. A. Goldberger and O. Duncan, 1–18. New York: Seminar Press.

Graber, H. 1976. *Wilderness as Sacred Space*. Washington, D.C.: Association of American Geographers.

Grossman, L. 1977. Man-environment relations in anthropology and geography. *Annals of the Association of American Geographers* 67:126–44.

Hall, C., and G. Lindzey. 1978. *Theories of Personality*, 3rd ed. New York: John Wiley.

Hindess, B., and P. Hirst. 1975. *Pre-Capitalist Modes of Production*. London: Routledge and Kegan Paul.

Keat, R., and J. Urry. 1975. *Social Theory as Science*. London: Routledge and Kegan Paul.

Kirk, G. S. 1970. *Myth: Its Meaning and Functions in Ancient and Other Cultures*. Cambridge: Cambridge University Press.

Kuhn, T. S. 1962. *The Structure of Scientific Revolutions*. Chicago: University of Chicago Press.

Leach, E. 1976. *Culture and Communications: The Logic by Which Symbols Are Connected*. Cambridge: Cambridge University Press.

Leiss, W. 1976. *The Limits to Satisfaction*. Toronto: University of Toronto Press.

Lévi-Strauss, C. 1963. *Structural Anthropology* (English trans.). New York: Basic Books.

Lovelock, J. 1979. *Gaia: A New Look at Life on Earth*. New York: Oxford University Press.

Mannheim, K. 1936. *Ideology and Utopia*. London: Routledge and Kegan Paul.

Marx, K. 1963. *The Eighteenth Brumaire of Napoleon Bonaparte*. New York: International Publishers.

———. 1967. *Capital*. Vol. 1. New York: Vintage Books.

Meyrowitz, J. 1985. *No Sense of Place: The Impact of Electronic Media on Social Behavior*. New York: Oxford University Press.

Michels, R. 1958. *Political Parties*. Glencoe, IL: The Free Press.

Nagel, T. 1986. *A View from Nowhere*. New York: Oxford University Press.

Relph, E. 1976. *Place and Placelessness*. London: Pion.

Sack, R. 1980. *Conceptions of Space in Social Thought: A Geographic Perspective*. Minneapolis, MN: University of Minnesota Press.

———. 1988. The consumer's world: Place as context. *Annals of the Association of American Geographers* 78:642–64.

Sahlins, M. 1981. *Historical Metaphors and Mythic Realities*. Ann Arbor, MI: University of Michigan Press.

———. 1985. *Islands of History*. Chicago: University of Chicago Press.

Schaeffer, F. 1975. *Pollution and the Death of Man: The Christian View of Ecology*. Wheaton, IL: Tyndale House Publishers.

Schmidt, A. 1971. *The Concepts of Nature in Marx*. London: New Left Books.

Schnaiberg, A. 1980. *The Environment: From Surplus to Scarcity*. New York: Oxford University Press.

Smith, N. 1984. *Uneven Development: Nature, Capital, and the Production of Space*. Oxford: Basil Blackwell.

Thompson, E. P. 1978. *The Poverty of Theory and Other Essays*. London: Merlin Press.

Tuan, Yi-Fu. 1968. Discrepancies between environmental attitude and behavior: Examples from Europe and China. *The Canadian Geographer* 12:176–91.

———. 1971. *Man and Nature*. Washington, D.C.: Association of American Geographers.

———. 1977. *Space and Place: The Perspective of Experience*. Minneapolis, MN: University of Minnesota Press.

Weber, M. 1947. *The Theory of Social and Economic Organization*. Glencoe, IL: The Free Press.

White, L. 1967. The historical roots of our ecologic crisis. *Science* 155:1203–1207. Reprinted in F. Schaefer. 1975. *Pollution and the Death of Man: The Christian View of Ecology*. Wheaton, IL: Tyndale House Publishers.

Williams, R. 1978. Problems of materialism. *New Left Review* 109:3–17.

Wilson, E. 1975. *Sociobiology*. Cambridge, MA: Harvard University Press.

Wittfogel, K. 1957. *Oriental Despotism*. New Haven, CT: Yale University Press.

41

The Realm of Social Relations: Production, Reproduction, and Gender in Environmental Transformations

CAROLYN MERCHANT

Whenever [man] plants his foot, the harmonies of nature are turned to discords. . . . Indigenous vegetable and animal species are extirpated and supplanted by others of foreign origin . . . with new and reluctant growth of vegetable forms, and with alien tribes of animals. These intentional changes and substitutions constitute indeed great revolutions.

MARSH (1864: 36)

About halfway through the past 300 years of great population and social change, George Perkins Marsh was able to observe the major environmental transformations of the earth through human action – transformations that have grown increasingly acute. For example, the massive colonization of overseas lands from the seventeenth through the nineteenth centuries by Europeans, accompanied by their livestock, crops, weeds, and diseases, caused *colonial* ecological revolutions in the lands of immigration. Beginning in the eighteenth century, industrialization and drains on Third World resources, both human and physical, accompanied *capitalist* ecological revolutions. Today, as the resource depletion and pollution associated with industrialization continue and as world population increases, doubling about every 30 years, *global* ecological revolution is taking place. These three phases of ecological revolution – colonial, capitalist, and global – involve transformations in the way people interact with their environments.

A number of theories have been proposed to explain the historical processes underlying such human–environment transformations. In this chapter, the strengths and weaknesses of those approaches that focus on the social relations of production, reproduction, and gender are explored briefly. A synthesis of these theories is also offered, using a dialectical approach to explain the three phases or types of ecological revolution of the past 300 years. Ecology, production, reproduction, and ideology are the key themes of this synthesis. Examples are used to illustrate the abstractions, especially drawing upon my own research on the environmental transformation of New England (Merchant 1989).

Theories of ecological transformation can appropriate methods from a number of disciplines or fields of study. The synthesis of these elements, however, should display three characteristics. First, they must be dynamic, to account for change in human-environment relations. Second, they must be able to handle specific and varying environments. Third, they must be able to explain complex changes in cultural wholes. In addition to these characteristics, a complete synthesis should incorporate the roles of science and technology and gender, as well as the elements traditionally included. A theoretical synthesis of this kind is attempted here.

Analytical Frameworks: Revolutions, Structures, and Systems

Kuhn's (1962) concept of paradigm change forms one useful backdrop for a theory of environmental transformations. It views science as both maintaining and revolutionizing human ways of representing the world. Scientific paradigms are structures of thought shared by scientists within which problems are solved. When a sufficient number of anomalies challenges the theory, new paradigms are constructed in a "scientific revolution." In the late 1960s, the "internalist" features of this concept were challenged by a revival of the social history of science that questioned the degree to which the development of science could be independent of economic or social activities (e.g., Basalla 1968), a subject not addressed in Kuhn's original study. Simultaneously, the environmental movement in the western world raised questions about the history and significance of attitudes and behaviors toward nature represented in scientific paradigms (Commoner 1972; Merchant 1980). When elaborated to include society and environment, Kuhn's concept of scientific revolutions can be expanded to one of "ecological revolutions" – of far-reaching changes in economy, society, and thought related to transformations in nature–society relations.

Kuhn argued that when a significant number of unexplainable anomalies accumulated within a long-accepted paradigm of "normal" science that a period of scientific revolution ensued, in which fundamental assumptions were challenged and a new explanatory framework emerged. By analogy, in an ecological revolution a number of external introductions or internal "contradictions" accumulate in a long-accepted "mode" of interaction between a society and its environment. A period of ecological revolution ensues, in which new nature-society relations emerge. Thus in colonial ecological revolutions a series of external introductions (e.g., biota and pathogens) into a given habitat break down indigenous modes of interacting with nature. In capitalist ecological revolutions internal contradictions (e.g., between land use and inheritance patterns), when combined with market incentives, may propel a society toward the industrial-capitalist mode of interaction. Today, an accumulating set of contradictions within the global capitalist mode of interaction (e.g., the greenhouse effect, ozone depletion, species extinctions, and population growth) may be initiating a global-ecological revolution.

Ecologically sensitive approaches to society-environment interactions draw upon ecology and systems theories as a point of departure. Cultural ecologists have been especially interested in the development of ways to examine human uses of and adaptations to various types of environments, both past and present. Steward's (1955) *Theory of Cultural Change*, with examples drawn from his work on the Shoshone Indians of the Great Plains of North America, dealt with the ways in which traditional societies adapted to such environmental features as topography, climate, and physical resources. In his scheme, technologies, economics, and population size are expressions of these adaptations – products of the interplay of the society with the habitats occupied. Cultural features, such as language, religion, and art were affected too, but could also diffuse from other cultures. Steward's approach worked best for relatively isolated societies characterized by long-term stablilty in both the human and physical realms; conditions of change were found more difficult to treat (Fig. 41.1).

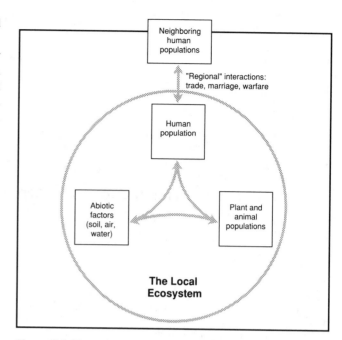

Figure 41.2 The ecosystem-based model of human ecology. Source: Rambo 1983: 14.

Rappaport (1968), drawing on structural-functionalist and ecological concepts, formalized an ecosystem approach that related culture to abiotic and biotic components of the environment as a spatially bounded unit. Cultural attributes were explained by their ecological survival value; even religious and ritualistic features were seen as a product of the ecologically adaptive mechanisms of that survival. His major test of the approach dealt with the Tsembaga of New Guinea, whose ritual warfare around pig populations was explained as a control mechanism to keep the human population in balance with the habitat (Fig. 41.2).

Ellen (1982) reviewed these and other cultural ecology- and ecosystem-based approaches, showing that each represented an advance over earlier ones, but arguing that a holistic approach had yet to be developed. This could be accomplished, according to him, by incorporating a materialist-ecological approach. Ellen's (1978) major example detailed the flow of energy and materials among the Nuaulu of eastern Indonesia, presuming that "[t]he material basis of human existence . . . underlies an adequate materialist explanation of human social relations and history of those relations" (Ellen 1982: 122). Organisms within an ecosystem are linked by transfers of energy, according to the laws of thermodynamics and the circulation of materials through biogeochemical cycles. Because of technology, the potential impacts on the environment of attempts by humans to supply energy are increased. This supply of energy allows the population and social formation to reproduce themselves (Ellen 1982: 100–101). Ecological reproduction results from species and population reproduction, whereas economic production creates value in order to reproduce social and economic formations (Ellen 1982: 130).

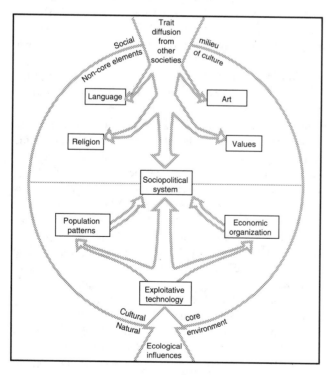

Figure 41.1 The model of cultural ecology. Source: Rambo 1983: 7.

Rambo (1983), using general systems theory, describes a unified model of human ecology as the interaction of two open systems – one social and one ecological – that receive inputs and outputs from one another. They exist in a complex, dynamic relationship with multicausal, multidirectional exchanges of energy, material, and information. Each system is open to external influences through diffusion, migration, and colonization. Changes in the system as a whole can be sudden and catastrophic (primary changes) or adaptive and incremental (secondary changes). The social system responds to the choices available to and the decisions of the individual actors, which if "correct," lead to survival and become institutionalized as social norms. Rambo's examples are drawn from studies of deforestation in Southeast Asia (Fig. 41.3). While dynamic in a systems sense, his approach is not well developed to explain environmental history or cultural evolution.

Bennett (1976) has offered an energy-output model that addresses these shortcomings. The ability to extract and transfer energy from the environment, he argues, has led to broad unidirectional trends toward growth. Human actions change situations of equilibrium to disequilibrium because, over the long haul, humans have opted to change the system by seeking new sources of fuel, food, medicines and space, rather than by controlling environmental change and limit population growth. Our present ecological transition is the result of "reducing human labor and hand tools and increasing powered machines" (Bennett 1976:51). In this scheme, historical changes in the nature-society relationships are the result of decisions to increase energy and goods (Fig. 41.4).

While each of these examples is helpful, each has inherent limitations for developing an integrative theory of environmental transformation. First, these approaches do not ad-

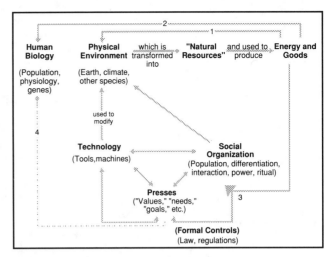

Figure 41.4 A paradigm of human (or cultural) ecology, emphasizing the output function. Source: Bennett 1976: 38.

equately specify the processes of social change that lead to environmental impacts, and do not account for the power relations that both maintain class structures and lead to social struggles that break them. Second, in discussing human action, they do not account for the inequalities created by class relations, inequalities that do not give all people within any system similar choices, including environmental ones. Third, these approaches assume the unity and structure of systems, perhaps not recognizing that, like the platonic form, a system is nothing more than a conceptual framework with which we interpret the world. Fourth, the use of structural-functionalism in many of these examples leads to approaches

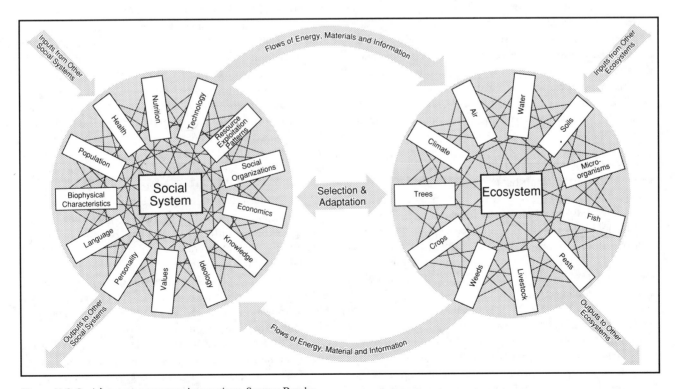

Figure 41.3 Social system-ecosystem interactions. Source: Rambo 1983: 26.

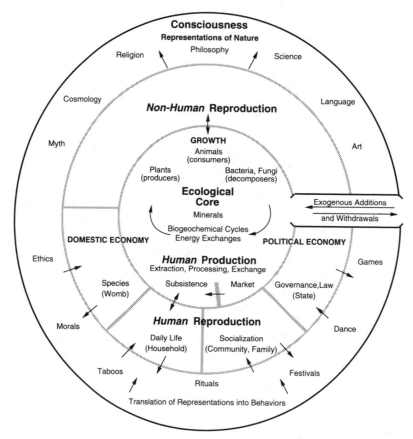

Figure 41.5 Conceptual framework for interpreting ecological transformations. Adapted from Merchant 1987.

that are ahistorical and do not account for the fact that environmental transformations are the product of decisions made in specific social systems and locational settings. Despite these criticisms, these approaches, combined with Kuhn's, serve as a base from which a more comprehensive and historical approach can be distilled. This approach is developed next by a consideration of the significance of the social relations of production, reproduction, and gender (Fig. 41.5).

Ecology and Production

An important contribution to this effort was made by Parsons (1977), who made clear the relevance of Marx's and Engels' insights into human–environment interactions, as well as the problems raised by their concept of the domination of nature through science and technology. Engels was especially sensitive to the ecological impacts of production. "There [was] devilishly little left of 'nature' at the time when Germanic peoples immigrated into it," he observed in 1878 (quoted in Parsons 1977: 141). Human activity continued to change the landscape, often with unforeseen side-effects for the production of subsistence. Nevertheless, it was only by continually increasing human control over natural processes by new modes of production that humanity could realize "true freedom." "The conditions of existence forming man's environment, which up to now have dominated man, at this

point pass under the dominion and control of man, who now for the first time becomes the real conscious master of Nature" (Parsons 1977: 141). The individual's control over the production process was the passage to human freedom; the domination of nature through science and technology offered the possibility of liberation from nature.

Marx and Engels were criticized during the 1970s for their advocacy of the domination of nature. Neo-Marxists, such as Herbert Marcuse, instead treated nature as an equal but opposing partner, while Marxist ecologists, such as Commoner (1971), argued that human production must operate with the limits of the laws of ecology and that science and technology must create sustainable relations with nature. Production and ecology are, in this view, the same, rather than hierarchically different, levels, changing the domination of nature to a relation of creative reciprocity between humans and the nonhuman world (Fig. 41.5).

Despite this concern, Marx's and Engels' concept of the inherent activity of nature is valuable for a theory of environmental transformations because it offers the possibility of making nature an actor on the stage of history – internally dynamic and responsive to human actions. In asserting the activity of nature as flux, tension, impulse, and change, Marx and Engels opposed their own dialectical materialism to mechanical (or metaphysical) materialism. The mechanistic science that had arisen in the seventeenth century analyzed nature as a collection of parts that were rearranged through the action of external forces. But this "... habit of observing natural objects and natural processes in their isolation," complained Engels, "detached [them] from the whole vast interconnection of things." It presented them "... not in their motion, but in their repose; not as essentially changing, but as fixed constants; not in their life, but in their death" (Parsons 1977: 130). The dialectic, in contrast, asserts the primacy of change over parts, of context over isolation, of internal dynamism over passivity. Out of conflicts and tensions within nature, new material combinations are formed. Causality is not linear and unidirectional, but reversible. "Causes and effects are constantly changing places, and what is now or here an effect becomes there and then a cause, and vice versa. ... Nature is the test of dialectics ... and in the last analysis Nature's process is dialectical and not metaphysical" (Parsons 1977: 131).

The mechanistic approach to nature can often lead to, for example, engineered structures such as factories that employ wage laborers and high-rise office buildings that house corporate managers that operate in isolation from their surroundings and are geared toward maximization of profits. The impact of effluents and pollutants on air, water, and humans is not integrated into factory design, and the impact of polluted, recirculated air on human health is not part of the office-planning process. The dialectical approach proposed here would start with the human – environment interaction as primary and would construct work and home places that sustain both human and environmental life.

In the Marxian view, humans express their "species being" in the activity of production. The mode of production, or economic base of the multileveled social formation, consists of the forces of production and the relations of production. The forces of production are the technologies and labor processes by which humans extract livelihoods from nature. The relations of production are human-to-human interactions, such as cooperation or exploitation. At a level once removed from the economic base of the social formation is the superstructure – the political–legal and ideological–symbolic structures. They are the human institutions and the forms of consciousness that are generated historically with the mode of production and function to support and maintain it. Economic revolution takes place when the forces of production conflict with the relations of production. The products are new ideologies and new forms of consciousness that support the new power relations of production (Marx 1968: preface).

This view offers a multitiered, dynamic approach to both history and ecology in which uneven development and major upheaval are more critical than continuous evolution. Periods of social transformation are explained as revolutions in modes of production, as in the transition from feudalism to capitalism in western Europe. By analogy, ecological revolutions can be characterized as fundamental changes in human–environment relations, in large part generated by such social changes.

Carr's (1977) study of the pastoral Dasanetch of Ethiopia demonstrates the utility of this framework for explaining ecological relationships. She identifies four major habitats used by the Dasanetch: plains, riverine lands, delta, and mesic lands. The pastoralists used them for stock rearing, horticulture, fishing, hunting and gathering, and settlement (their village is moved seasonally). This environmental–economic fabric was influenced by such "exogenous" factors as the flow of the Omo River and exchanges with other tribes.

This component-systems framework is analyzed by way of modes of production, defined as "... a recognizable set of relations (among producers and the means of production) of economic production and distribution of goods and services" (Carr 1977:237). To survive, the group needed not only to produce its means of subsistence, but additionally to reproduce the conditions that allow survival. The associated environmental and social complexes were both essential to the reproduction of the mode of production. The reproduction of the economic base "depends upon the social formation or society as a whole and the environment as a whole" (Carr 1977: 244). Therefore, the social arrangement of the Dasanetch was fundamental to its economic base and, ultimately, to the manner in which the Dasanetch perceived, used, and transformed their environment.

Carr's work on the synthesis of ecological ideas and Marxist concepts, some of which is under revision (C. Carr, personal communication), provides a starting point for the development of a more dynamic nature–society approach. First of all, this new formulation must not assume that change is even over time, for periods of slow evolutionary development may be punctuated by periods of major transformation in human–environment relationships. For example, Crosby's (1986) "ecological imperialism" identifies the sudden and dramatic changes wrought by associations of biota, pathogens, and people as introduced by European colonization of the world. Second, a means of relating human-induced transformations of the environment to other so-called revolutions in human history is needed. Examples include those associated with the scientific revolution of the sixteenth and seventeenth centuries (Merchant 1980), the industrial or capitalist revolutions in Europe and America in the eighteenth and nineteenth centuries, the introduction of western capitalism into the so-called Third World in the nineteenth and twentieth centuries, and long-term but regionally specific transformations from hunting–gathering to agricultural economies. Third, the formulation must be able to handle climatic and other "physical" changes that can trigger new human responses. Thus environmental devastations caused by natural catastrophes such as droughts, hurricanes, volcanos, and insect plagues, or by human induced crises such as wars, dam failures, or nuclear-power-plant accidents may lead to major reorganizations in society–environment interactions.

Environmental transformations with the characteristics just described are illustrated in several of the case studies in this volume and in the story of New England. Until the colonization of New England in the seventeenth century, Amerindians there were characterized by two broad modes of production: the gathering-hunting-fishing tribes of the north (today's Maine, New Hampshire, and Vermont) and the tribes to the south (Massachusetts, Connecticut, and Rhode Island), which added horticulture. Their ecological relations were initially disrupted by colonial settlers, who took heavy tolls on beaver and other animals for the fur trade and on forest habitats for wood products. The introduction of livestock, cultigens, weeds, and disease altered the land uses among the Indians and lowered their population numbers. The activities of the settlers were stimulated not only by the desire for land for subsistence but by their involvement in mercantile exchange (Cronon 1983; Merchant 1989) – issues of production, and, as shall be shown, reproduction. These changes constituted what I have called the colonial ecological revolution.

The economic transition to industrial capitalism in the nineteenth century, in part fueled by the availability of a wage-labor force of landless sons, single women, and immigrants, further altered the trajectory of ecological change in New England. Large dams for textile and iron mills halted the flow of migrating fish, and dyes and sewage polluted streams. Portable sawmills penetrated forests distant from navigable rivers, and railroads brought markets ever closer to the inland farmer. By midcentury, much of New England's forest had been lost to lumbering and farming. Again, the degree of ecological change exceeded what the subsistence of the population required; the economics of accumulation accounted for much of it.

The shift to global capitalism in twentieth-century New England has altered many of these transformations, even reversing some. Many of the mills are gone and agriculture is largely confined to dairying. As a result, the forests have returned. The subsistence of the region is now virtually all imported, making the region vulnerable to price and production fluctuations from afar. Outside the vast urban and suburban buildup of New England, which creates major problems of water supply and waste disposal, much improvement has occurred in the quality of once-degraded lakes, ponds, wetlands, and woodlands – features now critical to the quality of life that is expected by the inhabitants. The environments of New England today reflect an economy that does not rely on local production of food and fuel. But new problems have emerged. Acid precipitation now drifts from the industry of the Ohio River Valley, threatening the life of the regenerated forests of the region (Reidel 1982). Beyond New England and at a global scale, this international economy has propelled us into a global environmental transformation, the subject of this volume.

Reproduction and Gender

The relationships between production and ecology alone are insufficient to explain the complexities of decisions that drive environmental transformations. Issues arising from population changes, gender patterns, and political considerations also must be incorporated into the framework to understand fully those driving forces. One such attempt has been made by Harris (1980), who criticized Marx's system for not including a distinct "mode of reproduction." He reorganized Marx's economic base (mode of production) and superstructure (legal-political and ideological) into three levels: infrastructure, social structure, and superstructure. He divided the infrastructure into modes of production and reproduction,

the social structure into domestic or household economy and political economy, and the superstructure into behavior and ideology.

The mode of reproduction consisted of the technologies and sexual practices that maintained, limited, or increased human population. The latter was added to deal explicitly with issues of population pressures on land and production, as well as with their effects on social structures and ideologies. Why has global population increased over time? Why have some groups grown in numbers and others not? Harris argues that for most of human history people have used an array of malign techniques, such as senilicide, infanticide, killing female infants, assaults against pregnant women, and clitoridectomies as well as benign techniques, such as coitus interruptus, incest taboos, and delayed marriages, to control population growth, maintain high levels of subsistence, and conserve resources. Therefore, the mode of reproduction was fundamental to environmental transformations as it controlled population growth.

One step removed from direct interaction with the environment was social structure, and twice removed was the superstructure. These, in Harris's model, played the roles of maintaining and conserving the system as a whole. Changes in the infrastructure – major transformations in modes of production or reproduction – carried with them a high probability of changing the entire three-tiered system, whereas changes in the superstructure merely weakened resistance to this change. Harris's principle of cultural materialism asserted, then, that modes of production and reproduction *probablistically* determined the domestic political economy, which in turn, *probablistically* determined the behavioral and mental superstructures.

Cultural materialism is helpful for our synthesis for several reasons. Unlike systems models, it allows for historical weighting of the levels of the three-tiered system with respect to the immediacy of their impact on the environment and their roles in both change and legitimation. Thus humans using bulldozers and chain saws in land-clearing have a more immediate impact on the environment than do legislators formulating environmental policies. Policies must be translated from paper guidelines to physical behaviors before the environment experiences a change. Secondly, cultural materialism accepts a material basis for the physical world and culture, removing some of the problems associated with more abstract approaches. Thirdly, it specifically introduces population pressure and reproductive behavior as a problem for analysis and elaboration.

This approach, however, has been criticized on several grounds. Harris's view of population pressure has been seen as too close to "vulgar Malthusianism." That is, population growth in Harris's model is linked to genetic behavior – an abstract biological drive independent of cultural norms – and his controlling mechanisms are too simplistic and deterministic (e.g., Sahlins 1978). Further, if infrastructure gives rise to social structures, why do different social structures exist in technologically similar environments? Actual historical transformations are not explained, whereas too much emphasis is placed on the material conditions of a technology, such as irrigation, rather than on the social relations, such as the state bureaucracy (Friedman 1974).

Meillassoux (1981) expanded the Marxist meaning of reproduction as both biological and *social*. Here, the production and exchange of human energy is the key to reproduction, both intra- and intergenerational. Human energy, according to Meillassoux (1981: 50), is an advance over the Marxist concept of labor because "[it] covers all the energy produced by the metabolic effects of foodstuffs on the human organism. . . . Labor-power is only that fraction of human energy with exchange-value." In gathering, hunting, and fishing economies, the return from the land is instant food converted to human energy. In contrast, agrarian economies usually involve a period of nonfood production, in which accumulated food stores are consumed for energy, although this seasonality is absent in some parts of the tropics. Stored foods allow a lag between production and consumption, and during noncultivation periods energy is expended toward reproduction of the social relations within and between domestic communities. "It is evident that reproduction is the dominant preoccupation of these societies. All their institutions are organized to this purpose" (Meillassoux 1981: 38).

This energy circulates in the form of material products, and enough surplus product must be stored over time to allow reproduction. Poor harvest or extraction of surplus will stymie demographic growth. Only after the community maintains and reproduces its own subsistence can demographic growth or commercial development take place. In agrarian societies, production for use dominates, thus sustaining biological reproduction. The community as a reproducing unit is maintained by social reproduction. "The process of reproduction in the domestic community is achieved by means of very long-term commitments (vows, engagement, marriage, dowry, etc.)" (Meillassoux 1981: 39). These juridical structures result from the requirements of production and serve to perpetuate them.

Female exploitation, according to Meillassoux, is heightened in agrarian communities because women are necessary both for the conversion of the agricultural product into food and for procreation. As biological reproducers, women circulate either by forcible abduction by a neighboring community or peaceably through marriage. In either case, a woman is subordinate in juridical reproduction. Her value begins at puberty, when she becomes capable of bearing children; continues through motherhood, as the reproducer of social norms; and ends after menopause, unless she temporarily perpetuates the line of descent and property inheritance as a widow. Thus, women "are hidden behind men, behind fathers, brothers and/or husbands" (Meillassoux 1981: 75).

This approach, then, allows one to move from *gender relations* to reproduction to population and its impact on the environment. To date, however, these linkages have not been made, and Meillassoux's view of gender relations has been challenged by feminists for its assumption that female subordination is a given rather than a problem. In writing the history of environmental transformations, sensitivity to such issues can show that women are actors in their own societies,

rather than passive receivers of patriarchy (Mackintosh 1977; O'Laughlin 1977), and that their decisions are important to the ultimate human–environment relationship.

Environmental transformation can be linked to biological reproduction, which is linked to social reproduction. The last-named raises issues about socialization and politics. Giddens (1979) has developed a theory of the interaction between social structures and human agents that incorporates these factors. Socialization is an integral part of social reproduction and is institutionalized in three ways: interactions among people that take place daily, over lifespans, and over historic time spans. It involves a familiar repetition of practices in familiar settings (including the physical environment) by human agents. Socialization involves both the individual and the group, and the perceptions of both are continually transforming interpretations of their surroundings as they themselves are being transformed. Unfortunately for our purposes here, Giddens does not directly link socialization to environmental change. An example can be drawn from colonial New England. Boys were socialized by their fathers to assist in barn and field work, girls by their mothers to help in dairy, poultry, and textile production. Environmental impacts in each case were mediated by colonial farming practices – thus the male practice of grazing cattle and pigs in tillage plots after harvest added manure to the soil, while the female practice of tending poultry in orchards and gardens kept down insect pests and added manure. Socialization changed under capitalism. Young men were schooled in human intensive techniques of soil management and in agricultural specialization, including dairying and poultry raising, whereas young women worked in textile mills or were taught to emphasize indoor domestic work.

Peterson (1984) provides the rudiments for adding politics to social reproduction. In capitalist societies, the division of labor between sexes results in a situation in which men are responsible for and dominate the production of exchange commodities, and women are responsible for reproducing the work force and social relations. In this form of patriarchy, reproduction is subordinate to production. Peterson (1984: 6) argued that ". . . women's responsibilities for reproduction includes both the biological reproduction of the species (integenerational) and the intragenerational reproduction of the work force through unpaid labor in the home. Here too is included the reproduction of social relations – socialization." A taxonomy of this followed: issues related to the interests of (1) intergenerational reproduction, (2) intragenerational reproduction in the family and (3) in the public sector, and (4) reproduction workers (women) – the so-called women's liberation issues.

This taxonomy has been applied to issues of the environment through an examination of the politics of reproduction in the Swedish environmental movement (Peterson and Merchant 1986:472–74). Women's political involvement in biological reproduction is exemplified in their concern over radioactive damage to their reproductive organs and to children, leading to heightened activity in antinuclear campaigns. For example, 43% of Swedish women in contrast to only 21% of the men opposed the use of nuclear power in a

1980 national referendum on the subject. Women's political involvement in family reproduction is exemplified in improving the quality of food, clothing, and shelter for the family, opposing the use of pesticides and herbicides, and encouraging the use of cooperatives based on sustainable agriculture and the equitable distribution of food products. With respect to reproduction in the public sector, they protested changes that threatened their roles in reproducing the social system of the welfare state and the quality of the care provided. Finally, as reproduction workers, they are concerned about bringing more women into the environmental–science professions and about developing alternatives to the domination of nature through technology.

Peterson's taxonomy can be fused with the ideas of Meillassoux to apply to all types of political economies. A *sphere of reproduction* can be defined as having two biological and two social manifestations: (1) intergenerational reproduction of the species, and (2) intragenerational reproduction of daily life, (3) the reproduction of social norms within the family and community, and (4) of laws and politics within the public sector (Fig. 41.5). These manifestations can be linked directly to the physical environment. Biological reproduction and the social forces that maintain, limit, or increase population operate at a level once removed from immediate impact on the environment and are mediated by the production process. The legal–political framework that helps to reproduce and maintain the production systems is also on a level removed from immediate environmental impact. The reproduction of daily life and social norms are an integral part of production in precapitalist economies, but are separate from production in capitalist and socialist economies. Reproduction in this fourfold scheme is, therefore, one step removed from immediate interaction with the physical environment for most contemporary situations. Because the impacts of reproduction are mediated by production, environmental effects will differ in different types of economy.

The New England example illustrates the linkage between these four manifestations of reproduction and gender and human-environment relationships (Merchant 1989). About 300 years ago, New England's Indians were involved in production for the sake of reproducing the tribal whole. Gender roles and reproduction practices within the society maintained a population commensurate with the limits of the production–environment relationship. In the northern gathering, hunting, and fishing tribes, population was apparently limited to the technology–environment capacity of about 11,900 persons – a density of about 0.2 person/km^2; in contrast, the southern agricultural tribes supported some 65,000 individuals, or 2/km^2. The environmental impacts were obvious; a long-term sustainable system in which much more forest was cut at any one time in the south than in the north.

This situation changed with the arrival of the Europeans. Very rapidly, mercantile capitalism and private farming developed in association with an intergenerational reproduction dedicated to an expanding population for labor. Social and religious norms and legal–political frameworks developed

to support this purpose. The seventeenth and eighteenth centuries witnessed, therefore, considerable land-use changes and deforestation throughout the region. The nineteenth-century move to full-scale capitalism elaborated most of these trends, but also included water pollution, natural-resource management, and agricultural improvement. The twentieth century has witnessed major adjustments in gender and reproduction, as the global capitalist system no longer required large amounts of labor in the region; the related transformations of the environment are well known and already were discussed.

The key point here is that reproduction, interpreted as both biological and social, contributes to an understanding of how mechanisms once removed from the human–environment interface are critical to an understanding of how society and culture establish the means to sustain or change that interface.

Production and Reproduction in Tension

Given these explanatory categories of production, reproduction, and gender, what are the dynamics that drive change over time? Environmental transformations may be viewed as the results of interactions between a society's ecology and production and between its modes of production and reproduction. Marx and Engels discussed the reproduction of human beings as distinct from, but dialectically related to, the mode of production. As Engels (Parsons 1977) noted: "The determining factor in history is, in the last resort, the production and reproduction of immediate life . . . this itself is of a twofold character: on the one hand, the production of the means of subsistence . . . on the other, the production of human beings themselves." It follows from this point that population pressure on the environment is mediated by production. This view is not to be confused with Malthus's ([1798] 1986: chap 2) argument that population presses directly on the land because it has the capacity to grow faster than the technological ability to produce food. Marx and Engels argued that population presses on the land only through the mode of production, which involves much more than the mere technology of food production as detailed earlier. They showed how changes in these modes resulted in changes in the means of production and the overall social order, and how they led to differential adjustment by class. Marx and Engels believed that it was vital to understand the forces that drive technological change and to translate them into social conduct in order to understand nature–society relationships.

Again colonial New England provides an example. Because labor was scarce and land plentiful, a low person/land ratio existed. Hence, each family had to reproduce its own labor force, and population grew rapidly during the seventeenth and eighteenth centuries. Industrialization ultimately helped to bring about a demographic transition to smaller families, as children ceased to be an economic asset. In Sturbridge, Massachusetts, for instance, women marrying between 1730 and 1759 bore an average of 8.8 children, whereas those marrying between 1820 and 1839 bore an average of 5.3 children (Osterud and Fulton 1976). Nationwide, women who married in 1800 bore an average of 6.4 children, but in 1849 the figure was 4.9 children and in 1879 it was 2.8 children (Wells 1985). This demographic transition was aided by social-religious controls and the flow of information about a large number of family-planning practices (Mohr 1978).

Such gender relations of production and reproduction can be made dynamic and transformative, as shown by socialist–feminist scholarship. Bridenthal (1976) contends that changes in production give rise to changes in reproduction, creating tensions between them. For example, in colonial agrarian New England, production and reproduction were symbiotic (Bridenthal 1976; Merchant 1989). Women participated in both; children were socialized at home. But with the rise of industrial capitalism, production moved out of the home, and farms became specialized and mechanized. The symbiosis was broken. Unmarried women were employed outside the home, whereas married women remained within it. Thus, production became more public and reproduction more private, leading to their social and structural separation. The reproduction of daily life and the reproduction of social norms came into tension with the sphere of production – they separated under capitalism.

The rise of industrial capitalism also fueled tensions between intergenerational and legal–political reproduction and the sphere of production. Again we draw on examples from colonial New England. Inland farms had developed in a subsistence mode and required the reproduction of their own labor. Inheritance, however, tended to leave some sons without land, who became a general labor force. Hence, the tensions between farm-labor needs (production) and the juridical system (reproduction) created the needed labor for the transition to capitalist agriculture. The commercial boom of the 1790s and the interlinked transportation and market revolutions of the early nineteenth century made use of this labor pool to expand production, increasing marketable surplusses.

These shifts, of course, ultimately link to the way in which New England's rural landscape was used, creating a second dialectic in the relations between production and ecology (Merchant 1989). The colonial ecological revolution had introduced both the mercantile economy of the coast and the subsistence economy of the inland towns. Settlers used slash-and-burn agriculture that depleted soil fertility, requiring continual forest clearance for new plots. Old plots were seeded for pasture before they reverted to forest. The landscape was a mosaic of small fields within forests, polycultures, forests and stubble burning, and upland pastures. These methods reduced pest problems and helped to restore potassium in the tilled soils through pasturing cattle in the seeded meadows. With the move, however, to a capitalist agriculture, farmers increased their hectarage under cultivation, dramatically reducing forest cover. Although fertilizers helped to restore worn tillage, pasture quality deteriorated with the transfer of manure to hay production. With industrialization of textile production, sheep grazing increased, contributing further to pasture deterioration, while textile mills and dams polluted rivers with dyes and interfered with fish spawning. These changes, among others, constituted the "capitalist ecological" revolution, a 75-year period between the American Revolution and 1850.

Today a global ecological revolution may be occurring that may also be interpreted in the light of tensions between ecology and production and between reproduction and production. The new global economy, for example, transfers resource extraction to poorly developed regions with rapid population growth – regions in which domestic production conflicts with global market production. This is witnessed in the need for large farm families – as described for early colonial New England – a need now undertaken in a context of improved medical technology and leading to population increases. This population, in turn, provides both a demand and a cheap labor supply that fuels expanded production and contributes to environmental problems – the very ones documented in case studies dealing with the Gangetic Plain, Amazonia, Borneo, Nigeria, and the East African Highlands.

Science and Ideology

Ecological transformations are accompanied not only by major changes in the relationships of ecology, production, and reproduction, but also in the ways in which people perceive and represent the natural world through ideas such as science, myth, and religion (Fig. 41.5; see also Chap. 40). Social historians of science have focused on external causes for the rise of scientific ideas and on science as an ideological legitimation of the existing social order (Basalla 1968). Science – along with mythology, cosmology, religion, philosophy, language, and art – symbolizes nonhuman nature and legitimates particular human behaviors toward it. Science and ideology are socially mediated through ethics, morals, taboos, rituals, festivals, and games. Scientific, philosophical, and literary texts are sources of the ideas, symbols, and attitudes of the elite; the rituals and festivals of popular culture provide clues to those of the nonarticulate. These ideas, symbols, and other representations of reality are at a level twice removed from immediate impact on the environment (following Harris's superstructure).

How are ideas translated into ethics and behaviors that affect the environment? Berger and Luckmann (1966) argue that symbolic universes mediate between conceptual universes and social reality. Societies are influenced by symbols in which ideas are embedded (see chap. 40). Additionally, scientific descriptions of nature contain norms, or prescriptions for action. Cavell (1971) holds that normative meanings are contained within statements of existence – that is, "ought" and "is" are not separable. For example, the description of nature as a vast machine made of atomic parts facilitates the development of an ethic that people can manage, manipulate, and repair the environment, just as a mechanic repairs machines (Merchant 1980). Geertz (1973) argues that religious beliefs establish powerful moods and motivations that translate into social behavior. The New England Puritans' belief in success as an index to predestined salvation implied a life of hard work that resulted in clearing and "improving" the land through agriculture and artifact. Through symbols, norms, and religious beliefs, the sphere of ideas interacts with behaviors in the spheres of reproduction and production.

An environmental transformation may be accompanied by changes in the dominant ideology or world view for particular societies. Taylor (1973) holds that ideological frameworks "secrete" norms; intellectual frameworks give rise to a certain range of normative variations. When sufficiently powerful, frameworks can override social changes, and if weak or weakened, they themselves can be overridden. For example, the Puritans had a religious view–a transcendent God who preordained salvation – that held their communities together. But this view came into conflict with the needs of the new economy that emerged in the region; the fundamental changes were sufficient to weaken this world view, and it was supplanted by others.

The ideological superstructure both legitimates the levels of production and reproduction through ethical and power relations and responds to ecological, economic, social, and political changes. Even the forms of consciousness through which humans represent and interpret nonhuman nature may change. During the colonial ecological revolution, vision became dominant among the other senses. Daily life for most settlers was guided by imitative, oral, face-to-face transactions, but Puritans emphasized a transcendent God who sent down word in written form. Protestants learned to read so that they could interpret God's word for themselves. In turn, interpretations of the biblical word legitimated land clearing, "improvement" of the wilderness, and "civilization" of the Indians. The fur trader, lumber merchant, and banker viewed nature as a resource and commodity. Such changes from Puritan farmer to merchant-trader were part of the colonial ecological revolution.

Ideological frameworks are more than the ideas of controlling elites, however. They are also power structures. For example, shifts in scientific paradigms have at stake power over society and nature, as argued by Haraway (1983), because they are contests for power over the terms of the argument. Foucault (1980) has linked power, knowledge, and space in this manner. According to him, increasing power over space devalues and deadens it. Whereas space "used to belong to nature," when mapped by explorers and cartographers, catalogued and inventoried by traders and naturalists, and coded by militarists and computer scientists, it is controlled by an "eye of power" and subjected to unlimited surveillance. Foucault's model of the Panopticon of Jeremy Bentham, in which an entire prison can be surveyed from a single central tower by an overseer, translates to the concept of a cultural overseer. All things are made visible through the dominating, overseeing scrutiny that controls not only social institutions, such as schools, hospitals, and prisons, but also nature, resources, national parks, wild rivers, endangered whales, herds of wild antelope, migrating warblers, and indeed the "whole earth" itself through satellite surveillance (Associated Press 1985). The history of the "eye of power" over nature becomes a history of spaces, spatial arrangements, spatial metaphors (site, field, habitat, soil, and so on), strategies of control, and modes of mapping, tabulation, recording, classification, demarcation, and ordering.

The rise of mechanistic, quantitative consciousness is an ideological feature of the capitalist ecological revolution. The relations in this system emphasize efficient management and control of nature. With the development of Newtonian science and the use of perspective diagrams, the dominance of vision in the colonial era was integrated with numbering. The eye of empiricism and the disembodied mind's eye conspired to focus attention on the study of natural objects. The printing press and the rise of perspective art linked the mental to the material through what Latour (1986) calls "immutable mobiles." These mobiles are reductions of three-dimensional natural objects, such as stars, birds, rocks, and bones, to two-dimensional inscriptions, such as drawings, diagrams, lists, graphs, curves, texts, and archives. The latter allow the subject to be circulated unchanged among researchers, accumulated, arrayed in a single laboratory, superimposed, compared, and reconstructed as natural order. "The result is that we can work on paper with rulers and numbers, but still manipulate three-dimensional objects 'out there'. . . . Distant or foreign places and times [can] be gathered in one place in a form that allows all the places and times to be presented at once" (Latour 1986:29). The visual and material thus combine to produce power over nature through science.

A global ecological revolution is developing that may again alter our consciousness toward nature. This view has been stimulated not only by the warnings by the numerous "alternative" scientists concerned about a sustainable biosphere, but also by the apparent "actions" of nature to the long-term impacts of the capitalist ecological condition. These actions are well-known and are now having immediate impact on the people of the world as the almost weekly lead stories of national magazines in 1988 testify – the ozone hole over Antarctica, the impending "greenhouse effect," acid rain, and the unusable bays and shorelines of North America. One perspective argues that the global ecological revolution requires more than environmental reform. It requires a fundamental transformation in western epistemology, ontology, and ethics – a change from a mechanistic to an ecological consciousness rooted in species equality, appropriate technology, recycling, and bioregions (Devall and Sessions 1984).

This pending revolution has also been heralded by a spectrum of new sciences infused with assumptions based on nature's inherent activity, self-organization, permeable boundaries, and resilience. The Gaia hypothesis of Lovelock (1979) proposes that the earth's biota as a whole maintain an optimal chemical composition within the atmosphere and oceans that supports its life. The thermodynamics of Prigogine (Prigogine and Stengers 1984) contrasts the equilibrium and near-equilibrium dynamics of closed, isolated physical systems so common in the mechanistic model with open ecological and social systems, in which matter and energy are being exchanged constantly with their surroundings. The new physics of Bohm (1980) contrasts the older mechanistic picture of atomic fragmentation with a new philosophy of wholeness expressed in the unfolding and enfolding of moments within a "holomovement" – that is, process has primacy over parts. Chaos theory offers tools for describing complexity and turbulence, with the idea that nature as an actor offers surprises and catastrophes that cannot be predicted by linear equations and mechanistic descriptions (Gleick 1987).

Recognizing nature as an actor on the historical stage helps to show the instability of the "nature" that underlies many of science's major assumptions. Bird (1987) argues that science is actually engaged with "nature" in a process of negotiation for what counts as reality. Science does not achieve paradigmatic representations of a pristine nature behind human alterations of it, but engages with it in an ongoing historical process of negotiating representations of reality. These realities change over time, both materially (in that nature creates new species and ecological arrangements) and metaphorically (in that human images of it change). Humans transform nature through such activities as colonial additions and withdrawals of species, through industrial development of insecticides that creates mutant insects, or through genetic engineering of new bacteria. Humans thus alter the ecological webs in which they are embedded. Nature accommodates to these changes by adaptation and resilience or creates through mutation and evolution. Nature is, then, an actor both in the sense of a personified mother in precapitalist constructions or as in laws of ecology in modern constructions. It (she) engages with science by offering natural–technical objects prior to observation and experimentation and by resisting or accommodating to technological applications of laboratory "truths." Science is thus both a social negotiation for meaning, theory, and paradigm, and a political negotiation for power over what realities are to be seen and what metaphors may be used to describe them.

Summary

The concepts of ecology, production, reproduction, and ideology, together with their structural and dialectical relationships, help to illuminate the ways in which societies transform their environment over time and in turn are transformed by environmental change. Where human-environment transformations in specific habitats are relatively rapid (perhaps 50–100 years) and uneven, as in European colonial expansion or in change from agrarian to capitalist development, ecological revolutions – changes at all three structural levels – may be identified. Through dialectical interactions between a society's form of production and its local ecology and between its spheres of production and reproduction, its dominant world view and forms of consciousness are undermined and replaced. New forms of production, reproduction, and ideology arise that hold a culture together for another period of time. These themes must be understood if we are to understand adequately the transformation of the biosphere by human action.

References

Portions of this chapter appeared in Carolyn Merchant, 1987, "The theoretical structure of ecological revolutions," *Environmental Review*, 11, no. 4, Winter; and in Merchant, 1989, *Ecological Revolutions: Nature, Gender, and Science in New England*, Chapel Hill, NC: University of North Carolina Press. They are reprinted by permission.

Associated Press, 1985. Satellites serve as eyes on wildlife. *New York Times*, Sept. 22.

Basalla, G., ed., 1968. *The Rise of Modern Science: Internal or External Factors?* Lexington, MA: D.C. Heath.

Bennett, J. 1976. *The Ecological Transition: Cultural Anthropology and Human Adaptation*. New York: Pergamon Press.

Berger, P. L., and T. Luckmann. 1966. *The Social Construction of Reality*. Garden City, NY: Doubleday.

Berman, M. 1981. *The Reenchantment of the World*. Ithaca, NY: Cornell University Press.

Bird, E. A. R. 1987. The social construction of nature: Theoretical approaches to the history of environmental problems. *Environmental Review* 11, (4), Winter.

Bohm, D. 1980. *Wholeness and the Implicate Order*. Boston, MA: Routledge and Kegan Paul.

Bridenthal, R. 1976. The dialectics of production and reproduction in history. *Radical America* 10 (2), March-April: 3–11.

Briggs, J., and D. Peat. 1984. *The Looking Glass Universe: The Emerging Science of Wholeness*. New York: Simon and Schuster.

Carr, C. 1977. *Pastoralism in Crisis: The Dasanetch and Their Ethiopian Lands*. University of Chicago, Department of Geography.

Cavell, S., 1971. Must we mean what we say? In *Philosophy and Linguistics*, ed. C. Lyas. London: Macmillan.

Commoner, B. [1971] 1972. *The Closing Circle: Nature, Man, and Technology*. New York: Bantam.

Cronon, W. 1983. *Changes in the Land: Indians, Colonists, and the Ecology of New England*. New York: Hill and Wang.

Crosby, A. 1986. *Ecological Imperialism: The Biological Expansion of Europe, 900–1900*. New York: Cambridge University Press.

Devall, W., and G. Sessions. 1984. *Deep Ecology: Living as if Nature Mattered*. Salt Lake City, UT: Peregrine Smith Books.

Ellen, R. F. 1978. *Nuaulu Settlement and Ecology*. The Hague: Martinus Nijhoff.

——. 1982. *Environment, Subsistence, and System*. Cambridge: Cambridge University Press.

Engels, F. 1968. Origin of the family, private property, and the state. In *Selected Works*, ed. K. Marx and F. Engels. New York: International Publishers.

Foucault, M. 1980. Questions on geography. In *Power/Knowledge: Selected Interviews and Other Writings, 1972–1977*, ed. C. Gordon. New York: Pantheon.

Friedman, J. 1974. Marxism, structuralism, and vulgar materialism. *Man* 9:444–69.

Geertz, C. 1973. Religion as a cultural system. In *The Interpretation of Cultures*, ed. C. Geertz. New York: Basic Books.

Giddens, A. 1979. *Central Problems in Social Theory: Action, Structure, and Contradiction in Social Analysis*. Berkeley, CA: University of California Press.

Gleick, J. 1987. *Chaos*. New York: Viking.

Haraway, D. 1983. The contest for primate nature: Daughters of man-the-hunter in the field, 1960–1980. In *The Future of American Democracy*, ed. M. E. Kahn. Philadelphia: Temple University Press.

Harris, M. [1979] 1980. *Cultural Materialism: The Struggle for a Science of Culture*. New York: Vintage.

Havelock, E. 1963. *Preface to Plato*. Cambridge: Cambridge University Press.

Jantsch, E. 1980. *The Self-Organizing Universe*. New York: Pergamon.

Keller, E. F., and C. Grontkowski. 1983. The mind's eye. In *Discovering Reality*, ed. S. Harding and M. B. Hintikka. Dordrecht, Holland: D. Reidel.

Kuhn, T. 1970. *The Structure of Scientific Revolutions*, 2nd ed. Chicago: University of Chicago Press.

Latour, B. 1986. Visualization and cognition: Thinking with eyes and hands. In *Knowledge and Society: Studies in the Sociology of Culture, Past and Present*, Vol. 6:1–40.

Lovelock, J. 1979. *Gaia: A New Look at Life on Earth*. Oxford: Oxford University Press.

Mackintosh, M. 1977. Reproduction and patriarchy: A critique of Claude Meillassoux, "Femmes, Greniers et Capitaux." *Capital and Class* 2 (summer): 114–27.

Malthus, T. [1798] 1986. *An Essay on the Principle of Population*. Baltimore, MD: Penguin Books.

Marx, K. [1859] 1968. "Preface to a contribution to the critique of political economy. In *Selected Works*, K. Marx and F. Engels. New York: International Publishers.

Meek, R., ed. [1953] 1971. *Marx and Engels on the Population Bomb*. Berkeley, CA: Ramparts Press.

Meillassoux, C. [1975] 1981. *Maidens, Meal, and Money*. Cambridge: Cambridge University Press.

Merchant, C. 1980. *The Death of Nature: Women, Ecology, and the Scientific Revolution*. San Francisco: Harper and Row.

———. 1989. *Ecological Revolutions: Nature, Gender, and Science in New England*. Chapel Hill, NC: University of North Carolina Press.

Mohr, J. C. 1978. *Abortion in America: The Origins and Evolution of National Policy, 1800–1900*. New York: Oxford University Press.

O'Laughlin, B. 1977. Production and reproduction: Meillassoux's "Femmes, Greniers et Capitaux." *Critique of Anthropology* 2, no. 8 (Spring): 1–33.

Osterud, N., and J. Fulton. 1976. Family limitation and age at marriage: Fertility decline in Sturbridge, Massachusetts, 1730–1850. *Population Studies* 30 (5):481–94.

Parsons, H., ed. 1977. *Marx and Engels on Ecology*. Westport, CT: Greenwood Press.

Peterson, A. 1984. The gender-sex dimension in Swedish politics. *Acta Sociologica* 27 (1):3–17.

Peterson, A., and C. Merchant. 1986. "Peace with the Earth": Women and the environmental movement in Sweden. *Women's Studies International Forum* 9 (5–6):465–79.

Prigogine, I., and I. Stengers. 1984. *Order Out of Chaos: Man's New Dialogue With Nature*. Toronto: Bantam Books.

Rambo, A. T. 1983. *Conceptual Approaches to Human Ecology*. Research Report No. 14. Honolulu, HI: East-West Center.

Rappaport, R. 1968. *Pigs for the Ancestors: Ritual in the Ecology of a New Guinea People*. New Haven, CT: Yale University Press.

Reidel, C., ed. 1982. *New England's Prospects*. Hanover, NH: University Press of New England.

Sahlins, M. 1978. Culture as protein and profit. *New York Review of Books*, Nov. 13: 45–53.

Steward, J. 1955. *Theory of Culture Change*. Urbana, IL: University of Illinois Press.

Taylor, C. 1973. Neutrality in political science. In *The Philosophy of Social Explanation*, ed. A. Ryan. London: Oxford University Press.

Wells, R. 1985. *Uncle Sam's Family: Issues and Perspectives in American Demographic History*. Albany, NY: State of New York University Press.

42

The Realm of Cultural-Human Ecology: Adaptation and Change in Historical Perspective

KARL W. BUTZER

Cultural Ecology: The Relationships between Nature and Society

The social sciences are prone to an unusually high level of dialectic because much of their theory and method has been borrowed. This is especially true for studies of the interactions between people and their biophysical environment, which have a long history of borrowing directly from the natural sciences at virtually all conceptual levels. The inherent difficulties of transferring models and methods from the natural to the social sciences have fostered much controversy and created more than a little confusion. But these difficulties also have stimulated critical reappraisals of such methodologies, sharpening those approaches seeking to understand the complex interrelationships between nature and society that have so long appeared to be intractable.

Under the label of cultural (or human) ecology, research directed to society–environment interactions has attracted contributors from at least three of the social sciences. At one end of the spectrum, sociologists primarily are concerned with human behavior in complex social environments. They have contributed significantly to theory and to understanding the goal – conflicts of individuals, especially in urban contexts – but they also tend to ignore the biophysical environment. On more intermediate ground, anthropologists are preeminently interested in the processes and structures whereby relatively simple human groups match resources with their needs, and incorporate them into cultural behavior. Their contribution to understanding community behavior has been singularly important, although some anthropologists adhere too strongly to a material and biological paradigm, whereas others seem to ignore it. In addition, many anthropologists have been reluctant to deal with urban communities. At the other end of the spectrum, geographers tend to focus on a much broader sphere of interaction with respect to resources, emphasizing the spatial matrix of the cultural and biophysical environment. Sometimes lacking in cultural sophistication, they have, however, directed more attention to the broader systemic context of which small communities are part. Each viewpoint makes valuable contributions; each complements the others. It must also be emphasized that the disciplinary boundaries are indistinct in practice, with the proclivities of the individual investigator determining both the methods selected and the framework in which conclusions are offered.

In the broader context of an interdisciplinary cultural ecology, the interactions between people and their biophysical environment can be examined from several perspectives. Firstly, human actions and behavior can be taken into focus at different scales – as individuals, as small communities, or as larger social groups. Secondly, interactions can be studied in either a diachronic (historical and synthetic) fashion or in a synchronic (contemporary and analytical) mode. Thirdly, emphasis can be placed on normative, deductive patterns or on particularistic case studies that provide experience and draw attention to behavioral variety. Each perspective offers certain advantages, illuminating different facets of a complex subject.

Cultural ecology is obviously indebted to biological ecology, a paradigm that presents both advantages and inherent difficulties. Ecology allows a structured organization of unlike variables, emphasizes function and hence interchanges between component parts, and is amenable to systematic and nondeterministic study of interrelationships within an organic whole. It is less satisfactory in that it was developed for plants and animals, offers no niche for the role of culture and human cognition, and can lead to unfortunate analogies between human and animal behavior. Systems theory has great heuristic value for understanding complex interrelationships, feedback loops, and equilibrium states. The systems perspective allows projection of long-term environmental impacts, such as ecological "simplification" or "catastrophic" readjustment. Simulation is very difficult, however, and quantification rarely possible. Cybernetics also has been productive, because culture and technology can be compared with information. In this perspective, adaptive choices and cultural variety can be seen as key variables, with human cognition assuming primary importance.

Drawing upon these transferred and transformed paradigms, societies can be regarded as interlocking, human ecosystems. They operate on the basis of individual initiatives and actions, embodied in aggregate community behavior and institutional structures. Decisions are made with respect to alternative possibilities, within a social system characterized by established energy and information pathways, complicated by cooperation and competition at each trophic level, and screened by the experience and deeper values encoded in culture. At the individual level, built-it goal conflicts and human unpredictability represent powerful variables for change, whereas at the several community and institutional levels a range of negative feedbacks favors stability.

This view represents a heuristic model to understand social behavior, but its applicability is limited. Prediction, whether of long-term evolutionary change or of rapid modification, is difficult, even in probabilistic terms. Complex systems are almost impossible to simulate effectively, as exemplified by the failure of almost all economic prognoses. Retrodiction is almost as difficult, with past social behavior remarkably intractable to generally accepted explanation. Given these difficulties of comprehensive, normative study, cultural ecologists follow the precedent of biologists in focusing on small subsystems and a small range of variables in order to gain understanding of certain critical processes. The case study, typically directed toward a small, agricultural community, parallels the laboratory experiment of the natural scientist.

Cultural ecologists are therefore concerned with the role of people and the manipulation of resources within ecosystems, rather than the delineation or simulation of such systems as a whole (Butzer 1989). In their work:

1. Society and nature are seen as intimately interconnected, bound by complex, systemic interrelationships. Within that unified framework, particular attention is given to how people manage resources via a range of strategies in regard to diet, technology, settlement, reproduction, and system maintenance. The variability of the biophysical environment in time and space is an integral component of such research, as is the role of environmental constraints.
2. Cultural behavior and diversity are explicitly considered in their functional role and with respect to material and non-material culture. This consideration is normally achieved by in-depth field studies to gain a comprehensive understanding of how energy and information flows operate, how alternative options are developed and selected, and how process and form are interrelated. Empirical detail is crucial to such work, as is the connectivity between data and conclusions.
3. Food production is a fundamental theme, especially in relation to demographic variables and sustainability. Most studies in cultural ecology are in fact directed to rural and agricultural societies, and they generally exhibit a specific interest in understanding alternative outcomes and change, rather than causation or prediction.

In effect, the successful implementation of cultural ecology requires two kinds of expertise, namely sophistication in cultural matters and a solid background in one or more of the related, "hard" sciences. Intensive empirical research in a micro-setting is equally indispensable. Cultural ecology also employs both the synchronic and diachronic perspective with good results. The "contemporary" approach begins with a series of local case studies to develop a methodology, as successive examples offer more thematic insights at higher levels of generalization. Such synchronic work has been applied increasingly to a new view of Third World development. In contrast, the "historical" approach employs local studies to examine technological and related demographic changes over time so as to understand the dynamics of sociocultural adaptation and change. Such historical experience provides a different perspective on equilibrium properties and helps identify alternative scenarios relevant to contemporary problems. Although fundamentally different, these synchronic and diachronic methods are complementary.

Two methodological options are available. One is to develop a deductive model, such as would be appropriate in a general, positivistic work that seeks to create a measure of conceptual order and to direct research to specific, open questions (e.g., Adams 1988; Butzer 1982; Hawley 1986). Apart from being next to impossible to operationalize with quantitative data, however, deductive models are by their very purpose no more than simplified generalizations of reality. Beyond a certain point, they have little explanatory, let alone predictive value.

Models also can be used to formulate problems, develop field projects, and determine research design. In such a case, the empirical data generated by successive field seasons are used repeatedly to revise conceptual structures. The final model is as much a result of inductive as of deductive input, thus offering a better approximation of "reality." But even an inductive model of this type is ultimately limited to a particular scale, set by the initial assumptions and boundaries of the project. Because relationships are hierarchical, in that systems are both vertically and horizontally organized, examination must eventually be extended to higher orders of relationships. But assumptions, facts, or processes that may be valid at one scale may not be appropriate at another. To adjust the model so as to accommodate the open-ended, higher-order relationships integral to satisfactory interpretation is an awkward, if not impracticable task. It is more reasonable to reformulate and attack the problem at a different scale. In this way, different orders of relationships can be identified and discussed on their own terms.

The presentation that follows is structured around a brief case study that reveals and elucidates the complex web of interactions between a community and its environment by means of a culture ecological approach. This inductive micro-study of a small village in eastern Spain is used to delineate an informal model. That information is then discussed in higher-order context, and is generalized to derive a set of concepts and principles, valid or at least useful for meso-scale interpretation of sedentary, agricultural communities. Subsequently, we turn to macro-patterns that incorporate and reflect many of the same processes, but that must be reevaluated at this larger scale. Finally, the insights gained at both levels are examined for their potential to understand society–environment relationships in an era of accelerating transformation.

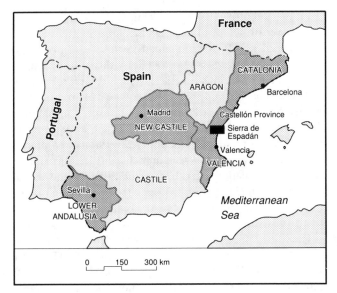

Figure 42.1 The Sierra de Espadán, Province of Castellón, Autonomous Region of Valencia. Shaded areas delineate the hinterlands of the four major cities of early modern Spain.

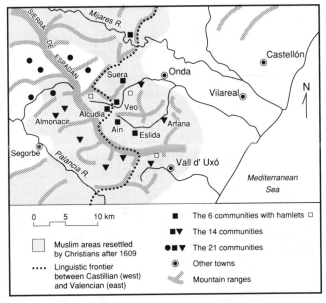

Figure 42.2 Aín, in the heart of the Sierra de Espadán. A Muslim population, speaking Arabic, remained in the central, shaded area until 1609. After resettlement by Christians, the linguistic frontier between Castilian, to the west, and Valencian (Catalan), to the east, consolidated about midway in the abandoned area.

Micro-Study As Laboratory: A Mountain Village in Eastern Spain[1]

Aín (formerly Ahín, pronounced *Ah-een*) is a village in the heart of the Sierra de Espadán, some 50 km north of Valencia, in eastern Spain (Figs. 42.1 and 42.2).[2] The Espadán is a cluster of rough mountains (maximum elevation 1,083 m), with narrow intersecting valleys at 300 to 500 m below the adjacent crests. The natural vegetation consisted of pine (*Pinus nigra, P. halepensis*) and cork oak (*Quercus suber*) forests, which palynology shows have been partially cleared or degraded since Bronze Age times (Butzer, Butzer, and

Mateu 1986; Butzer and Mateu n.d.). The climate is warm-temperate and subhumid, with 550–700 mm of rainfall, concentrated in the autumn (Quereda 1985); precipitation between late April and early October is inadequate for successful agriculture. Irrigation is desirable during the last six weeks of the winter-crop season and is essential for all summer crops.

Topography, soils, and water sources in the municipal lands of Aín (11.8 km²) and elsewhere in the Espadán require that irrigation be concentrated along the valley floors. Since runoff and stream discharge are intermittent, irrigation is linked to large springs and tends to be compartmentalized into autonomous or semiautonomous units. Unlike other municipalities, Aín is dependent on a single, unusually abundant and reliable spring (the origin of the Arabic toponym), which formerly irrigated a total of 30 ha (Catastro 1950). The remaining 302 ha of cultivated land was dry-farmed and much less productive; its average tax value per unit was only 12.5% that of irrigated land (see Catastro 1950).

Resettlement and Filling in: 1611–1700

The base line for this examination is given by the year 1609, when the 60 families of Muslims were expelled from Aín. The 16 or 17 Christian families who replaced them in 1611–12 settled in the core of the crumbling village, and the unoccupied areas were converted into corrals for livestock. Rebuilding included a different style of two- or three-story houses, with animal stalls at ground level, living quarters of 11–22 m² on the second floor, and possibly a partially open attic above for drying and storing food. The regional distribution of family names suggests that the new settlers were derived from both the Castilian-speaking area around Segorbe and the Valencian (Catalan)-speaking area north of Onda (see ARV 1646) (Fig. 42.2). The majority came from quite similar environments, where they had already had some 300 years of ecological experience.

Most of the Espadán belonged to the Duke of Segorbe (later, Medinaceli), and the contract terms for the permanent lease holds stipulated that one-eighth of all grains and fruits (one-ninth of vineyard produce) was to be paid as agricultural rent (ADM 1769; ARV 1814–16), in addition to a fixed sum per head for different types of livestock, fixed charges for pasturage on the mountain slopes (*monte*) or the gathering of deadwood for fuel, as well as tithes on the feudal monopolies (use of the grist mills, bread oven, oil press, and traffic in the town shop and butchery) (ADM 1613; Butzer et al. 1986). With administrative and some family ties to Segorbe, that city became the traditional market center for Aín.

Population growth during the first century of resettlement was slow (0.41% annual growth), and the community was not yet stable: of 19 family names in Aín 1646, nine had disappeared by 1750. The forests, destroyed in the fifteenth century, regenerated, soils stabilized, and stream channels were in equilibrium (Butzer and Mateu n.d.). In 1621, the duke complained that wheat was not being cultivated on unirrigated lands of the Espadán, reducing his revenues (ADM 1621). The pastures were used primarily (from November through

April) by transhumant herds from Aragón, in contract to the duke, with the effect that development of local livestock was impeded. However, the manure left by over 400 Aragonese sheep assured soil fertility for the cultivated, irrigated land.

Temporary abandonment after 1609 and the much smaller population during the first century of resettlement relaxed pressures on resources, allowing both cultivated and grazing land to revert to forest and favoring ecological recovery of an environment subject to increasing stress from the eleventh to the sixteenth centuries.

A Traditional Mediterranean Village: 1700–1830

During the eighteenth century, the population of Aín expanded rapidly (growth rate 1.06%), despite periodic bouts of high mortality (possibly due to typhoid and to other epidemics, one of them probably smallpox, which selectively affected children), as well as reduced birth rates after harvest failures due to drought, killing frosts, or locusts. The population doubled between 1700 and 1751, and trebled by 1787. Growth was not entirely autochthonous: 22 new family names appeared in Aín during the period 1667–1754, of which eight had not been present in the Espadán in 1646 (ARV 1646). These families were derived mainly from Valencian villages, most of them nearby. About 1700–1750, Aín crystallized as a stable, Valencian-speaking community. In 1737, it still was a very simple village with a town hall, two grist mills, a bread oven, and a jail. There were only farmers – no officials, no craftsmen – and the land was supremely poor, so that the village was exempt from some minor feudal dues (ARV 1737; 1765). New houses filled in the empty spaces on the streets of the old core, however, and new rooms (averaging 7.5 m² in area) were added to many existing homes, to accommodate the new families.

As pressure on resources increased, dry-farming of the lower slopes was begun. The Muslims had built no artificial terraces other than lynchets (berms), thus promoting massive soil erosion (Butzer et al. 1986). For the first time, now, complex terrace systems were constructed, primarily in areas that had grown over with cork oak since 1609; olive groves, figs, and vineyards were planted, and winter wheat was grown concomitantly on these terraced surfaces. Runoff was accelerated but little soil eroded, with the consequence that stream channels were incised in response to sediment starvation. A forest census of 1780 indicates that the proportion of oak to pine (3:1) in the municipal territory was exactly the same as about 1930 (Catastro 1950; Croix 1801), implying a similar forest cover, including 102 ha of pine, compared with only 40 ha in 1900 (Sarthou 1912: 909). By 1791, however, the former oak woodland was being converted to vineyards, fig orchards, and olive groves (Cavanilles 1797: 136), and by 1825 constant friction existed with neighboring Eslida over illegal collecting of deadwood (ARV 1831).

By the late 1700s, a new street had been laid out on the north end of town and new houses rapidly were built along it. In 1787–91 four craftsmen and two servants lived in town, and agriculture was flourishing (Castelló 1978: 347; Cavanilles 1797: 136). By the 1820s, three small distilleries for brandy also existed (Miñano 1826: I, 41).

At the end of the eighteenth century, Aín was in a severe resource crisis. Of the 61 households enumerated in 1787 (see Castelló 1978: 347), 10 represented day-laborers (jornaleros) without land of their own – presumably the younger sons of large families (see Vilar 1918: 149 on similar problems in Artana). More alarming is that 52% of the men over 25 years of age were unmarried, indicating a severe, involuntary curtailment of population growth, reflecting an inability to support families. Although the population estimate of Miñano (1826: I, 40–41) is of uncertain reliability, a stagnant or declining population after 1800 is indicated by the reconstructed population pyramid of 1860 (see Censo 1860: 168), which indicates few births or survivals among the cohorts of 1810–20.

Pieced together, the fragmentary evidence for taxation (Artana 1819; ARV 1814–16; Camarena 1966; Hacienda 1850; Madoz 1845–50; Miñano 1826; Vilar 1918: 210–12) shows that the villagers faced three major types of assessment:

1. the land rents to be paid to the duke at an average rate of 11.5–12% of annual farm production, plus additional charges for grazing, deadwood, and use of the monopolies;
2. two categories of tax to be paid to the government, the variations of which are not clear, from 2.6–5.5% in the smaller communities; and
3. a flat 10% of production to the church, plus "first fruits" of farm produce and animals.

These assessments totaled roughly 30% of income. Even allowing for underreporting, this was a high tax total because large fluctuations occurred from year to year, with some years producing barely enough for subsistence. That local food production was inadequate after poor harvests can be inferred from periodic grain purchases by villagers in Segorbe (Ballester 1832).

Although no quantitative data on agriculture in Aín exist for this period, an approximation can be made from those of neighboring places from 1794 to 1819 (Artana 1819; ARV 1814–16; Cavanilles 1795–97; Melía 1963; Vilar 1918: 210–11). The most important products were wheat and olive oil, of roughly equal value; at the second level were maize, figs, vegetables, and wine; and at a third, raisins and carobs. Only about 10% of the wheat represented the "soft" variety grown on irrigated land, and the ratio of wheat to maize typically was 2:1, suggesting that a good part of the irrigated land was occupied by maize. The primary irrigated vegetables were string beans and broad beans. Cork had not yet acquired economic significance, and transhumant herds outnumbered local goats and sheep by 3 to 1.

But fundamental socioeconomic change was imminent. During the ineffective French occupation of Castellón (1810–13), the Espadán villages were subject to arbitrary exactions by guerillas and French alike, but rents and dues were not collectible by the duke after 1811. Furthermore, feudal property rights were placed in question by a decree of the Spanish government in Cádiz (Blesa 1974). When reactionary government was restored in 1814, the Espadán villagers moved from passive acceptance of their poverty to a 20-year period of legal challenges to feudal control.

Aín immediately joined with Eslida, Alcudio de Veo, and Suera in refusing to deliver their annual rents in kind to the duke, leading to protracted but unsuccessful litigation before the high court in Valencia (ARV 1814–16). At the same time, Suera and Vall de Almonacir attempted to gain control of grazing rights to their *monte*; the suit was lost in 1817, but in 1832 the court was forced to void a pact by the council of Suera with the transhumant graziers on the municipal pastures, reaffirming the rights of the duke, who noted that many citizens were wont to use those pastures illegally (Blesa 1974). In 1830, Eslida and Aín lost another challenge, to the duke's right to charge a tax on the transport of produce and to his control over the permanent lease holds, specifically the right to one-tenth of the price on land transferred to a new owner (ARV 1830). Although a new law in 1837 abolished the minor feudal dues, including the "monopolies," it re-affirmed feudal property claims (Blesa 1974). But the spate of litigation by the feisty communities convinced the duke to sell out, and by 1852 he was no longer a major landholder (Picó 1975). In effect, during the 1840s, Aín had gained control of its own affairs, with at least the woodland held as private or communal property (see Hacienda 1850). The community opened its first school, with 20 to 30 pupils, at an annual cost of £12 3s sterling (Hacienda 1850; Madoz 1845: I, 165).

The period 1700–1830 represents a time of major, if incremental environmental transformation. Cultivation expanded and hillside terraces were widely implemented for the first time, representing a major work investment to create new orchards and fields, while assuring sustained yields. Forests receded on the lower slopes as a typical, Mediterranean agricultural landscape took shape. Population increased rapidly as long as more labor investment could provide sufficient food. Eventually the limits of growth, within the constraints of the feudal social order, were reached and the population leveled off. The several strands of information integrated here clearly show that demography is a critical variable in the processes of social readjustment and that it is a sensitive indicator of change. Beyond its intrinsic interest, demography thus becomes a major tool in diachronic cultural ecology.

Intensified Agriculture: 1830–1936

As the duke's authority crumbled, the villagers of Aín proceeded to develop the *monte* without permission. Annual records of 1841–47 (Hacienda 1850) show that cork production suddenly increased by 154% in 1844; since cork can first be harvested 12 years after planting, large stands of cork oak evidently had been planted in 1832. Aín was responding to the new demand for cork bottletops. Olive production increased 130% in the same year, and because new stands begin producing after six years, but only achieve full production after 20, olive groves were probably trebled in area during the 1830s. Productivity also was increased as better methods of pruning were introduced. By the end of the century, five oil presses were in operation. To provide more feed for pigs, the major source of meat, carob cultivation was expanded, complementing the acorns collected in the oak

woodland. Wheat production on unirrigated land was amplified by collecting water from minor springs into holding tanks, thence channeling it to small fields via shallow canals along the furrows of sloping terraces. Such micro-irrigation was limited to areas of 0.1 ha to 0.2 ha each (Butzer et al. 1985).

On the irrigated, prime bottom lands, maize was being displaced slowly to make more room for vegetables and summer wheat, as it lost favor as a human food and began to be used as animal feed. Processed wheat from 1841 to 1847 from the two major mills averaged 28,520 l. (26,920 bushels) a year, about 71.5 l. per person, presumably used for home consumption. This is 141 g of flour per person per day, or about 175 g of bread. With a population density up to 121 persons per km^2 of cultivable land, Aín was under intense pressure to feed its population, and the total tax load was increasing. Given that conversion from lease holds to private property involved long-term annual payments equivalent to the original agricultural rents paid to Segorbe, tax liabilities about 1850 were closer to 35%. One response to latent shortage appears to have been a shift to more animal protein, implied by the increase in pig feed and the increasing use of maize as fodder, primarily used for chickens and pigs. Conflicts with neighboring Eslida in 1825, 1827, and 1831 over the grazing of local sheep and goat herds (ARV 1831) also indicate that the citizens of Aín were expanding their livestock activities, and after 1860 the number of transhumant herders registered in the census reports declines. With more goats and sheep, the community was assured a larger supply of milk and cheese.

During the 1860s, phylloxera insects began destroying the roots of French grape vines, leading to increased demand for Valencian wine (Piqueras 1981). A decade later the citizens of Aín seized the opportunity and began to prepare vineyards on the communal grazing lands of the high mountain slopes. Small berms were constructed in the skeletal soils, the ditches were filled with mulch, and vines were planted in them. They did not compete with grazing, because the vines were dormant during the seven-month transhumant season. The practice also served as a means of soil conservation. By 1890, vineyards had expanded from about 20 ha to almost 250 ha, and Aín was marketing as much as 250,000 l. of table wine annually. Brandy was being made in two small distilleries. The remainder was carted to the coastal railroad stations or to the harbors. The resulting influx of capital transformed the village.

The other side of the coin was that the population exploded at an annual growth rate of 1.42% from 1825 to 1860. Growth then slowed dramatically to 0.33% from 1860 to 1877, however, and came to a complete halt by 1887, after which population began to decline. By now, the physical village had expanded to about its present configuration. It appears that severe curtailment of births was being practiced by the 1850s, because 78% of the men over 24 years of age were married in 1860 and yet there was no out-migration until about 1895. In addition to celibacy and prolonged periods of sexual abstinence, the widely known but rarely discussed "Catalan" method of contraception, namely interrupted coitus, was certainly being practiced. In other words, birth control was a significant factor in the attainment of zero growth in this strongly Catholic community during the second half of the nineteenth century.

Before the population began to decline, however, the density of use on the cultivated land reached 159 persons per km², a figure that can be compared with 246/km² for the Nile Valley in 1882, where 100% rather than 9% of the cultivated land was irrigated. Whereas the villages of the eighteenth century, under feudal control, had little opportunity to buy land, this situation changed in the 1840s. Those families that competed most successfully now enlarged their agricultural holdings and bought up most of the communal lands opened for purchase. By 1930, 21 of the wealthiest proprietors held an average of 55.5 land parcels each, controlling 35% of the private land, but for all 364 individual landowners, the average holding was only 9.0 parcels (see Catastro 1950). Many families were reduced to abject poverty, and a significant part of the population obviously did not share in the flush of wealth brought in by wine export. A strong sense of community persisted, however – to the point that differential wealth was a taboo subject for all our informants. This very reluctance to discuss inequity suggests that the structural changes in land distribution during the late 1800s did not sunder the sociocultural fabric.

The wine boom came to an abrupt halt in 1907, when phylloxera, relentlessly spreading from France into Spain, hit the local vineyards (Piqueras 1981: Fig. 26, Table 44). Once again, Aín had to confront a major crisis. In a series of town-council meetings, the leading citizens outlined and debated the options:

1. A return to a mixed agricultural–herding economy, much expanded by projected purchase of the grazing lands of adjacent communities;
2. Out-migration to the coastal, industrializing cities;
3. Systematic planting of cork oak to meet the growing demand for that commodity.

By 1910, the six largest herd owners in Aín together ran 260 sheep and 140 goats, some even hiring outside herders to tend them. With a total of nearly 1,000 head of stock (including pigs) in Aín, livestock production was high, yielding milk, cheese, meat, and wool, mostly sold to itinerant dealers. The herds were tightly controlled, and because owners were strictly liable for damage to private plantings or communal forest, no permanent ecological damage occurred. The absence of evidence for soil erosion is also explained, in part, by the belt of closed woodland or terraced fields immediately below the high slope pastures. But infringement on pastures of neighboring villages led to increasing litigation, and strategies were reevaluated.

Under the guidance of two progressive and well-informed town fathers, the council eventually decided to select the cork alternative. As the dying vineyards were abandoned on the upper slopes, the area of cork oak on the lower slopes was roughly trebled, to almost 350 ha.

The first financial returns on the cork oak plantings of 1915–18, however, could not be expected until 1927–30.

Because goats destroy young oak plants, the herds had to be cut back drastically, at high economic cost to the average citizen. For the poorer folk, work as domestic maids or industrial workers in Barcelona beckoned. The censuses show that 11 young people from Aín emigrated in the decade ending in 1900; by 1920 this number had swelled to 82, then 60 more by 1930, and 81 others by 1940. These numbers represent an average loss of six young adults per year from 1895 to 1940.

The cork venture also ran into trouble. An outside company moved into Eslida late in the 1920s, set up a processing plant, and established a monopoly for cork sales, attempting to buy out small local owners. As a result, Aín cork had great difficulty in getting sold in 1930, until the cork monopolists were bankrupted during the deepening economic depression that preceded the Spanish Civil War. Other market features were changing too. Prices for wheat were falling disastrously, and the poor quality of Spanish olive oil limited exports. By 1900, however, demand for almonds, cherries, and apples was growing. After 1920, olive groves were neglected increasingly and were even partially removed. Almonds were planted, and fruit trees began to appear on irrigated plots in place of summer wheat. Pine saplings began to recolonize the abandoned vineyards.

For all intents and purposes, Aín still appeared to be a thriving and diversified town. Business directories for the 1910s and 1920s confirm local information that there was a resident doctor, a nurse, and a pharmacy. There were two primary schools, one for boys and one for girls; a barbershop, a smithy, and a carpenter's workshop; a master stone mason, a resident mail-carrier, two millers, two olive-press operators, and eight part-time merchants for olive oil, cork, grain, and wine; a bottlecork factory, a factory for beeswax, a butchery, a tobacco shop, and two cafés. But the village was in obvious decline, with increasing poverty and a rapidly thinning labor force.

During the century following emancipation from feudal restrictions, Aín had embarked on a vigorous and flexible course of agricultural intensification, responding actively to market forces. Transformation of the environment into a primarily artificial landscape was completed. Yet this transformation was achieved without evident symptoms of degradation, demonstrating that sound management can contain the deleterious side effects of even such a fundamental, ecological transformation. But the costs in the social sphere were high: drastic demographic curtailment, increasing economic inequality, deepening poverty of the majority, and a community on the verge of disintegration.

Collapse and Simplification: After 1936

The Spanish Civil War placed Aín within Republican territory, but its citizens were ideologically divided, on economic lines (see Mirá 1974). In July 1938, the village was taken by Nationalist forces, but then remained under gunfire on the front for the last nine months of the War. With the men drafted into the Republican army, the women, children, and old folk were evacuated to Onda and elsewhere. After the War, until 1953, industrial activity was reduced and food was scarce. As a result, some emigrants returned to Aín, the population stabilized for 20 years, and farming was revitalized. But wartime depletion of the transhumant and local herds led to a shortage of manure and lower productivity. Chemical fertilizers were reluctantly brought into general use, but plant pests then became a major problem. Unarable land was restocked with *Pinus maritima* seedlings. Severe frosts in 1946 and 1956 badly damaged the olive and carob trees, as well as the surviving vineyards. By the 1960s, it was evident that agriculture was being simplified. Almond, cherry, apple, and pear trees were planted, but wheat farming was given up, the olive groves were neglected, and local herding was abandoned outright. However, the economy remained market-oriented – excessively so.

A striking ecological change was that the discharge of the minor springs began to decline in the 1920s, and ceased entirely during the 1960s. Since grazing had stopped almost completely, and grass or mulch cover currently is very good, and since woodland is now more extensive than at any time since the 1600s, the failure of the surface aquifers cannot be attributed to devegetation. Informants blame it on the decline of winter snowfall, noting that snow melts slowly and that most of its moisture percolates into the soil. The last major snows came in 1956, and autumn rains during the 1980s were not sufficient to generate temporary seepage in favored areas. A climatic shift to slightly warmer and drier conditions is indicated, but the result is that micro-irrigation is no longer possible.

From 1960 to 1980, Aín lost 43% of its population, and most of its younger people. The ratio of people older than 65 years to those under 15 (the index of aging) increased from 10% in the nineteenth century to 100% in 1950, 170% in 1970, and 391% in 1981. Major support for the senior citizens is provided by the generous social-security program.

The government made Aín accessible by an asphalt road, however, and provided electricity, piped water, and a sewage system in 1961–63. Physical deterioration stopped. A new plaza, a town hall, and a bar-as-social-center were built, and three small condominium structures provided summer homes for wealthy city folk. In summertime, Aín became filled with people – not casual vacationers, but old *emigrés* or their children and grandchildren returning home to their roots. As soon as residents who had moved to Valencia 30 years ago were able to buy cars, they returned to Aín on summer weekends, donned their farming clothes, and spent two days pruning olive trees or picking apples.

Aging widows today line up to pay the annual property tax on abandoned land with money sent by the children of relatives who moved to Barcelona before the Civil War. Some families occupy their apartments in Onda only on school days, preferring to live in Aín on weekends and during the vacations, while the men commute to industrial jobs. Prices for agricultural produce are unrealistically low, and even imported American almonds can be purchased more cheaply than they can be produced locally. In effect, the key impediments to permanent residence in the village are that agriculture cannot provide a living and that there are no schools. But the pace of community life continues to grow, so

that some young families have moved back, sending their children to school by bus as they drive to work in the city. Other younger men work in the coastal orange groves for eight months of the year, while young women paint tiles in the factories of Onda. Enough buildings are being remodeled to employ a full-time mason. The town council is active once more, mainly with younger adults, arriving at decisions through discussion and eventual consensus – the traditional way. The basic principle for all public behavior explicitly remains *comunidad* (community).

Aín today is very much alive, in the minds of hundreds of its citizens living in cities between Barcelona and Valencia, and for whom the people "back home" continue to act out a vital symbolic role. The ties are maintained through letters, transfers of money, visits, or part-time residence. Even the Sunday night train from Castellón to Barcelona is filled with interrelated Espadán people, dressed in "urban chic," giving proof of their sense of identity as they maintain relationships of support. As on earlier occasions, the citizens of Aín are again finding a way to cope with crisis, by adapting with the times, but without forgetting who they are.

During the past 50 years, the woodlands have thickened and matured, and are now closing in over vineyard furrows, abandoned fields, and crumbling terraces. The cycle of environmental transformation has been reversed, and agriculture has become a secondary occupation. Population has declined to the level of 1730. Aín's environment can no longer support its people, but the care that they have expended on its maintenance over almost four centuries remains apparent in the almost unscarred scenic beauty that now attracts vacationers. There is a lesson here: that socioeconomic circumstances can force people to alter, even transform, their environment; such changes, however, are not necessarily detrimental, and the complete replacement of a quasi-natural landscape by an agricultural one need not impair productivity, stability, or the capacity of the ecosystem to rebound to a more pristine state. The intensive, nineteenth-century land management of Aín probably could have been maintained indefinitely.

From Community to Open System: Aín in Context

The Espadán case study illustrates the level of resolution that can be achieved by historical cultural ecology in identifying constant reevaluation of agricultural and demographic strategies, community decision-making, the fine balance consistently maintained in ecological behavior, and the increasing influence of market prices on economic choices.

The demographic curve of Fig. 42.3 provides one measure of energy flow through time, with epidemics, harvest failures, and wars acting as external stochastic variables that temporarily affected energy flow, but did not determine its macropatterns. The various economic strategies and subordinate tactics experimented with, or implemented, over the generations represent those processes of cultural adaptation supporting this energy flow, matching energy needs with population. The other critical aspect of adaptation was the maintenance of some form of balance among population growth, resources,

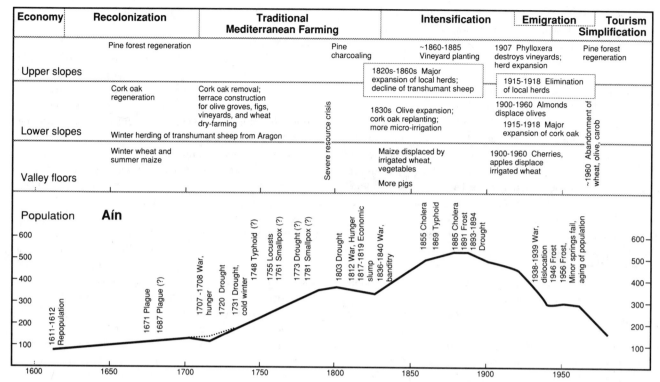

Figure 42.3 Population trends and changing adaptive strategies in Aín since 1610. The dashed line is probably more representative. Sources for population: 1646 (ARV 1646), 1692 (García Martínez 1974: II, App. 144), 1713 (Peña 1986), 1751 (ARV 1765), 1787 (Castelló 1978: 347), 1791 (Cavanilles 1795–97: 136), 1825 (Miñano 1826: I, 40), 1845 (Madoz 1845: I, 165), after 1857 (national censuses, Instituto Nacional de Estadística). A *padrón* of about 1737 (ARV 1737 and Camarena 1966) is omitted as patently too low. For 1646, 1692, 1713, 1765, and 1791 households are converted to inhabitants by factors of 4.4 to 5.0, derived from relationships established for the same *padrones* in villages where population totals were reconstructed from parish registers. For economic information, see text.

and agricultural productivity. Initially this balance was accomplished primarily by late marriage or celibacy, later by birth control, and ultimately by emigration. In the light of this fine-grained resolution, the debate as to whether population growth promotes intensification, or vice versa, becomes moot. Socioeconomic behavior as reflected in use and transformation of the environment is so intimately interlinked with population dynamics that the two become almost inseparable. Given the conservationist land management of Aín, the demographic trace of Fig. 42.3 indeed provides a surrogate for the direction and intensity of environmental transformation.

In effect, Fig. 42.3 represents the actual implementation of an inductive model, rather than an abstract heuristic device. But like all models, this one has its own structural limitations. By giving explicit, if general, attention to the market economy, the model does not assume a closed system. But it cannot accommodate the integration of Aín into a broader regional framework, as well as into the higher-order political economy of Spain, except as a microcosmic subsystem.

The adaptive histories of the different Espadán villages were to some extent unique (Table 42-1). Vall de Almonacir, located near Segorbe in much less rugged terrain, developed unusually rapidly, and intensified its vineyard potential a century earlier, to produce 250,000l. of wine by 1791. Outmigration to Segorbe is apparent as early as the 1780s, however, and population peaked early, about 1850. Eslida, on the other hand, developed more slowly than Aín,

Table 42-1 *Population Density in Three Municipalities, Sierra de Espadán (per square kilometer; parentheses indicate density on land cultivated in 1936).*

Year	Aín = 11.8 km²		Eslida = 17.0 km²		Vall de Almonacir = 20.7 km²	
1646	8.2	(29.4)	6.2	(14.8)	11.8	(28.8)
1692	9.9	(35.4)	8.8	(21.0)	20.1	(49.0)
1787	29.9	(107.0)	34.2	(81.7)	37.6	(91.7)
1848	33.8	(121.0)	38.0	(90.8)	49.7	(121.4)
1887	44.5	(159.3)	53.8	(128.6)*	40.1	(97.8)
1950	25.3	(90.6)	39.1	(93.4)	29.6	(72.2)

* Peak density for Eslida 57.5 (137.4) in 1910.

continued to grow until 1910, and subsequently declined less precipitously. Eslida had the disadvantage of depending on six relatively modest springs, which irrigated seven small units of prime land. But Eslida also lagged in intensifying land use on its remaining territory.

Nonetheless, aggregate demographic and adaptive behavior in the Espadán was basically similar, judging by grouped data from 6, 14, and 22 municipalities representing some 35,600 people in 1970 (Fig. 42.4). At all three scales, there was sustained growth until 1860, then stagnation, and finally massive out-migration and decline after 1910. The largest

Population (thousands)

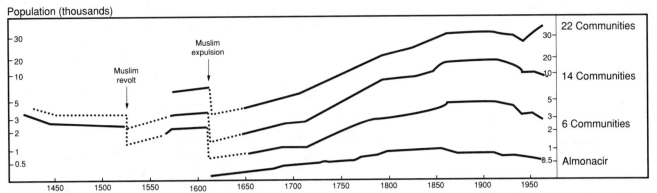

Figure 42.4 Population trends in the Sierra de Espadán since 1418. I = Vall de Almonacir, reliable data at 10-year intervals reconstructed from parish registers from 1611 to 1852, using family reconstitutions for selected years and net annual changes (courtesy of E. K. Butzer); after 1857, national censuses. II = 6 Espadán communities (Aín, Eslida, Alcudia with hamlet Xinquer, Veo with hamlet Benitandús, Suera, Fanzara (north of Mijares River), and Castro de Alfondeguilla (abandoned 1609). Sources as for Fig. 42.3; Butzer et al. 1986 for Muslim era. III = 14 Espadan communities, adding Alfondeguilla, Chóvar, Azuébar, Almedíjar, Vall de Almonacir, Algímia de Almonacir, Tales, and Artana. Sources as for II, except no data for 1751. IV = 21 Espadán communities, adding Vall d'Uxó, Castellnovo, Gaibiel, Matet, Pavias and Higueras, Torralba del Pinar, and Villalamur. Sources as for III. Logarithmic scale.

aggregate (IV) includes a town (Vall d'Uxó) on the periphery of the coastal plain, and shows renewed growth by 1950, supported by local industrialization and by inmigration. Comparisons with other historical studies of community demography and ecology (e.g., Adams and Kasakoff 1984; Netting 1984) extend such experience.

By including Muslim population trends during late medieval times, Fig. 42.4 also serves a retrospective purpose. Demographic recovery to the level of 1609 was achieved only between 1730 and 1770, and population levels comparable to those of 1415 were delayed until the early 1800s, just prior to the onset of intensification and increasing dependence on market forces. It could therefore be argued that the population of about 1800 approximates the "carrying capacity" of the Espadán, in terms of the technology, market access, and socially acceptable level of risk minimization of a traditional Mediterranean society. But the two-century struggle to regain this level required considerable labor investment and had high social costs. Population, as a surrogate for systemic energy, can be increased only by increasing per capita investment. To assume that acceptance of a new technology automatically leads to population growth ignores the human costs as well as individual and community decision-making.

The rebound to "carrying capacity" by the Christian resettlers of the Espadán, and subsequent intensification with maximum pressures on resources, were achieved without serious ecological repercussions. There was no soil loss, although channel scour, as a result of rapid runoff from terraced slopes and sediment starvation, did reduce the irrigation potential of larger floodplains farther downvalley. The vegetation cover remained reasonably intact and is now as good as at any point in the last millennium. This was no· mean feat, and must be attributed to the conservationist technology and behavior of the new colonists. It stands in stark contrast to the intense degradation of vegetation and destructive soil erosion unleashed by high population pressure during the fourteenth and fifteenth centuries, in the different social context of the original, Muslim inhabitants (Butzer et

al. 1986). The land-use practices of the two ethnic groups probably had diverged some centuries earlier, in different sociopolitical contexts or along different regional trajectories of trial and error. The Muslim minority, in particular, was faced with increasing uncertainty about its future, in a social environment of increasingly arbitrary repression after the 1360s (Butzer et al. 1986). There are, then, alternative modes of coping that involve different human investments and different optimization compromises, with distinct long-term implications.

Expanding the horizontal field from the Espadán to the broader region of Valencia, Fig. 42.5 shows a complex demographic trajectory, again as an index of socioeconomic and ecological change. After an impressive peak in 1418, population plummeted until 1475, then rose to recover its earlier density during the late 1500s. The loss of 130,000 Muslim inhabitants in 1609–10 had a catastrophic demographic impact, as did some 47,000 deaths during the plague of 1647–48 (two-thirds of these deaths were in the city of Valencia). The growth rate for 1692–1787 was 0.93% annually, regaining the population level of 1609 about 1740. From 1787 to 1900, growth remained strong (0.69% annually), even increasing thereafter (0.73%). By comparison, the growth rate of 22 Espadán communities for 1692–1787 was almost identical (0.96%), but faltering between 1787 and 1900 (0.48%). The spurt of growth from 1692 to 1787 was similar in Catalonia (0.67% annual growth), dampened in the hinterland of Sevilla (0.53% annually), and barely noticeable in the provinces around Madrid (0.19%). This pattern conforms to the established pattern of differential growth along the peripheries of the peninsula (Nadal 1984; Romero 1973).

Urban growth in all four cities lagged behind rural expansion. The urban population of Valencia, with respect to its region, declined steadily from 14% to 9% during the 1700s, rising minimally to 10% by 1870. Madrid finally began to boom in the 1830s, Barcelona about 1860, although Valencia and Sevilla grew only slowly until the 1930s. Rapid

Regional Population Growth   Population (thousands)

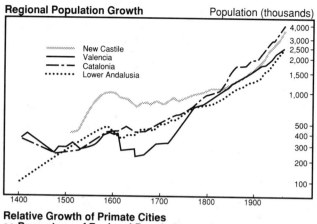

**Relative Growth of Primate Cities
as Percentage of Regional Population**

Percent

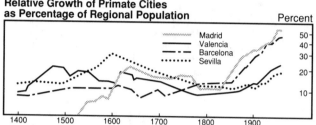

Figure 42.5 Population trends of major Spanish regions and their primate cities, 1400–1970. General sources: Censo 1787; Censo 1801; Domínguez 1970; Bustelo 1972; Romero, 1973; Kamen 1980; Nadal 1984; Molinié-Bertrand 1985; Arroyo 1986b; and national censuses since 1857. For 1830, a median value between Miñano 1826 and Moreau and Madoz 1835 was chosen. Population for Valencia reconstructed, using sample parishes (Castillo 1969; Casey 1979:5, Ortells et al. 1985; Arroyo 1986a; Butzer et al. 1986), from Casey 1979:11, Castelló 1978, and Pérez Puchal 1972. For Catalonia. after Nadal and Giralt 1960 and Nadal 1982, reconstructed with sample parishes. For New Castile and Lower Andalusia, reconstructed with sample parishes from Nadal 1984. For Madrid, see Ringrose 1969; since Toledo and Madrid competed as primate cities before 1600, the population of Toledo above a baseline 21,500 was added to Madrid. For Sevilla and Lower Andalusia before 1528, see Ponsot 1980.

rural expansion, in excess of urban growth, poses difficult problems of interpretation. Increasing urban demand was evidently not an independent stimulus for rural growth. Even during the earlier population surge of the sixteenth century, Valencia declined, Barcelona remained stagnant, Madrid lagged behind New Castile by 45 years, and only Sevilla outpaced the growth of Andalusia (Butzer 1988). In other words, rural Spain had a demographic and socioeconomic dynamism of its own, and one not always in phase with that of its leading cities. This situation should not be surprising for an agricultural nation, whose primary exports until the mid-nineteenth century were processed or raw farm products. Even the export wealth of Valencia at the end of the 1800s was almost exclusively agricultural.

The declining virulence of epidemics is frequently cited as a key factor in European population growth during the 1700s (Schofield 1985), but catastrophic mortalities from plague were mainly an urban phenomenon; although Pérez Moreda (1979, 1980) and Kamen (1980) suggest high rural mortalities in Castile resulting from plague in the 1600s, the Espadán evidence shows no impact of plague, typhoid, smallpox, or

cholera on growth at the decadal level since 1609. Whether personal hygiene and general sanitation were better in peripheral Spain than in the interior, or generally better during the nineteenth than during the seventeenth centuries, are debatable propositions. Whether rural nutritional levels were higher after 1700 or 1800 is not obvious from the Espadán data. Improved road networks reduced susceptibility to famine in northwestern Europe in the seventeenth and eighteenth centuries (Schofield 1985). In Spain better roads and formation of the Guardia Civil served to reduce banditry after 1750 (Ringrose 1970); but roads in the Espadán did not improve until the 1930s, and banditry (rarely directed at country folk) was more of a problem from 1836 to 40 than during the preceding century. Finally, the mercantilist policies and agrarian reforms of the later eighteenth century are commonly emphasized (Anes 1970, 1983; García Sanz 1974). But no agrarian reform occurred in the Espadán until the 1800s, and it had mixed blessings, whereas Bourbon mercantilism did not improve the market situation in Castellon,

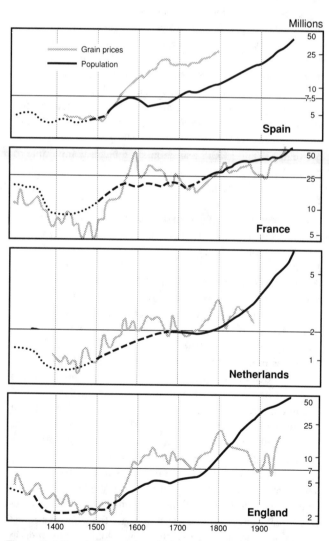

Figure 42.6 Population trends and grain prices in western Europe since 1400. In part after Hamilton 1934, 1936, 1947; Slicher van Bath 1963; Goy and LeRoy Ladurie 1972; Abel 1980; Grigg 1980; Wrigley and Schofield 1981; Day 1987.

Millions (logarithmic scale)

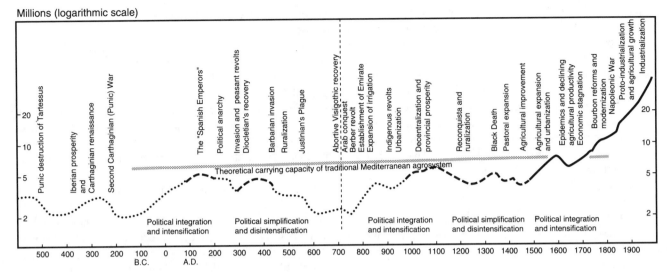

Figure 42.7 Long-term population trends of Spain (copyright 1988 Karl W. Butzer, with permission). For sources after 1400, see Figure 42.5. For the earlier period, population was estimated for ca. A.D. 150, 650, 1075, and 1300 on the basis of settlement reconstruction from archaeological and historical sources, town-site sizes, and regional economies; dotted lines are inferential.

although it did lead to higher and more consistent levels of taxation.

The macro-demographic pattern of Spain shows strong population growth during the 1500s (0.55%, 1528–91), possibly leading to a Malthusian crisis (Phillips 1987); during the 1600s decline occurred, but growth accelerated after 1700 (Fig. 42.6). This dynamism was closely paralleled throughout western Europe, a trend intriguingly matched by the price of grain (Fig. 42.7). The long-term price rises reflected inflationary pressures, although grain production increased from the late 1600s to the 1790s (Goy and LeRoy Ladurie 1972), except during spells of bad harvest weather (Butzer n.d.2; Pfister 1988). The growth surges of both the 1500s and the 1700s placed great pressure on resources throughout western Europe and led to accelerated agrarian change and environmental transformation. Whether population growth spurred productivity or vice versa is unclear.

The Espadán was always market-oriented in that olive oil and wine represented *the* traditional surplus until the mid-1800s, although some communities cultivated mulberry trees for silkworms and produced a little silk. Except for small quantities of silk, its produce did not reach the markets of Valencia, but only the small regional cities. While it is true that the economic well-being of Spain generally improved during the 1700s, it is not entirely clear why the trickle-down effect benefitted some rural sectors of the country and not others.

For Valencia the major growth factor was silk production from the 1750s to the 1790s, with perhaps half of the 700,000-kg yield of reeled and spun silk about 1790 exported (see Townsend 1791: 1634); silk manufacture employed perhaps 7,000 men (and an unknown number of women) in the capital and in numerous smaller places (Cavanilles 1795–97: 134–35; Censo 1801). Export was minimal in the subsequent war years, after which much of the Latin American market was lost. By

the 1840s, the silk industry was dead, throttled by French competition and silkworm blight. The other major Valencian exports – grapes and mediocre brandy (Townsend 1791: 1636–38) – encountered similar economic problems after 1790, creating a long period of economic stagnation. This may have indirectly inhibited population growth in the Espadán until the 1830s. By the 1840s, the role of market forces for the Espadán economy becomes apparent as Valencian agriculture began to intensify on a broad basis for export purposes (Garrabou 1985). But for the seventeenth and eighteenth centuries we are left with many unanswered questions.

A basic problem is that macro-economic theory is best suited to examine major trade networks and the role of urban-centered institutions. It neglects rural micro-histories by overemphasizing the role of a few national markets for agricultural commodity prices (compare Herr 1965 with Arroyo 1986b). In so doing, it underestimates the significance of agricultural innovation in general, and the complex local and regional patterns of rural socioeconomic behavior. That adaptive strategies and efficiency changed significantly in Aín since 1609 requires no elaboration. That the ecological behavior and, hence, optimization strategies of rural Castellón also evolved prior to 1609 is apparent from the stark contrast of Muslim and Christian land use.

We emphasize, rather than question the relevance of, national and international economies for understanding the Espadán. But, in contrast to the many good case histories for the rural economies of medieval Spain, and a comprehensive agricultural synthesis for the sixteenth century (Vassberg 1984), there is a dearth of inductive studies to verify and elucidate the generalizations currently offered for eighteenth- and nineteenth-century agriculture. This precludes a more satisfactory systemic interpretation.

A hierarchical model to elucidate the role of Aín within an open system would begin with the individual communities representing subsets within the socioeconomic matrix of the Espadán. Levels of interaction and reciprocity vary considerably between adjacent villages. Strong energy flows to the duke, the government, and the church were minimally reciprocated by economic and political stability, a little charity, and religious services. A random drain on productivity was engendered by poor weather and epidemics, with a more complex energizing role played by market forces. However, such a model, whether focused on exploitation or on economic theory, is not particularly productive. Far more significant are the conclusions that can be drawn from this discussion.

Deriving Basic Concepts and Principles

The preceding interpretation of the Espadán microstudy allows a number of general observations that can be explicated.

First, Adaptive decisions are consciously made by individuals, within the community context, as economic components are selected, rejected, or adjusted with respect to each other, in response to local needs and external demand.

Second, adaptation, at one scale or another, is an ongoing process of adjustment, as people cope with internal and external impulses, in the short or long term. The basic function of adaptation is to maintain a balance between population, resources, and productivity.[3]

Next, labor investment is the most flexible variable in meeting energy needs on a seasonal and year-to-year basis. Less flexible, but equally critical, are the population variables – nuptiality, natality, migration, mortality – ranging from voluntary to involuntary. Short-term adjustments serve as temporary expedients that alleviate periodic crises, but more fundamental responses include a generational time lag. Technology, in the broad sense, is a third option, but innovations may be inaccessible, socially unacceptable, or economically unfeasible, and they also require time and capital to implement with effect.

Fourth, population as a variable is subject to strong social controls (see Livi-Bacci 1968); birth rates are limited through celibacy, abstinence, or birth control, with emigration serving as the final safety valve. Self-regulation by net birth curtailment involves priorities and decisions on the one hand, and commonly requires personal or communal sacrifice on the other. As a result, curtailment carries human and social costs similar to those of mortality.

Fifth, agricultural intensification involves labor investment, innovation, and decision-making. The innovations are not necessarily unfamiliar. The novelty comes with the inclusion or reemphasis of such traits in the economic repertoire, as minor or major components of a highly dynamic continuum. "Conservative" innovations relate to productivity and can be accommodated within existing nutritional practices and market structures. More difficult are "progressive" innovations that require nutritional change, or the success of which depends upon sustained market demand. Most problematic in terms of both risk and social acceptance are unfamiliar innovations that affect diet or are controlled by fickle markets. Intensification must therefore also be viewed as a

continuum, some parts of which are integral to any systemic growth.

Sixth, as a means of socioeconomic behavior and adaptation, intensification is tightly interwoven with parallel strategies controlling population dynamics. The two processes are difficult to isolate in terms of cause and effect. In traditional societies, population can be increased only by increasing per capita investment of labor. It does not therefore follow that innovation will spur population growth, at least not without personal and group acceptance of the labor and other social costs.

Next, integral to community and individual behavior is a constant balancing between economic maximization and risk-minimization. Acutely dependent on the weather, markets, and political stability, traditional societies search for a mix of strategies that reduce risk to a socially acceptable minimum but that normally assure an adequate production of staple foods and marketable commodities. Plants, animals, and terrain with different susceptibilities to cold or warmth, drought or excess water, are blended. The resulting mini-max strategies, arrived at by trial and error, are "optimal" only in a particular social context and at a particular time. When intercommunity reciprocity, external maket centers, or rural bank credits are available, the margin of security may rise from one to two standard deviations of the inherent variability. The role of "big" government in providing emergency assistance, let alone subsidizing rural populations, is a recent innovation in industrial societies. The rural sector has always been the last to receive tangible returns for its taxes.

Eighth, ecological behavior is another facet of mini-max targeting, because it balances short- versus long-term needs, with some degree of appreciation for the hidden costs. Some rural communities appreciate that soil, water, and vegetation are interlinked and that they must be used with care and moderation if they are to serve family needs indefinitely. The roots of such knowledge may be quite ancient, but it is a pragmatic approach, strictly limited to those ecological components that are understood and that are believed to be critical for long-term optimization. Other rural communities either fail to grasp such ecological relationships or have different priorities. Confronted by repeated crises that they cannot control, they see labor investment in the future and good husbandry as immaterial for short-term survival, particularly if the sociopolitical context provides little hope for continuity in a troubled future.

Ninth, whether conservationist or exploitative farmers are cognizant of or interested in the precepts of academic elites is uncertain, at least in traditional societies, and one must distinguish between the ecological behavior of rural people and the abstract land ethic of the culture realm of which they are part. Only in more recent contexts, as new information is widely and rapidly disseminated, can rural communities begin to make more knowledgeable choices. In earlier times, a degree of ecologically sound behavior was learned painfully through trial and error, and then was encoded in a particular methodology of farming as the "correct" thing to do. Requisite to such traditional ecology is long-term experience in a particular environment and using a specific technology.

Great damage can be sustained when people are resettled in alien surroundings or when they begin to experiment with unfamiliar technologies. Another requisite is sociopolitical stability, specifically the prospect that particular parcels of land, leased or owned, will also serve the survival needs of their grandchildren and beyond. Conservationist behavior is learned and, because it is costly and pays only in the long run, it is not adopted or maintained readily or without protracted thought. Conservation is very difficult to impose "from above."

Next, traditional villages rarely are self-sufficient. Market demand is a very powerful variable, and rural communities have innumerable opportunities to estimate demand, as prices for what they sell or buy change rapidly during the course of the seasons, and from one year to the next. Not surprisingly, they shrewdly manipulate their own activities and "supply" accordingly. Whatever labor they invest beyond their subsistence needs is gauged by the prices they hope to receive, the tax demands they will face, and the likelihood that they will be able to sell everything they produce for the market.

Next, strong and sustained demand is as much an incentive for intensification as is the scarcity of staples for simple subsistence. But a seemingly insatiable market demand introduces a hazard, as short-term maximization becomes possible and increasingly attractive. When communities switch from a balanced optimization to a maximization strategy, they become increasingly vulnerable to the boom-and-bust cycles of the market and of the general, national economy, particularly if they neglect subsistence staples. An unstable equilibrium develops as market crops are switched repeatedly, even when they require long start-up periods. The probability of badly misjudging future market or weather trends increases, until the community spirals downward into a survival crisis. The coherence or continuity of the community may be destroyed, leading to an unhappy choice among undesirable alternatives: a hemorrhage of temporary or permanent emigration, or even abandonment. The individual survivors may maintain a semblance of social integrity as a diaspora, or they may lose their identity altogether in amorphous, periurban slums.

Finally, a surprising thread through all the decisions and adaptive choices that communities make over decades and centuries, both as a collection of individuals and as a whole, is that demographic behavior is not stereotypic. For one, stability or homeostasis may well be the exception rather than the rule in traditional societies. But, contrary to the projections and assumptions of global specialists, based on gross generalizations as to levels of "development" and religious bias, communities in the past and in the present adjust their demographic strategies constantly, as they attempt to match resources and needs. There may at times be inadequate information, so as to produce a lag in self-regulation, but more often than not, difficult social decisions repeatedly are made to bring human needs into line with local, regional, or national economic realities. Of course, mortality and emigration are included among these variables, complicating prospects and potentially leading to regional divergences in population trends. As long as emigration is a viable if undesirable option, it remains a major variable in the decisions made in regard to birth curtailment. But demographic strategies must be indeed accepted as strategies, not as unthinking, uninformed, primal behavior.

These inferences have been drawn from seven years of alternatingly living within and then reconstructing and reflecting on the historical trajectory of a little community. By learning to understand the options that confronted dead but very real people and the choices they might have made, the particularistic case study can be, and to some degree was, converted into a universal microcosm. The inferences are in varying measure normative, in that they find broad if fragmented support in numerous other studies, in both Western and non-Western societies. The themes selected and emphasized reflect a pragmatic cultural ecology, in which individuals and communities make conscious decisions with respect to their lifeways and lifestyles. The obvious limitations are those of economy and scale.

Aín was part of a rural society, which lived on the land and from the land; it was a small, but therefore functional, community. A transfer of the lessons learned to a complex urban-industrial society would raise major questions as to scale and appropriateness. But cultural ecology, as currently implemented, does not presume to tackle the problems of mega-societies singlehandedly. What it can do is contribute a particular kind of insight to an immensely difficult set of problems, for which none of the other social-science approaches is uniquely qualified either. That special expertise involves the systemic appreciation of socioeconomic behavior with respect to resources.

Prospects for Macro-Study

Macroscopic analysis of major historical trajectories is to some degree experimental in the social sciences. The task is so complex and intractable that research focuses on a small selection of variables, to derive interpretations that unduly reflect individual problem formulations and methodologies. But each different perspective enhances cumulative understanding.

For historical cultural ecology, the most informative variable to identify socioenvironmental stability or change is population. Demographic growth is rarely possible without improved technology or better social access to resources, or a combination of the two. Decline, on the other hand, points to fundamental social or environmental problems. Growth, stability, and decline also raise different questions about the quality of life. Historical demography, therefore, provides a sensitive index of general systemic "health" and potential pathologies, although diagnoses are not necessarily simple or unambiguous. It can, in fact, offer a valuable, macroscopic perspective on the exponential acceleration of demands placed on global resources during the past two centuries.

The prehistoric record includes some very long intervals of demographic steady state or homeostasis, but after about 35,000 years ago there is worldwide evidence for shifts into a trajectory of dynamic equilibrium, followed by increasing stability about 10,000 years ago (Butzer n.d. 1). At a slightly more restricted scale and with better resolution, archaeological estimates of population suggest an oscillating trend of net growth, characterized by cycles of growth, stability, and temporary decline during late prehistoric times (e.g., Van Andel and Runnels 1987). In the case of ancient Egypt, five such cycles (millennial waves) span the 3,500 years prior to A.D. 100, with net growth from less than 500,000 to over 7 million inhabitants (Butzer 1976, 1980), representing a density of about 250/km^2 on the irrigated alluvium. A similar pattern is apparent in Mesopotamia (chap. 40).

In Egypt, demographic growth was made possible by incremental improvements in water control, by enlargement of the repertoire of food staples to allow winter and summer cropping, by the inclusion of nitrogen-binding fodder plants, and by the addition of commercial crops. But growth always coincided with episodes of increasing governmental integration that evidently assured reasonably efficient and equitable "energy" pathways, linked with an active interchange of "information." Stabilization followed when productivity presumably no longer could be increased, given the available technology and institutional structures. Increasingly scarce resources now set off greater competition between social classes, to the point where existing institutions became ineffective. The societal system became metastable and vulnerable to perturbations, such as changes in flood volume or foreign relationships. A concatenation of crises triggered positive feedback loops that undermined the institutional structures, leading to systemic breakdown and demographic collapse (Butzer 1984).

The resulting demographic trajectory of ancient Egypt consequently represents an oscillating, dynamic equilibrium, made possible by an enlarging, technological repertoire. The superimposed cyclic fluctuations coincided with alternating trends of political integration and simplification. The technological and sociopolitical variables interlocked, to stimulate episodes of agricultural intensification with accelerated energy flows, followed by episodes of disintensification and atrophied energy exchange.

Drawing in the scale still further, Fig. 42.7 attempts to characterize the population of Spain over the past 2,000 years. Presumably, intensification to the level of the traditional Mediterranean agrosystem was completed in Roman times, by A.D. 150. Thereafter, population oscillated strongly, approximating the Roman level during the Islamic Middle Ages and by the late 1500s, with striking lows in the European "Dark Age" and again about 1400. An abortive, late medieval expansion was cut off by the Black Death. It appears that a population of about 7 million represented the carrying capacity of the traditional Mediterranean agrosystem, given the agricultural productivity of Spain within those parameters. Overall population density was 14 persons per km^2, rising to 30 or 40 per km^2 in the most intensified rural landscapes with limited irrigation (Butzer 1988). Again there is a notable correlation between population growth, agricultural intensification, and political integration, on the one hand, and decline, disintensification, and simplification, on the other.

The broad spectrum of demographic trends and cycles in human history shows that population is rarely stable. Technology and social organization set broad boundary conditions, but population approached these presumed limits only briefly, and under unusual politicoeconomic circumstances. For much of the time, systemic energy flux was well below capacity and relatively stagnant. The intriguing question of exactly which political and economic factors serve to accelerate growth or decline becomes particularly acute when comparing the broadly parallel patterns of demography and prices in western Europe since 1400 (Fig. 42.6). This problem of multiple feedbacks aside, the dramatic demographic cycles suggest that adaptive success in matching population with productivity was ephemeral in the long run. At some point, growth invariably led to metastable equilibrium, and it is uncertain whether political devolution facilitated collapse or whether socioeconomic stress facilitated political devolution. The matter of abrupt change and political or civilizational discontinuities is of more than metaphysical interest. Following a trajectory of sustained growth for almost 500 years, the possibility of drastic simplification seems almost unthinkable. But symptoms of latent instability are present in the modern, interdependent global economy, and the problem of matching population with resources is becoming ever more difficult.

Avenues for Contemporary Application

The purpose of historical studies is not to extrapolate from the past to predict future scenarios. The goal is to understand how communities and societies cope with crises or respond to change. Such an understanding is critical for effective policy formulation in regard to environmental management or the matching of resources with demands.

At the small scale, the case study in this chapter showed how people make collective and informed decisions, which weigh alternatives and which favor options most compatible with sociocultural integrity. Hägerstrand and Lohm (chap. 37) point out that environmental legislation in Sweden could be implemented only after the communities affected were properly informed, in order to convince them to comply. The U.S. effort in soil conservation has had a similar history.

One can also argue that individuals and communities, in the broad sense, can create pressures for government that lead to the formulation and passage of such legislation. But can one expect to see analogous developments in Third World countries, in which priorities and values are different? Success here ultimately requires that western advisers first learn the mini-max rationale of local traditional agriculture before they prescribe change, and that any changes incorporate and emphasize the best components of the traditional system (Knight 1974; Porter 1978). Change imposed from above, and in a cultural vacuum, will probably be ineffective or even ecologically disastrous.

Change is almost always costly in terms of labor or sociocultural dislocation or both. The relative costs and benefits of socioeconomic transformations affect successive generations differently. This disparity goes beyond the long-term investment of conservationist strategies in agriculture, in which the investments of one generation benefit the next. Industrialization and urbanization of western Europe since the late 1700s offer an equally valid example. While the first few generations of farmers turned factory workers paid a very high human price, later generations profited from a greater food supply and from better health care and education, although at the cost of some important cultural values, as community anchoring was lost. The present generation of urbanized Europeans and Americans exhibits blatant consumerism (chap. 40) in a deteriorating environment that threatens to impair the quality of life. Remedial environmental "clean-ups" are expensive, and better ecological behavior may require a curtailment of lifestyles, if future generations are to live more modestly but in better environmental surroundings. The present generation and the next will have to make difficult decisions: Will the population at large bear the high costs of the environmental transformations now underway, or will the few who have directed these transformations for the sake of immediate profits pay? A great deal of "information" will need to be expended before the average citizen can be convinced to make such a personal investment in the future.

Change will be even more difficult in the Third World, where local resource users have been impelled to adopt short-term exploitation strategies with respect to water, soil, and forest resources. Much of the stimulus and some of the agencies fueling this exploitation derive directly or indirectly from the same western entrepreneurs who have profited from degradation of the environment in the industrial world. In this vicious circle of economic and demographic pressures, under which traditional social values and integration are breaking down, Third World countries rarely have the resources to accommodate massive social readjustment, as dislocated people struggle to match expanding populations with deteriorating resources. Ultimately, faced with massive defaults on immense loans, international financial institutions will channel their losses back to middle-income taxpayers in the industrial world. Thus, willingly or not, the costs of remedial action on a global scale will most probably be born by the general population of the industrialized world. This double burden will not be accepted readily, and as time slips by, the ultimate costs increase exponentially.

Environmental degradation is a major hazard, both in times of population growth, while resources are prone to be overexploited, as well as in times of decline, if the better traits of husbandry are discarded. Prehistoric and historical studies show, however, that population numbers are not necessarily proportional to ecosystem stress. Often enough, relatively small populations have done great damage to the environment – sometimes to the point where a way of life has had to be given up, allowing the ecosystem to recuperate while the remaining human population is forced to reevaluate and reformulate its priorities and strategies (e.g., Butzer 1981; Butzer and Mateu n.d.; Van Andel and Runnels 1987). Similar processes can be observed in parts of the Third World today, as new technologies are introduced to unsuitable environments. Expansion or intensification have become counterproductive to sustainable growth in productivity, and traditional husbandry has been forfeited. Cultural preservation therefore becomes all the more imperative in the short- and medium-range view.

The contemporary crisis of population explosion, resource pressures, and environmental quality is unique in terms of its scale and universality. It also has been accompanied by an unprecedentedly rapid economic transformation, in that the majority of the people in urban-industrial societies are employed in the service sector, while per capita farm and factory productivity declines. We lack the long-term experience to judge whether this trend introduces new, latent problems for systemic equilibrium. At the same time, government itself has become a huge management machine, increasingly top-heavy, with dispersal of authority and decision-making among the broad ranks of a vast bureaucracy, far removed from community concerns and inputs, but increasingly vulnerable to special-interest groups. In response, information flows horizontally as much as it does vertically, while energy demands at the top, for nonproductive or inefficient goals and programs, continues to increase. Past experience warns that such "over-loaded" politicoeconomic structures are metastable (Butzer 1980; 1984; Cowgill 1988).

The great oscillations traced by historical demography through the many millennia of human experience were tightly linked with economic and political trends. The regularity of economic collapse and political simplification in the wake of each hemicycle of growth and integration is deeply disturbing. Devolution may not be certain, but it is probable. As steep as the human and social costs of accommodating growth evidently are, in the past as in the present, the price of devolution is difficult even to imagine.

Given the grim possibilities of catastrophic, downward readjustment, broader segments of society need to weigh the alternatives and to make informed decisions that will preserve the essentials of what is of highest sociocultural value. Given the level of "noise" incorporated in megasystems, this seems an almost insurmountable task. Our human experience suggests that information and responsibility are the most essential components for successful adaptation. The towering vertical structures of national societies are the most formidable obstacle to reimplementing "bottom-up" community response. The problem therefore seems to be systemic, rather than societal. The degree to which government can provide leadership, prove responsive to its constituencies, and reinvolve its diverse communities in decision-making will prove critical as to how or whether priorities can be revised and sociocultural values can be preserved.

Acknowledgments

Our debt is first and foremost to the people of Aín, for their interest and information. V. M. Rosselló Verger (Valencia) offered encouragement, advice, and constructive criticism. Partial financial support was given by the University of Chicago (1980), the Swiss Federal Institute of Technology at Zurich (1981), the National Science Foundation (Anthropology) (1982–83), the University Research Institute and the Dickson Professorship of the University of Texas at Austin (1985–87), and the Consellería de Cultura of the Autonomous Region of Valencia (1981–83, 1987). The *Catastro* of Aín was computer processed by James T. Abbott. Last but not least,

B. L. Turner II (Clark University) provided both challenge and feedback.

Notes

1. E. K. Butzer and J. F. Mateu collaborated in the preparation of this section.

2. The materials presented in this section are based on six field seasons, 1980–87, devoted to interdisciplinary, micro-regional study. The project was directed toward the history of settlement, demography, and land use over the past 800 years, and included intensive archival research and four excavation projects. Attention was focused on one corporate community, Aín, with supplementary work in nine other villages and two abandoned hamlets. Earlier publications, dealing with the medieval period, include Butzer and others (1985, 1986, 1989). The following synopsis is limited to the period after 1609, when the residual Muslim population of the area was expelled and entirely replaced by new Christian settlers. This unpublished segment of the project is based heavily on historical land-use study, ethnographic work, and analysis of the parish registers of four Espadán municipalities (Vall de Almonacir, 1611–1852; Alcudia de Veo, 1624–1723, 1833–70; Eslida, 1695–1742; and Aín confirmation records, 1737–54). Municipal archives of Aín were destroyed in 1936, but informants allowed a reconstruction of local events in Aín since about 1890, and families were reconstituted back to the mid-1800s from other sources. Partial documentation is available in several outside archives.

3. Implicit here is that adaptation represents continuous, complex adjustments, whether the long-term outcome be good or bad. It is a process, to be examined empirically, rather than a measure of success or failure.

References

Abel, W. 1980. *Agricultural Fluctuations in Europe from the Thirteenth to the Twentieth Centuries*. London: Methuen.

Adams, J. W., and A. B. Kasakoff. 1984. Ecosystems over time: the study of migration in "long run" perspective. In *The Ecosystem Concept in Anthropology*, ed. E. F. Moran, 205–24. Boulder, CO: Westview.

Adams, R. N. 1988. *The Eighth Day: Social Evolution as the Self-Organization of Energy*. Austin, TX: University of Texas Press.

Archivo de los Duques de Medinaceli, Sevilla. 1613. Estado de Segorbe, legajo 6, no. 3 (Carta Puebla de Vall d'Uxó y la Sierra de Eslida).

———. 1621. Estado de Segorbe, legajo 42, no. 2.

———. 1769. Estado de Segorbe, vol. 18–6 (1–2): 4–5 (1612 Carta Puebla for Eslida, Aín, Alcudia de Veo, Veo).

Anes Alvarez, G. 1970. *Las crísis agrarias en la España moderna*. Salamanca: Taurus.

———. 1983. *El Antiguo Regimen: los Borbones*, 6th ed. Madrid: Alianza Universidad – Alfaguera.

Arroyo Ilera, F. 1986a. Población y poblamiento en la Huerta de Valencia a fines de la Edad Media. *Cuadernos de Geografía* (Valencia) 39–40:125–55.

———. 1986b. Población y producción de la Corona de Castilla en el s. XVI, segun la recaudación de alcabalas y tercias reales. *Estudios Geográficos* 185:389–420.

Artana. 1819. Tax assessment by Gobernación de Castellón de la Plana for Villa de Artana. Document in municipal archive of Artana.

Archivo del Reino de Valencia. 1646. Section Generalidad, expedientes 4825–4829. For Aín, 4829, no. 76.

———. 1737 (?). Section Varia, libro 883, pp. 127v–128v for Aín.

———. 1765. Section Escribanía de Cámara, expediente 53, p. 65v (monopolies 1737), pp. 16v, 25v, 28v–29r (locusts, famine 1755), p. 97 (households 1751).

———. 1814–16. Section Escribanía de Cámara, expedientes 19, 32, and 190.

———. 1830. Section Escribanía de Cámara, expediente 3.

———. 1831. Section Escribanía de Cámara, expediente 161.

Ballester, M. 1832. Unpublished notebook of accounts and activities covering the years 1799–1826, concluded in Veo 1832.

Blesa Cuñat, A. 1974. Aportacion al estudio de los pleitos de señorío, posteriores al decreto de 1811. *Actas, Primer Congreso, Historia del País Valenciano*, vol. 4, 249–62. Valencia: Universidad de Valencia.

Bustelo García, F. 1972. La población española en la segunda mitad del siglo XVIII. *Moneda y Crédito* 123:53–104.

Butzer, K. W. 1976. *Early Hydraulic Civilization in Egypt: A Study in Cultural Ecology*. Chicago: University of Chicago Press.

———. 1980. Civilizations: Organisms or systems? *American Scientist* 68:517–23.

———. 1981. Rise and fall of Axum, Ethiopia: A geoarchaeological interpretation. *American Antiquity* 46:471–95.

———. 1982. *Archaeology as Human Ecology: Theory and Method for a Contextual Approach*. New York: Cambridge University Press.

———. 1984. Long-term Nile flood variation and political discontinuities in Pharaonic Egypt. In *From Hunters to Farmers*, ed. J. D. Clark and S. A. Brandt, 102–112. Berkeley, CA: University of California Press.

———. 1988. Cattle and sheep from Old to New Spain: Historical antecedents. *Annals, Association of American Geographers* 78:29–56.

———. 1989. Cultural ecology. In *Geography in America*, ed. G. Gaile and C. Willmott, 192–208. Columbus, OH: Merrill.

———. An Old World perspective on mid-Wisconsinan settlement of the Americas. In *The Peopling of the New World*, eds. T. Dillehay and D. Meltzer, in press.

———. Climate as a co-variable in historical process: The role of food stress and famine. In *The Engine of History*, ed. D. B. Dickson and P. J. Hugill. In preparation.

———. E. K. Butzer, and J. F. Mateu. 1986. Medieval Muslim communities of the Sierra de Espadán, Kingdom of Valencia, *Viator: Medieval and Renaissance Studies* 17:339–413.

———, J. F. Mateu, E. K. Butzer and P. Kraus. 1985. Irrigation agrosystems in eastern Spain: Roman or Islamic origins? *Annals, Association of American Geographers* 75:479–509.

———, J. F. Mateu, and E. K. Butzer. 1989. Orígenes de la distribución intercommunitaria del agua en la Sierra de Espadán (País Valenciano). *Los paisajes del agua*, ed. V. Rosselló Verger, 223–228. Valencia: Universidad de Valencia.

———, and J. F. Mateu, with L. Scott, Holocene environmental degradation and alluvial history in eastern Spain. In preparation.

Camarena Mahiques, J. 1966. *Padrón demográfico-económico del Reino de Valencia ?1735?*. Valencia: Universidad de Valencia, Seminario de Historia Moderna.

Casey, J. 1979. *The Kingdom of Valencia in the Seventeenth Century*. Cambridge: Cambridge University Press.

Castelló Traver, J. E. 1978. *El País Valenciana en el Censo de Floridablanca (1787): análisis demográfico, organisación y presentación de los datos locales*. Valencia: Institución Alfonso el Magnamino.

Castillo, A. 1969. La coyuntura de la economía Valenciana en los siglos XVI y XVII. *Anuario de Historia Económica y Social* 2:239–88.

Catastro. 1950. Catastro de Aín, file of 3412 cards, Ayuntamiento de Aín, collated 1950 as based on ownership and land use ca. 1920–1936. Computerized as a GIS file.

Cavanilles, A. J. [1795–97] 1972. *Observaciones sobre la historia natural, geografía, agricultura, población y frutos del Reyno de Valencia*, 2 vol. Facsimile reprint, Valencia: Artes Graficas Soler.

Censo, [1787] 1981. *Censo Español, executado de orden del Rey . . . por el Conde de Floridablanca . . . en el año 1787*. Reprinted Madrid: Instituto Nacional de Estadística.

———. 1801. *Censo de la población de España de el año de 1797*, *executado de Orden del Rey en el de 1801*. Madrid: Imprenta Real.

———. 1860. *Nomenclator de las poblaciones de España del año 1860*. Madrid: Instituto Nacional de Estadística.

Cowgill, G. L. 1988. Onward and upward with collapse. In *The Collapse of Ancient States and Civilizations*, ed. N. Yoffee and G. L. Cowgill, 244–76. Tucson, AZ: University of Arizona Press.

Croix y Vidal, J. de la. 1801. Memoria premiada que contiene la indicación de los montes del Reyno de Valencia. *Junta Publica, Real Socieded Económica de Amigos del País de Valencia* 163–267.

Day, J. *The Medieval Market Economy*. Oxford: B. Blackwell.

Domínguez Ortiz, A. 1970. *La Sociedad española en el siglo XVII*, 2 vols., 2d ed. Madrid: Consejo Superior de Investigaciones Científicas.

García Martínez, S. 1974. *Valencia bajo Carlos II*, 2 vols. Valencia: Universidad de Valencia, Departamento de Historia Moderna.

García Sanz, A. 1974. Agronomía y experiencias agronómicas en España durante la segunda mitad del siglo XVIII. *Moneda y Crédito* 131:29–54.

Garrabou, R. 1985. *Un fals dilema: modernitat o endarreriment de l'agricultura valenciana 1850–1900*. Valencia: Instituto Alfonso al Magnamino.

Goy, J., and E. LeRoy Ladurie. 1972. *Les fluctuations du produit de la dîme*. Paris: Mouton.

Grigg, D. G. 1980. *Population Growth and Agrarian Change: An Historical Perspective*. Cambridge: Cambridge University Press.

Hacienda. 1850. Datos estadísticos relativos a la Provincia de Castellón reunidos durante el gobierno del Sr. D. Ramón de Campoamor. Unpublished manuscript covering the years 1841–50 in the Archivo de la Delegación Provincial de Hacienda, Castellón.

Hamilton, E. J. 1934. *American Treasure and the Price Revolution in Spain, 1501–1650*. Cambridge, MA: Harvard University Press.

———. 1936. *Money Prices and Wages in Valencia, Aragon and Navarra (1351–1500)*. Cambridge, MA: Harvard University Press.

———. 1947. *War and Prices in Spain 1651–1800*. Cambridge, MA: Harvard University Press.

Hawley, A. H. 1986. *Human Ecology: A Theoretical Essay*. Chicago: University of Chicago Press.

Herr, R. 1965. *The Eighteenth-Century Revolution in Spain*, 2d ed. Princeton, NJ: Princeton University Press.

Kamen, H. 1980. *Spain in the Later Seventeenth Century 1665–1700*. New York: Longman.

Knight, C. G. 1974. *Ecology and Change: Rural Modernization in an African Community*. New York: Academic Press.

Livi-Bacci, M. 1968. Fertility and nuptiality changes in Spain from the late eighteenth to the early twentieth centuries. *Population Studies* 22: 83–102.

Madoz e Ibañez, P., ed. 1845–50. *Diccionario geográfico-estadístico-historico de España*, 16 vols. Madrid: P. Madoz y L. Sagastí.

Melía Tena, C. 1963. La economia de Castellón en tiempos de Cavanilles. *Boletín, Sociedad Castellonense de Cultura* 39:116–33.

Miñano, S. de. 1826. *Diccionario geográfico-estadístico de España y Portugal*, 11 vols. Madrid: Pierart-Peralta.

Mirá, J. F. 1974. *Un estudi d'antropología social al País Valencia: Vallalta i Miralcamp*. Barcelona: Edicions 62 (Miralcamp is the pseudonym for Tales).

Molinié-Bertrand, A. 1985. *Au siècle d'or: l'Espagne et ses hommes*. Paris: Economica.

Moreau de Jonnes, A., and P. Madoz e Ibañez. 1835. *Estadística de España*. Barcelona: Rivadeneyra.

Nadal Oller, J. 1982. La vrai richesse: les hommes. In *Histoire de la Catalogne*, ed. J. Nadal Farreras and P. Wolff, 61–90. Toulouse: Privat.

———. 1984. *Las población española (Siglos XVI a XX)*, rev. ed.

Barcelona: Ariel.

Nadal, J., and E. Giralt. 1960. *La population catalane de 1553 à 1717*. Paris: Ecole Pratique des Hautes Etudes.

Netting, R. M. 1984. Reflections on an Alpine village as ecosystem. In *The Ecosystem Concept in Anthropology*, ed. E. F. Moran, 225–35. Boulder, CO: Westview.

Ortells, V. M., R. Viruela, M. A. Badenes, and J. S. Bernat. 1985. Libros parroquiales para el estudio de la demografía historica de las comarcas meridionales de Castelló. *Estudis Castellonencs* 2:589–607.

Peña Gimeno, J. 1986. El Vezindario de Campoflorido. *Cuadernos de Geografía* (Valencia) 39–40:313–30.

Pérez Moreda, V. 1979. The intensity of the mortality crises in Spain: an outline of their regional differences over time. In *The Great Mortalities: Methodological Studies of Demographic Crises in the Past*, ed. H. Charbonneau and A. Larose, 179–98.

———. 1980. *Las crísis de mortalidad en la España Interior (Siglo XVI–XIX)*. Madrid: Siglo Veintiuno.

Pérez Puchal, P. 1972. La población del País Valenciano hasta la epoca estadística. *Cuadernos de Geografía* (Valencia) 10:1–30.

Pfister, C. 1988. Fluctuations climatiques et prix céréaliers en Europe du XVIe au XXe siècle. *Annales: Economies, Sociétés, Civilisations* 43:25–53.

Phillips, C. R. 1987. Time and duration: A model for the economy of early modern Spain. *American Historical Review* 92:531–62.

Picó, J. 1975. La burguesia valenciana en la segunda mitad del siglo XIX. *Revista Internacional de Sociología* 33:105–118.

Piqueras Haba, J. 1981. *La vid y el vino al País Valenciana (Geografía económica 1564–1980)*. Valencia: Institución Alfonso el Magnamino.

Ponsot, P. 1980. Un cas de croissance démographique précoce: La Basse-Andalousie au XVe et au début du XVIe siècle. *Annales de démographie Historique*, 143–50.

Porter, P. W. 1978. Geography as human ecology. *American Behavioral Scientist* 22:15–39.

Quereda Sala, J. 1985. Clima e hidrografía. In *La Provincia de Castellón de la Plana*, ed. T. Sanfeliu Montolío and others. 55–86. Madrid: Confederación Española de Cajas de Ahorro.

Ringrose, D. R. 1969. Madrid y Castilla, 1560–1850: Un capital nacional en una economía regional. *Moneda y Crédito* 111:65–122,

———. 1970. *Transportation and Economic Stagnation in Spain, 1750–1850*. Durham, NC: Duke University Press.

Romero de Solís, P. 1973. *La población española en los siglos XVIII y XIX: estudio de sociodemografía historica*. Madrid: Siglo Veintiuno.

Sarthou Carreres, C. 1912 (?). *Provincia de Castellón*. In *Geografía General del Reino de Valencia*, vol. 2 ed. F. Carreras y Candí. Barcelona: Alberto Martín.

Schofield, R. 1985. The impact of scarcity and plenty on population change in England, 1541–1871. In *Hunger and History*, ed. R. I. Rothberg and T. K. Raab, 67–94. Cambridge: Cambridge University Press.

Slicher van Bath, B. H. 1963. *The Agrarian History of Western Europe A.D. 500–1850*. London: Arnold.

Townsend, J. [1791] 1962. *A Journey through Spain in the Years 1786 and 1787*. Reprinted in Spanish in *Viajes de Extranjeros por España y Portugal*, vol. 3 (Siglo XVIII), trans. J. García Mercadal, 1354–660. Madrid: Aguilar.

Van Andel, T. H., and C. Runnels. 1987. *Beyond the Acropolis: A Rural Greek Past*. Stanford, CA: Stanford University Press.

Vassberg, D. E. 1984. *Land and Society in Golden Age Castile*. Cambridge: Cambridge University Press.

Vilar Pla, L. 1918. Historia de Artana. Unpublished manuscript in the municipal archive of Artana.

Wrigley, E. A., and R. S. Schofield. 1981. *The Population History of England, 1541–1871*. Cambridge, MA: Harvard University Press.

Postscript

MARTIN HOLDGATE

Imagine that it is now A.D. 2015. We have been meeting again in Worcester, Massachusetts, to look back at that remarkable symposium, "The Earth as Transformed by Human Action," convened in 1987, Clark University's centennial year. What would we feel in retrospect? How far would our perceptions and expectations of 1987 be likely to have been confirmed by the writings of time's moving finger?

I think that we shall see the late twentieth century as a time of reinterpretation of the human relationship with nature through the drawing together of many strands of culture, experience, and thought. One strand must be ecology, as a science that defines the structure of the diverse systems of interacting plants, animals, and decomposer organisms, and measures the flows of matter and energy within them. We shall, however, note a sea change in ecology itself. Academic ecology did not set out to interpret or serve the human situation, and indeed looked askance at agriculturalists and foresters who rightly posted claims to be the original applied ecologists. It looked even more sharply at certain geographers who borrowed its terms and applied them (more or less) in something called "human ecology." Yet ecology, with its capacity to interpret the complex interrelationships of life on the earth and to deal with variability and uncertainty, was drawn inexorably into the development of what we may, perhaps, one day see as "the service sciences."

Another strand has been public concern. It was fueled not so much by scientific analysis as by nature's manifestation of the unexpected in such things as the side-effects of beneficial pesticides on bird populations, the discovery that the supposedly inert halocarbons, invaluable as refrigerants and aerosol propellants, were knocking a rapidly widening hole in the earth's protective ozone layer, and the die-back of central European forests, in which two foundation stones of modern civilization, the automobile and the power station, were somehow incriminated through the pollution they caused. These were threats to the human life-support system, and in the late twentieth century people suddenly woke up and saw that despite a century and a half of confident industrialization, they still depended on the processes of uncontrolled nature

for their survival. They began to make a fuss about the environment.

In 1972, the first global Conference on the Human Environment was held at Stockholm. That marks a third strand – conferences. The late twentieth century has specialized in them. Stockholm was, however, a landmark on the road of conceptual convergence. The developed countries approached it with two dominant preoccupations: stopping pollution and saving the world's great natural features, such as the tropical rain forests. But the developing nations were unimpressed. They pointed out that they suffered from a graver pollution, "the pollution of poverty," and that while the rich countries had the wealth to clean up their own chemical pollution, the developing countries' dominant need was to develop their land to feed their peoples. The reconciliation came because both groups recognized that the wiser, more caring use of the natural environment was at the essential heart of development that would enhance the quality of human life. That theme was elaborated in the World Conservation Strategy, in the meeting that reviewed it in Ottawa in 1986, and in the Report of the World Commission on Environment and Development in 1987. The detached, top-down "first thinking" that focused on things rather than people, even if admirable and beautiful things like the great forests, has been replaced by what some have called "sustainable livelihood thinking." Conservation of soils, waters, the genetic richness of the planet, its natural beauty, and the biological profusion that contribute so much to life's quality has to be achieved as an integral component of the development process. Care for the environment has to be built into the fundamental policies of nations – their agriculture, industry, energy, and commerce – rather than treated as a cosmetic or a way of using land for which no more gainful purpose suggests itself.

The implications of this evolution in attitudes are profound. Those who organized the 1987 "ET" symposium and this volume clearly saw some of them. For example, if indeed environmental thinking is to pervade national thinking and to have as a central motive the enhancement of human life in a sustainable way, the insight of the social scientists is needed as well as the knowledge of the ecologists, chemists, physicists, and oceanographers. And if this broader scientific community is to respond, it must ensure that it works from the soundest knowledge base it can. It needs to take stock of the state of the oceans, airs, waters, and lands of our planet and the life they support. It needs to know the dynamics of flows and changes: the long-term cycles of climate; the fluxes of carbon, nitrogen, sulfur, phosphorus, and oxygen; and the rates at which people are altering the patterns of the earth. It needs to learn from success stories – and there are examples of good environmental management. Two other needs exist: to understand how people perceive their world, and to appreciate how to communicate the findings of the specialist to the citizens and to those who make decisions for the citizens. The structure of this volume responds to those needs, and demonstrates at the same time the need for different kinds of scientists to communicate better with one another.

What have we learned? I cannot summarize here more than 40 technical papers covering a wide range of topics and a time horizon of three centuries. But let me give you a personal flavor of some of the things that struck me, particularly looking forward to that hypothetical meeting the younger among us might hold in 2015.

First, we live on an intensely changeable planet. Its continents are in slow, inexorable movement. Its climate has changed so much that few places have not experienced alterations in mean temperature several degrees in magnitude within the past 10,000 years. Ice has several times flowed over the hills among which the symposium was held. We do not know for sure which of the changing patterns in planetary life are human-induced and which are natural. Even the oscillations in marine fish stocks that many of us were taught to link to human exploitation may have a substantial natural component.

Second, these systems of our planet are interconnected. We can read in this volume of the way our knowledge of the great elemental flows of carbon, nitrogen, sulfur, and phosphorus has been expanding so that we can describe their movement across the media of the environment and between different living species. We have learned also of their large-scale modification by humanity – industrial sulfur dioxide emissions now match the natural – and of how these flows interact. Nitrogen oxide interacts with hydrocarbon to produce ozone, and this, with sulfur dioxide, can have a more damaging effect on vegetation than either alone. We have to subdivide and classify nature, but this must never lead us to forget that many of our classifications are arbitrary, and for our own benefit. "What's the use of their having names," said Alice to the gnat, "if they don't answer to them?" "No use to them," replied the gnat. "But it's of use to the people that name them, I suppose?"

Whatever the importance of the natural, therefore, we cannot deny the reality and the scale of transformation by human agency. By A.D. 2015, carbon dioxide concentrations in the atmosphere will have risen to about 375 parts per million by volume, an increase of some 35% over the preindustrial background. We may already have an earth warmer on average by half a degree than it would have been without

the so-called greenhouse gases. By 2015, we can expect overall warmth to have increased appreciably, most markedly near the poles, and perhaps to be associated with greater variability in our climates. Expansion of the warmer seas is bound to raise the sea level – not much, but in a steady march toward perhaps half a meter of greater depth by the end of the century. We still lack the models that will allow prediction of what exactly will happen to the weather, but by 2015 we should have them. The issue will be what action we can and should take in response.

We are already acting to curb production of one greenhouse gas – the chlorofluorocarbons – not because of their potential climatic impact but because they are the agents of stratospheric ozone depletion. By 2015, I predict that their industrial use will have ceased and that they will have been replaced by substitutes. They will not, however, have gone from the planet. Even if we halve output within 5 years and end it in 15, there will be a lot of CFCs in the stratosphere for 60 years, doing damage there.

Rather similarly, by 2015 we can expect that all power stations that burn fossil fuels will have so-called acid-free technology: that is, they will emit very little of the sulfur and nitrogen oxides incriminated in acid rain. Nuclear power is by definition acid-free and emits no carbon dioxide, and assuming that people can be reassured as to the safety of its installations and waste outlets, it could contribute to the solution of both the acid rain and greenhouse gas problems. Tight checks on automobile emissions will help reverse the damage currently being exhibited by some European and North American forests. The acidified environment will not, however, be restored overnight. The pool of sulfate in certain soils, involved in the reactions that liberate toxic aluminum, will remain for decades.

I go into this detail to emphasize the complexity and the long lead times of nature. Environmental changes may build up over decades and take more than decades to reverse. We are reminded of this in the chapters on marine pollution, soils, the contamination of groundwater, and the problems of metals and other persistent pollutants, as well as those dealing with the atmosphere. The time involved in cleaning up a contaminated ocean could be immense. A precautionary approach is vital – one that analyzes the impact of possible actions and does not proceed unless good reason exists to believe that the consequences are acceptable. If we are to adopt this approach, however, we need good data, good models, good assessments, and convincing exposition of the results. Strengthening the global data base, as the UN Environmental Programme and others are seeking to do, is one crucial provision for a sustainable future.

The lands and fresh waters of the world are evidently under mounting pressure from the people that live in and use them. We are reminded in this volume that the world's human population, just past the 5-billion mark at the time of the symposium, would by 2025 hit 8.2 billion, on a moderate assumption, and would on that same assumption reach 10.4 billion, before it levels off in a century or so. But a global statistic, of course, covers immense regional variation, with near stability now in Europe (eastern and western) and North

America, and frightening growth rates of 4% or more in parts of Africa, where the land has scant capacity to sustain them. It is in the continents of fast-growing population that the world's great rain forests, the most complex ecosystems on earth, with literally thousands of species to the hectare, stand bare to the destroyer.

I have noted that we had to take proper account of the regional variability of our planet. This volume wisely does this through 12 case studies ranging from the mountains of Caucasia, Switzerland, and East Africa; through the plains of Russia, North America, and China; to the Amazonian, Malaysian, and Nigerian tropical lowlands.

What do we learn? I think, most importantly, that over-generalization is a deadly confusion. For example, the population-environment interaction has not proceeded through uniform growth everywhere. We are told of how, in times past, numbers fell in Mesopotamia and the Nile Valley as people's capacity to manage the land that sustained them declined. We are encouraged by the hope that many developed countries could create and maintain a stable balance between people and a high-quality environment. We learn also that some parts of the developing world, for example Malaysia, have a hope of passing through what I will call the "sustainable development transition" and achieving a balance, whereas for others the prospect looks grim. We are not so hopeful about the Amazonian rain forest.

We must be concerned about the process of transfer of technology to the developing world. Signs point to problems even worse than those of Victorian England at its foulest. Mexico City receives 1,500 immigrants from its nearby countryside every day. It is on course for 30 million inhabitants, in a smog-filled basin, on shrinking lake clays, where there is, in places, less than half a square meter of green space per inhabitant. The air-pollution problems we have overcome in the rich countries seem certain to recur in many Third World cities, to add their burden of ill health to the already frightful problems of poor shelter, no piped water, and inadequate sanitation and the diseases these bring. In some parts of the developing world, the political and administrative infrastructure is clearly inadequate to cope with stresses of this kind, and in some places, such as Ethiopia, environmental stresses are compounded by civil strife. In the future, the social pressure of burgeoning populations without hope could all too easily create further strife.

No volume can do everything. This one skates around what I, for my part, see as major problems – perhaps because they lie more in the sphere of policy than of evaluation, and environmental policy is my daily bread, even if I share with the authors the stimulus of intellectual curiosity. One crucial problem before the world is the so-called north-south divide (a phrase not prominent in these pages). It is the polarization of wealth between developed and developing countries, which has been aggravated by the crippling burden of debt. That debt means that developing countries have to export more and more produce – usually cash crops – onto a depressed world market, to service loan interest, at a time when they should be devoting all possible resources to sustainable development. Linked is the issue of technology

transfer to Third World countries, where ambivalence is obvious in public policy. Individual developed-country governments have imposed tight standards on their industries and made them internalize costs. They have enunciated the "polluter pays principle" as an agreed doctrine to prevent price cutting through subsidization. The danger is, however, that this principle increases the attractiveness of less stringently controlled, developing-country settings for industry. Many Third World governments – especially after the tragedy of Bhopal – have made it clear that they do not want to become "pollution havens" for dirty industry. This volume says enough, I think, to make it clear that if these problems are to be avoided, international agreement will be required, backed by technical assistance to help developing countries industrialize in a clean way.

It is easy to react to such problems with "top-down" solutions from an alien culture. But the world has had too much transfer of inappropriate technology from developed to developing countries. We have to recognize that sustainable development is about real people who interact with and shape the earth on a local scale. Such people do care about their environment. Often their traditional skills are adaptations learned over the centuries. While we need to transfer to them the best that science can offer, we need also the process some call "reverse learning," to find out how to blend the new and old and to develop approaches that will work because they are accepted among the people that sit under the trees by the well at sundown.

This whole question of securing environmentally sound development is inseparably tied up with economics, which is another issue that this volume skirts. Some environmentalists feel that the discipline of economics is so incapable of handling environmental considerations that the only thing to do is to abandon it altogether. In my view, this is not realistic. We live in a world in which governments, aid agencies, and even universities adopt cost-benefit analyses and seek value for money.   We have to find a way of improving the handling of environmental features in economic assessments. We need new systems for evaluating irreplaceable natural resources such as soils or genetic riches, for attaching a proper cost to their depletion, and for avoiding the distortion of discounting procedures that make them appear valueless 30 years ahead. The World Bank and the World Resources Institute have received this message, and I trust that by the hypothetical Clark Symposium of 2015, the whole issue will belong to history.

In summing up the 1955 conference on "Man's Role in Changing the Face of the Earth," Lewis Mumford said a number of crucial things that remain true today. One was that we must accept the limitations of nature. For example – and this is his illustration – "given the special role that sexuality and love play in human life, we might wish that nature – somewhere about the point where the structure of the frog was under consideration – had put the reproductive organs and the organs of excretion in different parts of the body" (Mumford 1956: 1141). But, as Mumford said, we cannot hope that this topographical mistake will be corrected, and in larger things we have to accept that we are a part of the natural order of creation and live the role as well as we can.

The "Earth Transformed" symposium asked some fundamental questions about the kind of theory of environmental transformation we need. It was suggested that three components are needed:

Understanding of what makes societies able to adapt;
Understanding of what makes them able to cope with the surprises with which nature is bound to confront us; and,
Understanding of the interactions between the various natural changes and human responses so that we do not manage ourselves into worse disaster.

For the goal must surely be so to understand the past that we can guide our diverse cultural selves to our diverse, sustainable, social, and economic futures.

My final point also comes from the 1955 conference. "Too much of our discussion here, I am afraid," said Mumford (1956: 1146), "has dealt with proposals for man's exercising control over nature without reference to the kind of control he must exercise over himself." Here we do not address much the issue of controlling nature. The ethic of our days is not one of domination. It is rather of interdependence. In our society today, many people recognize not only that we depend on the nature we misuse, but that other forms of life than our own have their own right to exist. We are together the product of processes that have been wrought since the origin of the universe. Perhaps this awareness lies behind the sensitivity that many people now feel to stories of environmental damage far away. In all strict logic, the loss of a species of bird on some small remote island matters little to the future of the world. Even the irreversible loss of soil and vegetation from some eroded African hillside is a small thing. Yet people grieve. Maybe we have learned that just as in John Donne's words, "any man's death diminishes me, because I am involved in mankind," so every loss that diminishes the diversity and beauty of the world makes us all truly the poorer. These feelings can not be embodied in the hard and brittle logic of science, but they may have truth of another kind, for all that. Certainly the sentiment would not surprise that great American, Chief Seattle, whose letter to the then President of the United States in 1855 is one of the most moving articulations of our interdependence with nature. "If all the beasts were gone, man would die from a great loneliness of spirit. For whatever happens to the beasts soon happens to man. All things are connected."

Reference

Mumford, L. 1956. Prospect. In *Man's Role in Changing the Face of the Earth*, ed. W. L. Thomas, Jr., 1141–52. Chicago: University of Chicago Press.

Index

(Page numbers in italics indicate material in tables or figures.)

DATE DUE